Western USA

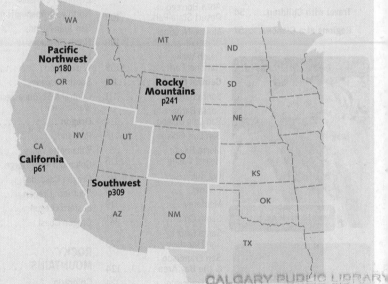

Pacific Northwest
p180

WA

OR

MT

ND

Rocky Mountains
p241

ID

SD

WY

NE

NV

UT

California
p61

CA

CO

KS

Southwest
p309

AZ

NM

OK

TX

THIS EDITION WRITTEN AND RESEARCHED BY

Amy C Balfour,

Sandra Bao, Michael Benanav, Greg Benchwick, Sara Benson,

Alison Bing, Celeste Brash, Lisa Dunford, Carolyn McCarthy,

Christopher Pitts, Brendan Sainsbury

PLAN YOUR TRIP

NATIVE AMERICANS P425

LAS VEGAS P314

ON THE ROAD

Contents

SPECIAL FEATURES

Welcome to Western USA

Landscapes and legends draw adventurers to the West, where a good day includes locavore dining, vineyard wine-sipping, cowboy history and outdoor fun.

Great Outdoors

Western landscapes are certainly inspiring, but it's the sound of adventure – splash! whoosh! kathunk! – that gives the scenery its punch. Surfers and beachcombers flock to the western coastline, which stretches north from the sunny shores of San Diego to the bluffs of central California and on to the rocky, mood-filled beaches of Oregon and Washington. Red rocks, plunging gorges and prickly-pear deserts lure hikers and bikers to the Southwest, where the biggest wonder is the 277-mile Grand Canyon. Meanwhile, in the Rockies, skiing, ice climbing and mountain-biking never looked so pretty.

Local Food & Wine

Famous local dishes include fish tacos in San Diego, Sonoran dogs in Tucson, steak in the Rockies, green chile sauces in New Mexico and wild salmon in the Pacific Northwest. Regional specialties are as diverse as the landscapes. One commonality? Chefs and consumers alike are focusing on fresh and locally grown food, a locavore trend that started in the West. This ecoconsciousness has been embraced by wine producers, who are increasingly implementing organic and biodynamic growing principles. And speaking of winemaking, Napa and Sonoma now share the spotlight with Washington, Oregon, central California and Arizona.

Urban Oases

Western cities have distinct personalities. In California there's the hey-bro friendliness of San Diego, the Hollywood flash of Los Angeles and the bohemian cool of San Francisco. Further north in Seattle, cutting-edge joins homegrown, often over a cup of joe. Cosmopolitan chic meets plucky frontier spirit in Denver, while patio preening and spa pampering give Phoenix a strangely compelling spoiled-girl vibe. And then there's Las Vegas, a glitzy neon playground where you can get hitched, spend your honeymoon in Paris and then bet the mortgage – all in the very same weekend.

Hands-On History

Museums? Save 'em for later. First you'll want to climb up a wooden ladder into a cliff dwelling, poke around the ruins of a Pony Express station, or simply join the congregation inside a 1700s Spanish mission. What else is there to see? Ancient petroglyphs. Abandoned mining towns. A former Titan Missile silo. Wander historic sites like these for up-close and evocative links to the region's not-so-long-ago past.

Why I Love Western USA

By Amy C Balfour, Author

After taking the Virginia bar exam in the 1990s, I drove west to clear my head and have some fun. My first glimpse of the Grand Canyon (not including a first look as a toddler) came after a mad dash from my car to Mather Point. I've been hooked on the West ever since. I subsequently spent seven years in Los Angeles, using the city as a launchpad for exploring Western beaches, deserts, mountains and some truly glorious national parks, not to mention lots of great restaurants. The West is a special place, worth an extended visit.

For more about our authors, see page 488

Above: Grand Canyon National Park (p348)

Western USA

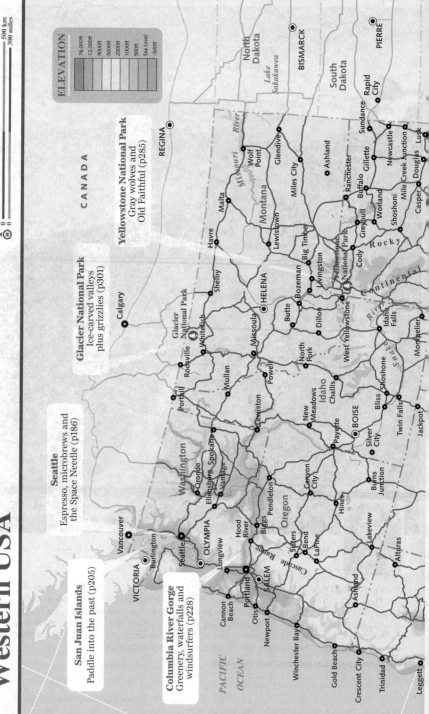

Seattle
Espresso, microbrews and
the Space Needle (p186)

San Juan Islands
Paddle into the past (p205)

Columbia River Gorge
Greenery, waterfalls and
windsurfers (p228)

Glacier National Park
Ice-carved valleys
plus grizzly (p301)

Yellowstone National Park
Gray wolves and
Old Faithful (p285)

ELEVATION

16,000ft
12,000ft
9000ft
5000ft
2000ft
1000ft
500ft
Sea Level
-500ft

500 km
300 miles

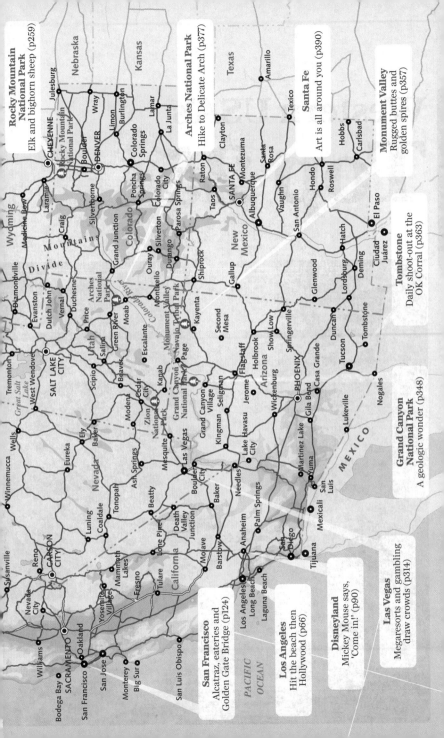

Western USA's
Top 25

Yellowstone National Park

1 What makes Yellowstone (p285) the quintessential national park? Geologic wonders for one thing, from geysers and hot springs to fumaroles and mud pots. There's also Mt Washburn, an impressive central peak with inspiring views from its summit. Add in a towering waterfall, a historic inn and an abundance of bison, elk, moose and bears, and you've described perfection. And don't forget the gray wolves; reintroduced in 1996 they now number about 80 in the park. Finally, America's first park has the one-and-only Old Faithful, a beloved geyser still blowing its top for appreciative crowds. Below left: Yellowstone National Park

San Francisco

2 Amid the fog and the clatter of old-fashioned trams, San Francisco's (p124) diverse neighborhoods invite long days of wandering, with great indie shops, world-class restaurants and bohemian nightlife. Highlights include peering into the cells at Alcatraz, strolling across the Golden Gate Bridge and dining inside the Ferry Building. And you must take at least one ride on the trolley. How cool is San Francisco? Trust us – turn that first corner to a stunning waterfront view, and you'll be hooked. Below: Powell cable car with Alcatraz in the distance

DOUGLAS STEAKLEY / GETTY IMAGES ©

SABRINA DALBESIO / GETTY IMAGES ©

California Wine Country

3 The rolling vineyards of Napa (p154), Sonoma (p156) and the Russian River Valley (p157) lure travelers north from San Francisco. Sample a world-class Cab in chichi Napa, enjoy a picnic in laid-back Sonoma, or cap off an outdoor adventure with a complex Pinot Noir near the Russian River. But wait, there's more: California has more than 100 recognized wine regions, including those east of Santa Barbara, in a bucolic area made famous by the 2004 wine-centric movie *Sideways*. Below: Napa Valley vineyard

Las Vegas

4 Just when you think you've got a handle on the West – majestic, sublime, soul-nourishing – here comes Vegas (p314) shaking her thing like a showgirl looking for trouble. Beneath the neon lights of the Strip, she puts on a dazzling show: dancing fountains, a spewing volcano, the Eiffel Tower. But she saves her most dangerous charms for the gambling dens – seductive lairs where the fresh-pumped air and bright colors share one goal: separating you from your money. Step away if you can for fine restaurants, Cirque du Soleil and the new Mob Museum.

Grand Canyon National Park

5 The sheer immensity of the Grand Canyon (p348) is what grabs you at first – a two-billion-year-old rip across the landscape that reveals the earth's geologic secrets with commanding authority. But it's Mother Nature's artistic touches, from sun-dappled ridges and crimson buttes to lush oases and a ribbonlike river, that hold your attention and demand your return. As Theodore Roosevelt said, this natural wonder is 'unparalleled throughout the rest of the world.' Or as we might say today, 'Whoa!'

Old West Towns

6 If you judge Old West towns by the quality of their nicknames, then Jerome, Arizona (p347), once known as 'The Wickedest Town in America,' and Tombstone, Arizona (p363), 'The Town Too Tough to Die,' are the most fascinating ex-mining towns in the West. In New Mexico, Silver City's moniker – 'The Richest Place on Earth' – isn't as snappy, but the town (p404) shares key traits with the others: a rough-and-tumble mining past, a remote location at the end of a scenic drive, and quirky citizens putting an Old West spin on B&Bs, saloons and museums. Top right: Jerome (p347)

Los Angeles

7 A perpetual influx of dreamers, go-getters and hustlers gives this shiny coastal city (p66) an energetic buzz. Learn the tricks of movie-making during a studio tour. Bliss out to acoustically perfect symphony sounds in the Walt Disney Concert Hall. Wander gardens and galleries at the hilltop Getty Center. And stargazing? Take in the big picture at the revamped Griffith Observatory or look for stylish, earthbound 'stars' at The Grove. Ready for your close-up darling? You will be – an hour on the beach practically guarantees that sun-kissed LA glow. Above: Hollywood Walk of Fame (p73)

Disneyland, California Adventure & Orange County

8 Inside Disneyland (p90), beloved cartoon characters waltz down Main Street USA, thrilling Space Mountain rockets through the darkness, and fireworks explode over Sleeping Beauty's castle. Next door, California Adventure (p91) showcases the best of the state with a re-created Hollywood back lot, a coastal boardwalk and a patio perfect for sipping California wines. Meanwhile, the Orange County (p92) coast lures travelers with upscale malls, bird-filled nature reserves and gorgeous beaches. Below: Laguna Beach (p92)

Yosemite National Park

9 Welcome to the park (p169) conservationist John Muir called his 'high pleasure ground' and 'great temple.' Meander through wildflower-strewn meadows in valleys carved by glaciers and earthquakes, and take in all of nature's majesty: the thunderous waterfalls that tumble over sheer cliffs; the enormous granite domes; or the ancient groves of giant sequoias, the planet's biggest trees. For the most sublime views, perch at Glacier Point (p170) on a full-moon night or drive the high country's dizzying Tioga Rd in summer. Right: Yosemite Falls

8

ANTHONY PIDGEON / GETTY IMAGES ©

RICHARD CUMMINS / GETTY IMAGES ©

Portland

10 How do you improve Portland (p213)? As the artsy characters in the indie series *Portlandia* might say – 'Put a bird on it!' The satiric show makes it clear that this is a quirky but loveable place: it's as friendly as a big town, and home to a mix of students, artists, cyclists, hipsters, young families, old hippies, ecofreaks and everything in between. There's great food, awesome music and plenty of culture, plus it's as sustainable as you can get. Come and visit, but be careful – like everyone else, you might just want to pack up and move here! Top right: Portland food carts (p220)

Route 66

11 As you step up to the counter at Seligman's Snow-Cap Drive In (p346), you know a prank is coming – a squirt of fake mustard, perhaps, or ridiculously incorrect change. Though it's all a bit hokey, you'd be disappointed if the owner forgot to 'get you.' It's these kitschy, down-home touches that make the 'Mother Road' (p35) – which crosses California, Arizona and New Mexico – so memorable. Begging burros, the Wigwam Motel, the neon signs of Tucumcari – a squirt of fake mustard beats a mass-consumption McBurger every time. Above: Wigwam Motel (p346), Route 66

ANN CECIL / GETTY IMAGES ©

Seattle

12 A cutting-edge Pacific Rim city with an uncanny habit of turning locally hatched ideas into global brands, Seattle (p186) has earned its place in the pantheon of 'great' US metropolises with a world-renowned music scene, a mercurial coffee culture and a penchant for internet-driven innovation. But, while Seattle's trendsetters rush to unearth the next big thing, city traditionalists guard its soul with distinct urban neighborhoods, a home-grown food culture, and what is arguably the nation's finest public market, Pike Place.
Above: Space Needle (p190)

Mt Rainier

13 When the skies are clear, Mt Rainier (p210) looms high over Seattle, creating an amazing backdrop to the Emerald City. Still very much a live volcano, the 14,411ft peak is the shining centerpiece of the Mt Rainier National Park, which offers a rare inland temperate rainforest, hikes through alpine wildflower meadows, and the famous 93-mile Wonderland Trail. If you're fit and adventurous enough, attempt to climb the peak itself; just be ready to traverse some of the largest glaciers outside Alaska.

San Juan Islands

14 Go back in time by hopping on a ferry to the San Juan Islands (p205), a low-key archipelago north of Puget Sound between Washington and Vancouver Island. Out of the more than 450 'islands' (most are only rocky promontories), only about 60 are inhabited and just four are regularly served by ferries. Nature is the main influence here and each island has its own personality, both geographic and cultural. What can you do here? Start with cycling, kayaking and spotting orcas – then just sit back and relax. Above: Orca breaching, San Juan Islands

Coastal Highways

15 Stunning highways track America's western coastline. In California, Hwy 1, Hwy 101 and I-5 pass dizzying sea cliffs, quaint beach towns and a handful of major cities: laid-back San Diego, rocker LA and beatnik San Francisco. North of the redwoods, Hwy 101 swoops into Oregon for windswept capes, rocky tide pools and, for *Twilight* fans, Ecola State Park (p238), the stand-in for werewolf haven La Push, Washington. Cross the Columbia River into Washington for wet-and-wild Olympic National Park (p201). Below: Hwy 1 near Montara

The Deserts

16 The humanlike saguaro cactus is one of the West's most enduring symbols. A denizen of the Sonoran Desert, it's a hardy survivor in a landscape harsh and unforgiving, yet also strangely beautiful. Four deserts – the Sonoran, Mojave, Chihuahuan and Great Basin – stretch across the Southwest (p309). Each is also home to an array of well-adapted reptiles, mammals and plants. It's this thriving diversity that makes a stroll through the desert a wondrous, one-of-a-kind experience. Bottom: Saguaro National Park (p359)

PLAN YOUR TRIP WESTERN USA'S TOP 25

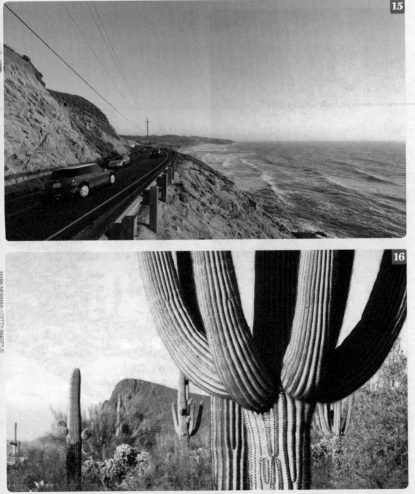

15

16

MARK NEWMAN / GETTY IMAGES ©

Native American History & Culture

17 The Southwest holds a fascinating array of Native American sites. To learn about America's earliest inhabitants, climb into the ancient cliff-top homes of Ancestral Puebloans in Colorado and New Mexico, or study petroglyphs in Sedona. For living cultures, visit Arizona's Navajo and Hopi nations. Here you'll discover that Native American art is not stuck in the past. While many designs have religious significance, the baskets, rugs and jewelry crafted today often put a fresh spin on the ancient traditions. Below: Navajo woman with turquoise jewelry

Rocky Mountain National Park

18 From behind the row of RVs growling along Trail Ridge Rd, Rocky Mountain National Park (p259) can look a bit overrun. But with hiking boots laced and the trail unfurling before you, the park's majestic, untamed splendor becomes unforgettably personal. From epic outings on the Continental Divide National Scenic Trail to family-friendly romps in the Bear Lake area, there's something here for people of every ability and ambition. With just the slightest effort, you'll feel like you have the place to yourself.

RUSSELL BURDEN / GETTY IMAGES ©

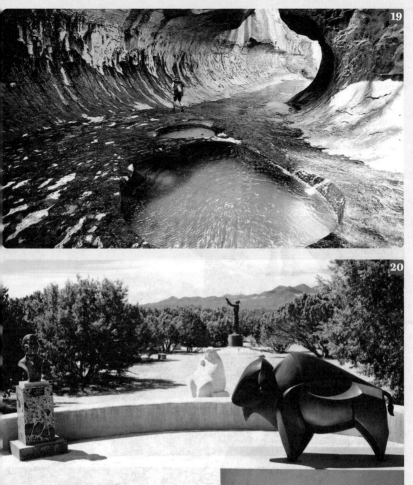

Zion & Bryce Canyon National Parks

19 Towering red rocks hide graceful waterfalls, narrow slot canyons and hanging gardens in Zion National Park (p382). This lush wonderland lies in the shadow of Angels Landing, which is the lofty terminus of the Angels Landing Trail. Photographers and view hounds should scoot north to Bryce Canyon National Park (p381), where golden-red rock spires shimmer like trees in a magical stone forest – a hypnotic, Tolkienesque place. Top: Zion National Park

Santa Fe & Taos

20 Santa Fe (p390) just celebrated her 400th birthday, but she's still kicking up her stylish heels like a teenager. On Friday nights, art lovers flock to Canyon Rd to gab with artists, sip wine and explore more than 75 galleries. Art and history partner up within the city's consortium of museums, and the food and the shopping are first rate, too. Artists also converge in gallery-filled Taos (p398) but the vibe is quirkier, with ski bums, off-the-grid Earthshippers and a few celebs keeping things offbeat. Above: View from visitor center at Allan Houser Sculpture Gardens, Santa Fe (p390)

Microbreweries

21 Microbreweries (p433) are a specialty of the West, and you'll find at least one in each of the outdoorsy towns from Moab to Missoula. Though specific to their home towns, these popular watering holes share a few commonalities: boisterous beer sippers, deep-flavored brews with locally inspired names, and cavernous drinking rooms that smell of sweat and adventure. And when it comes to memorable slogans, Wasatch Brew Pub & Brewery in Park City, Utah, earns kudos for its Polygamy Porter tagline: Why Have Just One?

Columbia River Gorge

22 Carved by the mighty Columbia as the Cascades were uplifted, the Columbia River Gorge (p228) is a geologic marvel. With Washington on its north side and Oregon on its south, the state-dividing gorge offers countless waterfalls and spectacular hikes, as well as an agricultural bounty of apples, pears and cherries. And if you're into windsurfing or kiteboarding, head straight to the sporty town of Hood River, ground zero for these extreme sports. Whether you're a hiker, apple lover or adrenaline junkie, the gorge delivers.

SHANNON NACE / GETTY IMAGES ©

FEARGUS COONEY / GETTY IMAGES ©

Boulder, CO

23 Tucked up against its signature Flatirons, Boulder (p255) has a sweet location and a progressive soul, which has attracted a groovy bag of entrepreneurs, hippies and hard-bodies. Packs of cyclists ride the Boulder Creek Bike Path, which links to an abundance of city and county parks purchased through a popular Open Space tax. The pedestrian-only Pearl St Mall is lively, especially at night, when students from the University of Colorado and Naropa University mingle and flirt. In many ways Boulder, not Denver, is the state's tourist hub.
Above: Pearl St Mall

Glacier National Park

24 Yep, the rumors are true. The namesake attractions at Glacier National Park (p301) are melting away. There were 150 glaciers in the area in 1850; today there are 25. But even without the giant ice cubes, Montana's sprawling national park is worthy of an in-depth visit. Road warriors can maneuver the thrilling 50-mile Going-to-the-Sun Road; wildlife-watchers can scan for elk, wolves and grizzly (but hopefully not too close); and hikers have 700 miles of trails, trees and flora – including mosses, mushrooms and wildflowers – to explore.

Monument Valley & Canyon de Chelly

25 'May I walk in beauty' is the final line of a famous Navajo prayer. Beauty takes many forms on the Navajos' sprawling reservation, but makes its most famous appearance at Monument Valley (p357), an otherworldly cluster of rugged buttes and stubborn towers. Beauty swoops in on the wings of birds at Canyon de Chelly (p356), a green valley where farmers till the land near age-old cliff dwellings. Elsewhere, beauty is in the connections, from the docent explaining Navajo clans, to the guide sharing photography tips in the flickering light of Antelope Canyon.

Need to Know

For more information, see Survival Guide (p450)

Currency
US dollars ($)

Language
English

Visas
Not required for citizens of Visa Waiver Program countries, but ESTA approval required (apply online in advance).

Money
ATMs widely available. Credit cards normally required for hotel reservations and car rentals.

Cell Phones
Only GSM multiband models will work in the USA. Coverage can be spotty in remote or mountainous areas.

Time
The 11 states in this guide are covered by Mountain Standard Time (Denver, Santa Fe, Phoenix) or Pacific Standard Time (Seattle, Los Angeles, San Francisco, Las Vegas). For details about Arizona hours, see p458.

When to Go

Seattle
GO Jun–Sep

Salt Lake City
GO Jan–Dec

San Francisco
GO May–Oct

Denver
GO May–Aug

Las Vegas
GO Jan–Dec

Los Angeles
GO Apr–Oct

Phoenix
GO Oct–May

Desert climate
Dry climate
Warm to hot summers, mild winters
Mild summers, cold winters

High Season
(Jun–Aug; Sep–Apr)

➡ Busiest season; sunny days, higher accommodation prices

➡ Clouds may blanket the southern coast during May and June

➡ Mountain high season January to March; deserts September to April

Shoulder
(Apr & May; Sep & Oct)

➡ Crowds and prices drop along the coast and in the mountains

➡ A good time to visit national parks, with milder temperatures

➡ Blooming spring flowers; fiery autumn colors

Low Season
(Nov–Mar)

➡ Accommodation rates drop by the coast

➡ Dark, wintery days, with snowfall in the north and heavier rains

Websites

American Southwest (www.americansouthwest.net) Parks and landscapes.

Lonely Planet (www.lonelyplanet.com/usa) Destination info, bookings and forums.

National Park Service (www.nps.gov) Information on national parks and monuments.

Recreation.gov (www.recreation.gov) Camping reservations on federally managed lands.

Roadside America (www.roadsideamerica.com) Find 'uniquely odd tourist attractions.'

Important Numbers

To call any regular number, dial the area code, followed by the 7-digit number.

USA Country Code	☏1
International Access Code	☏011
Emergency	☏911
National Sexual Assault Hotline	☏800-656-4673
Directory Assistance	☏411
Statewide Road Conditions	☏511

Exchange Rates

Australia	A$1	$0.94
Canada	C$1	$0.97
Euro zone	€1	$1.35
China	Y10	$1.63
Japan	¥100	$1.01
Mexico	MXN10	$0.77
New Zealand	NZ$1	$0.83
UK	£1	$1.60

For current exchange rates see www.xe.com.

Daily Costs

Budget: Less than $100

➡ Campgrounds and hostel dorms: $10-40

➡ Free activities (beach, park concerts): $0

➡ Food at markets, taquerias, sidewalk vendors: $3-12

➡ Bus, subway: $0-5

Midrange: $100-200

➡ Mom-and-pop motels, low-priced chains: $60-100

➡ Museums, national and state parks: $8-25

➡ Diners, good local restaurants: $8-35

➡ Car rental: from $33 per day, excluding insurance and gas

Top End: Over $200

➡ B&Bs, boutique hotels, resorts: from $185

➡ Meal in top restaurant: $25-75 plus wine

➡ Hiring an outdoor outfitter; top shows: from $100

➡ Rent a convertible: from $100 per day

Opening Hours

Opening hours vary throughout the year, with many attractions and visitor centers open longer hours in high season. We've provided high-season hours.

Banks 8:30am-4:30pm Monday to Thursday, to 5:30pm Friday (some 9am-noon Saturday)

Bars 5pm-midnight Sunday to Thursday, to 2am Friday & Saturday

Cafes 7:30am-8pm

Restaurants 11am-2:30pm, 5pm-9pm

Stores 10am-6pm Monday to Saturday, noon-5pm Sunday

Arriving in Western USA

Denver International Airport (DEN; p246) Ground Transportation Center is on the 5th level; buses available outside door 506 in West Terminal and door 511 in East Terminal, and cost $9 to $13 one way to Stapleton, downtown and suburbs. Taxis are around $60 to downtown Denver; shuttles to Denver area from $22.

Los Angeles International Airport (LAX; p88) Taxis from $30 to about $47 to downtown; door-to-door shuttles from $15 for shared ride; free Shuttle C to Metro Rail Green Line Station and Parking Lot C beside the LAX Transit Center; FlyAway bus to downtown LA is $7.

Seattle-Tacoma International Airport (SEA; p199) Light-rail trains run regularly from 4th floor of parking garage to downtown from 5am to 1am (fares $2 to $2.75); taxis available on 3rd floor of parking garage and cost $40 to downtown.

Getting Around

Car The best option for travelers who leave urban areas to explore national parks and more remote areas. Drive on the right.

Train Amtrak can be slow due to frequent delays, but trains are a convenient option for travel along the Pacific Coast. Cross-country routes to Chicago run from the San Francisco area and Los Angeles.

Bus Cheaper and slower than trains; can be a good option for travel to cities not serviced by Amtrak.

For much more on **getting around**, see p463

If You Like...

Geology

Grand Canyon A 277-mile river cuts through two-billion-year-old rocks, whose layered geological secrets are revealed within a mile-high stack. (p348)

Yellowstone National Park Massive geysers, rainbow-colored thermal pools and a supervolcano base – this 3472-sq-mile national park puts on a dazzling show. (p285)

Chiricahua National Monument A rugged wonderland of rock chiseled by rain and wind into pinnacles, bridges and balanced rocks. (p363)

Sand Dunes The white and chalky gypsum dunes at White Sands National Monument are mesmerizing. (p405)

Carlsbad Caverns Take a 2-mile walk along a subterranean passage to arrive in the great room – a veritable underground cathedral concealed in the massive cave system. (p407)

Volcanoes The earth's shifting crust formed powerful volcanoes in Washington, where you can hike around Mt Rainer or visit Mt St Helens to learn about its mighty 1980 eruption. (p210) (p211)

Old West Sites

The Southwest, particularly Arizona and New Mexico, is your best bet if you want to walk in the footsteps of cowboys and gunslingers at sites within a day's drive of each other.

Lincoln Billy the Kid's old stomping – and shooting – grounds during the Lincoln County War. (p406)

Tombstone Famous for the gunfight at the OK Corral, this dusty town is also home to Boothill Graveyard and the Bird Cage Theater. (p363)

Whiskey Row With sudsy aplomb, a block of Victorian-era saloons in downtown Prescott has survived fires, filmmakers and tourists. (p348)

Pony Express Stations Rte 50 across Nevada, known as the Loneliest Road, traces the route of the Pony Express; several crumbling changing stations line the highway. (p332)

Virginia City Site of the Comstock Lode silver strike, this hard-charging mining town gained notoriety in Mark Twain's semi-autobiographical book *Roughing It.* (p331)

Steam Train Channel the Old West on the steam-driven train that's chugged between Durango and Silverton for 125 years. (p279)

Film & TV Locations

Los Angeles Hollywood was born here, and today you can't throw a director's megaphone without hitting another celluloid site, from Mulholland Dr to Malibu. (p66)

Monument Valley Stride John Wayne tall beneath the iconic red monoliths that starred in seven of the Duke's beloved westerns. (p357)

Las Vegas Bad boys and their hijinks brought Sin City back to the big screen in *Ocean's Eleven* and *The Hangover.* (p314)

Moab & Around The directors of *Thelma & Louise* and *127 Hours* shot their most dramatic scenes in nearby parks. (p375)

Albuquerque Today, tax incentives lure production companies.

IF YOU LIKE...LAS VEGAS HISTORY

Get your mug shot taken and learn about Sin City's mafioso past at the new Mob Museum downtown, then stroll past iconic neon signs at the outdoor Neon Museum. (p319)

Albuquerque was the backdrop for the TV series *Breaking Bad*, and recent films shot in New Mexico include *Crazy Heart, Thor* and the Coen brothers' *True Grit*. (p384)

Fabulous Food

San Francisco An array of temptations awaits food-minded diners: real-deal taquerias and trattorias, top-notch Vietnamese, magnificent farmers markets and acclaimed chefs firing up the best of California cuisine. (p124)

Chez Panisse Chef Alice Waters revolutionized California cuisine in the '70s with seasonal Bay Area locavarian cooking. (p153)

Food Trucks LA sparked the mobile gourmet revolution, but the food truck craze has also taken hold in San Francisco and Portland. (p220)

Green Chiles The chiles grown in the town of Hatch are the pride of New Mexico. This spicy accompaniment is slathered over enchiladas, layered onto cheese-burgers and stirred into hearty stews. Try the green chile stew at Frontier in Albuquerque or test the heat at Horseman's Haven in Santa Fe. (p387) (p394)

Emerging Wine Regions

Verde Valley Wine Country Home to an up-and-coming Arizona wine trail that winds past wineries and vineyards in Cottonwood, Jerome and Cornville. (p342)

Willamette Valley Outside Portland, OR, this fertile region produces some of the tastiest Pinots Noir on the planet. (p225)

Walla Walla Washington's hot wine-growing region, with its namesake town as a very pretty centerpiece. (p212)

(Top) Monument Valley (p357), Arizona–Utah
(Bottom) Ferry Building Farmers Market (p142), San Francisco

Santa Barbara Wine Country

Large-scale winemaking has been going on here since the 1980s, and the climate is perfect for Pinots near the coast and further inland. (p111)

Hiking

Grand Canyon Rim to Rim Earn bragging rights on this classic 17-mile trek between the Grand Canyon's south and north rims. (p348)

Red Rock Country Hike to vortexes in Sedona, hoodoos in Bryce Canyon, and slender spans in Arches and Canyonlands National Parks. (p309)

Rocky Mountain National Park Longs Peak gets all the buzz but there are several loop trails best done in two or three nights; wildlife sightings are the norm here. (p259)

Wonderland Trail Circumnavigate Mt Rainier's lofty peak – it's 93 miles of spectacular nature. (p210)

Palm Springs & the Deserts Discover hidden palm-tree oases, stroll across salt flats or take a guided walk through Native American canyons. (p104)

Los Angeles Urban hiking doesn't get much better than this, with mountaintop trails overlooking the coast and a celeb-favored canyon trail near Hollywood. (p66)

National Parks

After camping in Yellowstone, Theodore Roosevelt said 'It was like lying in a great cathedral, far vaster and more beautiful than any built by the hand of man.' Similar praise could be applied to all of the great parks of the West, which are unique in their details but bound by their grandeur.

Yellowstone National Park The nation's first park is a stunner: lakes, waterfalls, mountains, wildlife galore and a cauldron of geysers and springs. (p285)

Grand Canyon National Park Two billion years of geologic history? Yeah, yeah, that's cool, but have you seen that view? (p348)

Glacier National Park Come for the glaciers, stay for the Going-to-the-Sun Road, the grand old lodges and the free-range wildlife. (p301)

Yosemite National Park Flanked by El Capitan and Half Dome, Yosemite Valley is indeed cathedral-like, but the lush Tuolomne backcountry will have you singing hallelujah, too. (p169)

Southern Utah Sorry, there's just too much red-rock goodness in Utah to narrow it down to one fave. Arches, Canyonlands, Bryce, Zion and Capitol Reef – see 'em all! (p375)

Weird Stuff

Route 66 This two-lane ode to Americana is dotted with wacky roadside attractions, especially in western Arizona. (p35)

Burning Man Festival A temporary city in the Nevada desert attracts 55,000 for a week of self-expression and blowing sand. (p328)

Roswell Did a UFO crash outside Roswell, New Mexico, in 1947? Museums and a UFO festival explore whether the truth is out there. (p407)

Seattle's Public Sculptures In Fremont, look for a car-eating troll, a human-faced dog, and some folks waiting, and waiting, for the train. (p186)

Venice Boardwalk Gawk at the human zoo, which includes chainsaw-jugglers, medical marijuana 'clinicians' and Speedo-clad snake-charmers. (p78)

Museums

Getty Center & Villa Art museums as beautiful as their ocean views in west LA and Malibu. (p76)

Los Angeles County Museum of Art More than 150,000 works of art spanning the ages and crossing all borders. (p74)

California Academy of Sciences SF's natural-history museum breathes 'green' in its ecocertified design, with a four-story rainforest and living roof. (p134)

Balboa Park Go all-day museum hopping in San Diego's favorite park where you can dive into top-notch art, history and science exhibitions. (p95)

Heard Museum Highlights the history and culture of Southwestern tribes. (p334)

Mini Time Machine Museum of Miniatures Exhibits get small at this new Tucson museum dedicated to miniatures, from doll houses to pocket dragons. (p359)

IF YOU LIKE...TO SCARE YOURSELF

Stand on the see-through panel that covers the 1910ft mining shaft at Audrey Headframe Park (p347) in Jerome, Arizona – and look down.

Roswell UFO Festival (p407), New Mexico

Historic Sites

Dinosaur National Monument OK, it may be a *prehistoric* site, but touching a 150-million-year-old fossil at one of the largest dinosaur fossil beds in North America is too cool to miss. (p374)

Mesa Verde Climb up to cliff dwellings that housed Ancestral Puebloans more than 700 years ago. (p277)

Manzanar National Historic Site WWII Japanese American internment camp interprets a painful chapter of the USA's collective past. (p176)

Little Bighorn Battlefield National Monument Native American battlefields where General George Custer made his famous 'last stand' against the Lakota Sioux. (p297)

Los Alamos The community that arose on this lonely mesa southwest of Santa Fe was top secret during WWII – a necessity for the scientists developing the atomic bomb. (p397)

Spas & Resorts

Truth or Consequences Built over hot springs adjacent to the Rio Grande, the bathtubs and pools here bubble with soothing, hydro-healing warmth. (p403)

Ten Thousand Waves The soaking tubs at this intimate Japanese spa are tucked on a woodsy hillside. (p392)

Phoenix & Scottsdale Honeymooners, families, golfers – there's a resort for every type of traveler within a few miles of Camelback Rd. (p334)

Las Vegas Encore, Bellagio, Wynn and other top hotels offer resortlike amenities. (p314)

Sheraton Wild Horse Pass Resort & Spa On the Gila Indian Reservation, this resort embraces its Native American heritage with style. (p339)

Month by Month

January

Ski resorts across the region bustle with guests. Palm Springs and southern deserts welcome travelers seeking warmer climes and saguaro-dotted landscapes.

☆ Tournament of Roses

This famous New Year's Day parade of flower-festooned floats, marching bands and prancing equestrians draws more than 100,000 spectators to Pasadena, CA, before the Rose Bowl college football game.

☆ Sundance Film Festival

Park City, UT, unfurls the red carpet for indie filmmakers, actors and moviegoers who flock to the mountain town in late January for a week of cutting-edge films.

🎭 Cowboy Poetry

Wranglers and ropers gather in Elvo, NV, for a week of poetry readings and folklore performances. Started in 1985, this event inspired cowboy poetry readings across the region.

February

It's the height of ski season, but there are plenty of distractions for those not swooshing down the slopes – low-desert wildflowers bloom, whales migrate off the California coast, and dude ranches saddle up in southern Arizona.

🎭 Carnival in Colorado

Mardi Gras meets the mountains in Breckenridge, where folks celebrate with a masquerade ball and a Fat Tuesday parade.

🎭 Tucson Gem & Mineral Show

At the largest mineral and gem show in the US, held the second full weekend in February, about 250 dealers sell jewelry, fossils, crafts and lots of rocks. Lecture seminars and a silent auction round out the weekend.

☆ Oregon Shakespeare Festival

In Ashland, tens of thousands of theater fans party with the Bard at this nine-month festival (that's right!) that kicks off in February and features world-class plays and Elizabethan drama.

🎭 Art Feast

Eat, drink and be merry while gallery hopping in Santa Fe, NM, during this weekend festival in late February, which warms up winter with fashion shows and wine tastings.

March

Ah spring, when a young man's fancy turns to thoughts of...beer! Jet skis! Parties! March is spring-break season, when hordes of college students converge on Arizona's lakes. Families ski or visit parks in warmer climes.

🏃 Spring Whale-Watching Week

Gray whales migrate along the Pacific Coast. Around Oregon's Depoe Bay, it's semi-organized, with docents and special viewpoints. Northward migration happens through June.

☆ Cactus League

Major league baseball fans head to southern Arizona in March and early April for the preseason Cactus League, when some of the best pro teams play ball in Phoenix and Tucson.

🎊 Frozen Dead Guy Days

Celebrate a cryogenically frozen town mascot, 'Grandpa Bredo,' in Nederland, CO, with a snowshoe race, a dead guy lookalike contest and copious beer drinking.

April

Migrating birds swoop into nature preserves in southern Arizona while wildflowers bloom in California's high deserts. In the mountains, it's shoulder season, meaning slightly lower room prices (except Easter weekend).

☆ Coachella Music & Arts Festival

Indie rock bands, cult DJs, superstar rappers and pop divas converge outside Palm Springs for a three-day musical extravaganza.

☆ Gathering of Nations

More than 3000 Native American dancers and singers from the US and Canada compete in this powwow in late April in Albuquerque, NM. There's also an Indian market with more than 800 artists and craftspeople.

May

Most national parks are ready for the summer crush, but with children still in school the masses don't show until Memorial Day weekend, the last weekend of the month.

🎊 Cinco de Mayo

Celebrate the victory of Mexican forces over the French army at the Battle of Puebla on May 5, 1862, with margaritas, music and merriment. Denver, Los Angeles and San Diego do it in style.

🏃 Bay to Breakers

Thousands run costumed, naked and/or clutching beer from Embarcadero to Ocean Beach in San Francisco on the third Sunday in May.

🎊 Boulder Creek Festival

Start the summer in the Rockies on Memorial Day weekend with food, drink, music, a rubber duck race and glorious sunshine. It closes with Bolder Boulder, a 10km race celebrated by screaming crowds.

June

High season begins for most of the West. Rugged passes are open, rivers are thick with snowmelt and mountain wildflowers are blooming. There may be gray fog (June gloom) over southern California beaches.

🎊 Pride Month

California's LGBTQ pride celebrations occur throughout June, with costumed parades, coming-out parties, live music and more. The biggest, bawdiest celebrations are in San Francisco and Los Angeles.

☆ Bluegrass in the Mountains

In mid-June, join 'Festivarians' for the high lonesome sounds of bluegrass in the mountain-flanked beauty of Telluride, CO.

July

Vacationers descend on beaches, theme parks, mountain resorts, and state and national parks. Broiling desert parks are best avoided.

🎊 Aspen Music Festival

From late June to mid-August, top-tier classical performers put on spectacular shows while students from orchestras led by sought-after conductors bring street corners to life with smaller groups.

🎊 Independence Day

Across the West, communities celebrate America's birth with rodeos, music festivals, parades and fireworks on July 4.

🍷 Oregon Brewers Festival

During this fun beer festival in Portland, about 80,000 microbrew lovers eat, drink and whoop it up on the banks of the Willamette River.

🎊 Comic-Con International

'Nerd Prom' is the alt-nation's biggest annual convention of comic-book geeks, sci-fi and animation lovers, and pop-culture memorabilia collectors. Held in San Diego late July.

August

Learn about Native American culture at art fairs, markets and ceremonial gatherings across the Southwest. Rodeos are popular in Colorado and Arizona.

🎊 Old Spanish Days Fiesta

A celebration of early ran-cho culture with parades, a rodeo, crafts exhibits and shows in Santa Barbara in early August.

👁 Perseids

Peaking in mid-August, these annual meteor show-ers are the best time to see shooting stars with your na-ked eye or a digital camera. For optimal viewing, head to the southern deserts.

☆ Santa Fe Indian Market

Santa Fe's most famous fes-tival is held the third week of August on the historic plaza where more than 1100 artists from 200 tribes and pueblos exhibit.

🎊 Hatch Chile Festival

On Labor Day weekend, the last weekend of the month, join 30,000 hot-pepper lov-ers in Hatch, NM, for a pa-rade, mariachi competition and chile-eating contests.

(Top) Willamette Valley (p225) winery, Oregon
(Bottom) Día de los Muertos celebrations

September

Summer's last hurrah is the Labor Day holiday weekend. It's a particularly nice time to visit the Pacific Northwest, where nights are cool and days are reliably sunny. Fall colors begin to appear in the Rockies.

☆ Burning Man

Outdoor celebration of self-expression known for elaborate art displays, an easygoing barter system, blowing sand and the final burning of the man. This temporary city rises in the Nevada desert the week before Labor Day.

♟ Great American Beer Festival

This three-day celebration of beer in Denver is so popular it always sells out in advance, with 600 US breweries getting in on the sudsy action. More than 2800 beers available.

☆ Bumbershoot

Seattle's biggest arts and cultural event hosts hundreds of musicians, artists, theater troupes and writers on two-dozen stages.

October

Shimmering aspens lure road-trippers to Colorado and northern New Mexico for the annual fall show. Watch for ghouls, ghosts and hard-partying maniacs as Halloween, on October 31, approaches.

🎈 International Balloon Fiesta

Look to the skies in early October for the world's biggest gathering of hot-air balloons in Albuquerque, NM.

🎈 Sedona Arts Festival

This fine-art show overflows with jewelry, ceramics, glass and sculptures in early October, when 125 artists exhibit their works at Sedona's Red Rock High School.

☆ Litquake

Author readings, discussions and literary events such as the legendary pub crawl in San Francisco in mid-October.

🎈 Halloween Carnival

Hundreds of thousands of costumed revelers come out to play in LA's West Hollywood LGBTQ neighborhood for all-day partying, dancing, kids' activities and live entertainment.

November

Temperatures drop across the West. Most coastal areas, deserts and parks are less busy, with the exception of the Thanksgiving holiday. Ski season begins.

🎈 Día de los Muertos

Mexican communities honor dead ancestors on November 2 with costumed parades, sugar skulls, graveyard picnics, candlelight processions and fabulous altars.

♟ Wine Country Thanksgiving

More than 150 wineries in the Willamette Valley open their doors to the public for three special days.

🎿 Yellowstone Ski Festival

Thanksgiving week celebration at West Yellowstone is a great time for ski buffs and newcomers alike. Highlights include ski clinics and gear demos. Nordic skiing kicks off around this time too.

December

'Tis the season for nativity scenes, holiday light shows and other celebrations of Christmas. The merriment continues through New Year's Eve. Expect crowds and higher prices at ski resorts.

☆ Holiday Light Displays

Communities decorate boats, parks and shopping malls with twinkling lights. In California, watch colorful boat parades in Newport Beach and San Diego, or drive past illuminated icons in LA's Griffith Park. The Desert Botanical Gardens are aglow in Phoenix, as is the Tlaquepaque Arts & Crafts Village in Sedona.

🎈 Snow Daze

Vail, CO, marks the opening of the mountain with a week-long festival featuring gear demos, parties and plenty of big-name live performances.

Itineraries

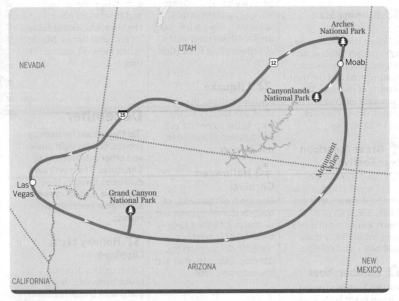

 Best of the Southwest

This tour spotlights the most iconic sites in the Southwest, looping past the region's most famous city, its biggest canyon and its most breathtaking red-rock scenery. Start in **Las Vegas** and spend a few days traveling the world on the Strip. When you've soaked up enough decadence, head east to canyon country – **Grand Canyon** country, that is. You'll want a couple of days to explore America's most famous park. For a once-in-a-lifetime experience, descend into the South Rim chasm on the back of a mule and spend the night at Phantom Ranch on the canyon floor.

From the Grand Canyon head northeast to **Monument Valley**, with scenery straight out of a Hollywood Western, to the national parks in Utah's southeast corner – they're some of the most visually stunning in the country. Hike the shape-shifting slot canyons of **Canyonlands National Park**, watch the sunset in **Arches National Park** or mountain bike slickrock outside **Moab**. Drive west on one of the most spectacular stretches of pavement, **Highway 12**, until it hooks up with I-15 and takes you back to Las Vegas.

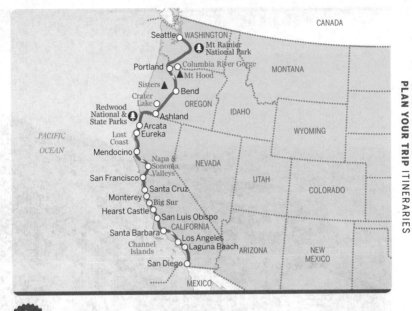

Winding Down the West Coast

3 WEEKS

Beach bums and nature lovers – this trip's for you. Kick off with fresh-roasted coffee in java-loving **Seattle** and check out the city's sprawling food markets, microbreweries and waterfront. Heading south, visit **Mt Rainier National Park**, with superb hiking and relaxing inns nestled beneath the snow-covered peak. Continue on to the cutting-edge city of **Portland**, known for its sprawling parks, eco-minded residents and progressive urbanism – plus food carts, coffeehouse culture and great nightlife. Embrace nature's bounty by driving east along the **Columbia River Gorge**, then turn south and make for **Mt Hood** for winter skiing or summer hiking. Further adventures await at the **Sisters**, a trio of 10,000ft peaks, and the striking blue waters of **Crater Lake**. Catch a Shakespearian play in sunny **Ashland**, then trade the mountains for the foggy coast. Enter California via Hwy 199 and stroll through the magnificent old-growth forests in **Redwood National and State Parks**.

Hug the coast as it meanders south through funky **Arcata** and seaside **Eureka**, lose yourself on the **Lost Coast**, and catch Hwy 1 through quaint **Mendocino**, where the scenic headlands and rugged shoreline make for a requisite wander.

For wine tasting with a photogenic backdrop, travel inland to the rolling vineyards of **Napa and Sonoma Valleys**, then continue south to romantically hilly, ever free-spirited **San Francisco**.

Return to scenic Hwy 1 through surf-loving **Santa Cruz**, stately bayfront **Monterey** and beatnik-flavored **Big Sur**. In no time, you'll reach the surreal **Hearst Castle** and laid-back, collegiate **San Luis Obispo**.

Roll into Mediterranean-esque **Santa Barbara**, and hop aboard a ferry in Ventura to the wildlife-rich **Channel Islands**. The pull from **Los Angeles** is strong. Go ahead – indulge your fantasies of Hollywood then cruise through LA's palm-lined neighborhoods. After racking up a few sins in the City of Angels, move south to wander the bluffs of **Laguna Beach**, then cruise into picture-perfect **San Diego.**

IMAGE SOURCE / GETTY IMAGES ©

Above: Big Sur (p117), California

Left: Mt Rainier National Park (p210), Washington

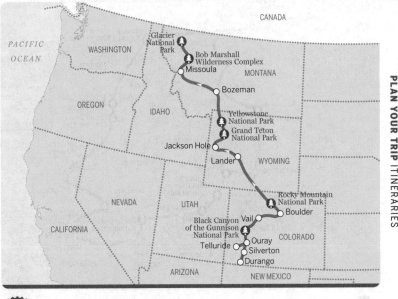

3 WEEKS Rocky Mountain High

Pack your bathing suit, mountain bike and hiking boots for this high-altitude cruise atop the Continental Divide; from here, rivers flow toward the west on one side and toward the east on the other.

Spend your first two days enjoying microbrews and single-track mountain-biking trails in **Durango**, the quintessential mountain town. From here, take the Million Dollar Hwy (Hwy 550) north through the San Juan Mountain range, sightseeing in **Silverton** and dipping into hot springs in **Ouray**. Take a side trip to **Telluride** for a festival – there's one almost every weekend in summer. From Montrose, drive east on Hwy 50, stopping at the **Black Canyon of the Gunnison National Park** to ogle the inky depths of the gorge before continuing to Hwy 24 north. Finish your first week in style with an overnight stay in ritzy **Vail**.

Enjoy kayaking, rock climbing and people-watching in high-energy **Boulder** then twist up to **Rocky Mountain National Park** to hike and horseback ride. While here, drive the thrilling Trail Ridge Rd through alpine vistas. Continue north on I-25. In Wyoming, take I-80 west to Hwy 287; follow this highway to **Lander** for rock climbing.

Continue north to **Jackson Hole**, another fun gateway town. Anchored by a central park surrounded by chic stores and cowboy bars, it's a good place to relax, catch a rodeo or spend the night before rafting the Snake River. From here, it's an easy glide north into **Grand Teton National Park**, a scenic spot for a lazy lake day and a mountain stroll. Next up is mighty **Yellowstone National Park**, where geysers, bison and hiking are highlights.

Start your last week with a drive on the gorgeous Beartooth Hwy, following it into Montana then hooking onto I-90 west to **Bozeman** and **Missoula**; both are good places to stock up before the final push. Serious nature awaits in the **Bob Marshall Wilderness Complex**, while **Glacier National Park** is a place to visit now – there are still some 25 glaciers hanging tight, but they may not be there for long. Scan for wildlife on a hike, then end with a drive on the stunning Going-to-the-Sun Road.

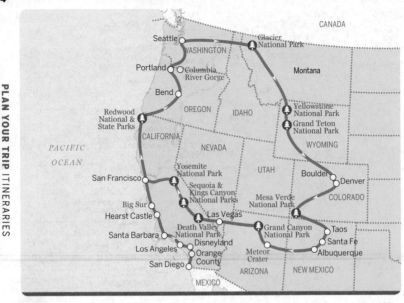

4 WEEKS Western US Grand Tour

This lasso loop takes in the highlights of the west as it rolls north along the California coast, cruises past the lush landscapes of the Pacific Northwest, the alpine villages of the Rockies and the glowing red-rock beauty of the Southwest, with a final swing back into California for a hit-parade tour of the state's national parks.

From sunny **San Diego**, follow Hwy 1 north through the surf-loving coastal villages of **Orange County**, detouring to **Disneyland** before driving into shiny **Los Angeles**. Continue up the coast on scenic Hwy 1, stopping to shop and sample wine in glossy **Santa Barbara**. Gawk at the gawdy **Hearst Castle** then continue north through woodsy **Big Sur**. Dine and shop then wander through Alcatraz in bohemian **San Francisco**. Return to Hwy 1 for the quirky towns dotting the northern California coast.

Check out the big trees in **Redwood National and State Parks** and continue into Oregon, taking time for outdoor fun in **Bend**. Soak in the greenery traveling west along the **Columbia River Gorge**, then spend a few days savoring brews and views in **Portland**. Zip up the Space Needle in **Seattle** and drive east into wide-open Montana, heading for the outdoor wonders of **Glacier National Park**. Continue south into **Yellowstone National Park** where Old Faithful still blasts regularly beside its namesake lodge. Swoosh below majestic peaks in **Grand Teton National Park** before swinging southeast through Wyoming's vast cowboy plains.

In Colorado, breathe deep in outdoorsy **Boulder** then embrace the charms of city life in bustling **Denver**. The mining towns of the San Juan Mountains are next, followed by **Mesa Verde National Park**. Just south in New Mexico, artist meccas **Taos** and **Santa Fe** are fab stops for one-of-a-kind gifts. Slurp green chile stew in **Albuquerque** and follow Route 66 west into Arizona, stopping at **Meteor Crater** before detouring north for **Grand Canyon National Park**. Continue west to **Las Vegas**, then drive into central California for **Death Valley National Park** and **Sequoia and Kings Canyon National Parks**, concluding with **Yosemite National Park**. Complete the loop with a glass of California wine in San Francisco.

Plan Your Trip

Route 66 & Scenic Drives

Silver, gold and other buried minerals drew prospectors to the West in the 19th century. Today, it's the scenic drives that consistently lure the masses. From desert backroads to coastal highways and mountain-hugging thrill rides, the West is chock-full of picturesque drives.

Route 66

'Get your kitsch on Route 66' might be a better slogan for the scrubby stretch of Mother Road running through California, Arizona and New Mexico. A wigwam motel. A meteor crater. Begging burros. And a solar-powered Ferris wheel overlooking the Pacific Ocean. It's a bit off the beaten path, but folks along the way will be very glad you're here.

Why Go

History, scenery and the open road. This alluring combination is what makes a Route 66 road trip so enjoyable. Navigators should note that I-40 and Route 66 overlap through much of New Mexico and Arizona.

In New Mexico, the neon signs of Tucumcari are a fun-loving welcome to the West. They also set the mood for adventure – the appropriate mood to have before dropping into the scuba-ready Blue Hole in Santa Rosa. Fuel up on lip-smacking green chile stew at Frontier in Albuquerque then grab a snooze at the 1937 El Rancho Motel (John Wayne slept here!) in Gallup.

In Arizona, swoop off the highway for a grand drive through Petrifed Forest National Park. First up? Sweeping views of the Painted Desert. Trade panoramas

Road-Trip Necessities

A prepared road-tripper is a happy road-tripper, especially in the West, with its lonely roads and unpredictable weather.

Make sure you have a spare tire and tool kit (eg jack, jumper cables, ice scraper), as well as emergency equipment in your vehicle; if you're renting a car, consider buying a roadside safety kit.

Bring good maps, especially if you're touring away from highways; don't depend on GPS units as they may not work in remote areas.

Carry extra water. You may need it if the car breaks down in the desert.

Fill up the tank regularly; gas stations can be few and far between in the West.

Always carry your driver's license and proof of insurance.

Best Roadside Dining

Turquoise Room, Route 66, Winslow, AZ

Hell's Backbone Grill, Hwy 12, Boulder, UT

Asylum Resturant, Hwy 89/89A, Jerome, AZ

Frontier, Route 66, Albuquerque, NM

Santa Barbara Shellfish Co, Pacific Coast Highway, Santa Barbara, CA

for close-up views in the southern section of the park, where fossilized 225-million-year-old logs are clustered just off the main park road. Spend the night in a concrete tipi in Holbrook, west of the park. Next stop is the 'Take It Easy' town of Winslow where there's a girl, my Lord, in a flatbed Ford... Snap a photo of the famous corner then savor a spectacular dinner in the Turquoise Room at La Posada Hotel. Meteor Crater, east of Flagstaff, is a mighty big hole in the ground – and a good place to slow down and catch your breath. From here, Route 66 parallels the train tracks into energetic Flagstaff, passing the wonderful Museum Club, a cabin-like roadhouse where everyone's having fun or is about to. Next up is Williams, a railroad town lined with courtyard motels and brimming with small-town charm.

Seligman is a quirky little village that greets travelers with retro motels, a roadkill cafe and a squirt of fake mustard at the Snow-Cap Drive In. Burma Shave signs share funny advice on the way to Grand Canyon Caverns, where you'll be lured 21 stories underground for a tour or possibly an overnight stay. From here, highlights include an eclectic general store in Hackberry, the Route 66 museum in Kingman and hay-loving burros in sun-baked Oatman.

Things stay sun-baked in California as the Mother Road swoops into the Mojave Desert and passes ghost towns heralded by lonesome railroad markers. In Victorville, the Brian Burger comes with a spicy kick at Emma Jean's Holland Burger Café. The vibe kicks up in stylish Pasadena before the road's final push to the Pacific. At the Santa Monica Pier, hop on the solar-powered Ferris wheel and celebrate your journey with a panoramic sunset view.

When to Go

The best time to travel Route 66 is from May to September, when the weather is warm and you'll be able to take advantage of more open-air activities.

The Route

This journey starts in Tucumcari, NM, then continues west through Arizona and California, roughly paralleling I-40 all the way to Barstow, CA. After Barstow, Route 66 south passes through San Bernardino on the I-15 before cutting west and heading into Pasadena. Follow I-110 to Santa Monica Blvd west to seaside Santa Monica.

Time & Mileage

➡ Time: You might be able to do this trip in two or three days if you rush, but plan for six and enjoy the drive

➡ Mileage: About 1250 miles, depending on segments driven

Pacific Coast Highway

Lovers, ramblers and bohemians, start your engines. The highways connecting Canada to Mexico on the West Coast were made for driving, including the especially scenic Pacific Coast Highway (PCH).

Why Go

This epic West Coast journey, which rolls through California, Oregon and Washington, takes in cosmopolitan cities, surf towns and charming coastal enclaves ripe for exploration. For many travelers, the

HISTORY OF ROUTE 66

Built in 1926, Route 66 stretched from Chicago to Los Angeles, linking a ribbon of small towns and country byways as it rolled across eight states. The road gained notoriety during the Great Depression, when migrant farmers followed it west from the Dust Bowl across the Great Plains. The nickname 'The Mother Road' first appeared in John Steinbeck's novel about the era, *The Grapes of Wrath*. Things got a little more fun after WWII, when newfound prosperity prompted Americans to get behind the wheel and explore, but just as things got going, the Feds rolled out the interstate system, which eventually caused the Mother Road's demise. The very last town on Route 66 to be bypassed by an interstate was Arizona's very own Williams, in 1984.

Scenic Drives

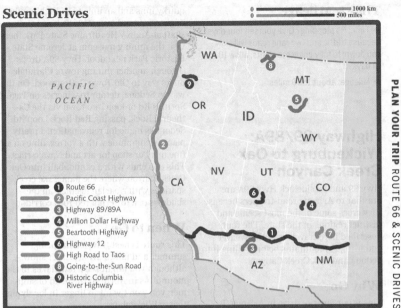

0 — 1000 km
0 — 500 miles

WA

MT

OR

ID

WY

NV

UT

CO

CA

AZ

NM

PACIFIC OCEAN

1 Route 66
2 Pacific Coast Highway
3 Highway 89/89A
4 Million Dollar Highway
5 Beartooth Highway
6 Highway 12
7 High Road to Taos
8 Going-to-the-Sun Road
9 Historic Columbia River Highway

biggest draw is the magnificent scenery: wild and remote beaches, cliff-top views overlooking crashing waves, rolling hills, and lush forests thick with redwoods and eucalyptus trees. But the route is not loved only for its looks. It's also got personality, offering beside-the-highway adventures for surfers, kayakers, scuba divers and hikers.

Highlights? Let's start with the cities. Coastal highways connect the dots between some of the West Coast's most striking municipalities, starting with surf-loving San Diego in Southern California and moving north through hedonistic Los Angeles and offbeat San Francisco. Way up north, take a worthwhile detour to artsy and alternative-minded Seattle, Washington.

If you want to bypass urban areas, it's easy to stick to the places in between. In southern California, PCH rolls past the almost-too-perfect beaches of California's Orange County ('the OC') and Santa Barbara (the 'American Riviera'). Further north, Hwy 1 passes wacky Santa Cruz (a university town and surfers' paradise), then redwood forests along the Big Sur coast and north of Mendocino. Hwy 1 cruises past the sand dunes, seaside resorts and fishing villages of coastal

Oregon; and finally, the wild lands of Washington's Olympic Peninsula, with its primeval rainforest and bucolic San Juan Islands, served by coastal ferries.

When to Go

There's no bad time of year to drive the route, although northern climes will be rainier and snowier during winter. Peak travel season is June through August, which isn't always the best time as many stretches of the coast are socked in by fog during early summer (locals call it 'June Gloom'). The shoulder seasons before Memorial Day (ie April and May) and after Labor Day (ie September and October) can be ideal, with sunny days, crisply cool nights and fewer crowds.

The Route

Highways stretch nearly 1500 miles from border to border – that is, from Tijuana, Mexico, to British Columbia, Canada. In California, the coastal route jumps between I-5, Hwy 101 and Hwy 1 (when in doubt, just hug the coast) before committing to Hwy 101 in Oregon and Washington.

Time & Mileage

➡ Time: No stopping? Give yourself four days because traffic and two-lane roads will slow you down; to fully enjoy the sights, allow 10 to 14 days

➡ Mileage: About 1500 miles

Highway 89/89A: Wickenburg to Oak Creek Canyon

Hwy 89 and its sidekick Hwy 89A are familiar to Arizona road-trippers because they cross some of the most scenic and distinct regions in the state. The route described here travels over the Weaver and Mingus mountains before rolling into Sedona and Oak Creek Canyon.

Why Go

This is our favorite drive in Arizona. It may not be the prettiest or the wildest, but there's a palpable sense of the Old West infusing the trip, like you've slipped through the swinging doors of history. But the route's not stuck in the 19th century. Far from it. Weekend art walks, a burgeoning wine trail, stylish indie-owned shops and restaurants all add some 21st-century sparkle. For those interested in cowboy history, Wickenburg and its dude ranches are a good place to spend some time. Hwy 89 leaves town via Hwy 93 and soon tackles the Weaver Mountains, climbing 2500ft in 4 miles. The road levels out at mountain-topping Yarnell, site of a devastating fire in the summer of 2013, then passes grassy buttes and grazing cattle in the Peeples Valley. From here, one highlight is Prescott's infamous Whiskey Row, home of the historic Palace Saloon. Thumb Butte is a hard-to-miss landmark west of downtown, and you'll pass the unusual boulders of Granite Dells on your way out of town.

Follow Hwy 89A to Jerome and hold on tight. This serpentine section of road brooks no distraction, clinging tight to the side of Mingus Mountain. If you dare, glance east for stunning views of the Verde Valley. The zigzagging reaches epic proportions in Jerome, a former mining town cleaved into the side of Cleopatra Hill. Pull over for art galleries, tasting rooms,

quirky inns and an unusually high number of ghosts. Stand over a 1910ft-long mining shaft at Audrey Headframe State Park then visit the mining museum at Jerome State Historic Park next door. Hwy 89A drops through another mining town, Clarkdale, on its way to Old Town Cottonwood. On the way to Sedona, detour to wineries on Page Springs Rd or loop into town via the Cathedral Rock, passing Red Rock Loop Rd. Sedona is made for rejuvenation, a pretty place to commune with a vortex, dine on a fine meal or shop for art and Navajo rugs. This trip ends with a cannonball into Oak Creek Canyon where the namesake creek sparkles with riparian lushness in the shadows of a towering red-rock corridor.

When to Go

This route is best traveled in spring, summer and fall to avoid winter snow – although you might see a few flakes in the mountains in April! In the dead of summer, you won't want to linger in low-lying, toasty Wickenburg.

The Route

From Wickenburg, follow Hwy 93 to Hwy 89 then drive north to Prescott. North of town, pick up Hwy 89A, following it to Sedona.

Time & Mileage

➡ Time: This route can be driven in a half-day, but we recommend two to three days for maximum enjoyment

➡ Mileage: 134 miles

Million Dollar Highway

Stretching between Ouray and Silverton in southern Colorado is one of the most gorgeous alpine drives in the US. Part of the 236-mile San Juan Skyway, this section of US 550 is known as the Million Dollar Highway because the road, they say, is filled with ore.

Why Go

Twenty-five miles of smooth, buttery pavement twists over three mountain passes, serving up views of Victorian homes, snow-capped peaks, mineshaft headframes

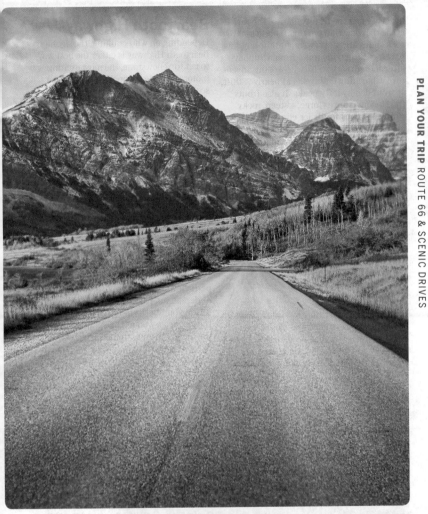

Above: Going-to-the-Sun Road, Glacier National Park (p301), Montana

Right: Route 66, Williams (p345), Arizona

KEVIN T LEVESQUE / GETTY IMAGES ©

and a gorge lined with rock. But the allure isn't just the beauty. Part of the thrill is the driving. Hairpin turns, occasional rock slides and narrow, mountain-hugging pavement flips this route from a Sunday-afternoon drive to a Nascar-worthy adventure. Charming Ouray sits at nearly 7800ft, surrounded by lofty peaks. It also fronts the Uncompahgre Gorge, a steep, rocky canyon famous for its ice climbing. While here, take a hike or soak in the town's hot springs. From Ouray, the Million Dollar Highway – completed in 1884 after three years of construction – hugs the side of the gorge, twisting past old mines that pock the mountainsides. Stay vigilant for the masochistic, spandex-clad cyclists pumping over the passes on the ribbon-thin road. In Silverton, step away from the car and enjoy the aspen-covered mountains or watch the steam-powered Durango & Silverton Narrow Gauge Railroad chug into town.

When to Go

Summer is the best time to visit. In winter, the highest pass sometimes closes and at other times you may need chains. You might even see snow on the ground in summer, though it likely won't be on the road.

The Route

From Ouray, follow Hwy 550 south to Silverton.

Time & Mileage

➡ Time: The drive can be done in a few hours, but give yourself a day to see the sights

➡ Mileage: 25 miles

Detour

The drive between Ouray and Telluride is 50 miles – if you take the paved route. If you're feeling adventurous (and have the right vehicle), consider the 16-mile road over Imogene Pass. On this old mining road you'll cross streams, alpine meadows and one of the state's highest passes. You'll also drive past an old mine. We should mention one thing: this 'short cut' takes three hours. Still game?

Beartooth Highway

Depending on who's talking, the sky-high Beartooth Highway is either the best way to get to Yellowstone, the most exciting motorcycle ride in the West or the most scenic highway in America. We'd say it was all three.

Why Go

Sometimes you just want to find a place so inspirational and beautiful that it'll make you pull over, leave your car, beat your chest (or shake out your hair) and yell 'Yeah!' In the West, that place is the Beartooth Highway.

From Red Lodge, Montana, this adventurous drive ascends Rock Creek Canyon's glaciated valley via a series of spaghetti-loop switchbacks, gaining an amazing 5000ft in elevation in just a few miles. Pull off at Rock Creek Vista Point Overlook for a short, wheelchair-accessible walk to superb views. The road continues up onto the high plateau, past 'Mae West Curve' and into Wyoming. Twin Lakes has views of the cirque as well as the ski lift that carries the daring to an extreme spring ski run. After a series of switchbacks, look northwest for the Hellroaring Plateau and the jagged Bears Tooth (11,612ft). The route, flanked by alpine tundra, crests at the Beartooth Pass West Summit, the highest point at 10,947ft. Fifteen-foot snowbanks may linger here as late as June (sometimes even July).

After passing more lakes, the road descends past Beartooth Butte, a huge lump of the sedimentary rock that once covered the Beartooths. The highway drops to several excellent fishing areas on the Clarks Fork, then re-enters Montana, reaching Cooke City via Colter Pass (8066ft). Yellowstone's northeast entrance is 4 miles from Cooke City.

When to Go

If you'd like to add some hiking to your driving, come in August. That's when the weather's typically the best for outdoor adventure.

The Route

From Red Lodge, follow Hwy 212 west – crossing into and out of Wyoming – to Cooke City, MT.

Time & Mileage

➡ Time: It's hard to zip through the twisty Beartooth Highway; allow at least an afternoon or morning to drive it

➡ Mileage: 68 miles

Highway 12

Arguably Utah's most diverse and stunning route, Hwy 12 winds through a remote and rugged canyon land, linking several national and state parks – and a few fantastic restaurants – in the state's red-rock center.

Why Go

With its mesmerizing mix of crimson canyons, sprawling deserts, thick forests and lofty peaks, Hwy 12 in remote southern Utah works well for adventurous explorers. The trip kicks off at Bryce Canyon National Park where the eye-catching gold-and-crimson spires set the stage for the color-infused journey to come.

Traveling east, the first highlight is Kodachrome Basin State Park, home to petrified geysers and dozens of red, pink and white sandstone chimneys – some nearly 170ft tall. Pass through tiny Escalante and then, 8 miles down the road, pull over for the view at Head of the Rocks Overlook, atop the Aquarius Plateau. From here you'll lord over giant mesas, towering domes, deep canyons and undulating slickrock, all unfurling in an explosion of color.

GOING-TO-THE-SUN ROAD: A LEGEND AND A LANDMARK

Going-to-the-Sun Road was named after Going-to-the-Sun Mountain. According to legend – or a story concocted in the 1880s – a deity of the Blackfeet Tribe once taught tribal members to hunt. After the lesson, he left an image of himself on the mountain as inspiration before he ascended to the sun. Today, the road is a National Historic Landmark and a National Civil Engineering Landmark, the only road in the country to hold both designations.

The adjacent Grand Staircase-Escalante National Monument is the largest park in the Southwest at nearly 1.9 million acres. The Lower Calf Creek Recreation Area, inside the park and beside Hwy 12, holds a picnic area and a pleasant campground. It's also the start of a popular 6-mile round-trip hike to the impressive 126ft Lower Calf Creek Falls. The razor-thin Hogback Ridge, between Escalante and Boulder, is pretty stunning, too.

The best section of the drive? Many consider it to be the switchbacks and petrified sand dunes between Boulder and Torrey. But it's not just about the views. In Boulder, treat your taste buds to a locally sourced meal at Hell's Backbone Grill, followed by homemade cookies and cakes at the Burr Trail Grill & Outpost, or enjoy a flavor-packed Southwestern dish at Cafe Diablo further north in Torrey.

When to Go

For the best weather and driving conditions – especially over 11,000ft Boulder Mountain – drive Hwy 12 between May and October.

The Route

From US Hwy 89 in Utah, follow Hwy 12 east to Bryce Canyon National Park. The road takes a northerly turn at Kodachrome Basin State Park then continues to Torrey.

Time & Mileage

➡ Time: Although the route could be driven in a few hours, two to three days will allow for a bit of exploration

➡ Mileage: 124 miles

High Road to Taos

This picturesque byway in northern New Mexico links Santa Fe to Taos, rippling through a series of adobe villages and mountain-flanked vistas in and around the Truchas Peaks.

Why Go

Santa Fe and Taos are well-known artists' communities, lovely places brimming with galleries, studios and museums. Two cities this stunning should be linked by an aesthetically pleasing byway, and the mountainous High Road to Taos obliges.

From Santa Fe follow Hwy 84/285 north. Exit onto Hwy 503 toward Nambe, where you can hike to waterfalls or simply meditate by the namesake lake. From here, the road leads north to picturesque Chimayo. Abandoned crutches line the wall in the Santuario de Chimayo, also known as 'The Lourdes of America.' In 1816 this two-towered adobe chapel was built over a spot said to have miraculous healing powers. Take some time to wander through the community, and admire the fine weaving and woodcarving in family-run galleries. Near Truchas, a village of galleries and century-old adobes, you'll find the High Road Marketplace. This co-operative on SR 676 sells a variety of artworks by area artists. Original paintings and carvings remain in good condition up Hwy 76 inside the Church of San José de Gracia, considered one of the finest surviving 18th-century churches in the USA.

Next is Picuris Pueblo, once one of the most powerful pueblos in the region. This ride ends at Penasco, a gateway to the Pecos Wilderness, which is also home to the engagingly experimental Penasco Theatre. From here, follow Hwys 75 and 518 into Taos.

When to Go

The high season is summer, but spring can be a nice time to see blooming flowers. Fall presents a show of colorful leaves. With mountains on the route, winter is not the best time to visit.

The Route

From Santa Fe, take 84/285 west to Pojoaque and turn right on Hwy 503, toward Nambe. From Hwy 503, take Hwy 76 to Hwy 75, then drive into Taos on Hwy 518.

Time & Mileage

➡ Time: Without stopping, this drive should take about a half day, but give yourself a full day if you want to shop and explore

➡ Mileage: 85 miles

Going-to-the-Sun Road

A strong contender for the most spectacular drive in America, the 53-mile Going-to-the-Sun Road is the only paved road through Glacier National Park in Montana.

Why Go

Glaciers! Grizzlies! A mountain-hugging marvel of modern engineering! Yep, the Going-to-the-Sun Road inspires superlatives and exclamation points. But the accolades are deserved. The road, completed in 1933, crosses a ruggedly beautiful alpine landscape, twisting and turning over a lofty Continental Divide that's usually blanketed in snow. From the park's west entrance, the road skirts the shimmering Lake McDonald. Ahead, the looming Garden Wall forms the 9000ft spine of the Continental Divide and separates the west side of the park from the east side. The road crosses the divide at Logan Pass (6880ft). From here, the 18.5-mile Highline Trail traces the park's mountainous backbone, with views of glaciated valleys, sawtooth peaks, wildflowers and wildlife. Oh, and the wildlife you might see? Mountain goats. Bighorn sheep. Moose. Maybe even a grizzly bear or an elusive wolverine. But save a few shots on your camera. After Logan Pass, the road passes Jackson Glacier Overlook, where you can bear witness to one of the park's melting monoliths. Experts say that at current global temperatures, all of the park's glaciers will be gone by 2020, so now is the time to visit.

When to Go

This snow-attracting route opens late and closes early, typically drivable between mid-June and mid-September. In 2011, due to an unusually heavy snowpack, the road didn't completely open until July 13.

The Route

From the west entrance of Glacier National Park, follow the Going-to-the-Sun Road east to St Mary.

Time & Mileage

➡ Time: It varies depending on conditions, but plan to spend at least a half-day on the drive

➡ Mileage: 53 miles

MORE SCENIC DRIVES

Hungry for more road trips? Here are a few more good ones.

Turquoise Trail, NM This back route between Tijeras, near Albuquerque, and Santa Fe, was a major trade route for several thousand years. Today it rolls past art galleries, shops (with turquoise jewelry) and a mining museum. From I-40, follow Hwy 14 north to I-25. Also see www.turquoisetrail.org.

Apache Trail, AZ This isn't your grandmother's Sunday-afternoon drive – unless your grandmother likes 45 miles of rabid road. From Apache Junction east of Phoenix, follow Hwy 88 past a kid-friendly ghost town, the wildflowers of Lost Dutchman State Park and three Salt River lakes. In the middle of it all? A snarling dirt section that drops 1000-plus feet in less than 3 miles. Hold tight!

Eastern Sierra Scenic Byway, CA From Topaz Lake, follow Hwy 395 south along the eastern flank of the mighty Sierra Nevada, ending at Little Lake. The region holds 14,000ft peaks, ice-blue lakes, pine forests, desert basins and hot springs.

Billy the Kid Highway, NM Named for the controversial outlaw famous for his role in the Lincoln County War, this lofty route loops through the mountains of central New Mexico. The road passes through the town of Lincoln, where Billy the Kid once shot his way out of the jail, and Capitan, site of the grave of Smokey the Bear.

Historic Columbia River Highway

Lush foliage and trailblazing history are highlights on US 30, a carefully planned byway that ribbons alongside the Columbia River Gorge east of Portland, Oregon.

Why Go

Look, there's a waterfall. And another waterfall. And another. Just how many waterfalls can one scenic highway hold? Quite a few if that road is the Historic Columbia River Hwy. The original route – completed in 1922 – connected Portland to the Dalles. The first paved road in the Pacific Northwest, it was carefully planned, built with the pleasure of driving in mind rather than speed. Viewpoints were carefully selected, and the stone walls and arching bridges stylishly complement the gorgeous scenery. Also notable is the history. Lewis and Clark traveled this route as they pushed toward the Pacific Ocean in 1805. Fifty years later, Oregon Trail pioneers ended their cross-country trek with a harrowing final push through the gorge's treacherous waters. Today, although sections of the original byway have been closed, or replaced by US 84, much of US 30 is still open for driving and some closed portions can be traversed by hiking or cycling. One roadside highlight is the Portland Women's Forum Park, which provides one of the best views of the gorge. Nearby, the 1916 Vista House, built to honor the Oregon Trail pioneers, now holds a visitor center. It's perched on Crown Point, a good viewpoint that also marks the western edge of the gorge. And those gushing cascades? For oohs and ahhs, don't miss Multnomah Falls, Oregon's tallest waterfall at 642ft.

When to Go

Waterfalls are at their peak February to May, while summer is great for hiking.

The Route

To reach the historic highway, take exit 17 or 35 off I-84 east of Portland and continue east. The western section of the original highway ends at Multnomah Falls. From here hop onto I-84 and continue east to exit 69 at Mosier where you can return to Hwy 30.

Time & Mileage

➡ Time: One day
➡ Mileage: 100 miles

Plan Your Trip

Western USA Outdoors

Adventure lovers, welcome to paradise. Whether you're a couch potato, a weekend warrior or an ironman (or maiden), the West has an outdoor activity for you. The best part? Your adventure will likely be accompanied by a stunning backdrop. Float on an inner tube, scan for hummingbirds, bounce over slickrock trails, swoosh down powdery slopes, surf curling waves or hike into the world's most famous canyon.

Ultimate Outdoor Experiences

Rafting the Colorado River through the Grand Canyon, AZ

Hiking the summit of Half Dome, Yosemite National Park, CA

Cycling Maroon Bells, Aspen, CO

Rock climbing in Joshua Tree National Park, CA

Scrambling at Angels Landing, Zion National Park, UT

Splashing in Havasu Falls, AZ

Skiing at Vail, CO

Touching a glacier, Glacier National Park, MT

Best Wildlife Watching

Bears: Glacier National Park, MT

Elk, bison and gray wolves: Yellowstone National Park, WY

Birds: Patagonia-Sonoita Creek Preserve, AZ

Whales and dolphins: Monterey Bay, CA

Camping

Campers are absolutely spoiled for choice in the West. Pitch a tent beside alpine lakes and streams in Colorado, sleep under saguaro cacti in southern Arizona or snooze on gorgeous strands of California sand.

Campground Types & Amenities

Primitive campsites Usually have fire pits, picnic tables and access to drinking water and vault toilets; most common in national forests (USFS) and on Bureau of Land Management (BLM) land.

Developed campgrounds Typically found in state and national parks, with more amenities, including flush toilets, barbecue grills and occasionally hot showers and a coin-op laundry.

RV (recreational vehicle) hookups and dump stations Available at many privately owned campgrounds, but only a few public-lands campgrounds.

Private campgrounds Cater mainly to RVers and offer hot showers, swimming pools, wi-fi and family camping cabins; tent sites may be few and uninviting.

WESTERN US NATIONAL PARKS

PARK	FEATURES	ACTIVITIES	BEST TIME
Arches	more than 2500 sandstone arches	scenic drives, day hikes	spring–fall
Bryce Canyon	brilliantly colored, eroded hoodoos	day and backcountry hikes, horseback riding	spring–fall
Canyonlands	epic Southwestern canyons, mesas and buttes	scenic viewpoints, back-country hikes, white-water rafting	spring–fall
Carlsbad Caverns	extensive underground cave system; free-tail bat colony	cave tours, backcountry hikes	spring–fall
Death Valley	hot, dramatic desert and unique ecology	scenic drives, day hikes	spring
Glacier	impressive glaciated landscape; mountain goats	day and backcountry hikes, scenic drives	summer
Grand Canyon	spectacular 277-mile-long, 1-mile-deep river canyon	day and backcountry hikes, mule trips, river running	spring–fall
Grand Teton	towering granite peaks; moose, bison, wolves	day and backcountry hikes, rock climbing, fishing	spring–fall
Sequoia & Kings Canyon	sequoia redwood groves, granite canyon	day and backcountry hikes, cross-country skiing	summer–fall
Mesa Verde	preserved Ancestral Puebloan cliff dwellings, historic sites, mesas and canyons	short hikes	spring–fall
Olympic	temperate rainforests, alpine meadows, Mt Olympus	day and backcountry hikes	spring–fall
Petrified Forest	fossilized trees, petroglyphs, Painted Desert scenery	day hikes	spring–fall
Redwood	virgin redwood forest, world's tallest trees; elk	day and backcountry hikes	spring–fall
Rocky Mountain	stunning peaks, alpine tundra, the Continental Divide; elk, bighorn sheep, moose, beavers	day and backcountry hikes, cross-country skiing	summer–fall
Saguaro	giant saguaro cactus, desert scenery	day and backcountry hikes	spring–fall
Yellowstone	geysers and geothermal pools, impressive canyon; prolific wildlife	day and backcountry hikes, cycling, cross-country skiing	year-round
Yosemite	sheer granite-walled valley, waterfalls, alpine meadows	day and backcountry hikes, rock climbing, skiing	year-round
Zion	immense red-rock canyon, Virgin River	day and backcountry hikes, canyoneering	spring–fall

Walk-in (environmental) sites Providing more peace and privacy; a few public-lands campgrounds reserve these for long-distance hikers and cyclists.

Rates & Reservations

Many public and private campgrounds accept reservations for all or some of their sites, while a few are strictly first-come, first-served. Overnight rates range from free for the most primitive campsites to $50 or more for pull-through RV sites with full hookups.

These agencies let you search for campground locations and amenities; check availability and reserve campsites online:

Recreation.gov (www.recreation.gov) Camping and cabin reservations for national parks, national forests, BLM land etc.

ReserveAmerica (www.reserveamerica.com) Reservations for state parks, regional parks and some private campgrounds across North America. See website for phone numbers by state.

Kampgrounds of America (KOA; ☑406-248-7444; www.koa.com) National chain of reliable but more expensive private campgrounds offering full facilities, including for RVs.

Hiking & Trekking

Good hiking trails are abundant in the West. Fitness is a priority throughout the region, and most metropolitan areas have at least one large park with trails. National parks and monuments are ideal for both short and long hikes. If you're hankering for nights in the wilderness beneath star-filled skies, however, plan on securing a backcountry permit in advance, especially in places like the Grand Canyon – spaces are limited, particularly during summer.

Hiking Resources

Wilderness Survival, by Gregory Davenport, is easily the best book on surviving nearly every contingency. Useful websites:

American Hiking Society (www.americanhiking. org) Links to local hiking clubs and 'volunteer vacations' building trails.

TOP TRAILS IN THE WEST

Ask 10 people for their top trail recommendations throughout the West and no two answers will be alike. The country is so varied and distances so enormous, there's little consensus. That said, you can't go wrong with the following all-star sampler.

South Kaibab/North Kaibab Trail, Grand Canyon, AZ (☑928-878-9378, 877-716-9378; www.destinationgrandcanyon.com; tours per person $50-350) A multiday cross-canyon tramp down to the Colorado River and back up to the rim.

Longs Peak Trail, Rocky Mountain National Park, CO (p259) Very popular 15-mile round-trip hike leads to the bouldery summit of Longs Peak (14,259ft) and its views of snow-capped summits.

Angels Landing, Zion National Park, UT (p382) After a heart-pounding scramble over a narrow, precipice-flanked strip of rock, the reward is a sweeping view of Zion Canyon. It's a 5-mile round-trip hike.

Mt Washburn Trail, Yellowstone National Park, WY (p288) From Dunraven Pass, this wildflower-lined trail climbs 3 miles to expansive views from the summit of Mt Washburn (10,243ft). Look for bighorn sheep.

Pacific Crest Trail (PCT; www.pcta.org) Follows the spines of the Cascades and Sierra Nevada, traipsing 2650 miles from Canada to Mexico, passing through six of North America's seven ecozones.

Half Dome, Yosemite National Park, CA (p169) Scary and strenuous, but the Yosemite Valley views and sense of accomplishment are worth it.

Enchanted Valley Trail, Olympic National Park, WA (p201) Magnificent mountain views, roaming wildlife and lush rainforests – all on a 13-mile out-and-back trail.

Great Northern Traverse, Glacier National Park, MT (www.nps.gov/glac) A 58-mile haul that cuts through the heart of grizzly country and crosses the Continental Divide.

The Big Loop, Chiricahua National Monument, AZ (p363) A 9.5-mile hike along several trails that winds past an 'army' of wondrous rock pillars in southeastern Arizona once used as a hideout by Apache warriors.

Tahoe Rim Trail, Lake Tahoe, CA (p177) This 165-mile all-purpose trail circumnavigates the lake from high above, affording glistening Sierra views.

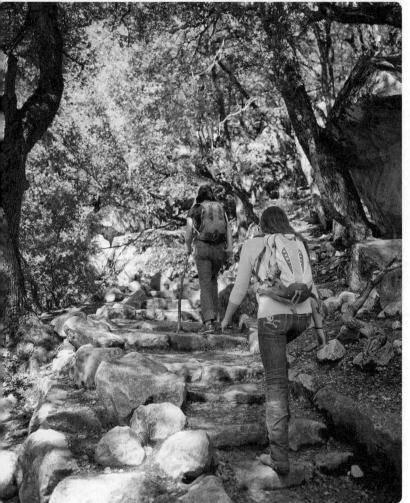

Above: Hiking to
Yosemite Falls,
Yosemite National Park
(p169), California

Right: Rock climbing,
Joshua Tree National
Park (p106), California

PANORAMIC IMAGES / GETTY IMAGES ©

Backpacker (www.backpacker.com) Premier national magazine for backpackers, from novices to experts.

Rails-to-Trails Conservancy (www.railstotrails. org) Converts abandoned railroad corridors into hiking and biking trails; publishes free trail reviews at www.traillink.com.

Survive Outdoors (http://www.surviveoutdoors. com) Dispenses safety and first-aid tips, plus helpful photos of dangerous critters.

Fees & Wilderness Permits

➡ State parks typically charge a daily entrance fee of $5 to $15; there's often a reduced fee, or no charge, if you walk or bike into these parks.

➡ National park entry averages $10 to $25 per vehicle for seven consecutive days; some national parks are free.

➡ For unlimited admission to national parks, national forests and other federal recreation lands for one year, buy an 'America the Beautiful' pass ($80).

➡ Often required for overnight backpackers and extended day hikes, wilderness permits are issued at ranger stations and park visitor centers. Daily quotas may be in effect during peak periods, usually late spring through early fall.

➡ Some wilderness permits may be reserved ahead of time, and very popular trails (eg Half Dome, Mt Whitney) may sell out several months in advance.

➡ You'll need a **National Forest Adventure Pass** ($5 per day, $30 per year) to park in some of southern California's national forests. To hike in the forest surrounding Sedona, AZ, you'll need to buy a **Red Rock Pass** (www. redrockcountry.org; $5/15 per day/week). Passes can be purchased at USFS ranger stations, kiosks (at some trailheads) and select local vendors.

Cycling

The popularity of cycling is growing by the day in the USA, with cities adding more cycle lanes and becoming more bike-friendly. An increasing number of greenways dot the countryside. You'll find diehard

---

MAD FOR MOUNTAIN BIKING

Mountain-biking enthusiasts will find trail nirvana in Boulder, CO, Moab, UT, Bend, OR, Ketchum, ID and Marin, CA, the latter being where Gary Fisher and Co bunny-hopped the sport forward by careening down the rocky flanks of Mt Tamalpais on home-rigged bikes. Other great destinations include the following:

Kokopelli's Trail, UT (http://www.blm.gov/ut/st/en/fo/moab/recreation/moun-tain_bike_trails/kokopelli_s_trail.html) One of the premier mountain-biking trails in the Southwest stretches 140 miles on mountainous terrain between Loma, CO, and Moab, UT. Other nearby options include the 206-mile, hut-to-hut ride between Tel-luride, CO, and Moab, UT, and the shorter but very challenging 38-mile ride from Aspen to Crested Butte – an equally stunning route.

Sun Top Loop, WA (www.visitrainier.com) A 22-mile ride with challenging climbs and superb views of Mt Rainier and surrounding peaks on the western slopes of Wash-ington's Cascade Mountains.

Downieville Downhill, Downieville, CA (www.sierracountychamber.com) Not for the faint of heart, this piney trail, located near its namesake Sierra foothill town in Tahoe National Forest, skirts river-hugging cliffs, passes through old-growth forest and drops 4200ft in under 14 miles.

McKenzie River Trail, Willamette National Forest, OR (www.fs.usda.gov/activity/willamette/recreation, www.mckenzierivertrail.com) Twenty-five miles of blissful single-track winding through deep forests and volcanic formations. The town of McKenzie is about 50 miles east of Eugene.

Porcupine Rim, Moab, UT (www.blm.gov/ut) A 30-mile loop from town, this vener-able high-desert romp features stunning views and hairy downhills. Difficult trail. Be prepared and bring lots of water.

enthusiasts in every town, and numerous outfitters offer guided trips for all levels and durations.

Many states offer social multiday rides, such as Ride the Rockies in Colorado. For a fee, you can join the peloton on a scenic, well-supported route; your gear is ferried ahead to that night's camping spot. Another standout ride is Arizona's Mt Lemmon, a thigh-zinging 28-mile climb from the Sonoran Desert floor to the 9157ft summit. You can also rent bikes on the South Rim of the Grand Canyon at Grand Canyon National Park. Ride to Hermit's Rest on the park's Hermit Rd and the ever-lengthening Greenway Trail.

Top Cycling Towns

San Francisco, CA A pedal over the Golden Gate Bridge lands you in the stunningly beautiful, and stunningly hilly, Marin Headlands.

Boulder, CO Outdoors-loving town with loads of great biking paths, including the 16-mile Boulder Creek Trail.

Portland, OR A trove of great cycling (on- and off-road) in the Pacific Northwest.

Los Angeles, CA Cycling on the surface streets isn't great, but the sunny South Bay Trail is a scenic, level bike path, running the length of the coast between Santa Monica and Redondo Beach to the south.

Surfing

The best surf in continental USA breaks off the coast of California. There are loads of options – from the funky and low-key Santa Cruz to San Francisco's Ocean Beach (a tough spot to learn!), or bohemian Bolinas, 30 miles north. South, you'll find strong swells and Santa Ana winds in San Diego, La Jolla, Malibu and Santa Barbara, all of which sport warmer waters, fewer sharks of the great white variety and a saucy SoCal beach scene; the best conditions are from September to November. Along the coast of Oregon and Washington are miles of crowd-free beaches and pockets of surfing communities.

Top California Surf Spots

Huntington Beach (aka Surf City, USA) is the quintessential surf capital, with perpetual sun and a 'perfect' break, particularly during winter when the winds are calm.

Huntington Beach, Orange County Surfer central is a great place to take in the scene – and some lessons.

Oceanside Beach, Oceanside One of SoCal's prettiest beaches boasts one of the world's most consistent surf breaks in summer. It's a family-friendly spot.

Rincon, Santa Barbara Arguably one of the planet's top surfing spots; nearly every major surf champion on the globe has taken Rincon for a ride.

Steamer Lane and Pleasure Point, Santa Cruz There are 11 world-class breaks, including the point breaks over rock bottoms, at these two sweet spots.

Swami's, Encinitas Located below Seacliff Roadside Park, this popular surfing beach has multiple breaks guaranteeing you some fantastic waves.

Rentals & Lessons

You'll find board rentals on just about every patch of sand where surfing is possible. Expect to pay about $30 per half-day for a board, with wetsuit rental another $10.

Two-hour group lessons for beginners start around $75 per person, while private, two-hour instruction costs $85 to $120. If you're ready to jump in the deep end, many surf schools offer pricier weekend surf clinics and week-long 'surfari' camps.

Stand-up paddle surfing (SUP) is easier to learn, and it's skyrocketing in popularity. You'll find similarly priced board-and-paddle rentals and lessons all along the coast, from San Diego to north of San Francisco Bay.

Surfing Resources

Surfline (www.surfline.com) Browse the comprehensive atlas, live webcams and surf reports for the lowdown from San Diego to Santa Barbara.

Surfer (www.surfermag.com) Orange County–based magazine website with travel reports, gear reviews, newsy blogs and videos.

Surfrider (www.surfrider.org) Enlightened surfers can join up with this nonprofit organization that aims to protect the coastal environment.

White-Water Rafting

There's no shortage of scenic and spectacular rafting in the West. In California, both the Tuolumne and American Rivers surge with moderate-to-extreme rapids, while in Idaho the Middle Fork of the Salmon River has it all: abundant wildlife, thrilling rapids, a rich history, waterfalls and hot springs. The North Fork of the Owyhee – which snakes from the high plateau of southwest Oregon to the rangelands of Idaho – is rightfully popular and features towering hoodoos. North of Moab, UT, look for wildlife on an easy float on the Colorado River or ramp it up several notches with a thrilling romp through Class V rapids and the red rocks of Canyonlands National Park.

To book a spot on the Colorado River through the Grand Canyon, the quintessential river trip, make reservations at least a year in advance. And if you're not after white-knuckle rapids, fret not – many rivers have sections suitable for peaceful float trips or inner-tube drifts that you can enjoy with a cold beer in hand.

Kayaking & Canoeing

For exploring flatwater (no rapids or surf), opt for a kayak or canoe. For big lakes and the sea coast use a sea kayak. Be aware that kayaks are not always suitable for carrying bulky gear.

For scenic sea kayaking, you can push into the surf just about anywhere off the California coast. Popular spots include La Jolla as well as the coastal state parks just north of Santa Barbara. In the Pacific Northwest, you can enjoy world-class kayaking in the San Juan Islands, the Olympic Peninsula and Puget Sound. There's a full-moon paddle in Sausalito's Richardson Bay, CA. Sea-kayak rentals average $20 to $40 for two hours. Reputable outfitters will make sure you're aware of the tide schedule and wind conditions of your proposed route.

White-water kayaking is also popular in the Pacific Northwest, where water tumbles down from the ice-capped volcanoes. Look for bald eagles on the Upper Sgakit River or slip through remote wilderness canyons on the Klickitat River. Close to Portland, try the Clackamas and the North Santiam. For urban white-water kayaking, you can't beat Colorado where white-water parks are de rigueur. There are relatively new parks in Boulder and Denver.

Kayaking & Canoeing Resources

American Canoe Association (www.american canoe.org) Organization supporting and providing information about canoeing and kayaking.

American Whitewater (www.americanwhitewater.org) Advocacy group for responsible recreation works to preserve America's wild rivers.

Canoe & Kayak (www.canoekayak.com) Special-interest magazine for paddlers.

Kayak Online (www.kayakonline.com) Advice for buying gear and helpful links to kayaking outfitters, schools and associations.

Skiing & Other Winter Sports

There are ski resorts in every western state, including Arizona. Colorado has some of the best skiing in the region, although California and Utah are both top-notch destinations for the alpine experience. The ski season typically runs from mid-December to April, though some resorts have longer seasons. In summer, many resorts offer mountain biking and hiking courtesy of chair lifts. Ski packages (including airfares, hotels and lift tickets) are easy to find through resorts, travel agencies and online travel booking sites; these packages can be a good deal if your main goal is to ski.

Wherever you ski, it won't come cheap. Find the best deals by going midweek, purchasing multiday tickets, heading to lesser-known 'sibling' resorts (like Alpine Meadows near Lake Tahoe) or checking out mountains that cater to locals including Santa Fe Ski Area and Colorado's Wolf Grade.

Top Ski Resorts

For snow, altitude and attitude Vail, CO; Squaw Valley, CA; Aspen, CO

For an unfussy scene and steep vertical chutes Alta, UT; Telluride, CO; Jackson, WY; Taos, NM

WHALE-WATCHING

Gray and humpback whales have the longest migrations of any mammal in the world – more than 5000 miles from the Arctic to Mexico, and back again. In the Pacific Northwest, most pass through from November to February (southbound) and March to June (northbound). Gray whales can be spotted off the California coast from December to April, while blue, humpback and sperm whales pass by in summer and fall. Bring binoculars! Top spots for whale-watching include the following:

Depoe Bay & Newport, OR Good whale-watching infrastructure; tour boats.

Long Beach & Westport, WA Scan from shore.

Puget Sound & San Juan Islands, WA Resident pods of orca.

Klamath River Overlook, CA Watch for whales from bluffs.

Point Reyes Lighthouse, CA Gray whales pass by in December and January.

Monterey, CA Whales can be spotted year-round.

Channel Islands National Park, CA Take a cruise or peer through the telescope on the visitor center tower.

Point Loma, CA Cabrillo National Monument is the best place in San Diego to watch gray-whale migration from January to March.

Snowboarding

On powdered slopes across the USA, snowboarding has become as popular as downhill skiing – all thanks to snow-surfing pioneer Jake Burton Carpenter, who set up a workshop in his Vermont garage and began to build snowboards in the mid-1970s. Snowboarders flock almost everywhere out West, including Sun Valley, Tahoe and Taos. For a fix during the summer months, head to Oregon's Mt Hood area, where several resorts offer snowboard camps.

Cross-Country Skiing & Snowshoeing

Most downhill ski resorts have cross-country (Nordic) ski trails. In winter, popular areas of national parks, national forests and city parks often have cross-country ski and snowshoe trails, and ice-skating rinks.

You'll find superb trail networks for Nordic skiers and snowshoers in California's Royal Gorge (North America's largest Nordic ski area) and Washington's sublime and crowd-free Methow Valley. Backcountry passionistas will be happily rewarded throughout the Sierra Nevada, with its many ski-in huts. There are more than 60 miles of trails around five ski-in huts in the San Juan Mountains in Colorado

(www.sanjuanhuts.com); the 10th Mountain Division Association manages more than two-dozen huts in the Rockies (www.huts.org). The South Rim of the Grand Canyon and the surrounding Kaibab National Forest are also pretty spots for wintery exploring.

Ski & Snowboard Resources

Cross-Country Ski Areas Association (www.xcski.org) Comprehensive information and gear guides for cross-country skiing and snowshoeing across North America.

Cross Country Skier (www.crosscountryskier.com) Magazine with Nordic-skiing news articles, online trail reports, and race and events information.

Powder (www.powdermag.com) Online version of *Powder* magazine for skiers.

Ski Resorts Guide (www.skiresortsguide.com) Comprehensive guide to resorts, with downloadable trail maps, lodging info and more.

SkiNet (www.skinet.com) Online versions of *Ski* and *Skiing* magazines.

SnoCountry Mountain Reports (www.snocountry.com) Snow reports for North America, plus events, news and resort links.

Rock Climbing & Canyoneering

In California, rock hounds test their mettle on the big walls, granite domes and boulders of world-class Yosemite National Park, where the climbing season lasts from April to October. Climbers also flock to Joshua Tree National Park, an otherworldly shrine in southern California's sun-scorched desert. There, amid craggy monoliths and the country's oldest trees, they make their pilgrimage on more than 8000 routes, tackling sheer vertical, sharp edges and bountiful cracks. For beginners, outdoor outfitters at both parks offer guided climbs and instruction.

In Zion National Park in Utah, multiday canyoneering classes teach the fine art of going *down:* rappelling off sheer sandstone cliffs into glorious red-rock canyons filled with trees. Some of the sportier pitches are made in dry suits, down the flanks of roaring waterfalls into ice-cold pools.

For ice climbing, try Ouray Ice Park in Ouray, off the Million Dollar Highway in southwest Colorado. Inside a narrow slot canyon, 200ft walls and waterfalls are frozen in thick sheets.

Other great climbing spots:

Grand Teton National Park, WY Good for climbers of all levels: beginners can take basic climbing courses and the more experienced can join two-day expeditions up to the top of Grand Teton itself; a 13,770ft peak with majestic views.

AND LET'S NOT FORGET...

ACTIVITY	WHERE?	WHAT?	MORE INFORMATION
Horseback riding	Southern Arizona dude ranches, AZ	Old West country (most ranches close in summer due to the heat)	www.azdra.com
	Grand Canyon South Rim, AZ	low-key trips through Kaibab National Forest; campfire rides	www.apachestables.com
	Santa Fe, NM	kids' rides; sunset rides	www.bishopslodge.com
	Telluride, CO	all-season rides in the hills	www.ridewithroudy.com
	Durango, CO	day rides and overnight camping in Weminuche Wilderness	www.vallecitolakeoutfitter.com
	Yosemite National Park, CA	rides in Yosemite Valley, Tuolumne Meadows and near Wawona	www.yosemitepark.com
	Florence, OR	romantic beach rides	www.oregonhorsebackriding.com
Diving	Blue Hole near Santa Rosa, NM	81ft-deep artesian well; blue water leads into a 131ft-long submerged cavern	www.santarosanm.org
	La Jolla Underwater Park, CA	beginner friendly; snorkelers enjoy nearby La Jolla Cove	www.sandiego.gov/lifeguards/beaches
	Channel Islands National Park, CA	kelp forests, sea caves off coastal islands	www.nps.gov/chis; www.islandpackers.com/watersports.html
	Point Lobos State Reserve, CA	fantastic shore diving; shallow reefs, caves, sea lions, seals, otters	www.mbdscuba.com
	Puget Sound, WA	clear water, diverse marine life (including giant octopus!)	www.underwatersports.com; www.pugetsounddivecharters.com
Hot-air ballooning	Sedona, AZ	float above red rock country; Champagne picnic	www.northernlightballoon.com
	Napa Wine Country, CA	colorful balloons float over vineyards	www.balloonrides.com; www.napavalleyballoons.com

City of Rocks National Reserve, ID More than 500 routes up wind-scoured granite and pinnacles 60 stories tall.

Bishop, CA This sleepy town in the Eastern Sierra is the gateway to excellent climbing in the nearby Owens River Gorge and Buttermilk Hills.

Red Rock Canyon, NV Ten miles west of Las Vegas is some of the world's finest sandstone climbing.

Rocky Mountain National Park, CO Offers alpine climbing near Boulder.

Flatirons, CO Also near Boulder, has fine multi-pitch ascents.

Climbing & Canyoneering Resources

American Canyoneering Association (www.canyoneering.net) An online canyons database with links to courses, local climbing groups and more.

Climbing (www.climbing.com) Cutting-edge rock-climbing news and information since 1970.

SuperTopo (www.supertopo.com) One-stop shop for rock-climbing guidebooks, free topo maps and route descriptions.

Plan Your Trip

Travel with Children

The West is extremely family friendly, with superb attractions for all ages: amusement parks, aquariums, zoos, science museums, adventurous campsites, hikes in wilderness reserves, boogie-boarding surf at the beach and leisurely bike rides through scenic forests. Most national and state parks gear some exhibits, trails and programs (junior ranger activities and the like) toward families with kids.

Best Regions for Kids in Western USA

Grand Canyon & Southern Arizona

Hike the Grand Canyon, splash in Oak Creek and ponder cacti outside Tucson. Water parks, dude ranches and ghost towns should keep kids entertained.

Los Angeles & Southern California

See celebrity handprints in Hollywood, take a studio tour in Burbank and hit the beach in Santa Monica. Orange County and San Diego have theme parks galore.

Colorado

The whole state is kid-friendly: museums in Denver, outdoor fun in the Rockies, rafting near Buena Vista and Salida, and ski resorts everywhere.

Western USA for Kids

Child- and family-friendly activities are listed throughout this book, and some major cities have a box devoted specifically to kids' activities. To find family-oriented sights and activities, accommodations, restaurants and entertainment, just look for the child-friendly icon (🔅).

Dining with Children

The US restaurant industry seems built on family-style service: children are not just accepted almost everywhere, but are usually encouraged by special children's menus with smaller portions and lower prices. In some restaurants children under a certain age even eat for free. Restaurants usually provide high chairs and booster seats. Some may also offer children crayons and puzzles.

Restaurants without children's menus don't necessarily discourage kids, though higher-end restaurants might; however, even at the nicer places, if you arrive early, you can usually eat without too much stress. You can ask if the kitchen will make a smaller order of a dish (check price), or if they will split a normal-size main dish between two plates for the kids.

Accommodations

Motels and hotels typically have rooms with two beds, which are ideal for families. Some also have roll-away beds or cribs that can be brought into the room for an extra charge (these are usually portable cribs, which may not work for all children). Some hotels offer 'kids stay free' programs, for children up to 12 or sometimes 18 years old. Many B&Bs don't allow children; ask when reserving. Most resorts are kid friendly and many offer children's programs, but ask when booking, as a few cater only to adults.

Babysitting

Resort hotels may have on-call babysitting services; otherwise, ask the front-desk staff or concierge to help you make arrangements. Always ask if babysitters are licensed and bonded, what they charge per hour per child, whether there's a minimum fee, and if they charge extra for transportation or meals. Most tourist bureaus list local resources for child care, plus recreation facilities, medical services and so on.

Discounts for Children

Child concessions often apply for tours, admission fees and transport, with some discounts as high as 50% off the adult rate. However, the definition of 'child' can vary from under 12 to under 16 years. Some popular sights also have discount rates for families. Most sights give free admission to children under two years.

Planning

Weather and crowds are all-important considerations when planning a Western US family getaway. The peak travel season is from June to August, when schools are out and the weather is warmest. Expect high prices and abundant crowds – meaning long lines at amusement and water parks, fully booked resort areas, and heavy traffic on the roads; reserve well in advance for popular destinations. The same holds true for winter resorts (eg the Rockies, Lake Tahoe) during the high season of January to March.

What to Pack

Bring lots of sunscreen, especially if you are planning on spending a lot of time outside.

For hiking, you'll need a front baby carrier (for children under one) or a backpack (for children up to about four years old) with a built-in shade top. These can be purchased or rented from outfitters throughout the region. Older kids need sturdy shoes and, for playing in streams, water sandals.

Other useful items are towels (for playing in water between destinations), rain gear, a snuggly fleece or heavy sweater (even in summer, desert nights can be cold), sun hats (especially if you are camping) and bug repellent.

To minimize concerns about bed configurations, it's a good idea to bring a portable crib for infants and sleeping bags for older children.

Children's Highlights

Outdoor Adventure

Yellowstone National Park (p285) Watch powerful geysers, spy on wildlife and take magnificent hikes.

Grand Canyon National Park (p348) Gaze across one of the earth's great wonders, followed by a hike, a ranger talk and biking.

Olympic National Park (p201) Explore the wild and pristine wilderness of one of the world's few temperate rainforests.

Oak Creek Canyon (p346; Hwy 89A NE Sedona) Swoosh over red rocks at Slide Rock State Park in Arizona.

Theme Parks

Disneyland (p90) It's the attention to detail that amazes most at Mickey Mouse's enchantingly imagined Disneyland, in the middle of Orange County, California.

SeaWorld (p98) Killer-whale shows, fun rides and loads of other amusements in San Diego's aquatic park.

ON THE ROAD & IN THE AIR

➡ Many public toilets have a baby-changing table (sometimes in men's toilets, too), and gender-neutral 'family' facilities appear in airports.

➡ Car-rental agencies should be able to provide an appropriate child seat, since these are required in every state, but you need to request it when booking and expect to pay around $10 more per day.

➡ Domestic airlines don't charge for children under two years. Those two or over must have a seat, and discounts are unlikely. Very rarely, some resort areas (such as Disneyland) offer a 'kids fly free' promotion. Amtrak and other train operators occasionally offer similar deals, with kids up to 15 riding free on various routes. Currently, children 15 years and younger enjoy 50% off the lowest Amtrak rail fare when they travel alongside a fare-paying adult.

Universal Studios (p74) Hollywood movie-themed action rides, special-effects shows and a studio back-lot tram tour in Los Angeles.

Aquariums & Zoos

Arizona-Sonora Desert Museum (p359) Coyotes, cacti and docent demonstrations are highlights at this indoor/outdoor repository of flora and fauna in Tucson.

Monterey Bay Aquarium (p119) Observe denizens of the deep next door to the California central coast's biggest marine sanctuary.

Aquarium of the Pacific (p79) High-tech aquarium at Long Beach houses critters from balmy Baja California to the chilly north Pacific, plus a shark lagoon.

Rainy-Day Activities

LA Museums See stars (the real ones) at LA's Griffith Observatory and dinosaur bones at the Natural History Museum of LA County and the Page Museum at the La Brea Tar Pits, then get hands-on at the amusing California Science Center.

SF Museums San Francisco's Bay Area is a mind-bending classroom for kids, especially at the interactive Exploratorium, multimedia Zeum and ecofriendly California Academy of Science.

Pacific Science Center (p193) Fascinating, hands-on exhibits at this center in Seattle, plus an IMAX theater, planetarium and laser shows.

Museum of Natural History & Science (p385) Check out the Hall of Jurassic Supergiants in Albuquerque.

Resources for Families

For all-round information and advice, check out Lonely Planet's *Travel with Children*. For outdoor advice, read *Kids in the Wild: A Family Guide to Outdoor Recreation* by Cindy Ross and Todd Gladfelter, and Alice Cary's *A Trailside Guide: Parents' Guide to Hiking & Camping*. Useful websites include **Family Travel Files** (www.thefamilytravelfiles.com), with ready-made vacation ideas, destination profiles and travel suggestions by age range; and **Kids.gov** (www.kids.gov), the eclectic, enormous national resource, where you can download songs and activities, and learn a bit about American history.

Regions at a Glance

What image comes to mind when someone mentions the West? A saguaro cactus, or maybe the OK Corral? Either would be accurate – for southern Arizona. But the West holds so much more. Lush forests in the Pacific Northwest. Sun-kissed beaches in California. Leafy single-track trails in the Rockies. Crimson buttes and hoodoos in Utah. There's a landscape for every mood and adventure.

Cultural travelers can explore Native American sites in Arizona and New Mexico. There's upscale shopping, fine dining and big-city bustle in Los Angeles, San Francisco and Seattle. Are you a history buff? Visit Mormon settlements in Utah, Spanish missions in California or Old West towns just about everywhere. Ready to let loose? Two words: Las Vegas.

California

Beaches
Outdoor Adventure
Food & Wine

Gorgeous Shores

With more than 1100 miles of coastline, California rules the sands: you'll find rugged, pristine beaches in the north and people-packed beauties in the south, with great surfing, sea kayaking or beach-walking all along the coast.

Romping Room

Swoosh down snowy slopes, raft on white-water rivers, kayak beside coastal islands, hike past waterfalls and climb boulders in the desert. The problem isn't choice in California, it's finding enough time to do it all.

King's Table

Fertile fields, talented chefs and an insatiable appetite for the new make California a major culinary destination. Browse local food markets, sample Pinot and Chardonnay at lush vineyards, and dine on farm-to-table fare.

p61

Pacific Northwest

Cycling
Food & Wine
National Parks

Pedal Power

Bicycle over paved, rolling roads in the tranquil San Juan Islands, cruise the bluff-dotted Oregon coast along Hwy 101 or pedal the streets of Portland, a city that embraces two-wheeled travel with loads of bike lanes, costumed theme rides and handcrafted bike shows.

Locavores & Oenophiles

'Up and coming' is the word used for Northwest cities such as Portland and Seattle, where chefs blend fish caught in local waters with vegetables harvested in the Eden-like valleys surrounding the Columbia River. Then there is Washington's wine, second only to California's.

Classic Playgrounds

The Northwest has four national parks, including three classics that were established near the turn of the 20th century – Olympic, Mount Rainier and Crater Lake – and the newest, the North Cascades.

p180

Rocky Mountains

Outdoor Adventure
Western Culture
Dramatic Landscapes

Rugged Fun

World-class skiing, hiking and cycling make the Rockies a top destination for adrenaline junkies. Everyone is welcome, with hundreds of races and group rides, and an incredible infrastructure of parks, trails and adventure huts.

Modern Cowboys

Once sporting Stetson cowboy hats and prairie dresses, today's freedom-loving Rocky folk are more often spotted in lycra, with mountain bike nearby, sipping a microbrew or latte at a sunny outdoor cafe. Hard playing and slow living still rule.

Alpine Wonderland

The snow-covered Rocky Mountains are pure majesty. With chiseled peaks, clear rivers and red-rock contours, the Rockies contain some of the world's most famous parks, and bucketloads of clean mountain air.

p241

Southwest

Natural Scenery
Native Cultures
Food

Red-Rock Country

The Southwest is famous for the jaw-dropping Grand Canyon, the dramatic red buttes of Monument Valley, the crimson arches of Moab and the fiery buttes of Sedona – just a few of many geographic wonders in and around the spectacular national parks and forests.

Pueblos & Reservations

Visiting the Hopi and Navajo Nations or one of the 19 New Mexico pueblos is a fine introduction to America's first inhabitants. This is your best bet for appreciating, and purchasing, native-made crafts.

Good Eats

Try chile-slathered chicken enchiladas in New Mexico, a messy Sonoran hotdog in Tucson or a hearty steak just about anywhere. In Vegas, stretch your fat pants and your budget at one of the extravagant buffets. For gourmands, off-the-Strip restaurants offer the most intriguing epicurean experiences.

p309

On the Road

California

Includes ➜

Best Places to Eat

➜ Benu (p142)

➜ Chez Panisse (p153)

➜ French Laundry (p156)

➜ George's at the Cove (p102)

➜ Bazaar (p84)

Best Places to Hike

➜ Yosemite National Park (p169)

➜ Sequoia & Kings Canyon National Parks (p173)

➜ Marin County (p151)

➜ Redwood National & State Parks (p161)

Why Go?

With bohemian spirit and high-tech savvy, not to mention a die-hard passion for the good life – whether that means cracking open a bottle of old-vine Zinfandel, climbing a 14,000ft peak or surfing the Pacific – California soars beyond any expectations sold on Hollywood's silver screens.

More than anything, California is iconic. It was here that the hurly-burly gold rush kicked off in the mid-19th century, poet-naturalist John Muir rhapsodized about the Sierra Nevada's 'range of light,' and Jack Kerouac and the Beat Generation defined what it really means to hit the road.

California's multicultural melting pot has been cookin' since this bountiful promised land was first staked out by Spain and Mexico. Today, waves of immigrants from around the world still look to find their own American dream on these palm-tree-studded Pacific shores.

Come see the future in the making in California. Then stay for the beaches.

When to Go
Los Angeles

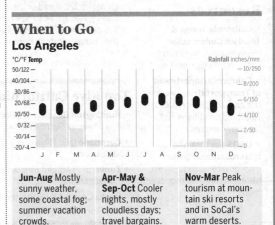

Jun–Aug Mostly sunny weather, some coastal fog; summer vacation crowds.

Apr–May & Sep–Oct Cooler nights, mostly cloudless days; travel bargains.

Nov–Mar Peak tourism at mountain ski resorts and in SoCal's warm deserts.

DON'T MISS

You can't leave California without hugging a tree! We suggest a coast redwood, which can live for 2000 years and grow to 379ft tall.

Fast Facts

➡ **Hub cities** Los Angeles (population 3,819,702), San Francisco (population 812,826)

➡ **Driving time** LA to San Francisco (5½ hours via inland I-5 & I-580 Fwys, 8½ hours via coastal Hwys 101 & 1)

➡ **Time zone** Pacific Standard

Did You Know?

Just a few of California's inventions: the internet and the iPad, power yoga and reality TV, the space shuttle and Mickey Mouse, the Cobb salad and the fortune cookie.

Resources

➡ **California Travel & Tourism Commission** (www.visitcalifornia.com) Official state tourism info.

➡ **California Department of Transportation** (www. dot.ca.gov/cgi-bin/roads. cgi) Road conditions and highway closures.

➡ **USGS Earthquake Hazards** (http://quake. usgs.gov/recenteqs/latest. htm) Real-time earthquake maps.

Getting There & Around

Los Angeles (LAX) and San Francisco (SFO) are major international airports. Small airports in San Diego, Orange County, Oakland, San Jose, Sacramento, Burbank, Long Beach and Santa Barbara handle primarily domestic flights.

Four long-distance Amtrak routes connect California with the rest of the USA: *California Zephyr* (Chicago–San Francisco Bay Area), *Coast Starlight* (Seattle–Los Angeles), *Southwest Chief* (Chicago–LA) and *Sunset Limited* (New Orleans–LA). Amtrak's intrastate routes include the *Pacific Surfliner* (San Diego–LA–Santa Barbara–San Luis Obispo), the *Capitol Corridor* (San Jose–Oakland–Berkeley–Sacramento) and the *San Joaquin* (Bakersfield to Oakland or Sacramento, with Yosemite Valley buses from Merced).

Greyhound buses travel to many corners of the state. But to really get out and explore, especially away from the coast, you'll need a car.

CALIFORNIA'S NATIONAL & STATE PARKS

Yosemite and Sequoia became California's first national parks in 1890, and today there are seven more: Kings Canyon, Death Valley, Joshua Tree, Channel Islands, Redwood, Lassen Volcanic and Pinnacles. The **National Park Service** (www.nps.gov) manages two dozen other historic sites, monuments, nature preserves and recreational areas statewide. Entry fees vary from nothing up to $25 per vehicle for a seven-day pass; campsites cost up to $20 nightly. **Recreation. gov** (☑ 877-444-6777, 518-885-3639; www.recreation.gov) handles camping reservations for all federal lands.

California's 280 **state parks** (☑ 800-777-0369, 916-653-6995; www.parks.ca.gov) are a diverse bunch – everything from marine preserves to redwood forests – protecting a third of the coastline and offering 3000 miles of hiking, biking and equestrian trails. Some state parks may be closed or have reduced opening hours due to budget cutbacks (call ahead or check the website). Day-use parking fees are $4 to $15, campsites $5 to $75 nightly. **ReserveAmerica** (☑ 800-444-7275; www.reserveamerica. com) handles state-park camping reservations.

Top Five California Beaches

➡ **Huntington Beach** (p92) Bonfires, beach volleyball and rolling waves in 'Surf City USA.'

➡ **Coronado** (p95) Sun yourself along San Diego's boundless Silver Strand.

➡ **Zuma** (p77) Aquamarine waters, frothy surf and tawny sand near Malibu.

➡ **Santa Cruz** (p121) Surf's up! And the beach boardwalk's carnival fun never stops.

➡ **Point Reyes** (p152) Wild, windy, walkable beaches for sunsets and wildlife watching.

History

By the time European explorers arrived in the 16th century, as many as 300,000 indigenous people called this land home. Spanish conquistadors combed through what they called Alta (Upper) California in search of a fabled 'city of gold,' but they left the territory virtually alone after failing to find it. Not until the Mission Period (1769–1833) did Spain make a serious attempt to settle the land; it established 21 Catholic missions – many founded by Franciscan priest Junípero Serra – and presidios (military forts) to deter the British and Russians.

After winning independence from Spain in 1821 Mexico briefly ruled California, but then was trounced by the fledgling United States in the Mexican War (1846–48). The discovery of gold just 10 days before the Treaty of Guadalupe Hidalgo was signed soon saw the territory's nonindigenous population quintuple to 92,000 by 1850, when California became the 31st US state. Thousands of imported Chinese laborers helped complete the transcontinental railroad in 1869, which opened up markets and further spurred migration to the Golden State.

The 1906 San Francisco earthquake was barely a hiccup as California continued to grow exponentially in size, diversity and importance. Mexican immigrants streamed in during the 1910–20 Mexican Revolution, and again during WWII, to fill labor shortages. Military-driven industries developed during wartime, while anti-Asian sentiments led to the unjust internment of many Japanese Americans, including at Manzanar in the Eastern Sierra.

California has long been a social pioneer thanks to its size, confluence of wealth, a diversity of immigration and technological innovation. Since the early 20th century, Hollywood has mesmerized the world with its cinematic dreams. Meanwhile, San Francisco reacted against the banal complacency of post-WWII suburbia with Beat poetry in the 1950s, hippie free love in the '60s and gay pride in the '70s. The internet revolution, initially spurred by high-tech visionaries in Silicon Valley, rewired the nation and led to a 1990s boom in overspeculated stocks.

When that tech bubble burst, plunging the state's economy into chaos, Californians blamed their Democratic governor, Gray Davis, and, in a controversial recall election, voted to give actor-turned-Republican Arnold Schwarzenegger (aka 'The Governator') a shot at fixing things. During the US recession that started in 2008, California's budget shortfalls caused another staggering

CALIFORNIA FACTS

Nickname Golden State

State motto Eureka ('I Have Found It')

Population 38 million

Area 155,779 sq miles

Capital city Sacramento (population 472,178)

Other cities Los Angeles (population 3,819,702), San Diego (population 1,326,179), San Francisco (population 812,826)

Sales tax 7.5%

Birthplace of Author John Steinbeck (1902–68), photographer Ansel Adams (1902–84), US president Richard Nixon (1913–94), pop-culture icon Marilyn Monroe (1926–62)

Home of The highest and lowest points in the contiguous US (Mt Whitney, Death Valley), world's oldest, tallest and biggest living trees (ancient bristlecone pines, coast redwoods and giant sequoias, respectively)

Politics Majority Democrat (multiethnic), minority Republican (mostly white), one in five Californians votes independent

Famous for Disneyland, earthquakes, Hollywood, hippies, Silicon Valley, surfing

Kitschiest souvenir 'Mystery Spot' bumper sticker

Driving distances Los Angeles to San Francisco 380 miles, San Francisco to Yosemite Valley 200 miles

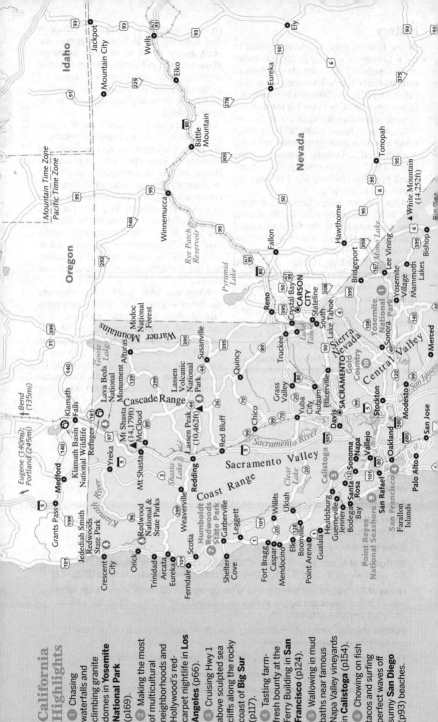

California Highlights

1 Chasing waterfalls and climbing granite domes in **Yosemite National Park** (p169).

2 Making the most of multicultural neighborhoods and Hollywood's red-carpet nightlife in **Los Angeles** (p66).

3 Cruising Hwy 1 above sculpted sea cliffs along the rocky coast of **Big Sur** (p117).

4 Tasting farm-fresh bounty at the Ferry Building in **San Francisco** (p124).

5 Wallowing in mud baths near famous Napa Valley vineyards in **Calistoga** (p154).

6 Chowing on fish tacos and surfing perfect waves off sunny **San Diego** (p93) beaches.

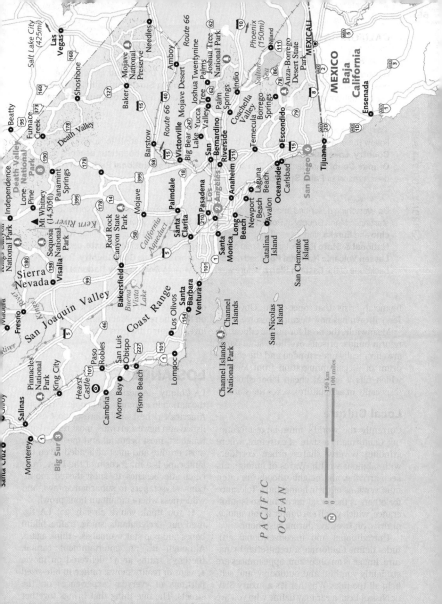

⑦ Craning your neck at the world's tallest trees along Avenue of the Giants in the **Humboldt Redwoods State Park** (p161).

⑧ Trekking across sand dunes and ambling Old West ghost towns in **Death Valley** (p109).

⑨ Spotting whales, seals and tule elk at **Point Reyes National Seashore** (p152).

⑩ Dipping into swimming holes and panning like a '49er in **Gold Country** (p165).

CALIFORNIA IN...

One Week

California in a nutshell: start in **Los Angeles**, detouring to **Disneyland**. Head up the breezy Central Coast, stopping in **Santa Barbara** and **Big Sur**, before getting a dose of big-city culture in **San Francisco**. Head inland to nature's temple, **Yosemite National Park**, then zip back to LA.

Two Weeks

Follow the one-week itinerary above, but at a saner pace. Add jaunts to NorCal's **Wine Country**; **Lake Tahoe**, perched high in the Sierra Nevada; the bodacious beaches of **Orange County** and laid-back **San Diego**; or **Joshua Tree National Park**, near the chic desert resort of **Palm Springs**.

One Month

Do everything described above, and more. From San Francisco, head up the North Coast, starting in Marin County at **Point Reyes National Seashore**. Stroll Victorian-era **Mendocino** and **Eureka**, find yourself on the **Lost Coast** and ramble through fern-filled **Redwood National & State Parks**. Inland, snap a postcard-perfect photo of **Mt Shasta**, detour to **Lassen Volcanic National Park** and ramble California's historic **Gold Country**. Trace the backbone of the **Eastern Sierra** before winding down into **Death Valley National Park**.

financial crisis that once-again Governor Jerry Brown has now begun to resolve.

Meanwhile, the need for public education reform builds, prisons overflow, state parks are chronically underfunded and the conundrum of illegal immigration from Mexico, which fills a critical cheap labor shortage (especially in agriculture), vexes the state.

Local Culture

Currently the world's ninth-largest economy, California is a state of extremes, where grinding poverty shares urban corridors with fabulous wealth. Waves of immigrants keep arriving, and neighborhoods are often mini versions of their homelands. Tolerance for others is the social norm, but so is intolerance, which you'll encounter if you smoke, or drive on freeways during rush hour.

Untraditional and unconventional attitudes define California, a trendsetter by nature. Image is an obsession, appearances are stridently youthful and outdoorsy, and self-help all the rage. Whether it's a luxury SUV or Nissan Leaf, a car may define who you are and how important you consider yourself to be, especially in SoCal (Southern California).

Think of California as the USA's most futuristic social laboratory. If technology identifies a new useful gadget, Silicon Valley will build it at light speed. If postmodern celebrities, bizarrely famous for the mere fact of being famous, make a fashion statement or get thrown in jail, the nation pays attention. No

other state's pop culture has as big an effect on how the rest of Americans work, play, eat, love, consume and, yes, recycle.

LOS ANGELES

LA County – America's largest – represents the nation in extremes. Its people are among America's richest and poorest, most established and newest arrivals, most refined and roughest, most beautiful and most botoxed, most erudite and most airheaded. Even the landscape is a microcosm of the USA, from cinematic beaches to snow-dusted mountains, skyscrapers to suburban sprawl, and wilderness where mountain lions prowl.

If you think you've already got LA figured out – celebutants, smog, traffic, bikini babes and pop-star wannabes – think again. Although it's an entertainment capital, the city's truths aren't delivered on movie screens or reality shows; rather, in bite-sized portions of everyday experiences on the streets. The one thing that brings together Angelenos is that they are seekers – or the descendants of seekers – drawn by a dream of fame, fortune or rebirth.

Now is an especially exciting time to visit LA: Hollywood and Downtown are undergoing an urban renaissance, and the art, music, food and fashion scenes are all in high gear. Chances are, the more you explore, the more you'll love 'La-La Land.'

History

The hunter-gatherer existence of the Gabrieleño and Chumash peoples ended with the arrival of Spanish missionaries and colonial pioneers in the late 18th century. Spain's first civilian settlement, El Pueblo de Nuestra Señora la Reina de Los Ángeles, remained an isolated farming outpost for decades after its founding in 1781. The city wasn't officially incorporated until 1850.

LA's population repeatedly swelled after the collapse of the California gold rush, the arrival of the transcontinental railroad, the growth of the citrus industry, the discovery of oil, the launch of the port of LA, the birth of the movie industry and the opening of the California Aqueduct. After WWII, the city's population doubled from nearly two million in 1950 to almost four million today.

LA's growth has caused problems, including suburban sprawl and air pollution – though, with aggressive enforcement, smog levels have fallen every year since records have been kept. Traffic, a fluctuating real-estate market and the occasional earthquake or wildfire remain nagging concerns but, with a diverse economy and decreasing crime rate, all things considered, LA's a survivor.

Sights

A dozen miles inland from the Pacific, Downtown LA combines history and highbrow arts and culture. Hip-again Hollywood awaits northwest of Downtown, while urban-designer chic and lesbi-gays rule West Hollywood. South of WeHo, Museum Row is Mid-City's main draw. Further west are ritzy Beverly Hills, Westwood near the UCLA campus and West LA. Beach towns include kid-friendly Santa Monica, boho Venice, star-powered Malibu and busy Long Beach. Upscale Pasadena lies northeast of Downtown.

Downtown

For decades, LA's historic core and main business and government district emptied out on nights and weekends. No more. Crowds fill performance and entertainment venues, and young professionals and artists have moved into new lofts, bringing bars, restaurants and art galleries. Don't expect Manhattan just yet; still, adventurous urbanites won't want to miss Downtown.

Downtown is most easily explored on foot combined with short subway and DASH minibus rides. Parking is cheapest (from $6 all day) around Little Tokyo and Chinatown.

EL PUEBLO DE LOS ANGELES & AROUND

Compact, colorful and car-free, this historic district is an immersion in LA's Spanish-Mexican roots. Its spine is Olvera St, a festive kitsch-o-rama where you can snap up handmade folkloric trinkets, then chomp on tacos or sugar-sprinkled churros.

'New' Chinatown is about a half-mile north along Broadway and Hill St, crammed with dim-sum parlors, herbal apothecaries, curio shops and Chung King Rd's edgy art galleries.

La Plaza de Cultura y Artes   MUSEUM
(Map p70; ☏213-542-6200; www.lapca.org; 501 N Main St; ⊙noon-7pm Wed-Mon) **FREE** Open

---

LOS ANGELES IN...

Distances are ginormous in LA, so allow extra time for traffic and don't try to pack too much into a day.

One Day

Fuel up for the day at the **Griddle Cafe** and then go star-searching on the **Hollywood Walk of Fame** along Hollywood Blvd. Up your chances of spotting actual celebs by hitting the fashion-forward boutiques on paparazzi-infested **Robertston Blvd**, or get a dose of nature at **Griffith Park**. Then drive west to the lofty **Getty Center** or head out to the **Venice Boardwalk** to see the seaside sideshow. Catch a Pacific sunset in **Santa Monica**.

Two Days

Explore rapidly evolving Downtown LA. Dig up its roots at **El Pueblo de Los Angeles**, then catapult to the future at dramatic **Walt Disney Concert Hall** topping the **Cultural Corridor**. Walk off lunch ambling between Downtown's historic buildings and nouveau art galleries nearby **Little Tokyo**. At South Park's glitzy **LA Live** entertainment center, romp through the multimedia **Grammy Museum**, then join real-life celebs cheering on the LA Lakers next door at **Staples Center**.

since 2010, La Plaza chronicles the Mexican-American experience in LA with exhibits about the city's history from the Zoot Suit Riots to the Chicana movement and Latino art. It adjoins 1822 La Placita (Map p70; www.laplacita.org; 535 N Main St) church.

Avila Adobe　　　　　　　　　　MUSEUM
(Map p70; ☎213-628-1274; http://elpueblo.lacity.org; Olvera St; ☉9am-4pm) FREE Claiming to be LA's oldest building, this 1818 ranch home is decorated with period furniture. A video gives history and highlights of the neighborhood.

Greater Los Angeles

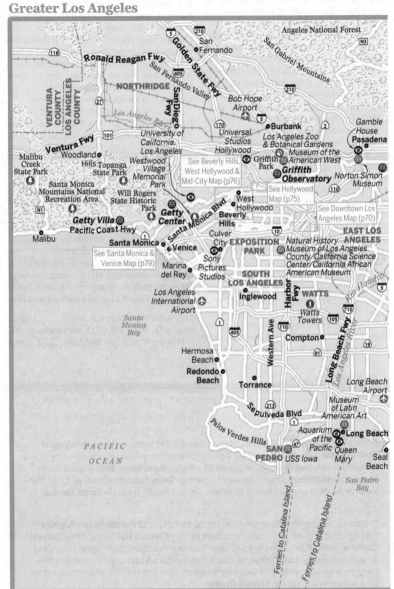

Union Station
LANDMARK

(Map p70; 800 N Alameda St; **P**) The last of America's grand rail stations (1939), Union Station's glamorous art-deco interior appears in *Blade Runner, 24, Speed* and many other films and TV shows. Parking costs from $2 for 20 minutes, $6 all day.

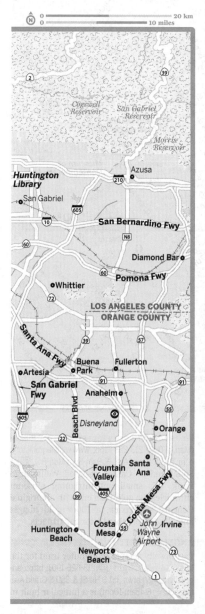

Chinese American Museum
MUSEUM

(Map p70; 213-485-8567; www.camla.org; Garnier Bldg, 425 N Los Angeles St; adult/child $3/2; 10am-3pm Tue-Sun) Small but smart, this museum inhabits a 19th-century Chinese merchant's building and community center, built before LA's Chinatown moved north.

CIVIC CENTER & CULTURAL CORRIDOR
North Grand Ave's 'Cultural Corridor' is anchored by the Music Center (Map p70; 213-972-7211; www.musiccenter.org; 135 N Grand Ave), where performing arts fill the Dorothy Chandler Pavilion, Mark Taper Forum and Ahmanson Theater.

★ Museum of Contemporary Art
MUSEUM

(MOCA; Map p70; 213-626-6222; www.moca. org; 250 S Grand Ave; adult/child $12/free, 5-8pm Thu free; 11am-5pm Mon & Fri, to 8pm Thu, to 6pm Sat & Sun) Housed in a building designed by Arata Isozaki, MOCA Grand Ave stages headline-grabbing special exhibits. Its permanent collection presents heavy hitters from the 1940s to the present. Parking at Walt Disney Concert Hall costs from $9 (cash only). MOCA has two other branches: the Geffen Contemporary in Little Tokyo and at West Hollywood's Pacific Design Center.

★ Walt Disney Concert Hall
CULTURAL BUILDING

(Map p70; info 213-972-7211, tickets 323-850-2000; www.laphil.org; 111 S Grand Ave; guided tours usually 10:30am & 12:30pm Tue-Sat; **P**) **FREE** Architect Frank Gehry's now-iconic 2003 building is a gravity-defying sculpture of curving and billowing stainless-steel walls that's home base for the Los Angeles Philharmonic (p86). Free tours are available subject to concert schedules, and walkways encircle the mazelike roof and exterior. Parking from $9 (cash only). Self-guided audio tours usually run between 10am and 2pm daily. Reservations are required for all tours.

Cathedral of Our Lady of the Angels
CHURCH

(Map p70; 213-680-5200; www.olacathedral.org; 555 W Temple St; 6:30am-6pm Mon-Fri, from 9am Sat, from 7am Sun; **P**) **FREE** Architect José Rafael Moneo mixed Gothic proportions with bold contemporary design for the main church of LA's Catholic Archdiocese. Built in 2002 it teems with art, and soft light through alabaster panes lends serenity. Tours (1pm Monday to Friday) and organ recitals (12:45pm Wednesday) are both free and popular.

Downtown Los Angeles

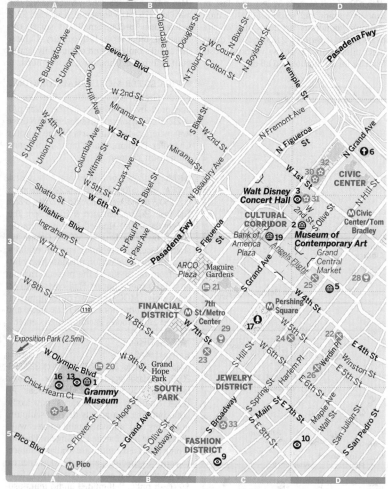

Weekday parking costs from $4 per 15 minutes (daily maximum $18) until 4pm, $5 flat-rate on weekends and holidays.

City Hall   LANDMARK
(Map p70; ☎213-978-1995; www.lacity.org; 200 N Spring St; ☉9am-5pm Mon-Fri) **FREE** Until the mid-1960s, no LA building stood taller than City Hall. This 1928 building, with its ziggurat-shaped top, cameoed in the *Superman* and *Dragnet* TV series and the 1953 sci-fi thriller *War of the Worlds*. Soak up views of the city and mountains from the observation deck. Weekday morning tours are free (reservations required).

Wells Fargo History Museum   MUSEUM
(Map p70; ☎213-253-7166; www.wellsfargohistory.com; 333 S Grand Ave; ☉9am-5pm Mon-Fri) **FREE** Sponsored by California-based Wells Fargo Bank, this small but intriguing museum chronicles the gold-rush era with an original Concord stagecoach, a 100oz gold nugget and all sorts of other historical artifacts.

ANGELS FLIGHT

Part novelty act, part commuter train for the lazy, Angels Flight (☎213-626-1901; http://angelsflight.org/; btwn 351 S Hill St & 350 S Grand Ave; fare 50¢; ☉6:45am-10pm) is a funicular built in

Downtown Los Angeles

1901 and billed as the 'shortest railway in the world' (298ft). The adorable cars chug up and down Bunker Hill's steep incline between Hill St and California Watercourt Plaza.

LITTLE TOKYO

Little Tokyo swirls with shopping arcades, Buddhist temples, public art, traditional gardens, authentic sushi bars and noodle shops and a branch of **MOCA** (Map p70; ☑213-626-6222; www.moca.org; 152 N Central Ave; adult/child $12/free; ☺11am-5pm Mon & Fri, to 8pm Thu, to 6pm Sat & Sun).

Japanese American National Museum   MUSEUM
(Map p70; ☑213-625-0414; www.janm.org; 100 N Central Ave; adult/child $9/5; ☺11am-5pm Tue-Wed & Fri-Sun, noon-8pm Thu) Get an in-depth look at the Japanese immigrant experience, including the painful chapter of WWII internment camps. Traveling exhibitions focus on Asian American art and civil rights. Check the online calendar for neighborhood

HISTORIC DOWNTOWN LA

At the center of Downtown's historic district, Pershing Square (Map p70; www.laparks. org/pershingsquare; 532 S Olive St) was LA's first public park (1866) and has been modernized many times since. Now encircled by high-rises, the park exhibits public art and hosts summer concerts and outdoor movie nights.

Nearby, some of LA's turn-of-the-last century architecture remains as it once was. Pop into the 1893 Bradbury Building (Map p70; www.laconservancy.org; 304 S Broadway; ⊘lobby usually 9am-5pm), whose dazzling galleried atrium cameoed in several hit movies, including *Blade Runner*, *(500) Days of Summer* and *The Artist*.

In the early 20th century, Broadway was a glamorous shopping and theater strip, where megastars such as Charlie Chaplin leapt from limos to attend premieres at lavish movie palaces. Some of these – such as the 1926 Orpheum Theater (Map p70; www. laorpheum.com; 842 S Broadway) – have been restored and once again host film screenings and events. Otherwise, the best way to get inside is with Los Angeles Conservancy (p80) on a weekend walking tour (reservations advised).

walking tours, film screenings, Japanese cooking classes and folkcraft workshops.

SOUTH PARK

South Park isn't actually a park but an emerging Downtown LA neighborhood around LA Live (Map p70; www.lalive.com; 800 W Olympic Blvd), a dining and entertainment hub where you'll find the Staples Center (p86) and the Nokia Theatre (Map p70; ☑213-763-6030; www.nokiatheatrelive.com; 777 Chick Hearn Court), home of the MTV Music Awards and *American Idol* finals. Parking at LA Live or in nearby private lots is expensive (flat-rate from $10 to $30).

★ Grammy Museum   MUSEUM
(Map p70; www.grammymuseum.org; 800 W Olympic Blvd; adult/child $13/11, after 6pm $8; ⊘11:30am-7:30pm Mon-Fri, from 10am Sat & Sun; ⋒) Music fans of all stripes will get lost in these mind-expanding interactive displays about the history of American music, where interactive sound booths let you and your entourage try mixing and remixing pop and rock hits, and singing and rapping with the stars.

EXPOSITION PARK & AROUND

Just south of the University of Southern California (USC) campus, this park has a full day's worth of kid-friendly museums. Outdoor landmarks include the Rose Garden (www. laparks.org; 701 State Dr; admission free; ⊘9am-sunset Mar 15–Dec 31) and the 1923 Los Angeles Memorial Coliseum, site of the 1932 and 1984 Summer Olympic Games. Parking costs from $8. From Downtown, take the Metro Expo Line or DASH minibus F.

★ Natural History
Museum of Los Angeles   MUSEUM
(☑213-763-3466; www.nhm.org; 900 Exposition Blvd; adult/child $12/5; ⊘9:30am-5pm; ⋒) Dinos to diamonds, bears to beetles, even an ultra-rare megamouth shark: this science museum will take you around the world and back millions of years in time. Great activities for kids include digging for fossils in the Discovery Center and gaping at gigantic skeletons in the recently reopened Dinosaur Hall.

California Science Center   MUSEUM
(☑film schedule 213-744-2109, info 323-724-3623; www.californiasciencecenter.org; 700 Exposition Park Dr; ⊘10am-5pm; ⋒) FREE A simulated earthquake, hatching baby chicks and a giant techno-doll named Tess bring out the kid in everyone at this great hands-on science museum. It's the new home of the retired Space Shuttle *Endeavour* (reservations are required for viewing). IMAX movies (adult/child $8.25/5) cap off an action-filled day.

California African
American Museum   MUSEUM
(☑213-744-7432; www.caamuseum.org; 600 State Dr; ⊘10am-5pm Tue-Sat, from 11am Sun) FREE Browse a handsome showcase of African American art, culture and history, focusing on California and the western US.

Watts Towers   MONUMENT
(www.wattstowers.org; 1727 E 107th St; adult/child $7/free; ⊘art center 10am-4pm Wed-Sat, from noon Sun; Ⓟ) South LA's beacon of pride, the world-famous Watts Towers are a huge

and fantastical free-form sculpture cobbled together from found objects – from 7-Up bottles to seashells and pottery shards – by folk artist Simon Rodia. Entry by guided tour only. Tours every 30 minutes; 10:30am to 3pm Thursday, Friday and Saturday, from 12:30pm Sunday.

◉ Hollywood

Just as aging movie stars get the occasional facelift, so has Hollywood. While it still hasn't recaptured its mid-20th century 'Golden Age' glamour, its modern seediness is disappearing. The Hollywood Walk of Fame (Map p75; www.walkoffame.com; Hollywood Blvd) honors over 2000 celebrities with stars embedded in the sidewalk.

The Metro Red Line stops beneath Hollywood & Highland (Map p75; ☑ 323-467-6412; www.hollywoodandhighland.com; 6801 Hollywood Blvd), a multistory mall with nicely framed views of the hillside Hollywood Sign, erected in 1923 as an advertisement for a land development called Hollywoodland. Validated mall parking costs $2 for two hours (daily maximum $13).

TCL Chinese Theatre   CINEMA
(Map p75; ☑ tour info 323-461-3331; 6925 Hollywood Blvd) Even the most jaded visitor may feel a thrill in Grauman's famous forecourt, where generations of screen legends have left their imprints in cement: feet, hands, dreadlocks (Whoopi Goldberg), and even magic wands (young stars of *Harry Potter* films). Actors dressed as Superman, Marilyn Monroe and the like pose for photos (for tips), and you may be offered free tickets to TV shows.

Dolby Theatre   THEATER
(Map p75; ☑ 323-308-6300; www.dolbytheatre.com; tour adult/child $17/12; ☺ tours usually 10:30am-4pm) Real-life celebs sashay along this theater's red carpet for the Academy Awards – columns with names of Oscar-winning films line the entryway. Pricey 30-minute tours take you inside the auditorium, VIP room and past an actual Oscar statuette.

Hollywood Forever Cemetery   CEMETERY
(☑ 323-469-1181; www.hollywoodforever.com; 6000 Santa Monica Blvd; ☺ 8am-5pm; P) Rock-and-roll faithful flock to the monument of Johnny Ramone at this historical boneyard, whose other famous residents include Rudolph Valentino, Cecil B DeMille and Bugsy Siegel. Check the online calendar of movie screenings and concerts (yes, really).

Hollywood Museum   MUSEUM
(Map p75; www.thehollywoodmuseum.com; 1660 N Highland Ave; adult/child $15/5; ☺ 10am-5pm Wed-Sun) Inside the art-deco Max Factor Building, this slightly musty 35,000-sq-ft shrine to the stars is crammed with kitsch, costumes, knickknacks and props from Marilyn Monroe to *Glee*.

◉ Griffith Park

America's largest urban park (☑ 323-913-4688; www.laparks.org/dos/parks/griffithpk; 4730 Crystal Springs Dr; ☺ 5am-10:30pm, trails sunrise-sunset; P ♿) FREE is five times the size of New York's Central Park, with an outdoor theater, zoo, observatory, museum, merry-go-round, antique and miniature trains, children's playgrounds, golf, tennis and over 50 miles of hiking paths, including to the original *Batman* TV series cave.

WORTH A TRIP

TOURING MOVIE & TV STUDIOS

Half the fun of visiting Hollywood is hoping you'll see stars. Up the odds by joining the studio audience of a sitcom or game show, which usually tape between August and March. For free tickets, contact Audiences Unlimited (☑ 818-260-0041; www.tvtickets.com).

For an authentic behind-the-scenes look, take a small-group shuttle tour at Warner Bros Studios (☑ 877-492-8687, 818-972-8687; www.wbstudiotour.com; 3400 W Riverside Dr, Burbank; tours from $49; ☺ 8:15am-4pm Mon-Sat, hours vary Sun) or Paramount Pictures (☑ 323-956-1777; www.paramount.com; 5555 Melrose Ave; tours from $48; ☺ tours 9:30am-2pm Mon-Fri, hours vary Sat & Sun), or a walking tour of Sony Pictures Studios (☑ 310-244-8687; www.sonypicturesstudiostours.com; 10202 W Washington Blvd; tour $35; ☺ tours usually 9:30am-2:30pm Mon-Fri). All of these tours show you around sound stages and backlots (outdoor sets), and inside wardrobe and make-up departments. Reservations are required (minimum-age restrictions apply); bring photo ID.

★ **Griffith Observatory** MUSEUM
(☎213-473-0800; www.griffithobservatory.org; 2800 E Observatory Rd; admission free, planetarium shows adult/child $7/3; ⊙noon-10pm Tue-Fri, from 10am Sat & Sun; **P**🚻) **FREE** Inside the iconic triple domes of this 1935 observatory are a state-of-the-art planetarium and the Leonard Nimoy Event Horizon multimedia theater. If nighttime skies are clear, you can often peer through public telescopes at heavenly bodies.

Los Angeles Zoo & Botanical Gardens ZOO
(☎323-644-4200; www.lazoo.org; 5333 Zoo Dr; adult/child $17/12; ⊙10am-5pm; **P**🚻) Make friends with 1100 finned, feathered and furry creatures at this conservation-oriented zoo, including in the Campo Gorilla Reserve and the Sea Life Cliffs, which replicate the California coast complete with harbor seals.

Museum of the American West MUSEUM
(☎323-667-2000; www.autrynationalcenter.org; 4700 Western Heritage Way; adult/child $10/4, 2nd Tue of month free; ⊙10am-4pm Tue-Fri, to 5pm Sat & Sun; **P**) Exhibits on the good, the bad and the ugly of America's westward expansion rope in even the most reluctant of cowpokes (lazy cowboys). Gems include a Colt firearms collection, an ornate saloon and Native American and California gold-rush relics.

⊙ West Hollywood

Welcome to the city of WeHo, where rainbow flags fly proudly over Santa Monica Blvd and celebs keep gossip rags happy by misbehaving at clubs on the fabled Sunset Strip. Boutiques along Robertson Blvd and Melrose Ave purvey sassy and ultrachic fashions for Hollywood royalty and celebutants. WeHo's also a hotbed of cutting-edge interior design, particularly along the Avenues of Art, Fashion & Design (www.avenueswh.com).

Pacific Design Center BUILDING
(PDC; Map p76; www.pacificdesigncenter.com; 8687 Melrose Ave; ⊙9am-5pm Mon-Fri) Some 120 galleries and showrooms fill the monolithic blue, green and red 'whales' of this Cesar Pelli–designed building, which houses a branch of MOCA (Map p76; ☎213-621-1741; www.moca.org; ⊙11am-5pm Tue-Fri, to 6pm Sat & Sun) **FREE**. Visitors can window-shop, though most sales are to the trade. Hourly parking from $6 (daily maximum $13).

⊙ Mid-City

Some of LA's best museums line 'Museum Row,' a short stretch of Wilshire Blvd east of Fairfax Ave.

★ **Los Angeles County Museum of Art** MUSEUM
(LACMA; Map p76; ☎323-857-6000; www.lacma.org; 5905 Wilshire Blvd; adult/child $15/free; ⊙11am-5pm Mon-Tue & Thu, to 9pm Fri, 10am-7pm Sat & Sun; **P**) One of the country's top art museums (and the largest in the western US), LACMA's seven buildings brim with paintings, sculpture and decorative arts: European masters such as Rembrandt, Cézanne and Magritte; ancient pottery from China, Turkey

---

DON'T MISS

UNIVERSAL STUDIOS HOLLYWOOD

Universal Studios Hollywood (www.universalstudioshollywood.com; 100 Universal City Plaza; admission from $80, child under 3yr free; ⊙ daily, hours vary; **P**🚻) first opened to the public in 1915, when studio head Carl Laemmle invited visitors at a quaint 25¢ each (including a boxed lunch) to watch silent films being made. Nearly a century later, Universal remains one of the world's largest movie studios.

Your chances of seeing an actual movie shoot are approximately nil at Universal's current theme park incarnation, yet generations of visitors have had a ball here. Start with the 45-minute narrated studio tour aboard a giant multicar tram that takes you past working soundstages, outdoor sets and King Kong 360, the planet's biggest 3D experience. Also prepare to survive a shark attack à la *Jaws*. It's cheesy but fun.

Among dozens of other attractions, take a motion-simulated romp on the Simpsons Ride, splash down among Jurassic Park dinosaurs or fight off Decepticons in Transformers: The Ride 3-D. The Special Effects Stage illuminates the craft of moviemaking. WaterWorld may have bombed as a movie, but the live action show based on it is a runaway hit, with stunts including giant fireballs and a crash-landing seaplane.

Self-parking is $15 (after 3pm $10), or arrive via the Metro Red Line.

Hollywood

and Iran; photographs by Ansel Adams; and a jewel-box of Japanese screen paintings and sculpture. Parking is $10.

Inside the Renzo Piano–designed **Broad Contemporary Art Museum** at LACMA are seminal pieces by Jasper Johns, Cindy Sherman and Ed Ruscha, and two gigantic works in rusted steel by Richard Serra. LACMA often has headline-grabbing touring exhibits too.

La Brea Tar Pits   ARCHAEOLOGICAL SITE
(Map p76) Between 11,000 and 40,000 years ago, tarlike bubbling crude oil trapped saber-toothed cats, mammoths and other extinct ice-age critters, which are still being excavated here. Check out their fossilized remains at the **Page Museum** (Map p76; ☎ 323-934-7243; www.tarpits.org; 5801 Wilshire Blvd; adult/child $12/5, 1st Tue of month Sep-Jun free; ⏱ 9:30am-5pm; 🅿 👶). New fossils are being discovered all the time, and an active staff of archaeologists works behind glass. Parking is $7 to $9 (cash only).

Petersen Automotive Museum   MUSEUM
(Map p76; www.petersen.org; 6060 Wilshire Blvd; adult/child $12/3; ⏱ 10am-6pm Tue-Sun; 🅿) A four-story ode to the auto, Petersen's exhibits shiny vintage cars galore, plus a fun LA streetscape showing how the city's growth has been shaped by traffic. Parking costs from $2 (maximum $12).

◎ Beverly Hills & Around

The mere mention of Beverly Hills conjures images of Maseratis, manicured mansions and megarich moguls. It's a stylish, sophisticated haven for the well-heeled and famous.

Hollywood

◎ Sights
1 Dolby Theatre A1
2 Hollywood Museum B1
3 TCL Chinese Theatre A1

🛌 Sleeping
4 Hollywood Roosevelt Hotel A1
5 Magic Castle Hotel A1
6 USA Hostels Hollywood B2

✴ Eating
7 Musso & Frank Grill B1
8 Umami Urban C2

✺ Entertainment
9 Arclight Cinemas C2
10 Egyptian Theater B1
11 Hotel Cafe C2
12 Upright Citizens Brigade
   Theatre D1

🛍 Shopping
13 Amoeba Music C2
14 Hollywood & Highland A1

Stargazers could take a guided bus tour to scout for stars' homes.

No trip to LA would be complete without a saunter along pricey, pretentious **Rodeo Drive**, a three-block ribbon where sample-size fembots browse for fashions from international houses – from Armani to Zegna – in couture-design stores. If the prices make you gasp, Beverly Dr, one block east, has more down-to-earth boutiques.

Several central municipal lots and garages offer two hours of free parking.

CALIFORNIA LOS ANGELES

Paley Center for Media   MUSEUM
(Map p76; 310-786-1000; www.paleycenter.
org; 465 N Beverly Dr; suggested donation adult/
child $10/5; noon-5pm Wed-Sun; P) TV and
radio addicts can indulge their passion at
this mind-boggling archive of TV and radio
broadcasts from 1918 through the internet
age. Pick your faves, grab a seat at a private
console and enjoy. Public programs include
lectures and screenings.

Annenberg Space for Photography MUSEUM
(www.annenbergspaceforphotography.org; 2000
Ave of the Stars; 11am-6pm Wed-Fri, 11am-7:30pm
Sat & 11am-6pm Sun; P) FREE See thought-

provoking rotating exhibitions inside the
camera-shaped interior of this museum just
west of Beverly Hills, among the skyscrapers
of Century City. Validated self-parking is
$3.50 from Wednesday to Friday ($1 after
4:30pm), $1 on weekends.

West LA

★**Getty Center**   MUSEUM
(310-440-7300; www.getty.edu; 1200 Getty
Center Dr, off I-405 Fwy; 10am-5:30pm Tue-Sun,
to 9pm Sat; P) FREE Triple delights: a stellar art collection from Renaissance masters

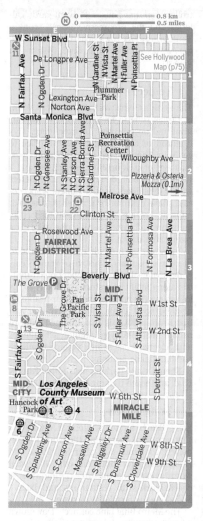

Beverly Hills, West Hollywood & Mid-City

edu; 10899 Wilshire Blvd; adult/child $10/free, Thu free; ⊙11am-8pm Tue-Fri, to 5pm Sat & Sun) has cutting-edge contemporary art exhibits; validated parking is $3.

Westwood Village Memorial Park CEMETERY (www.dignitymemorial.com; 1218 Glendon Ave; ⊙8am-dusk) Tucked among Westwood's high-rises, this postage-stamp-sized grave-yard is packed with such famous 6ft-under residents as Marilyn Monroe and Dean Martin. The gate is south of Wilshire Blvd, one block east of Westwood Blvd.

◎ Malibu

Hugging 27 spectacular miles of the Pacific Coast Hwy, Malibu has long been synonymous with surfing and Hollywood stars, but

to David Hockney, with Richard Meier's fabulous architecture and Robert Irwin's ever-changing gardens. On clear days, add breathtaking views of the city and ocean to the list. Crowds thin in the late afternoon. Parking is $15 (after 5pm $10).

**University of California,
Los Angeles** UNIVERSITY
(UCLA; www.ucla.edu; P) Westwood is dominated by the vast campus of prestigious UCLA, with its impressive botanical and sculpture gardens. The university's excellent **Hammer Museum** (http://hammer.ucla.

CALIFORNIA LOS ANGELES

it actually looks far less posh than glossy tabloids make it sound. Still, it has been celebrity central since the 1930s. Steven Spielberg, Barbra Streisand, Dustin Hoffman and other A-listers have homes here, and can sometimes be spotted shopping at the villagelike **Malibu Country Mart** (www. malibucountrymart.com; 3835 Cross Creek Rd) or more utilitarian **Malibu Colony Plaza** (www. malibucolonyplaza.com; 23841 W Malibu Rd).

One of Malibu's twin natural treasures is mountainous **Malibu Creek State Park** (☑818-880-0367; www.malibucreekstatepark.org; ☺dawn-dusk), a popular movie- and TV-filming location with hiking trails galore (parking $12). The other is a string of beaches, including aptly named **Surfrider** west of Malibu Pier, wilder **Point Dume State Beach** and family fave **Zuma Beach** (beach parking $10).

★**Getty Villa**   MUSEUM
(☑310-430-7300; www.getty.edu; 17985 Pacific Coast Hwy; ☺10am-5pm Wed-Mon; P) **FREE** Malibu's cultural star, this replica Roman villa is a fantastic showcase of Greek, Roman and Etruscan antiquities, embraced by peristyle and herb gardens. Admission is by timed ticket (no walk-ins, reservations required). Parking is $15.

◉ Santa Monica

The belle by the beach mixes urban cool with a laid-back vibe. Tourists, teens and street performers make car-free, chain-store-lined **Third Street Promenade** the most action-packed zone. For more local flavor, shop celeb-favored **Montana Avenue** or eclectic **Main Street**, backbone of the neighborhood once nicknamed 'Dogtown,' the birthplace of skateboard culture.

There's free 90-minute parking in most public garages downtown.

Santa Monica Pier   AMUSEMENT PARK
(Map p79; http://santamonicapier.org; all-day ride pass $13-20; P ♿) **FREE** Kids love the venerable pier, where attractions include a quaint carousel and a solar-powered Ferris wheel. Peer under the pier at the tiny **aquarium** (Map p79; ☑310-393-6149; www.healthebay.org; 1600 Ocean Front Walk; adult/child $5/free; ☺2-5pm Tue-Fri, 12:30-5pm Sat & Sun; ♿). Parking rates vary seasonally.

Bergamot Station Arts Center   ARTS CENTER
(www.bergamotstation.com; 2525 Michigan Ave; ☺10am-6pm Tue-Fri, 11am-5:30pm Sat; P) Art fans gravitate inland toward this former

trolley stop that houses 35 avant-garde galleries and the progressive **Santa Monica Museum of Art** (www.smmoa.org; 2525 Michigan Ave; donation adult/child $5/3; ☺11am-6pm Tue-Sat).

◉ Venice

The **Venice Boardwalk** (Ocean Front Walk) is a freak show, a human zoo, a wacky carnival and an essential LA experience. This cauldron of counterculture is the place to get your hair braided and a *qi gong* back massage, or pick up cheap sunglasses and a Rastafarian-colored-knit beret. Encounters with bodybuilders, hoop dreamers, a Speedo-clad snake charmer or a roller-skating Sikh minstrel are almost guaranteed, especially on sunny afternoons. Alas, the vibe gets creepy after dark.

To escape the hubbub, meander inland to the **Venice Canals**, a vestige of Venice's early days when Italian gondoliers poled tourists along artificial waterways. Today locals lollygag in rowboats in this flower-festooned neighborhood. Funky, hipper-than-ever **Abbot Kinney Blvd** is a palm-lined mile of restaurants, cafes, yoga studios, art galleries and eclectic shops selling vintage furniture and handmade fashions.

There's street parking near Abbot Kinney Blvd, and beach parking lots ($5 to $15).

◉ Long Beach

Long Beach stretches along LA County's southern flank, heralding the world's third-busiest container port after Singapore and Hong Kong. Its industrial edge has been worn smooth downtown – **Pine Ave** is chockablock with restaurants and bars – and along the restyled waterfront.

The Metro Blue Line connects Downtown LA with Long Beach in about an hour. **Passport** (www.lbtransit.com) minibuses shuttle around major tourist sights for free ($1.25 elsewhere in town).

Queen Mary   BOAT
(www.queenmary.com; 1126 Queens Hwy; tours adult/child from $14/7; ☺10am-6:30pm; P) Long Beach's 'flagship' is the grand (and supposedly haunted!) British ocean liner, which is permanently moored here. Larger and fancier than the *Titanic,* it transported royals, dignitaries, immigrants and troops during its 1001 Atlantic crossings between 1936 and 1964. Parking is $12.

Santa Monica & Venice

Santa Monica & Venice

◉ Sights
1 Santa Monica Pier.................................A2
2 Santa Monica Pier Aquarium A2

🛏 Sleeping
3 HI Los Angeles-Santa Monica............A2
4 Sea Shore Motel...................................A4
5 Viceroy A2

✕ Eating
6 Santa Monica Farmers Markets A1
7 Santa Monica Place A2

🍷 Drinking & Nightlife
8 Copa d'Oro...A2
9 Intelligentsia Coffeebar......................B5
10 Roosterfish A5

🛍 Shopping
11 Abbot Kinney Boulevard A5
12 Magellan...B1
13 Main Street...A3

and take a self-guided audio tour of this retired Pacific battleship, which transported FDR and General MacArthur during WWII and saw action in the Cold War. Parking from $1.

Museum of Latin American Art MUSEUM
(www.molaa.org; 628 Alamitos Ave; adult/child $9/free, Sun free; ⊙11am-5pm Wed-Sun, to 9pm Thu; 🅿) Although small, it's the only western US museum specializing in contemporary art from south of the border. The permanent collection highlights spirituality and landscapes, with colorful temporary exhibits and a sculpture garden out back.

◉ Pasadena

Below the lofty San Gabriel Mountains, this city drips with wealth and gentility, feeling a world apart from urban LA. It's known for its early 20th-century arts-and-crafts architecture and the Tournament of Roses Parade on New Year's Day.

Amble on foot around the shops, cafes, bars and restaurants of **Old Town Pasadena**, along Colorado Blvd east of Pasadena Ave. Metro Gold Line trains connect Pasadena and Downtown LA (30 minutes).

★Huntington Library MUSEUM, GARDEN
(☑626-405-2100; www.huntington.org; 1151 Oxford Rd, San Marino; adult weekday/weekend & hol $20/23, child $8, 1st Thu of month free; ⊙10:30am-4:30pm Wed-Mon Jun-Aug, noon-4:30pm Mon &

Aquarium of the Pacific AQUARIUM
(☑tickets 562-590-3100; www.aquariumofpacific.org; 100 Aquarium Way; adult/child $26/15; ⊙9am-6pm; 🚌) Let kids take a high-tech adventure through an underwater world where sharks dart, jellyfish dance and sea lions frolic. Validated parking is $8 to $15. *Queen Mary* or LA Zoo combination tickets are discounted for even less online.

USS Iowa MUSEUM, MEMORIAL
(☑877-446-9261; www.pacificbattleship.com; 250 S Harbor Blvd, Berth 87; adult/child $18/10; ⊙10am-5pm, from 9am Jun-Aug; 🅿) Near the port in San Pedro, step onto the gangway

Wed-Fri, from 10:30am Sat, Sun & hol Sep-May; P)
Its name is LA's biggest understatement.
While the Huntington does have a library of
rare books, including a Gutenberg Bible, it's
the masterful collection of European art and
exquisite gardens that make it a destination.
The Rose Garden blooms with over 1200 varieties
and the Desert Garden has Seussian-shaped
succulents. Free admission on first
Thursdays requires advance ticketing.

Gamble House ARCHITECTURE
(info 626-793-3334, tickets 800-979-3370; www.
gamblehouse.org; 4 Westmoreland Pl; tours adult/
child from $12.50/free; tours noon-3pm Thu-Sun,
gift shop 10am-5pm Tue-Sat, 11:30am-5pm Sun;
P) A masterpiece of California arts-and-crafts
architecture, the 1908 Gamble House
designed by architects Charles and Henry
Greene was Doc Brown's home in the movie
Back to the Future. Admission is only by
guided tour (reservations recommended).

Norton Simon Museum MUSEUM
(www.nortonsimon.org; 411 W Colorado Blvd; adult/
child $10/free; noon-6pm Wed-Mon, to 9pm Fri;
P) Stroll west of Old Town to visit Rodin's
The Thinker, a mere overture to the symphony
of European, Asian, modern and contemporary
art – even priceless prints and
photography – at this modest museum.

🏃 Activities

Cycling & In-line Skating
Get scenic exercise in-line skating or riding
along the paved South Bay Bicycle Trail,
which parallels the beach for most of the 22
miles between Santa Monica and Pacific Palisades.
Rental outfits are plentiful in beach
towns. Warning: it's crowded on weekends.

Hiking
Turn on your celeb radar while strutting it
with the hot bods along Runyon Canyon
Park above Hollywood. Griffith Park is
also laced with trails. For longer rambles,
head to the Santa Monica Mountains, where
Will Rogers State Historic Park, Topanga
State Park and Malibu Creek State Park
are all excellent gateways to beautiful terrain
(parking $8 to $12).

Swimming & Surfing
Top beaches for swimming are Malibu's
Zuma Beach, Santa Monica State Beach
and the South Bay's Hermosa Beach. Malibu's
Surfrider Beach is a legendary surfing
spot. Parking rates vary seasonally.

'Endless Summer' is, sorry to report, a
myth, so much of the year you'll want to
wear a wet suit in the Pacific. Water temperatures
become tolerable by June and peak
at about 70°F (21°C) in August and September.
Water quality varies; check the 'Beach
Report Card' at www.healthebay.org.

👉 Tours

⭐Esotouric BUS TOUR
(323-223-2767; www.esotouric.com; tours $58)
Hip, offbeat, insightful and entertaining
tours themed around famous crime sites
(Black Dahlia), literary lions (Chandler to
Bukowski) and LA's historic neighborhoods.

Los Angeles Conservancy WALKING TOUR
(info 213-430-4219, reservations 213-623-2489;
www.laconservancy.org; tours adult/child $10/5)
Thematic guided tours, mostly of Downtown
LA, focusing on architecture and history.
Check the website for self-guided audio
tours.

Museum of Neon Art BUS TOUR
(213-489-9918; http://neonmona.org; tours $55;
Sat Jun-Sep) Nighttime guided bus tours
that cruise the city's neon jungle, starting
from Downtown LA.

Melting Pot Tours WALKING TOUR
(800-979-3370; www.meltingpottours.com; tours
adult/child from $53/28) Eat your way through
the Original Farmers Market, Thai Town or
East LA's Latin flavors.

Dearly Departed BUS TOUR
(800-979-3370; www.dearlydepartedtours.com;
tours $45-75) Occasionally creepy, hilarious
'tragical' history tours of where famous stars
kicked the bucket.

🎉 Festivals & Events

Monthly street fairs for art-gallery hopping,
shopping and food-truck meet-ups include
Downtown LA Art Walk (www.downtownart
walk.com; 2nd Thu of month) and First Fridays
in Venice (1st Fri of month).

Tournament of Roses PARADE, SPORTS
(www.tournamentofroses.com) New Year's Day
cavalcade of flower-festooned floats along
Pasadena's Colorado Blvd, followed by the
Rose Bowl college football game.

Fiesta Broadway STREET FAIR
(http://fiestabroadway.la) Mexican-themed market
in Downtown LA, with performances by
Latino stars, on the last Sunday in April.

Watts Towers Day of the
Drum & Jazz Festivals ART, MUSIC

(http://wattstowers.org) Two days of drums circles, jazz jams and an arts-and-crafts fair in South LA during late September.

West Hollywood
Halloween Carnaval STREET FAIR

(www.visitwesthollywood.com) Eccentric, often NC17-rated costumes, live bands and DJs along Santa Monica Blvd on October 31.

🛏 Sleeping

For seaside life, base yourself in Santa Monica, Venice or Long Beach. Cool-hunters and party people will be happiest in Hollywood or WeHo; culture-vultures, in Downtown LA. Expect a lodging tax of 12% to 14%.

🛏 Downtown

Figueroa Hotel HISTORIC HOTEL **$$**
(Map p70; ☑213-627-8971, 800-421-9092; www.figueroahotel.com; 939 S Figueroa St; r $148-194, ste $225-265; P❄@🛜🏊🐕) A rambling 1920s oasis across from LA Live welcomes travelers with a richly tiled Spanish-style lobby that segues to a sparkling pool. Rooms are furnished in a global mash-up of styles (Morocco, Mexico, Zen), varying in size and configuration. Parking is $12.

Standard Downtown LA BOUTIQUE HOTEL **$$$**
(Map p70; ☑213-892-8080; http://standardhotels.com/downtown-la; 550 S Flower St; r $245-525; ste $1150-1300; P❄@🛜🏊🐕) This design-savvy hotel in a former office building goes for a young, hip and shag-happy crowd – the rooftop bar fairly pulses – so don't come here to get a solid night's sleep. Mod, minimalist rooms have platform beds and peek-through showers. Parking from $33.

🛏 Hollywood & West Hollywood

USA Hostels Hollywood HOSTEL **$**
(Map p75; ☑800-524-6783, 323-462-3777; www.usahostels.com; 1624 Schrader Blvd; dm $28-41, r without bath $81-104; ❄@🛜) Not for introverts, this energetic hostel puts you within steps of Hollywood's party circuit. Make new friends during BBQ and comedy nights, city tours or fruit-and-pancake breakfasts in the common kitchen.

★**Magic Castle Hotel** HOTEL **$$**
(Map p75; ☑323-851-0800; http://magiccastlehotel.com; 7025 Franklin Ave; r incl breakfast from $175; P❄@🛜🏊🐕) Walls are thin, but renovated

---

LOS ANGELES FOR CHILDREN

Keeping kids happy is child's play in LA. The sprawling Los Angeles Zoo (p74) in family-friendly Griffith Park (p73) is a sure bet. Dino-fans will dig the La Brea Tar Pits (p75) and the Natural History Museum (p72), while budding scientists crowd the California Science Center (p72). For under-the-sea creatures, head to the Aquarium of the Pacific (p79) in Long Beach, where teens might get a kick out of ghost tours of the *Queen Mary* (p78). The amusement park at Santa Monica Pier (p78) is fun for all ages. Activities for younger kids are more limited at tween/teen-oriented Universal Studios Hollywood (p74). In neighboring Orange County, Disneyland (p90) and Knott's Berry Farm (p90) are ever-popular theme parks.

---

apartments in this courtyard building come with contemporary furniture and attractive art, and suites have a separate living room. Complimentary snacks and access to a private club for magicians. Parking is $10.

Hollywood
Roosevelt Hotel BOUTIQUE HOTEL **$$$**
(Map p75; ☑323-466-7000, 800-950-7667; www.hollywoodroosevelt.com; 7000 Hollywood Blvd; r from $330; P❄@🛜🏊) Venerable historic hotel has hosted elite players since the first Academy Awards were held here in 1929. It pairs a palatial Spanish lobby with sleek Asian contemporary rooms, a glam pool scene and rockin' restos and lounges. Parking is $33.

London West Hollywood LUXURY HOTEL **$$$**
(Map p76; ☑866-282-4560; www.thelondonwesthollywood.com; 1020 N San Vicente Blvd; ste incl breakfast from $279; P❄@🛜🏊🐕) Gleaming like Harry Winston diamonds, just south of the Sunset Strip, the London dazzles with slick design, a swish restaurant by *Hell's Kitchen* chef Gordon Ramsay and a rooftop pool sporting panoramic views of the Hollywood Hills. Parking is $30.

🛏 Mid-City & Beverly Hills

StayOn Beverly HOSTEL **$**
(www.stayonbeverly.com; 4619 Beverly Blvd; r without bath $50-55; P❄🛜) In Koreatown, this Danish photographer's stripped-down

hostel is a tidy, secure base camp for backpackers and flashpackers. Ten basic rooms each have a mini fridge, with a shared microwave in the common coffee corner. Limited free self-parking.

Farmer's Daughter Hotel   MOTEL $$

(Map p76; 323-937-3930, 800-334-1658; www.farmersdaughterhotel.com; 115 S Fairfax Ave; r from $185; P❄@🗩🛇) Opposite the Original Farmers Market and CBS Studios, this perennial pleaser gets high marks for its sleek 'urban cowboy' look. Adventurous lovebirds, ask about the No Tell Room. Parking is $18.

Avalon Hotel   HOTEL $$$

(Map p76; 310-277-5221, 800-670-6183; www.viceroyhotelgroup.com/avalon; 9400 W Olympic Blvd; r from $210; ❄@🗩🛇🐾) Mid-century modern gets a 21st-century spin at this fashion-crowd fave, formerly Marilyn Monroe's pad in its apartment-building days. Today the beautiful, moneyed and metrosexual vamp it up in the buzzy resto-bar overlooking an hourglass-shaped pool. Parking is $30.

Santa Monica

★ HI Los Angeles-Santa Monica   HOSTEL $

(Map p79; 310-393-9913; www.hilosangeles.org; 1436 2nd St; dm $38-49, r without bath $99-159; ❄@🗩) Near the beach and Third Street Promenade, the location is the envy of much fancier places. Its 260 beds in single-sex dorms and bed-in-a-box doubles are clean and safe, and there are plenty of groovy public spaces to lounge or surf the web. All accommodation with shared bath.

Sea Shore Motel   MOTEL $$

(Map p79; 310-392-2787; www.seashoremotel.com; 2637 Main St; r from $110; P❄🗩) Clean, friendly, family-owned lodgings are two blocks from the beach and right on happening Main St (expect ambient noise). Spanish-tiled rooms are basic but attractive, and kitchen suites are roomy enough for families.

★ Viceroy   BOUTIQUE HOTEL $$$

(Map p79; 310-260-7500, 800-622-8711; www.viceroysantamonica.com; 1819 Ocean Ave; r from $350; P❄@🗩🛇🐾) Ignore the high-rise eyesore exterior to plunge headlong into *Top Design* judge Kelly Wearstler's campy 'Hollywood Regency' decor and color palette of dolphin gray to lime green. Lounge in poolside cabanas, Italian designer linens and a chic resto-bar. Parking is $35.

Long Beach

Hotel Varden   BOUTIQUE HOTEL $$

(562-432-8950, 877-382-7336; www.thevardenhotel.com; 335 Pacific Ave; r incl continental breakfast from $119; P❄@🗩🛇) Interior designers clearly had a modernist field day renovating the 35 diminutive rooms at this 1929 hotel: tiny desks, tiny sinks, lots of right angles, cushy beds, white, white and more white. It's two blocks west of hoppin' Pine Ave. Parking is $11.

Pasadena

Saga Motor Hotel   MOTEL $

(626-795-0431, 800-793-7242; www.thesagamotorhotel.com; 1633 E Colorado Blvd; r incl breakfast $79-99; P❄@🗩🛅) On historic Route 66, this midcentury modern 1950s motel has rooms that are spotless, even if they don't set new style standards. A heated pool ringed by chaises lets you soak up SoCal sunshine.

✕ Eating

LA's culinary scene is California's most vibrant and eclectic, from celebrity chefs whipping up farmers-market menus to down-home authentic global cuisine. With some 140 nationalities living in LA, ethnic neighborhoods for foodies to explore abound, including downtown's Little Tokyo and Chinatown, Mid-City's Koreatown, Thai Town east of Hollywood, East LA's Boyle Heights for Mexican flavors, the South Bay's Torrance for Japanese kitchens, and Monterey Park and Alhambra, east of Pasadena, for dim sum and regional Chinese cooking.

✕ Downtown

For cheap, fast meals-on-the-go, graze the international food stalls of the historic Grand Central Market (Map p70; www.grandcentralsquare.com; 317 S Broadway; ☺9am-6pm).

Philippe the Original   DINER $

(Map p70; 213-628-3781; www.philippes.com; 1001 N Alameda St; mains $4-10; ☺6am-10pm; P🛅) LAPD hunks, stressed-out attorneys and Midwestern vacationers chow down at this legendary 'home of the French dip sandwich,' dating back to 1908. Order your choice of meat on a crusty roll dipped in *jus,* and hunker down at community tables on the sawdust-covered floor. Cash only.

Gorbals
EASTERN EUROPEAN **$$**

(Map p70; ☑213-488-3408; www.thegorbalsla. com; 501 S Spring St; dishes $6-43; ☺lunch & dinner) *Top Chef* winner Ilan Hall tweaks traditional Jewish comfort food: bacon-wrapped matzo balls, potato latkes with smoked apple sauce, *gribenes* (chicken-skin cracklings) served BLT style. It's hidden at the back of the Alexandria Hotel lobby.

Nickel Diner
DINER **$$**

(Map p70; ☑213-623-8301; http://nickeldiner. com; 524 S Main St; mains $7-14; ☺8am-3:30pm Tue-Sun, 6-10:30pm Tue-Sat) In Downtown's historic theater district, this red-vinyl joint feels like a 1920s throwback. Ingredients are 21st-century, though: avocados stuffed with quinoa salad, 'lowrider' chili burgers and must-try doughnuts. Expect long waits.

Bäco Mercat
TAPAS **$$$**

(Map p70; ☑213-687-8808; http://bacomercat.com; 408 S Main St; small plates $8-19; ☺11:30am-2pm & 5:30-11pm Mon-Thu, 11:30-3pm & 5:30pm-midnight Fri & Sat, 11:30am-3pm & 5-10pm Sun) Daringly creative pan-Asian and Californian twists on traditional Spanish tapas flow out to outdoor patio tables at this elegant downtown kitchen. Specialty *bäco* (flatbread sandwiches) comes happily stuffed with anything from oxtail hash to pork carnitas.

Bottega Louie
ITALIAN **$$$**

(Map p70; ☑213-802-1470; www.bottegalouie. com; 700 S Grand Ave; mains $8-35; ☺8am-11pm Mon-Thu, 8am-midnight Fri, 9am-midnight Sat, 9am-11pm Sun) Louie's wide marble bar has become a magnet for the artsy loft set and office workers alike. The open-kitchen crew, in chef's whites, grills housemade sausage and wood-fired thin-crust pizzas in the white-on-white dining room. Always busy, always buzzy.

✕ Hollywood

Griddle Café
BREAKFAST **$$**

(Map p76; ☑323-874-0377; www.thegriddlecafe. com; 7916 W Sunset Blvd; mains $10-18; ☺7am-4pm Mon-Fri, from 8am Sat & Sun) Whimsically named sugar-bomb pancakes, giant-sized egg scrambles and French-press coffee pots keep the wooden tables and U-shaped counter full all day long at this pit-stop favored by Hollywood's young and tousled. Hungover hordes huddle outside on weekends.

Umami Urban
BURGERS **$$**

(Map p75; ☑323-469-3100; www.umami.com; 1520 N Cahuenga Blvd; mains $10-15; ☺11am-11pm Sun-Thu, to midnight Fri & Sat) Inside hip Space 15 Twenty shopping plaza, Umami elevates gourmet burgers with green Hatch chilies, smoked-salt onion strings and more. Order poutine fries, craft beers or peppermint lemonade on the side. Also in Los Feliz, Santa Monica, Westwood and Mid-City.

★ Pizzeria & Osteria Mozza
ITALIAN **$$$**

(☑323-297-0100; www.mozza-la.com; 6602 Melrose Ave; pizzas $11-20, dinner mains $27-38; ☺pizzeria noon-midnight daily, osteria 5:30-11pm Mon-Fri, 5-11pm Sat, 5-10pm Sun) Reserve weeks ahead for LA's hottest Italian eatery, run by celebrity chefs Mario Batali and Nancy Silverton. Two restaurants share the same building, with a wide-ranging traditional Italian menu at the osteria, and precision-made pizzas and savory antipasti inside the pizzeria.

Musso & Frank Grill
AMERICAN **$$$**

(Map p75; ☑323-467-7788; www.mussoandfrank. com; 6667 Hollywood Blvd; mains $9-45; ☺11am-11pm Tue-Sat) Hollywood history hangs thickly in the air at the boulevard's oldest eatery. Waiters balance platters of steaks, chops and other heart-attack dishes harking back to the days when cholesterol wasn't part of our vocabulary. Service is smooth, and so are the martinis.

✕ West Hollywood, Mid-City & Beverly Hills

Veggie Grill
VEGETARIAN **$**

(Map p76; ☑323-822-7575; www.veggiegrill.com; 8000 W Sunset Blvd; mains $7-10; ☺11am-11pm; ☑⬤) If crispy chickin' wings or a carne asada sandwich don't sound vegetarian, know that this darn tasty local chain uses seasoned vegetable proteins (mostly tempeh). Gluten-free and nut-free options are offered too. Also in Hollywood, Mid-City, Westwood, Santa Monica and Long Beach.

Original Farmers Market
MARKET **$**

(Map p76; www.farmersmarketla.com; 6333 W 3rd St; most mains $6-12; ☺9am-9pm Mon-Fri, to 8pm Sat, 10am-7pm Sun; P⬤) Although now heavily commercialized, the market still has a few worthy, budget-friendly eateries, most alfresco. Try Du-Par's classic diner, Cajun-style cooking at the Gumbo Pot or ¡Loteria! Mexican grill. Free two-hour validated parking.

★ **Night + Market** THAI $$
(Map p76; ☑ 310-275-9724; www.nightmarketla.
com; 9041 W Sunset Blvd; mains $10-19; ☺6-
10:30pm Tue-Sun, last order 9:45pm) Dying for
spicy-hot Thai food? Good, because that's
the only way you're going to get it at this
tiny Sunset Strip kitchen dishing up street
food like salt-crusted fish, duck larb and
'startled' grilled pork. Enter through Talesai
restaurant and duck behind the red curtain
by the bar.

★ **Bazaar** SPANISH $$$
(Map p76; ☑ 310-246-5555; www.thebazaar.com;
SLS Hotel, 465 S La Cienega Blvd; small plates $8-
42; ☺6-10:30pm Sun-Wed, to 11:30pm Thu-Sat)
Bazaar dazzles with over-the-top interior
design by Philippe Starck and 'molecular
gastronomic' tapas by José Andrés. Stuffed
piquillo peppers and sea-urchin sandwiches
explode with flavor in your mouth, or bite
into cotton-candy foie gras and Wagyu-beef
Philly cheese-steaks on 'air bread.'

✖ Malibu

Malibu Seafood SEAFOOD $
(☑ 310-456-3430; www.malibuseafood.com; 25653
Pacific Coast Hwy; most mains $8-15; ☺11am-8pm;
☐ ♿) Beloved by locals, this roadside seafood market grills tasty, simply prepared fish
fillets, baskets of fried seafood, sandwiches
and salads. Homemade tartar sauce and
clam chowder are both winners.

Paradise Cove Beach Cafe AMERICAN $$$
(☑ 310-457-2503; www.paradisecovemalibu.com;
28128 Pacific Coast Hwy; mains $11-36; ☺8am-
10pm; ☐ ♿) It's your movie-perfect image of
SoCal: stick your feet in the sand and knock
back piña coladas and fish tacos at this Cal-
ifornia-casual institution on a private beach
where *Beach Blanket Bingo* was filmed.
Four-hour validated parking $6.

✖ Santa Monica & Venice

★ **Santa Monica**
Farmers Markets MARKET $
(Map p79; www.smgov.net/portals/farmersmarket;
Arizona Ave, btwn 2nd & 3rd Sts; ☺8:30am-1:30pm
Wed, to 1pm Sat; ♿) ✎ Downtown Santa Mon-
ica's twice-weekly farmers market brings
out even star chefs to peruse a cornucopia of
fresh, often organic produce, while local res-
taurants set up stalls in the food tent. Main
St's Saturday morning market is more of a
community street fair.

Lemonade CALIFORNIAN $$
(http://lemonadela.com; 1661 Abbot Kinney Blvd;
small dishes $5-11; ☺11am-9pm) Look for an
imaginative seasonal line-up of deli salads,
such as butter lettuce with pink grapefruit;
seafood plates like seared tuna with watermelon radish; jerk pineapple chicken;
custom-made sourdough sandwiches; and
lotsa flavored lemonades – blueberry-mint!
Also in Downtown LA, Mid-City, Pasadena
and at LAX airport.

Santa Monica Place SHOPPING CENTER $$
(Map p79; www.santamonicaplace.com; 395 Santa
Monica Pl; ☺restaurants daily, hours vary; ♿) We
wouldn't normally eat at a mall, but this one
gets high marks for Latin-Asian fusion at
Zengo, Antica's wood-oven-fired pizzas and
M.A.K.E. raw vegan cuisine. Most 3rd-floor
restaurants have seating with views across
rooftops – some to the ocean – while market
stalls do everything from *salumi* to souf-
flés. Ground floor True Food Kitchen trends
healthy, vegetarian-friendly and gluten-free.

Father's Office PUB $$
(☑ 310-736-2224; www.fathersoffice.com; 1018
Montana Ave; dishes $5-15; ☺5-10pm Mon-Wed,
5-11pm Thu, 4-11pm Fri, noon-11pm Sat, noon-10pm
Sun) Everybody knows your name, or they
soon will, at this loud, elbow-to-elbow watering hole where barkeeps skillfully explain
dozens of beers on tap. Just don't ask for
substitutions on their decadent burgers. Bar
open till midnight or later daily. Second location in Culver City.

✖ Long Beach

George's Greek Café GREEK $$
(☑ 562-437-1184; www.georgesgreekcafe.com; 135
Pine Ave; mains $9-26; ☺10am-10pm Sun-Thu,
to 11pm Fri & Sat) George himself may greet
you at the entrance by the airy patio, in the
heart of Pine Ave's restaurant row. Locals
are addicted to the flaming *saganaki* (fried
cheese), fresh pita bread and lamb chops.

✖ Pasadena

Ración SPANISH $$
(☑ 626-396-3090; http://racionrestaurant.com;
119 W Green St; shared plates $5-27; ☺6-10pm Tue-
Thu, 6-11pm Fri, 11am-2pm & 5:30-11pm Sat, 11am-
2pm & 5:30-10pm Sun) Two blocks south of Old
Town Pasadena, this warm, streetfront tapas
bar lets you sample Basque-inspired dishes,
including house-cured charcuterie, imported cheeses and seasonal smoked vegetables.

🍸 Drinking

Hollywood has been legendary sipping territory since before the Rat Pack days, and the rockin' Sunset Strip is almost as much of a party zone as it was in the 1960s. Creative cocktails are the order of the day at the reinvented watering holes in Downtown LA and edgier neighborhoods. Beachside bars run the gamut from surfer dives and Irish-esque pubs to candlelit cocktail lounges.

⭐ **Edison** BAR
(Map p70; ☑213-613-0000; www.edisondowntown.com; 108 W 2nd St, off Harlem Pl; ☺5pm-2am Wed-Fri, from 7pm Sat) *Metropolis* meets *Blade Runner* at this industrial-chic basement boîte, where you'll be sipping hand-crafted cocktails surrounded by turbines and other machinery back from its days as a power plant. It's all tarted up with cocoa leather couches, three cavernous bars and a hoity-toity dress code.

Copa d'Oro BAR
(Map p79; www.copadoro.com; 217 Broadway, Santa Monica; ☺5:30pm-midnight Mon-Wed, to 2am Thu-Sat) A smooth, lamplit ambience will woo your sweetheart at this Santa Monica sanctuary. Artisanal cocktails draw from a well of top-end liquors and a farmers market's basket of fresh herbs, fruit and even veggies. Teetotaler? Ask for a fresh-pressed organic juice or homemade soda.

Seven Grand BAR
(Map p70; ☑213-614-0737; http://sevengrand-bars.com; 2nd fl, 515 W 7th St; ☺5pm-2am Mon-Wed, from 4pm Thu & Fri, from 7pm Sat) At Seven Grand, hipsters have invaded Mummy and Daddy's hunt club, amid tartan-patterned carpeting and deer heads on the walls. Whiskey is the drink of choice: choose from over 100 brands from Tennessee, Scotland, Ireland and Japan. There's an enforced dress code.

El Carmen BAR
(Map p76; 8138 W 3rd St; ☺5pm-2am Mon-Fri, from 7pm Sat & Sun) Mounted bull heads and *lucha libre* (Mexican wrestling) masks create an over-the-top 'Tijuana North' look that pulls in an entertainment-industry-heavy crowd. Swig happy-hour margaritas or peruse the 100-strong tequila and mezcal menu.

Intelligentsia Coffeebar CAFE
(Map p79; www.intelligentsiacoffee.com; 1331 Abbot Kinney Blvd; ☺6am-8pm Mon-Wed, to 11pm Thu & Fri, 7am-11pm Sat, 7am-8pm Sun; 🖥) In Venice's hip, architecturally minimalist monument to coffee, perfectionistic baristas never short you on foam or caffeine, and direct-trade beans are artfully roasted. Also in Silver Lake and Pasadena.

GAY & LESBIAN LA

'Boystown,' along Santa Monica Blvd in West Hollywood (WeHo), is gay ground zero, where dozens of high-energy bars, cafes, restaurants, gyms and clubs mostly cater to men. Silver Lake, LA's original gay enclave, has evolved from largely leather-and-Levi's to encompass multiethnic, metrosexual hipsters. Long Beach has a more laid-back gay community.

Out & About (www.outandabout-tours.com) Leads weekend walking tours of the city's lesbi-gay cultural landmarks. **LA Pride** (www.lapride.org) celebrations in mid-June attract hundreds of thousands of LGBT locals and out-of-town visitors for nonstop partying and a parade down Santa Monica Boulevard.

Abbey (Map p76; www.abbeyfoodandbar.com; 692 N Robertson Blvd; mains $9-13; ☺8am-2am) At WeHo's essential gay bar and restaurant, take your pick of preening on a leafy patio, in a slick lounge or on a dance floor, and enjoy flavored martinis and upscale pub grub. A dozen other bars and nightclubs are within walking distance.

Akbar (www.akbarsilverlake.com; 4356 W Sunset Blvd) Killer jukebox and a Los Feliz crowd that's been known to change from hour to hour – gay, straight or just hip, but not too-hip-for-you. Some nights the back room becomes a dance floor.

Roosterfish (Map p79; www.roosterfishbar.com; 1302 Abbot Kinney Blvd; ☺11am-2am) Venice's oldest gay bar has been serving men for over three decades. It's dark and divey yet chill, with a pool table and back patio.

☆ Entertainment

LA Weekly (www.laweekly.com) and the *Los Angeles Times* (www.latimes.com) have extensive entertainment listings. Buy tickets online, at the box office or through Ticketmaster (☎213-480-3232; www.ticketmaster.com). For discounted and half-price tickets, check Goldstar (www.goldstar.com) and ScoreBig (www.scorebig.com) for stage, concert, comedy and sports events, or LA Stage Alliance (www.lastagealliance.com) and Plays 411 (www.plays411.com) strictly for theater.

To confirm all your pre-conceived prejudices about LA, look no further than a velvet-roped nightclub in Hollywood. Come armed with a hot bod or a fat wallet to impress the goonish bouncers. Clubs are generally open from 9:30pm to 2am Thursdays to Sundays; cover charges average $20 (bring photo ID).

★ **Hollywood Bowl**   LIVE MUSIC

(☎323-850-2000; www.hollywoodbowl.com; 2301 N Highland Ave; ⊙Jun-Sep; ⊛) This historic outdoor amphitheater is the LA Phil's summer home and a stellar place to catch big-name rock, jazz, blues and pop acts. Come early for a preshow picnic (alcohol allowed).

Staples Center   SPECTATOR SPORTS, LIVE MUSIC

(Map p70; ☎213-742-7340; www.staplescenter.com; 1111 S Figueroa St; ⊛) Fans fill this flying-saucer-shaped home of the LA Lakers, Clippers and Sparks basketball teams, and Kings ice-hockey team. Headliners – Brunos Mars to Justin Bieber – also perform.

Los Angeles Philharmonic   ORCHESTRA

(Map p70; ☎323-850-2000; www.laphil.org; 111 S Grand Ave) The world-class LA Phil performs classics and cutting-edge works at Walt Disney Concert Hall (p69) under the baton of Venezuelan phenom Gustavo Dudamel.

★ **Upright Citizens Brigade Theatre**   COMEDY

(Map p75; ☎323-908-8702; http://losangeles.ucbtheatre.com; 5919 Franklin Ave; tickets $5-10) Founded in NYC by *Saturday Night Live* alum Amy Poehler and others, this sketch-comedy and improv club is frequented by Hollywood screenwriters and young TV stars.

★ **Egyptian Theater**   CINEMA

(Map p75; ☎323-466-3456; www.americancinematheque.com; 6712 Hollywood Blvd) Exotic 1922 movie house, home to the American Cinematheque, which presents arty retrospectives and Q&As with directors, writers and actors.

Actors' Gang Theater   THEATER

(www.theactorsgang.com; 9070 Venice Blvd, Culver City) Co-created by Tim Robbins, this socially mindful troupe wins awards for its bold reinterpretations of classic plays and new works pulled from ensemble workshops.

Arclight Cinemas   CINEMA

(Map p75; ☎323-464-1478; www.arclightcinemas.com; 6360 W Sunset Blvd; tickets $14-16) Star-sighting potential is exceptionally high at this state-of-the-art cineplex that has all-reserved seating (no late admission), at Hollywood's landmark Cinerama Dome.

House of Blues   LIVE MUSIC

(Map p76; ☎323-848-5100; www.hob.com; 8430 W Sunset Blvd) Despite a Disneyfied 'Mississippi blues shack' exterior, this Sunset Strip music hall books quality, and sometimes quirky, rock, hip-hop, jazz and blues acts.

Center Theatre Group   THEATER

(☎213-628-2772; www.centertheatregroup.org) Contemporary and classic plays and musicals, including Broadway touring productions, perform on three stages in Downtown LA and Culver City.

Largo at the Coronet   LIVE MUSIC, PERFORMING ARTS

(Map p76; ☎310-855-0530; www.largo-la.com; 366 N La Cienega Blvd) Pop-culture lab brings edgy comedy (Sarah Silverman), nouveau radio plays (*Thrilling Adventure Hour*) and indie bands to Mid-City's historic theatre.

Hotel Cafe   LIVE MUSIC

(Map p75; ☎323-461-2040; www.hotelcafe.com; 1623½ N Cahuenga Blvd; tickets $10-20) The 'it' place for handmade music is a social stepping stone for message-minded newbie balladeers. Get there early and enter from the alley.

Troubadour   LIVE MUSIC

(Map p76; ☎tickets 877-435-8949; www.troubadour.com; 9081 Santa Monica Blvd) Decades after catapulting Joni Mitchell and Tom Waits to stardom, this music hall is still great for catching tomorrow's headliners.

Los Angeles Opera   OPERA

(Map p70; ☎213-972-8001; www.laopera.com; 135 N Grand Ave, Dorothy Chandler Pavilion) Helmed by Plácido Domingo, this renowned ensemble plays it safe with crowd-pleasers like *Tosca*.

Will Geer's Theatricum Botanicum   THEATER

(☎310-455-3723; www.theatricum.com; 1419 N Topanga Canyon Blvd, Topanga; ⊛) Enchanting summer repertory in the woods for Shakespearean classics and family-friendly plays.

Dodger Stadium
BASEBALL

(☎866-363-4377; www.dodgers.com; 1000 Elysian Park Ave; ☺Apr-Sep) LA's Major League Baseball team plays within tobacco-spitting distance of downtown.

🔒 Shopping

Although Rodeo Drive is the most iconic strip in LA, the city abounds with other options for retail therapy. Besides those listed below, chain-free strips include **Main Street** (Map p79; btwn Bay & Marine Sts) in Santa Monica, **Abbot Kinney Boulevard** (Map p79) in Venice and **Vermont Avenue** (btwn Franklin & Prospect Aves) in Los Feliz.

Rodeo Drive
SHOPPING AREA

(Map p76; btwn Wilshire & Santa Monica Blvds) LA's most famous shopping street, in Beverly Hills.

Robertson Boulevard
SHOPPING AREA

(Map p76; btwn Beverly Blvd & 3rd St) Where fashionistas, and their paparazzi piranhas, flock to in Mid-City.

Montana Avenue
SHOPPING AREA

(btwn Lincoln Blvd & 20th St) Santa Monica's poshest shopping promenade.

Melrose Avenue
SHOPPING AREA

(Map p76; btwn San Vicente Blvd & La Brea Ave) In West Hollywood, Melrose Ave is still a fave of Gen-Y hipsters, including at **Melrose Trading Post** (Map p76; http://melrosetradingpost.org; Fairfax High School, 7850 Melrose Ave; admission $2; ☺9am-5pm Sun), a weekly flea market. Celebs are frequently sighted at **Book Soup** (Map p76; ☎310-659-3110; www.booksoup.com; 8818 W Sunset Blvd; ☺9am-10pm Mon-Sat, to 7pm Sun) on the Sunset Strip.

Amoeba Music
MUSIC

(Map p75; ☎323-245-6400; www.amoeba.com; 6400 W Sunset Blvd; ☺10:30am-11pm Mon-Sat, 11am-9pm Sun) Hollywood is ground zero for groovy tunes at this import from San Fran's Bay Area.

Sunset Junction
SHOPPING AREA

(Sunset Blvd, btwn Santa Monica & Griffith Park Blvds) Silver Lake, to the east of Hollywood, has cool kitsch, collectibles and emerging LA designers, especially around Sunset Junction.

Retro Row
SHOPPING AREA

(E 4th St, btwn Cherry & Junipero Aves) Long Beach's Retro Row brims with shops selling vintage clothing and mid-century furniture at prices from 'how much?' to '*how* much?'

IT'S A WRAP

Dress just like a movie star – in their actual clothes! Packed to the rafters, Mid-City's **It's a Wrap** (Map p76; ☎310-246-9727; www.itsawraphollywood.com; 1164 S Robertson Blvd; ☺10am-8pm Mon-Fri, 11am-6pm Sat & Sun) sells wardrobe castoffs – tank tops to tuxedos – worn by actors and extras working on TV or movie shoots. Tags are coded, so you'll be able to brag with the knowledge of which studio or show's clothing you're wearing. Original location in Burbank.

Distant Lands
BOOKS

(☎626-449-3220; www.distantlands.com; 20 S Raymond Ave; ☺10:30am-8pm Mon-Thu, to 9pm Fri & Sat, 11am-6pm Sun) Pasadena's Distant Lands bookshop is a treasure chest of travel guides and gadgets.

Rose Bowl Flea Market
MARKET

(www.rgcshows.com; 1001 Rose Bowl Dr, Pasadena; admission from $8; ☺9am-4:30pm 2nd Sun of month, last entry 3pm) There are more than 2500 vendors and 15,000 buyers here every month.

Fashion District
FASHION

(Map p70; www.fashiondistrict.org) Bargain hunters with couture taste head to Downtown LA's markets. The 100-block Fashion District is a head-spinning selection of samples, knockoffs and original designs at cut-rate prices; haggling is ubiquitous. Nearby, gold and diamonds are the main currency in the **Jewelry District** along Hill St.

Flower Market
MARKET

(Map p70; www.laflowerdistrict.com; Wall St; admission Mon-Fri $2, Sat $1; ☺8am-noon Mon, Wed & Fri, 6am-noon Tue, Thu & Sat) Downtown LA's flower market is the USA's largest, dating from 1919.

ℹ Information

DANGERS & ANNOYANCES

Crime rates are lowest in West LA, Beverly Hills, beach towns (except Venice and Long Beach) and Pasadena. Avoid walking alone and after dark around Downtown's 'Skid Row', roughly bounded by 3rd, Alameda, 7th and Main Sts.

INTERNET ACCESS

Coffee shops offer wi-fi with purchase (sometimes for free).

Los Angeles Public Library (☑213-228-7000; www.lapl.org; 630 W 5th St; ☺10am-8pm Mon-Thu, to 5:30pm Fri & Sat; @ 🕾) Free wi-fi and public internet terminals. Call or check the website for branch locations and hours.

Santa Monica Public Library (☑310-458-8600; www.smpl.org; 601 Santa Monica Blvd, Santa Monica; ☺10am-9pm Mon-Thu, to 5:30pm Fri & Sat, 1-5pm Sun; @ 🕾) Free wi-fi and public internet terminals.

MEDIA

KCRW 89.9 FM (www.kcrw.org) National Public Radio (NPR) station for cutting-edge music, news and public-affairs shows.

KPCC 89.3 FM (www.kpcc.org) NPR station airs BBC programming and intelligent SoCal talk shows.

LA Weekly (www.laweekly.com) Free alternative news, arts and entertainment weekly with a current-events calendar.

Los Angeles Magazine (www.lamag.com) Glossy lifestyle monthly has a useful restaurant guide.

Los Angeles Times (www.latimes.com) Pulitzer Prize–winning daily newspaper and info-packed website.

MEDICAL SERVICES

Cedars-Sinai Medical Center (☑310-423-3277; http://cedars-sinai.edu; 8700 Beverly Blvd, West Hollywood) Has a 24-hour emergency room.

MONEY

TravelEx (☑310-659-6093; www.travelex.com; US Bank, 8901 Santa Monica Blvd, West Hollywood; ☺9:30am-5pm Mon-Thu, 9am-6pm Fri, 9am-1pm Sat) Additional branches in Hollywood, Mid-City and Santa Monica open weekdays only.

TELEPHONE

LA County is covered by multiple area codes. Dial ☑1+(area code) before all local seven-digit numbers.

TOURIST INFORMATION

Beverly Hills Visitor Center (Map p76; ☑310-248-1015; www.lovebeverlyhills.com; 9400 S Santa Monica Blvd, Beverly Hills; ☺9am-5pm Mon-Fri, from 10am Sat & Sun)

Downtown LA Visitor Information Center (Map p70; http://discoverlosangeles.com; 800 N Alameda St, Union Station; ☺9am-5pm Mon-Fri)

Hollywood Visitor Information Center (Map p75; ☑323-467-6412; http://discoverlosangeles.com; Hollywood & Highland complex, 6801 Hollywood Blvd; ☺10am-10pm Mon-Sat, to 7pm Sun)

Santa Monica Visitor Center (Map p79; ☑800-544-5319, 310-393-7593; www.santamonica.com; 1920 Main St, Santa Monica; ☺9am-5:30pm Mon-Fri, to 5pm Sat & Sun) Additional info kiosks at Santa Monica Pier, Palisades Park and Third St Promenade.

WEBSITES

Daily Candy LA (www.dailycandy.com/los-angeles/) Little bites of LA style.

Discover Los Angeles (http://discoverlosangeles.com) Official tourist info site.

Experience LA (www.experiencela.com) Comprehensive cultural events calendar.

LAist (http://laist.com) Arts, entertainment, food, events and pop-culture gossip.

LA Observed (www.laobserved.com) News blog that often scoops mainstream media.

❶ Getting There & Away

AIR

LA's gateway hub is **Los Angeles International Airport** (LAX; ☑310-646-5252; www.lawa.org/lax; 1 World Way; 🕾), the USA's second busiest. The nine terminals are linked on the lower (arrivals) level by free shuttle bus A. Hotel and car-rental shuttles stop there as well.

Smaller **Long Beach Airport** and Burbank's **Bob Hope Airport** (BUR; ☑818-840-8840; www.burbankairport.com; 2627 N Hollywood Way) handle mostly domestic flights.

BUS

Greyhound's main **bus terminal** (☑213-629-8401; www.greyhound.com; 1716 E 7th St) is in an unsavory part of Downtown LA, so avoid arriving after dark. If you absolutely must, call a taxi from inside the bus terminal.

CAR

The usual international car-rental agencies have branches at LAX airport and throughout LA.

TRAIN

Long-distance Amtrak trains roll into Downtown LA's historic **Union Station** (☑800-872-7245; www.amtrak.com; 800 N Alameda St). *Pacific Surfliner* regional trains run southwards to San Diego ($37, 2¾ hours) and northwards to Santa Barbara ($25 to $30, three hours) and San Luis Obispo ($40, 5½ hours).

❶ Getting Around

TO/FROM THE AIRPORT

Door-to-door shared-ride vans operated by **Prime Time** (☑800-733-8267; www.primetimeshuttle.com) and **Super Shuttle** (☑800-258-3826; www.supershuttle.com) leave from the lower level of LAX terminals; typical destinations include Santa Monica ($19), Hollywood ($25) and Downtown LA ($16). **Disneyland Express** (☑714-978-8855; http://graylineanaheim. com; one way/round-trip $22/32; ☺7:30am-10:30pm) travels at least hourly between LAX and Disneyland-area hotels; a round-trip family pass costs $99.

Curbside dispatchers summon **taxis** at LAX. A flat fare applies to Downtown LA ($46.50) or Santa Monica ($30 to $35). Otherwise, metered fares (including $4 airport surcharge) average $45 to $55 for Hollywood and up to $95 to Disneyland, excluding tip.

LAX FlyAway Buses (☑866-435-9529; www. lawa.org; one way $7) depart LAX terminals every 30 minutes for Westwood ($10, 25 to 45 minutes) between 6am and 11pm daily, and 24 hours to Downtown LA's Union Station ($7, 30 to 50 minutes).

Other public transportation is slower and less convenient but cheaper. From the lower level outside any LAX terminal, catch a free shuttle bus C to the Metro Bus Center, a hub for buses serving all of LA; or take shuttle bus G to Aviation Station on the Metro Green Line light rail, then transfer at Willowbrook Station to the Blue Line, which connects Downtown LA and Long Beach.

CAR & MOTORCYCLE

Driving in LA doesn't need to be a hassle (a GPS device helps), but be prepared for some of the worst traffic in the country during weekday rush hours (roughly 7:30am to 9am and 4pm to 6:30pm).

Self-parking at motels is usually free; most hotels charge anywhere from $10 to $35. Valet parking at restaurants, hotels and nightspots is commonplace, with rates averaging $3 to $10.

PUBLIC TRANSPORTATION

If you're not in a hurry, public transportation suffices around – but not necessarily between – LA's most-touristed neighborhoods.

Local **DASH minibuses** (☑323-808-2273, 213-808-2273; www.ladottransit.com; fare 50¢; ☺6am-7pm) run around Downtown LA, Hollywood and Los Feliz. Santa Monica–based **Big Blue Bus** (☑310-451-5444; www.bigbluebus. com; fares from $1) covers much of West LA, including Westwood, Venice and LAX; its Rapid 10 Freeway Express connects Santa Monica with Downtown LA ($2, one hour).

Trip-planning help is available via LA's **Metro** (☑323-466-3876; www.metro.net), which operates 200 bus lines and the following six subway and light-rail lines:

Blue Line Downtown (7th St/Metro Center) to Long Beach

Expo Line Downtown (7th St/Metro Center) to Culver City, via Exposition Park

Gold Line Union Station to Pasadena and east LA

Green Line Norwalk to Redondo Beach

Purple Line Downtown to Koreatown

Red Line Downtown (Union Station) to North Hollywood, via Hollywood and Universal City

Metro train or bus fares are $1.50. On buses, bring exact change and ask the driver when boarding for a transfer. Note there are no free transfers between trains and buses. Metro 'TAP card' unlimited ride passes cost $5/20/75 per day/week/month. Purchase train tickets and TAP cards at vending machines inside train stations, or check www.metro.net for other locations.

TAXI

Except for taxis lined up outside airports, train and bus stations and major hotels, it's best to phone for a cab. Metered taxis charge $2.85 at flagfall, then $2.70 per mile. Taxis accept major credit cards, though sometimes grudgingly.

Checker (☑800-300-5007; http://ineed taxi.com)

Independent (☑800-521-8294; http://taxi 4u.com)

LOCAL KNOWLEDGE

CAR-FREE LA

'Nobody walks in LA,' the '80s band Missing Persons famously sang. That was then. Fed up with traffic, smog and high gas prices, the city that defined car culture is slowly developing an alt-transportation culture. Angelenos are moving into more densely populated neighborhoods where walking, cycling and taking public transit makes more sense.

The Metro Red Line subway connects Downtown LA with Koreatown, Hollywood and Universal Studios. Base yourself near one of its art-filled stations and you may not even need a car. Unlimited-ride tickets (per day $5) are a bargain; plus, given LA's legendary traffic, it's often faster to travel below ground than above.

While eventual plans call for a 'Subway to the Sea,' for now you'll be bussing it to Mid-City, Beverly Hills, Westwood and Santa Monica. From the Red Line (Wilshire/Vermont station) or Purple Line (Wilshire/Western station), transfer to Metro's Rapid 720 bus, making limited stops along Wilshire Blvd. For more information visit www.metro.net.

SOUTHERN CALIFORNIA COAST

Disneyland & Anaheim

The mother of all West Coast theme parks, aka the 'Happiest Place on Earth,' Disneyland is a parallel world that's squeaky clean, enchanting and wacky all at once. Smaller and somewhat more modest than Florida's Disney World, this was Walt Disney's original theme park. He famously dreamt of a 'magical park' where children and their parents could have fun together. For all his visions of waterfalls, castles and gigantic teacups, Disney was also a practical businessman, choosing to construct his fantasy land within easy reach of metropolitan LA.

Disneyland opened to great fanfare in 1955 and the workaday city of Anaheim grew up around it. Today the Disneyland Resort comprises the original theme park and newer California Adventure Park. Anaheim itself doesn't have much in the way of attractions outside the Disney juggernaut.

◉ Sights & Activities

You can see either theme park (☏714-781-4636; www.disneyland.com; 1313 Harbor Blvd; adult/child 3-9yr 1-day pass $92/86, 2-day park-hopper pass $210/197; ☉daily, seasonal hours vary) in a day, but going on all the rides requires at least two days, as waits for top attractions can be an hour or more. To minimize wait times, especially in summer, arrive midweek before the gates open, buy print-at-home tickets online and use the parks' Fastpass system, which pre-assigns boarding times at some rides and attractions. Check online for seasonal park hours and schedules of parades, shows and fireworks. Admission prices, contact information and opening hours are the same for both theme parks, although you'll need to buy a higher-priced park-hopper ticket to visit both parks rather than just one.

Disneyland Park THEME PARK
(☻) Spotless, wholesome Disneyland is still laid out according to Walt's original plans. Main Street USA, a pedestrian thoroughfare lined with old-fashioned ice-cream parlors and shops, is the gateway. At its far end is Sleeping Beauty Castle, an obligatory photo op and a central landmark worth noting – its towering blue turrets are visible from many areas.

The park's themed sections stuffed with rides and attractions radiate out from Sleeping Beauty Castle like spokes on a wheel. Although kids will make a beeline for the rides, adults may enjoy the antique photos and history exhibit just inside the main entrance at the Disneyland Story.

Your best bet for meeting princesses and other characters in costume is Fantasyland, home to the spinning teacups of Mad Tea Party, It's a Small World cruise and Peter Pan's Flight. For something a bit more fast-paced, head to the exhilarating Space Mountain roller coaster in Tomorrowland, where the Finding Nemo Submarine Voyage and Star Wars' Jedi Training Academy await.

The ever-popular Indiana Jones Adventure ride awaits in Adventureland. Nearby New Orleans Square offers several worthwhile attractions – the Haunted Mansion (not too scary for older kids) and Pirates of the Caribbean cruise, where cannons shoot

---

WORTH A TRIP

KNOTT'S BERRY FARM

What, Disney's not enough for you? Find even more thrill rides and cotton candy at Knott's Berry Farm (☏714-220-5200; www.knotts.com; 8039 Beach Blvd, Buena Park; adult/child $60/31; ☉from 10am daily, closing time varies seasonally 6-11pm; ☻). This Old West–themed amusement park teems with packs of speed-crazed adolescents testing their mettle on a line-up of rides. Gut-wrenchers include the Boomerang 'scream machine,' wooden GhostRider and 1950s-themed Xcelerator, while the single-digit-aged find tamer action at Camp Snoopy. From late September through October, the park transforms into Halloween-themed 'Knott's Scary Farm.'

When summer heat waves hit, jump next door to Soak City OC (☏714-220-5200; www.soakcityoc.com; 8039 Beach Blvd, Buena Park; adult/child 3-11yr $35/25; ☉10am-5pm, 6pm or 7pm mid-May–mid-Sep) water park. Save time and money by buying print-at-home tickets for both parks online. Parking is $15.

across the water, wenches are up for auction and the mechanical Jack Sparrow character is creepily lifelike. Big Thunder Mountain Railroad, another popular roller coaster, is in cowboy-themed Frontierland.

If you've got little ones in tow, you'll likely spend time at Mickey's Toontown and in Critter Country, where families can cool off on Splash Mountain's log-flume ride.

Disney's California Adventure THEME PARK

(DCA; 🚻) Disneyland resort's larger but less crowded park, DCA celebrates the natural and pop-cultural glories of the Golden State but lacks the density of attractions and depth of imagination. The best rides are Soarin' Over California, a virtual hang-glide; the famous Twilight Zone Tower of Terror, which drops you down an elevator chute; and Grizzly River Run, a white-water rafting ride.

Smaller children will love A Bug's Land and the Radiator Springs Racers, a slot-car roller coaster mimicking the Route 66 scenery of the *Cars* movie. Hang around Paradise Bay after dark to gawk at the World of Color light, sound and special-effects spectacular.

🛏 Sleeping

Chain motels and hotels are a dime a dozen in the surrounding city of Anaheim.

HI Fullerton HOSTEL $

(📞714-738-3721; www.hiusa.org; 1700 N Harbor Blvd, Fullerton; dm $24-27; ⊘mid-Jun–early Sep; ❄@🛜) About 6 miles north of Disneyland on an old dairy farm, this two-story hacienda houses 20 beds in mixed and single-sex dorms. Rates include continental breakfast. Public buses stop nearby.

Hotel Menage HOTEL $$

(📞714-758-0900; www.hotelmenage.com; 1221 S Harbor Blvd; r $100-200; @🛜🏊🚻❄) Off the I-5 Fwy, this stylish modern hotel pulls off an urbane atmosphere with leather headboards, plasma TVs and some sofa beds. The poolside tiki bar makes a relaxing respite after a day of running around Disney's 'Mouse House.'

Alpine Inn MOTEL $$

(📞714-772-4422; www.alpineinnanaheim.com; 715 W Katella Ave; r incl breakfast $79-149; ❄@🛜🏊🚻) Connoisseurs of kitsch will delight in this alpine chalet covered to the tippy-top of its A-framed rafters with artificial snow and icicles. Compact rooms have mod cons, but it's all about the convenient location outside Disneyland Resort's main gate.

Paradise Pier Hotel HOTEL $$$

(📞info 714-999-0990, reservations 714-956-6425; http://disneyland.disney.go.com/paradise-pier-hotel; 1717 S Disneyland Dr; d from $240; ❄@🛜🏊🚻) It's one big surfin' safari at the sun-dappled Paradise Pier Hotel, the brightest, happy-go-luckiest of the Disneyland Resort hotel trio, with splashy colors, Beach Boys tunes, upbeat staff and a rooftop pool deck with a waterslide and after-dark fireworks viewing. It's a 10-minute walk to Downtown Disney.

🍴 Eating & Drinking

There are dozens of dining options inside the theme parks; it's part of the fun to hit the walk-up food stands for treats like giant turkey legs and sugar-dusted churros.

For reservations or information on Disneyland Resort restaurants, call Disney Dining (📞714-781-3463; http://disneyland.disney.go.com/dining). No alcohol is allowed inside Disneyland Park; it's sold at DCA and Downtown Disney. Budget-conscious visitors and families with kids can store their own food and drinks (no glass) in the lockers ($7 to $15) along Disneyland's Main Street USA, DCA's Buena Vista Street and outside both parks' main entrance.

An open-air pedestrian mall adjacent to the parks, Downtown Disney (http://disneyland.disney.go.com/downtown-disney/; ⊘open daily, seasonal hours vary) has generic but family-friendly chain restaurants. The same is true of Anaheim GardenWalk (www.anaheimgardenwalk.com; 321 W Katella Ave; ⊘11am-9pm, some restaurants open later), an outdoor mall just east of the parks. If you want to steer clear of Mickey Mouse food, drive to retro-flavored Old Towne Orange (7 miles southeast), Little Arabia (3 miles west) or Little Saigon (12 miles southwest).

Earl of Sandwich DELI $

(www.earlofsandwichusa.com; Downtown Disney; dishes $2-8; ⊘8am-11pm Sun-Thu, to 12am Fri & Sat; 🚻) Lines are long, but worth it for Downtown Disney's best budget eats: hot and cold sandwiches, wraps, salads and soups that won't break the bank, and warm, oven-fresh cookies.

Café Orleans CAJUN, CREOLE $$

(Disneyland Park; mains $15-20; ⊘seasonal hours vary; 🚻) In Disneyland's New Orleans Sq, this cafeteria-style Southern restaurant dishes up bowls of jambalaya and gumbo, serves pan-fried Monte Cristo sandwiches and will shake up virgin mint-julep cocktails for customers. Reservations accepted.

Napa Rose

CALIFORNIAN $$$

(Grand Californian Hotel; mains $38-45, 4-course prix-fixe dinner from $90; ☺ 5:30-10pm; 🚗) Inside a soaring Craftsman-style dining room with colorful leaded-glass windows, Napa Rose is Disney's top-drawer restaurant. The chef's tasting menu exquisitely pairs seasonal ingredients with California-grown wines. Reservations essential.

Catal Restaurant & Uva Bar

MEDITERRANEAN $$$

(📞 714-774-4442; www.patinagroup.com/catal; Downtown Disney; mains breakfast $10-15, dinner $23-41; ☺ 8am-10pm; 🚗) Looking for something sophisticated yet unfussy? Share Mediterranean-inspired tapas and grill plates as you sip cocktails and craft beer in Downtown Disney. Book ahead, especially for balcony seating.

❶ Information

Stroller rentals ($15 per day) and drop-off pet kennels ($20 per day) are available outside the parks' main entrance.

Anaheim/Orange County Visitor & Convention Bureau (www.anaheimoc.org) Free travel-planning website and smartphone mobile app.

Disneyland City Hall (📞 714-781-4565; Main Street USA) One of several theme-park guest information centers, it offers foreign-currency exchange.

MousePlanet (www.mouseplanet.com) One-stop online resource for news, updates, trip planning and discussion boards.

MouseWait (www.mousewait.com) Free phone app with up-to-the-minute wait times and what's happening in the parks.

Touring Plans (http://touringplans.com) Online crowd calendar and free phone app with theme-park itineraries, wait times and restaurant menus.

❶ Getting There & Around

The Disneyland Resort is just off I-5 (Santa Ana Fwy), about 30 miles southeast of Downtown LA. As you approach the area, freeway signs indicate which exit ramps to take for Disney's theme parks, hotels or Anaheim's streets.

Amtrak trains between LA's Union Station ($14, 40 minutes) and San Diego ($28, two hours) stop almost hourly in Anaheim. The **train station** (📞 714-385-1448; 2150 E Katella Ave), next to Angel Stadium, is a quick bus or taxi ride east of Disneyland. **Metrolink** (📞 800-371-5465; www.metrolinktrains.com) commuter trains from LA's Union Station ($8.75, 45 minutes) stop at the same station.

Anaheim Resort Transit (ART; 📞 714-563-5287; www.rideart.org; day pass adult/child $5/2) provides frequent bus service between Disneyland Resort and many area hotels and motels.

A free tram connects Disneyland Resort's main parking garage (per day $15 to $20) and Downtown Disney, a short walk from the theme parks.

Orange County Beaches

If you've seen *The OC* or *Real Housewives*, you'll think that you already know what to expect from this giant quilt of suburbia connecting LA and San Diego, which lolls beside 42 miles of glorious coastline. In reality, Hummer-driving hunks and Botoxed beauties mix it up with hang-loose surfers and beatnik artists to give each of Orange County's beach towns a distinct vibe.

Just across the LA–OC county line, Seal Beach is old-fashioned and refreshingly noncommercial, with a quaint walkable downtown. Nine miles further south along the Pacific Coast Hwy (Hwy 1), Huntington Beach – aka 'Surf City, USA' – epitomizes SoCal's surfing lifestyle. Fish tacos and happy-hour specials abound at bars and cafes along downtown HB's Main St, not far from a shortboard-sized surfing museum (📞 714-960-3483; www.surfingmuseum.org; 411 Olive Ave; admission by donation; ☺ noon-5pm Sun & Mon, to 9pm Tue, to 7pm Wed-Fri, 11am-7pm Sat).

Next up is the ritziest of the OC's beach communities: yacht-filled Newport Beach. Families and teens steer toward Balboa Peninsula for its beaches, vintage wooden pier and quaint amusement center. From nearby the 1906 Balboa Pavilion, Balboa Island Ferry (www.balboaislandferry.com; 410 S Bay Front; adult/child $1/50¢, car incl driver $2; ☺ 6:30am-midnight Sun-Thu, to 2am Fri & Sat) shuttles across the bay to Balboa Island for strolls past historic beach cottages and boutiques along Marine Ave.

Continuing south, Hwy 1 zooms past the wild beaches of Crystal Cove State Park (📞 949-494-3539; www.parks.ca.gov; 8471 N Coast Hwy; per car $15, campsites $25-75) before winding downhill into Laguna Beach, the OC's most cultured and charming seaside community, where secluded beaches, glassy waves and eucalyptus-covered hillsides create a Riviera-like feel. Art galleries dot the narrow streets of the 'village' and the coastal highway, where the clifftop Laguna Art Museum (📞 949-494-8971; www.lagunaartmuseum.org; 307

Cliff Dr; adult/child $7/free; ⊘usually 11am-5pm Fri-Tue, to 9pm Thu) exhibits modern and contemporary Californian artworks. Soak up the natural beauty right in the center of town at Main Beach.

Another 10 miles south, detour inland to Mission San Juan Capistrano (☑949-234-1300; www.missionsjc.com; 26801 Ortega Hwy, San Juan Capistrano; adult/child $9/6; ⊘9am-5pm), one of California's most beautifully restored missions, with flowering gardens, a fountain courtyard and the charming 1778 Serra Chapel.

🛏 Sleeping & Eating

Oceanside motels and hotels along PCH (Hwy 1) charge surprisingly steep rates, especially on summer weekends. Dive inland near the freeways for better bargains.

★ **Crystal Cove Beach Cottages** CABIN $$
(☑reservations 800-444-7275; www.crystalcove beachcottages.com; 35 Crystal Cove, Newport Beach; r without bath $42-127, cottages $162-249; ⊘check-in 4-9pm; 🐾) To snag one of these historic mid-20th-century oceanfront cottages at Crystal Cove State Park, book on the first day of the month, seven months before your intended stay – or pray for last-minute cancellations.

Shorebreak Hotel BOUTIQUE HOTEL $$$
(☑714-861-4470; www.shorebreakhotel.com; 500 Pacific Coast Hwy, Huntington Beach; r $189-495; ✴@🛜🐾) Fashionably hip hotel livens things up with a surf concierge, beanbag chairs in the lobby and geometric-patterned rooms. Knock back sunset cocktails on the upstairs deck. Parking is $27.

Zinc Cafe & Market HEALTHY $
(www.zinccafe.com; 350 Ocean Ave, Laguna Beach; mains $6-11; ⊘market 7am-6pm, cafe until 4pm; 🐾) Maybe it's the happy-making tomato-colored walls or the open-air patio that draws the young and beautiful here. An all-vegetarian cafe menu ranges from breakfast quiche to pizzettes, garden-fresh salads and deli sandwiches for lunch.

Bear Flag Fish Company SEAFOOD $$
(☑949-673-3434; www.bearflagfishco.com; 407 31st St, Newport Beach; dishes $8-15; ⊘11am-9pm Tue-Sat, to 8pm Mon & Sun; 🐾) Seafood market dishes up spankin' fresh oysters, fish tacos, Hawaiian-style *poke* and more. Pick exactly what you want from the ice-cold display cases. Expect long lines. Cash only.

LAGUNA'S FESTIVAL OF ARTS

Hey, did that painting just move? Welcome to the Pageant of the Masters (☑800-487-3378; tickets from $15; ⊘8:30pm daily mid-Jul-Aug), in which elaborately costumed humans step into painstaking recreations of famous paintings on an outdoor stage. The pageant began in 1933 as a sideshow to Laguna Beach's Festival of Arts (www.foapom.com; admission $7-10; ⊘usually 10am-11:30pm Jul & Aug) and has been a prime attraction ever since. Our favorite part: watching the paintings deconstruct.

San Diego

San Diegans shamelessly promote their hometown as 'America's Finest City.' Smug? Maybe, but it's easy to see why: the weather is practically perfect, with coastal high temperatures hovering around 68°F (20°C) all year, and beaches are rarely more than a quick drive away. San Diego's population (1.3 million) makes it America's eighth-largest city and California's second-largest after LA, yet we're hard-pressed to think of a more laid-back metropolis anywhere.

The city grew by leaps and bounds during WWII, when the Japanese attack on Pearl Harbor prompted the US Navy to relocate the US Pacific Fleet from Hawaii to San Diego's natural harbor. The military, tourism, education and scientific research industries (especially medicine and oceanography), as well as high-tech ventures cropping up in inland valleys, have helped to shape the city. It all makes SD seem quintessentially all-American – its Mexico borderlands notwithstanding.

⊙ Sights

San Diego's compact downtown hinges on the historic Gaslamp Quarter, a beehive after dark. Coronado is reached via a stunning bridge to the southwest, while museum-rich Balboa Park (home of the San Diego Zoo) is north of downtown. Neighboring the park to the northwest is Hillcrest, the city's lesbigay hub, where everyone's welcome in the restaurants, cafes, bars and shops. Heading west is touristy Old Town and Mission Bay's aquatic playground.

Greater San Diego

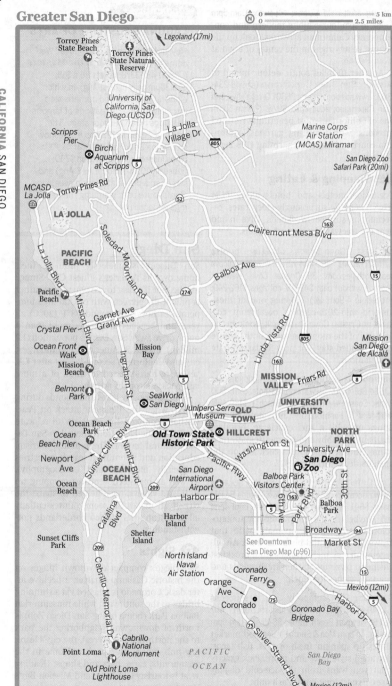

0 — 5 km
0 — 2.5 miles

Legoland (17mi)

Torrey Pines
State Beach

Torrey Pines
State Natural
Reserve

University of
California, San
Diego (UCSD)

La Jolla
Village Dr

Marine Corps
Air Station
(MCAS) Miramar

Scripps
Pier

Birch
Aquarium
at Scripps

San Diego Zoo
Safari Park (20mi)

805

5

MCASD
La Jolla

Torrey Pines Rd

52

LA JOLLA

Clairemont Mesa Blvd

163

**PACIFIC
BEACH**

Soledad Mountain Rd

Balboa Ave

274

15

La Jolla Blvd

Pacific
Beach

Mission Blvd

Garnet Ave
Grand Ave

274

Linda Vista Rd

Crystal Pier

Ocean Front
Walk

Mission
Beach

Mission
Bay

Ingraham St

163

Mission
San Diego
de Alcalá

805

Belmont
Park

5

**MISSION
VALLEY**

Friars Rd

8

SeaWorld
San Diego

Junípero Serra
Museum

**OLD
TOWN**

**UNIVERSITY
HEIGHTS**

Ocean Beach
Park

8

**Old Town State
Historic Park**

HILLCREST

**NORTH
PARK**

Ocean
Beach Pier

Sunset Cliffs Blvd

Nimitz Blvd

Washington St

University Ave

Newport
Ave

**OCEAN
BEACH**

San Diego
International
Airport

Pacific Hwy

**San Diego
Zoo**

30th St

Ocean
Beach

209

Harbor Dr

Balboa Park
Visitors Center

6th Ave

163

Park Blvd

Catalina Blvd

Harbor
Island

5

Balboa
Park

Sunset Cliffs
Park

Shelter
Island

Broadway

94

See Downtown
San Diego Map (p96)

Market St

209

North Island
Naval
Air Station

Cabrillo Memorial Dr

Coronado
Ferry

15

Orange
Ave

75

Mexico (12mi)

5

Coronado

Harbor Dr

Cabrillo
National
Monument

Coronado Bay
Bridge

Point Loma

75

Silver Strand Blvd

Old Point Loma
Lighthouse

*P A C I F I C

O C E A N*

*San Diego
Bay*

Mexico (12mi)

Cruising up the coast, Ocean Beach, Mission Beach and Pacific Beach live the laid-back SoCal dream, while La Jolla sits pretty and privileged. Further north, line up North County's eclectic beach towns: ritzy Del Mar, design-savvy Solana Beach, new-agey Encinitas and flowery Carlsbad, home of Legoland. The I-5 Fwy cuts through the region north–south.

Downtown & Embarcadero

In the 1860s, real-estate wrangling by developer Alonzo Horton created so-called 'New Town', which is Downtown San Diego today. The main street, 5th Ave, was once a notorious strip of saloons, gambling joints and bordellos known as Stingaree. These days, Stingaree has been beautifully restored and rechristened the Gaslamp Quarter, a heart-thumping playground of restaurants, bars, clubs, boutiques and galleries.

At downtown's northern edge, Little Italy (www.littleitalysd.com) has evolved into one of the city's hippest places to live, eat and shop. India St is the neighborhood's main drag.

★USS Midway Museum   MUSEUM
(Map p96; ☑619-544-9600; www.midway.org; 910 N Harbor Dr; adult/child $19/10; ☺10am-5pm, last entry 4pm; P☗) Step aboard the US Navy's longest-serving 20th-century aircraft carrier (1945–91). Self-guided audio tours take in berthing spaces, the galley, sick bay and the killer flight deck with its restored aircraft, including an F-14 Tomcat. Flight simulator experiences cost extra. Parking is $5 to $20.

★Maritime Museum   MUSEUM
(Map p96; ☑619-234-9153; www.sdmaritime.org; 1492 N Harbor Dr; adult/child $16/8; ☺9am-9pm late May-early Sep, to 8pm rest of year; ☗) The 1863 *Star of India* is one of seven historic sailing vessels open to the public at this museum. Don't miss clambering down inside the B-39 Soviet attack submarine. A 45-minute historical bay cruise costs just $5 extra.

Museum of Contemporary Art   MUSEUM
(MCASD Downtown; Map p96; ☑858-454-3541; www.mcasd.org; 1001 Kettner Blvd; adult/child $10/free, 5-7pm 3rd Thu of month free; ☺11am-5pm Thu-Tue, to 7pm 3rd Thu of month) MCASD emphasizes minimalist and pop art, plus conceptual and cross-border works. The 1100 Kettner Bldg is at the historic Santa Fe Depot. There's another branch in La Jolla (p99). Same ticket valid for seven-day admission to all.

Gaslamp Museum   MUSEUM
(Map p96; ☑619-233-4692; www.gaslampquarter.org; 410 Island Ave; adult/child $5/4; ☺10am-5pm Tue-Sat, noon-4pm Sun) Peruse the period exhibits inside this Victorian-era saltbox house that was the one-time home of William Heath Davis, the man credited with founding 'New Town.' Guided historical walking tours of the quarter usually depart at 11am Saturday (adult/child $15/free).

Petco Park   STADIUM
(Map p96; ☑619-795-5011; www.padres.com; 100 Park Blvd; tours adult/child/senior $11/7/8) In the Gaslamp Quarter's southeast corner stands the home of the San Diego Padres Major League Baseball (MLB) team. You can take a behind-the-scenes tour year-round. Call for tour schedules.

Coronado

Technically a peninsula, Coronado Island is joined to the mainland by a soaring boomerang-shaped bridge. The main draw here is the Hotel del Coronado (p100), known for its seaside Victorian architecture and illustrious guest book, which includes Thomas Edison, Brad Pitt and Marilyn Monroe (its exterior stood in for a Miami hotel in the classic flick *Some Like it Hot*).

The hourly Coronado Ferry (Map p96; ☑619-234-4111; www.sdhe.com; fare $4.25; ☺9am-10pm) departs from the Embarcadero's Broadway Pier (990 N Harbor Dr) and from Downtown's San Diego Convention Center. All ferries arrive on Coronado at the foot of 1st St, where Bikes & Beyond (☑619-435-7180; http://hollandsbicycles.com; 1201 1st St, Coronado; rental per hr/day from $7/25; ☺9am-sunset) rents cruisers and tandems, perfect for pedaling past Coronado's beaches sprawled south along the Silver Strand.

Balboa Park

Balboa Park is an urban oasis brimming with more than a dozen museums, gorgeous gardens and architecture, performance spaces and a zoo. Early 20th-century beaux arts and Spanish-Colonial buildings (the legacy of world's fairs) are grouped around plazas along east–west El Prado promenade.

Stop by the Balboa Park Visitors Center (p103) for maps, events information and discount attraction passes. Free parking lots off Park Blvd fill quickly on weekends.

Downtown San Diego

CALIFORNIA SAN DIEGO

From downtown, take MTS bus 7 ($2.25, 20 minutes). A free tram shuttles visitors around the park, but it's more enjoyable to stroll around the botanical gardens, past the Spreckels Organ Pavilion, the shops and galleries of the Spanish Village Art Center and the international-themed exhibitions cottages by the United Nations Building.

★ **San Diego Zoo** ZOO
(☎619-231-1515; www.sandiegozoo.org; 2920 Zoo Dr; adult/child $44/34; ☉9am-9pm mid-Jun–early Sep, to 5pm or 6pm rest of year; 🅿🚻) 🚲 If it slithers, crawls, stomps, swims, leaps or flies, chances are you'll find it in this world-famous zoo. It's home to more than 4000 animals representing 800-plus species in a beautifully landscaped setting, including the Australian Outback and Panda Canyon. Admission includes a narrated 35-minute double-decker-bus tour. For a wildlife viewing experience that's closer to the real thing, get a combo ticket to Escondido's San Diego Zoo Safari Park (p103).

Museum of Man MUSEUM
(☎619-239-2001; www.museumofman.org; Plaza de California, 1350 El Prado; adult/child $12.50/5; ☉10am-4:30pm) Topped by a dazzling blue-and-yellow-tiled tower, the churrigueresque California Building houses the Museum of Man, exhibiting world-class pottery, jewelry, baskets and anthropological artifacts from all around the Americas. Behind are the Old Globe theaters, an historic three-stage venue hosting a summer Shakespeare festival.

San Diego Air & Space Museum MUSEUM
(☎619-234-8291; www.sandiegoairandspace.org; 2001 Pan American Plaza; adult/child $18/7; ☉10am-5:30pm Jun-Aug, to 4:30pm Sep-May; 🚻) Highlights include the original Apollo 9 command module and a replica of Charles Lindbergh's *Spirit of St Louis*. Flight simulators entail a surcharge.

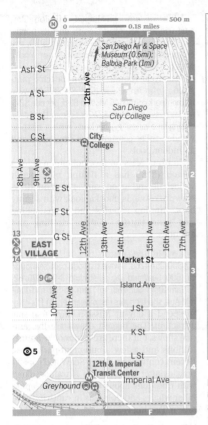

San Diego Natural History Museum MUSEUM
(☏ 619-232-3821; www.sdnhm.org; 1788 El Prado; adult/child $17/11; ◎10am-5pm; 👪) Dinosaur skeletons, glow-in-the-dark scorpions, ice-age fossils and nature-themed movies in a giant 3D cinema bring family crowds to 'The Nat.'

Timken Museum of Art MUSEUM
(☏ 619-239-5548; www.timkenmuseum.org; 1500 El Prado; ◎10am-4:30pm Tue-Sat, from 1:30pm Sun) **FREE** Small but exquisite museum showcases European and American heavyweights, from Rembrandt to Cézanne, and Western landscape painters.

San Diego Museum of Art MUSEUM
(☏ 619-232-7931; www.sdmart.org; 1450 El Prado; adult/child $12/4.50; ◎10am-5pm Mon-Tue & Thu-Sat, from noon Sun, also 5-9pm Thu Jun-Sep) SDMA gets accolades for its European old masters and curated collections of American and Asian art.

Mingei International Museum MUSEUM
(☏ 619-239-0003; www.mingei.org; 1439 El Prado; adult/child $8/5; ◎10am-4pm Tue-Sun; 👪) This museum exhibits stunning folk art, craft and design from around the globe, along with a colorful gift shop.

Reuben H Fleet Science Center MUSEUM
(☏ 619-238-1233; www.rhfleet.org; 1875 El Prado; adult/child $12/10, incl IMAX movie $16/13; ◎10am-5pm Mon-Thu, to 8pm Fri, to 7pm Sat, to 6pm Sun; 👪) Family-oriented hands-on science museum and IMAX movie theater near the fountain.

San Diego Model Railroad Museum MUSEUM
(☏ 619-696-0199; www.sdmrm.org; Casa de Balboa, 1649 El Prado; adult/child $8/free; ◎11am-4pm Tue-Fri, to 5pm Sat & Sun; 👪) The world's largest of its kind, with evocatively landscaped train sets.

◎ Old Town & Mission Valley
In 1769 a band of Spanish soldiers and missionaries, led by Franciscan friar Junípero Serra, founded the first of California's 21 historic mission churches on San Diego's

Presidio Hill. A small pueblo (village) grew up around it, but the spot turned out to be less than ideal for a mission. In 1774 the mission moved upriver, closer to a steady water supply and fertile land.

★ Old Town State Historic Park
HISTORIC SITE

(☑619-220-5422; www.parks.ca.gov; 4002 Wallace St; ⊙visitor center & museums 10am-4pm Oct-Apr, to 5pm May-Sep; Ⓟ) FREE This open-air park preserves five original adobe buildings and several recreated structures from the first pueblo, including a schoolhouse and newspaper office. Most buildings now contain museums, shops or restaurants. The visitor center offers free guided walking tours at 11am and 2pm daily.

Mission Basilica San Diego de Alcalá
CHURCH

(☑619-281-8449; www.missionsandiego.com; 10818 San Diego Mission Rd; adult/child $3/1; ⊙9am-4:45pm; Ⓟ) Secluded in a corner of what's now called Mission Valley, California's 'Mother of the Missions' hides beautifully restored buildings in bougainvillea gardens with views over the valley to the ocean.

Junípero Serra Museum
MUSEUM

(☑619-232-6203; www.sandiegohistory.org; 2727 Presidio Dr; adult/child $6/3; ⊙10am-4pm Sat & Sun mid-Sep–May, 10am-5pm Fri-Sun Jun–mid-Sep; Ⓟ♿) Atop Presidio Hill, in a handsome 1920s Spanish Revival building, multicultural historical exhibits highlight life during the city's rough-and-tumble early days.

◉ Point Loma

This pretty peninsula wraps around the entrance to crescent-shaped San Diego Bay.

Cabrillo National Monument
MONUMENT

(☑619-557-5450; www.nps.gov/cabr; 1800 Cabrillo Memorial Dr; per car $5; ⊙9am-5pm, last entry 4:30pm; Ⓟ) Soak up bay panoramas or go hiking and tide pooling at this monument, which honors the leader of the first Spanish exploration of the West Coast in 1542. The Old Point Loma Lighthouse (1854) here is now a tiny historical museum.

◉ Mission Bay & Beaches

San Diego's big three beach towns all have ribbons of hedonism where armies of tanned, taut bodies frolic in the sand.

West of amoeba-shaped Mission Bay, surf-friendly Mission Beach and its northern neighbor, Pacific Beach (aka 'PB'), are connected by car-free Ocean Front Walk, which swarms with skaters, joggers and cyclists year-round. Mission Beach's pintsized Belmont Park (☑858-458-1549; www.belmontpark.com; 3146 Mission Blvd; per ride $2-6, all-day pass adult/child $27/16; ⊙from 11am daily, closing time varies; Ⓟ) beckons with a historic wooden roller coaster, wave simulators and an indoor pool.

South of Mission Bay, bohemian Ocean Beach ('OB') has a fishing pier, beach volleyball and good surf. Its main drag, Newport Ave, is chockablock with scruffy bars, flip-flop eateries and shops selling surf gear, tattoos, vintage clothing and antiques.

SeaWorld San Diego
THEME PARK

(☑800-257-4268; www.seaworld.com/seaworld/ca; 500 SeaWorld Dr; adult/child 3-9yr $70/62; ⊙9am-10pm Sun-Thu, to 11pm Fri-Sat mid-Jun–mid-Aug, shorter hours rest of year; Ⓟ♿) It's easy to spend a day at Mission Bay's four-star attraction. The biggest draws are live animal shows, but there are also zoolike animal exhibits and a few amusement-park rides. Recent controversy about SeaWorld's safety policies after the death of a trainer, along with questions about the ethics of keeping killer whales and dolphins in captivity, have arisen. Parking is $15.

◉ La Jolla

Facing one of SoCal's loveliest sweeps of coastline, wealthy La Jolla (la-*hoy*-ah; Spanish for 'the jewel') possesses shimmering beaches and an upscale downtown filled with boutiques. Oceanfront diiversions include the Children's Pool (no longer for swimming, it's now home to barking sea lions), kayaking and exploring sea caves at La Jolla Cove and snorkeling at San Diego-La Jolla Underwater Park.

Torrey Pines State Natural Reserve
PARK

(☑858-755-2063; www.torreypine.org; 12600 N Torrey Pines Rd, La Jolla; per car $10; ⊙7:15am-dusk, visitor center 10am-4pm Oct-Apr, 9am-6pm May-Sep; Ⓟ) ✐ Up the coast near Del Mar, this wildlife reserve protects endangered Torrey pine trees and is perfect for oceanview hikes and bird-watching.

Birch Aquarium at Scripps   AQUARIUM

(✆858-534-3474; http://aquarium.ucsd.edu; 2300 Exhibition Way, La Jolla; adult/child $14/9.50; ⊙9am-5pm; Ⓟ♿) ✐ University-run ocean-front aquarium for kids uncovers tide-pool and kelp-forest displays, floating seahorses and a shark reef.

MCASD La Jolla   MUSEUM

(✆858-454-3541; www.mcasd.org; 700 Prospect St, La Jolla; adult/child $10/free, 5-7pm 3rd Thu of month free; ⊙11am-5pm Thu-Tue, to 7pm 3rd Thu of month) Sister venue of Downtown's contemporary art museum (same ticket valid for seven-day entry to both).

🏃 Activities

Surfing and windsurfing are both excellent, although in some areas territorial locals are a major irritation. For surf reports, call ✆619-221-8824.

Pacific Beach Surf School   SURFING

(✆858-373-1138; www.pbsurfshop.com; 4150 Mission Blvd; ⊙store 9am-7pm, lessons hourly until 4pm) Learn to hang 10 (private lesson $85) or just rent a board and wet suit (half-day from $35) at SD's oldest surf shop.

Surf Diva   SURFING

(✆858-454-8273; www.surfdiva.com; 2160 Avenida de la Playa; ⊙store 9am-5:30pm) In La Jolla, women board riders teach newbies how to shred with private lessons (from $75) and weekend clinics.

OEX Dive & Kayak   WATER SPORTS

(✆858-454-6195; www.oexcalifornia.com; 2243 Avenida de la Playa; ⊙9am-6pm Mon-Fri, from 8am Sat & Sun) For kayak, snorkel, scuba-diving and stand-up paddleboarding (SUP) rentals and guided tours, talk to La Jolla's one-stop resource. There is a second location at Mission Bay (✆619-866-6129; www.oexcalifornia. com; 1010 Santa Clara Pl; ⊙8am-6pm Mon-Fri, 9am-5pm Sat & Sun).

Hike, Bike, Kayak
San Diego   ADVENTURE SPORTS

(✆858-551-9510; www.hikebikekayak.com; 2216 Avenida de la Playa) Just what it says: hiking, cycling and kayaking tours, plus stand-up paddleboarding lessons and water-sports gear and bicycle rentals. Based in La Jolla.

☞ Tours

Another Side of San Diego   GUIDED TOUR

(Map p96; ✆619-239-2111; www.anothersideof-sandiegotours.com; 308 G St; tours from $30) Gaslamp Quarter food and history walking tours and Segway tours all over town.

Old Town Trolley Tours   TOUR

(✆888-910-8687; www.trolleytours.com; adult/child $36/18) Hop-on, hop-off narrated loop around the city's main tourist attractions.

🛏 Sleeping

Rates skyrocket in summer, especially by the beaches. Chain hotels and motels cluster inland off major freeways and in Mission Valley. Expect a 10.5% lodging tax.

🛏 Downtown

HI San Diego Downtown Hostel   HOSTEL $

(Map p96; ✆619-525-1531; www.sandiegohostels. org; 521 Market St; dm/d with shared bath incl breakfast from $31/75; ❄@🛜) At this well-run hostel inside a 19th-century hotel, there's loads of space to socialize. Dorms lack pizazz, but they're clean. Rates include a pancake breakfast. Quieter second location at Point Loma (✆619-223-4778; www.sandiego-hostels.org; 3790 Udall St; dm/r with shared bath incl breakfast $25/54; Ⓟ@🛜).

★USA Hostels San Diego   HOSTEL $

(Map p96; ✆800-438-8622, 619-232-3100; www. usahostels.com; 726 5th Ave; dm/r with shared bath incl breakfast from $30/71; @🛜) In a converted Victorian-era brothel, this Gaslamp hostel sports cheerful rooms, a shared kitchen and a lounge for chilling. Rates include a pancake breakfast. Taco dinners and Tijuana tours are cheap.

500 West Hotel   HOSTEL $

(Map p96; ✆info 619-234-5252, reservations 619-231-4092; www.500westhotelsd.com; 500 W Broadway; s/d with shared bath from $59/79; @🛜) Rooms are shoebox-sized and baths are down the hallway in this renovated 1920s YMCA, but hipsters on a budget love the bright decor, communal kitchen and fitness gym ($5).

★Hotel Indigo   BOUTIQUE HOTEL $$

(Map p96; ✆619-727-4000; www.hotelinsd. com; 509 9th Ave; r from $149; Ⓟ❄@🛜🏊🐾) ✐ San Diego's first hotel to be certified by Leadership in Energy & Environmental Design (LEED), this Gaslamp boutique hotel is smartly designed. Popping with vibrant color, room decor is contempo-chic, with huge floor-to-ceiling windows, rain showers and hardwood floors. Parking is $38. Second location in coastal Del Mar.

Hotel Vyant   B&B $$
(☑800-518-9930; www.hotelvyant.com; 505 W Grape St; r with/without bath from $149/109; ❄️🛜) This pretty Little Italy B&B is a charming place to hang your hat. Two dozen rooms all have inviting beds and bathrobes; deluxe rooms come with a whirlpool tub or kitchenette. Upgrade to an urban-chic apartment for a full kitchen.

🛏 Beaches

Pearl   MOTEL $$
(☑619-226-6100, 877-732-7574; www.thepearlsd. com; 1410 Rosecrans St; r from $130; P❄️🛜❄️) A mash-up of a boutique hotel and a 1960s motel, this swingin' crash-pad pulls in cool cats. Every sassy room comes with its own pet goldfish, and the tiniest digs have mirrored ceilings. Poolside movie nights and a cocktail bar keep things buzzing. Limited self-parking $10.

Best Western Island Palms   MOTEL $$
(☑800-922-2336, 619-222-0561; www.islandpalms .com; 2051 Shelter Island Dr; r from $149; P❄️@ 🛜❄️🛗) Gaze out over the bobbing boats of the marina at this tiki-inspired motor lodge on Shelter Island, right across the bay from Downtown. Say aloha to tropical-island style in crisp rooms with balconies swathed by sea breezes.

Ocean Beach Hotel   HOTEL $$
(☑619-223-7191; www.obhotel.com; 5080 Newport Ave; r from $100; ❄️🛜❄️) In surf-shabby OB, this remodeled courtyard hotel is across the street from the beach. Spotless guest rooms with mini fridges and microwaves are small and the French-provincial look is a tad dated.

⭐ **Hotel del Coronado**   LUXURY HOTEL $$$
(☑619-435-6611, 800-468-3533; www.hoteldel. com; 1500 Orange Ave; r from $325; P❄️@🛜❄️) San Diego's iconic hotel, the Del provides more than a century of star-spangled history, plus tennis courts, a spa, shops, splashy restaurants, manicured grounds and a white-sand beach. The original Victorian building lacks ocean views. Parking is $30.

Crystal Pier Hotel & Cottages   COTTAGE $$$
(☑800-748-5894, 619-483-6983; www.crystalpier. com; 4500 Ocean Blvd; d from $175; P🛜🛗) White clapboard, blue-shuttered cottages with kitchenettes – some built in the 1930s – sit right atop Pacific Beach's oceanfront Crystal Pier, offering one-of-a-kind sea views from private decks. Book up to 11 months in advance.

Tower23   BOUTIQUE HOTEL $$$
(☑866-869-3723; www.t23hotel.com; 723 Felspar St; r from $249; ❄️@🛜❄️) A mod and modernist showplace for an ubercool beach stay, this boxy, bold white hotel is splashed with lots of teals and mint blues – and a sense of humor. Catch sunset from the rooftop deck and cocktail bar. Parking is $20.

Inn at Sunset Cliffs   HOTEL $$$
(☑866-786-2453, 619-222-7901; www.innatsunsetcliffs.com; 1370 Sunset Cliffs Blvd; r/ste from $175/289; P❄️@🛜❄️🛗) Hear the surf crashing onto the rocky shore at this breezy 1960s oceanfront charmer wrapped around a flower-bedecked courtyard. Recently renovated rooms are light-filled but on the small side; some suites have a kitchen.

🍴 Eating

San Diego's dynamic dining scene caters to all tastes and budgets. Generally speaking, you'll find fine steakhouses and seafood institutions near Downtown's waterfront, boisterous gastropubs in the Gaslamp Quarter, casual seafood and burgers by the beach, hip kitchens in neighborhoods around Balboa Park, and tacos and margaritas, well, everywhere.

🍴 Downtown & Embarcadero

Neighborhood   PUB $$
(Map p96; www.neighborhoodsd.com; 777 G St; mains $7-14; ◷noon-midnight) More down-to-earth than other trendy gastropubs, this corner joint churns out crowd-pleasers like smoky chipotle burgers, kicky jalapeno mac 'n' cheese and hot dogs with braised pork and fried egg. Order a pint of microbrewed beer that's hoppy, fruity, malty or sour.

Underbelly   ASIAN, FUSION $$
(☑619-269-4626; 750 W Fir St; dishes $5-12; ◷11:30am-midnight) Off Little Italy's bustling strip of pizzerias and wine bars, this sleek noodle shop loads up steaming bowls of ramen with oxtail dumplings, hoisin-glazed short ribs and smoked brisket and bacon (vegetarian versions available). Two dozen craft beers on tap.

Cafe 21   BREAKFAST $$
(Map p96; ☑619-795-0721; www.cafe-21.com; 750 5th Ave; breakfast mains $9-15; ◷8am-10pm Sun-Thu, to 11pm Fri & Sat; 🛗) The Gaslamp's favorite brunch stop slings stuffed French

toast with agave cream cheese, fruit-topped pancakes and farm-fresh egg frittatas served in mini iron skillets. Housemade sangria rocks.

Island Prime
SEAFOOD, STEAKHOUSE $$$

(☑619-298-6802; www.islandprime.com; 880 Harbor Island Dr; mains restaurant $25-52, lounge $15-30; ⊘restaurant 5-9pm Sun-Thu, to 10pm Fri & Sat, lounge from 11:30am daily) The bay views are panoramic at this elegant seafood restaurant on Harbor Island, west of Downtown. Ever-popular dishes include the lobster BLT sandwich, seared tuna stack and shrimp with grits. Weekday happy hour in C Level lounge offers $5 'bites, brews and libations.'

Balboa Park & Around

★ Carnitas' Snack Shack
CALIFORNIAN, MEXICAN $

(http://carnitassnackshack.com; 2632 University Ave; mains $7-9; ⊘noon-midnight Wed-Mon; ⚑) Like a food truck that has rolled to a stop in happening North Park, this dressed-down shack has a daily-changing menu of all things porky: carnitas tacos, pork burgers with bacon jam, pork schnitzel sandwiches, pulled pork poutine with bacon crumble etc.

Bread & Cie
BAKERY, CAFE $

(www.breadandcie.com; 350 University Ave; mains $5-11; ⊘7am-7pm Mon-Fri, to 6pm Sat, 8am-6pm Sun; ℗) Crusty sandwiches, salads, French quiche and decadent pastries (try a ridiculously oversized *pain au chocolat*) make this busy bakery-cafe a Hillcrest institution. Free parking in rear lot.

★ Buona Forchetta
ITALIAN $$

(www.buonaforchettasd.com; 3001 Beech St; pizzas $7-15, small plates $5-13; ⊘5-10pm Sun & Tue-Thu, to 11pm Fri & Sat; ⚐) A gold-painted brick wood-fired oven custom-built in Italy delivers authentic Neapolitan pizzas straight to merrily jammed-together tables at this South Park trattoria with a dog-friendly patio. Leafy salads, handmade pasta and sweet *dolci* (desserts) are just as satisfying. No reservations.

Hash House a Go Go
AMERICAN $$

(☑619-298-4646; www.hashhouseagogo.com; 3628 5th Ave; mains breakfast $9-18, dinner $15-29; ⊘7.30am-2pm Mon-Fri, to 2:30pm Sat & Sun,

dinner 5:30-9pm Tue-Thu, to 9:30pm Fri-Sun; ⚑) This Hillcrest bungalow makes towering plates of 'twisted farm food': sausage-gravy pot pie, gianormous meatloaf sandwiches, tractor-wheel-sized pancakes and potato hash seven different ways. Come hungry for brunch.

★ Prado
CALIFORNIAN $$$

(☑619-557-9441; www.pradobalboa.com; House of Hospitality, 1549 El Prado; mains lunch $12-21, dinner $22-35; ⊘11:30am-3pm Mon-Fri, from 11am Sat & Sun, 5-9pm Sun & Tue-Thu, to 10pm Fri & Sat) This sought-after Balboa Park spot spices up fresh Cal-Mediterranean cuisine with Latin and Asian touches, from the seafood paella and chorizo pork burgers to chopped salads. Breezy outdoor seating and a colorfully tiled interior are equally inviting. Happy-hour food and drinks are a steal.

Beaches

South Beach Bar & Grille
SEAFOOD, MEXICAN $

(www.southbeachob.com; 5059 Newport Ave, Ocean Beach; most dishes $3-12; ⊘11am-2am) Maybe it's the lightly fried mahi and wahoo fish. Or the zippy white sauce. Or layered fresh cabbage and peppery tomato salsa. Whatever the secret, the fish tacos (discounted on Tuesdays) at this raucous beachside bar really stand out.

Hodad's
BURGERS $

(www.hodadies.com; 5010 Newport Ave, Ocean Beach; dishes $3-10; ⊘11am-9pm Sun-Thu, to 10pm Fri & Sat) OB's legendary burger joint serves great shakes, massive baskets of onion rings and paper-wrapped hamburgers. The walls are covered in license plates and your bearded, tattooed server might sidle right into your booth to take your order. Also has a branch in Downtown (Map p96; 945 Broadway Ave; ⊘11am-9pm Sun-Thu, to 10pm Fri & Sat).

Point Loma Seafoods
SEAFOOD $$

(http://pointlomaseafoods.com; 2805 Emerson St; dishes $3-16, mains $9-13; ⊘9am-7pm Mon-Sat, from 10am Sun; ℗⚑) Stroll up and order right at the counter inside this fish market, grill and deli with a sushi bar, where almost everything is fresh off the boat. It's a briny San Diego institution, with picnic tables outside.

★ **George's at the Cove** CALIFORNIAN $$$
(☑858-454-4244; www.georgesatthecove.com; 1250 Prospect St, La Jolla; mains $18-50; ☉11am-10pm Mon-Thu, to 11pm Fri-Sun) George's has graced just about every list of top restaurants in California, and chef Trey Foshee's Euro-Cal cuisine is as dramatic as the oceanfront location. Three venues allow you to enjoy it at stratospherically ascending price points: **George's Bar** (lunch mains $10-18), **Ocean Terrace** (dinner mains $18-35) and **California Modern** (dinner mains $30-50). Walk-ins welcome at the bar (hit happy hour from 3:30pm to 6:30pm weekdays).

🍷 Drinking & Entertainment

Downtown's Gaslamp Quarter has the rowdiest bars and hottest nightclubs. Check the *San Diego Reader* (www.sandiegoreader.com) or *U-T San Diego* (www.utsandiego.com) for the latest happenings around town. **Arts Tix** (Map p96; ☑858-381-5595; www.sdartstix.com; Lyceum Theatre, 79 Horton Plaza; ☉hours vary) sells half-price and discounted tickets to performing arts events, including plays, comedy shows, music concerts and more.

Prohibition LOUNGE
(Map p96; www.prohibitionsd.com; 548 5th Ave; ☉7pm-2am Wed-Sat) Sophisticated 1930s-style bar takes music and cocktails seriously. The house rules aren't a joke either: no cell phones at the bar and a strict dress code. Live jazz, blues, soul sounds or tiki tunes after 9pm.

Noble Experiment BAR
(Map p96; ☑619-888-4713; http://noble experimentsd.com; 777 G St; ☉7pm-2am Tue-Sun) Knock on the hidden door of this contempo speakeasy with gold skulls adorning the walls and a 400-strong cocktail list. Text a week ahead for a reservation and cryptic directions.

Hamilton's Tavern BAR
(http://hamiltonstavern.com; 1521 30th St; ☉3pm-2am Mon-Fri, from 1pm Sat & Sun; 🐾) Detour to the South Park 'hood and squeeze yourself onto a barstool at this low-key hangout with shuffleboard, pool, A+ pub grub and and a head-spinning menu of craft beers.

Tipsy Crow BAR
(Map p96; ☑619-338-9300; http://thetipsycrow.com; 770 5th Ave; ☉3pm-2am Mon-Fri, from noon Sat & Sun) In a historic Gaslamp building, this atmospheric watering hole has a loungelike 'Nest' (rumored to have been a brothel) and brick-walled 'Underground' dance floor with rockin' live bands and comedy acts.

Casbah LIVE MUSIC
(☑619-232-4355; www.casbahmusic.com; 2501 Kettner Blvd; tickets $5-45) MGMT, Liz Phair and the Smashing Pumpkins all rocked the funky Casbah on their way up the charts. Catch local bands and indie-rock headliners here and at the legendary **Belly Up** (☑858-481-8140; www.bellyup.com; 143 S Cedros Ave, Solana Beach; tickets $10-45) in Solana Beach.

DON'T MISS

SAN DIEGO'S MICROBREWERIES

San Diegans take their craft beers seriously – even at a dive bar, you might overhear local beer geeks debating the merits of 'hoppiness' and cask conditioning. Gargantuan to garage-sized microbreweries around the city specialize in all kinds of brews. Check out the following:

Stone Brewing Company (☑760-471-4999; www.stonebrew.com; 1999 Citracado Pkwy, Escondido; ☉tours noon-6pm daily) Take a tour ($3) before tasting the Oaked Arrogant Bastard Ale and Old Guardian Barley Wine.

Lost Abbey (☑800-918-6816; www.lostabbey.com; Suite 104, 155 Mata Way, San Marcos; ☉1-6pm Mon-Tue, to 9pm Wed & Fri, to 8pm Thu, 11:30am-8pm Sat, noon-7pm Sun) More than 20 brews ($1 per taste) are on tap in the tasting room, including the Belgian-style ales Judgment Day and Red Barn.

Green Flash (☑858-622-0085; www.greenflashbrew.com; 6550 Mira Mesa Blvd; ☉3-9pm Tue-Thu, to 10pm Fri, noon-9pm Sat, noon-6pm Sun) Sip American and Belgian ales ($1 per taste) in an outdoor beer garden; book ahead online for tours ($5).

AleSmith (☑858-549-9888; www.alesmith.com; 9366 Cabot Dr; ☉2-8pm Tue-Thu, to 9pm Fri, 11am-8pm Sat, 11am-6pm Sun) The Scotch ale Wee Heavy, citrusy Horny Devil and Speedway Stout ($1 to $2 per taste) are addictive.

La Jolla Playhouse THEATER
(☑ 858-550-1010; www.lajollaplayhouse.org; 2910 La Jolla Village Dr; tickets $15-70) Award-winning plays and world-premiere musicals that sometimes go on to shine brightly on Broadway take over multiple stages inside this coastal performing arts center.

ⓘ Information

INTERNET ACCESS

Coffee shops offer wi-fi with purchase (sometimes for free).

San Diego Public Library (☑ 619-236-5800; www.sandiego.gov/public-library; 820 E St; ☺ noon-8pm Mon & Wed, 9:30am-5:30pm Tue & Thu-Fri, 9:30am-2:30pm Sat, 1-5pm Sun; @ ⑤) Free wi-fi and public internet terminals. Call or check the website for branch locations.

MEDIA

San Diego Magazine (www.sandiegomagazine. com) Glossy monthly lifestyle magazine.

San Diego Reader (www.sandiegoreader.com) Free alternative weekly tabloid.

U-T San Diego (www.utsandiego.com) The city's major daily newspaper.

MEDICAL SERVICES

Scripps Mercy Hospital (☑ 619-294-8111; www.scripps.org; 4077 5th Ave) Has a 24-hour emergency room.

MONEY

TravelEx (www.travelex.com) Foreign currency-exchange services are at the airport (p103). Downtown (☑ 619-235-0901; www.travelex. com; 177 Horton Plaza; ☺ 10am-7pm Mon-Fri, to 6pm Sat, 11am-4pm Sun), Fashion Valley (☑ 619-542-1173; www.travelex.com; 7007 Friars Rd; ☺ 10am-9pm Mon-Sat, 11am-7pm Sun) and La Jolla (☑ 858-457-2412; www. travelex.com; University Town Centre, 4417 La Jolla Village Dr; ☺ 10am-7pm Mon-Fri, to 6pm Sat, 11am-4pm Sun).

TOURIST INFORMATION

Balboa Park Visitors Center (☑ 619-239-0512; www.balboapark.org; House of Hospitality, 1549 El Prado; ☺ 9:30am-4:30pm) Buy discounted one-day ($39) and seven-day (adult/child $39/27, including zoo $85/49) passports to park museums.

San Diego Visitor Information Centers (☑ 619-236-1212; www.sandiego.org) Downtown (Map p96; 1140 N Harbor Dr; ☺ 9am-5pm Jun-Sep, to 4pm Oct-May) La Jolla (☑ 858-454-5718; www.sandiego.org; 7966 Herschel Ave; ☺ 11am-6pm Jun-Sep, to 4pm Oct-May) Downtown's waterfront location sells discounted attraction and tour tickets.

WEBSITES

Gaslamp Quarter Association (http://gaslamp.org) Everything about the bustling Gaslamp Quarter, including parking tips.

San Diego Convention & Visitors Bureau (www.sandiego.org) Official tourist info site.

ⓘ Getting There & Away

Served mainly by domestic US and Mexico flights, **San Diego International Airport** (SAN; ☑ 619-400-2404; www.san.org; 3325 N Harbor Dr) sits 3 miles northwest of downtown.

Greyhound (Map p96; ☑ 619-515-1100; www. greyhound.com; 1313 National Ave) has hourly direct buses to Los Angeles ($19, two to three hours).

Amtrak (☑ 800-872-7245; www.amtrak.com) runs the *Pacific Surfliner* several times daily to Los Angeles ($37, 2¾ hours) and Santa Barbara ($41, 5¾ hours) from downtown's historic **Santa Fe Depot** (1055 Kettner Blvd).

Major international car-rental companies have desks at the airport. Smaller, independent **West Coast Rent a Car** (☑ 619-544-0606; http://sandiegoautos.org; 834 W Grape St; ☺ 9am-6pm Mon-Sat, to 5pm Sun) rents to under-25s, with free airport pick-ups.

ⓘ Getting Around

City buses ($2.25 to $2.50) and trolleys ($2.25), including south to the Mexico border, are operated by **Metropolitan Transit System** (MTS; ☑ 619-557-4555; www.sdmts.com). MTS's **Transit Store** (Map p96; ☑ 619-234-1060; 102 Broadway; ☺ 9am-5pm Mon-Fri) sells regional passes ($5/9/12/15 for one/two/three/four days); purchase one-day passes on-board buses.

MTS bus 992 ($2.25) runs every 15 to 30 minutes between the airport and downtown from 5am to 11pm daily. Airport shuttles such as the **Super Shuttle** (☑ 800-258-3826; www.supershuttle. com) charge $8 to $10 to downtown. An airport taxi to downtown averages $10 to $15, plus tip.

Metered taxis charge $2.80 at flag fall, then $3 per mile.

Around San Diego

San Diego Zoo Safari Park

Take a walk on the 'wild' side at this 1800-acre open-range zoo (☑ 760-747-8702; www. sdzsafaripark.org; 15500 San Pasqual Valley Rd; adult/child from $44/34, 2-day ticket incl San Diego Zoo $79/61; ☺ 9am-7pm late Jun–mid-Aug, to 5pm or 6pm rest of year; P ⊕). Giraffes graze, lions lounge and rhinos roam more or less freely on the valley floor. For that instant safari feel, board the Africa tram ride, which tours you around the second-largest continent in just 25 minutes.

The park is in Escondido, about 35 miles northeast of Downtown San Diego. Take the I-15 Fwy to the Via Rancho Pkwy exit, then follow the signs. Parking is $10.

Legoland

This fun fantasy theme park (☑760-918-5346; http://california.legoland.com; 1 Legoland Dr, Carlsbad; adult/child from $78/68; ☺daily mid-Mar–Aug, Wed-Sun only Sep–mid-Mar, seasonal hours vary; P) of rides, shows and attractions is mostly suited to the elementary-school set. Tots can dig for dinosaur bones, pilot helicopters and earn their driver's license. Families with young children can overnight in the brand-new, colorful Lego-themed hotel. From Downtown San Diego (about 33 miles), take the I-5 Fwy north to Carlsbad's Cannon Rd exit. Parking is $15.

PALM SPRINGS & THE DESERTS

From swanky Palm Springs to desolate Death Valley, Southern California's desert region swallows 25% of the entire state. At first what seems harrowingly barren may eventually be transformed in your mind's eye to perfect beauty: weathered volcanic peaks, booming sand dunes, purple-tinged mountains, cactus gardens, tiny wildflowers pushing up from hard-baked soil in spring, lizards scurrying beside colossal boulders, and in the night sky uncountable stars. California's deserts are serenely spiritual, surprisingly chic and ultimately irresistible, whether you're a bohemian artist, movie star, rock climber or 4WD adventurer.

Palm Springs

The Rat Pack is back, baby – or, at least, its hangout is. In the 1950 and '60s, Palm Springs (population 45,573), some 100 miles east of LA, was the swinging getaway of Sinatra, Elvis and other stars. Once the Rat Pack packed it in, however, Palm Springs surrendered to retirees in golf clothing. Recently a new generation has rediscovered the city's retro-chic charms: kidney-shaped pools, 'starchitect' bungalows, midcentury-modern boutique hotels and bars serving perfect martinis. Today retirees mix comfortably with hipsters and a significant lesbi-gay community.

◎ Sights & Activities

Palm Springs is the hub of the Coachella Valley, a string of desert towns along Hwy 111. In PS' compact downtown, one-way southbound Palm Canyon Dr is paralleled by northbound Indian Canyon Dr.

★Palm Springs Aerial Tramway   CABLE CAR
(☑888-515-8726; www.pstramway.com; 1 Tram Way; adult/child $24/17; ☺10am-8pm Mon-Fri, from 8am Sat & Sun, last tram down 9:45pm) Enjoy dizzying views as you're whisked 2.5 miles from sunbaked desert to a pine-scented alpine wonderland atop Mt San Jacinto. It gets chilly up here, so bring a jacket. Hiking trails wind through the adjacent wilderness, or rent snowshoes and cross-country skis at the Mountain Station's Winter Adventure Center (snowshoe/skis rental per day $18/21; ☺10am-4pm Thu-Fri & Mon, from 9am Sat & Sun, last rentals 2:30pm).

Living Desert Zoo & Gardens   ZOO
(☑760-346-5694; www.livingdesert.org; 47900 Portola Ave, Palm Desert, off Hwy 111; adult/child $17.25/8.75; ☺9am-5pm Oct-May, 8am-1:30pm Jun-Sep) ✐ At this engaging zoo off Hwy 111, kids can spy on North American and African wildlife, take a spin on the endangered species carousel and walk through a wildlife hospital. It's worth the 30-minute drive down-valley.

Palm Springs Art Museum   MUSEUM
(☑760-322-4800; www.psmuseum.org; 101 Museum Dr; adult/child $12.50/free, 4-8pm Thu free; ☺10am-5pm Tue-Wed & Fri-Sun, noon-8pm Thu) Downtown's art beacon views the evolution of American painting, sculpture, photography and architecture over the past century or so. Second location in Palm Desert.

Palm Springs Air Museum   MUSEUM
(☑760-778-6262; www.air-museum.org; 745 N Gene Autry Trail; adult/child $15/8; ☺10am-5pm) An exceptional collection of WWII aircraft, flight memorabilia and photos near the airport.

Tahquitz Canyon   HIKING
(☑760-416-7044; www.tahquitzcanyon.com; 500 W Mesquite Ave; adult/child $12.50/6; ☺7:30am-5pm Oct-Jun, Fri-Sun only Jul-Sep) Featured in Frank Capra's 1937 movie *Lost Horizon,* this canyon is famous for its seasonal waterfall and ancient rock art. Explore on your own or join a ranger-guided hike.

Indian Canyons
HIKING

(☑760-323-6018; www.indian-canyons.com; off S Palm Canyon Dr; adult/child $9/5, 90min guided hike $3/2; ☺8am-5pm Oct-Jun, Fri-Sun only Jul-Sep) Shaded by fan palms and flanked by soaring cliffs, these ancestral lands of the Cahuilla people are a desert hiker's delight, especially during spring wildflower blooms.

Knott's Soak City
SWIMMING

(☑760-327-0499; www.soakcityps.com; 1500 S Gene Autry Trail; adult/child $35/25; ☺hours vary, mid-Apr–early Oct) Keep cool on hot days with Knott's massive wave pool, towering water slides and tube rides. Buy discount tickets online. Parking is $12.

🛏 Sleeping

High-season winter rates are quoted below; rates drop midweek and during summer. Chain motels hug Hwy 111 southeast of downtown. Book ahead.

Caliente Tropics
MOTEL $

(☑800-658-6034, 760-327-1391; www.caliente-tropics.com; 411 E Palm Canyon Dr; r from $60; 🛜🅿️🐕🏊) Tiki-style motor lodge, where Elvis once frolicked poolside, shelters surprisingly spacious rooms with comfy beds.

★ Orbit In
BOUTIQUE HOTEL $$

(☑877-966-7248, 760-323-3585; www.orbitin.com; 562 W Arenas Rd; r incl breakfast from $149; ❄️🛜🏊) Swing back to the Rat Pack era at this quintessential mid-century modern property set around a saline pool and hot tub. Rooms sport designer furniture (Eames, Noguchi et al), while freebies include cocktail hour, daytime sodas and snacks, and cruiser bicycles to borrow.

Del Marcos Hotel
BOUTIQUE HOTEL $$

(☑800-676-1214, 760-325-6902; www.delmarcoshotel.com; 225 W Baristo Rd; r incl breakfast $139-189; ❄️🛜🏊🐕) At this 1947 gem designed by William F Cody, groovy tunes usher you toward a saltwater pool and ineffably chic rooms (some have kitchenettes) named for mid-century modern architectural luminaries. Complimentary beach cruisers for guests. No kids allowed.

Ace Hotel & Swim Club
HOTEL $$

(☑760-325-9900; www.acehotel.com/palmsprings; 701 E Palm Canyon Dr; r from $100; ❄️@🛜🏊🐕) Get all the sass *sans* attitude at this hipster hangout. Rooms (many with patios) sport a glorified cabana-shack look and are crammed with digerati lifestyle es-

sentials. Laughable karaoke, trivia and bingo nights, with DJs and live bands to boot.

El Morocco Inn & Spa
BOUTIQUE HOTEL $$$

(☑760-288-2527, 888-288-9905; www.elmoroccoinn.com; 66814 4th St, Desert Hot Springs; r incl breakfast $179-219; ❄️🛜🏊) Heed the call of the kasbah at this exotic adult-only hideaway whose 10 rooms wrap around a pool deck. Perks include a spa, natural-springs pool and homemade mint tea and 'Moroccotinis.' It's a 20-minute drive north of PS.

🍴 Eating

Some restaurants keep shorter hours and close for a few weeks in summer.

Tyler's Burgers
BURGERS $

(http://tylersburgers.com; 149 S Indian Canyon Dr; dishes $2-9; ☺11am-4pm Mon-Sat; 🧒) The best burgers in town. 'Nuff said. Expect a line.

Native Foods
VEGAN $

(☑760-416-0070; www.nativefoods.com; Smoke Tree Village, 1775 E Palm Canyon Dr; mains $8-11; ☺11am-9:30pm Mon-Sat; 🥗🧒) Organic, meatless and made-from-scratch salads, wraps and bowls that don't sacrifice a lick of taste.

★ Cheeky's
CALIFORNIAN $$

(☑760-327-7595; www.cheekysps.com; 622 N Palm Canyon Dr; mains $8-13; ☺8am-2pm Wed-Mon, last seating 1:30pm) 🍴 Waits can be oh-so long, but the seasonal and often organic farm-to-table menu dazzles with its witty inventiveness. Actual dishes change weekly, but tomatillo chilaquile plates, bacon 'flights' and pomegranate mimosas keep making appearances.

Sherman's   DELI, BAKERY $$
(☑760-325-1199; www.shermansdeli.com; 401 E Tahquitz Canyon Way; mains $8-18; ☺7am-9pm; ☷) With a breezy sidewalk patio, this 1950s kosher-style deli pulls in an all-ages crowd with its 40 sandwich varieties (great hot pastrami!), finger-lickin' rotisserie chicken and to-die-for pies. Also in Palm Desert (☑760-568-1350; www.shermansdeli.com; 73-161 County Club Dr; mains $8-18; ☺7am-9pm; ☷).

Trio   CALIFORNIAN $$$
(☑760-864-8746; www.triopalmsprings.com; 707 N Palm Canyon Dr; mains $13-29; ☺11am-10pm) The winning formula at this 1960s modernist space equals updated American comfort food (Yankee pot roast and mac 'n' cheese), eye-catching artwork and picture windows. Three-course prix-fixe dinner ($19) before 6pm.

Copley's   AMERICAN $$$
(☑760-327-9555; www.copleyspalmsprings.com; 621 N Palm Canyon Dr; mains $19-39; ☺from 5:30pm daily late Aug–mid-Jun, Tue-Sun only mid-Jun–early Jul, closed early Jul-Aug) Swoon-worthy American fare on the former Cary Grant estate. The 'Oh My Lobster Pot Pie' is unlikely to ever go out of style. Bring your sweetie and your platinum AmEx card.

🍷 Drinking & Entertainment

Arenas Rd, east of Indian Canyon Dr, is lesbi-gay nightlife central.

Koffi   CAFE
(www.kofficoffee.com; 1700 S Camino Real; ☺5:30am-7pm) Minimalist coffee shop for gourmet baked goods, organic coffee and handcrafted espresso drinks. Also downtown at 515 N Palm Canyon Dr.

Birba   BAR
(www.birbaps.com; 622 N Palm Canyon Dr; ☺5-11pm Sun & Wed-Thu, to midnight Fri & Sat) At this seductive cocktail lounge, floor-to-ceiling glass doors open onto a hedge-fringed patio with sunken fire pits.

Shanghai Red's   BAR
(www.fishermans.com; 235 S Indian Canyon Dr; ☺4pm-late Mon-Sat, from noon Sun) Behind a seafood shack, this courtyard watering hole has happy-hour drink specials and live blues music on Friday and Saturday nights.

🛍 Shopping

For art galleries, modern design stores and fashion boutiques, including fabulous Trina Turk (☑760-416-2856; www.trinaturk.com; 891 N Palm Canyon Dr; ☺10am-5pm Mon-Fri, to 6pm Sat, noon-5pm Sun), head 'Uptown' to North Palm Canyon Dr. If you're riding the retro wave, uncover treasures in thrift, vintage and consignment shops scattered around downtown and along Hwy 111. For a local version of Rodeo Dr, drive down-valley to Palm Desert's El Paseo.

ℹ Information

Desert Regional Medical Center (☑760-323-6511; www.desertregional.com; 1150 N Indian Canyon Dr) Has a 24-hour emergency room.

Palm Springs Library (www.palmspringsca.gov; 300 S Sunrise Way; ☺10am-5pm Wed-Sat, to 7pm Tue; @ ☏) Free wi-fi and public internet terminals.

Palm Springs Official Visitors Center (☑760-778-8418; www.visitpalmsprings.com; 2901 N Palm Canyon Dr; ☺9am-5pm) Inside a 1965 Albert Frey–designed gas station at the tramway turnoff, 3 miles northwest of downtown.

ℹ Getting There & Around

About 3 miles east of downtown, **Palm Springs International Airport** (PSP; ☑760-323-8299; www.palmspringsairport.com; 3400 E Tahquitz Canyon Way) is served by US and Canadian airlines; major car-rental agencies are on-site.

Thrice-weekly Amtrak trains to/from LA ($40, 2¾ hours) stop at the unstaffed, kinda-creepy North Palm Springs station, 6 miles north of downtown, as do several daily Greyhound buses to/from LA ($26, three hours).

SunLine (www.sunline.org; fare/day pass $1/3) runs slow-moving local buses throughout the valley.

Joshua Tree National Park

Like figments from a Dr Seuss book, whimsical-looking Joshua trees (actually tree-sized yuccas) welcome visitors to this wilderness park where the Sonora and Mojave Deserts converge. You'll find most of the main attractions, including all of the Joshua trees, in the park's northern half. 'J-Tree' is perennially popular with rock climbers and day hikers, especially in spring when the trees bloom with cream-colored flowers. The mystical quality of this stark, boulder-strewn landscape has inspired countless artists, most famously the rock band U2.

⊙ Sights & Activities

Dominating the north side of the park (☑760-367-5500; www.nps.gov/jotr; 7-day entry per car $15), the epic **Wonderland of Rocks** calls to climbers. Sunset-worthy **Keys View** overlooks the San Andreas Fault and, on clear days, as far as Mexico. For pioneer history, tour **Keys Ranch** (☑reservations 760-367-5555; www.nps.gov/jotr; adult/child $5/2.50; ⊙10am & 1pm late Sep-early Apr). Hikers seek out native desert fan-palm oases like **49 Palms Oasis** (3-mile round-trip) and **Lost Palms Oasis** (7.2-mile round-trip). Kid-friendly nature trails include **Barker Dam** (1.3-mile loop), which passes Native American petroglyphs; **Skull Rock** (1.5-mile loop); and **Cholla Cactus Garden** (0.25-mile loop). For a scenic 4WD route, tackle bumpy 18-mile **Geology Tour Road**, which is also open to mountain bikers.

🛏 Sleeping

The park itself only has camping. Bunches of independent and chain motels line Hwy 62.

Joshua Tree National
Park Campgrounds   CAMPGROUND $
(www.nps.gov/jotr; camping & RV sites $10-15; 🚻🐾) Of the park's nine campgrounds, only Cottonwood and Black Rock have potable water and flush toilets. Indian Cove and Black Rock accept **reservations** (☑518-885-3639, 877-444-6777; www.recreation.gov) from October to May. Other campgrounds are first-come, first-served, often filling by 10am in spring. **Joshua Tree Outfitters** (☑760-366-1848; www.joshuatreeoutfitters.com; 61707 Hwy 62) rents camping gear.

Harmony Motel   MOTEL $
(☑760-367-3351; www.harmonymotel.com; 71161 Hwy 62; r $65-90; 🅿@🛜🏊) Where U2 wrote its album *The Joshua Tree*, this minimalist motel is a bit designy, with oversized rooms and cabin decorated in a jumble of styles. There's a communal kitchenette and library.

★Kate's Lazy Desert   INN $$
(☑845-688-7200; www.lazymeadow.com; 58380 Botkin Rd, Landers; d $175-200; ❄🛜🏊🐾) Owned by Kate Pierson of the B-52s, this desert camp surrounds a petite pool. Six Airstream trailers are kitted out with a kitchenette and fanasta-pop design, from groovy tiki to woodsy lodge kitsch. It's a 30-minute drive north of Yucca Valley, near the wacky **Integratron** (☑760-364-3126; www.integratron.com; 2477 Belfield Boulevard, Landers; sound baths $20-80).

WORTH A TRIP

PIONEERTOWN
About 4.5 miles northwest of Yucca Valley, **Pioneertown** was built as a Hollywood movie set in 1946, and it hasn't changed much since. On Mane St, witness mock gunfights at 2:30pm on Saturdays from April to October. Enjoy BBQ, cheap beer and live music at honky-tonk **Pappy & Harriet's Pioneertown Palace** (☑760-365-5956; www.pappy-andharriets.com; 53688 Pioneertown Rd; mains $8-29; ⊙11am-2am Thu-Sun, from 5pm Mon). Snooze at the **Pioneertown Motel** (☑760-365-7001; www.pioneertown-motel.com; 5040 Curtis Rd; r $70-120; ❄🛜🐾), where old-time movie stars once slept. Simple rooms are crammed with Western-themed memorabilia.

Spin & Margie's Desert Hide-a-Way   INN $$
(☑760-366-9124; www.deserthideaway.com; 64491 Hwy 62; ste $135-175; ❄🛜) Not far from the park, this hacienda-style inn encloses five boldly colored kitchenette suites with striking design using corrugated tin, old license plates and cartoon art. Two-night minimum stay required.

🍴 Eating & Drinking

Natural Sisters Cafe   VEGETARIAN $
(☑760-366-3600; 61695 Hwy 62, Joshua Tree; dishes $4-8; ⊙7am-7pm; 🛜🐾) Fill up on fruit smoothies, garden-fresh salads, tofu wraps, vegan curries and homemade kombucha at this much-adored J-Tree cafe.

★Palm Kabob House   MIDDLE EASTERN $$
(☑760-362-8583; 6341 Adobe Rd, Twentynine Palms; mains $6-14; ⊙11am-9pm; 🐾🅿) Hustle over to near Twentynine Palms' marine base for home-baked pita bread, lamb or chicken shwarma, refreshingly cool eggplant dip and vegetable salads.

Pie for the People   PIZZERIA $$
(http://pieforthepeople.com; 61740 Hwy 62, Joshua Tree; pizzas $13-25; ⊙11am-9pm Mon-Thu, to 10pm Fri & Sat, to 8pm Sun; 🅿) Chew thin-crust NYC-style pizzas, calzones and other stuff-your-face Italian-American fare, just outside the park.

Ma Rouge   CAFE
(www.marouge.net; 55844 Hwy 62, Yucca Valley; ⊙7am-6pm) Swing by this community coffee house for organic coffee, espresso and baked goods.

❶ Information

Pick up park information at NPS visitor centers at **Joshua Tree** (6554 Park Blvd; ⊘8am-5pm), **Oasis** (74485 National Park Dr; ⊘8am-5pm) and **Cottonwood** (Cottonwood Springs, 8 miles north of I-10 Fwy; ⊘9am-3pm) and at **Black Rock Nature Center** (9800 Black Rock Canyon Rd; ⊘8am-4pm Sat-Thu, noon-8pm Fri Oct-May ; ⊞). There are no park facilities aside from restrooms. Get gas and stock up in the three desert communities linked by the Twentynine Palms Hwy (Hwy 62) along the park's northern boundary: down-to-earth Yucca Valley, which has the most services (banks, supermarkets, post office, public library with free wi-fi and internet terminals etc); beatnik Joshua Tree, where outdoor outfitters cluster; and Twentynine Palms, home of the USA's largest marine base.

Anza-Borrego Desert State Park

Shaped by an ancient sea and tectonic forces, Anza-Borrego is the largest state park in the USA outside Alaska. Cradling the park's only commercial hub – tiny Borrego Springs (pop 3429) – are 600,000 acres of mountains, canyons and badlands; a fabulous variety of plants and wildlife; and intriguing historical relics of Native American tribes, Spanish explorers and gold-rush pioneers. Wildflower blooms (usually from late February through April – call ☏760-767-4684 for updates) bring the biggest crowds, right before Hades-like heat makes daytime exploring dangerous.

◎ Sights & Activities

Two miles west of Borrego Springs, the park **visitor center** (☏760-767-4205; www.parks. ca.gov; 200 Palm Canyon Dr; ⊘9am-5pm Oct-May, Sat & Sun only Jun-Sep) has natural-history exhibits, informational handouts and updates on road conditions. Driving through the park is free, but if you camp, hike or picnic, a day-use parking fee (per car $5 to $8) applies. You'll need 4WD to tackle the 500 miles of backcountry dirt roads. If you'll be hiking or mountain biking, pack extra water.

Park highlights include: **Fonts Point** desert lookout; **Clark Dry Lake** for birding; **Elephant Tree Discovery Trail** near Split Mountain's wind caves; and **Blair Valley**, with its Native American pictographs and *morteros* (grinding stones). Further south, soak in hot-springs pools at **Agua Caliente County Park** (☏760-765-1188; www.sdcounty. ca.gov/parks/; 39555 Rte S2; entry per car $5; ⊘9:30am-5pm Sep-May).

🍴 Sleeping & Eating

Free backcountry camping without a permit is permitted anywhere in the park, as long as you're at least 100ft from water or roads (no campfires or gathering of vegetation).

For country-style B&Bs and famous apple pie, the gold-mining town of **Julian** (www. julianca.com) is a 30-mile drive southwest of Borrego Springs.

Anza-Borrego Desert State Park Campgrounds ⸻ CAMPGROUND **$**
(☏reservations 800-444-7275; www.reserveamerica.com; tent/RV sites $25/35; ⊞❄) Book ahead for campsites at busy Borrego Palm Canyon Campground, 3 miles northwest of Borrego Springs, or smaller but shadier Tamarisk Grove (nonpotable water only), 12 miles south near Hwy 78.

Borrego Springs Motel ⸻ MOTEL **$**
(☏760-767-4339; www.borregospringsmotel.com; 2376 Borrego Springs Rd; r $75-95; ⊘late Sep-early Jun; ❄❅❄❄) ✎ Just north of in-town Christmas Circle, this refurbished 1940s motel (now solar-powered) has eight spic-and-span, spartan rooms with deluxe mattresses. Go stargazing by the outdoor fire pit.

SALTON SEA & SALVATION MOUNTAIN

East of Anza-Borrego and south of Joshua Tree awaits a most unexpected sight: the **Salton Sea** (http://salton-sea.ca.gov), California's largest lake, which sits in the middle of its biggest desert. After the Colorado River flooded in 1905, it took 1500 workers and half a million tons of rock to put it back on course. With no natural outlet, the artificial lake's surface is 220ft below sea level and its waters 30% saltier than the Pacific – an environmental nightmare that's yet to be cleaned up.

An even stranger sight near the lake's eastern shore is **Salvation Mountain** (www.salvationmountain.us), a 50ft-high hill of hand-mixed clay blanketed in colorful acrylic paint and found objects, and inscribed with Christian messages. It's the vision of folk artist Leonard Knight. It's in Niland, about 3 miles east of Hwy 111, via Main St and Beal Rd.

Borrego Valley Inn   INN $$$
(☑800-333-5810, 760-767-0311; www.borregoval-leyinn.com; 405 Palm Canyon Dr; r incl breakfast $180-280; ✳️🛜❄️) An intimate adults-only spa resort sports 15 elegant adobe-style rooms (some with kitchenettes) accented with Southwestern decor, plus two pools (one clothing-optional) and an outdoor hot tub.

Carlee's Place   AMERICAN $$
(660 Palm Canyon Dr; mains lunch $7-14, dinner $12-23; ⊙11am-9pm) Join locals for OK bar-and-grill food, pool tables and crazy karaoke.

❶ Information

Borrego Springs has banks with ATMs, gas stations, a post office, supermarket and public library with free wi-fi and internet terminals, all on Palm Canyon Dr.

Mojave National Preserve

If you're on a quest for the 'middle of no-where,' you may find it in Mojave National Preserve (☑760-252-6100; www.nps.gov/moja) FREE a 1.4-million-acre jumble of sand dunes, Joshua trees, volcanic cinder cones and habitats for desert tortoises, jack rabbits and coyotes. No gas is available here.

Southeast of Baker and the I-15 Fwy, Kel-baker Rd crosses a ghostly landscape of cin-der cones before arriving at Kelso Depot, a 1920s Mission Revival–style railroad station. It now houses the park's main visitor cent-er (☑760-252-6108; ⊙9am-5pm Fri-Tue), which has excellent natural and cultural history ex-hibits, and an old-fashioned lunch counter. It's another 11 miles southwest to 'singing' Kelso Dunes. When wind conditions are right, they emanate low-pitched vibrations caused by shifting sands – running downhill can jump-start the effect.

From Kelso Depot, the Kelso–Cima Rd takes off northeast. After 19 miles, Cima Rd slingshots northwest toward I-15 around Cima Dome, a 1500ft-high hunk of granite with crusty lava outcroppings, whose slopes are home to the world's largest Joshua tree forest. For close-ups, summit Teutonia Peak (3 miles round-trip); the trailhead is 6 miles northwest of Cima.

Further east, Mojave Rd is a scenic back-door route to first-come, first-served camp-grounds (tent sites $12) with potable water at Mid Hills (no RVs) and Hole-in-the-Wall. The campgrounds bookend a rugged 12-mile scenic drive along Wild Horse Canyon

Rd, ending near Hole-in-the-Wall visitor center (☑760-252-6104; ⊙9am-4pm Wed-Sun Oct-Apr, 10am-4pm Sat May-Sep) and the slot-canyon Rings Loop Trail. Both of these dirt roads usually don't require 4WD.

🛏 Sleeping & Eating

Free backcountry and roadside camping is permitted throughout the preserve in already impacted areas; ask at the visitor center or consult the free park newspaper.

For historical ambience, Hotel Nipton (☑760-856-2335; http://nipton.com; 107355 Nip-ton Rd; cabins/r with shared bath from $65/80; ⊙reception 8am-6pm; 🛜) encompasses a century-old adobe villa with rustic rooms and tent cabins in a remote railway outpost, northeast of the preserve. Check in at the trading post next to Mexican American Oa-sis (dishes $5-10; ⊙usually 11am-6pm Sun-Fri, to 8pm Sat) cafe.

Off I-15, Baker (35 miles northwest of Kelso) is the nearest town with bare-bones motels and fast food, while state-line Primm, NV (50 miles northeast) has well-worn casi-no hotels and restaurants by an outlet mall.

Death Valley National Park

The name itself evokes all that is harsh and hellish – a punishing, barren and lifeless place of Old Testament severity. Yet closer inspection reveals nature puts on a spec-tacular show here, with water-sculpted can-yons, windswept sand dunes, palm-shaded oases, jagged mountains and wildlife aplen-ty. It's also a land of superlatives, holding the US records for the hottest temperature (134°F/57°C), lowest point (Badwater, 282ft below sea level) and largest national park outside Alaska (more than 5000 sq miles). Peak tourist season is when spring wildflo-wers bloom.

◉ Sights & Activities

From Furnace Creek, the central hub of the park (☑760-786-3200; www.nps.gov/deva; 7-day entry per car $20), drive southeast up to Zabriskie Point for spectacular sunset views across the valley and golden badlands eroded into waves, pleats and gullies. Twen-ty miles southeast at Dante's View, you can simultaneously spot the highest (Mt Whit-ney, 14,505ft) and lowest (Badwater) points in the contiguous USA.

Badwater itself, a timeless landscape of crinkly salt flats, is 17 miles south of Furnace Creek. Along the way, Golden Canyon and Natural Bridge are easily explored on short hikes from roadside parking lots. A 9-mile detour along Artists Drive through a narrow canyon is best in late afternoon when the eroded hillsides erupt in fireworks of color.

Northwest of Furnace Creek, near Stovepipe Wells Village, trek across the Saharanesque Mesquite Flat sand dunes – magical during a full moon – and scramble along the smooth marble walls of Mosaic Canyon.

About 35 miles north of Furnace Creek is whimsical Scotty's Castle (☑reservations 877-444-6777; www.recreation.gov; tours adult/child from $15/7.50; ☺grounds 7am-5:30pm, tour times vary), where tour guides in historical character dress bring to life the Old West tales of con-man 'Death Valley Scotty' (reservations advised). Five miles west of Grapevine junction, circumambulate volcanic Ubehebe Crater and its younger sibling.

In summer, stick to paved roads (dirt roads can quickly overheat vehicles), limit your exertions and visit higher-elevation areas: for example, the scenic drive up Emigrant Canyon, starting 8 miles west of Stovepipe Wells, passing turnoffs to ghost towns and ending with a 3-mile unpaved stretch up to the historic beehive-shaped Charcoal Kilns. Nearby is the trailhead for the 8.4-mile round-trip hike up Wildrose Peak (9064ft). At the park's western edge, utterly remote Panamint Springs offers panoramic vistas and a 2-mile round-trip hike to tiny Darwin Falls.

WORTH A TRIP

RHYOLITE

Four miles west of Beatty, NV, look for the turnoff to the ghost town of Rhyolite (www.rhyolitesite.com; off Hwy 374; ☺sunrise-sunset) FREE, which epitomizes the hurly-burly, boom-and-bust story of so many Western gold-rush mining towns. Don't miss the 1906 'bottle house' or the skeletal remains of a three-story bank. Next door is the bizarre Goldwell Open Air Museum (www.goldwellmuseum.org; off Hwy 374; ☺24hr) FREE of trippy art installations begun by Belgian artist Albert Szukalski in 1984.

Activities offered at the Ranch at Furnace Creek include horseback riding, golf, mountain biking and hot-springs pool swimming.

🛏 Sleeping & Eating

In-park lodging is often booked solid in springtime when campgrounds fill by midmorning, especially on weekends. Backcountry camping (no campfires) is allowed in previously impacted sites 2 miles away from any paved road and developed or dayuse area, and 100yd from water sources; pick up free permits at the visitor center.

The closest town with cheaper lodging is Beatty, NV (40 miles northeast of Furnace Creek); accommodations are more plentiful in Las Vegas, NV (120 miles southeast) and Ridgecrest, CA (120 miles southwest).

Death Valley National Park Campgrounds CAMPGROUND $
(www.nps.gov/deva; campsites free-$30; 🚻🐾) Of the park's nine campgrounds, only Furnace Creek accepts reservations (☑518-885-3639, 877-444-6777; www.recreation.gov) and only from mid-October to mid-April. In summer, Furnace Creek is first-come, first-served, and the only other campgrounds open are Mesquite Spring, near Scotty's Castle, and those along Emigrant Canyon Rd (high-clearance 4WD may be required). Other valley-floor campgrounds – including RV-oriented Stovepipe Wells and Sunset, and shadier tent-friendly Texas Springs – are open October to April.

Ranch at Furnace Creek MOTEL, CABINS $$
(☑760-786-2345, 800-236-7916; www.furnacecreekresort.com; Hwy 190; d $139-219; 🌡🛜🏊🐾) Tailor-made for families, this rambling resort offers lodge rooms awash in desert colors, with French doors opening onto porches or patios, as well as duplex cabins. The ranch encompasses a natural spring-fed pool, golf course and tennis courts. The 49'er Cafe (mains $10-25) cooks up decent American standards, or grab beers and pizza at Corkscrew Saloon.

Cynthia's HOSTEL, INN $$
(☑760-852-4580; www.discovercynthias.com; 2001 Old Spanish Trail Hwy, Tecopa; dm $22-25, r $75-140, tipi $165; ☺check-in 3-8pm; 🛜) Match your budget to your bed: eclectic-looking private rooms and dorm beds come in vintage trailers with common kitchens, or camp out at China Ranch in a Native American-style tipi with thick rugs, a fire pit and

king-sized bed. Reservations essential. It's in the hot-springs town of Tecopa, 70 miles southeast of Furnace Creek.

Stovepipe Wells Village MOTEL $$
(☑760-786-2387; www.escapetodeathvalley.com; Hwy 190; RV sites $33, r $95-160; ❄@ 🛜🐾🐕🐶) Spruced-up rooms lay out quality linens beneath cheerful Native American bedspreads. The small pool is cool, while a cowboy-style saloon and restaurant deliver three square yet unmemorable meals a day (mains $6 to $23).

Inn at Furnace Creek HOTEL $$$
(☑800-236-7916, 760-786-2345; www.furnacecreekresort.com; Hwy 190; r/ste from $345/450; ☺mid-Oct–mid-May; ❄🛜🐾) Enjoy languid valley views while lounging by the spring-fed pool or when you roll out of bed and pull back the curtains at this minimalist 1927 mission-style hotel. The upscale restaurant (dress code at dinner) is only recommended for its Sunday brunch buffet ($25). Come for sunset cocktails on the terrace.

ℹ Information

Purchase a seven-day entry pass ($20 per car) at self-service pay stations throughout the park. For a free map and newspaper, show your receipt at the **visitor center** (☑760-786-3200; www.nps.gov/deva; ☺8am-5pm) in Furnace Creek, where you'll also find a general store, gas station, post office, ATM, laundromat and showers. Stovepipe Wells Village, a 30-minute drive northwest, has a general store, gas station, ATM and showers. Panamint Springs, on the park's western edge, has an ATM, gas, wi-fi, snacks and drinks. Cell-phone reception is spotty to nonexistent in the park.

CENTRAL COAST

No trip to California would be worth its salt without a jaunt along the surreally scenic Central Coast. Among California's most iconic roads, Hwy 1 skirts past posh Santa Barbara, retro Pismo Beach, collegiate San Luis Obispo, fantastical Hearst Castle, soul-stirring Big Sur, cutesy Carmel, down-to-earth Monterey and hippie Santa Cruz, often within view of the Pacific. Slow down – this idyllic coast deserves to be savored, not gulped. Incidentally, that same advice goes for award-winning locally grown wines too.

Santa Barbara

Life is sweet in Santa Barbara, a coastal Shangri-La where the air is redolent of citrus and jasmine, flowery bougainvillea drapes whitewashed buildings with Spanish red-tiled roofs, and it's all cradled by pearly beaches – just ignore those pesky oil derricks out to sea. Downtown's main drag, State St, abounds with bars, cafes, theaters and boutiques.

◉ Sights

Mission Santa Barbara CHURCH
(www.santabarbaramission.org; 2201 Laguna St; adult/child $5/1; ☺9am-4:15pm) Established in 1786, California's hilltop 'Queen of the Missions' was the only one to escape secularization under Mexican rule. Look for Chumash artwork inside the vaulted church, unusually topped by twin bell towers, and a moody cemetery out back.

Santa Barbara Museum of Art MUSEUM
(www.sbma.net; 1130 State St; adult/child $10/6, 5-8pm Thu free; ☺11am-5pm Tue-Wed & Fri-Sun, to 8pm Thu) Downtown galleries house an impressive, tightly edited collection of contemporary California artists, modern masters including Matisse and Chagall, 20th-century photography and Asian art, plus provocative special exhibits.

County Courthouse HISTORIC BUILDING
(☑805-962-6464; www.sbcourts.org; 1100 Anacapa St; ☺8am-4:45pm Mon-Fri, from 10am Sat & Sun) **FREE** Built in Spanish-Moorish revival style, it's an absurdly beautiful place to stand trial. Marvel at hand-painted ceilings and intricate murals, then climb the *Vertigo*-esque clock tower for panoramic views. Free tours given daily (call for schedules).

Santa Barbara Historical Museum MUSEUM
(www.santabarbaramuseum.com; 136 E De La Guerra St; donations welcome; ☺10am-5pm Tue-Sat, from noon Sun) **FREE** Around a romantic cloistered adobe courtyard, peruse a fascinating mishmash of memorabilia, including Chumash woven baskets. Learn about odd historical footnotes, like the city's involvement in toppling the last Chinese monarchy.

Santa Barbara Maritime Museum MUSEUM
(www.sbmm.org; 113 Harbor Way; adult/child $7/4, 3rd Thu of month free; ☺10am-5pm, to 6pm late May-early Sep; 🐾) Set by the harbor, this

OFF THE BEATEN TRACK

IF YOU HAVE A FEW MORE DAYS

Remote, rugged Channel Islands National Park (www.nps.gov/chis) earns the nickname 'California's Galápagos' for its unique wildlife. These islands offer superb snorkeling, scuba diving and sea kayaking. Spring, when wildflowers bloom, is a gorgeous time to visit; summer and fall can be bone-dry, and winter stormy.

Anacapa, an hour's boat ride from the mainland, is the best island for day-tripping, with easy hikes and unforgettable views. Santa Cruz, the biggest island, is for overnight camping excursions, kayaking and hiking. Other islands require longer channel crossings and multiday trips. San Miguel is often shrouded in fog. Tiny Santa Barbara supports seabird and seal colonies. So does Santa Rosa, which also protects Torrey pines and Chumash archaeological sites.

Boats leave from Ventura Harbor, off Hwy 101, where the park's visitor center (☑805-658-5730; 1901 Spinnaker Dr, Ventura; ☺8:30am-5pm) has info and maps. The main tour-boat operator is Island Packers (☑805-642-1393; www.islandpackers.com; 1691 Spinnaker Dr; cruises adult/child from $36/26); book ahead. Primitive island campgrounds require reservations; book through Recreation.gov (p62) and bring food and water.

two-story exhibition hall celebrates the town's briny history with yesteryear artifacts, documentary videos and hands-on and virtual-reality exhibits.

Santa Barbara Botanic Garden   GARDEN
(www.sbbg.org; 1212 Mission Canyon Rd; adult/child $8/4; ☺9am-6pm, to 5pm Nov-Feb; 🖪) Uphill from the mission, this garden devoted to California's native flora meanders beside rolling trails past cacti and wildflowers. Nearby is a natural-history museum for kids.

🏃 Activities

Overlooking busy municipal beaches, 1872 Stearns Wharf is the West's oldest continuously operating wooden pier, strung with touristy shops and restaurants. Outside town off Hwy 101, bigger palm-fringed state beaches (www.parks.ca.gov; entry per car $10; ☺8am-sunset) await at Carpinteria, 12 miles east, and El Capitan and Refugio, over 20 miles west of town.

Santa Barbara Sailing Center   WATER SPORTS
(☑800-350-9090, 805-962-2826; www.sbsail.com; off Harbor Way; kayak/SUP rentals from $10/15, cruises/tours from $25/50) Rent kayaks or join a paddling tour, sign up for sailing classes or take a whale-watching or sunset cocktail cruise.

Channel Islands Outfitters   WATER SPORTS
(☑rentals 805-617-3425, tours 805-899-4925; www.channelislandso.com; 117b Harbor Way; surfboard/kayak/SUP rentals from $10/25/40) Friendly kayaking, surfing and stand-up

paddle boarding (SUP) outfitter also leads coastal kayaking tours.

Wheel Fun   CYCLING
(www.wheelfunrentalssb.com; 22 State St & 23 E Cabrillo Blvd; 1hr/half-day bicycle rentals from $9/24; ☺8am-8pm, to 6pm Nov-Feb) Pedal along the paved recreational trail connecting miles of beautiful beaches.

Santa Barbara
Adventure Co   WATER SPORTS, CYCLING
(☑877-885-9283, 805-884-9283; www.sbadventureco.com; 720 Bond Ave; tours/lessons from $49/109) Take a kayak or cycling tour or a traditional board-surfing or SUP lesson.

🛌 Sleeping

Hello, sticker shock: even basic motel rooms can command over $200 in summer. Less expensive motels line upper State St, north of downtown, and Hwy 101. Make reservations (☑800-444-7275; www.reserveamerica.com; campsites $10-70; 🖪🐾) for state-park campgrounds outside town.

Santa Barbara Auto Camp   CAMPGROUND $$
(☑888-405-7553; http://sbautocamp.com; 2717 De La Vina St; trailer q $139-199; 🏵🛜🐾🐾) 🖉
Slumber inside a vintage Airstream trailer decked out with minimalist mod decor, sustainable design features, a full kitchen, redwood deck and outdoor BBQ grill. Book far ahead (two-night minimum stay).

Agave Inn   MOTEL $$
(☑805-687-6009; http://agaveinnsb.com; 3222 State St; r from $119; 🏵🛜) This affordable gem has arty panache and personality, with its

'Mexican pop meets modern' motif. Family-sized rooms have kitchenettes. Thin walls and limited parking.

Marina Beach Motel
MOTEL $$

(☎877-627-4621, 805-963-9311; www.marina-beachmotel.com; 21 Bath St; r incl breakfast $150-210; ❋ 🐾 🛜 🐾) Old-fashioned one-story motor lodge, a short walk from the beach, has been all done up inside with crisp linens and plantation shutters. Some rooms have kitchenettes. Free bikes to borrow.

El Capitan Canyon
CABINS, CAMPGROUND $$$

(☎866-352-2729, 805-685-3887; www.elcapitancanyon.com; 11560 Calle Real, off Hwy 101; safari tents $155, cabins from $225; 🛜 🐾 🐾) 🐾 Go 'glamping' in this car-free zone near El Capitan State Beach, a 30-minute drive west of town via Hwy 101. Safari tents are rustic, while creekside cedar cabins come with dreamy beds and outdoor fire pits.

Spanish Garden Inn
BOUTIQUE HOTEL $$$

(☎805-564-4700; www.spanishgardeninn.com; 915 Garden St; d incl breakfast from $319; ❋ @ 🛜 🐾) Elegant Spanish Revival–style hotel downtown harbors two dozen romantic luxury rooms and suites facing a gracious fountain courtyard. Concierge services are top-notch.

✗ Eating

Silvergreens
CALIFORNIAN $

(www.silvergreens.com; 791 Chapala St; dishes $4-10; ⊙7am-10pm Mon-Fri, from 8am Sat & Sun; 🐾) 🐾 Who says fast food can't be fresh and tasty? With the tag line 'Eat smart, live well,' this sun-drenched cafe makes nutritionally sound salads, soups, sandwiches, burgers, breakfast burritos and much more.

Lilly's Taquería
MEXICAN $

(http://lillystacos.com; 310 Chapala St; items from $1.75; ⊙10:30am-9pm Sun-Mon & Wed-Thu, to 10pm Fri & Sat) There's almost always a line out the door, so be snappy with your order – locals will fight for these authentic street tacos, especially with *adobada* (marinated pork) or *lengua* (beef tongue).

Olio Pizzeria
ITALIAN $$

(☎805-899-2699; www.oliopizzeria.com; 11 W Victoria St; mains $9-18; ⊙11:30am-9pm Sun-Thu, to 10pm Fri & Sat) Convivial, high-ceilinged pizzeria with a happening wine bar sets out a tempting selection of crispy pizzas, imported cheeses and meats, traditional antipasti and *dolci* (desserts).

Santa Barbara Shellfish Company
SEAFOOD $$

(www.sbfishhouse.com; 230 Stearns Wharf; dishes $3-16; ⊙11am-9pm) 'From sea to skillet to plate' best describes this end-of-the-wharf crab shack that's more of a counter joint. Great crab cakes, ocean views and the same location for 30 years.

🍷 Drinking & Entertainment

Nightlife orbits lower State St. You can ramble between a dozen wine-tasting rooms along the city's Urban Wine Trail (www.urbanwinetrailsb.com). The free alt-weekly *Santa Barbara Independent* (www.independent.com) has an entertainment calendar.

Brewhouse
BREWERY

(www.brewhousesb.com; 229 W Montecito St; ⊙11am-11pm Sun-Thu, to midnight Fri & Sat; 🛜) Rowdy dive down by the railroad tracks crafts its own unique small-batch beers and has rockin' live music from Wednesday to Saturday nights.

Soho
LIVE MUSIC

(☎805-962-7776; www.sohosb.com; Suite 205, 1221 State St; tickets $5-30) Unpretentious brick room located upstairs behind a McDonald's has live bands almost nightly, from indie rock, folk and world beats to jazz and blues.

ℹ Information

Santa Barbara Car Free (www.santabarbaracarfree.org) Eco-travel tips and discounts.

Santa Barbara Visitors Center (☎805-965-3021; www.santabarbaraca.com; 1 Garden St; ⊙9am-5pm Mon-Sat, from 10am Sun, to 4pm Nov-Jan) Maps and self-guided tour brochures by the waterfront.

ℹ Getting There & Around

From the **train station** (209 State St) south of downtown, Amtrak trains roll toward LA ($25 to $30, three hours) and San Luis Obispo ($28 to $34, 2¾ hours). From a downtown **bus station** (☎805-965-7551; 224 Chapala St), Greyhound has a few daily buses to LA ($19, two to three hours) and via San Luis Obispo ($28, two hours) to Santa Cruz ($53, six hours) and San Francisco ($57, nine hours).

Metropolitan Transit District (MTD; ☎805-963-3366; www.sbmtd.gov) runs city-wide buses ($1.75) and electric shuttles (50¢) between downtown's State St and Stearns Wharf and along beachfront Cabrillo Blvd.

Santa Barbara to San Luis Obispo

You can speed up to San Luis Obispo in less than two hours along Hwy 101, or take all day detouring to wineries, historical missions and hidden beaches.

A scenic backcountry drive north of Santa Barbara follows Hwy 154, where you can go for the grape in the wine country (www. sbcountywines.com) of the Santa Ynez and Santa Maria Valleys. For eco-conscious vineyard tours, ride along with Sustainable Vine (805-698-3911; www.sustainablevine.com; tour $125) , or just follow the pastoral Foxen Canyon Wine Trail (www.foxencanyonwinetrail.com) north to cult winemakers' vineyards. In the town of Los Olivos, where two dozen more wine-tasting rooms await, Los Olivos Cafe & Wine Merchant (805-688-7265; www.losolivoscafe.com; 2879 Grand Ave; mains $12-29; 11:30am-8:30pm) is a charming Cal-Mediterranean bistro with a wine bar.

Further south, the Danish-immigrant village of Solvang (www.solvangusa.com) is aflutter with kitschy windmills and fairytale-esque bakeries. Fuel up on buffalo chicken breakfast biscuits, cinnamon-cumin pork-belly sandos and organic Thai salads at Succulent Cafe & Trading Company (805-691-9235; www.succulentcafe.com; 1555 Mission Dr; breakfast & lunch mains $8-12; 9am-1pm & 11am-3pm Wed-Sun, 5:30-9pm Thu-Sat) . For a picnic lunch or BBQ takeout, swing into El Rancho Marketplace (www.elranchomarket.com; 2886 Mission Dr; 6am-10pm), east of Solvang's 19th-century Spanish mission (805-688-4815; www.missionsantaines.org; 1760 Mission Dr; adult/child $5/free; 9am-4:30pm). West of Hwy 101 in Buellton, Avant (www.avantwines.com; 35 Industrial Way; 11am-9pm) wine bar and Figueroa Mountain Brewing Co (www.figmtnbrew.com; 45 Industrial Way; 4-9pm Mon-Thu, from 11am Fri-Sun) are side-street locals' hangouts.

Follow Hwy 246 about 15 miles west of Hwy 101 to La Purísima Mission State Historic Park (www.lapurisimamission.org; 2295 Purisima Rd; entry per car $6; 9am-5pm, guided tour 1pm). Exquisitely restored, it's one of California's most evocative Spanish Colonial missions, with flowering gardens, livestock pens and adobe buildings. South of Lompoc off Hwy 1, Jalama Rd travels 14 twisting miles to windswept Jalama Beach County Park (805-736-3616; www.sbparks.org; 9999

Jalama Rd; per car $10). Book ahead for its crazy-popular campground (http://sbparks.org/reservations; tent/RV sites $28/43, cabins $110-210), where newly built, simple wooden cabins have kitchenettes.

Heading north on Hwy 1, rough-and-tumble Guadalupe is the gateway to North America's largest coastal dunes, where the Lost City of DeMille (www.lostcitydemille.com), a movie set from The Ten Commandments (1923), lies buried beneath the sands. Scenes from Hidalgo (2004) and Pirates of the Caribbean: At World's End (2007) were also filmed here. The best dunes access is west of town via Hwy 166.

Where Hwy 1 rejoins Hwy 101, Pismo Beach has a long, lazy stretch of sand and a butterfly grove (www.monarchbutterfly.org; Hwy 1) FREE, where migratory monarchs perch in eucalyptus trees from late October to February. Adjacent North Beach Campground (800-444-7275; www.reserveamerica.com; Hwy 1; campsites $35;) offers beach access and hot showers. Dozens of motels and hotels stand by the ocean and along Hwy 101, but rooms fill quickly, especially on weekends. Pismo Lighthouse Suites (805-773-2411, 800-245-2411; www.pismolighthousesuites.com; 2411 Price St; ste incl breakfast from $219;) has everything vacationing families need, from kitchenette suites to a life-sized outdoor chessboard; ask about off-season discounts. Nearby Pismo's seaside pier, Old West Cinnamon Rolls (www.oldwestcinnamon.com; 861 Dolliver St; items $3-5; 6:30am-5:30pm) is gooey goodness. Uphill at the Cracked Crab (www.crackedcrab.com; 751 Price St; mains $9-53; 11am-9pm Sun-Thu, to 10pm Fri & Sat;), make sure you don a plastic bib before a fresh bucket o' seafood gets dumped on your butcher-paper-covered table.

The nearby town of Avila Beach has a sunny waterfront promenade, an atmospherically creaky old wooden fishing pier and a historical lighthouse (hiking info 805-541-8735, trolley tour 855-533-7843; www.sanluislighthouse.org; entry per hiker $5, trolley tour $20; Sat only, reservations required). Back toward Hwy 101, pick juicy berries or apples and feed the goats at Avila Valley Barn (http://avilavalleybarn.com; 560 Avila Beach Dr; 9am-6pm;) farmstand, then do some stargazing from a private redwood hot tub at Sycamore Mineral Springs (805-595-7302; www.sycamoresprings.com; 1215 Avila Beach Dr; 1hr per person $13.50-17.50; 8am-midnight, last reservation 10:45pm).

San Luis Obispo

Halfway between LA and San Francisco, San Luis Obispo is a low-key place. But CalPoly university students inject a healthy dose of hubbub into the streets, pubs and cafes, especially during the weekly **farmers market** (⊙6-9pmThu; ⊞) 🖉, which turns downtown's Higuera St into a carnival with live music and sidewalk BBQs. Like several other California towns, SLO grew up around a Spanish Catholic **mission** (⊒805-543-6850; www.missionsanluisobispo.org; 751 Palm St; donation $2; ⊙9am-5pm, to 4pm early Nov–mid-Mar), founded in 1772 by Junípero Serra. These days, SLO is just a grape's throw from thriving **Edna Valley wineries** (www.slowine.com), known for crisp Chardonnay and smooth Pinot Noir.

🛏 Sleeping

SLO's motel row is north of downtown along Monterey St. Chain motels line Hwy 101.

HI Hostel Obispo   HOSTEL **$**
(⊒805-544-4678; www.hostelobispo.com; 1617 Santa Rosa St; dm $25-28, r from $55; ⊙check-in 4:30-10pm; @🖂) 🖉 Solar-powered hostel inhabits a cozy Victorian near the train station. Amenities include a common kitchen and bike rentals (from $10 per day). No credit cards or curfew; BYOT (bring your own towel). All accommodation with shared bath.

Peach Tree Inn   MOTEL **$$**
(⊒805-543-3170,   800-227-6396; www.peachtreeinn.com; 2001 Monterey St; r incl breakfast $70-175; ✳@🖂⊞) Folksy, nothing-fancy motel rooms are relaxing, especially those set creekside or with rocking chairs overlooking a rose garden. Hearty continental breakfasts include homemade breads.

Madonna Inn   HOTEL **$$$**
(⊒805-543-3000; www.madonnainn.com; 100 Madonna Rd; r $189-309; ✳@🖂✳) Fantastically campy, this garish confection is visible from Hwy 101. Overseas tourists, vacationing Midwesterners and irony-loving hipsters adore the 110 themed rooms – including the rock-walled Caveman and hot-pink Floral Fantasy (gawk at photos online).

🍴 Eating & Drinking

Downtown abounds with cafes, restaurants, wine bars, brewpubs and the USA's first solar-powered cinema, **Palm Theatre** (⊒805-541-5161; www.thepalmtheatre.com; 817 Palm St; tickets $5-8) 🖉, screening indie flicks.

Firestone Grill   BARBECUE **$**
(www.firestonegrill.com; 1001 Higuera St; dishes $4-10; ⊙11am-10pm Sun-Wed, to 11pm Thu-Sat; ⊞) Sink your teeth into an authentic Santa Maria–style tri-tip BBQ sandwich on a toasted garlic roll, or a chopped Cobb steak salad.

Sidecar   CALIFORNIAN **$$**
(⊒805-540-5340; http://sidecarslo.com; 1127 Broad St; mains $7-22; ⊙11am-11pm Mon-Fri, from 10am Sat & Sun) 🖉 Pull out a chair around a 1950s dinette table and feast on a creative chef's seasonal menu of local farm and ranch goodness. Weekend brunch is sociable, and so is the regional wine list.

Big Sky Café   CALIFORNIAN **$$**
(www.bigskycafe.com; 1121 Broad St; mains $9-20; ⊙7am-9pm Mon-Thu, to 10pm Fri, 8am-10pm Sat, 8am-9pm Sun; 🖉) 🖉 With the tagline 'analog food for a digital world,' this airy, sustainable-minded cafe gets top marks for market-fresh breakfasts (served until 1pm daily), healthy big-plate dinners and homemade soups and baskets of cornbread.

❶ Information

San Luis Obispo Car Free (http://slocarfree.org) Eco-travel tips and discounts.

Visitor Center (⊒805-781-2777; www.visitslo.com; 895 Monterey St; ⊙10am-5pm Sun-Wed, to 7pm Thu-Sat) Downtown near Higuera St.

PINNACLES NATIONAL PARK

Named for the towering spires that rise abruptly out of the chapparal-covered hills, **Pinnacles National Park** (⊒831-389-4485; www.nps.gov/pinn; 5000 Hwy 146, Paicines; per car $5) is a study in geologic drama, with craggy monoliths, sheer-walled canyons and ancient volcanic remnants. Besides hiking and rock climbing, the park's biggest attractions are talus caves and endangered California condors. Visit during spring or fall – summer heat and humidity are extreme. A family **campground** (⊒877-444-6777; www.recreation.gov; tent/RV sites $23/36; ✳⊞✳) is situated near the park's east entrance, off Hwy 25 northwest of King City, a two-hour drive north of San Luis Obispo.

ℹ Getting There & Around

Amtrak trains from Santa Barbara ($28 to $34, 2¾ hours) and LA ($40, 5½ hours) arrive at SLO's **train station** (1011 Railroad Ave), 0.6 miles southeast of downtown. Inconveniently stopping 2.5 miles southwest of downtown off Hwy 101, **Greyhound** (1460 Calle Joaquin) has a few daily buses to Santa Barbara ($28, two hours), LA ($40, five hours), Santa Cruz ($42, four hours) and San Francisco ($53, seven hours).

Operated by **SLO Regional Transit Authority** (☑ 805-541-2228; www.slorta.org; fares $1.50-3, day pass $5), county-wide buses with limited weekend services converge on downtown's **transit center** (cnr Palm & Osos Sts).

Morro Bay to Hearst Castle

A dozen miles northwest of SLO via Hwy 1, Morro Bay is a sea-sprayed fishing town where Morro Rock, a volcanic peak jutting up from the ocean floor, is your first hint of the coast's upcoming drama. (Never mind those powerplant smokestacks obscuring the views.) Hop aboard a cruise or rent kayaks along the Embarcadero, packed with touristy shops, cafes and bars. A classic seafood shack, Giovanni's (www.giovannisfishmarket.com; 1001 Front St; mains $6-17; ☉ 11am-6pm; ⊕) cooks killer garlic fries and fish-and-chips. Midrange motels cluster uphill off Harbor and Main Sts and along Hwy 1.

Nearby are fantastic state parks for coastal hikes and camping (☑ 800-444-7275; www.reserveamerica.com; campsites $5-50; ⊕ ⛲). South of the Embarcadero, Morro Bay State Park (☑ 805-772-2694; www.parks.ca.gov; admission free, museum entry adult/child $2/free) has a natural-history museum and heron rookery. Further south in Los Osos, west of Hwy 1, wilder Montaña de Oro State Park (www.parks.ca.gov; Pecho Valley Rd) **FREE** features coastal bluffs, tide pools, sand dunes, peak hiking and mountain-biking trails. Its Spanish name ('mountain of gold') comes from native California poppies that blanket the hillsides in spring.

Heading north of downtown Morro Bay along Hwy 1, surfers love the Cal-Mexican Taco Temple (2680 Main St; mains $8-15; ☉ 11am-9pm Mon & Wed-Sat, to 8:30pm Sun), a cash-only joint, and Ruddell's Smokehouse (www.smokerjim.com; 101 D St; dishes $4-16; ☉ 11am-6pm), serving smoked-fish tacos by the beach in Cayucos. Vintage motels

line Cayucos' Ocean Ave, including the cute, family-run Seaside Motel (☑ 805-995-3809; www.seasidemotel.com; 42 S Ocean Ave; d $80-160; 🐾), offering kitchenettes. Inhabiting a historic sea captain's home, Cass House Inn (☑ 805-995-3669; http://casshouseinn.com; 222 N Ocean Ave; r incl breakfast $175-365; 🐾) has plush rooms, some with soaking tubs and antique fireplaces to ward off chilly coastal fog, and an elegant, seasonally inspired French-Californian restaurant (4-course prix-fixe menu $68; ☉ 5:30pm-7:30pm Thu-Mon) downstairs.

North of Harmony (population: just 18 souls), Hwy 46 leads east into the vineyards of Paso Robles wine country (www.pasowine.com). Further north along Hwy 1, quaint Cambria has lodgings along unearthly pretty Moonstone Beach, where the Blue Dolphin Inn (☑ 805-927-3300, 800-222-9157; www.cambriainns.com; 6470 Moonstone Beach Dr; r incl breakfast from $179; 🐾⛲) offers crisp, modern rooms with romantic fireplaces. Inland, HI Cambria Bridge Street Inn (☑ 805-927-7653; www.bridgestreetinncambria.com; 4314 Bridge St; dm $25-28, r $49-75, all with shared bath; ☉ check-in 5pm-9pm; 🐾) sleeps like a hostel but feels like a grandmotherly B&B, while the retro Cambria Pines Motel (☑ 866-489-4485, 805-927-4485; www.cambriapalmsmotel.com; 2662 Main St; r $89-139; ☉ check-in 3pm-9pm; 🐾⊕⛲) has clean-lined rooms, some with kitchenettes. An artisan cheese and wine shop, Indigo Moon (☑ 805-927-2911; www.indigomooncafe.com; 1980 Main St; mains lunch $9-14, dinner $14-35; ☉ 10am-9pm) has breezy bistro tables and market-fresh salads and sandwiches at lunch. With a sunny patio and take-out counter, Linn's Easy as Pie Cafe (www.linnsfruitbin.com; 4251 Bridge St; mains $7-12; ☉ 10am-6pm; ⊕) is famous for its olallieberry pie.

About 10 miles north of Cambria, hilltop Hearst Castle (☑ reservations 800-444-4445; www.hearstcastle.org; 750 Hearst Castle Rd; tours adult/child from $25/12; ☉ usually 9am-sunset) is California's most famous monument to wealth and ambition. William Randolph Hearst, the newspaper magnate, entertained Hollywood stars and royalty at this fantasy estate dripping with European antiques, accented by shimmering pools and surrounded by flowering gardens. Try to make tour reservations in advance, especially for Christmas holiday evening living-history programs.

Across Hwy 1, overlooking a historic whaling pier, Sebastian's Store (442 Slo San Simeon Rd; mains $6-12; ☉ 11am-5pm Wed-Sun, deli closes 4pm) sells Hearst Ranch beef burgers and giant sandwiches for impromptu beach picnics. Five miles back south along Hwy 1, past a forgettable row of budget and mid-range motels in San Simeon, Hearst San Simeon State Park (800-444-7275; www. reserveamerica.com; campsites $5-35;) has primitive and developed creekside campsites.

Heading north, Point Piedras Blancas is home to an enormous elephant seal colony that breeds, molts, sleeps, frolics and, occasionally, goes aggro on the beach. Keep your distance from these wild animals, who move faster on the sand than you can. The signposted vista point, 4.5 miles north of Hearst Castle, has interpretive panels. Seals haul out year-round, but the frenzied birthing and mating season runs from January through March, aptly peaking on Valentine's Day. Nearby, the 1875 Piedras Blancas Light Station (805-927-7361; www.piedrasblancas. org; tours adult/child $10/5; tours usually 9:45am Mon-Sat mid-Jun–Aug, Tue, Thu & Sat Sep–mid-Jun) is an outstandingly scenic spot; call ahead to check tour schedules and meeting points.

Big Sur

Much ink has been spilled extolling the raw beauty and energy of this 100-mile stretch of craggy coastline sprawling south of Monterey Bay. More a state of mind than a place you can pinpoint on a map, Big Sur has no traffic lights, banks or strip malls. When the sun goes down, the moon and stars are the only illumination – if summer fog hasn't extinguished them, that is.

Lodging, food and gas are all scarce and pricey in Big Sur. Demand for rooms is high year-round, especially on weekends, so book ahead. The free Big Sur Guide (www.bigsur-california.org), an info-packed newspaper, is available everywhere along the way. Note the day-use parking fee ($10) charged at Big Sur's state parks is valid for same-day entry to all.

It's about 25 miles from Hearst Castle to blink-and-you-miss-it Gorda, home of Tree-bones Resort (877-424-4787, 805-927-2390; www.treebonesresort.com; 71895 Hwy 1; d with shared bath incl breakfast from $199;), which offers back-to-nature clifftop yurts and a small locavarian restaurant (dinner mains $24-33; noon-2pm & 5:30pm-8pm) and sushi bar. Basic USFS campgrounds (877-444-6777, 518-885-3639; www.recreation. gov; campsites $22;) are just off Hwy 1 at Plaskett Creek and Kirk Creek.

Ten miles north of Lucia is the new-agey Esalen Institute (831-667-3047; www. esalen.org; 55000 Hwy 1), famous for its esoteric workshops and ocean-view hot-springs baths. By reservation, you can frolic nekkid in the latter from 1am to 3am nightly ($25, credit cards only). It's surreal.

Another 3 miles north, Julia Pfeiffer Burns State Park hides one of California's only coastal waterfalls, 80ft-high Mc-Way Falls; the viewpoint is reached via a quarter-mile stroll. Two more miles north, a steep dirt trail descends from a hairpin turn on Hwy 1 to Partington Cove, a raw and breathtaking spot where crashing surf salts your skin – but swimming isn't safe, sorry.

Seven miles further north, nestled among redwoods and wisteria, quaint Deetjen's Restaurant (831-667-2378; www.deetjens. com; Deetjen's Big Sur Inn, 48865 Hwy 1; dinner mains $24-38; 8am-noon Mon-Fri, to 12:30pm Sat & Sun, 6-9pm daily) serves country-style comfort fare. Just north, the beatnik Henry Miller Memorial Library (831-667-2574; www.henrymiller.org; 48603 Hwy 1; 11am-6pm Wed-Mon) is the heart and soul of Big Sur bohemia, with a jam-packed bookstore, live-music concerts and DJs, open-mike nights and outdoor film screenings. Opposite, food takes a back seat to dramatic ocean views at clifftop Nepenthe (831-667-2345; www. nepenthebigsur.com; 48510 Hwy 1; mains $15-42; 11:30am-4:30pm & 5-10pm), meaning 'island of no sorrow.' Its Ambrosia burger is mighty.

Heading north, Big Sur Station (831-667-2315; www.fs.usda.gov/lpnf/; 8am-4pm, closed Mon & Tue Oct-Apr) can clue you in about hiking trails and camping options. Rangers issue overnight parking ($5) and campfire permits (free) for backpacking trips into Ventana Wilderness, including the popular 10-mile one-way hike to Sykes Hot Springs.

---

❶ DRIVING HWY 1

Navigating the narrow two-lane highway through Big Sur can be slow going. Allow at least 2½ hours to drive nonstop between Hearst Castle and Monterey Bay, much more if you stop to explore. Driving after dark can be risky and, more to the point, it's futile because you'll miss all the scenery. Watch out for cyclists and use signposted road-side pullouts to let faster-moving traffic pass. For updates on road conditions, call 800-427-7623.

On the opposite side of Hwy 1 just south, turn onto obscurely marked Sycamore Canyon Rd, which drops two narrow, twisting miles to crescent-shaped **Pfeiffer Beach** (per car $5; ⊘9am-8pm), with a towering offshore sea arch and strong currents too dangerous for swimming. Dig down into the sand – it's purple!

Next up, **Pfeiffer Big Sur State Park** is crisscrossed by sun-dappled trails through redwood forests, including the 1.4-mile round-trip to seasonal Pfeiffer Falls. Make **campground** (☑800-444-7275; www.reserveamerica.com; campsites $35-50; 🖶🐾) reservations or stay at the rambling, old-fashioned **Big Sur Lodge** (☑800-424-4787, 831-667-3100; www.bigsurlodge.com; 47225 Hwy 1; d $205-365; 🐾🖶), which has rustic duplex cottages (some with kitchens and wood-burning fireplaces), a simple **restaurant** (mains $10-27; ⊘8-11:30am & noon-10pm) and a well-stocked general store.

Most of Big Sur's commercial activity is concentrated just north along Hwy 1, including private campgrounds with rustic cabins, motels, restaurants, gas stations and shops. **Glen Oaks Motel** (☑831-667-2105; www. glenoaksbigsur.com; 47080 Hwy 1; d from $225; 🐾), a redesigned 1950s redwood-and-adobe motor lodge, rents snug rooms and cabins with gas fireplaces. Nearby, the Big Sur River Inn's **general store** (http://bigsurriverinn.com; 46840 Hwy 1; mains $6-9; ⊘11am-7pm) hides a burrito and fruit-smoothie bar at the back, while **Maiden Publick House** (☑831-667-2355; Hwy 1; ⊘3pm-2am Mon-Fri, from noon Sat & Sun) pulls off an encyclopedic beer menu and live-music jams. Back south, near the post office, grab a sandwich from **Big Sur Deli** (http://bigsurdeli.com; 47520 Hwy 1; dishes $1.50-7; ⊘7am-8pm), attached to the laid-back **Big Sur Taphouse** (www.bigsurtaphouse.com; 47520 Hwy 1; ⊘noon-10pm Mon-Thu, to midnight Fri & Sat, 10am-10pm Sun; 🐾), a craft beer bar with pub grub, board games and sports TVs.

Heading north again, don't skip **Andrew Molera State Park**, a gorgeous trail-laced pastiche of grassy meadows, waterfalls, ocean bluffs and rugged beaches. Learn all about endangered California condors at the park's **Discovery Center** (☑831-624-1202; www.ventanaws.org; ⊘10am-4pm Sat & Sun late May-early Sep; 🖶) **FREE**; book ahead for popular bird-tracking tours ($50). From the dirt parking lot, a 0.4-mile trail leads to a first-come, first-served primitive **campground** (www.parks.ca.gov; tent sites $25).

Six miles before landmark Bixby Creek Bridge, you can tour 1889 **Point Sur Lightstation** (☑831-625-4419; www.pointsur.org; adult/child from $12/5). Check online or call for tour schedules, including seasonal moonlight walks, and directions to the meeting point. Arrive early because space is limited (no reservations).

Carmel

Once a bohemian artists' seaside resort, quaint Carmel-by-the-Sea now has the well-manicured feel of a country club. Simply plop down in any cafe and watch the parade of behatted ladies toting fancy-label shopping bags and dapper gents driving top-down convertibles along Ocean Ave, the village's slow-mo main drag.

◉ Sights & Activities

Often foggy, municipal **Carmel Beach** is a gorgeous white-sand crescent, where pampered pups excitedly run off-leash.

★**Point Lobos State Natural Reserve**   PARK
(www.pointlobos.org; Hwy 1; per car $10; ⊘8am-7pm, closes 30min after sunset early Nov–mid-Mar) They bark, they bray, they bathe and they're fun to watch – sea lions are the stars here, 4 miles south of town, where a dramatically rocky coastline offers excellent tide-pooling. The full perimeter hike is 6 miles, but shorter walks take in Bird Island, Piney Woods and the Whalers Cabin. Show up early on weekends since parking is limited.

San Carlos Borroméo de Carmelo Mission   CHURCH
(www.carmelmission.org; 3080 Rio Rd; adult/child $6.50/2; ⊘9:30am-5pm Mon-Sat, from 10:30am Sun) A mile south of downtown, this gorgeous mission is an oasis of calm and solemnity, ensconced in flowering gardens. Its stone basilica is filled with original art, while a separate chapel holds the memorial tomb of California's peripatetic mission founder Junípero Serra.

Tor House   HISTORIC BUILDING
(☑831-624-1813; www.torhouse.org; 26304 Ocean View Ave; adult/child $10/5; ⊘10am-3pm Fri & Sat) Even if you've never heard of 20th-century poet Robinson Jeffers, a pilgrimage to his handbuilt house with its Celtic-inspired Hawk Tower offers fascinating insights into bohemian Old Carmel. Admission only by guided tour (reservations essential).

✖ Eating & Drinking

Bruno's Market & Deli
DELI, MARKET $

(www.brunosmarket.com; cnr 6th & Junípero Aves; sandwiches $6-9; ⏰7am-8pm) Pick up a saucy tri-trip beef sandwich and all the other accoutrements for a beach picnic.

Mundaka
SPANISH $$

(✆831-624-7400; www.mundakacarmel.com; San Carlos St, btwn Ocean & 7th Aves; small plates $7-20; ⏰5:30-10pm Sun-Wed, to 11pm Thu-Sat) This courtyard hideaway is a svelte escape from Carmel's stuffy 'newly wed and nearly dead' crowd. Take Spanish tapas plates for a spin and sip housemade sangria while DJs spin or flamenco guitarists play.

Katy's Place
AMERICAN $$

(http://katysplacecarmel.com; Mission St, btwn 5th & 6th Aves; mains $11-21; ⏰7am-2pm; 🐾) In a cutesy cottage, this popular breakfast kitchen cooks 16 different kinds of eggs Benedict, from crab-meat to spicy Cajun, along with equally filling omelettes, fruit-topped pancakes, chef's salads and club sandwiches.

Monterey

Working-class Monterey is all about the sea. It lures visitors with a top-notch aquarium that's a veritable temple to Monterey Bay's underwater universe. A National Marine Sanctuary since 1992, the bay begs for exploration by kayak, boat, scuba or snorkel. Meanwhile, downtown's historic quarter preserves California's Spanish and Mexican roots. Don't waste too much time on touristy Fisherman's Wharf or Cannery Row. The latter was immortalized by novelist John Steinbeck back when it was the hectic, smelly epicenter of the sardine-canning industry, which was Monterey's lifeblood until the 1950s.

◎ Sights

★ Monterey Bay Aquarium
AQUARIUM

(✆info 831-648-4800, tickets 866-963-9645; www.montereybayaquarium.org; 886 Cannery Row; adult/child $35/22; ⏰9:30am-6pm Mon-Fri, to 8pm Sat & Sun Jun-Aug, 10am-5pm or 6pm daily Sep-May; 🐾) 🌿 Give yourself at least half a day to see sharks and sardines play hide-and-seek in kelp forests, observe the antics of frisky otters, meditate upon psychedelic jellyfish and get touchy-feely with sea cucumbers, bat rays and other tide-pool creatures. Feeding times are the most fun. To avoid the biggest crowds, get tickets in advance and arrive when the doors open.

Monterey State Historic Park
HISTORIC SITE

(✆audio tour 831-998-9458; www.parks.ca.gov) Downtown, Old Monterey boasts a cluster of lovingly restored 19th-century brick-and-adobe buildings, including novelist Robert Louis Stevenson's one-time boarding house and the Cooper-Molera Adobe, a sea captain's home. Admission to the gardens is free, but individual buildings' opening hours, admission fees and tour schedules vary. Pick up walking-tour maps and check current schedules at the Pacific House (✆831-649-7118; www.parks.ca.gov; 20 Custom House Plaza; admission $3, incl walking tour $5; ⏰10am-4pm Fri-Mon), a multicultural historical museum.

Museum of Monterey
MUSEUM

(✆831-372-2608; http://museumofmonterey.org; 5 Custom House Plaza; admission $5; ⏰10am-7pm Tue-Sat & noon-5pm Sun late May-early Sep, 10am-5pm Wed-Sat & noon-5pm Sun early Sep-late May) Near the waterfront, this voluminous modern exhibition hall illuminates Monterey's helter-skelter past, from its Spanish colonial mission days to the roller-coaster rise and fall of the local sardine industry. Gems include the ship-in-a-bottle collection and historic Fresnel lens from Point Sur Lightstation.

Point Pinos Lighthouse
LIGHTHOUSE

(✆831-648-3176; www.pointpinos.org; 90 Asilomar Ave, Pacific Grove; adult/child $2/1; ⏰1-4pm Thu-Mon) The West Coast's oldest continuously operating lighthouse has been warning ships off this peninsula's hazardous point since 1855. Inside are exhibits on its history and its failures: local shipwrecks.

Monarch Grove Sanctuary Park
PARK

(www.ci.pg.ca.us; off Ridge Rd, Pacific Grove; ⏰dawn-dusk) FREE Between October and February, over 25,000 migratory monarch butterflies cluster in a thicket of eucalyptus trees off Lighthouse Ave.

✚ Activities

Diving and snorkeling reign supreme, although the water is rather frigid, even in summer. Year-round, Fisherman's Wharf is a launchpad for whale-watching trips. Rent a bicycle or walk the paved Monterey Peninsula Recreation Trail, which edges the coast past Cannery Row, ending at Lovers Point in Pacific Grove. The overhyped 17-Mile Drive (www.pebblebeach.com; per car/bicycle $10/free) toll road connects Monterey and Pacific Grove with Carmel-by-the-Sea.

Adventures by the Sea   WATER SPORTS, CYCLING
(☑831-372-1807; http://adventuresbythesea.com; 299 Cannery Row; rental per day kayak or bicycle $30, SUP set $50) Stop by for bicycle and water-sports gear rentals, SUP lessons ($60) and kayaking tours (from $60). Also downtown at 210 Alvarado St.

Monterey Bay Kayaks   KAYAKING
(☑800-649-5357; www.montereybaykayaks.com; 693 Del Monte Ave; rental per day kayak or SUP set from $30) Kayak and SUP rentals, paddling lessons (from $50) and tours (from $50) of Monterey Bay and Elkhorn Slough, including sunrise and full-moon trips.

Sanctuary Cruises   WHALE-WATCHING
(☑831-917-1042; www.sanctuarycruises.com; adult/child $50/40) 🚢 Departing from Moss Landing, over 20 miles north of Monterey, this biodiesel boat runs whale-watching tours year-round (reservations essential).

Seven Seas Scuba   SCUBA DIVING
(☑831-717-4546; http://sevenseasscuba.com; 225 Cannery Row; snorkel/scuba rental package per day $35/65) Call ahead for scuba equipment rental and guided bayshore dives ($50 to $100), including at Point Lobos.

🛏 Sleeping

Skip the frills and save a bunch of dough at motels along Munras Ave south of downtown, or on N Fremont St east of Hwy 1. For camping, drive south to Big Sur.

HI Monterey Hostel   HOSTEL $
(☑831-649-0375; www.montereyhostel.org; 778 Hawthorne St; dm $27-35, r from $99; ⊙check-in 4-10pm; @🛜) Four blocks from Cannery Row, this simple, clean hostel is just the ticket for backpackers on a budget (reservations strongly recommended). Take MST bus 1 from downtown's Transit Plaza. All accommodation with shared bath.

Asilomar Conference Grounds   LODGE $$
(☑888-635-5310, 831-372-8016; www.visitasilomar.com; 800 Asilomar Ave; r incl breakfast $115-175; @🛜🏊🍴) This coastal state-park lodge preserves buildings designed by architect Julia Morgan, of Hearst Castle fame. Historic rooms are small and thin-walled, but charming nonetheless. The lodge's fireside rec room has pool tables and bicycle rentals.

Monterey Hotel   HISTORIC HOTEL $$
(☑800-966-6490, 831-375-3184; www.monterey hotel.com; 406 Alvarado St; r $80-195; 🛜) Right downtown, this quaint 1904 edifice harbors small, somewhat noisy renovated rooms sporting reproduction Victorian furniture. No elevator. Parking is $17.

InterContinental–Clement   HOTEL $$$
(☑866-781-2406, 831-375-4500; www.icthe clementmonterey.com; 750 Cannery Row; r from $220; ✳@🛜🏊🍴) Like an upscale version of a millionaire's seaside clapboard house, this resort presides over Cannery Row. For utmost luxury, book an ocean-view suite with a private balcony and fireplace. Parking is $21.

🍴 Eating & Drinking

Restaurants, bars and live-music venues line Cannery Row and downtown's Alvarado St.

First Awakenings   DINER $$
(www.firstawakenings.net; American Tin Cannery, 125 Oceanview Blvd; mains $6-13; ⊙7am-2pm Mon-Fri, to 2:30pm Sat & Sun; 🍴) Sweet and savory creative breakfasts and lunches, bottomless pitchers of coffee and an outdoor patio make this hideaway cafe in a mall near the aquarium worth finding.

Cannery Row Brewing Co   PUB $$
(☑831-643-2722; www.canneryrowbrewing company.com; 95 Prescott Ave; mains $8-18; ⊙11:30am-11pm, bar till midnight Sun-Thu, 2am Fri & Sat) Dozens of craft beers from around the world pull raucous crowds into this bar-and-grill, with roaring fire pits on the back deck. Decent burgers, barbecue, salads and garlic fries.

★ Passionfish   SEAFOOD $$$
(☑831-655-3311; www.passionfish.net; 701 Lighthouse Ave; mains $16-26; ⊙5-9pm Sun-Thu, to 10pm Fri & Sat) Eureka! Finally, a perfect, chef-owned seafood restaurant where the sustainable fish is dock-fresh, every preparation fully flavored and the wine list affordable. Reservations strongly recommended.

East Village Coffee Lounge   CAFE
(www.eastvillagecoffeelounge.com; 498 Washington St; ⊙6am-late Mon-Fri, from 7am Sat & Sun) Sleek coffeehouse with a liquor license and live-music, DJ and open-mike nights.

ℹ Information

Monterey Visitors Center (☑877-666-8373, 831-657-6400; www.seemonterey.com; 401 Camino El Estero; ⊙9am-6pm Mon-Sat, to 5pm Sun, closes 1hr earlier Nov-Mar) Ask for a free *Monterey County Literary & Film Map*.

ⓘ Getting There & Around

Regional and local **Monterey-Salinas Transit** (MST; ☎ 888-678-2871; www.mst.org; fares $1.50-3, day pass $10) buses converge on downtown's **Transit Plaza** (cnr Pearl & Alvarado Sts), including routes to Pacific Grove, Carmel, Big Sur (summer only) and Salinas (for Greyhound bus and Amtrak train connections). In summer, free trolleys shuttle between downtown Monterey and Cannery Row and around Pacific Grove.

Santa Cruz

SoCal beach culture meets NorCal counterculture in Santa Cruz. The university student population makes this old-school radical town youthful, hip and lefty-political. Some worry that Santa Cruz's weirdness quotient is dropping, but you'll disagree when you witness the freak show (and we say that with love, man) along Pacific Ave downtown.

⊙ Sights & Activities

Most of the action takes place by Main Beach, a mile south of downtown. Locals favor less-trampled beaches off E Cliff Dr.

Santa Cruz Beach Boardwalk   AMUSEMENT PARK
(☎ 831-423-5590; www.beachboardwalk.com; 400 Beach St; rides $3-6, all-day pass $32; ⊙ daily late May-early Sep, off-season hours vary; ▣) A short walk from the municipal wharf, this slice of Americana is the West Coast's oldest beachfront amusement park, boasting the 1924 Giant Dipper roller coaster and 1911 Looff carousel. Show up in summer for free concerts and outdoor movies.

Santa Cruz State Parks   PARK
(www.thatsmypark.org; per car $8-10; ⊙ sunrise-sunset) Streamside trails through coast redwood forests await at Henry Cowell Redwoods and Big Basin Redwoods State Parks, off Hwy 9 north of town in the Santa Cruz Mountains, and the Forest of Nisene Marks State Park, off Hwy 1 south near Aptos. For mountain biking, explore Wilder Ranch State Park, off Hwy 1 northbound.

Santa Cruz Surfing Museum   MUSEUM
(www.santacruzsurfingmuseum.org; 701 W Cliff Dr; admission by donation; ⊙ 10am-5pm Wed-Mon Jul 4-early Sep, noon-4pm Thu-Mon early Sep-Jul 3) About a mile southwest of the wharf, the old lighthouse is packed with memorabilia, including vintage redwood boards. It overlooks experts-only Steamers Lane and beginners' Cowells, both popular surf breaks.

Natural Bridges State Beach   BEACH
(www.parks.ca.gov; 2531 W Cliff Dr; per car $10; ⊙ 8am-sunset) This pretty beach bookends a scenic coastal cycling path about 3 miles southwest of the wharf. There are tide pools to explore and leafy trees where monarch butterflies roost from October to February.

Seymour Marine Discovery Center   MUSEUM
(☎ 831-459-3800; http://seymourcenter.ucsc.edu; end of Delaware Ave; adult/child $6/4; ⊙ 10am-5pm Tue-Sat, from noon Sun; ▣) ⊘ University-run Long Marine Lab has cool interactive science exhibits for kids, including touch tanks. Look for the world's largest blue-whale skeleton outside.

Sanctuary Exploration Center   MUSEUM
(☎ 831-421-9993; http://montereybay.noaa.gov; 35 Pacific St; ⊙ 10am-5pm Wed-Sun; ▣) ⊘ FREE Virtually journey into the kelp forests and submarine canyons of Monterey Bay National Marine Sanctuary at this educational mini museum down by the wharf.

Venture Quest   KAYAKING
(☎ 831-425-8445, 831-427-2267; www.kayaksantacruz.com; Municipal Wharf; kayak rentals from $30) Experience the craggy coastline on sea-cave and wildlife-watching kayak tours (adult/child from $60/35), including moonlight paddles and excursions to Elkhorn Slough.

Roaring Camp Railroads   TRAIN RIDES
(☎ 831-335-4484; www.roaringcamp.com; adult/child from $26/19; ▣) For family fun, hop aboard a narrow-gauge steam train up into the redwoods or a standard-gauge train leaving from the beach boardwalk.

O'Neill Surf Shop   SURFING
(☎ 831-475-4151; www.oneill.com; 1115 41st Ave; wetsuit/surfboard rental $10/20; ⊙ 9am-8pm Mon-Fri, from 8am Sat & Sun) Head east to Capitola to this internationally renowned surfboard maker's mothership store. There's a smaller downtown branch at 110 Cooper St.

Santa Cruz Surf School   SURFING
(☎ 831-426-7072; www.santacruzsurfschool.com; 131 Center St; group/private lesson from $90/120; ▣) Friendly folks can teach you how to get out there on the waves (surfboard and wetsuit rental included with lessons).

🛏 Sleeping

Motels border Ocean St near downtown, Mission St by the university campus and Hwy 1 heading south. Make reservations for state-park campgrounds (☑800-444-7275; www.reserveamerica.com; campsites $35-65; 🛗🐾) at beaches off Hwy 1 and in forests off Hwy 9.

HI Santa Cruz Hostel   HOSTEL $

(☑831-423-8304; www.hi-santacruz.org; 321 Main St; dm $26-29, r $60-110; ⊙check-in 5pm-10pm; 📶) Budget overnighters dig this cute hostel at the Carmelita Cottages in a flowery garden setting, two blocks from the beach. All accommodations come with shared bath. Make reservations. Parking is $2.

Adobe on Green B&B   B&B $$

(☑831-469-9866; www.adobeongreen.com; 103 Green St; r incl breakfast $149-219; 🛜) 🐾 Peace and quiet are the mantras here. Your hosts are practically invisible, but their thoughtful touches are everywhere: from boutique amenities inside airy solar-powered rooms to breakfast spreads from organic gardens.

Pelican Point Inn   INN $$

(☑831-475-3381; www.pelicanpointinn-santacruz.com; 21345 E Cliff Dr; ste $109-199; 🛜🛗🐾) Ideal for families, these roomy apartment-style lodgings near kid-friendly Twin Lakes Beach are equipped with everything you'll need for a lazy beach vacation, including kitchenettes. Expect some noise.

Dream Inn   HOTEL $$$

(☑866-774-7735,   831-426-4330;   www.dreaminnsantacruz.com; 175 W Cliff Dr; r $200-380; ❄📶🛜🐾) Overlooking the wharf from its hillside perch, this retro-chic boutique hotel is as stylish as Santa Cruz gets. Rooms have all mod cons, while the beach is just steps away. Hit happy hour at the bar inside oceanview Aquarius Restaurant. Parking is $24.

🍴 Eating

Downtown is chockablock with just-OK cafes. Cruise Mission St near the university campus and 41st Ave in neighboring Capitola for cheaper takeout and international eats.

Picnic Basket   DELI, BAKERY $

(http://thepicnicbasketsc.com; 125 Beach St; items $3-8; ⊙7am-9pm, shorter hours off-season; 🛗) Locavores' kitchen across the street from the beach boardwalk makes creative sandwiches, soups, fruit sodas and baked goodies from scratch.

Penny Ice Creamery   DESSERT $

(http://thepennyicecreamery.com; 913 Cedar St; items $2-4; ⊙noon-11pm) 🐾 Artisanal ice-cream shop dreams up zany flavors using local, often organic ingredients like avocado, Meyer lemon and wildflower honey.

Hula's Island Grill   FUSION $$

(☑831-426-4852; www.hulastiki.com; 221 Cathcart St; dinner mains $11-20; ⊙11:30am-9:30pm Sun & Tue-Thu, to 11pm Fri & Sat, 4:30pm-9:30pm Mon) Sip a tropical cocktail at the tiki bar inside this faux lil' grass shack with glowing lanterns. Fish tacos, macadamia-nut-encrusted ahi (tuna) and luau pork plates will sate big kahunas.

Laili   AFGHAN $$$

(☑831-423-4545; www.lailirestaurant.com; 101 Cooper St; dinner mains $13-26; ⊙11:30am-3pm & 5-10pm) Taste the flavors of the Silk Road at this chic, high-ceilinged dining room: pomegranate eggplant, lamb kabobs, lentil-yogurt soup and savory flatbreads are all delish.

Soif   BISTRO $$$

(☑831-423-2020; www.soifwine.com; 105 Walnut Ave; small plates $5-17, mains $19-26; ⊙5-9pm Sun-Thu, to 10pm Fri & Sat) Downtown wine shop caters to bon vivants with a heady selection of 45 international wines by the glass paired with a sophisticated, seasonally driven Euro-Cal menu.

🍷 Drinking & Entertainment

Downtown is jam-packed with bars, live-music lounges, low-key nightclubs and coffeehouses. Check the free *Santa Cruz Weekly* (www.santacruzweekly.com) tabloid for more venues and current events.

Santa Cruz Mountain Brewing   BREWERY

(www.scmbrew.com; 402 Ingalls St; ⊙noon-10pm) Bold, organic brews are poured west of downtown off Mission St, squeezed between Santa Cruz Mountains winery tasting rooms.

Caffe Pergolesi   CAFE

(www.theperg.com; 418 Cedar St; ⊙7am-11pm; 🛜) On a leafy sidewalk verandah, discuss art and conspiracy theories over strong coffee, organic juices or beer.

Surf City Billiards & Café   BAR

(http://surfcitybilliardscafe.com; 931 Pacific Ave; ⊙5pm-midnight Sun-Thu, to 2am Fri & Sat) For shooting stick, dartboards, big-screen TVs and darn good pub grub.

Catalyst

LIVE MUSIC

(☑831-423-1338; www.catalystclub.com; 1011 Pacific Ave) Over the years, this landmark concert venue downtown has put cutting-edge national acts up on stage, from Nirvana to the Cold War Kids.

ℹ Information

KPIG 107.5 FM Plays the classic Santa Cruz soundtrack – think Bob Marley, Janis Joplin and Willie Nelson.

Santa Cruz Visitor Center (☑800-833-3494, 831-425-1234; www.santacruzca.org; 303 Water St; ⊗9am-4pm Mon-Fri, 10am-3pm Sat & Sun; 🛜)

ℹ Getting There & Away

Regional **Santa Cruz Metro** (☑831-425-8600; www.scmtd.com; fare/day pass $2/6) buses converge on downtown's **Metro Center** (920 Pacific Ave). From there, Greyhound operates a few daily buses to San Francisco ($16, three hours), San Luis Obispo ($42, four hours), Santa Barbara ($53, six hours) and LA ($59, nine hours). Daily during summer and on weekends in fall, a trolley (25¢) shuttles between downtown and the wharf.

Santa Cruz to San Francisco

Far more scenic than any freeway, this curvaceous 70-mile stretch of coastal Hwy 1 is bordered by wild beaches, organic farm stands and sea-salted villages, all scattered like loose diamonds in the rough.

About 20 miles northwest of Santa Cruz, **Año Nuevo State Park** (☑tour reservations 800-444-4445; www.parks.ca.gov; entry per car $10, tour per person $7; ⊗8:30am-5pm, last entry 3:30pm Apr-Aug, to 4pm, last entry 3pm Sep-Nov, tours only mid-Dec–Mar) is home base for the world's largest mainland breeding colony of northern elephant seals. Call ahead to reserve a 2½-hour, 3-mile guided walking tour, given during the cacophonous winter birthing and mating season.

On a quiet windswept coastal perch further north, green-business-certified **HI Pigeon Point Lighthouse Hostel** (☑650-879-0633; www.norcalhostels.org/pigeon; 210 Pigeon Point Rd; dm $26-30, r $75-180, all with shared bath; ⊗check-in 3:30pm-10:30pm; @🛜🛖) 🏄 inhabits the historic lightkeepers' quarters; it's popular, so book ahead. For more creature comforts, sleep in a tent bungalow or cozy fireplace cabin at **Costanoa** (☑877-262-7848, 650-879-1100; www.costanoa.com; 2001 Rossi Rd; tent/cabin with shared bath from $89/179; 🛜🛖).

Five miles north of Pigeon Point, **Pescadero State Beach** (www.parks.ca.gov; per car $8; ⊗8am-sunset) attracts beachcombers and birders to its marshy nature preserve nearby. For picnic supplies, head a few miles inland to Pescadero village and the bakery-deli at **Arcangeli Grocery Co** (www.normsmarket.com; 287 Stage Rd; ⊗10am-6pm). Nearby family-owned **Harley Farms Cheese Shop** (☑650-879-0480; www.harleyfarms.com; 250 North St; ⊗10am-5pm Thu-Sun; 🛖) 🏄 offers goat-dairy farm tours by reservation.

Another 15 miles north, busy Half Moon Bay is bordered by 4-mile-long **Half Moon Bay State Beach** (www.parks.ca.gov; per car $10; 🛖) and scenic **campsites** (☑800-444-7275; www.reserveamerica.com; campsites $35-50). Get out on the water with **Half Moon Bay Kayak** (☑650-773-6101; www.hmbkayak.com; Pillar Point Harbor; kayak rentals/tours from $25/75). For oceanfront luxury, the **Inn at Mavericks** (☑650-728-1572; www.innatmavericks.com; 364 Princeton Ave; r from $209; 🛜🐾) has spacious, romantic roosts. It overlooks Pillar Point Harbor, which has a decent brewpub with a sunset-view patio. In Half Moon Bay's quaint downtown, homey cafes, restaurants and eclectic shops line Main St, just inland from Hwy 1. **Flying Fish Grill** (☑650-712-1125; www.flyingfishgrill.net; 211 San Mateo Rd; dishes $5-17; ⊗11am-8:30pm Wed-Mon; 🛖) is the tastiest seafood shack around.

North of the harbor off Hwy 1, follow the signs to **Moss Beach Distillery** (www.mossbeachdistillery.com; 140 Beach Way; ⊗noon-8:30pm Sun-Thu, to 9pm Fri & Sat), a historic bootleggers' joint with a dog-friendly ocean-view deck for sunset drinks. Just north, **Fitzgerald Marine Reserve** (www.fitzgeraldreserve.org; end of California Ave; ⊗8am-sunset; 🛖) **FREE** protects tide pools teeming with colorful sea life; time your visit for low tide. Another mile north, ecofriendly **HI Point Montara Lighthouse Hostel** (☑650-728-7177; www.norcalhostels.org/montara; 16th St & Hwy 1; dm $27-30, r $74-110, all with shared bath; ⊗check-in 3:30pm-10:30pm; @🛜🛖) 🏄 fronts a small private beach (reservations essential). From there, it's less than 20 miles to San Francisco via Pacifica and the Devil's Slide Tunnels.

SAN FRANCISCO & THE BAY AREA

San Francisco

If you've ever wondered where the envelope goes when it's pushed, here's your answer. Psychedelic drugs, newfangled technology, gay liberation, green ventures, free speech and culinary experimentation all became mainstream long ago in San Francisco. After 160 years of booms and busts, losing your shirt has become a favorite local pastime at the clothing-optional Bay to Breakers race, Pride Parade and hot Sundays on Baker Beach. So long, inhibitions; hello, San Francisco.

History

Before gold changed everything, San Francisco was a hapless Spanish mission built by conscripts from the Native American Ohlone and Miwok communities. Without immunity to European diseases, some 5000 of these native builders fell sick and died; they are buried beside the aptly named 18th-century Mission Dolores, 'Mission of Sorrows'.

In 1849 the gold rush turned a 800-person village into a port city of 100,000 prospectors, con artists, prostitutes and honest folk. Panic struck when Australian gold flooded the market in 1854. Frustrated miners rioted against San Francisco's Chinese community, who from 1877 to 1943 were restricted to living and working in Chinatown by anti-Chinese laws. Chinese laborers were left with few options in the 1860s to '90s besides dangerous work building railroads for San Francisco's robber barons, who dynamited, mined and clear-cut across the Golden West, and built grand Nob Hill mansions.

The city's lofty ambitions came crashing down in 1906, when earthquake and fire reduced the city to rubble. San Franciscans rebuilt an astounding 15 buildings per day. By 1915, the rebuilt city hosted the Panama-Pacific International Expo in grand style.

During WWII, soldiers accused of homosexuality and insubordination were dismissed in San Francisco, cementing the city's counterculture reputation. The Summer of Love brought free food, love and music to the hippie Haight, and enterprising gay activists founded an out-and-proud community in the Castro.

San Francisco's unconventional thinking spawned the web in the mid-1990s, and is behind today's boom in social media, mobile apps and biotech. Congratulations: you're just in time for San Francisco's next wild ride.

◉ Sights

Let San Francisco's 43 hills and more than 80 arts venues stretch your legs and your imagination, and deliver breathtaking views. Downtown sights are within walking distance of Market St, but keep your city smarts and wits about you, especially around South of Market (SoMa) and the Tenderloin (5th to 9th Sts).

SAN FRANCISCO IN...

One Day

Since the Gold Rush, San Francisco adventures have started in **Chinatown**, where you can still find hidden fortunes – in cookies, that is. Beat it to **City Lights Bookstore** to revel in Beat poetry, then pass **Transamerica Pyramid** en route to dumplings at **City View**. Hit downtown **galleries**, then head to the **Asian Art Museum**, where art transports you across centuries and oceans within an hour. Take a spooky night tour of **Alcatraz**, then make your escape from the island prison in time for dinner at the **Ferry Building** before you hit the dance floor in **SoMa** clubs.

Two Days

Start your day amid mural-covered garage doors lining **Balmy Alley**, then window-shop to **826 Valencia** for pirate supplies and ichthyoid antics in the Fish Theater. Break for burritos, then hoof it to the Haight for flashbacks at vintage boutiques and the Summer of Love site: **Golden Gate Park**. Glimpse Golden Gate Bridge views atop **MH de Young Museum**, take a walk on the wild side inside **California Academy of Sciences**, then dig into organic Cal-Moroccan feasts at **Aziza**.

San Francisco & the Bay Area

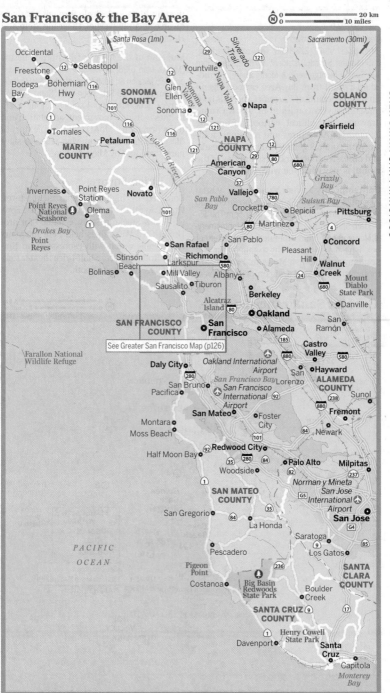

◉ SoMa

Cartoon Art Museum MUSEUM
(Map p128; ☑ 415-227-8666; www.cartoonart.org; 655 Mission St; adult/student $7/5; ⊙11am-5pm Tue-Sun; Ⓜ Montgomery, Ⓑ Montgomery) Founded on a grant from Bay Area cartoon legend Charles M Schultz of *Peanuts* fame, this bold museum covers comics from '70s R Crumb drawings to political cartoons from the *Economist*. At lectures and openings, mingle with comic legends, Pixar studio heads, and obsessive collectors. First Tuesday of the month is 'pay what you wish' entry.

Contemporary Jewish Museum MUSEUM
(Map p128; ☑ 415-344-8800; www.thecjm.org; 736 Mission St; adult/child $10/free, after 5pm Thu $5; ⊙11am-5pm Fri-Tue, 1-8pm Thu; Ⓜ Montgomery, Ⓑ Montgomery) That upended brushed-steel box isn't a sculpture, but a gallery for the Contemporary Jewish Museum. Exhibits are thoughtfully curated and compelling, investigating ideas and ideals through artists as diverse as Andy Warhol, Gertrude Stein and Harry Houdini.

Museum of the African Diaspora MUSEUM
(MoAD; Map p128; ☑ 415-358-7200; www.moadsf. org; 685 Mission St; adult/student/child $10/5/free; ⊙11am-6pm Wed-Sat, noon-5pm Sun; Ⓜ Montgomery, Ⓑ Montgomery) Exploring four main themes – origins, movement, adaptation and transformation – MoAD tells the epic story of diaspora, including a moving video of slave narratives, told by Maya Angelou.

◉ Union Square

Bordered by high-end department stores, Union Sq (at the intersection of Geary, Powell, Post & Stockton Sts) was named for pro-Union Civil War rallies held here 150 years ago. People-watch with espresso from Emporio Rulli, and score half-price theater tickets at TIX Bay Area's booth.

Greater San Francisco

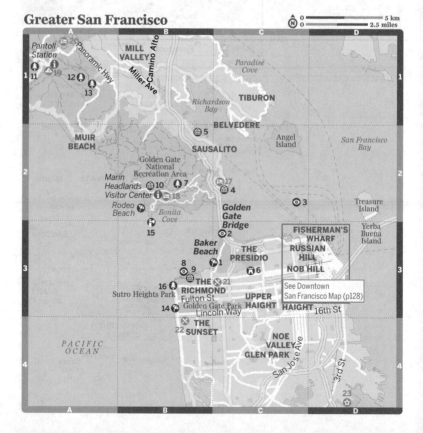

See Downtown San Francisco Map (p128)

Powell St Cable Car Turnaround   LANDMARK
(Map p128; cnr Powell & Market Sts; Ⓜ Powell,
Ⓑ Powell) Cable cars can't go backwards, so
cable-car operators turn them by hand on a
revolving platform at the terminus of Powell St lines. Powell-Mason cars are quickest
to the Wharf, but Powell-Hyde cars traverse
more terrain and hills.

◉ Civic Center

Asian Art Museum   MUSEUM
(Map p128; ☑ 415-581-3500; www.asianart.org; 200
Larkin St; adult/student/child $12/8/free, 1st Sun
of month free; ⊘ 10am-5pm Tue-Sun, to 9pm Thu
Feb-Sep; Ⓜ Civic Center, Ⓑ Civic Center) Imagina-
tions race from ancient Persian miniatures
to cutting-edge Japanese fashion through
three floors spanning 6000 years of Asian
arts. Besides the largest collection outside
Asia – 18,000 works – the museum offers
excellent programs, from shadow-puppet
shows to mixers with cross-cultural DJ
mash-ups.

City Hall   HISTORICAL BUILDING
(Map p128; ☑ art exhibit info 415-554-6080, tour
info 415-554-6023; www.ci.sf.ca.us/cityhall; 400
Van Ness Ave; ⊘ 8am-8pm Mon-Fri, tours 10am,
noon & 2pm; ♿; Ⓜ Civic Center, Ⓑ Civic Center)
FREE That mighty beaux-arts dome covers San Francisco's grandest ambitions and
swinging tendencies. Designed in 1915 to
outclass Paris and outsize Washington, DC's
capitol dome, San Francisco's Rotunda remained unsteady until its retrofit after the
city's 1989 earthquake, which enabled the
dome to swing on its base.

◉ Financial District

Suits abound, but the 'FiDi' has redeeming
quirks such as a redwood grove sprouted
from whaling ships below rocket-shaped
Transamerica Pyramid (Map p128; www.the
pyramidcenter.com; 600 Montgomery St; ⊘ 9am-
6pm Mon-Fri; Ⓜ Embarcadero, Ⓑ Embarcadero).
Eccentric art collectors descend from hilltop
mansions for First Thursday gallery openings
at **14 Geary**, **49 Geary** and **77 Geary**, which
are all run by the **San Francisco Art Dealers
Association** (SFADA; www.sfada.com; ⊘ gallery
openings 10:30am-5:30pm Tue-Fri, 11am-5pm Sat).

Ferry Building   LANDMARK
(Map p128; ☑ 415-983-8000; www.ferrybuilding-
marketplace.com; Market St & the Embarcadero;
⊘ 10am-6pm Mon-Fri, 9am-6pm Sat, 11am-5pm
Sun; ☐ 2, 6, 9, 14, 21, 31, Ⓜ F, J, K, L, M, N, T) Hedonism thrives at this transit hub turned gourmet emporium, where foodies happily miss
their ferries while slurping local oysters and
bubbly. Star chefs are spotted at the Tuesday, Thursday and Saturday farmers market
(p142) year-round.

◉ Chinatown

Since 1848 this community has survived riots,
earthquakes, bootlegging gangsters and politicians' attempts to relocate it down the coast.

**Chinese Historical
Society of America**   MUSEUM
(CHSA; Map p128; ☑ 415-391-1188; www.chsa.org;
965 Clay St; adult/child $5/2, 1st Thu of month free;
⊘ noon-5pm Tue-Fri, 11am-4pm Sat; ☐ 1, 30, 45,
🚋 California St) Picture what it was like to be

Greater San Francisco

Downtown San Francisco

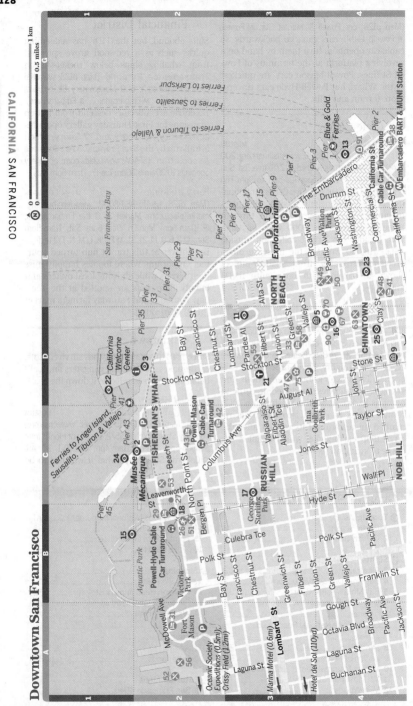

1 km
0.5 miles

Ferries to Larkspur
Ferries to Sausalito
Ferries to Tiburon & Vallejo

San Francisco Bay

Pier 1
Blue & Gold
Ferries
13

The Embarcadero
Drumm St
Commercial St
California St
Cable Car Turnaround
Embarcadero BART & MUNI Station
Pier 2
38

Broadway
Pacific Ave
Walton Park
Jackson St
Washington St
California St

Pier 7
Pier 9
Pier 17
Pier 15
Pier 19
Pier 23
Pier 29
Pier 27
Pier 31
Pier 33
Pier 35

Exploratorium
1

49
50
23

Alta St
NORTH
BEACH
Green St
Vallejo St
5
70
63
48
41

Francisco St
Chestnut St
Lombard St
Pardee Al
Filbert St
Union St
33
55
58
CHINATOWN
90
16
67
25
Clay St
9

Bay St
Stockton St

California
Welcome
Center
22
3

FISHERMAN'S
WHARF
Beach St
North Point St
43
Powell-Mason
Cable Car
Turnaround
42
Columbus Ave
21
47
75
Stone St
John St

Pier 43
Pier 41

Ferries to Angel Island,
Sausalito, Tiburon & Vallejo

24
Musée 2
Mécanique

Pier 45

53
29
26
51
18
George
Sterling
Park
17
RUSSIAN
HILL

Valparaiso St
Filbert Tce
Aladdin Tce
Ina
Coolbrith
Park
Taylor St

August Al

Jones St

Wall Pl
NOB HILL

Leavenworth St
Bergen Pl
Culebra Tce
Polk St
Hyde St
Pacific Ave

15

Powell-Hyde Cable
Car Turnaround
Victoria
Park
Bay St
Francisco St
Chestnut St
Greenwich St
Filbert St
Union St
Green St
Vallejo St
Franklin St

Aquatic Park

McDowell Ave
Fort Mason
31
52
56

Oceanic Society
Expeditions (0.5mi);
Crissy Field (1.2mi)

Marina Motel (0.6mi)
Lombard St
Hotel del Sol (110yd)

Polk St
Gough St
Octavia Blvd
Broadway
Pacific Ave
Jackson St
Laguna St
Buchanan St

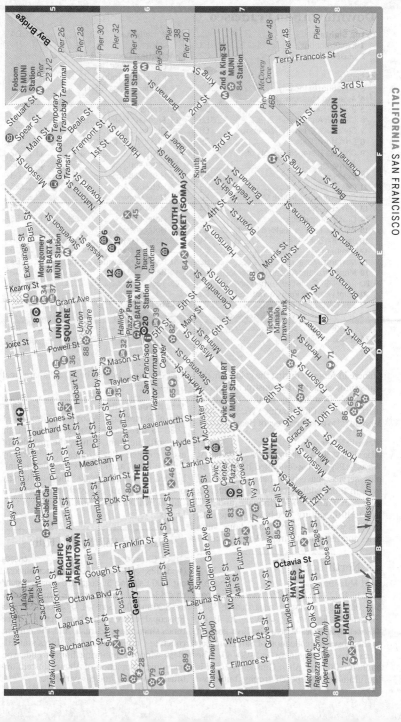

Bay Bridge

Pier 26
Pier 28
Pier 30
Pier 32
Pier 34
Pier 36
Pier 38
Pier 40
Pier 48
Pier 50

Folsom St MUNI Station
Pier 22 1/2

Steuart St
Spear St
Main St
Golden Gate Transit
Temporary Transbay Terminal
Beale St
Fremont St
1st St
Mission St
Howard St
Natoma St

Brannan St MUNI Station
2nd & King St MUNI Station

Terry Francois St
Pier McCovey Cove
Pier 46B
3rd St

Branton St
King St
Tabor Pl
Stillman St
2nd St
3rd St
4th St

MISSION BAY

Channel St
Berry St
Townsend St

SOUTH OF MARKET (SOMA)

Exchange St
Bush St
Montgomery St BART & MUNI Station
Jessie St
Stevenson St
Natoma St
Minna St

Welsh St
Freelon St
Brannan St
King St
Channel St
Bluxome St

Yerba Buena Gardens

Kearny St
Grant Ave
UNION SQUARE
Union Square
4th St
5th St
Mary St
6th St
Clementina St
Folsom St
Harrison St
Bryant St

Morris St
7th St

Powell St BART & MUNI Station
San Francisco Visitor Information Center
Hallidie Plaza
Mason St
Taylor St
Derby St
Geary St
O'Farrell St

Victoria Manalo Draves Park
Heron St
Homer St

Joice St
Powell St
Cable Car Center
5th St
Market St
Stevenson St
Mission St
Minna St
7th St
8th St

THE TENDERLOIN
Jones St
Touchard St
Sutter St
Post St
Meacham Pl
Leavenworth St
Hyde St
McAllister St
Civic Center BART & MUNI Station
Grace St
9th St
10th St

PACIFIC HEIGHTS & JAPANTOWN
California St Cable Car Turnaround
Sacramento St
Clay St
Pine St
Bush St
Larkin St
Polk St

CIVIC CENTER
Civic Center Plaza
Redwood St
Larkin St
McAllister St
Grove St
Ivy St
Elm St
Minna St
Howard St
11th St
12th St
Mission (1mi)

Washington St
Lafayette Park
Sacramento St
Octavia Blvd
California St
Laguna St
Franklin St
Gough St
Fern St
Ellis St
Willow St
Eddy St
Golden Gate Ave
Fell St
Hickory St
Page St
Rose St

HAYES VALLEY
Octavia St
Jefferson Square
Ash St
Fulton St
Hayes St
Hayes St
Linden St
Lily St

Tataki (0.4mi)
Geary Blvd
Buchanan St
Sutter St
Post St
Turk St
Laguna St
Webster St
Grove St
Fillmore St
Chateau Tivoli (20yd)

LOWER HAIGHT
Metro Hotel; Ragazza (0.25mi); Oak St (0.25mi); Upper Haight (0.7mi)
Castro (1mi)

Downtown San Francisco

Chinese in America during the gold rush, the transcontinental railroad construction or San Francisco's Beat heyday in this 1932 landmark, built as Chinatown's YWCA by Julia Morgan (also chief architect of Hearst Castle).

Waverly Place   STREET
(Map p128; 🚌30, 🚋California St, Powell-Mason) At Waverly Place's flag-festooned historic temples, services have been held since 1852 – even in 1906, while altars were smoldering after San Francisco's earthquake and fire. Due to 19th-century race-based restrictions, temples were built atop barber shops, laundries and restaurants lining Waverly Place.

North Beach

Beat Museum   MUSEUM
(Map p128; ☎1-800-537-6822; www.kerouac.com; 540 Broadway; admission adult/student $8/5; ⊗10am-7pm Tue-Sun; 🖥; 🚌10, 12, 30, 41, 45, 🚋Powell-Hyde, Powell-Mason) The Beat goes on at this obsessive collection of San Francisco literary-scene ephemera c 1950–69. The banned edition of Allen Ginsberg's *Howl* is the ultimate free-speech trophy, but those

Jack Kerouac bobble-head dolls are real head-shakers.

Jack Kerouac Alley   STREET
(Map p128; btwn Grant & Columbus Aves; 🚌1, 10, 12, 30, 45, 🚋Powell-Hyde, Powell-Mason) 'The air was soft, the stars so fine, the promise of every cobbled alley so great...' This ode by *On the Road* author Jack Kerouac is embedded in his namesake alley, a fittingly poetic and slightly seedy shortcut between Chinatown bars and North Beach via City Lights.

Russian Hill & Nob Hill

Grace Cathedral   CHURCH
(Map p128; ☎415-749-6300; www.gracecathedral.org; 1100 California St; suggested donation adult/child $3/2, Sun services free; ⊗8am-6pm, services 8:30am & 11am Sun; 🚌1, 🚋California St) This Episcopal church has been rebuilt three times since the gold rush, and the current concrete Gothic cathedral features stained-glass windows honoring human endeavor, including a depiction of Albert Einstein uplifted in swirling nuclear particles.

Lombard St   STREET

(Map p128; 900 block of Lombard St; 🚋 Powell-Hyde) You've probably already seen Lombard Street's flower-lined switchbacks, made famous by Hitchcock's Vertigo and notorious in Tony Hawk's Pro Skater video game. In the 1920s, Lombard St's natural 27% grade was too steep for automobiles to ascend – so local property owners added eight turns to this redbrick street.

⊙ Fisherman's Wharf

★**Exploratorium**   MUSEUM

(Map p128; ☎415-528-4444; www.exploratorium.edu; Pier 15; adult/child $25/19, Thu evening $15; ☺10am-5pm Tue-Sun, to 10pm Wed, adults over-18yr only Thu 6pm-10pm; 🚹; Ⓜ F) 🍃 Hear salt sing, stimulate your appetite with color, and find out what cows see, through hands-on exhibits by MacArthur Genius grant-winners. Manhattan Project nuclear physicist Frank Oppenheimer founded the Exploratorium in 1969 to explore science and human perception, and you might experience '60s flashbacks as you grope through the Tactile Dome.

★**Musée Mécanique**   AMUSEMENT PARK

(Map p128; www.museemechanique.org; Pier 45, Shed A; ☺10am-7pm; 🚹; 🚌47, 🚋Powell-Mason, Powell-Hyde, Ⓜ F) Where else can you guillotine a man for a quarter? Here, creepy 19th-century arcade games such as macabre French Execution compete for your spare change with the diabolical Ms Pac-Man.

Maritime Museum   MUSEUM

(Aquatic Park Bathhouse; Map p128; www.maritime.org; 900 Beach St; ☺10am-4pm; 🚹; 🚌19, 30, 47, 🚋Powell-Hyde) FREE A monumental hint to sailors needing a scrub, the ship-shape 1939 streamline moderne Aquatic Park Bathhouse is decked out with a playful seal sculpture by Beniamino Bufano, Hilaire Hiler's underwater murals, Richard Ayer's reliefs, and veranda mosaics and a carved slate doorway by pioneering African American artist Sargent Johnson.

USS Pampanito   HISTORIC SITE

(Map p128; ☎415-775-1943; www.maritime.org/pamphome.htm; Pier 45; adult/child $12/6; ☺9am-8pm Thu-Tue, to 6pm Wed; 🚹; 🚌19, 30, 47, 🚋Powell-Hyde, Ⓜ F) Explore a restored WWII submarine that survived six tours of duty, while you listen to

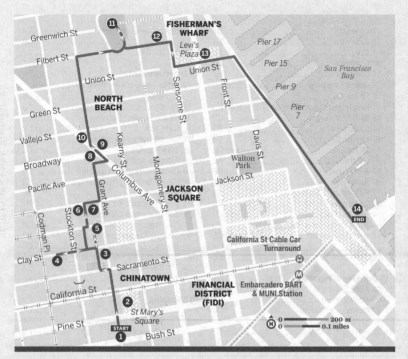

City Walk
Chinatown to the Waterfront

START CHINATOWN'S DRAGON GATE
FINISH FERRY BUILDING
LENGTH 1.8 MILES; 4½ HOURS

Discover revolutionary plots, find hidden fortunes, see controversial art and go gourmet with Gandhi. Starting at ❶ **Chinatown's Dragon Gate**, head past Grant St's gilded dragon lamps to ❷ **Old St Mary's Square**, site of a brothel leveled in the 1906 fire. Today, renegade skateboarders turn different kinds of tricks under the watchful eye of Beniamino Bufano's 1929 statue of Chinese revolutionary Sun Yat-Sen. Pass flag-festooned temple balconies along ❸ **Waverly Place**, then head to the ❹ **Chinese Historical Society of America** (p127) museum, in the majestic Chinatown YWCA built by Julia Morgan.

Enter ❺ **Spofford Alley**, where mahjong tiles click, Chinese orchestras play and beauticians gossip over blow-dryers – hard to believe this is where Prohibition bootleggers fought turf wars, and Sun Yat-Sen plotted the 1911 overthrow of China's last dynasty at No

36. Once packed with brothels, ❻ **Ross Alley** turned movie star as a location for *Karate Kid II* and *Indiana Jones and the Temple of Doom*. At No 56, make a fortune and watch it get folded into a warm cookie at ❼ **Golden Gate Fortune Cookie Factory**.

Back on Grant, take a shortcut through ❽ **Jack Kerouac Alley** (p130), where the binge-prone author often wound up *On the Road*. Stop by ❾ **City Lights** (p149) bookstore on Columbus Ave, champion of Beat poetry and free speech, and savor free verse with espresso at ❿ **Caffe Trieste** at 601 Vallejo St, under the Sicilian mural where Francis Ford Coppola wrote *The Godfather* script.

Climb to ⓫ **Coit Tower** (p133) for viewing-platform panoramas and 1930s lobby murals. Take ⓬ **Filbert St Steps** downhill past wild parrots and hidden cottages to ⓭ **Levi's Plaza**, named for the denim inventor. Head right on Embarcadero to the ⓮ **Ferry Building** (p127) for lunch Bayside, with a gaunt bronze Gandhi peeking over your shoulder.

sub-mariners' tales of stealth mode and sudden attacks in a riveting audio tour ($2) that makes surfacing afterwards a relief.

Hyde Street Pier Historic Ships HISTORIC SITE
(Map p128; ☑415-447-5000; www.nps.gov/safr; 499 Jefferson St, at Hyde St; adult/child $5/free; ☺9am-5pm; Ⓜ F, ⓖPowell-Hyde) Tour 19th-century ships moored here as part of the Maritime National Historical Park, including triple-masted 1886 Balclutha and 1890 steamboat Eureka; summer sailing trips are available aboard elegant 1891 schooner Alma (☺Jun-Nov; adult/child $40/20).

Sea Lions at Pier 39 OUTDOORS
(Map p128; ☑981-1280; www.pier39.com; Beach St & the Embarcadero, Pier 39; ☺ Jan-Jul; ⓖ15, 37, 49, F) Since California law requires boats to make way for marine mammals, yacht owners relinquish valuable slips to hundreds of sea lions who 'haul out' onto the docks from January to July, and whenever else they feel like sunbathing.

⊙ The Marina & Presidio

★Crissy Field PARK
(www.crissyfield.org; 1199 East Beach; Ⓟ; ⓖ30, PresidioGo Shuttle) The Presidio's army airstrip has been stripped of asphalt and re-invented as a haven for coastal birds, kite fliers and windsurfers enjoying sweeping views of Golden Gate Bridge.

★Baker Beach BEACH
(Map p126; ☺sunrise-sunset; Ⓟ; ⓖ29, PresidioGo Shuttle) Unswimmable waters but unbeatable views of the Golden Gate make this former Army beachhead San Francisco's tanning location of choice, especially the clothing-optional north end – at least until the afternoon fog rolls in.

⊙ The Mission

★Balmy Alley STREET ART
(☑415-285-2287; www.precitaeyes.org; btwn 24th & 25th Sts; ⓖ10, 12, 27, 33, 48, Ⓑ24th St Mission) Inspired by Diego Rivera's 1930s San Francisco murals and outraged by US foreign policy in Central America, Mission artists set out in the 1970s to transform the political landscape, one mural-covered garage door at a time.

Dolores Park PARK
(www.doloresparkworks.org; Dolores St, btwn 18th & 20th Sts; ⓖ⛹; ⓖ14, 33, 49, Ⓑ16th St Mission, Ⓜ J) Semiprofessional tanning, taco picnics

and a Hunky Jesus Contest every Easter: welcome to San Francisco's sunny side. Dolores Park has something for everyone, from tennis and political protests to the Mayan pyramid playground.

★826 Valencia CULTURAL SITE
(☑415-642-5905; www.826valencia.org; 826 Valencia St; ☺ noon-6pm; ⛹; ⓖ14, 33, 49, Ⓑ16th St Mission, Ⓜ J) The eccentric Pirate Supply Store sells eye patches, scoops from an actual tub o' lard, and McSweeney's literary magazines to support a teen-writing nonprofit organization and the Fish Theater. It's a shop, but really it's much more than that. There's even a vat of sand where kids can rummage for buried pirates' booty.

Mission Dolores CHURCH
(Misión San Francisco de Asís; ☑415-621-8203; www.missiondolores.org; 3321 16th St; adult/child $5/3; ☺9am-4pm Nov-Apr, to 4:30pm May-Oct; ⓖ22, 33, Ⓑ16th St Mission, Ⓜ J) The city's oldest building and its namesake, whitewashed adobe Misión San Francisco de Asís was founded in 1776 and rebuilt in 1782 with conscripted Ohlone and Miwok labor – note the ceiling patterned after native baskets.

⊙ The Castro

GLBT History Museum MUSEUM
(☑415-777-5455; www.glbthistory.org/museum; 4127 18th St; admission $5; ☺11am-7pm Mon-Sat, noon-5pm Sun; Ⓜ Castro) America's first gay-history museum showcases Harvey Milk's

---

COIT TOWER

Adding an exclamation mark to San Francisco's landscape, Coit Tower (Map p128; ☑415-362-0808; http://sfrecpark.org/destination/telegraph-hill-pioneer-park/coit-tower; Telegraph Hill Blvd; elevator entry (nonresident) adult/child $7/5; ☺10am-5:30pm Mar-Sep, 9am-4:30pm Oct-Feb; ⓖ39) offers views worth shouting about – especially after you climb the giddy, steep Filbert St steps to get here. Check out 360-degree views of downtown from the viewing platform, and wrap-around 1930s lobby murals glorifying San Francisco workers – once denounced as communist but now a beloved landmark. To glimpse murals hidden inside Coit Tower's stairwell, take free docent-led tours at 11am Saturdays.

SAN FRANCISCO NEIGHBORHOODS IN A NUTSHELL

North Beach Poetry and parrots, sidewalk cafes, Italian restaurants.

Fisherman's Wharf Sea-lion antics, vintage video games, and getaways to and from Alcatraz.

Downtown & the Financial District Glossy flagship stores and top-chef bistros, gallery openings and clearance sales.

Chinatown Pagoda roofs, dim sum, and fortunes made and lost in historic alleyways.

Hayes Valley & Civic Center Grand buildings and great performances, foodie finds and local designs.

Tenderloin Theater district, Skid Row, dive bars and noodle shops.

SoMa Where high technology meets higher art, and everyone gets down and dirty on the dance floor.

Mission A book in one hand, a burrito in the other, murals all around.

Castro Out and proud with samba whistles, rainbow flags and policy platforms.

Haight Sixties flashbacks, alternative fashion, free music and pricey skateboards.

Japantown & the Fillmore Sushi, shopping and rock at the Fillmore.

Marina & the Presidio Boutiques, organic dining, nature and nudity at a former army base.

Golden Gate Park & Around San Francisco's mile-wide wild streak, surrounded by gourmet surfer hangouts.

---

campaign literature, matchbooks from long-gone bathhouses, audiovisual interviews with Gore Vidal and pages of the 1950s penal code banning homosexuality.

◉ The Haight

Alamo Square Park   PARK
(Hayes & Scott Sts; 🚲; 🚌 5, 21, 22, 24) **FREE**
Summit Alamo Sq to see downtown framed by gabled Victorian rooflines and wind-sculpted pines. Pastel 'Painted Lady' Victorian mansions along eastside Postcard Row pale in comparison to colorful neighbors, including gilded green 1889 Westerfield House, which survived tenancies by czarist bootleggers, hippie communes, even tower rituals by Church of Satan founder Anton LaVey.

Haight & Ashbury   LANDMARK
(🚌 6, 33, 37, 43, 71) The legendary psychedelic '60s intersection remains a counterculture magnet, where you can sign Green Party petitions, commission poems, hear Hare Krishna on keyboards and Bob Dylan on banjo. The clock overhead always reads 4:20 – better known in herbal circles as International Bong-Hit Time.

◉ Golden Gate Park & Around

San Francisco was way ahead of its time in 1865, when the city voted to turn 1017 acres of sand dunes into the world's largest city stretch of green, Golden Gate Park. Tenacious park architect William Hammond Hall ousted hotels and casinos for this nature preserve. The park ends at Ocean Beach (Map p126; ☑ 415-561-4323; www.parksconservancy.org; Great Hwy; ☉ sunrise-sunset; 🚌 5, 18, 31, Ⓜ N), where Cliff House restaurant overlooks the splendid ruin of Sutro Baths (Map p126; www.nps.gov/goga/historyculture/sutro-baths.htm; Point Lobos Ave; ☉ sunrise-sunset; visitor center hours 9am-5pm; 🅿; 🚌 5, 31, 38) *FREE*. Follow the partly paved trail around Lands End for shipwreck sightings and Golden Gate Bridge views.

California Academy of Sciences   MUSEUM
(☑ 415-379-8000; www.calacademy.org; 55 Music Concourse Dr; adult/child $35/25, discount with Muni ticket $3; ☉ 9:30am-5pm Mon-Sat, 11am-5pm Sun; 🚼; 🚌 5, 6, 31, 33, 44, 71, Ⓜ N) *Architect Renzo Piano's LEED-certified green building houses 38,000 weird and wonderful animals, with a four-story rainforest and aquarium under a 'living roof' of California wildflowers. After the penguins nod off to

sleep, the wild rumpus starts at kids-only Academy Sleepovers and over-21 NightLife Thursdays.

MH de Young Museum MUSEUM
(☑ 415-750-3600; www.famsf.org/deyoung; 50 Hagiwara Tea Garden Dr; adult/child $10/6, discount with Muni ticket $2, 1st Tue of month free, online booking fee $1 per ticket; ⊙ 9:30am-5:15pm Tue-Sun, to 8:45pm Fri mid-Jan–Nov; ☐ 5, 44, 71, Ⓜ N) Follow sculptor Andy Goldsworthy's sidewalk fault line into Herzog & de Meuron's sleek copper-clad building, and broaden your artistic horizons with Oceanic ceremonial masks and sculptor Al Farrow's cathedrals built from bullets.

Legion of Honor MUSEUM
(Map p126; ☑ 415-750-3600; http://legionofhonor.famsf.org; 100 34th Ave; adult/child $10/6, discount with Muni ticket $2, 1st Tue of month free; ⊙ 9:30am-5:15pm Tue-Sun; 🚹; ☐ 1, 18, 38) A museum as eccentric and illuminating as San Francisco itself, the Legion showcases a wildly eclectic collection, ranging from Monet water lilies to John Cage soundscapes, ancient Iraqi ivories and R Crumb comics.

Conservatory of Flowers NATURAL SITE
(☑ info 415-831-2090; www.conservatoryofflowers.org; 100 John F Kennedy Dr; adult/child $7/5; ⊙ 10am-4:30pm Tue-Sun; ☐ 71, Ⓜ N) This recently restored 1878 Victorian greenhouse is home to outer-space orchids, contemplative floating lilies and creepy carnivorous plants that reek of insect belches.

Japanese Tea Garden GARDEN
(☑ tea ceremony reservations 415-752-1171; www.japaneseteagardensf.com; 75 Hagiwara Tea Garden Dr; adult/child $7/5, before 10am Mon, Wed & Fri free; ⊙ 9am-6pm Mar-Oct, to 4:45pm Nov-Feb; ☐ 5, 44, 71, Ⓜ N) Since 1894, this picturesque 5-acre garden and bonsai grove has blushed with cherry blossoms in spring and turned flaming red with maple leaves in fall. Lose all track of time in the meditative Zen Garden.

San Francisco Botanical Garden GARDEN
(Strybing Arboretum; ☑ 415-661-1316; www.strybing.org; 1199 9th Ave; adult/child $7/5, 2nd Tue of month free; ⊙ 9am-6pm Apr-Oct, to 5pm Nov-Mar, bookstore 10am-4pm; 🚹; ☐ 6, 43, 44, 71, Ⓜ N) ✈ Sniff your way around the world inside this 55-acre garden. Almost anything grows in the peculiar microclimates of this corner of Golden Gate Park, from South African savannah grasses to Japanese magnolias.

◉ San Francisco Bay

★ Golden Gate Bridge BRIDGE
(Map p126; www.goldengatebridge.org/visitors; off Lincoln Blvd; northbound free, southbound toll $6; ☐ 28, all Golden Gate Transit buses) San Francisco's 1937 suspension bridge was almost nixed by the navy in favor of yellow-striped concrete pylons. Instead, engineer Joseph B Strauss, architects Gertrude and Irving Murrow and daredevil workers created an International Orange deco icon. The southbound toll is billed electronically to your vehicle's license plate; for details, see www.goldengate.org/tolls.

🏃 Activities

★ Kabuki Springs & Spa SPA
(Map p128; ☑ 415-922-6000; www.kabukisprings.com; 1750 Geary Blvd; admission $25; ⊙ 10am-9:45pm, co-ed Tue, women-only Wed, Fri & Sun, men-only Mon, Thu & Sat; ☐ 22, 38) Scrub down with salt in the communal steam room, soak in the hot pool, take the cold plunge and reheat in the sauna. Silence sets a meditative mood – if you hear the gong, it means shhhh!

DON'T MISS

ALCATRAZ

Over 150 years, Alcatraz (Map p126; ☑ Alcatraz Cruises 415-981-7625; www.alcatrazcruises.com; day tours adult/child/family $30/18/92, night tours adult/child $37/22; ⊙ call center 8am-7pm, ferries depart Pier 33 half-hourly 9am-3:55pm, night tours 6:10pm & 6:45pm) has been the nation's first military prison, a maximum-security penitentiary housing A-list criminals including Al Capone, and hotly disputed Native American territory. No prisoners escaped Alcatraz alive, but since importing guards and supplies cost more than putting up prisoners at the Ritz, the prison was closed in 1963.

Day visits include the cruise to and from the penitentiary and captivating audio tours with prisoners and guards recalling life on 'the Rock,' while night tours are led by a park ranger; reserve tickets at least two weeks ahead.

Alcatraz

Book a ferry from Pier 33 and ride 1.5 miles across the bay to explore America's most notorious former prison. The trip itself is worth the money, providing stunning views of the city skyline. Once you've landed at the **Ferry Dock & Pier 1**, you begin the 580-yard walk to the top of the island and prison; if you're out of shape, there's a twice-hourly tram.

As you climb toward the **Guardhouse 2**, notice the island's steep slope; before it was a prison, Alcatraz was a fort. In the 1850s, the military quarried the rocky shores into near-vertical cliffs. Ships could then only dock at a single port, separated from the main buildings by a sally port (a drawbridge and moat in what became the guardhouse). Inside, peer through floor grates to see Alcatraz' original prison.

Volunteers tend the brilliant **Officer's Row Gardens 3** – an orderly counterpoint to the overgrown rose bushes surrounding the burned-out shell of the **Warden's House 4**. At the top of the hill, by the front door of the **Main Cellhouse 5**, beauty shots unfurl all around, including a **view of the Golden Gate Bridge 6**. Above the main door of the administration building, notice the **historic signs & graffiti 7**, before you step inside the dank, cold prison to find the **Frank Morris cell 8**, former home to Alcatraz' most notorious jail-breaker.

TOP TIPS

➡ Book at least two weeks prior for self-guided daytime visits, longer for ranger-led night tours. For info on garden tours, see www.alcatraz gardens.org.

➡ Be prepared to hike; a steep path ascends from the ferry landing to the cell block. Most people spend two to three hours on the island. You need only reserve for the outbound ferry; take any ferry back.

➡ There's no food (just water) but you can bring your own; picnicking is allowed at the ferry dock only. Dress in layers as weather changes fast and it's usually windy.

JOHN A VLAHIDES ©

Historic Signs & Graffiti
During their 1969–71 occupation, Native Americans graffitied the water tower: 'Home of the Free Indian Land.' Above the cellhouse door, examine the eagle-and-flag crest to see how the red-and-white stripes were changed to spell 'Free.'

Warden's House
Fires destroyed the warden's house and other structures during the Indian Occupation. The government blamed the Native Americans; the Native Americans blamed agents provocateurs acting on behalf of the Nixon Administration to undermine public sympathy.

Parade Grounds

DAVID CLAPP / GETTY IMAGES ©

Ferry Dock & Pier
A giant wall map helps you get your bearings. Inside nearby Bldg 64, short films and exhibits provide historical perspective on the prison and details about the Indian Occupation.

View of Golden Gate Bridge

The Golden Gate Bridge stretches wide on the horizon. Best views are from atop the island at Eagle Plaza, near the cellhouse entrance, and at water level along the Agave Trail (September to January only).

Main Cellhouse

During the mid-20th century, the maximum-security prison housed the day's most notorious troublemakers, including Al Capone and Robert Stroud, the 'Birdman of Alcatraz' (who actually conducted his ornithology studies at Leavenworth).

Power House

Recreation Yard　**Water Tower**

Officers' Club

6

5

8

7

Lighthouse

3

4

2

Guard Tower

1

Frank Morris Cell

Peer into cell 138 on B-Block to see a re-creation of the dummy's head that Frank Morris left in his bed as a decoy to aid his notorious – and successful – 1962 escape from Alcatraz.

Guardhouse

Alcatraz' oldest building dates to 1857 and retains remnants of the original drawbridge and moat. During the Civil War the basement was transformed into a military dungeon – the genesis of Alcatraz as prison.

Officer's Row Gardens

In the 19th century soldiers imported topsoil to beautify the island with gardens. Well-trusted prisoners later gardened – Elliott Michener said it kept him sane. Historians, ornithologists and archaeologists choose today's plants.

DON'T MISS

JAPANTOWN & PACIFIC HEIGHTS

Atop every Japantown sushi counter perches a *maneki neko*, the porcelain cat with one paw raised in permanent welcome: you are invited for shopping at New People (p149), shiatsu massages at Kabuki Springs & Spa (p135), eco-entertainment at Sundance Kabuki Cinema (p148), world-class jazz at Yoshi's (p147) or mind-blowing rock at the Fillmore (p147).

★ **18 Reasons** COOKING
(☎415-568-2710; www.18reasons.org; 3674 18th St; classes & events $5-35; ☺varies by event; 🖈; 🚊22, 33, 🅼J) 🍴 Deliciously educational events: shochu tastings, knife-skills and cheese-making workshops, and California cuisine classes. Mingle at family-friendly Wednesday soup suppers and Thursday happy hours.

Blazing Saddles CYCLING
(Map p128; ☎415-202-8888; www.blazingsaddles. com; 2715 Hyde St; bike rental per hour $8-15, per day $32-88; electric bikes per day $48-88; ☺8am-7:30pm; 🖈; 🚋Powell-Hyde) Convenient for biking the Embarcadero or to the Golden Gate Bridge, this outfit offers electric bikes, rentals with packs and bungee cords, and 24-hour return service.

👉 Tours

★ **Precita Eyes Mission Mural Tours** TOUR
(☎415-285-2287; www.precitaeyes.org; adult $15-20, child $5; ☺see website calendar for tour dates; 🖈) Muralists lead two-hour tours on foot or bicycle covering 60 to 70 murals in a six-to-10-block radius of mural-bedecked Balmy Alley; proceeds fund mural upkeep at this community arts nonprofit.

Chinatown Alleyway Tours TOUR
(☎415-984-1478; www.chinatownalleywaytours. org; adult/student $18/12; ☺11am Sat & Sun; 🖈) Neighborhood teens lead two-hour community nonprofit tours for up-close-and-personal peeks into Chinatown's past (weather permitting). Book five days ahead or pay double for Saturday walk-ins; cash only.

Oceanic Society Expeditions TOUR
(☎415-474-3385; www.oceanicsociety.org; 3950 Scott St; whale-watching trips per person $120-125; ☺office 8:30am-5pm Mon-Fri, trips Sat & Sun; 🚊30) Naturalist-led weekend boating day-trips depart from Yacht Harbor. Kids must be 10 years or older. Reservations required.

Public Library City Guides TOUR
(www.sfcityguides.org; donations/tips welcome) **FREE** Volunteer local historians lead non-profit tours organized by neighborhood and theme: Gold Rush Downtown, Secrets of Fisherman's Wharf, Telegraph Hill Stairway Hike and more.

🎉 Festivals & Events

Chinese New Year Parade CULTURE
(www.chineseparade.com; ☺Feb) Chase the 200ft dragon, and see lion dancers and toddler kung-fu classes parade through Chinatown.

SF International Film Festival FILM
(www.sffs.org; ☺Apr) Stars align and directors launch premieres at the nation's oldest film festival.

Bay to Breakers SPORT
(www.baytobreakers.com; race registration $58-90; ☺May) Run costumed from Embarcadero to Ocean Beach on the third Sunday in May, while joggers dressed as salmon run upstream.

Carnaval CULTURE
(www.carnavalsf.com; ☺May) Brazilian, or just faking it with a wax and a tan? Shake your tail feathers in the Mission on the last weekend of May.

SF Pride Celebration CULTURE
(☺Jun) A day isn't enough to do San Francisco proud: June begins with **International LGBT Film Festival** (www.frameline.org), and goes out in style the last weekend with Pink Saturday's **Dyke March** (www.dykemarch.org) and the frisky, million-strong **Pride Parade** (www.sfpride.org).

Folsom Street Fair STREET FAIR
(www.folsomstreetfair.com; ☺Sep) Work that leather look and enjoy public spankings for local charities at this adults-only bondage festival. Runs the last weekend of September.

Hardly Strictly Bluegrass MUSIC
(www.strictlybluegrass.com; ☺Oct) San Francisco celebrates Western roots with three days of free Golden Gate Park concerts and headliners ranging from Elvis Costello to Gillian Welch in early October.

Litquake LITERATURE
(www.litquake.com; ⊙ Sep) Score signed books and grab drinks with authors afterwards.

Green Festival CULTURE
(www.greenfestivals.org; ⊙ mid-Nov) Energy-saving spotlights are turned on green cuisine, technology, fashion and booze for three days in mid-November.

🛌 Sleeping

San Francisco is the birthplace of the boutique hotel, which offers stylish rooms for a price: $120 to $200 midrange, plus 15.5% hotel tax (hostels exempt) and $35 to $50 for overnight parking. For vacancies and deals, check San Francisco Visitor Information Center's reservation line (p150), Bed & Breakfast San Francisco (✆ 415-899-0060; www.bbsf.com) and Lonely Planet (http://hotels.lonelyplanet.com).

🛌 Union Square & Civic Center

★ **Orchard Garden Hotel** BOUTIQUE HOTEL **$$**
(Map p128; ✆ 888-717-2881, 415-399-9807; www.theorchardgardenhotel.com; 466 Bush St; r $189-259; ❋ @ 🛜 🛜; 🚌 2, 3, 30, 45, Ⓑ Montgomery) 🍃 San Francisco's first all-green-practices hotel uses sustainably grown wood, chemical-free cleaning products and luxe recycled fabrics in its soothingly quiet rooms. Don't miss the sunny rooftop terrace.

Hotel Rex BOUTIQUE HOTEL **$$**
(Map p128; ✆ 415-433-4434, 800-433-4434; www.jdvhotels.com; 562 Sutter St; r $159-229; ❋ @ 🛜 🛜; 🚋 Powell-Hyde, Powell-Mason, Ⓜ Powell, Ⓑ Powell) 🍃 French gramophone lobby music conjures New York's Algonquin in the 1920s, and handsome guest rooms feature hand-painted lampshades, local art and plush beds with crisp linens and down pillows. Street-facing rooms are bright but noisy; request air-con.

Hotel Triton BOUTIQUE HOTEL **$$**
(Map p128; ✆ 800-800-1299, 415-394-0500; www.hoteltriton.com; 342 Grant Ave; r $175-275, ste $350; ❋ @ 🛜 🛜 🛜; Ⓜ Montgomery, Ⓑ Montgomery) 🍃 Beyond the colorful, comic-bookish lobby are hip rooms with San Francisco–centric details – such as wallpaper of Kerouac's *On the Road* – plus ecofriendly amenities, shag-worthy beds and unlimited ice cream. Don't miss tarot-card readings and chair massages during nightly wine hour.

Hotel Zetta HOTEL **$$**
(Map p128; ✆ 855-212-4187, 415-543-8555; www.hotelzetta.com; 55 5th St; r $189-249; ❋ @ 🛜 🛜 🛜; Ⓑ Powell St, Ⓜ Powell St) 🍃 Opened in 2013, this eco-conscious downtower caters to play-hard techies; there's billiards, shuffleboard and a Plinko wall above the art-filled lobby. Bigger-than-average rooms have padded black-leather headboards, low-slung platform beds and web-enabled flat-screen TVs.

Golden Gate Hotel HOTEL **$$**
(Map p128; ✆ 800-835-1118, 415-392-3702; www.goldengatehotel.com; 775 Bush St; r with/without bath $175/115; @ 🛜; 🚌 2, 3, 🚋 Powell-Hyde, Powell-Mason) Like an old-fashioned pension, this 1913 Edwardian hotel has kindly owners and homey mismatched furniture.

SAN FRANCISCO FOR CHILDREN

Although it has the least kids per capita of any US city – according to recent San Francisco SPCA data, there are 32,000 more dogs than children in town – San Francisco is packed with attractions for kids, including Golden Gate Park, Exploratorium, California Academy of Sciences, Cartoon Art Museum and Musée Mécanique. For babysitting, **American Child Care** (✆ 415-285-2300; www.americanchildcare.com; 580 California St, Suite 1600) charges $20 per hour plus gratuity; four-hour minimum.

The **Children's Creativity Museum** (Map p128; ✆ 415-820-3320; www.zeum.org; 221 4th St; admission $11; ⊙ 10am-4pm Wed-Sun Sep-May, Tue-Sun Jun-Aug; 🛜; Ⓜ Powell, Ⓑ Powell) has technology that's too cool for school: robots, live-action video games, DIY music videos and 3D animation workshops with Silicon Valley innovators.

At **Aquarium of the Bay** (Map p128; www.aquariumofthebay.com; Pier 39; adult/child/family $18/10/50; ⊙ 9am-8pm summer, 10am-6pm winter; 🛜; 🚌 49, 🚋 Powell-Mason, Ⓜ F), glide through glass tubes underwater on conveyer belts as sharks circle overhead.

Fire Engine Tours (Map p128; ✆ 415-333-7077; www.fireenginetours.com; departs Beach St, at the Cannery; adult/child $50/30; ⊙ tours depart 9am, 11am, 1pm, 3pm) are hot stuff: take a 75-minute, open-air vintage fire-engine ride over Golden Gate Bridge.

Rooms are small but comfortable; most have private baths. Homemade cookies and a resident kitty-cat provide comfort after sightseeing.

Hotel Abri
HOTEL $$

(Map p128; ☑ 415-392-8800, 888-229-0677; www.hotelabrisf.com; 127 Ellis St; r $169-249; ❄ @ 🕙 🐾; Ⓜ Powell, Ⓑ Powell) Contemporary chic, with bold black-and-tan motifs, pillow-top beds with feather pillows, iPod docks, flat-screen TVs and big workstations. Few bathrooms have tubs, but rainfall showerheads compensate.

Hotel des Arts
ART HOTEL $$

(Map p128; ☑ 800-956-4322, 415-956-3232; www.sfhoteldesarts.com; 447 Bush St; r with bath $119-159, without bath $79-99; 🕙; Ⓜ Montgomery, Ⓑ Montgomery) A budget hotel for art freaks, with jaw-dropping murals by underground artists. Downsides: thin linens, earplugs possibly needed, and rooms with private bath require seven-night stays.

★ Hotel Monaco
BOUTIQUE HOTEL $$

(Map p128; ☑ 415-292-0100, 866-622-5284; www.monaco-sf.com; 501 Geary St; r $179-269; ❄ @ 🕙 🐾; 🖵 38, 🚋 Powell-Hyde, Powell-Mason) 🍴 Snazzy Monaco gets the details right: colorful guest rooms offer high-thread-count sheets, ergonomic workspaces and ample closet space. Extras include spa with Jacuzzi, gym, evening wine and bicycles.

Financial District & North Beach

San Remo Hotel
HOTEL $

(Map p128; ☑ 800-352-7366, 415-776-8688; www.sanremohotel.com; 2237 Mason St; d with shared bath $79-129; @ 🕙 🐾; 🖵 30, 47, 🚋 Powell-Mason) One of the city's best-value spots, this 1906 inn is an old-fashioned charmer with vintage furnishings. Bargain rooms face the corridor; family suites accommodate up to five. No elevator.

Pacific Tradewinds Hostel
HOSTEL $

(Map p128; ☑ 888-734-6783, 415-433-7970; www.sanfranciscohostel.org; 680 Sacramento St; dm $30; @ 🕙; 🖵 1, 🚋 California St, Ⓑ Montgomery) San Francisco's smartest-looking all-dorm hostel has a blue-and-white nautical theme, fully equipped kitchen, spotless glass-brick showers, no lockout time and great service. No elevator means hauling bags up three flights.

★ Hotel Bohème
BOUTIQUE HOTEL $$

(Map p128; ☑ 415-433-9111; www.hotelboheme.com; 444 Columbus Ave; r $174-224; @ 🕙; 🖵 10, 12, 30, 41, 45) A love letter to the Beat era, with moody orange, black and sage-green color schemes nodding to the 1950s, parasol lights and vintage photos. Rooms are smallish and some face noisy Columbus Ave, but you're in the heart of vibrant North Beach.

Hotel Vitale
BOUTIQUE HOTEL $$$

(Map p128; ☑ 888-890-8688, 415-278-3700; www.hotelvitale.com; 8 Mission St; r from $255; ❄ @ 🕙 🐾; Ⓜ Embarcadero, Ⓑ Embarcadero) Tinted glass disguises a fashion-forward hotel, with up-to-the-minute luxuries: 450-thread-count sheets, on-site spa with rooftop hot tubs, and some rooms that offer spectacular bridge views.

Fisherman's Wharf & The Marina

★ HI San Francisco Fisherman's Wharf
HOSTEL $

(Map p128; ☑ 415-771-7277; www.sfhostels.com; Bldg 240, Fort Mason; r $65-100; P @ 🕙; 🖵 28, 30, 47, 49) A former army hospital building offers bargain-priced private rooms and dorms (some co-ed) with four to 22 beds and a huge kitchen. No curfew, but no heat during the day: bring warm clothes. Limited free parking.

Hotel del Sol
MOTEL $$

(☑ 415-921-5520, 877-433-5765; www.thehoteldelsol.com; 3100 Webster St; d $189-269; P ❄ @ 🕙 🐾 🐾; 🖵 22, 28, 30, 43) 🍴 A spiffy, kid-friendly, tropical-themed 1950s motor lodge, with palm-lined central courtyard and heated outdoor pool. Family suites have trundle beds and board games. Free parking.

Tuscan Inn
BOUTIQUE HOTEL $$

(Map p128; ☑ 800-648-4626, 415-561-1100; www.tuscaninn.com; 425 North Point St; r $169-299; ❄ @ 🕙 🐾 🐾; 🖵 47, 🚋 Powell-Mason, Ⓜ F) 🍴 Managed by fashion-forward Kimpton, the Tuscan's spacious jewel-toned rooms have more character than most chain-hotel digs. Kids love in-room Nintendo; parents love afternoon wine hours.

Marina Motel
MOTEL $$

(☑ 800-346-6118, 415-921-9406; www.marinamotel.com; 2576 Lombard St; r $139-199; P 🕙 🐾; 🖵 28, 30, 41, 43, 45) The vintage 1939 Marina has a Spanish-Mediterranean look, with a bougainvillea-lined courtyard. Rooms are homey and well maintained, and some have full kitchens (extra $10 to $20).

⭐ **Argonaut Hotel** BOUTIQUE HOTEL **$$$**
(Map p128; ☎866-415-0704, 415-563-0800; www.argonauthotel.com; 495 Jefferson St; r $205-325, with view $305-550; ✳🖤📶❄; 🚇19, 47, 49, 🚋Powell-Hyde) ✎ Built as a cannery in 1908, Fisherman's Wharf's best inn has wooden beams, exposed brick walls, and an over-the-top nautical theme that includes porthole-shaped mirrors. Ultracomfy beds and iPod docks are standard, though some rooms are tiny, with limited sunlight – pay extra for a mesmerizing bay view.

🛏 The Mission

Inn San Francisco B&B **$$**
(☎415-641-0188, 800-359-0913; www.innsf.com; 943 S Van Ness Ave; r incl breakfast $185-295, with shared bath $135-185, cottage $325-385; 🅿@📶; 🚇14, 49) ✎ An impeccably maintained 1872 Italianate-Victorian mansion, this inn has period antiques, fresh-cut flowers and fluffy feather beds; some have Jacuzzi tubs. Outside there's an English garden and a redwood hot tub. Limited parking: reserve ahead. No elevator.

🛏 The Castro

Parker Guest House B&B **$$**
(☎888-520-7275, 415-621-3222; www.parkerguesthouse.com; 520 Church St; r incl breakfast $159-269; @📶; 🚇33, Ⓜ J) The Castro's stateliest gay digs occupy two side-by-side Edwardian mansions sharing a garden and steam room. Rooms have supercomfortable beds and down duvets; bath fixtures gleam. No elevator.

🛏 The Haight

Metro Hotel HOTEL **$**
(☎415-861-5364; www.metrohotelsf.com; 319 Divisadero St; r $88-138; @📶; 🚇6, 24, 71) A central Haight hotel providing cheap, clean rooms with private bath and garden patio. Ragazza pizzeria (p144) is downstairs. No elevator.

Red Victorian Bed, Breakfast & Art B&B **$**
(☎415-864-1978; www.redvic.net; 1665 Haight St; r incl breakfast $159-189, without bath $99-139; 📶; 🚇33, 43, 71) ✎ The trippy '60s live at this 1904 Victorian, with room themes that include Sunshine, Flower Children and Sum-

mer of Love. Only four of the 18 rooms have private baths; but all include breakfast in organic Peace Café downstairs.

Chateau Tivoli B&B **$$**
(☎800-228-1647, 415-776-5462; www.chateautivoli.com; 1057 Steiner St; r incl breakfast $170-215, without bath $115-135, ste $275-300; 📶; 🚇5, 22) This glorious chateau off Alamo Sq once hosted Isadora Duncan and Mark Twain, and shows character with turrets, cornices, woodwork and, rumor has it, the ghost of a Victorian opera diva. No elevator; no TVs.

🍴 Eating

Hope you're hungry – there are 10 times more restaurants per capita in San Francisco than in any other US city. Most of San Francisco's top restaurants are quite small, so reserve ahead. For bargain eats, hit Mission taquerias, Chinatown dim-sum joints and North Beach delis.

🍴 SOMA, Union Square & Civic Center

Saigon Sandwich Shop VIETNAMESE **$**
(Map p128; ☎415-474-5698; saigon-sandwich.com; 560 Larkin St; sandwiches $3.50; ⏱7am-5pm; 🚇19, 31) Wait on a sketchy sidewalk for baguettes piled high with your choice of roast pork, chicken, pâté, meatballs and/or tofu, plus pickled carrots, cilantro, jalapeño and onion.

Brenda's French Soul Food CREOLE, SOUTHERN **$$**
(Map p128; ☎415-345-8100; www.frenchsoulfood.com; 652 Polk St; mains lunch $9-13, dinner $11-17; ⏱8am-3pm Mon & Tue, to 10pm Wed-Sat, to 8pm Sun; 🚇19, 31, 38, 47, 49) Chef–owner Brenda Buenviaje serves Cal-Creole classics, including Hangtown fry (eggs with bacon and fried oysters), shrimp-stuffed po' boys, fried chicken with collard greens, hot-pepper jelly and watermelon sweet tea.

⭐ **Rich Table** CALIFORNIAN **$$$**
(Map p128; ☎415-355-9085; http://richtablesf.com; 199 Gough St; meals $30-40; ⏱5:30-10pm Sun-Thu, to 10:30pm Fri-Sat; 🚇5, 6, 21, 47, 49, 71, Ⓜ Van Ness) ✎ Licking plates is the obvious move after finishing apricot soup with pancetta and rabbit canneloni with nasturtium cream. Co-chefs/co-owners/spouses Sarah and Evan Rich invent playful Californian food such as the Dirty Hippie: silky

goat-buttermilk panna cotta topped with nutty hemp. Book two to four weeks ahead (call the restaurant directly).

Sweet Woodruff　　　CAFE, CALIFORNIAN $$
(Map p128; ☑ 415-292-9090; www.sweetwoodruffsf.com; 798 Sutter St; dishes $8-13; ⏰11am–9:45pm; ☐2, 3, 27) ✐ Little sister to Michelin-starred Sons & Daughters, this storefront cafe uses seasonal-regional ingredients for small plates such as roasted padron peppers with fromage blanc and sea-urchin baked potatoes with bacon. There's no waiter service and no stove – just an oven, hot plate and imagination.

Zero Zero　　　PIZZA $$
(Map p128; ☑ 415-348-8800; www.zerozerosf.com; 826 Folsom St; pizzas $10-19; ⏰ 11:30am-2:30pm & 5:30-10pm Mon-Thu, to 11pm Fri, 11:30am-11pm Sat, 11:30am-10pm Sun; Ⓜ Powell, Ⓑ Powell) Neapolitan pizza credentials – '00' flour is used for Naples' famous puffy-edged crust – with inspired San Francisco–themed toppings. The cross-town, cross-cultural Geary includes Manila clams, bacon and chilies, and the crowd-pleasing Castro comes turbo-loaded with housemade sausage.

★**Benu**　　　CALIFORNIAN, FUSION $$$
(Map p128; ☑ 415-685-4860; www.benusf.com; 22 Hawthorne St; mains $26-42; ⏰5:30-10pm Tue-Sat; ☐10, 12, 14, 30, 45) San Francisco has refined fusion cuisine over 150 years, but no one rocks it quite like chef-owner Corey Lee (formerly of Napa's French Laundry), who remixes local, sustainable fine-dining staples and Pacific Rim flavors with a SoMa DJ's finesse. Dungeness crab and black-truffle custard bring such outsize flavor to faux-shark's-fin soup, you'll swear there's Jaws in there.

★**Jardinière**　　　CALIFORNIAN $$$
(Map p128; ☑ 415-861-5555; www.jardiniere.com; 300 Grove St; mains $19-37; ⏰5-10:30pm Tue-Sat, to 10pm Sun & Mon; ☐5, 21, 47, 49, Ⓜ Van Ness) ✐ Iron Chef, Top Chef Master and James Beard Award winner Traci des Jardins has a particular flair with California's organic vegetables, free-range meats and sustainably caught seafood. Housemade tagliatelle is lavished with bone marrow and velvety scallops are topped with satiny sea urchin. On Mondays $49 scores you three decadent courses with wine pairings.

Financial District, Chinatown & North Beach

★**Liguria Bakery**　　　BAKERY $
(Map p128; ☑ 415-421-3786; 1700 Stockton St; focaccia $4-5; ⏰8am-1pm Mon-Fri, from 7am Sat; ☑ ♿; ☐8X, 30, 39, 41, 45, 🚋 Powell-Mason) Bleary-eyed art students and Italian grandmothers line up by 8am for cinnamon-raisin focaccia hot from the 100-year-old oven, leaving 9am dawdlers a choice of tomato or classic rosemary/garlic and 11am stragglers out of luck. Cash only.

FIVE TASTY REASONS TO MISS THAT FERRY

When it comes to California dining, you'll be missing the boat unless you stop for local specialties at the Ferry Building:

➡ Today's catch at **Hog Island Oyster Company** (Map p128; ☑ 415-391-7117; www.hogislandoysters.com; 1 Ferry Bldg; 6 oysters $16-20; ⏰11:30am-8pm Mon-Fri, 11am-6pm Sat & Sun; Ⓜ Embarcadero, Ⓑ Embarcadero) ✐, including $1 oysters at happy hour.

➡ Gourmet picnic supplies from the **farmers market** (Map p128; ☑ 415-291-3276; www.cuesa.org; ⏰10am-2pm Tue & Thu, from 8am Sat) – especially 4505 artisan meats, Donna's tamales and Namu Gaji's Korean tacos.

➡ Iron Chef Traci des Jardins' *nuevo* Mexican street eats at **Mijita** (Map p128; ☑ 415-399-0814; www.mijitasf.com; 1 Ferry Bldg; dishes $4-8; ⏰10am-7pm Mon-Thu, to 8pm Fri-Sat, 8:30am-3pm Sun; ☑ ♿; Ⓜ Embarcadero, Ⓑ Embarcadero).

➡ Free-range beef burgers and sweet-potato fries at **Gott's Roadside** (Map p128; www.gotts.com; 1 Ferry Bldg; burgers $8-11; ⏰10:30am-10pm; ♿; Ⓜ Embarcadero, Ⓑ Embarcadero) ✐

➡ Cal-Vietnamese Dungeness crab over cellophane noodles at Charles Phan's family-operated **Slanted Door** (Map p128; ☑ 415-861-8032; www.slanteddoor.com; 1 Ferry Bldg; lunch $15-28, dinner $19-42; ⏰11am-2:30pm & 5:30-10pm Mon-Sat, 11:30-3pm & 5:30-10pm Sun; Ⓜ Embarcadero, Ⓑ Embarcadero).

City View
CHINESE $

(Map p128; ☑415-398-2838; 662 Commercial St; dishes $3-8; ⊙11am-2:30pm Mon-Fri, from 10am Sat & Sun; ☒8X, 10, 12, 30, 45, ☐California St) Take your seat in the sunny dining room and take your pick from carts loaded with delicate shrimp and leek dumplings, garlicky Chinese broccoli, tangy spare ribs, coconut-dusted custard tarts and other tantalizing dim sum.

Cinecittà
PIZZA $

(Map p128; ☑415-291-8830; www.cinecittaristaurant.com; 663 Union St; pizza $12-15; ⊙noon-10pm Sun-Thu, to 11pm Fri & Sat; ☑☑; ☒8X, 30, 39, 41, 45, ☐Powell-Mason) Follow tantalizing aromas into this 22-seat eatery for thin-crust Roman pizza, including the classic Travestere (fresh mozzarella, arugula and prosciutto) and Neapolitan O Sole Mio (capers, olives, mozzarella and anchovies). Local brews are on tap, house wine is $5 from 3pm to 7pm, and house-made tiramisu is SF's best.

★Cotogna
ITALIAN $$

(Map p128; ☑415-775-8508; www.cotognasf.com; 470 Pacific Ave; mains $14-26; ⊙11:30am-11:30pm Mon-Sat, 11:30am-2:30pm & 5-9pm Sun; ☑; ☒10, 12) Since chef-owner Michael Tusk won the James Beard Award for best chef, bookings are coveted at rustic Italian Cotogna (and fancier sister-restaurant Quince) for pristine pastas, toothsome wood-fired pizzas and rotisserie-caramelized meats.

Z & Y
CHINESE $$

(Map p128; ☑415-981-8988; www.zandyrestaurant.com; 655 Jackson St; mains $9-18; ⊙11am-10pm Mon-Thu, to 11pm Fri-Sun; ☒8X, ☐Powell-Mason, Powell-Hyde) Sensational Szechuan dishes that go down in a blaze of glory: spicy pork dumplings, heat-blistered string beans, housemade tantan noodles with peanut-chili sauce, and fish poached in flaming chili oil and buried under red Szechuan chili peppers. Go early; expect a wait.

Ristorante Ideale
ITALIAN $$

(Map p128; ☑415-391-4129; www.idealeristorante.com; 1315 Grant Ave; pasta $15-18; ⊙5:30-10:30pm Mon-Thu, to 11pm Fri-Sat, 5-10pm Sun; ☒8X, 10, 12, 30, 41, 45, ☐Powell-Mason) Roman chef Maurizio Bruschi serves authentic *bucatini ammatriciana* (tube pasta with tomato-pecorino sauce and house-cured pancetta), and ravioli and gnocchi that are both handmade and housemade ('of course!'). Ask the Tuscan staff to recommend well-priced wine, and everyone goes home happy.

★Coi
CALIFORNIAN $$$

(Map p128; ☑415-393-9000; www.coiristorant.com; 373 Broadway; set menu $175; ⊙5:30-10pm Wed-Sat; ☑; ☒8X, 30, 41, 45, ☐Powell-Mason) ✔ Chef-owner Daniel Patterson's imaginative eight-course tasting menu is like licking the California coastline: purple ice-plant petals are strewn atop warm duck's tongue, and wild-caught Monterey Bay abalone appears in a tidepool of pea shoots, inducing a uniquely Golden State of bliss.

★ Fisherman's Wharf & the Marina

Off the Grid
FOOD TRUCK $

(Map p128; www.offthegridsf.com; dishes $5-10; ⊙5-10pm Fri; ☒22, 28) Thirty food trucks circle their wagons at Fort Mason for mobile gourmet feasts. Arrive before 6:30pm or expect 20-minute waits for Chairman Bao's clam-shell buns with duck and mango, Roli Roti's free-range herbed roast chicken, and dessert from the Crème Brûlée Man. Cash only.

In-N-Out Burger
BURGERS $

(Map p128; ☑800-786-1000; www.in-n-out.com; 333 Jefferson St; meals under $10; ⊙10:30am-1am Sun-Thu, to 1:30am Fri & Sat; ☑; ☒30, 47, ☐Powell-Hyde) Prime chuck beef processed on site, plus fries and shakes made with ingredients you can pronounce, all served by employees paid a living wage. Order yours off the menu 'animal style' – cooked in mustard with grilled onions.

★Greens
VEGETARIAN, CALIFORNIAN $$

(Map p128; ☑415-771-6222; www.greensrestaurant.com; Bldg A, Fort Mason Center, cnr Marina Blvd & Laguna St; lunch $15-17, dinner $17-24; ⊙11:45am-2:30pm & 5:30-9pm Tue-Fri, from 11am Sat, 10:30am-2pm & 5:30-9pm Sun, 5:30-9pm Mon; ☑; ☒28) ✔ Career carnivores won't realize there's zero meat in the hearty black-bean chili with crème fraîche and pickled jalapeños or in the roasted eggplant panini packed with ingredients mostly grown on a Zen organic farm. Enjoy takeout on a wharfside bench; reserve ahead for weekend dinners or Sunday brunch.

★Gary Danko
CALIFORNIAN $$$

(Map p128; ☑415-749-2060; www.garydanko.com; 800 North Point St; 3-/5-course menu $73/107; ⊙5:30-10pm; ☒19, 30, 47, ☐Powell-Hyde) Smoked-glass windows prevent passersby from tripping over their tongues at the sight of James Beard Award–winning feasts: roasted lobster with trumpet mushrooms, blushing duck breast and rhubarb compote, lavish cheeses and trios of crèmes brûlées. Reservations required.

✕ The Mission

★ La Taqueria
MEXICAN $

(☑ 415-285-7117; 2889 Mission St; burritos $6-8; ⏱ 11am-9pm Mon-Sat, to 8pm Sun; ⵌ; 🚇 12, 14, 48, 49, Ⓑ 24th St Mission) The definitive burrito at La Taqueria has no debatable saffron rice, spinach tortilla or mango salsa, just perfectly grilled meats, slow-cooked beans and classic *tomatillo* or *mesquite* salsa wrapped in a flour tortilla. Spicy pickles and *crema* (Mexican sour cream) complete the burrito bliss.

★ Namu Gaji
KOREAN, CALIFORNIAN $$

(☑ 415-431-6268; www.namusf.com; 499 Dolores St; small plates $8-22; ⏱ 11:30am-10pm Tue-Thu, to 11pm Fri & Sat; 🚇 22, 33, Ⓜ J, Ⓑ 16th St Mission) ◢ San Francisco's unfair culinary advantages – organic local ingredients, Silicon Valley inventiveness and Pacific Rim roots – are showcased in Namu's Korean-inspired soul food. Menu standouts include ultrasavory shiitake-mushroom dumplings, tender marinated beef tongue, and Marin Sun Farms grass-fed steak atop sizzling rice served in a stone pot.

★ Commonwealth
CALIFORNIAN $$$

(☑ 415-355-1500; www.commonwealthsf.com; 2224 Mission St; small plates $11-16; ⏱ 5:30-10pm Sun-Thu, to 11pm Fri & Sat; ⵌ; 🚇 14, 22, 33, 49, Ⓑ 16th St Mission) California's most imaginative farm-to-table dining isn't in some quaint barn but in a converted cinderblock Mission dive. Here chef Jason Fox serves green strawberries and black radishes with fennel pollen,

GOURMET TO GO

Bi-Rite (☑ 415-241-9760; www.biritemarket.com; 3639 18th St; sandwiches $7-10; ⏱ 9am-9pm; ⵌ; 🚇 14, 22, 33, 49, Ⓑ 16th St Mission) Nemesis of grocery budgets and ally of foodies best at reheating, the Bi-Rite store in the Mission area displays artisan chocolates, sustainable cured meats and organic fruit like jewels, with dazzling California wine-and-cheese selections. Get deli sandwiches to go to Dolores Park.

and poached oysters atop foraged succulents and rhubarb ice. Savor the $75 prix-fixe knowing $10 is donated to charity.

✕ The Castro

Chilango
MEXICAN $$

(☑ 415-552-5700; www.chilangorestaurantsf.com; 235 Church St; dishes $8-12; ⏱ 11am-10pm; Ⓜ Church) ◢ Upgrade from taqueria to sit-down restaurant at this casual Mexican spot that uses all-organic ingredients in filet-mignon tacos, chicken *mole* (cocoa-based sauce) and succulent carnitas (roast pork).

Starbelly
CALIFORNIAN, PIZZA $$

(☑ 415-252-7500; www.starbellysf.com; 3583 16th St; dishes $6-19; ⏱ 11:30am-11pm Sun-Thu, to midnight Fri & Sat; Ⓜ Castro) ◢ Nab a spot on the heated garden patio for *salumi* (Italian cured meat), market-fresh salads, scrumptious pâté, roasted mussels with housemade sausage and thin-crust pizzas.

★ Frances
CALIFORNIAN $$$

(☑ 415-621-3870; www.frances-sf.com; 3870 17th St; mains $27-28; ⏱ 5-10.30pm Tue-Sun; Ⓜ Castro) Chef-owner Melissa Perello's daily menus showcase bright, seasonal flavors and luxurious textures: cloudlike sheep's milk ricotta gnocchi with crunchy breadcrumbs and broccolini, grilled calamari with preserved Meyer lemon, and Sonoma artisan wine on tap.

✕ The Haight

★ Rosamunde Sausage Grill
FAST FOOD $

(Map p128; ☑ 415-437-6851; http://rosamunde sausagegrill.com; 545 Haight St; sausages $4-6; ⏱ 11:30am-10pm; 🚇 6, 22, 71, Ⓜ N) Impress a dinner date on the cheap: load up classic Brats or duck-fig links with complimentary roasted peppers, grilled onions, wholegrain mustard and mango chutney. Enjoy with your choice from 100 beers at Toronado, next door.

Ragazza
PIZZA $$

(☑ 415-255-1133; www.ragazzasf.com; 311 Divisadero St; pizza $13-18; ⏱ 5-10pm Mon-Thu, to 10:30 Fri & Sat; ⵌ; 🚇 6, 21, 24, 71) 'Girl' is what the name means, as in, 'Oooh, *girl,* did you try the potato-leek pizza?!' Artisan *salumi* is the star of many Ragazza pies, from the Amatriciana with pecorino, bacon and egg to the pork belly with Calabrian chili and beet greens. Arrive early to nab garden patio tables.

Magnolia Brewpub
CALIFORNIAN, AMERICAN $$

(☑415-864-7468; www.magnoliapub.com; 1398 Haight St; mains $11-20; ⊙11am-midnight Mon-Thu, to 1am Fri, 10am-1am Sat, to midnight Sun; ☐6, 33, 43, 71) ✒ Organic pub grub and home-brew samplers keep conversation flowing at communal tables, while grass-fed Prather Ranch burgers satisfy stoner appetites in the booths – it's like the Summer of Love all over again, only with better food.

Japantown & Pacific Heights

Benkyodo
JAPANESE $

(Map p128; ☑415-922-1244; www.benkyodocompany.com; 1747 Buchanan St; dishes $1-10; ⊙8am-5pm Mon-Sat; ☐2, 3, 22, 38) The perfect retro lunch counter cheerfully serves an old-school egg-salad sandwich or pastrami for $5, but the real draw is the $1.25 *mochi* (Japanese filled rice cake) made in-house daily – come early for popular flavors including green tea and chocolate-filled strawberry. Cash only.

Tataki
JAPANESE, SUSHI $$

(☑415-931-1182; www.tatakisushibar.com; 2815 California St; dishes $12-20; ⊙11:30am-2pm & 5:30-10:30pm Mon-Thu, to 11:30pm Fri, 5-11:30pm Sat, 5-9:30pm Sun; ☐1, 24) ✒ Pioneering sushi chefs Kin Lui and Raymond Ho rescue dinner and the oceans with sustainable delicacies: silky Arctic char drizzled with yuzu-citrus replaces at-risk wild salmon; and the Golden State Roll features spicy, line-caught scallop, Pacific tuna, organic-apple slivers and edible 24-carat gold.

State Bird Provisions
CALIFORNIAN $$

(Map p128; ☑415-795-1272; statebirdsf.com; 1529 Fillmore St; ⊙5:30pm-10pm Mon-Thu, to 11pm Fri-Sat; ☐22, 38) Forget Kentucky-fried: San Francisco prefers its poultry creative, locally sourced and dim-sum-sized. Pumpkin seeds and baguette crumbs are secrets to the golden state bird (quail), the signature of this high-concept, low-key California cuisine hot spot, which was the 2013 James Beard Award winner for best new restaurant in America. Reserve ahead or join the 5pm bar-seat line.

The Richmond

★Outerlands
CALIFORNIAN $$

(Map p126; ☑415-661-6140; www.outerlandssf.com; 4001 Judah St; sandwiches & small plates $8-9, mains $12-27; ⊙11am-3pm & 6-10pm Tue-Fri, 10am-3pm & 5:30-10pm Sat & Sun; 🚼; ☐18, Ⓜ N) ✒ When windy Ocean Beach leaves you feeling shipwrecked, drift into this beach-shack bistro for organic California comfort food. Brunch demands Dutch pancakes in iron skillets with housemade ricotta, lunch brings $12 grilled artisan cheese combos with farm-inspired soup, and slow-cooked lamb shoulder slouches on flatbread at dinner. Reserve ahead.

★Aziza
MOROCCAN, CALIFORNIAN $$$

(Map p126; ☑415-752-2222; www.aziza-sf.com; 5800 Geary Blvd; mains $16-29; ⊙5:30-10:30pm Wed-Mon; ☐1, 29, 31, 38) Chef Mourad Lahlou's inspiration is Moroccan, his ingredients organic Californian, and his flavors out of this world: Sonoma duck confit melts into caramelized onion inside flaky pastry *basteeya*, while saffron infuses slow-cooked local lamb atop barley.

🍷 Drinking & Nightlife

For a pub crawl, your best bets are North Beach saloons or Mission bars around Valencia and 16th St. Top chefs serve craft cocktails downtown, Hayes Valley has wine bars and the Tenderloin mixes dives with speakeasies. The Castro has historic gay bars and SoMa has leather bars, while Marina bars are preppy and straight, and Haight bars draw mixed alterna-crowds.

★Bar Agricole
BAR

(Map p128; ☑415-355-9400; www.baragricole.com; 355 11th St; ⊙6-10pm Sun-Wed, to late Thu-Sat; ☐9, 12, 27, 47) Drink your way to a history degree with well-researched cocktails: Bellamy Scotch Sour with egg whites passes the test, but Tequila Fix with lime, pineapple gum and hellfire bitters earns honors. For its modern design with natural materials and a sleek deck, Agricole won a James Beard Award.

★Smuggler's Cove
BAR

(Map p128; ☑415-869-1900; www.smugglerscovesf.com; 650 Gough St; ⊙5pm-1:15am; ☐5, 21, 49, Ⓜ Van Ness) Yo-ho-ho and a bottle of rum...or perhaps you'll try a Dead Reckoning with Angostura bitters, Nicaraguan rum, tawny port and vanilla liqueur, unless someone will share the flaming Scorpion Bowl? With 400 rums and 70 cocktails gleaned from rum-running around the world, you won't be dry-docked long.

★ **Comstock Saloon** BAR

(Map p128; ☑415-617-0071; www.comstocksaloon. com; 155 Columbus Ave; ☺4pm-2am Sat-Thu, from noon Fri; ☐8X, 10, 12, 30, 45, ☐Powell-Mason) Welcome to the Barbary Coast, where cocktails at this Victorian saloon remain period-perfect: Pisco Punch is made with pineapple gum, and martini-precursor Martinez features gin, vermouth, bitters and maraschino liqueur. Call ahead to claim booths or tufted-velvet parlour seating.

★ **Toronado** PUB

(Map p128; ☑415-863-2276; www.toronado.com; 547 Haight St; ☺11:30am-2am; ☐6, 22, 71, Ⓜ N) Glory hallelujah, beer-lovers: your prayers have been heard with 50-plus beers on tap and hundreds more bottled, including spectacular seasonal microbrews. Bring cash. Order sausages from Rosamunde next door to accompany ale made by Trappist monks.

★ **Specs Museum Cafe** BAR

(Map p128; ☑415-421-4112; 12 William Saroyan Pl; ☺5pm-2am; ☐8X, 10, 12, 30, 41, 45, ☐Powell-Mason) What do you do with a drunken sailor? Here's your answer. The walls are plastered with Merchant Marine mementos, and you'll be plastered too if you try to keep up with the salty old-timers holding court in back. Your order is obvious: pitcher of Anchor Steam, coming right up.

★ **Elixir** BAR

(☑415-522-1633; www.elixirsf.com; 3200 16th St; ☺3pm-2am Mon-Fri, noon-2am Sat & Sun; ☐16th St Mission) ✐ Do the planet a favor and have a drink at San Francisco's first certified-green bar in an actual 1858 Wild West saloon. Elixir serves knock-out cocktails made with farm-fresh organic mixers and small-batch spirits that will get you air-guitar-rocking to the killer jukebox.

GAY/LES/BI/TRANS SAN FRANCISCO

Doesn't matter where you're from, who you love or who's your daddy: if you're here, and queer, welcome home. The Castro is the heart of the gay cruising scene, but South of Market (SoMa) has thump-thump clubs. The Mission is the preferred 'hood of alt-chicks, trans FTMs (female-to-males) and flirty femmes. *Bay Area Reporter* (aka BAR; www.ebar.com) covers community news and listings; *San Francisco Bay Times* (www. sfbaytimes.com) also has good resources for transsexuals; free mag *Gloss Magazine* (www.glossmagazine.net) covers nightlife. For roving dance parties, check Honey Soundsystem (Map p128; www.honeysoundsystem.com); Juanita More (www.juanita-more.com); and Sisters of Perpetual Indulgence (www.thesisters.org). San Francisco is home to some top GLBT venues.

Stud (Map p128; ☑415-252-7883; www.studsf.com; 399 9th St; admission $5-8; ☺5pm-3am; ☐12, 19, 27, 47) Join parties in-progress since 1966: Meow Mix Tuesday drag variety shows; Wednesday raunchy comedy; and Friday 'Some-thing' parties with midnight drag, pool-table crafts and dance beats.

Aunt Charlie's (Map p128; ☑415-441-2922; www.auntcharlieslounge.com; 133 Turk St; admission $5; Ⓜ Powell, Ⓑ Powell) Divey Aunt Charlie's brings vintage pulp-fiction covers to life with drag Hot Boxxx Girls Friday and Saturday nights (call for reservations) and Thursday's Tubesteak Connection ($5), featuring vintage porn and '80s disco.

EndUp (Map p128; www.theendup.com; 401 6th St; admission $5-20; ☺10pm-4am Mon-Thu, 11pm-11am Fri, 10pm Sat-4am Mon; ☐12, 27, 47) Anyone on the streets after 2am weekends is subject to the magnetic pull of the EndUp's marathon dance sessions and gay Sunday tea dances, in full force since 1973.

Lexington Club (☑415-863-2052; www.lexingtonclub.com; 3464 19th St; ☺3pm-2am; ☐14, 33, 49, Ⓑ 16th St Mission) San Francisco's all-grrrrl bar can be cliquish, so compliment someone on her skirt (she designed it herself) or tattoo (ditto) and mention you're un-defeated at pinball, pool or thumb-wrestling. When she wins (because she's no stranger to the Lex), pout and maybe she'll buy you a $4 beer.

Cafe Flore (☑415-621-8579; www.cafeflore.com; 2298 Market St; ☺7am-midnight Sun-Thu, to 2am Fri & Sat; ☎; Ⓜ Castro) You haven't done the Castro till you've unwound on Flore's sunny patio. Great happy-hour drink specials, such as two-for-one margaritas. Wi-fi weekdays only, no electrical outlets.

Zeitgeist
BAR

(☑ 415-255-7505; www.zeitgeistsf.com; 199 Valencia St; ⊙ 9am-2am; 🚌 22, 49, Ⓑ 16th St Mission) You've got two seconds flat to order one of 40 beers on draft from tough-gal barkeeps used to putting macho bikers in their place. Regulars head straight to the bar's huge graveled beer garden to sit at long picnic tables to smoke. Bring cash for the bar and for late-night food vendors who circulate.

Trick Dog
BAR

(☑ 415-471-2999; www.trickdogbar.com; 3010 20th St; ⊙ 3pm-2am; 🚌 12, 14, 49) Choose your drink by Pantone-paint-swatch color: Razzle Dazzle Red gets you local Hangar One vodka with house cordials, strawberries and lime, while Gypsy Tan means Rittenhouse rye with Fernet, lemon-ginger and nutmeg.

El Rio
CLUB

(☑ 415-282-3325; www.elriosf.com; 3158 Mission St; admission $3-8; ⊙ 1pm-2am; 🚌 12, 14, 27, 49, Ⓑ 24th St Mission) The DJ mix at El Rio takes its cue from the patrons: eclectic, fearless, funky and sexy, no matter your orientation. Powerful margaritas will get you bopping to disco-post-punk mashups and flirting shamelessly in the back garden. Cash only.

☆ Entertainment

TIX Bay Area (Map p128; www.tixbayarea.org) sells last-minute theater tickets half-price. Other event listings are covered in *7x7* magazine (www.7x7.com), *SF Bay Guardian* (www.sfbg.com) newspaper, *SF Weekly* (www.sfweekly.com) newspaper and Squid List (www.squidlist.com/events) blog.

Live Music

★ SFJAZZ Center
JAZZ

(Map p128; ☑ 866-920-5299; www.sfjazz.org; 201 Franklin St; ⊙ showtimes vary; 🚌 5, 7, 21, Ⓜ Van Ness) Jazz greats coast-to-coast and further afield from Argentina to Yemen are showcased at America's newest, largest, LEED-certified green jazz center. The San Francisco Jazz Festival takes place here in July, but year-round the calendar features such legends as McCoy Tyner, Regina Carter, Bela Flek and Tony Bennett (who left his heart here, after all). Upper-tier cheap seats are more like stools, but offer clear stage views.

Fillmore Auditorium
LIVE MUSIC

(Map p128; ☑ 415-346-6000; http://thefillmore.com; 1805 Geary Blvd; admission $15-50; ⊙ box office 10am-4pm Sun, 7:30-10pm show nights; 🚌 22, 38) Jimi Hendrix, Janis Joplin, the Doors – they all played the Fillmore. Now you might catch the Indigo Girls, Duran Duran or Tracy Chapman in the historic 1250-capacity standing-room theater; don't miss the '60s psychedelic posters in the upstairs gallery.

Slim's
LIVE MUSIC

(Map p128; ☑ 415-255-0333; www.slims-sf.com; 333 11th St; tickets $12-30; ⊙ 5pm-2am; 🚌 9, 12, 27, 47) Guaranteed good times by Gogol Bordello, Tenacious D and the Expendables fit the bill at this midsized club, owned by R&B star Boz Skaggs. Shows are all-ages, though shorties may have a hard time seeing once the floor starts bouncing. Reserve dinner for $25, and score seats on the small balcony.

Mezzanine
LIVE MUSIC

(Map p128; ☑ 415-625-8880; www.mezzaninesf.com; 444 Jessie St; admission $10-40; Ⓜ Powell, Ⓑ Powell) Big nights come with bragging rights at the Mezzanine, which has one of the city's best sound systems. Crowds are hyped for alt-bands, breakthrough hip-hop and R&B shows by Wyclef Jean, Quest Love, Method Man, Nas and Snoop Dogg.

Great American Music Hall
LIVE MUSIC

(Map p128; ☑ 415-885-0750; www.gamh.com; 859 O'Farrell St; admission $12-35; ⊙ box office 10:30am-6pm Mon-Fri & on show nights; 🚌 19, 38, 47, 49) Once a bordello, the rococo Great American Music Hall has a balcony with table seating, a top-notch sound system, and reasonable food and drinks. Music ranges from alt-rock and metal to jazz and bluegrass.

Yoshi's
JAZZ, LIVE MUSIC

(Map p128; ☑ 415-655-5600; www.yoshis.com; 1300 Fillmore St; ⊙ shows 8pm and/or 10pm Tue-Sun, dinner Tue-Sun; 🚌 22, 31) San Francisco's definitive jazz club draws the world's top talent, and hosts appearances by the likes of Leon Redbone and Nancy Wilson, along with occasional classical and gospel acts. Students: ask about half-priced tickets.

Cafe du Nord/Swedish American Hall
LIVE MUSIC

(☑ 415-861-5016; www.cafedunord.com; 2170 Market St; cover varies; Ⓜ Church) Rockers, chanteuses, comedians, raconteurs and burlesque acts perform nightly at this former basement speakeasy with bar and showroom, and the joint still looks like it did in the '30s.

Drag

Cat Club
DRAG

(Map p128; www.catclubsf.com; 1190 Folsom St; admission after 10pm $5; ⏰9pm-3am Tue-Sun; Ⓜ Civic Center, Ⓑ Civic Center) You never really know your friends till you've seen them belt out A-ha's 'Take on Me' at 1984, Cat Club's Thursday-night retro dance party. Tuesdays it's karaoke, Wednesdays Bondage-a-Go-Go, Fridays Goth, and Saturdays '90s power pop – but confirm online, lest you dress the wrong part.

DNA Lounge
DRAG

(Map p128; www.dnalounge.com; 375 11th St; admission $3-25; ⏰9pm-3am Fri & Sat, other nights vary; 🚌12, 27, 47) One of San Francisco's last megaclubs hosts live bands, mash-up dance party Bootie, epic drag at Trannyshack, and Monday's 18-and-over Goth Death Guild. Early arrivals may hear crickets.

AsiaSF
DRAG CABARET

(Map p128; ☎415-255-2742; www.asiasf.com; 201 9th St; per person from $39; ⏰7-11pm Wed & Thu, 7pm-2am Fri, 5pm-2am Sat, 7-10pm Sun, reservation line 1-8pm; Ⓜ Civic Center, Ⓑ Civic Center) Cocktails and Asian-inspired dishes are served with sass and a secret: your servers are drag stars. Every hour, they dance atop the bar, while gaggles of girlfriends squeal and straight blushing businessmen play along. Once inspiration and drinks kick in, everyone mixes it up on the downstairs dance floor.

Classical Music & Opera

★ Davies Symphony Hall
CLASSICAL MUSIC

(Map p128; ☎415-864-6000; www.sfsymphony.org; 201 Van Ness Ave; Ⓜ Van Ness, Ⓑ Civic Center) Home of nine-time Grammy-winning San Francisco Symphony, conducted with verve by Michael Tilson Thomas. The season runs September to July.

★ San Francisco Opera
OPERA

(Map p128; ☎415-864-3330; www.sfopera.com; War Memorial Opera House, 301 Van Ness Ave; tickets $10-350; Ⓑ Civic Center, Ⓜ Van Ness) San Francisco has been obsessed with opera since the gold rush, and it remains a staple from July to December. Tuesdays attract local socialites, when you can spot fabulous gowns and tuxedos. After 10am, the box office sells 150 standing-room spots ($10; cash only); snag empty seats after intermission.

San Francisco Ballet
DANCE

(Map p128; ☎415-861-5600, tickets 415-865-2000; www.sfballet.org; War Memorial Opera House, 301 Van Ness Ave; tickets $10-120; Ⓜ Van Ness) The San Francisco Ballet is America's oldest ballet company and the first to premier the *Nutcracker*. The company regularly performs at War Memorial Opera House.

Theater

★ American Conservatory Theater
THEATER

(ACT; Map p128; ☎415-749-2228; www.act-sf.org; 415 Geary St; 🚌38, 🚋 Powell-Mason, Powell-Hyde) Breakthrough shows begin at ACT's turn-of-the-century Geary Theater, which has launched Tony Kushner's *Angels in America* and Robert Wilson's *Black Rider,* with a libretto by William S Burroughs and music by the Bay Area's own Tom Waits. ACT's **Strand Theater** (1127 Market St) is scheduled to open late 2014.

Beach Blanket Babylon
CABARET

(BBB; Map p128; ☎415-421-4222; www.beachblanketbabylon.com; 678 Green St; admission $25-100; ⏰shows 8pm Wed, Thu & Fri, 6:30pm & 9:30pm Sat, 2pm & 5pm Sun; 🚌8X, 🚋 Powell-Mason) Snow White searches for Prince Charming in San Francisco: what could possibly go wrong? The Disney-gone-drag musical-comedy cabaret has been running since 1974, but topical jokes keep it outrageous and wigs as big as parade floats are gasp-worthy.

Cinemas

★ Castro Theatre
CINEMA

(☎415-621-6120; www.thecastrotheatre.com; 429 Castro St; adult/child $11/8.50; ⏰Tue-Sun; Ⓜ Castro) The Mighty Wurlitzer organ rises from the deco movie palace's orchestra pit before evening shows, ending with (sing along, now): 'San Francisco open your Golden Gate/ You let no stranger wait outside your door...'

★ Roxie Cinema
CINEMA

(☎415-863-1087; www.roxie.com; 3117 16th St; regular screening/matinee $10/7; 🚌14, 22, 33, 49, Ⓑ 16th St Mission) A little neighborhood non-profit cinema with major international clout for indie premieres, controversial films and documentaries banned elsewhere. No ads; personal introductions to every film.

Sundance Kabuki Cinema
CINEMA

(Map p128; ☎415-929-4650; www.sundancecinemas.com; 1881 Post St; adult $9.50-15, child $9; 🚌2, 3, 22, 38) 🌿 A multiplex initiative by Robert Redford's Sundance Institute,

Kabuki features big-name flicks and festivals, served with local chocolates and booze. And it's green, with recycled-fiber seating.

Sports

San Francisco Giants BASEBALL
(Map p128; http://sanfrancisco.giants.mlb.com; AT&T Park; tickets $5-135) Watch and learn how the World Series is won – bushy beards, women's underwear and all.

San Francisco 49ers FOOTBALL
(Map p126; ☑415-656-4900; www.sf49ers.com; Levi's Stadium from 2014; tickets $25-100 at www.ticketmaster.com; ☒T) The 49ers were the National Football League dream team from 1981 to 1994, claiming five Superbowl championships. After decades shivering through games and a fumbled bid for the 2012 Superbowl, the 49ers have a new home in 2014: Santa Clara's brand-new Levi's Stadium.

🔒 Shopping

★City Lights BOOKS
(Map p128; ☑415-362-8193; www.citylights.com; 261 Columbus Ave; ☉10am-midnight; ☒8X, 10, 12, 30, 41, 45, ☒Powell-Mason, Powell-Hyde) 'Abandon all despair, all ye who enter,' orders the sign by the door to City Lights bookstore by founder and San Francisco poet laureate Lawrence Ferlinghetti. This commandment is easy to follow when you're upstairs in the sunny **Poetry Room**, with freshly published verse, designated **Poet's Chair** and views over Jack Kerouac Alley.

★New People CLOTHING, GIFTS
(Map p128; www.newpeopleworld.com; 1746 Post St; ☉noon-7pm Mon-Sat, to 6pm Sun; ☒2, 3, 22, 38) Wall-to-wall *kawaii* (cuteness): Japanimation T-shirts; *Alice in Wonderland*–inspired Lolita fashions at 2nd-floor **Baby the Stars Shine Bright**; ninja shoes with contemporary graphics at **Sou-Sou**; contemporary art at **Superfrog Gallery**; and tea cakes at **Crown & Crumpet**.

★Betabrand CLOTHING
(☑800-694-9491; www.betabrand.com; 780 Valencia St; ☉11am-6pm Fri-Sat, noon-6pm Sun; ☒14, 22, 33, 49, ☒16th St Mission) Crowd-source fashion decisions at Betabrand, where experimental designs are put to an online vote, and winners are produced in limited editions: lunch-meat-patterned socks, reversible smoking jackets, disco-ball windbreakers and bike-to-work pants with reflective-strip cuffs.

ℹ️ Information

EMERGENCY & MEDICAL SERVICES

American College of Traditional Chinese Medicine (☑415-282-9603; www.actcm.edu; 450 Connecticut St; ☉8:30am-9pm Mon-Thu, 9am-5:30pm Fri & Sat; ☒10, 19, 22) Acupuncture, herbal remedies and other traditional Chinese medical treatments provided at low cost.

Haight Ashbury Free Clinic (☑415-762-3700; www.healthright360.org; 558 Clayton St; ☉by appointment; ☒6, 33, 37, 43, 71, ☒N) Clinic whose services are offered by appointment only; provides substance abuse and mental-health services.

Police, Fire & Ambulance (☑911, nonemergency 311)

San Francisco General Hospital (☑emergency 415-206-8111, main hospital 415-206-8000; www.sfdph.org; 1001 Potrero Ave; ☉24hr; ☒9, 10, 33, 48) Provides care to uninsured patients, including psychiatric care; no documentation required beyond ID.

Trauma Recovery & Rape Treatment Center (☑415-437-3000; www.traumarecoverycenter.org) A 24-hour hotline.

Walgreens (☑415-861-3136; www.walgreens.com; 498 Castro St, cnr 18th St; ☉24hr; ☒24, 33, 35, ☒F, K, L, M) Pharmacy and over-the-counter meds; dozens of locations citywide.

BEST SHOPPING AREAS

All those rustic-chic dens, well-stocked cupboards and fabulous outfits don't just pull themselves together – San Franciscans scoured their city for it all. Here's where to find what:

Hayes Valley Local and independent designers, home design, sweets, shoes.

Valencia St Bookstores, local design collectives, art galleries, vintage whatever.

Haight St Head shops, music, vintage, skate, snow and surf gear.

Upper Fillmore & Union Sts Date outfits, girly accessories, wine and design.

Powell & Market Sts Department stores, megabrands, discount retail, Apple store.

Grant St From Chinatown souvenirs to eccentric North Beach boutiques.

Ferry Building Local food, wine and kitchenware.

INTERNET ACCESS

San Francisco has free wi-fi hot spots citywide – locate one nearby with www.openwifispots.com. Connect for free in Union Sq, most cafes and hotel lobbies.

Apple Store (www.apple.com/retail/sanfrancisco; 1 Stockton St; ☉9am-9pm Mon-Sat, 10am-8pm Sun; @ 🛜; Ⓜ Powell St) Free wi-fi and internet terminal usage.

San Francisco Main Library (www.sfpl.org; 100 Larkin St; ☉10am-6pm Mon & Sat, 9am-8pm Tue-Thu, noon-5pm Fri & Sun; @ 🛜; Ⓜ Civic Center) Free 15-minute internet terminal usage; spotty wi-fi access.

MEDIA

KALW 91.7 FM (www.kalw.org) National Public Radio (NPR) affiliate.

KPFA 94.1 FM (www.kpfa.org) Alternative news and music.

KPOO 89.5 FM (www.kpoo.com) Community radio with jazz, R & B, blues and reggae.

KQED 88.5 FM (www.kqed.org) NPR and Public Broadcasting (PBS) affiliate offering podcasts and streaming video.

San Francisco Bay Guardian (www.sfbg.com) San Francisco's free, alternative weekly covers politics, theater, music, art and movie listings.

San Francisco Chronicle (www.sfgate.com) Main daily newspaper with news, entertainment and event listings.

MONEY

Bank of America (www.bankamerica.com; 1 Market Plaza; ☉9am-6pm Mon-Fri)

POST

Rincon Center Post Office (Map p128; ☑800-275-8777; www.usps.gov; 180 Steuart St; ☉8am-6pm Mon-Fri, 9am-2pm Sat; Ⓜ Embarcadero, Ⓑ Embarcadero) Postal services, plus historic murals in historic wing.

TOURIST INFORMATION

San Francisco Visitor Information Center (Map p128; ☑415-391-2000, events hotline 415-391-2001; www.onlyinsanfrancisco.com; Market & Powell Sts, lower level, Hallidie Plaza; ☉9am-5pm Mon-Fri, to 3pm Sat & Sun; 🚠 Powell-Mason, Powell-Hyde, Ⓜ Powell St, Ⓑ Powell St) Provides practical information for tourists, publishes glossy tourist-oriented booklets and runs a 24-hour events hotline.

WEBSITES

The global social media platforms **Craigslist** (http://sfbay.craigslist.org), **Twitter** (www.twitter.com) and **Yelp** (www.yelp.com) were all invented in San Francisco and are city institutions; check them out for news on pop-up shops, free shows, bar and restaurant reviews and the like.

❶ Getting There & Away

AIR

San Francisco International Airport (SFO; www.flysfo.com) is 14 miles south of downtown off Hwy 101 and accessible by Bay Area Rapid Transit (BART). **Oakland International Airport** (OAK; ☑510-563-3300; www.oaklandairport.com) serves primarily domestic destinations and is located about a 50-minute drive or BART ride across the Bay from San Francisco.

BUS

Until 2017, San Francisco's intercity hub remains the **Temporary Transbay Terminal** (Map p128; Howard & Main Sts), where you can catch buses on **AC Transit** (☑511; www.actransit.org) to the East Bay, **Golden Gate Transit** (Map p128; www.goldengatetransit.org) north to Marin and Sonoma Counties, and SamTrans south to Palo Alto and the Pacific coast. **Greyhound** (☑800-231-2222; www.greyhound.com) buses leave daily for Los Angeles ($59, eight to 12 hours), Truckee near Lake Tahoe ($31, 5½ hours) and other destinations.

TRAIN

Amtrak (☑800-872-7245; www.amtrakcalifornia.com) offers rail passes that are good for seven days of travel in California within a 21-day period (from $159). *Coast Starlight*'s spectacular 35-hour run from Los Angeles to Seattle stops in Oakland, and *California Zephyr* takes its sweet time (51 hours) from Chicago to Oakland. Both have sleeping cars and dining/lounge cars with panoramic windows. Amtrak runs free shuttle buses to San Francisco's Ferry Building and CalTrain station.

CalTrain (www.caltrain.com; cnr 4th & King Sts) connects San Francisco with Silicon Valley hubs and San Jose.

❶ Getting Around

For Bay Area transit options, departures and arrivals, call ☑511 or check www.511.org.

TO/FROM SAN FRANCISCO INTERNATIONAL AIRPORT

A taxi to downtown San Francisco costs $35 to $50.

BART (Bay Area Rapid Transit; www.bart.gov; one way $8.25) Fast 30-minute ride to/from downtown San Francisco from/to SFO BART station of the International Terminal.

SamTrans (www.samtrans.com; one way $5) Express bus KX takes about 30 minutes to reach Temporary Transbay Terminal.

SuperShuttle (☑800-258-3826; www.supershuttle.com) Shared van rides to downtown San Francisco for $17.

TO/FROM OAKLAND INTERNATIONAL AIRPORT

From Oakland International Airport, take the AirBART shuttle ($3) to Coliseum station to catch BART to downtown San Francisco ($3.85); take a shared van to downtown for $27 to $35 with SuperShuttle; or or pay $55 to $70 for a taxi to San Francisco destinations.

BOAT

Blue & Gold Ferries (Map p128; www.blueand-goldfleet.com) operates the Alameda–Oakland ferry from Pier 41 and the Ferry Building. **Golden Gate Ferry** (www.goldengateferry.org) runs from the Ferry Building to Sausalito and Larkspur in Marin County.

CAR

Avoid driving in San Francisco if possible: street parking is elusive and meter readers are ruthless. Downtown parking lots are at Embarcadero Center, 5th and Mission Sts, Union Sq, and Sutter and Stockton Sts. National car-rental agencies have airport and downtown offices.

PUBLIC TRANSPORTATION

MUNI (Municipal Transit Agency; ☑511; www.sfmta.com) operates bus, streetcar and cable-car lines; *MUNI Street & Transit Map* is available free online. Standard fare for buses or streetcars is $2; cable-car fare is $6. **MUNI Passport** (1/3/7 days $14/22/28) allows unlimited travel on all MUNI transportation, including cable cars; it's sold at San Francisco Visitor Information Center and Union Sq's TIX Bay Area kiosk. **City Pass** (www.citypass.com; adult/child $84/59) covers Muni and admission to four attractions.

BART links San Francisco with the East Bay and runs beneath Market St, down Mission St, south to SFO and Millbrae, where it connects with CalTrain.

TAXI

Fares run about $2.75 per mile; meters start at $3.50.

DeSoto Cab (☑415-970-1300)

Green Cab (☑415-626-4733; www.626green.com) Fuel-efficient hybrids; worker-owned collective.

Luxor (☑415-282-4141)

Yellow Cab (☑415-333-3333)

Marin County

Majestic redwoods cling to coastal hills just across the Golden Gate Bridge in wealthy, laid-back Marin (www.visitmarin.org). The southernmost town, Sausalito, is a tiny bayside destination for bike trips over the bridge (take the ferry back to San Francisco). Near the harbor, the San Francisco Bay-Delta Model (Map p126; ☑415-332-3871; www.spn.usace.army.mil; 2100 Bridgeway Blvd, Sausalito; admission by donation; ⊙9am-4pm Tue-Fri, 10am-5pm Sat & Sun late May-early Sep, 9am-4pm Tue-Sat early Sep-late May; ⚑) is a way-cool giant hydraulic recreation of the entire bay and delta.

Marin Headlands

These windswept, rugged headlands are laced with hiking trails, providing panoramic views of the city and bay. To find the visitor center (Map p126; ☑415-331-1540; www.nps.gov/goga/marin-headlands.htm; Fort Barry, Bldg 948; ⊙9:30am-4:30pm Sat-Mon Apr-Sep), take the Alexander Ave exit after crossing north over the Golden Gate Bridge, turn left under the freeway onto Bunker Rd then follow the signs.

Nearby attractions include Point Bonita Lighthouse (Map p126; www.nps.gov/goga/pobo.htm; off Field Rd; ⊙12:30-3:30pm Sat-Mon) FREE, Rodeo Beach and the educational Marine Mammal Center (Map p126; ☑415-289-7325; www.tmmc.org; 2000 Bunker Rd; admission by donation; ⊙10am-5pm; ⚑) ☞ at Fort Cronkite. East of Hwy 101 at Fort Baker, the interactive Bay Area Discovery Museum (Map p126; ☑415-339-3900; www.baykidsmuseum.org; 557 McReynolds Rd, Sausalito; admission $11, 1st Wed of month free; ⊙9am-5pm Tue-Sun; ⚑) is awesome for kids.

Near the visitor center, eco-conscious HI Marin Headlands Hostel (Map p126; ☑415-331-2777; www.norcalhostels.org/marin; Fort Barry, Bldg 941; dm $26-30, r withouth bath $72-92; @) ☞ occupies two historic 1907 buildings on a forested hill, with private rooms in a former officer's house. For historical luxury, book a fireplace room with bay views at Fort Baker's LEED-certified Cavallo Point (Map p126; ☑415-339-4700, 888-651-2003; www.cavallopoint.com; 601 Murray Circle; r from $379; ❈ 🖤 🈳 ⚑ 🛍) ☞ lodge.

Mt Tamalpais State Park

Majestic Mt Tam (2571ft) is a woodsy playground for hikers and mountain bikers. Mt Tamalpais State Park (Map p126; ☑415-388-2070; www.friendsofmttam.org; per car $8) encompasses 6300 acres of parklands and over 200 miles of trails; don't miss driving up to East Peak Summit lookout. Panoramic Hwy climbs from Hwy 1 through the park to Stinson Beach, a mellow seaside town with a sandy crescent-shaped beach.

Park headquarters are at **Pantoll Station** (Map p126; ☑415-388-2070; 801 Panoramic Hwy, Mill Valley; ☺8am-7pm Fri-Sun, shorter hr winter;), the nexus of many trails, with a first-come, first-served **campground** (Map p126; tent sites $25). Book far ahead for a rustic cabin (no electricity or running water) or walk-in campsite at **Steep Ravine** (☑800-444-7275; www.reserveamerica.com; tent site $25, cabin $100), off Hwy 1 south of Stinson Beach. Or hike in with food, a sleeping bag and a towel to off-the-grid **West Point Inn** (Map p126; ☑info 415-388-9955, reservations 415-646-0702; www.westpointinn.com; 100 Old Railroad Grade Fire Rd, Mill Valley; r per adult/child $50/25); reservations required.

Muir Woods National Monument

Wander among an ancient stand of the world's tallest trees at 520-acre **Muir Woods National Monument** (Map p126; ☑415-388-2595; www.nps.gov/muwo; Muir Woods Rd, Mill Valley; adult/child $7/free; ☺8am-7:30pm, closes earlier mid-Sep–mid-Mar), 10 miles northwest of the Golden Gate Bridge. Easy hiking trails loop past thousand-year-old redwoods at Cathedral Grove. By the entrance, a **cafe** serves light lunches and drinks. Come midweek to avoid crowds; otherwise arrive early morning or late afternoon. Take Hwy 101 to the Hwy 1 exit, then follow the signs.

The **Muir Woods Shuttle** (Marin Transit Bus 66; ☑415-455-2000; www.goldengatetransit.org; round-trip adult/child $5/free) operates weekends and holidays from early May through late October, running every 10 to 20 minutes from Marin City, with limited connections to Sausalito's ferry terminal.

Point Reyes National Seashore

The windswept peninsula of **Point Reyes National Seashore** (www.nps.gov/pore) juts 10 miles out to sea on an entirely different tectonic plate, protecting over 100 sq miles of beaches, lagoons and forested hills. A mile west of Olema, **Bear Valley Visitor Center** (☑415-464-5100; www.nps.gov/pore; ☺10am-5pm Mon-Fri, from 9am Sat & Sun) has maps, information and natural-history displays. The 0.6-mile **Earthquake Trail**, which crosses the San Andreas Fault zone, starts nearby.

Crowning the peninsula's westernmost tip, **Point Reyes Lighthouse** (end of Sir Francis Drake Blvd; ☺2:30pm-4pm Thu-Mon, weather permitting) **FREE** is ideal for winter whale-watching. Off Pierce Point Rd, the 9.5-mile round-trip **Tomales Point Trail** rolls atop blustery bluffs past herds of tule elk to the peninsula's northern tip. Paddling Tomales Bay gets you up close to seabirds and seals; **Blue Waters Kayaking** (☑415-669-2600; www.bwkayak.com; rentals/tours from $50/70;) launches from Inverness and Marshall (reserve in advance).

Nature lovers bunk at the only in-park lodging, **HI Point Reyes Hostel** (☑415-663-8811; www.norcalhostels.org/reyes; 1390 Limantour Spit Rd; dm $24, r without bath $82-120; ☺check-in 2:30pm-10pm; @) , 8 miles inland from the visitor center. By marshy wetlands, **Motel Inverness** (☑866-453-3839, 415-236-1967; www.motelinverness.com; 12718 Sir Francis Drake Blvd; r $99-190;) sports spiffy rooms and a fireplace lounge with pool tables. The **West Marin Chamber of Commerce** (☑415-663-9232; www.pointreyes.org) checks availability at cozy inns, cottages and B&Bs.

Two miles north of Olema, the tiny town of **Point Reyes Station** has heart-warming bakeries, cafes and restaurants. Gather a picnic lunch at **Tomales Bay Foods & Cowgirl Creamery** (www.cowgirlcreamery.com; 80 4th St; sandwiches $6-12; ☺10am-6pm Wed-Sun;) or revel in handmade, seasonal Cal-Italian cuisine at **Osteria Stellina** (☑415-663-9988; http://osteriastellina.com; 11285 Hwy 1; mains $14-24; ☺11:30am-2:30pm & 5-9pm;) .

Berkeley

Not much has changed since the 1960s heyday of anti–Vietnam War protests – except the bumper stickers: 'No Blood for Oil' has supplanted 'Make Love Not War.' You can't walk around nude on campus anymore, but 'Berserkeley' remains the Bay Area's radical hub, crawling with university students, scoffing skateboarders and aging Birkenstock-shod hippies.

⊙ Sights & Activities

Leading to the campus's south gate, **Telegraph Avenue** is as youthful and gritty as San Francisco's Haight St, packed with cafes, cheap eats, bookshops and music stores.

University of California, Berkeley   UNIVERSITY
(www.berkeley.edu) One of the country's top universities, 'Cal' is home to over 35,000 diverse, politically conscious students. The **Visitor Services Center** (☑510-642-5215;

http://visitors.berkeley.edu; 101 Sproul Hall; ☺ tours usually 10am Mon-Sat, 1pm Sun) leads free campus tours (reservations required). Ride the elevator to the top of the landmark 1914 **Campanile** (Sather Tower; adult/child $2/1; ☺ 10am-3:45pm Mon-Fri, to 4:45pm Sat, 10am-1:30pm & 3-4:45pm Sun; ♿). The **Bancroft Library** displays the small gold nugget that kicked off California's gold rush in 1848.

UC Berkeley Art Museum   MUSEUM
(☎ 510-642-0808; www.bampfa.berkeley.edu; 2626 Bancroft Way; adult/child $10/7; ☺ 11am-5pm Wed-Sun) Eleven galleries showcase a wide range of works, from ancient Chinese to cutting-edge contemporary American art. Across the street, its **Pacific Film Archive** (PFA; ☎ 510-642-5249; www.bampfa.berkeley.edu; 2575 Bancroft Way; adult/child $9.50/6.50) screens independent and avant-garde films. Both are scheduled to move to a new location on Oxford St, between Center and Addison Sts.

Tilden Regional Park   PARK
(www.ebparks.org/parks/tilden) Up in the Berkeley Hills, escape on 40 miles of hiking and biking trails, with botanical gardens, swimming at Lake Anza and a merry-go-round and a steam train for kiddos.

🛏 Sleeping

Motels line University Ave west of campus.

YMCA   HOSTEL $
(☎ 510-848-6800; www.ymca-cba.org/downtown-berkeley; 2001 Allston Way; s/d without bath from $49/81; @ 🛜 🏊) The recently remodeled 100-year-old downtown 'Y' is Berkeley's best budget option. Rates for austere private rooms include pool, fitness center and kitchen access.

Downtown Berkeley Inn   MOTEL $$
(☎ 510-843-4043;   www.downtownberkeleyinn.com; 2001 Bancroft Way; r from $109; P ❄ 🛜) Showing off elements of boutique style, this 27-room motel has good-sized rooms with modern amenities. Free parking.

Hotel Durant   BOUTIQUE HOTEL $$$
(☎ 510-845-8981; www.hoteldurant.com; 2600 Durant Ave; r $195-309; P @ 🏊) 🍴 A block from campus, the lobby of this 1928 hotel is cheekily adorned with embarrassing yearbook photos, while smallish rooms have bongs repurposed into bedside lamps. Parking is $16 (free for hybrid cars).

🍴 Eating

Cream   DESSERTS $
(www.creamnation.com; 2399 Telegraph Ave; items $2-4; ☺ noon-midnight Mon-Wed, to 2am Thu-Fri, 11am-2am Sat, 11am-11pm Sun) Crazily creative ice-cream sandwiches let you mix and match your own flavors – salted caramel with snickerdoodles, anyone? Cash only.

Cheese Board Pizza   PIZZERIA $
(http://cheeseboardcollective.coop; 1512 Shattuck Ave; slice/half pizza $2.50/10; ☺ 11:30am-3pm & 4:30-8pm Tue-Sat; 🍴 ♿) Sit down for a slice of crispy one-option-per-day veggie pizza at this worker-owned collective, where live music often plays at night.

Bette's Oceanview Diner   DINER $$
(www.bettesdiner.com; 1807 4th St; mains $6-13; ☺ 6:30am-2:30pm Mon-Fri, to 4pm Sat & Sun) At this buzzing breakfast spot near the I-80 Fwy, table waits can be long, but it's worth it for baked souffle pancake perfection.

★**Chez Panisse**   CALIFORNIAN $$$
(☎ cafe 510-548-5049, restaurant 510-548-5525; 1517 Shattuck Ave; cafe dinner mains $18-29, restaurant prix-fixe dinner $65-100; ☺ cafe 11:30am-2:45pm & 5-10:30pm Mon-Thu, to 3pm & to 11:30pm Fri & Sat; restaurant seatings 6-6:30pm & 8:30-9:15pm Mon-Sat) 🍴 Genuflect at the culinary temple of Alice Waters: the birthplace of California cuisine remains at the pinnacle of Bay Area dining. Book one month ahead for its seasonally inspired prix-fixe restaurant menu (no substitutions) or upstairs at the à la carte cafe.

🍷 Drinking & Entertainment

Caffe Strada   CAFE
(2300 College Ave; ☺ 6am-midnight; 🛜) Caffeine-wired students mob the outdoor patio to study, ardently talk philosophy or flirt.

Freight & Salvage Coffeehouse   LIVE MUSIC
(☎ 510-644-2020; http://thefreight.org; 2020 Addison St; tickets $5-30) Originating in the radical '60s era, this legendary club stages all-ages shows of traditional folk and world music.

Berkeley Repertory Theatre   THEATER
(☎ 510-647-2949; www.berkeleyrep.org; 2025 Addison St; tickets $35-100) Highly respected company has produced bold versions of classical and contemporary plays since 1968.

❶ Getting There & Around

AC Transit (p150) runs local buses around Berkeley ($2.10) and to Oakland ($2.10) and San Francisco ($4.20). **BART** (☑ 511, 510-465-2278; www.bart.gov) trains connect downtown Berkeley, a short walk from campus, with Oakland ($1.75) and SF ($3.70).

NORTHERN CALIFORNIA

The Golden State goes wild in Northern California, with coast redwoods swirled in fog and Wine Country vineyards and mud-bath wallows. Befitting this dramatic meeting of land and water is an unlikely melange of local residents: timber barons and hippie tree huggers, dreadlocked Rastafarians and biodynamic ranchers, pot farmers and political radicals of every stripe. Come for the scenery, but stay for the top-notch wine and farm-to-fork restaurants, along with misty hikes among the world's tallest trees, a nekkid hot-springs soak and rambling conversations that begin with 'Hey, dude!' and end hours later.

Wine Country

A patchwork of vineyards stretches from sunny inland Napa to windy coastal Sonoma – California's premier wine-growing region. Napa has art-filled tasting rooms by big-name architects, with prices to match. In down-to-earth Sonoma, you may drink in a shed and meet the vintner's dog. Wine Country is at least an hour's drive north of San Francisco via Hwy 101 or I-80.

Napa Valley

Over 200 wineries crowd 30-mile-long Napa Valley along three main routes. Traffic-jammed on weekends, Hwy 29 is lined with blockbuster wineries. Running parallel, Silverado Trail moves faster, passing boutique winemakers, bizarre architecture and cult-hit Cabernet Sauvignon. West toward Sonoma, Hwy 121 (Carneros Hwy) has landmark vineyards specializing in sparkling wines and Pinot Noir.

At the southern end of the valley, Napa – the valley's workaday hub – lacks rusticity, but has trendy restaurants and tasting rooms downtown. Stop by the Napa Valley Welcome Center (☑ 855-333-6272, 707-251-5895; www.visitnapavalley.com; 600 Main St; ☺ 9am-5pm Sep-Apr, 9am-5pm Mon-Thu, to 6pm Fri-Sun May-Oct) for wine-tasting passes and winery maps.

Heading north on Hwy 29, the former stagecoach stop of tiny Yountville has more Michelin-starred eateries per capita than anywhere else in the USA. Another 10 miles north, traffic rolls to a stop in charming St Helena – the Beverly Hills of Napa – where there's genteel strolling and shopping, if you can find parking, that is.

At the valley's northern end, folksy Calistoga – Napa's least-gentrified town – is home to hot-spring spas and mud-bath emporiums using volcanic ash from nearby Mt St Helena.

◉ Sights & Activities

Most Napa wineries require reservations. Book one appointment, then build your day around it. Plan to visit no more than a few tasting rooms each day.

⭐**Hess Collection**   WINERY, GALLERY
(☑ 707-255-8584; www.hesscollection.com; 4411 Redwood Rd, Napa; tasting $10; ☺ 10am-5pm) ✿
Northwest of downtown Napa, this sustainable winery pairs monster Cabernet with blue-chip modern art by Robert Rauschenberg and others. Reservations suggested.

⭐**di Rosa Art +
Nature Preserve**   GALLERY, GARDEN
(☑ 707-226-5991; www.dirosaart.org; 5200 Hwy 121, Napa; admission $5, tours $12-15; ☺ 10am-4pm Wed-Sun, to 6pm Wed-Sun Apr-Oct) When you notice scrap-metal sheep grazing Carneros vineyards, you've spotted one of the best collections of modern NorCal art anywhere. Reservations advised for tours.

Frog's Leap   WINERY
(☑ 707-963-4704; www.frogsleap.com; 8815 Conn Creek Rd, Rutherford; tasting $15, incl tour $20; ☺ 10am-4pm; 🅿🅰🅶) ✿ Meandering paths wind through gardens surrounding an 1884 barn at this LEED-certified winery, pouring stand-out Sauvignon Blanc and Cabernet. Book tours in advance.

Pride Mountain   WINERY
(☑ 707-963-4949; www.pridewines.com; 3000 Summit Trail, St Helena; tasting $10, incl tour $15-75; ☺ by appointment) Cult-favorite Pride straddles the Sonoma–Napa border and makes stellar Cabernet, Merlot, Chardonnay and Viognier at an unfussy hilltop estate with spectacular picnicking.

Casa Nuestra
WINERY

(☑ 866-844-9463; www.casanuestra.com; 3451 Silverado Trail, St Helena; tasting $10; ☺ by appointment) ✐ A peace flag and portrait of Elvis greet you at this tiny solar-powered winery, known for growing unusual varietals. Goats frolic beside the picnic area.

Castello di Amorosa
WINERY, CASTLE

(☑ 707-967-6272; www.castellodiamorosa.com; 4045 Hwy 29, Calistoga; admission & tasting $18-28, incl guided tour $33-69; ☺ 9:30am-6pm, to 5pm Nov-Feb) Tour a recreated 13th-century Tuscan castle, complete with a dungeon tasting room stocked with Italian varietals.

Indian Springs Spa
SPA

(☑ 707-942-4913; www.indianspringscalistoga. com; 1712 Lincoln Ave, Calistoga; ☺ by appointment 9am-8pm) Book ahead for a volcanic-mud bath at Calistoga's original 19th-century mineral-springs resort. Treatments include access to spring-fed pools.

🛏 Sleeping

The valley's best values are midweek at Napa's less-than-exciting motels.

Bothe-Napa Valley State Park Campground
CAMPGROUND $

(☑ 800-444-7275; www.reserveamerica.com; 3801 Hwy 128, Calistoga; camping & RV sites $35; ▨▨▨) Hillside campsites with a summertime swimming pool, coin-op hot showers and hiking trails beneath moss-covered oaks await.

Chablis Inn
MOTEL $$

(☑ 707-257-1944; www.chablisinn.com; 3360 Solano Ave, Napa; r $105-179; ▨@▨▨) On Napa's suburban strip, these crisp, modern rooms are spacious and don't cut corners – some even have jetted tubs for couples.

EuroSpa & Inn
MOTEL $$

(☑ 707-942-6829; www.eurospa.com; 1202 Pine St, Calistoga; r incl breakfast $145-195; ▨▨▨) Immaculate single-story motel on a quiet side street has just 13 rooms with two-person whirlpool tubs and gas fireplaces. Skip the on-site spa, though.

★ Indian Springs Resort
RESORT $$$

(☑ 707-942-4913; www.indianspringscalistoga. com; 1712 Lincoln Ave, Calistoga; r/cottage from $199/229; ▨@▨▨▨) At Calistoga's most harmonious hot-springs resort, charming bungalows (some with kitchens) face a

broad lawn with rustling palm trees, shuffleboard and bocce courts, hammocks and BBQ grills. Bicycles are free for pampered guests to borrow.

🍴 Eating

Many Wine Country restaurants keep shorter hours in winter and spring.

Oxbow Public Market
MARKET $

(☑ 707-226-6529; www.oxbowpublicmarket.com; 644 1st St, Napa; dishes from $3; ☺ 9am-7pm Mon-Sat, 10am-5pm Sun) ✐ Oxbow showcases sustainably produced artisanal foods by 20-plus vendors. Feast on Hog Island oysters, Model Bakery muffins, Ca' Momi's crispy pizzas or Three Twins organic ice cream.

Gott's Roadside
AMERICAN $$

(☑ 707-963-3486; http://gotts.com; 933 Main St, St Helena; dishes $3-14; ☺ 7am-9pm, to 10pm May-Sep; ⊞) A 1950s drive-in diner with 21st-century sensibilities: burgers are all-natural beef, organic chicken or sushi-grade tuna, with sides like chili-dusted sweet-potato fries and handmade milkshakes.

Oakville Grocery
DELI, MARKET $$

(☑ 707-944-8802; www.oakvillegrocery.com; 7856 Hwy 29, Oakville; sandwiches $9-14; ☺ 6:30am-5pm) Pick up picnic staples or grab a gourmet meal on the go, with specialty sandwiches crafted from locally made artisanal ingredients and decadent desserts. Second location in downtown Healdsburg.

Wine Spectator Greystone Restaurant
CALIFORNIAN $$$

(☑ 707-967-1010; www.ciarestaurants.com; 2555 Main St, St Helena; dinner mains $22-34; ☺ 11:30am-2:30pm & 5-9pm Mon-Fri, 11:30am-9pm Sat, noon-7:15pm Sun; ☎) An 1889 stone chateau houses the Culinary Institute of America's fine-dining restaurant, bakery-cafe and gadget-filled shop. Book ahead for weekend cooking demos and wine-tasting classes.

Ad Hoc
CALIFORNIAN $$$

(☑ 707-944-2487; www.adhocrestaurant.com; 6476 Washington St, Yountville; prix-fixe dinner from $52; ☺ 5-10pm Wed-Sun, plus 10am-1pm Sun) Don't ask for a menu at chef Thomas Keller's dressed-down 'experimental' kitchen. Changing daily, a four-course family-style dinner allows no substitutions (except for dietary restrictions), but none are needed – every dish is comforting, fresh and spot-on.

★ **French Laundry**   CALIFORNIAN $$$
(☑707-944-2380; www.frenchlaundry.com; 6640 Washington St, Yountville; prix-fixe dinner $270; ⊙seatings 11am-1pm Fri-Sun & 5:30pm-9:15pm daily) Sparkling with three Michelin stars, the French Laundry is a high-wattage culinary experience, full of whimsy and wit. Book exactly two months ahead: call at 10am (or try OpenTable.com at midnight). If you can't score a reservation, console yourself at chef Thomas Keller's nearby note-perfect French brasserie **Bouchon** or with pastries from **Bouchon Bakery**.

Sonoma Valley

More laid-back, less commercial than Napa, Sonoma Valley enfolds over 70 wineries off Hwy 12 – and, unlike in Napa, most welcome picnicking. Note there are actually three Sonomas: the town, the valley and the county.

◉ Sights & Activities

Downtown Sonoma was once the capital of the short-lived Bear Flag Republic. Today **Sonoma Plaza** – the state's largest town square – is bordered by chic boutiques, historical buildings and a **visitor center** (☑866-996-1090, 707-996-1090; www.sonomavalley.com; 453 1st St E; ⊙9am-5pm Mon-Sat, from 10am Sun).

Jack London State Historic Park   PARK
(☑707-938-5216; www.jacklondonpark.com; 2400 London Ranch Rd, Glen Ellen; per car $8, tour adult/child $4/2; ⊙9:30am-5pm Thu-Mon) Obey the call of the wild where adventurer-novelist Jack London built his dream house – it burned on the eve of completion in 1913. Tour the writer's original cottage or browse memorabilia inside the small museum standing in a redwood grove. Twenty miles of hiking and mountain-biking trails weave through the park's 1400 hilltop acres.

★ **Bartholomew Park Winery**   WINERY
(☑707-939-3024; www.bartpark.com; 1000 Vineyard Lane, Sonoma; tasting $10, incl tour $20; ⊙11am-4:30pm) ❀ In a 400-acre nature preserve that's perfect for picnicking, the family-owned vineyards originally cultivated in 1857 are now organic-certified, yielding citrus-sunshine Sauvignon Blanc and smoky-midnight Merlot.

Gundlach-Bundschu Winery   WINERY
(☑707-939-3015; www.gunbun.com; 2000 Denmark St, Sonoma; tasting $10, incl tour $20-50; ⊙11am-4:30pm, to 5:30pm Jun–mid-Oct) ❀ West of downtown, this sustainable winery dating from 1858 looks like a storybook castle. Winemakers craft legendary Tempranillo and signature Gewürztraminer.

Kunde   WINERY
(☑707-833-5501; www.kunde.com; 9825 Hwy 12, Kenwood; tasting & tour $10-40; ⊙10:30am-5pm) ❀ Make reservations for a sustainable vineyard tour, guided hike or mountain-top tasting of estate-grown Cabernet, Zinfandel and Sauvignon Blanc.

Kaz Winery   WINERY
(☑707-833-2536; www.kazwinery.com; 233 Adobe Canyon Rd, Kenwood; tasting $5; ⊙11am-5pm Fri-Mon, by appointment Tue-Thu; ⚑⚑) ❀ Veer off Hwy 12 for offbeat, organically grown, cult-favorite wines, poured at a wooden barrel-top bar inside a barn.

Ravenswood Winery   WINERY
(☑707-933-2332; www.ravenswoodwinery.com; 18701 Gehricke Rd, Sonoma; tasting $10, incl tour $15; ⊙10am-4:30pm) With the slogan 'no wimpy wines,' this buzzing tasting room pours a full slate of Zinfandels. Novices welcome.

Cornerstone Sonoma   GARDENS
(☑707-933-3010; www.cornerstonegardens.com; 23570 Arnold Dr, Sonoma; ⊙10am-4pm) **FREE** There's nothing traditional about this avante-garde tapestry of landscaped gardens, 5 miles south of downtown Sonoma.

🛏 Sleeping

At the valley's north end, Santa Rosa has more budget-saving motels and hotels.

Sugarloaf Ridge State Park   CAMPGROUND $
(☑800-444-7275; www.reserveamerica.com; 2605 Adobe Canyon Rd, Kenwood; camping & RV sites $35; ⚑⚑) Near mid-valley wineries, camp-sites laze in a stream-fed hillside meadow by forested hiking trails. Coin-op hot showers available.

Sonoma Hotel   HISTORIC HOTEL $$
(☑800-468-6016, 707-996-2996; www.sonomahotel.com; 110 W Spain St, Sonoma; r incl breakfast

$115-240) Old-fashioned rooms squeeze inside this 19th-century plaza landmark. No elevator or parking lot. Two-night minimum stay most weekends

Beltane Ranch
B&B $$$
(☎707-996-6501; www.beltaneranch.com; 11775 Hwy 12, Glen Ellen; d incl breakfast $150-265; 🛜) Wide porches are dotted with swings and white wicker chairs at this cheerful lemon-yellow 1890 ranch house and cottage surrounded by pasturelands. No phones or TVs.

Gaige House Inn
B&B $$$
(☎800-935-0237, 707-935-0237; www.gaige.com; 13540 Arnold Dr, Glen Ellen; d incl breakfast from $275; 🛜🞉🞉) Near vineyards, Asian-chic rooms and fireplace suites adorn a historic home, with pebbled meditation courtyards out by the pool. Sister inns in Sonoma, Healdsburg and Yountville.

✖ Eating

Fremont Diner
AMERICAN $$
(☎707-938-7370; http://thefremontdiner.com; 2698 Fremont Dr, Sonoma; breakfast & lunch mains $6-14; ⊗8am-3pm Mon-Wed, to 9pm Thu-Sun; 🞉) ✐ Feast on Southern-inspired, farm-to-table cooking at this down-home diner with picnic tables outside. Arrive early to avoid long waits.

Fig Cafe & Winebar
FRENCH $$
(☎707-938-2130; www.thefigcafe.com; 13690 Arnold Dr, Glen Ellen; mains $10-20; ⊗10am-3pm Sat & Sun, 5:30pm-9pm daily) Imagine French-inspired comfort food like steamed mussels and duck cassoulet in a convivial room with vaulted wooden ceilings. Even better: no reservations or corkage fee.

Red Grape
ITALIAN $$
(☎707-996-4103; http://theredgrape.com; 529 1st St W, Sonoma; mains $10-20; ⊗11:30am-10pm; 🞉) At this sunlight-filled pizzeria, thin-crust pies topped with locally made cheeses, panini sandwiches and pasta shake hands with small-production Sonoma wines.

★ Cafe La Haye
CALIFORNIAN $$$
(☎707-935-5994; www.cafelahaye.com; 140 E Napa St, Sonoma; mains $20-30; ⊗5:30pm-9pm Tue-Sat) ✐ This tiny bistro with an open kitchen creates earthy New American dishes from ingredients all sourced within 60 miles. Tables are squeezed together elbow-to-elbow. Book ahead.

Russian River Valley

Redwood trees tower over small wineries in the Russian River Valley, about 75 miles northwest of San Francisco (via Hwys 101 and 116), in western Sonoma County.

Famous for its apple orchards and farm-tour trails, Sebastopol has a New Age spiritual aura, with downtown bookshops, art galleries and boutiques and antiques stores further south. Have a pint and pub grub in the beer garden at Hopmonk Tavern (☎707-829-9300; www.hopmonk.com; 230 Petaluma Ave; mains $12-23; ⊗11:30am-9pm Sun-Wed, to 9:30pm Thu-Sat, bar till 1:30am; 🛜), shaking with world beats at night. Four miles northwest, Willow Wood Market Cafe (☎707-823-0233; www.willowwoodgraton.com; 9020 Graton Rd, Graton; most mains $7-17; ⊗8am-9pm Mon-Sat, to 3pm Sun; 🞉) cooks comfort-food breakfasts and hot, haute sandwiches at lunch.

Guerneville is the main river beach town, buzzing with Harleys and gay-friendly honky-tonks. Explore old-growth redwoods at Armstrong Redwoods State Reserve (☎707-869-2015; www.parks.ca.gov; 17000 Armstrong Woods Rd; per car $8; ⊗8am-sunset; 🞉), next to no-reservations Bullfrog Pond Campground (www.stewardsofthecoastandredwoods.org; campsites $25; 🞉🞉). Paddle downriver, past herons and otters, with Burke's Canoe Trips (☎707-887-1222; www.burkescanoetrips.com; 8600 River Rd, Forestville; canoe rental incl shuttle $60). Head southeast to sip bubbly at the outdoor hilltop tasting bar at Iron Horse Vineyards (☎707-887-1507; www.ironhorsevineyards.com; 9786 Ross Station Rd, Sebastopol; tasting $15, incl tour $20; ⊗10am-4:30pm). Other excellent wineries are scattered along rural Westside Rd, which follows the river to Healdsburg. Guerneville's visitor center (☎877-644-9001, 707-869-9000; www.russianriver.com; 16209 1st St; ⊗10am-5pm) offers winery maps and lodging info. The town's best eats are at California-smart Boon Eat + Drink (☎707-869-0780; http://eatatboon.com; 16248 Main St; dinner mains $15-26; ⊗11am-3pm Mon-Tue & Thu-Fri, 5-9pm Mon-Fri, 10am-3pm & 5-10pm Sat & Sun), which manages the boutique Boon Hotel + Spa (☎707-869-2721; www.boonhotels.com; 14711 Armstrong Woods Rd; r $165-275; 🛜🞉🞉) ✐, a minimalist green oasis with a saline pool.

The aptly named 10-mile Bohemian Hwy winds south of the river to tiny Occidental, where Howard Station Cafe (www.

howardstationcafe.com; 3811 Bohemian Hwy; mains $6-11; ⊘ 7am-2:30pm Mon-Fri, to 3pm Sat & Sun; 🔊🐾) serves hearty breakfasts like blueberry cornmeal pancakes (cash only) and Barley & Hops Tavern (☑707-874-9037; www.barleynhops.com; 3688 Bohemian Hwy; ⊘ 4-9:30pm Mon-Wed, 11am-9:30pm Thu & Sun, to 10pm Fri & Sat) pours craft beers. It's another three miles south to Freestone, home of the phenomenal bakery Wild Flour Bread (www.wildflourbread.com; 140 Bohemian Hwy; items from $3; ⊘ 8:30am-6pm Fri-Mon) and invigorating cedar-enzyme baths at Osmosis (☑707-823-8231; www.osmosis.com; 209 Bohemian Hwy; ⊘ by appointment) spa.

Healdsburg to Boonville

More than 100 wineries dot the valleys within a 20-mile radius of Healdsburg, where upscale eateries, wine-tasting rooms and stylish hotels surround a Spanish-style plaza. For tasting passes and maps, drop by the visitor center (☑800-648-9922, 707-433-6935; www.healdsburg.org; 217 Healdsburg Ave; ⊘9am-5pm Mon-Fri, to 3pm Sat, 10am-2pm Sun). Dine with California-chic locavores on the leafy patio at Barndiva (☑707-431-0100; www.barndiva.com; 231 Center St; dinner mains $25-36; ⊘noon-2pm Wed-Sat, 11am-2pm Sun & 5:30pm-9:30pm Wed-Sun, to 10pm Fri & Sat), or grab lunch near the Alexander Valley's vineyards at country-style Jimtown Store (☑707-433-1212; www.jimtown.com; 6706 Hwy 128; sandwiches $6-14; ⊘ 7:30am-4pm Mon-Thu, to 5pm Fri-Sun). Afterward bed down at old-fashioned L&M Motel (☑707-433-6528; www.landmmotel.com; 70 Healdsburg Ave; r $85-165; 🌸🛜🌊🔊🐾) or retro-romantic Healdsburg Modern Cottages (☑866-964-0110; www.healdsburgcottages.com; 425 Foss St; d from $250; 🌸🛜🌊).

Picture-perfect farmstead wineries await discovery in Dry Creek Valley, west of Hwy 101 from Healdsburg. Pedal a bicycle out to taste Zinfandel at Truett Hurst Vineyards (☑707-433-9545; www.truetthurst.com; 5610 Dry Creek Rd; tastings $5-10; ⊘10am-5pm) 🐾 and Bella Vineyards & Wine Caves (☑707-473-9171; www.bellawinery.com; 9711 West Dry Creek Rd; tasting $10; ⊘ 11am-4:30pm), or motor toward the Russian River and biodynamic Porter Creek Vineyards (☑707-433-6321; www.portercreekvineyards.com; 8735 Westside Rd; tasting $10; ⊘10:30am-4:30pm) 🐾 for Pinot Noir and Viognier poured at a bar made from a bowling-alley lane.

North of Healdsburg, follow Hwy 128 through the Anderson Valley, known for its fruit orchards and stand-out winemakers like Navarro (☑707-895-3686; www.navarrowine.com; 5601 Hwy 128, Philo; ⊘9am-5pm, to 6pm May-Sep) and Husch (☑800-554-8724; www.huschvineyards.com; 4400 Hwy 128, Philo; ⊘10am-5pm). Outside Boonville, which has roadside cafes, bakeries, delis and ice-cream shops, brake for disc-golf and beer at solar-powered Anderson Valley Brewing Company (☑707-895-2337; www.avbc.com; 17700 Hwy 253; ⊘11am-6pm Sat-Thu, to 7pm Fri, tours 1:30pm & 3:30pm daily, closed Tue & Wed Jan-Mar) 🐾.

❶ Getting There & Around

Getting to and around Wine Country by public transportation is slow, but just possible.

For Napa, take **Vallejo Baylink Ferry** (☑877-643-3779; www.baylinkferry.com) from San Francisco's Ferry Building ($13, one hour). In Vallejo, connect with Napa Valley's **Vine Transit** (☑707-251-2800; www.ridethevine.com) buses to Napa ($1.50 to $3.25, 40 to 55 minutes), with limited onward connections to Yountville, St Helena and Calistoga. Alternatively, take BART to El Cerrito del Norte station, then connect on weekdays with Vine Transit bus 29 to Napa ($3.25, 1¼ hours); on weekends, transfer to **SolTrans** (☑707-648-4666; www.soltransride.com) bus 80 to Vallejo ($1.75, 25 minutes), then catch Vine Transit bus 11 to Napa ($1.50, 55 minutes).

For Sonoma, **Greyhound** (☑800-231-2222; www.greyhound.com) buses connect San Francisco and Santa Rosa ($24, 1¾ hours). **Golden Gate Transit** (☑415-455-2000, 511; http://goldengate.org) also links San Francisco to Santa Rosa ($10.75, two to three hours). From Santa Rosa, **Sonoma County Transit** (☑800-345-7433, 707-576-7433; www.sctransit.com) buses connect to Sonoma ($3.05, 70 minutes) via Sonoma Valley towns.

Rent bicycles (per day $30 to $85) from **Napa River Vélo** (☑707-258-8729; www.naparivervelo.com; 680 Main St, Napa), **Wine Country Cyclery** (☑707-966-6800; www.winecountrycyclery.com; 262 W Napa St, Sonoma), **Calistoga Bike Shop** (☑707-942-9687; www.calistogabikeshop.com; 1318 Lincoln Ave, Calistoga) or **Spoke Folk Cyclery** (☑707-433-7171; www.spokefolk.com; 201 Center St, Healdsburg).

North Coast

Metropolitan San Francisco, only a few hours behind in the rearview mirror, feel eons away from the frothing, frigid crash of Pacific tide and two-stoplight towns on this jagged edge of the continent. Valleys of redwoods brush up against the moody ocean waves and rural farms here on California's North Coast, home to hippies, hoppy microbrews and, most famously, the tallest trees on earth. The winding coastal drive gets more rewarding with every gorgeous, white-knuckled mile of narrow highway.

Bodega Bay to Fort Bragg

Compared with the famous Big Sur coast, the serpentine stretch of Hwy 1 up the North Coast is more challenging, remote and *real*: it passes farms, fishing towns and hidden beaches. Drivers use roadside pull-outs to scan the hazy Pacific horizon for migrating whales and to amble the coastline dotted with rock formations and relentlessly pounded by the surf. The 110-mile stretch from Bodega Bay to Fort Bragg takes at least three hours of nonstop driving; at night in the fog, it takes steely nerves and much, much longer.

Bodega Bay, the first pearl in a string of sleepy fishing towns, was the setting for Hitchcock's terrifying 1963 psycho-horror flick *The Birds*. Today the skies are free from bloodthirsty gulls, but you'd best keep an eye on that picnic basket as you explore the arched rocks, secret coves and wildflower-covered bluffs of Sonoma Coast State Park (www.parks.ca.gov; per car $8), with beaches rolling even beyond Jenner, 10 miles north. Bodega Bay Charters (707-875-3495; http://bodegacharters.com; Eastshore Rd) runs winter whale-watching trips (adult/child $50/35). Bodega Bay Surf Shack (707-875-3944; http://bodegabaysurf.com; 1400 N Hwy 1; surfboard/wet-suit/kayak rentals from $17/17/45) rents surfboards, wet-suits and kayaks. Landlubbers hike Bodega Head or saddle up horses at Chanslor Riding Stables (707-785-8849; www.chanslorranch.com; 2660 N Hwy 1; rides from $40).

Where the wide, lazy Russian River meets the Pacific, there isn't much to do in Jenner, a cluster of shops and restaurants dotting coastal hills. Informative volunteers protect the resident colony of harbor seals at the river's mouth during pupping season, between March and August.

Twelve miles north of Jenner, the salt-weathered structures of Fort Ross State Historic Park (707-847-3286; www.fortrossstatepark.org; 19005 Hwy 1; per car $8; 10am-4pm Sat & Sun, also 10am-4pm Fri late May-early Sep) preserve an 1812 trading post and Russian Orthodox church. It's a quiet place, but the history is riveting: this was once the southernmost extent of Tsarist Russia's North American trading expeditions. The small, wood-scented museum offers historical exhibits and respite from the windswept cliffs.

Seven miles further north, Salt Point State Park (707-847-3321; per car $8; visitor center 10am-3pm Sat & Sun Apr-Oct) abounds with hiking trails and tide pools and has two campgrounds (800-444-7275; www.reserveamerica.com; campsites $35, walk-in tent sites $25). At neighboring Kruse Rhododendron State Reserve, pink blooms spot the misty green woods in springtime. Cows graze the surrounding rock-strewn fields on the bluffs heading north to Sea Ranch, where public-access hiking trails lead from roadside parking lots downhill to pocket beaches.

Two miles north of Point Arena town, detour to wind-battered Point Arena Lighthouse (707-882-2777; www.pointarenalighthouse.com; 45500 Lighthouse Rd; adult/child $7.50/1; 10am-3:30pm, to 4:30pm late May-early Sep), built in 1908. Ascend 145 steps to inspect the flashing Fresnel lens and get jaw-dropping coastal views. Eight miles north of the Little River crossing at Hwy 128 is Van Damme State Park (707-937-5804; www.parks.ca.gov; per car $8), where the popular 5-mile round-trip Fern Canyon Trail passes through a lush river canyon with young redwoods, continuing another mile each way to a pygmy forest. The park's campground (800-444-7275; www.reserveamerica.com; walk-up/drive-in sites $25/35) has coin-op hot showers.

In Mendocino, a historical village perched on a gorgeous headland, baby boomers stroll around New England saltbox and water-tower B&Bs, quaint shops and art galleries. Wilder paths pass berry brambles, wildflowers and cypress trees standing guard over rocky cliffs and raging surf at Mendocino Headlands State Park (www.parks.ca.gov) FREE. Ask at the Ford House Museum & Visitor Center (707-537-5397; http://mendoparks.org; 735 Main St; 11am-4pm) about guided weekend wildlife-watching walks. Just south of town, paddle your way up the Big River tidal estuary with Catch a Canoe & Bicycles Too! (707-937-0273; www.catchacanoe.com; Stanford Inn, 44850 Comptche-Ukiah Rd; kayak & canoe rental adult/child from $28/14; 9am-5pm).

Medocino's scrappy sister city, Fort Bragg is trying to lure some of the well-heeled weekenders 10 miles further north, but it still has a way to go. You'll find cheap gas here and the historic Skunk Train (707-964-6371; www.skunktrain.com; foot of Laurel St; adult/child from $20/10;) whose diesel and steam engines make diverting half-day excursions through the woods.

Sleeping

Every other building in Mendocino seems to be a B&B; there are dozens to choose from, but always book ahead. Fort Bragg, just 10 miles north, has plenty of motels.

Gualala Point Regional Park CAMPGROUND $
(http://parks.sonomacounty.ca.gov; 42401 Highway 1, Gualala; camp sites & RV sites $30-45;) Shaded by redwoods and fragrant California bay laurel trees, a short trail connects this creekside campground to the windswept beach. Choose a drive-up campsite or secluded hike-in tent site. Coin-op hot showers available.

Andiorn CABIN $$
(800-955-6478, 707-937-1543; http://theandiorn.com; 6051 N Hwy 1, Little River; most cabins $109-199;) This cluster of 1950s roadside cottages is a refreshingly playful after the cabbage-rose and lace aesthetic of Mendocino. Duplex cabins come with complementary whimsical themes; some have kitchenettes and fireplaces.

Mar Vista Cottages CABIN $$$
(877-855-3522, 707-884-3522; www.marvistamendocino.com; 35101 S Hwy 1, Gualala; cottages $175-295;) These renovated 1930s cottages with kitchens are a simply restful seaside escape at Anchor Bay. Linens are line-dried over lavender, guests harvest their own dinner from the organic vegetable garden and chickens cluck around the grounds, laying the next morning's breakfast. Two-night minimum.

Brewery Gulch Inn B&B $$$
(800-578-4454, 707-937-4752; www.brewerygulchinn.com; 9401 N Hwy 1, Mendocino; d incl breakfast $245-495;) Just south of Mendocino, this serene, eco-conscious inn wins hearts that crave luxury, with modern fireplace rooms and hosts who pour heavily at wine hour and leave sweets for midnight snacking. Cooked-to-order breakfasts are served in a small dining room overlooking the distant sea.

Eating & Drinking

Even small coastal towns usually have a bakery, deli, natural-foods market and a few roadside cafes and restaurants.

Spud Point Crab Company SEAFOOD $
(www.spudpointcrab.com; 1910 Westshore Rd, Bodega Bay; dishes $4-11; 9am-5pm;) Classic dockside seafood shack makes salty-sweet crab sandwiches and *real* clam chowder to eat at picnic tables overlooking the marina.

Franny's Cup & Saucer BAKERY $
(www.frannyscupandsaucer.com; 213 Main St, Point Arena; items from $2; 8am-4pm Wed-Sat) Fairytale patisserie pops colorful fresh berry tarts, handmade cookies and rich chocolate confections into petite shopfront windows.

GoodLife Cafe CAFE $
(http://goodlifecafemendo.com; 10485 Lansing St, Mendocino; items $3-10; 8am-4pm) Strong organic espresso, buttery baked goods, savory empandas, from-scratch soups and fresh salads and juices will wake you up.

Piaci Pub & Pizzeria ITALIAN $$
(www.piacipizza.com; 120 W Redwood Ave, Fort Bragg; mains $8-18; 11am-9:30pm Mon-Thu, to 10pm Fri & Sat, 4-9:30pm Sun) Chat up locals while downing microbrews and wood-fired brick-oven pizzas, calzones and focaccia topped with 'adult' flavors like pesto-chevre and proscuitto-potato. It's tiny, loud and fun.

Café Beaujolais CALIFORNIAN $$$
(707-937-5614; www.cafebeaujolais.com; 961 Ukiah St, Mendocino; dinner mains $23-35; 11:30am-2:30pm Wed-Sun, dinner from 5:30pm daily) Mendocino's iconic, beloved country Cal-French restaurant occupies an 1893 farmhouse restyled into a chic dining room, perfect for holding hands by candlelight. Refined and inspired, the locally sourced menu merrily changes with the seasons.

North Coast Brewing Co BREWERY
(707-964-3400; www.northcoastbrewing.com; 444 N Main St, Fort Bragg; 4-9:30pm Wed-Thu & Sun, to 10pm Fri & Sat) Overpriced fish-and-chips and garlicky waffle fries are not up to the same standard as the stellar handcrafted brews like Red Seal Ale and Belgian-style 'Brother Thelonious' poured in the taproom.

Getting There & Around

Neither Greyhound nor Amtrak serves towns along Hwy 1. **Mendocino Transit Authority** (MTA; 800-696-4682; www.mendocinotransit.org) bus 65 travels daily between Fort Bragg and Santa Rosa ($21, 2½ hours) via Ukiah; from Santa Rosa, catch hourly **Golden Gate Transit** (☑ 415-455-2000; http://goldengate.org) bus 101 to San Francisco ($10.75, 2¾ hours). On weekdays, MTA bus 60 shuttles several times between Fort Bragg and Mendocino ($1.25, one hour), with one onward connection to Point Arena and Gualala.

Ukiah to Garberville

While the coastal Hwy 1 route is ideal for dawdling, much of the traffic on inland Hwy 101 is rushing toward remote regions beyond the 'Redwood Curtain.' Diversions along the way include the down-home vineyards around Ukiah, bounteous redwood forests north of Leggett and the abandoned wilds of the Lost Coast.

Although **Ukiah** is mostly a place to gas up or get a bite, nearby **Vichy Springs Resort** (☑ 707-462-9515; www.vichysprings.com; 2605 Vichy Springs Rd; 2hr/day pass $30/50) offers North America's only naturally carbonated mineral baths (swimwear required).

Just north of tiny **Leggett** on Hwy 101, you can take a dip or fish in the Eel River at **Standish-Hickey State Recreation Area** (☑ 707-925-6482; www.parks.ca.gov; 69350 Hwy 101; per car $8; 🐾), where 9 miles of hiking trails traipse through virgin and second-growth redwoods; look for the 225ft-tall Miles Standish tree. Seven miles south of **Garberville** on Hwy 101, **Richardson Grove State Park** (☑ 707-247-3318; www.parks.ca.gov; per car $8) protects 2000 acres of old-growth redwood forest. Both parks have developed **campgrounds** (☑ 800-444-7275; www.reserveamerica.com; campsites $35-45; 🐾🐕).

The **Lost Coast** tops any dedicated hiker's itinerary, offering the most rugged coastal backpacking in California. It became 'lost' when the highway bypassed the mountains of the King Range, which rise 4000ft within several miles of the ocean, leaving the region largely undeveloped. From Garberville, it's 23 miles along a rough road to **Shelter Cove**, the main supply point but little more than a seaside subdivision with a general store, cafes and motels. Heed 'no trespassing' signs before wandering off-trail, lest you encounter extremely territorial farmers of the region's illicit cash crop, marijuana.

Along Hwy 101, 82-sq-mile **Humboldt Redwoods State Park** (www.humboldtredwoods.org) **FREE** protects some of the world's oldest redwoods and has 80% of the world's tallest 137 trees. Magnificent groves rival those in Redwood National Park, a long drive further north. Even if you don't have time to hike, at least drive the awe-inspiring **Avenue of the Giants**, a 32-mile, two-lane road parallel to Hwy 101. Book ahead for **campsites** (☑ 800-444-7275; www.reserveamerica.com; campsites $20-35; 🐾). Get hiking info and maps at the **visitor center** (☑ 707-946-2263; ⊘ 9am-5pm Apr-Oct, 10am-4pm Nov-Mar).

🛌 Sleeping & Eating

Campgrounds and RV parks are plentiful along Hwy 101, where every one-horse town guarantees at least a natural-foods store with a deli, a drive-thru espresso stand, a hippie-owned cafe and a handful of motels. Woodsy cabin resorts and aging motels along Avenue of the Giants are mostly mediocre at best.

Benbow Inn   HISTORIC HOTEL **$$$**
(☑ 707-923-2124, 800-355-3301; www.benbowinn.com; 445 Lake Benbow Dr, Garberville; r/cottage from $180/230; ✳🐾🐕) With almost comically highbrow decor, this 1926 Tudor-style manor is nevertheless a memorable getaway. There's complimentary afternoon tea service and decanted sherry in each room. The white-tablecloth restaurant and wood-paneled bar are inviting on foggy evenings.

Ardella's   DINER **$**
(77 S Main St, Willits; mains $6-11; ⊘ 7am-2:45pm Wed-Sat, 8am-2pm Sun; 🐾) On Hwy 101, hippie hitchhikers, truckers and tourists all pat their bellies after gobbling giant omelets, potato hashes, gourmet salads and homemade soups like curried carrot-ginger. Cash only.

ℹ Getting There & Around

Daily Greyhound buses connect San Francisco with Ukiah ($43, three hours), Willitts ($43, 3½ hours) and Garberville ($58, 5½ hours). **Redwood Transit System** (☑ 707-443-0826; www.hta.org; 🐾) operates infrequent weekday buses between Garberville and Eureka ($5, 1¾ hours).

Eureka to Crescent City

Past the strip malls that sprawl from its edges, the heart of **Eureka** is Old Town, abounding with fine Victorians buildings, antique shops and restaurants. Cruise the harbor aboard the blue-and-white 1910 Madaket (707-445-1910; www.humboldtbay maritimemuseum.com; tour from $10; Jun-early Oct), departing from the foot of C St; sunset cocktail cruises serve from the state's smallest licensed bar. The visitor center (800-356-6381, 707-442-3738; www.eurekachamber.com; 2112 Broadway; 8:30am-5pm Mon-Fri;) is on Hwy 101, south of downtown.

On the north side of Humboldt Bay, Arcata is a patchouli-dipped hippie haven of radical politics. Biodiesel-fueled trucks drive in for the weekly farmers market (www.humfarm.org; Arcata Plaza; 9am-2pm mid-Apr–mid-Oct;) on the central plaza, surrounded by art galleries, shops, cafes and bars. Make reservations to soak at Finnish Country Sauna & Tubs (707-822-2228; http://cafemokkaarcata.com; cnr 5th & J Sts; 30min per adult/child $10/2; noon-11pm Sun-Thu, to 1am Fri & Sat). Northeast of downtown is the Humboldt State University (www.humboldt.edu) campus.

A working fishing town 16 miles north of Arcata, Trinidad sits on a bluff overlooking a breathtakingly beautiful harbor. Stroll sandy beaches or take short hikes around Trinidad Head after meeting tide-pool critters at the HSU Telonicher Marine Laboratory (707-826-3671; www.humboldt.edu/marinelab; 570 Ewing St; donation $1; 9am-4:30pm Mon-Fri, plus noon-4pm Sat & Sun mid-Sep–mid-May;). Heading north of town, Patrick's Point Dr is dotted with forested campgrounds, cabins and lodges. Patrick's Point State Park (707-677-3570; www.parks.ca.gov; 4150 Patrick's Point Dr; per car $8) has stunning rocky headlands, beachcombing, wildlife-watching and an authentic reproduction of a Yurok village. The park's campgrounds (800-444-7275; www.reserveamerica.com; campsites $35-45;) offer coin-op hot showers.

Heading north, Hwy 101 passes Redwood National Park's Thomas H Kuchel Visitor Center (707-465-7765; www.nps.gov/redw; Hwy 101, Orick; 9am-5pm, to 4pm Nov-Mar;). Together, the national park and three state parks – Prairie Creek, Del Norte and Jedediah Smith – are a World Heritage site containing over 40% of all remaining old-growth redwood forests. The national park is free, while some state-park areas have an $8 day-use parking fee and also developed campgrounds (800-444-7275; www.reserveamerica.com; campsites $35;).

This patchwork of state and federally managed land stretches all the way north to the Oregon border, interspersed with several towns. Furthest south, you'll first encounter Redwood National Park, where a 1-mile nature trail winds through Lady Bird Johnson Grove. Pick up a first-come, first-served permit (free) back at the Thomas H Kuchel Visitor Center to visit Tall Trees Grove, home to some of the world's tallest trees.

Six miles north of Orick, the 10-mile Newton B Drury Scenic Parkway runs parallel to Hwy 101 through Prairie Creek Redwoods State Park. Roosevelt elk graze in the pastoral meadow outside the visitor center (707-488-2039; www.parks.ca.gov; 9am-5pm May-Oct, 10am-4pm Nov-Apr), where several sunlight-dappled hiking trails begin. Three miles back south, unpaved Davison Rd heads northwest to Gold Bluffs Beach, dead-ending at lush Fern Canyon, which cameoed in the Lost World: Jurassic Park.

North of tiny Klamath, Hwy 101 passes the Trees of Mystery (800-638-3389; www.treesofmystery.net; 15500 Hwy 101; adult/child $15/8; 8am-6:30pm Jun-Aug, 9:30am-4:30pm Sep-May;), a kitschy roadside attraction with aerial tram rides. Next up, Del Norte Coast Redwoods State Park preserves virgin redwood groves and 8 miles of unspoiled coastline. The 5-mile round-trip Damnation Creek Trail careens over 1000ft downhill past skyscraping redwoods to a hidden rocky beach, best visited at low tide. The trailhead is at a parking turn-out on Hwy 101 near Mile 16.

Sprawling over a crescent-shaped bay, Crescent City is a drab little town, but it's the only sizable coastal settlement north of Arcata. More than half the town was destroyed by a tidal wave in 1964 and rebuilt with utilitarian architecture. When the tide's out, you can walk across to the 1856 Battery Point Lighthouse (707-467-3089; www.delnortehistory.org; adult/child $3/1; 10am-4pm Wed-Sun Apr-Oct) from the south end of A St.

Jedediah Smith Redwoods State Park is the northernmost park in the system, 5 miles beyond Crescent City. The redwood stands here are so dense that there are few trails, but a couple of easy hikes start near riverside swimming holes along Hwy 199 and rough, unpaved Howland Hill Rd, an 11-mile scenic drive. The park visitor center (707-458-3496; www.parks.ca.gov; Hwy 199, Hiouchi; 9am-5pm mid-May-mid-Sep) has maps and information.

🛏 Sleeping & Eating

A mixed bag of motels are scattered along Hwy 101, including in Eureka, Arcata and Crescent City. Arcata has the biggest variety of dining options, from organic juice bars and vegan cafes to Californian and world-fusion bistros.

Requa Inn B&B $$
(📞707-482-1425; www.requainn.com; 451 Requa Rd, Klamath; r $119-199; 📶) Built in 1914, this simple inn caters to outdoorsy types, with a big breakfast and old-fashioned rooms overlooking the river. No TVs or phones.

Carter House Inns B&B $$$
(📞800-404-1390, 707-444-8062; http://carter-house.com; 301 L St, Eureka; r incl breakfast $189-385; 📶🐾) The cushiest option near Eureka's Old Town are these lovingly tended Victorians. Many of the rooms and suites have romantic fireplaces. Evening wine and hors d'oeuvres and milk with cookies are complimentary. Seasonal Cal-French cuisine at the hotel's **Restaurant 301** (dinner mains $20-30; ⊙6-9pm) is the most haute dining around.

Wildberries Marketplace MARKET, DELI $
(www.wildberries.com; 747 13th St, Arcata; sandwiches $4-10; ⊙6am-midnight; 🚗) Step inside the North Coast's best natural-foods grocery store, with a healthy-minded deli and fruit-smoothie bar. Stock up on snacks and drinks for beach picnics and trailside lunches.

Samoa Cookhouse AMERICAN $$
(📞707-442-1659; www.samoacookhouse.net; 908 Vance Ave, Samoa; all-you-can-eat meals $11-16; ⊙7am-9pm; 🚗) On Humboldt Bay's Samoa Peninsula, this popular dining hall was originally built for an 1890s lumber camp. Today road-trippers and hippies stuff themselves at long red-checked oilcloth-covered tables. Kids eat for half-price.

Lost Coast Brewery BREWERY $$
(📞707-445-4480; www.lostcoast.com; 617 4th St, Eureka; mains $9-15; ⊙11am-10pm Sun-Thu, to 11pm Fri & Sat; 📶🚗) At this legendary North Coast brewery, the Downtown Brown and Great White beers are worth stopping for, but the kitchen turns out only so-so wings, nachos and other pub grub. True beer geeks should also visit Fortuna's organic Eel River Brewing, Arcata's Redwood Curtain Brewing, McKinleyville's Six Rivers Brewery and Blue Lake's Mad River Brewing Company.

ℹ Getting There & Around

Arcata's **Greyhound depot** (925 E St) has daily buses to San Francisco ($57, seven hours) via Eureka, Garberville, Willits and Ukiah. Several daily **Redwood Transit System** (📞707-443-0826; www.hta.org) buses stop in Eureka and Arcata on the Trinidad–Scotia route ($2.75, 2½ hours).

Sacramento

California's first nonmission European settlement, the state capital is an anomalous place: the first city to shoot up during the gold-rush era is flat and fairly bland, with shady trees, withering summer heat and jammed highways.

In 1839 eccentric Swiss immigrant John Sutter built a fort here. Once gold was discovered in the nearby Sierra foothills in 1848, the town's population boomed. After much legislative waffling, Sacramento eventually became California's capital in 1854.

Old Sacramento remains a visitor's magnet – a riverside area with raised wooden sidewalks that can feel like a ye olde tourist trap. More interesting food and culture are hidden on the grid of streets downtown and in Midtown, where a fledgling arts scene quietly defies the city's reputation as a cow town.

◉ Sights

California Museum MUSEUM
(www.californiamuseum.org; 1020 O St; adult/child $8.50/6; ⊙10am-5pm Mon-Sat, from noon Sun) This modern museum is home to the California Hall Of Fame – perhaps the only place to simultaneously encounter Amelia Earhart, Cesar Chavez and Mark Zuckerburg. The exhibit 'California Indians: Making A Difference' covers the traditions and culture of indigenous tribes, past and present.

California State Capitol HISTORIC BUILDING
(📞916-324-0333; http://capitolmuseum.ca.gov; 1315 10th St; ⊙8am-5pm Mon-Fri, from 9am Sat & Sun, tours hourly 9am-4pm) **FREE** The 19th-century state capitol is a white jewel rising from the manicured Capitol Mall. Inside are California art and history exhibits and period-furnished chambers. The Assembly and Senate rooms are open to the public.

California State Railroad Museum MUSEUM
(📞916-445-6645; www.californiastaterailroadmuseum.org; 125 I St; adult/child $10/5, incl train ride $20/10; ⊙10am-5pm, train rides hourly Apr-Sep;

⚐) Step aboard dozens of meticulously restored beasts of steam and diesel by the river in Old Sacramento (www.oldsacramento.com), a walkable district of historical buildings and tiny museums.

Sutter's Fort State Historic Park
HISTORIC SITE

(☑916-445-4422; www.parks.ca.gov; 2701 L St; adult/child $5/3; ☺10am-5pm) Within the walls of this restored fort, the original cannon and a working ironsmith are straight out of the 1850s. Next door is the tiny but fascinating California State Indian Museum (☑916-324-0971; www.parks.ca.gov; 2618 K St; adult/child $3/2; ☺10am-5pm Wed-Sun).

Crocker Art Museum
MUSEUM

(☑916-264-5423; www.crockerartmuseum.org; 216 O St; adult/child $10/5; ☺10am-5pm Tue-Wed & Fri-Sun, to 9pm Thu) Adjoining the handsome residence of a 19th-century California Supreme Court judge, modern galleries highlight early and contemporary California art.

🍴 Sleeping & Eating

Sacramento's hotels cater to business travelers, so look for weekend bargains. The freeways and suburbs around the city are glutted with chain lodgings. For more restaurants and bars, make for Midtown, especially J St east of 16th St.

HI Sacramento Hostel
HOSTEL $

(☑916-443-1691; http://norcalhostels.org/sac; 925 H St; dm $30-36, r with/without bath from $76/58; ☺check-in 2pm-10pm; @ 🛜) A short walk from the capitol, this restored Victorian mansion has common areas of nearly B&B quality, spacious dorms and staff who know about local nightlife.

Delta King
B&B $$

(☑800-825-5464, 916-444-5464; www.deltaking.com; 100 Front St; d incl breakfast from $139; ✳🛜) Snuggle into compact rooms aboard the *Delta King*, a 1927 paddle-wheeler docked in Old Sacramento. The boat has a nautical-themed bar and restaurant. Parking is $18.

Citizen Hotel
BOUTIQUE HOTEL $$$

(☑info 916-447-2700, reservations 916-492-4460; www.jdvhotels.com; 926 J St; r $139-269; ✳@🛜🐾) Elegant rooms at this 1920s downtown office building are lovely with luxurious linens, bold-patterned fabrics and iPod docking stations. Little touches make a big impression: vintage political cartoons adorn-

ing the walls and political movies to borrow. On the ground floor, Grange (☑916-492-4450; www.grangesacramento.com; 926 J St; dinner mains $19-39; ☺6:30-10:30am & 11:30am-2pm Mon-Fri, 8am-2pm Sat & Sun, 5:30pm-10pm Mon-Thu, to 11pm Fri & Sat, to 10pm Sun; 🛜) cooks California farm-to-table fare. Hotel parking is $25.

La Bonne Soupe Cafe
DELI $

(☑916-492-9506; 920 8th St; items $4-8; ☺11am-3pm Mon-Fri) Divinely epicurean sandwiches and scratch soups, all handmade with love by a chef, bring downtown office workers to line up out the door.

Tower Cafe
ECLECTIC $$

(☑916-441-0222; www.towercafe.com; 1518 Broadway; mains $7-18; ☺8am-10pm Sun-Thu, to 11pm Fri & Sat) Best bet for big ol' breakfasts – custardy French toast topped with fruit, or chorizo sausage with eggs – at a 1938 art-deco movie theater.

Mulvaney's B & L
CALIFORNIAN $$$

(☑916-441-6022; www.mulvaneysbl.com; 1215 19th St; dinner mains $26-38; ☺11:30am-2:30pm Tue-Fri, 5-10pm Tue-Sat) Arguably the classiest restaurant in town, here inside an 1890s fire house a hyper-seasonal, European-touched menu changes every single day.

🍷 Drinking & Entertainment

Temple Coffee
CAFE

(www.templecoffee.com; 1010 9th St; ☺6am-11pm; 🛜) 🌿 Sip sustainably sourced, locally roasted coffee at communal wooden tables.

Rubicon Brewing Company
BREWERY

(☑916-448-7032; www.rubiconbrewing.com; 2004 Capitol Ave; ☺11am-11:30pm Mon-Thu, to 12:30am Fri & Sat, to 10pm Sun) The place for award-winning ales, hot wings and brewhouse chili-cheese fries.

Sacramento River Cats
SPORTS

(www.milb.com; Raley Field, 400 Ballpark Dr; tickets $5-65; ☺Apr-Sep) Minor-league baseball team plays at Raley Field, with dazzling views of Tower Bridge.

ℹ️ Getting There & Around

About 11 miles northwest of downtown off I-5, Sacramento International Airport (☑919-929-5411; www.sacairports.org; 6900 Airport Blvd) is served mainly by domestic flights.

From downtown's train station (☑877-974-3322; www.capitolcorridor.org; 401 I St), Amtrak runs frequent *Capitol Corridor* trains to/from the San Francisco Bay Area ($28 to $38, 90 minutes to three hours); twice-daily *San Joaquin* trains, with onward bus connections to Yosemite Valley ($37, five hours); and daily long-distance *Coast Starlight* and *California Zephyr* trains. **Greyhound** (420 Richards Blvd) has several daily buses to San Francisco ($27, two hours) and Los Angeles ($78, 7½ to nine hours).

Sacramento Regional Transit (www.sacrt. com; fare/day pass $2.25/6) runs a bus and light-rail system around town.

Gold Country

Hard to believe, but this is where it all began – the quiet hill towns and drowsy oaklined byways of Gold Country belie the wild, chaotic, often violent establishment of California. After a glint caught James Marshall's eye in Sutter's Creek in 1848, the gold rush brought a 300,000-stong stampede of '49ers to these Sierra foothills. The frenzy paid little heed to the starched moral decorum of Victorian society, and traces of its lawless boom towns and environmental havoc remain today.

Traveling here might be a thrill ride for history buffs – the fading historical markers tell tales of bloodlust and banditry – but more tactile pleasures await the traveler willing to plunge into a swimming hole, rattle down a mountain-biking trail or go white-water rafting in the icy currents of the American, Stanislaus and Tuolumne Rivers. Based in the Central Valley, **All-Outdoors California Whitewater Rafting** (☏800-247-2387; www.aorafting.com) outfits a variety of day and overnight rafting trips for all skill levels from spring through fall.

Hwy 50 divides the Northern and Southern Mines. Winding Hwy 49, which connects everything, has plenty of pull-outs and vistas of the surrounding hills. **The Gold Country Visitors Association** (www.calgold. org) has many more touring ideas.

Northern Mines

Known as the 'Queen of the Northern Mines,' **Nevada City** has narrow streets gleaming with lovingly restored buildings, tiny theaters, art galleries, cafes and shops. The **visitor center** (☏530-265-2692; www. nevadacitychamber.com; 132 Main St; ☉9am-5pm Mon-Fri, 11am-4pm Sat, 11am-3pm Sun) dispenses information and self-guided walking-tour maps. On Hwy 49, **Tahoe National Forest Headquarters** (☏530-265-4531; www.fs.usda.

gov/tahoe; 631 Coyote St; ☉8am-4:30pm Mon-Fri) provides camping, hiking and mountain-biking information and wilderness permits.

Four miles south, **Grass Valley** is Nevada City's functional sister, where artists, hippies and ranchers get their trucks' oil changed. Just over a mile east of Hwy 49, **Empire Mine State Historic Park** (☏530-273-8522; www.empiremine.org; 10791 E Empire St; adult/child $7/3; ☉10am-5pm) marks the site of one of the richest mines in California. From 1850 to 1956 it produced more than 5.6 million ounces of gold – about $5 billion in today's market.

When it's sweltering hot outside during summer, if you see a line of cars parked roadside along Hwy 49, that's your signal to discover a swimming hole. One of the best is where the North and South forks of the American River join up, a few miles east of **Auburn**, an I-80 pit stop about 25 miles south of Grass Valley.

Coloma is where California's gold rush started. Riverside **Marshall Gold Discovery State Historic Park** (☏530-622-3470; www.parks.ca.gov; per person/car $6/8; ☉park 8am-5pm, to 7pm late May-early Sep, museum 10am-3pm, to 4pm Mar-Nov; ♿) pays tribute to James Marshall's riot-inducing discovery, with a replica of Sutter's Mill, restored buildings and gold-panning opportunities. There's a hilltop monument to Marshall himself, who, in one of the many ironic twists of the gold rush, died as a penniless ward of the state.

🛏 Sleeping & Eating

Nevada City boasts the biggest spread of restaurants and historical B&Bs. Motels speckle Hwy 49 in Grass Valley and I-80 in Auburn.

Broad Street Inn   INN $$
(☏530-265-2239; www.broadstreetinn.com; 517 E Broad St, Nevada City; r $110-120; ❄☎🖥) ✿ Unlike dozens of frilly bed-and-breakfasts in Gold Country, this sun-drenched, six-room inn keeps things refreshingly simple with modern, brightly furnished rooms.

Outside Inn   MOTEL, CABIN $$
(☏530-265-2233; www.outsideinn.com; 575 E Broad St, Nevada City; r $79-155, cottage $200; ❄☎🖥♿🐾) More fun than any ho-hum chain are these knotty-pine-walled themed rooms (some with kitchenettes), BBQ grills and friendly owners who are outdoor enthusiasts.

Treats
DESSERT **$**

(http://treatsnevadacity.com; 110 York St, Nevada City; items $2-5; ⊙noon-9pm Sun-Thu, to 10pm Fri & Sat, shorter hr winter; 🖈) Handmade, often organic ice cream, seasonal sorbets and other cool treats.

Ikedas
MARKET **$**

(www.ikedas.com; 13500 Lincoln Way, Auburn; items from $3; ⊙8am-7pm, to 8pm Sat & Sun) Off I-80 north of downtown Auburn, Tahoe-bound travelers stop for fresh fruit, homemade pies and picnic fixin's.

Ike's Quarter Cafe
CREOLE, CALIFORNIAN **$$**

(✐530-265-6138; www.ikesquartercafe.com; 401 Commercial St, Nevada City; mains $7-15; ⊙8am-3pm Wed-Mon; 🖈) Dig into gut-busting breakfasts like the 'Hangtown Fry,' a gold miners' mess of cornmeal-crusted oysters and bacon, or N'awlins-style fare like muffaletta sandwiches on the fountain patio. Cash only.

Southern Mines

The towns of the Southern Mines – from Placerville to Sonora – receive less traffic and their dusty streets have a whiff of Wild West, today evident in the motley assortment of Harley riders, gold prospectors (still!) and outsider winemakers who populate them. Some, like Plymouth (Ole Pokerville) and Mokelumne Hill, are virtual ghost towns, slowly crumbling into photogenic oblivion. Others, like Sutter Creek, Murphys and Angels Camp, are gussied-up showpieces of Victorian Americana. Get off the beaten path at family-run vineyards and subterranean caverns, where geological wonders reward those willing to navigate the touristy gift shops above ground.

A short detour off Hwy 49 is Columbia State Historic Park (✐209-588-9128; www.parks.ca.gov; 11255 Jackson St, Columbia; ⊙museum 9am-4:30pm Apr-Oct, from 10am Nov-Mar; 🖈) **FREE**, which preserves four square blocks of authentic 1850s buildings complete with shopkeepers and street musicians in period costumes; it's crazy-busy with school-kids panning for gold. Also near Sonora, Railtown 1897 State Historic Park (✐209-984-3953; www.railtown1897.org; 18115 5th Ave, Jamestown; museum adult/child $5/3, incl train ride $15/8; ⊙9:30am-4:30pm Apr-Oct, 10am-3pm Nov-Mar, train rides 11am-3pm Sat & Sun Apr-Oct; 🖈) offers excursion trains through the surrounding hills where Hollywood Westerns including *High Noon* were filmed.

🛏 Sleeping & Eating

Lacy B&Bs, cafes and ice-cream parlors are in nearly every town. Busy Sonora, just over an hour's drive from Yosemite National Park, and Placerville have the most motels.

Indian Grinding Rock State Historic Park Campground
CAMPGROUND **$**

(www.parks.ca.gov; 14881 Pine Grove-Volcano Rd, Pine Grove; camping & RV sites $30; ⊙mid-Mar–Sep; 🖈🐕) Around 10 miles northeast of Sutter Creek, this pastoral state-park campground has 22 sites set among trees (no reservations) and coin-op hot showers.

Gunn House Hotel
HISTORIC HOTEL **$$**

(✐209-532-3421; www.gunnhousehotel.com; 286 S Washington St, Sonora; r incl breakfast $79-115; ❋🐕) For an alternative to cookie-cutter chains, this historic hotel hits the sweet spot. B&B-esque rooms feature period decor. On summer evenings, sink back into rocking chairs on the front porch.

City & Fallon Hotels
HISTORIC HOTEL **$$**

(✐800-532-1479; www.briggshospitalityllc.com; 22768 Main St, Columbia; r incl breakfast without bath $105-175; ❋🛜) Twin restored period hotels in historic Columbia town are decked out with museum-quality pieces. After dark, shoot whiskey at What Cheer Saloon or watch plays at the Fallon's repertory theater.

Volcano Union Inn
HISTORIC HOTEL **$$**

(✐209-296-7711; www.volcanounion.com; 21375 Consolation St, Volcano; r incl breakfast $119-149; ❋❋🛜) Of a quartet of lovingly updated rooms with crooked floors, two have street-facing balconies. Downstairs, Union Pub (mains $10-19; ⊙5-8pm Thu & Mon, 3-9pm Fri, noon-9pm Sat, 10am-8pm Sun) has billiards, shuffleboard, darts and gourmet pub grub.

Cozmic Café & Pub
HEALTHY **$**

(www.ourcoz.com; 594 Main St, Placerville; items $4-10; ⊙7am-6pm Tue & Wed, to 8pm Thu-Sun; 🛜✐) Grab tables *inside* a historic mining tunnel at Placerville's funky organic, health-conscious cafe. There are microbrews on tap and live music on weekends.

Magnolia Cafe
CAFE **$$**

(✐209-728-2186; www.magnoliacafemurphys.com; 64 Mitchler St, Murphys; mains $7-13; ⊙8am-3pm Wed-Sun) Breakfast on chef Devon's chorizo-egg tortas and vanilla-bean French toast, or Asian-spiced pulled-pork burritos and classic steak sandwiches with mustard aioli at lunch.

★ **Taste** CALIFORNIAN $$$
(☑209-245-3463; www.restauranttaste.com;
9402 Main St, Plymouth; dinner mains $27-43;
⊙11:30am-2pm Sat & Sun, dinner from 5pm Thu
& Fri, 4:30pm Sat & Sun) The antidote to Gold
Country's dependence on burgers, Taste
plates artful, fresh, seasonal dishes with
European influences that pair well with
wines from Amador County's vineyards.

❶ Getting There & Around

A patchwork of public buses sporadically serves
some towns. For the Northern Mines, **Gold
Country Stage** (☑888-660-7433, 530-477-
0103; www.mynevadacounty.com; fares $1.50-
3) buses link Nevada City, Grass Valley and
Auburn, while **Placer County Transit** (☑530-
885-2877; www.placer.ca.gov/transit; fare
$1.25) buses connect Auburn with Sacramento.
Among the Southern Mines, weekday-only
Amador Transit (☑209-267-9395; http://ama-
dortransit.com; fares $1-2) runs buses between
Sutter Creek and Sacramento, Jackson and
Plymouth. **Calaveras Transit** (☑209-754-4450;
http://transit.calaverasgov.us; fare $2) buses
serve Angels Camp, Jackson and Murphys.
Tuolumne County Transit (☑209-532-0404;
www.tuolumnecountytransit.com; fare $1.50)
buses and trolleys loop between Sonora, Colum-
bia and Jamestown.

Northern Mountains

Remote, empty and eerily beautiful, these
are some of California's least-visited wild
lands, an endless show of geological won-
ders, alpine lakes, rushing rivers and high
desert. The major peaks – Lassen, Shasta
and the Trinity Alps – have few geological
features in common, but all offer backcoun-
try camping under starry skies. Isolated
towns dotting the region aren't attractions,
but are handy resupply points for wilder-
ness adventures.

Redding to Yreka

Much of the drive north of Redding is domi-
nated by Mt Shasta, a 14,179ft snow-capped
goliath at the southern end of the volcan-
ic Cascades Range. It rises dramatically,
fueling the anticipation felt by outdoor
enthusiasts who seek to climb its slopes. A
helpful pit stop just off I-5 is the Califor-
nia Welcome Center (☑800-474-2784, 530-
365-1180; www.shastacascade.com; 1699 Hwy 273,
Anderson; ⊙9am-5pm Mon-Sat, 10am-4pm Sun),

12 miles south of Redding at the Shasta Out-
lets mall.

Don't believe the tourist brochures; Red-
ding, the region's largest city, is a snooze.
The best reason to detour off I-5 is the
Sundial Bridge, a glass-bottomed pedes-
trian marvel designed by Spanish architect
Santiago Calatrava. It spans the Sacramen-
to River at Turtle Bay Exploration Park
(☑800-887-8532; www.turtlebay.org; 844 Sundial
Bridge Dr; adult/child $14/10, after 3:30pm $9/5;
⊙9am-5pm Mon-Sat & 10am-5pm Sun, closes
1hr earlier Oct-Mar; ❸), a kid-friendly science
center with botanical gardens.

About 6 miles west of Redding along Hwy
299, explore a genuine gold-rush town at
Shasta State Historical Park (☑520-243-
8194; www.parks.ca.gov; museum adult/child $3/2;
⊙10am-5pm Fri-Sun). Two miles further west,
Whiskeytown National Recreation Area
(☑530-246-1225; www.nps.gov/whis; per car $5;
⊙visitor center 9am-5pm late May-early Sep,
10am-4pm early Sep-late May) FREE is home to
Whiskeytown Lake, with sandy beaches, wa-
terfall hikes and water-sports and camping
opportunities.

At Weaverville, another 35 miles west
of Whiskeytown, Joss House State His-
toric Park (☑530-623-5284; www.parks.ca.gov;
cnr Hwy 299 & Oregon St; tour adult/child $4/2;
⊙10am-5pm Thu-Sun, hourly tours until 4pm) pre-
serves an 1874 Chinese immigrant temple.
Weaverville Ranger Station (☑530-623-
2121; www.fs.usda.gov/stnf; 360 Main St; ⊙8am-
4:30pm Mon-Fri) issues backcountry permits
for the near-pristine wilderness of the sur-
rounding Trinity Alps.

North of Redding, I-5 crosses deep-blue
Shasta Lake, California's biggest reservoir,
formed by towering Shasta Dam (☑530-
275-4463; www.usbr.gov/mp/ncao/shasta/; 16349
Shasta Dam Blvd; ⊙visitor center 8am-5pm, tours
9am-3pm) FREE and surrounded by shoreline
hiking trails and RV campgrounds. High in
the limestone megaliths at the lake's north-
ern end are the prehistoric caves of Lake
Shasta Caverns (☑800-795-2283, 530-238-
2341; http://lakeshastacaverns.com; 20359 Shasta
Caverns Rd; adult/child $24/14; ⊙tours 9am-4pm
late May-early Sep, to 3pm Apr-late May & Sep,
10am-2pm Oct-Mar; ❸), where guided tours
include a catamaran ride.

Another 35 miles north on I-5, Dunsmuir
is a teeny historic railroad town with vi-
brant cafes and art galleries in its quaint
downtown. If for no other reason, stop to
fill your bottle from the public fountains:

Dunsmuir claims to have the best H_2O on earth. Just south off I-5, **Castle Crags State Park** (☑ 530-235-2684; www.parks.ca.gov; per car $8) shelters forested **campsites** (☑ 800-444-7275; www.reserveamerica.com; campsites $15-30; 🚻 🐕). Be awed by stunning views of Mt Shasta from the summit of the 5.4-mile round-trip **Crags Trail**.

Ten miles north of Dunsmuir, **Mt Shasta town** lures climbers, New Age hippies and back-to-nature types, all of whom revere the majestic mountain looming overhead. The **Everitt Memorial Hwy** ascends the mountain to a perfect sunset-watching perch at almost 8000ft; simply head east from town on Lake St and keep going 14 more miles. For experienced mountaineers only, climbing the peak above 10,000ft requires a Summit Pass ($20), available from **Mt Shasta Ranger Station** (☑ 530-926-4511; www.fs.usda.gov/stnf; 204 W Alma St; ⏱ 8am-4:30pm Mon-Fri), which has weather reports and sells topographic maps. Stop by downtown's **Fifth Season** (☑ 530-926-3606; http://thefifthseason.com; 300 N Mt Shasta Blvd) outdoor-gear shop for equipment rentals. **Shasta Mountain Guides** (☑ 530-926-3117; http://shastaguides.com) offers multiday mountaineering trips (from $500).

🛏 Sleeping & Eating

Roadside motels are abundant in all parts but the remote northeast. Redding has the most chain motels and hotels, clustered near major highways. Campgrounds are abundant, especially on public lands.

McCloud River Mercantile Hotel   INN $$
(☑ 530-964-2330; www.mccloudmercantile.com; 241 Main St, McCloud; r $139-250; 🛜) Guests are greeted with fresh flowers and can drift to sleep on feather beds after soaking in clawfoot tubs. Exposed brick and antique accents are a perfect marriage of preservationist class and modern panache. The 1930s soda fountain downstairs cooks country-style breakfasts and lunches (mains $6 to $10). It's about 10 miles east of Mt Shasta town off Hwy 89.

Railroad Park Resort   INN, CAMPGROUND $$
(☑ 530-235-4440, 800-974-7245; www.rrpark.com; 100 Railroad Park Rd, Dunsmuir; tent/RV sites from $29/37, d $115-150; 🚿 🛜 🏊 🚻 🐕) The most memorable overnight stay is inside a wood-paneled caboose, off I-5 just south of town.

Sengthongs   THAI, VIETNAMESE $$
(☑ 530-235-4770; http://sengthongs.com; 5855 Dunsmuir Ave, Dunsmuir; mains $11-20; ⏱ usually 5-8:30pm Thu-Sun) Beloved long-running Southeast Asian restaurant hosts live music a few doors down in its Blue Sky Room.

Café Maddalena   BISTRO $$$
(☑ 530-235-2725; www.cafemaddalena.com; 5801 Sacramento Ave, Dunsmuir; mains $14-25; ⏱ 5-10pm Thu-Sun Feb-Nov) Chef-owner Bret LaMott maintains this cozy riverfront restaurant's stellar reputation with Mediterranean specialties and a well-stocked wine bar. Reservations recommended.

❶ Getting There & Around

Amtrak's *Coast Starlight* trains stop in Redding and Dunsmuir, incovneniently in the middle of the night. Greyhound buses serve Redding and Weed. **Siskiyou County STAGE** (☑ 800-247-8243, 530-842-8295; www.co.siskiyou.ca.us/GS/stage.aspx; fares $2.50-4) buses run up and down I-5 several times daily, connecting Dunsmuir, Mt Shasta and Weed.

Northeast Corner

Site of California's last major Native American conflict and a half-million years of volcanic destruction, **Lava Beds National Monument** (☑ 530-667-8113; www.nps.gov/labe; 7-day entry per car $10) is a peaceful monument to centuries of turmoil. This park's got it all: lava flows, craters, cinder and spatter cones, and more than 500 lava tubes. It was the site of the Modoc War, and Native American petroglyphs are etched into cave walls. Pick up info, maps and flashlights for spelunking at the **visitor center** (☑ 530-667-8113; 1 Indian Well, Tulelake; ⏱ 8am-6pm late May-early Sep, 8:30am-5pm mid-Sep–mid-May). Nearby is the park's **campground** (campsites $10), where basic sites accommodate tents and small RVs; drinking water is available.

Just north, the **Klamath Basin National Wildlife Refuge Complex** (www.fws.gov/klamathbasinrefuges) comprises six separate refuges. This is a prime stopover on the Pacific Flyway and an important wintering site for bald eagles. The **visitor center** (☑ 530-667-2231; 4009 Hill Rd, Tulelake; ⏱ 8am-4:30pm Mon-Fri, 9am-4pm Sat & Sun) is off Hwy 161, about 4 miles south of the Oregon border. Self-guided 10-mile auto tours of the Lower Klamath and Tule Lake reserves provide excellent birding opportunities. For gas, food and lodging, drive into Klamath Falls, OR.

The **Modoc National Forest** (☑530-233-5811; www.fs.usda.gov/modoc) blankets over 3000 sq miles of northeastern California. Camping is free and reservations are not accepted, although campfire permits are required. **Medicine Lake**, about an hour's drive southwest of Lava Beds National Monument, is a pristine, gleaming blue crater lake surrounded by pine forest, hulking volcanic formations and cool, secluded campgrounds. Further east is landmark **Glass Mountain**, where Native Americans quarried jet-black obsidian. East of Cedarville via Hwy 299, near the Nevada border, the high desert of **Surprise Valley** is a gateway to the wild **Warner Mountains** – possibly California's least-visited range.

Quietly impressive **Lassen Volcanic National Park** (☑530-595-4444; www.nps.gov/lavo; 7-day entry per car $10) has hydrothermal sulfur pools, boiling mud pots and steaming pools, as glimpsed from the **Bumpass Hell** boardwalk. At 10,462ft, **Lassen Peak** is the world's largest plug-dome volcano. The park has two entrances: an hour's drive east of Redding off Hwy 44, near popular **Manzanita Lake Campground** (☑877-444-6777; www.recreation.gov; campsites $10-18, cabins $59-84); and northwest of Lake Almanor off Hwy 89, by the **Kohm Yah-ma-nee Visitor Center** (☑530-595-4480; www.nps.gov/lavo; ☉9am-5pm, closed Tue & Wed Nov-Mar). Hwy 89 through the park is typically snow-free and open to cars from May or June through October or November (snowshoes and cross-country skis permitted in winter).

SIERRA NEVADA

The mighty Sierra Nevada – baptized the 'Range of Light' by naturalist John Muir – is California's backbone. This 400-mile phalanx of craggy peaks, chiseled and gouged by glaciers and erosion, both welcomes and challenges outdoor-sports enthusiasts. Cradling three national parks (Yosemite, Sequoia and Kings Canyon), the Sierra is a spellbinding wonderland of superlative wilderness, embracing the contiguous USA's highest peak (Mt Whitney), North America's tallest waterfall (Yosemite Falls) and the world's oldest and biggest trees (ancient bristlecone pines and giant sequoias, respsectively).

Yosemite National Park

There's a reason why everybody's heard of it: the granite-peak heights are dizzying, the mist from thunderous waterfalls drenching, the Technicolor wildflower meadows amazing and the majestic silhouettes of El Capitan and Half Dome almost shocking against a crisp blue sky. It's a landscape of dreams, surrounding oh-so-small people on all sides.

Then, alas, the hiss and belch of another tour bus, disgorging dozens, rudely breaks the spell. While staggering crowds can't be ignored, these rules will shake most of 'em:

➡ Avoid summer in the valley. Spring's best, especially when waterfalls gush in May. Autumn is blissfully peaceful, and snowy winter days can be magical too.

➡ Park your car and leave it – simply by hiking a short distance up almost any trail, you'll lose the car-dependent hordes.

➡ Forget jet lag. Get up early, or go for moonlit hikes with stargazing.

◉ Sights

The main entrances to the **park** (☑209-372-0200; www.nps.gov/yose; 7-day entry per car $20) are at Arch Rock (Hwy 140), Wawona (Hwy 41) and Big Oak Flat (Hwy 120 west). Tioga Pass (Hwy 120 east) is open only seasonally.

◉ Yosemite Valley

From the ground up, this dramatic valley cut by the meandering Merced River is song-inspiring: rippling green meadow-grass; stately pines; cool, impassive pools reflecting the looming granite monoliths; and cascading

---

❶ IMPASSABLE TIOGA PASS

Hwy 120 is the only road connecting Yosemite National Park with the Eastern Sierra, climbing through Tioga Pass (9945ft). Most maps mark this road 'closed in winter,' which, while literally true, is also misleading. Tioga Rd is usually closed from the first heavy snowfall in October or November, not reopening until May or June. If you are planning a trip through Tioga Pass in spring, you'll likely be out of luck. Call ☑209-372-0200 or check www.nps.gov/yose/planyourvisit/conditions.htm for current road conditions.

ribbons of glacially cold white-water. Often overrun and traffic-choked, Yosemite Village is home to the park's main visitor center (p172), museum, photography gallery, general store and many more services. Curry Village is another valley hub, offering public showers and outdoor equipment rental and sales, including for camping.

Spring snowmelt turns the valley's famous waterfalls into thunderous cataracts; most are reduced to a mere trickle by late summer. Yosemite Falls is North America's tallest, dropping 2425ft in three tiers. A wheelchair-accessible trail leads to the bottom of this cascade or, for solitude and different perspectives, you can trek the grueling switchback trail to the top (7.2 miles round-trip). No less impressive are other waterfalls around the valley. A strenuous granite staircase beside Vernal Fall leads you, gasping, right to the waterfall's edge for a vertical view – look for rainbows in the clouds of mist.

You can't ignore the valley's monumental El Capitan (7569ft), an El Dorado for rock climbers. Toothed Half Dome (8842ft) soars above the valley as Yosemite's spiritual centerpiece. The classic panoramic photo op is at Tunnel View on Hwy 41 as you drive into the valley. Early or late in the day during spring or early summer, hike 2 miles round-trip from the eastern valley floor out to Mirror Lake to catch the ever-shifting reflection of Half Dome in the still waters.

Glacier Point

Rising 3200ft above the valley floor, dramatic Glacier Point (7214ft) practically puts you at eye level with Half Dome. It's about an hour's drive from Yosemite Valley up Glacier Point Rd (usually open from late May into November) off Hwy 41, or a strenuous hike along the Four Mile Trail (actually, 4.8 miles one way) or the less-crowded, waterfall-strewn Panorama Trail (8.5 miles one way). To hike one-way downhill from Glacier Point, reserve a seat on the hikers' shuttle bus (p173).

Wawona

At Wawona, almost an hour's drive south of Yosemite Valley, drop by the Pioneer Yosemite History Center, with its covered bridge, pioneer cabins and historic Wells Fargo office. Further south, wander giddily around towering Mariposa Grove, home of the Grizzly Giant and other giant sequoias. Free shuttle buses run to the grove from Wawona from spring through fall; in winter, the access road is usually closed to vehicles, but you can snowshoe along it.

Tuolumne Meadows

A 90-minute drive from Yosemite Valley, high-altitude Tuolumne Meadows (pronounced *twol*-uh-mee) draws hikers, backpackers and climbers to the park's northern wilderness. The Sierra Nevada's largest subalpine meadow (8600ft), it's a vivid contrast to the valley, with wildflower fields, azure lakes, ragged granite peaks and polished domes, and cooler temperatures. Hikers and climbers have a paradise of options; swimming and picnicking by lakes are also popular. Access is via scenic Tioga Rd (Hwy 120), which is only open seasonally (see p169), following a 19th-century wagon road and older Native American trading route. West of Tuolumne Meadows and Tenaya Lake, stop at Olmsted Point for epic vistas of Half Dome.

Hetch Hetchy

It's the site of perhaps the most controversial dam in US history. Despite not existing

---

DON'T MISS

SUPERSIZED FORESTS

In California you can stand under the world's oldest trees (ancient bristlecone pines) and its tallest (coast redwoods), but the record for biggest in terms of volume belongs to giant sequoias (*Sequoiadendron giganteum*). They grow only on the western slope of the Sierra Nevada range and are most abundant in Sequoia, Kings Canyon and Yosemite National Parks. John Muir called them 'Nature's forest masterpiece,' and anyone who's ever craned their neck to take in their soaring vastness has probably done so with the same awe. These trees can grow to over 300ft tall and 100ft in circumference, protected by bark up to 2ft thick. The Giant Forest Museum (p173) in Sequoia National Park has exhibits about the trees' unusual ecology.

in its natural state, Hetch Hetchy Valley remains pretty and mostly crowd-free. It's a 40-mile drive northwest of Yosemite Valley. A 5.4-mile round-trip hike across the dam and through a tunnel to the base of Wapama Falls lets you get thrillingly close to an avalanche of water crashing down into the sparkling reservoir. In spring, you'll get drenched.

🏃 Activities

With over 800 miles of varied hiking trails, you're spoiled for choice. Easy valley-floor routes can get jammed; escape the teeming masses by heading up. The ultimate hike summits Half Dome (14 miles round-trip), but be warned: it's very strenuous, and advance permits (www.nps.gov/yose/planyourvisit/hdpermits.htm; from $12.50) are required even for day hikes. It's rewarding to hike just as far as the top of Vernal Fall (3 miles round-trip) or Nevada Fall (5.8 miles round-trip) via the Mist Trail. A longer, alternate route to Half Dome follows a more gently graded section of the long-distance John Muir Trail.

For overnight backpacking trips, wilderness permits (☑ 209-372-0826; www.nps.gov/yose/planyourvisit/wildpermits.htm; from $10) are required year-round. A quota system limits the number of hikers leaving from each trailhead. Make reservations up to 24 weeks in advance, or try your luck at the Yosemite Valley Wilderness Center or another permit-issuing station, starting at 11am on the day before you want to hike.

Yosemite Mountaineering School　　　ROCK CLIMBING
(☑ 209-372-8344;　www.yosemitemountaineering.com; Curry Village; ⊙ Apr-Oct) With sheer spires, polished domes and soaring monoliths, Yosemite is rock-climbing nirvana. YMS offers topflight instruction for novice to advanced climbers, plus guided climbs and equipment rental. During summer, it also operates at Tuolumne Meadows.

Badger Pass　　　SKIING, SNOWBOARDING
(☑ 209-372-8430; www.badgerpass.com; lift ticket adult/child $42/23; ⊙ 9am-4pm mid-Dec–Mar) Gentle slopes are perfect for beginner skiers and snowboarders. Cross-country skiers can glide along 25 miles of groomed tracks and 90 miles of marked trails, which are also open to snowshoers. Equipment rental and lessons available for all ages.

🛏 Sleeping & Eating

Concessionaire DNC (☑ 801-559-4884; www.yosemitepark.com) has a monopoly on park lodging and eating establishments, including ho-hum food courts and snack bars. Lodging reservations (up to 366 days in advance) are essential during peak season (May through September). During summer, DNC sets up simple canvas-tent cabins at riverside Housekeeping Camp (d from $95) in Yosemite Valley; busy Tuolumne Meadows Lodge (d from $120), a 90-minute drive from the valley; and quieter White Wolf Lodge (d from $120) off Tioga Rd, an hour away from the valley.

Curry Village　　　CABINS $$
(d without bath from $95; 🛜 ♨ 🚻) With a nostalgic summer-camp atmosphere, Curry Village has hundreds of helter-skelter cabins scattered beneath towering evergreens in Yosemite Valley. Soft-sided tent cabins resemble Civil War army barracks with scratchy wool blankets. Solid-wood cabins are smaller but cozy.

Wawona Hotel　　　HISTORIC HOTEL $$
(r with/without bath incl breakfast from $225/155; 🛜 ♨) Filled with character, this Victorian-era throwback has wide porches, manicured lawns, tennis courts and a golf course. Half the thin-walled rooms share baths. The dining room serves three just-OK meals a day (dinner mains $19 to $34). Wawona is about a 45-minute drive south of the valley.

Ahwahnee Hotel　　　HISTORIC HOTEL $$$
(r from $470; @ 🛜 ♨) Sleep where Steve Jobs, Eleanor Roosevelt and JFK bedded down at this national historic landmark, built in 1927. Sit a spell by the roaring fireplace beneath soaring sugar-pine timbers. Skip the formal dining room, serving overpriced California fare (dinner mains $26 to $46), for cocktails at the lobby bar instead.

Yosemite Lodge at the Falls　　　LODGE $$$
(r from $220; @ 🛜 ♨ 🚻) 🐾 Spacious motel rooms come with ecofriendly upgrades and patios or balconies overlooking Yosemite Falls, meadows or the parking lot. Fork into sustainably caught river trout and organic veggies at the lodge's Mountain Room (dinner mains $18 to $35), open nightly (no reservations). For a beer and small bites, the next-door lounge has a convivial fireplace.

Degnan's Deli & Loft　　　　DELI, PIZZERIA **$$**
(mains $8-12; ⊙ deli 7am-5pm year-round, pizzeria usually 5-9pm Apr-Sep; 🖶) Grab a deli sandwich and bag of chips downstairs before hitting the trail. After dark, head upstairs for cold brewskies and crispy pizzas.

🛏 Outside Yosemite National Park

Gateway towns that have a mixed bag of motels, hotels, lodges and B&Bs include Fish Camp, Oakhurst, El Portal, Midpines, Mariposa, Groveland and Lee Vining.

★Yosemite Bug
Rustic Mountain Resort　　　HOSTEL, CABINS **$**
(☑866-826-7108, 209-966-6666; www.yosemite-bug.com; 6979 Hwy 140, Midpines; dm $23-26, tent cabins $45-75, r with/without bath from $75/65; ⊙ cafe 7am-4pm & 6-8:30pm; @🛜🖶) 🥾 Tucked into the forest about 30 miles west of Yosemite Valley, this mountain hostelry hosts globetrotters who dig the clean rooms, low-key spa, shared kitchen access and laundry. The cafe's fresh, organic and vegetarian-friendly meals (mains $5 to $18) get raves.

★Evergreen
Lodge Resort　　　CABINS, CAMPGROUND **$$$**
(☑209-379-2606; www.evergreenlodge.com; 33160 Evergreen Rd, Groveland; tents $80-120, cabins $210-380; @🛜🏊🖶) 🥾 Near Hetch Hetchy, this woodsy 1920s resort welcomes families and couples with its prefurnished tents and comfy mountain cabins. Outdoor recreational activities abound, with equipment rentals and nightly s'mores in the rec room. There's a general store, a tavern with a pool table and a country restaurant (dinner mains $18 to $30) serving three hearty meals a day.

❶ Information

Yosemite Village, Curry Village and Wawona stores all have ATMs. Drivers should fill up before entering the park. High-priced gas is sold at Wawona and Crane Flat year-round and at Tuolumne Meadows in summer. Cell-phone service is spotty throughout the park. Unreliable pay-as-you-go internet kiosks are available next to Degnan's Deli and at Yosemite Lodge, which offers slow fee-based wi-fi.

Wawona Branch Library (www.mariposalibrary.org; Chilnualna Falls Rd; ⊙1-6pm Mon-Fri, 10am-3pm Sat late May-early Sep, noon-5pm Mon, Wed & Fri, 10am-3pm Sat early Sep-late May; @) Free public internet terminals.

Yosemite Medical Clinic (☑209-372-4637; 9000 Ahwahnee Dr; ⊙9am-7pm daily late May-late Sep, 9am-5pm Mon-Fri late Sep-late May) Urgent-care clinic in Yosemite Valley.

Yosemite Valley Branch Library (www.mariposalibrary.org; Girls Club Bldg, 9000 Cedar Ct; ⊙9am-noon Mon, 8:30am-12:30pm Tue, 3-7pm Wed & 4-7pm Thu; @) Free public internet terminals.

Yosemite Valley Visitor Center (☑209-372-0200; www.nps.gov/yose; ⊙9am-6pm, to 5pm

---

CAMPING IN YOSEMITE

From March through October, many park campgrounds require **reservations** (☑518-885-3639, 877-444-6777; www.recreation.gov), which are available starting five months in advance. Campsites routinely sell out online within *minutes*. All campgrounds have bearproof lockers and campfire rings; most have potable water.

In summer, most campgrounds are noisy and booked to bulging, especially **North Pines** (campsites $20; ⊙Apr-Oct; 🖶🏕), **Lower Pines** (campsites $20; ⊙Apr-Oct; 🖶🏕) and year-round **Upper Pines** (campsites $20; 🖶🏕) in Yosemite Valley; **Tuolumne Meadows** (campsites $20; ⊙mid-Jul-late Sep; 🖶🏕) off Tioga Rd, a 90-minute drive from the valley; and riverside **Wawona** (campsites $20; 🖶🏕), under an hour's drive from the valley.

Year-round **Camp 4** (shared tent sites per person $5), a rock-climber's hangout in the valley; **Bridalveil Creek** (campsites $14; ⊙mid-Jul-early Sep), a 45-minute drive from the valley off Glacier Point Rd; and **White Wolf** (campsites $14; ⊙Jul-mid-Sep; 🏕), an hour's drive from the valley off Tioga Rd, are all first-come, first-served and often full before noon, especially on weekends.

Looking for a quieter, more rugged experience? Try the primitive campgrounds (no potable water) at **Tamarack Flat** (tent sites $10; ⊙Jul-Sep), **Yosemite Creek** (tent sites $10; ⊙Jul-mid-Sep; 🏕) and **Porcupine Flat** (campsites $10; ⊙Jul-Sep; 🏕) off Tioga Rd. They're all first-come, first-served.

in winter) Smaller visitor centers at Wawona, Tuolumne Meadows and Big Oak Flat are open seasonally.

Yosemite Valley Wilderness Center (🖉20 9-372-0826; www.nps.gov/yose; ☉8am-5pm May-Oct, 7:30am-5pm Jul & Aug) Backcountry permits and bear-canister rentals also available seasonally at Wawona, Tuolumne Meadows and Big Oak Flat.

❶ Getting There & Around

The nearest Greyhound and Amtrak stations are in Merced. **YARTS** (🖉877-989-2787; www. yarts.com) buses travel year-round from Merced to Yosemite Valley via Hwy 140, stopping at towns along the way. In summer, YARTS buses run from Yosemite Valley to Mammoth Lakes via Tuolumne Meadows along Hwy 120. One-way fares (including park entry fee) are $12.50 from Merced, $18 from Mammoth Lakes.

Free shuttle buses loop around Yosemite Valley and, in summer, the Tuolumne Meadows and Wawona/Mariposa Grove areas. **DNC** (🖉209-372-4386; www.yosemitepark.com) runs hikers' buses from the valley to Tuolumne Meadows (one way/round-trip $15/23) and Glacier Point (one way/round-trip $25/41). Valley bike rentals (per hour/day $11/32) are available seasonally at Yosemite Lodge and Curry Village.

In winter, highways to the parks are kept open (except Tioga Rd/Hwy 120, see p169), although snow chains may be required at any time. During ski season, a free twice-daily shuttle bus connects Yosemite Valley with Badger Pass.

Sequoia & Kings Canyon National Parks

In these neighboring parks, giant sequoia trees are bigger – up to 30 stories high! – and more numerous than anywhere else in the Sierra Nevada. Tough and fire-charred, they'd easily swallow two freeway lanes each. Giant, too, are the mountains – including Mt Whitney (14,505ft), the tallest peak in the lower 48 states. Finally, there is the deep Kings Canyon, carved out of granite by ancient glaciers and a powerful river. For quiet, solitude and close-up sightings of wildlife, including black bears, hit the trail and lose yourself in peaceful wilderness.

❖ Sights

Sequoia was designated a national park in 1890; Kings Canyon, in 1940. Though distinct, the two parks (🖉559-565-3341; www. nps.gov/seki; 7-day entry per car $20) operate as one unit with a single admission fee. From the south, Hwy 198 enters Sequoia National Park beyond the town of Three Rivers at Ash Mountain, then ascends the zigzagging Generals Hwy to Giant Forest. From the west, Hwy 180 enters Kings Canyon National Park near Grant Grove, then plunges down into the canyon to Cedar Grove.

❖ Sequoia National Park

We dare you to try hugging the trees in **Giant Forest**, a 3-sq-mile grove that protects the park's most gargantuan specimens – the world's largest – the **General Sherman Tree**. With sore arms and sticky sap fingers, lose the crowds by venturing onto the network of forested hiking trails (bring a map).

Giant Forest Museum   MUSEUM
(🖉559-565-4480; Generals Hwy; ☉9am-4:30pm or 6pm mid-May–mid-Oct; 🖫) A short drive or shuttle ride south of Lodgepole Village, this tiny museum has exhibits on giant sequoia ecology and wildlife conservation. For 360° panoramic mountain views, climb the steep quarter-mile staircase up **Moro Rock** off Crescent Meadow Rd nearby.

Crystal Cave   CAVE
(🖉info 559-565-3759; www.sequoiahistory.org; Crystal Cave Rd; tours adult/child from $15/8; ☉mid-May–Nov; 🖫) Discovered in 1918, this cave protects marble formations estimated to be 10,000 years old. First-come, first-served tickets for the 45-minute introductory tour are only available in person at the Lodgepole and Foothills visitor centers, *not* at the cave. Bring a jacket.

Mineral King   HISTORIC SITE
(Mineral King Rd) Take a detour to Mineral King Valley (7500ft), a late-19th-century mining and logging camp ringed by craggy peaks and alpine lakes. The 25-mile one-way scenic drive – navigating almost 700 hairraising hairpin turns – is usually open from mid-May to late October.

❖ Kings Canyon National Park & Scenic Byway

Just north of Grant Grove Village, **General Grant Grove** brims with majestic giants. Beyond, Hwy 180 begins its 30-mile descent into **Kings Canyon**, serpentining past chiseled rock walls laced with waterfalls. The road meets the Kings River, its roar ricocheting off granite cliffs soaring over 8000ft high, making this one of North America's deepest canyons. The scenic byway past Hume Lake to Cedar Grove Village is usually closed from mid-November through mid-April.

Cedar Grove
OUTDOORS

Cedar Grove Village is the last outpost of civilization before the rugged grandeur of the Sierra Nevada backcountry begins. Hike from Roads End, with its river beach and summertime swimming holes, to roaring Mist Falls (8.4 miles round-trip). Popular with birders, an easy 1.5-mile nature trail loops around Zumwalt Meadow, just west of Roads End.

Boyden Cavern
CAVE

(www.boydencavern.com; Hwy 180; tours adult/ child from $13/8; ⊙ May–mid-Nov; ⛟) While its smaller and less impressive than Sequoia National Park's Crystal Cave, tours of the beautiful and whimsical formations here require no advance tickets.

🏃 Activities

Hiking is why people come here – with over 850 miles of marked trails to prove it. Cedar Grove and Mineral King offer the best backcountry access. Trails usually begin to open by early summer, though there's hiking year-round in the Foothills area. Overnight backcountry trips require wilderness permits (☑ 559-565-3766; www.nps.gov/seki/plan-yourvisit/backpacking.htm; per trip $15), subject to a quota system from late May through late September, so reserve in advance.

In summer, cool off by swimming in Hume Lake, on national forest land off Hwy 180, and at riverside swimming holes in

> **DON'T MISS**
>
> ## TOP SIERRA NEVADA SCENIC DRIVES
>
> **Tioga Road** (Hwy 120) Yosemite's rooftop of the world
>
> **Generals Highway** (Hwy 198) Historic byway past giant sequoias
>
> **Kings Canyon Scenic Byway** (Hwy 180) Drop into one of North America's deepest canyons
>
> **Mineral King Rd** Wind up into a high Sierra valley
>
> **Eastern Sierra Scenic Byway** (US 395) Where snowy mountains overshadow the desert

both parks. In winter, you can cross-country ski or snowshoe among giant sequoias; equipment rental is available at Grant Grove Village and Wuksachi Lodge. For groomed cross-country ski trails and other winter sports, visit old-fashioned Montecito Sequoia Lodge, off the Generals Hwy between the two parks.

🍴 Sleeping & Eating

Camping reservations (☑ 518-885-3639, 877-477-6777; www.recreation.gov) are accepted only during summer at Lodgepole and Dorst Campgrounds in Sequoia National Park. The parks' dozen other developed campgrounds (campsites $10 to $20) are first-come, first-served. Lodgepole, Azalea, Potwisha and South Fork are open year-round. Overflow camping is available in the surrounding Sequoia National Forest.

The markets in Grant Grove, Lodgepole and Cedar Grove have limited groceries. Lodgepole and Cedar Grove also have snack bars serving basic, budget-friendly meals; Grant Grove has a simple restaurant, seasonal pizzeria and espresso cart.

Outside Sequoia's southern entrance, mostly well-worn independent and chain motels, rustic cabins and down-home eateries line Hwy 198 through Three Rivers town.

John Muir Lodge & Grant Grove Cabins
LODGE, CABINS $$

(☑ 559-335-5500, 866-522-6966; www.sequoia-kingscanyon.com; Hwy 180; cabins without bath $65-95, r $120-190; ⛟🐾) In Grant Grove Village, this woodsy lodge has amply sized, if generic-looking, rooms and a fireplace lobby with board games. Oddly assorted cabin types range from thin-walled canvas tents to historical cabins.

Cedar Grove Lodge
LODGE $$

(☑ 559-335-5500, 866-522-6966; www.sequoia-kingscanyon.com; Hwy 180; r $129-135; ⊙ mid-May–early Oct; ✳🐾) The almost two dozen motel-style rooms with shared porches overlooking the Kings River are simple and worn, but they're your best option down canyon.

Montecito Sequoia Lodge
LODGE $$

(☑ 559-565-3388, 800-227-9900; www.mslodge.com; 63410 Generals Hwy; cabins with/without bath from $ 159/79, r $99-249; ⛟🐾) Family camps keep things raucous all summer long. In winter, go ice-skating and snow tubing. Basic lodge rooms and rustic cabins are midway between the parks. Rates include meals.

Wuksachi Lodge LODGE $$$
(☑559-565-4070, 866-807-3598; www.visitsequoia.com; 64740 Wuksachi Way, off Generals Hwy; r from $225; 🛜) Don't be misled by the grand lobby because oversized motel-style rooms here are nothing to brag about. The upscale **Peaks Restaurant** (☑559-565-4070; www.visitsequoia.com; dinner mains $17-32; ☺breakfast, lunch & dinner daily, seasonal hr vary) is hit-or-miss (dinner reservations required). If you've got stamina, hike 11.5 miles each way to the lodge's **Bearpaw High Sierra Camp** (☑866-807-3598, 801-559-4930; www.visitsequoia.com; tent cabin incl all meals s/d $175/225; ☺mid-Jun–mid-Sep), which books up far in advance.

❶ Information

Lodgepole Village and Grant Grove Village are the parks' main commerical hubs. Both have visitor centers, post offices, markets, ATMs, coin-op laundry and public showers (summer only).

Lodgepole Visitor Center (☑559-565-4436; ☺9am-4:30pm or 6pm daily, shorter winter hr) in Lodgepole Village, **Foothills Visitor Center** (☑559-565-4212; ☺8am-4:30pm) at Ash Mountain and **Kings Canyon Visitor Center** (☑559-565-4307; ☺8am or 9am to 4:30pm or 5pm, shorter winter hr) in Grant Grove stay open year-round. **Cedar Grove Visitor Center** (☑559-565-4307; ☺8am or 9am to 4:30pm or 5pm late May-early Sep) in Kings Canyon and **Mineral King Ranger Station** (☑559-565-3768; ☺8am-4pm late May-early Sep) in Sequoia are open seasonally. Check the free park newspaper for other visitor services.

Expensive gas is available at Hume Lake (year-round) and Stony Creek (summer only) outside the park boundaries on national forest land.

❶ Getting There & Around

From late May to early September, free buses loop around the Giant Forest and Lodgepole Village areas of Sequoia National Park, while the **Sequoia Shuttle** (☑877-287-4453; www.sequoiashuttle.com) links the park to Three Rivers and Visalia (round-trip fare including park entry fee $15, reservations required), with onward connections to Amtrak from Visalia. Kings Canyon National Park has no public transportation.

Eastern Sierra

Vast, empty and majestic, here jagged peaks plummet down into the Great Basin desert, a dramatic juxtaposition that creates a potent scenery cocktail. Hwy 395 runs the entire length of the Sierra Nevada, with

turnoffs leading to pine forests, wildflower-strewn meadows, placid lakes, hot springs and glacier-gouged canyons. Hikers, backpackers, mountain bikers, fishers and skiers all escape here. The main visitor hubs are Mammoth Lakes and Bishop.

At **Bodie State Historic Park** (☑760-647-6445; www.bodiefoundation.org; Hwy 270; adult/child $7/5; ☺9am-6pm mid-May–Oct, to 3pm Nov–mid-May), a gold-rush ghost town is preserved in a state of 'arrested decay.' Weathered buildings sit frozen in time on a dusty, windswept plain. To get there, head east for 13 miles (the last three unpaved) on Hwy 270, about 7 miles south of Bridgeport. The access road is closed by snow during winter.

Further south at **Mono Lake** (www.monolake.org), unearthly tufa towers rise from the alkaline water like drip sandcastles. Off Hwy 395, **Mono Basin Scenic Area Visitor Center** (☑760-647-3044; ☺8am-5pm Apr–Nov) has excellent exhibits and schedules of guided walks and talks. The best photo ops are from the south shore's **South Tufa Area** (adult/child $3/free). From the nearby town of Lee Vining, Hwy 120 heads west into Yosemite National Park via seasonal Tioga Pass (p169).

Continuing south on Hwy 395, detour along the scenic 16-mile **June Lake Loop** or push on to **Mammoth Lakes**, a popular four-seasons resort guarded by 11,053ft **Mammoth Mountain** (☑800-626-6684; www.mammothmountain.com; 10001 Minaret Rd), a top-notch skiing area. The slopes morph into a mountain-bike park in summer, when there's also camping, fishing and day hiking around Mammoth Lakes Basin and Reds Meadow. Nearby are the 60ft-high basalt columns of **Devils Postpile National Monument** (☑760-934-2289; www.nps.gov/depo; shuttle day pass adult/child $7/4; ☺late May-Oct), formed by volcanic activity. Hot-springs fans can soak in primitive pools off Benton Crossing Rd or view the geysering water at **Hot Creek Geological Site** (www.fs.usda.gov/inyo; Hot Creek Hatchery Rd; ☺sunrise-sunset) **FREE**, both off Hwy 395 southeast of town. The in-town **Mammoth Lakes Welcome Center & Ranger Station** (☑866-466-2666; www.visitmammoth.com; 2510 Main St; ☺8am-5pm) has helpful maps and information.

Further south, Hwy 395 descends into the Owens Valley, soon arriving in frontier-flavored **Bishop**, whose minor attractions include art galleries and a historical **railroad** museum ([📞] 760-873-5950; www.lawsmuseum. org; Silver Canyon Rd; donation $5; ⊙10am-4pm; [🐾]). Bishop is the main gateway for pack-horse trips and access to the best fishing and rock climbing in the entire Eastern Sierra.

Budget a half-day for the thrilling drive up to the Ancient Bristlecone Pine Forest ([📞] 760-873-2500; www.fs.usda.gov/inyo; per car $6; ⊙ usually mid-May–Nov). These gnarled, otherworldly looking trees are found above 10,000ft on the slopes of the White Mountains, where you'd think nothing could grow. The oldest tree – called Methuselah – is estimated to be over 4700 years old. The road (closed by snow in winter and spring) is paved to the visitor center at Schulman Grove, where hiking trails await. From Hwy 395 in Big Pine, take Hwy 168 east for 13 miles, then head upll another 10 miles on White Mountain Rd.

Hwy 395 barrels south to Independence and Manzanar National Historic Site ([📞] 760-878-2194; www.nps.gov/manz; 5001 Hwy 395, Independence; ⊙dawn-dusk, visitor center 9am-4:30pm) [FREE], which memorializes the war relocation camp where some 10,000 Japanese Americans were unjustly interned during WWII following the attack on Pearl Harbor. Interpretive exhibits and a short film vividly chronicle life at the camp, marked by a short self-guided auto tour route.

Further south in Lone Pine, you will finally catch a glimpse of 14,505ft Mt Whitney (www.fs.usda.gov/inyo), the highest mountain in the lower 48 states. The heart-stopping, 12-mile scenic drive up Whitney Portal Road (closed in winter) is spectacular. Climbing the peak is hugely popular, but requires a permit (www.recreation.gov; per person

TOP EASTERN SIERRA OUTDOOR SPOTS

Bodie State Historic Park (p175) An eerie gold-rush ghost town.

Mono Lake (p175) Unearthly, mysterious-looking mineral formations.

Mammoth Mountain (p175) Lofty winter sports and mountain biking.

Ancient Bristlecone Pine Forest (p176) Earth's oldest living trees.

Manzanar National Historic Site (p176) Uncensored history of WWII-era internment camps.

$15) issued on a lottery basis. West of Lone Pine, the bizarrely shaped boulders of the Alabama Hills have enchanted the makers of Hollywood Westerns. Peruse vintage memorabilia and movie posters at the Museum of Lone Pine Film History ([📞] 760-876-9909; www.lonepinefilmhistorymuseum.org; 701 S Main St; adult/child $5/free; ⊙10am-6pm Mon-Wed, to 7pm Thu-Sat, to 4pm Sun). South of town, the Eastern Sierra InterAgency Visitor Center ([📞] 760-876-6222; www.fs.fed.us/r5/inyo; Hwys 395 & 136; ⊙8am-5pm) issues wilderness permits, dispenses outdoor-recreation information and sells books and maps.

🛏 Sleeping

The Eastern Sierra is freckled with campgrounds; backcountry camping requires a wilderness permit, reservable in advance and available at ranger stations. Bishop, Lone Pine and Bridgeport have the most motels. Mammoth Lakes has a few motels and dozens of inns, B&Bs and condo and vacation rentals. Reservations are essential everywhere in summer.

El Mono Motel MOTEL $
([📞] 760-647-6310; www.elmonomotel.com; 51 Hwy 395, Lee Vining; r with/without bath from $89/69; ⊙mid-May–Oct; [📶]) Neighboring a coffee shop, snug motel rooms nearby Mono Lake are a short drive from Yosemite National Park's Tioga Pass entrance.

Whitney Portal Hostel HOSTEL $
([📞] 760-876-0030; www.whitneyportalstore.com; 238 S Main St, Lone Pine; dm/q $25/84; [❄][📶][🐾]) Carpeted bunk-bed rooms at this ultrabasic hostel are popular launchpads for Whitney summit hikes. Public showers ($5) available.

★ Tamarack Lodge LODGE, CABINS $$
([📞] 800-626-6684, 760-934-2442; www.tamaracklodge.com; 163 Twin Lakes Rd, Mammoth Lakes; r with/without bath from $149/99, cabins from $169; [@][📶][🐾]) ✦ Since 1924, this heart-warming lakeside resort has rented lodge rooms and cabins with kitchens, ranging from rustic to deluxe – some have wood-burning fireplaces.

Dow Hotel & Dow Villa Motel HOTEL, MOTEL $$
([📞] 800-824-9317, 760-876-5521; www.dowvillamotel.com; 310 S Main St, Lone Pine; r $85-150, without bath $70; [❄][@][📶][❄][🐾]) John Wayne and Errol Flynn are among the movie stars who have slept at this 1922 hotel, restored with rustic charm. Modern motel rooms are a mite more comfortable.

✖ Eating & Drinking

Good Life Café
AMERICAN $

(http://mammothgoodlifecafe.com; 126 Old Mammoth Rd, Mammoth Lakes; mains $7-10; ⊙ 6:30am-3pm) Stomach-stuffing breakfasts, brawny burgers and Cal-Mexican burritos, healthy veggie wraps and big salad bowls keep this spot with a sunny patio packed.

Raymond's Deli
DELI $

(http://raymondsdeli.com; 206 N Main St, Bishop; items $5-9; ⊙ 10am-5:30pm; 🖉) A brash den of kitsch and pinball, Raymond's makes over-stuffed sandwiches with names like 'When Pigs Fly' and 'Flaming Farm.' Kick back with California craft beers.

★ Whoa Nellie Deli
CALIFORNIAN $$

(🖉 760-647-1088; Tioga Gas Mart, 22 Vista Point Rd, off Hwy 120, Lee Vining; mains $7-20; ⊙ 7am-9pm late Apr-early Nov; 🖬) Great food in a gas station? Really, you gotta try chef Matt Toomey's amazing roadside kitchen, dishing up fish tacos, wild buffalo meatloaf and bar-becue ribs.

Skadi
EUROPEAN $$$

(🖉 760-934-3902; http://skadirestaurant.com; 587 Old Mammoth Rd, Mammoth Lakes; mains $24-32; ⊙ 5:30-9:30pm) As you gaze out at dreamy mountain vistas, feast on Scandinavian 'alpine cuisine' – like roasted crispy-skin salmon and juniper-spiced duck breast with lingonberries – with stellar wines.

Mammoth Brewing
Company Tasting Room
BREWERY

(www.mammothbrewingco.com; 94 Berner St, Mammoth Lakes; ⊙ 10am-6pm) Sample a dozen brews on tap for free, then buy take-home bottles of IPA 395 or Double Nut Brown.

Looney Bean Coffee
CAFE

(www.looneybean.com; 399 N Main St, Bishop; ⊙ 6am-6pm Mon-Sat, 7am-5pm Sun; 🖀) Lo-cal hangout for freshly roasted brews, fruit smoothies and baked goods. Also in Mammoth Lakes.

Lake Tahoe

Shimmering in myriad blues and greens, Lake Tahoe is the nation's second-deepest lake. Driving around its spellbinding 72-mile scenic shoreline gives you quite a workout behind the wheel. The north shore is quiet and upscale; the west shore, rugged and old-timey; the east shore, undeveloped; and the

south shore, busy with families and flashy casinos. The horned peaks surrounding the lake (elevation 6225ft), which straddles the California–Nevada state line, are year-round outdoor playgrounds.

Tahoe gets packed in summer, on winter weekends and over holidays, when reservations are essential. Lake Tahoe Visitors Authority (🖉 800-288-2463; www.tahoesouth.com) and North Lake Tahoe Visitors' Bureau (🖉 888-434-1262; www.gotahoenorth.com) run multiple visitor information centers. There's camping in state parks (🖉 800-444-7275; www.reserveamerica.com; campsites $35-50; 🖬 🖀) and on USFS lands (🖉 877-444-6777, 518-885-3639; www.recreation.gov; campsites $20-40; 🖬 🖀).

South Lake Tahoe & West Shore

With retro motels and eateries lining busy Hwy 50, South Lake Tahoe gets crowded. Gambling at Stateline's casino hotels, just across the Nevada border, attracts thou-sands, as does the world-class ski resort of Heavenly (🖉 775-586-7000; www.skiheavenly.com; 3860 Saddle Rd; 🖬). In summer, a trip up Heavenly's gondola (adult/child $38/20) guarantees fabulous views of the lake and Desolation Wilderness, a starkly beauti-ful landscape of raw granite peaks, glacier-carved valleys and alpine lakes that's a fa-vorite of hikers. Get maps, information and wilderness permits (🖉 877-444-6777; www.recreation.gov; per adult $5-10) from the USFS Taylor Creek Visitor Center (🖉 530-543-2674; www.fs.usda.gov/ltbmu; Hwy 89; ⊙ daily late May–Oct, hr vary). It's 3 miles north of the 'Y' intersection of Hwys 50/89, at Tallac His-toric Site (Tallac Rd; entry free, tour adult/child $5/3; ⊙ 10am-4:30pm mid-Jun-Sep, Fri & Sat only late May–mid-Jun; 🖀), preserving early-20th-century vacation estates.

From sandy, swimmable Zephyr Cove across the Nevada border or the in-town Ski Run Marina, Lake Tahoe Cruises (🖉 800-238-2463; www.zephyrcove.com; adult/child from $47/10) ply the 'Big Blue' year-round. Back on shore, boutique-chic motels include the Alder Inn (🖉 530-544-4485; www.thealderinn.com; 1072 Ski Run Blvd; r $85-229; 🖀 🖀) and the hip Basecamp Hotel (🖉 530-208-0180; http://basecamphotels.com; 4143 Cedar Ave; r incl breakfast $115-239; 🖀 🖀), which has a rooftop hot tub and communal fire pits. Fuel up at vegetarian-friendly Sprouts (3123 Harrison Ave; mains $6-10; ⊙ 8am-9pm; 🖉), a natural-foods cafe, or with a peanut-butter-topped burger and garlic fries at the Burger Lounge (☑530-542-2010; www.burgerloungeintahoe.com; 717 Emerald Bay Rd; items $4-9; ⊙10am-8pm, shorter hr Oct-May; ⛄).

Hwy 89 threads northwest along the thickly forested west shore to Emerald Bay State Park (☑530-541-6498; www.parks.ca.gov; per car $8-10; ⊙daily late May-Sep), where granite cliffs and pine trees frame a sparkling fjordlike inlet. A 1-mile trail leads steeply downhill to Vikingsholm Castle (tours adult/child $10/8; ⊙10:30am or 11am-4pm daily late May-Sep). From this 1920s Scandinavian-style mansion, the Rubicon Trail ribbons 4.5 miles north along the lakeshore past petite coves to DL Bliss State Park (☑530-525-7277; www.parks.ca.gov; per car $10; ⊙usually late May-Sep; ⛄), offering sandy beaches. Further north, Tahoma Meadows B&B Cottages (☑866-525-1533, 530-525-1553; www.tahomameadows.com; 6821 W Lake Blvd, Homewood; cottages incl breakfast $109-199; ⛄⛄⛄) rents darling country cabins.

North & East Shores

The north shore's commercial hub, Tahoe City is great for grabbing supplies and renting outdoor gear. It's not far from Squaw Valley USA (☑800-403-0206; www.squaw.com; 1960 Squaw Valley Rd, Olympic Valley; ⛄), a megasized ski resort that hosted the 1960 Winter Olympics. Après-ski crowds gather at woodsy Bridgetender Tavern (www.tahoebridgetender.com; 65 W Lake Blvd; mains $8-12; ⊙11am-11pm, to midnight Fri & Sat) back in town. In the morning, gobble eggs Benedict with house-smoked salmon at down-home Fire Sign Cafe (www.firesigncafe.com; 1785 W Lake Blvd, Sunnyside; mains $7-11; ⊙7am-3pm; ⛄), 2 miles south along the lakeshore.

In summer, swim or kayak at Tahoe Vista or Kings Beach. Overnight at Franciscan Lakeside Lodge (☑800-564-6754, 530-546-6300; http://franciscanlodge.com; 6944 N Lake Blvd, Tahoe Vista; d $95-285; ⛄⛄⛄), where simple cabins, cottages and suites have kitchenettes, or at well-kept, compact Hostel Tahoe (☑530-546-3266; http://hostel tahoe.com; 8931 N Lake Blvd, Kings Beach; dm $32, r $65-80; ⊙check-in 4-7pm; @⛄). East of Kings Beach's casual lakeside eateries, Hwy 28 barrels into Nevada. You can catch a live-music show at Crystal Bay Club Casino (☑775-833-6333; www.crystalbaycasino.com; 14 Hwy 28, Crystal Bay), but, for more happening bars and bistros, drive further to Incline Village.

With pristine beaches, lakes and miles of multi-use trails, Lake Tahoe-Nevada State Park (http://parks.nv.gov; per car $7-12) is the east shore's biggest draw. Summer crowds splash in the turquoise waters of Sand Harbor. The 13.5-mile Flume Trail, a mountain biker's holy grail, ends further south at Spooner Lake. Back in Incline Village, Flume Trail Bikes (☑775-298-2501; www.flume trailtahoe.com; 1115 Tunnel Creek Rd; bike rental per day $35-90, shuttle $10-15) offers bicycle rentals and trailhead shuttles.

Truckee & Around

North of Lake Tahoe off I-80, Truckee is not in fact a truck stop but a thriving mountain town, with coffee shops, trendy boutiques and dining in downtown's historical district. Ski bums have several area resorts to pick from, including glam Northstar-at-Tahoe (☑800-466-6784; www.northstarat tahoe.com; 5001 Northstar Dr; ⛄); kid-friendly Sugar Bowl (☑530-426-9000; www.sugarbowl. com; 629 Sugar Bowl Rd, Norden; ⛄), cofounded by Walt Disney; and Royal Gorge (☑530-426-3871; www.royalgorge.com; 9411 Pahatsi Rd, Soda Springs; ⛄), paradise for cross-country skiers.

West of Hwy 89, Donner Summit is where the infamous Donner Party became trapped during the fierce winter of 1846-47. Fewer than half survived – some by cannibalizing their dead friends. The grisly tale is chronicled at the museum inside Donner Memorial State Park (www. parks.ca.gov; Donner Pass Rd; per car $8; ⊙museum 10am-5pm, closed Tue & Wed Sep-May; ⛄), where Donner Lake is popular with swimmers and paddlers.

Do-it-yourself hikers and skiers who don't mind doing small chores stay at the Sierra Club's rough-hewn Clair Tappan Lodge (☑800-679-6775, 530-426-3632; www. sierraclub.org/outings/lodges/ctl; 19940 Donner Pass Rd, Norden; dm incl meals adult/child from $60/30; ⛄) outside town. On the outskirts of Truckee, green-certified Cedar House Sport Hotel (☑866-582-5655, 530-582-5655; www.cedarhousesporthotel.com; 10918 Brockway Rd; r incl breakfast $170-290; ⛄⛄) ⊘ offers stylish boutique rooms and an outdoor hot tub. Down pints of 'Donner Party Porter' at Fifty Fifty Brewing Co (www.fifty fiftybrewing.com; 11197 Brockway Rd; ⊙11am-9pm, to 9:30pm Fri & Sat) ⊘.

❶ Getting There & Around

South Tahoe Express (☎ 866-898-2463, 775-325-8944; www.southtahoeexpress.com; one way/round-trip $30/53) runs several daily shuttles from Nevada's Reno-Tahoe International Airport to Stateline. **North Lake Tahoe Express** (☎ 866-216-5222, 775-786-3706; www.north-laketahoeexpress.com; one way/round-trip $45/85) connects Reno's airport with Truckee, Northstar, Squaw Valley and north-shore towns.

Truckee's **Amtrak depot** (10065 Donner Pass Rd) has daily trains to Sacramento ($50, 4½ hours) and Reno ($16, 1½ hours), and twice-daily Greyhound buses to Reno ($18, one hour), Sacramento ($45, 2½ hours) and San Francisco ($41, six hours). Amtrak buses connect Sacramento with South Lake Tahoe ($34, 2½ hours).

Tahoe Area Regional Transit (TART; ☎ 800-736-6365, 530-550-1212; www.placer.ca.gov/tart; fare/day pass $1.75/3.50) operates local buses from Truckee around the north and west shores. South Lake Tahoe is served by **BlueGO** (☎ 530-541-7149; www.bluego.org; fare/day pass from $2/5) buses. BlueGO's summer-only Nifty 50 trolley heads up the west shore to Tahoma, connecting with TART.

If you're driving, tire chains are often required in winter on I-80, US 50 and other mountain highways, which may close temporarily due to heavy snow.

Pacific Northwest

Best Places to Eat

➡ Cascina Spinasse (p196)

➡ Saffron Mediterranean Kitchen (p213)

➡ Ox (p220)

➡ New Sammy's Cowboy Bistro (p234)

Best Places to Stay

➡ Sun Mountain Lodge (p208)

➡ Kennedy School (p219)

➡ Oxford Hotel (p231)

➡ Hotel Five (p193)

Why Go?

As much a state of mind as a geographical region, the US's northwest corner is a land of subcultures and new trends, where evergreen trees frame snow-dusted volcanoes, and inspired ideas scribbled on the back of napkins become tomorrow's business start-ups. You can't peel off the history in layers here, but you *can* gaze wistfully into the future in fast-moving, innovative cities such as Seattle and Portland, which are sprinkled with food carts, streetcars, microbreweries, green belts, coffee connoisseurs and weird urban sculpture.

Ever since the days of the Oregon Trail, the Northwest has had a hypnotic lure for risk takers and dreamers, and the metaphoric carrot still dangles. There's the air, so clean they ought to bottle it; the trees, older than many of Rome's Renaissance palaces; and the end-of-the-continent coastline, holding back the force of the world's largest ocean. Cowboys take note; it doesn't get much more 'wild' or 'west' than this.

When to Go

Seattle

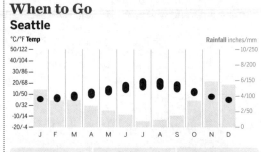

Jan–Mar Most reliable snow cover for skiing in the Cascades and beyond.

May Festival season: Portland Rose, Seattle International Film Festival, Oregon Shakespeare.

Jul–Sep The best hiking months in between the spring snowmelt and the first fall flurries.

Grunge & Other Subcultures

Synthesizing Generation X angst with a questionable approach to personal hygiene, grunge first dive-bombed onto Seattle's music scene in the early 1990s like a clap of thunder on an otherwise dry and sunny afternoon. The anger had been fermenting for years. Hardcore punk originated in Portland in the late 1970s, led by resident contrarians the Wipers, whose antifashion followers congregated in legendary dive bars such as Satyricon. Another musical blossoming occurred in Olympia, where DIY-merchants Beat Happening invented 'lo-fi' and coyly mocked the corporate establishment. Scooping up the fallout of a disparate youth culture, Seattle quickly became grunge's pulpit, spawning bands such as Pearl Jam, Soundgarden and Alice in Chains. The genre went global in 1991 when Nirvana's *Nevermind* album knocked Michael Jackson off the number-one spot, but the movement was never meant to be successful and the kudos quickly killed it. Since the mid '90s the Pacific Northwest has kept its subcultures largely to itself, though the music's no less potent or relevant.

MICROBREWERIES

'Beer connoisseurship' is a nationwide phenomenon these days, but the campaign to put a dash of flavor into commercially brewed beer was first ignited in the Pacific Northwest in the 1980s.

One of America's first microbreweries was the mercurial Cartwright Brewing Company, set up in Portland in 1980. The nation's first official brewpub was the now defunct Grant's, which opened in the Washington city of Yakima in 1982. The trend went viral in 1984 with the inauguration of Bridgeport Brewing Company in Portland, followed a year later by Beervana's old-school brewing brothers Mike and Brian McMenamin, whose quirky beer empire still acts as a kind of personification of the craft-brewing business in the region.

Today, Washington and Oregon operate nearly 300 microbreweries (Portland alone has more than 50). These take classic, natural ingredients – malt, hops and yeast – to produce high-quality beer in small batches.

Best State Parks

→ **Moran State Park** Orcas Island

→ **Ecola State Park** Cannon Beach

→ **Deception Pass State Park** Whidbey Island

→ **Fort Worden State Park** Port Townsend

→ **Lime Kiln Point State Park** San Juan Island

→ **Cape Perpetua State Park** Near Yachats

→ **Smith Rock State Park** Near Bend

PACIFIC NORTHWEST

DON'T MISS

Between them, the states of Washington and Oregon harbor four of the US's most spectacular national parks: Mt Rainier (established 1899), Crater Lake (1902), Olympic (1938) and North Cascades (1968).

Fast Facts

→ **Hub cities** Seattle (621,000), Portland (594,000)

→ **Distances from Seattle** Portland (172 miles), Vancouver BC (140 miles)

→ **Time zone** Pacific Standard

Did You Know?

Over the winter of 1998–99, the Mt Baker ski resort in northwest Washington received 1140in of snow in a single season, the largest annual snowfall ever recorded.

Resources

→ **Washington State Parks & Recreation Commission** (www.parks.wa.gov)

→ **Oregon State Parks & Recreation Dept** (www.oregonstateparks.org)

→ **Washington State Tourism Office** (www.tourism.wa.gov)

→ **Oregon Tourism Commission** (www.traveloregon.com)

Pacific Northwest Highlights

1 Cycling and kayaking around the quieter corners of the **San Juan Islands** (p205).

2 Exploring the gorgeous **Oregon Coast** (p237), from scenic Astoria to balmy Port Orford.

3 Admiring trees older than Europe's Renaissance castles in Washington's **Olympic National Park** (p201).

4 Watching the greatest outdoor show in the Pacific Northwest in Seattle's theatrical **Pike Place Market** (p186).

5 Walking the green and serene neighborhoods of **Portland** (p213), energized by beer, coffee and food-cart treats.

6 Witnessing the impossibly deep blue waters and scenic panoramas of **Crater Lake National Park** (p232).

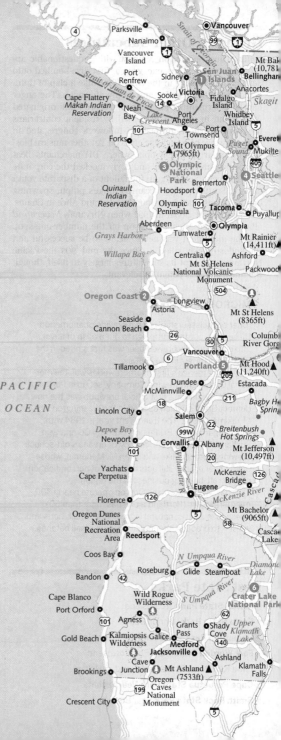

History

Native American societies, including the Chinook and the Salish, had long-established coastal communities by the time Europeans arrived in the Pacific Northwest in the 18th century. Inland, on the arid plateaus between the Cascades and the Rocky Mountains, the Spokane, Nez Percé and other tribes thrived on seasonal migration between river valleys and temperate uplands.

Three hundred years after Columbus landed in the New World, Spanish and British explorers began probing the northern Pacific coast, seeking the fabled Northwest Passage. In 1792 Captain George Vancouver was the first explorer to sail the waters of Puget Sound, claiming British sovereignty over the entire region. At the same time, an American, Captain Robert Gray, found the mouth of the Columbia River. In 1805 the explorers Lewis and Clark crossed the Rockies and made their way down the Columbia to the Pacific Ocean, extending the US claim on the territory.

In 1824 the British Hudson's Bay Company established Fort Vancouver in Washington as headquarters for the Columbia region. This opened the door to waves of settlers but had a devastating impact on the indigenous cultures, which were assailed by European diseases and alcohol.

In 1843 settlers at Champoeg, on the Willamette River south of Portland, voted to organize a provisional government independent of the Hudson's Bay Company, thereby casting their lot with the US, which formally acquired the territory from the British by treaty in 1846. Over the next decade, some 53,000 settlers came to the Northwest via the 2000-mile Oregon Trail.

Arrival of the railroads set the region's future. Agriculture and lumber became the pillars of the economy until 1914, when WWI and the opening of the Panama Canal brought increased trade to Pacific ports. Shipyards opened along Puget Sound, and the Boeing aircraft company set up shop near Seattle.

Big dam projects in the 1930s and '40s provided cheap hydroelectricity and irrigation. WWII offered another boost for aircraft manufacturing and shipbuilding, and agriculture continued to thrive. In the postwar period, Washington's population, especially around Puget Sound, grew to twice that of Oregon.

In the 1980s and '90s, the economic emphasis shifted with the rise of the high-tech industry, embodied by Microsoft in Seattle and Intel in Portland.

Hydroelectricity production and massive irrigation projects along the Columbia, however, have threatened the river's ecosystem in the past few decades and logging has also left its scars. But the region has reinvigorated its eco credentials by attracting some of the country's most environmentally conscious companies and its major cities are among the greenest in the US. It stands at the forefront of US efforts to tackle climate issues.

Local Culture

The stereotypical image of a Pacific Northwesterner is a casually dressed, latte-supping urbanite who drives a Prius, votes Democrat and walks around with an unwavering diet

THE PACIFIC NORTHWEST IN...

Four Days

Hit the ground running in **Seattle** to see the main sights, including Pike Place Market and the Seattle Center. On day three, head down to **Portland**, where you can be like the locals and cycle to bars, cafes, food carts and shops.

One Week

Add a couple highlights like **Mt Rainier**, **Olympic National Park**, the **Columbia River Gorge** and **Mt Hood**. Or explore the spectacular Oregon Coast (try the **Cannon Beach** area) or the historic seaport of **Port Townsend** on the Olympic Peninsula.

Two Weeks

Crater Lake is unforgettable, and can be combined with a trip to **Ashland** and its Shakespeare Festival. Don't miss the ethereal **San Juan Islands** up near the watery border with Canada, or **Bend**, the region's biggest outdoor draw. If you like wine, Washington's **Walla Walla** is your mecca, while the **Willamette Valley** is Oregon's Pinot Noir paradise.

of Nirvana-derived indie rock programmed into their iPod. But, as with most fleeting regional generalizations, the reality is far more complex.

Noted for their sophisticated cafe culture and copious microbrew pubs, the urban hubs of Seattle and Portland are the Northwest's most emblematic cities. But head east into the region's drier and less verdant interior, and the cultural affiliations become increasingly more traditional. Here, strung out along the Columbia River Valley or nestled amid the arid steppes of southeastern Washington, small towns host raucous rodeos, tourist centers promote cowboy culture, and a cup of coffee is served 'straight up' with none of the chai lattes and frappés that are par for the course in Seattle.

In contrast to the USA's hardworking eastern seaboard, life out West is more casual and less frenetic than in New York or Boston. Idealistically, Westerners would rather work to live than live to work. Indeed, with so much winter rain, the citizens of the Pacific Northwest will dredge up any excuse to shun the nine-to-five treadmill and hit the great outdoors a couple of hours (or even days) early. Witness the scene in late May and early June, when the first bright days of summer prompt a mass exodus of hikers and cyclists making enthusiastically for the national parks and wilderness areas for which the region is justly famous.

Creativity is another strong Northwestern trait, be it redefining the course of modern rock music or reconfiguring the latest Microsoft computer program. No longer content to live in the shadow of California or Hong Kong, the Pacific Northwest has redefined itself internationally in recent decades through celebrated TV shows (*Frasier* and *Portlandia*, for example), iconic global personalities (Bill Gates) and a groundbreaking music scene that has spawned everything from grunge rock to riot grrrl feminism.

Tolerance is widespread in Pacific Northwestern society, from recreational drug use to gay rights to physician-assisted suicide. Commonly voting Democrat in presidential elections, the population has also enthusiastically embraced the push for 'greener' lifestyles in the form of extensive recycling programs, 'sustainable' restaurants and biodiesel whale-watching tours. An early exponent of ecofriendly practices, former Seattle mayor Greg Nickels has become a leading spokesperson on climate change, while progressive Portland regularly features at the top of America's most sustainable and bike-friendly cities.

❶ Getting There & Around

AIR

Seattle-Tacoma International Airport (p199), aka 'Sea-Tac' and Portland International Airport (p224) are the main airports for the region, serving many North American and a few international destinations.

BOAT

Washington State Ferries (WSF; p199) links Seattle with Bainbridge and Vashon Islands. Other WSF routes cross from Whidbey Island to Port Townsend on the Olympic Peninsula, and from Anacortes through the San Juan Islands to Sidney, BC. Victoria Clipper (p199) operates services from Seattle to Victoria, BC, and ferries to Victoria also operate from Port Angeles. **Alaska Marine Highway** (AMHS; ☑ 800-642-0066; www.ferryalaska.com) ferries go from Bellingham, WA, to Alaska.

BUS

Greyhound (www.greyhound.com) provides service along the I-5 corridor from Bellingham in northern Washington down to Medford in southern Oregon, with connecting services across the US and Canada. East–west routes fan out toward Spokane, Yakima, the Tri-Cities (Kennewick, Pasco and Richland in Washington), Walla Walla and Pullman in Washington, and Hood River and Pendleton in Oregon. Private bus companies service most of the smaller towns and cities across the region, often connecting to Greyhound or Amtrak.

CAR

Driving your own vehicle is by far the most convenient way of touring the Pacific Northwest. Major and minor rental agencies are commonplace throughout the region. The I-5 is the major north–south artery. In Washington I-90 heads east from Seattle to Spokane and into Idaho. In Oregon I-84 branches east from Portland along the Columbia River Gorge to link up with Boise in Idaho.

TRAIN

Amtrak (www.amtrak.com) runs train services north (to Vancouver, Canada) and south (to California) linking Seattle, Portland and other major urban centers with the Cascades and Coast Starlight routes. The famous Empire Builder heads east to Chicago from Seattle and Portland (joining up in Spokane).

WASHINGTON

Divided in two by the spinal Cascade Mountains, Washington isn't so much a land of contrasts as a land of polar opposites. Centered on Seattle, the western coastal zone is wet, urban, liberal and famous for its fecund evergreen forests; splayed to the east between the less celebrated cities of Spokane and Yakima, the inland plains are arid, rural, conservative and covered by mile after mile of scrublike steppe.

Of the two halves it's the west that harbors most of the quintessential Washington sights, while the more remote east is less heralded, understated and full of surprises.

WASHINGTON FACTS

Nickname Evergreen State

Population 6,897,000

Area 71,342 sq miles

Capital city Olympia (population 47,266)

Other cities Seattle (population 620,778), Spokane (population 210,103), Yakima (population 92,512), Bellingham (population 81,862), Walla Walla (population 32,148)

Sales tax 6.5%

Birthplace of Singer and actor Bing Crosby (1903–77), guitarist Jimi Hendrix (1942–70), computer geek Bill Gates (b 1955), political commentator Glen Beck (b 1964), musical icon Kurt Cobain (1967–94)

Home of Mt St Helens, Microsoft, Starbucks, Nordstrom, Evergreen State College

Politics Democrat governor, Democrat senators, Democrat in presidential elections since 1988

Famous for Grunge rock, coffee, *Grey's Anatomy*, *Twilight*, volcanoes, apples, wine, precipitation

State vegetable Walla Walla sweet onion

Driving distances Seattle to Portland 174 miles, Spokane to Port Angeles 365 miles

Seattle

Combine the brains of Portland, OR, with the beauty of Vancouver, BC, and you'll get something approximating Seattle. It's hard to believe that the Pacific Northwest's largest metropolis was considered a 'secondary' US city until the 1980s, when a combination of bold innovation and unabashed individualism turned it into one of the dot-com era's biggest trendsetters, spearheaded by an unlikely alliance of coffee-supping computer geeks and navel-gazing musicians. Reinvention is the buzzword these days in a city where grunge belongs to the history books and Starbucks now competes among a cavalcade of precocious indie coffee providers eking out their market position.

Surprisingly elegant in places and coolly edgy in others, Seattle is notable for its strong neighborhoods, top-rated university, monstrous traffic jams and proactive city mayors who harbor green credentials. Although it has fermented its own pop culture in recent times, it has yet to create an urban mythology befitting Paris or New York, but it does have 'the Mountain.' Better known as Rainier to its friends, Seattle's unifying symbol is a 14,411ft mass of rock and ice, which acts as a perennial reminder to the city's huddled masses that raw wilderness and potential volcanic catastrophe are never far away.

👁 Sights

👁 Downtown

⭐ **Pike Place Market**　　　　MARKET
(www.pikeplacemarket.org; btwn Virginia St & Union St & 1st Ave & Western Ave; ⊙9am-6pm Mon-Sat, to 5pm Sun; 🚇Westlake) 🍴 Take a bunch of small-time businesses and sprinkle them liberally around a spatially challenged waterside strip amid crowds of old-school bohemians, new-wave restaurateurs, tree-huggers, bolshie students, artists, urban buskers and artisans. The result: Pike Place Market, a cavalcade of noise, smells, personalities, banter and urban theater that's almost London-like in its cosmopolitanism. In operation since 1907, Pike Place is Seattle in a bottle, a wonderfully 'local' experience that highlights the city for what it really is: all-embracing, eclectic and proudly singular.

WORTH A TRIP

PIONEER SQUARE

Pioneer Sq is Seattle's oldest quarter, which isn't saying much if you're visiting from Rome or London. Most of the buildings here date from just after the 1889 fire (a devastating inferno that destroyed 25 city blocks, including the entire central business district), and are referred to architecturally as Richardsonian Romanesque, a red-brick revivalist style in vogue at the time. In the early years, the neighborhood's boom-bust fortunes turned its arterial road, Yesler Way, into the original 'skid row' – an allusion to the skidding logs that were pulled downhill to Henry Yesler's pier-side mill. When the timber industry fell on hard times, the road became a haven for the homeless and its name subsequently became a byword for poverty-stricken urban enclaves countrywide.

Thanks to a concerted public effort, the neighborhood avoided being laid to waste by the demolition squads in the 1960s and is now protected in the Pioneer Sq–Skid Rd Historic District.

The quarter today mixes the historic with the seedy, while harboring art galleries, cafes and nightlife. Its most iconic building is the 42-story **Smith Tower** (cnr 2nd Ave S & Yesler Way; observation deck adult/child $7.50/5; ⊙10am-dusk), completed in 1914 and, until 1931, it was the tallest building west of the Mississippi. Other highlights include the 1909 **Pergola**, a decorative iron shelter reminiscent of a Parisian Metro station, and **Occidental Park**, containing totem poles carved by Chinook artist Duane Pasco.

Klondike Gold Rush National Historical Park (www.nps.gov/klse; 117 S Main St; ⊙9am-5pm; 🚇 International District/Chinatown) is a shockingly good museum eloquently run by the US National Park Service. It's full of exhibits, photos and news clippings from the 1897 Klondike gold rush, when a Seattle-on-steroids acted as a fueling depot for prospectors bound for the Yukon in Canada. It would cost $10 anywhere else; in Seattle it's free!

Seattle Art Museum   MUSEUM

(SAM; www.seattleartmuseum.org; 1300 1st Ave; adult/child $17/11; ⊙10am-5pm Tue, Wed, Sat & Sun, to 9pm Thu & Fri; 🚇University St) While it can't be compared with the big guns in New York and Chicago, Seattle Art Museum is no slouch and is constantly updating. Over the last decade, it has added more than 100,000 sq ft to its gallery space and acquired about $1 billion worth of new art, including works by Zurbarán and Murillo. The museum is known for its extensive Native American artifacts and work from the local Northwest school, in particular by Mark Tobey (1890-1976). Modern American art is also well represented.

Belltown   NEIGHBORHOOD

Where industry once fumed, glassy condos now rise in the thin walkable strip of Belltown. The neighborhood gained a reputation for trend-setting nightlife in the 1990s and two of its bar-clubs, the Crocodile (p197) and Shorty's (p196), can still claim legendary status. Then there are the restaurants – more than 100 of them – and not all are prohibitively expensive. Belltown covers an area of roughly 10 blocks by six blocks, sandwiched in between downtown and the Seattle Center.

Olympic Sculpture Park   PARK, SCULPTURE

(2901 Western Ave; ⊙sunrise-sunset; 🚌13) **FREE**

Hovering above train tracks, in an unlikely oasis between the water and busy Elliott Ave, is the 8.5-acre, $85-million Olympic Sculpture Park. Worth a visit just for its views of the Olympic Mountains over Elliott Bay, the park has begun to grow into its long-range plan by filling a former brownfield industrial site with vibrant art and plant life.

◉ International District

For 'international' read Asian. East of Pioneer Sq, the shops and businesses are primarily Chinese, Vietnamese and Filipino.

Wing Luke Asian Museum   MUSEUM

(www.wingluke.org; 719 S King St; adult/child $12.95/8.95; ⊙10am-5pm Tue-Sun; 🚇Chinatown/International District E) Relocated and refurbished in 2008, the Wing Luke examines Asian and Pacific American culture, focusing on prickly issues such as Chinese settlement in the 1880s and Japanese internment camps in WWII. There are also art exhibits and a preserved immigrant apartment. Guided tours are available and recommended.

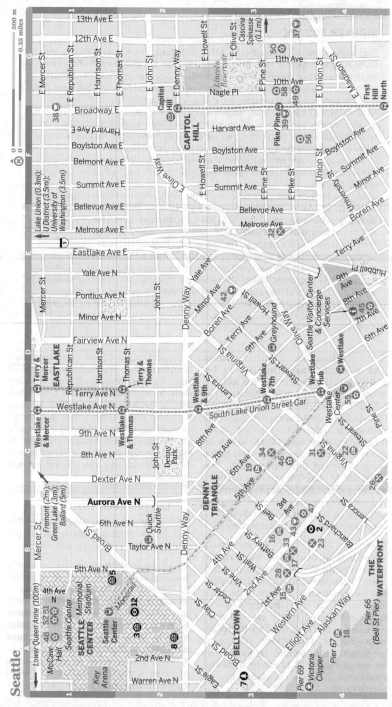

Seattle

PACIFIC NORTHWEST SEATTLE

500 m
0.25 miles

13th Ave E
12th Ave E
E Mercer St
E Republican St
E Harrison St
E Thomas St
E John St
E Denny Way
E Howell St
E Olive St
Cascina
Spirasse (0.1mi)
37
50
11th Ave
10th Ave
58
Nagle Pl
Lincoln
Reservoir
49
E Pine St
E Union St
E Madison St
First
Hill
North

38
Broadway E
Harvard Ave E
Capitol
Hill
CAPITOL HILL
Harvard Ave
Pike/Pine
39
56
E Pine St
E Pike St
Union St
Boylston Ave
Summit Ave
Minor Ave
Boren Ave

Boylston Ave E
Belmont Ave E
Summit Ave E
Bellevue Ave E
Melrose Ave E
E John St
E Olive Way
E Howell St
Boylston Ave
Belmont Ave
Summit Ave
Bellevue Ave
Melrose Ave
32
University St
Terry Ave

Eastlake Ave E
Yale Ave N
Pontius Ave N
Minor Ave N
Fairview Ave N
Mercer St
John St
Denny Way
Yale Ave
Minor Ave
Howell St
42
Boren Ave
Terry Ave
9th Ave
Olive Way
Greyhound
Seattle Visitor Center
& Concierge
Services
9th
Ave
8th Ave
7th Ave
6th Ave
45
Hubbell Pl

EASTLAKE
Terry &
Mercer
Republican St
Harrison St
Terry Ave N
Thomas St
Terry &
Thomas
Westlake &
Thomas
Westlake Ave N
Westlake &
9th
Lenora St
Virginia St
Stewart St
Westlake &
7th
Westlake
Hub
Westlake
Center
55
Pine St

Westlake & Mercer
Westlake Ave N
9th Ave N
8th Ave N
Dexter Ave N
John St
Denny
Park
South Lake Union Street Car
8th Ave
7th Ave
6th Ave
5th Ave
19
34
46
31
26
DENNY
TRIANGLE
Virginia St
Stewart St
Pine St

Aurora Ave N
Mercer St
Fremont (2mi);
Green Lake (3mi);
Ballard (5mi)
6th Ave N
Taylor Ave N
Broad St
Denny Way
Quick
Shuttle
Bell St
3rd
Ave
47
43
2
23
Blanchard St
Lenora St

5th Ave N
4th Ave
N
Lower Queen Anne (100m)
48
52 51
McCaw
Hall
Seattle Center
Memorial Stadium
Monorail
Seattle
Center
5
12
3
8
2nd Ave N
Warren Ave N
Key
Arena
SEATTLE
CENTER
16
33
17
28
15
Battery St
Wall St
Vine St
Cedar St
4th Ave
5th Ave
Blanchard St
2nd Ave
1st Ave
Western Ave
Elliott Ave
Alaskan Way
BELLTOWN
Clay St
Broad St
Eagle St
7
Victoria Clipper
Pier 69
Pier 67
Pier 66
(Bell St Pier)
18
THE
WATERFRONT

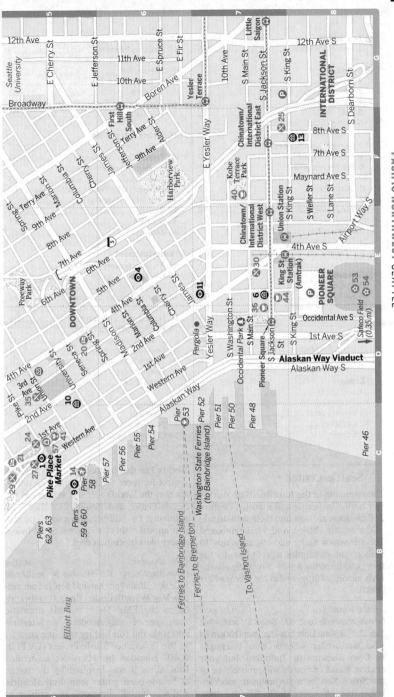

Seattle

◉ Seattle Center

The remnants of the futuristic 1962 World's Fair hosted by Seattle and subtitled Century 21 Exposition are now into their sixth decade at the Seattle Center. And what remnants! The fair was a major success, attracting 10 million visitors, running a profit (rare for the time) and inspiring a skin-crawlingly kitschy Elvis movie, *It Happened at the World's Fair* (1963).

Space Needle
LANDMARK

(www.spaceneedle.com; 400 Broad St; adult/child $19/12; ◷9:30am-11pm Sun-Thu, 9am-11:30pm Fri & Sat, 9am-11pm Sun; Ⓜ Seattle Center) You might be from Alabama or Timbuktu, but your abiding image of Seattle will probably be of the Space Needle, a streamlined, modern-before-its-time tower built for the 1962

World's Fair that has been the city's defining symbol for more than 50 years. The needle anchors the World's Fair site, now called the Seattle Center, and, despite its rather steep admission fee, still persuades over one million annual visitors to ascend to its flying-saucer-like observation deck.

EMP Museum
MUSEUM

(www.empsfm.org; 325 5th Ave N; adult/child $20/14; ◷10am-7pm Jun–mid-Sep, to 5pm mid-Sep–May; Ⓜ Seattle Center) Recently rebranded as the EMP Museum, this dramatic marriage of supermodern architecture and rock-and-roll history was inaugurated as the Experience Music Project (EMP) in 2000. Founded by Microsoft co-creator Paul Allen, it was inspired by the music of Seattle-born guitar icon Jimi Hendrix and was initially intended as a tribute to

Hendrix alone, although the collection has since expanded to include other local musicians.

Chihuly Garden & Glass MUSEUM
(206-753-3527; www.chihulygardenandglass.com; 305 W Harrison St; adult/child $19/12; ⊙11am-7pm Sun-Thu, to 8pm Fri & Sat; MSeattle Center) It's not every year that a city of Seattle's size adds a museum of such high quality to its list of urban attractions. Reinforcing the metropolis's position as the Venice of North America, this exquisite expose of the life and work of dynamic local glass sculptor Dale Chihuly requires a sharp intake of breath on first viewing. It opened in May 2012, and has quickly become a top city icon to rival the Space Needle.

Capitol Hill

Millionaires mingle with goth musicians in irreverent Capitol Hill, a well-heeled but liberal neighborhood rightly renowned for its fringe theater, alternative music scene, indie coffee bars, and vital gay and lesbian culture. You can take your dog for a herbal bath here, go shopping for ethnic crafts on Broadway, or blend in (or not) with the young punks and the old hippies on the eclectic Pike-Pine Corridor. The junction of Broadway and E John St is the nexus from which to navigate the quarter's various restaurants, brewpubs, boutiques and dingy, but not dirty, dive bars.

Fremont

Fremont pitches young hipsters among old hippies in an unlikely urban alliance, and vies with Capitol Hill as Seattle's most irreverent neighborhood. It's full of junk shops, urban sculpture and a healthy sense of its own ludicrousness.

Public Sculpture MONUMENT
Public art has never been as provocative as it is in Fremont. Look out for Waiting for the Interurban (cnr N 34th St & Fremont Ave N), a cast-aluminum statue of people awaiting a train that never comes: the Interurban linking Seattle and Everett stopped running in the 1930s (it started up again in 2001 but the line no longer passes this way). Check out the human face on the dog; it's Armen Stepanian, once Fremont's honorary mayor, who made the mistake of objecting to the sculpture. Equally eye-catching is the Fremont Troll (cnr N 36th St & Troll Ave), a scary-

looking 18ft troll crushing a Volkswagen Beetle in its left hand. The Fremont Rocket (cnr Evanston Ave & N 35th St) is a rocket that was found lying around in Belltown in 1993 and that now sticks out of a building – mmm, interesting. Fremont's most controversial art is the statue of Lenin (cnr N 36th St & Fremont PI N) salvaged from Slovakia after it was toppled during the 1989 revolution. Even if you hate the politics, you have to admire the art – and the audacity!

The U District

U-dub, a neighborhood of young, studious out-of-towners, places the beautiful, leafy University of Washington campus next to the shabbier 'Ave,' an eclectic strip of cheap boutiques, dive bars and ethnic restaurants.

University of Washington UNIVERSITY
(www.washington.edu; 70) Founded in 1861, Seattle's university is almost as old as the city itself and is ranked highly worldwide (the prestigious *Times Higher Education* magazine listed it 24th in the world in 2013). The present-day 700-acre campus that sits at the edge of Lake Union, about 3 miles northeast of downtown, is flecked with stately trees and beautiful architecture, and affords wondrous views of Mt Rainier framed by fountains and foliage.

Burke Museum MUSEUM
(www.burkemuseum.org; cnr 17th Ave NE & NE 45th St; adult/child $10/7.50; ⊙10am-5pm; 70) Of the University of Washington's two on-site museums, the Burke is the best. The main collection has an impressive stash of fossils

including a 20,000-year-old sabre-toothed cat. Equally compelling is the focus on 17 different Native American cultures.

◉ Ballard

A former seafaring community with a strong Scandinavian heritage, Ballard still feels like a small town engulfed by a bigger city. Traditionally gritty, no-nonsense and uncommercial, it's slowly being condo-ized, but remains a good place to down a microbrew or see a live band.

Hiram M Chittenden Locks GARDENS
(3015 NW 54th St; ⊙locks 24hr, ladder & gardens 7am-9pm, visitor center 10am-6pm May-Sep; ▣62) Seattle shimmers like an impressionist painting on sunny days at the Hiram M Chittenden Locks. Here, the fresh waters of Lake Washington and Lake Union that flow through the 8-mile-long Lake Washington Ship Canal drop 22 feet into salt-water Puget Sound. On the southern side of the locks you can view a fish ladder from underwater glass-sided tanks. Flanking Carl English Jr Botanical Gardens on the northern side is a small museum and a visitors center documenting the history of the locks.

DON'T MISS

DISCOVERY PARK

A former military installation that has been transformed into a wild coastal park, Discovery Park (www.seattle.gov/parks/environment/discovery.htm; ▣33) is a relatively recent addition to the city landscape – it wasn't officially inaugurated until 1973 and the American military finally left in 2012. Comprising the largest green space in the city, the park's 534 acres are laced with cliffs, meadows, sand dunes, forest and beaches, all of which provide a welcome breathing space for hemmed-in Seattleites and a vital corridor for wildlife. For a map of the park's trail and road system, stop by the Discovery Park Environmental Learning Center (☑206-386-4236; 3801 W Government Way; ⊙8:30am-5pm) near the Government Way entrance. The park is located five miles northwest of downtown Seattle in the neighborhood of Magnolia. To get there, catch bus 33 from 3rd Ave & Union St downtown.

⭐ Activities

Cycling

A cycling favorite, the 16.5-mile Burke-Gilman Trail winds from Ballard to Log Boom Park in Kenmore on Seattle's Eastside. There, it connects with the 11-mile Sammamish River Trail, which winds past the Chateau Ste Michelle winery in Woodinville before terminating at Redmond's Marymoor Park.

More cyclists pedal the popular loop around Green Lake, situated just north of Fremont and 5 miles north of the downtown core. From Belltown, the 2.5-mile Elliott Bay Trail runs along the Waterfront to Smith Cove.

Get a copy of the *Seattle Bicycling Guide Map,* published by the City of Seattle's Transportation Bicycle & Pedestrian Program (www.cityofseattle.net/transportation/bikemaps.htm) online or at bike shops.

For bicycle rentals and tours, try Recycled Cycles (www.recycledcycles.com; 1007 NE Boat St; rentals per 6/24hr $20/40; ⊙10am-8pm Mon-Fri, to 6pm Sat & Sun; ▣; ▣66), a friendly U District shop that also rents out chariots and trail-a-bike attachments for kids, or SBR Seattle Bicycle Rental & Tours (☑800-349-0343; www.seattlebicyclerentals.com; Pier 58; rental per hr/day $10/40; ⊙11am-7pm Wed-Mon; ▣University St), which offers reasonable rates and daily tours (book online).

Water Sports

Seattle is not just on a network of cycling trails. With Venice-like proportions of downtown water, it is also strafed with kayak-friendly marine trails. The Lakes to Locks Water Trail links Lake Sammamish with Lake Washington, Lake Union and – via the Hiram M Chittenden Locks – Puget Sound. For launching sites and maps, check the website of the Washington Water Trails Association (www.wwta.org).

Northwest Outdoor Center Inc (www.nwoc.com; 2100 Westlake Ave N; kayaks per hr $14-22; ▣62) on Lake Union rents kayaks, and offers tours and instruction in sea and white-water kayaking.

☞ Tours

Seattle Free Walking Tours WALKING TOUR
(www.seattlefreewalkingtours.org) A nonprofit set up by a couple of world travelers and Seattle residents in 2012. These intimate two-hour tours meet daily at 11am on the corner of Western Ave and Virginia St. If

SEATTLE FOR CHILDREN

Make a beeline for the Seattle Center, preferably on the monorail, where food carts, street entertainers, fountains and green space will make the day fly by. One essential stop is the Pacific Science Center (www.pacsci.org; 200 2nd Ave N; adult/child exhibits-only $18/13, with IMAX $22/17; ⊙10am-5pm Mon-Fri, to 6pm Sat & Sun; Ⓜ Seattle Center), which entertains and educates with virtual-reality exhibits, laser shows, holograms, an IMAX theater and a planetarium – parents won't be bored either.

Downtown on Pier 59, Seattle Aquarium (www.seattleaquarium.org; 1483 Alaskan Way, Pier 59; adult/child $19/12; ⊙9:30am-5pm; 📭; ⓡ University St) is a fun way to learn about the natural world of the Pacific Northwest. Even better is Woodland Park Zoo (📭20 6-684-4800; www.zoo.org; 5500 Phinney Ave N; adult/child Oct-Apr $12.50/8.75, May-Sep $18.75/11.75; ⊙9:30am-4pm Oct-Apr, to 6pm May-Sep; 📭; 🚌5) in the Green Lake neighborhood, one of Seattle's greatest tourist attractions and consistently rated as one of the top 10 zoos in the country.

you have a rip-roaring time (highly likely), there's a suggested $15 donation.

Seattle by Foot
WALKING TOUR

(📭206-508-7017; www.seattlebyfoot.com; tours $20-25) This company runs a handful of tours including the practically essential Coffee Crawl, which will ply you liberally with caffeine while explaining the nuances of latte art and dishing the inside story on the rise of Starbucks. It costs $25 including samples. Registration starts at 9.50am from Thursday to Sunday outside Seattle Art Museum.

Savor Seattle
FOOD TOUR

(📭206-209-5485; www.savorseattletours.com; tours $59.99) These guys lead a handful of gastronomic tours, the standout being the two-hour Booze-n-Bites that runs daily at 4pm from the corner of Western Ave & Virginia St.

🎉 Festivals & Events

Seattle International Film Festival
FILM

(SIFF; www.siff.net; tickets $13-30; ⊙mid-May) The city's biggest film festival uses a half-dozen cinemas around town but also has its own dedicated cinema in McCaw Hall's Nesholm Family Lecture Hall.

Seafair
WATER

(www.seafair.com; ⊙Jul/Aug) Huge crowds attend this festival held on the water, which includes hydroplane races, a torchlight parade, an air show, music and a carnival.

Bumbershoot
MUSIC, LITERATURE

(www.bumbershoot.com; ⊙Sep) A major arts and cultural event at Seattle Center on the Labor Day weekend in September, with live music, author readings and lots of unclassifiable fun.

🛏 Sleeping

From mid-November through to the end of March, most downtown hotels offer Seattle Super Saver Packages – generally 50% off rack rates, with a coupon book for savings on dining, shopping and attractions. Make reservations online at www.seattlesuper saver.com.

★Moore Hotel
HOTEL $

(📭206-448-4851; www.moorehotel.com; 1926 2nd Ave; s/d with shared bath $68/80, with private bath $85/97; 🛜; ⓡWestlake) Old-world and allegedly haunted, the Moore nonetheless has a friendly front desk and a prime location. If that doesn't swing you, the price should. There's a cute little cafe on the premises and the divey Nitelite Lounge next door. You can practically hold your breath and walk to Pike Place Market from here.

City Hostel Seattle
HOSTEL $

(📭206-706-3255; www.hostelseattle.com; 2327 2nd Ave; 6-/4-bed dm $28/32, d $73, all incl breakfast; @🛜; ⓡRapid Ride D-Line) 🌿 Sleep in an art gallery for peanuts – in Belltown, no less. That's the reality in this new 'art hostel', which will make your parent's hostelling days seem positively spartan by comparison. Aside from arty dorms, expect a common room, hot tub, in-house movie theater (with free DVDs) and all-you-can-eat breakfast.

★Hotel Five
BOUTIQUE HOTEL $$

(📭206-441-9785; www.hotelfiveseattle.com; 2200 5th Ave; r from $165; 🅿🌀🛜; 🚌13) This wonderful reincarnation of the old Ramada Inn on Fifth Ave in Belltown mixes retro '70s furniture with sharp color accents to produce something that is dazzlingly modern. And it's functional, too. The ultracomfortable beds could be nominated as a valid cure for insomnia, while the large reception area invites lingering, especially when they lay out the complimentary cupcakes and coffee in the late afternoon.

★ **Maxwell Hotel** BOUTIQUE HOTEL $$
(☑206-286-0629; www.themaxwellhotel.com; 300 Roy St; r from $179; P❄@🛜🏊; ⬚ Rapid Ride D-Line) A gorgeous boutique hotel that graces the Lower Queen Anne neighborhood, the Maxwell's huge designer-chic lobby is enough to make anyone dust off their credit card. Look out for periodic offers online.

Ace Hotel HOTEL $$
(☑206-448-4721; www.acehotel.com; 2423 1st Ave; r with shared/private bath $109/199; P🛜; ⬚13) Emulating (almost) its hip Portland cousin, the Ace sports minimal, futuristic decor (everything's white or stainless steel, even the TV), antique French army blankets, condoms instead of pillow mints and a copy of the *Kama Sutra* instead of the Bible. Parking costs $15.

Belltown Inn HOTEL $$
(☑206-529-3700; www.belltown-inn.com; 2301 3rd Ave; s/d $159/164; P❄@🛜; ⬚Rapid Ride D-Line) Can it be true? The Belltown is such a bargain and in such a prime location that it's hard to believe it hasn't accidentally floated over from a smaller, infinitely cheaper city. But no: clean functional rooms, handy kitchenettes, roof terrace, free bikes and – vitally important – borrow-and-return umbrellas are all yours for the price of a posh dinner.

Mediterranean Inn HOTEL $$
(☑206-428-4700; www.mediterranean-inn.com; 425 Queen Anne Ave N; r from $159; P❄@; ⬚Rapid Ride D-Line) There's something about the surprisingly un-Mediterranean Med Inn that just clicks. Maybe it's the handy cusp-of-Belltown location, or the genuinely friendly staff, or the kitchenettes in every room, or the small downstairs gym or the surgical cleanliness. Don't try to define it – just go there and soak it up.

★ **Edgewater** HOTEL $$$
(☑206-728-7000; www.edgewaterhotel.com; Pier 67, 2411 Alaskan Way; r 420-750; P❄@🛜; ⬚13) Fame and notoriety has stalked the Edgewater. Perched over the water on a pier, it was once the hotel of choice for every rock band that mattered, including the Beatles, the Rolling Stones and, most infamously, Led Zeppelin, who took the 'you can fish from the hotel window' advertising jingle a little too seriously and filled their suite with sharks.

Hotel Monaco BOUTIQUE HOTEL $$$
(☑206-621-1770; www.monaco-seattle.com; 1101 4th Ave; d/ste $339/399; P@🛜🐾; ⬚University St) 🐾 Whimsical, with dashes of European elegance, the downtown Hotel Monaco is worthy of all four of its illustrious stars. Bed down amid the stripy wallpaper and heavy drapes.

Inn at the Market BOUTIQUE HOTEL $$$
(☑206-443-3600; www.innatthemarket.com; 86 Pine St; r with/without water view $370/255; P❄🛜; ⬚Westlake) The only hotel lodging in venerable Pike Place Market, this elegant 70-room boutique hotel has large rooms, many of which enjoy views onto market activity and Puget Sound. Parking costs $20.

🍴 Eating

The best budget meals are to be found in Pike Place Market. Take your pick from fresh produce, baked goods, deli items and takeout ethnic foods.

★ **Top Pot Hand-Forged Doughnuts** CAFE $
(www.toppotdoughnuts.com; 2124 5th Ave; doughnuts from $1.50; ⏱6am-7pm; ⬚13) Top Pot is to doughnuts what champagne is to wine – a different class. And its cafes – especially this one in an old car showroom with floor-to-ceiling library shelves and art-deco signage – are equally legendary. The coffee's pretty potent, too.

★ **Piroshky Piroshky** BAKERY $
(www.piroshkybakery.com; 1908 Pike Pl; snacks $2-7; ⏱8am-6:30pm Oct-Apr, from 7:30am May-Sep; ⬚Westlake) Proof that not all insanely popular Pike Place holes-in-the-wall go global (à la Starbucks), Piroshky is still knocking out its delectable mix of sweet and savory Russian pies and pastries in a space barely big enough to swing a small kitten. Join the melee and order one 'to go.'

★ **Salumi** SANDWICHES $
(www.salumicuredmeats.com; 309 3rd Ave S; sandwiches $7-10; ⏱11am-4pm Tue-Fri; ⬚International District/Chinatown) The queue outside Salumi has long been part of the sidewalk furniture. This place has even formed its own community of chatterers, food bloggers, Twitter posters and gourmet-sandwich aficionados who compare notes. The fact that it's owned

by the father of celebrity chef Mario Batali probably helps.

★ Pie
PIES $

(☑ 206-436-8590; www.sweetandsavorypie.com; 3515 Fremont Ave N; pies $5.95; ☺ 9am-9pm Mon-Thu, to 2am Fri & Sat, 10am-6pm Sun; 🚇 26) 🚶 It's as simple as P-I-E. Bake fresh pies daily on-site, stuff them with homemade fillings (sweet and savory) and serve them in a cool, bold-colored Fremont cafe. The pies are ideal for a snack lunch, or you can double up and get a sweet one for desert, too.

★ Green Leaf
VIETNAMESE $

(☑ 206-340-1388; www.greenleaftaste.com; 418 8th Ave S; pho $7.95, specials $11.95; ☺ 11am-10pm; 🚇 Chinatown/International District E) As narrow as a railway carriage and as crowded as a pub full of Sounders supporters, Green Leaf shoots out rapid-fire dishes from its tiny kitchen to its shiny black tables. People shout about the huge bowls of traditional or vegetarian pho (noodle soup) and a swoon-inducing version of *bahn xeo* – a sort of cross between a pancake and an omelet.

Crumpet Shop
CRUMPETS $

(1503 1st Ave; crumpets $3-6; ☺ 7am-5pm; 🚇 Westlake) Take a treasured British culinary invention (the crumpet) and give it a distinct American twist (ridiculously lavish toppings) and you've got another reason to have your breakfast or lunch in Pike Place Market.

Macrina
BAKERY $

(☑ 206-448-4032; 2408 1st Ave; pastries $2-3.75; ☺ 7am-7pm; 🚇 13) That snaking queue is there for a reason – damned good artisan bread (you can watch through the window as the experts roll out the dough). There are two options and two lines at Macrina. One for the fantastic takeout bakery (possibly the best in Seattle); the other for the sit-down cafe with its so-good-it-could-be-Paris sandwiches, soups and other such snacks. Join the pilgrimage.

Lowells
DINER $

(www.eatatlowells.com; 1519 Pike Pl; mains $6-9; ☺ 7am-6pm; 🚇 Westlake) Fish and chips is a simple meal often done badly – but not here. Slam down your order for Alaskan cod at the front entry and take it up to the top floor for delicious views over Puget Sound. Lowells also serves corned-beef hash and an excellent clam chowder.

★ Serious Pie
PIZZA $$

(www.tomdouglas.com; 316 Virginia St; pizzas $16-18; ☺ 11am-11pm; 🚇 Westlake) It's an audacious move to take the down-to-earth Italian pizza and give it a gourmet spin, but local culinary phenomenon Tom Douglas pulls off the trick with casual aplomb. In the crowded confines of Serious Pie, you can enjoy beautifully blistered pizza bases topped by such unconventional ingredients as clams, kale, potato, apples, pistachio and more. It's seriously good!

★ Wild Ginger
ASIAN $$

(www.wildginger.net; 1401 3rd Ave; mains $15-28; ☺ 11am-3pm & 5-11pm Mon-Sat, 4-9pm Sun; 🚇 University St) Food from around the Pacific Rim – via China, Indonesia, Malaysia, Vietnam and Seattle, of course – is the wide-ranging theme at this highly popular downtown fusion restaurant. The signature fragrant duck goes down nicely with a glass of Riesling. The restaurant also provides food for the swanky Triple Door (☑ 206-838-4333; www.thetripledoor.net; 216 Union St; 🚇 University St) club downstairs.

★ Toulouse Petit
CAJUN $$

(☑ 206-432-9069; 601 Queen Anne Ave N; mains $13-17; ☺ 8am-2am; 🚇 13) Something of a Seattle phenomenon, Toulouse Petit is hailed for its generous happy hours, cheap brunches and rollicking atmosphere – it's perennially (and boisterously) busy. Somewhere underneath all this cacophony is the specialty food, which pays more than a passing nod to the 'Big Easy' (aka New Orleans).

360 Local
NORTHWEST $$

(☑ 206-441-9360; www.local360.org; cnr 1st Ave & Bell St; mains $16-26; ☺ 11am-late Mon-Fri, 8am-late Sat & Sun; 🚇 13) 🚶 Snaring 90% of its ingredients from within a 360-mile radius, this new restaurant follows it ambitious 'locavore' manifesto pretty rigidly. The farms where your meat was reared are displayed on the daily blackboard menu and the restaurant's wood-finish interior looks like a rustic barn. With such a fertile hinterland to draw upon the food is pretty special; try the rabbit, the oysters or the chickpea cake.

Le Pichet
FRENCH $$

(www.lepichetseattle.com; 1933 1st Ave; lunch/mains $9/18; ☺ 8am-midnight; 🚇 Westlake) Say *bienvenue* to Le Pichet just up from Pike Place Market, a very French bistro with pâtés, cheeses, wine, chocolate and a refined Parisian feel. An economical way to impress a date.

★Cascina Spinasse   ITALIAN $$$

(☑206-251-7673; www.spinasse.com; 1531 14th Ave; 2-course meal $40; ☺5-10pm Sun-Thu, to 11pm Fri & Sat; ☐11) Behind the rather fussy lace curtains hides what is possibly the finest new restaurant in Seattle. Spinasse specializes in cuisine of the Piedmont region of northern Italy. This means delicately prepared ravioli, buttery risottos (enhanced with stinging nettles, no less), rabbit meatballs and roasted artichokes.

★Sitka & Spruce   NORTHWEST $$$

(☑206-324-0662; www.sitkaandspruce.com; 1531 Melrose Ave E; small plates $8-24; ☺11:30am-2pm & 5:30-10pm; ☐10) Now in a new location in the Capitol Hill 'hood, this small-plates fine-diner has won acclaim for its casual vibe, constantly changing menu, good wine selection and involved chef-owner (he'll be the guy who brings bread to your table). All the ingredients are obtained from local producers, and the idea is to assemble a meal out of a bunch of different taster-sized dishes.

Tavolàta   ITALIAN $$$

(☑206-838-8008; 2323 2nd Ave; meals $40-75; ☺5-11pm; ☐13) Eating around a large communal table was once something you did reluctantly in youth hostels, but lately it's been deemed trendy, which is why it's become a feature in cool restaurants in Belltown such as Tavolàta, owned by top Seattle chef Ethan Stowell. Decor is industrial Belltown, but the menu is more Italian trattoria (homemade pasta) with some Northwestern inflections (nettles).

🍷 Drinking & Nightlife

Starbucks is the tip of the iceberg when it comes to coffee culture in Seattle; the city has spawned plenty of smaller indie chains, many with their own roasting rooms. Look out for Uptown Espresso, Caffe Ladro and Espresso Vivace.

You'll find cocktail bars, dance clubs and live music on Capitol Hill. The main drag in Ballard has brick taverns both old and new, filled with the hard-drinking older set in daylight hours and indie rockers at night. Belltown has gone from grungy to shabby chic, and has the advantage of many drinking holes neatly lined up in rows.

Zeitgeist   CAFE

(www.zeitgeistcoffee.com; 171 S Jackson St; ☺6am-7pm Mon-Fri, from 8am Sat & Sun; 🔊; ☐Pioneer Sq) Listen. The comforting buzz of conver-

sation! People actually talk in the attractive exposed-brick confines of Zeitgeist – they're not all glued to their laptops. Bolstered by tongue-loosening doses of caffeine, you can join them discussing the beautiful smoothness of your *doppio macchiato* or the sweet intensity of your to-die-for almond croissant.

★Pike Pub & Brewery   BREWERY

(www.pikebrewing.com; 1415 1st Ave; ☺11am-midnight; ☐University St) Leading the way in the microbrewery revolution, this brewpub was an early starter, opening in 1989 underneath Pike Place Market. Today it continues to serve sophisticated pub food and hop-heavy beers in a neoindustrial multilevel space that's a beer nerd's heaven. The brewery runs free tours daily at 2pm.

★Espresso Vivace at Brix   CAFE

(www.espressovivace.com; 532 Broadway E; ☺6am-11pm; ☐60) Loved in equal measure for its no-nonsense walk-up stand on Broadway and this newer cafe (a large retro place with a beautiful streamline moderne counter), Vivace is known to have produced some of the Picassos of latte art. But it doesn't just offer pretty toppings. Many of Seattle's coffee experts rate the espresso shots as the best in the city.

★Fremont Brewing   BREWERY

(www.fremontbrewing.com; 3409 Woodland Park Ave N; ☺11am-7pm Mon-Wed, to 8pm Thu-Sat, to 6pm Sun; ☐26) No conventional bar (this, after all, is Fremont!), this 2008-inaugurated brewery has what is called an 'Urban Beer Garden'; ie you sit at a couple of communal tables in the brewery and enjoy samples of what are quickly being hailed as some of the finest microbrews in the city.

★Shorty's   BAR

(www.shortydog.com; 2222 2nd Ave; ☺noon-2am; ☐13) Shorty's is all about beer, pinball and music, which is punk and metal mostly. A remnant of Belltown's grungier days that refuses to become an anachronism, it keeps the lights low (to cover the grime?) and the music loud. Pinball machines are built into every table and very basic snacks (hot dogs, nachos) soak up the beer.

★Noble Fir   BAR

(☑206-420-7425; www.thenoblefir.com; 5316 Ballard Ave NW; ☺4-11pm Mon-Wed, to 1am Thu-Sat, noon-11pm Sun; ☐17) Possibly the first bar devoted to the theme of wilderness hiking, the Noble Fir is a bright, shiny, new Ballard spot with an epic beer list that might just make you want to abandon all your plans for outdoor adventure. Should your resolve begin to flag, head to the back corner, where there's a library of activity guides and maps that will reinspire you.

Elysian Brewing Company BREWERY
(www.elysianbrewing.com; 1221 E Pike St; ⊘11:30am-2am; 🚇Pike-Pine) The Elysian's huge windows are great for people-watching – or being watched. This is one of Seattle's best brewpubs, and is loved in particular for its spicy pumpkin beers. The same folks also run the Tangletown Pub near Green Lake.

Panama Hotel Tea & Coffee House CAFE
(607 S Main St; ⊘8am-7pm Mon-Sat, from 9am Sun; 🚇Chinatown/International District W) The Panama, a historic 1910 building containing the only remaining Japanese bathhouse in the US, doubles as a memorial to the neighborhood's Japanese residents forced into internment camps during WWII. The beautifully relaxed cafe has a wide selection of teas and is one of the few places in Seattle to sell Lavazza Italian coffee.

Caffè Umbria CAFE
(www.caffeumbria.com; 320 Occidental Ave S; ⊘6am-6pm Mon-Fri, from 7am Sat, 8am-5pm Sun; 🚇Pioneer Sq) Umbria has a European flavor with its 8oz cappuccinos, chatty clientele, pretty Italianate tiles and baguettes so fresh they must have been teleported over from Milan. Ideal for Italio-philes and Starbucks-phobes.

Blue Moon BAR
(712 NE 45th St; ⊘2pm-late; 🚇66) A legendary counterculture dive near the university that first opened in 1934 to celebrate the repeal of the prohibition laws, the Blue Moon makes much of its former literary patrons: doyens Dylan Thomas, Allen Ginsberg and Tom Robbins get mentioned a lot.

Re-Bar GAY
(www.rebarseattle.com; 1114 Howell St; 🚇70) This storied dance club, where many of Seattle's defining cultural events have happened (such as Nirvana album releases), welcomes gay, straight, bi or undecided revelers to its lively dance floor. It's in the Denny Triangle.

Neighbours GAY
(www.neighboursnightclub.com; 1509 Broadway Ave E; 🚇Pike-Pine) Check out the always-packed dance factory for the gay club scene and its attendant glittery straight girls.

☆ Entertainment

Consult the *Stranger, Seattle Weekly* or the daily papers for listings. Tickets for big events are available at TicketMaster (www.ticketmaster.com). Tickets can be picked up at branches of Fred Meyer electronics stores. Local addresses are listed on the Ticket-Master website.

Live Music

★Crocodile LIVE MUSIC
(www.thecrocodile.com; 2200 2nd Ave; 🚇13) Nearly old enough to be called a Seattle institution, the Crocodile is a clamorous 560-capacity music venue that first opened in 1991, just in time to grab the coattails of the grunge explosion. Everyone who's anyone in Seattle's alt-music scene has since played here, including a famous occasion in 1992 when Nirvana appeared unannounced on a bill supporting Mudhoney.

Neumo's LIVE MUSIC
(www.neumos.com; 925 E Pike St; 🚇Pike-Pine) A punk, hip-hop and alternative-music venue that counts Radiohead and Bill Clinton (not together) among its former guests, Neumo's (formerly known as Moe's) fills the big shoes of its original namesake. Yes, it can get hot, and yes, mid-show it's a long walk to the toilets; but that's rock and roll.

Tractor Tavern LIVE MUSIC
(🖉206-789-3599; www.tractortavern.com; 5213 Ballard Ave NW; 🚇17) The premier venue for folk and acoustic music, the elegant Tractor Tavern in Ballard also books local songwriters and regional bands such as Richmond Fontaine, plus touring acts like John Doe and Wayne Hancock. It's a gorgeous room, usually with top-quality sound.

Cinema

Northwest Film Forum CINEMA
(www.nwfilmforum.org; 1515 12th Ave; 🚇Pike-Pine) A film arts organization whose two-screen cinema offers impeccable programming, from restored classics to cutting-edge independent and international films. It's in Capitol Hill, of course!

Cinerama CINEMA
(www.cinerama.com; 2100 4th Ave; 🚇13) Possibly Seattle's most popular theater, Cinerama is one of only three of its type left in the world (with a giant curved three-panel screen). Regular renovations, the latest in 2010, have kept it up to date. It presents a good mix of new releases and 70mm classics.

Performing Arts

★ A Contemporary Theatre   THEATRE
(ACT; www.acttheatre.org; 700 Union St; 🚇 University St) One of the three big companies in the city, ACT fills its $30-million home at Kreielsheimer Place with performances by Seattle's best thespians and occasional big-name actors. Terraced seating surrounds a central stage and the interior has gorgeous architectural embellishments.

Intiman Theater Company   THEATRE
(☎ 206-269-1900; www.intiman.org; 201 Mercer St; ⊙ ticket office noon-5pm Tue-Sun; Ⓜ Seattle Center) In a shocking move, Seattle's Tony Award-winning Intiman Theater abruptly closed in April 2011, a victim of the financial crisis. But city icons aren't allowed to die. The theater raised the $1 million necessary for a heroic reopening in 2012 and is back doing what it does best: magnificent stagings of Shakespeare and Ibsen. Time for another Tony?

Seattle Opera   CLASSICAL MUSIC
(www.seattleopera.org; Ⓜ Seattle Center) Features a program of four or five full-scale operas every season at Seattle Center's McCaw Hall, including Wagner's *Ring* cycle that draws sellout crowds in summer.

On the Boards   THEATRE
(☎ 206-217-9888; www.ontheboards.org; 100 W Roy St; 🚌 13) *The* place for avant-garde performance art, the nonprofit On the Boards makes its home at the intimate Behnke Center for Contemporary Performance in the Lower Queen Anne neighborhood. It showcases some innovative and occasionally weird dance and music.

Pacific Northwest Ballet   DANCE
(www.pnb.org; Ⓜ Seattle Center) The foremost dance company in the Northwest puts on more than 100 shows a season September through June at Seattle Center's McCaw Hall.

Sport

Seattle Mariners   BASEBALL
(www.mariners.org; tickets $7-60) Established in 1977 but yet to appear in a World Series, the Mariners make their home at Safeco Field.

Seattle Seahawks   FOOTBALL
(www.seahawks.com; tickets $42-95) Runners up to Pittsburgh Steelers in the 2006 Super Bowl, the Seahawks play at CenturyLink Field.

Seattle Sounders   SOCCER
(☎ 206-622-3415; www.seattlesounders.net; tickets from $37) Share CenturyLink with the Seahawks. The Sounders are the best supported team in Major League Soccer with average gate attendance of 43,000.

🔒 Shopping

The main big-name shopping area is downtown between 3rd and 6th Aves and University and Stewart Sts. Pike Place Market is a maze of arts-and-crafts stalls, galleries and small shops. Pioneer Sq and Capitol Hill have locally owned gift and thrift shops. There are many only-in-Seattle shops that are worth seeking out.

Elliott Bay Book Company   BOOKS
(www.elliottbaybook.com; 1521 10th Ave; ⊙ 10am-10pm Mon-Fri, to 11pm Sat, 11am-9pm Sun; 🚇 Pike-Pine) Perish the day when e-books render bookstores obsolete. What will happen to the Saturday-afternoon joy of Elliott Bay books, where 150,000 titles inspire author readings, discussions, reviews and hours of serendipitous browsing?

★ DeLaurenti's   FOOD
(☎ 206-622-0141; cnr 1st Ave & Pike Pl; ⊙ 9am-6pm Mon-Sat, 10am-5pm Sun; 🚇 University St) DeLaurenti's is a mandatory market stop for the Italian chef or continental food enthusiast. Not only is there a stunning selection of cheese, sausages, ham and pasta, but there's also the largest selection of capers, olive oil and anchovies that you're likely to find this side of Genoa.

★ Bop Street Records   MUSIC
(www.bopstreetrecords.com; 2220 NW Market St; ⊙ noon-8pm Tue-Wed, to 10pm Thu-Sat, to 5pm Sun; 🚌 17) What is probably the most impressive collection of vinyl you're ever likely to see lines the heavily stacked shelves of Bop Street Records, in the north Seattle neighborhood of Ballard. The collection of half-a-million records covers every genre – there's even old-school 78s.

Babeland   ADULT
(www.babeland.com; 707 E Pike St; ⊙ 11am-10pm Mon-Sat, noon-7pm Sun; 🚇 Pike-Pine) Remember those pink furry handcuffs and that glass dildo you needed? Well, look no further.

ℹ Information

EMERGENCY & MEDICAL SERVICES
45th St Community Clinic (☎ 206-633-3350; 1629 N 45th St) Medical and dental services.

Harborview Medical Center (☎206-731-3000; 325 9th Ave) Full medical care, with emergency room.

Seattle Police (☎206-625-5011)

Washington State Patrol (☎425-649-4370) The local traffic police.

KEXP 90.3 FM Legendary independent music and community station.

Seattle Times (www.seattletimes.com) The state's largest daily paper.

The Stranger (www.thestranger.com) Irreverent weekly edited by Dan Savage of 'Savage Love' fame.

MONEY

Travelex-Thomas Cook Currency Services Airport (◷6am-8pm); Westlake Center (400 Pine St, Level 3; ◷9:30am-6pm Mon-Sat, 11am-5pm Sun) The booth at the main airport terminal is behind the Delta Airlines counter.

American Express (Amex; 600 Stewart St; ◷8:30am-5:30pm Mon-Fri)

POST

Post Office (301 Union St; ◷8:30am-5:30pm Mon-Fri)

TOURIST INFORMATION

Seattle Visitor Center & Concierge Services (☎206-461-5840; www.visitseattle.org; Washington State Convention Center, E Pike St & 7th Ave; ◷9am-5pm)

ⓘ Getting There & Away

AIR

Seattle-Tacoma International Airport (Sea-Tac; ☎206-787-5388; www.portseattle.org/sea-tac; 17801 International Blvd), 13 miles south of Seattle on I-5, has daily services to Europe, Asia, Mexico and points throughout the USA and Canada, with frequent flights to and from Portland, OR, and Vancouver, BC.

BOAT

Victoria Clipper (www.clippervacations.com) operates several high-speed passenger ferries to Victoria, BC, and to the San Juan Islands. It also organizes package tours that can be booked in advance through the website. Victoria Clipper runs from Seattle to Victoria up to six times daily (round-trip adult/child $149/74.50).

Washington State Ferries (WSF; www.wsdot.wa.gov/ferries) includes maps, prices, schedules, trip planners and weather updates on its website, plus estimated waiting times for popular routes. Fares depend on the route, vehicle size and trip duration, and are collected either for round-trip or one-way travel depending on the departure terminal.

BUS

Various intercity coaches serve Seattle at different drop-off points.

Greyhound (www.greyhound.com; 811 Stewart St; ◷6am-midnight) connects Seattle with cities all over the country, including Chicago ($228 one way, two days, two daily), Spokane ($51, eight hours, three daily), San Francisco ($129, 20 hours, three daily) and Vancouver, BC ($32, four hours, five daily). The company has its own terminal in the Denny Triangle within easy walking distance to downtown.

Fast and efficient **Quick Shuttle** (www.quickcoach.com; ☎) has 5 to 6 daily buses to Vancouver ($43). Pickup is at the Best Western Executive Inn in Taylor Ave N near the Seattle Center. Grab the monorail or walk to downtown. Free on-board wi-fi.

Bellair Airporter Shuttle (www.airporter.com) runs buses to Yakima, Bellingham and Anacortes and stops at King Street station (for Yakima) and the downtown Convention Center (for Bellingham and Anacortes).

TRAIN

Amtrak (www.amtrak.com) serves Seattle's **King Street Station** (303 S Jackson St; ◷6am-10:30pm, ticket counter 6:15am-8pm). Three main routes run through town: the Amtrak Cascades (connecting Vancouver, Seattle, Portland and Eugene); the very scenic Coast Starlight (connecting Seattle, Oakland and Los Angeles) and the Empire Builder (a cross-continental roller coaster to Chicago).

Chicago, IL (from $227, 46 hours, daily)

Oakland, CA ($131, 23 hours, daily)

Portland, OR ($25, three to four hours, five daily)

Vancouver, BC ($30, three to four hours, five daily)

ⓘ Getting Around

TO/FROM THE AIRPORT

There are a number of options for making the 13-mile trek from the airport to downtown Seattle. The most efficient is via the new light-rail service run by Sound Transit (p200).

Shuttle Express (☎800-487-7433; www.shuttleexpress.com) has a pickup and drop-off point on the 3rd floor of the airport garage; its charges approximately $18 and is handy if you have a lot of luggage.

Taxis are available at the parking garage on the 3rd floor. The average fare to downtown is $42.

CAR & MOTORCYCLE

Trapped in a narrow corridor between mountains and sea, Seattle is a horrendous traffic bottleneck and its nightmarish jams are famous. I-5 has a high-occupancy vehicle lane for vehicles carrying two or more people. Otherwise, try to work around the elongated 'rush hours.'

PUBLIC TRANSPORTATION

Buses are operated by **Metro Transit** (www.metro.kingcounty.gov), part of the King County Department of Transportation. Fares cost a flat $2.50 (off-peak $2.25).

The **Seattle Street Car** (www.seattlestreetcar.org) runs from the Westlake Center to Lake Union along a 2.6-mile route. There are 11 stops allowing interconnections with numerous bus routes. A second route from Pioneer Square via First Hill to Capitol Hill opens in 2014.

Seattle's Link Light Rail run by **Sound Transit** (www.soundtransit.org), operates between Sea-Tac Airport and downtown (Westlake Center) every 15 minutes between 5am and midnight. The ride takes 36 minutes and costs $3. There are additional stops in Pioneer Sq and the International District.

TAXI

All Seattle taxi cabs operate at the same rate, set by King County; $2.50 at meter drop, then $2.70 per mile.

Orange Cab Co (206-444-0409; www.orangecab.net)

Yellow Cab (206-622-6500; www.yellowtaxi.net)

Around Seattle

Olympia

Small in size but big in clout, state capital Olympia is a musical, political and outdoor powerhouse. Look no further than the streetside buskers on 4th Ave belting out acoustic grunge, the smartly attired bureaucrats marching across the lawns of the state legislature, or the Gore-Tex-clad outdoor fiends overnighting before sorties into the Olympic Mountains. Progressive Evergreen State College has long lent the place an artsy turn (creator of the *Simpsons,* Matt Groening studied here), while the dive bars and secondhand guitar shops of downtown provided an original pulpit for riot grrrl music and grunge.

Sights & Activities

Washington State Capitol LANDMARK
(8am-4:30pm) FREE Looking like a huge Grecian temple, the Capitol complex, set in a 30-acre park overlooking Capitol Lake, dominates the town. The campus' crowning glory is the magnificent Legislative Building (1927) topped by a 287ft dome that is only slightly smaller than its namesake in Washington, DC. Free guided tours are available.

State Capital Museum MUSEUM
(211 W 21st Ave; admission $2; 10am-4pm Tue-Fri, from noon Sat) Preserves the general history of Washington State, from the Nisqually tribe to the present day.

Olympia Farmers Market MARKET
(700 Capitol Way N; 10am-3pm Thu-Sun Apr-Oct, Sat & Sun Nov-Dec) At the north end of Capitol Way, this is one of the state's best markets, with fresh local produce, crafts and live music.

Sleeping & Eating

Phoenix Inn Suites HOTEL $$
(360-570-0555; www.phoenixinn.com; 415 Capitol Way N; r $139-179;) The town's most upmarket accommodations is slick, efficient and well tuned to dealing with demanding state government officials.

Traditions Cafe & World Folk Art AMERICAN $
(www.traditionsfairtrade.com; 300 5th Ave SW; sandwiches $8.25; 9am-6pm Mon-Fri, 10am-5pm Sat & Sun;) Your fair-trade hippy enclave of yummy salads, sandwiches (meat, veggie and vegan), a few Mexican and Italian plates for good measure, coffee and a selection of herbal teas. Also pop into the eclectic folk art store attached.

Drinking & Nightlife

The city's never-static music scene still makes waves on 4th Ave at the retrofitted **4th Avenue Tavern** (210 4th Ave E) or the graffiti-decorated **Le Voyeur** (404 4th Ave E), an anarchistic, vegan-friendly dive bar with a busker invariably guarding the door. Try the most famous locally roasted coffee at **Batdorf & Bronson** (Capitol Way S; 6am-7pm Mon-Fri, 7am-6pm Sat & Sun) .

Fish Tale Brew Pub BREWERY
(515 Jefferson St) Fish Brewing has a classic selection of organic beers, hard ciders and India Pale Ales making it one of Washington's best-known microbreweries.

Burial Grounds CAFE
(406 Washington St SE; specialty lattes $3.50; 10am-12am Mon-Sat, to 10pm Sun) Order fantastic coffee drinks such as the Zombie Attacker Latte (two shots with nutmeg and almond), which comes with a skeleton head drawn in the foam. The goth decor looks like a horror-movie-obsessed teenager's bedroom.

ℹ️ Information

The **State Capitol Visitor Center** (cnr 14th Ave & Capitol Way; ⊙ 10am-2pm Oct-Apr, till 4pm May-Sep) offers information on the capitol campus, the Olympia area and Washington State.

Olympic Peninsula

Surrounded on three sides by sea and exhibiting many of the characteristics of a full-blown island, the remote Olympic Peninsula is about as 'wild' and 'west' as America gets. What it lacks in cowboys it makes up for in rare, endangered wildlife and dense primeval forest. The peninsula's roadless interior is largely given over to the notoriously wet Olympic National Park, while the margins are the preserve of loggers, Native American reservations and a smattering of small but interesting settlements, most notably Port Townsend. Equally untamed is the western coastline, America's isolated end point, where the tempestuous ocean and misty old-growth Pacific rainforest meet in aqueous harmony.

Olympic National Park

Declared a national monument in 1909 and a national park in 1938, the 1406-sq-mile Olympic National Park (www.nps.gov/olym) shelters one of the world's only temperate rainforests and a 57-mile strip of Pacific coastal wilderness that was added in 1953. Opportunities for independent exploration abound, with activities from hiking and fishing to kayaking and skiing.

EASTERN ENTRANCES

The graveled Dosewallips River Rd follows the river from US 101 (turn off approximately 1km north of Dosewallips State Park) for 15 miles to Dosewallips Ranger Station, where hiking trails begin; call ☑ 360-565-3130 for road conditions. Even hiking smaller portions of the two long-distance paths, including the 14.9 mile Dosewallips River Trail, with views of glaciated Mt Anderson, is reason enough to visit the valley. Another eastern entry for hikers is the Staircase Ranger Station (☑ 360-877-5569; ⊙ May-Sep), just inside the national-park boundary, 15 miles from Hoodsport on US 101. Two state parks along the eastern edge of the national park are popular with campers: Dosewallips State Park (☑ 888-226-7688; tent/RV sites $23/32) and Lake Cushman State Park

(☑ 888-226-7688; tent/RV sites $22/28). Both have running water, flush toilets and some RV hookups. Reservations are accepted.

NORTHERN ENTRANCES

The park's easiest – and hence most popular – entry point is at Hurricane Ridge, 18 miles south of Port Angeles. At the road's end, an interpretive center gives a stupendous view of Mt Olympus (7965ft) and dozens of other peaks. The 5200ft altitude can mean you'll hit inclement weather and the winds here (as the name suggests) can be ferocious. Aside from various summer trekking opportunities, the area maintains one of only two US national-park-based ski runs, operated by the small, family-friendly Hurricane Ridge Ski & Snowboard Area (www.hurricaneridge.com; 🚠).

Popular for boating and fishing is Lake Crescent, the site of the park's oldest and most reasonably priced lodge (☑ 360-928-3211; www.olympicnationalparks.com; 416 Lake Crescent Rd; lodge r $153, cottages $162-300; ⊙ May-Oct; P ✳ 🛜). Delicious sustainable food is served in the lodge's ecofriendly restaurant. From Storm King Information Station (☑ 360-928-3380; ⊙ May-Sep) on the lake's south shore, a 1-mile hike climbs through old-growth forest to Marymere Falls.

Along the Sol Duc River, the Sol Duc Hot Springs Resort (☑ 360-327-3583; www.northolympic.com/solduc; 12076 Sol Duc Hot Springs Rd, Port Angeles; RV sites $36, r $172-210; ⊙ late Mar-Oct; ✳ 🈺) 🖋 has lodging, dining, massage and, of course, hot-spring pools (adult/child $10/7.50), as well as great day hikes.

WESTERN ENTRANCES

Isolated by distance and home of one of the country's rainiest microclimates, the Pacific

---

ℹ️ WASHINGTON STATE DISCOVER PASS

For parking access to millions of acres of Washington State's recreational lands from State Parks to trail heads, you'll need to buy a Discover Pass (one day/annual $10/30). Passes are available from vending machines at many of the larger parking lots they serve and at state-park headquarters 'when staff is available,' or with a 10% service fee online (www.fishhunt.dfw.wa.gov).

side of the Olympics remains the wildest. Only US 101 offers access to its noted temperate rainforests and untamed coastline. The Hoh River Rainforest, at the end of the 19-mile Hoh River Rd, is a Tolkienesque maze of dripping ferns and moss-draped trees. The Hoh Visitor Center and Campground (☑360-374-6925; campsites $12; ☺9am-6pm Jul & Aug, to 4:30pm Sep-Jun) has information on guided walks and longer backcountry hikes. There are no hookups or showers; first come, first served.

A little to the south lies Lake Quinault, a beautiful glacial lake surrounded by forested peaks. It's popular for fishing, boating and swimming, and is punctuated by some of the nation's oldest trees. Lake Quinault Lodge (☑360-288-2900; www.olympicnational-parks.com; 345 S Shore Rd; r $202-305; ✳🛜✉), a luxury classic of 1920s 'parkitecture,' has a heated pool and sauna, a crackling fireplace and a memorable dining room. For a cheaper sleep nearby, try the ultrafriendly Quinault River Inn (☑360-288-2237; www.quinaultriverinn.com; 8 River Dr; r $79-119; ✳🛜) in Amanda Park, a favorite with anglers.

A number of short hikes begin just outside the Lake Quinault Lodge, or you can try the longer Enchanted Valley Trail, a medium-grade 13-miler that begins from the Graves Creek Ranger station at the end of South Shore Rd and climbs up to a large meadow resplendent with wildflowers and copses of alder trees.

ⓘ Information

The park entry fee is per person/vehicle $5/15, valid for one week, payable at park entrances. Many park visitor centers double as United States Forestry Service (USFS) ranger stations, where you can pick up permits for wilderness camping (per group $5, valid up to 14 days, plus $2 per person per night).

Forks Visitor Information Center (1411 S Forks Ave; ☺10am-4pm) Suggested itineraries and seasonal information.

Olympic National Park Visitor Center (3002 Mt Angeles Rd, Port Angeles; ☺9am-5pm) The best overall center is situated at the Hurricane Ridge gateway, a mile off Hwy 101 in Port Angeles.

Wilderness Information Center (3002 Mt Angeles Rd, Port Angeles; ☺7:30am-6pm Sun-Thu, to 8pm Fri & Sat May-Sep, 8am-4:30pm daily Oct-Apr) Directly behind the Olympic National Park Visitor Center; you'll find maps, permits and trail information.

Port Townsend

Historical relics are rare in the Pacific Northwest, which makes time-warped Port Townsend all the more fascinating. Small, nostalgic and culturally vibrant, this showcase of 1890s Victorian architecture is the 'New York of the West that never was,' a one-time boomtown that went bust at the turn of the 20th century, only to be rescued 70 years later by a group of farsighted locals. Port Townsend today is a buoyant blend of inventive eateries, elegant fin de siècle hotels and quirky annual festivals.

⊙ Sights

Jefferson County Historical Society Museum　MUSEUM
(210 Madison St; adult/12yr & under $4/1; ☺11am-4pm Mar-Dec) The local historic society runs this well-maintained exhibition area that includes mock-ups of an old courtroom and jail cell, along with the full lowdown on the rise, fall and second coming of this captivating port town.

Fort Worden State Park　PARK
(www.parks.wa.gov/fortworden; 200 Battery Way) This attractive park located within Port Townsend's city limits is the remains of a large fortification system constructed in the 1890s. The extensive grounds and array of historic buildings have been refurbished in recent years into a lodging, nature and historical park. The Commanding Officer's Quarters (admission $4; ☺10am-5pm daily Jun-Aug, 1-4pm Sat & Sun Mar-May & Sep-Oct), a 12-bedroom mansion, is open for tours, and part of one of the barracks is now the Puget Sound Coast Artillery Museum (admission $2; ☺11am-4pm Tue-Sun), which tells the story of early Pacific coastal fortifications.

Hikes lead along the headland to Point Wilson Lighthouse Station and some wonderful windswept beaches.

🛏 Sleeping

Palace Hotel　HISTORIC HOTEL $
(☑360-385-0773; www.palacehotelpt.com; 1004 Water St; r $59-109; ✳🛜) Built in 1889, this beautiful Victorian building is a former brothel that was once run by the locally notorious Madame Marie, who managed her business from the 2nd-floor corner suite. It's been reincarnated as an attractive

period hotel with antique furnishings and claw-foot baths.

Waterstreet Hotel   HOTEL $

(☑ 360-385-5467; www.waterstreethotelport-townsend.com; 635 Water St; r $60-160; ❀❋☎) Of Port Townsend's old dockside hotels, the easy-on-the-wallet Waterstreet has to be the best bargain in town. A multitude of rooms can accommodate between two and six people. Some have shared bathrooms.

✖ Eating

Waterfront Pizza   PIZZERIA $$

(951 Water St; large pizzas $11-21) This buy-by-the-slice outlet inspires huge local loyalty and will satisfy even the most querulous of Chicago-honed palates. The secret: crisp sourdough crusts, or creative but not over-stacked toppings? Who knows.

★ Sweet Laurette Cafe & Bistro   FRENCH $$

(1029 Lawrence St; mains $12-28; ☺8am-5pm Wed & Thu, to 9pm Fri & Sat, to 3pm Sun) This adorable French shabby-chic cafe serves breakfast, lunch & dinner in the bistro, and delicious coffee and pastries between meal times.

❶ Information

To get the lowdown on the city's roller-coaster boom-bust history, call in at the **visitor center** (www.ptchamber.org; 2437 E Sims Way; ☺9am-5pm Mon-Fri, to 4pm Sat & Sun).

❶ Getting There & Away

Port Townsend can be reached from Seattle by a ferry-bus connection; from Colman Dock in Seattle take the ferry across to Bainbridge Island. From here, catch bus 90 to Poulsbo and then bus 7 to Port Townsend. **Washington State Ferries** (☑ 206-464-6400; www.wsdot.wa.gov/ferries) goes to and from Coupeville on Whidbey Island (car and driver $10.25/foot passenger $3.10, 35 minutes).

Port Angeles

Despite the name, there's nothing Spanish or particularly angelic about Port Angeles, propped up by the lumber industry and backed by the steep-sided Olympic Mountains. Rather than visiting to see the town per se, people come here to catch a ferry for Victoria, BC, or plot an outdoor excursion into the nearby Olympic National Park. The visitor center (www.portangeles.org; 121 E Railroad Ave; ☺8am-8pm mid-May–mid-Oct, 10am-4pm mid-Oct–mid-May) is adjacent to the ferry terminal. For information on the national park, the Olympic National Park Visitor Center (p202) is just outside town.

The Olympic Discovery Trail (www.olympic discoverytrail.com) ✐ is a 30-mile off-road hiking and cycling trail between Port Angeles and Sequim, starting at the end of Ediz Hook, the sand spit that loops around the bay. Bikes can be rented at Sound Bikes & Kayaks (www.soundbikekayaks.com; 120 Front St; bike rental per hr/day $9/30)

Port Angeles' most comfortable accommodations is the Olympic Lodge (☑360-452-2993; www.olympiclodge.com; 140 Del Guzzi Drive; r from $119; ❋@☎❀), which offers a swimming pool, on-site bistro, so-clean-they-seem-new rooms and complimentary cookies and milk. Backpackers will find their happiness at the new, well run and social Toadlily House (☑360-797-3797; www.toadlilyhouse.com; 105 E 5th St; per person $25; ☎).

★ Bella Italia (118 E 1st St; mains $12-20; ☺from 4pm) has been around a lot longer than Bella, the heroine of the *Twilight* saga, but its mention in the book as the place where Bella and Edward Cullen go for their first date has turned an already popular restaurant into an icon. Try the clam linguine, chicken marsala or smoked duck breast.

The Coho Vehicle Ferry (www.cohoferry. com; passenger/car $15.50/55) runs to/from Victoria, BC, and the crossing takes 1½ hours. Olympic Bus Lines (www.olympic-buslines.com) runs twice daily to Seattle ($39) from the public transit center at the corner of Oak and Front Sts. Clallam Transit (www. clallamtransit.com) buses go to Forks and Sequim, where they link up with other transit buses, enabling you to circumnavigate the whole Olympic Peninsula.

Northwest Peninsula

Several Native American reservations cling to the extreme northwest corner of the continent, and are welcoming to visitors. The small weather-beaten settlement of Neah Bay on Hwy 112 is home to the Makah Indian Reservation, whose Makah Museum (www.makah. com; 1880 Bayview Ave; admission $5; ☺10am-5pm) displays artifacts from one of North America's most significant archaeological finds from the 500-year-old Makah village of Ozette. Several miles beyond the museum, a short boardwalk trail leads to stunning Cape Flattery, a 300ft promontory that marks the most northwesterly point in the lower 48 states.

THE TWILIGHT ZONE

A small lumber town on Hwy 101, Forks was little more than a speck on the map when Stephenie Meyer set her now famous *Twilight* vampire novels here in 2003. Once the *Twilight* film franchise began around 2008, Forks apparently saw a 600% rise in tourism, although now that the book and movie series are complete those numbers are falling. Many of the visitors are wide-eyed under 15 year olds who are more than a little surprised to find out what Forks really is: chillingly ordinary (and wet).

Vampire fans can get into fantasy-Forks at a few *Twilight* merchandise shops or on daily Twilight Tours (adult/child $39/25; ⊘8am, 11:30am, 3pm & 6pm) that visit most of the places mentioned in Meyer's books.

Other areas to pick up the Twilight trail include film and book locations such as Port Angeles, Ecola State Park, Silver Falls State Park and the werewolf lair of La Push (actually a Quileute Indian Reservation where in real local legend the people were changed into humans from wolves).

Convenient to the Hoh River Rainforest and the Olympic coastline is Forks, a one-horse lumber town that's now more famous for its *Twilight* paraphernalia. It's a central town for exploring Olympic National Park. A good accommodation choice is the Miller Tree Inn (☑360-374-6806; www.millertreeinn. com; 654 E Division St; r $115-230; 🐾🐕).

Northwest Washington

Wedged between Seattle, the Cascades and Canada, northwest Washington draws influences from three sides. Its urban hub is collegiate Bellingham, while its outdoor highlight is the pastoral San Juan Islands, an extensive archipelago that glimmers like a sepia-toned snapshot from another era. Anacortes is the main hub for ferries to the San Juan Islands and Victoria, BC.

Whidbey Island

While not as detached (there's a bridge connecting it to adjacent Fidalgo Island at its northernmost point) or nonconformist as the San Juans, life is almost as slow, quiet and pastoral on Whidbey Island. Having six state parks is a bonus, along with a plethora of B&Bs, two historic fishing villages (Langley and Coupeville), famously good clams and a thriving artist's community.

Deception Pass State Park (☑360-675-2417; 41229 N State Hwy 20) straddles the eponymous steep-sided water chasm that flows between Whidbey and Fidalgo Islands, and incorporates lakes, islands, campsites and 27 miles of hiking trails.

Ebey's Landing National Historical Reserve (www.nps.gov/ebla; ⊘8am-5pm mid-Oct–Mar, 6:30am-10pm Apr–mid-Oct) FREE comprises 17,400 acres encompassing working farms, sheltered beaches, two state parks and the town of Coupeville. This small settlement is one of Washington's oldest towns and has an attractive seafront, antique stores and a number of old inns, including the Coupeville Inn (☑800-247-6162; www.thecoupe-villeinn.com; 200 Coveland St; r with/without balcony incl breakfast $150/110; 🐾🐕), which bills itself as a French-style motel (if that's not an oxymoron), with fancy furnishings and a substantial breakfast. For the famous fresh local clams, head to Christopher's (☑360-678-5480; www.christophersonwhidbey.com; 103 NW Coveland St; mains $15-23; ⊘11:30am-2pm Mon-Fri, 12-2:30pm Sat & Sun, nightly from 5pm).

Washington State Ferries (WSF; www.wsdot.wa.gov/ferries) link Clinton to Mukilteo (car and driver $8, foot passenger free, 20 minutes, every 30 minutes) and Coupeville to Port Townsend (car and driver $10.25, foot passenger $3.10, 35 minutes, every 45 minutes). Free Island Transit buses (www.islandtransit.org) 🚌 run the length of Whidbey every hour daily, except Sundays, from the Clinton ferry dock.

Bellingham

Welcome to a green, liberal and famously livable settlement that has taken the libertine, nothing-is-too-weird ethos of Oregon's 'City of Roses' and given it a peculiarly Washingtonian twist. Mild in both manners and weather, the 'city of subdued excitement,' as a local mayor once dubbed it, is an unlikely alliance of espresso-supping students, venerable retirees, all-weather triathletes and placard-waving peaceniks. Publications such as *Out-*

side Magazine have consistently lauded it for its abundant outdoor opportunities.

Activities

Bellingham offers outdoor activities by the truckload. Whatcom Falls Park is a natural wild region that bisects Bellingham's eastern suburbs. The change in elevation is marked by four sets of waterfalls, including Whirlpool Falls, a popular summer swimming hole. The substantial intra-urban trails extend south as far as Larabee State Park, with a popular 2.5-mile section tracking Bellingham's postindustrial waterfront. Fairhaven Bike & Mountain Sports (www.fairhavenbike.com; 1103 11th St) rents bikes from $40 a day and has all the info (and maps) on local routes.

Victoria/San Juan Cruises (www.whales. com; 355 Harris Ave) has whale-watching trips to the San Juan Islands. Boats leave from the Bellingham Cruise Terminal in Fairhaven.

Sleeping

Guesthouse Inn — MOTEL $
(☎360-671-9600; www.bellinghamvaluinn.com; 805 Lakeway Dr; r from $95; ❉🐾) The clean, personable Guesthouse Inn is just off I-5 and an easy 15-minute walk from downtown Bellingham. The Vancouver–Seattle Bellair Airporter Shuttle (p199) stops here, making it an ideal base for overnighters who want to explore the Bellingham area.

★ Hotel Bellwether — BOUTIQUE HOTEL $$$
(☎360-392-3100; www.hotelbellwether.com; 1 Bellwether Way; r $165-284, lighthouse from $398; ❉🐾🐾) Bellingham's finest and most charismatic hotel is positioned on the waterfront and offers views of the whale-like hump of Lummi Island. Its crowning glory is the celebrated 900-sq-ft lighthouse condominium, a converted three-story lighthouse with a wonderful private lookout.

Eating

Old Town Cafe — CAFE $
(316 W Holly St; mains $6-9; ⊙6.30am-3pm) This is a classic bohemian breakfast haunt where you can get to know the locals over fresh pastries, espresso and an excellent huevos rancheros. Wandering musicians sometimes drop by to enhance the happy-go-lucky atmosphere.

★ Pepper Sisters — MODERN AMERICAN $$
(www.peppersisters.com; 1055 N State St; mains $9-16; ⊙from 5pm Tue-Sun; 🐾) People travel from far and wide to visit this cult restaurant with its bright turquoise booths. Try the cilantro-and-pesto quesadillas, blue-corn *rellenos* (stuffed peppers) and potato-garlic burritos.

ℹ Information

The best downtown tourist information can be procured at the **Visitor Info Station** (www. downtownbellingham.com; 1304 Cornwall St; ⊙9am-6pm).

ℹ Getting There & Away

Alaska Marine Highway (AMHS; www.dot. state.ak.us/amhs; 355 Harris Ave) ferries go to Juneau (60 hours) and other southeast Alaskan ports (from $326 without car). The Bellair Airporter Shuttle (p199) runs to Sea-Tac Airport ($34), with connections en route to Anacortes and Whidbey Island.

San Juan Islands

Take the ferry west out of Anacortes and you'll feel like you've dropped off the edge of the continent. A thousand metaphoric miles from the urban inquietude of Puget Sound, the nebulous San Juan archipelago conjures up Proustian flashbacks from another era and often feels about as American as – er – Canada (which surrounds it on two sides).

There are 172 landfalls in this expansive archipelago but unless you're rich enough to charter your own yacht or seaplane, you'll be restricted to seeing the big four – San Juan, Orcas, Shaw and Lopez Islands – all served daily by Washington State Ferries. Communally, the islands are famous for their tranquility, whale-watching opportunities, sea kayaking and seditious nonconformity.

A great way to explore the San Juans is by sea kayak or bicycle. Expect a guided half-day trip to cost from $45 to $65. Cycling-wise, Lopez is flat and pastoral and San Juan is worthy of an easy day loop, while Orcas offers the challenge of undulating terrain and a steep 5-mile ride to the top of Mt Constitution.

ℹ Getting There & Around

Airlines serving the San Juan Islands include **San Juan Airlines** (www.sanjuanairlines.com) and **Kenmore Air** (www.kenmoreair.com).

Washington State Ferries (WSF; www.wsdot. wa.gov/ferries) leave Anacortes for the San Juans; some continue to Sidney, BC, near Victoria. Ferries run to Lopez Island (45 minutes), Orcas Landing (60 minutes) and Friday Harbor on San Juan Island (75 minutes). Fares vary by season; the cost of the entire round-trip is collected on westbound journeys only (except those returning from Sidney, BC). To visit all the islands, it's cheapest to go to Friday Harbor first and work your way back through the other islands.

Shuttle buses ply Orcas and San Juan Island in the summer months.

San Juan Island

San Juan Island is the archipelago's unofficial capital, a harmonious mix of low forested hills and small rural farms that resonate with a dramatic and unusual 19th-century history. The only real settlement is Friday Harbor, where the chamber of commerce (www.sanjuanisland.org; 135 Spring St; ⊙10am-5pm Mon-Fri, to 4pm Sat & Sun), home to the visitor center, sits inside a small mall off the main street.

◉ Sights & Activities

San Juan Island
National Historical Park HISTORIC SITE
(www.nps.gov/sajh; ⊙8:30am-4pm, visitor center 8:30am-4:30pm Thu-Sun, daily Jun-Sep) FREE
San Juan Island hides one of the 19th-century's oddest political confrontations, the so-called 'Pig War' between the USA and Britain. This curious 19th-century cold war standoff is showcased in two historical parks on either end of the island that once housed opposing American and English military encampments. On the island's southern flank, the American Camp hosts the small visitor center, the remnants of a fort, desolate beaches and a series of interpretive trails. At the opposite end of the island, English Camp, 9 miles northwest of Friday Harbor, contains the remains of the 1860s-era British military facilities.

Lime Kiln Point State Park PARK
(⊙8am-5pm mid-Oct–Mar, 6:30am-10pm Apr–mid-Oct) The Clinging to San Juan Island's rocky west coast, this beautiful park overlooks the deep Haro Strait and is, reputedly, one of the best places in the world to view whales from the shoreline.

🛏 Sleeping & Eating

There are hotels, B&Bs and resorts scattered around the island, but Friday Harbor has the highest concentration.

Wayfarer's Rest HOSTEL $
(☑360-378-6428; 35 Malcolm St; dm $35, r $65-80; 🛜) The island's only backpacker hostel is a short hike from the ferry terminal. Budget

travelers will love its comfortable dorms and cheap private rooms, but beware – it gets busy.

Roche Harbor Resort RESORT $$
(☑800-451-8910; www.rocheharbor.com; Roche Harbor; r with shared bath $149, 1- to 3-bedroom condos $275-450, 2-bedroom townhouses $499; ❄🛜❄) Located on the site of the former lime kiln and estate of limestone king John McMillin, this seaside 'village' is a great getaway. The centerpiece is the old Hotel de Haro, where the pokey rooms are enlivened by the fact that John Wayne once brushed his teeth here.

Juniper Lane Guest House INN $$
(☑360-378-7761; www.juniperlaneguesthouse.com; 1312 Beaverton Valley Rd; r $85-135; 🛜) The handful of wood-paneled rooms here are decorated with a colorful and eclectic assortment of refurbished or recycled art and furnishings. The result is a sublimely cozy and livable hybrid of an upscale backpackers and an inn.

Market Chef DELI $
(225 A St; ⊙10am-6pm) Several hundred locals can't be wrong, can they? The 'Chef's' specialty is deli sandwiches, and very original ones at that. Join the queue and watch staff prepare the goods with fresh, local ingredients.

Orcas Island

Precipitous, unspoiled and ruggedly beautiful, Orcas Island is the San Juans' emerald icon, excellent for hiking and, more recently, gourmet food. The ferry terminal is at Orcas Landing, 8 miles south of the main village, Eastsound.

On the island's eastern lobe is Moran State Park (⊙6:30am-dusk Apr-Sep, from 8am Oct-Mar), dominated by Mt Constitution (2409ft), with 40 miles of trails and an amazing 360-degree mountaintop view.

Kayaking in the calm island waters is a real joy here. Shearwater (www.shearwaterkayaks.com; 138 North Beach Rd, Eastsound) has the equipment and know-how. Three-hour guided trips start at $75.

🛏 Sleeping

Doe Bay Village Resort
& Retreat HOSTEL, RESORT $
(☑360-376-2291; www.doebay.com; dm $55, cabin d from $90, yurts from $120; 🛜) The Doe Bay has the atmosphere of an artists' com-

mune cum hippie retreat. Accommodations include sea-view campsites, a small hostel with dormitory and private rooms, and various cabins and yurts, most with views of the water.

Golden Tree Hostel HOSTEL $

(☑ 360-317-8693; www.goldentreehostel.com; 1159 North Beach Rd, Eastsound; dm/d with shared bath $38/88; @☎) An 1890s-era heritage mansion with a hip remodel, and a hot tub and sauna out back. Immaculate six-bed single-sex dorms and bright private rooms.

Outlook Inn HOTEL $

(☑ 360-376-2200; www.outlookinn.com; 171 Main St, Eastsound; r with shared/private bath from $79/119; ☎) The Outlook Inn (1888) is an island institution that has kept up with the times by expanding into a majestic white (but still quite small) bayside complex. Also on-site is the fancy New Leaf Cafe.

✖ Eating & Drinking

★ Mijita's MEXICAN $$

(310 A St, Eastsound; mains $13-22; ⊘4-9pm Wed-Sun) Ooh and aah over the Mexican native chef's family recipes, such as slow-braised short ribs with blackberry mole or the vegetarian quinoa cakes with mushrooms, chevre, almonds and *pipian* (Mexican piquant sauce).

Island Hoppin' Brewery BREWERY

(www.islandhoppinbrewery.com; 33 Hope Lane, Eastsound; ⊘4-9pm Tue-Sun) This is *the* place to go to enjoy six changeable brews on tap while making friends with those islanders who enjoy beer. There's often live music on weekends.

Lopez Island

If you're going to Lopez – or 'Slow-pez,' as locals prefer to call it – take a bike. With its undulating terrain and salutation-offering locals (who are famous for their three-fingered 'Lopezian wave'), this is the ideal cycling isle. A leisurely pastoral spin can be tackled in a day, with good overnight digs available next to the marina in the **Lopez Islander Resort** (☑ 800-736-3434; www.lopezfun.com; Fisherman Bay Rd; r from $139; ☎☒), which has a restaurant, gym and pool and offers free parking in Anacortes (another incentive to dump the car). If you prefer cycleless, call up **Village Cycles** (☑ 360-468-4013; www.villagecycles.net; 9 Old Post Rd; rentals per hour/day from $7/30;

⊘10am-4pm Wed-Sun), which can deliver a bicycle to the ferry terminal for you.

North Cascades

Geologically different from their southern counterparts, the North Cascade Mountains are peppered with sharp, jagged peaks, copious glaciers and a preponderance of complex metamorphic rock. Thanks to their virtual impregnability, the North Cascades were an unsolved mystery to humans until relatively recently. The first road was built across the region in 1972 and, even today, it remains one of the Northwest's most isolated outposts.

Mt Baker

Rising like a ghostly sentinel above the sparkling waters of upper Puget Sound, Mt Baker has been mesmerizing visitors to the Northwest for centuries. A dormant volcano that last belched smoke in the 1850s, this haunting 10,781ft peak shelters 12 glaciers, and in 1999 registered a record-breaking 95ft of snow in one season.

Well-paved Hwy 542, known as the Mt Baker Scenic Byway, climbs 5100ft to **Artist Point**, 56 miles from Bellingham. Near here you'll find the **Heather Meadows Visitor Center** (Mile 56 Mt Baker Hwy; ⊘8am-4:30pm May-Sep) and a plethora of varied hikes including the 7.5-mile Chain Lakes Loop that leads you around a half-dozen lakes surrounded by huckleberry meadows.

Receiving more annual snow than any ski area in North America, the **Mt Baker Ski Area** (www.mtbakerskiarea.com) has 38 runs, eight lifts and a vertical rise of 1500ft. The resort has gained something of a cult status among snowboarders, who have been coming here for the Legendary Baker Banked Slalom every January since 1985.

On the 100 or so days a year when Baker breaks through the clouds, the views from the deck at the **Inn at Mt Baker** (☑ 360-599-1359; www.theinnatmtbaker.com; 8174 Mt Baker Hwy; r $155-165; ☎), seven miles east of Maple Falls, are stunning. On your way up the mountain, stop for a bite at authentic honky-tonk bar and restaurant **Graham's** (9989 Mt Baker Hwy; mains $4-14; ⊘dinner Mon-Sun, breakfast & lunch Sat & Sun; hours vary) and grab trail munchies at **Wake & Bakery** (6903 Forest St, Glacier; munchies from $4; ⊘7:30am-5pm), both in the town of Glacier.

Leavenworth

Blink hard and rub your eyes. This isn't some strange Germanic hallucination. This is Leavenworth, a former lumber town that underwent a Bavarian makeover back in the 1960s after the rerouting of the cross-continental railway threatened to put it permanently out of business. Swapping wood for tourists, Leavenworth today has successfully reinvented itself as a traditional Romantische Strasse village, right down to the beer, sausages and the lederhosen-loving locals (25% of whom are German). The classic *Sound of Music* mountain setting helps, as does the fact that Leavenworth serves as the main activity center for sorties into the nearby Alpine Lakes Wilderness.

The Leavenworth Ranger Station (600 Sherbourne St; ☺ 7:30am-4:30pm daily mid-Jun–mid-Oct, from 7:45am Mon-Fri mid-Oct–mid-Jun) can advise on the local outdoor activities. Highlights include the best climbing in the state at Castle Rock in Tumwater Canyon, about 3 miles northwest of town off US 2.

The Devil's Gulch is a popular off-road mountain bike trail (25 miles, four to six hours). Local outfitters Der Sportsmann (☎ 509-548-5623; www.dersportsmann.com; 837 Front St; One-day bike/cross-country ski rentals from $25/14; ☺ 9am-6pm) rents mountain bikes from $25 a day.

🛏 Sleeping & Eating

Hotel Pension Anna   HOTEL $$
(☎ 509-548-6273; www.pensionanna.com; 926 Commercial St; r incl breakfast $155-250, chapel ste $240-360) The most authentic Bavarian hotel in town; each room is decorated in imported Austrian decor and the European-inspired breakfasts may induce joyful yodels. The adjacent St Joseph's chapel (which the owners rescued and moved here in 1992) is perfect for families.

Enzian Inn   HOTEL $$
(☎ 509-548-5269; www.enzianinn.com; 590 Hwy 2; d $110-205, ste $215-375; ☎ ☒) Taking the German theme up a notch, the Enzian goes way beyond the call of duty with an 18-hole putting green, a racquetball court, a sunny breakfast room and a lederhosen-clad owner who entertains guests with an early morning blast on the alphorn.

★ München Haus   GERMAN $
(www.munchenhaus.com; 709 Front St; snacks from $6; ☺ 11am-11pm May-Oct, closed Mon-Fri Nov-Apr; ☻) An alfresco beer garden that serves the best charbroiled Bavarian sausages this side of Bavaria.

Lake Chelan

Long, slender Lake Chelan is central Washington's water playground. Lake Chelan State Park (☎ 509-687-3710; S Lakeshore Rd; tent/RV sites $23/32) has 144 campsites; a number of lakeshore campgrounds are accessible only by boat. If you'd rather sleep in a real bed, try the great-value Midtowner Motel (☎ 509-682-4051; www.midtowner.com; 721 E Woodin Ave; r $65-120; ☒ @ ☎ ☒) in town. The town of Chelan, at the lake's southeastern tip, is the primary base for accommodations and services, and has a USFS ranger station (428 Woodin Ave). Several wineries have also opened in the area and many have excellent restaurants. Try Tsillan Cellars (www.tsillancellars.com; 3875 Hwy 97A; ☺ noon-5pm Sun-Thu, to 6pm Fri & Sat).

Link Transit (www.linktransit.com) buses connect Chelan with Wenatchee and Leavenworth ($1).

Beautiful Stehekin, on the northern tip of Lake Chelan, is accessible only by boat (www.ladyofthelake.com; round-trip from Chelan $39), seaplane (www.chelanairways.com; round-trip from Chelan $159) or a long hike across Cascade Pass, 28 miles from the lake. You'll find lots of information about hiking, campgrounds and cabin rentals at www.stehekin.com. Most facilities are open from mid-June to mid-September.

Methow Valley

The Methow's combination of powdery winter snow and abundant summer sunshine has transformed the valley into one of Washington's primary recreation areas. You can bike, hike and fish in summer, and cross-country ski on the second-biggest snow trail network in the US in winter.

The 200km of trails are maintained by the nonprofit organization Methow Valley Sport Trails Association (MVSTA; www.mvsta.com; 209 Castle Ave, Winthrop) ☻, which, in the winter, provides the most comprehensive network of hut-to-hut (and hotel-to-hotel) skiing in North America. An extra blessing is that few people seem to know about it. For classic accommodations and easy access to the skiing, hiking and cycling trails, decamp at the exquisite Sun Mountain Lodge (☎ 509-996-2211; www.sunmountainlodge.com;

Box 1000, Winthrop; r $175-375, cabins $150-750; ☉closed 21 Oct-7 Dec; ❄☏❆), 10 miles west of the town of Winthrop. While the rooms and facilities are cozy cabin-style (including a lot of taxidermy), it's the views from up here and the endless choice of hiking and cross-country skiing trails surrounding the resort that make it so special.

North Cascades National Park

Even the names of the lightly trodden and dramatic mountains in North Cascades National Park (www.nps.gov/noca) sound wild and untamed: Desolation Peak, Jagged Ridge, Mt Despair and Mt Terror. Not surprisingly, the region offers some of the best backcountry adventures outside of Alaska.

The North Cascades Visitor Center (502 Newhalem St; ☉9am-4:30pm mid-Apr–Oct, closed Mon-Fri Nov-Mar) ✐, in the small settlement of Newhalem on Hwy 20, is the best orientation point for visitors and is staffed by expert rangers who can enlighten you on the park's highlights.

Built in the 1930s for loggers working in the valley that was soon to be flooded by Ross Dam, the floating cabins at the Ross Lake Resort (☏206-386-4437; www.rosslakeresort.com; cabins $155-315; ☉mid-Jun–Oct) on the eponymous lake's west side are the state's most unique accommodations. There's no road in – guests can either hike the 2-mile trail from Hwy 20 or take the resort's tugboat-taxi-and-truck shuttle from the parking area near Diablo Dam.

Northeastern Washington

Spokane

Washington's second-biggest population center is one of the state's latent surprises and a welcome break after the treeless monotony of the eastern scablands. Situated at the nexus of the Pacific Northwest's so-called 'Inland Empire,' this understated yet confident city sits clustered on the banks of the Spokane River, close to where British fur traders founded a short-lived trading post in 1810.

Though rarely touted in national tourist blurbs, Spokane hosts the world's largest mass participation running event (May's annual Bloomsday).

◉ Sights & Activities

Riverfront Park   PARK
(www.spokaneriverfrontpark.com; ▦) On the former site of Spokane's 1974 World's Fair, park highlights include a 17-point sculpture walk, plenty of bridges and trails to satisfy the city's plethora of amateur runners and Spokane Falls, a gushing combination of scenic waterfalls and rapids. There are various viewing points over the river, including a short gondola ride (☉11am-6pm Sun-Thu, to 10pm Fri & Sat Apr-Sep) that takes you directly above the falls. Walkers and joggers crowd the interurban Spokane River Centennial Trail (www.spokanecentennialtrail.org), which extends for 37 miles to the Idaho border and beyond. The park also includes an ice-skating rink, IMAX theater and carousel; check the website for details.

**Northwest Museum of
Arts & Culture**   MUSEUM
(www.northwestmuseum.org; 2316 W 1st Ave; adult/child $7/5; ☉10am-5pm Wed-Sun) Encased in a striking state-of-the-art building in the posh Browne's Addition neighborhood, the museum has – arguably – one of the finest collections of indigenous artifacts in the Northwest.

⌷ Sleeping & Eating

Hotel Ruby   BOUTIQUE MOTEL $
(☏509-747-1041; www.hotelrubyspokane.com; 901 W 1st Ave; r $68-110; ❄☏❆) This basic motel with a hip red-and-black color scheme has an unbeatable downtown location opposite the Davenport.

★ Davenport Hotel   HISTORIC HOTEL $$
(☏509-455-8888; www.thedavenporthotel.com; 10 S Post St; Davenport Hotel/Davenport Tower r from $130/120; ❄☏❆) A historic Spokane landmark (opened in 1914) that is considered one of best hotels in the US. If you can't afford a room, linger in the exquisite lobby. The adjacent Davenport Tower is the modern version of all this glam with a surprisingly sophisticated safari theme.

★ Mizuna   FUSION $$
(☏509-747-2004; 214 N Howard St; mains lunch/dinner $10/28; ☉11am-10pm Mon-Sat, 4-10pm Sun; ✐) A well-lit, antique brick building, with simple wood furniture, and tables topped with fresh flowers. Dishes such as lemongrass green curry with scallops and clams or equally good vegetarian specialties are washed down with exquisite wines. Heaven.

WORTH A TRIP

GRAND COULEE DAM

While the more famous Hoover Dam (conveniently located between Las Vegas and the Grand Canyon) gets around 1.6 million visitors per year, the much larger (four times) and arguably more significant Grand Coulee Dam (inconveniently located far from everything) gets only a trickle of tourism. It's the largest concrete structure in the US and also the largest producer of electricity in the US.

The **Grand Coulee Visitor Arrival Center** (☑509-633-9265; ⊙9am-5pm) details the history of the dam and surrounding area with movies, photos and interactive exhibits, while free guided **tours** of the facility run on the hour from 10am until 5pm (from May to September) and involve taking a glass-walled elevator 465ft down an incline into the Third Power Plant, where you can view the tops of the generators from an observation deck.

Similarly spectacular is the nightly **laser show** (⊙May-Sep after dark) – purportedly the world's largest – which illustrates the history of the Columbia River and its various dams against a gloriously vivid backdrop.

🍷 Drinking & Entertainment

With a vibrant student population based at Gonzaga University, Spokane has a happening nighttime scene.

Northern Lights Brewing Company BREWERY
(www.northernlightsbrewing.com; 1003 E Trent Ave) You can sample the locally handcrafted ales at Spokane's best microbrewery, near the university campus.

Bing Crosby Theater THEATER
(www.mettheater.com; 901 W Sprague Ave) The former Met, now named after local hero Bing, presents concerts, plays, film festivals and the Spokane Opera in a fairly intimate setting.

ℹ Information

Spokane Area Visitor Information Center (www.visitspokane.com; 201 W Main Ave at Browne St; ⊙8:30am-5pm Mon-Fri, 9am-6pm Sat & Sun) keeps a raft of information.

ℹ Getting There & Away

Buses and trains depart from the **Spokane Intermodal Transportation Station** (221 W 1st Ave). **Amtrak** (www.amtrak.com) has a daily service on the esteemed Empire Builder route to Seattle ($53, 7½ hours), Portland ($53, 9½ hours) and Chicago ($163, 45 hours).

South Cascades

The South Cascades are taller but less clustered than their northern counterparts, extending from Snoqualmie Pass east of Seattle down to the mighty Columbia River on the border with Oregon. The highpoint in more ways than one is 14,411ft Mt Rainier. Equally compelling for different reasons is Mt St Helens (8365ft), still recovering from a devastating 1980 volcanic eruption. Lesser-known Mt Adams (12,276ft) is notable for the huckleberries and wildflowers that fill its grassy alpine meadows during the short but intense summer season.

Mt Rainier National Park

The USA's fourth-highest peak (outside Alaska), majestic Mt Rainier is also one of its most beguiling. Encased in a 368-sq-mile national park (the world's fifth national park when it was inaugurated in 1899), the mountain's snowcapped summit and forest-covered foothills harbor numerous hiking trails, huge swaths of flower-carpeted meadows and an alluring conical peak that presents a formidable challenge for aspiring climbers.

Mt Rainier National Park (www.nps.gov/mora; entry per pedestrian/car $5/15) has four entrances. Call ☑800-695-7623 for road conditions. The National Park Service (NPS) website includes downloadable maps and descriptions of 50 park trails. The most famous trail is the hardcore, 93-mile-long Wonderland Trail that completely circumnavigates Mt Rainier and takes around 10 to 12 days to tackle.

For overnight trips, you'll need a wilderness camping permit (free) from ranger stations or visitor centers. The six campgrounds in the park have running water and toilets, but no RV hookups. Reservations at **park campsites** (☑800-365-2267; www.mount.rainier.national-park.com/camping.htm; reserved campsites $12-15) are strongly advised during summer months and can be made up to two months in advance by phone or online.

Evergreen Escapes (www.evergreenescapes.com; 10hr tour $195) runs deluxe and eco-minded guided bus tours from Seattle.

NISQUALLY ENTRANCE

The busiest and most convenient gate to Mt Rainier National Park, Nisqually lies on Hwy 706 via Ashford, near the park's southwest corner. It's open year-round. Longmire, 7 miles inside the Nisqually entrance, has a **museum and information center** (⊘9am-6pm Jun-Sep, to 5pm Oct-May) FREE, a number of important trailheads, and the rustic **National Park Inn** (☑360-569-2275; www.guestservices.com/rainier; r with shared/private bath $116/164, units $244; P❄) complete with an excellent restaurant. More hikes and interpretive walks can be found 12 miles further east at loftier Paradise, which is served by the informative **Henry M Jackson Visitor Center** (☑360-569-2211, ext 2328; Paradise; ⊘10am-7pm daily Jun-Oct, 10am-5pm Sat & Sun Oct-Dec), and the vintage **Paradise Inn** (☑360-569-2275; www.mtrainierguestservices.com; r with shared/private bath from $69/114; ⊘May-Oct), a historic 'parkitecture' inn constructed in 1916 and long part of the national park's fabric. Climbs to the top of Rainier leave from the inn; excellent four-day guided ascents are led by **Rainier Mountaineering Inc** (www.rmiguides.com; 30027 SR706 E, Ashford; 4-day ascent $991).

OTHER ENTRANCES

The three other entrances to Mt Rainier National Park are **Ohanapecosh**, via Hwy 123 and accessed via the town of Packwood, where lodging is available; **White River**, off Hwy 410, which literally takes the high road (6400ft) to the beautiful viewpoint at the **Sunrise Lodge Cafeteria** (☑360-569-2425; snacks $5-7; ⊘10am-7pm Jun 30-Sep 16); and remote **Carbon River** in the northwest corner, which gives access to the park's inland rainforest.

Mt St Helens National Volcanic Monument

What it lacks in height, Mt St Helens makes up for in fiery infamy – 57 people perished on the mountain when it erupted with a force of 1500 atomic bombs on May 18, 1980. The cataclysm began with an earthquake measuring 5.1 on the Richter scale, which sparked the biggest landslide in human history and buried 230 sq miles of forest under millions of tons of volcanic rock and ash. Today it's a fascinating landscape of recovering forests, new river valleys and ash-covered slopes. There's an $8 fee to enter the monument.

For those without a car, Mt St Helens can be seen on a day trip by bus from Portland with **Eco Tours of Oregon** (www.ecotours-oforegon.com; 3127 SE 23rd Ave, Portland; $59.50). If traveling independently, there are three entrances to the mountain, and plenty of short and long hikes along the way. From around mid-June through September, Hwy 25 opens up and links the Eastside and Southeastern entrances.

NORTHEAST ENTRANCE

From the main northeast entrance on Hwy 504, your first stop should be the **Silver Lake Visitor Center** (3029 Spirit Lake Hwy; admission $3; ⊘9am-5pm), which has films, exhibits and free information about the mountain (including trail maps). For a closer view of the destructive power of nature, venture to the **Johnston Ridge Observatory** (⊘10am-6pm mid-May–late Oct), situated at the end of Hwy 504, which looks directly into the mouth of the crater.

A welcome stop in an accommodations-lite area, the **Eco Park Resort** (☑360-274-6542; www.ecoparkresort.com; 14000 Spirit Lake Hwy; campsites $20, yurts $75, cabins $100-110) offers seven rooms in a large house opposite the Silver Lake Visitor Center.

SOUTHEASTERN & EASTSIDE ENTRANCES

The southeastern entrance via the town of **Cougar** on Hwy 503 holds some serious lava terrain, including the two-mile-long **Ape Cave** lava tube, which you can explore year-round but be prepared for chill as it remains a constant 41°F (5°C). Bring two light sources per adult or rent lanterns at **Apes' Headquarters** (8303 Forest Rd; ⊘10:30am-5pm Jun-Sep) for $5 each.

The eastside entrance is the most remote but the harder-to-reach **Windy Ridge** viewpoint on this side gives you a palpable, if eerie, sense of the destruction from the blast – it's often closed until June. A few miles down the road you can descend 600ft on the 1-mile-long **Harmony Trail** (hike 224) to Spirit Lake.

Central & Southeastern Washington

The sunny, dry near-California-looking central and southeastern parts of Washington harbor one not-so-secret weapon: wine. The fertile land that borders the Nile-like Yakima and Columbia River valleys is awash with enterprising new wineries producing quality grapes that now vie with the Napa and Sonoma Valleys for national recognition. Yakima and its more attractive cousin Ellensburg once held the edge, but nowadays the real star is Walla Walla, where talented restaurateurs and a proactive local council are crafting a wine destination par excellence.

Yakima & Ellensburg

Situated in its eponymous river valley, the city of Yakima is a rather bleak trading center that doesn't really live up to its 'Palm Springs of Washington' tourist label. The main reason to stop here is to visit one of the numerous wineries that lie between Yakima and Benton City; pick up a map at the Yakima Valley Visitors & Convention Bureau (www.visityakima.com; 10 N 8th St; ☉9am-5pm Mon-Sat, 10am-4pm Sun).

A better layover is Ellensburg, a diminutive settlement 36 miles to the northwest that juxtaposes the state's largest rodeo (each Labor Day) with a town center that has more coffee bars per head than anywhere else in the world (allegedly). Grab your latte at local roaster D&M Coffee (www.dmcoffee.com; 301 N Pine St; ☉7am-5pm) 🍴 and overnight at centrally located and charming

Victorian Guesthouse Ellensburg (☑509-962-3706; www.guesthouseellensburg.com; 606 Main St; r $145), which also runs the excellent Yellow Church Cafe (www.yellowchurchcafe.com; 111 S Pearl St; brunch $8-10, dinner $13-23; ☉11am-8pm Mon-Fri, 8am-8pm Sat & Sun).

Greyhound (www.greyhound.com) services both cities with buses to Seattle, Spokane and points in between.

Walla Walla

Over the last decade, Walla Walla has converted itself from an obscure agricultural backwater, famous for its sweet onions and large state penitentiary, into the hottest wine-growing region outside of California. While venerable Marcus Whitman College is the town's most obvious cultural attribute, you'll also find zany coffee bars here, along with cool wine-tasting rooms, fine Queen Anne architecture, and one of the state's freshest and most vibrant farmers markets.

◉ Sights

You don't need to be sloshed on wine to appreciate Walla Walla's historical and cultural heritage. Its Main St has won countless historical awards, and to bring the settlement to life, the local chamber of commerce (www.wallawalla.org; 29 E Sumach St; ☉8:30am-5pm Mon-Fri, 9am-4pm Sat & Sun May-Sep) has concocted some interesting walking tours, complete with leaflets and maps. For information on the region's wine culture, check out Walla Walla Wine News (www.wallawallawinenews.com).

DON'T MISS

YAKIMA VALLEY WINE TOUR

If you find yourself driving between Ellensburg and Walla Walla, do yourself a favor along the way and do some swish-and-spit wine tasting; it sounds unappealing but this is the way the pros do it and it will keep you legal. The Yakima Valley AVA (American Viticultural Area) is the oldest, largest and most diverse in the state. You'll find www.wineyakimavalley.org is a top resource for finding great wineries.

Bonair Winery (www.bonairwine.com; 500 S Bonair Rd, Zillah; ☉10am-5pm) In the Rattlesnake Hills near Zillah; has lovely gardens and is a laid-back place to sample luscious reds.

Terra Blanca (www.terrablanca.com; 34715 N DeMoss Rd , Benton City; ☉11am-6pm) Majestically located up on Red Mountain with views over the valley, this is one of the fanciest vineyards in the region, and perfect for sipping sweet dessert wines on the patio.

Maison Bleue (☑509-378-6527; www.mbwines.com; 357 Port Ave, Studio D, Prosser; ☉by appointment) By appointment only, these lauded Rhone-style wines can be tasted in Vinter's Village in Prosser. The village isn't a scenic stop, but the wines are great.

Fort Walla Walla Museum
MUSEUM

(755 Myra Rd; adult/child $7/3; ⊙10am-5pm; ☑) A pioneer village of 17 historic buildings, with the museum housed in the old cavalry stables. There are collections of farm implements, ranching tools and what could be the world's largest plastic replica of a mule team.

Waterbrook Wine
WINERY

(www.waterbrook.com; 10518 W US 12; ⊙11am-6pm Mon-Thu, till 8pm Fri & Sat) The pondside patio of this large winery situated about 10 miles west of town is a great place to imbibe a long selection of wines on a sunny day. Outrageously good tacos (two for $6) are served on Fridays and Saturdays.

Amavi Cellars
WINERY

(3796 Peppers Bridge Rd; ⊙10am-4pm) South of Walla Walla amid a scenic spread of grape and apple orchards, you can sample some of the most talked-about wines in the valley (try the Syrah and Cabernet Sauvignon). The classy yet comfortable outdoor patio has views of the Blue Mountains.

🛏 Sleeping & Eating

Colonial Motel
MOTEL $

(☑509-529-1220; www.colonial-motel.com; 2279 Isaacs Ave; r from $70; ✸🐾) A simple family-run motel halfway to the airport, the Colonial is welcoming and bike-friendly, with safe cycle storage and plenty of local maps.

Marcus Whitman Hotel
HOTEL $$

(☑509-525-2200; www.marcuswhitmanhotel.com; 6 W Rose St; r $119-325; ✸🐾☎) In keeping with the settlement's well-preserved image, this red-bricked 1928 beauty has been elegantly renovated with ample rooms kitted out in rusts and browns, and embellished with Italian-crafted furniture.

Graze
CAFE $

(5 S Colville St; sandwiches from $8; ⊙10am-7:30pm Mon-Sat, to 3:30pm Sun; ✍) Have your amazing sandwiches packed for your picnic or eat them at the simple cafe. Try the butternut squash panini with mozzarella, roasted garlic, sage and provolone or the flank steak torta with pickled jalapenos, avocado, tomato, cilantro and chipotle dressing.

★ Saffron Mediterranean Kitchen
MEDITERRANEAN $$$

(☑509-525-2112; www.saffronmediterraneankitchen. com; 125 W Alder St; mains $15-27; ⊙2-10pm, to 9pm in winter) Saffron takes seasonal, local ingredients and turns them into pure gold. The Med-inspired menu lists dishes such as pheasant, ricotta gnocchi, amazing flatbreads and weird yogurt-cucumber combo soups that could stand up against anything in Seattle.

ℹ Getting There & Away

Alaska Airlines services **Walla Walla Regional Airport** (www.wallawallaairport.com) with four daily flights to Seattle.

Greyhound (www.greyhound.com) buses run once daily to Seattle via Yakima and Ellensburg; change buses in Pasco for buses east to Spokane and beyond.

OREGON

It's hard to slap a single characterization onto Oregon's geography and people. Its landscape ranges from rugged coastline and thick evergreen forests to barren, fossil-strewn deserts, volcanoes and glaciers. As for its denizens, you name it – Oregonians run the gamut from pro-logging conservatives to tree-hugging liberals, and everything in between. What they all have in common is an independent spirit, a love of the outdoors and a fierce devotion to where they live.

Portland

Call it what you want – PDX, Stumptown, City of Roses, Bridge City, Beervana or Portlandia – Portland positively rocks. It's a city with a vibrant downtown, pretty residential neighborhoods, ultragreen ambitions and zany characters. Here, liberal idealists outnumber conservative stogies, Gore-Tex jackets are acceptable in fine restaurants and everyone supports countless brewpubs, coffeehouses, knitting circles, lesbian potlucks and eclectic book clubs. Portland is an up-and-coming destination that has finally arrived, and makes for an appealing, can't-miss stop on your adventures in the Pacific Northwest.

◎ Sights

◎ Downtown

★ Tom McCall Waterfront Park
PARK

This sinuous, 2-mile-long park flanks the west bank of the Willamette River and is both an unofficial training ground for lunchtime runners and a commuter path for the

OREGON FACTS

Nickname Beaver State

Population 3,900,000

Area 95,998 sq miles

Capital city Salem (population 157,000)

Other cities Portland (population 594,000), Eugene (population 157,000), Bend (population 78,000)

Sales tax Oregon has no sales tax

Birthplace of President Herbert Hoover (1874–1964), writer and merry prankster Ken Kesey (1935–2001), actor and dancer Ginger Rogers (1911–95), *The Simpsons* creator Matt Groening (b 1954), filmmaker Gus Van Sant (b 1952)

Home of Oregon Shakespeare Festival, Nike, Crater Lake

Politics Democratic governor, Democrat majorities in Congress, Democrat in Presidential elections since 1984

Famous for Forests, rain, microbrew, coffee, Death with Dignity Act

State beverage Milk (dairy's big here)

Driving You can't pump your own gas in Oregon; Portland to Eugene 110 miles, Portland to Astoria 96 miles

is embellished by the Portlandia statue, representing the Goddess of Commerce (and the second-largest hammered-copper statue in the US – after the Statue of Liberty).

Oregon Historical Society   MUSEUM
(☑ 503-222-1741; www.ohs.org; 1200 SW Park Ave; adult/child 6-18yr $11/5; ⊙10am-5pm Mon-Sat, noon-5pm Sun) Along the tree-shaded South Park Blocks sits the state's primary history museum, which dedicates most of its space to the story of Oregon and the pioneers who made it. There are interesting sections on Native American tribes and the travails of the Oregon Trail.

Portland Art Museum   MUSEUM
(☑ 503-226-2811; www.portlandartmuseum.org; 1219 SW Park Ave; adult/child $15/free; ⊙10am-5pm Tue, Wed & Sat, to 8pm Thu & Fri, noon-5pm Sun) Right on the South Park Blocks, the art museum's excellent exhibits include Native American carvings, Asian and American art, and English silver. The museum also houses the Whitsell Auditorium, a first-rate theater that frequently screens rare or international films.

Aerial Tram   CABLE CAR
(www.gobytram.com; 3303 SW Bond Ave; round-trip $4; ⊙5:30am-9:30pm Mon-Fri, 9am-5pm Sat) Portland's aerial tram runs from the south Waterfront (there's a streetcar stop) to Marquam Hill. The tram runs along a 3300ft line up a vertical ascent of 500ft. The ride takes three minutes. The tram opened in 2007, smashing its budget predictions and causing much public controversy.

◉ Old Town & Chinatown

The core of rambunctious 1890s Portland, the once-notorious Old Town used to be the lurking grounds of unsavory characters, but today disco queens outnumber drug dealers. It's one of the livelier places in town after dark, when nightclubs and bars open their doors and hipsters start showing up.

Shanghai Tunnels   HISTORIC SITE
(www.shanghaitunnels.info; adult/child $13/8) Running beneath Old Town's streets is this series of underground corridors through which, in the 1850s, unscrupulous people would kidnap or 'shanghai' drunken men and sell them to sea captains looking for indentured workers. Tours run Fridays and Saturdays at 6:30pm and 8pm. Book online.

city's avid army of cyclists. It's also a great spot for picnics, and hosts large summertime festivals.

★**Pioneer Courthouse Square**   LANDMARK
Portland's downtown hub, this people-friendly brick plaza attracts tourists, sunbathers, lunching office workers, buskers and the odd political activist. Formerly a parking lot, and before that a posh hotel, the square today hosts concerts, festivals, rallies and farmers markets. Across 6th Ave is the muscular Pioneer Courthouse, the oldest federal building in the Pacific Northwest.

Portland Building   LANDMARK
(cnr SW 5th Ave & SW Main St) In a downtown devoid of big skyscrapers, the city's signature structure is the Portland Building, designed in 1980 by Michael Graves. A triumph of postmodernism to some, but a mine of user-unfriendliness to others, the 15-story block

Chinatown

NEIGHBORHOOD

The ornate **Chinatown Gates** (cnr W Burnside St & NW 4th Ave) defines the southern edge of Portland's Chinatown, which has a few token Chinese restaurants (most are on 82nd Ave over to the east). The main attraction here is the **Classical Chinese Garden** (☑ 503-228-8131; www.lansugarden.org; 239 NW Everett St; adult/child $8/7; ☺ 10am-6pm), a wonderfully tranquil block of reflecting ponds and manicured greenery.

Saturday Market

MARKET

(☑ 503-222-6072; www.portlandsaturdaymarket. com; SW Ankeny St & Naito Pkwy; ☺ 10am-5pm Sat, 11am-4:30pm Sun Mar-Dec) The best time to hit the river for a walk is on a weekend to catch this famous market, which showcases handicrafts, street entertainers and food booths.

Skidmore Fountain

FOUNTAIN

(SW 1st Ave & Ankeny St) Located beneath the Burnside Bridge, the Victorian-era Skidmore Fountain (1888) was idealistically designed with three 'drinking' tiers; the top for humans, the middle for horses and the lowest for dogs.

◉ The Pearl District & Northwest

The Pearl District

NEIGHBORHOOD

(www.explorethepearl.com) Northwest of downtown, the Pearl District is an old industrial quarter that has transformed its once grotty warehouses into expensive lofts, upscale boutiques and creative restaurants. On the first Thursday of every month, the zone's abundant **art galleries** extend their evening hours and the area turns into a fancy street party of sorts. The **Jamison Square Fountain** (810 NW 11th Ave) is one of its prettier urban spaces, and don't miss the **Museum of Contemporary Craft** (☑ 503-223-2654; www. museumofcontemporarycraft.org; 724 NW Davis St; admission $4; ☺ 11am-6pm Tue-Sat, to 8pm 1st Thu of every month), which has many fine ceramics.

Northwest 23rd Ave

NEIGHBORHOOD

NW 23rd Ave ('Trendy-third') is an upscale shopping street, near the West Hills area, that brims with clothing boutiques, home decor shops and cafes. The restaurants here – including some of Portland's finest – lie along parallel NW 21st Ave. This is a great neighborhood for strolling, window-shopping, coffee breaks and looking at lovely arts-and-crafts houses.

◉ West Hills

Behind downtown Portland is the West Hills area, known for its exclusive homes, huge parks and – if you're lucky – peek-a-boo views of up to five Cascade volcanoes.

★ Forest Park

PARK

(www.forestparkconservancy.org) Not many cities have more than 5000 acres of temperate rainforest within their limits, but then not many cities are like Portland. Abutting the more manicured Washington Park to the west is the far wilder Forest Park, whose dense foliage harbors plants, animals and an avid hiking fraternity. The **Portland Audubon Society** (☑ 503-292-6855; www.audubonportland.org; 5151 NW Cornell Rd; ☺ 9am-5pm, nature store 10am-6pm Mon-Sat, till 5pm Sun) maintains a bookstore, wildlife rehabilitation center and 4 miles of trails within its Forest Park sanctuary.

The main sight in the park is the **Pittock Mansion** (☑ 503-823-3623; www.pittockmansion.org; 3229 NW Pittock Dr; adult/child 6-18yr $8.50/5.50, grounds free; ☺ 11am-4pm), a mansion built in 1914 by Henry Pittock, who revitalized the Portland-based Oregonian newspaper. It's worth visiting the grounds just to check out the spectacular views – bring a picnic.

Washington Park

PARK

(www.washingtonparkpdx.org) West of Forest Park, extensive Washington Park contains several attractions within its 400 acres of greenery. **Hoyt Arboretum** (☑ 503-865-8733; www.hoytarboretum.org; 4000 Fairview Blvd; ☺ trails 6am-10pm, visitor center 9am-4pm Mon-Fri, 11am-3pm Sat & Sun) FREE showcases more than 1000 species of native and exotic trees and has 12 miles of walking trails. It's prettiest in the fall. The **International Rose Test Gardens** (☑ 503-823-3636; www.rosegardenstore.org/rose-gardens.cfm; 400 SW Kingston Ave; ☺ 7:30am-9pm) FREE has fine city views and is the centerpiece of Portland's famous rose blooms; there are more than 500 types on show here. Further uphill is the **Japanese Garden** (☑ 503-223-1321; www.japanesegarden.com; 611 SW Kingston Ave; adult/child 6-17yr $9.50/6.75; ☺ noon-7pm Mon, 9am-7pm Tue-Fri & Sun, 9am-9pm Sat), another oasis of tranquility.

◉ Northeast & Southeast

Across the Willamette River from downtown is the **Lloyd Center**, Oregon's largest shopping mall and where notorious ice-queen Tonya Harding first learned to skate in the rink here. A few blocks to the southwest are the unmissable glass towers of the **Oregon Convention Center**, and nearby is **Moda Center** (previously called the Rose Garden Arena) – home of professional basketball team the Trailblazers.

Further up the Willamette, **N Mississippi Avenue** used to be full of run-down buildings but is now a hot spot of trendy shops and eateries. Northeast is artsy **NE Alberta Street**, a long ribbon of art galleries, boutiques and cafes (don't miss Last Thursday street-art event here, taking place

Portland

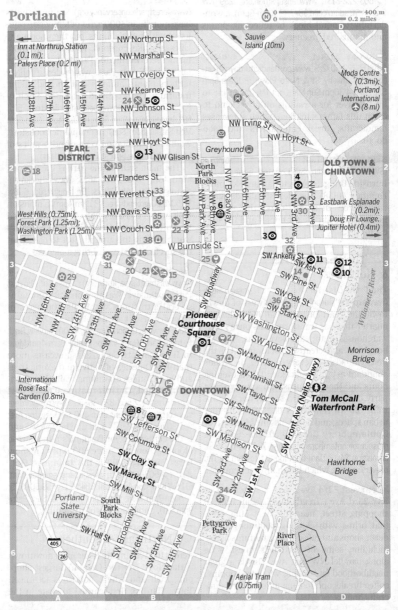

on the last Thursday of each month). SE Hawthorne Boulevard (near SE 39th Ave) is affluent hippy territory, with gift stores, cafes, coffeeshops and two branches of Powell's bookstores. One leafy mile to the south, SE Division Street has become a foodie destination, with plenty of excellent restaurants, bars and pubs. The same is true of E Burnside at NE 28th Avenue, though it has a more concentrated and upscale feel.

🏃 Activities

Hiking

The best hiking is found in Forest Park (p215), which harbors an unbelievable 80 miles of trails and often feels more like Mt Hood's foothills than Portland's city limits. The park's Wildwood Trail starts at the Hoyt Arboretum and winds through 30 miles of forest, with many spur trails that allow for loop hikes. Other trailheads into Forest Park are located at the western ends of NW Thurman and NW Upshur Sts.

Cycling

Portland has been voted the 'most bike-friendly city in the US' several times in the media by the likes of CNN Travel, NBC News and *Bicycling Magazine*. There are many streets that cater to bicycles, and drivers are used to watching out for cyclists. Riding along downtown riverside paths is a great way to see the city.

To the east the Springwater Corridor starts near the Oregon Museum of Science & Industry (as an extension of the Eastbank Esplanade) and goes all the way to the suburb of Boring – 21 miles away. In the northwest, Leif Erikson Drive is an old logging road leading 11 miles into Forest Park and offering occasional peeks over the city.

For scenic farm country, head to Sauvie Island, 10 miles northwest of downtown Portland. This island is prime cycling land – it's flat, has relatively little traffic and much of it is wildlife refuge.

For bike rental, try Waterfront Bicycle Rentals (📞503-227-1719; www.waterfrontbikes.com; 10 SW Ash St; per day $40). Good cycling maps can be found at the tourist office and any bike store.

Kayaking

Situated close to the confluence of the Columbia and Willamette Rivers, Portland has miles of navigable waterways. Portland

---

Portland

◉ Top Sights
1 Pioneer Courthouse Square	C4
2 Tom McCall Waterfront Park	D4

◎ Sights
3 Chinatown Gates	C3
4 Classical Chinese Gardens	D2
5 Jamison Square Fountain	B1
6 Museum of Contemporary Craft	C2
7 Oregon Historical Society	B5
8 Portland Art Museum	B5
9 Portland Building	C5
10 Saturday Market	D3
11 Shanghai Tunnels	D3
12 Skidmore Fountain	D3
13 The Pearl District	B2

✛ Activities, Courses & Tours
14 Pedal Bike Tours	D3

😴 Sleeping
15 Ace Hotel	B3
16 Crystal Hotel	B3
17 Heathman Hotel	B4
18 Northwest Portland Hostel	A2

✕ Eating
19 Andina	B2
20 Jake's Famous Crawfish	B3
21 Kenny & Zuke's	B3
22 Little Big Burger	B3
23 Nong's Khao Man Gai	B3
24 Piazza Italia	B1

🍷 Drinking & Nightlife
25 Bailey's Taproom	C3
26 Barista	B2
27 Departure Lounge	C4

🎭 Entertainment
28 Arlene Schnitzer Concert Hall	B4
29 Artists Repertory Theatre	A3
30 CC Slaughters	D2
31 Crystal Ballroom	B3
32 Dante's	C3
Darcelle XV	(see 30)
33 Jimmy Mak's	B2
34 Keller Auditorium	C5
35 Portland Center Stage	B3
36 Silverado	C3

🛍 Shopping
37 Pioneer Place	C4
38 Powell's City of Books	B3

Kayak Company (☑503-459-4050; www.portlandkayak.com; 6600 SW Macadam Ave) offers kayaking rentals, instruction and tours including a three-hour circumnavigation of Ross Island on the Willamette River. For rentals, instruction and wildlife-based tours around Sauvie Island, try **Scappoose Bay Kayaking** (☑503-397-2161; www.scappoosebaykayaking.com; 57420 Old Portland Rd), located in Scappoose, which is 20 miles northwest of Portland.

☞ Tours

Pedal Bike Tours   BICYCLE TOUR
(☑503-243-2453; www.pedalbiketours.com; 133 SW 2nd Ave) Bike tours with all sorts of themes – history, food carts, beer– and options to head to the coast or gorge.

Portland Walking Tours   WALKING TOUR
(☑503-774-4522; www.portlandwalkingtours.com) Food, chocolate, underground and even ghost-oriented tours.

Forktown   FOOD TOUR
(☑503-234-3663; www.forktown.com) Experience Stumptown's neighborhood eateries from the point of view of your tastebuds.

Pubs of Portland Tours   BEER TOUR
(☑512-917-2464; www.pubsofportlandtours.com) Visit several breweries and brewpubs with guides who will educate you on the beer-brewing process, various styles of beer and, essentially, how to taste the stuff.

⚞ Festivals & Events

Portland Rose Festival   ROSE FESTIVAL
(www.rosefestival.org; ☉late May–mid-Jun) Rose-covered floats, dragon-boat races, fireworks, roaming packs of sailors and the crowning of a Rose Queen combine to make this Portland's biggest celebration.

Oregon Brewers Festival   BEER FESTIVAL
(www.oregonbrewfest.com; ☉Jul & Dec) Quaff microbrews during the summer (late July) in Tom McCall Waterfront Park and during the winter (early December) at Pioneer Courthouse Sq.

Bite of Oregon   FOOD FESTIVAL
(www.biteoforegon.com; ☉early Aug) All the food (and beer) you could think of consuming, much of it from great local restaurants – and some of it from Portland's now-famous food carts. Good microbrews, too. Bite of Oregon benefits Special Olympics Oregon.

Art in the Pearl   ART FESTIVAL
(www.artinthepearl.com; ☉first Mon in Sep & weekend prior) On Labor Day weekend, more than 100 carefully selected artists come together to show and sell their fine works. Plenty of food and live music.

🛏 Sleeping

Reserve ahead in summer.

Hawthorne Portland Hostel   HOSTEL $
(☑503-236-3380; www.portlandhostel.org; 3031 SE Hawthorne Blvd; dm $28, d with shared bath $60; ☺@�🐾) ✎ This ecofriendly hostel has good vibes and a great Hawthorne location. Private rooms are decent and dorms spacious. There are summertime open-mic nights in the grassy backyard, and bike rentals available. The Hawthorne is very environmentally conscious; it composts and recycles, uses rainwater to flush toilets and has a nice eco-roof. Discounts are available to those bike touring; non-HI members pay $3 extra.

Northwest Portland Hostel   HOSTEL $
(☑503-241-2783; www.nwportlandhostel.com; 425 NW 18th Ave; dm $20-29, d with shared bath $65; ☺❈@☑) Perfectly located between the Pearl District and NW 21st and 23rd Aves, this friendly and clean hostel takes up four old buildings and features plenty of common areas (including a small deck) and bike rentals. Dorms are spacious and private rooms can be as nice as in hotels, though all share outside bathrooms. Non-HI members pay $3 extra.

★ Ace Hotel   BOUTIQUE HOTEL $$
(☑503-228-2277; www.acehotel.com; 1022 SW Stark St; d with shared/private bath from $135/185; ☺❈@☑) Portland's trendiest place to sleep is this unique hotel fusing classic, industrial, minimalist and retro styles. From the photo booth and sofa lounge in its lobby to the recycled fabrics and furniture in its rooms, the Ace makes the warehouse-feel work. A Stumptown coffee shop on the premises adds even more comfort. Parking costs $25.

Crystal Hotel   HOTEL $$
(☑503-972-2670; www.mcmenamins.com/CrystalHotel; 303 SW 12th Ave; r $85-165; ❈☑) Room furnishings that blend Grateful Dead–inspired psychedelia with the interior of a Victorian boudoir can only mean one thing. Welcome to the latest McMenamins hotel, filled with 51 guestrooms (the cheapest with

bathrooms down the hall), each 'inspired' by a song. A wondrous saltwater soaking pool lies in the basement.

Jupiter Hotel
BOUTIQUE MOTEL $$

(☑503-230-9200; www.jupiterhotel.com; 800 E Burnside; d from $159; ❂❀🛜❂) The hippest hotel in town, this slick, remodeled motel is within walking distance of downtown and right next to Doug Fir Lounge (p222), a top-notch live-music venue. Standard rooms are tiny – go for the Metropolitan instead, and ask for a pad away from the bamboo patio if you're more into sleeping than staying up late. Kitchenettes and bike rentals available; walk-ins after midnight get a discount.

Clinton St Guesthouse
GUESTHOUSE $$

(☑503-234-8752; www.clintonstreetguesthouse.com; 4220 SE Clinton St; d $100-145; ❂❀🛜) Four simple but beautiful rooms (two with shared bathroom) are on offer in this lovely arts-and-crafts house in a residential neighborhood. Furnishings are elegant, the linens luxurious and your hosts gracious. Located in a great residential neighborhood with many restaurants within walking distance.

★McMenamins Edgefield
HOTEL $$

(☑503-669-8610; www.mcmenamins.com/54-edgefield-home; 2126 SW Halsey St, Troutdale; dm $30, d with shared bath $70-115, with private bath $120-155; ❂❀🛜) This former county poor farm, restored by the McMenamin brothers, is now a one-of-a-kind 38-acre hotel complex with a dizzying variety of services. Taste wine and homemade beer, play golf, watch movies, shop at the gift store, listen to live music, walk the extensive gardens and eat at one of its restaurants. It's about a 20-minute drive east from downtown.

★Kennedy School
HOTEL $$

(☑503-249-3983; www.mcmenamins.com; 5736 NE 33rd Ave; d $115-155; ❂🛜) This Portland institution, a former elementary school, is now home to a hotel (yes, the bedrooms are converted classrooms), a restaurant, several bars, a microbrewery and a movie theater. There's a soaking pool, and the whole school is decorated with mosaics, fantasy paintings and historical photographs.

Inn at Northrup Station
BOUTIQUE HOTEL $$

(☑503-224-0543; www.northrupstation.com; 2025 NW Northrup St; d from $174; ❂❀@) Almost over the top with its bright color scheme and funky decor, this supertrendy hotel boasts huge artsy suites, many with patio or balcony, and all with kitchenettes or full kitchens. There's a cool rooftop patio with plants, and complimentary streetcar tickets are included (the streetcar runs just outside).

Heathman Hotel
LUXURY HOTEL $$$

(☑503-241-4100; www.heathmanhotel.com; 1001 SW Broadway; d from $249; ❀@🛜❂) A Portland institution, the Heathman has top-notch services and one of the best restaurants in the city. Rooms are elegant, stylish and luxurious, and the location is very central. It also hosts high tea in the afternoons, jazz in the evenings and has a library stocked with signed books by authors who have stayed here. Parking costs $32.

✖ Eating

Portland's rapidly evolving food scene tore up the rule book years ago and has branched out into countless genres and subgenres. Vegetarianism is well represented, as is brunch, Asian fusion and the rather loose concept known as 'Pacific Northwest.' Then there are the city's famous food carts, representing dozens of cuisines and quirky food niches.

Little Big Burger
BURGERS $

(☑503-274-9008; www.littlebigburger.com; 122 NW 10th Ave; burgers $4; ⊙11am-10pm) A simple six-item menu takes fast food to the next level with mini-burgers made from prime ingredients. Try a beef burger topped with cheddar, Swiss, chevre or blue cheese, served with a side of truffled fries, and wash it down with a gourmet root-beer float. There are several locations; check the website.

Pok Pok
THAI $$

(☑503-232-1387; www.pokpokpdx.com; 3226 SE Division St; mains $11-16; ⊙11:30am-10pm) Spicy Thai street food with a twist draws crowds of flavor-seekers to this famous eatery; don't miss the renowned chicken wings. To endure the inevitably long wait, try a tastier-than-it-sounds drinking vinegar at the restaurant's nearby bar, Whiskey Soda Lounge. There's a second location at 1469 NE Prescott St.

Navarre
EUROPEAN $$

(☑503-232-3555; www.navarreportland.blogspot.com; 10 NE 28th Ave; small plates $4-8, large plates $10-18; ⊙4:30-10:30pm Mon-Thu, till 11:30pm Fri, 9:30am-11:30pm Sat, till 10:30pm Sun) The paper menu at this industrial-elegant restaurant lists various small plates (don't call them tapas), which rotate daily – though a few popular dishes are fixed commodities. Expect a simple and truly delicious approach to crab cakes, lamb and roasted veggies. Weekend brunch is just as good.

Piazza Italia
ITALIAN $$

(☎ 503-478-0619; www.piazzaportland.com; 1129 NW Johnson St; pasta $13-17; ⊙ 11:30am-3pm & 5-9pm Mon-Thu, till 10pm Fri-Sun) Remember that great *ragù* (meat sauce) you last had in Bologna or those memorable *vongole* (clams) you once polished off in Sicily? Well, you'll find them here in this highly authentic restaurant that succeeds where so many fail: replicating the true essence of Italian food in North America.

Pambiche
CUBAN $$

(☎ 503-233-0511; www.pambiche.com; 2811 NE Glisan St; mains $12-17; ⊙ 11am-10pm Mon-Thu, to midnight Fri, 9am-midnight Sat, to 10pm Sun) Portland's best Cuban food served in a riotously colorful atmosphere. All your regular favorites including *ropa vieja* (shredded beef in a tomato sauce) are available, and leave room for dessert. Happy hour is a good deal (2pm to 6pm Monday to Friday, 10pm to midnight Friday and Saturday). Be prepared to wait for dinner.

Kenny & Zuke's
DELI $$

(☎ 503-222-3354; www.kennyandzukes.com; 1038 SW Stark St; sandwiches $10-15; ⊙ 7am-8pm Mon-Thu, till 10pm Fri, 8am-10pm Sat, till 8pm Sun) The only place in the city for real Jewish deli food: bagels, pickled herring, homemade pickles and latkes. But the real draw is the house pastrami, cut to order and gently sandwiched in one of the best Reubens you'll ever eat. Bustles for breakfast, too. Also in North Portland.

★ Ox
STEAKHOUSE $$$

(☎ 503-284-3366; www.oxpdx.com; 2225 Martin Luther King Jr Blvd; mains $19-38; ⊙ 5-10pm Tue-Sun) Currently Portland's most popular restaurant, this is an upscale Argentine-inspired steakhouse (who said Portland is all vegetarian?). Go for the 'Gusto' (grass-fed beef rib-eye for $38) or, if there are two of you, the *asado* is a good choice for trying many different cuts ($60). Reserve ahead and bring your wallet.

Paley's Place
FRENCH, FUSION $$$

(☎ 503-243-2403; www.paleysplace.net; 1204 NW 21st Ave; mains $23-36; ⊙ 5:30-10pm Mon-Thu, till 11pm Fri & Sat, 5-10pm Sun) 🍴 Established by Vitaly and Kimberly Paley, this is one of Portland's premier restaurants, offering a creative blend of French and Pacific Northwest cuisines. Whether you're enjoying seared Alaskan halibut or crispy sweetbreads with fava-bean puree, you can count on fresh ingredients and excellent service.

Andina
PERUVIAN $$$

(☎ 503-228-9535; www.andinarestaurant.com; 1314 NW Glisan St; lunch mains $14-17, dinner mains $22-30; ⊙ 11:30am-2:30pm & 5-9:30pm Sun-Thu, till

PORTLAND'S FOOD CARTS

One of the most fun ways to explore Portland's cuisine is to eat at a food cart. These semipermanent kitchens-on-wheels inhabit parking lots around town and are usually clustered together in 'pods,' often with their own communal tables, ATMs and portaloos. As many of the owners are immigrants (who can't afford a hefty restaurant start-up), the carts are akin to an international potluck.

Food-cart locations vary, but the most significant cluster is on the corners of SW Alder St and SW 9th Ave. For a current list and some background information, see www.foodcartsportland.com. Highlights in a highly competitive field:

Nong's Khao Man Gai (☎ 971-255-3480; www.khaomangai.com; SW 10th & SW Alder St; mains $7; ⊙ 10am-4pm Mon-Fri) Tender poached chicken with rice. That's it – and enough. Also at 411 SW College St and 609 SE Ankeny St.

Viking Soul Food (www.vikingsoulfood.com; 4262 SE Belmont Ave; mains $5-6; ⊙ noon-8pm Tue-Thu, 11:30am-9:30pm Fri & Sat, 11:30am-8:30pm Sun) Delicious sweet and savory wraps.

Rip City Grill (www.ripcitygrill.com; cnr SW Moody & Abernathy, south waterfront; sandwiches $5-7; ⊙ 10am-2pm Mon-Fri) The tri-tip steak sandwich is not to be missed.

Thrive Pacific NW (www.thrivepacificnw.com; mains $5-8) Organic, free-range and gluten-free exotic food bowls. See the website for changing location and hours.

Pepper Box (www.pepperboxpdx.com; 2737 NE Martin Luther King Jr Blvd; tacos & quesadillas $3.50-4; ⊙ 9am-2pm Tue-Fri, till 1pm Sat) Awesome breakfast tacos and fancy quesadillas.

10:30pm Fri & Sat) A modern take on traditional Peruvian food produces delicious mains such as quinoa-crusted scallops on a bed of wilted spinach, or slow-cooked lamb shank in cilantro-and-black-beer sauce. For lighter fare, hit the bar for tapas, great cocktails and Latin-inspired live music.

Jake's Famous Crawfish
SEAFOOD $$$

(☑503-226-1419; 401 SW 12th Ave; lunch mains $10-16, dinner mains $19-39; ⊖11:30am-10pm Mon-Thu, till midnight Fri & Sat, 3-10pm Sun) Some of Portland's best seafood can be found here within an elegant old-time atmosphere. The oysters are divine, the crab cakes a revelation and the macadamia-crusted wild halibut your ticket to heaven. Come at happy hour for more-affordable treats.

Drinking & Nightlife

Portland is famous for its coffee, and boasts more than 50 breweries within its borders – more than any other city on earth. It also offers a wide range of excellent bars, from dive bars to hipster joints to pubs and ultramodern lounges. You'll never get thirsty in these parts.

★Barista
CAFE

(☑503-274-1211; www.baristapdx.com; 539 NW 13th Ave; ⊖6am-6pm Mon-Fri, 7am-6pm Sat & Sun) One of Portland's best coffee shops is owned by award-winning barista Billy Wilson and known for its lattes. It sources its beans from specialty roasters. Also at 529 SW 3rd Ave and 1725 NE Alberta St.

Amnesia Brewing
BREWERY

(☑503-281-7708; www.amnesiabrews.com; 832 N Beech St; ⊖3pm-midnight Mon, noon-midnight Tue-Sun) This brewery, located on hip Mississippi Street (though its official address is Beech St), has picnic tables out front and a very casual feel. For excellent (and despite the name, memorable) beer, try the Desolation IPA, Amnesia Brown or Wonka Porter. An outdoor grill offers burgers and sausages, and there's live music on weekends.

Horse Brass Pub
PUB

(☑503-232-2202; www.horsebrass.com; 4534 SE Belmont St; ⊖11am-2:30am) Portland's most authentic English pub, cherished for its dark-wood atmosphere, excellent fish and chips, and about four dozen beers on tap. Play some darts, watch soccer on TV and just take it all in.

Coava Coffee
CAFE

(☑503-894-8134; www.coavacoffee.com; 1300 SE Grand Ave; ⊖6am-6pm Mon-Fri, 7am-6pm Sat, 8am-6pm Sun) The decor takes the concept of 'neo-industrial' to extremes, but most people love that – and Coava delivers where it matters. Their pour-over makes for a fantastic cup of java, and their espressos are exceptional, too.

Bailey's Taproom
BREWERY

(☑503-295-1004; www.baileystaproom.com; 213 SW Broadway; ⊖2pm-midnight) Unique and popular beer bar offering a rotation selection of 20 eclectic beers from Oregon and beyond. Cool digital menu board lets you know all about the beers, and how much of each is left. No food served, but you can bring something in from outside.

Belmont Station
BREWERY

(☑503-232-8538; www.belmont-station.com; 4500 SE Stark St; ⊖noon-11pm) More than 20 excellent rotating taps in a simple 'biercafé' with sidewalk seating. Attached to one of the city's best bottle shops, which sells more than 1200 beers and offers a small discount if customers pay in cash.

Departure Lounge
BAR

(☑503-802-5370; www.departureportland.com; 525 SW Morrison St; ⊖4pm-midnight Sun-Thu, to 1am Fri & Sat) This rooftop restaurant-bar (atop the 15th floor of the Nines Hotel) fills a deep downtown void: a cool bar with unforgettable views. The vibe is distinctly spaceship LA, with mod couches and sleek lighting. For something different, try the spicy tasho macho cocktail.

Ristretto Roasters
CAFE

(☑503-288-8667; www.ristrettoroasters.com; 3808 N Williams Ave; ⊖6:30am-6pm Mon-Sat, 7am-6pm Sun) Medium-roast, small-batch and single-origin coffee beans that result in a mellow, subtle cup of java. Free cuppings (tasting sessions) Fridays at 1pm. Also at 555 NE Couch St and 2181 NW Nicolai St (in a cool Schoolhouse Electric building).

Breakside Brewery
BREWERY

(☑503-719-6475; www.breakside.com; 820 NE Dekum St; ⊖3-10pm Mon-Thu, noon-11pm Fri & Sat, noon-10pm Sun) More than 20 taps of some of the most experimental, tasty beer you'll ever drink, laced with fruits, vegetables and spices. Past beers have included a Meyer lemon kolsch, mango IPA and a beet beer with ginger. For dessert, pray they have the

GAY & LESBIAN PORTLAND

For current listings, see *Just Out*, Portland's free gay biweekly. Stark St, around SW 10th St, has several edgy gay bars.

CC Slaughters (☑503-248-9135; www.ccslaughterspdx.com; 219 NW Davis St) Popular and long-running nightclub with big, loud dance floor, laser light show and DJs. There's a Sunday night drag show and fun themed nights. The relaxed lounge is good for conversation.

Darcelle XV (☑503-222-5338; www.darcellexv.com; 208 NW 3rd Ave; ⊙shows Wed-Sat) Portland's Vegas-style cabaret show, featuring glitzy drag queens in big wigs, fake jewelry and over-stuffed bras. Male strippers perform at midnight on Friday and Saturday.

Silverado (☑503-224-4493; www.silveradopdx.com; 318 SW 3rd Ave) Almost nightly stripper shows (Monday is karaoke) catering to men. Mixed crowd, cheap drinks, potential groping and muscled dancers, so bring plenty of dollar bills and expect a wild time.

salted-caramel milk stout. Good food and nice outdoor seating, too.

Stumptown Coffee Roasters CAFE
(☑503-230-7702; www.stumptowncoffee.com; 4525 SE Division St; ⊙6am-7pm Mon-Fri, 7am-7pm Sat & Sun) The first microroaster to put Portland on the coffee map, and still its most famous coffee shop. Stumptown is proud to deal directly with coffee farmers to ensure quality beans. See the website for other Portland (and US) locations.

Green Dragon BREWERY
(☑503-517-0660; www.pdxgreendragon.com; 928 SE 9th Ave; ⊙11am-11pm Sun-Wed, to 1am Thu-Sat) Although it is owned by Rogue Breweries, Green Dragon serves a whopping 62 guest taps – and it's an eclectic mix to boot. It has decent pub-fare food, too. Located in an echoey eastside warehouse space; sit on the patio on warm days.

Rontoms BAR
(☑503-236-4536; 600 E Burnside St; ⊙4:30pm-2:30am) First the downside of this trendy-industrial bar – the food's just ok, the service can be mediocre, and if you're not a hipster you might feel out of place. But if it's a nice

day, the large patio in back is the place to be. It's at the corner of E Burnside and 6th (too cool for a sign).

Hopworks Urban Brewery BREWERY
(☑503-232-4677; www.hopworksbeer.com; 2944 SE Powell Blvd; ⊙11am-11pm Sun-Thu, till midnight Fri & Sat) ◢ Organic beers made with local ingredients, served in an ecobuilding with bicycle frames above the bar. Good selection of food in a family-friendly atmosphere; the back deck can't be beat on a warm day. Also at 3947 N Williams Ave.

Sterling Coffee Roasters CAFE
(www.sterlingcoffeeroasters.com; 417 NW 21st Ave; ⊙7am-4pm Mon-Fri, 8am-4pm Sat & Sun) Very small but elegant coffee shop that roasts complex, flavorful beans. Simple menu, great cappuccino and espresso, and knowledgeable baristas. Also at 1951 W Burnside (where it's called Coffeehouse Northwest).

☆ Entertainment

The best guide to local entertainment is the free *Willamette Week* (www.wweek.com), which comes out on Wednesday and lists theater, music, clubs, cinema and events in the metro area. Also, try the *Portland Mercury* (www.portlandmercury.com).

For summer outdoor concerts, check what's happening at the Oregon Zoo.

Live Music

Doug Fir Lounge LIVE MUSIC
(☑503-231-9663; www.dougfirlounge.com; 830 E Burnside St) Paul Bunyan meets the Jetsons at this ultratrendy venue. Doug Fir books edgy, hard-to-get talent, drawing crowds from tattooed youth to suburban yuppies. Their decent restaurant has long hours; located next to the rock-star quality Jupiter Hotel.

Dante's LIVE MUSIC
(☑503-345-7892; www.danteslive.com; 350 W Burnside St) This steamy red bar books vaudeville shows along with national acts such as the Dandy Warhols and Concrete Blonde. Drop in on Sunday night for the eclectic Sinferno Cabaret.

Crystal Ballroom LIVE MUSIC
(☑503-225-0047; www.mcmenamins.com; 1332 W Burnside St) Major acts have played at this large and historic ballroom, including the Grateful Dead, James Brown and Jimi Hendrix. The 'floating' dance floor makes dancing a balancing act. If you like '80s music, head to Lola's Room downstairs on Friday nights.

Mississippi Studios
LIVE MUSIC

(☑503-288-3895; www.mississippistudios.com; 3939 N Mississippi Ave) Intimate venue good for checking out budding acoustic talent, along with more established alternative musical groups. Excellent sound system. There's a good restaurant-bar with patio next door.

Jimmy Mak's
LIVE MUSIC

(☑503-295-6542; www.jimmymaks.com; 221 NW 10th Ave; ⊙music from 8pm) Stumptown's premier jazz venue, which also serves excellent Mediterranean food in their fancy dining room. There's a casual bar with pool tables and darts in the basement.

Cinema

Kennedy School
CINEMA

(☑503-249-3983; www.mcmenamins.com; 5736 NE 33rd Ave) McMenamins' premier Portland venue; watch $3 movies in the old school gym.

Bagdad Theater
CINEMA

(☑503-249-7474; www.mcmenamins.com; 3702 SE Hawthorne Blvd) An awesome McMenamins venue that shows bargain flicks.

Laurelhurst Theater
CINEMA

(☑503-232-5511; www.laurelhursttheater.com; 2735 E Burnside St) Great gourmet pizza-and-microbrew theater with nearby nightlife.

Cinema 21
CINEMA

(www.cinema21.com; 616 NW 21st Ave) This is Portland's premier art-house and foreign-film theater.

Performing Arts

Portland Center Stage
THEATER

(☑503-445-3700; www.pcs.org; 128 NW 11th Ave) The city's main theater company now performs in the Portland Armory – a newly renovated Pearl District landmark with state-of-the-art features.

Arlene Schnitzer Concert Hall
CLASSICAL MUSIC

(☑503-228-1353; www.pcpa.com/schnitzer; 1037 SW Broadway) The Oregon Symphony performs in this beautiful, if not acoustically brilliant, downtown venue.

Artists Repertory Theatre
THEATER

(☑503-241-1278; www.artistsrep.org; 1515 SW Morrison St) Some of Portland's best plays, including regional premiers, are performed in two intimate theaters.

Keller Auditorium
THEATER

(☑503-248-4335; www.pcpa.com/keller; 222 SW Clay St) The Portland Opera and Oregon Ballet Theatre stage performances here, and it's also home to some Broadway productions.

Sports

Portland's Trailblazers play at Moda Center (☑503-235-8771; www.rosequarter.com; 300 N Winning Way). The city's A-League soccer teams are the Timbers (www.portlandtimbers.com), who play at Jeld-Wen Field along with their female counterparts, the Thorns (www.portlandtimbers.com/thornsfc), who won their leagues' inaugural championship in 2013. Other major sports teams include the Winter Hawks (www.winterhawks.com), who play ice-hockey at Moda Center, and Rose City Rollers (www.rosecityrollers.com), a roller-derby team who play at The Hanger in Oaks Amusement Park.

🛍 Shopping

Portland's downtown shopping district extends in a two-block radius from Pioneer Courthouse Sq and hosts all of the usual suspects. Pioneer Place (☑503-228-5800; www.pioneerplace.com; 700 SW 5th Ave; ⊙10am-8pm Mon-Sat, 11am-6pm Sun), a fancy mall, is east of the square. The Pearl District is dotted with high-end galleries, boutiques and home-decor shops. On weekends, you can visit the quintessential Saturday Market (p215) by the Skidmore Fountain. For a pleasant, upscale shopping street, head to NW 23rd Ave.

DON'T MISS

POWELL'S CITY OF BOOKS

You remember bookstores, don't you? Well they haven't all disappeared. Enter Powell's City of Books (☑503-228-4651; www.powells.com; 1005 W Burnside St; ⊙9am-11pm), an empire of reading that takes up a whole city block on multiple stories, and once claimed to be 'the largest independent bookstore in the world.' Don't miss it during your Portland tenure; it's a local institution, tourist attraction and a worthy place to hang out for a few hours (it'll take you that long to get through it). There are other branches around town and at the airport, but none as large.

Eastside has lots of trendy shopping streets that also host restaurants and cafes. SE Hawthorne Blvd is the biggest, N Mississippi Ave is the most recent and NE Alberta St is the most artsy and funky. Down south, Sellwood is known for its antique shops.

❶ Information

EMERGENCY & MEDICAL SERVICES

Legacy Good Samaritan Medical Center (☎503-413-7711; www.legacyhealth.org; 1015 NW 22nd Ave)

Portland Police (☎503-823-0000; www.portlandoregon.gov/police; 1111 SW 2nd Ave)

INTERNET ACCESS

Backspace (☎503-248-2900; www.backspace.bz; 115 NW 5th Ave; ⊙7am-midnight Mon-Fri, 10am-midnight Sat & Sun) Youth-oriented hangout with arcade games, coffee, long hours and even live music.

Central Library (☎503-988-5123; www.multcolib.org; 801 SW 10th Ave) Downtown; for other branches check the website.

MEDIA

KBOO 90.7 FM (www.kboo.fm) Progressive local station run by volunteers; alternative news and views.

Portland Mercury (www.portlandmercury.com) Free local sibling of Seattle's the *Stranger*.

Willamette Week (www.wweek.com) Free weekly covering local news and culture.

MONEY

Travelex (⊙5:30am-4:30pm) Downtown (900 SW 6th Ave); Portland International Airport (☎503-281-3045; ⊙5:30am-4:30pm) Foreign-currency exchange.

POST

Post Office (☎503-525-5398; www.usps.com; 715 NW Hoyt St; ⊙8am-6:30pm Mon-Fri, 8:30am-5pm Sat) This is the main branch, but there are many others around Portland.

TOURIST INFORMATION

Portland Oregon Visitors Association (www.travelportland.com; 701 SW 6th Ave; ⊙8:30am-5:30pm Mon-Fri, 10am-4pm Sat, till 2pm Sun) In Pioneer Courthouse Sq. There's a small theater with a 12-minute film about the city, and Tri-Met bus and light-rail offices inside.

USEFUL WEBSITES

Oregon Live (www.oregonlive.com) *The Oregonian's* website, with news, sports and entertainment.

Portland Food & Drink (www.portlandfoodanddrink.com) Unbiased reviews of Portland's restaurants, along with specialty articles.

Portland Monthly (www.portlandmonthlymag.com) *Portland Monthly* magazine's website features interesting local content.

Travel Portland (www.travelportland.com) What to do, where to go, how to save.

❶ Getting There & Away

AIR

Portland International Airport (PDX; ☎503-460-4234; www.flypdx.com; 7000 NE Airport Way) Portland International Airport has daily flights all over the US, as well as several international destinations. It's situated just east of I-5 on the banks of the Columbia River (a 20-minute drive from downtown heading northeast via the Steel Bridge). Amenities include money changers, restaurants, bookstores (including three Powell's branches) and business services such as free wi-fi.

BUS

Greyhound (☎503-243-2361; www.greyhound.com; 550 NW 6th Ave) Greyhound connects Portland with cities along I-5 and I-84. Destinations include Chicago, Boise, Denver, San Francisco, Seattle and Vancouver, BC.

Bolt Bus (☎877-265-8287; www.boltbus.com) If you're traveling between Portland, Seattle and Vancouver, BC, try Bolt Bus, which provides service in large buses with wi-fi and power outlets.

TRAIN

Amtrak (☎503-273-4865; www.amtrak.com; 800 NW 6th Ave) Amtrak offers services up and down the West Coast. The *Empire Builder* travels to Chicago, the *Cascades* goes to Vancouver, BC, and the *Coast Starlight* runs between Seattle and LA.

❶ Getting Around

TO/FROM THE AIRPORT

Portland International Airport (PDX) is about 10 miles northeast of downtown, next to the Columbia River. Tri-Met's light-rail MAX line takes about 40 minutes to get from downtown to the airport. If you prefer a bus, **Blue Star** (☎503-249-1837; www.bluestarbus.com) offers shuttle services between PDX and several downtown stops.

Taxis charge around $34 from the airport to downtown (not including tip).

BICYCLE

It's easy riding a bicycle around Portland, often voted 'the most bike-friendly city in America.'

Rental companies include **Clever Cycles** (☑503-334-1560; www.clevercycles.com/rentals; 900 SE Hawthorne Blvd) and Waterfront Bicycle Rentals (p217).

PUBLIC TRANSPORTATION

Portland has a good public-transportation system, which consists of local buses, streetcars and the MAX light-rail. All are run by **TriMet** (☑503-238-7433; www.trimet.org; 701 SW 6th Ave), which has an information center at Pioneer Courthouse Sq.

Tickets for the transportation systems are completely transferable within two hours of the time of purchase. Buy tickets for local buses from the fare machines as you enter; for streetcars, you can buy tickets either at streetcar stations or on the streetcar itself. Tickets for the MAX must be bought from ticket machines at MAX stations (before you board); there is no conductor or ticket seller on board (but there are enforcers).

If you're a night owl, be aware that there are fewer services at night, and only a few run past 1am; check the website for details on specific lines.

CAR

Most major car-rental agencies have outlets both downtown and at Portland International Airport (PDX). Many of these agencies have added hybrid vehicles to their fleets. **Zipcar** (www.zipcar.com) is a popular car-sharing option, but there are many. For cheap parking downtown, see www.portlandoregon.gov/transportation/35272.

CHARTER SERVICE

For custom bus or van charters and tours, try **EcoShuttle** (☑503-548-4480; www.ecoshuttle.net). Vehicles are run on 100% biodiesel.

PEDICAB

For an ecofriendly option, there are several pedicab operators in town, including **PDX Pedicab.** (☑503-828-9888; www.pdxpedicab.com) Bicycle pedicabs come with 'drivers' that pedal you around downtown.

TAXI

Cabs are available 24 hours by phone. Downtown, you can often just flag them down. Try **Broadway Cab** (☑503-333-3333; www.broadwaycab.com) or **Radio Cab** (☑503-227-1212; www.radiocab.net).

Willamette Valley

The Willamette Valley, a fertile 60-mile-wide agricultural basin, was the Holy Grail for Oregon Trail pioneers who headed west more than 150 years ago. Today it's the state's breadbasket, producing more than 100 kinds of crops – including renowned Pinot Noir grapes (see p225). Salem, Oregon's capital, is about an hour's drive from Portland at the northern end of the Willamette

WILLAMETTE VALLEY WINE COUNTRY

Just a hour's drive from Portland is the Willamette Valley, home to hundreds of wineries producing world-class tipples, especially Pinot Noir. McMinnville, Newberg and Dundee provide many of this region's services, which include some very fine restaurants, shops, B&Bs and wine-tasting rooms. Check out www.willamettewines.com for more information on the region's wineries.

Meandering through plush green hills on winding country roads from one wine-tasting room to another is a delightful way to spend an afternoon (just make sure you designate a driver). If you'd rather go on a tour, Grape Escape (☑503-283-3380; www.grapeescapetours.com) offers some good ones. If you like to bicycle, Portland-based Pedal Bike Tours (p218) runs five-hour bike tours.

For something more cerebral, head to McMinnville's Evergreen Aviation Museum (☑503-434-4180; www.evergreenmuseum.org; 500 NE Captain Michael King Smith Way; adult/child 5-16yr $25/23 (incl 3-D movie); ☺9am-5pm; ⊞) and check out Howard Hughes' Spruce Goose, the world's largest wood-framed airplane. There's also a replica of the Wright brothers' *Flyer,* along with a 3-D theater and – oddly enough – an excellent water park.

For an interesting place to stay, head to McMenamins Hotel Oregon (☑503-472-8427; www.mcmenamins.com; 310 NE Evans St, McMinnville; d $75-145; ⊛✿☎☎), an older building renovated into a charming hotel. It has a wonderful rooftop bar. And for a spectacular restaurant experience, consider Joel Palmer House (☑503-864-2995; www.joelpalmerhouse.com; 600 Ferry St, McMinnville; prix fixe $49-80; ☺4:30-9:30pm Tue-Sat) ✐; its dishes are peppered with wild mushrooms collected locally by the chefs.

Valley, and most of the other attractions in the area make easy day trips as well. Toward the south is Eugene, a dynamic college town worth a few days of exploration.

Salem

Oregon's legislative center (not the Salem associated with witches, which is in Massachusetts) is renowned for its cherry trees, art-deco capitol building and Willamette University.

Willamette University's Hallie Ford Museum of Art (900 State St; admission adult/ under 12yr $3/free; ⊙10am-5pm Tue-Sat, from 1pm Sun) showcases the state's best collection of Pacific Northwest art, including an impressive Native American gallery.

The Oregon State Capitol (900 Court St NE) FREE, built in 1938, looks like a background prop from a lavish Cecil B DeMille movie; free tours are offered. Rambling 19th-century Bush House (☎503-363-4714; www.salemart.org; 600 Mission St SE; adult/child 6-15yr $6/3; ⊙1-4pm Wed-Sun, closed Jan & Feb) is an Italianate mansion now preserved as a museum with historic accents, including original wallpapers and marble fireplaces.

You can get oriented at the Visitors Information Center (www.travelsalem.com; 181 High St NE; ⊙8:30am-5pm Mon-Fri, 10am-4pm Sat).

Salem is served daily by Greyhound (☎503-362-2428; www.greyhound.com; 500 13th St SE) buses and Amtrak (☎503-588-1551; www.amtrak.com; 500 13th St SE) trains.

Eugene

Eclectic Eugene – also known as 'Tracktown' – is full of youthful energy and liberal politics, and famous for its track-and-field champions (Nike was born here, after all). And while the city maintains a working-class base in timber and manufacturing, some unconventional citizens live here as well, from ex-hippie activists to eco-green anarchists to upscale entrepreneurs to high-tech heads.

Eugene offers a great art scene, exceptionally fine restaurants, boisterous festivals, miles of riverside paths and several lovely parks. It's an awesome place to be, for both energetic visitors and those lucky enough to settle here.

◉ Sights

Alton Baker Park PARK
(100 Day Island Rd) This popular 400-acre riverside park is heaven for cyclists and joggers. It provides access to the Ruth Bascom Riverbank Trail System, a 12-mile cycleway that flanks both sides of the Willamette. The park is divided roughly in half, demarcating wild and manicured areas. Abutting the Willamette River, it connects to the city's wider trail network via three footbridges. Just northwest of Alton Baker Park and on the opposite side of the river, Skinner Butte (682ft) is a landmark hill replete with lawns, hiking trails and a prime city view.

WORTH A TRIP

HOT SPRINGS

Oregon has an abundance of hot springs and there some not far from Salem. A couple of hours' drive east of the city is Bagby Hot Springs (www.bagbyhotsprings.org; per person $5), a rustic hot spring with various wood tubs in semiprivate bathhouses. It's reachable via a 1.5 mile lovely hiking trail. From Estacada, head 26 miles south on Hwy 224. This road turns into Forest Rd 46; keep going straight for 3.5 more miles, then turn right onto Forest Rd 63 and go 3.6 miles to USFS Rd 70. Turn right again and go about 6 miles to the parking area.

There's another good soak at Terwilliger Hot Springs (aka Cougar Hot Springs), a beautiful cluster of terraced outdoor pools framed by large rocks ($6 per person fee). They're rustic but well maintained, with the hottest on top. From the parking lot, you'll have to walk 0.25 miles to the springs. To get here, turn south onto Aufderheide Scenic Byway from Hwy 126 and drive 7.5 miles.

For something more developed, check out Breitenbush Hot Springs (☎503-854-7174; www.breitenbush.com), a fancier spa with massages, yoga and vegetarian food. Breitenbush is east of Salem on Hwy 46, just past the town of Detroit.

University of Oregon

UNIVERSITY

(☑541-346-1000; www.uoregon.edu) Established in 1872, the University of Oregon is the state's foremost institution of higher learning, with a focus on the arts, sciences and law. The campus is filled with historic ivy-covered buildings and includes a **Pioneer Cemetery**, with tombstones that give vivid insight into life and death in the early settlement. A campus highlight is the **Jordan Schnitzer Museum of Art** (☑541-346-3027; www.jsma.uoregon.edu; 1430 Johnson Lane; admission adult/child $5/free; ⊙11am-5pm Tue-Sun, till 8pm Wed), which offers a rotating permanent collection of world-class art from Korean scrolls to Rembrandt paintings. The **Museum of Natural and Cultural History** (☑541-346-3024; http://natural-history.uoregon. edu; 1680 E 15th Ave; adult/3-18yr $3/2, free Wed; ⊙11am-5pm Wed-Sun) is also worth a visit for its Native American exhibits.

🛏 Sleeping

Eugene has all the regular chain hotels and motels. Prices rise sharply during key football games and graduation.

Campus Inn

MOTEL $

(☑541-343-3376; www.campus-inn.com; 390 E Broadway; d $70-80; ⊛❄@🕾🐾) Very pleasant motel with spacious business-style rooms and simple yet stylish decor. Get the $10 upgrade for a bigger bed and more space. Small gym, communal Jacuzzi and upstairs outside patio available.

Eugene Whiteaker Hostel

HOSTEL $

(☑541-343-3335; www.eugenehostels.com; 970 W 3rd Ave; dm incl breakfast $25, r incl breakfast $40-70; ⊛@🕾) Casual hostel in an old rambling house. Artsy vibe, nice front and back patios to hang out in, and a free simple breakfast. Campsites are available ($15 per person), and there's an annex down the street.

★ C'est La Vie Inn

B&B $$

(☑541-302-3014; www.cestlavieinn.com; 1006 Taylor St; d $150-170; ⊛❄@🕾) This gorgeous Victorian house, run by a friendly French woman and her American husband, is a neighborhood show-stopper. Beautiful antique furniture fills the living and dining areas, while the three tastefully appointed rooms offer comfort and luxury. Also available is an amazing suite with kitchenette ($260).

🍴 Eating

Sweet Life Patisserie

CAFE, BAKERY $

(☑541-683-5676; www.sweetlifedesserts.com; 755 Monroe St; pastries $2-5; ⊙7am-11pm Mon-Fri, from 8am Sat & Sun) 🌱 Eugene's best dessert shop; think pecan sticky buns, savory croissants and *pain au chocolat*. Even the day-old pastries it often sells off half-price are delicious. Organic coffee, too.

Belly Taquería

MEXICAN $

(☑541-687-8226; www.eatbelly.com; 291 E 5th Ave; tacos $3-4, tostadas $5-6; ⊙5-9pm Mon-Thu, till 10pm Fri & Sat) Corn tortilla tacos are on tap here – order the *carnitas* (slow-cooked pork), *camarones* (shrimp), scallops (beer-battered and fried) or *lengua* (tongue – don't knock it till you try it).

★ Beppe & Gianni's Trattoria

ITALIAN $$

(☑541-683-6661; www.beppeandgiannis.net; 1646 E 19th Ave; mains $15-25; ⊙5-9pm Sun-Thu, to 10pm Fri & Sat) One of Eugene's most beloved restaurants and certainly its favorite for Italian food. Homemade pastas are the real deal here, and the desserts are excellent. Expect a wait.

McMenamins North Bank

AMERICAN $$

(☑541-343-5622; www.mcmenamins.com; 22 Club Rd; mains $9-20; ⊙11am-11pm Sun-Thu, to midnight Fri & Sat) Gloriously located on the banks of the mighty Willamette, this pub-restaurant boasts some of the best views in Eugene. Grab a riverside patio table on a warm, sunny day and order a cheeseburger with the Hammerhead ale – you can't get more stylin'.

ℹ Information

For information, try the **Visitor Center** (www. eugenecascadecoast.org; 754 Olive St; ⊙8am-5pm Mon-Fri).

ℹ Getting There & Around

Eugene's **Amtrak station** (☑541-687-1383; www.amtrak.com; cnr E 4th Ave & Willamette St) runs daily trains to Vancouver, BC, and LA, and everywhere in between on its *Cascade* and *Coast Starlight* lines. **Greyhound** (☑541-344-6265; www.greyhound.com; 987 Pearl St) runs north to Salem and Portland, and south to Grants Pass and Medford. **Porter Stage Lines** (www. kokkola-bus.com) runs a daily bus from outside the train station to the coast.

Local bus service is provided by **Lane Transit District** (☑541-682-6100; www.ltd.org; 3500

E 17th Ave). For bike rentals, try **Paul's Bicycle Way of Life** (152 W 5th St; ⊙ 9am-7pm Mon-Fri, 10am-5pm Sat & Sun).

Columbia River Gorge

The fourth-largest river in the US by volume, the mighty Columbia runs 1243 miles from Alberta, Canada, into the Pacific Ocean just west of Astoria. For the final 309 miles of its course, the heavily dammed waterway delineates the border between Washington and Oregon and cuts though the Cascade Mountains via the spectacular Columbia River Gorge. Showcasing numerous ecosystems, waterfalls and magnificent vistas, the land bordering the river is protected as a National Scenic Area and is a popular sporting nexus for windsurfers, cyclists, anglers and hikers.

Not far from Portland, Multnomah Falls is a huge tourist draw, while Vista House offers stupendous gorge views. And if you want to stretch your legs, the Eagle Creek Trail is the area's premier tromp – provided you don't get vertigo!

Hood River & Around

Famous for its surrounding fruit orchards and wineries, the small town of Hood River – 63 miles east of Portland on I-84 – is also a huge mecca for windsurfing and kiteboarding. Strong river currents, prevailing westerly winds and the vast Columbia River provide the perfect conditions for these wind sports.

◉ Sights & Activities

In operation since 1906, the 22-mile Mount Hood Railroad (☑ 800-872-4661; www.mthoodrr.com; 110 Railroad Ave) was built to transport lumber to the Columbia River. Today, it transports tourists beneath Mt Hood's snowy peak and past fragrant orchards on summer excusions. Reserve in advance.

Want to go wine tasting? Not far away is Cathedral Ridge Winery (☑ 800-516-8710; www.cathedralridgewinery.com; 4200 Post Canyon Dr).

To partake in Hood River's wind sports, contact Hood River Waterplay (☑ 541-386-9463; www.hoodriverwaterplay.com; Port of Hood River Marina) for rentals and classes. There's also great mountain biking in the area; head to Discover Bicycles (☑ 541-386-4820; www.discoverbicycles.com; 210 State St; ⊙ 10am-6pm Mon-Sat, till 5pm Sun) for information and rentals.

🛏 Sleeping & Eating

Inn of the White Salmon   INN, HOSTEL **$$**
(☑ 509-493-2335; www.innofthewhitesalmon.com; 172 West Jewett Blvd; d $129-189; ⊜ ❀ 🛜) Over in White Salmon, Washington is this very pleasant and contemporary 18-room inn with comfortable rooms and a lovely patio-garden out back. There's also a very nice eight-bed dorm room available (single bunk $29, queen bunk for two $40), along with a common-use kitchenette area.

Hood River Hotel   HISTORIC HOTEL **$$**
(☑ 541-386-1900; www.hoodriverhotel.com; 102 Oak St; d $99-179; ⊜ ❀ 🛜 ❀) Located in downtown Hood River, this fine 1913 hotel offers comfortable old-fashioned rooms with tiny baths. The suites have the best amenities and views. Kitchenettes available.

Double Mountain Brewery   BREWPUB **$**
(☑ 541-387-0042; www.doublemountainbrewery.com; 8 4th St; sandwiches $7.50-10, pizzas $16-22; ⊙ 11:30am-11pm Sun-Thu, till midnight Fri & Sat) This popular Hood River brewpub-restaurant is great for a tasty sandwich, excellent brick-oven pizza and home-brewed beer. Live music on weekends.

❶ Information

For information head to the **chamber of commerce** (☑ 541-386-2000; www.hoodriver.org; 720 E Port Marina Dr; ⊙ 9am-5pm Mon-Fri year-round, 10am-5pm Sat & Sun Apr-Oct).

❶ Getting There & Away

Hood River is connected to Portland by daily **Greyhound** (☑ 541-386-1212; www.greyhound.com; 110 Railroad Ave) buses. **Amtrak** (www.amtrak.com) runs on the Washington side.

Oregon Cascades

The Oregon Cascades offer plenty of dramatic volcanoes that dominate the skyline for miles around. Mt Hood, overlooking the Columbia River Gorge, is the state's highest peak, and has year-round skiing plus a relatively straightforward summit ascent. Tracking south you'll pass Mt Jefferson and the Three Sisters before reaching Crater Lake, the ghost of erstwhile Mt Mazama that collapsed in on itself after blowing its top approximately 7000 years ago.

Mt Hood

The state's highest peak, Mt Hood (11,240ft) pops into view over much of northern Oregon whenever there's a sunny day, exerting an almost magnetic tug on skiers, hikers and sightseers. In summer, wildflowers bloom on the mountainsides and hidden ponds shimmer blue, making for some unforgettable hikes; in winter, downhill and cross-country skiing dominates people's minds and bodies.

Mt Hood is accessible year-round from Portland on US 26 and from Hood River on Hwy 35. Together with the Columbia River Hwy, these routes comprise the Mt Hood Loop, a popular scenic drive. Government Camp is at the pass over Mt Hood, and is the center of business on the mountain.

🏃 Activities

Skiing

Hood is rightly revered for its skiing. There are six ski areas on the mountain, including Timberline (☑503-272-3158; www.timberlinelodge.com; lift ticket adult/child 15-17/child 7-14 $68/56/42), which lures snow-lovers with the only year-round skiing in the US. Closer to Portland, Mt Hood SkiBowl (☑503-272-3206; www.skibowl.com; lift ticket adult/child 7-12 $49/30) is no slacker either. It's the nation's largest night-ski area and popular with city slickers who ride up for an evening of powder play from the metro zone. The largest ski area on the mountain is Mt Hood Meadows (☑503-337-2222; www.skihood.com; lift ticket adult/child 7-14 $74/39) and the best conditions usually prevail here.

Hiking

The Mt Hood National Forest protects an astounding 1200 miles of trails. A Northwest Forest Pass ($5) is required at most trailheads.

One popular trail loops 7 miles from near the village of Zigzag to beautiful Ramona Falls, which tumbles down mossy columnar basalt. Another heads 1.5 miles up from US 26 to Mirror Lake, continues 0.5 miles around the lake, then tracks 2 miles beyond to a ridge.

The 41-mile Timberline Trail circumnavigates Mt Hood through scenic wilderness. Noteworthy portions include the hike to McNeil Point and the short climb to Bald Mountain. From Timberline Lodge, Zigzag Canyon Overlook is a 4.5-mile round-trip. At research time, however, part of the trail was washed out, with no timetable for when it would be repaired.

Climbing Mt Hood should be taken seriously, as deaths do occur. Dog-owners are able to bring their dogs along. The climb can be done in a long day. Contact Timberline Mountain Guides (☑541-312-9242; www.timberlinemtguides.com) for guided climbs.

🍴 Sleeping & Eating

Reserve campsites (☑877-444-6777; www.reserveusa.com; campsites $12-18) in summer. Streamside campgrounds Tollgate and Camp Creek are on US 26. Large and popular Trillium Lake has great views of Mt Hood.

Huckleberry Inn   INN $
(☑503-272-3325; www.huckleberry-inn.com; 88611 E Government Camp Loop; r $85-180; ☺🐾🛜) You'll find simple and comfortably rustic rooms here, including a bunk room that sleeps up to 14. The inn is in a great central location in Government Camp, and has a casual restaurant (which doubles as the hotel's reception). Holiday rates go up by 20%.

★Timberline Lodge   LODGE $$
(☑800-547-1406; www.timberlinelodge.com; d $115-290; ☺🛜🏊) More a community treasure than a hotel, this gorgeous historic wood gem from the 1930s offers a variety of rooms, from bunk rooms that sleep up to 10 to deluxe fireplace rooms. Huge wooden beams tower over multiple fireplaces, there's a year-round heated outdoor pool, and the ski lifts are close by. Enjoy awesome views of Mt Hood, access to nearby hiking trails, and the use of two bars and a good dining room. Not to be missed.

★Rendezvous Grill & Tap Room   AMERICAN $$
(☑503-622-6837; www.rendezvousgrill.net; 67149 E US 26, Welches; lunch mains $9-16, dinner mains $13-22; ⏰11:30am-9pm) This excellent restaurant is in a league of its own. Outstanding dishes include citrus-curry wild salmon and char-grilled pork chop with apple-fennel chutney. Lunch means gourmet sandwiches, burgers and salads on the outdoor patio.

Ice Axe Grill   BREWPUB $$
(☑503-272-3172; www.iceaxegrill.com; 87304 E Government Camp Loop, Government Camp; mains $12-18; ⏰11am-10pm) Government Camp's only brewery-restaurant, the Ice Axe offers a friendly, family-style atmosphere and pub

fare including good pizzas, shepherd's pie and upscale burgers. There are veggie chili and lentil burgers, too.

ℹ Information

If you're approaching from Hood River, visit the **Hood River Ranger Station** (☎ 541-352-6002; 6780 Hwy 35, Parkdale; ⊙ 8am-4:30pm Mon-Fri). The **Zigzag Ranger Station** (☎ 503-622-3191; 70220 E Hwy 26; ⊙ 7:45am-4:30pm Mon-Sat) is more handy for Portland arrivals. **Mt Hood Information Center** (☎ 503-272-3301; 88900 E US 26; ⊙ 9am-5pm) is in Government Camp. The weather changes quickly here; carry chains in winter.

ℹ Getting There & Away

From Portland, Mt Hood is one hour (56 miles) by car along Hwy 26. Alternatively, you can take the prettier and longer approach via Hwy 84 to Hood River, then Hwy 35 south (1¾ hours, 95 miles). The **Central Oregon Breeze** (☎ 800-847-0157; www.cobreeze.com) shuttle between Bend and Portland stops briefly at Government Camp, 6 miles from the Timberline Lodge. There are regular **shuttles** (www.skihood.com) from Portland to the ski areas during the winter.

Sisters

Straddling the Cascades and high desert, where mountain pine forests mingle with desert sage and juniper, is the darling town of Sisters. Once a stagecoach stop and a trade town for loggers and ranchers, today Sisters is a bustling tourist destination whose main street is lined with boutiques, art galleries and eateries housed in Western-facade buildings. Visitors come for the mountain scenery, spectacular hiking, fine cultural events and awesome climate – there's plenty of sun and little precipitation here. And while the town's atmosphere is a bit upscale, people are still friendly and the back streets are still undeveloped enough that deer are often seen nibbling in neighborhood garden plots.

At the southern end of Sisters, the city park has camp sites ($15) but no showers. For ultracomfort, bag a room in the luxurious Five Pine Lodge (☎ 866-974-5900; www.fivepinelodge.com; 1021 Desperado Trail; d $170-257, cabins $179-317; ❄✿❀✿✿). On the quieter and cheaper side is Sisters Motor Lodge (☎ 541-549-2551; www.sistersmotorlodge.com; 511 W Cascade St; r $119-225; ❄✿✿✿), offering 11 cozy rooms with homey decor (and some with kitchenettes).

For great gourmet treats head to Porch (☎ 541-549-3287; www.theporch-sisters.com; 243 N Elm St; small plates $6-12, mains $15-17; ⊙ 5-9pm Tue-Sat), which offers morsels such as truffle fries and creamy butternut-squash risotto. Three Creeks Brewing (☎ 541-549-1963; www.threecreeksbrewing.com; 721 Desperado Ct; ⊙ 11:30am-10pm Sun-Thu, till 11pm Fri & Sat) is the place to go for home brew and pub grub.

For local orientation, see the chamber of commerce (☎ 541-549-0251; www.sisterscountry.com; 291 Main St; ⊙ 10am-4pm Mon-Sat).

Valley Retriever (www.kokkola-bus.com/VRBSchedule.html) buses connect Sisters with Bend, Newport, Corvallis, Salem, McMinnville and Portland; they stop at the corner of Cascade and Spruce Sts.

Bend

Bend is where all outdoor-lovers should live – it's an absolute paradise. You can ski fine powder in the morning, paddle a kayak in the afternoon and take in a game of golf into the evening. Or would you rather go mountain biking, hiking, mountaineering, stand-up paddleboarding, fly-fishing or rock climbing? It's all close by, and top-drawer. Plus, you'll probably be enjoying it all in great weather, as the area gets nearly 300 days of sunshine each year.

With the lovely Deschutes River carving its way through the heart of the city, Bend also offers a vibrant and attractive downtown area full of shops, galleries and upscale dining. South of downtown, the Old Mill District has been renovated into a large shopping area full of brand-name stores, fancy eateries and modern movie theaters. Bend has also become a beer-lover's dream; it has more than a dozen breweries and per capita more than any other city in Oregon.

◉ Sights

★ **High Desert Museum**　　　　MUSEUM
(☎ 541-382-4754; www.highdesertmuseum.org; 59800 S US 97; adult/child 5-12yr May-Oct $15/9, Nov-Apr $12/7; ⊙ 9am-5pm; 🚗) Don't miss this excellent museum about 3 miles south of Bend on US 97. It charts the exploration and settlement of the West, using re-enactments of a Native American camp, a hard-rock mine and an old Western town. The region's natural history is also explored; kids love the live snake, tortoise and trout exhibits, and watching the birds of prey and otters is always fun.

⚡ Activities

Cycling

Bend is a mountain-biking paradise, with hundreds of miles of awesome bike trails to explore. For a good bike-trails map, get the *Bend, Central Oregon Mountain Biking and XC Skiing* map ($12), available at the Visit Bend tourist office and elsewhere.

The king of Bend's mountain-biking trails is Phil's Trail network, which offers a variety of excellent fast single-track forest trails just minutes from town. If you want to catch air, don't miss the Whoops Trail.

Cog Wild (www.cogwild.com; 255 SW Century Dr) offers bike rentals, along with organized tours and shuttles out to the best trailheads.

Rock Climbing

About 25 miles northeast of Bend lies Smith Rock State Park (☎800-551-6949; www.ore-gonstateparks.org; 9241 NE Crooked River Dr; day use $5), where 800ft cliffs over the Crooked River offer gorgeous lead and trad climbing. The park's 1800-plus routes are among the best in the nation. Guides can be procured through Smith Rock Climbing Guides Inc (www.smithrockclimbingguides.com).

Skiing

Bend hosts Oregon's best skiing 22 miles southwest of the town at the glorious Mount Bachelor Ski Resort (☎800-829-2442; www.mtbachelor.com; lift tickets adult/child 6-12yr/child 13-18yr $59/36/49), famous for its 'dry' powdery snow, long season (until late May) and ample terrain (it's the largest ski area in the Pacific Northwest). The mountain has long advocated cross-country skiing in tandem with downhill, and maintains 35 miles of groomed trails.

🛏 Sleeping

Mill Inn   INN $
(☎877-748-1200, 541-389-9198; www.millinn.com; 642 NW Colorado Ave; dm $35, d incl breakfast $90-130; ❄🖥) A 10-room boutique hotel with small, classy rooms decked out in velvet drapes and comforters; four share outside bathrooms. Full breakfast and hot tub use is included, and there's a nice back patio and basement recreation room. Budget travelers should go for the one (tight) dorm room.

★McMenamins Old
St Francis School   HOTEL $$
(☎541-382-5174; www.mcmenamins.com; 700 NW Bond St; d $135-175, cottages $185-395; ❄✳🖥) One of McMenamins' best venues, this old schoolhouse has been remodeled into a classy 19-room hotel. Two rooms have side-by-side clawfoot tubs, and the fabulous tiled saltwater Turkish bath is worth the stay alone, though nonguests can soak for $5. A restaurant-pub, three other bars, a cinema and creative artwork complete the picture.

★Oxford Hotel   BOUTIQUE HOTEL $$$
(☎877-440-8436; www.oxfordhotelbend.com; 10 NW Minnesota Ave; d $289-549; ❄✳🖥) 🅿 Bend's premier and very popular boutique hotel. The smallest rooms are huge (470 sq ft) and decked out with eco-features including soy-foam mattresses and cork flooring. High-tech aficionados will love the iPod docks and smart-panel work desk. Suites with kitchen and steam shower are available, and the basement restaurant is slick.

🍴 Eating & Drinking

★Chow   AMERICAN $$
(☎541-728-0256; www.chowbend.com; 1110 NW Newport Ave; mains $8-14; ⊙7am-2pm) 🅿 The signature poached-egg dishes here are spectacular and beautifully presented, served with sides such as crab cakes, house-cured ham and corn-meal-crusted tomatoes (don't miss their homemade hot sauces). Or try the caramelized banana French toast, or bacon biscuits with thyme. Gourmet sandwiches and salads are available for lunch, with many vegetables grown in the garden. Good cocktails, too.

Jackson's Corner   AMERICAN $$
(☎541-647-2198; www.jacksonscornerbendor.com; 845 NW Delaware Ave; mains $10-26; ⊙7am-9pm; 🖲) This homey corner restaurant has a market-like feel and is very popular with families. Homemade pizzas and pastas are always tasty, as are the organic salads (add on chicken, steak or prawns). There's a kids menu, and outside seating for sunny days; just remember to order at the counter first.

Deschutes Brewery
& Public House   BREWERY
(☎541-382-9242; www.deschutesbrewery.com; 1044 NW Bond St; ⊙11am-11pm Mon-Thu, till midnight Fri & Sat, till 10pm Sun) Bend's first microbrewery serves up handcrafted beers, including Mirror Pond Pale Ale, Black Butte Porter and Obsidian Stout, and plenty of food at their beautiful huge two-story restaurant with balcony seating. Free daily tours run every hour from 1pm tp 4pm at the plant, located at 901 SW Simpson Ave.

Crux BREWERY

(☑541-385-3333; www.cruxfermentation.com; 50 SW Division St; ⊙11:30am-10pm Tue-Sun) Bend's latest brewpub darling, located in an industrial neighborhood (don't let the 'private road' signs put you off). It has an awesome casual atmosphere. Fermentation tanks behind glass windows house the unique, experimental beers. There's outdoor seating, it's family-friendly and has a good range of foods made with beer.

❶ Information

For local information, see the **Visit Bend** (☑800-949-6086; www.visitbend.com; 750 NW Lava Rd; ⊙9am-5pm Mon-Fri, 10am-4pm Sat) tourist office.

❶ Getting There & Away

Central Oregon Breeze (p230) offers transport to Portland two or more times daily. Connect to Sisters, Willamette Valley destinations and the coast with Valley Retriever (p230) and **Porter Stage Lines** (www.kokkola-bus.com/PSLSchedule.html).

High Desert Point (www.highdesert-point.com) buses link Bend with Chemult, where the nearest train station is located (65 miles south). High Desert Point also has bus services to Eugene, Ontario and Burns.

Cascades East Transit (www.cascadeseast-transit.com) is the regional bus company in Bend, covering La Pine, Mt Bachelor, Sisters, Prineville and Madras. It also provides bus transport within Bend.

Newberry National Volcanic Monument

Newberry National Volcanic Monument (day use $5) showcases 400,000 years of dramatic seismic activity. Start your visit at the Lava Lands Visitor Center (☑541-593-2421; 58201 S Hwy 97; ⊙9am-5pm mid-June to Labor Day weekend, limited hours off-season), 13 miles south of Bend. Nearby attractions include Lava Butte, a perfect cone rising 500ft, and Lava River Cave, Oregon's longest lava tube. Four miles west of the visitor center is Benham Falls, a good picnic spot on the Deschutes River.

Newberry Crater was once one of the most active volcanoes in North America, but after a large eruption a caldera was born. Close by are Paulina Lake and East Lake, deep lakes rich with trout, while looming above is 7985ft Paulina Peak.

Crater Lake National Park

It's no exaggeration: Crater Lake is so blue, you'll catch your breath. And if you get to see it on a calm day, the surrounding cliffs are reflected in those deep waters like a mirror. It's a stunningly beautiful sight. Crater Lake is Oregon's only national park (entry costs $10 per vehicle).

The secret lies in the water's purity. No rivers or streams feed the lake, meaning its content is made up entirely of rain and melted snow. It is also exceptionally deep – at 1949ft, it's the deepest lake in the US. The classic tour is the 33-mile rim drive (open from approximately June to mid-October), but there are also exceptional hiking and cross-country skiing opportunities. Note that because the area receives some of the highest snowfalls in North America, the rim drive and north entrance are sometimes closed up until early July.

You can stay from late May to mid-October at the Cabins at Mazama Village (☑541-830-8700; www.craterlakelodges.com; d $140; ⊖) or the majestic and historic Crater Lake Lodge (☑888-774-2728; www.craterlakelodges.com; d $165-292; ⊖ 🛜), opened in 1915. Campers head to Mazama Campground (☑888-774-2728; www.craterlakelodges.com; tent/RV sites from $21/29; 🛜 🛉).

For more information, head to Steel Visitor Center (☑541-594-3100; ⊙9am-5pm May-Oct, 10am-4pm Nov-Apr).

Southern Oregon

With a warm and sunny climate that belongs in nearby California, southern Oregon is the state's banana belt. Rugged landscapes, scenic rivers and a couple of attractive towns top the highlights list.

Ashland

Oregon was unknown territory to the Elizabethan explorers of William Shakespeare's day, so it might seem a little strange to find that the pretty settlement of Ashland in southern Oregon has established itself as the English playwright's second home. The irony probably wouldn't have been lost on Shakespeare himself. 'All the world's a stage,' the great Bard once opined, and fittingly people come from all over to see Ashland's famous Shakespeare Festival, which has been held here under various guises since

OREGON SHAKESPEARE FESTIVAL

One of southern Oregon's highlights is Ashland's wildly popular Oregon Shakespeare Festival (OSF). Despite being deeply rooted in Shakespearean and Elizabethan drama, the festival also features plenty of revivals and contemporary theater from around the world.

Productions run from February to October in three theaters near Main and Pioneer Sts: the outdoor Elizabethan Theatre (open from June to October), the Angus Bowmer Theatre and the intimate Thomas Theatre. Children under six are not allowed. There are no performances on Mondays.

Performances sell out quickly; obtain tickets at www.osfashland.org. The box office (☎541-482-4331; 15 S Pioneer St; tickets $25-95) also has last minute tickets. Be sure to book backstage tours (adult/child 6-17yr $15/11) well in advance.

Check the OSF Welcome Center (76 N Main St; ⏰10am-6pm Tue-Sun) for other events, which may include scholarly lectures, play readings, concerts and preshow talks.

the 1930s. The 'festival' moniker is misleading; the shows here are a semipermanent fixture occupying nine months of the annual town calendar and attracting up to 400,000 theater-goers per season.

Even without the shows, Ashland is an attractive town, propped up by various wineries, upscale B&Bs and fine restaurants.

◉ Sights & Activities

Lithia Park   PARK
(59 Winburn Way) Adjacent to Ashland's three splendid theaters (one of which is outdoors) lies one of the loveliest city parks in Oregon, whose 93 acres wind along Ashland Creek above the center of town. Unusually, the park is in the National Register of Historic Places and is embellished with fountains, flowers, gazebos and an ice-skating rink (winter only).

Schneider Museum of Art   MUSEUM
(☎541-552-6245; www.sou.edu/sma; 1250 Siskiyou Blvd; suggested donation $5; ⏰10am-4pm Mon-Sat) Like all good Oregonian art museums, this one's on the local university campus and displays a fine collection of paintings, sculptures and artifacts.

Jackson Wellsprings   SPA
(☎541-482-3776; www.jacksonwellsprings.com; 2253 Hwy 99; ⏰8am-midnight, shorter hours winter) For a good soak, try this casual New Age–style place, which maintains an 85°F (29°C) mineral-fed swimming pool and 103°F (39°C) private soaking tubs. It's about a mile north of town.

Mt Ashland Ski Resort   SKI RESORT
(☎541-482-2897; www.mtashland.com; lift pass adult/child 7-12yr $43/33) Powdery snow is surprisingly abundant at this resort 18 miles

southwest of Ashland on Mt Ashland (7533ft), which has some excellent advanced terrain.

Siskiyou Cyclery   BICYCLE RENTAL
(☎541-482-1997; www.siskiyoucyclery.com; 1729 Siskiyou Blvd; ⏰10am-6pm Mon-Sat, 11am-4pm Sun) Pedal-pushers can rent a bike here and explore the countryside on the semi-completed Bear Creek Greenway, a 21-mile bike path between Ashland and the town of Central Point.

🛏 Sleeping

Reserve ahead in summer when the thespians descend in droves.

Manor Motel   MOTEL $
(☎541-482-2246; www.manormotel.net; 476 N Main St; d $87-129; ❀❄🐾📶) Cute motel with 12 pleasant rooms and one- and two-bedroom units near downtown; kitchenettes available. The Garden Suite has its own private garden.

Ashland Hostel   HOSTEL $
(☎541-482-9217; www.theashlandhostel.com; 150 N Main St; dm $28, d $45-94; ❀❄📶) Central and somewhat upscale hostel (shoes-off inside!). Most private rooms share bathrooms; some are connected to dorms. Hangout spaces include the cozy basement living room and shady front porch. No alcohol or smoking on premises; call ahead as reception times are limited.

Ashland Commons   APARTMENTS, HOSTEL $
(☎541-482-6753; www.ashlandcommons.com; 437 Williamson Way; dm $26, s $45-65, d $60-80; ❀❄📶) Interesting dorm or private-room accommodations, provided within three large apartments. All vary in atmosphere, and are either two- or four-bedroom, with

kitchen and living areas. Great for large groups, as entire apartments can be rented.

The Palm
BOUTIQUE HOTEL $$

(☑541-482-2636; www.palmcottages.com; 1065 Siskiyou Blvd; d $98-239; ❄✴🐾🐕🐾) Fabulous small motel remodeled into 16 charming garden cottage rooms and suites (some with kitchens). It's an oasis of green on a busy avenue, complete with grassy lawns and a saltwater pool. A house harbors three large suites ($299).

Columbia Hotel
HOTEL $$

(☑541-482-3726; www.columbiahotel.com; 262 1/2 E Main St; d $89-179; ❄✴🐾) Awesomely located 'European-style' hotel – which means most rooms share outside bathrooms. It's the best deal in downtown Ashland, with 24 quaint vintage rooms (no TVs), a nice lobby and a thick historic feel. The rooms are on the 2nd floor and there's no elevator.

🍴 Eating & Drinking

There are plenty of great eating choices in Ashland, which levies a 5% restaurant tax. Dinner reservations in summer are a good idea at the fancier spots.

★ Morning Glory
CAFE $

(☑541-488-8636; www.morninggloryrestaurant.com; 1149 Siskiyou Blvd; mains $11-13; ⊙8am-1:30pm) This colorful, casual cafe is one of Ashland's best breakfast joints. Creative dishes include the Alaskan crab omelet, vegetarian hash with roasted chilis and shrimp cakes with poached eggs. For lunch there's gourmet salad and sandwiches. Go early or late to avoid a long wait.

Ashland Food Cooperative
SELF-CATERING $

(☑541-482-2237; www.ashlandfood.coop; 237 N 1st St; ⊙7am-9pm) Head to this awesome food co-op if you've scored a kitchenette in your hotel room. All the typical healthy foods are available, and there's a small cafe-deli and to-go food bar.

★ New Sammy's Cowboy Bistro
FRENCH, AMERICAN $$$

(☑541-535-2779; 2210 S Pacific Hwy, Talent; mains $25-28, prix fixe $45; ⊙noon-1:30 & 5-9pm Wed-Sun) 🌿 One of Oregon's best restaurants has only a handful of tables and a spectacular wine selection. Mains are few but the flavor combinations can be incredible; many vegetables come from the garden outside. Located in Talent, about 2 miles north of Ashland. Reserve a week in advance for dinner.

Caldera Tap House
BREWPUB

(☑541-482-4677; www.calderabrewing.com; 31 Water St; ⊙2pm-close) Popular, casual brewpub with outdoor decks under a street overpass. Typical pub grub accompanied by award-winning ales and lagers; live music two to three times per week. Also has a fancier restaurant at 590 Clover St.

ℹ Information

For information, visit the **Chamber of Commerce** (☑541-482-3486; www.ashlandchamber.com; 110 E Main St; ⊙9am-5pm Mon-Fri).

Jacksonville

This small but endearing former gold-prospecting town is the oldest settlement in southern Oregon and a National Historic Landmark. The main drag is lined with well-preserved buildings dating from the 1880s, now converted into boutiques and galleries. Music-lovers shouldn't miss the September Britt Festival (www.brittfest.org; ⊙Jun-Sep), a world-class musical experience with top-name performers. Seek more enlightenment at the Chamber of Commerce (☑541-899-8118; www.jacksonvilleoregon.org; 185 N Oregon St; ⊙10am-5pm Mon-Fri, till 3pm Sat & Sun).

Jacksonville is full of fancy B&Bs; for budget motels head 6 miles east to Medford. The Jacksonville Inn (☑541-899-1900; www.jacksonvilleinn.com; 175 E California St; d $159-199; ❄✴🐾🐕🐾) is the most pleasant abode, shoe-horned downtown in an 1863 building with regal antique-stuffed rooms. There's a fine restaurant on-site.

Wild Rogue Wilderness

Situated between the town of Grants Pass on I-5 and Gold Beach on the Oregon coast, the aptly named Wild Rogue Wilderness is anchored by the turbulent Rogue River, which cuts through 40 miles of untamed, roadless canyon. The area is known for challenging white-water rafting (classes III and IV) and long-distance hikes.

The humble city of Grants Pass is the gateway to adventures along the Rogue. For information, the chamber of commerce (☑541-450-6180; www.visitgrantspass.org; 1995 NW Vine St; ⊙8am-5pm Mon-Fri) is right off I-5, exit 58. For raft permits and backpacking advice, contact the Bureau of Land Management's Smullin Visitors Center (☑541-479-3735; www.blm.gov/or/resources/recreation/rogue;

14335 Galice Rd, Galice; ⊙ 7am-3pm) in Galice, 16 miles northwest of Grants Pass.

Rafting the Rogue is legendary, but not for the faint of heart; a typical trip takes three days and costs upward of $780. A good outfitter is **Rogue Wilderness Adventures** (✆ 800-336-1647; www.wildrogue.com; 325 Galice Rd, Merlin). Kayaking the river is equally exhilarating; for instruction and guidance, contact **Sundance Kayak** (✆ 541-386-1725; www.sundancekayak.com).

Another highlight of the region is the 42-mile **Rogue River Trail**, once a supply route from Gold Beach. The full trek takes four to five days; day hikers might aim for Whiskey Creek Cabin, a 6-mile round-trip from the Grave Creek trailhead. The trail is dotted with rustic lodges ($110 to $160 per person including meals; reservations required) – try **Black Bar** (✆ 541-479-6507; www.blackbarlodge.com; Merlin). There are also primitive campgrounds along the way.

North Umpqua River

This 'Wild and Scenic' river boasts world-class fly-fishing, fine hiking and serene camping. The 79-mile **North Umpqua Trail** begins near Idleyld Park, three miles east of Glide, and passes through Steamboat en route to the Pacific Crest Trail. A popular sideline is pretty **Umpqua Hot Springs**, east of Steamboat near Toketee Lake. Not far away, stunning, two-tiered **Toketee Falls** (113ft) flows over columnar basalt, while **Watson Falls** (272ft) is one of the highest waterfalls in Oregon. For information, stop by Glide's **Colliding Rivers Information Center** (✆ 541-496-0157; 18782 N Umpqua Hwy, Glide; ⊙ 9am-5pm May-Sep). Adjacent is the **North Umpqua Ranger District** (✆ 541-496-3532; 18782 N Umpqua Hwy; ⊙ 8am-4:30pm Mon-Fri).

Between Idleyld Park and Diamond Lake are dozens of riverside campgrounds; these include lovely **Susan Creek** and primitive **Boulder Flat** (no water). Area accommodations fill up quickly in summer; try the log-cabin-like rooms at **Dogwood Motel** (✆ 541-496-3403; www.dogwoodmotel.com; 28866 N Umpqua Hwy; d $70-75; ❄ ✽ 🛜 🐾).

Oregon Caves National Monument

This very popular cave (there's only one) lies 19 miles east of Cave Junction on Hwy 46. Three miles of passages are explored via 90-minute cave tours that include 520 rocky steps and dripping chambers running along the River Styx. Dress warmly, wear shoes with good traction and be prepared to get dripped on.

Cave Junction, 28 miles south of Grants Pass on US 199 (Redwood Hwy), provides the region's services – though the best area sleeps are at the **Holiday Motel** (✆ 541-592-3003; 24810 Redwood Hwy; d $68-78; ❄ ✽ 🛜), two miles north in Kerby. For fancy lodgings right at the cave there's the impressive **Oregon Caves Chateau** (✆ 541-592-3400; www.oregoncaveschateau.com; 20000 Caves Hwy; r $109-199; ⊙ mid-May to late Sep; ❄); grab a milkshake at the old-fashioned soda fountain here. Campers should head to **Cave Creek Campground** (✆ 541-592-4000; campsites $10), 14 miles up Hwy 46, about 4 miles from the cave.

Eastern Oregon

Oregon east of the Cascades bears little resemblance to its wetter western cohort, either physically or culturally. Few people live here – the biggest town, Pendleton, numbers only 20,000 – and the region hoards high plateaus, painted hills, alkali lake beds and the country's deepest river gorge.

John Day Fossil Beds National Monument

Within the soft rocks and crumbly soils of John Day country lies one of the world's greatest fossil collections, laid down between six and 50 million years ago. Roaming the forests at the time were nimravids (false saber-toothed cats), pint-sized horses, bear-dogs and other early mammals.

The national monument includes 22 sq miles at three different units: Sheep Rock Unit, Painted Hills Unit and Clarno Unit. Each has hiking trails and interpretive displays. To visit all of the units in one day requires quite a bit of driving, as more than 100 slow miles of curvy roads separate the fossil beds – it's best to take it easy and spend the night somewhere.

Visit the excellent **Thomas Condon Paleontology Center** (✆ 541-987-2333; www.nps.gov/joda; 32651 Hwy 19, Kimberly; ⊙ 10am-5pm, occasionally closed due to short staffing), 2 miles north of US 26 at the **Sheep Rock Unit**. Displays include a three-toed horse and petrified dung-beetle balls, along with many other fossils and geologic history exhibits. If you feel like walking, take the short hike up the Blue Basin Trail.

The Painted Hills Unit, near the town of Mitchell, consists of low-slung, colorfully banded hills formed about 30 million years ago. Ten million years older is the Clarno Unit, which exposes mud flows that washed over an Eocene-era forest and eroded into distinctive, sheer white cliffs topped with spires and turrets of stone.

Rafting is popular on the John Day River, the longest free-flowing river in the state. Oregon River Experiences (☑800-827-1358; www.oregonriver.com) offers trips of up to five days. There's also good fishing for smallmouth bass and rainbow trout; find out more at the Oregon Department of Fish & Wildlife (www.dfw.state.or.us).

Most towns in the area have at least one hotel; these include the atmospheric Historic Oregon Hotel (☑541-462-3027; 104 E Main St; dm $20, d $45-69; 🐾) in Mitchell and economical Dreamers Lodge (☑800-654-2849; 144 N Canyon Blvd; d from $63; 😊❄🐾🐕) in the town of John Day (which has most of the area's services). There are several public campgrounds in the area, including Lone Pine and Big Bend (camp sites $5) on Hwy 402.

Wallowa Mountains Area

The Wallowa Mountains, with their glacier-hewn peaks and crystalline lakes, are among the most beautiful natural areas in Oregon. The only drawback is the large number of visitors who flock here in summer, especially to the pretty Wallowa Lake area. Escape them all on one of several long hikes into the nearby Eagle Cap Wilderness area, such as the 6-mile one-way jaunt to Aneroid Lake or the 8-mile trek on the Ice Lake Trail.

Just north of the mountains, in the Wallowa Valley, Enterprise is a homely backcountry town with several motels such as the Ponderosa (☑541-426-3186; 102 E Greenwood St; d $70-80; ❄🐾🐕). If you like beer and good food, don't miss the town's microbrewery, Terminal Gravity Brewing (☑541-426-3000; www.terminalgravitybrewing. com; 803 SE School St; mains $9-12; ☉11am-9pm Sun-Tue, till 10pm Wed-Sat). Just 6 miles south of Enterprise's fancy cousin, the upscale town of Joseph. Expensive bronze galleries and artsy boutiques line the main strip, along with some good eateries.

Hells Canyon

North America's deepest river gorge (yes – even deeper than the Grand Canyon when measured from the highest mountain peak) provides visitors with some wild and scenic vistas. The mighty Snake River has taken 13 million years to carve its path through the high plateaus of eastern Oregon to its present depth of 8000ft. The canyon itself is a true wilderness bereft of roads but open to the curious and the brave.

For perspective, drive 30 miles northeast from Joseph to Imnaha, where a slow-going 24-mile gravel road leads up to the excellent lookout at Hat Point. From here you can see the Wallowa Mountains, Idaho's Seven Devils, the Imnaha River and the wilds of the canyon itself. This road is open from late May until snowfall; give yourself two hours each way for the drive.

For white-water action and spectacular scenery, head down to Hells Canyon Dam, 25 miles north of the small community of Oxbow. A few miles past the dam, the road ends at the Hells Canyon Visitor Center (☑541-785-3395; ☉8am-4pm May-Sep), which has good advice on the area's campgrounds and hiking trails. Beyond here, the Snake River drops 1300ft in elevation through wild rapids accessible only by jet boat or raft. Hells Canyon Adventures (☑800-422-3568; www.hellscan-yonadventures.com) is the main operator running raft trips and jet-boat tours from May through September (reservations required).

The area has many campgrounds. Just outside Imnaha is the huntsman-style Imnaha River Inn (☑866-601-9214; www. imnahariverinn.com; 73946 Rimrock Rd; s/d from $70/130), a B&B replete with Hemingway-esque animal trophies, while Oxbow has the good-value Hells Canyon B&B (☑541-785-3373; www.hcbb.us; 49922 Homestead Rd; d $80; 😊❄🐾). For more services, head to the towns of Enterprise, Joseph and Halfway.

Steens Mountain & Alvord Desert

The highest peak in southeastern Oregon, Steens Mountain (9773ft) is part of a massive, 30-mile-long fault-block range that was formed about 15 million years ago. On the western slope of the range, Ice Age glaciers bulldozed trenches that formed massive U-shaped gorges and hanging valleys. To the east, 'the Steens' – as the range is usually referred to as – drop off to the Alvord Desert, 5000ft below.

Beginning in Frenchglen (population 12), the gravel 56-mile Steens Mountain Loop Rd is Oregon's highest road and offers the range's best sights with its awesome overlooks, and also has access to camping and hiking trails. You'll see sagebrush, bands of junipers and aspen forests, and finally fragile rocky tundra at the top. Kiger Gorge viewpoint is especially stunning; it's 25 miles up from Frenchglen. It takes about two hours all the way around if you're just driving through, but you'll want to see the sights so give yourself much more time. You can also see the eastern side of the Steens via the Fields-Denio road, which goes through the Alvord Desert between Hwys 205 and 78. Take a full tank of gas and plenty of water, and be prepared for weather changes at any time of year.

Frenchglen has the charming Frenchglen Hotel (☎ 541-493-2825; fghotel@yahoo.com; 39184 Hwy 205, Frenchglen; d $75-115; ☺ mid-Mar–Oct; ☻❄❅), with its small dining room (reserve for dinners), a small store with seasonal gas pump and not much else. There are camping options on the Steens Mountain Loop Rd, such as the BLM's pretty Page Springs, open year-round. A few other campgrounds (sites $6 to $8), further into the loop, are very pleasant but accessible in summer only. Water is available at all of these campgrounds. Free backcountry camping is also allowed in the Steens.

Oregon Coast

Thanks to a farsighted government in the 1910s, Oregon's 363-mile Pacific Coast was set aside as public land. This magnificent littoral is paralleled by US 101, a scenic highway that winds its way through towns, resorts, state parks (more than 70 of them) and wilderness areas. Everyone from campers to gourmet-lovers will find a plethora of ways to enjoy this exceptional region.

Astoria

Astoria sits at the 5-mile-wide mouth of the Columbia River and was the first US settlement west of the Mississippi. The city has a long seafaring history and has seen its old harbor, once home to poor artists and writers, attract fancy hotels and restaurants in recent years. Inland are many historical houses, including lovingly restored Victorians – a few converted into romantic B&Bs.

⊙ Sights

Adding to the city's scenery is the 4.1-mile Astoria-Megler Bridge, the longest continuous truss bridge in North America, which crosses the Columbia River into Washington State. See it from the Astoria Riverwalk, which follows the trolley route. Pier 39 is an interesting covered wharf with an informal cannery museum and a couple places to eat.

★ Columbia River
Maritime Museum   MUSEUM
(☑ 503-325-2323; www.crmm.org; 1792 Marine Dr; adult/child 6-17yr $12/5; ☺ 9:30am-5pm) Astoria's seafaring heritage is well interpreted at this wave-shaped museum. It's hard to miss the Coast Guard boat, frozen in action, through the huge outside window. Other exhibits highlight the salmon-packing industry, local lighthouses and the river's commercial history; also check out the Columbia River Bar exhibit and 3-D theater.

Flavel House   HISTORIC BUILDING
(www.cumtux.org; 441 8th St; adult/child 6-17yr $5/4; ☺ 10am-5pm) The Queen Anne Flavel House was built by Captain George Flavel, one of Astoria's leading citizens during the 1880s.

Astoria Column   LANDMARK
(☑ 503-325-2963; www.astoriacolumn.org; Coxcomb Hill; parking $1) Rising high on Coxcomb Hill, the Astoria Column (1926) is a 125ft tower painted with scenes from the westward sweep of US exploration and settlement. The top of the column (up 164 steps) offers excellent views over the area.

Fort Stevens State Park   PARK
(☑ 503-861-1671; www.oregonstateparks.org; 100 Peter Iredale Rd, Hammond; day use $5) Ten miles west of Astoria, this park holds the historic military installation that guarded the mouth of the Columbia River. Near the Military Museum (☑ 503-861-2000; ☺ 10am-6pm May-Sep, to 4pm Oct-Apr) FREE are gun batteries dug into sand dunes – interesting remnants of the fort's mostly demolished military buildings. There's a popular beach at the small Peter Iredale 1906 shipwreck, plus camping and 12 miles of paved bike trails.

🛌 Sleeping & Eating

Norblad Hotel & Hostel   HOTEL, HOSTEL $
(☑ 503-325-6989; www.norbladhotel.com; 443 14th St; dm $30, d $59-89; ☻❅❆) This central option offers six simple but elegant private

LEWIS & CLARK: JOURNEY'S END

In November 1805 William Clark and fellow explorer Meriwether Lewis of the Corps of Discovery staggered, with three dozen others, into a sheltered cove on the Columbia River, 2 miles from the present-day Astoria-Megler Bridge, completing what was indisputably the greatest overland trek in US history.

After the first truly democratic ballot in US history (in which a woman and a black slave both voted), the party elected to make their bivouac 5 miles south of Astoria at Fort Clatsop, where the Corps spent a miserable winter in 1805–06. Today this site is called the Lewis and Clark National & State Historical Parks (www.nps.gov/lewi), where you'll find a reconstructed Fort Clatsop, along with a visitor's center and historical reenactments in summer.

rooms, most with shared bathroom and one with en-suite ($74). There are also several dorm rooms and a communal kitchen. Some have flat-screen TVs and glimpses of the river.

★ **Commodore Hotel** BOUTIQUE HOTEL **$$**
(☎503-325-4747; www.commodoreastoria.com; 258 14th St; d with shared/private bath from $89/149; ☻☎) Hip travelers should beeline to this slick and trendy hotel, which offers small, chic, minimalist rooms. Choose either private bathrooms or go euro-style (sinks in rooms but baths down the hall). Great living room–style lobby with attached cafe. Room 309 has the best river view.

Blue Scorcher Bakery Café CAFE **$**
(☎503-338-7473; www.bluescorcher.com; 1493 Duane St; mains $7-13; ☻8am-5pm; ☑⊞) ✐ Artsy, organic co-op cafe and bakery. Tasty salads, sandwiches, pizza and egg dishes for breakfast. Vegetarian friendly; doughnut-free.

Fort George Brewery BREWPUB **$$**
(☎503-325-7468; www.fortgeorgebrewery.com; 1483 Duane St; mains $9-14; ☻11am-11pm Mon-Thu, till midnight Fri & Sat, noon-11pm Sun) Atmospheric brewery-restaurant in a historic building – this was the original settlement site of Astoria. Today you can get gourmet burgers, homemade sausages, organic salads and a few eclectic dishes. Afternoon brewery tours on weekends.

❶ Information

Find local information head to the **visitor center** (www.oldoregon.com; 111 W Marine Dr; ☻9am-5pm).

❶ Getting There & Away

Twice-daily **Northwest Point** (☎503-484-4100; www.northwest-point.com) buses head to Seaside, Cannon Beach and Portland. **Sunset Empire Transit** (☎503-861-7433; www.ridethe-bus.org; 900 Marine Dr) provides local transport; buses also head to Warrenton, Cannon Beach and Seaside.

Cannon Beach

Charming Cannon Beach is one of the most popular and upscale beach resorts on the Oregon coast. The streets are full of boutiques and galleries, and lined with colorful flowers. Lodging is pricy, and the streets are jammed; on a warm sunny Saturday, you'll spend a good chunk of time just finding a parking spot.

❂ Sights & Activities

Photogenic Haystack Rock, a 295ft sea stack, is the most spectacular landmark on the Oregon coast and accessible from the beach at low tide. Birds cling to its ballast cliffs and tide pools ring its base.

The coast to the north, protected inside Ecola State Park (☎503-436-2844; day use $5), is the Oregon you may have already visited in your dreams: sea stacks, crashing surf, hidden beaches and gorgeous pristine forest. The park is 1.5 miles from town and is crisscrossed by paths, including part of the Oregon Coast Trail, which leads over Tillamook Head to the town of Seaside.

The Cannon Beach area is good for surfing, though not the beach itself. The best spots are Indian Beach in Ecola State Park, 3 miles to the north, and Oswald West State Park, 10 miles south. Cleanline Surf Shop (www.cleanlinesurf.com; 171 Sunset Blvd) is a friendly local shop that rents out boards and mandatory wetsuits.

⊯ Sleeping & Eating

Cannon Beach Hotel HISTORIC HOTEL **$$**
(☎503-436-1392; www.cannonbeachhotellodgings.com; 1116 S Hemlock St; d incl breakfast $139-269; ☻☎) A classy, centrally located hotel with 10 rooms. Standards are lovely but very small; even the regular suites are tight. A good breakfast at the onsite cafe is included.

Blue Gull Inn Motel
MOTEL $$

(☑800-507-2714; www.haystacklodgings.com; 487 S Hemlock St; d $119-219; ❄🐾🅿) Some of the more affordable rooms in town, with comfortable atmosphere and toned-down decor. Kitchenette and Jacuzzi units available. Run by Haystack Lodgings.

Sleepy Monk Coffee
CAFE $

(☑503-436-2796; www.sleepymonkcoffee.com; 1235 S Hemlock St; ⊙8am-2pm Mon & Tue, till 4pm Fri-Sun) 🍃 For organic, certified fair-trade coffee, try this little coffee shop on the main street. It also runs the Irish Table, an excellent restaurant in the same building.

★Newman's at 988
FRENCH, ITALIAN $$$

(☑503-436-1151; www.newmansat988.com; 988 S Hemlock St; mains $22-36; ⊙5:30-9pm daily Jul 1-Oct 15, Tue-Sun Oct 16-Jun 30) Small but quality restaurant on the main drag. Award-winning chef John Newman delivers a fusion of French and Italian dishes. Desserts are sublime.

ℹ Information

For information try the **Chamber of Commerce** (☑503-436-2623; www.cannonbeach.org; 207 N Spruce St; ⊙10am-5pm).

ℹ Getting There & Away

Northwest Point (www.northwest-point.com) buses head from Astoria to Portland (and vice versa) every morning, stopping at Cannon Beach; buy tickets at the Beach Store, next to Cannon Beach Surf.

The **Cannon Beach Shuttle** (☑503-861-7433; www.ridethebus.org), also known as 'The Bus,' runs the length of Hemlock St to the end of Tolovana Beach; the schedule varies seasonally. Both buses go to Seaside and Astoria, too.

Wave buses (www.tillamookbus.com) service Manzanita and Lincoln City several times daily.

Newport

Home to Oregon's largest commercial fishing fleet, Newport is a lively tourist city with fine beaches and a world-class aquarium. In 2011 it became the host of NOAA, the National Oceanic and Atmospheric Administration. Good restaurants – along with some tacky attractions, gift shops and barking sea lions – abound in the historic bay-front area, while bohemian Nye Beach has galleries and a friendly village atmosphere. The area was first explored in the 1860s by fishing crews who found oyster beds at Yaquina Bay.

The world-class **Oregon Coast Aquarium** (☑541-867-3474; www.aquarium.org; 2820 SE Ferry Slip Rd; adult/child 13-17yr/child 3-12yr $18.95/16.95/11.95; ⊙9am-6pm; 🚼) is an unmissable attraction, featuring a sea-otter pool, surreal jellyfish tanks and Plexiglas tunnels through a shark tank. Nearby, the **Hatfield Marine Science Center** (☑541-867-0100; www.hmsc.oregonstate.edu; 2030 SE Marine Science Dr; ⊙10am-5pm; 🚼) **FREE** is much smaller but still worthwhile. For awesome tide-pooling and views, don't miss the **Yaquina Head Outstanding Area** (☑541-574-3100;

WORTH A TRIP

SCENIC DRIVE: THREE CAPES

Cape Meares, Cape Lookout and Cape Kiwanda, about halfway between Cannon Beach and Newport, are some of the coast's most stunning headlands, strung together on a slow, winding and sometimes bumpy 40-mile alternative to US 101. It's a worthwhile drive, though in March 2013 a section of road north of Cape Meares began sinking and was closed. Repairs are ongoing, so you might have to drive to Cape Meares via Netarts and Oceanside, then backtrack.

The forested headland at **Cape Meares** offers good views from its lighthouse, which is 38ft tall (Oregon's shortest). Short trails lead to Oregon's largest Sitka spruce and the 'Octopus Tree,' another Sitka shaped like a candelabra.

A panoramic vista atop sheer cliffs that rise 800ft above the Pacific makes **Cape Lookout State Park** a highlight. In winter, the end of the cape, which juts out nearly a mile, is thronged with whale-watchers. There are wide sandy beaches, hiking trails and a popular campground near the water.

Finally there's **Cape Kiwanda**, a sandstone bluff that rises just north of the little town of Pacific City. You can hike up tall dunes, or drive your truck onto the beach. It's the most developed of the three capes, with plenty of services nearby. Don't miss **Pelican Brewpub** (Cape Kiwanda; mains $12-32; ⊙8am-10pm Sun-Thu, till 11pm Sat & Sun) if you like beer. Watch the dory fleet launch their craft or, after a day's fishing, land as far up the beach as possible.

750 NW Lighthouse Dr; admission $7; ☺ sunrise-sunset, interpretive center 10am-6pm), site of the coast's tallest lighthouse and an interesting interpretive center.

Campers can head to large and popular South Beach State Park (☎ 541-867-4715; www.oregonstateparks.org; tent sites/RV sites/yurts $21/27/40; ☒), two miles south on US 101. Book-lovers can stay at the Sylvia Beach Hotel (☎ 541-265-5428; www.sylvia-beachhotel.com; 267 NW Cliff St; d incl breakfast $115-220; ☺), which has simple but comfy rooms, each named after a famous author; reservations are mandatory.

For great seafood, head to Local Ocean Seafoods (☎ 541-574-7959; www.localocean.net; 213 SE Bay Blvd; mains $11-23; ☺ 11am-8:30pm Sun-Thu, till 9pm Fri & Sat) ✐ – especially lovely for lunch, when the glass walls open to the port.

Get information at the chamber of commerce (☎ 541-265-8801; www.newportchamber.org; 555 SW Coast Hwy; ☺ 8am-5pm Mon-Fri, 10am-3pm Sat).

Yachats & Around

One of the Oregon coast's best-kept secrets is the neat and friendly little town of Yachats (ya-hots). People come here and to the small remote inns and B&Bs just south of town to get away from it all, which isn't hard to do along this relatively undeveloped coast.

Three miles south, lofty Cape Perpetua was first sighted by Captain Cook in 1778. Volcanic intrusions have formed a beautifully rugged shoreline, with dramatic features such as the Devil's Churn, where powerful waves crash through a 30ft inlet. For an easy hike, take the paved Captain Cook Trail (1.2-mile round trip) down to tide pools near Cooks Chasm, where at high tide the geyser-like spouting horn blasts water out of a sea cave. For information head to the Cape Perpetua Visitor Center (☎ 541-547-3289; www.fs.usda.gov/siuslaw; ☺ 10am-4pm daily Mar-May & Sept-Oct, to 5pm daily Jun-Aug, closed Tue Nov-Feb).

South 15 miles on US 101 is the almost-tourist trap but fun Sea Lion Caves (☎ 541-547-3111; www.sealioncaves.com; 91560 US 101; adult/child 6-12yr $14/8; ☺ 9am-6pm), a noisy grotto filled with sea lions, accessed via an elevator.

Camp at Beachside State Park (☎ 800-551-6949; www.oregonstateparks.org; tent sites/RV sites/yurts $21/26/40; ☒), five miles north of Yachats on US 101. The Ya'Tel Motel (☎ 541-547-3225; www.yatelmotel.com; cnr US 101 & 6th St; d $64-84; ☺@☎☒) is a good, inexpensive place to sleep, and for snacks there's the Green Salmon Coffee House (☎ 541-547-4409; www.thegreensalmon.com; 220 US 101; mains $7-11; ☺ 7:30am-2pm; ✐).

Oregon Dunes National Recreation Area

Stretching for 50 miles between Florence and Coos Bay, the Oregon Dunes form the largest expanse of coastal dunes in the USA. They tower up to 500ft and undulate inland as far as three miles to meet coastal forests, harboring curious ecosystems that sustain an abundance of wildlife. Hiking trails, bridle paths, and boating and swimming areas are available, but avoid the stretch south of Reedsport as noisy dune buggies dominate. For tourist info, head to the Oregon Dunes National Recreation Area's headquarters (☎ 541-271-3495; www.fs.usda.gov/siuslaw; 855 Highway Ave; ☺ 8am-4:30pm Mon-Fri, to 4pm Sat & Sun) in Reedsport.

State parks with camping include popular Jessie M Honeyman (☎ 800-452-5687, 541-997-3641; www.oregonstateparks.org; 84505 US 101 S; tent sites/RV sites/yurts $21/26/39; ☒), 3 miles south of Florence, and pleasant Umpqua Lighthouse (☎ 800-452-5687, 541-271-4118; www.oregonstateparks.org; 460 Lighthouse Rd; tent sites/RV sites/yurts/cabins/deluxe yurts $19/24/36/39/76; ☒), 4 miles south of Reedsport. There's plenty of other camping in the area, too.

Port Orford

Occupying a rare natural harbor and guarding spectacular views, the scenic hamlet of Port Orford sits on a headland wedged between two magnificent state parks. Cape Blanco State Park, nine miles to the north, is the second most-westerly point in continental USA. As well as hiking, visitors can tour the Cape Blanco Lighthouse (☎ 541-332-2207; www.oregonstateparks.org; US 101; admission $2; ☺ 10am-3:30pm Wed-Mon) built in 1870; it's the oldest and highest operational lighthouse in Oregon.

Six miles south of Port Orford, in Humbug Mountain State Park, mountains and sea meet in aqueous disharmony with plenty of angry surf. You can climb the 1750ft peak on a 3-mile trail through old-growth cedar groves.

For an affordable stay try Castaway-by-the-Sea Motel (☎ 541-332-4502; www.castawaybythesea.com; 545 W 5th St; d $85-145; ☺@☎☒). Food here means a visit to slick Redfish (☎ 541-336-2200; www.redfishportorford.com; 517 Jefferson St; mains $21-29; ☺ 11am-9pm Mon-Fri, 9am-9pm Sat & Sun) ✐ for the freshest seafood in town.

Rocky Mountains

Best Places to Eat

➜ Root Down (p252)

➜ Salt (p257)

➜ Rickshaw (p306)

➜ Pine Creek Cookhouse (p269)

➜ Silk Road (p299)

Best Places to Stay

➜ Curtis (p250)

➜ Boise Guest House (p304)

➜ Chautauqua Lodge (p256)

➜ Alpine House (p293)

➜ Old Faithful Inn (p289)

Why Go?

The high backbone of the lower 48, the Rockies are nature on steroids, with rows of snowcapped peaks, rugged canyons and wild rivers running buckshot over the Western states. With its beauty and vitality, it's no wonder that 100 years ago, it beckoned ailing patients with last-ditch hopes for cures.

The healing power of the Rocky Mountains persists. You can choose between tranquility (try Wyoming, the USA's most under-populated state) and adrenaline (measured in vertical drop). Locals love a good frozen, wet or mud-spattered adventure and, with plenty of climbing, skiing and white-water paddling, it's easy to join in. Afterwards, relax by soaking in hot springs under a roof of stars, sipping cold microbrews or feasting farm-to-table style.

Lastly, don't miss the supersized charms of Yellowstone, Rocky Mountain, Grand Teton and Glacier national parks, where the big five (grizzly bears, moose, bison, mountain lions and wolves) still roam wild.

When to Go

Denver

°C/°F Temp — Rainfall inches/mm

Jun-Aug Long days of sunshine ideal for cycling, hiking, farmers markets and summer festivals.

Sep & Oct Fall foliage coincides with terrific lodging deals.

Jan & Feb Snow dusted peaks, powdery slopes, après-ski parties deluxe.

DON'T MISS

Don a Stetson hat and gallop the sagebrush wilderness of Wyoming or Montana. Guest ranches offer memorable summer rides in the Rockies.

Fast Facts

➡ **Hub city** Denver (population 600,000)

➡ **Mountains** Colorado has the most summits over 14,000ft in the continental US

➡ **Time zone** Mountain (two hours behind NYC)

Did You Know?

Pitch your tent in Yellowstone National Park and you'll be sleeping atop one of the world's largest supervolcanoes. It's active every 640,000 years: an eruption is due soon – give or take 10,000 years.

Resources

➡ **Denver Post** (www.denverpost.com) The region's top newspaper

➡ **5280** (www.5280.com) Denver's best monthly magazine

➡ **Discount Ski Rental** (www.rentskis.com) At major resorts

➡ **14ers** (www.14ers.com) Resource for hikers climbing the Rockies' highest summits

Getting There & Around

Denver (DEN) has the only major international airport in the region. Both Denver and Colorado Springs offer flights on smaller planes to Jackson, WY, Boise, ID, Bozeman, MT, Aspen, CO, and other destinations.

Two Amtrak train routes pass through the region. *California Zephyr,* traveling daily between Emeryville, CA and Chicago, IL, has six stops in Colorado, including Denver, Fraser-Winter Park, Glenwood Springs and Grand Junction. *Empire Builder* runs daily from Seattle, WA, or Portland, OR, to Chicago, IL, with 12 stops in Montana (including Whitefish and East and West Glacier) and one stop in Idaho at Sandpoint.

Greyhound travels some parts of the Rocky Mountains. But to really get out and explore you'll need a car.

NATIONAL PARKS

The region is home to some of the USA's biggest national parks. In Colorado, **Rocky Mountain National Park** offers awesome hiking through alpine forests and tundra. There's also the Sahara-like wonder of **Great Sand Dunes National Park** and **Mesa Verde National Park**, an archaeological preserve with elaborate cliff-side dwellings.

Wyoming has **Grand Teton National Park**, with dramatic craggy peaks, and **Yellowstone National Park**, the country's first national park, a true wonderland of volcanic geysers, hot springs and forested mountains. In Montana, **Glacier National Park** features high sedimentary peaks, small glaciers and lots of wildlife, including grizzly bears. Idaho is home to **Hells Canyon National Recreation Area**, where the Snake River carves the deepest canyon in North America. **National Park Service** (NPS; www.nps.gov) also manages over two dozen other historic sites, monuments, nature preserves and recreational areas in Idaho.

Best in Outdoor Instruction

With plenty of wilderness and tough terrain, the Rockies are a natural school for outdoor skills, and a perfect place to observe nature in action.

➡ **Chicks with Picks** (p274) Fun ice-climbing clinics for women, by women.

➡ **Yellowstone Institute** (www.yellowstoneassociation.org) Study wolves, ecology or arts with experts in the park.

➡ **Teton Science Schools Ecology** (p292) Best for kids; both about nature and experiencing it.

➡ **Colorado Mountain School** (p261) Climb a peak safely or learn belay skills.

History

Before the late 18th century, when French trappers and Spaniards stepped in, the Rocky Mountain area was a land of many tribes, including the Nez Percé, the Shoshone, the Crow, the Lakota and the Ute.

Meriwether Lewis and William Clark claimed enduring fame after the USA bought almost all of present-day Montana, Wyoming and eastern Colorado in the 1803 Louisiana Purchase. Their epic survey covering 8000 miles in three years. Their success urged on other adventurers, setting migration in motion. Wagon trains voyaged to the Rockies right into the 20th century, only temporarily slowed by the completion of the Transcontinental Railroad across southern Wyoming in the late 1860s.

To accommodate settlers, the US purged the western frontier of the Spanish, British and, in a truly shameful era, most of the Native American population. The government signed endless treaties to defuse Native American objections to increasing settlement, but always reneged and shunted tribes onto smaller reservations. Gold-miners' incursions into Native American territory in Montana and the building of US Army forts along the Bozeman Trail ignited a series of wars with the Lakota, Cheyenne, Arapaho and others.

ROCKY MOUNTAINS IN...

Two Weeks

Start your Rocky Mountain odyssey in the **Denver** area. Go tubing, vintage-clothes shopping or biking in outdoor-mad, boho **Boulder**, then soak up the liberal rays eavesdropping at a sidewalk cafe. Enjoy the vistas of the **Rocky Mountain National Park** before heading west on I-70 to play in the mountains around **Breckenridge**, which also has the best beginner slopes in Colorado. Go to ski and mountain bike mecca **Steamboat Springs** before crossing the border into Wyoming.

Your first stop in the state should be **Lander**, rock-climbing destination extraordinaire. Continue north to chic **Jackson** and the majestic **Grand Teton National Park** before hitting iconic **Yellowstone National Park**. Save at least three days for exploring this geyser-packed wonderland.

Cross the state line into 'big sky country' and slowly make your way northwest through Montana, stopping in funky **Bozeman** and lively **Missoula** before visiting **Flathead Lake**. Wind up your trip in Idaho. If it's summer, you can paddle the wild whitewater of **Hells Canyon National Recreation Area** before continuing to up-and-coming **Boise**. End your trip with a few days skiing **Sun Valley** and partying in **Ketchum**. The town and ski resort, despite being *the* winter playground *du jour* for Hollywood, are refreshingly unpretentious.

One Month

With a month on your hands, you can really delve into the region's off-the-beaten-path treasures. Follow the two-week itinerary, but dip southwest in Colorado – an up-and-coming wine region – before visiting Wyoming. Ride the 4WD trails around **Ouray**. Be sure to visit **Mesa Verde National Park** and its ancient cliff dwellings.

In Montana, you'll want to get lost backpacking in the **Bob Marshall Wilderness Complex** and visit **Glacier National Park** before the glaciers disappear altogether. In Idaho, spend more time playing in **Sun Valley** and be sure to explore the shops, pubs and yummy organic restaurants in delightful little **Ketchum**. With a one-month trip, you also have time to drive along a few of Idaho's fantastically remote scenic byways. Make sure you cruise Hwy 75 from Sun Valley north to **Stanley**. Situated on the wide banks of the Salmon River, this stunning mountain hamlet is completely surrounded by national forest land and wilderness areas. Wild good looks withstanding, Stanley is also blessed with world-class trout fishing and mild to wild rafting. Take Hwy 21 from Stanley to Boise. This scenic drive takes you through miles of dense ponderosa forests, and past some excellent, solitary riverside camping spots – some of which come with their own natural hot-springs pools.

Rocky Mountains Highlights

❶ Spotting bears, bison and geysers at **Yellowstone National Park** (p285).

❷ Reveling in Hollywood gone cowboy in the party resort of **Aspen** (p267).

❸ Hiking and climbing the craggy wilderness of **Grand Teton National Park** (p290).

❹ Paddling top-notch white water at the **Middle Fork of the Salmon River** (p307).

❺ Getting your groove on in the outdoor mecca of **Boulder** (p255).

❻ Roaming the San Juan's picturesque Wild West towns of **Southern Colorado** (p263).

200 km
100 miles

Saskatchewan

CANADA

Milk River

North Dakota

Central Time
Mountain Time

Fort Peck Indian Reservation

Glendive

Yellowstone River

Powder River

South Dakota

Rapid City

Devil's Tower National Monument ❶

Black Hills

Sheridan
Buffalo
Gillette

Wyoming

Bighorn Mountains

Thermopolis

Dubois

Wind Riv.

Cody

Absaroka Beartooth Wilderness

West Yellowstone

Yellowstone National Park ❶

Yellowstone Lake

Grand Teton National Park ❸

Jackson

Teton Range

Idaho Falls

Crow Indian Reservation

Billings

Livingston

Red Lodge

Bozeman

Butte

HELENA

Great Falls

Montana

Lewistown

Jordan

Fort Peck Lake

Fort Belknap Indian Reservation

Missouri River

Blackfeet Indian Reservation

Glacier National Park ❼

East Glacier

West Glacier

Whitefish

Kalispell

Rocky Mountain Front

Bob Marshall Wilderness Complex ❹

Seeley-Swan Valley

Flathead Lake

Polson

Alberta

Continental Divide

British Columbia

Idaho Panhandle

Sandpoint

Lake Pend Oreille

Coeur d'Alene

Coeur d'Alene Lake

Wallace

Moscow

Lewiston

Spokane

Washington

Snake River

Oregon

BOISE

Idaho

Mountain Time
Pacific Time

Selway-Bitterroot Wilderness Area

Salmon River

Frank Church-River of No Return Wilderness Area

Middle Fork of the Salmon River ❹

Salmon River Scenic Byway

Challis

Stanley

Sawtooth Wilderness Area

Ketchum

Sun Valley ❽

Bitterroot Range

Continental Divide

Madison Valley

Rocky Mountains

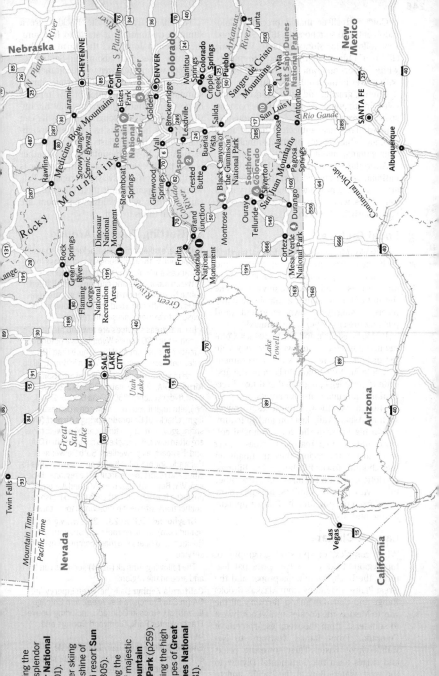

7 Enjoying the untamed splendor of **Glacier National Park** (p301).

8 Powder skiing in the sunshine of classic ski resort **Sun Valley** (p305).

9 Scaling the heights of majestic **Rocky Mountain National Park** (p259).

10 Roaming the high desertscapes of **Great Sand Dunes National Park** (p281).

Gold and silver mania preceded Colorado's entry to statehood in 1876. Statehood soon followed for Montana (1889), Wyoming (1890) and Idaho (1890). Along with miners, white farmers and ranchers were the people with power in the late 19th century.

Mining, grazing and timber played major roles in regional economic development, sparking growth for financial and industrial support. They also subjected the region to boom-and-bust cycles by unsustainable resource management.

After the economy boomed post-WWII, national parks started attracting vacationers. Tourism is now a leading industry in all four states, with the military a close second, particularly in Colorado.

Local Culture

The Rocky Mountain states tout a particular brand of freedom echoed in the vast and rugged landscape. There's lots of public land for many uses and rules are few – just take the out-of-bound skiing available at many resorts. Using your own judgment (and pushing the envelope) is encouraged.

It also boasts live and let live values. Coloradans may be split on whether they vote red or blue, but most balk at a government mandate. In 2013, Colorado became the first state to have legal, regulated and taxed recreational marijuana use for adults.

Though even the wealthiest resort towns, such as Aspen, Vail, Jackson and Ketchum, took a big hit with the 2008 financial collapse and ensuing real-estate woes, along with most of the region, they are finally on the rebound. Towns like blue-collar Billings, patriotic Colorado Springs and every other town with military families, are on a slow mend from the human toll of the campaigns in Iraq and Afghanistan.

Land & Climate

While complex, the physical geography of the region divides into two principal features: the Rocky Mountains proper and the Great Plains. Extending from Alaska's Brooks Range and Canada's Yukon Territory all the way to Mexico, the Rockies sprawl northwest to southeast, from the steep escarpment of Colorado's Front Range westward to Nevada's Great Basin. Their towering peaks and ridges form the Continental Divide: to the west, waters flow to the Pacific, and to the east, toward the Atlantic and the Gulf of Mexico.

For many travelers, the Rockies are a summer destination. It starts to feel summery around June, and the warm weather generally lasts until about mid-September (though warm outerwear is recommended for evenings in mountain towns during summer). The winter, which brings in packs of powder hounds, doesn't usually hit until late November, though snowstorms can start in the mountains as early as September. Winter usually lasts until March or early April. In the mountains, the weather is constantly changing (snow in summer is not uncommon), so always be prepared. Fall, when the aspens flaunt their fall gold, and early summer, when wildflowers bloom, are wonderful times to visit.

ℹ Getting There & Around

Travel here takes time. The Rockies are sparsely developed, with attractions spread across long distances and linked by roads that meander between mountains and canyons. With limited public transportation, touring in a private vehicle is best. After all, road-tripping is one of the reasons to explore this scenic region.

In rural areas services are few and far between – the I-80 across Wyoming is a notorious offender. It's not unusual to go more than 100 miles between gas stations. When in doubt, fill up.

The main travel hub is **Denver International Airport** (☑ information 303-342-2000; www.flydenver.com; 8500 Peña Blvd; ⊙24hrs; ⓢ), although if you are coming on a domestic flight, check out **Colorado Springs Airport** (www.springsgov.com/airportindex.aspx) as well: fares are often lower, it's quicker to navigate than DIA and it's nearly as convenient. Both Denver and Colorado Springs offer flights on smaller planes to cities and resort towns around the region – Jackson, WY, Boise, ID, Bozeman, MT, and Aspen, CO, are just a few options. Salt Lake City, UT, also has connections with destinations in all four states.

Greyhound (☑ 800-231-2222; www.greyhound.com) has fixed routes throughout the Rockies, and offers the most comprehensive bus service.

The following Amtrak (p254) services run to and around the region:

California Zephyr Daily between Emeryville, CA (in San Francisco Bay Area), and Chicago, IL, with six stops in Colorado, including Denver, Fraser-Winter Park, Glenwood Springs and Grand Junction.

Empire Builder Runs daily from Seattle, WA, or Portland, OR, to Chicago, IL, with 12 stops in Montana (including Whitefish and East and West Glacier) and one stop in Idaho at Sandpoint.

COLORADO

From double-diamond runs to stiff espressos, Colorado is all about vigor. This is also the state graced with the greatest concentration of high peaks – dubbed 14ers for their height of 14000ft. But it isn't all about the great outdoors. Universities and high-tech show the state's industrious side, though even workaholics might call in sick when snow starts falling.

It's no wonder that the sunny state attracts so many East Coasters and Californians. Latinos also have answered the calling to shore up a huge hospitality industry. And while much of the state is considered conservative, there is common ground in everyone's mad love for the outdoors and a friendly, can-do ethos that inspires.

ℹ Information

Colorado Road Conditions (☑ 877-315-7623; www.state.co.us) Highway advisories.

Colorado State Parks (☑ 303-470-1144; www. parks.state.co.us) Tent and RV sites cost from $10 to $24 per night, depending on facilities. Rustic cabins and yurts are also available in some parks and those with wood-burning stoves may be available year-round. Advance reservations for specific campsites are taken, but subject to a $10 nonrefundable booking fee. Reservation changes cost $6.

Colorado Travel & Tourism Authority (☑ 800-265-6723; www.colorado.com) State-wide tourism information.

Denver Post (www.denverpost.com) Denver's major daily newspaper.

Denver

Denver's mile-high gravity is growing, pulling all objects in the Rocky Mountain West toward her glistening downtown towers, hopped-up brewpubs, hemped-out cannabis dispensaries, trails, toned-and-tanned mountain warriors, and growing western cosmopolitanism that's fostered a burgeoning arts scene, and brought great restaurants and hip bars to a cow-town gone world-wide crazy.

While most of the tourist action centers on the Downtown and Lower Downtown (LoDo) Districts, travelers in the know are heading out to neighborhoods like Highlands, Washington Park, Cherry Creek, Five Points, South Santa Fe and the River North (RiNo) to dive into the spirited heart of Denver's ever-expanding culture club.

Top that off with back-door service to the Rocky Mountains, one of the best off-road bike trail systems in the USA, and plenty of parks, open spaces, riverfronts and sunshiney perches for a sky-high psychedelic carpet ride.

◉ Sights & Activities

★ **Denver Art Museum**   MUSEUM
(DAM; ☑ ticket sales 720-865-5000; www.denverartmuseum.org; 100 W 14th Ave; adult/child/student $13/5/10, 1st Sat of each month free; ⊙ 10am-5pm Tue-Thurs, 10am-8pm Fri, 10am-5pm Sat-Sun; 🅿 ♿; 🚉 9, 16, 52, 83L RTD) 🍴 The DAM is home to one of the largest Native American art collections in the USA, and puts on special avant-garde multimedia exhibits. The Western American Art section of the permanent collection is justifiably famous. This isn't your Momma's museum, and the best part of a visit is diving into the interactive exhibits – kids love this place.

COLORADO FACTS

Nickname Centennial State

Population 5 million

Area 104,247 sq miles

Capital city Denver (population 566,974)

Other cities Boulder (population 91,500), Colorado Springs (population 372,400)

Sales tax 2.9% state tax, plus individual city taxes

Birthplace of Ute tribal leader Chief Ouray (1833–80); South Park creator Trey Parker (b 1969); actor Amy Adams (b 1974); climber Tommy Caldwell (b 1978)

Home of Naropa University (founded by Beat poets), powder slopes, boutique beers

Politics Swing state

Famous for Sunny days (300 per year), the highest altitude vineyards and longest ski run in the continental USA

Kitschiest souvenir Deer-hoof bottle openers

Driving distances Denver to Vail 100 miles, Boulder to Rocky Mountain National Park 38 miles

Denver

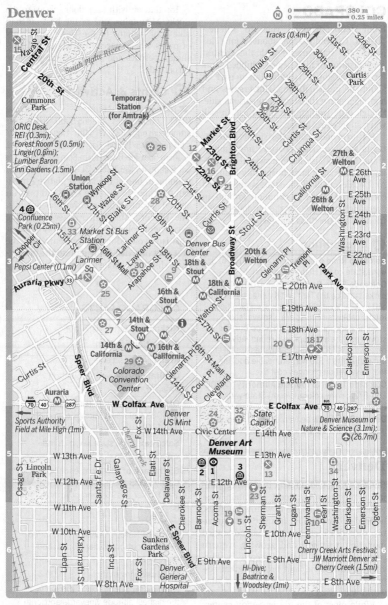

The landmark $110-million Frederic C Hamilton wing, designed by Daniel Libeskind, is quite simply awesome. Whether you see it as expanding crystals, juxtaposed mountains or just architectural indulgence, it's an angular modern masterpiece. If you think the place looks weird from the outside, look inside: shapes shift with each turn thanks to a combination of design and uncanny natural-light tricks.

Denver

ROCKY MOUNTAINS DENVER

Clyfford Still Museum
MUSEUM

(☑720-354-4880; www.clyffordstillmuseum.org; 1250 Bannock St; adult/child $10/3; ⊙10am-5pm, till 8pm Fri) Dedicated exclusively to the work and legacy of 20th century American Abstract Expressionist, Clyfford Still, this fascinating museum's collection includes over 2400 works by the powerful and narcissistic master of bold. When he died in 1980, in his will Still insisted that his body of work only be exhibited in a singular space. So Denver built him a museum.

History Colorado Center
MUSEUM

(☑303-447-8679; www.historycoloradocenter. org; 1200 Broadway; adult/student/child $10/8/8; ⊙10am-5pm Mon-Sat, noon-5pm Sun; P) Discover Colorado's frontier roots and high-tech modern triumphs at this sharp, smart and charming museum. There are plenty of interactive exhibits, including a Jules Verne-esque 'Time Machine' that you push across a giant map of Colorado to explore seminal moments in the Centennial State's history.

★ Confluence Park
PARK

(2200 15th St; ♿; ◙10 RTD) ⊘FREE Where Cherry Creek and Platte River meet is the nexus and plexus of Denver's sunshine loving culture. It's a good place for an afternoon picnic, and there's a short white-water park for kayakers and tubers.

Head south from here along the Cherry Creek trail and you can get all the way to Cherry Creek Shopping Center and beyond to Cherry Creek Reservoir. If you go Southwest along the Platte Trail, you'll eventually ride all the way to Chatfield Reservoir. By heading north, and connecting to the Clear Creek Trail, you can get to Golden.

Museum of Contemporary Art
GALLERY

(☑303-298-7554; www.mcadenver.org; 1485 Delgany St; adult/student/child/after 5pm $8/5/1/5; ⊙noon-7pm Tue-Thu, noon-8pm Fri, 10am-7pm Sat-Sun; P; ◙6 RTD) This space was built with interaction and engagement in mind, and Denver's home for contemporary art can be provocative, delightful or a bit disappointing, depending on the show.

Denver Museum of Nature & Science
MUSEUM

(☑303-370-6000; www.dmns.org; 2001 Colorado Blvd; museum adult/child $13/8, IMAX $10-8, Planitarium $5/4; ⊙9am-5pm; P ♿; ◙20, 32, 40 RTD) The Denver Museum of Nature & Science is located on the eastern edge of City Park. This classic natural science museum has excellent temporary exhibits, plus those cool panoramas we all loved as kids. The IMAX theater and Gates Planetarium are especially fun.

WORTH A TRIP

BEST MILE HIGH DAY HIKES

There are literally hundreds of day hikes within an hour of Denver. Many people choose to head up to Boulder's Mountain Parks or Colorado Springs for a day.

Jefferson County Open Space Parks (www.jeffco.us/openspace; ♿) Top picks include Matthews Winters, Mount Falcon, Elk Meadow and Lair o' the Bear.

Golden Gate Canyon State Park (☎303-582-3707; www.parks.state.us/parks; 92 Crawford Gulch Road, Golden; entrance/camping $7/24; ⊙5am-10pm) Located halfway between Denver and Nederland, this massive 12,000-acre state park can be reached in about 45 minutes from downtown Denver.

Staunton State Park (☎303-816-0912; www.parks.state.co.us/parks) Colorado's newest state park sits on a historic ranch site 40 miles west of Denver. It is accessed from Hwy 285 between Conifer and Bailey.

Waterton Canyon (☎303-634-3745; www.denverwater.org/recreation/watertoncanyon; Kassler Center) South of the city, just west of Chatfield Reservoir, this pretty canyon has an easy 6.5-mile trail to the Strontia Springs Dam. From there, the **Colorado Trail** (CTF; ☎303-384-3729; www.coloradotrail.org; PO Box 260876; ⊙9am-5pm Mon-Fri) will take you all the way to Durango!

Buffalo Creek Mountain Bike Area (www.frmbp.org; Pine Valley Ranch Park) If you're into single-track mountain biking, this area has about 40 miles of bike trails.

✦ Festivals & Events

Cinco de Mayo　　　　CULTURAL
(www.cincodemayodenver.com; ⊙May; ♿) **FREE**
Enjoy salsa music and margaritas at one of the country's biggest Cinco de Mayo celebrations, held over two days on the first weekend in May.

Cherry Creek Arts Festival　　ARTS
(www.cherryarts.org; cnr Clayton St & E 3rd Ave; ♿) A sprawling celebration of visual, culinary and performing arts where a quarter of a million visitors browse the giant block party.

Taste of Colorado　　　　FOOD
(☎303-295-6330; www.atasteofcolorado.com; Civic Center Park; ♿) Food stalls of over 50 restaurants; there's also booze, live music, and arts-and-crafts vendors at this Labor Day festival.

Great American Beer Festival　　BEER
(☎303-447-0816; www.greatamericanbeerfestival.com; 700 14th St; $75; ⊙early Sept; ♿; ☐101 D-Line, 101 H-Line, ☐1, 8, 30, 30L, 31, 48 RTD) ✇ Colorado has more microbreweries than any other US state, and this hugely popular event in early September sells out in advance.

🛏 Sleeping

Besides the places mentioned here, there are chain and independent motels throughout the city, with rooms starting at $75. Save big with the online aggregators. Denver's hostels tend to cater more to transients than backpackers.

Denver International Youth Hostel HOSTEL $
(☎303-832-9996; www.youthhostels.com/denver; 630 E 16th Ave; dm $19; ℗@🛜; ☐15, 15L, 20 RTD) If cheap really matters then the Denver International Youth Hostel might be the place for you. It's basic and vaguely chaotic, but has a ramshackle charm and a great downtown location. All dorms have attached bathroom facilities and the common area in the basement has a large-screen TV, library and computers for guests to use.

11th Avenue Hotel　　　　HOTEL $
(☎303-894-0529; www.11thavenuehotel.com; 1112 Broadway; dm $19-22, r with/without bath $45/39; ⊖❄🛜) This budget hotel has a good location for art lovers in the Golden Triangle district. The lobby looks vaguely like something from a Jim Jarmusch movie. The upstairs rooms, some with attached bathrooms, are bare but clean. It's safe, secure and a decent place for budget travelers.

★**Curtis**　　　BOUTIQUE HOTEL $$
(☎303-571-0300; www.thecurtis.com; 1405 Curtis St; d $159-279; ⊖❄@🛜; ☐15 RTD) It's like stepping into a doobop Warhal wonderworld at this temple to post-modern pop culture. Attention to detail – be it through the service or the decor in the rooms – is paramount at the Curtis, a one of a kind hotel in Denver.

There are 13 themed floors and each is devoted to a different genre of American pop culture. Rooms are spacious and very mod without being too out there to sleep. The hotel's refreshingly different take on sleeping may seem too kitschy for some – you can get a wake up call from Elvis – but if you're tired of the same old international brands and looking for something different, this joint in the heart of downtown might be your tonic.

★ Queen Anne Bed & Breakfast Inn
B&B **$$**

(☎303-296-6666; www.queenannebnb.com; 2147 Tremont Pl; r incl breakfast $135-215; P❀❉✿) Soft chamber music wafting through public areas, fresh flowers, manicured gardens and evening wine tastings create a romantic ambience at this ecoconscious B&B in two late-1800s Victorian homes. Featuring period antiques, private hot tubs and exquisite hand-painted murals, each room has its own personality.

Green features include mattresses made from recycled coils and green-tea insulation, organic fabrics (just like the delicious full breakfast), and products and produce purchased from local merchants when possible. They even have free bikes.

Patterson Historic Inn
HISTORIC HOTEL **$$**

(☎303-955-5142; www.pattersoninn.com; 420 E 11th Ave; r incl breakfast from $169; ❉@✿) This 1891 Grande Dame was once a Senator's home. It's now one of the best historic bed-and-breakfasts in town. The gardens are limited, but the Victorian charm, sumptuous breakfast, and well appointed chambers in this nine-room château will delight. Rooms come with modern touches like silk robes, down comforters and flat-screens.

Lumber Baron Inn Gardens
B&B **$$**

(☎303-477-8205; www.lumberbaron.com; 2555 W 37th Ave; r $149-239; P❀❉✿; 🚌38 RTD) Murder mystery dinners and romance-inducing suites make this elegantly quirky B&B in the cooled-out Highlands neighborhood stand out from the pack – even the locals choose to stay here for a weekend mystery getaway! The five suites are all different, although all feature Jacuzzis and giant plasma TVs.

Brown Palace Hotel
HISTORIC HOTEL **$$$**

(☎303-297-3111; www.brownpalace.com; 321 17th St; r from $299; P❀❉@✿) Standing agape under the stained-glass crowned atrium, it's clear why this palace is shortlisted among the country's elite historic hotels. There's deco artwork, a four-star spa, imported marble, and staff who discretely float down the halls.

The rooms, which have been hosting presidents since Teddy Roosevelt's days, have the unique elegance of a distant era, but can be a bit small by modern standards.

JW Marriott Denver at Cherry Creek
HOTEL **$$$**

(☎303-316-2700; www.jwmarriottdenver.com; 150 Clayton Ln; d from $245; P❀❉✿❉; 🚌1, 2, 3, 46 RTD) Spacious digs come with high-thread count sheets, plump beds and marble bathrooms featuring top class soaps and shampoos. The onsite bar is also quite cool – you might even spot a Denver Bronco... Local artwork and colorful blown glass grace lobbies and rooms.

Hotel Monaco
BOUTIQUE HOTEL **$$$**

(☎303-296-1717, 800-990-1303; www.monaco-denver.com; 1717 Champa St; r from $127; P❀❉✿❉; 🚌0, 6, 30, 30L, 31, 36, 48, 52 RTD) This ultrastylish boutique is a favorite with the celebrity set. Modern rooms blend French and art-deco styles – think bold colors and fabulous European-style feather beds. Don't miss the evening 'Altitude Adjustment Hour,' when guests enjoy free wine and five-minute massages. The place is 100% pet-friendly; staff will even deliver a named goldfish to your room upon request!

✕ Eating

While the downtown restaurants offer the greatest depth and variety in Denver, insiders head to strollable neighborhoods like Highlands, Cherry Creek, South Pearl Street, Uptown, Five Points, Washington Park and Old Town Littleton, where little five-block commercial strips hold some of Denver's best eateries. Check out www.5280.com or www.diningout.com/denver for new eats.

Snooze
BREAKFAST **$**

(☎303-297-0700; www.snoozeeatery.com; 2262 Larimer St; mains $6-12; ⏱6:30am-2:30pm Mon-Fri, 7am-2:30pm Sat & Sun; ❉❉) This retostyled cheery breakfast-and-brunch spot is one of the hottest post-party breakfast joints in town. It dishes up spectacularly crafted breakfast burritos and a smokin' salmon benedict. The coffee's always good, but you have the option of an early-morning Bloody Mary. The wait can be up to an hour on weekends!

City O' City
VEGETARIAN, VEGAN $

(☑303-831-6443; www.cityocitydenver.com; 206 E 13th Ave; mains $8-15; ⊙7am-2am Mon-Fri, 8am-2am Sat, 8am-midnight Sun; ☑⏹; ⛒2, 9, 52 RTD) ⚑ This popular vegan/vegetarian restaurant mixes stylish decor with an innovative spin on greens, grains, faux meat and granola. The menu offers tapa boards, big salads, some good trans-national noodle dishes and the best vegan pizza pie in D-Town.

Buenos Aires Pizzeria
ARGENTINEAN $

(☑303-296-6710; www.bapizza.com; 1307 22nd St; empanadas $2.50, mains $6-10; ⊙11:30am-10pm Tues-Sat, noon-8pm Sun) An authentic taste of Argentina in the heart of cow-town Colorado, this wide-angled pizzeria looks and feels like the real-deal Holyfield. You can either pig out on two or three empanadas (stuffed pastries) or dig into yummy sandwiches, above average pizza and pasta. Alas, no steaks.

★Beatrice & Woodsley
TAPAS $$

(☑303-777-3505; www.beatriceandwoodsley. com; 38 S Broadway; small plates $9-13; ⊙5-11pm Mon-Fri, 10am-2pm, 5-10pm Sat-Sun; ⛒0 RTD) Beatrice and Woodsley is the most artfully designed dining room in Denver. Chainsaws are buried into the wall to support shelves, there's an aspen growing through the back of the dining room and the feel is that of a mountain cabin being elegantly reclaimed by nature. The menu of small plates is whimsical and Continental inspired.

★Steuben's Food Service
AMERICAN $$

(☑303-803-1001; www.steubens.com; 523 E 17th Ave; mains $8-21; ⊙11am-11pm Sun-Thu, 11am-midnight Fri & Sat; ⏹) ⚑ Although styled as a midcentury drive-in, the upscale treatment of comfort food (mac and cheese, fried chicken, lobster rolls) and the solar-powered kitchen demonstrate Steuben's contemporary smarts. In summer, open garage doors lining the street create a breezy atmosphere and after 10pm they have the most unbeatable deal around: a burger, hand-cut fries and beer for $5.

★Root Down
MODERN AMERICAN $$$

(☑303-993-4200; www.rootdowndenver.com; 1600 W 33rd Ave; small plates $7-17, mains $18-28; ⊙5-10pm Sun-Thu, 5-11pm Fri & Sat, brunch 10am-2:30pm Sat & Sun; ☑) ⚑ In a converted gas station, chef Justin Cucci has undertaken one of the city's most ambitious culinary concepts, marrying sustainable 'field-to-fork' practices, high-concept culinary fusions and a low-impact, energy efficient ethos. The menu changes seasonally, but consider yourself lucky if it includes the sweet-potato falafel or hoisin-duck confit sliders.

★Rioja
MODERN AMERICAN $$$

(☑303-820-2282; www.riojadenver.com; 1431 Larimer St; mains $18-29; ⊙11:30am-2:30pm Wed-Fri, 10am-2:30pm Sat & Sun, 5-10pm Mon-Sun; ⚒☑; ⛒2, 12, 15, 16th St Shuttle) This is one of Denver's most innovative restaurants. Smart, busy and upscale, yet relaxed and casual – just like Colorado – Rioja features modern cuisine inspired by Italian and Spanish traditions and powered by modern culinary flavors.

🍷 Drinking

Top nightlife districts include Uptown for gay bars and a young professional crowd, LoDo for loud sports bars, heavy drinking and dancing, River North for hipsters, Lower Highlands for an eclectic mix and sweet decks, Cherry Creek over 35s, and Broadway and Colfax for old school wannabees.

★Forest Room 5
BAR

(☑303-433-7001; www.forestroom5.com; 2532 15th St; ⊙4pm-2am) One of the best damned bars in Denver, this LoHi (that's Lower Highlands) juggernaut has an outdoor patio with fire circles (where you can smoke!), streams and a funked-out Airstream.

Linger
LOUNGE

(☑303-993-3120; www.lingerdenver.com; 2030 W 30th Ave; mains $8-14; ⊙11:30am-2:30pm, 4pm-2am Tues-Sat, 10am-2:30pm Sun) This rambling LoHi complex sits in the former Olinger mortuary. Come nighttime, they black out the 'O' and it just becomes Linger. The light-up-the-night rooftop bar has a replica of the RV made famous by the Bill Murray smash *Stripes*.

Bar Standard
CLUB

(☑303-534-0222; www.coclubs.com; 1037 Broadway; ⊙8pm-2am Fri & Sat; ⛒0 RTD) It's ice cold without the attitude, and when the right DJ is on the tables it can be some of the best dancing in town.

The attached Milk Bar takes a page from Anthony Burgess' classic *A Clockwork Orange*.

Tracks
GAY

(☑303-863-7326; www.tracksdenver.com; 3500 Walnut St; ⊙9pm-2am Fri & Sat, hrs vary Sun-Thu) Denver's best gay dance club has an 18-and-up night on Thursdays, Friday drag shows, and lesbian nights (just once a month).

Denver Wrangler · GAY

(☑303-837-1075; www.denverwrangler.com; 1700 Logan St; ⊙11am-2am; ☐101 RTD) Though it attracts an amiable crowd of gay male professionals after work, the central location endows Denver's premiere bear bar.

Great Divide Brewing Company · BREWPUB

(www.greatdivide.com; 2201 Arapahoe St; ⊙2-8pm Mon & Tue, 2-10pm Wed-Sat) This excellent local brewery does well to skip the same old burger menu and the fancy digs to keep its focus on what it does best: crafting exquisite beer.

Ace · BAR

(☑303-800-7705; www.acedenver.com; 501 E 17th Ave; ⊙11am-midnight Mon-Fri, 2pm-midnight Sat-Sun) The best ping-pong bar in Denver - street rules apply.

Matchbox · BAR

(www.matchboxdenver.com; 2625 Larimer St; ⊙4pm-2am Mon-Fri, noon-2am Sat-Sun) Located in the ever-hip RiNo (River North) art district, this hole-in-the-wall appeals to the thick-glasses and blue-jeans crowd.

The Church · CLUB

(www.coclubs.com; 1160 Lincoln St) The Church has three dance floors, acrobats, a couple of lounges and even a sushi bar!

☆ Entertainment

To find out what's happening with music, theater and other performing arts, pick up a free copy of Westword (www.westword.com).

★Denver Performing Arts Complex · PERFORMING ARTS

(☑720-865-4220; www.artscomplex.com; cnr 14th & Champa St) This massive complex – one of the largest of its kind – occupies four city blocks and houses several major theaters, including the historic Ellie Caulkins Opera House and the Seawell Grand Ballroom. It's also home to the Colorado Ballet, Denver Center for the Performing Arts, Opera Colorado and the Colorado Symphony Orchestra.

★El Chapultepec · LIVE MUSIC

(☑303-295-9126; www.thepeclodo.com; 1962 Market St; ⊙7am-2am, music from 9pm) This smoky old-school jazz joint attracts a diverse mix of people. Since it opened in 1951 Frank Sinatra, Tony Bennett and Ella Fitzgerald have played here, as have Jagger and Richards.

Red Rocks Amphitheatre · CONCERT VENUE

(☑303-640-2637; www.redrocksonline.com; 18300 W Alameda Pkwy; ⊙5am-11pm; ⊕) Red Rocks Amphitheatre is set between 400ft-high red sandstone rocks 15 miles southwest of Denver. Acoustics are so good many artists record live albums here.

Hi-Dive · LIVE MUSIC

(☑303-733-0230; www.hi-dive.com; 7 S Broadway) Local rock heroes and touring indie bands light up the stage at the Hi-Dive, a venue at the heart of Denver's local music scene.

Grizzly Rose · LIVE MUSIC

(☑303-295-1330; www.grizzlyrose.com; 5450 N Valley Hwy; ⊙from 6pm Tue-Sun; ⊕) This is one kick-ass honky-tonk – 40,000 sq ft of hot live music – attracting real cowboys from as far as Cheyenne.

Bluebird Theater · LIVE MUSIC

(☑303-377-1666; www.bluebirdtheater.net; 3317 E Colfax Ave; ⊕; ☐15, 15L RTD) This medium-sized theater is general admission standing-room, and has terrific sound and clear sight lines from the balcony.

Ogden Theatre · LIVE MUSIC

(☑303-832-1874; www.ogdentheatre.net; 935 E Colfax Ave; ⊕; ☐15 RTD) One of Denver's best live-music venues.

Comedy Works · COMEDY

(☑303-595-3637; www.comedyworks.com; 1226 15th St; ☐6, 9, 10, 15L, 20, 28, 32, 44, 44L RTD) Denver's best comedy club occupies a basement space in Larimer Sq (enter down a set of stairs at the corner of Larimer and 15th).

Lannie's Clocktower Cabaret · CABARET

(☑303-293-0075; www.lannies.com; 1601 Arapahoe St; tickets $25-40; ⊙1-5pm Tue, to 11pm Wed-Thu, 1pm-1:30am Fri & Sat; ☐Arapahoe) Bawdy, naughty and strangely romantic, Lannie's Clocktower Cabaret is a wild child standout among LoDo's rather straight-laced (or at least straight) night spots.

Coors Field · BASEBALL

(☑800-388-7625; www.mlb.com/col/ballpark/; 2001 Blake St; ⊕) The Colorado Rockies play baseball at the highly rated Coors Field. Tickets for the outfield – The Rockpile – cost $4. Not a bad deal.

Sports Authority Field at Mile High · STADIUM

(☑720-258-3000; www.sportsauthorityfieldatmile high.com; 1701 S Bryant St; ⊕) The much-lauded

Denver Broncos football team and the Denver Outlaws lacrosse team play at Mile High Stadium, 1 mile west of downtown.

Pepsi Center   STADIUM
(☑ 303-405-1111; www.pepsicenter.com; 1000 Chopper Circle) The mammoth Pepsi Center hosts the Denver Nuggets basketball team, the Colorado Mammoth of the National Lacrosse League and the Colorado Avalanche hockey team.

🛍 Shopping

Head to the pedestrian mall on 16th Street or LoDo for downtown shopping. Cherry Creek, Highlands Square and South Broadway are other top shopping districts.

★ Tattered Cover Bookstore   BOOKS
(www.tatteredcover.com; 1628 16th St; ⊗ 6:30am-9pm Mon-Fri, 9am-9pm Sat, 10am-6pm Sun) There are plenty of places to curl up with a book in Denver's beloved independent bookstore, one of two locations in the Denver area.

★ REI   OUTDOOR EQUIPMENT
(Recreational Equipment Incorporated; ☑ 303-756-3100; www.rei.com; 1416 Platte St; 🚲) In addition to top outdoor gear, it has a rental department, maps and a climbing wall.

Wax Trax Records   MUSIC
(☑ 303-831-7246; www.waxtraxrecords.com; 638 E 13th Ave; 🚌 2, 10, 15, 15L RTD) Your best spot for vinyl.

ℹ Information

Visitors & Convention Bureau Information Center (☑ 303-892-1112; www.denver.org; 1600 California St; 🕿 🚲; 🚋 California)

ORIC Desk (Outdoor Recreation Information Center; ☑ REI main line 303-756-3100; www.oriconline.org; 1416 Platte St; 🚲) For outdoor trips, hit this desk inside the REI store.

Police Headquarters (☑ 720-913-2000; 1331 Cherokee St)

Post Office (www.usps.com; 951 20th St; ⊗ 8am-6:30pm Mon-Fri, 9am-6:30pm Sat) Main branch.

University of Colorado Hospital (☑ 720-848-0000; www.uch.edu; 12605 E 16th Ave, Aurora; ⊗ 24hr) Emergency services.

ℹ Getting There & Away

Denver International Airport (p246) is served by around 20 airlines and offers flights to nearly every major US city. Located 24 miles east of downtown, DIA is connected with I-70 exit 238

by 12-mile-long Peña Blvd. Tourist and airport information is available at a **booth** (☑ 303-342-2000) in the terminal's central hall.

Greyhound buses stop at **Denver Bus Center** (☑ 303-293-6555; 1055 19th St), which runs services to Boise (from $151, 19 hours), Los Angeles (from $125, 22 hours) and other destinations.

The **Colorado Mountain Express** (CME; ☑ 800-525-6363; www.coloradomountainexpress.com; 🕿) has shuttle service from DIA, downtown Denver or Morrison to Summit County, including Breckenridge and Keystone ($35-$49, 2.5 hours) and Vail ($45-$82, 3 hours).

Amtrak's *California Zephyr* runs daily between Chicago and San Francisco via Denver. Trains arrive and depart from a **Temporary Station** (1800 21st St) behind Coors Field until light-rail renovations at **Union Station** (☑ Amtrak 303-534-2812; www.denverunionstation.org; cnr 17th & Wynkoop Sts; 🚌 31X, 40X, 80X, 86X, 120X RTD) finish in 2014. **Amtrak** (☑ 800-872-7245; www.amtrak.com) can also provide schedule information and train reservations.

ℹ Getting Around

TO/FROM THE AIRPORT

All transportation companies have booths near the baggage-claim area. Public **Regional Transit District** (RTD; ☑ 303-299-6000; www.rtd-denver.com) runs a SkyRide service to the airport from downtown Denver hourly ($9 to $13, one hour). RTD also goes to Boulder ($13, 1½ hours) from the **Market Street Bus Station** (cnr 16th & Market Sts). **Shuttle King Limo** (☑ 303-363-8000; www.shuttlekinglimo.com) charges $65 for rides from DIA to destinations in and around Denver. **SuperShuttle** (☑ 303-370-1300; www.supershuttle.com) offers shared van services (from $22) between the Denver area and the airport.

BICYCLE

BikeDenver.org (www.bikedenver.org) or **City of Denver** (www.denvergov.org) have downloadable bike maps for the city.

Denver B-Cycle (denver.bcycle.com) is the first citywide bicycle-share program in the US. Directions are given at the over 80 stations found throughout the city. Rentals under 30 minutes are free. Helmets are not included, and not required in Denver.

CAR & MOTORCYCLE

Street parking can be a pain, but there are slews of pay garages in downtown and LoDo. Nearly all the major car-rental agencies have counters at DIA, a few have offices in downtown Denver.

RTD provides public transportation throughout the Denver and Boulder area. Free shuttle buses operate along the 16th St Mall. RTD's light rail line currently has six lines servicing 46 stations. Fares are $2.25 for one to two stops, $4 for three fare zones, and $5 for all zones.

TAXI
For 24-hour cab service:
Metro Taxi (☎303-333-3333; www.metrotaxi denver.com)
Yellow Cab (☎303-777-7777; www.denver yellowcab.com)

Boulder

Tucked against the Flatirons' cragged and near-vertical rockface, this idyllic town has a sweet location and a palpable idealism that's a magnet to entrepreneurs, athletes, hippies and hard-bodies. It's also home to the University of Colorado and the Beat-founded, Buddhist-leaning Naropa University.

Boulder's mad love of the outdoors was officially legislated in 1967, when it became the first US city to tax itself specifically to preserve open space. Thanks to such vision, packs of cyclists whip up and down the Boulder Creek corridor, which links city and county parks those taxpayer dollars have purchased. The pedestrian-only Pearl St Mall is lively and perfect for strolling, especially at night, when residents peruse until the wee hours.

In many ways it is Boulder, not Denver, that is the region's tourist hub. The city is about the same distance from Denver International Airport, and staying here puts you closer to local trails in the foothills, as well as the big ski resorts west on I-70 and Rocky Mountain National Park.

◎ Sights & Activities

Boulder's two areas to see and be seen are the downtown Pearl St Mall and the University Hill district (next to campus), both off Broadway, though The Hill is rarely the haunt of anyone over 25. Overlooking the city from the west are the Flatirons, an eye-catching rock formation.

★**Chautauqua Park**   PARK
(www.chautauqua.com; 900 Baseline Rd; admission free; ⛟HOP 2) **FREE** This historic landmark park is the gateway to Boulder's most magnificent slab of open space (we're talking about the Flatirons), and it also has a wide,

lush lawn that attracts picnickers. It gets copious hikers, climbers and trail runners. World-class musicians perform each summer at the auditorium and there's a quality restaurant at the dining hall.

Boulder Creek Bike Path   CYCLING
(admission free; ☉24 hr; ⛿) **FREE** The most utilized commuter bike path in town, this fabulously smooth and mostly straight creekside concrete path follows Boulder Creek from Foothill Parkway all the way to the split of Boulder Canyon and Four Mile Canyon Rd west of downtown – a total distance of over 5 miles one-way. The path also feeds urban bike lanes that lead all over town.

Eldorado Canyon State Park   OUTDOORS
(☎303-494-3943; ☉visitor center 9am-5pm) One of the country's most favored rock-climbing areas, offering class 5.5 to 5.12 climbs and some nice hiking trails. The park entrance is on Eldorado Springs Dr, west of Hwy 93. Information is available from Boulder Rock Club.

University Bicycles   CYCLING
(www.ubikes.com; 839 Pearl St; 4hr rental $15; ☉10am-6pm Mon-Sat, 10am-5pm Sun) Plenty of places rent bicycles to cruise around town, but U Bikes has the widest range of rides and the most helpful staff.

Boulder Rock Club   ROCK CLIMBING
(☎303-447-2804; http://boulderrockclub.com; 2829 Mapleton Ave; day pass adult/child $17/10; ☉8am-10pm Mon, 6am-11pm Tue-Thu, 8am-11pm Fri, 10am-8pm Sat & Sun; ⛿) Climb indoors at

---

THE THOUSAND-YEAR FLOOD

It came after a drought that followed the worst wildfire in Colorado history. On September 12, 2013, the Front Range woke up to flooding canyons and inundations that isolated mountain communities. Eight people died and thousands lost their homes. A disaster of this magnitude is considered a thousand-year flood, with a 0.1% probability in any given year. The month's 17in of rainfall blasted September's usual 1.7in average. Now cited as the second-largest natural disaster in US history, after Hurricane Katrina, it will take years to recover from. The affected area was roughly the size of Connecticut. Losses were estimated at $2 billion.

this massive warehouse full of artificial rock faces cragged with ledges and routes. The auto-belay system allows solo climbers an anchor. The staff are a great resource for local climbing routes and tips too.

✦ Festivals & Events

Boulder Creek Festival
MUSIC, FOOD

(☎303-449-3137; www.bceproductions.com; Canyon Blvd, Central Park; ☺May; ⚐; ⊟206, JUMP) FREE Billed as the kick-off to summer and capped with the fabulous Bolder Boulder, this massive Memorial Day weekend festival has 10 event areas featuring more than 30 live entertainers and 500 vendors. With food and drink, music and sunshine, what's not to love?

Bolder Boulder
ATHLETICS

(☎303-444-7223; www.bolderboulder.com; adult from $59; ☺May; ⚐) Held in a self-consciously hyper athletic town, this is the biggest foot race within the city limits. It doesn't take itself too seriously – spectators scream, there are runners in costume, and live music plays throughout the course. It's held on Memorial Day.

🛏 Sleeping

Boulder has dozens of options – drive down Broadway or Hwy 36 to take your pick. Booking online usually scores the best discounts.

Boulder Outlook
HOTEL $

(☎303-443-3322, 800-542-0304; www.boulderoutlook.com; 800 28th St; d incl breakfast $89-99; P❋☎🐾🏊) ✎ Boulder's first zero-waste hotel is just off the highway at the south end of town, with easy access from Denver, and has funky colors, a sustainability focus and pet-friendly atmosphere. Strangely, motel-style rooms with outdoor access are less expensive than their main building counterparts. There's a dimly-lit indoor pool and climbing wall.

The onsite restaurant and bar often hosts blues bands.

★ Chautauqua Lodge
HISTORIC HOTEL $$

(☎303-442-3282; www.chautauqua.com; 900 Baseline Rd; r from $73; cottages $125-183; P❋☎🐾; ⊟HOP 2) Adjoining beautiful hiking trails to the Flatirons, this leafy neighborhood of cottages is our top pick. It has contemporary rooms and one- to three-bedroom cottages with porches and beds with patchwork quilts. It's perfect for families and pets. All have full kitchens, though the wraparound porch of the Chautauqua Dining Hall is a local favorite for breakfast.

Hotel Boulderado
BOUTIQUE HOTEL $$$

(☎303-442-4344; www.boulderado.com; 2115 13th St; r from $264; P❋☎🐾; ⊟HOP, SKIP) With over a century of service, the charming Boulderado is a National Registered Landmark and a romantic getaway. Think Victorian elegance and antique-filled rooms. The stained glass atrium and glacial water fountain accent the lobby, usually awash with jazz music.

St Julien Hotel & Spa
HOTEL $$$

(☎720-406-9696, reservations 877-303-0900; www.stjulien.com; 900 Walnut St; r from $309; P❋🐾@☎🏊) In the heart of downtown, Boulder's finest four-star is modern and refined, with photographs of local scenery and cork walls that warm the room ambiance. With fabulous Flatiron views, the back patio hosts live world music, jazz concerts and wild salsa parties. Rooms are plush, and so are the robes.

🍴 Eating

Boulder's dining scene has dozens of great options. Most are centered on the Pearl Street Mall, while bargains are more likely to be found on the Hill. Between 3:30pm and 6:30pm nearly every restaurant in the city features a happy hour with some kind of amazing food and drink special. It's a great way to try fine dining on a budget – check websites for details.

Spruce Confections
BAKERY $

(☎303-449-6773; 767 Pearl St; cookies from $3.25; ☺6:30am-6pm Mon-Fri, 7am-6pm Sat & Sun; ⚐; ⊟206) Boulder's go-to bakehouse has sinful scones and breakfast lattes. Come for lunch for good homemade soups and salads.

Dish
SANDWICHES $

(☎720-565-5933; www.dishgourmet.com; 1918 Pearl St; mains $10; ☺9am-6pm Mon-Fri, 11am-4pm Sat; ⚐; ⊟204, HOP) Bank lines flank this gourmet deli at lunchtime. At $10, the sandwiches are hardly cheap but they are satisfying. Think roasted turkey carved in chunks, pate, natural beef, slow-cooked brisket and baguettes smothered with butter and top-tier cheeses.

Zoe Ma Ma
CHINESE $

(2010 10th St; mains $5-13; ⊙11am-10pm Sun-Thu, 11am-11pm Fri & Sat; 🚌206, SKIP, HOP) 🅿 At Boulder's hippest noodle bar you can slurp and munch fresh street food at a long outdoor counter. Mama, the Taiwanese matriarch, is on hand, cooking and chatting up customers in her Croc sandals. Organic noodles are made from scratch, as are the garlicky melt-in-your mouth pot stickers.

The Sink
PUB $

(www.thesink.com; 1165 13th St; mains $5-12; ⊙11am-2am, kitchen to 10pm; 📶; 🚌203, 204, 225, DASH, SKIP) Dim and graffiti-scrawled, the Sink has been a Hill classic since 1923 and once Robert Redford worked here. Colorful characters cover the cavernous space – the scene alone is almost worth a visit. Almost. Once you've washed back the legendary Sink burger with a slug of a local microbrew, you'll be glad you stuck around.

Alfalfa's
SELF-CATERING $

(www.alfalfas.com; 1651 Broadway St; ⊙7:30am-10pm; 🚌AB, B, JUMP, SKIP) A small, community-oriented natural market with a wonderful selection of prepared food ($1 to $16) and an inviting indoor-outdoor dining area to enjoy it in.

Cafe Aion
SPANISH $$

(🕿303-993-8131; www.cafeaion.com; 1235 Pennsylvania Ave; tapas $5-13; ⊙11am-10pm Tues-Fri, 9am-3pm Sat-Sun; 🚌203, 204, 225, DASH, SKIP) Original and unpretentious, this side street cafe mimics the relaxed rhythms of Spain with fresh tapas and delectable house-made sangria. Papas bravas have the perfect crisp, and grilled spring onions and dolmas are springtime-fresh. Check out the all-evening happy hour on Tuesday.

Lucile's
CAJUN $$

(🕿303-442-4743; www.luciles.com; 2142 14th St; mains $8-14; ⊙7am-2pm Mon-Fri, from 8am Sat & Sun; 🖶; 🚌205, 206, HOP) 🅿 This New Orleans–style diner has perfected breakfast; the Creole egg dishes (served over creamy spinach alongside cheesy grits or perfectly blackened trout) are all-stars. Start with the chicory coffee and an order of beignets. Their homemade jam is perfect on a steaming biscuit.

★ Salt
MODERN AMERICAN $$$

(🕿303-444-7258; www.saltboulderbistro.com; 1047 Pearl St; mains $14-28; ⊙11am-10pm Mon-Wed, to 11pm Thu-Sat, 10am-10pm Sun; 🖶; 🚌208, HOP, SKIP) While farm-to-table is

FOODIE FINDS IN THE ROCKIES

Start by digging into regional *Edible* (www.ediblecommunities.com) magazines online – a great resource for farmers markets and innovative eats. There are editions for the Front Range and Aspen.

Boulder is worth a stop since being named America's Foodiest Small Town, according to *Bon Appetit*. At Kitchen (p257) Monday is community night, which means shared tables and a homegrown five-course meal served family-style, with 20% of proceeds going to charity. Go behind the scenes with **Local Table Tours** (🕿303-909-5747; www.localtabletours.com; tours $25-70), a tour presenting a smattering of great local cuisine and inside knowledge on food and wine or coffee and pastries. The cocktail crawl is a hit.

For fine dining in a warehouse or an airplane hangar, Denver's Hush (www.hushdenver.com) sponsors fun pop-up dinners with top regional chefs, by invitation only – make contact online.

ubiquitous in Boulder, this spot surpasses expectations. The sweet pea ravioli with lemon *buerre blanc* and shaved radishes is a feverish delight. But Salt also knows meat: local and grass-fed, basted, braised and slow roasted to utter perfection. When in doubt, ask – the servers really know their stuff.

It also has one of Boulder's best happy hours, with bargain bites. The house mixologist has repeatedly won the competition for Boulder's best.

Kitchen
MODERN AMERICAN $$$

(🕿303-544-5973; www.thekitchencafe.com; 1039 Pearl St; mains $18-32; 📶; 🚌206, HOP) 🅿 Clean lines and fresh farmers-market ingredients provide the building blocks at Boulder's most lauded kitchen. Think tapas of roasted root vegetables, shaved prosciutto and mussels steamed in wine and cream. The pulled-pork sandwich rocks, but save room for the sticky toffee pudding.

A younger crowd gathers at the more casual upstairs bar and the Kitchen Next Door, with cheaper eats (mains $10).

🍷 Drinking & Entertainment

Playboy didn't vote CU the best party school for nothing – the blocks around the Pearl St Mall and the Hill churn out fun, with many restaurants doubling as bars or turning into all-out dance clubs come 10pm.

★ **Mountain Sun Pub & Brewery**   BREWERY
(1535 Pearl St; ⊙ 11am-1am; ᴥ; 🖥 HOP, 205, 206) Boulder's favorite brewery serves a rainbow of brews from chocolaty to fruity, and packs in an eclectic crowd of yuppies, hippies and everyone in between. Walls are lined with tapestries, there are board games to amuse you and the pub grub (especially the burgers) is delicious. There's usually live music of the bluegrass and jam-band variety on Sunday and Monday nights. Second location 627 S Broadway.

Bitter Bar   COCKTAIL BAR
(☑ 303-442-3050; www.thebitterbar.com; 835 Walnut St; cocktails $9-15; ⊙ 5pm-12am Mon-Thur, 5pm-2am Fri-Sat; 🖥 HOP) A chic Boulder speakeasy where killer cocktails – such as the scrumptious lavender-infused Blue Velvet – make the evening slip happily out of focus. The patio is great for conversation and their monthly classes buy you the know-how to mix two drinks that would make a Mad Man weep. There's live music at 9pm on Thursday.

> **WORTH A TRIP**
>
> ## SUSTAINABLE BREWS
>
> **New Belgium Brewing Co** (☑ 800-622-4044; www.newbelgium.com; 500 Lined St; ⊙ guided tours 10am-6pm, Tue-Sat) **FREE** satisfies beer connoisseurs with its hearty Fat Tire Amber Ale, and diverse concoctions like 1554, Trippell and Sunshine Wheat. Recognized as one of the world's most environmentally conscious breweries, a 100,000kw turbine keeps it wind-powered. The brewery also sponsors cool events such as bike-in cinema and ski resort scavenger hunts. It's in the college town of Fort Collins (home to Colorado State University), a worthwhile 46-mile drive north of Boulder on I-25 – especially if you're heading to Wyoming. Reserve tickets online – these popular tours include complimentary tasting of the flagship and specialty brews.

Boulder Dushanbe Teahouse   TEAHOUSE
(☑ 303-442-4993; 1770 13th St; mains $8-19; ⊙ 8am-10pm; 🖥 203, 204, 205, 206, 208, 225, DASH, JUMP, SKIP) Step into this incredible Tajik work of art – a gift from Boulder's sister city (Dushanbe, Tajikistan). Incredible craftsmanship and meticulous painting envelop the vibrant multicolored interior. The international fare is sadly less notable than the setting, but it's perfect for tea.

Boulder Theater   CINEMA, MUSIC
(☑ 303-786-7030; www.bouldertheatre.com; 2032 14th St) This old movie theater-turned-historic venue brings in slightly under-the-radar acts like jazz great Charlie Hunter, the madmen rockers of Gogol Bordello and West African divas, Les Nubians. But it also screens classic films and short-film festivals that can and should be enjoyed with a glass of beer.

🛍 Shopping

Boulder has great shopping and galleries. The outdoor 29th St Mall, with a movie theatre, just off 28th St between Canyon and Pearl St, is a more recent addition.

Pearl Street Mall   MALL
The main feature of downtown Boulder is the Pearl Street Mall, a vibrant pedestrian zone filled with kids' climbing boulders and splash fountains, bars, galleries and restaurants.

Momentum   HANDICRAFTS
(www.ourmomentum.com; 1625 Pearl St; ⊙ 10am-7pm Tue-Sat, 11am-6pm Sun) 🌿 The kitchen sink of unique global gifts – Zulu wire baskets, fabulous scarves from India, Nepal and Ecuador – all handcrafted and purchased at fair value from disadvantaged artisans. Every item purchased provides a direct economic lifeline to the artists.

Common Threads   CLOTHING
(www.commonthreadsboulder.com; 2707 Spruce St; ⊙ 10am-6pm Mon-Sat, noon-5pm Sun) Vintage shopping at its most haute couture, this fun place is where to go for secondhand Choos and Prada purses. The shop is a pleasure to browse, with clothing organized by color and type on visually aesthetic racks, just like a big-city boutique. Also runs clothes-making courses.

Boulder Bookstore   BOOKS
(www.boulderbookstore.indiebound.com; 1107 Pearl St; 🛜 ᴥ) Boulder's favorite indie bookstore has a huge travel section downstairs and hosts readings and workshops.

ℹ Information

Boulder Visitor Center (☑303-442-2911; www.bouldercoloradousa.com; 2440 Pearl St; ⊙8:30am-5pm Mon-Thu, 8:30am-4pm Fri) Offers information and internet access.

ℹ Getting There & Around

Boulder has fabulous public transportation, with services extending as far away as Denver and its airport. Ecofriendly buses are run by **RTD** (☑303-299-6000; www.rtd-denver.com; per ride $2-4.50; ⛟). Maps are available at **Boulder Station** (cnr 14th & Walnut Sts). RTD buses (route B) operate between Boulder Station and Denver's Market St Bus Station ($5, 55 minutes). RTD's SkyRide bus (route AB) heads to Denver International Airport ($13, one hour, hourly). **SuperShuttle** (☑303-444-0808; www. supershuttle.com; one-way around $27) provides hotel ($27) and door-to-door ($34) shuttle service from the airport.

For two-wheel transportation, **Boulder B-Cycle** (boulder.bcycle.com; 24-hr rental $7) is a new citywide program with townie bikes available at strategic locations, but riders must sign up online first.

Northern Mountains

With one foot on either side of the continental divide and behemoths of granite in every direction, Colorado's Northern Mountains offer out-of-this-world alpine adventures, laid-back skiing, kick-butt hiking and biking, and plenty of rivers to raft, fish and float as you stare into the big-blue arching Colorado sky.

Rocky Mountain National Park

Rocky Mountain National Park showcases classic alpine scenery, with wildflower meadows and serene mountain lakes set under snowcapped peaks. There are over 4 million visitors annually, but many stay on the beaten path. Hike an extra mile and enjoy the incredible solitude. Elk are the park's signature mammal – you will even see them grazing on hotel lawns, but also keep an eye out for bighorn sheep, moose, marmots and black bear.

◉ Sights & Activities

With over 300 miles of trail, traversing all aspects of its diverse terrain, the park is suited to every hiking ability.

Those with the kids in tow might consider the easy hikes in the Wild Basin to Calypso

Falls or to Gem Lakes in the Lumpy Ridge area, or the trail to Twin Sisters Peak south of Estes Park, while those with unlimited ambition, strong legs and enough trail mix will be lured by the challenge of summiting Longs Peak.

Regardless, it's best to spend at least one night at 7000ft to 8000ft prior to setting out to allow your body to adjust to the elevation. Before July, many trails are snowbound and high water runoff makes passage difficult.

In the winter, avalanches are a hazard.

★**Moraine Park Museum**   MUSEUM
(☑970-586-1206; Bear Lake Rd; ⊙9am-4:30pm Jun-Oct) Built by the Civilian Conservation Corps in 1923 and once the park's proud visitors lodge, this building has been renovated in recent years to host exhibits on geology, glaciers and wildlife.

🛏 Sleeping & Eating

The only overnight accommodations in the park are at campgrounds. Dining options and the majority of motel or hotel accommodations are around Estes Park or Grand Lake, located on the other side of the Trail Ridge Road Pass (open late May to October).

You will need a backcountry permit to stay outside developed park campgrounds. None of the campgrounds have showers, but they do have flush toilets in summer and outhouse facilities in winter. Sites include a fire ring, picnic table and one parking spot.

Olive Ridge Campground   CAMPGROUND $
(☑303-541-2500; campsites $19; ⊙mid-May–Nov) This well-kept USFS campground has access to four trailheads: St Vrain Mountain, Wild Basin, Longs Peak and Twin Sisters. In the summer it can get full, though sites are mostly first come, first served.

Longs Peak Campground   CAMPGROUND $
(☑970-586-1206; MM 9, State Hwy 7; campsites $20; ℗) This is the base camp of choice for the early morning ascent of Longs Peak. There are no reservations, but if you're planning to bag Longs Peak after sleeping here, get here early one day before the climb.

Moraine Park Campground   CAMPGROUND $
(☑877-444-6777; www.recreation.gov; off Bear Lake Rd; summer campsites $20) In the middle of a stand of ponderosa pine forest off Bear Lake Road, this is the biggest of the park's campgrounds.

Reservations are accepted and recommended from the end of May through to the end of September; other times of the year the campground is first come, first served. At night in the summer, there are numerous ranger-led programs in the ampitheater.

Aspenglen Campground CAMPGROUND $

(☑877-444-6777; www.recreation.gov; State Hwy 34; campsites summer $20) With only 54 sites, this is the smallest of the park's reservable camping. There are many tent-only sites, including some walk-ins.

Timber Creek Campground CAMPGROUND $

(Trail Ridge Rd, US Hwy 34; campsites $20) This campground has 100 sites and remains open through winter. No reservations accepted. The only established campground on the west side of the park, it's 7 miles north of Grand Lake.

Glacier Basin Campground CAMPGROUND $

(☑877-444-6777; www.recreation.gov; off Bear Lake Rd; campsites summer $20) This developed campground has a large area for group camping and accommodates RVs. It is served by the shuttle buses on Bear Lake Rd throughout the summer. Make reservations through the website.

❶ Information

For private vehicles, the park entrance fee is $20, valid for seven days. Individuals entering the park on foot, bicycle, motorcycle or bus pay $10 each. All visitors receive a free copy of the park's information brochure, which contains a good orientation map and is available in English, German, French, Spanish and Japanese.

Backcounty permits ($20 for a group up to 12 people for seven days) are required for overnight stays in the 260 designated backcountry camping sites in the park. They are free between November 1 and April 30. Phone reservations can be made only from March 1 to May 15. Reservations by snail mail or in person are accepted via the **Backcountry Office**. (☑970-586-1242; www.nps.gov/romo).

A bear box to store your food is required if you are staying overnight in the backcountry (established campsites already have them). These can be rented for around $3 to $5 per day from REI (p254) or the **Estes Park Mountain Shop** (☑970-586-6548; www.estesparkmountain-shop.com; 2050 Big Thompson Ave; 2-person tent $10, bear box $3 per night; ⊙8am-9pm).

Alpine Visitor Center (www.nps.gov/romo; Fall River Pass; ⊙10:30am-4:30pm late May–mid-Jun, 9am-5pm late Jun-early Sep, 10:30am-4:30pm early Sep–mid-Oct; ⓓ) The views from this popular visitors center and souvenir store at 11,796ft, and right in the middle of the park, are extraordinary.

Beaver Meadows Visitor Center (☑970-586-1206; www.nps.gov/romo; US Hwy 36; ⊙8am-9pm late Jun-late Aug, to 4:30pm or 5pm rest of year; ⓓ) The primary visitors center and best stop for park information if you're approaching from Estes Park.

Kawuneeche Visitor Center (☑970-627-3471; 16018 US Hwy 34; ⊙8am-6pm last week May-Labor Day, 8am-5pm Labor Day-Sep, 8am-4:30pm Oct-May; ⓓ) This is the main visitors center on the west side of the park, offering a film about the park, ranger-led walks and discussions, backcountry permits and family activities.

❶ Getting There & Away

Trail Ridge Rd (US 34) is the only east–west route through the park and is closed in winter. The most direct route from Boulder follows US 36 through Lyons to the east entrances.

There are two entrance stations on the east side, Fall River (US 34) and Beaver Meadows (US 36). The Grand Lake Station (also US 34) is the only entry on the west side. Year-round access is available through Kawuneeche Valley along the Colorado River headwaters to Timber Creek Campground. The main centers of visitor activity on the park's east side are the Alpine Visitor Center, high on Trail Ridge Rd and Bear Lake Rd, which leads to campgrounds, trailheads and the Moraine Park Museum.

North of Estes Park, Devils Gulch Rd leads to several hiking trails. Further out on Devils Gulch Rd, you pass through the village of Glen Haven to reach the trailhead entry to the park along the North Fork of the Big Thompson River.

❶ Getting Around

In summer a free shuttle bus operates from the Estes Park Visitor Center multiple times daily, bringing hikers to a park-and-ride location where you can pick up other shuttles. The year-round option leaves the Glacier Basin parking area toward Bear Lake, in the parks lower elevations. During the summer peak, a second shuttle operates between Moraine Park campground and the Glacier Basin parking area. Shuttles run on weekends only from mid-August through September.

Estes Park

It's no small irony that becoming a nature-lovers hub has turned the gateway to one of the most pristine outdoor escapes in the US into kind of Great Outdoors Disney. And while there are plenty of T-shirt shops and mountain kitsche, a nice river runs through town, it has cool parks, decent restaurants and a haunted hotel.

🏃 Activities

★Colorado Mountain School

ROCK CLIMBING

(☑800-836-4008; www.totalclimbing.com; 341 Moraine Ave; half-day guided climbs per person from $125) There's no better resource for climbers in Colorado. Basic courses, such as Intro to Rock Climbing, are a great way for novices to deeply experience the Rockies, more experienced climbers can hire guides to take them up some of the radical neighboring peaks. It has an stay on-site in dorm lodging.

🛏 Sleeping

Estes Park's dozens of hotels fill up fast in summer. There are some passable budget options but the many lovely area campgrounds are the best-value.

Try the **Estes Park Visitor Center** (☑970-577-9900; www.estesparkresortcvb.com; 500 Big Thompson Ave; ⊗9am-8pm Jun-Aug, 8am-5pm Mon-Fri, 9am-5pm Sat, 10am-4pm Sun Sep-May), just east of the US 36 junction, for help with lodging; note that many places close in winter.

Total Climbing Lodge

HOSTEL $

(☑303-447-2804; www.totalclimbing.com; 341 Moraine Ave; dm $25; P⊖@🛜) A bustling hub of climbers, lodging here is the best dorm option in town. Expect simple pine bunks, a ping-pong table and a laid-back vibe.

Estes Park Hostel

HOSTEL $

(☑970-237-0152; www.estesparkhostel.com; 211 Cleave St; dm/s/d $26/38/52; 🛜) This hostel, with a handful of shared rooms and simple privates, isn't going into history books as the plushest digs ever, but there's a kitchen on site, and Terri, the owner, is helpful. The price is right too.

★YMCA of the Rockies – Estes Park Center

RESORT $$

(☑970-586-3341; www.ymcarockies.org; 2515 Tunnel Rd; r & d from $109, cabins from $129; P⊖❄🛜🏊) Estes Park Center is not your typical YMCA boarding house. Instead it's a favorite vacation spot. There are upmarket motel-style accommodations and cabins set on hundreds of acres of high alpine terrain. Book ahead.

Riversong

BOUTIQUE HOTEL $$

(☑970 586 4666; www.romanticriversong.com; 1766 Lower Broadview Dr; d from $165; P⊖) Tucked down a dead-end dirt road overlooking the Big Thompson River, Riversong offers nine romantic rooms with private bath in an arts-and-crafts-style mansion. The minimum stay is two nights, and prices vary by amenities. West of town take Moraine Ave, turn onto Mary's Lake Rd and take the first right.

Stanley Hotel

HOTEL $$$

(☑970-577-4000; www.stanleyhotel.com; 333 Wonderview Ave; r from $199; P🛜🏊) The white Georgian Colonial Revival hotel stands in brilliant contrast to the towering peaks of Rocky Mountain National Park framing the skyline. A favorite local retreat, this best-in-class hotel served as the inspiration for Stephen King's famous cult novel *The Shining*. Rooms are decorated to retain some of the Old West feel while still ensuring all the creature comforts.

🍴 Eating

Estes Park Brewery

BREWERY

(www.epbrewery.com; 470 Prospect Village Dr; ⊗11am-2am Mon-Sun) The town's brewpub serves pizza, burgers and wings, and at least eight different house beers, in a big, boxy room resembling a cross between a classroom and a country kitchen. Pool tables and outdoor seating keep the place rocking late into the night.

Ed's Cantina & Grill

MEXICAN $$

(☑970-586-2919; www.edscantina.com; 390 E Elkhorn Ave; mains $9-13; ⊗11am-late daily, from 8am-10pm Sat & Sun; 🍴) With an outdoor patio right on the river, Ed's is a great place to kick back with a margarita and one of the daily $3 blue-plate specials (think fried, rolled tortillas) with shredded pork and guacamole). Serving Mexican and American staples, the restaurant is in a retro-mod space with leather booth seating and a bold primary color scheme. The bar is in a separate room with light-wood stools featuring comfortable high backs.

ℹ Getting There & Away

From Denver International Airport, **Estes Park Shuttle** (☑970-586-5151; www.estesparkshuttle.com) runs four times daily to Estes Park (one-way/return $45/85).

Steamboat Springs

With luxuriant tree-skiing, top-notch trails for mountain-biking and a laid-back Western feel, Steamboat beats out other ski towns in both real ambience and offerings.

Its historic center is cool for rambling, its hot springs top off a hard day of play, and locals couldn't be friendlier.

◉ Sights & Activities

Steamboat Mountain Resort   SNOW SPORTS
(☑ticket office 970-871-5252; www.steamboat. com; lift ticket adult/child $94/59; ☉ticket office 8am-5pm) Known for a 3600ft vertical drop, excellent powder and trails for all levels, this is the main draw for winter visitors, offering some of the best skiing in the US. In the ski area there are (overpriced) food and equipment vendors galore.

★Strawberry Park Hot Springs HOT SPRING
(☑970-870-1517; www.strawberryhotsprings. com; 44200 County Rd; per day adult/child $10/5; ☉10am-10:30pm Sun-Thu, to midnight Fri & Sat; ☻) 🏊 Steamboat's favorite hot springs are actually outside the city limits, but offer great back-to-basics relaxation. Water is 104°F in these tasteful stone pools formed by cascading drops. To stay over, choose from camping or rustic cabins. There's no electricity (you get gas lanterns) and you'll need your own linens.

Be sure to reserve. Weekend reservations require a two-night stay. Note that the thermal pools are clothing optional after dark.

Orange Peel Bikes   BICYCLE RENTAL
(☑970-879-2957; www.orangepeelbikes.com; 1136 Yampa St; bike rental per day $20-65; ☉10am-6pm Mon-Fri, to 5pm Sat; ☻) Stop by the coolest bike shop in town to pick up a cruiser or top-line mountain bike. They have a great biking map, and plenty of info on the best spots to ride, including Emerald Mountain (just out of town), Spring Creek, Mad Creek and Red Dirt. Families can rent cruisers and do the 7-mile-trail that follows the Yampa near town.

Bucking Rainbow
Outfitters   RAFTING, FISHING
(☑970-879-8747; www.buckingrainbow.com; 730 Lincoln Ave; inner tubes $17, rafting $43-100, fishing $150-340; ☉daily) This excellent outfitter offers rafting trips on the Yampa, Platte, Eagle and Elk Rivers (Class II-IV), tubes and shuttle services for the relatively flat section of the Yampa in town, fishing year round and plenty more.

Old Town Hot Springs   HOT SPRING
(☑970-879-1828; www.oldtownhotsprings.org; 136 Lincoln Ave; adult/child $16/9, waterslide $6;

☉5:30am-10pm Mon-Fri, 7am-9pm Sat, 8am-9pm Sun; ☻) Right in the center of town, the mineral water here is warmer than most in the area. The springs recently underwent a $5-million renovation and now there's a new pool, a pair of 230ft-long waterslides and, perhaps coolest of all, an aquatic climbing wall! Kids will dig it!

🍽 Sleeping & Eating

There are plenty of places to sleep; contact Steamboat Central Reservations (☑877-783-2628; www.steamboat.com; Mt Werner Circle, off Gondola Sq) for condos and other options near the ski area.

Hotel Bristol   HOTEL $$
(☑970-879-3083; www.steamboathotelbristol. com; 917 Lincoln Ave; d $129-149; ☻☎) The elegant Hotel Bristol has small, but sophisticated, Western digs, with dark-wood and brass furnishings and Pendleton wool blankets on the beds. There's a ski shuttle, a six-person indoor Jacuzzi and a cozy restaurant.

The Boathouse   MODERN AMERICAN $$
(☑970-879-4797; 609 Yampa; $12-20; ☉restaurant 11am-10pm, bar to 1am) You can't beat the view from the riverfront deck, and the creative menu takes you across continents with innovative plates such as 'When Pigs Fly,' a piquant pork-chop-wasabi invention. Great for afternoon cloud-watching.

Carl's Tavern   AMERICAN $$
(☑970-761-2060; www.carlstavern.com; 700 Yampa Ave; $14-31) This local's favorite has great pub grub, a happening patio, live music, cool waitstaff, and a raucous spirit that will get your hear thumping.

❶ Information

Steamboat Springs Visitor Center (☑970-879-0880; www.steamboat-chamber.com; 125 Anglers Drive; ☉8am-5pm Mon-Fri, 10am-3pm Sat)

❶ Getting There & Away

Buses between Denver and Salt Lake City stop at the **Greyhound Terminal** (☑800-231-2222; www.greyhound.com; 1505 Lincoln Ave), about half a mile west of town. **Steamboat Springs Transit** (☑970-879-3717, for pick-up in Mountain Area 970-846-1279; http://steamboat-springs.net) runs free buses between Old Town and the ski resort year-round. Steamboat is 166 miles northwest of Denver via US 40.

Central Colorado

Colorado's central mountains are well known for their plethora of world-class ski resorts, sky-high hikes and snow-melt rivers. To the southeast is Colorado Springs and Pikes Peak, which anchor the southern Front Range.

Winter Park

Less than two hours from Denver, unpretentious Winter Park is a favorite ski resort with Front Rangers, who flock here from as far away as Colorado Springs to ski fresh tracks each weekend. Beginners can frolic on miles of powdery groomers while experts test their skills on Mary Jane's world-class bumps. Most services are along US 40 (the main drag), including the visitor center (☑970-726-4118; www.winterpark-info.com; 78841 Hwy 40; ⊙9am-5pm daily).

South of town, Winter Park Resort (☑970-726-1564; www.winterparkresort.com; Hwy 40; lift ticket adult/child $104/62; ⊞) covers five mountains and has a vertical drop of more than 2600ft. Experts love it here because more than half of the runs are geared solely for highly skilled skiers. It also has 45 miles of lift-accessible mountain-biking trails (www.trestlebikepark.com; day pass adult/child $39/29; ⊙mid-Jun–mid-Sep) connecting to a 600-mile trail system running through the valley.

★Devil's Thumb Ranch (☑800-933-4339; www.devilsthumbranch.com; 3530 County Rd 83; bunkhouse $100-180, lodge $240-425, cabins from $365; ⊞⊜⊠⊠) ∅, with a cowboy chic lodge and cabins alongside a 65-mile network of trails, makes an ultra-romantic getaway for the active-minded. Geothermal heat, reclaimed wood and low-emission fireplaces make it green. It's ideal for cross-country skiing and horseback rides (☑970-726-5632; www.devilsthumbranch.com; 3530 County Rd 83; trail passes adult/child $20/8, horseback riding $95-175; ⊞) in the high country.

The best deal around is the friendly Rocky Mountain Chalet (☑970-726-8256; www.therockymountainchalet.com; 15 Co Rd 72; dm $30, r summer/winter $89/149; ℗⊛⊜), with plush, comfortable doubles, dorm rooms and a sparkling kitchen.

For inspired dining, Tabernash Tavern (☑970-726-4430; www.tabernashtavern.com; 72287 US Hwy 40; mains $20-34; ⊙5-9pm Tue-Sat) ∅ whets the appetite with buffalo rib ragout or venison burgers. Reserve ahead. It's north of town.

Breckenridge & Around

Set at 9600ft, at the foot of a marvelous range of treeless peaks, Breck is a sweetly surviving gold-mining town with a lovely national historic district. With down-to-earth grace, the town boasts family-friendly ski runs that don't disappoint and always draw a giddy crowd. If you should happen to grow restless, there are five great ski resorts and outlet shopping less than an hour away.

⚡ Activities

Breckenridge Ski Area   SNOW SPORTS
(☑800-789-7669; www.breckenridge.com; lift ticket adult/child $115/68; ⊙8:30am-4pm Nov–mid-Apr; ⊞) Spans five mountains and features some of the best beginner and intermediate terrain in the state (the green runs are

ROCKY MOUNTAINS CENTRAL COLORADO

THE ROCKIES FOR POWDER HOUNDS

Well worth the five-hour road trip from Denver, Crested Butte promises deep powder and lovely open terrain next to a mining outpost re-tooled to be one of Colorado's coolest small towns.

If you're short on travel time, go directly to Summit County. Use lively Breckenridge as your base and conquer five areas on one combo lift ticket, including the mastodon resort of Vail, our favorite for remote back bowl terrain, and the ultralocal and laid-back Arapahoe Basin Ski Area. A-Basin stays open into June, when spring skiing means tailgating with beer and barbecue in between slush runs.

From Crested Butte, you can head a little further south and ski the slopes at Telluride; from Summit County and Vail, Aspen is nearby. Both are true old gold towns. Be sure to devote at least a few hours to exploring Aspen's glitzy shops and Telluride's down-to-earth bars for a real local vibe in a historic Wild West setting.

From Aspen, catch a local flight up to Jackson Hole Mountain Resort to do some real vertical powder riding in the Grand Tetons.

flatter than most in Colorado), as well as killer steeps and chutes for experts, and a renowned snowboard park.

Arapahoe Basin Ski Area
SNOW SPORTS

(☑970-468-0718; www.arapahoebasin.com; Hwy 6; lift adult/child 6-14yr $79/40; ⊙9am-4pm Mon-Fri, from 8:30 Sat & Sun) North America's highest resort, about 12 miles from Breck, is smaller, less commercial and usually open until at least mid-June! Full of steeps, walls and backcountry terrain, it's a local favorite because it doesn't draw herds of package tourists.

Peak 8 Fun Park
AMUSEMENT PARK

(☑800-789-7669; www.breckenridge.com; Peak 8; day pass 3-7yr/8yr & up $34/68; ⊙9:30am-5:30pm mid-Jun–mid-Sep; 🖼) With a laundry list of made-for-thrills activities, including a big-air trampoline, climbing wall, mountain-bike park (rental half/full day $49/59) and the celebrated SuperSlide – a luge-like course taken on a sled at exhilarating speeds. Get the day pass, do activities à la carte or simply take a scenic ride up the chair lift (without/with bike $10/17).

★ Festivals & Events

Ullr Fest
CULTURE

(www.gobreck.com; ⊙early to mid-January) The Ullr Fest celebrates the Norse god of winter with a wild parade and four-day festival featuring a twisted version of the Dating Game, an ice-skating party and a bonfire.

International Snow Sculpture Championship
ART

(www.gobreck.com; ⊙mid-Jan; 🖼) Sculptors from around the world descend on Breck to create meltable masterpieces. It starts in mid-January and lasts for two weeks on Riverwalk.

🛏 Sleeping

For upscale slope-side rentals, contact Great Western Lodging (☑888-453-1001; www.gw-lodging.com; 322 N Main St; condos summer/winter from $125/275; P ❋ 🐾). Campers can look for USFS campgrounds (☑877-444-6777; www.recreation.gov) outside of town.

Fireside Inn
B&B, HOSTEL $

(☑970-453-6456; www.firesideinn.com; 114 N French St; summer/winter dm $30/41, summer/winter d $101/140; P ❋ @ 🐾) The best deal for budget travelers in Summit County, this chummy hostel and B&B is a find. All guests can enjoy the chlorine-free barrel hot tub and resident snuggly dog. The English hosts are delight and very helpful with local information. It's a 10-minute walk to the gondola in ski boots.

★ Abbet Placer Inn
B&B $$

(☑970-453-6489; www.abbettplacer.com; 205 S French St; r summer $99-179, winter $119-229; P ❋ @ 🐾) This violet house has five large rooms decked-out with wood furnishings, iPod docks and fluffy robes. It's very low key. The warm and welcoming hosts cook big breakfasts, and guests can enjoy a lovely outdoor Jacuzzi deck and use of a common kitchenette. The top-floor room has massive views of the peaks from a private terrace. Check-in is from 4pm to 7pm.

✗ Eating & Drinking

Clint's Bakery & Coffee House
CAFE $

(131 S Main St; sandwiches $4.95-7.25; ⊙7am-8pm; 🐾 🖼) Brainy baristas steam up a chalkboard full of latte and mocha flavors and dozens of loose-leaf teas. If you're hungry, the downstairs bagelry (which closes at 3pm) stacks burly sandwiches and tasty breakfast bagels with egg and ham, lox, sausage and cheese.

WORTH A TRIP

THE VAGABOND RANCH

Moose outnumber people at the remote Vagabond Ranch (☑303-242-5338; www.vagabondranch.com; per person $50; 🖼), a fine backcountry spot in Colorado's pristine Never Summer Range. By backcountry we mean a 3-mile dirt access road – it can be driven in summer but you'll need to park the car and ski or snowmobile in for winter fun.

Ringed by high peaks and ponderosa forest, this former stagecoach stop features a smattering of comfortable cabins – ranging from rustic to elegant – at 9000ft. Features include chef-worthy cooking facilities, firewood, a hot tub, solar power and composting toilets. Like any ski hut, lodgings may be shared, but couples or groups can book privates (we recommend the retro-gorgeous Parkview for couples). Dedicated trails are groomed in winter for cross-country skiing or snowmobiling. It also hosts yoga and meditation retreats.

It's 22 miles from Granby (near Winter Park).

CLIMBING YOUR FIRST 14ER

Known as Colorado's 'easiest' 14er, Quandary Peak (www.14ers.com; County Rd 851), near Breckenridge, is the state's 15th-highest peak at 14,265ft. Though you will see plenty of dogs and children, easiest may be misleading – the summit remains three grueling miles from the trailhead. Go between June and September.

The trail ascends to the west; after about 10 minutes of moderate climbing, follow the right fork to a trail junction. Head left, avoiding the road, and almost immediately you will snatch some views of Mt Helen and Quandary (although the real summit is still hidden).

Just below timberline you'll meet the trail from Monte Cristo Gulch – note it so you don't take the wrong fork on your way back down. From here it's a steep haul to the top. Start early and aim to turn around by noon, as afternoon lightning is typical during summer. It's a 6-mile round-trip, taking roughly between seven and eight hours. To get here, take Colorado 9 to County Rd 850. Make a right and turn right again onto 851. Drive 1.1 miles to the unmarked trailhead. Park parallel on the fire road.

Hearthstone　　　　　MODERN AMERICAN **$$$**
(☑970-453-1148; hearthstonerestaurant.biz; 130 S Ridge St; mains $26-44; ☉4pm-late; 🖼) 🖋
One of Breck's favorites, this restored 1886 Victorian churns out creative mountain fare such as blackberry elk and braised buffalo ribs with tomatillos, roasted chiles and polenta. Fresh and delicious, it's worth a splurge, or hit happy hour (4pm to 6pm) for $5 plates paired with wine. Reserve.

Downstairs at Eric's　　　　　BAR
(www.downstairsaterics.com; 111 S Main St; ☉11am-midnight; 🖼) Downstairs at Eric's is a Breckenridge institution. Locals flock to this game-room-style basement joint for the brews, burgers and delicious mashed potatoes. There are over 100 beers (20 on tap) to choose from.

🛍 Shopping

Outlets at Silverthorne　　　　　CLOTHING
(www.outletsatsilverthorne.com; ☉10am-8pm Mon-Sat, 10am-6pm Sun) Located 15 minutes from Breckenridge, just off I-70, are three shopping villages of designer brand stores with discount prices. Brands include Calvin Klein, Nike, Levi's, Gap and many others.

ℹ Information

Visitor Center (☑877-864-0868; www.go-breck.com; 203 S Main St; ☉9am-9pm; 🖼🖼) Partly set in a 19th-century cabin, with plenty of info and a small but interesting museum.

ℹ Getting There & Around

Breckenridge is about 80 miles from Denver, 9 miles south of I-70 on Hwy 9.

Colorado Mountain Express (☑800-525-6363; www.coloradomountainexpress.com; adult/child $70/36; 🖥) runs shuttles between Breckenridge and Denver International Airport.

Free buses (www.townofbreckenridge.com; ☉8am-11:45pm) run along four routes throughout town.

To get between Breckenridge, Keystone and Frisco, hop on free **Summit Stages buses** (☑970-668-0999; www.summitstage.com; 150 Watson Ave). To get to Vail, take the **Fresh Tracks shuttle** (☑970-453-4052; www.fresh-trackstransportation.com; $20 one-way).

Vail

Darling of the rich and sometime famous, Vail resembles an elaborate adult amusement park, with everything man-made from the golf greens down to the indoor waterfalls. It's compact and highly walkable, but the location (I-70 runs alongside) lacks the natural drama of other Rocky Mountain destinations. That said, no serious skier would dispute its status as the best ski resort in Colorado, with its powdery back bowls, chutes and wickedly fun terrain.

◉ Sights & Activities

Colorado Ski Museum　　　　　MUSEUM
(www.skimuseum.net; 3rd fl; ☉10am-5pm; 🖼) **FREE** Humble but informative, this museum takes you from the invention of skiing to the trials of the Tenth Mountain Division, a decorated WWII alpine unit that trained in these mountains. There are also hilarious fashions from the past, as well as the fledgling Colorado Ski and Snowboard Hall of Fame. It's located at the exit of the Vail Village parking garage.

★**Vail Mountain** SNOW SPORTS

(☎970-754-8245; www.vail.com; lift ticket adult/child $129/89; ⊗9am-4pm Dec–mid-Apr; ⊕) Vail Mountain is our favorite in the state, with 5289 skiable acres, 193 trails, three terrain parks and some of the highest lift-ticket prices in the country. If you're a Colorado ski virgin, it's worth paying extra to start here – especially on a sunny, blue, fresh-powder day. Multiday tickets are good at four other resorts. The mountaintop Adventure Ridge has child-friendly winter and summer sports and is slated to morph into the much larger Epic Discovery (www.epicdiscovery.com) in summer 2015.

Holy Cross Wilderness HIKING

(☎970-827-5715; www.fs.usda.gov/whiteriver; 24747 US Hwy 24, Minturn; ⊗9am-4pm Mon-Fri) Consult rangers for hiking tips. The strenuous Notch Mountain Trail affords great views of Mt of the Holy Cross (14,005ft), or very experienced hikers can climb the mountain itself (a class 2 scramble) via Half Moon Pass Trail.

Vail to Breckenridge Bike Path CYCLING

(www.fs.usda.gov) This paved car-free bike path stretches 8.7 miles from East Vail to the top of Vail Pass (elevation gain 1831ft), before descending 14 miles into Frisco (nine more if you go all the way to Breckenridge). If you're only interested in the downhill, hop on a shuttle from a bike rental shop (☎970-476-5385; www.bikevalet.net; 520 E Lionshead Cir; bike rental per day from $30; ⊗10am-5pm; ⊕) and enjoy the ride back to Vail.

⌂ Sleeping

Vail is as expensive as Colorado gets, and lodging – generally private condo rentals – is very hit or miss.

Gore Creek Campground CAMPGROUND $

(☎877-444-6777; www.recreation.gov; Bighorn Rd; campsites $18; ⊗mid-May–Sep; ⊛) At the end of Bighorn Rd, this campground has 25 first-come, first-served tent sites with picnic tables and pit toilets nestled in the woods by Gore Creek. It's 6 miles east of Vail Village via exit 180 (East Vail) off I-70.

★**Minturn Inn** B&B $$

(☎970-827-9647; www.minturninn.com; 442 Main St; r summer/winter from $100/150; P☎; ♿ECO) If you don't need to be at the heart of the action, the rustic Minturn Inn should be your pick. Set in a 1915 log-hewn building in Minturn (8 miles from Vail), this cozy B&B lays on the mountain charm with handcrafted log beds, river-rock fireplaces and antlered decor. Reserve one of the newer River Lodge rooms for private Jacuzzi access.

★**The Sebastian** HOTEL $$$

(☎800-354-6908; www.thesebastianvail.com; 16 Vail Rd; r summer/winter from $230/500; P☀☎☲⊛) Deluxe and modern, this sophisticated hotel showcases tasteful contemporary art and an impressive list of amenities from a mountainside ski valet to spectacular pool area with hot tubs frothing and spilling over like champagne. Given the prices in Vail, the Sebastian certainly offers the most bang for your buck, but you'll need to reserve months in advance for the best rates.

✖ Eating & Drinking

★**Yellowbelly** SOUTHERN $

(www.yellowbellychicken.com; unit 14, 2161 N. Frontage Rd; $10 plates; ⊗11am-8:30pm; ☲Vail Transit) It may be hidden in a West Vail strip mall, but man is this chicken good. We could tout the healthy angle (free-range, no GMOs, veggie-fed birds), but it's the dynamite gluten-free batter that earns this place its stars. Spicy, tender pieces of chicken come with two sides (brussel slaw, citrus quinoa, mac and cheese) and a drink; alternatively, order an entire rotisserie bird for the whole gang.

★**bōl** MODERN AMERICAN $$

(☎970-476-5300; www.bolvail.com; 141 E Meadow Dr; mains $14-28; ⊗5pm-1am, from 2pm in winter; ☎☲⊛) Half hip -atery, half space-age bowling alley, bōl is hands down the funkiest hangout in Vail. You can take the kids bowling in the back ($50 per hour), but it's the surprisingly eclectic menu that's the real draw: creations range from a filling chicken paillard salad with gnocchi to shrimp and grits with grapefruit. Prices are relatively affordable by Vail standards. Reserve.

Matsuhisa JAPANESE $$$

(☎970-476-6628; www.matsuhisavail.com; 141 E Meadow Dr; mains $29-39, 2 piece sushi $8-12; ⊗6-10pm) Legendary chef Nobu Matsuhisa has upped Vail's gastronomic standards with this modern, airy space, set at the heart of the Solaris complex. Expect traditional sushi and tempura alongside his signature new-style sashimi – Matsuhisa opened his first restaurant in Peru, and continues to incorporate South American influences into his cuisine. Star dishes include black cod with miso and scallops with jalapeño salsa. Reserve.

Los Amigos BAR

(400 Bridge St; ⊘11:30am-9pm) If you want views, tequila, and rock and roll with your après-ski ritual, come to Los Amigos. The Mexican food is decent at best, but the happy hour prices and slope-side seating more than make up for any culinary shortcomings.

❶ Information

Vail Visitor Center (✆970-479-1385; www.visitvailvalley.com; 241 S Frontage Rd; ⊘8:30am-5:30pm winter, till 8pm summer; ⊚) A second office is located in Lionshead Village.

❶ Getting There & Around

Eagle County Airport (✆970-328-2680; www.flyvail.com; 219 Eldon Wilson Drive), 35 miles west of Vail, has services to destinations across the country (many of which fly through Denver) and rental car counters.

Colorado Mountain Express (✆800-525-6363; www.coloradomountainexpress.com; ⊚) shuttles run to/from Denver International Airport ($92) and Eagle County Airport ($51). Greyhound buses stop at the **Vail Transportation Center** (✆970-476-5137; 241 S Frontage Rd) en route to Denver ($33, 2½ hours) or Grand Junction ($28, three hours).

Vail's **free buses** (www.vailgov.com; ⊘6:30am-1:50am) shuttle between West Vail, Lionshead and Vail Village; most have ski/bike racks. **Regional buses** (ECO; www.eaglecounty.us; per ride $4, $7 to Leadville) also run to Beaver Creek, Minturn and Leadville. To get to Breckenridge and other Summit County resorts, take the Fresh Tracks shuttle (p265).

Compact Vail Village, filled with upscale restaurants, bars and boutiques, is traffic free. Motorists must park in the public parking garage ($25 per day in winter, free in summer) before entering the pedestrian mall area near the chairlifts. Lionshead is a secondary base area about half a mile to the west; it also has a parking garage (same rates). It has direct lift access and is usually less crowded.

Aspen

Immodestly posh Aspen is Colorado's glitziest high-octane resort, playing host to some of the wealthiest skiers in the world. The handsome, historic red-brick downtown is as alluring as the glistening slopes, but Aspen's greatest asset is its magnificent scenery. The stunning alpine environment – especially during late September and October, when the aspen trees put on a spectacular display – just adds extra sugar to an already sweet cake.

◉ Sights & Activities

★ Aspen Center for Environmental Studies WILDLIFE RESERVE

(ACES; ✆970-925-5756; www.aspennature.org; Hallam Lake, 100 Puppy Smith St; ⊘9am-5pm Mon-Fri; P ⊛) **FREE** The Aspen Center for Environmental Studies is a 22-acre (10-hectare) wildlife sanctuary that hugs the Roaring Fork River. It has three other locations throughout the region and runs guided hikes, birding programs and snowshoe tours year-round. Great for families.

Aspen Art Museum MUSEUM

(✆970-925-8050; www.aspenartmuseum.org; cnr East Hyman Ave & Spring St; ⊘10am-6pm Tue-Sat, to 7pm Thu, noon-6pm Sun) **FREE** No permanent collection here, just edgy, innovative contemporary exhibitions. Its brand-new home was under construction at press time; it's expected to open in summer 2014, with gorgeous rooftop views. Art lovers will not leave disappointed.

★ Aspen Mountain SNOW SPORTS

(✆800-525-6200; www.aspensnowmass.com; lift ticket adult/child $117/82; ⊘9am-4pm Dec–mid-Apr; ⊛) The Aspen Skiing Company runs the area's four resorts – Aspen (intermediate/expert), Snowmass (longest vertical drop in the US), Buttermilk (beginner/terrain parks) and the Highlands (expert) – which are spread out through the valley and connected by free shuttles. Both Aspen and Snowmass are open in summer (lift ticket adult/child $28/11) for sightseeing, mountain biking and kids activities.

Maroon Bells WILDERNESS AREA

If you have but one day to enjoy a slice of the pristine, you'd be wise to spend it in the shadow of Colorado's most iconic peaks. Hikes

---

DON'T MISS

CYCLING TO MAROON BELLS

According to the Aspen cycling gurus, the most iconic road-bike ride in Aspen is the one to the stunning Maroon Bells. The climb is 11 lung-wrenching miles to the foot of one of the most picturesque wilderness areas in the Rockies. If you crave sweet, beautiful pain, rent two-wheelers at **Aspen Bike Tours** (✆970-925-9169; www.aspenbikerentals.com; 430 S Spring St; half/full day adult from $33/40, child $22/29; ⊘9am-6pm; ⊛).

range from the popular 1.8-mile-long excursion (Crater Lake) to more serious challenges like Buckskin Pass (12,462ft). To get here, you'll need to catch a **shuttle** (Aspen Highlands; adult/child $6/4; ⊙9am-4:30pm daily Jun 15-Aug, Fri-Sun Sep-Oct 6) from the Highlands.

The access road is only open to vehicle traffic ($10) from 5pm to 9am and is not plowed in winter. It can get awfully crowded, so if you prefer solitude, check out the Hunter-Fryingpan Wilderness near Basalt.

Ashcroft Ski Touring   SNOW SPORTS
(☑970-925-1971; www.pinecreekcookhouse.com/tours; 11399 Castle Creek Rd; adult/child $15/10; 🖐) Twenty miles of groomed Nordic trails through 600 acres of subalpine country with a truly spectacular backdrop. You can rent gear and sign up for various lessons and tours. Shuttles ($35) to/from Aspen are available.

✺✲ Festivals

Aspen Music Festival   MUSIC
(☑970-925-9042; www.aspenmusicfestival.com; ⊙Jul & Aug) Every summer classical musicians from around the world come to play, perform and learn from the masters of their craft.

🛏 Sleeping

Aspen is popular year-round. Reserve well in advance. The **Aspen Ranger District** (☑970-925-3445; www.fs.usda.gov/whiteriver; 806 W Hallam St; ⊙8am-4:30pm Mon-Fri) operates some-twenty **campgrounds** (☑877-444-6777; www.recreation.gov; campsites $15-21) in the Maroon Bells, Independence Pass and Hunter-Fryingpan wilderness areas.

WORTH A TRIP

SCENIC DIVE: INDEPENDENCE PASS

Looming at 12,095ft, Independence Pass on **Hwy 82** is one of the more high-profile passes along the Continental Divide. The views along the narrow ribbon of road range from pretty to stunning to downright cinematic, and by the time you glimpse summer snowfields just below knife-edged peaks, you'll be living in your own IMAX film. Stop at the ghost town of **Independence** (www.aspenhistorysociety.com; suggested donation $3; ⊙10am-6pm mid-Jun–Aug) FREE on the way up. **Hwy 82** is only open from late May to October.

St Moritz Lodge   HOSTEL $
(☑970-925-3220; www.stmoritzlodge.com; 334 W Hyman Ave; dm summer/winter $60/66, d summer $130-269, winter $155-299; P❄@🌐≋) St Moritz is the best no-frills deal in town. Perks include a heated outdoor pool and grill overlooking Aspen Mountain, and a lobby with games, books and a piano. The European-style lodge offers a wide variety of options, from quiet dorms to two-bedroom condos. The cheapest options share bathrooms. There's a kitchen downstairs.

Annabelle Inn   HOTEL $$
(☑877-266-2466; www.annabelleinn.com; 232 W Main St; r incl breakfast summer/winter from $169/199; P❄@🌐) Personable and unpretentious, the cute and quirky Annabelle Inn resembles an old-school European-style ski lodge in a central location. Rooms are cozy and come with flat-screen TVs and warm duvets. You can also enjoy after-dark ski video screenings from the upper-deck hot tub (one of two on the property).

★ Limelight Hotel   HOTEL $$$
(☑800-433-0832; www.limelighthotel.com; 355 S Monarch St; r summer/winter from $245/395; P❄🌐≋🌐) Sleek and trendy, the Limelight's brick-and-glass modernism reflects Aspen's effortless alpine chic vibe. Rooms are spacious and have their perks: gas fireplaces, leather furnishings and mountain views from the balconies and rooftop terraces. In addition to the ski valet and shuttle services, you can also catch live music most winter nights in the lobby's Italian kitchen. Breakfast is included.

🍴 Eating & Drinking

★ Justice Snow's   PUB $$
(☑970-429-8192; www.justicesnows.com; 328 E Hyman Ave; mains $10-22; ⊙11am-2am; 🌐✐) 🅿 Located in the historic Wheeler Opera House, Justice Snow's is a retro-fitted old saloon that marries antique wooden furnishings with a deft modern touch. Although nominally a bar – the speakeasy cocktails give the place its soul – the affordable and locally sourced menu ($10 gourmet burger! in Aspen!) is what keeps the locals coming back.

The Meatball Shack   ITALIAN $$$
(☑970-925-1349; www.themeatballshack.com; 312 S Mill Rd; lunch $13, dinner $21-28; ⊙11:30am-11:30pm; 🖐) 🅿 Helmed by Florentine chef Eddie Baida and NYC transplant Michael Gurtman, the shack specializes in – you

guessed it – fettuccine and meatballs (*nonna*'s, chicken or veal). It's quite the happening place come evening, but forget about the scene for a minute and concentrate on what's on your plate: this is some of the best Italian fare in the Rockies.

★ **Pine Creek Cookhouse**　　AMERICAN **$$$**
(☑970-925-1044; www.pinecreekcookhouse.com; 12700 Castle Creek Rd; lunch and summer dinner mains $13-41, winter dinner prix-fixe with ski tour/sleigh $90/110; ◷11:30am-2:30pm daily, 2:30-8:30pm Wed-Sun Jun-Sep, seatings at noon & 1:30pm daily, plus 7pm Wed-Sun Dec-Mar; ☑ ♿) 🍃 This log-cabin restaurant, located 1.5 miles past the Ashcroft ghost town at the end of Castle Creek Rd (about 30 minutes from Aspen), boasts the best setting around. In summer you can hike here; in winter it's cross country skis or horse-drawn sleigh in the shadow of glorious white-capped peaks. Sample alpine delicacies like house-smoked trout, buffalo tenderloin and grilled elk brats.

★ **Aspen Brewing Co**　　BREWERY
(www.aspenbrewingcompany.com; 304 E Hopkins Ave; ◷noon-late daily; 🐾) With six signature flavors and a sun-soaked balcony facing the mountain, this casual spot is definitely the place to unwind after a hard day's play. Brews range from the flavorful This Year's Blonde and high-altitude Independence Pass Ale (its IPA) to the mellower Conundrum Red Ale and the chocolatey Pyramid Peak Porter.

Woody Creek Tavern　　PUB
(☑970-923-4585; www.woodycreektavern.com; 2 Woody Creek Plaza, 2858 Upper River Rd; ◷11am-10pm) Formerly one of Hunter S Thompson's favorite watering holes, this funky tavern is well worth the 8-mile trek from Aspen. The lunch menu features organic salads, low-fat but juicy burgers and popular Mexican food including some quality guacamole. The dinner menu is less imaginative, but there's plenty of alcohol. Eleven gallons of margaritas a day can't be wrong.

ⓘ Information

Aspen Visitor Center (☑970-925-1940; www.aspenchamber.org; 425 Rio Grande Pl; ◷8:30am-5pm Mon-Fri)

ⓘ Getting There & Around

Four miles north of Aspen on Hwy 82, **Aspen-Pitkin County Airport** (☑970-920-5380; www.aspenairport.com; 233 E Airport Rd; 🐾) has direct flights from Denver, Los Angeles, Dallas and Chicago. **Colorado Mountain Express** (☑800-525-6363; www.coloradomountainexpress.com; adult/child $118/61; 🐾) runs frequent shuttles to/from Denver International Airport ($118, three hours).

Roaring Fork Transit Agency (www.rfta.com) buses connect Aspen with all four ski areas (free) and runs free trips to and from Aspen-Pitkin County Airport.

If you're driving, it's easiest to park in the public garage ($15 per day) next to the Aspen Visitor Center on Rio Grande Pl.

Salida

Blessed with one of the state's largest historic downtowns, Salida is not only a charming spot to explore, it also has an unbeatable location, with the Arkansas River on one side and the intersection of two mighty mountain ranges on the other. The plan of attack here is to raft, bike or hike during the day, then come back to town to refuel with grilled buffalo ribs and a cold IPA at night.

🏃 Activities

Most rafting companies are based just south of Buena Vista (25 miles north of Salida), near where Hwys 24 and 285 diverge.

Buffalo Joe's Whitewater Rafting　　RAFTING
(☑866-283-3563; www.buffalojoe.com; 113 N Railroad St; half/full day adult $64/98, child $54/78; ◷May-Sep; ♿) One of the top river outfitters, this shop is located in downtown Buena Vista.

River Runners　　RAFTING
(☑800-723-8987; www.riverrunnersltd.com; 24070 Co Rd 301; half/full day adult $60/98, child $50/88; ◷May-Sep; ♿) Another recommended river outfitter based in both Buena Vista and the Royal Gorge.

Absolute Bikes　　BICYCLE RENTAL
(☑719-539-9295; www.absolutebikes.com; 330 W Sackett Rd; bike rental $40-80, tours from $90; ◷9am-7pm; ♿) From the Monarch Crest and Rainbow Trails to across-the-river cruising. Maps, gear, advice, guided tours and rentals.

🛏 Sleeping

The Arkansas Headwaters Recreation Area operates six campgrounds (bring your own water) along the river. The nicest is **Hecla Junction** (☑800-678-2267; http://coloradostateparks.reserveamerica.com; Hwy 285, MM135; $16 per site; 🎫), located north of Salida. Reserve in summer.

ROCKY MOUNTAINS CENTRAL COLORADO

RAFTING THE ARKANSAS RIVER

The headwaters of the Arkansas is Colorado's most popular stretch of river for rafters and kayakers, with everything from extreme rapids to mellow flatwater. Although most rafting companies cover the river from Leadville to the Royal Gorge, the most popular trips descend Brown's Canyon, a 22-mile stretch that includes class III/IV rapids. If you're with young kids or just looking for something mellower, Bighorn Sheep Canyon is a good bet. Those after more of an adrenaline rush can head upstream to the Numbers or downstream to the Royal Gorge, both of which are class IV/V.

Water flow varies by season, so time your visit for early June for a wilder ride – by the time August rolls around, the water level is usually pretty low. If you're rafting with kids, note that they need to be at least six years old and weigh a minimum 50 pounds.

★ **Simple Lodge & Hostel**　　HOSTEL **$**
(☑719-650-7381; www.simplelodge.com; 224 E 1st St; dm/d/q $24/55/76; [P][含][🐾]) If only Colorado had more spots like this. Run by a super-friendly husband-wife team (Jon and Julia), this hostel is simple but stylish, with a fully stocked kitchen and comfy communal area that feels just like home. It's a popular stopover for touring cyclists following the coast-to-coast Hwy 50.

✖ Eating & Drinking

★ **Amícas**　　PIZZA, MICROBREWERY **$$**
(www.amicassalida.com; 136 E 2nd St; pizzas & paninis $8.10-11.55; ⊙11:30am-9pm; [🖉][📶]) Thin-crust woodfired pizzas and six microbrews on tap? Amícas can do no wrong. This laid-back, high-ceilinged hangout (formerly a funeral parlor) is the perfect spot to replenish all those calories you burned off during the day. Savor a Michelangelo (pesto, sausage and goat cheese) or Vesuvio (artichoke hearts, sun-dried tomatoes, roasted peppers) alongside a cool glass of Headwaters IPA.

Fritz　　TAPAS **$$**
(☑719-539-0364; http://thefritzdowntown.com; 113 East Sackett St; tapas $4-8, mains $9-14; ⊙11am-2am; [含]) This fun and funky riverside watering hole serves up clever American-style tapas. Think Mac and three-cheese with bacon, fries with truffle aioli, shrimp curry and even bone marrow with red onion jam. It also does a mean grass-fed beef burger and other sandwiches at lunch. Good selection of beers on tap.

ℹ Information

USFS Ranger Office (☑719-539-3591; www.fs.usda.gov; 5575 Cleora Rd; ⊙8am-4:30pm Mon-Fri) Located east of town off Hwy 50, with info on hiking and camping in the Collegiates and northern Sangre de Cristo ranges.

ℹ Getting There & Away

Salida is located at the intersection of Hwys 285 and 50, west of Cañon City and south of Leadville. You'll need your own car to get here.

Colorado Springs

The site of one of the country's first destination resorts, Colorado Springs sits at the foot of majestic Pikes Peak. Pinned down with four military bases and recently beset by a series of devastating summer wildfires, the city has evolved into a strange and sprawling quilt of neighborhoods – visitors can best come to grips with the layout by dividing it in three. From east to west along Hwy 24 is the downtown district, an odd mix of fine art, Olympic dreams and downbeat desperation; Old Colorado City, whose Old West brothels and saloons now host restaurants and shops; and new agey Manitou Springs, whose mountainside location makes it the most visitor-friendly part of town.

⊙ Sights & Activities

★ **Pikes Peak**　　MOUNTAIN
(☑719-385-7325; www.springsgov.com; highway per adult/child $12/5; ⊙7:30am-8pm Jun-Aug, 7:30am-5pm Sep, 9am-3pm Oct-May; [📶]) Originally known as the Mountain of the Sun by the Ute, Pikes Peak (14,110ft) may not be the tallest of Colorado's 54 14ers, but it's certainly the most famous. Maybe because it's the only one with a train to the top? Or perhaps because the views from the summit inspired Katherine Bates to write the lyrics for *America the Beautiful* in 1893?

In all likelihood, its location as the easternmost 14er – rising 7400ft straight up from the plains – has contributed significantly to its renown. Today, over half a million visitors ascend its summit every year. The cog railway (☎719-685-5401; www.cograilway.com; 515 Ruxton Ave; round-trip adult/child $35/19; ☺8am-5:20pm May-Oct, reduced hours rest of year; 🚹) leaves from Manitou Springs (about three hours 10 minutes round-trip), while the Pikes Peak Highway (about five hours round trip) climbs 19 miles to the top from Hwy 24 west of town. For an entirely different experience, consider hiking up (p271) instead.

Garden of the Gods   PARK
(www.gardenofgods.com; 1805 N 30th St; ☺5am-11pm May-Oct, 5am-9pm Nov-Apr; 🅿🚹) **FREE** This gorgeous vein of red sandstone (about 290 million years old) appears elsewhere along Colorado's Front Range, but the exquisitely thin cathedral spires and mountain backdrop of the Garden of the Gods are particularly striking. Explore the network of paved and unpaved trails, enjoy a picnic and watch climbers test their nerve on the sometimes flaky rock.

In the summer, Rock Ledge Ranch (www.rockledgeranch.com; adult/child $8/4; ☺10am-5pm Wed-Sat Jun–mid-Aug; 🚹), a living history museum near the park entrance, is worth a visit for those interested in the lives of Native Americans and 19th-century homesteaders in the region.

★ Colorado Springs

Fine Arts Center   MUSEUM
(FAC; ☎719-634-5583; www.csfineartscenter.org; 30 W Dale St; adult/student $10/8.50; ☺10am-5pm Tue-Sun; 🅿) A sophisticated collection with terrific Latin American art, Mexican clay figures, Native American basketry and quilts, wood-cut prints and abstract work from local artists. One of Colorado's best fine arts museums.

US Air Force Academy   MILITARY ACADEMY
(☎719-333-2025; www.usafa.af.mil; I-25 exit 156B; ☺visitor center 9am-5pm; 🅿) **FREE** One of the highest-profile military academies in the country, a visit to this campus offers a limited but nonetheless fascinating look into the lives of an elite group of cadets. The visitor center provides general background on the academy; from here you can walk over to the dramatic chapel (1963) or embark on a driving tour of the grounds. The entrance is via the North Gate, 14 miles north of Colorado Springs.

Barr Trail   HIKING
(www.barrcamp.com; Hydro Dr) The tough 12.5-mile Barr Trail ascends Pikes Peak with a substantial 7400ft of elevation gain. Most hikers split the trip into two days, stop-ping to overnight at Barr Camp, the halfway point. If you're interested in doing it as a day hike, you can buy a one-way ticket up to Barr Camp ($22; first or last departure only) from the Cog Railway. The trailhead is just above the Manitou Springs cog railway depot; parking is $5.

🎉 Festivals & Events

Colorado Balloon Classic   BALLOONING
(www.balloonclassic.com; 1605 E Pikes Peak Ave; ☺Labor Day weekend; 🚹) For nearly 40 years running, hot-air ballooners, both amateur and pro, have been launching Technicolor balloons just after sunrise for three straight days over the Labor Day weekend. You'll have to wake with the roosters to see it all, but it's definitely worth your while.

🛏 Sleeping

Barr Camp   CAMPGROUND $
(www.barrcamp.com; tent sites $12, lean-tos $17, cabin dm $28; 🐾) At the halfway point on the Barr Trail, about 6.5 miles from the Pikes Peak summit, you can pitch a tent, shelter in a lean-to or reserve a bare-bones cabin. There's drinking water and showers; dinner ($8) is available Wednesday to Sunday. Reservations are essential and must be made online in advance. It's open year-round.

Mining Exchange   HOTEL $$
(☎719-323-2000; www.wyndham.com; 8 S Nevada Ave; r $135-200; 🅿❄🖥) Opened in 2012 and set in the turn-of-the-century bank where Cripple Creek prospectors once traded in their gold for cash (check out the vault door in the lobby), the Mining Exchange takes the prize for Colorado Spring's most stylish hotel. Twelve-foot-high ceilings, exposed brick walls and leather furnishings make for an inviting, contemporary feel, though its downtown location lacks the charm of Manitou Springs. Excellent-value rates.

Two Sisters Inn   B&B $$
(☎719-685-9684; www.twosisinn.com; 10 Otoe Pl, Manitou Springs; r without bath $79-94, with bath $135-155; 🅿❄🖥) A longtime favorite among B&B aficionados, this place has five rooms (including the honeymoon cottage out back) set in a rose-colored Victorian home, built in 1919 by two sisters. It was originally a boarding house for schoolteachers and has been an inn since 1990. There's a magnificent stained-glass front door and an 1896 piano in the parlor; it has won awards for its breakfast recipes.

WORTH A TRIP

CRIPPLE CREEK CASINOS

Just an hour from Colorado Springs yet worlds away, Cripple Creek hurls you back into the Wild West of lore. This once lucky lady produced a staggering $413 million in gold by 1952.

The booze still flows and gambling still thrives, but yesteryear's saloons and brothels are now modern casinos. If you're more interested in the regional history or simply need a break from the slots, check out the **Heritage Center** (www.visitcripplecreek.com; 9283 Hwy 67; ☉ 8am-7pm; 🖈), the popular **gold mine tour** (www.goldminetours.com; 9388 Hwy 67; adult/child $18/10; ☉ 8:45am-6pm mid May–Oct; 🖈) and the **narrow gauge railroad** (http://cripplecreekrailroad.com; Bennet Ave; adult/child $13/8; ☉ 10am-5pm mid-May–mid-Oct; 🖈🐾) to historic Victor.

Cripple Creek is 50 miles southwest of Colorado Springs on scenic Hwy 67. For an even more impressive drive, check out the old Gold Camp Rd (Hwy 336) out of Victor on the way home. It's unpaved and narrow, but provides spectacular views. It takes about 90 minutes down to the Springs. Alternatively, catch the **Ramblin' Express** (📞 719-590-8687; www.ramblinexpress.com; round-trip tickets $25; ☉ departures 7am-midnight Wed-Sun) from Colorado Springs' 8th St Depot.

Broadmoor   RESORT $$$
(📞 855-634-7711; www.broadmoor.com; 1 Lake Ave; r from $280-500; 🅿️❄️🛜🏊🐾) One of the top five-star resorts in the US, the 744-room Broadmoor sits in a picture-perfect location against the blue-green slopes of Cheyenne Mountain. Everything here is exquisite: acres of lush grounds and a lake, a glimmering pool, world-class golf, myriad bars and restaurants, an incredible spa and ubercomfortable guest rooms (which, it must be said, are of the 'grandmother' school of design).

There's a reason that hundreds of Hollywood stars, A-list pro athletes and nearly every president since FDR have made it a point to visit.

🍴 Eating & Drinking

Shuga's   CAFE $
(www.shugas.com; 702 S Cascade St; dishes $8-9; ☉ 11am-midnight; 🛜🐾) If you thought Colorado Springs couldn't be hip, stroll to Shuga's, a southern-style cafe with a knack for knockout espresso drinks and hot cocktails. Cuter than buttons, this little white house is decked out in paper cranes and red vinyl chairs. There's also patio seating. The food – brie BLT on rosemary toast, Brazilian coconut shrimp soup – comforts and delights. Don't miss vintage-movie Saturdays.

⭐ Marigold   FRENCH $$
(📞 719-599-4776; www.marigoldcafeandbakery.com; 4605 Centennial Blvd; lunch $8.25-11, dinner $9-19; ☉ 11am-2:30pm & 5pm-9pm Mon-Sat, bakery 8am-9pm) Way out by the Garden of the Gods is this buzzy French bistro and bakery that's easy on both the palate and the wallet. Feast on delicacies such as snapper Marseillaise, garlic and rosemary rotisserie chicken, and gourmet salads and pizzas, and be sure to leave room for the double (and triple!) chocolate mousse cake and lemon tarts.

Adam's Mountain Cafe   MODERN AMERICAN $$
(📞 719-685-1430; www.adamsmountain.com; 934 Manitou Ave; mains $9-19; ☉ 8am-3pm daily, 5-9pm Tue-Sat; 🛜🚲🐾) In Manitou Springs, this slow-food cafe makes a lovely stop. Breakfast includes orange-almond French toast and huevos rancheros (eggs and beans on a tortilla). Lunch and dinner are more eclectic with offerings such as Moroccan chicken, pasta gremolata and grilled watermelon salad. The interior is airy and attractive with marble floors and exposed rafters, and there's patio dining and occasional live music too.

Jake & Telly's   GREEK $$
(📞 719-633-0406; www.greekdining.com; 2616 W Colorado Ave; lunch $9-12, dinner $16-24.50; ☉ 11:30am-9pm daily; 🛜🐾) One of the best choices in Old Colorado City, this eatery looks slightly touristy – lots of Greek monument murals on the walls and themed music on the stereo – but the food is absolutely delicious. It does a nice Greek-dip sandwich as well as traditional dishes such as souvlaki, dolmadas and spanakopita. It's set on a 2nd-story terrace above a magic wand shop.

⭐ Swirl   WINE BAR
(www.swirlwineemporium.com; 717 Manitou Ave; ☉ noon-10pm Sun-Thu, to midnight Fri & Sat) Behind a stylish bottle shop in Manitou Springs, this nook bar is intimate and cool.

The garden patio has dangling lights and vines while inside are antique armchairs and a fireplace. If you're feeling peckish, sample the tapas and homemade pasta.

Bristol Brewing Co BREWERY
(www.bristolbrewing.com; 1604 S Cascade Ave; ⊙11am-10pm; 🐾) Although a bit out of the way in south Colorado Springs, this brewery – which in 2013 spearheaded a community center in the shuttered Ivywild Elementary School – is worth seeking out for its Laughing Lab ale and Blue Star–inspired pub grub. Other back-to-school tenants include a bakery, deli, cafe, art gallery and movie theater in the former gym.

ⓘ Information

Colorado Springs Convention and Visitors Bureau (☑719-635-7506; www.visitcos.com; 515 S Cascade Ave; ⊙8:30am-5pm; 🐾)

ⓘ Getting There & Around

Colorado Springs Municipal Airport (☑719-550-1900; www.springsgov.com; 7770 Milton E Proby Parkway; 🐾) is a viable alternative to Denver. The **Yellow Cab** (☑719-777-7777) fare from the airport to the city center is $30.

Buses between Cheyenne, WY, and Pueblo, CO, stop daily at **Greyhound** (☑719-635-1505; 120 S Weber St). **Mountain Metropolitan Transit** (www.springsgov.com; per trip $1.75, day pass $4) maps for all local buses; find information online.

All street parking is meter only; if you have your own wheels, bring lots of quarters.

Southern Colorado

Home to the dramatic San Juan and Sangre de Cristo mountain ranges, Colorado's bottom half is just as pretty as its top, has fewer people and is filled with stuff to see and do.

Crested Butte

Powder-bound Crested Butte has retained its rural character better than most Colorado ski resorts. Remote, and ringed by three wilderness areas, this former mining village is counted among Colorado's best ski resorts (some say it's *the* best). The old town center features beautifully preserved Victorian-era buildings refitted with shops and businesses. Strolling two-wheel traffic matches its laid-back, happy attitude.

Most everything in town is on Elk Ave, including the **visitor center** (☑970-349-

6438; www.crestedbuttechamber.com; 601 Elk Ave; ⊙9am-5pm).

★**Crested Butte Mountain Resort** (☑970-349-2222; www.skicb.com; 12 Snowmass Rd; lift ticket adult/child $98/54; 🅿) sits 2 miles north of the town at the base of the impressive mountain of the same name, surrounded by forests, rugged mountain peaks and the West Elk, Raggeds and Maroon Bells-Snowmass Wilderness Areas. The scenery is breathtakingly beautiful. It caters mostly to intermediate and expert riders.

Crested Butte is also a **mountain-biking** mecca, full of excellent high-altitude single-track trails. For maps, information and mountain-bike rentals, visit the **Alpineer** (☑970-349-5210; www.alpineer.com; 419 6th St; bike rental per day $20-55; 🅿).

Crested Butte International Hostel (☑970-349-0588, toll-free 888-389-0588; www.crestedbuttehostel.com; 615 Teocalli Ave; dm $35, d shared bath $89, r $99-109; 🐾) is one of Colorado's nicest hostels. The best private rooms have their own baths. Dorm bunks come with reading lamps and lockable drawers. The communal area is mountain rustic with a stone fireplace and comfortable couches. Rates vary dramatically by season, with fall being cheapest.

With phenomenal food, the funky-casual **Secret Stash** (☑970-349-6245; www.thesecretstash.com; 303 Elk Ave; mains $8-20; ⊙8am-late; 🅿🐾) is adored by locals, who also dig the original cocktails. The house specialty is pizza; its Notorious Fig (with prosciutto, fresh figs and truffle oil) won the World Pizza Championship. Breakfast is best enjoyed at **Izzy's** (218 Maroon Ave; mains $7-9; ⊙7am-1pm Wed-Mon), where fresh bagels, eggs and latkes are served at crowded picnic tables.

The original **Montanya** (130 Elk; snacks $3-12; ⊙11am-9pm) distillery has moved here, with wide acclaim. Its basiltini, made with basil-infused rum, fresh grapefruit and lime, will have you levitating. For music, lively **Eldo Brewpub** (☑970-349-6125; www.eldobrewpub.com; 215 Elk Ave; cover charge varies; ⊙3pm-late, music from 10:30pm; 🅿) is one of the town's most popular microbreweries, it also hosts the most out-of-town bands. Check out the great deck.

Crested Butte's air link to the outside world is **Gunnison County Airport** (☑970-641-2304), 28 miles south of the town. Shuttle **Alpine Express** (☑970-641-5074; www.alpineexpressshuttle.com; per person $34) goes to Crested Butte; reserve ahead in summer.

The free **Mountain Express** (☑970-349-7318; www.mtnexp.org) connects Crested Butte with Mt Crested Butte every 15 minutes in winter, less often in other seasons; check times at bus stops.

Ouray

With gorgeous ice falls draping the box canyon and soothing hot springs that dot the valley floor, Ouray is a privileged place for nature, even for Colorado. For ice-climbers it's a world-class destination, but hikers and 4WD fans can also appreciate its rugged (and sometimes stunning) charms. The town is a well-preserved quarter-mile mining village sandwiched between imposing peaks.

Between Silverton and Ouray, US 550 is one of the state's most memorable drives and is paved, but the road is scary in rain or snow, so take extra care.

🏃 Activities

The visitor center is at the hot-springs pool. Check out their leaflet on an excellent walking tour that takes in two-dozen buildings and houses constructed between 1880 and 1904.

Ouray Ice Park   ICE CLIMBING
(☑970-325-4061; www.ourayicepark.com; Hwy 361; ⊗7am-5pm mid-Dec–March; 🚹) **FREE** Enthusiasts from around the globe come to ice climb at the world's first public ice park, spanning a 2-mile stretch of the Uncompahgre Gorge. The sublime (if chilly) experience offers something for all skill levels.

★**Chicks with Picks**   COURSE, CLIMBING
(☑970-316-1403, office 970-626-4424; www.chickswithpicks.net; 163 County Rd 12) Arming women with ice tools and crampons, this group of renowned women athletes gives excellent instruction for all-comers (beginners included) in rock climbing, bouldering and ice climbing. Programs are fun and change frequently, with multiday excursions or town-based courses. The climbing clinics also go on the road all over the US.

Ouray Hot Springs   HOT SPRINGS
(☑970-325-7073; www.ourayhotsprings.com; 1220 Main St; adult/child $12/8; ⊗10am-10pm Jun-Aug, noon-9pm Mon-Fri & 11am-9pm Sat & Sun Sep-May; 🚹) For a healing soak, try the historic Ouray Hot Springs. The natural spring water is free of the sulfur smells plaguing other hot springs around here, and the pool features a variety of soaking areas at temperatures ranging from 96° to 106°F (35.5° to 41°C). The complex also offers a gym and massage service.

San Juan
Mountain Guides   ROCK CLIMBING, SKIING
(☑800-642-5389, 970-325-4925; www.ourayclimbing.com; 725 Main St; 🚹) Ouray's own professional guiding and climbing group is certified with the International Federation of Mountain Guides Association (IFMGA). It specializes in ice and rock climbing and wilderness backcountry skiing.

DON'T MISS

SCENIC DRIVE: SAN JUAN MOUNTAIN PASSES

With rugged peaks and deep canyon drops, the scenery of the San Juan mountain range is hard to beat. Suitable for all vehicles, the **Million Dollar Highway** (US 550) takes its name from the valuable ore in the roadbed. But the scenery is also golden – the paved road clings to crumbly mountains, passing old mine-head frames and big alpine scenery.

A demanding but fantastic drive, the 65-mile **Alpine Loop Backcountry Byway** (www.alpineloop.com) begins in **Ouray** and travels east to **Lake City** – a wonderful mountain hamlet worth a visit – before looping back to its starting point. Along the way you'll cross two 12,000ft mountain passes and swap pavement and people for solitude, spectacular views and abandoned mining haunts. You'll need a high-clearance 4WD vehicle and some off-road driving skills to conquer this drive; allow six hours.

Spectacular during autumn for the splendor of its yellow aspens, **Ophir Pass** connects Ouray to Telluride via a former wagon road. The moderate 4WD route passes former mines, with a gradual ascent to 11,789ft. To get there, drive south of Ouray on Hwy 550 for 18.1 miles to the right-hand turnoff for National Forest Access, Ophir Pass.

As with all 4WD routes and mountain passes, check for road closures before going. The road is scary in rain or snow, so take extra care.

✪ Festivals & Events

Ouray Ice Festival ICE CLIMBING
(☑ 970-325-4288; www.ourayicefestival.com; donation for evening events; ☉ Jan; ⛑) The Ouray Ice Festival features four days of climbing competitions, dinners, slide shows and clinics in January. There's even a climbing wall set up for kids. You can watch the competitions for free, but to check out the various evening events you will need to make a donation to the ice park. Once inside you'll get free brews from popular Colorado microbrewer New Belgium.

🛏 Sleeping & Eating

**Amphitheater Forest
Service Campground** CAMPGROUND $
(☑ 877-444-6777; http://www.recreation.gov; US Hwy 550; tent sites $16; ☉ Jun-Aug) With great tent sites under the trees, this high-altitude campground is a score. On holiday weekends a three-night minimum applies. South of town on Hwy 550, take a signposted left-hand turn.

★ Wiesbaden HOTEL $$
(☑ 970-325-4347; www.wiesbadenhotsprings.com; 625 5th St; r $132-347; ⊜ 🐾🈂) Few hotels can boast their own natural indoor vapor cave (long ago used by Chief Ouray). This quirky New Age inn charms with quilted bedcovers, free organic coffee and a spacious outdoor hot-spring pool. Guests can use the Aveda salon or book a private, clothing-optional soaking tub with a waterfall ($35 per hour).

Box Canyon Lodge & Hot Springs LODGE $$
(☑ 970-325-4981, 800-327-5080; www.boxcanyon-ouray.com; 45 3rd Ave; r $110-165, apt $278-319; 🐾)
⌔ With geothermal heat, these pine-board rooms are toasty and spacious. A set of outdoor spring-fed barrel hot tubs are perfect for a romantic stargazing soak. Book well ahead.

**Buen Tiempo Mexican
Restaurant & Cantina** MEXICAN $$
(☑ 970-325-4544; 515 Main St; mains $7-20; ☉ 6-10pm; ⌖) From the chili-rubbed sirloin to the *posole* (hearty hominy soup) served with warm tortillas, Buen Tiempo delivers. Start with one of its signature margaritas, served with chips and spicy homemade salsa.

❶ Information

Visitor Center (☑ 970-325-4746; www.ouray-colorado.com; 1220 Main St; ☉ 9am-5pm)

❶ Getting There & Away

Ouray is 24 miles north of Silverton along US 550 and best reached by private vehicle.

Telluride

Surrounded on three sides by mastodon peaks, exclusive Telluride feels cut off from the hubbub of the outside world, and it often is. Once a rough mining town, today it's dirtbag-meets-diva – mixing the few who can afford the real estate with those scratching out a slope-side living for the sport of it. The town center still has palpable old-time charm and the surroundings are simply gorgeous.

Colorado Ave, also known as Main St, is where you'll find most businesses. From downtown you can reach the ski mountain via two lifts and the gondola. The latter also links Telluride with Mountain Village, the true base for the Telluride Ski Area. Located 7 miles from town along Hwy 145, Mountain Village is a 20-minute drive east, but is only 12 minutes away by gondola (free for foot passengers).

🏃 Activities

Telluride Ski Resort SNOW SPORTS
(☑ 970-728-7533, 888-288-7360; www.telluride-skiresort.com; 565 Mountain Village Blvd; lift tickets $98) Covering three distinct areas, Telluride Ski Resort is served by 16 lifts. Much of the terrain is for advanced and intermediate skiers, but there's still ample choice for beginners.

✪ Festivals & Events

★ Mountainfilm FILM
(www.mountainfilm.org; ☉ Memorial Day weekend, May) A four-day screening of outdoor adventure and environmental films on Memorial Day weekend.

Telluride Bluegrass Festival MUSIC
(☑ 800-624-2422; www.planetbluegrass.com; 4-day pass $195; ☉ late Jun) A wild frolic held in June, with all-day and evening music, food stalls and local microbrews. Camping is popular during the festival. Check out the website for info on sites, shuttle services and combo ticket-and-camping packages – it's all very organized!

Telluride Film Festival FILM
(☑ 603-433-9202; www.telluridefilmfestival.com) National and international films are premiered throughout town in early September, and the event attracts big-name stars. For more information on the relatively complicated pricing scheme, visit the film festival website.

ROCKY MOUNTAINS SOUTHERN COLORADO

Sleeping

Telluride's lodgings can fill quickly, and for the best rates it's best to book online. Unless you're planning to camp, however, don't expect budget deals. Telluride's activities and festivals keep it busy year-round. For vacation rentals, the most reputable agency is **Telluride Alpine Lodging** (☑888-893-0158; www.telluridelodging.com; 324 W Colorado Ave).

Telluride Town Park Campground   CAMPGROUND $

(☑970-728-2173; 500 E Colorado Ave; campsite with/without vehicle space $23/15; ☺mid-May–mid-Oct; ☎) Right in the center of town, these 20 sites have access to showers, swimming and tennis. It fills up quickly in the high season. For other campgrounds within 10 miles of town, check with the visitor center. 'Walk-in' camping spots don't have space for a car, but you can park your car in an adjacent lot.

Victorian Inn   LODGE $$

(☑970-728-6601; www.victorianinntelluride.com; 401 W Pacific Ave; r incl breakfast from $124; ⊜☀☎) The smell of fresh cinnamon rolls greets visitors at one of Telluride's better deals, offering comfortable rooms (some with kitchenettes), and a hot tub and dry sauna in a nice garden area. Staff are friend-

ly and guests get lift-ticket discounts. Kids aged 12 and under stay free, and you can't beat the downtown location.

Hotel Columbia   HOTEL $$$

(☑970-728-0660, toll-free 800-201-9505; www.columbiatelluride.com; 300 W San Juan Ave; d/ste from $175/305; ℗⊜☀☎☒) Locally owned and operated, this stylish hotel pampers guests. The gondola is across the street, so leave your gear in the ski and boot storage and head directly to a room with espresso maker, fireplace and heated tile floors. With shampoo dispensers and recycling, it's also pretty ecofriendly. Other highlights include a rooftop hot tub and fitness room.

Eating & Drinking

For the best deals, look for food carts serving Mediterranean food, hot dogs, tacos and coffee on Colorado Ave.

★La Cocina de Luz   MEXICAN, ORGANIC $$

(www.lacocinatelluride.com; 123 E Colorado Ave; mains $9-19; ☺9am-9pm; ☑) 🍴 As they lovingly serve two Colorado favorites (organic and Mexican), it's no wonder that the lunch line runs deep at this healthy taqueria. Delicious details include a salsa and chip bar, handmade tortillas and margaritas with organic lime and agave nectar. Vegan, gluten-free options too.

The Butcher & The Baker   CAFE $$

(☑970-728-3334; 217 E Colorado Ave; mains $10-14; ☺7am-7pm Mon-Sat, 8am-2pm Sun; ☒) 🍴 Two veterans of upscale local catering started this heartbreakingly cute cafe, and no one beats it for breakfast. Organic ingredients and locally sourced meats make it a cut above. The to-go sandwiches are the best bet for a gourmet meal on the trail.

Brown Dog Pizza   PIZZA $$

(☑970-728-8046; www.browndogpizza.net; 10 E Colorado Ave; pizzas $10-22; ☺11am-10pm) The pizza? It's thin crust and fair enough, but the crowd makes the place interesting. Ten minutes after you belly up to the bar for a slice and a cheap pint of Pabst, you'll be privy to all the local dirt. Among the most affordable meals on the strip.

New Sheridan Bar   BAR

(☑970-728-3911; www.newsheridan.com; 231 W Colorado Ave; ☺5pm-2am) Mixes real local flavor with the see-and-be-seen crowd. Most of this historic bar survived the waning mining fortunes even as the adjoining hotel sold off

---

WORTH A TRIP

COLORADO HUT TO HUT

An exceptional way to enjoy hundreds of miles of single-track in summer or virgin powder slopes in winter, **San Juan Hut Systems** (☑970-626-3033; www.sanjuanhuts.com; per person $30) continues the European tradition of hut-to-hut adventures with five backcountry mountain huts. Bring just your food, flashlight (torch) and sleeping bag: amenities include padded bunks, propane stoves, wood stoves for heating and firewood.

Mountain-biking routes go from Durango or Telluride to Moab, winding through high alpine and desert regions. Or pick one hut as your base for a few days of backcountry skiing or riding. There's terrain for all levels, though skiers should have knowledge of snow and avalanche conditions. If not, go with a guide.

The website has helpful tips and information on rental skis, bikes and (optional) guides based in Ridgway or Ouray.

chandeliers to pay the bills. Look for the bullet holes in the wall.

There COCKTAIL BAR
(☑ 970-728-1213; http://therebars.com; 627 W Pacific Ave; appetizers from $4; ☺ 5pm-12am Mon-Fri, 10am-3pm Sat-Sun) A hip social alcove for cocktails and nibbling, plus weekend brunch. For those with a bigger appetite, there's shareable entrees. East-meets-West in yummy lettuce wraps, duck ramen and sashimi tostadas, paired with original hand-shaken drinks. We liked the jalapeño kiss.

☆ Entertainment

Fly Me to the Moon Saloon LIVE MUSIC
(☑ 970-728-6666; 132 E Colorado Ave; ☺ 3pm-2am) Let your hair down and kick up your heels to the tunes of live bands at this saloon, the best place in Telluride to groove to live music.

Sheridan Opera House THEATER
(☑ 970-728-4539; www.sheridanoperahouse.com; 110 N Oak St; ⊕) This historic venue has a burlesque charm and is always the center of Telluride's cultural life.

❶ Information

Visitor Center (☑ 888-353-5473, 970-728-3041; www.telluride.com; 398 W Colorado Ave; ☺ 9am-5pm)

❶ Getting There & Around

Commuter aircraft serve the mesa-top **Telluride Airport** (☑ 970-778-5051; www.tellurideairport.com; Last Dollar Rd) 5 miles east of town on Hwy 145. If the weather is poor, flights may be diverted to Montrose, 65 miles north. For car rental, National and Budget both have airport locations.

In ski season Montrose Regional Airport, 66 miles north, has direct flights to and from Denver (on United), Houston, Phoenix and limited cities on the East Coast.

Shared shuttles by **Telluride Express** (☑ 970-728-6000; www.tellurideexpress.com) go from the Telluride Airport to town or Mountain Village for $15. Shuttles between the Montrose Airport and Telluride cost $50.

Mesa Verde National Park

Shrouded in mystery, Mesa Verde, with its cliff dwellings and verdant valley walls, is a fascinating, if slightly eerie, national park to explore. It is here that a civilization of Ancestral Puebloans appears to have vanished in AD 1300, leaving behind a complex civilization

DON'T MISS

TELLURIDE'S GREAT OUTDOORS

Sure, the festivals are great, but there's much more to a Telluride summer.

Mountain biking
Follow the River Trail from Town Park to Hwy 145 for 2 miles. Join Mill Creek Trail west of the Texaco gas station; it climbs and follows the contour of the mountain and ends at the Jud Wiebe Trail (hikers only).

Hiking
Just over 2 miles, Bear Creek Trail ascends 1040ft to a beautiful cascading waterfall. From here you can access the strenuous Wasatch Trail, a 12-mile loop that heads west across the mountains to Bridal Veil Falls – Telluride's most impressive waterfalls. The Bear Creek trailhead is at the south end of Pine St, across the San Miguel River.

Cycling
A 31-mile (one-way) trip, Lizard Head Pass features amazing mountain panoramas.

of cliff dwellings, some accessed by sheer climbs. Mesa Verde is unique among parks for its focus on preserving this civilization's cultural relics so that future generations may continue to interpret the puzzling settlement, and subsequent abandonment, of the area.

Mesa Verde rewards travelers who set aside a day or more to take the ranger-led tours of Cliff Palace and Balcony House, explore Wetherill Mesa or participate in one of the campfire programs. But if you only have time for a short visit, check out the Chapin Mesa Museum and walk through the Spruce Tree House, where you can climb down a wooden ladder into the cool chamber of a kiva (ceremonial structure, usually partly underground).

◉ Sights & Activities

Chapin Mesa Museum MUSEUM
(☑ 970-529-4475; www.nps.gov/meve; Chapin Mesa Rd; admission included with park entry; ☺ 8am-6:30pm Apr–mid-Oct, 8am-5pm mid-Oct–Apr; ⊕ ⊕) A good first stop, with detailed dioramas and exhibits pertaining to the park. When park headquarters are closed on weekends, staff at the museum provide information.

Chapin Mesa
ARCHEOLOGICAL SITE

The largest concentration of Ancestral Puebloan sites is at Chapin Mesa, where you'll see the densely clustered Far View Site and the large Spruce Tree House, the most accessible of sites, with a paved half-mile round-trip path.

If you want to see Cliff Palace or Balcony House, the only way is through an hour-long ranger-led tour booked in advance at the visitor center ($3). These tours are extremely popular; go early in the morning or a day in advance to book. Balcony House requires climbing a 32ft and 60ft ladder – those with medical problems should skip it.

Wetherill Mesa
ARCHEOLOGICAL SITE

This is the second-largest concentration. Visitors may enter stabilized surface sites and two cliff dwellings, including the Long House, open late May to August. South from Park Headquarters, the 6-mile Mesa Top Road connects excavated mesa-top sites, accessible cliff dwellings and vantage points to view inaccessible dwellings from the mesa rim.

★ Aramark Mesa Verde
HIKING

(970-529-4421; www.visitmesaverde.com; adult $42-48) Highly recommended, these backcountry ranger tours are run through the park concessionaire. Backcountry hikes sell out fast, since they provide exclusive access to Square House (via an exposed one-mile hike) and Spring House (an eight-hour, 8-mile hike), but make very personalized trips to excavated pit homes, cliff dwellings and the Spruce Tree House daily from May to mid-October. Tickets available only online.

🍴 Sleeping & Eating

The nearby towns of Cortez and Mancos have plenty of midrange places to stay; inside the park there's camping and a lodge.

Morefield Campground
CAMPGROUND $

(970-529-4465; www.visitmesaverde.com; North Rim Rd; tent/RV site $29/37; ⊙May–early-Oct; 🐕) 🍴 Deluxe campers will dig the big canvas tents kitted out with two cots and a lantern. The park's camping option, located 4 miles from the entrance gate, also has 445 regular tent sites on grassy grounds conveniently located near Morefield Village. The village has a general store, gas station, restaurant, free showers and laundry. Free evening campfire programs take place nightly from Memorial Day (May) to Labor Day (September) at the Morefield Campground Amphitheater.

Far View Lodge
LODGE $$

(970-529-4421, toll-free 800-449-2288; www.visitmesaverde.com; North Rim Rd; r $115-184; ⊙mid-Apr–Oct; P⊛❄) Perched on a mesa top 15 miles inside the park entrance, this tasteful Pueblo-style lodge has 150 rooms, some with kiva fireplaces. Standard rooms don't have air con (or TV) and summer daytimes can be hot. The Southwestern-style kiva rooms are a worthwhile upgrade, with balconies, pounded copper sinks and bright patterned blankets. You can even bring your dog for an extra $10 per night.

Far View Terrace Café
CAFE $

(970-529-4421, toll-free 800-449-2288; www.visitmesaverde.com; North Rim Rd; dishes from $5; ⊙7-10am, 11am-3pm & 5-8pm May–mid-Oct; 🍴🐕) Housed in Far View Lodge, this self-service place offers reasonably priced meals. Don't miss the house special – the Navajo Taco.

Metate Room
MODERN AMERICAN $$$

(800-449-2288; www.visitmesaverde.com; North Rim Rd; mains $15-28; ⊙5-7:30pm year-round, & 7-10am Apr–mid-Oct; 🍴🐕) 🍴 Featuring lovely views, this innovative restaurant in the Far View Lodge offers regional flavors with some innovation, serving dishes such as cinnamon chili pork, elk shepherd's pie and trout crusted in pine nuts. You can also get local Colorado beers.

ℹ Information

The park entrance is off US 160, midway between Cortez and Mancos. New in 2012, the **Mesa Verde Visitor and Research Center** (800-305-6053, 970-529-5034; www.nps.gov/meve; North Rim Rd; ⊙8am-7pm daily Jun-early Sep, 8am-5pm early Sep–mid-Oct, closed mid-Oct–May; 🐕), located near the entrance, has information and news on park closures (many areas are closed in winter). It also sells tickets for **tours** ($3) of the magnificent Cliff Palace or Balcony House.

Durango

An archetypal old Colorado mining-town, Durango is a regional darling that is nothing short of delightful. Its graceful hotels, Victorian-era saloons and tree-lined streets of sleepy bungalows invite you to pedal around soaking up all the good vibes. There is plenty to do outdoors. Style-wise, Durango is torn between its ragtime past and a cool, cutting-edge future where townie bikes, caffeine and farmers markets rule.

The town's historic central precinct is home to boutiques, bars, restaurants and theater halls. Foodies will revel in the innovative organic and locavore fare that is making it the best place to eat in the state. But the interesting galleries and live music, combined with a relaxed and congenial local populace, also make it a great place to visit.

Activities

Mountain Biking
CYCLING

From steep single-track to scenic road rides, Durango is a national hub for mountain biking. The easy Old Railroad Grade Trail is a 12.2-mile loop that uses both US Hwy 160 and a dirt road following the old railway tracks. From Durango take Hwy 160 west through the town of Hesperus. Turn right into the Cherry Creek Picnic Area, where the trail starts. For something a bit more technical, try Dry Fork Loop, accessible from Lightner Creek just west of town. It has some great drops, blind corners and vegetation. Cycling shops on Main or Second Ave rent out mountain bikes.

★ Durango & Silverton Narrow Gauge Railroad
RAILWAY

(☑970-247-2733, toll-free 877-872-4607; www.durangotrain.com; 479 Main Ave; adult/child return from $85/51; ☺departure at 8am, 8:45am, 9:30am; ⊕) Riding the Durango Silverton Narrow Gauge Railroad is a Durango must. These vintage steam locomotives have been making the scenic 45-mile trip north to Silverton (3½ hours each way) for over 125 years. The dazzling journey allows two hours for exploring Silverton. This trip operates only from May through October. Check online for different winter options.

Durango Mountain Resort
SNOW SPORTS

(☑970-247-9000; www.durangomountainresort.com; 1 Skier Pl; lift tickets adult/child from $75/45; ☺mid-Nov–Mar; ⊕) Also known as Purgatory, this resort, 25 miles north on US 550, offers 1200 skiable acres of varying difficulty and boasts 260in of snow per year. Two terrain parks offer plenty of opportunities for snowboarders to catch big air. Check local grocery stores and newspapers for promotions and two-for-one lift tickets.

Sleeping

Hometown Hostel
HOSTEL $

(☑970-385-4115; www.durangohometownhostel.com; 736 Goeglein Gulch Rd; dm $28; ☺reception 3:30-8pm; P@☎) The bee's knees of hostels, this suburban-style house sits on the winding road up to the college, next to a convenient bike path. A better class of backpackers, it's all-inclusive, with linen, towels, lockers and wi-fi. There are two single-sex dorms and a larger mixed dorm, and a great common kitchen and lounge area. Room rates fall with extended stays.

Adobe Inn
MOTEL $

(☑970-247-2743; www.durangohotels.com; 2178 Main Ave; d $84; ⊕❉@☎) Locally voted the best value lodging, this friendly motel gets the job done with clean, decent rooms and friendly service. You might even be able to talk them into giving their best rate if you arrive late night. Check out their Durango tip sheet.

★ Rochester House
HOTEL $$

(☑970-385-1920, toll-free 800-664-1920; www.rochesterhotel.com; 721 E 2nd Ave; d $169-229; ⊕❉☎) Influenced by old Westerns (movie posters and marquee lights adorn the hallways), the Rochester is a little bit of old Hollywood in the new West. It's linked to smaller accommodations, Leland House, across the street, where all guests check in. Rooms in both are spacious but slightly worn, some with kitchenettes. Still, you can't beat the cool townie bikes, available for guests to take spins around town. Pet rooms come with direct access outside.

Strater Hotel
HOTEL $$$

(☑970-247-4431; www.strater.com; 699 Main Ave; d $197-257; ⊕❉@☎) The past lives large in this historical Durango hotel with walnut antiques, hand-stenciled wallpapers and relics ranging from a Stradivarius violin to a gold-plated Winchester. But we can boast about the friendly staff, who go out of their way to resolve guests' queries. Rooms lean toward the romantic, with comfortable beds amid antiques, crystal and lace. The hot tub is a romantic plus (reserved by the hour) as is the summertime melodrama (theater) the hotel runs. In winter, rates drop by more than 50%, making it a virtual steal. Look online.

Eating & Drinking

Durango has a fantastic dining scene, especially strong on organic and locally sourced foods. Get a local dining guide (available in most hostels and at the visitors center) for all the options. It's also home to a slew of breweries.

Homeslice
PIZZERIA $

(☑970-259-5551; http://homeslicedelivers.com; 441 E College Ave; slice $4; ☺11am-10pm) Locals pile into this no-frills pizza place for thick pies with bubbly crust, sriracha sauce on the side. There's patio seating, gluten-free crust options and salads too.

Durango Diner
DINER $$

(☑970-247-9889; www.durangodiner.com; 957 Main Ave; mains $7-18; ☺6am-2pm Mon-Sat, 6am-1pm Sun; ☑⛄) Enjoy the open view of the griddle at this lovable greasy spoon with monstrous plates of eggs, smothered burritos or French toast. It's a local institution.

Jean Pierre Bakery
FRENCH, BAKERY $$

(☑970-247-7700; www.jeanpierrebakery.com; 601 Main Ave; mains $9-22; ☺8am-9pm; ☑⛄) This French patisserie has tempting delicacies made from scratch. Prices are dear, but the soup-and-sandwich lunch special, with a sumptuous French pastry (we recommend the sticky pecan roll), is a good deal.

East by Southwest
FUSION, SUSHI $$

(☑970-247-5533; http://eastbysouthwest.com; 160 E College Dr; sushi $4-13, mains $12-24; ☺11:30am-3pm, 5-10pm Mon-Sat, 5-10pm Sun; ☑⛄) Low-lit but vibrant, this is a worthy local favorite. Skip the standards for goosebump-good house favorites like sashimi with jalapeño and rolls with mango and wasabi honey. Fish is fresh and sustainably sourced. An extensive fusion menu also offers Thai, Vietnamese and Indonesian, well matched with creative martinis and sake cocktails. For a deal, hit the happy-hour food specials (5pm to 6:30pm).

Steamworks Brewing
BREWERY

(☑970-259-9200; www.steamworksbrewing.com; 801 E 2nd Ave; mains $10-15; ☺11am-midnight Mon-Thur, 11am-2am Fri-Sun) DJs and live music pump up the volume at this industrial micro-brewery with high sloping rafters and metal pipes. College kids fill the large bar area, but there's also a separate dining room with a Cajun-influenced menu.

Diamond Belle Saloon
BAR

(☑970-376-7150; www.strater.com; 699 Main Ave; ☺11am-late; ⛄) A rowdy corner of the historic Strater Hotel, this elegant old-time bar has waitresses dressed in vintage Victorian garb and flashing fishnets, and live ragtime that keeps out-of-town visitors packed in – standing room only at happy hour (4pm to 6pm daily). The food is below average.

🛈 Information

Visitor Center (☑800-525-8855; www.durango.org; 111 S Camino del Rio) South of town at the Santa Rita exit from US 550.

🛈 Getting There & Around

Durango-La Plata County Airport (DRO; ☑970-247-8143; www.flydurango.com; 1000 Airport Rd) is 18 miles southwest of Durango via US 160 and Hwy 172. Greyhound buses run daily from the **Durango Bus Center** (☑970 259 2755; 275 E 8th Ave), north to Grand Junction and south to Albuquerque, NM.

Check **Durango Transit** (☑970-259-5438; www.getarounddurango.com) for local travel information. Durango buses are fitted with bicycle racks. It's free to ride the red T shuttle bus that circulates Main St.

Durango is at the junction of US 160 and US 550, 42 miles east of Cortez, 49 miles west of Pagosa Springs and 190 miles north of Albuquerque.

Silverton

Ringed by snowy peaks and steeped in sooty tales of a tawdry mining town, Silverton seems more at home in Alaska than the lower 48. But here it is. Whether you're into snowmobiling, powder skiing, fly-fishing, beer on tap or just basking in some very high-altitude sunshine, Silverton delivers.

It's a two-street town, but only one is paved. The main drag, Greene St, is where you'll find most businesses. Notorious Blair St, still unpaved, runs parallel to Greene and is a blast from the past. During the silver rush, Blair St was home to thriving brothels and boozing establishments.

🏃 Activities

In summer, Silverton has some of the west's best 4WD trails. Traveling in modified Chevy Suburbans without the top, **San Juan Backcountry** (☑970-387-5565; toll-free 800-494-8687; www.sanjuanbackcountry.com; 1119 Greene St; 2hr tours adult/child $60/40; ☺May-Oct; ⛄) offers both tours and rental jeeps.

🛏 Sleeping & Eating

Red Mountain Motel & RV Park
MOTEL, CAMPGROUND $$

(☑970-382-5512, toll-free 800-970-5512; www.redmtmotelrvpk.com; 664 Greene St; motel r from $110, cabins from $120, tent/RV sites $22/38; ☺year-round; ᴘ☺ᴙ) Campers can try Red Mountain Motel & RV Park, a pet-friendly place that stays open year-round.

Inn of the Rockies at the
Historic Alma House
B&B $$

(☑970-387-5336, toll-free 800-267-5336; www.innoftherockies.com; 220 E 10th St; r incl breakfast $109-173; P ⊝ ❋) Splurge for romance here with an outdoor hot tub and New Orleans–inspired breakfast.

Stellar
ITALIAN $$

(☑970-387-9940; 1260 Blair St; mains $8-20; ⊗4pm-9:30pm; ☒) Your best bet for a sit-down meal is Stellar, an atmospheric pizzeria with full bar and beer on tap. Go for the lasagna if it isn't sold out.

⬤ Drinking

★ Montanya Distillers
BAR

(www.montanyadistillers.com; 1309 Greene St; mains $6-13; ⊗12pm-10pm) The town has its share of Western-style saloons, but for something original seek out Montanya Distillers, a smart bar with rooftop summer seating and exotic cocktails crafted with homemade syrups and award-winning rum. Organic tamales and other yummy edibles are served.

ⓘ Getting There & Away

Silverton is 50 miles north of Durango and 24 miles south of Ouray off US 550.

Great Sand Dunes National Park

Landscapes collide in a shifting sea of sand at **Great Sand Dunes National Park** (☑719-378-6399; www.nps.gov/grsa; 11999 Hwy 150; adult/child $3/free; ⊗visitor center 8:30am-6:30pm summer, shorter hours rest of year), making you wonder whether a spaceship has whisked you to another planet. The 55-sq-mile dune park – the tallest sand peak rises 700ft above the valley floor – is squeezed between the jagged 14,000ft peaks of the Sangre de Cristo and San Juan Mountains and flat, arid scrub-brush of the San Luis Valley.

Plan a visit to this excellent-value national park ($3 admission is a steal) around a full moon. Stock up on supplies, stop by the visitor center for your free backcountry camping permit and hike into the surreal landscape to set up camp in the middle of nowhere (bring plenty of water). You won't be disappointed.

There are numerous **hiking trails**, like the half-mile **Zapata Falls** (BLM road 5415), reached through a fun slot canyon (wear grippy shoes, you may be in standing water). And there's always **sandboarding**, where you ride a snowboard down the dunes, though it's best left to those who already snowboard.

The most popular month to visit is June, when Medano Creek is flowing and kids get a natural refreshment by wading in. Be sure to bring lots of water. Walking in loose sand is difficult, and summer temperatures on the dunes can exceed 130°F (54°C).

🛏 Sleeping

Pinyon Flats Campground
CAMPGROUND $

(☑888-448-1474; www.recreation.gov; Great Sand Dunes National Park; campsites $20; ☒) In the national park, Pinyon Flats has 88 sites and year-round water.

Zapata Falls Campground
CAMPGROUND $

(www.fs.usda.gov; BLM road 5415; campsites $11; ⊗year-round; ☒) With awesome valley panoramas, the more secluded Zapata Falls lies seven miles south via a steep 3.6-mile dirt access road. Bring your own water.

Zapata Ranch
RANCH $$$

(☑719-378-2356; www.zranch.org; 5303 Hwy 150; d with full board $300) Ideal for horse-riding enthusiasts, the exclusive Zapata Ranch is a working cattle and bison ranch set amid groves of cottonwood trees. Owned and operated by the Nature Conservancy, the main inn is a refurbished 19th-century log structure, with distant views of the sand dunes.

ⓘ Getting There & Away

The national park is about 35 miles northeast of Alamosa and 250 miles south of Denver. From Denver, take I-25 south to Hwy 160 west and turn onto Hwy 150 north. There is no public transportation.

WYOMING

With wind, restless grasses and wide blue skies, the most sparsely populated state offers solitude to spare. Called the 'Bunchgrass edge of the World' by writer Annie Proulx, Wyoming may be nuzzled in the bosom of America, but it's emptiness that defines it.

Though steeped in ranching culture – just see the line of Stetsons at the local credit union – Wyoming is the number-one coal producer in the US, and is also big in natural gas, crude oil and diamonds. Deeply conservative, its propensity toward industry has sometimes made it an uneasy steward of the land.

But wilderness may be Wyoming's greatest bounty. Its northwestern corner is home to the magnificent national parks of Yellowstone and Grand Teton. Chic Jackson and

ROCKY MOUNTAINS SOUTHERN COLORADO

WYOMING FACTS

Nickname Equality State

Population 576,000

Area 97,100 sq miles

Capital city Cheyenne (population 60,100)

Sales tax 4%

Birthplace of Artist Jackson Pollock (1912-1956)

Home of Women's suffrage, coal mining, geysers, wolves

Politics Conservative to the core

Famous for Rodeo, ranches, former Vice President Dick Cheney

Kitschiest souvenir Fur jock strap from a Jackson boutique

Driving distances Cheyenne to Jackson 440 miles

progressive Lander make great bases for epic hiking, climbing and skiing. For a truer taste of Western life, check out the plain prairie towns of Laramie and Cheyenne.

ℹ Information

Even on highways, distances are long, with gas stations few and far between. Driving hazards include frequent high gusty winds and fast-moving snow squalls that can create whiteout blizzard conditions. If the weather gets too rough, the highway patrol will shut the entire interstate until it clears.

Wyoming Road Conditions (☎307-772-0824, 888-996-7623; www.wyoroad.info)

Wyoming State Parks & Historic Sites (☎307-777-6323; www.wyo-park.com; admission $6, historic site $4, campsite per person $17) Wyoming has 12 state parks. Camping reservations are taken online or over the phone.

Wyoming Travel & Tourism (☎800-225-5996; www.wyomingtourism.org; 1520 Etchepare Circle)

Cheyenne

Many a country tune has been penned about Wyoming's state capital and largest city, though Cheyenne is more like the Hollywood Western *before* the shooting begins – that is, until Frontier Days festival, a raucous July celebration of cowboy fun. At the junction of I-25 and I-80, it's an obvious pit stop.

◉ Sights & Activities

Cheyenne Gunslingers WILD WEST SHOW
(☎800-426-5009; www.cheyennegunslingers.com; cnr W 15th at Pioneer Ave; ⊙noon Sat & 6pm Thu-Fri Jun, 6pm Mon-Fri, 12pm Sat Jul; ☻) **FREE** A nonprofit group of actors who puts on a lively, if not exactly accurate Old West show – from near hangings to slippery jailbreaks. Stars include corrupt judges, smiling good guys and, of course, the bad-ass villains.

Frontier Days Old West Museum MUSEUM
(☎307-778-7290; www.oldwestmuseum.org; 4601 N Carey Ave; adult/child $10/5; ⊙8am-6pm Mon-Fri, 9am-5pm Sat & Sun summer, 9am-5pm Mon-Fri, 10am-5pm Sat & Sun winter) For a peek into the pioneer past, visit the lively Frontier Days Old West Museum at I-25 exit 12. It is chock-full of rodeo memorabilia – from saddles to trophies. For the audio tour, call ☎307-316-0071.

★ Festivals & Events

★ **Cheyenne Frontier Days** RODEO
(☎1-800-227-6336; www.cfdrodeo.com; 4501 N Carey Ave; admission free-$32; ⊙July; ☻) If you've never seen a steer wrestler leap into action, this very Western event is bound to brand an impression. Beginning in late July, Wyoming's largest celebration features 10 days of rodeos, concerts, dances, air shows, and chili cook-offs. Free events include morning 'slack' rodeos, pancake breakfasts and parades. There's also an art sale and 'Indian village.'

⌂ Sleeping & Eating

Reservations are a must during Frontier Days, when rates double and everything within 50 miles is booked; see www.cheyenne.org/availability for bookings. The cheapest motels line noisy Lincolnway (I-25 exit 9).

Nagle Warren Mansion Bed & Breakfast B&B $$
(☎307-637-3333; www.naglewarrenmansion.com; 222 E 17th St; r incl breakfast from $155; ☷☎☻) This lavish spread is a fabulous find. In a quickly-going-hip neighborhood, this historic 1888 house is decked out with late-19th-century regional antiques. Spacious and elegant, the mansion boasts a hot tub, a reading room tucked into a turret and classic 1954 Schwinn bikes for cruising. Jim, the owner, entertains with his deep knowledge of local history.

It's worth stopping at the excellent art gallery next door.

Tortilla Factory
MEXICAN $

(715 S Greeley Hwy; mains $3-10; ⊘6am-8pm Mon-Sat, 8am-5pm Sun) A delicious Mexican dive serving homemade tamales for $1.50, and authentic classics such as shredded-beef tacos and huevos rancheros.

Shadows Pub & Grill
BREWERY $

(Depot Station; mains $8-15; ⊘11am-11pm Mon-Thur, 11am-1am Fri-Sat, 11am-9pm Sun) It's hard to beat the ambience at this handsome brick brewpub at the 1860s Union Pacific depot. The pub fare is standard, but there's ample patio seating for sunny days and good microbrews on tap.

🛍 Shopping

Boot Barn
CLOTHING, SOUVENIRS

(1518 Capitol Ave; ⊘9am-9pm Mon-Sat, 9am-6pm Sun) If you are hankering after a Stetson hat, rhinestone belt-buckle or authentic cowboy boots, look no further. This hub of Western wear is full of gems.

ℹ Information

Cheyenne Visitor Center (☑307-778-3133; www.cheyenne.org; 1 Depot Sq; ⊘8am-7pm Mon-Fri, 9am-5pm Sat, 11am-5pm Sun, closed weekends in winter) A great resource.

ℹ Getting There & Around

Cheyenne Airport (CYS; ☑307-634-7071; www.cheyenneairport.com; 200 E 8th Ave) has daily flights to Denver. Greyhound buses depart from the **Black Hills Stage Lines** (☑307-635-1327; www.blackhillsstagelines.com; 5401 Walker Rd) daily for Billings, MT, ($84, 9½ hours) and Denver, CO ($31, 2¾ hours), among other destinations.

On weekdays, the **Cheyenne Transit Program** (☑307-637-6253; adult $1, 6-18yr 75¢; ⊘service 6am-7pm Mon-Fri, 10am-5pm Sat) operates six local bus routes. Also, **Cheyenne Street Railway Trolley** (☑800-426-5009; 121 W 15th St; adult/child $10/5; ⊘May-Sep) takes visitors on tours through downtown.

Laramie

Home to the state's only four-year university, Laramie can be both hip and boisterous, a vibe missing from most Wyoming prairie towns. Worth exploring is the small historic downtown, a lively five-block grid of attractive two-story brick buildings with hand-painted signs and murals pushed up against the railroad tracks.

For an infusion of culture, check out one of the museums on the University of Wyoming (UW) campus, the newly refurbished **Geological Museum** (☑307-766-2646; www.uwyo.edu/geomuseum; Hwy 287 at I-80; ⊘10am-4pm Tues-Fri, 10am-3pm Sat-Sun) **FREE** features an impressive collection of dinosaur remains, including those of a Tyrannosaurus rex. If you're traveling with the kids (or just feel like one), stop by the **Wyoming Frontier Prison** (☑307-745-616; www.wyomingfrontierprison.org; 975 Snowy Range Rd; adult/child $7/6; ⊘8am-5pm; 🖘), a curious restoration of an early prison and frontier town.

There are numerous cheap sleeps off I-80 at exit 313. With landscaped gardens, lauded homemade granola and three snug rooms, **Mad Carpenter Inn** (☑307-742-0870; madcarpenter.com; 353 N 8th St; r incl breakfast $95-125; 🖘) has warmth to spare. A serious game room features billiards and table tennis. In town, the **Gas Lite Motel** (☑307-742-6616; 960 N 3rd St; r $61; ❀🖘🖳🐾) relies on an outrageously kitsch setup (think cowboy cutouts and plastic horses) to sell its well-priced and pet-friendly digs.

With superlative brews, **Coal Creek Coffee Co** (110 E Grand Ave; mains $3-6; ⊘6am-10pm; 🖘) is modern and stylish, with Fair Trade roasts and tasty sandwiches (eg bluecheese and portobello panini). Doubtless the healthiest food for miles, **Sweet Melissa's** (213 S 1st St; mains $8-10; ⊘11am-9pm Mon-Sat; 🖉) does good down-home vegetarian. It's packed at lunchtime.

For live country music and beer, favorite dive **Old Buckhorn Bar** (☑307-742-3554; 114 Ivinson St; ⊘9am-midnight Sun-Wed, 9am-2am Thur-Sat) is Laramie's oldest standing bar. Check out the hand-scratched graffiti and old condom dispenser in the bathroom.

Located 4 miles west of town via I-80 exit 311, **Laramie Regional Airport** (☑307-742-4164) has daily flights to Denver ($98 one-way). **Greyhound** (☑307-742-5188) buses stop at the **Diamond Shamrock gas station** (1952 Banner Road). Fill up your tank (and tummy) in Laramie; heading west on I-80, the next services aren't for 75 miles.

Lander

Lander just might be the coolest little one-street town in Wyoming – and there are many of those. Just a stone's throw from the Wind River Reservation, it's a rock-climbing and mountaineering mecca in a friendly and unpretentious foothills setting. It is also home to **NOLS** (www.nols.edu; 284 Lincoln St.), the National Outdoor Leadership School, a renowned outdoor school that leads trips around the world and locally into the Wind River Range.

The **Lander Visitor Center** (☑ 307-332-3892; www.landerchamber.org; 160 N 1st St; ☺ 9am-5pm Mon-Fri) is a good source of general information. If you've come to hike, camp or climb, you're best popping into **Wild Iris Mountain Sports** (☑ 307-332-4541; 166 Main St), a gear shop offering good advice and rental climbing or snow shoes. Pick up their cheat sheet with local tips. If you want to check out the single-track trails outside town, head to **Gannett Peak Sports** (351B Main Street; ☺ 10am-6pm Mon-Fri, 9am-5pm Sat).

The beautiful **Sinks Canyon State Park** (☑ 307-332-3077; 3079 Sinks Canyon Rd; admission $6; ☺ visitor center 9am-6pm Jun-Aug), 6 miles south of Lander, features a curious underground river. Flowing through a narrow canyon, the Middle Fork of the Popo Agie River disappears into the soluble Madison limestone called the Sinks and returns warmer a quarter-mile downstream in a pool called the Rise. The scenic **campgrounds** (campsites $17) come highly recommended by locals.

Chain hotels line Main St, but for a deal try the locally owned **Holiday Lodge** (☑ 307-332-2511; www.holidaylodgelander.com; 210 McFarlane Dr; camping $10 per person, r incl breakfast from $50; ✷ ☎). The look might say 1961, but it's scrubbed shiny and friendly, with thoughtful extras like an iron, makeup remover and sewing kits. Recommended riverside camping includes breakfast and showers.

Decompress from long hours of travel or adventure at the backyard patio of **Gannett Grill** (☑ 307-332-8227; 128 Main St; mains $6-9; ☺ 11am-9pm), a local institution, where you take a microbrew from the **Lander Bar** (☑ 307-332-8228; 126 Main St; mains $6-9; ☺ 11am-late) next door and wander back to your shady picnic table to dine on local beef burgers, crisp waffle fries and stone-oven pizzas. If you're feeling fancy, try the adjoining **Cowfish**, a more upscale dinner offering from the same folks. There's live music many nights.

Grab your coffee at chic **Old Town Coffee** (300 Main St; ☺ 7am-7pm; ☎) where each cup is brewed to order, as stiff as you like it.

Wind River Transportation Authority (☑ 307-856-7118; www.wrtabuslines.com) provides bus service to Jackson ($160) and other destinations; check the website for schedules.

Cody

Raucous Cody revels in its Wild West image (it's named after legendary showman William 'Buffalo Bill' Cody). With a staged streak of yeehaw, the town happily relays yarns (not always the whole story, mind you) about its past. Summer is high season, and Cody puts on quite an Old West show for the throngs of visitors making their way to Yellowstone National Park, 52 miles to the west. From Cody, the approach to geyserland through the Wapiti Valley is dramatic to say the least. President Teddy Roosevelt once said this stretch of pavement was 'the most scenic 50 miles in the world.'

The **visitor center** (☑ 307-587-2777; www.codychamber.org; 836 Sheridan Ave; ☺ 8am-6pm Mon-Sat, 10am-3pm Sun Jun-Aug, 8am-5pm Mon-Fri Sep-May) is the logical starting point.

Cody's major tourist attraction is the superb **Buffalo Bill Historical Center** (www.bbhc.org; 720 Sheridan Ave; adult/child $18/10; ☺ 8am-6pm May-Oct, 10am-5pm Nov, Mar & Apr, 10am-5pm Thu-Sun Dec-Feb). A sprawling complex of five museums, it showcases everything Western: from posters, grainy films and other lore pertaining to Buffalo Bill's world-famous Wild West shows, to galleries showcasing frontier artwork and a museum dedicated to Native Americans. Its Draper Museum of Natural History is a great primer for the Yellowstone ecosystem, with information on everything from wolves to grizzlies.

Also popular is the **Cody Nite Rodeo** (www.codystampederodeo.com; 519 West Yellowstone Ave; adult/child 7-12 yr $18/8), which giddy-ups nightly from June to August.

The lovely **Chamberlin Inn** (☑ 307-587-0202; 1032 12th St.; d/ste $185/325) offers an elegant downtown retreat. Built by ol' Bill himself in 1902, **Irma Hotel** (☑ 307-587-4221; www.irmahotel.com; 1192 Sheridan Ave; mains $8-23; ✷) is now better known for its restaurant – the ornate cherrywood was a gift from Queen Victoria. Gunfights break out nightly at 6pm in front of the hotel from June through September.

The **Silver Dollar Bar** (1313 Sheridan Ave; mains $7-12; ☺ 11am-12pm) is a historic watering hole with live music nightly on the outdoor deck. It serves epic burgers and has pool tables.

Yellowstone Regional Airport (COD; www.flyyra.com) is 1 mile east of Cody and runs daily flights to Salt Lake City and Denver.

Yellowstone National Park

They grow their critters and geysers big up in Yellowstone, America's first national park and Wyoming's flagship attraction. From shaggy grizzlies to oversized bison and magnificent packs of wolves, this park boasts the lower 48's most enigmatic concentration of wildlife. Throw in half the world's geysers, the country's largest high-altitude lake and a plethora of blue-ribbon rivers and waterfalls, all sitting pretty atop a giant supervolcano, and you'll quickly realize you've stumbled across one of Mother Nature's most fabulous creations.

When John Colter became the first white man to visit the area in 1807, the only inhabitants were Tukadikas (aka Sheepeaters), a Shoshone Bannock people who hunted bighorn sheep. Colter's reports of exploding geysers and boiling mud holes (at first dismissed as tall tales) brought in expeditions and tourism interest eagerly funded by the railroads. The park was established in 1872 (as the world's first) to preserve Yellowstone's spectacular geography: the geothermal phenomena, the fossil forests and Yellowstone Lake.

The 3472-sq-mile park is divided into five distinct regions (clockwise from the north): Mammoth, Roosevelt, Canyon, Lake and Geyser Countries.

Of the park's five entrance stations, only the North Entrance, near Gardiner, MT, is open year-round. The others, typically open May to October, offer access from the northeast (Cooke City, MT), east (Cody, WY), south (Grand Teton National Park) and west (West Yellowstone, MT). The park's main road is the 142-mile Grand Loop Rd scenic drive.

◎ Sights & Activities

Just sitting on the porch of the Old Faithful Inn with a cocktail in hand waiting for Old Faithful geyser to erupt could be considered enough activity by itself but there's plenty else to keep you busy here, from hiking and backpacking to kayaking and fly-fishing. Most park trails are not groomed, but unplowed roads and trails are open for cross-country skiing.

Yellowstone is split into five distinct regions, each with unique attractions. Upon entering the national park you'll be given a basic map and a park newspaper detailing the excellent ranger-led talks and walks (well worth attending). All the visitor centers have information desks staffed by park rangers who can help you tailor a hike to your tastes, from great photo spots to best chance of spotting a bear.

Geyser Country   GEYSER, HIKING
With the densest collection of geothermal features in the park, Upper Geyser Basin contains 180 of the park's 250-odd geysers. The most famous is Old Faithful, which spews from 3700 to 8400 gallons of water 100ft to 180ft into the air every 1½ hours or so. For an easy walk, check out the predicted eruption times at the brand new visitor center and then follow the easy boardwalk trail around the Upper Geyser Loop. The park's most beautiful thermal feature is Grand Prismatic Spring in the Midway Geyser Basin. The Firehole and Madison Rivers offer superb fly-fishing and wildlife viewing.

Mammoth Country   GEYSER, HIKING
Known for the geothermal terraces and elk herds of historic Mammoth and the hot springs of Norris Geyser Basin, Mammoth Country is North America's most volatile and oldest-known continuously active thermal area. The peaks of the Gallatin Range rise to the northwest, towering above the area's lakes, creeks and numerous hiking trails.

Roosevelt Country   HIKING
Fossil forests, the commanding Lamar River Valley and its tributary trout streams, Tower Falls and the Absaroka Mountains'

❶ BEAT THE CROWDS

Yellowstone's wonderland attracts up to 30,000 visitors daily in July and August and over three million gatecrashers annually. Avoid the worst of the crowds with the following advice:

➡ Visit in May, September or October for decent weather and few people; or even in winter.

➡ Ditch 95% of the crowds by hiking a backcountry trail. Lose 99% by camping in a backcountry site (permit required).

➡ Mimic the wildlife and be most active in the golden hours after dawn and before dusk.

➡ Pack lunch for one of the park's many scenic picnic areas and eat lodge dinners late (after 9pm).

➡ Make reservations for park lodging months in advance and book concession campgrounds *at least* the day before.

Yellowstone & Grand Teton National Parks

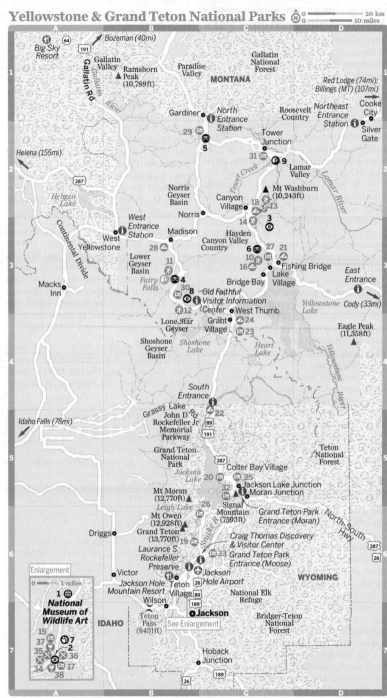

Yellowstone & Grand Teton National Parks

ROCKY MOUNTAINS YELLOWSTONE NATIONAL PARK

craggy peaks are the highlights of Roosevelt Country, the park's most remote, scenic and undeveloped region. Several good hikes begin near **Tower Junction**.

Canyon Country   LOOKOUT, HIKING

A series of scenic overlooks linked by hiking trails highlight the colorful beauty and grandeur of the Grand Canyon of the Yellowstone and its impressive **Lower Falls**. South Rim Dr leads to the canyon's most spectacular overlook, at **Artist Point**. **Mud Volcano** is Canyon Country's primary geothermal area.

Lake Country   LAKE, BOATING

Yellowstone Lake, the centerpiece of Lake Country and one of the world's largest alpine lakes, is a watery wilderness lined with volcanic beaches and best explored by boat or sea kayak. Rising east and southeast of the lakes, the wild and snowcapped Absaroka Range hides the wildest lands in the lower 48, perfect for epic backpacking or horseback trips.

Hiking Trails   HIKING

Hikers can explore Yellowstone's backcountry from more than 92 trailheads that give access to 1100 miles of hiking trails. A free backcountry-use permit, which is available at visitor centers and ranger stations, is required for overnight trips. Backcountry camping is allowed in 300 designated sites, 60% of which can be reserved in advance by mail; a $25 fee applies to all bookings that are more than three days in advance.

After much heated debate and a narrowly avoided fistfight, we have settled on the following as our favorite five-day hikes in the park.

➜ **Lone Star Geyser Trail**

A good family hike or bike ride along an old service road to a geyser that erupts every three hours. Start at the Kepler Cascades parking area, southeast of the Old Faithful area (5 miles, easy).

➜ **South Rim Trail**

A web of interconnected trails that follows the spectacular Yellowstone Canyon rim past the Lower Falls to scenic Artists Point then Lily Pad Lake, returning to Uncle Tom's trailhead via thermal areas and Clear Lake (3.5 miles, easy).

➡ Mt Washburn

A fairly strenuous uphill hike from Dunraven Pass trailhead to a mountaintop fire tower, for 360-degree views over the park and nearby bighorn sheep (6.4 miles, moderate).

➡ Elephant Back Mountain

An 800ft climb from near Lake Hotel to a panoramic viewpoint over Yellowstone Lake (3.5 miles, moderate).

➡ Fairy Falls

Climb off-trail to a viewpoint over spectacular Grand Prismatic Spring and then hike through lodgepole forest to the falls, before continuing on to beautiful Imperial Geyser (6 miles, easy).

Cycling   CYCLING

Cyclists can ride on public roads and a few designated service roads, but not on the backcountry trails. The best season is April to October, when the roads are usually snow-free. From mid-March to mid-April the Mammoth–West Yellowstone park road is closed to cars but open to cyclists, offering a long but stress-free ride.

Yellowstone Raft Company   ADVENTURE TOUR
(☎800-858-7781; www.yellowstoneraft.com; halfday adult/child $40/30) There is exhilarating white water through Yankee Jim Canyon on the Yellowstone River just north of the park boundary in Montana. This company offers a range of guided adventures out of Gardiner starting in late May.

🛏 Sleeping

NPS and private campgrounds, along with cabins, lodges and hotels, are all available in the park. Reservations are essential in summer. Contact the park concessionaire Xanterra (☎307-344-5395; www.yellowstonenationalparklodges.com) to reserve a spot at its campsites, cabins or lodges.

Plentiful accommodations can also be found in the gateway towns of Cody, Gardiner and West Yellowstone.

The best budget options are the seven NPS–run campgrounds (campsites from $15-20) in Mammoth (campsites $14; ⊙year-round), Tower Fall, Indian Creek, Pebble Creek, Slough Creek, Norris and Lewis Lake, which are first-come, first-served. Xanterra runs five more campgrounds (listed below; reservations accepted, $20 to $45 per night), all with cold-water bathrooms, flush toilets and drinking water. RV sites with hookups are available at Fishing Bridge.

Xanterra-run cabins, hotels and lodges are spread around the park and are open from May or June to October. Mammoth Hot Springs Hotel and Old Faithful Snow Lodge are the exceptions; these are also open mid-December through March. All places are nonsmoking and none have air con or TV. Where wi-fi is available, it costs extra.

Bridge Bay Campground   CAMPGROUND $
(campsite $21) Near the west shore of Yellowstone Lake, popular with boaters, and with 425 sites for tents and RVs.

WHERE THE BEARS & BISON ROAM...

Along with the big mammals – grizzly, black bear, moose and bison – Yellowstone is home to elk, pronghorn antelope and bighorn sheep. Wolves have been part of the national park since reintroduction in 1996, though they are now legally hunted outside park boundaries. Native to the area, both wolves and bison nearly met extinction by the end of the last century because of hunting and human encroachment. While their numbers have resurged, taking them off the endangered species list means they may yet be hunted out of the park.

In Yellowstone's heart between Yellowstone Lake and Canyon Village, Hayden Valley is your best all-round bet for wildlife viewing. For the best chances of seeing wildlife, head out at dawn or dusk and stakeout a turnout anywhere off the Grand Loop Rd. Bring patience and binoculars, a grizzly just might wander into your viewfinder, or perhaps you'll spy a rutting elk or hear the bugle of a solitary moose reaching the river for a drink.

Lamar Valley, in the northeast, is where wolves were first reintroduced and ground zero for spotting them. Ask rangers where packs are most active or attend a wolf-watching (or other) excursion with the recommended Yellowstone Institute (www.yellowstoneassociation.org). Hearing howls echo across the valley at dusk is a magical, primeval experience.

Canyon Campground   CAMPGROUND $
(campsite $25.50) Centrally located, with pay showers and coin laundry nearby. There are 250 sites for tents and RVs.

Fishing Bridge RV Park   CAMPGROUND $
(campsite $45) Full hook-ups for hard-shell RVs only ($37). Pay showers and coin laundry. There are 325 sites.

Grant Village Campground   CAMPGROUND $
(campsite $25.50) On Yellowstone Lake's southwest shore, it has 400 sites for tents and RVs. Pay showers and coin laundry nearby.

Madison Campground   CAMPGROUND $
(☑ 307-344-7311; www.yellowstonenationalpark-lodges.com; campsite $21; ⊘ early May-late Oct) The closest campground to Old Faithful, with 250 sites for tents and RVs.

Old Faithful Lodge Cabins   CABIN $
(cabins $69-115) Views of Old Faithful; simple, rustic cabins.

Roosevelt Lodge Cabins   CABIN $$
(☑ 866-439-7375; www.yellowstonenationalpark-lodges.com; cabins $69-115; ☷) These cabins are good for families. With a cowboy vibe, the place offers nightly 'Old West dinner cookouts,' during which guests travel by horse or wagon to a large meadow 3 miles from the lodge for open-air buffets (book ahead).

Lake Lodge Cabins   CABIN $$
(cabins $75-188) The main lodge boasts a large porch with lakeside mountain views and a cozy room with two fireplaces. Choose from rustic 1920s wooden cabins or more modern motel-style modules.

Old Faithful Snow Lodge   HOTEL $$
(cabins $99-155, r from $229; ☏) A stylish modern option that combines timber-lodge style with modern fittings and park motifs.

★ **Old Faithful Inn**   HOTEL $$
(☑ 866-439-7375; www.yellowstonenationalpark-lodges.com; old house d with shared/private bath from $103/140, standard from $164; ⊘ early May-early Oct) Next to the signature geyser, this grand inn is the most requested lodging in the park. A national historic landmark, it features an immense timber lobby, with huge stone fireplaces and sky-high knotted-pine ceilings. Rooms come in all price ranges, and many of the most interesting historic rooms share baths. Public areas offer plenty of allure.

It's worth staying two nights to soak up the atmosphere.

Lake Yellowstone Hotel   HOTEL $$
(☑ 866-439-7375; www.yellowstonenationalpark-lodges.com; cabins $130, r $149-299; ⊘ mid-May-Sep) Oozing grand 1920s Western ambience, this romantic, historic hotel is a classy option. It has Yellowstone's most divine lounge, which was made for daydreaming, with big picture windows overlooking the lake, ample natural light and a live string quartet playing in the background. Rooms are well appointed, cabins more rustic.

Canyon Lodge & Cabins   CABIN $$
(cabins $99-188, r $185) Clean and tidy in a central locale.

Mammoth Hot Springs
Hotel & Cabins   HOTEL $$
(cabins $86-229, r with/without bath $123/87; ☏) Wide variety of sleeping options; elk are often seen grazing on the front lawn.

Grant Village   HOTEL $$
(r $155) Near the southern edge of the park, it offers comfortable but dull motel-style rooms. Two nearby restaurants have fabulous lake views.

🍴 Eating

Snack bars, delis, burger counters and grocery stores are scattered around the park. In addition, most of the lodges offer breakfast buffets, salad bars, and lunch and dinner in formal dining rooms. Food, while not always exceptional, is quite good considering how many people the chef is cooking for, and not too overpriced for the exceptional views.

★ **Lake Yellowstone**
Hotel Dining Room   AMERICAN $$$
(☑ 307-344-7311; mains $13-33; ⊘ 6:30-10am, 11:30am-2:30pm, 5-10pm; ☝) Keep one unwrinkled outfit to dine in style at the dining room of the Lake Yellowstone Hotel, the best in the park. Lunch options include Montana lamb sliders, lovely salads and bison burgers. Local and gluten-free options. Dinner consists of heavier fare, with reservations highly recommended.

Old Faithful Inn Dining Room   AMERICAN $$$
(☑ 307-545-4999; dinner mains $13-29; ⊘ 6:30-10:30am, 11:30am-2:30pm, 5-10pm; ☝) The buffets here will maximize your time spent geyser gazing but the à la carte options are more innovative, think elk burgers, bison pot roast and the ever-popular pork osso bucco. With gluten-free options. Reservations recommended.

WORTH A TRIP

SCENIC DRIVE: THE ROOF OF THE ROCKIES

The most scenic route into Yellowstone Park, Beartooth Highway (www.beartoothhighway.com; US 212; ☉ Jun–mid-Oct) connects Red Lodge to Cooke City and Yellowstone's north entrance by an incredible 68-mile journey alongside 11,000ft peaks and wildflower-sprinkled alpine tundra. It's been called both American's most scenic drive and its premier motorcycle ride. There are a dozen USFS campgrounds (reservations for some accepted at www.recreation.gov) along the highway, four within 12 miles of Red Lodge.

❶ Information

The park is open year-round, but most roads close in winter. Park entrance permits (hiker/vehicle $12/25) are valid for seven days for entry into both Yellowstone and Grand Teton National Parks. Summer-only visitor centers are evenly spaced every 20 to 30 miles along Grand Loop Rd.

Albright Visitors Center (☏ 307-344-2263; www.nps.gov/yell; ☉ 8am-7pm Jun-Sep, 9am-5pm Oct-May) Serves as park headquarters. The park website is a fantastic resource.

❶ Getting There & Away

The closest year-round airports are: Yellowstone Regional Airport (COD) in Cody (52 miles); Jackson Hole Airport (JAC) in Jackson (56 miles); Gallatin Field Airport (BZN) in Bozeman, MT (65 miles); and Idaho Falls Regional Airport (IDA) in Idaho Falls, ID (107 miles). The airport (WYS) in West Yellowstone, MT, is usually open June to September. It's often more affordable to fly into Billings, MT (170 miles), Salt Lake City, UT (390 miles) or Denver, CO (563 miles) and rent a car.

There is no public transportation to or within Yellowstone National Park.

Grand Teton National Park

With its jagged, rocky peaks, cool alpine lakes and fragrant forests, the Tetons rank among the finest scenery in America. Directly south of Yellowstone, Grand Teton National Park has 12 glacier-carved summits, which frame the singular Grand Teton (13,770ft). For mountain enthusiasts, this sublime and crazy terrain is thrilling. Less crowded than Yellowstone, the Tetons also have plenty of tranquility, along with wildlife such as bear, moose, grouse and marmot.

The park has two entrance stations: Moose (south), on Teton Park Rd west of Moose Junction; and Moran (east), on US 89/191/287 north of Moran Junction. The park is open year-round, although some roads and entrances close from around November to May 1, including part of Moose-Wilson Rd, restricting access to the park from Teton Village.

🏃 Activities

With 200 miles of hiking trails you can't really go wrong. Consult at the visitor center where you can grab a hiking map. A free backcountry-use permit, also available here, is required for overnight trips. The Tetons are also known for excellent short-route rock climbs as well as classic longer routes to summits like Grant Teton, Mt Moran and Mt Owen.

Fishing is another draw, with several species of whitefish and cutthroat, lake and brown trout thriving in local rivers and lakes. Get a license at the Moose Village store, Signal Mountain Lodge or Colter Bay Marina.

Cross-country skiing and snowshoeing are the best ways to take advantage of park winters. Pick up a brochure detailing routes at Craig Thomas Discovery & Visitor Center.

Jenny Lake Ranger Station   ROCK CLIMBING
(☏ 307-739-3343; ☉ 8am-6pm Jun-Aug) For climbing information.

Exum Mountain Guides   ROCK CLIMBING
(☏ 307-733-2297; www.exumguides.com) For instruction and guided climbs.

🛏 Sleeping

Three different concessionaires run the park's six campgrounds. Demand is high from early July to Labor Day. Most campgrounds fill by 11am (Jenny Lake fills much earlier; Gros Ventre rarely fills up). Colter Bay and Jenny Lake have tent-only sites reserved for backpackers and cyclists.

Climbers' Ranch   CABIN $
(☏ 307-733-7271; www.americanalpineclub.org; Teton Park Rd; dm $25; ☉ Jun-Sep) Started as a refuge for serious climbers, these rustic log cabins run by the American Alpine Club are now available to hikers who can take advantage of the magnificent in-park location. There is a bathhouse with showers and a sheltered cook station with locking bins for coolers. Bring your own sleeping bag and pad (bunks are bare, but still a steal).

Flagg Ranch Resorts
CAMPGROUND **$**
(www.flaggranch.com; 2-person campsites $35)
Accepts online reservations for Flagg Ranch
campground, and also has cabins. Forever
Resorts manages Signal Mountain and Lizard Creek campgrounds in the park.

Grand Teton Lodge
Company
ACCOMMODATIONS SERVICES **$**
(☑ 307-543-2811; www.gtlc.com; campsites $21)
Runs most of the park's private lodges,
cabins and the campgrounds of Colter Bay,
Jenny Lake and Gros Ventre. Call for last-
minute cancellations, though it's best to
reserve ahead, as nearly everything is completely booked by early June. Each lodge has
an activity desk.

Colter Bay Village
CABIN **$$**
(☑ 307-543-2811; www.gtlc.com; tent cabins $57,
cabins with bath $135-239, without bath $73; ☉ Jun-
Sep) Half a mile west of Colter Bay Junction,
the village has two types of accommoda-
tions. Tent cabins (June to early September)
are very basic structures with bare bunks
and shared bathrooms in a separate build-
ing. At these prices, you're better off camp-
ing. The log cabins, some original, are much
more comfortable and a better deal; they're
available late May to late September.

Signal Mountain Lodge
CAMPGROUND, LODGE **$$**
(☑ 307-543-2831; www.signalmtnlodge.com; camp-
sites $21, r $194-230, cabins $156-185; ☉ May–mid-
Oct) This spectacularly located place at the
edge of Jackson Lake offers cozy, well-appointed cabins and rather posh rooms with
stunning lake and mountain views.

★ Jenny Lake Lodge
LODGE **$$$**
(☑ 307-733-4647; www.gtlc.com; Jenny Lake; cabins
incl half board $655; ☉ Jun-Sep) Worn timbers,
down comforters and colorful quilts imbue
this elegant lodging off Teton Park Rd with a
cozy atmosphere. It doesn't come cheap, but
includes breakfast, a five-course dinner, bi-
cycle use and guided horseback riding. Rainy
days are for hunkering down at the fireplace
in the main lodge with a game or book from
the stacks. The log cabins sport a deck but no
TVs or radios (phones on request).

Jackson Lake Lodge
LODGE **$$$**
(☑ 307-543-2811; www.gtlc.com; r & cabins $249-
335; ☉ Jun-Sep; ☎☒☀) With soft sheets,
meandering trails for long walks and enormous picture windows framing the lumi-
nous peaks, this lodge is the perfect place to
woo. Yet, you may find the 348 cinder-block

cottages generally overpriced. Has a heated
pool and pets are OK.

Spur Ranch Log Cabins
CABIN **$$$**
(☑ 307-733-2522; www.dornans.com; cabins $185-
265; ☉ year-round) Gravel paths running
through a broad wildflower meadow link
these tranquil duplex cabins on the Snake
River in Moose. Lodgepole-pine furniture,
Western styling and down bedding create a
homey feel, but the views are what make it.

✖ Eating
Colter Bay Village, Jackson Lake Lodge,
Signal Mountain and Moose Junction have
several reasonably priced cafes for breakfast
and fast meals.

Pioneer Grill
DINER **$$**
(☑ 307-543-1911; Jackson Lake Lodge; mains $9-
23; ☉ 6am-10:30pm; ☗) A casual classic with
leatherette stools lined up in a maze, the
Pioneer serves up wraps, burgers and salads.
Kids adore the hot fudge sundaes. A takeout
window serves boxed lunches (order a day
ahead) and room-service pizza for pooped
hikers (5pm to 9pm).

Mural Room
MODERN AMERICAN **$$$**
(☑ 307-543-1911; Jackson Lake Lodge; mains $22-
40; ☉ 7am-9pm) With stirring views of the
Tetons, gourmet selections include game
dishes and imaginative creations like trout
wrapped in sushi rice with sesame seeds.
Breakfasts are very good; dinner reserva-
tions are recommended.

Peaks
AMERICAN **$$$**
(☑ 307-543-2831; Signal Mountain Lodge; meals
$18-31) Dine on selections of cheese and fruit,
local free-range beef, and organic polenta
cakes. Small plates, like wild game sliders,
are also available. While the indoor ambience
is rather drab, the patio seating, starring sunsets over Jackson Lake and top-notch huckleberry margaritas, gets snapped up early.

Jenny Lake Lodge
Dining Room
MODERN AMERICAN **$$$**
(☑ 307-543-3352; breakfast $24, lunch mains
$12-15, dinner prix-fixe $85; ☉ 7am-9pm) A real
splurge, this may be the only five-course wil-
derness meal of your life, but it's well worth
it. For breakfast, crab-cake eggs benedict is
prepared to perfection. Trout with polenta
and crispy spinach satisfies hungry hikers,
and you can't beat the warm atmosphere
snuggled in the Tetons. Dress up in the
evening, when reservations are a must.

ROCKY MOUNTAINS GRAND TETON NATIONAL PARK

ℹ Information

Park permits (hiker/vehicle $12/25) are valid for seven days for entry into both Yellowstone and Grand Teton National Parks. It's easy to stay in one park and explore the other in the same day.

Craig Thomas Discovery & Visitor Center
(📞307-739-3399, backcountry permits 307-739-3309; Teton Park Rd; ⊗8am-7pm Jun-Aug, 8am-5pm rest of year) Located in Moose.

Laurance S Rockefeller Preserve Center
(📞307-739-3654; Moose-Wilson Rd; ⊗8am-6pm Jun-Aug, 9am-5pm rest of year) This recent addition gives information about the new and highly recommended Rockefeller Preserve, a less crowded option for hiking, located 4 miles south of Moose.

Park Headquarters (📞307-739-3600; www.nps.gov/grte; ⊗8am-7pm Jun-Aug, 8am-5pm rest of year) Shares a building with the Craig Thomas center.

Jackson

Technically this is Wyoming, but you'll have a hard time believing it. With a median age of 32, this Western town has evolved into a mecca for mountain lovers, hard-core climbers and skiers, easily recognizable as sunburned baristas. The upswing of being posh and popular? Jackson is abuzz with life: trails and outdoor opportunities abound. Fresh sushi is flown in daily and generous pursestrings support a vigorous cultural life. Skip the souvenirs and remember why you came to Jackson in the first place: to visit its glorious backyard, Grand Teton National Park.

👁 Sights

Downtown Jackson has a handful of historic buildings.

★**National Museum of Wildlife Art**   MUSEUM
(📞307-733-5771; www.wildlifeart.org; 2820 Rungius Rd; adult/child $12/6; ⊗9am-5pm) If you visit one area museum, make it this one. Major works by Bierstadt, Rungius, Remington and Russell that will make your skin prickle. The discovery gallery has a kids' studio for drawing and print rubbing that adults plainly envy. Check the website for summer film series and art-class schedules.

Center for the Arts   ARTS CENTER
(📞307-733-4900; www.jhcenterforthearts.org; 240 S Glenwood S) One-stop shopping for culture, attracting big-name concert acts and featuring theater performances, classes, art exhibits and events. Check the calendar of events online.

National Elk Refuge   WILDLIFE RESERVE
(📞307-733-9212; www.fws.gov/nationalelkrefuge; Hwy 89; horse-drawn sleigh ride adult/child $18/14; ⊗8am-5pm Sep-May, 8am-7pm Jun-Aug, horse-drawn sleigh ride 10am-4pm mid-Dec–Mar) **FREE** Protects thousands of migrating wapiti from November to March. A 45-minute horse-drawn sleigh ride is a highlight of a winter visit.

Town Square Shoot-out   WILD WEST SHOW
(⊗6.15pm Mon-Sat summer; 🚻) **FREE** In summer this hokey tourist draw takes place at 6:15pm Monday to Saturday.

🏃 Activities

★**Jackson Hole Mountain Resort**   SNOW SPORTS
(📞307-733-2292; www.jacksonhole.com; lift ticket adult/child $99/59) One of the country's top ski destinations, Jackson Hole Mountain Resort boasts the USA's greatest continuous vertical rise – from the 6311ft base at Teton Village to the 10,450ft summit of Rendezvous Mountain. Terrain is mostly advanced, boasting lots of fluffy powder and rocky ledges made for jumping. Tickets are slightly discounted online.

When the snow melts, the resort runs a plethora of summertime activities; check the website for details.

📖 Courses

Teton Science Schools Ecology   SCIENCE SCHOOL
(📞307-733-1313; www.tetonscience.org) No one beats this nonprofit for fun experiential education, with programs ranging from GPS scavenger hunts to ecology expeditions. Make inquiries through the website.

🛏 Sleeping

Jackson has plenty of lodging options, both in town and around the ski hill. Reservations are essential in summer and winter.

Hostel   HOSTEL $
(📞307-733-3415; www.thehostel.us; 3315 Village Dr; dm/d $34/99; ⊗closed fall & spring shoulder seasons; @) Teton Village's only budget option, this old ski lodge offers private doubles and bunk-bed rooms with renovated showers for up to four. The spacious lounge with fireplace is ideal for movies or Scrabble tournaments and there's a playroom for tots. Guests can use a microwave and outdoor grill, coin laundry and a ski-waxing area.

Buckrail Lodge
MOTEL $

(☑ 307-733-2079; www.buckraillodge.com; 110 E Karnes Ave; r from $93; ✳🌫) Spacious and charming log-cabin-style rooms, this steal is centrally located, with ample grounds and an outdoor Jacuzzi.

Golden Eagle Motor Inn
MOTEL $$

(☑ 307-733-2042; 325 E Broadway; r $148; ✹) Super-friendly and just far enough out of the fray, this refurbished motel with friendly hosts is a reliable choice in the center.

Alpine House
B&B $$$

(☑ 307-739-1570; www.alpinehouse.com; 285 N Glenwood St; d $250, cottage $450; @) Two former Olympic skiers have infused this downtown home with sunny Scandinavian style and personal touches like great service and a cozy mountaineering library. Amenities include plush robes, down comforters, a shared Finnish sauna and an outdoor Jacuzzi. Save your appetite for the creative breakfast options such as poached eggs over ricotta with asparagus or multigrain French toast.

🍴 Eating & Drinking

Jackson is home to Wyoming's most sophisticated and exotic food. Many restaurants double as bars, with the real deals dished out for happy hour.

★ Coco Love
DESSERT $

(☑ 307-733-3253; 55 N Glenwood Dr; desserts $5-8; ☯ 9am-8pm) Master dessert chef Oscar Ortega shows off his French training with a pastry case of exquisite object d'art desserts and handmade chocolates that make you quiver in delight. Do it.

Pica's Mexican Taqueria
MEXICAN $$

(1160 Alpine Lane; mains $7-15; ☯ 11:30am-9pm Mon-Fri, 11am-4pm Sat & Sun; ☷) Cheap and supremely satisfying, with Baja tacos wrapped in homemade corn tortillas or *cochinita pibil* (chili-marinated pork), served with Mexican sodas. Locals love this place; it's the best value around.

Pizzeria Caldera
PIZZERIA $$

(☑ 307-201-1472; 20 West Broadway; pizzas $12-16; ☯ 11am-9:30pm; ☷) 🍴 Fresh and unpretentious, this upstairs pizzeria serves their pies on the thinner side. Try topping yours with briny kalamata olives or fragrant bison sausage with sage, which begs one of the beers on tap. Salads use locally-grown arugula and beets.

Bubba's Bar-B-Que
BARBECUE $$

(☑ 307-733-2288; 100 Flat Creek Dr; mains $6-20; ☯ 7am-10pm; ☷) Get the biggest, fluffiest breakfast biscuits for miles at this friendly and energetic bring-your-own-bottle (BYOB) eatery. Later on, it's got a decent salad bar, and serves up a ranch of ribs and racks.

★ Snake River Grill
MODERN AMERICAN $$$

(☑ 307-733-0557; 84 E Broadway; mains $21-52; ☯ from 5:30pm) With a roaring stone fireplace, an extensive wine list and snappy

ROCKY MOUNTAINS JACKSON

IF YOU HAVE A FEW MORE DAYS

Wyoming is full of great places to get lost, sadly there are too many for us to elaborate on in this guide, but we'll prime you with a taster.

With vast grassy meadows, seas of wildflowers and peaceful conifer forests, the **Bighorn Mountains** in north-central Wyoming are truly awe-inspiring. Factor in gushing waterfalls and abundant wildlife and you've got a stupendous natural playground with hundreds of miles of marked trails.

Rising a dramatic 1267ft above the Belle Fourche River, the nearly vertical monolith of **Devil's Tower National Monument** is an awesome site. Known as Bears Lodge by some of the 20-plus Native American tribes who consider it sacred, it's a must-see if you are traveling between the Black Hills (on the Wyoming–South Dakota border) and the Tetons or Yellowstone.

West of Laramie, the lofty national forest stretching across **Medicine Bow Mountains** and **Snowy Range** is a wild and rugged place, perfect for multiday hiking and camping trips.

Nestled in the shadow of the Bighorn Mountains, **Sheridan** boasts century-old buildings once home to Wyoming cattle barons. It's popular with adventure fanatics who come to play in the Bighorns.

white linens, this grill creates notable American haute cuisine. Start with tempura string beans with spicy sriracha dipping sauce. The crispy pork falls off the bone and grilled elk chops show earthy goodness. Splurge-desserts like crème brulée or homemade ice cream easily satisfy two.

★ **Stagecoach Bar** BAR
(☑ 307-733-4407; 5755 W Hwy 22, Wilson) Wyoming has no better place to shake your booty. 'Mon-day' means reggae, Thursday is disco night and every Sunday the house band croons country-and-western favorites until 10pm. Worth the short drive to Wilson (just past the Teton Village turnoff).

Snake River Brewing Co BREWPUB
(☑ 307-739-2337; 265 S Millward St; ☉ 11:30am-midnight) With an arsenal of 22 microbrews crafted on the spot, some award-winning, it's no wonder that this is a favorite rendezvous spot. Food includes wood-fired pizzas and pasta (mains $6 to $18). Happy hour is from 4pm to 6pm.

Million Dollar Cowboy Bar BAR
(25 N Cache Dr) Touristy to the gills, but tempting nonetheless. Plunk your hind quarters on a saddle stool in this dark chop house, an obligatory stop on the Western tour. On weekends the dance floor sparks up and karaoke drones.

❶ Information

Jackson Hole Wyoming (www.jacksonholenet.com) A good website for information on the area.
Valley Bookstore (125 N Cache St) Sells regional maps.
Visitor Center (☑ 307-733-3316; www.jacksonholechamber.com; 532 N Cache Dr; ☉ 9am-5pm)

❶ Getting There & Around

Jackson Hole Airport (JAC; ☑ 307-733-7682) is 7 miles north of Jackson off US 26/89/189/191 within Grand Teton National Park. Daily flights serve Denver, Salt Lake City, Dallas and Houston, while weekend flights connect Jackson with Chicago.
Alltrans' Jackson Hole Express (☑ 307-733-3135; www.jacksonholebus.com) buses provide a shuttle to Grand Teton National Park ($14 per day) and the airport ($16). It also departs at 6:30am daily from Maverik County Store (cnr Hwy 89 S and S Park Loop Rd) for Salt Lake City ($70, 5½ hours).

MONTANA

Maybe it's the independent frontier spirit, wild and free and oh-so American, that earned Montana its 'live and let live' state motto. The sky seems bigger and bluer. The air is crisp and pine-scented. From its mountains that drop into undulating ranchlands to brick brewhouses and the shaggy grizzly found lapping at an ice-blue glacier lake, Montana brings you to that euphoric place, naturally. And then it remains with you long after you've left its beautiful spaces behind.

❶ Information

Montana Fish, Wildlife & Parks (☑ 406-444-2535; http://fwp.mt.gov) Camping in Montana's 24 state parks costs around $15/23 per night for residents/nonresidents, while RV hookup sites (where available) cost an additional $5. Make reservations at ☑ 1-855-922-6768 or http://montanastateparks.reserveamerica.com.
Montana Road Conditions (☑ 800-226-7623, within Montana 511; www.mdt.mt.gov/travinfo)
Travel Montana (☑ 800-847-4868; www.visitmt.com)

Bozeman

In a gorgeous locale, surrounded by rolling green hills, pine forests and snowcapped peaks, Bozeman is the defending title holder of Coolest Town in Montana. Brick buildings with brewpubs and boutiques line historic Main St, mashing bohemian style up against cowboy cool and triathlete verve. A prime location up against the Bridger and Gallatin mountains makes it one of the very best outdoor towns in the West.

◎ Sights & Activities

Museum of the Rockies MUSEUM
(☑ 406-994-2251; www.museumoftherockies.org; 600 W Kagy Blvd; adult/child $14/10; ☉ 8am-8pm; ⬆) Montana State University's (MSU) museum is the most entertaining in Montana and shouldn't be missed, with stellar dinosaur exhibits, early Native American art and laser planetarium shows.

★ **Bridger Bowl Ski Area** SNOW SPORTS
(☑ 406-587-2111; www.bridgerbowl.com; 15795 Bridger Canyon Rd; day lift ticket adult/child under 12yr $49/16; ☉ mid-Dec–Mar) Only in Bozeman would you find a nonprofit ski resort. But this excellent community-owned

ROCKY MOUNTAINS BOZEMAN

facility, 16 miles north of Bozeman, is just that. It's known for its fluffy, light powder and unbeatable prices – especially for children under 12.

🛏 Sleeping

The full gamut of chain motels lies north of downtown on 7th Ave, near I-90. There are more budget motels east of downtown on Main St, with rooms starting at around $50, depending on the season.

Bear Canyon Campground   CAMPGROUND $
(☑ 800-438-1575; www.bearcanyoncampground.com; tent sites $20, RV sites $28-33; ☉ May–mid-Oct; ☎ ⊠) Three miles east of Bozeman off I-90 exit 313, Bear Canyon Campground is on top of a hill with great views of the surrounding valley. There's even a pool.

Howlers Inn   B&B $$
(☑ 406-586-0304; www.howlersinn.com; 3185 Jackson Creek Rd; d incl breakfast $110-150, 2-person cabin $195; ☎) Wolf-watchers will love this beautiful sanctuary 15 minutes outside of Bozeman. Rescued captive-born wolves live in an enclosed 4-acre area, supported by profits of the B&B. There's three spacious Western-style rooms in the main lodge and a two-bedroom cabin. With luck, you will drift off to sleep serenaded by howls. Take exit 319 off I-90.

Lewis & Clark Motel   MOTEL $$
(☑ 800-332-7666; www.lewisandclarkmotelbozeman.com; 824 W Main St; r weekend/weekday $159/99; ❋ ☎) For a drop of Vegas in your Montana, stay at this flashy, locally owned motel. The large rooms have floor-to-ceiling front windows and the piped 1950s music adds to the retro Rat Pack vibe. With hot tub and steam room.

🍴 Eating & Drinking

As a college town, Bozeman has no shortage of student-oriented cheap eats and enough watering holes to quench a college football team's thirst. Nearly everything is located on Main St.

La Tinga   MEXICAN $
(12 E Main St; mains $1.50-7; ☉ 8:30am-2:30pm) Simple, cheap and authentic, La Tinga is no-frills dining at its tastiest. The tiny order-at-the-counter taco joint makes a delicious version of the Mexican pork dish it is named after, and lots of freshly made tacos starting at just $1.50, or choose the daily lunch combo deal for less than $7.

Community Co-Op   SUPERMARKET $
(www.bozo.coop; 908 W Main; mains $5-10; ☉ 7am-10pm Mon-Sat, 8am-10pm Sun; ☎ ✈) ✒ This beloved local is the best place to stock up on organic and bulk foods, as well as hot meals, salads and soups to eat in or take away. The W Main branch has a great organic coffeehouse upstairs.

Plonk   WINE BAR $$
(www.plonkwine.com; 29 E Main St; dinner mains $13-32; ☉ 11:30am-midnight) Where to go for a drawn-out three-martini, gossipy lunch? Plonk serves a wide-ranging menu from light snacks to full meals, mostly made from local organic products. In summer the entire front opens up and cool breezes enter the long building, which also has a shotgun bar and pressed-tin ceilings.

John Bozeman's Bistro   AMERICAN $$
(☑ 406-587-4100; www.johnbozemansbistro.com; 125 W Main St; mains $14-34; ☉ 11:30am-2:30pm, 5-9:30pm Tues-Sat; ☑) Bozeman's best

---

MONTANA FACTS

Nickname Treasure State, Big Sky Country

Population 1,005,000

Area 145,552 sq miles

Capital city Helena (population 28,600)

Other cities Billings (population 105,600), Missoula (67,300), Bozeman (38,000)

Sales tax No state sales tax

Birthplace of Movie star Gary Cooper (1901–61), motorcycle daredevil Evel Knievel (1938–2007), actress Michelle Williams (1980)

Home of Crow, Blackfeet and Salish Native Americans

Politics Republican ranchers and oil-men generally edge out the Democratic students and progressives of left-leaning Bozeman and Missoula

Famous for Fly-fishing, cowboys and grizzly bears

Random fact Some Montana highways didn't have a speed limit until the 1990s!

Driving distances Bozeman to Denver 695 miles, Missoula to Whitefish 136 miles

DON'T MISS

FLY-FISHING IN BIG SKY

Ever since Robert Redford and Brad Pitt made it look sexy in the 1992 classic, *A River Runs Through It,* Montana has been closely tied to fly-fishing cool. Whether you are just learning or a world-class trout wrangler, the wide, fast rivers are always spectacularly beautiful and filled with fish. Although the film – and book it is based on – is set in Missoula and the nearby Blackfoot River, the movie was actually shot around Livingston and the Yellowstone and Gallatin Rivers.

For DIY trout fishing, the Gallatin River, 8 miles southwest of Bozeman along Hwy 191, has the most accessible, consistent angling spots, closely followed by the beautiful Yellowstone River, 25 miles east of Bozeman in the Paradise Valley.

For the scoop on differences between rainbow, brown and cutthroat trout – as well as flies, rods and a Montana fishing license – visit Bozeman Angler (406-587-9111; www. bozemanangler.com; 23 E Main St; 9:30am-5:30pm Mon-Sat, 10am-3pm Sun). Owned by a local couple for nearly two decades, the downtown shop runs a great introduction-to-fly-fishing class ($125 per person, casting lessons $40 per hour) on the second Saturday of the month between May and September.

restaurant offers Thai, Creole and pan-Asian slants on the cowboy dinner steak, plus starters like lobster chowder and a weekly 'superfood' special, featuring especially nutritious seasonal vegetarian fare.

Molly Brown   BAR
(www.mollybrownbozeman.com; 703 W Babcock) Popular with local MSU students, this noisy dive bar offers 20 beers on tap and eight pool tables for getting your game on.

Zebra Cocktail Lounge   LOUNGE
(406-585-8851; 15 N Rouse St; 8pm-2am) Inside the Bozeman Hotel, this place is the epicenter of the local live music scene, strong on club and hip-hop.

ℹ Information

Visitor Center (406-586-5421; www.bozemanchamber.com; 1003 N 7th Ave; 8am-5pm Mon-Fri) Information on lodging and area attractions.

ℹ Getting There & Away

Gallatin Field Airport (BZN; 406-388-8321; www.bozemanairport.com) is 8 miles northwest of downtown. **Karst Stage** (406-556-3540; www.karststage.com) runs buses daily, December to April, from the airport to Big Sky ($51, one hour) and West Yellowstone ($102, two hours); summer service is by reservation only.

Rimrock Stages buses depart from the **bus depot** (406-587-3110; www.rimrocktrailways.com; 1205 E Main St), half a mile from downtown, and service all Montana towns along I-90.

Gallatin & Paradise Valleys

Outdoor enthusiasts could explore the expansive beauty around the Gallatin and Paradise Valleys for days. Big Sky Resort (800-548-4486; www.bigskyresort.com; lift ticket adult $89), with multiple mountains, 400in of annual powder and Montana's longest vertical drop (4350ft), is one of the nation's premier downhill and cross-country ski destinations, especially now it has merged with neighboring Moonlight Basin. Lift lines are the shortest in the Rockies, and if you are traveling with kids then Big Sky is too good a deal to pass up – children under 10 ski free, while even your teenager saves $20 off the adult ticket price. In summer it offers gondola-served hiking and mountain biking.

For backpacking and backcountry skiing, head to the Spanish Peaks section of the Lee Metcalf Wilderness. It covers 389 sq miles of Gallatin and Beaverhead National Forest land west of US 191. Numerous scenic USFS campgrounds snuggle up to the Gallatin Range on the east side of US 191.

Twenty miles south of Livingston, off US 89 en route to Yellowstone, unpretentious Chico Hot Springs (406-333-4933; www.chicohotsprings.com; 2-person cabin $225, main lodge r $55-93; 8am-11pm;) has garnered quite a following in the last few years, even attracting celebrity residents from Hollywood. Some come to soak in the swimming-pool-sized open-air hot pools (admission for nonguests $7.50), others come for the lively bar hosting swinging country-and-western dance bands on weekends. The on-site restaurant (mains $20 to $32) is known for fine steak and seafood. You can stay here overnight, too. It's not called Paradise Valley for nothing.

Absaroka Beartooth Wilderness

The fabulous, vista-packed Absaroka Beartooth Wilderness covers more than 943,377 acres and is perfect for a solitary adventure. Thick forests, jagged peaks and marvelous, empty stretches of alpine tundra are all found in this wilderness, saddled between Paradise Valley in the west and Yellowstone National Park in the south. The thickly forested Absaroka Range dominates the area's west half and is most easily reached from Paradise Valley or the Boulder River Corridor. The Beartooth Range's high plateau and alpine lakes are best reached from the Beartooth Hwy south of Red Lodge. Because of its proximity to Yellowstone, the Beartooth portion gets two-thirds of the area's traffic.

A picturesque old mining town with fun bars and restaurants and a good range of places to stay, Red Lodge offers great day hikes, backpacking and, in winter, skiing right near town. The Red Lodge Visitor Center (✐406-446-1718; www.redlodge.com; 601 N Broadway Ave; ⊙8am-6pm Mon-Fri, 9am-5pm Sat & Sun) has information on accommodations.

Billings

It's hard to believe laid-back little Billings is Montana's largest city. The friendly oil and ranching center is not a must-see but makes for a decent overnight pit stop. The historic downtown is hardly cosmopolitan, but has its own unpolished charm.

Road-weary travelers will appreciate the downtown Dude Rancher Lodge (✐800-221-3302; www.duderancherlodge.com; 415 N 29th St; d from $89; @ 🛜), a fine and friendly motel with groovy oak furniture dating back to the 1940s, Western-styling, flat-screen TVs and in-room coffee.

With a hefty dose of Martha Stewart, plush Harper & Madison (✐406-281-8550; 3115 10th Av N; mains $4-10; ⊙7am-6pm Mon-Fri, 7am-1pm Sat) does some brisk business. It's no wonder with the excellent coffee, homemade quiches and gourmet pressed sandwiches. If you're rushing to hit the road, grab some French pastries to go.

The upscale Walkers Grill (www.walkersgrill.com; 2700 1st Ave N; tapas $8-14; mains $17-33; ⊙5-10pm) offers good grill items and fine tapas at the bar, with sophisticated Western decor. For classic dive ambience, check out Angry Hank's (✐(406) 252-3370; 2405 1st Ave N; ⊙4-8pm Mon-Sat), a former auto repair shop turned popular tap room and brewery.

Logan International Airport (BIL; www.flybillings.com), 2 miles north of downtown, has direct flights to Salt Lake City, Denver, Minneapolis, Seattle, Phoenix and destinations within Montana. The bus depot (✐406-245-5116; 2502 1st Ave N; ⊙24hr) has services to Bozeman ($30, three hours) and Missoula ($61, eight hours).

Helena

With one foot in cowboy legend (Gary Cooper was born here) and the other in the more hip, less stereotypical lotus land of present-day Montana, diminutive Helena is one of the nation's smallest state capitals (population 28,000), a place where white-collared politicians draft legislation, while white-knuckle

---

WORTH A TRIP

CUSTER'S LAST STAND

The best detour from Billings is to the Little Bighorn Battlefield National Monument (✐406-638-3224; www.nps.gov/libi; admission per car $10; ⊙8am-9pm), 65 miles outside town in the arid plains of the Crow (Apsaalooke) Indian Reservation. Home to one of the USA's best-known Native American battlefields, this is where General George Custer made his famous 'last stand.'

Custer, and 272 soldiers, messed one too many times with Native Americans (including Crazy Horse of the Lakota Sioux), who overwhelmed the force in a (frequently painted) massacre. A visitor center tells the tale or, better, take one of the five daily tours with a Crow guide through Apsaalooke Tours (✐406-638-3897; apsaalooketourism@gmail.com; ⊙Memorial Day-Labor Day). The entrance is a mile east of I-90 on US 212. If you're here for the last weekend of June, the Custer's Last Stand Reenactment (www.custerslaststand.org; adult/child $20/10) is an annual hoot, 6 miles west of Hardin.

adventurers race into the foothills to indulge in that other Montana passion.

Back in town, half hidden among the Gore-tex and outdoor outfitters, you will find an unexpected Gallic-inspired neo-Gothic cathedral. Another pleasant surprise is the artsy pedestrian-only shopping quarter.

◉ Sights & Activities

Many of Helena's sites are free, including the elegant old buildings along Last Chance Gulch (Helena's pedestrian shopping district), and the sights covered here.

State Capitol   LANDMARK
(cnr Montana Ave & 6th St; ⊙8am-6pm Mon-Fri) This grand neoclassical building was completed in 1902 and is known for its beacon-like dome, richly decorated with gold-rimmed paintings inside.

Cathedral of St Helena   CHURCH
(530 N Ewing St) Rising like an apparition from old Europe over the town is this neo-Gothic cathedral completed in 1914. Highlights include the baptistry, organ and intricate stained-glass windows.

Holter Museum of Art   MUSEUM
(www.holtermuseum.org; 12 E Lawrence St; ⊙10am-5.30pm Tue-Sat, noon-4pm Sun) FREE Exhibits modern pieces by Montana artists.

Mt Helena City Park   OUTDOORS
Nine hiking and mountain-biking trails wind through Mt Helena City Park, including one that takes you to the 5460ft-high summit of Mt Helena.

🛏 Sleeping & Eating

East of downtown near I-15 is a predictable string of chain motels. Most rooms are $70 to $95, and come with free continental breakfast, pool and Jacuzzi.

Sanders   B&B $$
(☑406-442-3309; www.sandersbb.com; 328 N Ewing St; r incl breakfast $130-145; ❇) A historic B&B with seven elegant guest rooms, a wonderful old parlor and a breezy front porch. Each bedroom is unique and thoughtfully decorated, it's run by a relative of the Ringling Brothers Circus family, with appropriate memorabilia.

Fire Tower Coffee House   CAFE, BREAKFAST $
(www.firetowercoffee.com; 422 Last Chance Gulch; breakfast $4-9; ⊙6.30am-6pm Mon-Fri, 8am-3pm Sat; 🛜) The hub for coffee, light meals and live music on Friday evening. The breakfast menu features granola and breakfast burritos, while lunch has a wholesome and interesting sandwich selection.

ℹ Information
Helena Visitor Center (☑406-442-4120; www.helenachamber.com; 225 Cruse Ave; ⊙8am-5pm Mon-Fri)

ℹ Getting There & Around
Two miles north of downtown, **Helena Regional Airport** (HNL; www.helenaairport.com) operates flights to most other airports in Montana, as well as to Salt Lake City, Seattle and Minneapolis. Rimrock Trailways leave from Helena's **Transit Center** (630 N Last Chance Gulch; ⊙2-4pm, 8-9pm) where at least daily buses go to Missoula ($25, 2¼ hours), Billings ($52, 4¾ hours) and Bozeman ($22, two hours).

Missoula

Outsiders in Missoula usually spend the first 30 minutes wondering where they took a wrong turn; Austin, Texas? Portland, Oregon? Canada, perhaps? The confusion is understandable given the city's lack of standard Montana stereotypes. There's no Wild West saloons here and even fewer errant cowboys. Instead, Missoula is a refined university city with ample green space and abundant home pride.

Not surprisingly, its metro-west bounty is contagious. Though among the fastest growing cities in the US, sensible planning means that Missoula rarely feels clamorous. The small traffic-calmed downtown core broadcasts an interesting array of historic buildings, and bicycle transportation is ever hip.

◉ Sights

Missoula is a great city for walking, especially in the spring and summer, when enough people emerge onto the streets to give it a definable metro personality.

Smokejumper Visitor Center   MUSEUM
(W Broadway; ⊙10am-4pm Jun-Aug) FREE Located seven miles west of downtown is this active base for the heroic men and women who parachute into forests to combat raging wildfires. Its visitor center has thought-provoking audio and visual displays that do a great job illustrating the life of the Western firefighter.

Missoula Art Museum MUSEUM
(www.missoulaartmuseum.org; 335 North Pattee; ⊙10am-5pm Mon-Thu, 10am-3pm Fri-Sun) FREE
All hail a city that encourages free-thinking art and then displays it in a plush new building that seamlessly grafts a sleek contemporary addition onto a 100-year-old library.

🏃 Activities

Clark Fork River Trail System CYCLING, HIKING
Sitting astride the Clark Fork River, Missoula has been bequeathed with an attractive riverside trail system punctuated by numerous parks. Caras Park is the most central and active green space with over a dozen annual festivals and a unique hard-carved carousel.

Mount Sentinel HIKING
A steep switchback trail from behind the football stadium leads up to a concrete whitewashed 'M' (visible for miles around) on 5158ft Mt Sentinel. Tackle it on a warm summer's evening for glistening views of this much-loved city and its spectacular environs.

★ Adventure Cycling HQ CYCLING
(www.adventurecycling.org; 150 E Pine St; ⊙8am-5pm Mon-Fri, open Sat Jun-Aug) 🖉 The HQ for America's premier nonprofit bicycle travel organization is something of a pilgrimage site for cross-continental cyclists, many of whom plan their route to pass through Missoula. Staff offer a warm welcome and plenty of cycling information.

Fly-fishing FISHING
A River Runs Through It was set here (although it was filmed outside Bozeman) and fly-fishers will find some of the best angling in the state. Rock Creek, 21 miles east, is a designated blue-ribbon trout stream and the best year-round fishing spot.

🛏 Sleeping

Mountain Valley Inn MOTEL $
(☎800-249-9174; www.mountainvalleyinnmissoula.com; 420 W Broadway; d from $79; P ❋ ☎) Offering a good deal for the downtown location, the Mountain Valley pulls few surprises, but delivers where it matters – clean rooms and a polite welcome.

Goldsmith's Bed & Breakfast B&B $$
(☎406-728-1585; www.missoulabedandbreakfast.com; 809 E Front St; r $124-169; ❋ @) A delightful riverside B&B. The wraparound deck is the perfect place to kick back with other guests or a good novel. Comfy Victorian-style rooms are

simply lovely. Some come with private decks, river views, fireplaces and reading nooks.

🍴 Eating & Drinking

Liquid Planet CAFE $
(www.liquidplanet.com; 223 N Higgins; mains $4-9) 🖉 Started by a university professor in 2003, this sustainable coffeehouse and wine outlet proffers handwritten recommendations for every bottle. Coffee beans are also thoughtfully deconstructed. For smoothies, teas and pastries, you're on your own.

★ Silk Road INTERNATIONAL $$
(www.silkroadcatering.com; 515 S Higgins; tapas $4-12; ⊙5-10pm) Spanning global dishes from the Ivory Coast to Piedmont, Silk Road takes on lesser-known world cuisine and, more often than not, nails it. Dishes are tapas-sized, allowing you to mix and match. A warm welcome and an ambience of cushions and candlelit tapestries set the scene.

Caffe Dolce MODERN AMERICAN $$
(☎406-830-3055; www.caffedolcemissoula.com; cnr Brooks & Beckwith; mains $11-30; ⊙7am-9pm Mon-Thur, 7am-10pm Fri, 8am-9pm Sat, 8am-3pm Sun) In a stately stone building, this chic newcomer is abuzz with well-clad Missoulans getting their fix of gelato, pastries, wine and gorgeous salads. Dinner can be pricey but exotic pizzas like the salty fig and proscuitto offer a lighter, cheaper option. Coffee is a serious business here, and it deals in the best Montana roasters. With patio seating. It's located after the bridge going north of downtown.

Iron Horse Brewpub BREWERY
(www.ironhorsebrewpub.com; 501 N Higgins St; ⊙11:30am-late) Rather swanky for a brewpub, the Iron Horse includes a plush upstairs bar complete with a saltwater aquarium. It's popular with students for its microbrews and traditional American pub grub.

❶ Information

Visitor Center (☎406-532-3250; www.missoulacvb.org; 101 E Main St; ⊙8am-5pm Mon-Fri)

❶ Getting There & Around

Missoula County International Airport (MSO; www.flymissoula.com) is 5 miles west of Missoula on US 12 W.

Greyhound buses serve most of the state and stop at the **depot** (1660 W Broadway), 1 mile west of town. **Rimrock Trailways** (www.rimrocktrailways.com) buses, connecting to Kalispell, Whitefish, Helena and Bozeman, also stop here.

Flathead Lake

The largest natural freshwater lake west of the Mississippi, sitting not an hour's drive from Glacier National Park, completes western Montana's embarrassment of natural lures. The lake's north shore is dominated by the nothing-to-write-home-about city of Kalispell; far more interesting is the southern end embellished by the small polished settlement of Polson, which sits on the Flathead Indian Reservation. There's a visitor center (www.polsonchamber.com; 418 Main St; ☺9am-5pm Mon-Fri) and a handful of accommodations here including the lakeside Kwataqnuk Resort (☑406-883-3636; www.kwataqnuk.com; 49708 US 93; r from $130; ⓟ✳☎☀), an above-average Best Western with a boat dock, indoor and outdoor pools and a relatively innocuous game room. Directly opposite, the lurid pink Betty's Diner (49779 US 93; meals $10-15) delivers salt-of-the-earth American food with customary Montana charm. From town you can walk 2 miles south along a trail starting on 7th Ave E to the mind-boggling Miracle of America Museum (www.miracleofamericamuseum.org; 58176 Hwy 93; admission $5; ☺8am-8pm). At turns random and fascinating, it consists of 5 acres cluttered with the leftovers of American history. Wander past weird artifacts including the biggest buffalo (now stuffed) ever recorded in Montana.

Flathead Lake's eastern shore is kissed by the mysterious Mission Mountains while the west is a more pastoral land of apple orchards and grassy hills. To get the best all-round view, hit the water. Soloists can kayak or canoe the conceptual Flathead Lake Marine Trail, which links various state parks and campsites (☑406-751-4577; tent sites from $10) around the lake. The nearest site to Polson is Finley Point 5.5 miles away by water.

Lake cruises (www.kwataqnuk.com) are run out of the Kwataqnuk Resort in Polson. The 1½ hour Bay Cruise leaves daily at 10:30am and costs $15. Summer dining cruises leave at 4pm on Wednesdays and Saturdays (cost per person is $30).

Bob Marshall Wilderness Complex

Away from the Pacific coast, America's northwest harbors some of the most lightly populated areas in the lower 48. Point in question: the Bob Marshall Wilderness Complex, an astounding 2344 sq miles of land strafed with 3200 miles of trails including sections that are a 40-mile slog from the nearest road. And you thought the US was car-obsessed.

Running roughly from the southern boundary of Glacier National Park in the north to Rogers Pass (on Hwy 200) in the south, there are actually three designated wilderness areas within the complex: Great Bear, Bob Marshall and Scapegoat. On the periphery the complex is buffered with national-forest lands offering campgrounds, road access to trailheads and quieter country when 'the Bob' (as locals and park rangers call it) hosts hunters in fall.

The main access point to the Bob from the south is from Hwy 200 via the Monture Guard Station Cabin (cabins $60), on the wilderness perimeter. To reach it you'll need to drive 7 miles north of Ovando and snowshoe or hike the last mile to your private abodes at the edge of the gorgeous Lewis and Clark Range. Contact the USFS about reservations.

Other Bob access points include the Seeley-Swan Valley in the west, Hungry Horse Reservoir in the north and the Rocky Mountain Front in the east. The easiest (and busiest) access routes are from the Benchmark and Gibson Reservoir trailheads in the Rocky Mountain Front.

Trails generally start steep, reaching the wilderness boundary after around 7 miles. It takes another 10 miles or so to really get into the Bob's heart. Good day-hikes run from all sides. Two USFS districts tend to the Bob, Flathead National Forest Headquarters (☑406-758-5208; www.fs.fed.us/r1/flathead; 650 Wolfpack Way; ☺8am-4:30pm Mon-Fri) and Lewis & Clark National Forest Supervisors (☑406-791-7700; www.fs.fed.us/r1/lewis-clark; 1101 15th St N; ☺8am-4:30pm Mon-Fri).

Whitefish

One square mile of rustic Western chic, tiny Whitefish (population 8000) easily charms. Once sold as the main gateway to Glacier National Park, this charismatic and caffeinated New West town would merit a long-distance trip itself. Aside from grandiose Glacier (an easy day's cycling distance), Whitefish is home to an attractive stash of restaurants, a historic railway station that doubles up as a museum (www.stumptownhistoricalsociety.org; 500 Depot St; ☺10am-4pm Mon-Sat) FREE and underrated Whitefish Mountain Resort (✆406-862-2900; www.bigmtn.com), known as Big Mountain until 2008, guards 3000 acres of varied ski terrain and offers night skiing on weekends. In the summer there's lift-assisted mountain biking and zip lines.

Check with the Whitefish Visitor Center (www.whitefishvisit.com; 307 Spokane Ave; ⏰9am-5pm Mon-Fri) for more info on activities.

A string of chain motels lines US 93 south of Whitefish, but the savvy dock in town at the cheerful Downtowner Inn (✆406-862-2535; www.downtownermotel.cc; 224 Spokane Ave; d $123; ❇🐾) with a gym, a Jacuzzi and a morning bagel bar. The more upmarket Pine Lodge (✆406-862-7600; www.thepinelodge.com; 920 Spokane Ave; d from $145; P❇🐾🐾), offers deep discounts outside the peak seasons. Decent restaurants and bars abound, though most locals will point you in the direction of the Buffalo Café (www.buffalocafewhitefish.com; 514 3rd St E; breakfast $7-10), a breakfast and lunch hot spot. Later check out The Great Northern Brewing Co (✆406-863-1000; www.greatnorthernbrewing.com; 2 Central Ave; ⏰tours 1pm & 3pm Mon-Thu), with factory tours and sampling.

Amtrak stops daily at Whitefish's railroad depot (✆406-862-2268; 500 Depot St; ⏰6am-1:30pm, 4:30pm-midnight) en route to West Glacier ($7, 30 minutes) and East Glacier ($15, two hours). Rimrock Trailways (www.rimrocktrailways.com) runs daily buses to Kalispell and Missoula from the same location.

Glacier National Park

Few of the world's parks of great natural wonders can emulate the US national park system, and few national parks are as magnificent and pristine as Glacier. Created in 1910 during the first flowering of the American conservationist movement, Glacier ranks with Yellowstone, Yosemite and the Grand Canyon.

It is renowned for its historic 'parkitecture' lodges, spectacular arterial road (the Going-to-the-Sun Road), and intact pre-Columbian ecosystem. This is the only place in the lower 48 states where grizzly bears still roam in abundance and smart park management has kept the place accessible yet, at the same time, authentically wild (there is no populated town site à la Banff or Jasper). Among a slew of outdoor attractions, the park is particularly noted for its hiking, wildlife-spotting, and sparkling lakes, ideal for boating and fishing.

Although Glacier's tourist numbers are relatively high (two million a year), few visitors stray far from the Going-to-the-Sun Road and almost all visit between June and September. Choose your moment and splendid isolation is yours for the taking. The park remains open year-round; however, most services are open only from mid-May to September.

Glacier's 1562 sq miles are divided into five regions, each centered on a ranger station: Polebridge (northwest); Lake McDonald (southwest), including the West Entrance and Apgar village; Two Medicine (southeast); St Mary (east); and Many Glacier (northeast). The 50-mile Going-to-the-Sun Road is the only paved road that traverses the park.

❍ Sights & Activities

Going-to-the-Sun Road   OUTDOORS
(⏰mid-Jun–late Sep) A strong contender for the most spectacular road in America, the 53-mile Going-to-the-Sun Road is a national historic landmark, flanked by hiking trails and a mountain pass, served by a free shuttle

The road skirts near shimmering Lake McDonald before angling sharply to the Garden Wall – the main dividing line between the west and east sides of the park. At Logan Pass you can stroll 1.5 miles to Hidden Lake Overlook; heartier hikers can try the 7.5-mile Highline Trail. The shuttle stops on the western side of the road at the trailhead for Avalanche Lake, an easy 4-mile return hike to a stunning alpine lake in a cirque beautified with numerous weeping waterfalls.

Many Glacier   HIKING
Anchored by the historic 1915 Many Glacier Lodge and sprinkled with more lakes than glaciers, this picturesque valley on the park's east side has some tremendous hikes, some of which link to the Going-to-the-Sun Road. A favorite is the 9.4-mile (return) Iceberg Lake Trail, a steep but rewarding jaunt through flower meadows and pine forest to an iceberg infested lake.

Glacier Park Boat Co   BOATING, HIKING
(✆406-257-2426; www.glacierparkboats.com; St Mary Lake cruise adult/child $25/12) Rents out kayaks and canoes, and runs popular lake cruises from five locations in Glacier National Park. Also offers guided hikes.

📖 Sleeping

There are 13 NPS campgrounds (☎406-888-7800; http://reservations.nps.gov; tent & RV sites $10-23) and seven historic lodges in the park, which operate between mid-May and the end of September. Of the sites, only Fish Creek and St Mary can be reserved in advance (up to five months). Sites fill by mid-morning, particularly in July and August.

Glacier also has seven historic lodges dating from the early 1900s.

★ Many Glacier Hotel   HOTEL $$

(☎406-732-4411; www.glacierparkinc.com; r $163-250; ⊙mid-Jun–mid-Sep; 🛜) Modeled after a Swiss chalet, this national historic landmark on Swiftcurrent Lake is the park's largest hotel, with 208 rooms featuring panoramic views. Evening entertainment, a lounge and fine-dining restaurant specializing in fondue all add to the appeal.

Lake McDonald Lodge   HOTEL $$

(☎406-888-5431; www.glacierparkinc.com; cabin/lodge r from $137/79; ⊙May-Sep; 🛜) 🅿 Built in 1913, this old hunting lodge is adorned with stuffed-animal trophies and exudes relaxation. The 100 rooms are lodge, chalet or motel style. Nightly park-ranger talks and lake cruises add a rustic ambience. There's a restaurant and pizzeria.

Glacier Park Lodge   HOTEL $$

(☎406-226-5600; www.glacierparkinc.com; r $152-235; ⊙late May-Sep) 🅿 The park's flagship lodge is a graceful, elegant place featuring interior balconies supported by Douglas fir timbers and a massive stone fireplace in the lobby. It's an aesthetically appealing, historically charming and very comfortable place to stay. Pluses include nine holes of golf and cozy reading nooks.

Rising Sun Motor Inn   MOTEL $$

(☎406-732-5523; www.glacierparkinc.com; r $134-142; ⊙late May-early Sep) One of two classic 1940s-era wooden motels, the Rising Sun lies on the north shore of St Mary Lake in a small complex that includes a store, restaurant and boat launch. The rustic rooms and cabins offer everything an exhausted hiker could hope for.

🍴 Eating

In summer there are grocery stores with limited camping supplies in Apgar, Lake McDonald Lodge, Rising Sun and at the Swiftcurrent Motor Inn. Most lodges have on-site restaurants. Dining options in West Glacier and St Mary offer mainly hearty hiking fare.

Polebridge Mercantile   BAKERY, SUPERMARKET $

(Polebridge Loop Rd, North Fork Valley; snacks $4; ⊙8am-6pm May-Nov; 🛜) Come here for the cinnamon buns, known to pump a good couple of hours into tired hiking legs.

Park Café   AMERICAN $

(www.parkcafe.us; US 89, St. Mary; breakfast $7-12; ⊙7am-10pm Jun-Sep) Offers hearty breakfasts and comes recommended for the homemade pies topped with whipped cream or ice cream.

Ptarmigan Dining Room   INTERNATIONAL $$$

(Many Glacier Lodge; mains $15-32; ⊙6:30am-9:30pm, mid-Jun–early Sep) With its lakeside views, this is the most refined of the lodge restaurants, also serving wine and microbrews.

ℹ Information

Visitor centers and ranger stations in the park sell field guides and hand out hiking maps. Those at Apgar and St Mary are open daily May to October; the visitor center at Logan Pass is open when the Going-to-the-Sun Road is open. The Many Glacier, Two Medicine and Polebridge Ranger Stations close at the end of September. **Park headquarters** (☎406-888-7800; www.nps.gov/glac; ⊙8am-4:30pm Mon-Fri), in West Glacier between US 2 and Apgar, is open year-round.

Entry to the park (hiker/vehicle $12/25) is valid for seven days. Day-hikers don't need permits, but overnight backpackers do (May to October only). Half of the permits are available on a first-come, first-served basis from the **Apgar Backcountry Permit Center** (permits per person per day $4; ⊙May 1-Oct 31), St Mary Visitor Center, and the Many Glacier, Two Medicine and Polebridge ranger stations.

The other half can be reserved at the Apgar Backcountry Permit Center, St Mary and Many Glacier visitor centers and Two Medicine and Polebridge ranger stations.

ℹ Getting There & Around

Amtrak's Empire Builder train stops daily at West Glacier (year-round) and East Glacier Park (April to October) on its route between Seattle and Chicago. **Glacier National Park** (www.nps.gov/glac) runs shuttles (adult/child $10/5) from Apgar Village to St Mary over Going-to-the-Sun Road from July 1 to Labor Day. **Glacier Park, Inc** (www.glacierparkinc.com) offers the East Side Shuttle (adult/child $10/5) on the eastern side of the park with daily links to Waterton (Canada), Many Glacier, St Mary, Two Medicine and East Glacier.

IDAHO

Famous for not being particularly famous, the nation's 43rd state is a pristine wilderness of Alaskan proportions, rudely ignored by passing traffic heading west to Seattle or east to Montana. In truth, much of this lightly trodden land is little changed since the days of Lewis and Clark, including a vast 15,000-sq-km 'hole' in the middle of the state which is bereft of roads, settlements, or any other form of human interference.

Flatter, dryer southern Idaho is dominated by the Snake River, deployed as a transportation artery by early settlers on the Oregon Trail and tracked today by busy Hwy 84. But, outside of this narrow populated strip, the Idaho landscape is refreshingly free of the soulless strip-mall, fast-food infestations so ubiquitous elsewhere in the US.

Boise

Understated, underrated and underappreciated, Idaho's state capital (and largest city) gets little name recognition from people outside the northwest. The affable downtown surprises blinkered outsiders with the modest spirit of an underdog. Cool surprises include Basque culture, a grandiose Idaho capitol building and a fair number of well-heeled bars and Parisian-style bistros. With a university campus to boot and a 'city of trees' moniker, it's not just a marketing ploy. Boise leaves a poignant and lasting impression – primarily because it's not supposed to.

◉ Sights & Activities

Delve into the main business district, bounded by State, Grove, 4th and 9th Sts.

★ **Basque Block**   NEIGHBORHOOD
(www.thebasqueblock.com)   Unbeknownst to many, Boise harbors one of the largest Basque populations outside Spain. European émigrés first arrived in the 1910s to work as Idaho shepherds. Elements of their distinct culture can be glimpsed along Grove St between 6th St and Capitol Blvd.

Sandwiched between the ethnic taverns, restaurants and bars is the **Basque Museum & Cultural Center** (www.basquemuseum. com; 611 Grove St; adult/senior & student $5/4; ⊙10am-4pm Tue-Fri, 11am-3pm Sat), a commendable effort to unveil the intricacies of Basque culture and how it was transposed

6000 miles west to Idaho. Language lessons in Euskara, Europe's oldest language, are held here, while next door in the **Anduiza Fronton Building** (619 Grove St) there's a Basque handball court where aficionados play the traditional sport of *pelota*.

Idaho State Capitol   LANDMARK
The joy of US state capitol buildings is that visitors can admire some of the nation's best architecture for free. The Boise building, constructed from native sandstone, celebrates the neoclassical style in vogue when it was built in 1920. It was extensively refurbished in 2010 and is now heated with geothermal hot water.

Boise River & Greenbelt   PARK, MUSEUM
🖋 Laid out in the 1960s, the tree-lined riverbanks of the Boise River protect 30 miles of vehicle-free trails. It personifies Boise's 'city of trees' credentials, with parks, museums and river fun.

The river is insanely popular for its floating and tubing. The put-in point is **Barber Park** (Eckert Rd; tube rental $12) 6 miles east of downtown. It's a 5-mile float to the take-out

IDAHO FACTS

Nickname Gem State

Population 1,596,000

Area 83,570 sq miles

Capital city Boise (population 210,100)

Other cities Idaho Falls (population 57,600)

Sales tax 6%

Birthplace of Lewis and Clark guide Sacagawea (1788–1812); politician Sarah Palin (b 1964); poet Ezra Pound (1885–1972)

Home of Star garnet, Sun Valley ski resort

Politics Reliably Republican with small pockets of Democrats, eg Sun Valley

Famous for Potatoes, wilderness, the world's first chairlift

North America's deepest river gorge Idaho's Hells Canyon (7900 ft deep)

Driving distances Boise to Idaho Falls 280 miles, Lewiston to Coeur d'Alene 116 miles

point at Ann Morrison Park. There are four rest-stops en route and a shuttle bus ($3) runs from the take-out point.

The most central and action-packed space on the Greenbelt, 90-acre Julia Davis Park contains the **Idaho State Historical Museum** (610 N Julia Davis Dr; adult/child $5/3; ⊘9am-5pm Tue-Fri, 11am-5pm Sat) with well thought-out exhibits on Lewis and Clark; and the **Boise Art Museum** (www.boiseart-museum.org; 670 N Julia Davis Dr; adult/senior & student $6/3; ⊘10am-5pm Tue-Sat, noon-5pm Sun). There's also a pretty outdoor rose garden.

Ridge to Rivers Trail System HIKING
(www.ridgetorivers.org) More rugged than the greenbelt are the scrub- and brush-covered foothills above town offering 75 miles of scenic, sometimes strenuous hiking and mountain-biking routes. The most immediate access from downtown is via Fort Boise Park on E Fort St, five blocks southeast of the state capitol building.

🛏 Sleeping

Here are three true gems.

Leku Ona HOTEL $
(☎ 208-345-6665; www.lekuonaid.com; 117 S 6th St; r $65-85; 🖧) Run by a Basque-born immigrant, this central boarding house has seen some wear. The downtown location can be noisy on weekends, but it certainly is economical. The restaurant next door serves delicious *pintxos* (Basque tapas).

⭐ **Boise Guest House** GUESTHOUSE $$
(☎ 208-761-6798; boiseguesthouse.com; 614 North 5th St; suites $89-119; 🖧🍴) The dearest home away from home, this artist-owned guesthouse has a handful of stylin' suites with kitchens and living areas. Whimsical and well thought-out, it's decked out in lovely decor with good books on the shelf and appealing local art. The free cruiser bikes (with handlebar streamers – hello!) encourage further exploration.

Modern Hotel BOUTIQUE MOTEL $$
(☎ 208-424-8244; www.themodernhotel.com; 1314 W Grove St; d incl breakfast from $99; P❄🖧) Making an oxymoron (a boutique motel!?) into a fashion statement, the Modern Hotel offers retro-trendy minimalist rooms and a slavishly hip bar slap-bang in the middle of downtown. The power showers are huge and the service is five-star.

🍴 Eating & Drinking

Restaurants and nightspots are found downtown in the brick-lined pedestrian plaza of the Grove, and the gentrified former warehouse district between 8th St and Idaho Ave. Count on some exciting Basque specialties, authentic bistros and exceptional bars.

⭐ **Fork** MODERN AMERICAN $$
(☎ 207-287-1700; www.boisefork.com; 199 North 8th St; mains $8-29; ⊘11am-10pm; 🖉) Twenty years ago, this kind of upscale green-boosted menu would have been Idaho heresy. No more. Down-home starts with cast- iron-fried chicken with waffles and balsamic maple syrup. But there's also heaping salads and braised greens in addition to local meat and many regionally-sourced ingredients. Don't even think of skipping the rosemary parmesean fries. So popular, service can be slow.

Vietnam Pho Nouveau VIETNAMESE $$
(☎ 208-367-1111; www.phonouveau.com; 780 West Idaho St; mains $9-15; ⊘11am-9:30pm Mon-Thur, 11am-10:30pm Sat, 12-8:30pm Sun) A small, smart cafe oozing understated cool, it's Boise's happy destination for Asian comfort food. Dig into *bun* (a big bowl of noodles with grilled meat and plenty of greens), lily blossom salad with tender shredded pork, or Saigon crepes.

Grape Escape WINE BAR $$
(800 W Idaho St; appetizers $7-11, mains $11-18; ⊘11am-close) Sit alfresco and enjoy your Pinot Noir with light supper fare (bruschetta, salads and highly creative pizzas) while logging the ubiquity of downtown cyclists, closet intellectuals and bright young things out for an early evening aperitif. The wine menu is almost as good as the people-watching. With jazz Sundays.

**Bittercreek Ale House
& Red Feather Lounge** MODERN AMERICAN $$
(www.justeatlocal.com; 246 N 8th St; mains $7-15; ⊘11:30am-late) These adjoining restaurants offer lively, intimate environs and lots of personality. They also serve wholesome, usually locally produced food with an emphasis on sustainable growth. The nouveau-American menu features a good selection of vegetarian options. The more polished Red Feather does delicious wood-oven pizza.

Order one of the whiskey cocktails that are made using an old-fashioned pre-Prohibition-era recipe.

Bar Gernika   PUB

(www.bargernkia.com; 202 S Capitol Blvd; lunch $8-10; ☺ 11am-midnight Mon-Thu till 1am Fri & Sat) *Ongi etorri* (welcome) to the Basque block's most accessible pub-tavern with a menu that leans heavily on old-country favorites such as lamb kebab, chorizo and beef tongue (Saturdays only). Pair your meal with a 20oz Guinness or regional microbrew. It's a true only-in-Boise kind of place.

Bardenay   PUB

(www.bardenay.com; 610 Grove St; mains $8-18; ☺ 11am-late) Bardenay was the USA's very first 'distillery-pub,' and remains a one-of-a-kind watering hole. Today it serves its own home-brewed vodka, rum and gin in casual, airy environs. It gets consistently good reviews.

ℹ Information

Visitor Center (☎ 208-344-7777; www.boise.org; 250 S. 5th St, Ste. 300; ☺ 10am-5pm Mon-Fri, 10am-2pm Sat Jun-Aug, 9am-4pm Mon-Fri Sep-May) Stop by the visitor center.

ℹ Getting There & Around

Boise Municipal Airport (BOI; I-84 exit 53) has daily flights to Denver, Las Vegas, Phoenix, Portland, Salt Lake City, Seattle and Spokane. Greyhound services depart from the **bus station** (1212 W Bannock St) with routes fanning out to Spokane, Pendleton and Portland, and Twin Falls and Salt Lake City.

Ketchum & Sun Valley

In one of Idaho's most stunning natural locations sits a piece of ski history. Sun Valley was the first purpose-built ski resort in the US, hand-picked by Union Pacific Railroad scion William Averell Harriman (after an exhaustive search) in the 1930s and publicized by glitterati Ernest Hemingway, Clark Gable and Gary Cooper. When Sun Valley opened in 1936 it sported the world's first chairlift and a showcase 'parkitecture' lodge that remains its premier resort.

Sun Valley has kept its swanky Hollywood clientele and extended its facilities to include the legendary Bald Mountain, yet it remains a refined and pretty place (no fast-food joints or condo sprawl here). Highly rated nationwide, the resort is revered for its reliably good snow, big elevation drop and almost windless weather. The adjacent village of Ketchum, 1 mile away, holds a rustic beauty despite the skiing deluge. Heming-

way made it prime territory for fishing and hunting, though these days fat tires are the summer rage.

🏃 Activities

Main St between 1st and 5th Sts is where you'll find nearly all the businesses. Sun Valley and its lodge is 1 mile to the north and easily walkable. Twelve miles south of Ketchum, also on Hwy 75, is Hailey, another delightful small town with a bar scene.

Wood River Trail   HIKING, CYCLING

There are numerous hiking and mountain biking trails around Ketchum and Sun Valley, as well as excellent fishing spots. The Wood River Trail is the all-connecting artery linking Sun Valley with Ketchum and continuing 32 bucolic miles south down to Bellevue via Hailey. Bikes can be hired from **Pete Lane's** (bikes per day $35) in the mall next to the Sun Valley Lodge.

Sun Valley Resort   SNOW SPORTS

(www.sunvalley.com; adult/child Bald Mountain $95/54, Dollar Mountain $54/39) Famous for its light, fluffy powder and celebrity guests, the dual-sited resort comprises advanced-terrain **Bald Mountain** and easier-on-the-nerves **Dollar Mountain**, which also has a **tubing hill**. In summer, take the chairlift to the top of either mountain (adult/child ride $15/10), and hike or cycle down. Facilities are predictably plush.

🛏 Sleeping

In summer, there is free camping on Bureau of Land Management (BLM) land very close to town, see the visitor center for details.

Lift Tower Lodge   MOTEL $

(☎ 208-726-5163; 703 S Main St; r $89-109; P ☎) Lifelong members of the hoi polloi can hobnob with millionaires and decamp afterwards to this friendly and economical small motel on the cusp of Ketchum with firm quilted beds. A landmark exhibition chairlift (c 1939) is lit up after dark.

Tamarack Lodge   HOTEL $$

(☎ 208-726-3344; www.tamaracksunvalley.com; 500 E Sun Valley Rd; r $149-169; ❄ ☎ ☒) Tasteful rooms complete with fireplace, balcony and many amenities are offered at this well-maintained lodge. Sterling service, a Jacuzzi and indoor pool are definite assets. Discounts are often available midweek and off-season.

HEMINGWAY: THE FINAL DAYS

Although Sun Valley and Ketchum never featured explicitly in the work of Ernest Miller Hemingway, the globe-trotting author had a deep affection for the area. He became a frequent visitor following its development as a ski resort in the late 1930s. Legend has it that he completed his Spanish Civil War masterpiece *For Whom the Bell Tolls* in room 206 of the Sun Valley Lodge in between undertaking fishing and hunting excursions with friends such as Gary Cooper and Clark Gable.

In the 1940s and '50s, Hemingway migrated south to Key West and Cuba. After the Cuban revolution in 1959, Hemingway's Havana house was expropriated and the author moved permanently to Idaho. Increasingly paranoid and in declining physical and mental health, on July 2, 1961, Hemingway took his favorite gun, walked out onto the porch of his home off Warm Springs Rd and blew his brains out at age 61.

There is a surprising (and refreshing) lack of hullaballoo surrounding Hemingway in Ketchum. You'll have to look hard to find the small, pretty cemetery half a mile north of the center on Hwy 75, where he is buried alongside his granddaughter Margaux. Pennies, cigars and the odd bottle of liquor furnish his simple grave. Hemingway's house is out of bounds to the public but a monument honors him near Trail Creek, 1 mile beyond the Sun Valley Lodge. In Ketchum, his favorite drinking holes were the Casino Club (p306) and the Alpine Club, now known as Whiskey Jacques (208-726-5297; 251 Main St; cover up to $5; 4pm-2am).

Sun Valley Lodge
HOTEL $$$

(208-622-2001; www.sunvalley.com; 1 Sun Valley Rd; r $287-405; ❀@🛜🏊) Hemingway completed *For Whom the Bell Tolls* in this swank 1930s-era beauty and the place has lost little of its luxurious pre-war sheen. Old-fashioned elegance is the lure in comfortable rooms that sometimes feel a little small by today's standards. Amenities include a fitness facility, game room, bowling alley and sauna. There's also a ski shuttle and children's program.

🍴 Eating & Drinking

Despo's
MEXICAN $

(208-726-3068; 211 4th St; mains $7-14; 11:30am-10pm Mon-Sat) Locals dig this healthy Mexican joint, even if it isn't the most authentic. Everything is fresh, salads huge, and homemade salsas (warm, hot and smokin') are worthy.

★ Rickshaw
ASIAN $$

(www.eat-at-rickshaw.com; 460 Washington Ave N; small plates & mains $4-15; 5:30-10.30pm Tue-Sat, 5:30-9.30pm Sun) Small and crooked as an actual rickshaw, welcoming and with the vitality of a busy thoroughfare, this red-hot fusion restaurant turns out A-plus versions of street food from Vietnam, Thailand, Korea and Indonesia. Tender short ribs with a jalapeno-cilantro glaze are maddeningly wonderful. From green curry to cashew stir fry, the default here is spicy. A must.

Glow
VEGAN $$

(380 Washington #105; mains $7-12; 10am-6pm Mon-Fri, 10am-5pm Sat) A pleasure palace for raw and vegan dining. With a laundry list of smoothies, chia pudding for breakfast, organic salads, blended soups and (thank God) handmade raw chocolates, you too might glow. The crowd: perfect, Sun Valley types in yoga pants.

Pioneer Saloon
STEAKHOUSE $$$

(www.pioneersaloon.com; 320 N Main St; mains $9-29; 5:30-10pm) Around since the 1950s and originally an illicit gambling hall, the Pio is an unashamedly Western den decorated with deer heads, antique guns, bullet boards and – oh yes – good food too, as long as you like beef and trout. All dinners are guaranteed.

Casino Club
BAR

(220 N Main St) In a ski resort less than 75 years old, this dive bar is the oldest thing still standing from days of yore. It has witnessed everything from gambling fist fights, to psychedelic hippies, to the rise and fall of Ernest Hemingway, to tattooed men on Harleys riding through the front door.

ℹ️ Information

Sun Valley/Ketchum Visitors Center (208-726-3423; www.visitsunvalley.com; 491 Sun Valley Rd; 6am-7pm) Staffed only from 9am-6pm, you can still come in and get maps and brochures before and after hours as it smartly doubles as a Starbucks cafe.

ⓘ Getting There & Around

The region's airport, **Friedman Memorial Airport** (www.flyfma.com) in Hailey is 12 miles south of Ketchum. **A-1 Taxi** (☑ 208-726-9351; www.a1sunvalley.com) offers transportation. **Sun Valley Express** (www.sunvalleyexpress.com) operates a daily shuttle between Sun Valley and Boise Airport in both directions ($65 one-way).

Stanley

Backed by the ragged Sawtooths, Stanley (population 100), with its gravel roads, log homes and rusted iron sheds might be the most scenic small town in America. Surrounded by protected wilderness and national-forest land, the remote outpost sits in the crook of the Salmon River, miles from anywhere. Here the high summer twilight stretches past 10pm and the roaring creek lulls you to sleep.

🏃 Activities

Middle Fork of the Salmon   RAFTING

Stanley is the jumping-off point for rafting the legendary Middle Fork of the Salmon. Billed as the 'last wild river,' it's part of the longest undammed river system outside Alaska. Full trips last six days and allow you to float for 106 miles through the 300 or so rapids (class I to IV) of the 2.4-million-acre Frank Church–River of No Return Wilderness, miles from any form of civilization.

Main Fork of the Salmon   RAFTING

(🖈) For more affordable, albeit slightly less dramatic, white-water action than Middle Fork, do a DIY float trip down the Main Fork of the Salmon in a raft or inflatable kayak. There are 8 miles of quiet water, starting in Stanley, with views of the Sawtooth Mountains you can't see from the road. Bring fishing gear.

ROCKY MOUNTAINS STANLEY

DON'T MISS

CENTRAL IDAHO'S SCENIC BYWAYS

Goodbye suburban strip malls, hello unblemished wilderness. All three roads into the remote Idahoan outpost of Stanley are designated National Scenic Byways (it's the only place in the US where this happens). Considering there are only 125 such roads in the country, it means 2.4% of American's prettiest pavement runs through bucolic Stanley.

Sawtooth Scenic Byway

Following the Salmon River along Hwy 75 north from Ketchum to Stanley this 60-mile drive is gorgeous, winding through a misty, thick ponderosa pine forest – where the air is crisp and fresh and smells like rain and nuts – before ascending the 8701ft **Galena Summit**. From the overlook at the top, there are views of the glacially carved Sawtooth Mountains.

Ponderosa Pine Scenic Byway

Hwy 21, between Stanley and Boise, is so beautiful it will be hard to reach your destination because you'll want to stop so much. From Stanley the trees increase in density, until you find yourself cloaked in pine – more Pacific Northwest than classic Rockies. With frequent bursts of rain, the roadway can feel dangerous. Even in late May the snowfields stretch right down to the highway.

Two of the road's many highlights are **Kikham Creek Hot Springs** (parking $6; ⊘ 6am-10pm), 6 miles east of Lowman, a primitive campground and natural hot springs boiling out of the creek; and the old restored gold rush town of **Idaho Falls**.

Salmon River Scenic Byway

Northeast of Stanley, Hwy 75 and US 93 make up another scenic road that runs beside the Salmon River for 161 miles to historic **Lost Trail Pass** on the Montana border, the point where Lewis and Clark first crossed the continental divide in 1805. Much of the surrounding scenery has changed little in over 200 years.

Fly Fishing
FISHING

(⊙Mar-Nov) The Salmon and surrounding mountain lakes have epic trout fishing from March until November, with late June to early October best for dry fly-fishing. The eight species of local trout include the mythical steelhead, which measure up to 40in. These fish travel 900 miles from the Pacific Ocean at winter's end, arriving near Stanley in March and April.

☞ Tours

White Otter
RAFTING

(☑208-788-5005; www.whiteotter.com; 100 Yankee Fork Road and Hwy 75, Sunbeam, ID; half-day adult/child $75/55) The sole rafting outfit that's locally run, White Otter is recommended for fun class III day trips. It also arranges float trips in inflatable kayaks.

Solitude River Trips
RAFTING

(☑800-396-1776; www.rivertrips.com; 6-day trip $2185; ⊙Jun-Aug) Offers top-notch multiday trips on the famed Middle Fork of the Salmon. Camping is riverside and guides cook excellent food.

Silver Creek Outfitters
FISHING

(☑207-622-5282; www.silver-creek.com; 1 Sun Valley Rd) Run out of Sun Valley, Silver Creek does custom trips to the Salmon and remote river spots, only accessible via drift boat or float tube.

🛏 Sleeping & Eating

There are about half a dozen hotels in Stanley, all done in traditional pioneer log-cabin style. During the short summer season a couple of restaurants open up.

Sawtooth Hotel
HOTEL $

(☑208-721-2459; www.sawtoothhotel.com; 755 Ace of Diamonds St; d with/without bath $100/70; 🕾) Set in a nostalgic 1931 log motel, the Sawtooth updates the slim comforts of yesteryear, but keeps the hospitality effusively Stanley-esque. Six rooms are furnished old-country style, two with private bathrooms. Room No 9 is the fave. Don't expect TVs or room phones, but count on home-spun dining that is exquisite.

★ Stanley Baking Co
BAKERY, BREAKFAST $

(www.stanleybakingco.com; 250 Wall St; breakfast & lunch $3-10; ⊙7am-2pm May-Oct) After having lumbered the world with unhealthy delights, this middle-of-nowhere bakery and brunch spot is a godsend. Operating for five months of the year out of a small log cabin, Stanley Baking Co is the only place in town where you're likely to see a queue. The reason: off-the-ratings-scale homemade baked goods and oatmeal pancakes.

Idaho Panhandle

Idaho grabbed the long, skinny spoon-handle that brushes up against Canada in an 1880's land dispute with Montana. Yet in both looks and attitude, the area has more in common with the Pacific Northwest than the Rockies. Spokane, a few miles west in Washington, acts as the regional hub and most of the panhandle observes Pacific Standard Time.

Near the Washington border, fast-growing Coeur d'Alene (population 44,000) is an extension of the Spokane metro area and the panhandle's largest town. There's a rather tacky boardwalk waterfront and one of those Anywhere USA–type golf and spa resorts. The adjacent lake is ideal for water-based activities like standup paddling. The Coeur d'Alene Visitors Bureau (☑877-782-9232; www.coeurdalene.org; 105 N 1st; ⊙10am-5pm Tue-Sat) has further information. Lodgers can count on the quirky pink-door Flamingo Motel (☑208-664-2159; www.flamingomotel-idaho.com; 718 Sherman Ave; d/ste $100/170; ❄), a retro 1950s throwback with themed rooms like English Garden and Americana. The best coffee is at Java on Sherman (324 Sherman, Coeur d'Alene; mains $4-9; ⊙6am-7pm), also serving good breakfasts and sandwiches.

Sandpoint, on Lake Pend Oreille, is the nicest panhandle town. Set in a gorgeous wilderness locale surrounded by mountains, it also sports Idaho's only serviceable Amtrak train station, an attractive historic building dating from 1916. The *Empire Builder,* running daily between Seattle/Portland and Chicago, stops here.

You can soak up Idaho's largest lake from the Pend Oreille Scenic Byway (US 200), which hugs the north shore. Eleven miles northwest of town is highly rated Schweitzer Mountain Resort (www.schweitzer.com; ski tickets adult/child $68/50), lauded for its tree-skiing, with mountain biking in summer.

The best accommodation bargain for miles around is the clean, friendly mom-and-pop-run Country Inn (☑208-263-3333; www.countryinnsandpoint.com; 470700 Hwy 95; s/d $64/80; 🕾❄), 3 miles south of Sandpoint.

Southwest

Best Places to Eat

➡ Elote Cafe (p347)

➡ Hell's Backbone (p380)

➡ Love Apple (p400)

➡ Cafe Roka (p364)

➡ Raku (p323)

Best Places to Stay

➡ Ellis Store Country Inn (p407)

➡ El Tovar Hotel (p352)

➡ Motor Lodge (p348)

➡ St Regis Deer Valley (p372)

➡ Vdara (p320)

Why Go?

The Southwest is America's untamed backyard, where life plays out before a stunning backdrop of red rocks, lofty peaks, shimmering lakes and deserts dotted with saguaros (cacti). Reminders of the region's multicultural beginnings and hardscrabble past dot the landscape, from curious pictographs and abandoned cliff dwellings to crumbling missions and rusty mining towns. Today, history-making continues, with astronomers and rocket builders peering into star-filled skies while artists and entrepreneurs flock to urban centers and quirky mountain towns, energizing the region.

The best part for travelers? A splendid network of scenic drives linking the most beautiful and iconic sites. But remember: it's not just iconic, larger-than-life landscapes that make a trip through the Southwest memorable. Study that saguaro up close. Ask a Hopi artist about his craft. Savor some green-chile stew. It's the tap-you-on-the-shoulder moments you may just cherish the most.

When to Go

Las Vegas

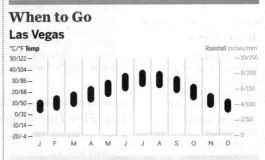

Jan Ski near Taos and Flagstaff. In Park City, hit the slopes and the Sundance Film Festival.

Jun–Aug High season for exploring national parks in New Mexico, Utah and northern Arizona.

Sep–Nov Hike to the bottom of the Grand Canyon or gaze at bright leaves in northern New Mexico.

DON'T MISS

A hike in the desert. Your choices? The Sonoran, Chihuahuan and Great Basin.

Fast Facts

➡ **Hub cities** Las Vegas (population 596,400), Phoenix (population 1.4 million), Salt Lake City (population 189,314)

➡ **Las Vegas to Grand Canyon National Park South Rim** 280 miles

➡ **Los Angeles to Albuquerque** 670 miles

➡ **Time zones** Nevada (Pacific), Arizona (Mountain, does not observe DST), Utah (Mountain), New Mexico (Mountain)

Did You Know?

Flash floods can occur from mid-July to early September. Avoid camping on sandy washes and canyon bottoms; don't drive across flooded roads. If hiking, move quickly to higher ground.

Resources

➡ **Public Lands Information Center** (www.publiclands.org) Descriptions, maps and book recommendations.

➡ **Grand Canyon Association** (www.grandcanyon.org) Extensive online bookstore.

➡ **Recreation.gov** (www.recreation.gov) Reservations for camping and activities at nationally run outdoor areas.

Getting There & Around

Las Vegas' McCarran International Airport and Phoenix' Sky Harbor International Airport are the region's busiest airports, followed by the airports serving Salt Lake City, Albuquerque and Tucson.

Greyhound stops at major points within the region but doesn't serve all national parks or off-the-beaten-path towns such as Moab. In larger cities, bus terminals can be in less-safe areas of town. Private vehicles are often the only means to reach out-of-the-way towns, trailheads and swimming spots.

Amtrak train service is much more limited than the bus system, although it does link many major cities and offers bus connections to others (including Santa Fe and Phoenix). The *California Zephyr* crosses Utah and Nevada; the *Southwest Chief* stops in Arizona and New Mexico; and the *Sunset Limited* traverses southern Arizona and New Mexico.

NATIONAL & STATE PARKS

Containing 50 national parks and monuments, the Southwest is a scenic and cultural jackpot. Add several stunning state parks, and, well, you might need to extend your trip.

One of the most deservedly popular national parks is Arizona's Grand Canyon National Park (p348). Other Arizona parks include Monument Valley Navajo Tribal Park (p357), a desert basin with towering sandstone pillars and buttes; Canyon de Chelly National Monument (p356), with ancient cliff dwellings; Petrified Forest National Park (p357), with its odd mix of Painted Desert and fossilized logs; and Saguaro National Park (p359), with pristine desert and giant cacti.

The southern red-rock Canyon Country in Utah includes five national parks: Arches (p377), Canyonlands (p378), Zion (p382), Bryce Canyon (p381) and Capitol Reef (p379), which offers exceptional wilderness solitude. Grand Staircase-Escalante National Monument (p380) is a mighty region of undeveloped desert. New Mexico boasts Carlsbad Caverns National Park (p407) and the mysterious Chaco Culture National Historic Park (p401). In Nevada, Great Basin National Park (p332) is a rugged, remote mountain oasis. For more information, check out the National Park Service website (www.nps.gov).

Top Five Day Hikes

➡ **Angels Landing** Zion National Park, UT

➡ **Winsor Trail** Santa Fe, NM

➡ **Navajo Loop** Bryce Canyon National Park, UT

➡ **South Kaibab Trail to Cedar Ridge** (p349) South Rim, Grand Canyon, AZ

➡ **Cape Final** North Rim, Grand Canyon, AZ

History

By about AD 100, three dominant cultures had emerged in the Southwest: the Hohokam, the Mogollon and the Ancestral Puebloans (formerly known as the Anasazi).

The Hohokam lived in the Arizona deserts from 300 BC to AD 1450, and created an incredible canal irrigation system, earthen pyramids and a rich heritage of pottery. Archaeological studies suggest that a cataclysmic event in the mid-15th century caused a dramatic decrease in the Hohokam's population, most notably in larger villages. Though it's not entirely clear what happened or where they went, the oral traditions of local tribes suggest that some Hohokam remained in the area and that members of these tribes are their descendants. From 200 BC to AD 1450 the Mogollon lived in the central mountains and valleys of the Southwest, and left behind what are now called the Gila Cliff Dwellings.

The Ancestral Puebloans left the richest heritage of archaeological sites, such as that at Chaco Culture National Historic Park. Today descendants of the Ancestral Puebloans are found in the Pueblo groups throughout New Mexico. The Hopi are descendants, too, and their village Old Oraibi may be the oldest continuously inhabited settlement in North America.

In 1540 Francisco Vásquez de Coronado led an expedition from Mexico City to the Southwest. Instead of riches, his party found Native Americans, many of whom were then killed or displaced. More than 50 years later, Juan de Oñate established the first capital of New Mexico at San Gabriel. Great bloodshed resulted from Oñate's attempts to control Native American pueblos, and he left in failure in 1608. Santa Fe was established as the new capital around 1610.

Development in the Southwest expanded rapidly during the 19th century, mainly due to railroad and geological surveys. As the US pushed west, the army forcibly removed whole tribes of Native Americans in often horrifyingly brutal Indian Wars. Gold and silver mines drew fortune seekers, and practically overnight the lawless mining towns of the Wild West mushroomed. Capitalizing on the development, the Santa Fe Railroad lured an ocean of tourists to the West.

Modern settlement is closely linked to water use. Following the Reclamation Act of 1902, huge federally funded dams were built to control rivers, irrigate the desert and encourage development. Rancorous debates and disagreements over water rights are ongoing, especially with the phenomenal boom in residential development. Other big issues today are illegal immigration and fiscal solvency.

Local Culture

The Southwest is one of the most multicultural regions of the country, encompassing a rich mix of Native American, Hispanic and Anglo populations. These groups have all influenced the area's cuisine, architecture and arts, and the Southwest's vast Native American reservations offer exceptional opportunities to learn about Native American culture and history. Visual arts are a strong force as well, from the art colonies dotting New Mexico to the roadside kitsch on view in small towns everywhere.

NEVADA

Nevada has a devil-may-care exuberance that's dangerously intoxicating – and sometimes a little bit wacky. Here, dazzling replicas of the Eiffel Tower, the Statue of Liberty and an Egyptian pyramid rise from the desert. Cowboys gather to recite poetry. Artists build a temporary city on a windswept playa. An Air Force base inspires alien conspiracies. And smack in the middle of it all is a lonely tree, its branches draped in sneakers tossed by mischievous road trippers.

On the map, the state is a vast and mostly empty stretch of desert, dotted with former mining towns that have traded pickaxes for slot machines. The mother lode is Las Vegas, an over-the-top place where people still catch gold fever. In the west, adventure outfitters are staking their claims on new treasures: gorgeous scenery and outdoor fun, which beckon from the Sierra Nevada mountains.

The first state to legalize gambling, Nevada is loud with the chime of slot machines singing out from gas stations, supermarkets and hotel lobbies. There's no legally mandated closing time for bars, and in rural areas, legalized brothels and hole-in-the-wall casinos sit side by side with Mormon and cowboy culture.

Our advice? Never ask 'Why?' Just embrace the state's go-for-broke joie de vivre.

Southwest Highlights

1 Stroll the Rim Trail at **Grand Canyon National Park** (p348).

2 Live your own John Wayne Western in northeastern Arizona's **Monument Valley** (p357).

3 Practice your fast draw in dusty **Tombstone** (p363).

4 Gallery-hop and jewelry-shop on the stylish streets of **Santa Fe** (p390).

5 Sled down a shimmering sand dune at **White Sands National Monument** (p405).

6 Wander a wonderland of stalactites at **Carlsbad Caverns National Park** (p407).

7 Live the high life on Las Vegas' **Strip** (p317).

8 Drive through flaming-red sandstone formations in **Valley of Fire State Park** (p327).

9 Ski incredible terrain and enjoy chichi nightlife in **Park City** (p370).

10 Explore a majestic canyon and climb Angels Landing at **Zion National Park** (p382).

SOUTHWEST IN...

One Week

Museums and a burgeoning arts scene set an inspirational tone in **Phoenix**, an optimal springboard for exploring. In the morning, follow Camelback Rd into **Scottsdale** for top-notch shopping and gallery-hopping in Old Town. Drive north to **Sedona** for spiritual recharging before pondering the immensity of the **Grand Canyon**. From here, choose either bling or buttes. For bling, detour onto **Route 66**, cross the new bridge beside **Hoover Dam** then indulge your fantasies in **Las Vegas**. For buttes, drive east from the Grand Canyon into the Navajo country, cruising beneath the giant rock formations in **Monument Valley Navajo Tribal Park**, then stepping back in time at stunning **Canyon de Chelly National Monument**.

Two Weeks

Start in glitzy **Las Vegas** before kicking back in funky **Flagstaff** and peering into the abyss at **Grand Canyon National Park**. Check out collegiate **Tucson** or frolic among cacti at **Saguaro National Park**. Watch the gunslingers in **Tombstone** before settling into Victorian **Bisbee**.

Secure your sunglasses for the blinding dunes of **White Sands National Monument** in nearby New Mexico then sink into **Santa Fe**, a magnet for art-lovers. Explore a pueblo in **Taos** and watch the sunrise at awesome **Monument Valley Navajo Tribal Park**. Head into Utah for the red-rock national parks, **Canyonlands** and **Arches**. Do the hoodoos at **Bryce Canyon** then pay your respects at glorious **Zion**.

ⓘ Information

Prostitution is illegal in Clark County (which includes Las Vegas) and Washoe County (which includes Reno), although there are legal brothels in many of the smaller counties.

Nevada is on Pacific Standard Time and has two areas codes: Las Vegas and vicinity is ☎702, while the rest of the state is ☎775.

Nevada Commission on Tourism (☎800-638-2328; www.travelnevada.com) Sends free books, maps and information on accommodations, campgrounds and events.

Nevada Department of Transportation (☎in-state 511, 877-687-6237; www.nvroads.com) For up-to-date road conditions.

Nevada Division of State Parks (☎775-684-2770; www.parks.nv.gov; 901 S Stewart St, 5th fl, Carson City; ◷8am-5pm Mon-Fri) Camping in state parks ($10 to $15 per night) is first-come, first-served. You can pick up maps and brochures at this office.

Las Vegas

Ah, Vegas. A dazzling rhinestone of a city where you can sip champagne inside a three-story chandelier. You can also travel the world in a day, gliding through the canals of Venice, climbing the Eiffel Tower and crossing the Brooklyn Bridge. It's a slice of desert that's transformed itself into one of the most lavish places on earth, nothing is halfway – even the illusions.

A city of multiple personalities, Las Vegas has been reinventing itself since the days of the Rat Pack. To grab your attention, not to mention your cash, the old is constantly torn down for the new. Once-famous signs collect dust in a neon boneyard while the clang of construction echoes over the Strip. The horizon is ever-evolving. But it's a different story inside the casinos, where time seems to stand still. There are no clocks, just fresh-pumped air, endless buffets and ever-flowing drinks.

Sin City's reach is all-inclusive. Hollywood bigwigs gyrate at A-list ultralounges, while college kids seek cheap debauchery and grandparents whoop it up at the penny slots. You can sip designer martinis as you sample the apex of world-class cuisine or wander the casino floor with a 3ft-high cocktail tied around your neck.

History

Contrary to popular legend, there was much more at the dusty crossroads than a gambling parlor and some tumbleweeds the day mobster Ben 'Bugsy' Siegel rolled in and erected a glamorous tropical-themed casino, the Flamingo, under the searing sun.

Speared into the modern era by the completion of a railroad that linked up Salt Lake City to Los Angeles in 1902, Las Vegas boomed in the 1920s thank to federally sponsored construction projects. The legalization of gambling in 1931 carried Vegas through the Great Depression, WWII brought a huge air-force base and aerospace bucks, plus a paved highway to Los Angeles. Soon after, the Cold War justified the Nevada Test Site. It proved to be a textbook case of 'any publicity is good publicity': monthly aboveground atomic blasts shattered casino windows downtown while the city's official Miss Mushroom Cloud mascot promoted atomic everything in tourism campaigns.

A building spree sparked by the Flamingo in 1946 led to mob-backed tycoons upping the glitz ante at every turn. Big-name entertainers like Frank Sinatra, Liberace and Sammy Davis Jr arrived on stage at the same time as topless French showgirls.

The high-profile purchase of the Desert Inn in 1966 by eccentric billionaire Howard Hughes gave the gambling industry a much-needed patina of legitimacy. The debut of the MGM Grand in 1993 signaled the dawn of the corporate mega-resort era.

An oasis in the middle of a final frontier, Sin City continues to exist chiefly to satisfy the desires of visitors. Hosting 39.7 million people a year, until recently Las Vegas was the engine of North America's fastest-growing metropolitan area. The housing crisis hit residents here especially hard, but construction has picked up on the Strip and the Downtown Project is revitalizing the Fremont area.

◎ Sights

Roughly 4 miles long, the Strip, aka Las Vegas Blvd, is the center of gravity in Sin City. Circus Circus Las Vegas caps the north end and Mandalay Bay is at the south end, near the airport. Whether you're walking or driving, distances on the Strip are deceiving; a walk to what looks like a nearby casino usually takes longer than expected.

Downtown Las Vegas is the original town center and home to the city's oldest hotels and casinos: expect a retro feel, cheaper drinks and lower table limits. Its main drag is fun-loving Fremont St, a four-block stretch of casinos and restaurants covered by a dazzling canopy that runs a groovy light show every evening.

Major tourist areas are safe. However, Las Vegas Blvd between downtown and the Strip gets shabby, and Fremont St east of downtown is rather unsavory, although that's beginning to change, with new bars and restaurants opening their doors.

At press time, the $550 million LINQ shopping and entertainment district on the central Strip planned to open soon. LINQ's calling card is the 550ft-tall High Roller, billed as the world's tallest Ferris wheel. Projections aren't as certain for Skyvue, a 500ft-tall Ferris wheel (and electronic billboard) at the south end of the Strip across from Mandalay Bay. Construction has stagnated, and there are rumors of financial problems.

Openings are ongoing in the Fremont East neighborhood, where the online retailing giant Zappos is moving its headquarters. Zappos CEO Tony Hsieh, through

NEVADA FACTS

Nickname Silver State

Population 2.76 million

Area 109,800 sq miles

Capital city Carson City (population 54,800)

Other cities Las Vegas (population 596,400), Reno (population 227,000)

Sales tax 6.85%

Birthplace of Patricia Nixon (b 1912), Andre Agassi (b 1970), Greg LeMond (b 1961)

Home of The slot machine, Burning Man

Politics Nevada has six electoral votes – the state went for Obama in the 2012 presidential election, but it is split evenly in sending elected officials to Washington; US Senate Majority Leader Harry Reid (D) is Nevada's best-known politician

Famous for The 1859 Comstock Lode (the country's richest known silver deposit), legalized gambling and prostitution (outlawed in certain counties), and liberal alcohol laws allowing 24-hour bars

Best Las Vegas T-Shirt "I saw nothing at the Mob Museum."

Driving distances Las Vegas to Reno: 452 miles, Great Basin National Park to Las Vegas: 313 miles

Las Vegas

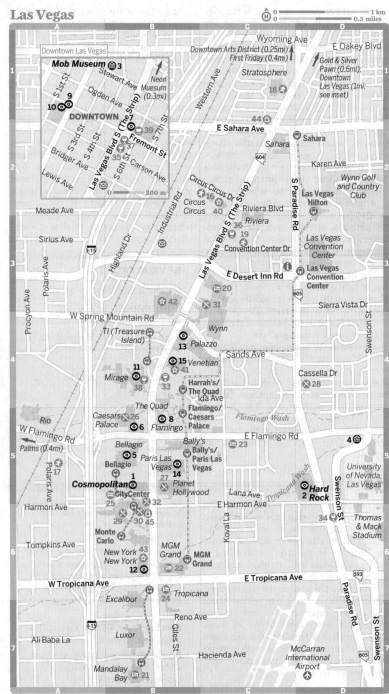

Las Vegas

his Downtown Project initiative, has injected hundreds of millions of dollars into community-based projects to revitalize the neighborhood.

⊙ The Strip

★ **Cosmopolitan**   CASINO
(www.cosmopolitanlasvegas.com; 3708 Las Vegas Blvd S; ⊙24hr) The twinkling three-story chandelier inside this sleek addition to the Strip isn't a piece of contemporary art only to be ogled. It's a step-inside, sip-a-swanky-cocktail and survey-your-domain kind of place, worthy of your wildest fairy tale. And

Cinderellas, you simply must step into the Roark Gourley–designed giant slipper for an Instagrammy moment. A bit much? Not really. It's all pure fun, and the Cosmopolitan manages to avoid utter pretension, despite the near-constant wink-wink moments, from the Art-o-Matics (vintage cigarette machines hawking local art not nicotine) to the hidden pizza joint.

★ **Hard Rock**   CASINO
(www.hardrockhotel.com; 4455 Paradise Rd; ⊙24hr) This casino hotel has got the moves like Jagger – getting older, but still strutting across the stage like a pouty-lipped bad boy.

Fresh off a $750 million expansion that added two new towers, the tres-hip Hard Rock is still luring them in with concerts, attitude and a very impressive collection of rock and roll memorabilia. Highlights include Jim Morrison's handwritten lyrics to one of the Doors' greatest hits and leather jackets from a who's who of famous rock stars. The Joint concert hall, Vanity Nightclub and 'Rehab' summer pool parties at Paradise Beach attract a pimped-out, sex-charged crowd flush with celebrities.

Bellagio
CASINO

(www.bellagio.com; 3600 Las Vegas Blvd S; ⊘24hr) The Bellagio dazzles with Tuscan architecture and an 8.5-acre artificial lake, complete with don't-miss choreographed dancing fountains. Look up as you enter the lobby: the stunning ceiling is adorned with a backlit glass sculpture composed of 2000 handblown flowers by renowned artist Dale Chihuly. The Bellagio Gallery of Fine Art (adult/student/child $16/11/free; ⊘10am-8pm) showcases temporary exhibits by top-notch artists. The Bellagio Conservatory & Botanical Gardens (⊘24hr) FREE features changing exhibits throughout the year.

Caesars Palace
CASINO

(www.caesarspalace.com; 3570 Las Vegas Blvd S; ⊘24hr) Forget Caesar. It's King Minos who springs to mind at this sprawling, labyrinth-like Greco-Roman fantasyland where maps are few (and not oriented to the outside). The interior is captivating, however, with marble reproductions of classical statuary, including a not-to-be-missed 4-ton Brahma

shrine near the front entrance. Towering fountains, goddess-costumed cocktail waitresses and the swanky haute-couture Forum Shops all up the glitz. And the minotaur? It's the new Bacchanal Buffet. But it can never be slayed.

Venetian
CASINO

(www.venetian.com; 3355 Las Vegas Blvd S; gondola ride adult/private $19/76; ⊘24hr) Hand-painted ceiling frescoes, roaming mimes, gondola rides and full-scale reproductions of famous Venice landmarks are found at the romantic Venetian. Next door, the Palazzo (www.palazzo.com; 3325 Las Vegas Blvd S) exploits a variation on the Italian theme with a luxurious but less interesting effect.

Mirage
CASINO

(www.mirage.com; 3400 Las Vegas Blvd S; ⊘24hr) A domed atrium filled with jungle foliage and soothing cascades captures the imagination at this tropically themed wonderland. Circling the atrium is a vast Polynesian-themed casino, which places gaming areas under separate roofs to evoke intimacy, including a popular high-limit poker room. Pause by the front desk for the 20,000-gallon saltwater aquarium, with 60 species of critters hailing from Fiji to the Red Sea. Out front in the lagoon, a fiery faux volcano erupts hourly after dark until midnight.

Paris-Las Vegas
CASINO

(www.parislv.com; 3655 Las Vegas Blvd S; ⊘24hr) Evoking the gaiety of the City of Light, Paris Las Vegas strives to capture the essence of the grand dame by re-creating her land-

---

LAS VEGAS FOR CHILDREN

With its recent focus on adult-oriented fun – marked by the now-iconic slogan 'What happens in Vegas stays in Vegas' – the city isn't a great choice for families. People under 21 can walk through most casinos on their way to shops, shows and restaurants but they cannot stop. Policies vary on whether under-21s must be accompanied by an adult, but younger children should always be with an adult for safety reason. Some casinos prohibit strollers.

If you do land in Sin City with the kids, don't abandon all hope. The Circus Circus (www.circuscircus.com; 2880 Las Vegas Blvd S; ⊘24hr; 🚻) hotel complex is all about kiddie fun, and its Adventuredome (www.adventuredome.com; day pass over/under 48in tall $28/17, per ride $5-8; ⊘hour vary; 🚻) is a 5-acre indoor theme park with rock climbing, bumper cars and a new 70mph roller coaster, the El Loco, which is set to open by the end of 2013. The Midway (⊘11am-midnight; 🚻) FREE features animals, acrobats and magicians performing on center stage.

If your kids are literally bouncing off the walls, take them to the trampoline-filled Skyzone (www.skyzone.com/LasVegas; 4915 Steptoe St; 30 min/60 min $9/12; ⊘2-8pm Mon-Thu, 2-10pm Fri, 10am-9pm Sat, 11am-8pm Sun) where such behavior is encouraged.

marks. Fine likenesses of the Opéra, the Arc de Triomphe, the Champs-Élysées, the soaring Eiffel Tower and even the Seine frame the property.

Flamingo   CASINO
(www.flamingolasvegas.com; 3555 Las Vegas Blvd S; ⊙24hr) The Flamingo is quintessential vintage Vegas. Weave through the slot machines to the **Wildlife Habitat** (3555 S Las Vegas Blvd; ⊙8am-dusk) **FREE** to see the flock of Chilean flamingos that call these 15 tropical acres home.

New York-New York   CASINO
(www.newyorknewyork.com; 3790 Las Vegas Blvd S; ⊙24hr) A mini metropolis featuring scaled-down replicas of the Empire State Building, the Statue of Liberty, a September 11 memorial, and the Brooklyn Bridge. There's also a classic roller coaster with a drop of 144ft (tickets $14).

⊙ Downtown & Off the Strip

★Mob Museum   MUSEUM
(☑702-229-2734; www.themobmuseum.org; 300 Stewart Ave; adult/child $20/14; ⊙10am-7pm Sun-Thu, to 8pm Fri & Sat) Bugs. Lucky. Whitey. Yeah goombah, all the boys are hanging out at downtown's new mob museum, which fills three floors in the old federal building. The fascinating, often lurid, exhibits trace the development of organized crime in America and look at the mob's connection to Las Vegas. Learn how money is laundered, listen in on a wiretap, get your mug shot taken and catch your breath in front of the bullet-and-blood-ridden wall that backed the victims of the 1929 St Valentine's Day Massacre.

Plan to spend several hours here. The museum is not appropriate for children.

★Neon Museum   MUSEUM
(☑702-387-6366; www.neonmuseum.org; 770 Las Vegas Blvd N; day tour adult/child $18/12; night tour $25/22; ⊙9-10am & 7:30-9pm Jun-Aug, extended daytime hours beginning at 10am rest of the year) A tour of the neon boneyard here is a fun stroll through Sin City's 'electrifying' past. Guides share stories about the city's former bigwigs as you walk past the gaudy signs that fronted their casinos, from Binion's to the Stardust. The new visitor center is housed in the lobby of the La Concha Motel, a striking mid-city modern structure that was saved from demolition in 2005 and moved here. All tours are guided, and they sell out quickly, so reserve beforehand online. At press time, the museum was offering evening tours on a trial basis, when a few of the signs are illuminated. There are no afternoon tours in the summer due to the heat. Call ahead to confirm tour times, which change seasonally.

The museum also has a public-art component, with a series of restored vintage signs scattered across downtown. This 'urban gallery' is best viewed at night when the neon blazes. Most of these signs are on Las Vegas Blvd between Fremont St and Washington Ave.

Atomic Testing Museum   MUSEUM
(www.atomictestingmuseum.org; 755 E Flamingo Rd; adult/child $14/11; ⊙10am-5pm Mon-Sat, noon-5pm Sun) Recalling an era when the word 'atomic' conjured modernity and mystery, the Smithsonian-run Atomic Testing Museum remains an intriguing testament to the period when the fantastical – and destructive – power of nuclear energy was tested just outside Las Vegas. Don't skip the deafening Ground Zero Theater, which mimics a concrete test bunker.

Fremont Street Experience   PLAZA
(www.vegasexperience.com; Fremont St, btwn Main St & Las Vegas Blvd; ⊙hourly 7pm-midnight) A four-block pedestrian mall topped by an arched steel canopy and filled with computer-controlled lights, the multi-sensory Fremont Street Experience, between Main St and Las Vegas Blvd, has re-energized downtown. Every evening, the canopy transforms into a six-minute light-and-sound show enhanced by 550,000 watts of wraparound sound. Bands play on several stages and zipliners whizz past overhead after stepping off Slotzilla, a 12-story slot machine scheduled to open soon.

Golden Nugget   CASINO
(www.goldennugget.com; 129 E Fremont St; ⊙24hr) This casino hotel has set the downtown benchmark for extravagance since opening in 1946. It's currently earning wows for its three-story waterslide, which drops through a 200,000-gallon shark tank. No brass or cut glass was spared inside the swanky but lovely casino, known for its nonsmoking poker room and the RUSH Lounge, where live local bands play. The gigantic 61lb Hand of Faith, the world's largest gold nugget, is around the corner from the hotel lobby.

Downtown Arts District ARTS

On the **First Friday** (www.firstfridaylasvegas.com; ⏱5-11pm) of each month, 10,000 art-lovers, hipsters, indie musicians and hangers-on descend on Las Vegas' downtown arts district for gallery openings, performance art, live bands and tattoo artists. The action revolves around S Casino Center Blvd between Colorado Ave and California Ave, northwest of the Stratosphere. Activities have also extended to Fremont East.

🏃 Activities

For area hiking and biking trails, check out the Neon to Nature listings on www.gethealthyclarkcountry.org.

Qua Baths & Spa SPA

(✆866-782-0655; www.harrahs.com/qua-caesars-palace; 3570 Las Vegas Blvd S, Caesars Palace; ⏱6am-8pm) Social spa-going is encouraged in the tea lounge, herbal steam room and arctic ice room, where dry-ice snowflakes fall.

Desert Adventures KAYAKING, HIKING

(✆702-293-5026; www.kayaklasvegas.com; 1647 Nevada Hwy, Suite A, Boulder City; trips from $149) With Lake Mead and Hoover Dam just 30 minutes away, would-be river rats should check out Desert Adventures for guided half-, full- and multiday kayaking adventures. Hiking and horseback-riding trips, too.

Escape Adventures MOUNTAIN BIKING

(✆800-596-2953; www.escapeadventures.com; 10575 Discovery Dr; trips incl bike from $129) The source for guided mountain-bike tours of Red Rock Canyon State Park.

🛏 Sleeping

Rates rise and fall dramatically. Some hotel websites feature calendars listing day-by-day room rates. Most of the hotels on the Strip are now adding a daily resort fee. These daily fees are noted below.

🏨 The Strip

★**Vdara** HOTEL **$$**

(✆702-590-2767; www.vdara.com; 2600 W Harmon Ave; r $159-196; [P][🐾][🛜][🏊]) Cool sophistication and warm hospitality merge easily at Vdara, a no-gaming, all-suites hotel in the new CityCenter complex. With earth-toned walls, chocolate-brown furniture and riparian green pillows, the suites have a soothing 'woodland' appeal, apropos for a LEED-certified property. If you're nice, you might score a room with a view of Bellagio's dancing waters. The hotel is near the Bellagio monorail stop. Resort fee is $28.

Tropicana CASINO HOTEL **$$**

(✆702-739-2222; www.troplv.com; 3801 Las Vegas Blvd S; r from $129, ste from $229; [P][❄][@][🛜][🏊]) After a multi-million-dollar renovation this

---

LAS VEGAS: HIGH-OCTANE THRILLS

Driving Hop into a race car at **Richard Petty Driving Experience** (✆800-237-3889; www.drivepetty.com; 6975 Speedway Blvd, Las Vegas Motor Speedway, off I-15 exit 54; ride-alongs from $99; drives from $449; ⏱hour vary) or careen around the track in a souped-up go-kart at **Fast Lap** (✆702-736-8113; www.fastlaplv.com; 4288 S Polaris; per race $25; ⏱10am-11pm Mon-Sat, 10am-10pm Sun).

Indoor Skydiving No time to jump from a plane? Enjoy the thrill without the altitude at **Vegas Indoor Skydiving** (✆702-731-4768; www.vegasindoorskydiving; 200 Convention Center Dr; single flight $85; ⏱9.45am-8pm).

Shooting If you're dying to fire a sub-machine gun or feel the heft of a Glock in your hot little hands, visit the high-powered **Gun Store** (✆702-454-1110; www.thegunstorelasvegas.com; 2900 E Tropicana Ave; from $99; ⏱9am-6:30pm; [🚌]201), with an indoor video training range.

Stratosphere Atop this 110-story **casino** (✆702-380-7777; www.stratospherehotel.com; Stratosphere, 2000 Las Vegas Blvd S; elevator adult/concession $18/15, incl 3 thrill rides $33, all-day pass $34, SkyJump from $110; underground rail Sahara) you can ride a roller coaster, drop 16 stories on the Big Shot, spin above thin air, or plummet 108ft over the edge.

Ziplining Whoosh over Bootleg Canyon on four separate ziplines with **Flightlinez** (✆702-293-6885; www.flightlinezbootleg.com; 1152 Industrial Rd, Boulder City; adult/child $159/99; ⏱7am-5pm). You'll drop 11 stories over throngs of tourists from the 12-story Slotzilla, set to open on Fremont St.

retro property, which has kept the Strip's tropical love going since 1953, just got cool again. The vibe is finger-snappin' hip, but still inviting, with a bright, monochromatic color scheme, lush, relaxing gardens and earth-toned, breezy rooms and bi-level suites. Resort fee is $20.

MGM Grand
CASINO HOTEL $$

(☑702-891-7777, 800-929-1111; www.mgmgrand. com; 3799 Las Vegas Blvd S; r from $122, ste from $150; P✳@🗐🏊) With more than 5000 rooms, this green leviathan is one of the world's largest hotels, but is bigger better? That depends, but top-drawer restaurants, a sprawling pool complex and a monorail station always make it a good bet – if you can find your room. Standard rooms have blah decor, so stay in the minimalist-modern West Wing instead. Try the Signature Suites for more space, high thread counts and a kitchenette. Resort fee is $28.

Caesars Palace
CASINO HOTEL $$

(☑866-227-5938; www.caesarspalace.com; 3570 Las Vegas Blvd S; r from $197; P✳@🏊) Send away the centurions and decamp in style – Caesars' standard rooms are some of the most luxurious in town. Resort fee is $25.

Cosmopolitan
CASINO HOTEL $$$

(☑702-698-7000; www.cosmopolitanlasvegas. com; 3708 Las Vegas Blvd S; r/ste from $320/470; P✳@🗐🏊) This place is like Hogwarts for hipsters, an uber-trendy warren tantalizing guests with magically impressive details and fun surprises. The wonder starts in the lobby where digitally enhanced columns display eye-catching backdrops. Rooms preen with mod designs, but the real delight is to stumble from your room at 1am to play pool in the upper lobbies before going on a mission to find the 'secret' pizza joint. Resort fee is $25.

Mandalay Bay
CASINO HOTEL $$$

(☑702-632-7777, 877-632-7800; www.mandalaybay.com; 3950 Las Vegas Blvd S; r $141-291; P✳@🗐🏊) The ornately appointed rooms here have a South Seas theme, and the amenities include floor-to-ceiling windows and luxurious bathrooms. Swimmers will swoon over the pool complex, with a sand-and-surf beach. Resort fee is $28.

Encore
CASINO HOTEL $$$

(☑702-770-8000; www.encorelasvegas.com; 3121 Las Vegas Blvd S; r/ste from $303/449; P✳@🗐🏊) Classy and playful rather than overblown and opulent – even people cheering

at the roulette table clap with more elegance. The rooms are studies in subdued luxury. Resort fee is $28.

Downtown & Off The Strip

Downtown hotels are generally less expensive than those on the Strip.

Main Street Station
CASINO HOTEL $

(☑800-713-8933, 702-387-1896; www.mainstreetcasino.com; 200 N Main St; r from $50; P✳🗐) For one of the best deals out there, try this 17-floor downtown hotel with marble-tiled foyers and Victorian sconces in the hallways. The classically styled rooms lack 'oomph,' but they do come with plantation shutters and comfy beds. The Mob Museum and Fremont St are within walking distance, and there's a microbrewery on-site.

Golden Nugget
CASINO HOTEL $$

(☑800-846-5336, 702-385-7111; www.goldennugget.com; 129 E Fremont St; r $99-239, ste $179-269; P✳@🗐🏊) Rooms feel swankier in the Gold and Rush Towers, but the vibe is still nice in the more traditionally decored Carson Tower. Outside, enjoy the lavish pool area, or brave the three-story water slide, which plunges through a shark tank.

Platinum Hotel
BOUTIQUE HOTEL $$

(☑702-365-5000, 877-211-9211; www.theplatinumhotel.com; 211 E Flamingo Rd; r from $152; P✳@🗐🏊🏋) Just off the Strip, the coolly modern rooms at this non-gaming property are comfortable, spacious and full of nice touches – many have fireplaces and all have kitchens and Jacuzzi tubs. The Strip is a 10 to 15-minute walk. One-time pet fee of $75.

Hard Rock
CASINO HOTEL $$$

(☑800-473-7625, 702-693-5000; www.hardrockhotel.com; 4455 Paradise Rd; r $122-399; P✳@🗐🏊) Everything about this boutique hotel spells stardom. French doors reveal skyline and palm tree views, and brightly colored Euro-minimalist rooms feature souped-up stereos and plasma TVs. While we dig the jukeboxes in the HRH All-Suite Tower, the standard rooms are nearly as cool. The hottest action revolves around the lush Beach Club.

Red Rock Resort
RESORT $$$

(☑702-797-7777; www.redrock.sclv.com; 11011 W Charleston Blvd; r $140-380; P✳@🗐🏊) If you're planning to hike in Red Rock Canyon, this oasis-like resort 15 miles west of the Strip is a stylish place to rest beforehand.

Rooms are comfy, spacious and well-appointed, with forest greens, deep browns and lots of pillows. On-site you'll find a bowling alley and a movie theater. There's free transportation to and from the Strip and the airport.

✗ Eating

Sin City is an unmatched eating adventure. Reservations are a must for fancier restaurants.

✗ The Strip

On the Strip itself, cheap eats beyond fast-food joints are hard to find.

Secret Pizza   PIZZA $
(3708 Las Vegas Blvd S, Cosmopolitan; slice $5, pizza $25; ⊙11:30am-3am) There's an unmarked pizza joint hidden deep within Cosmopolitan. We're not going to reveal its exact location because, well, where's the fun in that? But if you're craving a late-night slice of New York pizza, go to the third level and look for the narrow hallway between the other eateries. Or just join the queue of over-imbibers already waiting.

Earl of Sandwich   SANDWICHES $
(www.earlofsandwichusa.com; 3667 Las Vegas Blvd S, Planet Hollywood; mains under $7; ⊙24hr) Yes, calm down, we know it's a chain. But you know what? The sandwiches are tasty, the prices are easy on the wallet and it's in a convenient central Strip location. And everybody seems to like it.

WORTHY INDULGENCES: BEST BUFFETS

Extravagant all-you-can-eat buffets are a Sin City tradition. Three of the best include:

Bacchanal Buffet (www.caesarspalace.com; 3570 Las Vegas Blvd S, Caesars Palace; breakfast $20, lunch $30, dinner $40)

Wicked Spoon Buffet (www.cosmopolitanlasvegas.com; 2708 Las Vegas Blvd S, Cosmopolitan; brunch $33, dinner $41)

Buffet Bellagio (☏702-693-7111; www.bellagio.com; Bellagio, 3600 Las Vegas Blvd S; breakfast $18, lunch $22, dinner $33)

Todd English PUB   PUB $$
(www.toddenglishpub.com; 3720 Las Vegas Blvd S, Crystals; mains $16-24; ⊙11am-2am Mon-Fri, 9:30am-2am Sat & Sun) A rollicking City Center venture from Bostonian chef Todd English, PUB is a strangely fun cross between a British pub and a frat party, with creative sliders, an 80+ beer list that includes English pub classics, and an interesting promotion: if you drink your beer in less than seven seconds, it's on the house.

Society Café   CAFE $$
(www.wynnlasvegas.com; 3121 Las Vegas Blvd S, Encore; breakfast $14-22, lunch $14-24, dinner $15-39; ⊙7am-11pm Sun-Thu, 7am-11:30pm Fri & Sat; ⚲) A slice of reasonably priced culinary heaven amid Encore's loveliness. The basic cafe here is equal to fine dining at other joints. There's a short list of vegan options on all menus.

Social House   JAPANESE $$
(☏702-736-1122; www.socialhouselv.com; 3720 Las Vegas Blvd S, Crystals Mall, CityCenter; lunch prix fixe $20, sushi $6-24, mains $22-38; ⊙5-10pm Mon-Thu, noon-11pm Fri & Sat, noon-10pm Sun) Nibble on creative dishes inspired by Japanese street food in one of the Strip's most serene yet sultry dining rooms. Watermarked scrolls, wooden screens, and loads of dramatic red and black conjure visions of Imperial Japan, while the sushi and steaks are totally contemporary.

Joël Robuchon   FRENCH $$$
(☏702-891-7925; www.mgmgrand.com; 3799 Las Vegas Blvd S, MGM Grand; mains $135-175, menu per person $120-420; ⊙5:30-10pm Sun-Thu, to 10:30pm Fri & Sat) A once-in-a-lifetime culinary experience; block off a solid three hours and get ready to eat your way through the multicourse seasonal menu of traditional French fare. Next door at L'Atelier de Joël Robuchon (☏702-891-7358; www.mgmgrand.com; 3799 Las Vegas Blvd S, MGM Grand; mains $41-97; ⊙5-11pm), you can belly up to the counter for a slightly more economical but still delicious meal.

Picasso   FRENCH $$$
(☏702-693-8865; www.bellagio.com; 3600 Las Vegas Blvd S, Bellagio; prix-fixe menu $115; ⊙5:30-9:30pm Wed-Mon) Why yes, I would like to dine with Picasso tonight – or a least one of his paintings. But the art isn't just on the wall at chef Julian Serrano's swanky French restaurant, where dishes on the four-course prix-fixe menu are masterworks themselves. Servings are small, but you should leave

satisfied after several courses. Desserts are spectacular.

Gordon Ramsay Steak
STEAKHOUSE $$$

(☑ 877-346-4642; www.parislasvegas.com; 3655 Las Vegas Blvd S, Paris; mains $32-63; ☺ 4:30-10:30pm, bar to midnight Fri & Sat) For a top-notch steak, leave Paris and the Eiffel Tower behind and stroll through 'the chunnel' to Gordon Ramsay's new steakhouse. Ribboned in red and and domed by a jaunty Union Jack, this is one of the top seats in town. No reservation? Sit at the bar, where the knowledgable bartenders will explain the cuts and their preparations. And definitely say yes to the side of bread. Fish, chops and one lonely chicken dish round out the a la carte menu.

Sage
AMERICAN $$$

(☑ 702-590-8690; www.arialasvegas.com; 3730 Las Vegas Blvd S, Aria; mains $35-54; ☺ 5-11pm Mon-Sat) Acclaimed chef Shawn McClain meditates on the seasonally sublime with global inspiration and artisanal, farm-to-table ingredients in one of Vegas' most drop-dead gorgeous dining rooms. Don't miss the inspired seasonal cocktails doctored with housemade liqueurs, French absinthe and fruit purees.

DOCG Enoteca
ITALIAN $$$

(☑ 877-893-2003; www.cosmopolitanlasvegas.com; 3708 Las Vegas Blvd S, Cosmopolitan; mains $22-45; ☺ 6-11pm) Order to-die-for fresh pasta or a wood-fired pizza in the stylish enoteca (wine shop)–inspired room that feels like you've joined a festive dinner party. Or head next door to sexy Scarpetta (☑ 877-893-2003; www.cosmopolitalasvegas.com; 3708 Las Vegas Blvd S; mains $24-55; ☺ 6-11pm), which offers a more intimate, upscale experience by the same fantastic chef, Scott Conant.

✗ Downtown & Off The Strip

For gourmands, off the Strip is where dining gets really interesting. Downtown's restaurants offer better value than those on the Strip, and new eateries are popping up in the E Fremont St neighborhood.

The Asian restaurants on Spring Mountain Rd in Chinatown are also good budget options, with lots of vegetarian choices.

★Raku
JAPANESE $$

(☑ 702-367-3511; www.raku-grill.com; 5030 W Spring Mountain Rd; small plates $2-18, mains $8-19; ☺ 6pm-3am Mon-Sat) Japanese owner-

chef Mitsuo Edo crafts small plate dishes that simmer with delicate, exquisite flavors. You'll find yourself ordering just one more thing – again and again – from the menu of grilled meats, homemade tofu and seasoned vegetables. Try one of the tofu and the kobe beef with wasabi. Raku is a 15-minute cab ride from the Strip. Make reservations or angle for a seat at the small bar.

★Lotus of Siam
THAI $$

(☑ 702-735-3033; www.saipinchutima.com; 953 E Sahara Ave; mains $9-30; ☺ 11:30am-2:30pm Mon-Fri, buffet to 2pm, 5:30-10pm daily) The top Thai restaurant in the US? According to *Gourmet Magazine,* this is it. One bite of simple pad Thai – or any of the exotic northern Thai dishes – nearly proves it.

Firefly
TAPAS $$

(www.fireflylv.com; 3824 Paradise Rd; small dishes $4-10, large dishes $12-20; ☺ 11:30am-2am Sun-Thu) A meal at Firefly can be twice as fun as an overdone Strip restaurant, and half the price. Is that why it's always hopping? Nosh on traditional Spanish tapas, while the bartender pours sangria and flavor-infused *mojitos.*

Eat
BREAKFAST, AMERICAN $$

(☑ 702-534-1515; www.facebook.com/eatdowntownlv; 707 Carson Ave; breakfast $8-20, lunch $9-25; ☺ 8am-3pm Mon-Fri, to 2pm Sat & Sun) What makes newcomer Eat so special? Community spirit and down-home cooking are what first leap to mind. Trust us, you'll feel compelled to share 'ooohs' and 'aahhs' with fellow diners when a humongous serving of chicken-fried steak lands at the adjacent table. With a concrete floor and spare decor, it can get loud, but that just adds to the fun as folks chow down on beignets, truffled egg sandwiches, and shrimp and grits.

The restaurant is a collaboration between chef Natalie Young, a veteran of Las Vegas kitchens, and the Downtown Project, led by Zappo's CEO Tony Hsieh.

Pink Taco
MEXICAN $$

(www.hardrockhotel.com; 4455 Paradise Rd, Hard Rock; mains $14-21; ☺ 11am-10pm Sun-Thu, to late Fri & Sat) Whether it's the $5 margarita happy hour, the leafy poolside patio, or the friendly rock and roll clientele, Pink Taco always feels like a worthwhile party.

Hugo's Cellar
STEAK, SEAFOOD $$$

(Four Queens; ☑ 702-385-4011; www.hugoscellar.com; 702 Fremont St; mains $37-60; ☺ 5:30-

EMERGENCY ARTS

A coffee shop, an art gallery, studios, and a de facto community center of sorts, all under one roof and right smack downtown? The Emergency Arts (www.emergencyartslv.com; 520 Fremont St) building, also home to Beat Coffeehouse (www.thebeatlasvegas. com; sandwiches $6-8; ☉ 7am-midnight Mon-Fri, 9am-midnight Sat, 9am-5pm Sun; ☎) is a friendly bastion of laid-back cool and strong coffee where vintage vinyl spins on old turntables. If you're aching to meet some savvy locals who know their way around town, this is your hangout spot.

10:30pm) This is old-school Vegas, but in a good way. In a dark and clubby space beneath the Four Queens, Hugo's Cellar is a return to the days when service was king. Ladies are given a rose, salads are tossed beside the table and the service is attentive but not intrusive. Party like it's 1959 with veal Oscar, beef Wellington and cherries jubilee.

🍸 Drinking

Loads of new and interesting bars are opening on E Fremont St. Zip down Slotzilla then walk over. Definitely worth a wander.

🍸 The Strip

★ **Chandelier Bar**   BAR
(www.cosmopolitanlasvegas.com; 3708 Las Vegas Blvd S, Cosmopolitan; ☉ varies by floor, 24hr for 1st fl) In a city full of lavish hotel lobby bars, this one pulls out all the stops. Kick back with the Cosmopolitan hipsters and enjoy the curiously thrilling feeling that you're tipsy inside a giant crystal chandelier.

Mix   LOUNGE
(www.mandalaybay.com; 3950 Las Vegas Blvd S, 64th fl, THEhotel at Mandalay Bay; cover after 10pm $20-25; ☉ 5pm-1am Sun-Wed, to 2am Thu, to 3am Fri & Sat) The place to grab sunset cocktails. The glassed-in elevator has amazing views, and that's before you even glimpse the mod interior design and soaring balcony.

Rhumbar   COCKTAIL BAR
(☎ 702 792-7615; www.mirage.com; 3400 Las Vegas Blvd S, Mirage; ☉ 1pm-midnight Sun-Thu, 1pm-2am Fri & Sat) Minty mojitos and frozen daiquiris

are pure mixology magic at this Caribbean-flavored bar and cigar lounge. Rhumbar is handy to the Mirage's south entrance. Chill at breezy, beachy open-air lounge tables on the chic Strip-view patio.

Parasol Up – Parasol Down   BAR, CAFE
(www.wynnlasvegas.com; 3131 Las Vegas Blvd S, Wynn; ☉ 11am-2am, to 4am Fri & Sat at Parasol Up) Unwind with a fresh fruit *mojito* by the soothing waterfall at the Wynn to experience one of Vegas' most successful versions of paradise.

Carnaval Court   BAR
(☎ 702-369-5000;   www.harrahslasvegas.com; 3475 Las Vegas Blvd S, outside Harrah's; cover varies; ☉ 11am-3am) Bartenders juggle fire for raucous crowds at this outdoor bar. Live pop and rock cover bands tear up the stage at night, but all eyes are on the hot bods at the bar. Party on, dudes.

🍷 Downtown & Off the Strip

Want to chill out with the locals? Head to one of their go-to favorites. New bars and and cafes are opening along E Fremont St, making it the number one alternative to the Strip.

Griffin   BAR
(☎ 702-382-0577; 511 E Fremont St; cover $5-10; ☉ 5pm-3am Mon-Fri, 7pm-3am Sat, 8pm-2am Sun) Escape from the casinos' clutch and imbibe at this indie joint, a short walk along the less illuminated side of Fremont St. Crackling fireplaces, leather booths and an almost unbearably cool jukebox make this dark and cozy spot popular with rebels, hipster sweethearts and surely an in-the-know vampire or two.

Commonwealth   COCKTAIL BAR
(www.commonwealthlv.com; 525 E Fremont St; ☉ 6pm-2am Wed-Fri, 8pm-2am Sat & Sun) This new cocktail bar might be a little too hip for laid-back E Fremont St, but whoa, its Steampunk interior is worth a look. Softly glowing chandeliers. Saloon-style bar. Victorian-era bric-a-brac. Enjoy your tipple. It also has a rooftop bar and, we hear, a secret bar within the bar.

Downtown Cocktail Room   LOUNGE
(☎ 702-880-3696; www.downtownlv.net; 111 Las Vegas Blvd S; cover free-$10; ☉ 4pm-2am Mon-Fri, 7pm-2am Sat) With a retro cocktail list you must take seriously, this speakeasy with sateen pillows and suede-covered couches

feels decades removed from the old-school carpet joints on Fremont St. In true Prohibition-era style, the entrance is disguised.

Fireside Lounge
COCKTAIL BAR

(www.peppermilllasvegas.com; 2985 Las Vegas Blvd S, Peppermill; ⊙24hr) The Strip's most unlikely romantic hideaway is inside a retro coffee shop. Courting couples flock here for the low lighting, sunken fire pit and cozy nooks built for supping on multistrawed tiki drinks.

Double Down Saloon
BAR

(www.doubledownsaloon.com; 4640 Paradise Rd; no cover; ⊙24hr) You can't get more punk rock than a dive whose tangy, blood-red house drink is named 'Ass Juice' and where the noon to 5pm happy hour means everything in the bar is two bucks. Killer jukebox, cash only.

☆ Entertainment

Las Vegas has no shortage of entertainment on any given night, and **Ticketmaster** (☑800-745-3000; www.ticketmaster.com) sells tickets for pretty much everything. **Tix 4 Tonight** (☑877-849-4868; www.tix4tonight.com; 3200 Las Vegas Blvd S, Fashion Show; ⊙10am-8pm) offers half-price tickets for a limited lineup of same-day shows and small discounts on 'always sold-out' shows.

Nightclubs & Live Music

In 2012, seven of the 10 highest-earning nightclubs in the US were in Vegas, with both XS and Marquee earning more than $80 million each. Admission prices to nightclubs vary wildly based on the mood of door staff, male-to-female ratio, and how crowded the club is that night. Avoid waiting in line by booking ahead with the club VIP host. Most bigger clubs have someone working the door in the late afternoon and early evening. Your hotel concierge will also typically have free passes for clubs, or be able to make reservations. Also consider bottle service. It usually waives cover charges and waiting in line.

XS
CLUB

(www.xslasvegas.com; 3131 Las Vegas Blvd S, Encore; cover $20-50; ⊙9:30pm-4am Fri & Sat, 10:30pm-4am Sun & Mon) The only club where we've seen club-goers jump in the pool to dance (and not be thrown out by the bouncers), XS is a Vegas favorite with a more diverse crowd (read: you won't feel outta place if you're over 30) than most. Dress up or you won't get in.

Marquee
CLUB

(www.cosmopolitanlasvegas.com; 3708 Las Vegas Blvd, Cosmopolitan) When someone asks what the coolest club in Vegas is, Marquee is the undisputed answer. Celebrities (we spotted Macy Gray as we danced through the crowd), an outdoor beach club, hot DJs and that certain *je ne sais quoi* that makes a club worth the line.

Tao
CLUB

(www.taolasvegas.com; 3355 Las Vegas Blvd S, Venetian; ⊙lounge 5pm-midnight Sun-Thu, to 1am Thu-Sat, nightclub 10pm-5am) Some Vegas clubbing aficionados claim that Tao has reached a been-there-done-that saturation point. Newbies, however, still gush at the decadent details and libidinous vibe: from the giant gold Buddha to the near-naked go-go girls languidly caressing themselves in rose petal-strewn bathtubs.

Stoney's Rockin' Country
LIVE MUSIC

(www.stoneysrockincountry.com; 6611 Las Vegas Blvd S; cover free-$20; ⊙7pm-2am Sun-Wed, to 3am Thu-Sat) This fun-lovin' country-western bar recently moved closer to the Strip. Dance lessons are offered every night of the week, with two-stepping on Tuesdays at 7:30pm. On Fridays, chicks wearing Daisy Dukes and cowboy boots get in free. On Saturdays, come for the $15 all-you-can-drink drafts.

Production Shows

There are hundreds of shows to choose from in Vegas. Any Cirque du Soleil show tends to be an unforgettable experience.

★LOVE
PERFORMING ARTS

(☑800-963-9634, 702-792-7777; www.cirquedusoleil.com; tickets $99-150; ⊙7pm & 9:30pm Thu-Mon; ⊞) This show at the Mirage is a popular addition to the Cirque du Soleil lineup; locals who have seen many Cirque productions come and go say it's the best.

Zumanity
PERFORMING ARTS

(☑702-740-6815; www.cirquedusoleil.com; tickets $76-138) A sensual and sexy adult-only show at New York-New York.

La Rêve
LIVE PERFORMANCE

(☑888-320-7110; www.wynnlasvegas.com; 3131 Las Vegas Blvd S, Wynn; tickets from $105; ⊙7pm & 9:30pm Fri-Tue) Aquatic acrobatic feats are the centerpiece of La Rêve, which means 'The Dream' in French. The theater holds a one-million-gallon swimming pool and performers must be scuba-certified. Note that cheaper seats are in the 'splash zone.'

House of Blues
LIVE MUSIC

(702-632-7600; www.hob.com; 3950 Las Vegas Blvd S, Mandalay Bay) Blues is the tip of the hog at this Mississippi Delta juke joint, showcasing modern rock, pop and soul.

Shopping

Bonanza Gift Shop
SOUVENIRS

(www.worldslargestgiftshop.com; 2440 Las Vegas Blvd S; 8am-midnight) More than 40,000 sq ft of...stuff! The best place for only-in-Vegas kitsch souvenirs.

Gold & Silver Pawn
JEWELRY

(702-385-7912; http://gspawn.com; 713 Las Vegas Blvd S; shop 9am-9pm, night window 9pm-9am) As seen on the reality-TV hit series *Pawn Stars*, this humble-looking storefront has untold treasures inside, from Wild West shotguns and restored 1950s classic cars to vintage Vegas casino and autographed star memorabilia. Line up outside by the red-velvet rope.

Fashion Show Mall
MALL

(www.thefashionshow.com; 3200 Las Vegas Blvd S; 10am-9pm Mon-Sat, 11am-7pm Sun) Nevada's biggest and flashiest mall.

Forum Shops
MALL

(www.caesarspalace.com; 3570 Las Vegas Blvd S, Caesars Palace; 10am-11pm Sun-Thu, to midnight Fri & Sat) Upscale stores in an air-conditioned version of Ancient Rome.

The Shops at Crystals
MALL

(www.crystalsatcitycenter.com; 3720 Las Vegas Blvd S; 10am-11pm Sun-Thu, to midnight Fri & Sat) From Assouline to Versace, this posh new mall beside Aria preens with more than 40 luxury shops.

Grand Canal Shoppes
MALL

(www.thegrandcanalshoppes.com; 3355 Las Vegas Blvd S, Venetian; 10am-11pm) Italianate indoor luxury mall with gondolas.

Shoppes at the Palazzo
MALL

(www.theshoppesatthepalazzo.com; 3327 Las Vegas Blvd S, Palazzo; 10am-11pm Sun-Thu, to midnight Fri & Sat) Sixty international designers flaunt their goodies.

Information

EMERGENCY & MEDICAL SERVICES

Gamblers Anonymous (855-222-5542; www.gamblersanonymous.com) Assistance with gambling concerns.

Police (702-828-3111; www.lvmpd.com)

Sunrise Hospital & Medical Center (702-731-8000; www.sunrisehospital.com; 3186 S Maryland Pkwy) Children's hospital and 24-hour emergency room.

University Medical Center (702-383-2000, emergency 702-383-2661; www.umcsn.com; 1800 W Charleston Blvd; 24hr) Nevada's most advanced trauma center, and 24-hour emergency department.

INTERNET ACCESS & MEDIA

Wi-fi is available in most hotel rooms (about $10 to $25 per day, sometimes included in the 'resort fee') and there are internet kiosks with attached printers in most hotel lobbies.

Eater Vegas (www.vegas.eater.com) News about Sin City's chefs and new restaurants, with a regularly updated list of the city's top 38 eateries.

Las Vegas Review-Journal (www.lvrj.com) Daily paper with a weekend guide, *Neon*, on Friday.

Las Vegas Weekly (www.lasvegasweekly.com) Free weekly with good entertainment and restaurant listings.

Vegas Chatter (www.vegaschatter.com) The latest on what's happening in Vegas, from restaurant openings to the hottest pools.

MONEY

Every hotel-casino and bank and most convenience stores have an ATM. The ATM fee at most casinos is around $5. Best to stop at off-Strip banks if possible.

Travelex Currency Services (702-369-2219; 3200 Las Vegas Blvd S, Fashion Show; 10am-9pm Mon-Sat, 11am-7pm Sun) Changes currencies at Fashion Show Mall.

POST

Post office (www.usps.com; 201 Las Vegas Blvd S; 9am-5pm Mon-Fri) Downtown.

TOURIST INFORMATION

Las Vegas Tourism (www.onlyinvegas.com) Official tourism website.

Las Vegas Visitor Information Center (LVCVA | Las Vegas Convention & Visitors Authority; 702-892-7575, 877-847-4858; www.visitlasvegas.com; 3150 Paradise Rd; 8am-5:30pm Mon-Fri) Free local calls, internet access and maps galore.

Las Vegas.com (www.lasvegas.com) Travel services.

Vegas.com (www.vegas.com) Travel information with booking service. Also lists kid-friendly attractions.

Getting There & Around

Just south of the major Strip casinos and easily accessible from I-15, **McCarran International**

Airport (LAS; ☑ 702-261-5211; www.mccarran. com; 5757 Wayne Newton Blvd; ✈) has direct flights from many US cities, and some from Canada and Europe. Most domestic flights arrive in Terminal 1. International flights arrive in the new Terminal 3. **Bell Trans** (☑ 702-739-7990; www.bell-trans.com) offers a shuttle service ($7) between the airport and the Strip. Fares to downtown destinations are slightly higher. At the airport, exit at door 9 near baggage claim to find the Bell Trans booth.

Most of the attractions in Vegas have free self-parking and valet parking available (tip $2). Fast, fun and fully wheelchair accessible, the **mono-rail** (www.lvmonorail.com; 1 ride $5, 24/72hr pass $12/28, child under 6yr free; ☉ 7am-midnight Mon, to 2am Tue-Thu, to 3am Fri-Sun) connects the Sahara Station (closest to Circus Circus) to the MGM Grand, stopping at major Strip megaresorts along the way. The **Deuce** (☑ 702-228-7433; www.rtcsouthernnevada. com; 2/24hr pass $6/8), a local double-decker bus, runs frequently 24 hours daily between the Strip and downtown.

Around Las Vegas

Red Rock Canyon
National Conservation Area   PARK
(☑ 702-515-5350;   www.redrockcanyonlv.org; day-use per car/bicycle $7/3; ☉ scenic loop 6am-8pm Apr-Sep, earlier Oct-Mar, visitor center 8am-4:30pm) This dramatic park is the perfect antidote to Vegas' artificial brightness. A 23-mile drive west of the Strip, the canyon is actually more like a valley, with the steep, rugged red-rock escarpment rising 3000ft on its western edge. There's a 13-mile scenic loop with access to hiking trails and first-come, first-served camping (September to May) 2 miles east of the visitor center. The 2.5-mile round-trip hike to Calico Tanks climbs through the red rocks and ends with a lofty view of Las Vegas.

Lake Mead & Hoover Dam   LAKE, HISTORIC SITE
Lake Mead and Hoover Dam are the most-visited sites within the Lake Mead National Recreation Area (☑ park information desk 702-293-8906, visitor center 702-293-8990; www.nps. gov/lake; car/bicycle $10/5; ☉ 24hr, visitor center 9am-4:30pm Wed-Sun), which encompasses 110-mile-long Lake Mead, 67-mile-long Lake Mohave and many miles of desert around the lakes. The excellent Alan Bible Visi-tor Center (☑ 702-293-8990; www.nps.gov/ lake; Lakeshore Scenic Dr, off US Hwy 93; ☉ 9am-4:30pm), on Hwy 93 halfway between Boul-der City and Hoover Dam, has information

on recreation and desert life. Here, hikers and cyclists can pick up a map of the River Mountains Loop Trail (www.rivermountains-trail.com), which offers 32-miles of hiking and biking around the lake. From the visi-tor center, North Shore Rd and Lakeshore Rd wind around the lake and make a great scenic drive. Lakeshore Rd stretches all the way to Valley of Fire Hwy, which leads to the stunning Valley of Fire State Park.

Straddling the Arizona–Nevada border, the graceful curve and art-deco style of the 726ft Hoover Dam (☑ 866-730-9097, 702-494-2517; www.usbr.gov/lc/hooverdam; Hwy 93; visitor center $8, incl power-plant tour adult/child $11/9, all-inclusive tour $30; ☉ 9am-6pm, last ticket sold 5:15pm) contrasts superbly with the stark landscape. Don't miss a stroll over the new Mike O'Callaghan-Pat Tillman Memorial Bridge, which features a pedestrian walk-way with perfect views upstream of Hoover Dam. Not recommended for anyone with vertigo. Parking for access to the bridge is off Hwy 172/Hoover Dam Access Rd. Visi-tors can either take the 30-minute power plant tour (adult/child $11/9) or the more in-depth, one-hour Hoover Dam tour (no children under 8yr; tours $30). If you're inter-ested in history and construction, spring for the longer tour.

Tickets for both tours are sold at the visi-tor center. Tickets for the power plant tour only can be purchased online.

Nearby Boulder City was home to the men and women who built the dam. Today, the inviting downtown is a nice place to grab a meal or spend the night. Center-of-the-action Milo's (www.miloswinebar.com; 538 Nevada Hwy; mains $9-13; ☉ 11am-10pm Sun-Thu, to midnight Fri & Sat) serves fresh sandwiches, salads and gourmet cheese plates at side-walk tables outside its wine bar. Around the corner is the pleasant Boulder Dam Hotel

---

VALLEY OF FIRE STATE PARK

A masterpiece of desert scenery filled with psychedelically shaped sandstone outcroppings, this park (☑ 702-397-2088; www.parks.nv.gov/parks/valley-of-fire-state-park; per vehicle $10; ☉ visitor center 8:30am-4:30pm) is a great escape 55 miles from Vegas. Hwy 169 runs right past the visitor center, which has hiking and camping (tent/RV sites $20/30) information and excellent desert-life exhibits.

WORTH A TRIP

BURNING MAN

For one week at the end of August, Burning Man (www.burningman.com; admission $380) explodes onto the sunbaked Black Rock Desert, and Nevada sprouts a third major population center – Black Rock City. An experiential art party (and alternative universe) that climaxes in the immolation of a towering stick figure, Burning Man is a whirlwind of outlandish theme camps, dust-caked bicycles, bizarre bartering, costume-enhanced nudity and a general relinquishment of inhibitions.

(☑702-293-3510; www.boulderdamhotel.com; 1305 Arizona St; r incl breakfast $72-89, ste $99; ✳@🖘), where the rate includes made-to-order breakfasts and admission to the onsite Boulder City/Hoover Dam museum.

Western Nevada

A vast and mostly undeveloped sagebrush steppe, the western corner of the state is carved by mountain ranges and parched valleys. It's the place where modern Nevada began with the discovery of the famous Comstock silver lode in and around Virginia City. This part of the state lures visitors today with outdoor adventure in the form of hiking, biking, and skiing on its many mountains. Contrasts here are as extreme as the weather: one moment you're driving through a quaint historic town full of grand homes built by silver barons, and the next you spot a tumbleweed blowing by a homely little bar that turns out to be the local (and legal) brothel.

Reno

In downtown Reno you can gamble at one of two-dozen casinos in the morning then walk down the street and shoot rapids at the Truckee River Whitewater Park. These contrasts are what makes 'The Biggest Little City in the World' so interesting – it's holding tight to its gambling roots but also earning kudos as a top-notch basecamp for outdoor adventure. The Sierra Nevada Mountains and Lake Tahoe are less than an hour's drive away, and the region is teaming with lakes, trails and ski resorts.

☉ Sights

The downtown Riverwalk District (www.renoriver.org) hugs the Truckee River. Kayakers and inner tubers ride the rapids in the whitewater park that stretches east from Wingfield Park to Virginia St.

National Automobile Museum MUSEUM

(☑775-333-9300; www.automuseum.org; 10 S Lake St; adult/child $10/4; ⊙9:30am-5:30pm Mon-Sat, 10am-4pm Sun; 🖘) Stylized street scenes illustrate a century's worth of automobile history at this engaging car museum. The collection is enormous and impressive, with one-of-a-kind vehicles, including a 1928 Model A Ford given to Mary Pickford by Douglas Fairbanks and a 1935 Dusenburg owned by Sammy Davis Jr. Rotating exhibits bring in all kinds of souped-up or fabulously retro rides.

Nevada Museum of Art MUSEUM

(☑775-329-3333; www.nevadaart.org; 160 W Liberty St; adult/child $10/1; ⊙10am-5pm Wed-Sun, 10am-8pm Thu) In a sparkling building inspired by the geological formations of the Black Rock Desert north of town, a floating staircase leads to galleries showcasing temporary exhibits and images related to the American West. Climb to the roof for a view of the Sierras. Great cafe for postcultural refueling.

Virginia Street

Wedged between the I-80 and the Truckee River, downtown's N Virginia St is casino central. South of the river it continues as S Virginia St. All of the following hotel-casinos are open 24 hours.

Circus Circus CASINO

(www.circusreno.com; 500 N Sierra St; 🖘) The most family-friendly of the bunch, it has free circus acts to entertain kids beneath a giant, candy-striped big top, which also harbors a gazillion carnival and video games.

Silver Legacy CASINO

(www.silverlegacyreno.com; 407 N Virginia St) A Victorian-themed place, it's easily recognized by its white landmark dome, where a giant mock mining rig periodically erupts into a tame sound-and-light show.

Eldorado
CASINO

(www.eldoradoreno.com; 345 N Virginia St) The Eldorado has a kitschy Fountain of Fortune that probably has Italian sculptor Bernini spinning in his grave.

Harrah's
CASINO

(www.harrahsreno.com; 219 N Center St) Founded by Nevada gambling pioneer William Harrah in 1946, it's still one of the biggest and most popular casinos in town.

🏃 Activities

Reno is a 30- to 60-minute drive from Tahoe ski resorts, and many hotels and casinos offer special stay and ski packages.

Truckee River
Whitewater Park
WATER SPORTS

(www.reno.gov) Mere steps from the casinos, the park's Class II and III rapids are gentle enough for kids riding inner tubes, yet sufficiently challenging for professional freestyle kayakers. Two courses wrap around Wingfield Park, a small river island that hosts free concerts. **Tahoe Whitewater Tours** (☑ 775-787-5000; www.gowhitewater.com) and **Wild Sierra Adventures** (☑ 866-323-8928; www.wildsierra.com) offer kayak trips and lessons.

Historic Reno
Preservation Society
WALKING TOUR

(☑ 775-747-4478; www.historicreno.org; tours $10) Dig deeper with a walking or cycling tour highlighting subjects including architecture, politics and literary history.

🛏 Sleeping

Lodging rates vary widely depending on the day of the week and local events. Sunday through Thursday are generally the best; Friday is more expensive and Saturday can be as much as triple the midweek rate.

In summer, there's gorgeous high-altitude camping at **Mt Rose** (☑ 877-444-6777; www.recreation.gov; Hwy 431; RV & tent sites $17-50).

Sands Regency
CASINO HOTEL $

(☑ 775-348-2200; www.sandsregency.com; 345 N Arlington Ave; r Sun-Thu from $29, Fri & Sat $69; P ✳ 🛜 🐾 🏊) The exterior is a little tired, but rooms are fine, decked out in a cheerful tropical palette of upbeat blues, reds and greens. Empress Tower rooms are best. A good deal.

Wildflower Village
MOTEL, B&B $

(☑ 775-747-8848; www.wildflowervillage.com; 4395 W 4th St; hostel $30, motel $55, B&B $125;

P ✳ @ 🛜) This welcoming artists' colony on the west edge of town has a tumbledown yet creative vibe. Murals decorate the facade of each room, and you can hear the freight trains rumble on by. Has three types of rooms: hostel, motel and B&B.

★ Peppermill
CASINO HOTEL $$

(☑ 866-821-9996, 775-826-2121; www.peppermillreno.com; 2707 S Virginia St; r/ste Sun-Thu from $70/130, Fri & Sat from $170/200; P ✳ @ 🛜 🏊) Now awash in Vegas-style opulence, the popular Peppermill boasts Tuscan-themed rooms in its newest 600-room tower, and has almost completed a plush remodel of its older rooms. The three sparkling pools (one indoor) are dreamy, with a full spa on hand. Geothermal energy powers the resort's hot water and heat.

🍴 Eating

Reno's dining scene goes far beyond the casino buffets.

Peg's Glorified Ham & Eggs
DINER $

(www.eatatpegs.com; 420 S Sierra St; breakfast $9-14, lunch $8-12; ⊙ 6:30am-2pm; 🚼) Locally regarded as the best breakfast in town, Peg's offers tasty grill food that's not too greasy. Look for the mint-and-white striped awning.

★ Old Granite Street Eatery
AMERICAN $$

(☑ 775-622-3222; www.oldgranitestreeteatery.com; 243 S Sierra St; lunch $9-14, dinner $11-26; ⊙ 11am-11pm Mon-Thu, 11am-midnight Fri, 10am-midnight Sat, 10am-4pm Sun) A lovely place for organic and local comfort food, old-school artisanal cocktails and seasonal craft beers, this antique-strewn hot spot enchants diners with its stately wooden bar, water served in old liquor bottles and its lengthy seasonal menu.

> ℹ **RENO AREA TRAIL INFORMATION**
>
> For extensive information on regional hiking and biking trails, including the Mt Rose summit trail and the Tahoe-Pyramid Bikeway, download the **Truckee Meadows Trails Guide** (www.reno.gov/Index.aspx?page=291). You can pick up a copy of the guide at the **Galena Creek Visitor Center** (www.galenacreekvisitorcenter.org; 18250 Mt Rose Hwy; ⊙ 9am-6pm Tue-Sun) at Galena Creek Regional Park, where you'll find three of the trails that are included in the guide.

SOUTHWEST WESTERN NEVADA

No reservation? Check out the iconic rooster and pig murals and wait for seats at a 'community table' fashioned from a barn door.

Silver Peak Restaurant & Brewery PUB $$
(124 Wonder St; mains lunch $8.25-11, dinner $9.25-22; ☺ restaurant 11am-10pm Sun-Thu, to 11pm Sat & Sun, pub open 1hour later) Casual and pretense-free, this place hums with the chatter of happy locals settling in for a night of micro-brews and great eats, from pizza with pesto shrimp to spinach and ricotta ravioli to filet mignon. In the heart of the downtown Riverwalk District.

🍺 Drinking

Great Basin Brewing Co BREWERY $$
(www.greatbasinbrewingco.com; 5525 S Virginia St; mains $8-19; ☺ 11am-midnight Sun-Thu, 11am-1:30am Fri & Sat) There's a debate in town over who brews the best beer, Great Basin or Silver Peak. We're not picking sides, but we give extra points to Great Basin for its outdoorsy ambience, which includes a mountain scene splashed across the wall. Serves five flagship beers with 13 seasonal brews. Also has a nice selection of Belgian ales. It's 3 miles south of downtown on Virginia St.

Imperial Bar & Lounge BAR
(150 N Arlington Ave; ☺ 11am-2am Fri & Sat, to 10pm Sun-Thu) A classy bar inhabiting a relic of the past, this building was once an old bank, and in the middle of the wood floor you can see cement where the vault once stood. Sandwiches and pizzas go with 16 beers on tap and a buzzing weekend scene.

Jungle Java & Jungle Vino CAFE, WINE BAR
(www.javajunglevino.com; 246 W 1st St; ☺ coffee 6am-midnight, wine 3pm-midnight Mon-Fri, noon-midnight Sat & Sun; ☎) A side-by-side coffee shop and wine bar with a cool mosaic floor and an internet cafe all rolled into one.

☆ Entertainment

The free weekly **Reno News & Review** (www.newsreview.com) is your best source for listings.

Edge CLUB
(www.edgeofreno.com; 2707 S Virginia St, Pepper-mill; admission $10-20; ☺ from 9pm Thu & Sat, from 7pm Fri) The Peppermill reels in the night-hounds with a big glitzy dance club, where go-go dancers, smoke machines and laser lights may cause sensory overload. If so, step outside to the patio and relax in front of cozy fire pits.

Knitting Factory LIVE MUSIC
(☎ 775-323-5648; http://re.knittingfactory.com; 211 N Virginia St) This mid-sized venue opened in 2010, filling a gap in Reno's music scene with mainstream and indie favorites.

ⓘ Information

An information center sits near the baggage claim at Reno-Tahoe International Airport, which also has free wi-fi.

Reno-Sparks Convention & Visitors Authority Visitor Center (☎ 775-682-3800; www.visitrenotahoe.com; 135 N Sierra St; ☺ 9am-6pm) Inside the RENO eNVy store (get it?) in the Riverwalk District. Has brochures and maps and free parking with validation. Also has an airport desk.

ⓘ Getting There & Away

About 5 miles southeast of downtown, **Reno-Tahoe International Airport** (RNO; www.renoairport.com; ☎) is served by most major airlines.

The **North Lake Tahoe Express** (☎ 866-216-5222; www.northlaketahoeexpress.com) operates a shuttle ($45 one-way, about six to eight daily, 3:30am to midnight) to and from the airport to multiple North Shore Lake Tahoe locations including Truckee, Squaw Valley and Incline Village. Reserve in advance.

To reach South Lake Tahoe (weekdays only), take the wi-fi-equipped **RTC Intercity bus** (www.rtcwashoe.com) to the Nevada DOT stop in Carson City ($4, one hour, six per weekday) and then the **BlueGo** (www.bluego.org) 21X bus ($2 with RTC Intercity transfer, one hour, five to six daily) to the Stateline Transit Center.

Greyhound (☎ 775-322-2970; www.grey-hound.com; 155 Stevenson St) buses run daily service to Truckee, Sacramento and San Francisco ($11 to $41, five to seven hours), as does the once-daily westbound *California Zephyr* train route operated by **Amtrak** (☎ 800-872-7245, 775-329-8638; 280 N Center St). The train is slower and more expensive, but also more scenic and comfortable, with a bus connection from Emeryville for passengers to San Francisco ($60, eight hours).

ⓘ Getting Around

The casino hotels offer frequent free airport shuttles for their guests.

Local **RTC Ride buses** (☎ 775-348-7433; www.rtcwashoe.com; per ride $2, daily pass pre-paid/on-board $4/5) blanket the city, and most routes converge at the RTC 4th St Station downtown. Useful routes include the RTC Rapid line for Center St and S Virginia St, 11 for Sparks and 19 for the airport. The free Sierra Spirit bus, which has wi-fi, loops around all major downtown landmarks – including the casinos and the university – every 15 minutes from 7am to 7pm.

Carson City

This underrated town is an easy drive from Reno or Lake Tahoe, and it's a perfect stop for lunch and a stroll around the quiet, old-fashioned downtown.

The Kit Carson Blue Line Trail passes pretty historic buildings on pleasant tree-lined streets. Pick up a copy of the trail map at the visitor center (800-638-2321, 775-687-7410; www.visitcarsoncity.com; 1900 S Carson St; 8am-5pm Mon-Fri, 9am-5pm Sat & Sun), a mile south of downtown, or download it from the visitor center website.

Anchoring downtown is the 1870 Nevada State Capitol (cnr Musser & Carson; 8am-5pm Mon-Fri) FREE, where you might spot the governor himself chatting with one of his constituents. There's a small museum with state-related paraphernalia on the 2nd floor – check out that elk-antler chair. Ouch! Train buffs shouldn't miss the Nevada State Railroad Museum (775-687-6953; www.museuems.nevadaculture.org; 2180 S Carson St; adult/child $6/free; 9am-5pm Fri-Mon), which displays some 65 train cars and locomotives from the 1800s to the early 1900s.

Grab lunch at fetching Comma Coffee (www.commacoffee.com; 312 S Carson St; breakfast $6-8, lunch $8-10; 7am-8pm Mon & Wed-Thu, to 10pm Tue, Fri & Sat) and eavesdrop on the politicians. Or spend the evening at the locally owned microbrewery, High Sierra Brewing Company (www.highsierrabrewco.com; 302 N Carson St; mains $9-17; 11am-10pm Sun-Thu, to 2am Fri & Sat), for great beer and burgers.

Hwy 395/Carson St is the main drag. For hiking and camping information in the area, stop by the United States Forest Service (USFS) Carson Ranger District Office (775-882-2766; 1536 S Carson St; 8am-4:30pm Mon-Fri).

Virginia City

The discovery of the legendary Comstock Lode in 1859 sparked a silver bonanza in the mountains 25 miles south of Reno. During the 1860s gold rush, Virginia City was a high-flying, rip-roaring Wild West boomtown. Newspaperman Samuel Clemens, alias Mark Twain, spent some time in this raucous place during its heyday; years later his eyewitness descriptions of mining life were published in a book called *Roughing It*.

The high-elevation town is a National Historic Landmark, with a main street of Victorian buildings, wooden sidewalks and some hokey but fun museums. To see how the mining elite lived, stop by the Mackay Mansion (775-847-0173; 129 South D St; adult/child $5/free; 10am-5pm in summer, vary in winter) and the Castle (B St). Mark Twain's desk and, er, toilet, are among a haphazard collection of artifacts in the Mark Twain Museum at The Territorial Enterprise (53 South C St; adult/child $4/3; 10am-5pm) in the old newspaper press room. The basement level space survived the devastating 1878 town fire.

Locals agree that the best food in Virginia City is probably at Cafe del Rio (www.cafedelriovc.com; 394 S C St; dinner $19-15, brunch $9.25-14; 11am--8pm Wed-Sat, 10am-7pm Sun), serving a nice blend of *nuevo* Mexican and good cafe food, including breakfast. Wet your whistle at the longtime family-run Bucket of Blood Saloon (www.bucketofbloodsaloonvc.com; 1 S C St; 9am-7pm Sun-Thu, to 9pm Fri & Sat), which serves up beer and 'bar rules' at its antique wooden bar ('If the bartender doesn't laugh, you are not funny').

The main drag is C St, where you'll find the visitor center (800-718-7587, 775-847-7500; www.visitvirginiacitynv.com; 86 S C St; 10am-5pm).

Nevada Great Basin

A trip across Nevada's Great Basin is a serene, almost haunting experience. But those on the quest for the 'Great American Road Trip' will relish the fascinating historic towns and quirky diversions tucked away along lonely desert highways.

Along I-80

Heading east from Reno, Winnemucca, 150 miles to the northeast, is the first worthwhile stop. It boasts a vintage downtown and a number of Basque restaurants, along with a yearly Basque festival. For information, stop by the Winnemucca Visitor Center (775-623-5071, 800 962 2638; www.winnemucca.com; 30 W Winnemucca Blvd; 8am-5pm Mon-Fri). Check out the displays here, like a buckaroo (cowboy) hall of fame and big-game museum. Don't miss the Griddle (www.thegriddlecom; 460 W Winnemucca Blvd; mains $10-15; 6am-2pm), one of Nevada's

CATHEDRAL GORGE STATE PARK

Awe, then *ahhh*. Cathedral Gorge State Park (☎775-728-4460; www.parks.nv.gov/parks/cathedral-gorge; Hwy 93; entry $7, tent & RV sites $17; ☺visitor center 9am-4:30pm) really does feel like you've stepped into a magnificent, many-spired cathedral, albeit one whose dome is a view of the sky. Sleep under the stars at the first-come, first-served tent & RV sites ($17) set amid badlands-style cliffs.

best retro cafes, serving up fantastic breakfasts, diner classics and homemade desserts since 1948.

The culture of the American West is most diligently cultivated in Elko. Aspiring cowboys and cowgirls should visit the Western Folklife Center (www.westernfolklife.org; 501 Railroad St; adult/child $5/1; ☺10am-5:30pm Mon-Fri, 10am-5pm Sat), which offers art and history exhibits, musical jams, dance nights and also hosts the popular Cowboy Poetry Gathering each January. Elko also holds a National Basque Festival every July 4, with games, traditional dancing and a 'Running of the Bulls' event. If you've never sampled Basque food, the best place in town for your inaugural experience is the Star Hotel (www.elkostarhotel.com; 246 Silver St; lunch $6-12, dinner $15-32; ☺11am-2pm & 5-9pm Mon-Fri, 4:30-9:30pm Sat), a family-style supper club located in a circa-1910 boardinghouse for Basque sheepherders.

Along Highway 50

In Nevada, the transcontinental Hwy 50 is better known by its nickname, 'The Loneliest Road in America.' It cuts across the heart of the state, connecting Carson City in the west to Great Basin National Park in the east. It was once part of the Lincoln Hwy and follows the route of the Overland Stagecoach, the Pony Express and the first transcontinental telegraph line. Towns are few, and the only sounds are the hum of the engine or the whisper of wind.

About 25 miles southeast of Fallon, the Sand Mountain Recreation Area (☎775-885-6000; www.blm.gov/nv; admission free for brief, non-motorized use; ☺24hr) FREE is worth a stop for a look at its 600ft sand dune and

the ruins of a Pony Express station. Just east, enjoy a juicy burger at an old stagecoach stop, Middlegate Station (42500 Austin Hwy) then toss your sneakers onto the new Shoe Tree on the north side of Hwy 50 just ahead (the old one was cut down).

A fitting reward for surviving Hwy 50 is the awesome, uncrowded Great Basin National Park (☎775-234-7331; www.nps.gov/grba; ☺24hr) FREE. Near the Nevada–Utah border, it's home to 13,063ft Wheeler Peak, which rises abruptly from the desert. Hiking trails near the summit take in superb country with glacial lakes, ancient bristlecone pines and even a permanent ice field. In summer, the Great Basin Visitor Center (☎775-234-7331; www.nps.gov/grba; ☺8am-4:30pm Jun-Aug), just north of the town of Baker, is the place to get oriented.

For a 60- or 90-minute guided tour of the caves here, which are richly decorated with rare limestone formations, head to the year-round Lehman Caves Visitor Center (☎775-234-7331, tour reservations 775-234-7517; www.nps.gov/grba; adult $8-10, child $4-5; ☺8am-4:30 pm, tours 8:30am-4pm) five miles outside of Baker. Reservations recommended. In warmer months, drive 12 scenic miles to the Wheeler Peak summit. There are five first-come, first-served developed campgrounds (☎775-234-7331; www.nps.gove/grba; primitive camping free, tent & RV sites $12) in the park.

Along Highway 95

Hwy 95 runs roughly north–south through the western part of the state; the southern section is starkly scenic as it passes the Nevada Test Site (where more than 720 nuclear weapons were exploded in the 1950s).

Along Highways 375 & 93

Hwy 375 is dubbed the 'Extraterrestrial Hwy' because of the huge number of UFO sightings along this stretch and because it intersects Hwy 93 near top-secret Area 51, part of Nellis Air Force Base and a supposed holding area for captured UFOs. Some people may find Hwy 375 more unnerving than the Loneliest Road; it's a desolate stretch of pavement and cars are few and far between. In the tiny town of Rachel, on Hwy 375, Little A'Le'Inn (☎775-729-2515; www.littlealeinn.com; 1 Old Mill Rd, Alamo; RV sites with hookups $15, r $35-150; ☺restaurant 8am-9pm; ✳☎☺☺) accommodates earthlings and aliens alike, and sells extraterrestrial souvenirs. Probings not included.

ARIZONA

The nation's 6th-largest state is dotted with stunning works of nature: the Grand Canyon, Monument Valley, the Chiricahua Mountains, and the red rocks of Sedona, to name a few. In the shadows of these icons, a compelling cast of settlers and explorers tried to tame Arizona's wilds, building prehistoric irrigation canals through desert scrub, mapping the labyrinth of canyons and mining the state's underground riches. Gorgeous backroads link these natural and historic sites, making Arizona a prime destination for roadtrippers.

Greater Phoenix, ringed by mountains, is one of the biggest metro areas in the Southwest. It has the eateries, sights and glorious spas you'd expect in a spot that stakes its claim on rest and renewal. Tucson is the funky, artsy gateway to southern Arizona's astronomical and historical sights. Only 60 miles from the Mexican border, it embraces its cross-border heritage.

History

Arizona was the last territory in the Lower 48 to become a state, and it celebrated its centennial in 2012. Why did it take so long for a territory filled with copper and ranchland to join the Union? Arizonans were seen as troublemakers by the federal government, and for years acquiring their riches wasn't worth the potential trouble.

Cynics might say that Arizonans are still making trouble. In 2010, Arizona's legislature passed the most restrictive anti-immigration law in the nation, known as SB 1070. The controversial bill was passed soon after the mysterious shooting death of a popular rancher near the Mexican border.

The US Supreme Court recently struck down several sections of the hot-button law but retained the provision stating that an officer can try to determine the immigration status of a person who as been stopped, as long as the officer has a reasonable suspicion that the person is here illegally. At press time, implementation of the provision is facing legal challenge.

The state was shaken in 2011 by the shooting of Democratic Congresswoman Gabrielle Giffords during a public appearance. She was critically injured and six bystanders and staff members were killed.

An ongoing statewide fiscal crisis led to deep cuts for the state park system, forcing many parks to join forces with non-profit groups and local governments for funding.

ℹ Information

Arizona is on Mountain Standard Time but is the only western state that does not observe daylight saving time from spring to early fall. The exception is the Navajo Reservation, which *does* observe daylight saving time.

Generally speaking, lodging rates in southern Arizona (including Phoenix, Tucson and Yuma) are much higher in winter and spring, which are considered the 'high season.' Great deals are to be had in the hot areas at the height of summer.

Arizona Department of Transportation (☑ in-state 511, 888-411-7623; www.az511.com) Updates on road conditions and traffic statewide, with links to weather and safety information.

Arizona Office of Tourism (☑ 602-364-3700; www.arizonaguide.com) Free state information.

Arizona Public Lands Information Center (☑ 602-417-9200; www.publiclands.org) Information about USFS, NPS, Bureau of Land Management (BLM) and state lands and parks.

Arizona State Parks (☑ 602-542-4174; www.azstateparks.com) Fifteen state parks have

---

ARIZONA FACTS

Nickname Grand Canyon State

Population 6.5 million

Area 113,637 sq miles

Capital city Phoenix (population 1.48 million)

Other cities Tucson (population 524,000), Flagstaff (population 67,400), Sedona (population 10,000)

Sales tax 6.6%

Birthplace of Apache chief Geronimo (1829–1909), political activist Cesar Chavez (1927–93), singer Linda Ronstadt (b 1946)

Home of Sedona New Age movement, mining towns turned art colonies

Politics Majority vote Republican

Famous for Grand Canyon, saguaro cacti

Best souvenir Pink cactus-shaped neon lamp from roadside stall

Driving distances Phoenix to Grand Canyon Village: 235 miles, Tucson to Sedona: 230 miles

campgrounds. Online reservations are available for all of them, with a $5 reservation fee. (campsites $15 to $50, cabins and yurts $35 to $75).

Phoenix

Despite the heat, Phoenix has a bit of spring in its step. The city, which is hosting the 2015 Super Bowl, is welcoming guests these days to its new downtown dining-and-entertainment district, Cityscape. And the city-to-airport rail line, the SkyTrain, opened ahead of schedule.

Several 'towns' make up the region known as Greater Phoenix, which is the largest urban area in the Southwest. The City of Phoenix, with its downtown high-rises and top-notch museums, is the patriarch of the bunch. Scottsdale is the stylish big sister who married up, Tempe the good-natured but occasionally rowdy college kid, and Mesa is the brother who wants a quiet life in the suburbs. And mom? She left for Flagstaff in June because it's just too darn hot.

How hot? In summer temperatures reach above 110°F (43°C). Resort rates drop dramatically, which is great for travelers on a budget, but the most popular time to visit is winter and spring, when pleasant days prevail.

◉ Sights

Greater Phoenix, also known as the Valley of the Sun, is ringed by mountains that range from 2500ft to more than 7000ft in elevation. Central Ave runs north–south through Phoenix, dividing west addresses from east addresses; Washington St runs

CACTUS LEAGUE SPRING TRAINING

Before the start of the major league baseball season, teams spend March in Arizona (Cactus League) and Florida (Grapefruit League) auditioning new players, practicing and playing games. Tickets are cheaper (from about $8 to $10 depending on venue), the seats better, the lines shorter and the games more relaxed. Check www.cactus-league.com for schedules and links for purchasing tickets, or www.visitphoenix.com for a summary of team and ticket information.

west–east, dividing north addresses from south addresses.

Scottsdale, Tempe and Mesa are east of the airport. Scottsdale Rd runs north–south between Scottsdale and Tempe. The airport is 3 miles southeast of downtown.

◎ Phoenix

★ Heard Museum   MUSEUM
(☑ 602-252-8848; www.heard.org; 2301 N Central Ave; adult/child 6-12 yr & student/senior $18/7.50/13.50; ⊙ 9:30am-5pm Mon-Sat, 11am-5pm Sun; ⊛) This private museum opened in 1929 when Dwight and Maie Bartlett Heard decided to share their extensive collection of Native American artifacts. Today, across 10 galleries, the museum displays Native American art, textiles, and ceramics, and spotlights Native American history and traditions. The focus is Southwestern tribes.

Check out the kachina (Hopi spirit doll) collection as well as the 'Boarding School Experience' gallery, a moving look at the controversial federal policy of removing Native American children from their families and sending them to remote boarding schools to Americanize them.

Musical Instrument Museum   MUSEUM
(☑ 480-478-6000; www.themim.org; 4725 E Mayo Blvd; adult $18, teen 13-19 yr $14, child $10; ⊙ 9am-5pm Mon-Sat, 10am-5pm Sun, to 9pm first Fri of the month) From Ugandan thumb pianos to Hawaiian ukuleles to an Indonesian gong, the ears have it at this new museum that celebrates the world's musical instruments. More than 200 countries and territories are represented within five regional galleries, where music and video performances automatically start as you stop beside individual displays.

The free-to-use wireless headsets are a necessity, but they are very easy to operate. Just don't walk too quickly between the Alice Cooper exhibit and the Fife & Drums display in the United States gallery – your head will spin! To get to the museum from downtown, follow Hwy 51 north to Hwy 101 east. From 101, take exit 31. Turn right onto N Tatum Blvd and then turn right just ahead and you're there.

★ Desert Botanical Garden   GARDENS
(☑ 480-941-1225; www.dbg.org; 1201 N Galvin Pkwy; adult/child/student/senior $18/8/10/15; ⊙ 8am-8pm Oct-Apr, 7am-8pm May-Sep) On 145 acres, this inspirational garden is a refresh-

ing place to reconnect with nature and offers a great introduction to desert plant life. Looping trails lead past an astonishing variety of desert denizens arranged by theme, including a desert wildflower loop and a Sonoran Desert nature loop. Check for special seasonal events like the summer flashlight tours (7pm Tuesday and Saturday June to August).

★ Phoenix Art Museum   MUSEUM
(☑602-257-1222; www.phxart.org; 1625 N Central Ave; adult/child 6-17yr/student/senior $15/6/10/12, free 3-9pm Wed & 1st Fri of the month 6-10pm; ⊙10am-9pm Wed, 10am-5pm Thu-Sat, noon-5pm Sun; ⊕) The Phoenix Art Museum is Arizona's premier repository of fine art. Galleries include works by Claude Monet, Diego Rivera and Georgia O'Keeffe. Landscapes in the Western American gallery set the tone for adventure.

◉ Scottsdale

Scottsdale's main draw is its popular shopping districts, which include Old Town, known for its early-20th-century buildings (and others built to look old), and the adjacent Arts District. The neighborhoods are stuffed with art galleries, clothing stores for the modern cowgirl, and some of the best eating and drinking in the Valley of the Sun.

Taliesin West   ARCHITECTURE
(☑480-860-2700; www.franklloydwright.org; 12621 Frank Lloyd Wright Blvd; ⊙9am-4pm Tue & Wed Jul & Aug) Taliesin West was Frank Lloyd Wright's desert home and studio, built between 1938 and 1940. Still home to an architecture school and open to the public for guided tours, it's a prime example of organic architecture with buildings incorporating elements and structures found in surrounding nature. To see the house and grounds, you must take a tour. The 90-minute Insights Tour (adult/4-12yr/student & senior $32/17/28; ⊙half-hourly 9am-4pm Nov–mid-Apr, hourly 9am-4pm mid-Apr–Oct) is both informative and quick-moving. Shorter and longer tours are also available; see website for prices and times.

◉ Tempe

Founded in 1885 and home to around 58,000 students, Arizona State University (ASU; www.asu.edu) is the heart and soul of Tempe. The Gammage Auditorium (☑box

SCENIC DRIVES: ARIZONA'S BEST
....

Oak Creek Canyon A thrilling plunge past swimming holes, rockslides and crimson canyon walls on Hwy 89A between Flagstaff and Sedona.

Hwy 89/89A Wickenburg to Sedona The Old West meets the New West on this lazy drive past dude ranches, mining towns, art galleries and stylish wineries.

Patagonia–Sonoita Scenic Road This one's for the birds, and those who like to track them, in Arizona's southern wine country on Hwys 82 and 83.

Kayenta–Monument Valley Become the star of your own Western on an iconic loop past cinematic red rocks in Navajo country just off Hwy 163.

Vermilion Cliffs Scenic Road A solitary drive on Hwy 89A through the Arizona Strip linking condor country, the North Rim and Mormon hideaways.

office 480-965-3434, tours 480-965-6912; www.asugammage.com; cnr Mill Ave & Apache Blvd; tickets from $20; ⊙1-4pm Mon-Fri Oct-May) was Frank Lloyd Wright's last major building.

Easily accessible by light-rail from downtown Phoenix, Mill Avenue, Tempe's main drag, is packed with chain restaurants, themed bars and other collegiate hangouts. While visiting, it's worth checking out Tempe Town Lake (www.tempe.gov/lake), an artificial lake with boat rides and paths perfect for strolling or biking its fringes. At Cox Splash Playground (⊙10am-7pm Apr-Sep; ⊕) at the beach park, kids love to frolic under the oversized sprinklers.

◉ Mesa

Founded by Mormons in 1877, low-key Mesa is one of the fastest-growing cities in the nation and is the third-largest city in Arizona, with a population of 452,000.

Arizona Museum of
Natural History   MUSEUM
(☑480-644-2230; www.azmnh.org; 53 N MacDonald St; adult/child 3-12yr/student/senior $10/6/8/9; ⊙10am-5pm Tue-Fri, 11am-5pm Sat, 1-5pm Sun; ⊕) Worth a trip if your kids are into dinosaurs (aren't they all?). In addition

Phoenix

to the multilevel Dinosaur Mountain, there are loads of life-sized casts of the giant beasts plus a touchable Apatosaurus thighbone. Other exhibits highlight Arizona's colorful past, from a prehistoric Hohokam village to an eight-cell territorial jail.

🏃 Activities

Find trail information for Piestewa Peak, South Mountain Park, Camelback Park and others at http://phoenix.gov/recreation/rec/ parks/preserves/index.html.

Piestewa Peak/Dreamy Draw Recreation Area   HIKING
(☑602-261-8318; www.phoenix.gov/parks; Squaw Peak Dr, Phoenix; ⊙trails 5am-11pm, last entry 6:59pm) Previously known as Squaw Peak, this easy-to-access viewpoint was renamed for local Native American soldier Lori Piestewa, killed in Iraq in 2003. The trek to the 2608ft summit is hugely popular and

the saguaro-dotted park can get jammed on winter weekends. Dogs are allowed on some trails.

South Mountain Park   HIKING
(☑602-262-7393; 10919 S Central Ave, Phoenix; ⊙5am-11pm, last entry 6:59pm) The 51-mile trail network (leashed dogs allowed) dips through canyons, over grassy hills and past granite walls, offering city views and access to Native American petroglyphs.

Cactus Adventures   BIKING
(☑480-688-4743; www.cactusadventures.com; half-day rental from $45; ⊙hours vary) Cactus Adventures rents bikes and offers guided hiking and biking tours. Will deliver bikes to South Mountain trailhead or Arizona Grand Resort; flexible with pick-up times for bikes.

Ponderosa Stables   HORSEBACK RIDING
(☑602-268-1261; www.arizona-horses.com; 10215 S Central Ave, Phoenix; 1/2hr rides $33/55;

Camelback Mountain Echo
Canyon Recreation Area
16
Camelback Rd
37
22
33
7
17
14 10
30
27
Indian School Rd
Osborn Rd
Jokake Rd
56th St
52nd St
Arizona Canal
76th St
68th St
Scottsdale Rd

1
Desert
Botanical
Garden
Papago
Park &
Golf Course
Roosevelt St
McKellips Rd
Curry Rd
Mill Ave
Galvin Pkwy

8
3rd St
5th St
TEMPE
Tempe Town Lake
11

52nd St
Priest Dr
Hardy Dr
20
6
5
Apache Blvd
28
E 8th St

⊙6am-5pm Jun-Sep, 8am-5pm rest of year) This outfitter leads rides through South Mountain Park. Reservations required for most trips.

Tours

Arizona Detours SIGHTSEEING
(☑866-438-6877; www.detoursaz.com) Leads day tours to far-flung locations such as Tombstone (adult/child $145/75) and the Grand Canyon (adult/child $155/90), and a half-day Phoenix/Scottsdale tour (adult/child $80/45).

Arizona Outback Adventures HIKING
(☑480-945-2881; www.aoa-adventures.com; 16447 N 91st St, Scottsdale) Offers half-day trips for hiking ($95, minimum two people), mountain biking ($115, minimum two people), and Salt River kayaking ($150, minimum two people).

⚞ Festivals & Events

Tostitos Fiesta Bowl SPORTS
(☑480-350-0911; www.fiestabowl.org) Held in early January at the University of Phoenix Stadium in Glendale, this football game is preceded by massive celebrations and parades.

Sleeping

Greater Phoenix is well stocked with hotels and resorts, but you won't find many B&Bs or cozy inns. Prices plummet in the scorching summer, a time when Valley residents take advantage of super-low prices at their favorite resorts.

Phoenix

HI Phoenix Hostel HOSTEL $
(☑602-254-9803; www.phxhostel.org; 1026 N 9th St; dm from $20, s/d $37/47; ⊛@⏾) This inviting 14-bed hostel sits in a working-class residential neighborhood and has relaxing garden nooks. The owners are fun, and they know Phoenix. Check-in is from 8am to 10am (until noon Friday and Saturday) and 5pm to 10pm. Closed July and August. No credit cards.

Budget Lodge Downtown MOTEL $
(☑602-254-7247; www.blphx.com; 402 W Van Buren St; r incl breakfast $60-67; ⓟ⊛⏾) In the heart of downtown, this simple, two-story motel is a clean, low-cost place to lay your head, and it provides the most important amenities: a microwave and fridge in every room, and complimentary breakfast.

Aloft Phoenix-Airport HOTEL $$
(☑602-275-6300; www.aloftphoenixairport.com; 4450 E Washington St; r $109-149; ⓟ@⏾⏾⏾) Rooms blend a pop-art sensibility with the cleanest edges of modern design. The hotel is near Tempe and across the street from the Pueblo Grand Museum. No extra fee for pets.

Palomar Phoenix HOTEL $$$
(☑877-488-1908, 602-253-6633; www.hotelpalomar-phoenix.com; 2 E Jefferson St; r $349-359; ⓟ⊛⏾⏾⏾) Shaggy pillows, antler-shaped lamps and portraits of blue cows. Yep, whimsy takes a stand at the new, 242-room Palomar, and we like it. Rooms, which are larger than average, pop with modern style and come with a yoga mat and animal-print robes. You can relax in style at the

SOUTHWEST PHOENIX

Phoenix

3rd-floor outdoor pool and lounge, with nice views of downtown. The hotel anchors the new CityScape dining and entertainment district. Rates are slightly lower on weekends.

Royal Palms Resort & Spa   RESORT $$$

(☑ 602-840-3610; www.royalpalmsresortandspa. com; 5200 E Camelback Rd; r $333-423, ste from $342-519; 🅿 ❋ @ 🛜 🏊 🐾) This posh boutique resort at the base of Camelback Mountain is a hushed and elegant place, dotted with Spanish Colonial villas, flower-lined walkways, and palms imported from Egypt. Pets are pampered with soft beds, personalized biscuits and walking services. There's a $34 daily resort fee.

🛏 Scottsdale

Sleep Inn   HOTEL $$

(☑ 480-998-9211; www.sleepinnscottsdale.com; 16630 N Scottsdale Rd; r incl breakfast $139-159; 🅿 ❋ @ 🛜 🐾) This outpost of the national chain in North Scottsdale wins points for its extensive breakfast, friendly staff and proximity to Taliesin West. Rooms have microwaves and refrigerators.

Saguaro Inn   HOTEL $$

(☑ 480-308-1100; www.jdvhotels.com; 4000 N Drinkwater Blvd; r $189; 🅿 ❋ 🛜 🏊 🐾) Embrace your inner hipster at this candy-bright hideaway beside Old Town. The vibe skews young and attention to detail may sometimes be lacking, but the location is great, palm trees surround the pool and the rate is lower than neighborhood competitors.

★ Hotel Valley Ho   BOUTIQUE HOTEL $$$

(☑ 480-248-2000; www.hotelvalleyho.com; 6850 E Main St; r $249-299, ste $399-509; 🅿 ❋ @ 🛜 🏊 🐾) Everything's swell at the Valley Ho, a jazzy joint that once bedded Bing Crosby, Natalie Wood and Janet Leigh. Today, bebop music, upbeat front staff and the 'ice fireplace' recapture the Rat Pack–era vibe, and the theme travels well to the balconied rooms. Pets stay free; wi-fi is complimentary for 12 hours per day.

Bespoke Inn, Cafe & Bicycles   B&B $$$

(☑ 480-664-0730; www.bespokeinn.com; 3701 N Marshall Way; r from $299; 🅿 ❋ 🛜 🏊 🐾) Ooh la la. Are we in the French countryside or downtown Scottsdale? At this breezy new B&B guests can sip coffee in the chic cafe, loll in the infinity edge pool, or pedal the neighborhood on Pashley city bikes. Rooms are plush with handsome touches like handcrafted furniture and nickel bath fixtures. Gourmet breakfasts are served around a communal farm table. From $199 in summer.

Boulders RESORT $$$
(✆480-488-9009; www.theboulders.com; 34631 N Tom Darlington Dr, Carefree; casitas $319-369, villas $599-1149; P✿@⊛⊠) Blending nearly imperceptibly into a landscape of natural rock formations, this escape-the-city retreat is simultaneously sumptuous and laid-back. Everything here is calculated to take the edge off travel. Extra stressed? Enjoy a session at the ultraposh on-site spa. Daily resort fee is $30. Weekend rates can drop as low as $125 in summer.

Tempe

Best Western Inn of Tempe HOTEL $
(✆480-784-2233; www.innoftempe.com; 670 N Scottsdale Rd; r incl breakfast $89-99; P✿@ ⊛⊠) This well-kept, helpful hotel is within walking distance of Tempe Town Lake and close to ASU and lively Mill Ave. Has 24-hour airport shuttle.

★**Sheraton Wild Horse Pass Resort & Spa** RESORT $$$
(✆602-225-0100; www.wildhorsepassresort.com; 5594 W Wild Horse Pass Blvd, Chandler; r $209-279, ste $284-520, mains $44-54; P✿@⊛⊠) Scan the horizon for the namesake wild horses at this striking property, designed by the Gila River tribe as a luxurious place to soak up the best of Native American healing and wisdom. This oasis has comfortable rooms, spacious common areas, fine dining, two 18-hole golf courses, an equestrian center, tennis courts, a spa and a water slide modeled after Hohokam ruins.

✖ Eating

The Phoenix-Scottsdale area has the largest selection of restaurants in the Southwest. To sample a variety of Arizona's finest foods, stop by Food Truck Friday (www.phxstreetfood.org; 721 N Central ave, Phoenix Public Market, downtown; ⊙11am-1:30pm Fri) at the Phoenix Public Market downtown.

★**Matt's Big Breakfast** BREAKFAST $
(✆602-254-1074; www.mattsbigbreakfast.com; 825 N 1st St, at Garfield St; breakfast $5-10, lunch $7-10; ⊙6:30am-2:30pm) Matt re-opened his legendary breakfast joint in a bigger location down the block from its old digs, but folks still cluster on the sidewalk to wait for a table. Regular menu items are great, but daily specials, such as eggs scrambled with peppers and chorizo into fluffy-spicy-ohmygoodness on a bed of mouth-watering crispy homefries, are supremely yummy.

Tee Pee Mexican Food MEXICAN $
(✆602-956-0178; www.teepeemexicanfood.com; 4144 E Indian School Rd; mains $5-14; ⊙11am-10pm Mon-Sat, to 9pm Sun) If you like piping-hot plates piled high with cheesy, messy American-style Mexican fare then grab a booth at this 40-year-old fave. When George W Bush ate here in 2004, he ordered two cheese and onion enchiladas, rice and beans – now called the Presidential Special.

La Grande Orange Grocery CAFE $
(www.lagrandeorangegrocery.com; 4410 N 40th St; breakfast under $8, lunch $7-9, pizza $12-15; ⊙cafe 6:30am-10pm, pizzeria from 4pm Mon-Thu, from 11am Fri & Sat) Take away a muffin and coffee for breakfast, pop in for a guacamole BLT at lunch or nibble margherita pizza at dinner. This bustling gourmet market, bakery, cafe and pizzeria sits at the corner of 40th St and and E Campbell Ave.

★**Dick's Hideaway** NEW MEXICAN $$
(✆602-241-1881; http://richardsonsnm.com; 6008 N 16th St; breakfast $5-20, lunch $12-16, dinner $12-35; ⊙7am-midnight Sun-Wed, to 1am Thu-Sat) Grab a table beside the bar or join the communal table in the side room and settle in for hearty servings of savory, chile-slathered enchiladas, tamales and other New Mexican cuisine. We especially like the Hideaway for breakfast, when the Bloody Marys arrive with a shot of beer. The unmarked entrance is between the towering shrubs.

Pizzeria Bianco PIZZERIA $$
(✆602-258-8300; www.pizzeriabianco.com; 623 E Adams St; pizza $12-16; ⊙11am-9pm Mon, 11am-10pm Tue-Sat) The dining room is small and the menu short, but flavors are big and savory at this famed eatery run by James Beard winner Chris Bianco. In thin crust, wood-fired pies include the Rosa, with red onion, parmesan, rosemary and Arizona pistachios, and the Wiseguy with wood-roasted onions, house-smoked mozzarella and fennel sausage.

SOUTHWEST PHOENIX

Beckett's Table NEW AMERICAN $$
(☑602-954-1700; www.beckettstable.com; 3717 E
Indian School Rd; mains $13-21; ⏰5-10pm Tue-Sat,
5-9pm Sun) Enjoy a country supper in the
village's most stylish barn, complete with
concrete floor, trussed beams and wooden
accents. The urban farm concept really
shines as you savor chef Justin Beckett's locally sourced dishes, from tender pork *osso
bucco* to short ribs with mashed potatoes.
Don't miss the bacon cheddar biscuit with
candied jalapeno apple butter. Dining solo?
Join the conversation at the black-walnut
communal table.

Durant's STEAKHOUSE $$$
(☑602-264-5967; 2611 N Central Ave; lunch $10-
30, dinner $20-50; ⏰11am-4pm Mon-Fri, dinner
daily) This dark and manly place is a gloriously old-school steakhouse. You will get
steak. It will be big and juicy. There will
be a potato. The ambience is awesome
too: cozy red-velvet booths and the sense
the Rat Pack is going to waltz in at any
minute.

PHOENIX FOR CHILDREN

Wet 'n' Wild Phoenix (☑623-201-
2000; www.wetnwildphoenix.com; 4243
W Pinnacle Peak Rd, Glendale; over/under
42in tall $39/30, senior $30; ⏰10am-6pm
Sun-Wed, 10am-10pm Thu-Sat, varies May,
Aug & Sep; ♿) water park has pools,
tube slides, wave pools, waterfalls and
floating rivers. It's in Glendale, 2 miles
west of I-17 at exit 217.

At the re-created 1880s frontier
town **Rawhide Western Town &
Steakhouse** (☑480-502-5600; www.
rawhide.com; 5700 W N Loop Rd, Chandler;
admission free, per attraction or show $5,
unlimited day pass $15; ⏰5-10pm Wed-
Sun, varies seasonally; ♿), about 20
miles south of Mesa, kids can enjoy all
sorts of hokey-but-fun shenanigans.
The steakhouse has rattlesnake for
adventurous eaters.

Arizona Science Center (☑602-
716-2000; www.azscience.org; 600 E
Washington St; adult/child 3-17 yr/senior
$15/11/13; ⏰10am-5pm; ♿) is a high-
tech temple of discovery; there are
more than 300 hands-on exhibits and a
planetarium.

Scottsdale

Sugar Bowl ICE CREAM $
(☑480-946-0051; www.sugarbowlscottsdale.com;
4005 N Scottsdale Rd; ice cream $2.25-9, mains $6-
12; ⏰11am-10pm Sun-Thu, 11am-midnight Fri & Sat;
♿) This pink-and-white Valley institution
has been working its ice-cream magic since
the '50s. For more substantial fare, there's a
whole menu of sandwiches and salads.

The Mission MEXICAN $$
(☑480-636-5005; www.themissionaz.com; 3815
N Brown Ave; lunch $9-12, dinner $12-32; ⏰11am-
3pm & 5-10pm Sun-Thu, to 11pm Fri & Sat) With
its dark interior, glowing votives and religious icons, this *nuevo* Latin spot looks very
15th-century, but sunny patios with orange
umbrellas keep the vibe light. For a satisfying lunch, try the steak taco with green chile
salsa, avocado and tecate-marinated beef.
The guacamole is made table-side. Margaritas and mojitos round out the fun.

Herb Box AMERICAN $$
(☑480-289-6160; www.theherbbox.com; 7134 E
Stetson Dr; lunch $10-19, dinner $15-28; ⏰lunch
daily, dinner Tue-Sat) It's not just about sparkle and air kisses at this chichi bistro. It's
also about fresh, regional ingredients, artful
presentation and attentive service.

Tempe

★ Essence CAFE $
(☑480-966-2745; 825 W University Dr; breakfast
$5-9, lunch $7.25-9; ⏰7am-3pm Mon-Sat; ♿) This
breezy box of deliciousness serves egg dishes
and French toast at breakfast, and salads,
gourmet sandwiches and a few Mediterranean specialties at lunch. The iced caramel
coffee and the macaroons make a nice mid-
afternoon reward.

★ Kai Restaurant NATIVE AMERICAN $$$
(☑602-225-0100; www.wildhorsepassresort.com;
5594 W Wild Horse Pass Blvd, Chandler; mains $44-
54, tasting menus $135-$225; ⏰5-9pm Tue-Thu,
to 9:30pm Fri & Sat) Simple ingredients from
mainly Native American farms and ranches
are turned into something extraordinary.
Dinners are like fine tapestries with dishes –
such as the pecan-crusted Colorado lamb
with native seeds mole – striking just the
right balance between adventure and comfort. Dress nicely (no shorts or hats). It's at
the Sheraton Wild Horse Pass Resort & Spa
on the Gila River Indian Reservation. Kai
closes for one month in August.

🍷 Drinking

Scottsdale has the greatest concentration of trendy bars and clubs; Tempe attracts the student crowd.

★ Postino Winecafé Arcadia   WINE BAR
(www.postinowinecafe.com; 3939 E Campbell Ave, at 40th St, Phoenix; ⏰ 11am-11pm Mon-Thu, 11am-midnight Fri, 9am-midnight Sat, 9am-10pm Sun) This convivial, indoor-outdoor wine bar is a perfect gathering spot for a few friends ready to enjoy the good life, but solos will do fine too. Highlights include the misting patio, rave-inducing bruschetta and $5 wines by the glass from 11am to 5pm.

Edge Bar   BAR
(5700 E McDonald Dr, Sanctuary on Camelback Mountain, Paradise Valley) Enjoy a sunset 'on the edge' at this stylish cocktail bar perched on the side of Camelback Mountain at the Sanctuary resort. No room outside? The equally posh, big-windowed Jade Bar should do just fine. Complimentary valet.

Four Peaks Brewing Company   BREWERY
(📞 480-303-9967; www.fourpeaks.com; 1340 E 8th St, Tempe; ⏰ 11am-2am Mon-Sat, 10am-2am Sun) So this is where everybody is. Beer-lovers are in for a treat at this quintessential neighborhood brewpub in a cool Mission Revival–style building.

Rusty Spur Saloon   BAR
(📞 480-425-7787; www.rustyspursaloon.com; 7245 E Main St, Scottsdale; ⏰ 10am-1am Sun-Thu, to 2am Fri & Sat) Nobody's putting on airs at this fun-lovin', pack-'em-in-tight country bar where the grizzled Budweiser crowd gathers for cheap drinks and twangy country bands; check the website to see who's playing. It's in an old bank building that closed during the Depression.

☆ Entertainment

The Phoenix Symphony Orchestra (📞 administration 602-495-1117, box office 602-495-1999; www.phoenixsymphony.org; 75 N 2nd St, box offices 1 N 1st St, 75 N 2nd St) performs at Symphony Hall (75 N 2nd St). In 2013, the Arizona Opera (📞 602-266-7464; www.azopera.com; 1636 N Central Ave) moved into a new opera hall across the street from the Phoenix Art Museum

The men's basketball team, the Phoenix Suns (📞 602-379-7900; www.nba.com/suns; 201 E Jefferson St, Phoenix), and the women's team, the Phoenix Mercury (📞 602-252-9622; www.

wnba.com/mercury; 201 E Jefferson St, Phoenix), play at the US Airways Center. The Arizona Cardinals (📞 602-379-0101; www.azcardinals.com; 1 Cardinals Dr, Glendale) football team plays in Glendale at the new University of Phoenix Stadium, which will host the Super Bowl in 2015. The Arizona Diamondbacks (📞 602-462-6500; www.arizona.diamondbacks.mlb.com; 401 E Jefferson St, Phoenix) play baseball at Chase Field.

Rhythm Room   LIVE MUSIC
(📞 602-265-4842; www.rhythmroom.com; 1019 E Indian School Rd, Phoenix; ⏰ doors usually open 7:30pm) Some of the Valley's best live acts take the stage at this small venue, where you pretty much feel like you're in the front row of every gig. It tends to attract more local and regional talent than the big names, which suits us just fine.

Char's Has the Blues   BLUES
(📞 602-230-0205; www.charshastheblues.com; 4631 N 7th Ave, Phoenix; Mon-Wed no cover, Thu & Sun $3, Fri & Sat $7; ⏰ 8pm-1am Sun-Wed, 7:30pm-1am Thu-Sat) Dark and intimate, but very welcoming, this blues and R & B cottage packs 'em in with solid acts most nights of the week, but somehow still manages to feel like a well-kept secret.

BS West   GAY
(📞 480-945-9028; www.bswest.com; 7125 E 5th Ave, Scottsdale; ⏰ 2pm-2am) A high-energy gay video bar and dance club in the Old Town Scottsdale area. This place has go-go dancers and hosts karaoke on Sundays.

🛍 Shopping

The valley has several notable shopping malls. For more upscale shopping, visit the Scottsdale Fashion Square (www.fashionsquare.com; 7014 E Camelback, at Scottsdale Rd, Scottsdale; ⏰ 10am-9pm Mon-Sat, 11am-6pm Sun) and the even more exclusive Biltmore Fashion Park (www.shopbiltmore.com; 2502 E Camelback Rd, at 24th St, Phoenix; ⏰ 10am-8pm Mon-Sat, noon-6pm Sun). In northern Scottsdale, the outdoor Kierland Commons (www.kierlandcommons.com; 15205 N Kierland Blvd, Scottsdale; ⏰ 10am-8pm Mon-Thu, 10am-9pm Sat, noon-6pm Sun) pulls in the crowds.

Heard Museum Shop & Bookstore   ARTS & CRAFTS
(www.heardmuseumshop.com; 2301 N Central Ave, Phoenix; ⏰ shop 9:30am-5pm, from 11am Sun, bookstore 9:30am-5:30pm Mon-Sat, to 5pm Sun) Has a range of books about Native Americans,

and a reliable and expansive selection of Native American arts and crafts, including jewelry and kachina dolls.

ⓘ Information

EMERGENCY & MEDICAL SERVICES

Banner Good Samaritan Medical Center (☑602-839-2000; www.bannerhealth.com; 1111 E McDowell Rd, Phoenix) Has a 24-hour emergency room.

Police (☑602-262-6151; http://phoenix.gov/police; 620 W Washington St, Phoenix)

INTERNET RESOURCES & MEDIA

Arizona Republic (www.azcentral.com) Arizona's largest newspaper; publishes a free entertainment guide, *Calendar*, every Thursday.

Burton Barr Central Library (☑602-262-4636; www.phoenixpubliclibrary.org; 1221 N Central Ave, Phoenix; ◎9am-5pm Mon, Fri & Sat, 9am-9pm Tue-Thu, 1-5pm Sun; ☎) Free internet access.

KJZZ 91.5 FM (http://kjzz.org) National Public Radio (NPR).

Phoenix New Times (www.phoenixnewtimes.com) The major free weekly; lots of event and restaurant listings.

POST

Downtown Post Office (☑602-253-9648; 522 N Central Ave, Phoenix; ◎9am-5pm Mon-Fri)

TOURIST INFORMATION

Downtown Phoenix Visitor Information Center (☑877-225-5749; www.visitphoenix.com; 125 N 2nd St, Suite 120; ◎8am-5pm Mon-Fri) The Valley's most complete source of tourist information.

Mesa Convention & Visitors Bureau (☑800-283-6372, 480-827-4700; www.visitmesa.com; 120 N Center St, Mesa; ◎8am-5pm Mon-Fri)

Scottsdale Convention & Visitors Bureau (☑800-782-1117, 480-421-1004; www.experiencescottsdale.com; 4343 N Scottsdale Rd, Suite 170; ◎8am-5pm Mon-Fri) Inside the Galleria Corporate Center. Very helpful staff. Pick up the free Desert Discovery Guide for a good list of area trails.

Tempe Convention & Visitors Bureau (☑866-914-1052, 480-894-8158; www.tempetourism.com; 51 W 3rd St, Suite 105; ◎8:30am-5pm Mon-Fri)

ⓘ Getting There & Around

Sky Harbor International Airport (☑602-273-3300; http://skyharbor.com; 3400 E Sky Harbor Blvd; ☎) is 3 miles southeast of downtown Phoenix and served by 17 airlines, including United, American, Delta and British Airways. Its three terminals (Terminals 2, 3 and 4; Terminal 1 was demolished in 1990) and the parking lots are linked by the free 24-hour Airport Shuttle Bus. The free **Phoenix Sky Train**, which began operating in 2013, currently runs between the economy parking lot, Terminal 4 and the METRO light-rail station at 44th St and E Washington St.

Greyhound (☑602-389-4200; www.greyhound.com; 2115 E Buckeye Rd) runs buses to Tucson ($21 to $23, two hours, eight daily), Flagstaff ($38, three hours, five daily), Albuquerque

---

VERDE VALLEY WINE TRAIL

Vineyards, wineries and tasting rooms have opened their doors along Hwy 89A and I-17, bringing a dash of style and energy to Cottonwood, Jerome and Cornville.

In Cottonwood, you can float to Verde River–adjacent **Alcantara Vineyards** (www.alcantaravineyard.com; 3445 S Grapevine Way) then stroll through Old Town where two new tasting rooms, **Arizona Stronghold** (www.azstronghold.com; 1023 N Main St; tastings $9; ◎noon-7pm Sun-Thu, to 9pm Fri & Sat) and **Pillsbury Wine Company** (www.pillsburywine.com; 1012 N Main St; ◎11am-6pm Sun-Thu, 11am-8pm Fri), sit across from each other on Main St. Art, views and wine-sipping converge in Jerome, where there's a tasting room on every level of town, starting with **Cellar 433** (www.bittercreekwinery.com; 240 Hull Ave; ◎11am-5pm Mon-Wed, 11am-6pm Thu-Sun) near the chamber of commerce visitor center. From there, stroll up to **Caduceus Cellars** (www.caduceus.org; 158 Main St; ◎11am-6pm Sun-Thu, to 8pm Sun) then end with a final climb to **Jerome Winery** (☑928-639-9067; 403 Clark St; ◎11am-5pm Mon-Thu, 11am-8pm Sat, 11am-4pm Sun Jun-Aug, shorter hours Sep-May) with its inviting patio.

Three wineries with tasting rooms hug a short stretch of Page Springs Rd east of Cornville: bistro-housing **Page Springs Cellars** (www.pagespringscellars.com; 1500 N Page Springs Rd; wine tasting $10; ◎11am-7pm Mon-Wed, to 9pm Thu-Sun), welcoming **Oak Creek Vineyards** (www.oakcreekvineyards.net; 1555 N Page Springs Rd; wine tasting $5; ◎10am-6pm) and mellow-rock-playing **Javelina Leap Vineyard** (www.javelinaleapwinery.com; 1565 Page Springs Rd; wine tasting $8; ◎11am-5pm).

($78 to $85, 10 to 12½ hours, seven daily) and Los Angeles ($38, seven to eight hours, eight daily). Valley Metro's No 13 buses link the airport and the Greyhound station.

Valley Metro (☑ 602-253-5000; www.valley-metro.org; tickets $2) operates buses all over the Valley and a 20-mile light-rail line linking north Phoenix with downtown Phoenix, Tempe/ASU and downtown Mesa. Fares for light-rail and bus are $2 per ride (no transfers) or $4 for a day pass. Buses run daily at intermittent times. **FLASH buses** (www.tempe.gov) operate daily around ASU and downtown Tempe, while the **Scottsdale Trolley** (www.scottsdaleaz.gov/trolley; ⊗ 11am-6pm Fri-Wed, to 9pm Thu during Artwalk) loops around downtown Scottsdale, both at no charge.

Flagstaff

Flagstaff's laid-back charms are myriad, from its pedestrian-friendly historic downtown crammed with eclectic vernacular architecture and vintage neon to its high-altitude pursuits such as skiing and hiking. Locals are generally a happy, athletic bunch, skewing more toward granola than gunslinger. Northern Arizona University (NAU) gives Flagstaff its college-town flavor, while its railroad history still figures firmly in the town's identity. Throw in a healthy appreciation for craft beer, freshly roasted coffee beans and an all-round good time and you have the makings of a town you want to slow down and savor.

⊙ Sights

With its cultural sites, historic downtown and access to outdoorsy pursuits, it's easy to fall for Flagstaff. Pick up walking-tour maps for Route 66 and haunted buildings at the visitor center.

Museum of Northern Arizona   MUSEUM
(☑ 928-774-5213; www.musnaz.org; 3101 N Fort Valley Rd; adult/child/senior $10/6/9; ⊗ 9am-5pm) For a helpful primer about the region, stop here. Three miles north of downtown, the museum spotlights local geology, biology and arts as well as Native American anthropolopgy, with exhibits spotlighting archaeology, history and customs of local tribes.

Lowell Observatory   OBSERVATORY
(☑ 928-233-3212; www.lowell.edu; 1400 W Mars Hill Rd; adult/child $12/5; ⊗ 9am-10pm Jun-Aug, shorter hour Sep-May) This observatory witnessed the first sighting of Pluto in 1920. Weather permitting, there's nightly stargazing,

helped by the fact that Flagstaff is the first International Dark Sky city in the world. Day tours are offered from 1pm to 4pm.

**Walnut Canyon
National Monument**   CANYON
(☑ 928-526-3367; www.nps.gov/waca; 7-day admission adult/child $5/free; ⊗ 8am-5pm May-Oct, 9am-5pm Nov-Apr) Sinagua cliff dwellings are set in the nearly vertical walls of a small limestone butte amid a forested canyon at this worth-a-trip monument. A short hiking trail descends past many cliff-dwelling rooms. The monument is 11 miles southeast of Flagstaff, off I-40 exit 204.

⚑ Activities

Alpine Pedaler   CYCLING
(☑ 928-213-9233; www.alpinepedaler.com; per person $25) Hop on the bus – or should we say communal bicycle – to pedal to downtown bars. This 15-seater makes pub crawling a whole lot easier. Tours are two hours.

Humphreys Peak   HIKING
The state's highest mountain (12,663ft) is a reasonably straightforward, though strenuous, hike in summer. The trail, which begins in the Arizona Snowbowl, winds through forest, eventually coming out above the beautifully barren tree line. The distance is 4.5 miles one-way; allow six to eight hours round-trip.

Arizona Snowbowl   SKIING
(☑ 928-779-1951; www.arizonasnowbowl.com; Hwy 180 & Snowbowl Rd; lift ticket adult/child $55/15; ⊗ 9am-4pm) Six lifts service 40 runs and a snowboarding park at elevations between 9200ft and 11,500ft. You can ride the chairlift (adult/child $15/10) in summer.

⊨ Sleeping

Flagstaff provides the widest variety of lodging choices in the region. Unlike in southern Arizona, summer is high season here.

**Grand Canyon
International Hostel**   HOSTEL $
(☑ 928-779-9421; www.grandcanyonhostel.com; 19½ S San Francisco St; dm $22-24, r without bath room $44-56, both incl breakfast; ❄ @ ⧉) A site along Flagstaff's Route 66 walking tour, this historic property now holds a hostel. Run by friendly people, dorms are clean and small. There's a kitchen, laundry facilities and tours to the Grand Canyon and Sedona. It's one block from the Amtrak station, and guests are fetched from the Greyhound bus

for free. This hostel gets more traffic than sister-property Dubeau Hostel.

Dubeau Hostel
HOSTEL $

(☑ 928-774-6731; www.grandcanyonhostel.com; 19 W Phoenix St; dm $22-24, r $48-68, both incl breakfast; P ❋ @ ☎) Run by the Grand Canyon International Hostel folks. The private rooms are like basic hotel rooms, with refrigerators and bathrooms with showers, but at half the price. The quieter of the two hostels.

Hotel Monte Vista
HOTEL $$

(☑ 928-779-6971; www.hotelmontevista.com; 100 N San Francisco St; d $65-110, ste $120-140; ☎) Feather lampshades, vintage furniture, bold colors and old-fashioned layouts – things are historically frisky in the 50 rooms and suites here, which are named for the film stars who slept in them. Ask for a quiet room if you're opposed to the live music that may drift up from Monte Vista Lounge. For the supernaturally curious, there's a ghost information sheet at the front desk.

Drury Inn & Suites
HOTEL $$

(☑ 928-773-4900; www.druryhotels.com; 300 S Milton Rd; r incl breakfast $155-165, ste $200; P ❋ @ ☎ ☒ ❋) The stone columns in the lobby set an adventurous mood at this six-story, LEED-certified property, but the deal clincher is the hearty Kickback happy hour which serves up complimentary beer and wine (with a limit) and a hearty spread of appetizers. The free breakfast is also filling. All rooms have a microwave and refrigerator. Pets are $10 per day.

✗ Eating

Wander around downtown and you'll stumble on plenty of eating options.

Diablo Burger
BURGERS $

(www.diabloburger.com; 120 N Leroux St; mains $10-13.25; ⊙ 11am-9pm Mon-Wed, 11am-10pm Thu-Sat) The cheddar-topped Blake at this gourmet burger joint gives a nod to New Mexico with Hatch chile mayo and roasted green chilies. Diablo uses locally sourced, antibiotic-free beef and fresh cut, deep-fried frites with dipping sauce. The place is tiny, four tables inside and a few bar seats (serves wine and beer), so come early.

Beaver Street Brewery
BREWPUB $$

(www.beaverstreetbrewery.com; 11 S Beaver St; lunch $8-13, dinner $10-20; ⊙ 11am-11pm Sun-Thu, to midnight Fri & Sat; ☷) This bustling brewpub does bar food right, offering delicious pizzas, burgers and salads. It usually has five handmade beers on tap and some seasonal brews. Surprisingly, it's very family friendly.

Criollo Latin Kitchen
FUSION $$

(☑ 928-774-0541; www.criollolatinkitchen.com; 16 N San Francisco St; lunch $8-17, dinner $10-22, brunch $8-10; ⊙ 11am-9pm Mon-Thu, 11am-10pm Fri, 9am-10pm Sat, 9am-9pm Sun) This Latin fusion spot has a romantic, industrial setting for cozy cocktail dates and delectable late-night small plates. The blue-corn blueberry pancakes make a strong argument for showing up for Sunday brunch. Food is sourced locally and sustainable when possible.

☙ Drinking & Entertainment

Follow the 1-mile Flagstaff Ale Trail (www.flagstaffaletrail.com) to sample craft beer at downtown breweries and a pub or two.

★ Museum Club
BAR

(☑ 928-526-9434; www.themuseumclub.com; 3404 E Rte 66; ⊙ 11am-2am) This honky-tonk roadhouse has been kickin' up its boot heels since 1936. Inside what looks like a huge log cabin you'll find a large wooden dance floor, animals mounted on the walls and a sumptuous elixir-filled mahogany bar. The origins of its name? In 1931 it housed a taxidermy museum.

Macy's
CAFE

(www.macyscoffee.net; 14 S Beaver St; mains under $8; ⊙ 6am-8pm; ☎) Macy's delicious house-roasted coffee has kept Flagstaff buzzing for over 30 years. Tasty vegetarian menu includes many vegan choices, with traditional cafe grub.

Cuvee 928
WINE BAR

(☑ 928-214-9463; www.cuvee928winebar.com; 6 E Aspen Ave; ⊙ 11:30am-9pm Mon-Thu, to 10pm Fri & Sat, 10am-3pm Sun) With a central location on Heritage Sq, and patio seating, this wine bar is a pleasant venue for people-watching.

Charly's Pub & Grill
LIVE MUSIC

(☑ 928-779-1919; www.weatherfordhotel.com; 23 N Leroux St; ⊙ 8am-10pm) This restaurant at the Weatherford Hotel has live music on the weekends. Its fireplace and brick walls provide a cozy setting for the blues, jazz and folk played here. Upstairs, stroll the wraparound verandah outside the popular 3rd-floor Zane Grey Ballroom.

ℹ Information

Visitor Center (☎800-842-7293, 928-774-9541; www.flagstaffarizona.org; 1 E Rte 66; ⊙8am-5pm Mon-Sat, 9am-4pm Sun) Inside the historic Amtrak train station.

ℹ Getting There & Around

Flagstaff Pulliam Airport is 4 miles south of town off I-17. **US Airways** (☎800-428-4322; www.usairways.com) offers several daily flights between Pulliam Airport and Phoenix Sky Harbor International Airport. **Greyhound** (☎800-231-2222, 928-774-4573; www.greyhound.com; 880 E Butler Ave) stops in Flagstaff en route to/from Albuquerque, Las Vegas, Los Angeles and Phoenix. **Arizona Shuttle** (☎800-888-2749, 928-226-8060; www.arizonashuttle.com) has shuttles that run to the park (one-way $29), Sedona (one-way $25) and Phoenix Sky Harbor Airport (one-way $45).

Operated by **Amtrak** (☎800-872-7245, 928-774-8679; www.amtrak.com; 1 E Rte 66; ⊙3am-10:45pm), the Southwest Chief stops at Flagstaff on its daily run between Chicago and Los Angeles.

Central Arizona

This part of Arizona draws people year-round for outdoor fun and is an oasis for summer visitors searching for cooler climes. After Phoenix, the land gains elevation, turning from high rolling desert to jagged hills covered in scrubby trees. Farther north still, mountains punctuate thick stands of pine.

Williams

Affable Williams, 60 miles south of Grand Canyon Village and 35 miles west of Flagstaff, is a gateway town with character. Classic motels and diners line Route 66, and the old-school homes and train station give a nod to simpler times.

Most tourists visit to ride the turn-of-the-19th-century Grand Canyon Railway (☎800-843-8724, 928-635-4253; www.thetrain.com; Railway Depot, 233 N Grand Canyon Blvd; round trip adult/child from $75/45; ▥) to the South Rim; departs Williams 9:30am, returns at 5:45pm. Even if you're not a train buff, a trip is a scenic stress-free way to visit the Grand Canyon. Characters in period costumes provide historical and regional narration, and banjo folk music sets the tone. There's also a wildly popular Polar Express service (adult/child from $32/18) from November through early January, ferrying pajama-clad kids to

ARIZONA'S QUIRKIEST SLEEPS

➡ **Wigwam Motel** (p346) Concrete teepee.

➡ **Bisbee Grand Hotel** (p364) Covered wagon.

➡ **Red Garter Bed & Bakery** (p345) An 1897 bordello.

➡ **Jerome Grand Hotel** (p348) Former mining hospital.

➡ **Shady Dell RV Park** (p364) Retro Airstream.

➡ **Canyon Motel & RV Park** (p345) Santa Fe train caboose.

➡ **Grand Canyon Caverns** (p346) Underground cavern.

the 'North Pole' to visit Santa. Kids and pre-teens will most enjoy Bearizona (☎928-635-2289; www.bearizona.com; 1500 E Rte 66; adult/child/under 4yr $20/10/free; ⊙8am-6pm Jun–mid-Aug, hours vary rest of year), an awesomely named drive-through wildlife park where visitors drive themselves past gray wolves, bison, bighorn sheep and black bears. Stop by the Fort Bearizona walking area for an up-close look at younger bears.

The Red Garter Bed & Bakery (☎928-635-1484; www.redgarter.com; 137 W Railroad Ave; d $135-160; ▣☎) is an 1897 bordello turned B&B where the ladies used to hang out the windows to flag down customers. The four rooms have nice period touches and the downstairs bakery has good coffee. The funky little Grand Canyon Hotel (☎928-635-1419; www.thegrandcanyonhotel.com; 145 W Rte 66; dm $40, r without bathroom $67, r with bathroom $74-125; ⊙Mar-Nov; ▣@☎) has small themed rooms and a six-bed dorm room; no TVs. You can sleep inside a 1929 Santa Fe train caboose or a Pullman railcar at the Canyon Motel & RV Park (☎928-635-9371; www.thecanyonmotel.com; 1900 E Rodeo Rd, Williams; RV sites $35-38, cottages $74-78, train cars $78-160; ▣☎▨), just east of downtown.

Sedona

Nestled amid majestic red sandstone formations at the southern end of Oak Creek Canyon, Sedona attracts artists, spiritual seekers, hikers and cyclists, and day-trippers from Phoenix fleeing the oppressive heat. Many New Age types believe that this area is the center of vortexes that radiate the earth's power, and Sedona's combination of scenic beauty and mysticism draws throngs of tourists year-round. New Age businesses dot downtown, along with galleries and gourmet restaurants, while the surrounding canyons offer excellent hiking and mountain biking.

In the middle of town, the 'Y' is the landmark junction of Hwys 89A and 179. Businesses are spread along both roads.

◉ Sights & Activities

New Agers believe Sedona's rocks, cliffs and rivers radiate Mother Earth's mojo. The world's four best-known vortexes are here: Bell Rock near Village of Oak Creek east of Hwy 179, Cathedral Rock near Red Rock Crossing, Airport Mesa along Airport Rd, and Boynton Canyon. Airport Rd is also a great location for watching the Technicolor sunsets.

Coconino National Forest PARK
(Red Rock Visitor Contact Center; ☑ 928-203-7500; www.redrockcountry.org/recreation; 8375 Hwy 179; ⊙ 8am-5pm) The best way to explore the area is by hiking, biking or horseback riding in the surrounding forest. Many day-use and parking areas require a Red Rock Pass ($5/15 per day/week), which can be purchased at most area stores and lodgings, and self-serve kiosks at popular sites.

For a map of local trails, download the Red Rock Country map (www.redrockcountry.org/maps/index.shtml) or pick up a free copy at the helpful USFS visitor center just south of the Village of Oak Creek.

The most scenic spots are along Hwy 89A north of Sedona, which snakes alongside Oak Creek through the heavily visited Oak Creek Canyon, and the drive between Sedona and the Village of Oak Creek to the south.

Chapel of the Holy Cross CHURCH
(☑ 928-282-4069; www.chapeloftheholycross.com; 780 Chapel Rd; ⊙ 9am-5pm Mon-Sat, 10am-5pm Sun) FREE Situated between spectacular, statuesque red-rock columns 3 miles south of town, this modern, nondenominational chapel was built in 1956 by Marguerite Brunwig Staude in the tradition of Frank Lloyd Wright.

Slide Rock State Park PARK
(☑ 928-282-3034; www.azstateparks.com/Parks/SLRO; 6871 N Hwy 89A; per car Memorial Day-Labor Day $20, Sep-May $10; ⊙ 8am-7pm Memorial Day-Labor Day, 8am-5pm Sep-May) Swoosh down big rocks into cool creek water at Oak Creek Canyon's star attraction, or walk the hiking trails.

Pink Jeep Tours DRIVING TOUR
(☑ 928-282-5000; www.pinkjeeptours.com; 204 N Hwy 89A) Many companies offer 4WD tours,

ROADSIDE ATTRACTIONS ON ROUTE 66

Route 66 enthusiasts will find 400 miles of pavement stretching across Arizona, including the longest uninterrupted portion of old road left in the country, between Seligman and Topock. The Mother Road (www.azrt66.com) connects the dots between gun-slinging Oatman, Kingman's mining settlements, Williams' 1940s-vintage downtown, and Winslow's windblown streets, with plenty of kitschy sights, listed here from west to east, along the way.

Wild Burros of Oatman Mules beg for treats in the middle of the road.

Grand Canyon Caverns & Inn (☑ 928-422-3223; www.gccaverns.com; Route 66, Mile 115; 1hr tour adult/child $19/13, r $85, campsites $15-30; ⊙ 8am-6pm May-Sep, 10am-4pm Oct-Apr) A guided tour 21 stories underground loops past mummified bobcats, civil-defense supplies and a $800 motel room.

Burma Shave signs Red-and-white ads from a bygone era between Grand Canyon Caverns and Seligman.

Seligman's Snow-Cap Drive In Prankish burger and ice-cream joint open since 1953.

Meteor Crater (☑ 928-289-5898; www.meteorcrater.com; adult/child/senior $16/8/15; ⊙ 7am-7pm Jun–mid-Sep, 8am-5pm mid-Sep–May) A 550ft-deep pockmark that's nearly 1 mile across, near Flagstaff.

Wigwam Motel (☑ 928-524-3048; www.galerie-kokopelli.com/wigwam; 811 W Hopi Dr, Holbrook; r $56-62; ❋) Concrete wigwams with hickory logpole furniture in Holbrook.

but Pink Jeep Tours has a great reputation and a vast variety of outings.

Sedona Bike & Bean   MOUNTAIN BIKING
(☑ 928-284-0210; www.bike-bean.com; 75 Bell Rock Plaza; 2hr/half-/full day from $30/40/50) A mountain-bike rental place near trails for hiking, biking and vortex-gazing. Also serves coffee.

🛏 Sleeping

Sedona hosts many beautiful B&Bs, creek-side cabins, motels and full-service resorts.

Dispersed camping is not permitted in Red Rock Canyon. The USFS (☑ 877-444-6777; www.recreation.gov; campsites $18) runs campgrounds, none with hookups, along Hwy Alt 89 in Oak Creek Canyon. All are nestled in the woods just off the road. It costs $18 to camp, and you don't need a Red Rock Pass. Reservations are accepted for all campgrounds except Pine Flat East. Six miles north of town, Manzanita has 19 sites, showers and is open year-round; 11.5 miles north, Cave Springs has 78 sites, and showers; Pine Flat East and Pine Flat West, 12.5 miles north, together have 58 sites, with 18 reservable.

Star Motel   MOTEL $
(☑ 928-282-3641; www.starmotelsedona.com; 295 Jordan Rd; r $80-100) Low rates, warm hospitality and a prime uptown location are the big draw at the retro Star Motel. You won't find candy on your pillow, but the bed is clean, the shower strong and the refrigerator handy for chilling those sunset beers.

Cozy Cactus   B&B $$$
(☑ 928-284-0082; www.cozycactus.com; 80 Canyon Circle Dr; r incl breakfast $190-290; ❇@🛜) This five-room, recently revamped B&B is particularly well suited to adventure-loving types ready to enjoy the great outdoors. The Southwest-style abode bumps up against a National Forest trail and is just around the bend from cyclist-friendly Bell Rock Pathway.

🍴 Eating & Drinking

Coffee Pot Restaurant   BREAKFAST $
(☑ 928-282-6626; www.coffeepotsedona.com; 2050 W Hwy Alt 89; mains $6-14; ⊙6am-2pm; 🔲) The go-to breakfast and lunch joint for decades, it's always busy. Meals are reasonably priced and the selection is huge – 101 types of omelet, for a start.

Sedona Memories   DELI $
(☑ 928-282-0032; 321 Jordan Rd; sandwiches under $7; ⊙10am-2pm Mon-Fri) This tiny local spot assembles gigantic sandwiches on slabs of homemade bread, with several vegetarian options. Cash only.

★ Elote Cafe   MEXICAN $$$
(☑ 928-203-0105; www.elotecafe.com; 771 Hwy 179, King's Ransom Hotel; mains $17-26; ⊙5pm-late Tue-Sat) Arrive early for some of the best, most authentic Mexican food you'll find in the region, with unusual traditional dishes you won't find elsewhere, such as the fire-roasted corn with lime and cotija cheese, or tender, smoky pork cheeks. No reservations.

Oak Creek Brewery & Grill   PUB
(☑ 928-282-3300; www.oakcreekpub.com; 336 Hwy 179; beers $5.75; ⊙11:30am-8:30pm; 🛜) For an outdoor town, Sedona is surprisingly short on microbreweries. Fortunately, this spacious brewpub at Tlaquepaque Village will satisfy your post-hike drinking needs. The menu includes upmarket pub-style dishes. Oak Creek also runs a low-frills brewery (☑ 928-204-1300; www.oakcreekbrew.com; 2050 Yavapai Dr; ⊙4-10pm Mon-Thu, noon-midnight Fri-Sun) in West Sedona; it's open later than the brewpub and has live music regularly.

ℹ Information

Sedona Chamber of Commerce Visitor Center (☑ 800-288-7336, 928-282-7722; www.visitsedona.com; 331 Forest Rd, Uptown Sedona; ⊙8:30am-5pm Mon-Sat, 9am-3pm Sun) Has tourist information and last-minute hotel bookings.

ℹ Getting There & Around

The **Sedona-Phoenix Shuttle** (☑ 800-448-7988, 928-282-2066; www.sedona-phoenix-shuttle.com; one-way/return $50/90) runs between Phoenix Sky Harbor International Airport and Sedona eight times daily. For Jeep rentals, try **Barlow Jeep Rentals** (☑ 800-928-5337, 928-282-8700; www.barlowjeeprentals.com; 3009 W Hwy 89A; ⊙8am-6pm summer, 9am-5pm winter).

Jerome

The childhood game Chutes and Ladders comes to mind on a stroll up and down the stairways of Jerome, a historic mining town clinging to the side of Cleopatra Hill – not always successfully as evidenced by the crumbling Sliding Jail. Shabbily chic, this resurrected ghost town was known as the 'Wickedest Town in the West' during its late-1800s mining heyday, but today its historic buildings have been lovingly restored and turned into galleries, restaurants, B&Bs and wine-tasting rooms.

Feeling brave? Stand on the glass platform covering the 1910ft mining shaft at Audrey Headframe Park (55 Douglas Rd; ⊗8am-5pm) FREE – it's longer than the Empire State Building by 650ft! Just ahead is the excellent Jerome State Historic Park (☑928-634-5381; www.azstateparks.com; adult/child $5/2; ⊗8:30am-5pm), which preserves the 1916 mansion of mining mogul Jimmy 'Rawhide' Douglas and spotlights the town's mining past.

A community hospital during the town's mining years, the Jerome Grand Hotel (☑928-634-8200; www.jeromegrandhotel.com; 200 Hill St; r $120-205, ste $270-460; ❉⊛) plays up its past with hospital relics in the hallways and an entertaining ghost tour that kids will enjoy. Wi-fi is available in the lobby only. The adjoining Asylum Restaurant (☑928-639-3197; www.theasylum.biz; 200 Hill St; lunch $10-16, dinner $20-32; ⊗11am-9pm), with its valley and red-rock views, is a breathtaking spot for a fine meal and glass of wine. Downtown, the popular Spirit Room Bar (☑928-634-8809; www.spiritroom.com; 166 Main St; ⊗10:30am-1am) is the town's liveliest watering hole. For wine drinkers, there are three tasting rooms just a few steps away.

Step into the Flatiron Café (☑928-634-2733; www.theflatironjerome.com; 416 Main St; breakfast $3-11, lunch $8-10; ⊗8am-4pm Wed-Mon) at the Y intersection for a savory gourmet breakfast or lunch. Its specialty coffees are delicious.

The chamber of commerce (☑928-634-2900; www.jeromechamber.com; Hull Ave, Hwy 89A north after the Flatiron Café split; ⊗10am-3pm), inside a small trailer, offers tourist information on the local attractions and art scene.

Prescott

With a historic Victorian-era downtown and a colorful Wild West history, Prescott feels like the Midwest meets cowboy country. Residents are a diverse mix of retirees, artists and families looking for a taste of yesteryear's wholesomeness. The town boasts more than 500 buildings on the National Register of Historic Places and is the home of the world's oldest rodeo. Along the plaza is Whiskey Row, an infamous strip of old saloons that still serve up their fair share of booze.

Just south of downtown, the fun-loving Motor Lodge (☑928-717-0157; www.themotorlodge.com; 503 S Montezuma St; r $99-119, ste $149, apt $159; ❉⊛) welcomes guests with 12 snazzy bungalows arranged around a central driveway – it's indie lodging at its best.

For breakfast, mosey into the friendly Lone Spur Café (☑928-445-8202; www.thelonespur.com; 106 W Gurley St; breakfast & lunch $8-17, dinner $14-24; ⊗8am-2pm daily, 4:30-8pm Fri), where you always order your breakfast with a biscuit and a side of sausage gravy. Portions are huge, and there are three bottles of hot sauce on every table. Cajun and Southwest specialties spice up the menu at welcoming Iron Springs Cafe (☑928-443-8848; www.ironspringscafe.com; 1501 Iron Springs Rd; brunch $10-13, lunch $10-15, dinner $10-21; ⊗8am-8pm Wed-Sat, 9am-2pm Sun), which sits inside an old train station 3 miles northwest of downtown.

On Whiskey Row, the Palace (☑928-541-1996; www.historicpalace.com; 120 S Montezuma St; lunch $9-12, dinner $16-27; ⊗lunch & dinner, bar opens at 11am) is an atmospheric place to drink; you enter through swinging saloon doors into a big room anchored by a Brunswick bar (saved during a 1900 fire).

The chamber of commerce (☑800-266-7534, 928-445-2000; www.visit-prescott.com; 117 W Goodwin St; ⊗9am-5pm Mon-Fri, 10am-2pm Sat & Sun) has tourist information, including a handy walking tour pamphlet ($1) of historical Prescott.

Prescott Transit Authority (☑928-445-5470; www.prescotttransit.com; 820 E Sheldon St) runs buses to/from Phoenix airport (one-way adult/child $30/17, two hours, eight daily). Also offers a local taxi service.

Grand Canyon National Park

Mather Point, near the park's southern entrance, is usually packed elbow-to-elbow with a global array of photo-snapping tourists. But even with the crowds, there's a sense of communal wonder that keeps the scene polite. The sheer immensity of the canyon grabs you first, followed by the dramatic layers of rock, which pull you in for a closer look. Next up are the artistic details – rugged plateaus, crumbly spires, maroon ridges – that flirt and catch your eye as shadows flicker across the rock.

Snaking along its floor are 277 miles of the Colorado River, which has carved the canyon over the past six million years and exposed rocks up to two billion years old – half the age of the earth.

The two rims of the Grand Canyon offer quite different experiences; they lie more than 200 miles apart by road and are rarely visited on the same trip. Most visitors choose the South Rim with its easy access, wealth of services and vistas that don't disappoint. The quieter North Rim has its own charms; at 8200ft elevation (1000ft higher than the South Rim), its cooler temperatures support wildflower meadows and tall, thick stands of aspen and spruce.

June is the driest month, July and August the wettest. January has average overnight lows of 13°F (-11°C) to 20°F (-7°C) and daytime highs around 40°F (4°C). Summer temperatures inside the canyon regularly soar above 100°F (38°C). While the South Rim is open year-round, most visitors come between late May and early September. The North Rim is open from mid-May to mid-October.

ℹ Information

The most developed area in the **Grand Canyon National Park** (☑ 928-638-7888; www.nps.gov/grca; entrance ticket vehicles/cyclists & pedestrians $25/12) is Grand Canyon Village, 6 miles north of the South Rim Entrance Station. The North Rim has one entrance, which is 30 miles south of Jacob Lake on Hwy 67; continue another 14 miles south to the actual rim. The North Rim and South Rim are 215 miles apart by car, 21 miles on foot through the canyon, or 10 miles as the condor flies.

The park entrance ticket is valid for seven days and can be used at both rims.

All overnight hikes and backcountry camping in the park require a permit. The **Backcountry Information Center** (☑ fax 928-638-2125 928-638-7875; ☺ 8am-noon & 1-5pm, phone staffed 1-5pm Mon-Fri) accepts applications for backpacking permits ($10, plus $5 per person per night) starting four months before the proposed month. Your chances are decent if you apply early (four months in advance for spring and fall) and provide alternative hiking itineraries. Reservations are accepted in person or by mail or fax. For more information see www.nps.gov/grca/planyourvisit/backcountry-permit.htm.

If you arrive without a permit, head to the backcountry office, by Maswik Lodge, to join the waiting list.

As a conservation measure, note that the park no longer sells bottled water. Instead, fill your thermos at water filling stations along the rim or at Canyon View Marketplace. Water bottles constituted 20% of the waste generated in the park.

VISITOR CENTERS

In addition to the visitor centers listed below, information is available inside the park at **Yavapai Museum of Geology** (☺ 8am-7pm Mar-Nov, to 6pm Dec-Feb), **Verkamp's Visitor Center** (☺ 8am-7pm Mar-Nov, to 6pm Dec-Feb), **Kolb Studio** (☑ 928-638-2771; Grand Canyon Village; ☺ 8am-7pm Mar-Nov, to 6pm Dec-Feb), **Tusayan Ruin & Museum** (☑ 928-638-2305; ☺ 9am-5pm) and **Desert View Information Center** (☑ 928-638-7893; ☺ 9am-5pm).

Grand Canyon Visitor Center (www.nps.gov/grca; South Rim; ☺ 8am-5pm Mar-Nov, from 9am Dec-Feb) Three hundred yards behind Mather Point, a large plaza holds the visitor center and the Books & More Store. Outdoor bulletin boards display information about trails, tours, ranger programs and the weather. The center's bright, spacious interior includes a ranger-staffed information desk, a theater and a lecture hall, where rangers offer daily talks.

National Geographic Visitor Center (☑ 928-638-2468; www.explorethecanyon.com; 450 Hwy 64, Tusayan; adult/child $14/11; ☺ 8am-10pm Mar-Oct, 10am-8pm Nov-Feb) In Tusayan, 7 miles south of Grand Canyon Village; pay your $25 vehicle entrance fee here and spare yourself a potentially long wait at the park entrance, especially in summer. The IMAX theater screens the terrific 34-minute film *Grand Canyon – The Hidden Secrets*.

The North Rim Visitor Center (p354) is adjacent to the Grand Canyon Lodge, with maps, books, trail guides and current conditions.

South Rim

To escape the throngs, visit during fall or winter, especially on weekdays. You'll also gain some solitude by walking a short distance away from the viewpoints on the Rim Trail or by heading into the canyon itself.

⊙ Sights & Activities

Driving & Hiking

A scenic route follows the rim on the west side of Grand Canyon Village along Hermit Rd. Closed to private vehicles March through November, the 7-mile road is serviced by the free park shuttle bus; cycling is encouraged because of the relatively light traffic. Stops offer spectacular views, and interpretive signs explain canyon features.

Hiking along the South Rim is among park visitors' favorite pastimes, with options

Grand Canyon National Park

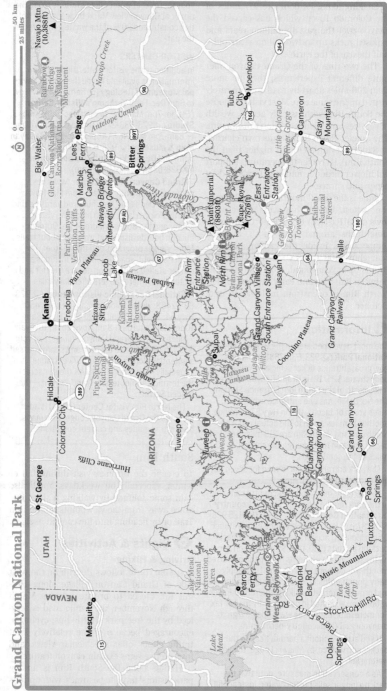

50 km
25 miles

Navajo Mtn
(10,388ft)

Rainbow
Bridge
National
Monument

Navajo Creek

Moenkopi

264

Big Water

Glen Canyon National
Recreation Area

Page

Antelope Canyon

Tuba
City

89A

Lees Ferry

Bitter
Springs

Marble
Canyon

Little Colorado
River Gorge

Gray
Mountain

89

Paria Canyon–
Vermilion Cliffs
Wilderness

Navajo Bridge
Interpretive Center

Cameron

89 Alt

Colorado River

89

Paria Plateau

Point Imperial
(8803ft)

Bright Angel Point

Cape Royal
(7876ft)

East
Entrance
Station

Kaibab
National
Forest

Kanab

Jacob
Lake

Kaibab Plateau

67

North Rim
(8803ft)

North Rim
Entrance
Station

Grand Canyon
National Park

Grandview
Lookout
Tower

180

Fredonia

Grand Canyon Village

South Entrance Station

Tusayan

64

Valle

Arizona
Strip

Kaibab
National
Forest

Supai

Tapeats
Creek

Bright
Angel
Area

Havasu
Canyon

Hualapai
Hilltop

Coconino Plateau

Grand Canyon
Railway

Hildale

Colorado City

389

Pipe Spring
National Monument

Kanab
Creek

Grand Canyon

Tuweep

18

St George

Hurricane Cliffs

ARIZONA

Tuweep

Tuweep
Overlook

Diamond Creek
Campground

Grand Canyon
Caverns

66

UTAH

Peach
Springs

Truxton

Mesquite

15

NEVADA

Lake Mead
National
Recreation
Area

Pearce
Ferry

Grand Canyon
West & Skywalk

Pierce Ferry Rd

Diamond
Bar Rd

Music Mountains

Red
Lake
(dry)

Stockton Hill Rd

Dolan
Springs

Lake
Mead

for every skill level. The Rim Trail is the most popular, and easiest, walk in the park. It dips in and out of the scrubby pines of Kaibab National Forest and connects a series of scenic points and historical sights over 13 miles. Portions are paved, and every viewpoint is accessed by one of the three shuttle routes. The new Trail of Time exhibit borders the Rim Trail just west of Yavapai Geology Museum. Here, every meter along the trail represents one million years of geologic history, with exhibits providing the details.

Desert View Drive starts to the east of Grand Canyon Village and follows the canyon rim for 26 miles to Desert View, the east entrance of the park. Pullouts offer spectacular views, and interpretive signs explain canyon features and geology.

The most popular of the corridor trails is the beautiful Bright Angel Trail. The steep and scenic 8-mile descent to the Colorado River is punctuated with four logical turnaround spots. Summer heat can be crippling; day hikers should either turn around at one of the two resthouses (a 3- to 6-mile round-trip) or hit the trail at dawn to safely make the longer hikes to Indian Garden and Plateau Point (9.2 and 12.2 miles round-trip respectively). Hiking to the river in one day should not be attempted. In 2013 the park spruced up the Bright Angel Trailhead by adding a shaded plaza, new restrooms and a stone trailhead marker. These improvements are just west of Bright Angel Lodge.

The South Kaibab is arguably one of the park's prettiest trails, combining stunning scenery and unobstructed 360-degree views with every step. Steep, rough and wholly exposed, summer ascents can be dangerous, and during this season rangers discourage all but the shortest day hikes – otherwise it's a grueling 12.6-mile round-trip to the river and back. Turn around at Cedar Ridge, (about 3 miles round-trip), perhaps the park's finest short day hike.

Individuals and groups who prefer a more in-depth experience while giving something back can apply for various programs with Grand Canyon Volunteers (☏ 928-774-7488; www.gcvolunteers.org). Multiday regional programs include habitat assessments, wildlife monitoring and botany training.

Cycling

Bright Angel Bicycles BICYCLE RENTAL
(☏ 928-638-3055; www.bikegrandcanyon.com; 10 S Entrance Rd, Grand Canyon Visitor Center; full-day adult/child $40/30; ◷ 8am-6pm May-Oct, 10am-4pm Nov, Mar-Apr & Oct) Renting 'comfort cruiser' bikes, the friendly folks here custom-fit each bike to the individual. Rate includes helmet. Also rents wheelchairs ($10 per day).

☞ Tours

Xanterra
(☏ 303-297-2757, 888-297-2757; www.grandcanyonlodges.com) Park tours are run by Xanterra, which has information desks at Bright Angel (p352), Maswik (p352) and Yavapai (p352) lodges. Various daily bus tours (tickets from $22) are offered.

Due to erosion concerns, half-day mule rides into the canyon from the South Rim are not offered and the NP has limited inner-canyon mule rides to those traveling all the way to Phantom Ranch. Rather than going below the rim, three-hour day trips ($123) now take riders along the rim, through the ponderosa, piñon and juniper forest to the Abyss overlook. Overnight trips (one/two people $507/895, year-round) and two-night trips (one/two people $714/1192, November to March) follow the Bright Angel Trail to the river, travel east on the River Trail and cross the river on the Kaibab Suspension Bridge. Riders spend the night at Phantom Ranch.

If you arrive at the park and want to join a mule trip the following day, ask about availability at the transportation desk at Bright Angel Lodge.

⌷ Sleeping

Advance or same-day reservations are required for the South Rim's six lodges, which are operated by Xanterra (☏ 888-297-2757, 303-297-2757; www.grandcanyonlodges.com). Use this phone number to make advance reservations (highly recommended) at any of the places (although its best to call Phantom Ranch directly) listed here. For same-day reservations or to reach a guest, call the South Rim switchboard (☏ 928-638-2631). If you can't find accommodations in the national park, try Tusayan (at South Rim Entrance Station), Valle (31 miles south), Cameron (53 miles east) or Williams (about 60 miles south).

All campgrounds and lodges are open year-round except Desert View.

Phantom Ranch CABIN $
(☏ reservations 888-297-2727; dm $46, cabin $148; ◷ year-round; ❄) It's not the Four Seasons, but this summer-campy complex has

SOUTHWEST GRAND CANYON NATIONAL PARK

undeniable charm. Perched beside Phantom Creek at the bottom of the canyon, the ranch has basic cabins sleeping four to 10 people and segregated dorms. Call at the first of the month for reservations 13 months ahead. The canteen serves family-style meals (breakfast from $21, dinner $29 to $44). No overnight reservation? Stop by the Bright Angel Lodge transportation desk to get on the waiting list, then show up at the desk at 6:30am the following morning to try to snag any canceled bunks.

Desert View Campground
CAMPGROUND $

(campsites $12; ☉ May–mid-Oct) Near the East Entrance Station, 26 miles east of Grand Canyon Village, this first-come, first-served campground is a quieter alternative to Mather. A small cafeteria/snack shop serves meals.

Mather Campground
CAMPGROUND $

(☎ 877-444-6777; www.recreation.gov; Grand Canyon Village; campsites $18; ☉ year-round) Well-dispersed, relatively peaceful sites amid pine and juniper trees. There are pay showers and laundry facilities nearby, drinking water, toilets, grills and a small general store. First-come, first-served during winter months.

Trailer Village
CAMPGROUND $

(☎ 888-297-2757, same-day reservations 928-638-2631; www.xanterra.com; Grand Canyon Village; campsites $35; ☉ year-round) Camp here if everywhere else is full. You can reserve well in advance or same day. Managed by Xanterra.

Bright Angel Lodge
LODGE $$

(www.grandcanyonlodges.com; Grand Canyon Village; r without/with bathroom $83/94, suites $185-362, cabins $120-340; ☉ year-round; ❈ @ ☏) The log-and-stone Bright Angel offers historic charm and refurbished rooms, the cheapest of which have shared bathrooms. Don't expect a TV in these very basic rooms (think university dorm room), but rim cabins have better views than TV.

Maswik Lodge
LODGE $$

(Grand Canyon Village; r South/North $92/176, cabins $94; ☉ year-round; ❈ @ ☏) Set away from the rim, Maswik is comprised of 16 modern, two-story buildings. Rooms at Maswik North have private patios, air-con, cable TV and forest views; those at Maswik South are smaller with fewer amenities and more forgettable views. Cabins are available in summer only.

Kachina & Thunderbird Lodges
LODGE $$

(Grand Canyon Village; r streetside/rimside $180/191; ☉ year-round; ❈) Decent motel-style rooms in a central location. Some have canyon views.

Yavapai Lodge
LODGE $$

(Grand Canyon Village; r West/East $125/166; ☉ Apr-Oct; ❈ ☏) Basic lodging amid peaceful piñon and juniper forest. No air-conditioning in Yavapai West.

★ El Tovar Hotel
LODGE $$$

(Grand Canyon Village; r $183-281, ste $348-440; ❈ ☏) Open since 1905, this dark-timbered lodge encourages lingering, even if you're not a guest. Inviting porches wrap around the rambling structure and the lobby has plenty of comfy seats – better for gazing at the impressive collection of animal mounts. These public spaces show the lodgelike, genteel elegance of the park's heyday. The standard rooms are small but first-class. Suites are fantastic.

🍴 Eating & Drinking

Maswik Cafeteria
CAFETERIA $

(Maswik Lodge; mains $7-15; ☉ 6am-10pm) A cafeteria-style place.

Yavapai Cafeteria
CAFETERIA $

(Yavapai Lodge; breakfast $6-10, lunch & dinner $5-11; ☉ 6:30am-8pm) Cafeteria food, service and seating.

Canyon Village Marketplace
MARKET $

(Market Plaza; ☉ 8am-7pm) Stock up on groceries or hit the deli (8am to 6pm).

★ El Tovar Dining Room
INTERNATIONAL $$$

(El Tovar; ☎ 928-638-2631, ext 6432; breakfast $9-13, lunch $10.25-16, dinner $17.25-33; ☉ 6:30-10:45am, 11:15am-2pm & 4:30-10pm) A stone's throw from the canyon's edge, it has the best views of any restaurant in the state, if not the country. The grand stone and dark-oak dining room warms the soul like an upscale lodge of yore, and the food, especially the steaks, makes the trip worthwhile. If you're not seated near a window, head to the verandah of the El Tovar Lounge afterward for a guaranteed Grand Canyon vista.

Arizona Room
AMERICAN $$$

(Bright Angel Lodge; lunch $8-12, dinner $8-28; ☉ 11:30am-3pm Mar-Oct & 4:30-10pm Mar-Dec) 🍃 Antler chandeliers hang from the ceiling and picture windows overlook the canyon. Mains include steak, chicken and fish dishes. No reservations; there's often a wait.

Bright Angel Bar BAR
(Bright Angel Lodge; mains $4-9; ⏰11:30am-10pm) Come here for your post-hike beer and burger. It's a fun place to relax at night when the lack of windows and dark decor aren't such a big deal. Some evenings there might be musical entertainment. The bar is beside the charmless Bright Angel Restaurant.

❶ Getting There & Around

Most people arrive at the canyon in private vehicles or on a tour. Parking can be a chore in Grand Canyon Village. Under the Park-n-Ride program, summer visitors can buy a park ticket at the National Geographic Visitor Center, park their vehicle at a designated lot, then hop aboard a free **park shuttle** (⏰8am-9:30pm mid-May–early Sep) that follows the Tusayan Route to the Grand Canyon Visitor Center inside the park. Park passes are also OK for this option. The trip takes 20 minutes, and the first bus departs from Tusayan at 8am. The last bus from the park leaves at 9:30pm.

Inside the park, free park shuttles operate along three routes: around Grand Canyon Village, west along Hermits Rest Route and east along Kaibab Trail Route. Buses typically run at least twice per hour, from one hour before sunset to one hour afterward.

A free shuttle runs from Bright Angel Lodge during the summer months, the **Hiker's Express** (⏰4am, 5am & 6am Jun-Aug. 5am, 6am & 7am May & Sep) has pickups at the Backcountry Information Center and Grand Canyon Visitor Center, and then heads to the South Kaibab trailhead.

North Rim

Head here for blessed solitude; of the park's 4.4 million annual visitors, only 400,000 make the trek to the North Rim. Meadows are thick with wildflowers and dense clusters of willowy aspen and spruce trees, and the air is often crisp, the skies big and blue.

Facilities on the North Rim are closed from mid-October to mid-May, although you can drive into the park and stay at the campground until the first snow closes the road from Jacob Lake.

Call the **North Rim Switchboard** (☎928-638-2612) to reach facilities on the North Rim.

◉ Sights & Activities

The short and easy paved trail (0.5 miles) to **Bright Angel Point** is a canyon must. Beginning from the back porch of Grand Canyon Lodge, it goes to a narrow finger of an overlook with fabulous views.

The **North Kaibab Trail** is the North Rim's only maintained rim-to-river trail and connects with trails to the South Rim. The first 4.7 miles are the steepest, dropping 3050ft to **Roaring Springs** – a popular all-day hike. If you prefer a shorter day hike below the rim, walk just 0.75 miles down to **Coconino Overlook** or 2 miles to the **Supai Tunnel** to get a taste of steep inner-canyon hiking. The 28-mile round-trip to the Colorado River is a multiday affair. For a ranger-recommended short hike that works well for families, try the 4-mile round-trip **Cape Final** trail, which leads through ponderosa pines to sweeping views of the eastern Grand Canyon area.

RAFTING THE COLORADO RIVER

A boat trip down the Colorado is an epic, adrenaline-pumping adventure. The biggest single drop at Lava Falls plummets 37ft in just 300yd. But the true highlight is experiencing the Grand Canyon by looking up, not down from the rim. Its human history comes alive in ruins, wrecks and rock art. Commercial trips run from three days to three weeks and vary in the type of watercraft used. At night you camp under stars on sandy beaches (gear provided). It takes about two or three weeks to run the entire 279 miles of river through the canyon. Shorter sections of around 100 miles take four to nine days. Space is limited and the trips are popular, so book as far in advance as possible – although you might luck out and find a last-minute bargain on a rafting company Facebook page.

Arizona Raft Adventures (☎800-786-7238, 928-526-8200; www.azraft.com; 6-day Upper Canyon hybrid trips/paddle trips $2025/2125, 10-day Full Canyon motor trips $2965)

Arizona River Runners (☎800-477-7238, 602-867-4866; www.raftarizona.com; 6-day Upper Canyon oar trip $1925, 8-day Full Canyon motor trip $2650)

Canyon Trail Rides (☑435-679-8665; www.
canyonrides.com; ☺mid-May–mid-Oct) offers
one-hour ($40) and half-day ($80, minimum age 10 years) mule trips. Of the half-
day trips, one is along the rim and the other
drops into the Canyon on the North Kaibab
Trail.

🛌 Sleeping

Accommodations are limited to one lodge
and one campground. If these are booked,
try your luck 80 miles north in Kanab, UT,
or 84 miles northeast in Lees Ferry. There
are also campgrounds in the Kaibab National Forest north of the park.

North Rim Campground   CAMPGROUND $
(☑928-638-7814, 877-444-6777; www.recreation.
gov; tent sites $6-18, RV sites $18-25; ☺mid-May–
Oct; 🐾) This campground, 1.5 miles north of
Grand Canyon Lodge, offers pleasant sites
on level ground blanketed in pine needles.
There is water, a store, a snack bar and coin-
operated showers and laundry facilities, but
no hookups. Hikers and cross-country skiers can use the campground during winter
months if they have a backcountry permit.
Reservations accepted.

Grand Canyon Lodge   LODGE $$
(☑advance reservations 877-386-4383, reserva-
tions outside USA 480-337-1320, same-day reserva-
tions 928-638-2611; www.grandcanyonlodgenorth.
com; r $124, 2-person cabins $124-192, extra guest
over 15yr $10; ☺mid-May–mid-Oct; 🐾) Made of
wood, stone and glass, the lodge enjoys a
lofty perch beside the rim. Rustic yet mod-
ern cabins make up the majority of accom-
modations. The most expensive cabins offer
two rooms, a porch and beautiful rim views.
The canyon views from the Sun Room are
stunning, the lobby regal. Reserve far in
advance.

🍴 Eating & Drinking

The lodge will prepare sack lunches ($12),
ready for pickup as early as 5:30am, for
those wanting to picnic on the trail. Place
your order the day before. For sandwiches,
pizza and breakfast burritos, try Deli in the
Pines (mains $4-8; ☺7am-9pm mid-May–mid-
Oct), also at the Lodge.

★ **Grand Canyon Lodge**
Dining Room   AMERICAN $$
(☑928-638-2611, 928-645-6865 call Jan 1-Apr 15
for next season; www.grandcanyonlodgenorth.com;
breakfast $7-12, lunch & dinner $12-30; ☺6:30-

10am, 11:30am-2:30pm & 4:45-9:45pm mid-May–
mid-Oct) The windows are so huge that you
can sit anywhere and get a good view. The
menu includes rainbow trout, bison flank
steak, several vegetarian dishes and Arizo-
na-crafted mircrobrews. Dinner reservations are required. Next door is the atmospheric Rough Rider Saloon (snacks $2-5;
☺breakfast 5:30am-10:30am, drinks & snacks
11:30am-10:30pm), full of memorabilia from
the country's most adventurous president.
Come here for coffee, pastries and breakfast
burritos in the morning and saloon drinks
later in the day.

Grand Canyon
Cookout Experience   AMERICAN $$
(adult/child/child   under   6yr $30/15/free;
☺6:15pm Jun-Sep; 🍴) This chuck-wagon-
style cookout featuring barbecue and corn-
bread is more of an event than a meal. Kids
love it. Make arrangements at the Grand
Canyon Lodge.

ℹ️ Information

North Rim Visitor Center (☑928-638-7864;
www.nps.gov/grca; North Rim; ☺8am-6pm
mid-May–mid-Oct, 9am-4pm Oct 16-31) Sitting
beside Grand Canyon Lodge, this is the place
to get information about the park. It's also the
starting point for ranger-led nature walks and
evening programs.

ℹ️ Getting There & Around

The **Transcanyon Shuttle** (☑877-638-2820,
928-638-2820; www.trans-canyonshuttle.com;
one-way/return $85/160; ☺May 15-Oct 31)
departs daily from Grand Canyon Lodge for the
South Rim (five hours) and is perfect for rim-to-
rim hikers. Reserve at least one or two weeks in
advance. A complimentary hikers' shuttle to the
North Kaibab Trail departs at both 5:45am and
7:10am from Grand Canyon Lodge. You must
sign up for it at the front desk 24 hours ahead; if
no one signs up, it will not run.

Around the
Grand Canyon

Havasu Canyon

In a hidden valley with stunning, spring-fed
waterfalls and azure swimming holes, this is
one of the most beautiful spots in the region.
It's also hard to reach, but the hike down
and back up is what makes the trip unique –
and a bit of an adventure.

Located on the Havasupai Indian Reservation, Havasu Canyon is about 195 miles west of the South Rim. The four falls lie 10 miles below the rim, accessed via a moderately challenging hiking trail, and trips require an overnight stay in the nearby village of Supai.

Supai offers two sleeping options and reservations must be secured before starting out. There's a $35 entrance fee for all overnight guests. The Havasupai Campground (☑928-448-2180, 928-448-2141, 928-448-2121; www.havasupai.nsn.gov.tourism.html; Havasupai Tourist Enterprise, PO Box 160, Supai, AZ 86435; per night per person $17), 2 miles north of Supai, has primitive campsites along a creek. In addition, every camper must pay a $5 environmental fee. The Havasupai Lodge (☑928-448-2111; www.havasupai-nsn.gov/tourism.html; PO Box 159, Supai, AZ 86435; r $145; ✳) has motel rooms with canyon views but no phones or TVs. Check in by 5pm, when the lobby closes. A village cafe serves meals and accepts credit cards.

Continue through Havasu Canyon to the waterfalls and blue-green swimming holes. If you don't want to hike to Supai, call the lodge or campground to arrange for a mule or horse (round-trip to lodge/campground $135/197) to carry you there. Rides depart from Hualapai Hilltop, where the hiking trail begins. The road to Hualapai Hilltop is 7 miles east of Peach Springs off Route 66. Look for the marked turnoff and follow the road for 62 miles.

Grand Canyon West

Grand Canyon West is not part of Grand Canyon National Park, which is about 215 driving miles to the east. Run by the Hualapai Nation, the remote site is 70 miles northeast of Kingman, and the last 9 miles are unpaved and unsuitable for RVs.

Grand Canyon Skywalk   PARK
(☑928-769-2636; www.grandcanyonwest.com; per person $88; ⊙7am-7pm Apr-Sep, 8am-5pm Oct-Mar) A slender see-through glass horseshoe levitates over a 4000ft chasm of the Grand Canyon. The only way to visit is to purchase a package tour. A hop-on, hop-off shuttle travels the loop road to scenic points along the rim. Tours can include lunch, horse-drawn wagon rides from an ersatz Western town, and informal Native American performances.

Northeastern Arizona

Between the brooding buttes of Monument Valley, the blue waters of Lake Powell and the fossilized logs of the Petrified Forest National Park are photogenic lands locked in ancient history. Inhabited by Native Americans for centuries, this region is largely made up of reservation land called Navajo Nation, which spills into surrounding states. The Hopi reservation is here as well, completely surrounded by Navajo land.

Lake Powell

The country's second-largest artificial reservoir and part of the Glen Canyon National Recreation Area (☑928-608-6200; www.nps.gov/glca; 7-day pass per vehicle $15), Lake Powell stretches between Utah and Arizona. Set amid striking red-rock formations, sharply cut canyon and dramatic desert scenery, it's water-sports heaven.

South of the lake and looking out over a pleasant stretch of the Colorado River is Lee's Ferry (www.nps.gov/glca; tent & RV sites $12), a very scenic stopover with first-come, first served camping.

HOPI NATION

Descendants of the Ancestral Puebloans, the Hopi are one of the most untouched tribes in the United States. Their village of Old Oraibi may be the oldest continuously inhabited settlement in North America.

Hopi land is surrounded by the Navajo Nation. Hwy 264 runs past the three mesas (First, Second and Third Mesa) that form the heart of the Hopi reservation. On Second Mesa, some 10 miles west of First Mesa, the Hopi Cultural Center Restaurant & Inn (☑928-734-2401; www.hopiculturalcenter.com; Hwy 264; r $95-110, breakfast $5-15, lunch $8-20, dinner $13-20; ⊙breakfast, lunch, dinner) is as visitor-oriented as things get on the Hopi reservation. It provides food and lodging, and there's the small Hopi Museum (☑928-734-6650; adult/child $3/1; ⊙8am-5pm Mon-Fri, 9am-3pm Sat), filled with historic photographs and introductory cultural exhibits.

Photographs, sketching and recording are not allowed.

The region's central town is Page, and Hwy 89 forms the main strip. The Carl Hayden Visitor Center (☑928-608-6404; www.nps.gov/glca; Hwy 89; ☉8am-6pm Jun-Aug, shorter hours rest of year) is located at Glen Canyon Dam, 2.5 miles north of Page. Tours (☑928-608-6072; www.glencanyonnha. org; adult/child $5/2.50) run by the Glen Canyon Natural History Association take you inside the dam.

To visit photogenic Antelope Canyon (www.navajonationparks.org/htm/antelopecanyon. htm), a stunning sandstone slot canyon with two main parts, you must join a tour. Upper Antelope Canyon is easier to navigate and more touristed. Several tour companies offer trips into Upper Antelope Canyon; expect a bumpy ride and a bit of a cattle call; try Roger Ekis's Antelope Canyon Tours (☑928-645-9102; www.antelopecanyon.com; 22 S Lake Powell Blvd; adult/child 5-12yr from $35/25). The more strenuous Lower Antelope Canyon sees much smaller crowds.

A deservedly popular hike is the 1.5 mile roundtrip trek to Horseshoe Bend, where the river wraps around a dramatic stone outcropping to form a perfect U. The trailhead is south of Page off Hwy 89, across from mile marker 541.

Chain hotels line Hwy 89 in Page and a number of independent places line 8th Ave. The revamped Lake Powell Motel (☑928-645-3919; www.powellmotel.com; 750 S Navajo Dr; r $69-159; ☉Apr-Oct; ❇☎), formerly Bashful Bob's, was originally constructed to house Glen Canyon Dam builders. Four units here have kitchens, and book up quickly. A fifth, smaller room is typically held for walk-ups.

For breakfast in Page, the Ranch House Grille (www.ranchhousegrille.com; 819 N Navajo Dr; mains $7-16; ☉6am-3pm) has good food, huge portions and fast service. The murals of local landcapes are impressive inside Bonkers (www.bonkerspagaz.com; 810 N Navajo

---

ⓘ HIGHWAY 89

Travelers should note that the 24-mile stretch of Hwy 89 between Page and Bitter Springs, which is just south of Lees Ferry, closed in February 2013 after a landslide buckled the road. Beginning in August 2013, drivers will be rerouted to Navajo Route 20, which has been paved and renamed 89T. It is the most direct route until 89A re-opens.

Dr; mains $9-22; ☉from 4pm Mon-Sat), which serves satisfying steaks, seafood, pasta and a few burgers and sandwiches.

Navajo Nation

The wounds are healing but the scars remain on Arizona's Navajo lands, a testament to the forced relocation of thousands of Native Americans to reservations.

Amid the isolation is some of North America's most spectacular scenery, including Monument Valley and Canyon de Chelly. Cultural pride remains strong and many still speak Navajo as their first language. The Navajo rely heavily on tourism; visitors can help keep their heritage alive by staying on reservation land or purchasing their renowned crafts. Stopping at roadside stalls is a nice way for personal interaction and making sure money goes straight into the artisan's pocket.

Unlike Arizona, the Navajo Nation observes Mountain daylight saving time. During summer, the reservation is one hour ahead of Arizona.

For details about hiking and camping, and required permits, visit www.navajonationparks.org.

CAMERON

Cameron is the gateway to the east entrance of the Grand Canyon's South Rim, but the other reason people come here is for Cameron Trading Post (www.camerontradingpost. com), just north of the Hwy 64 turnoff to the Grand Canyon. Food, lodging, a gift shop and a post office are in this historic settlement. It's one of the few worthwhile stops on Hwy 89 between Flagstaff and Page.

CANYON DE CHELLY NATIONAL MONUMENT

This many-fingered canyon (pronounced *duh-shay*) contains several beautiful Ancestral Puebloan sites important to Navajo history, including ancient cliff dwellings. Families still farm the land, wintering on the rims then moving to hogans on the canyon floor in spring and summer. The canyon is private Navajo property administered by the NPS. Enter hogans only with a guide and don't photograph people without their permission.

The only lodging in the park is Sacred Canyon Lodge (☑800-679-2473; www.sacred-canyonlodge.com; r $122-129, ste $178, cafeteria mains $5-17; breakfast, lunch & dinner; ❇@☎❇), formerly Thunderbird Lodge. It has comfortable rooms and an inexpensive cafeteria serving Navajo and American meals. The nearby Navajo-run campground has about 90 sites on a first-come, first-served basis ($10), with water but no showers.

The Canyon de Chelly **visitor center** (☑928-674-5500; www.nps.gov/cach; ☺8am-5pm) is 3 miles from Rte 191 in the small village of Chinle. Two scenic drives follow the canyon's rim. For travel within the canyon, stop by the visitor center for a list of tour companies; this list is also on the park website.

FOUR CORNERS NAVAJO TRIBAL PARK

Don't be shy: do a spread eagle at the **four corners marker** (☑928-871-6647; www.navajonationparks.org; admission $3; ☺8am-7pm May-Sep, 8am-5pm Oct-Apr), the middle-of-nowhere landmark that's looking spiffy after a 2010 renovation of the central plaza. The only spot in the US where you can straddle four states – Arizona, New Mexico, Colorado, and Utah – it makes a good photograph, even if it's not 100% accurate. According to government surveyors, the marker is almost 2000ft east of where it should be (but it is the legally recognized border point, regardless).

MONUMENT VALLEY NAVAJO TRIBAL PARK

With flaming-red buttes and impossibly slender spires bursting to the heavens, the Monument Valley landscape off Hwy 163 has starred in countless Hollywood Westerns and looms large in many a road-trip daydream.

For up-close views of the towering formations, you'll need to visit the **Monument Valley Navajo Tribal Park** (☑435-727-5874; www.navajonationparks.org/htm/monumentvalley.htm; adult/child $5/free; ☺drive 6am-8:30pm May-Sep, 8am-4:30pm Oct-Apr, visitor center 6am-8pm May-Sep, 8am-5pm Oct-Apr), where a rough and unpaved scenic driving loop covers 17 miles of stunning valley views. You can drive it in your own vehicle or take a tour (1½ hours $75, 2½ hours $95) through one of the kiosks in the parking lot (tours enter areas private vehicles can't).

Inside the tribal park is the **View Hotel at Monument Valley** (☑435-727-5555; www.monumentvalleyview.com; Hwy 163; r $209-265, ste $299-329; ❈@☎). Built in harmony with the landscape, the sandstone-colored hotel blends naturally with its surroundings,

and most of the 96 rooms have private balconies facing the monuments. The Navajo-based specialties at the adjoining restaurant (mains $10 to $30, no alcohol) are mediocre, but the red-rock panorama is stunning. Wi-fi is available in the lobby. A gift shop and small museum are within the hotel complex. At press time the campground was closed for construction.

The historic **Goulding's Lodge** (☑435-727-3231; www.gouldings.com; r $205-242, tent sites $26, RV sites $5, cabins $92; ❈☎❈❈), just across the border in Utah, offers lodge rooms, camping and small cabins. Book early for summer. In Kayenta, 20 miles south, there are a handful of okay hotels. Try the **Wetherill Inn** (☑928-697-3231; www.wetherillinn.com; 1000 Main St/Hwy 63; r incl breakfast $136; ❈@☎❈) if everything in Monument Valley is booked.

Winslow

'Standing on a corner in Winslow, Arizona, such a fine sight to see...' Sound familiar? Thanks to the Eagles' twangy 1970s tune 'Take It Easy,' otherwise nondescript Winslow has earned its wings in pop-culture heaven. A small **park** (www.standinonthecorner.com; 2nd St) on Route 66 at Kinsley Ave pays homage to the band.

Just 50 miles east of Petrified Forest National Park, Winslow is a good regional base. Old motels border Route 66, and eateries sprinkle the downtown. The inviting 1929 **La Posada** (☑928-289-4366; www.laposada.org; 303 E 2nd St; r $119-169; ❈☎❈) is a restored hacienda designed by star architect du jour Mary Jane Colter. Elaborate tilework, glass-and-tin chandeliers, Navajo rugs and other details accent its palatial Western-style elegance. The on-site restaurant, the much-lauded **Turquoise Room** (www.theturquoiseroom.net; La Posada; breakfast $8-12, lunch $9-13, dinner $19-40; ☺7am-9pm), serves the best meals between Flagstaff and Albuquerque; dishes have a neo-Southwestern flair.

Petrified Forest National Park

The multicolored Painted Desert here is strewn with fossilized logs predating the dinosaurs. This **national park** (☑928-524-6228; www.nps.gov/pefo; vehicle/walk-in, bicycle & motorcycle $10/5; ☺7am-8pm Jun & Jul, shorter hour Aug-May) is an extraordinary site. The hard-to-miss **visitor center** is just half a

SOUTHWEST NORTHEASTERN ARIZONA

mile north of I-40 and has maps and information on guided tours and science lectures.

The park straddles I-40 at exit 311, 25 miles east of Holbrook. From this exit, a 28-mile paved park road offers a splendid scenic drive. There are no campsites, but a number of short trails, ranging from less than a mile to 2 miles, pass through the best stands of petrified rock and ancient Native American dwellings in the park. Those prepared for rugged backcountry camping need to pick up a free permit at the visitor center.

Western Arizona

The Colorado River is alive with sun worshippers at Lake Havasu City, while Route 66 offers well-preserved stretches of classic highway near Kingman. South of the I-10, the wild, empty landscape is among the most barren in the West. If you're already here, there are some worthwhile sites, but there's nothing worth planning an itinerary around unless you're a Route 66 or boating fanatic.

Kingman & Around

Faded motels and gas stations galore grace Kingman's main drag, but several turn-of-the-19th-century buildings remain. If you're following the Route 66 trail (aka Andy Devine Ave here) or looking for cheap lodging, it's worth a stroll.

Pick up maps and brochures at the historic Powerhouse Visitor Center (☑ 866-427-7866, 928-753-6106; www.gokingman.com; 120 W Andy Devine Ave; ☺ 8am-5pm), which has a small but engaging Route 66 museum (☑ 928-753-9889; www.kingmantourism.org; 120 W Andy Devine Ave; adult/child/senior $4/free/3; ☺ 9am-5pm).

A cool neon sign draws road-trippers to the Hilltop Motel (☑ 928-753-2198; www.hilltopmotelaz.com; 1901 E Andy Devine Ave; r $44; ✳@☎✉☘) on Route 66. Rooms are a bit of a throwback, but are well kept, and the views are superb. Pets (dogs only) stay for $5. As rednecks, we can confirm that the pork at Redneck's Southern Pit BBQ (www.redneckssouthernpitbbq.com; 420 E Beale St; mains $5-22; ☺ 11am-8pm Tue-Sat; ⛶) is tasty, but Southerners rarely use the word 'sammich,' as displayed on the menu. 'Big ole tater,' however, is fine.

Lake Havasu City

When the city of London auctioned off its 1831 bridge in the late 1960s, developer Robert McCulloch bought it, took it apart, shipped it, and then reassembled it at Lake Havasu City, which sits along a dammed-up portion of the Colorado River. The place attracts hordes of young spring-breakers and weekend warriors who come to play in the water and party hard. An 'English Village' of pseudo-British pubs and tourist gift shops surrounds the bridge and houses the visitor center (☑ 928-855-5655; www.golakehavasu.com; 422 English Village; ☺ 9am-5pm; ☎) where you can pick up tourist information and access the internet.

The hippest hotel in town is Heat (☑ 928-854-2833; www.heathotel.com; 1420 N McCulloch Blvd; r $209-299, ste $249-439; ✳☎), a slick boutique property where the front desk doubles as a bar. Rooms are contemporary and most have private patios with views of London Bridge. For a hearty, open-air breakfast, rise and shine at the Red Onion (☑ 928-505-0302; www.redonionhavasu.com; 2013 N McCulloch Blvd; mains $7-12; ☺ 7am-2pm), a popular eatery where the menu is loaded with omelets and diet-busting fare. For microbrews and good pub grub, try the Barley Brothers (☑ 928-505-7837; www.barleybrothers.com; 1425 N McCulloch Blvd; mains $9-24; ☺ 11am-9pm Sun-Thu, to 10pm Fri & Sat), which has great views of the lake.

Tucson

Arizona's second-largest city is set in the Sonoran Desert, full of rolling, sandy hills and crowds of cacti. The vibe here is ramshackle-cool and cozy compared with the shiny vastness of Phoenix. A college town, Tucson (the 'c' is silent) is home turf to the 40,000-strong University of Arizona (U of A) and was an artsy, dress-down kind of place before that was the cool thing to be. Eclectic shops and scores of funky restaurants and bars flourish in this arid ground. Tucsonans are proud of the city's geographic and cultural proximity to Mexico (65 highway miles south); more than 35% of the population is of Mexican or Central American descent.

◉ Sights & Activities

Downtown Tucson and the historic district are east of I-10 exit 258. About a mile northeast of downtown is the U of A campus; 4th Ave is the main drag here, packed with cafes, bars and interesting shops. For downtown's historic highlights, pick up a Presidio Trail walking tour map at the visitor center (p362).

Saguaro National Park   PARK

(☑ Tucson Mountain District 520-733-5158, headquarters 520-733-5100; www.nps.gov/sagu; 2700 N Kinney Rd, western district; 7-day pass per vehicle/bicycle $10/5; ⊙ vehicles sunrise-sunset, walkers & cyclists 24hr) This prickly canvas of green cacti and desert scrub is split in half by 30 miles of freeway and farms. Both sections sit at the edges of Tucson, but are still officially within the city.

You'll have a nice time exploring in either section, but if you want to make a day of it, head to **Saguaro West** (Tucson Mountain District), where you'll find several fun activities in and around the park. For maps and ranger-led programs, stop at the **Red Hills Visitor Center** (☑ 520-733-5158; 2700 N Kinney Rd; ⊙ 9am-5pm), which is also the starting point for the **Cactus Garden Trail**, a short, wheelchair-accessible path with interpretive signs for many of the park's cacti. The **Bajada Loop Drive**, an unpaved 6-mile loop that begins 1.5 miles west of the visitor center, provides fine views of cactus forests, several picnic spots and access to trailheads.

Saguaro East is 15 miles east of downtown. The **visitor center** (☑ 520-733-5153; 3693 S Old Spanish Trail; ⊙ 9am-5pm) has information about day hikes, horseback riding and backcountry camping. Backcountry camping requires a permit ($6 per site per day) and must be obtained by noon on the day of your hike. This section of the park has about 130 miles of hiking and 5.3 miles of mountain biking. The meandering 8-mile **Cactus Forest Scenic Loop Drive**, a paved road open to cars and bicycles, provides access to picnic areas, trailheads and viewpoints.

★**Arizona-Sonora Desert Museum**   MUSEUM

(☑ 520-883-2702; www.desertmuseum.org; 2021 N Kinney Rd; adult/child Sep-May $14.50/5, Jun-Aug $12/4; ⊙ 8:30am-5pm Oct-Feb) This tribute to the Sonoran Desert is one part zoo, one part botanical garden and one part museum – a trifecta that'll keep young and old entertained for easily half a day. All sorts of desert denizens, from precocious coatis to playful prairie dogs, make their home in natural enclosures hemmed in by invisible fences. The grounds are thick with desert plants,

MINI TIME MACHINE MUSEUM OF MINIATURES

'Meddle ye not in the affairs of Dragons, for ye are crunchy and tasteth good with condiments,' reads the sign beside the Pocket Dragons, one of several magical creatures inhabiting the Enchanted Realm gallery at this gobsmackingly fun **museum** (www.theminitimemachine.org; 4455 E Camp Lowell Rd; adult/child $9/6; ⊙ 9am-4pm Tue-Sat, noon-4pm Sun; 🚹). Here you can walk over a snowglobe-y Christmas village, peer into intricate mini-homes built in the 1700s and 1800s, and search for the tiny inhabitants of a magical tree. This is a great museum for families and for adults who still have a sense of fun.

To get here from downtown, follow E Broadway Blvd east 3.5 miles. Turn left onto N Alvernon Way and drive 3 miles to E Fort Lowell Rd, which turns into Camp Lowell. Turn right and continue almost 1 mile.

and docents are on hand to answer questions and give demonstrations. Strollers and wheelchairs are available, and there's a gift shop, art gallery, restaurant and cafe. Hours vary seasonally.

Old Tucson Studios   FILM LOCATION

(☑ 520-883-0100; www.oldtucson.com; 201 S Kinney Rd; adult/child $17/11; ⊙ hours vary; 🚹) A few miles southeast of the Arizona-Sonora Desert Museum, Old Tucson Studios was an actual Western film set. Today it's a Western theme park with shootouts and stagecoach rides. Call or check website for opening hours.

Pima Air & Space Museum   MUSEUM

(☑ 520-574-0462; www.pimaair.org; 6000 E Valencia Rd; adult/child/senior & military $16/9/13; ⊙ 9am-5pm, last admission 4pm; 🚗) An SR-71 Blackbird spy plane and JFK's Air Force One are among the stars at this private aircraft museum, home to 300 'birds.' Hardcore plane-spotters should book ahead for the 90-minute bus tour of the nearby 309th **Aerospace Maintenance & Regeneration Center** (AMARG; adult/child $7/4; ⊙ Mon-Fri, departure times vary seasonally) – aka the 'boneyard' – where almost 4000 aircraft are mothballed. Book through the Pima Air & Space Museum.

✿ Festivals & Events

Fiesta de los Vaqueros RODEO
(Rodeo Week; ☑ 520-741-2233; www.tucsonrodeo.
com; ☉ last week of Feb) This huge nonmotor-
ized parade with Western-themed floats is a
locally famous spectacle.

🛏 Sleeping

Lodging prices vary considerably, with lower rates in summer and fall. To sleep under
stars and saguaros, try **Gilbert Ray Campground** (☑ 520-877-6000; www.pima.gov/nrpr/
camping; Kinney Rd; tent/RV sites $10/20) near
the western district of Saguaro National
Park.

Roadrunner Hostel & Inn HOSTEL $
(☑ 520-940-7280; www.roadrunnerhostelinn.com;
346 E 12th St; dm/r incl breakfast $22/45; ✸ @ 🛜)
This comfortable hostel within walking distance of the arts district has a large kitchen,
free coffee and waffles in the morning, and
a big-screen TV for watching movies. Dorms
close between noon and 3pm for cleaning.
Takes cash and traveler's checks only.

Quality Inn Flamingo Hotel MOTEL $
(☑ 520-770-1910;   www.flamingohoteltucson.
com; 1300 N Stone Ave; r incl breakfast $65-80;
✸ @ 🛜 ⛑) Though not as spiffy as it used
to be, this motel retains its great 1950s Rat
Pack vibe. And the fact that Elvis slept here
doesn't hurt. Rooms have stylish striped
bedding, comfy beds and flat-screen plasma
TVs. Pets stay for $20 per day.

★ Catalina Park Inn B&B $$
(☑ 520-792-4541; www.catalinaparkinn.com; 309
E 1st St; r $140-170; ☉ closed Jul & Aug; ✸ @ 🛜)
Style, hospitality and comfort merge seam-
lessly at this inviting B&B just west of the
University of Arizona. Hosts Mark Hall
and Paul Richard have poured their hearts
into restoring this 1927 Med-style villa, and
their efforts are on display in the six guest
rooms, from the oversized and over-the-top
peacock-blue-and-gold Catalina Room to the
white and uncluttered East Room with an
iron canopy bed.

Hotel Congress HISTORIC HOTEL $$
(☑ 520-622-8848; www.hotelcongress.com; 311 E
Congress St; r $89-129; ℗ ✸ @ 🛜 ⛑) A little bit
hip, a little bit historic and whole lotta fun,
the Congress is a nonstop buzz of activity,
mostly because of its popular bar, restaurant
and nightclub. Infamous bank robber John
Dillinger and his gang were captured here in

1934 – check out the wall of photos and articles beside the lobby. Many rooms have period furnishings, rotary phones and wooden
radios – but no TVs. Ask for a room at the far
end of the hotel if you're noise-sensitive. Pets
stay for $10 per night.

**Windmill Inn at
St Philips Plaza** HOTEL $$
(☑ 520-577-0007;   www.windmillinns.com;
4250 N Campbell Ave; r incl breakfast $120-134;
✸ @ 🛜 ⛑) This modern, friendly place
wins kudos for spacious two-room suites (no
charge for kids under 18 years of age), free
continental breakfast, a lending library, a
heated pool and free bike rentals. Pets stay
free.

Arizona Inn RESORT $$$
(☑ 800-933-1093, 520-325-1541; www.arizonainn.
com; 2200 E Elm St; r $329-399, ste $459-579;
✸ @ 🛜 ⛑) The mature gardens and old Arizona grace provide a respite not only from
city life but also from the 21st century. Sip
coffee on the porch, take high tea in the
library, lounge by the small pool or join a
game of croquet, then retire to rooms fur-
nished with antiques. The on-site spa is our
favorite in town.

🍴 Eating

Your best bet for great food at good prices
is 4th Ave; we've listed some of Tucson's
standouts.

Mi Nidito MEXICAN $
(☑ 520-622-5081; www.minidito.net; 1813 S 4th Ave;
mains $6-13; ☉ lunch & dinner Wed-Sun) The wait
is worth it at this bustling spot (My Little
Nest), where Bill Clinton's order has become
the signature president's plate: a heaping
mound of tacos, tostadas, burritos, enchiladas etc – groaning under melted cheese.
Also give the prickly pear cactus chile or the
birria (spicy, shredded beef) a whirl.

★ Cafe Poca Cosa SOUTH AMERICAN $$
(☑ 520-622-6400; www.cafepocacosatucson.com;
110 E Pennington St; lunch $12-15, dinner $18-26;
☉ 11am-9pm Tue-Thu, to 10pm Fri & Sat) At this
award-winning Nuevo-Mexican bistro, a
chalkboard menu circulates between tables
because dishes change twice daily. It's all
freshly prepared, innovative and beautifully
presented. The undecided can't go wrong
by ordering the Plato Poca Cosa and letting
chef Suzana D'avila decide. Great margari-
tas, too.

Cup Cafe
AMERICAN, GLOBAL **$$**

(☑520-798-1618; www.hotelcongress.com/food; 311 E Congress St; breakfast $7-12, lunch $10-12, dinner $13-23; ⊙7am-10pm Sun-Thu, to 11pm Fri & Sat; ☑) Wine-bottle chandeliers above. Penny-tiled floor below. And 'Up on Crippled Creek' on the speakers. Yep, we're gonna like it here. In the morning, choices include a Creole dish with andouille sausage, eggs and potatoes, as well as cast-iron baked eggs with Gruyere cheese. There's a global mix of dishes for lunch and dinner, with a decent selection of vegetarian entrees. The coffee is excellent.

Lovin' Spoonfuls
VEGAN **$$**

(☑520-325-7766; 2990 N Campbell Ave; breakfast $7-9, lunch $6-8, dinner $8-12; ⊙9:30am-9pm Mon-Sat, 10am-3pm Sun; ☑) Burgers, country-fried chicken, a BLT, salads... The menu here reads like a typical cafe, but there's one big difference: no animal products find their way into this vegan haven.

Hub Restaurant & Creamery
AMERICAN **$$**

(☑520-207-8201; www.hubdowntown.com; 266 E Congress Ave; lunch $9-16, dinner $10-21; ⊙11am-midnight Sun-Wed, to 2am Thu-Sat) Upscale comfort food is the name of the game here, plus a few sandwiches and salads. If you don't want a meal, pop in for a scoop of flavor-packed gourmet ice cream – bacon scotch anyone?

El Charro Café
MEXICAN **$$**

(☑520-622-1922; www.elcharrocafe.com; 311 N Court Ave; lunch $6-10, dinner $7-18; ⊙lunch & dinner) The Flin family has been making innovative Mexican food at this busy hacienda since 1922. It's famous for the *carne seca*, sundried lean beef that's been reconstituted, shredded and grilled with green chile and onions.

🍷 Drinking & Entertainment

Downtown 4th Ave, near 6th St, is the happening bar-hop spot, and there are a number of nightclubs on downtown Congress St.

Che's Lounge
BAR

(☑520-623-2088; 350 N 4th Ave; ⊙noon-2am) A slightly skanky but hugely popular watering hole that rocks with live music Saturday nights. And it never charges a cover.

Thunder Canyon Brewery
MICROBREWERY

(www.thundercanyonbrewery.com; 220 E Broadway Blvd; ⊙11am-11pm Sun-Wed, to 2am Thu-Sat) This cavernous new microbrewery, within walking distance of Hotel Congress, serves its own brews as well as beer from other breweries. Forty beers on tap.

Chocolate Iguana
COFFEE SHOP

(www.chocolateiguanaon4th.com; 500 N 4th Ave; ⊙7am-8pm Mon-Thu, 7am-10pm Fri, 8am-10pm Sat, 9am-6pm Sun) For coffee-lovers and chocoholics, this is the place.

Club Congress
LIVE MUSIC

(☑520-622-8848; www.hotelcongress.com; 311 E Congress St; cover free-$24) Live and DJ music are found at this very popular place that's sometimes a rock hangout and sometimes a dance club. The crowd depends on the night, but it's almost always a happening place.

ⓘ Information

EMERGENCY & MEDICAL SERVICES

Police (☑520-791-4444; http://cms3.tucsonaz.gov; 270 S Stone Ave)

Tucson Medical Center (☑520-327-5461; www.tmcaz.com/TucsonMedicalCenter; 5301 E Grant Rd) Has 24-hour emergency services.

INTERNET ACCESS

Joel D Valdez Main Library (☑520-594-5500; 101 N Stone Ave; ⊙9am-8pm Mon-Wed, 9am-6pm Thu, 9am-5pm Fri, 10am-5pm Sat, 1-5pm Sun; 🛜) Free internet, including wi-fi.

MEDIA

Arizona Daily Star (http://azstarnet.com) The Tucson region's daily newspaper.

Tucson Weekly (www.tucsonweekly.com) A free weekly full of entertainment and restaurant listings.

POST

Post office (☑520-629-9268; 825 E University Blvd, Suite 111; ⊙8am-5pm Mon-Fri, 9am-12:30pm Sat)

HOT DIGGETY DOG

Tucson's signature 'dish' is the Sonoran hot dog, a tasty example of what happens when Mexican ingredients meet America's processed meat and penchant for excess. The ingredients? A bacon-wrapped hot dog layered with tomatillo salsa, pinto beans, shredded cheese, mayo, ketchup or mustard or both, chopped tomatoes and onions. We like 'em at **El Guero Canelo** (www.elguerocanelo.com; 5201 S 12th Ave; Sonoran hot dog $3).

TOURIST INFORMATION

Tucson Convention & Visitors Bureau
(☑800-638-8350, 520-624-1817; www.visit-tucson.org; 100 S Church Ave; ☉9am-5pm Mon-Fri, to 4pm Sat & Sun) Ask for its free *Official Destination Guide.*

ⓘ Getting There & Around

Tucson International Airport (☑520-573-8100; www.flytucson.com; 7250 S Tucson Blvd) is 15 miles south of downtown. **Arizona Stagecoach** (☑520-889-1000; www.azstagecoach.com) runs shared van service with fares for about $25 between downtown and the airport. **Greyhound** (☑520-792-3475; www.greyhound.com; 471 W Congress St) runs buses to Phoenix ($21 to $23, two hours, daily) and other destinations. The station is on the western end of Congress St, 3 miles from downtown. **Amtrak** (☑800-872-7245, 520-623-4442; www.amtrak.com; 400 E Toole Ave) is across from Hotel Congress and has train services to Los Angeles (from $56, 10 hours, three weekly) on the Sunset Limited.

The **Ronstadt Transit Center** (215 E Congress St, cnr Congress St & 6th Ave) is the major downtown transit hub. From here **Sun Tran** (☑520-792-9222; www.suntran.com) buses serve metropolitan Tucson (day pass $3.50).

Around Tucson

The places listed here are less than 1½ hours' drive from town and make great day trips.

West of Tucson

You want wide solitude? Follow Hwy 86 west from Tuscon into some of the emptiest parts of the Sonoran Desert – except for the ubiquitous green-and-white border patrol trucks.

The lofty **Kitt Peak National Observatory** (☑520-318-8726; www.noao.edu/kpno; Hwy 86; visitor center by donation; ☉9am-4pm) west of Sells features the largest collection of optical telescopes in the world. Guided tours (adult/child $9.75/4.25 November to May, $7.75/3.25 June to October, at 10am, 11:30am and 1:30pm) last about an hour. Book two to four weeks in advance for the worthwhile nightly observing program (adult/child $49/45; no programs from mid-July through August because of monsoon season). Clear, dry skies equal an awe-inspiring glimpse of the cosmos. Dress warmly, buy gas in Tucson (the nearest gas station is 30 miles from the observatory) and note that children under eight years of age are not allowed at the evening program for safety reasons. The picnic area

draws amateur astronomers at night. It's about a 75-minute drive from Tucson.

If you truly want to get away from it all, you can't get much further off the grid than the huge and exotic **Organ Pipe Cactus National Monument** (☑520-387-6849; www.nps.gov/orpi; Hwy 85; per vehicle $8; ☉visitor center 8:30am-4:30pm) along the Mexican border. It's a gorgeous, forbidding land that supports an astonishing number of animals and plants, including 28 species of cacti, first and foremost its namesake organ-pipe. A giant columnar cactus, it differs from the more prevalent saguaro in that its branches radiate from the base. The 21-mile **Ajo Mountain Drive** takes you through a spectacular landscape of steep-sided, jagged cliffs and rock tinged a faintly hellish red. There are 208 first-come, first-served sites at **Twin Peaks Campground** (www.nps.gov/orpi; tent/RV sites $12) by the visitor center.

South of Tucson

South of Tucson, I-19 is the main route to Nogales and Mexico. Along the way are several interesting stops.

The striking **Mission San Xavier del Bac** (☑520-294-2624; www.patronatosanxavier.org; 1950 W San Xavier Rd; donations appreciated; ☉museum 8:30am-5pm, church 7am-5pm), 9 miles south of downtown Tucson, is Arizona's oldest European building still in use. It's a graceful blend of Moorish, Byzantine and late Mexican Renaissance architecture with an unexpectedly ornate interior.

At exit 69, 16 miles south of the mission, the **Titan Missile Museum** (☑520-625-7736; www.titanmissilemuseum.org; 1580 W Duval Mine Rd, Sahuarita; adult/child/senior $9.50/6/8.50; ☉8:45am-5pm) features an underground launch site for Cold War–era intercontinental ballistic missiles. Tours are chilling and informative.

If history or shopping for crafts interest you, head 48 miles south of Tucson to the small village of **Tubac** (www.tubacaz.com), with more than 100 galleries, studios and shops.

Patagonia & the Mountain Empire

This lovely riparian region, sandwiched between the Mexican border and the Santa Rita and Patagonia Mountains, is one of the shiniest gems in the Arizona jewel box. It's a tranquil destination for bird-watching and wine tasting.

Bird-watchers and nature-lovers wander the gentle trails at the **Patagonia-Sonoita Creek Preserve** (☑520-394-2400; www.nature.org/arizona; 150 Blue Heaven Rd; admission $6; ☉6:30am-4pm Wed-Sun Apr-Sep, 7:30am-4pm Wed-Sun Oct-Mar), an enchanting creekside willow and cottonwood forest managed by the Nature Conservancy. The peak migratory seasons are April through May, and late August to September. For a leisurely afternoon of wine tasting, head to the villages of **Sonoita** and **Elgin** north of Patagonia (see www.arizonavinesandwines.com). The big-sky views are terrific.

If you stick around for dinner, try the fantastic gourmet pizzas at **Velvet Elvis** (☑520-394-2102; www.velvetelvispizza.com; 292 Naugle Ave, Patagonia; mains $10-26; ☉11:30am-8:30pm Thu-Sat, to 7:30pm Sun). Salute the old West and its simple charms at the **Stage Stop Inn** (☑520-394-2211; www.stagestophotelpatagonia.com; 303 McKeown, Patagonia; s $79, d $89-99, ste $109; 🖥🚳🐾), where rooms surround a central courtyard and pool. The stage coach did indeed stop here on the Butterfly Trail.

A small **visitor center** (☑888-794-0060; www.patagoniaaz.com; 307 McKeown Ave, Patagonia; ☉10am-5pm Mon-Thu & Sat, 11am-4pm Fri) is tucked inside Mariposa Books & More in Patagonia.

Southeastern Arizona

Chockablock with places that loom large in the history of the Wild West, southern Arizona is home to the wonderfully preserved mining town of Bisbee, the OK Corral in Tombstone, and a wonderland of stone spires at Chiricahua National Monument.

Kartchner Caverns State Park

The emphasis is on education at **Kartchner Caverns State Park** (☑information 520-586-4100, reservations 520-586-2283; http://azstateparks.com; Hwy 90; park entrance per vehicle/bicycle $6/3, Rotunda Tour adult/child $23/13, Big Room Tour mid-Oct–mid-Apr $23/13; ☉8am-5pm Jun-Sep, 7am-6pm Oct-May), a 2.5-mile wet limestone fantasia of rocks. Two guided tours explore different areas of the caverns, which were 'discovered' in 1974. The Rotunda/Throne Room Tour is open year-round; the Big Room Tour closes in mid-April for five months to protect the migratory bats

that roost here. The park is 9 miles south of Benson, off I-10 at exit 302. The $6 entrance fee is waived for reserved tour tickets.

Chiricahua National Monument

The towering rock spires at remote but mesmerizing **Chiricahua National Monument** (☑520-824-3560; www.nps.gov/chir; Hwy 181; adult/child $5/free) in the Chiricahua Mountains sometimes rise hundreds of feet high and often look like they're on the verge of tipping over. The **Bonita Canyon Scenic Drive** takes you 8 miles to Massai Point (6870ft) where you'll see thousands of spires positioned on the slopes like some petrified army. There are numerous hiking trails, but if you're short on time, hike the **Echo Canyon Trail** at least half a mile to the Grottoes, an amazing 'cathedral' of giant boulders where you can lie still and enjoy the wind-caressed silence. The monument is 36 miles southeast of Willcox off Hwy 186/181.

Tombstone

In Tombstone's 19th-century heyday as a booming mining town the whiskey flowed and six-shooters blazed over disputes large and small, most famously at the OK Corral. Now a National Historic Landmark, it attracts hordes of tourists to its old Western buildings, stagecoach rides and gunfight reenactments.

And yes, you must visit the **OK Corral** (☑520-457-3456; www.ok-corral.com; Allen St btwn 3rd & 4th Sts; admission $10, without gunfight $6; ☉9am-5pm), site of the legendary gunfight where the Earps and Doc Holliday took on the McLaurys and Billy Clanton on October 26, 1881. The McClaurys and Clanton now rest at the **The Boot Hill Graveyard** on Hwy 80 north of town. Also make time for the dusty **Bird Cage Theater** (☑520-457-3421; 517 E Allen St; adult/child/senior $10/8/9; ☉9am-6pm), a one-time dance hall and saloon now crammed with historic odds and ends. And a merman.

The **Visitor & Information Center** (☑520-457-3929; www.tombstonechamber.com; cnr 395 E Allen & 4th Sts; ☉9am-5pm) has walking maps and local recommendations.

Bisbee

Oozing old-fashioned ambience, Bisbee is a former copper-mining town that's now a delightful mix of aging Bohemians, elegant buildings, sumptuous restaurants and charming hotels. Most businesses are found in the Historic District (Old Bisbee), along Subway and Main Sts.

To burrow under the earth in a tour led by the retired miners who worked here, take the Queen Mine Tour (☑ 520-432-2071; www.queenminetour.com; 478 Dart Rd, off Hwy 80; adult/child $13/5.50; ⊙ tours 9am-3:30pm; ⊛). Right outside of town, check out the Lavender Pit, an ugly yet impressive testament to strip mining.

Rest your head at Shady Dell RV Park (☑ 520-432-3567; www.theshadydell.com; 1 Douglas Rd; rates $87-145, closed early Jul–mid-Sep; ⊛), a kitschy trailer park extraordinaire. Everything's done up with fun, retro furnishings. Swamp coolers provide cold air. You can sleep in a covered wagon at the quirky but fun Bisbee Grand Hotel (☑ 520-432-5900; www.bisbeegrandhotel.com; 61 Main St, Bisbee; r incl breakfast $89-175; ⊛ ⊜), which brings the Old West to life (or maybe it never died) with Victorian-era decor and a kick-up-your-spurs saloon.

For good eats, stroll up Main St and pick a restaurant – you can't go wrong. For fine American food, try stylish Cafe Roka (☑ 520-432-5153; www.caferoka.com; 35 Main St; dinner $17-24; ⊙ 5-9pm Thu-Sat), where four-course dinners include salad, soup, sorbet and a rotating choice of crowd-pleasing mains. Continue up Main St for wood-fired pizzas and punk-rock style at Screaming Banshee Pizza (☑ 520-432-1300; 200 Tombstone Canyon Rd; pizzas $7-15; ⊙ 4-9pm Tue & Wed, 11am-10pm Thu-Sat, 11am-9pm Sun). Bars cluster in Brewery Gulch, at the south end of Main St.

The visitor center (☑ 520-432-3554; www.discoverbisbee.com; 478 Dart Rd; ⊙ 8am-5pm Mon-Fri, 10am-4pm Sat & Sun), in the Queen Mine Tour Building just south of downtown, is a good place to start.

UTAH

Shhhhh, don't tell. We wouldn't want word to get out that this oft-overlooked state is really one of nature's most perfect playgrounds. Utah's rugged terrain comes ready-made for hiking, biking, rafting, rappelling, rock climbing, skiing, snowboarding, snow riding, horseback riding, four-wheel driving... Need we go on?

More than 65% of the state's lands are public, including 12 national parks and monuments – a dazzling display of geology that leaves many awestruck. Southern Utah is a seemingly endless expanse of sculpted sandstone desert, its red-rock country defined by soaring Technicolor cliffs, spindles and spires. The 11,000ft-high forest- and snow-covered peaks of the Wasatch and other mountains and valleys dominate northeastern Utah.

Across the state you'll find well-organized towns with pioneer-era buildings dating to when the first Mormon settlers arrived; still today, church members make up more than 50% of the wonderfully polite population. Rural towns may be quiet and conservative, but the rugged beauty has attracted many outdoorsy, independent thinkers as well. Salt Lake and Park cities especially have vibrant nightlife and foodie scenes.

So come wonder at the roadside geologic kaleidoscope, hike out into the vast expanses or enjoy a great craftworks micro-brew. Just don't tell your friends: we'd like to keep this secret to ourselves.

History

Traces of the Ancestral Puebloan (or Anasazi) and Fremont people, this land's earliest human inhabitants, can today be seen in the rock art and ruins they left behind. But it was the modern Ute, Paiute and Navajo tribes who were living here when settlers of European heritage arrived in large numbers. Led by second church president, Brigham Young, Mormons fled to this territory to escape religious persecution starting in the late 1840s. They set about attempting to settle every inch of their new land, no matter how inhospitable, which resulted in skirmishes with Native Americans – and more than one abandoned ghost town.

For nearly 50 years after the United States acquired the Utah Territory from Mexico, petitions for statehood were rejected as a result of the Mormon practice of polygamy (taking multiple wives), which was illegal in the US. Tension and prosecutions grew until 1890, when Mormon leader Wilford Woodruff had a divine revelation and the church officially discontinued the practice. Utah became the 45th state in 1896. The modern Mormon church, now called the Church of Jesus Christ of Latter-Day Saints (LDS) continues to exert a strong influence here.

ⓘ Information

Note that it can be difficult to change currency outside Salt Lake City, but ATMs are widespread.

Utah Office of Tourism (☏800-200-1160; www.utah.com) Publishes the free *Utah Travel Guide*; runs several visitor centers statewide.

Utah State Parks & Recreation Department (☏801-538-7220; www.stateparks.utah.gov) Produces comprehensive guide to the 40-plus state parks; available online and at visitor centers.

ⓘ Getting There & Away

Salt Lake City (SLC) has the state's only international airport. It may be cheaper to fly into Las Vegas (425 miles south) and rent a car.

ⓘ Getting Around

You will need a private vehicle to get around anywhere besides SLC and Park City. Utah towns are typically laid out in a grid with streets aligned north–south or east–west. There's a zero point in the town center at the intersection of two major streets (often called Main St and Center St). Addresses and numerical street names radiate out from this point, rising by 100 with each city block. Thus, 500 South 400 East will be five blocks south and four blocks east of the zero point. The system is complicated to explain, but thankfully it's quite easy to use.

Salt Lake City

Snuggled up against the soaring peaks of the Wasatch Mountains, Salt Lake City is a small town with just enough edge to satisfy city slickers. Yes, it is the Mormon equivalent of Vatican City, but Utah's capital city is quite modern. A redeveloped downtown and local foodie scene balance out the city's charming anachronisms.

◉ Sights & Activities

Top church-related sights cluster near downtown's zero point: the corner of S Temple (east–west) and Main St (north–south). See those 132ft-wide streets? They were originally built so that four oxen pulling a wagon could turn around.

Don't forget that just 45 minutes away, world-class hiking, climbing and snow sports await in the Wasatch Mountains (p370).

UTAH FACTS

Nickname Beehive State

Population 2.85 million

Area 82,169 sq miles

Capital city Salt Lake City (population 189,314), metro area (1.2 million)

Other cities St George (population 75,561)

Sales tax 5.95%

Birthplace of Entertainers Donny (b 1957) and Marie (b 1959) Osmond, beloved bandit Butch Cassidy (1866–1908)

Home of 2002 Winter Olympic Games

Politics Mostly conservative

Famous for Mormons, red-rock canyons, polygamy

Best souvenir Wasatch Brew Pub & Brewery T-shirt: 'Polygamy Porter – Why Have Just One?'

◉ Temple Square Area

Temple Square PLAZA
(www.visittemplesquare.com; cnr S Temple & N State Sts; ☺grounds 24hr, visitor centers 9am-9pm) **FREE** The city's most famous sight, a 10-acre square filled with stunning LDS architecture, flower gardens and fountains, is certainly awe-inspiring. Disarmingly nice LDS-member 'sister' and 'brother' volunteers answer questions and lead free 30-minute grounds tours from the visitor centers, just inside the two entrances (on S and N Temple).

Lording over the square, the 210ft-tall **Salt Lake Temple** is at its most ethereal when lit up at night. Atop the tallest spire stands a statue of the angel Moroni, who appeared to first LDS prophet, Joseph Smith, and led him to the Book of Mormon. The Temple and its ceremonies are private, open only to LDS members. In addition to the sights listed, the square also contains a church history museum, Joseph Smith theater and restaurants.

Tabernacle RELIGIOUS
(http://mormontabernaclechoir.org; Temple Sq; ☺9am-9pm) **FREE** This domed, 1867 auditorium – with a massive 11,000-pipe organ –

SALT LAKE CITY FOR CHILDREN

Young and old alike appreciate the attractions in the University-Foothill District, but there are also a couple of kid-specific sights to see.

Discovery Gateway (www.childmuseum.org; 444 W 100 South; admission $8.50; ⊘10am-6pm Mon-Thu, 10am-8pm Fri & Sat, noon-6pm Sun; 🚻) is an enthusiastic, hands-on children's museum. The mock network-news desk in the media zone is particularly cool for budding journos.

More than 800 animals inhabit zones like the Asian Highlands on the landscaped 42-acre grounds of **Hogle Zoo** (www.hoglezoo.org; 2600 E Sunnyside Ave; adult/child $13/10; ⊘9am-5pm; 🚻). Daily animal-encounter programs help kids learn more about their favorite species.

has incredible acoustics. A pin dropped in the front can be heard in the back, almost 200ft away. Free organ recitals are held here at noon Monday through Saturday. For more on the famous choir performances, see Entertainment.

Beehive House　　　　　　　HOUSE
(☑801-240-2671; www.visittemplesquare.com; 67 E South Temple St; ⊘9am-8:30pm Mon-Sat) **FREE** The Beehive House was Brigham Young's main home during his tenure as governor and church president in Utah. The required tours begin on your arrival and vary in the amount of historic house detail versus religious education offered.

Family History Library　　　　LIBRARY
(www.churchhistory.org; 35 N West Temple St; ⊘8am-5pm Mon, 8am-9pm Tue-Fri, 9am-5pm Sat) **FREE** Investigating your ancestors? This incredible library contains more than 3.5 million genealogy-related microfilms, microfiches, books and other records gathered from more than 110 countries.

⊙ Greater Downtown

Utah State Capitol　　　　HISTORIC BUILDING
(www.utahstatecapitol.utah.gov; 350 N State St; ⊘building 7am-8pm Mon-Fri, 8am-6pm Sat & Sun, visitor center 8:30am-5pm Mon-Fri) **FREE** Inside the 1916 State Capitol, colorful Works Progress Administration (WPA) murals of pioneers, trappers and missionaries adorn the dome. Free, hourly guided tours (9am to 5pm, Monday to Friday) start at the 1st-floor visitor center; self-guided tours are also available.

City Creek　　　　　　　PLAZA
(www.shopcitycreekcenter.com; Social Hall Ave, btwn Regent & Richards Sts) Smack dab in the middle of the city you'll find this 20-acre

pedestrian plaza fraught with pleasant fountains and outdoor fireplaces, plus a whole host of restaurants and an indoor-outdoor mall.

⊙ University-Foothill District & Beyond

★**Natural History Museum of Utah**　　　　　MUSEUM
(http://umnh.utah.edu; 301 Wakara Way; adult/child $11/6; ⊘10am-5pm Thu-Tue, 10am-8pm Wed) The stunning architecture of the Rio Tinto Center forms a multistory indoor 'canyon' that showcases exhibits to great effect. Walk up through the layers as you explore both indigenous peoples' and natural history.

The Past Worlds paleontological displays are the most impressive. You get an incredible perspective from beneath, next to, and above a vast collection of dinosaur fossils – one that represents the full breadth of pre-history.

This Is the Place Heritage Park　　　　HISTORIC SITE
(www.thisistheplace.org; 2601 E Sunnyside Ave; adult/child $10/7; ⊘9am-5pm Mon-Fri, 10am-5pm Sat; 🚻) A 450-acre park marks the spot where Brigham Young uttered the fateful words, 'This is the place.' The centerpiece is a living-history village where, June through August, costumed docents depict mid-19th-century life. Admission includes a tourist train ride and activities. During the off-season guests can wander the village at reduced rates.

Red Butte Garden　　　　GARDEN
(www.redbuttegarden.org; 300 Wakara Way; adult/child $10/6; ⊘9am-7:30pm) Both landscaped and natural gardens cover the lovely 150, trail-accessible acres of Red Butte Gardens in the Wasatch foothills. Check online to see

who's playing at the popular, outdoor summer concert series also held here.

Church Fork Trail
HIKING

(Millcreek Canyon, off Wasatch Blvd; day-use $3) Looking for the nearest workout with big views? Hike the 6-mile round-trip, pet-friendly trail up to Grandeur Peak (8299ft). Millcreek Canyon is 13.5 miles southwest of downtown.

👉 Tours

Utah Heritage Foundation
WALKING TOURS

(☑ 801-533-0858; www.utahheritagefoundation. com; tours per person $5-20) The local heritage society offers walking tours of different neighborhoods, as well as 'Thirst Fursday' pub crawls. For do-it-yourselfers, detailed self-guided walking-tour brochures are available online (or at the city visitor center).

🛏 Sleeping

Downtown, rates vary greatly depending on local events and daily occupancy. Cheaper chain motels cluster off I-80: near the airport and south in suburban Midvale. Outside ski season, prices plunge at Wasatch Mountain resorts, about 45 minutes from downtown.

Crystal Inn & Suites
MOTEL $

(☑ 800-366-4466, 801-328-4466; www.crystal-innsaltlake.com; 230 W 500 South; r incl breakfast $78-120; P ❀ @ 🛜 ☲) Utah-owned, multistory motel with a super-friendly staff and loads of free amenities (including a huge, hot breakfast buffet).

Avenues Hostel
HOSTEL $

(☑ 801-539-8888, 801-359-3855; www.saltlake-hostel.com; 107 F St; dm $18, s/d without bathroom $40/46, with bathroom $56/60; ❀ @ 🛜) Well-worn hostel, a bit halfway house–like with long-term residents. But it has a convenient location.

★ Inn on the Hill
INN $$

(☑ 801-328-1466; www.inn-on-the-hill.com; 225 N State St; r incl breakfast $135-220; P ❀ @ 🛜) Exquisite woodwork and Maxfield Parrish Tiffany glass are just some of the adornments in this sprawling 1906 Renaissance Revival mansion turned inn. Guest rooms are classically comfortable, not at all stuffy, and you have the run of two patios, a billiard room, a library and a dining room. High above Temple Sq, expect great views – and an uphill hike back from town.

Peery Hotel
HOTEL $$

(☑ 801-521-4300, 800-331-0073; www.peeryhotel. com; 110 W 300 South; r $90-130; P ❀ @ 🛜) This stately historic hotel (1910) has a great location in the Broadway Ave entertainment district, within walking distance of restaurants, bars and theaters. Expect upscale conveniences such as Egyptian-cotton robes, iPod docking stations and Tempurpedic mattresses.

SVEA
B&B $$

(☑ 801-832-0970; www.svea.us; 720 Ashton Ave; r incl breakfast $155-165; P ❀ 🛜) Both elegant and eclectic, the 1890s Victorian house that contains this B&B has a few odd angles and room configurations. Continental breakfast arrives in a basket at your door daily.

Grand America
HOTEL $$$

(☑ 800-621-4505; www.grandamerica.com; 555 S Main St; r $199-289; P ❀ @ 🛜 ☲) Italian marble bathrooms, English wool carpeting, tasseled damask draperies and other cushy details decorate SLC's most luxurious hotel. If that's not enough to spoil you, there's always afternoon high tea or the lavish Sunday brunch.

🍴 Eating

Many of Salt Lake City's bountiful assortment of ethnic and organically minded restaurants are within the downtown core. There's also a good collection (Middle Eastern, a noodle house, upscale new American, a cafe...) at 9th and 9th (cnr 900 East and 900 South Sts).

POLYGAMY TODAY

Though the Mormon church eschewed plural marriage in 1890, there are unaffiliated offshoot sects that still believe it is a divinely decreed practice. Most of the roughly 7000 residents in Hilldale-Colorado City on the Utah–Arizona border are polygamy-practicing members of the Fundamentalist Church of Jesus Christ of Latter-Day Saints (FLDS). Walk into a Walmart in Washington or Hurricane and the shoppers you see in pastel-colored, prairie-style dresses – with lengthy braids or elaborate up-dos – are likely sister wives. Other, less-conspicuous polygamy-practicing sects are active in the southern parts of the state as well.

Lion House Pantry Restaurant AMERICAN $
(www.templesquarehospitality.com; 63 E South
Temple St; meals $7-13; ⊙11am-8pm Mon-Sat)
Down-home, carb-rich cafeteria cookin' just
like your Mormon grandmother made. Several of Brigham Young's wives used to live in
this historic house (including this author's
great-great-great grandmother).

Ekamai Thai THAI $
(http://ekamaithai.com/; 336 W 300 South; dishes
$6-9; ⊙11am-9pm Mon-Sat) In nice weather
you can enjoy this tasty Thai curry takeaway at the patio tables outside.

★ Tin Angel MODERN AMERICAN $$
(http://thetinangel.com; 365 W 400 South; small
plates & sandwiches $10-16, dinner mains $19-25;
⊙11am-3pm & 5-10pm Mon-Sat) Using ingredients from local growers, the chef melds
different cuisines to create fresh, new American flavors. Think wild boar ribs with gorgonzola gnocchi. Vintage china and local art
lining the walls give this great little place an
even more eclectic vibe.

Red Iguana MEXICAN $$
(www.rediguana.com; 736 W North Temple; mains
$8-16; ⊙11am-10pm) Ask for a sample plate of
mole if you can't decide which of the seven
chile- and chocolate-based sauces sounds
best. Really, you can't go wrong with any of
the thoughtfully flavored Mexican food at
this always-packed, family-run restaurant.

Squatters Pub Brewery AMERICAN $$
(www.squatters.com; 147 W Broadway; dishes $10-
22; ⊙11am-midnight Sun-Thu, to 1am Fri & Sat)
Come for an Emigration Pale Ale, stay for

the blackened tilapia salad. The lively pub
atmosphere here is always fun.

Copper Onion INTERNATIONAL $$$
(☑801-355-3282; www.thecopperonion.com; 111
E Broadway Ave; brunch & small plates $7-15, dinner mains $22-29; ⊙11am-3pm & 5-10pm) Locals
keep the Copper Onion bustling at lunch, at
dinner, at weekend brunch, at happy hour
in the bar... And for good reason: small
plates like wagyu beef tartare and pasta carbonara call out to be shared. Design-driven
rustic decor provides a convivial place to
enjoy it all.

Takashi JAPANESE $$$
(☑801-519-9595; 18 W Market St; rolls $10-18,
mains $18-30; ⊙11:30am-2pm & 5:30-10pm Mon-
Sat) The best of a number of surprisingly
good sushi restaurants in landlocked Salt
Lake; even LA restaurant snobs rave about
the excellent rolls at oh-so-chic Takashi.

🍷 Drinking & Nightlife

Epic Brewing Company CAFE
(www.epicbrewing.com; 825 S State St; ⊙11am-
9pm Mon-Thu, 10am-11pm Fri & Sat, 11am-7pm
Sun) Utah's first full-strength beer brewery.
You have to order something small to eat
(Utah law) at this small tasting counter, but
then staff pour samples ($0.40 to $1) and
full glasses of their 30 ales, IPAs, lagers and
stouts.

Gracie's BAR
(326 S West Temple; ⊙11am-2am) Even with two
levels and four bars, this upscale hang-out
still gets crowded. The two sprawling patios

CAN I GET A DRINK IN UTAH?

Absolutely. Although there are still a few unusual liquor laws on the books, regulations
have relaxed somewhat in recent years. Private club memberships are no more: a 'bar'
is now a bar (no minors allowed), and you don't have to order food to consume alcohol in one of them. These are few and far between though. Most establishments, even
brewpubs, are 'restaurants', where you have to order something small to imbibe alcohol.
Also note that not all restaurants have full liquor licenses; many sell only wine and beer.

Remaining rules to remember:

➡ You must be actually dining at a fully licensed restaurant to order any alcoholic
drink there.

➡ Mixed drinks and wine are available only after noon. In bars and restaurants, beer can
be served from 10am.

➡ Packaged liquor can only be sold at state-run liquor stores (closed on Sundays), some
beer is sold in convenience stores.

➡ Most beer you get here does not exceed 3.2% alcohol content by weight (a typical
Budweiser is 5%).

are the best place to kick back. Live music or DJs most nights.

Beerhive Pub PUB
(128 S Main St; ⊘noon-1am) More than 200 beer choices, including many Utah-local microbrews, are wedged into this small downtown bar.

Coffee Garden CAFE
(895 E 900 South; ⊘6am-11pm Sun-Thu, 6am-midnight Fri & Sat; 🛜) Amazing baked goods and great coffee in one of SLC's most character-filled neighborhood coffeehouses.

☆ Entertainment
Music
A complete list of local music is available online at www.cityweekly.net. Orchestra, organ, choir and other LDS-linked performances are listed at www.mormontabernacle-choir.org.

Mormon Tabernacle Choir LIVE MUSIC
(☑801-570-0080; www.mormontabernaclechoir.org) **FREE** Hearing the world-renown Mormon Tabernacle choir is a must-do during any SLC visit. A live, half-hour choir broadcast goes out every Sunday at 9:30am. Doors open at 8:30am and tickets are free, but guests may be seated by 9:15am.

September through November and January through May, attend the broadcast in person at the Tabernacle. From June to August and in December, to accommodate larger crowds, the choir performs at the 21,000-seat LDS Conference Center. Public rehearsals are held at the Tabernacle year round from 8pm to 9pm on Thursdays.

Theater
The Salt Lake City Arts Council provides a complete cultural events calendar on its website (www.slcgov.com/city-life/ec). Local venues include Abravanel Hall (www.slcfa.org; 123 W South Temple St), Capitol Theater (http://theatresaltlakecity.com; 50 W 200 South) and the Rose Wagner Performing Arts Center (www.slcfa.org; 138 W 300 South). You can reserve through ArtTix (☑888-451-2787, 801-355-2787; www.arttix.org).

Sports
Energy Solutions Arena STADIUM
(☑801-355-7328; www.energysolutionsarena.com; 301 W South Temple St) Utah Jazz, the men's professional basketball team, play at this downtown stadium – as does the indoor soccer league. Concerts are held here, too.

THE BOOK OF MORMON, THE MUSICAL
Singing and dancing Mormon missionaries have been lighting up Broadway since 2011. But rumor has it that *The Book of Mormon*, the musical, may actually open in Salt Lake City before the 10-years-down-the-road date originally forecast. This light-hearted satire about brothers and sisters on their mission trip in Uganda came out of the comic minds that created the *Avenue Q* musical and the animated TV series *South Park*. No wonder people laughed them all the way to nine Tony Awards. The LDS church's official response? Actually quite measured, though it was made clear that their belief is that while the *Book*, the musical, can entertain you, the Book, the scripture, can change your life.

Maverik Center STADIUM
(☑tickets 800-745-3000; www.maverikcenter.com; 3200 S Decker Lake Dr, West Valley City) The International Hockey League's Utah Grizzlies play 8.5 miles outside town.

🛍 Shopping
City Creek (p366) is the indoor-outdoor mall of choice for big-name-brand shopping downtown. A small but interesting array of boutiques line up along Broadway Avenue (300 South), between 100 and 300 East. A few crafty shops can be found on the 300 block of W Pierpont Avenue.

ℹ Information
EMERGENCY & MEDICAL SERVICES
Salt Lake Regional Medical Center (☑801-350-4111; www.saltlakeregional.com; 1050 E South Temple; ⊘ emergency24hr)

INTERNET ACCESS
Main Library (www.slcpl.org; 210 E 400 South; ⊘9am-9pm Mon-Thu, 9am-6pm Fri & Sat, 1-5pm Sun; 🛜) Free wi-fi and computer internet access.

MEDIA
City Weekly (www.cityweekly.net) Free alternative weekly with restaurant and entertainment listings.
Salt Lake Tribune (www.sltrib.com) Utah's largest-circulation paper; entertainment section lists eateries and events.

GREAT SALT LAKE

Once part of prehistoric Lake Bonneville, Great Salt Lake today covers 2000 sq miles and is far saltier than the ocean; you can easily float on its surface. The pretty, 15-mile-long **Antelope Island State Park** (☑801-773-2941; http://stateparks.utah.gov; Antelope Dr; day use per vehicle $9, tent & RV sites without hookups $13; ☺7am-10pm Jul-Sep, 7am-7pm Oct-Jun), 40 miles northwest of SLC, has nice hiking and the best beaches for lake swimming (though at low levels they're occasionally smelly). It's also home to one of the largest bison herds in the country. A basic campground operates year-round. Six of the 26 sites are available first-come, first-served, the rest by reservation.

MONEY

Wells Fargo (www.wellsfargo.com; 79 S Main St; ☺9am-6pm Mon-Fri, 9am-3pm Sat) Currency-exchange services.

TOURIST INFORMATION

Public Lands Information Center (☑801-466-6411; www.publiclands.org; REI Store, 3285 E 3300 South; ☺10:30am-5:30pm Mon-Fri, 9am-1pm Sat) Recreation information for the Wasatch-Cache National Forest; located inside the REI store.

Visit Salt Lake (☑801-534-4900; www.visit-saltlake.com; visitor center 90 S West Temple, Salt Palace Convention Center; ☺9am-6pm Mon-Fri, 9am-5pm Sat & Sun) Large office with lots of brochures and gift shop.

WEBSITES

Downtown SLC (www.downtownslc.org) Arts, entertainment and business information about the downtown core.

❶ Getting There & Away

AIR

A new terminal is in the planning stages, but for now the **Salt Lake City International Airport** (SLC; www.slcairport.com; 776 N Terminal Dr), 5 miles northwest of downtown, has mostly domestic flights except for a few jaunts to Canada and Mexico. **Delta** (☑800-221-1212; www.delta.com) is the main SLC carrier.

BUS

Greyhound (☑800-231-2222; www.greyhound.com; 300 S 600 West) connects SLC with Southwestern towns such as Las Vegas, NV ($86, eight hours), and Denver, CO ($114, 10 hours).

TRAIN

Traveling between Chicago and Oakland/Emeryville, the *California Zephyr* from **Amtrak** (☑800-872-7245; www.amtrak.com) stops daily at **Union Pacific Rail Depot** (340 S 600 West). Scheduled delays can be substantial, and trains depart at odd hours, but you can connect with destinations such as Denver ($150, 15 hours) and Reno, NV ($68, 10 hours).

❶ Getting Around

TO/FROM THE AIRPORT

In 2013 the **Utah Transit Authority** (UTA; www.rideuta.com; one-way $2) completed a 6-mile TRAX light-rail extension that connects the airport with the Energy Solutions Arena stop (green line). Bus 453 also connects the airport with downtown.

Express Shuttle (☑800-397-0773; www.xpressshuttleutah.com) shared van service costs about $16 to downtown; a taxi will run you roughly $25

PUBLIC TRANSPORTATION

Utah Transit Authority (p370) continues to expand its TRAX light-rail system. The seven stops in the center of downtown SLC are a fare-free zone and are on all three, color-coded lines. During ski season UTA buses serve the local ski resorts (one-way $4.50).

Park City & the Wasatch Mountains

Utah has awesome skiing, some of the best anywhere in North America. Its fabulous low-density, low-moisture snow – between 300in and 500in annually – and thousands of acres of high-altitude terrain helped earn Utah the honor of hosting the 2002 Winter Olympics. The Wasatch Mountain Range, which towers over SLC, is home to numerous ski resorts, abundant hiking, camping and mountain biking – not to mention chichi Park City with its upscale amenities and famous film festival.

Salt Lake City Resorts

On the western side of the Wasatch mountain range, the four impressive snow-sport resorts in Little Cottonwood and Big Cottonwood Canyons lie within 40 minutes' drive of downtown SLC. All have lodging and dining facilities. A one- to 10-day **Super**

Pass (www.visitsaltlakecity.com/ski/superpass; 3-day pass adult/child $219/114) offers ski access to all resorts (one per day) plus round-trip transportation from SLC.

For a full list of summer hiking and biking trails, see www.utah.com/saltlake/hiking.htm.

BIG COTTONWOOD CANYON

Solitude   SNOW SPORTS
(☑ 801-534-1400; www.skisolitude.com; 12000 Big Cottonwood Canyon Rd; day lift ticket adult/child $72/46) Exclusive, European-style village surrounded by excellent snow-sport terrain. The Nordic Center has cross-country skiing in winter and nature and mountain-biking trails in summer.

Brighton Resort   SNOW SPORTS
(☑ 800-873-5512; www.brightonresort.com; 12601 Big Cottonwood Canyon Rd; day lift ticket adult/child $57/31) Small but stellar slopes where all of SLC learned to ski and snowboard. Brighton is still an old-school, family and first-timer favorite.

LITTLE COTTONWOOD CANYON

Snowbird   SNOW SPORTS
(☑ 800-232-9542; www.snowbird.com; Hwy 210, Little Cottonwood Canyon; day lift ticket adult/child $65/42) Biggest and busiest of SLC's snow-sport resorts, Snowbird has all-round great snow riding – think steep and deep. Numerous lift-assist summer hiking trails; aerial tramway runs year-round.

Alta Ski Area   SKIING
(☑ 800-258-2716; www.alta.com; Highway 210, Little Cottonwood Canyon; day lift ticket adult/child $65/42) A laid-back choice exclusive to skiers. No snowboarders affecting snow cover here. Enjoy summer hiking among the hundreds of wildflowers in Albion Basin.

Park City

A mere 35 miles east of SLC via I-80, Park City (elevation 6900ft) first skyrocketed to international fame when it hosted the downhill, jumping and sledding events at the 2002 Winter Olympics. The Southwest's most popular ski destination is still home to the US ski team. Come summer, residents (population 7873) gear up for hiking and mountain biking among the nearby peaks.

The town itself – a silver-mining community during the 19th century – has an attractive main street lined with upscale galleries, shops, hotels, restaurants and bars. Despite the spread of prefab condos across the valley, the setting remains relatively charming. Winter (roughly late December through March) is high season. In other months, businesses may close various days and resorts operate limited facilities.

⊙ Sights

Park City Museum   MUSEUM
(www.parkcityhistory.org; 528 Main St; adult/child $10/4; ⊙ 10am-7pm Mon-Sat, noon-6pm Sun) A well-staged, interactive museum touches on the highlights of the town's history as a mining boomtown, hippie hang-out and premier ski resort.

Utah Olympic Park   ADVENTURE SPORTS
(☑ 435-658-4200; http://utaholympiclegacy.com; 3419 Olympic Pkwy; tours adult/child $10/7; ⊙ 10am-6pm, tours 11am-4pm) **FREE** Tour the 2002 Olympic ski-jumping, bobsledding, skeleton, Nordic combined and luge facilities, check out the free ski museum, and if you're lucky, watch the pros practice during a freestyle show (summer and winter; $10). Activities (rates $15 to $200 per ride) include a winter/summer bobsled, an alpine slide, zip lines and a chair lift.

⭐ Activities

In addition to snow sports, each area resort has posh lodging close to the slopes, abundant eateries and various summer activities, including mountain-bike rental and lift-assist hiking. More than 300 miles of interconnecting hiking/biking trails crisscross area mountains; maps are available from the visitor center or online at http://mountaintrails.org. Two of the newer trails to open, **Armstrong** (4 miles; Park City Mountain Resort

---

SCENIC DRIVE: MIRROR LAKE HIGHWAY

This alpine route, also known as Hwy 150, begins about 12 miles east of Park City in Kamas and climbs to elevations of more than 10,000ft as it winds the 65 miles into Wyoming. The highway provides breathtaking mountain vistas, passing scores of lakes, campgrounds and trailheads in the **Uinta-Wasatch-Cache National Forest** (www.fs.usda.gov/uwcnf). Note that sections may be closed to traffic into late spring due to heavy snowfall; check online.

trailhead) and **Pinecone Ridge** (4 miles) combine for excellent mountain biking.

Park City

Mountain Resort
ADVENTURE SPORTS

(☑435-649–8111; www.parkcitymountainresort. com; 1310 Lowell Ave; day lift ticket adult/child $80/50) Family-friendly, super-central Park City Mountain Resort has activities galore: more than 3300 acres of skiable terrain, snow-tubing, an alpine coaster, year-round in-town lift, summer trails, a zip line...

Deer Valley
ADVENTURE SPORTS

(☑800-424-3337; www.deervalley.com; Deer Valley Dr; day lift ticket adult/child $100/64) The area's most exclusive resort is known as much for its superb dining and luxury hilltop hotels, such as the St Regis, as it is for the meticulously groomed, capacity-controlled slopes and ski valets. No snowboarding.

Canyons
ADVENTURE SPORTS

(☑888-226-9667; www.thecanyons.com; 4000 Canyons Resort Dr; day lift ticket adult/child $80/60) The largest resort in Utah, with a year-round gondola, encompasses nine mountain peaks, five bowls and three terrain parks. In summer there are guided hiking and mountain biking in addition to zip-line tours.

★ Festivals & Events

Sundance Film Festival
FILM

(☑888-285-7790; www.sundance.org/festival) Independent films, their makers, movie stars and fans fill the town to bursting for 10 days in late January. Passes, ticket packages and the few individual tickets sell out well in advance; plan ahead.

🛏 Sleeping

More than 100 condos, hotels and resorts rent rooms in Park City; none are dirt cheap. For complete listings, check www.visitparkcity.com. High-season winter rates are quoted below (minimum stays may be required); prices drop by half or more out of peak season. Better deals are to be found at chain motels at the intersection of I-40 and Hwy 248, and in SLC.

Chateau Apres Lodge
HOSTEL $

(☑800-357-3556, 435-649-9372; www.chateauapres.com; 1299 Norfolk Ave; dm $40, d/q $125/175; 🛜) The only budget-ish accommodation in town is this very basic, 1963 lodge – with a 1st-floor dorm – near the town ski lift. Reserve ahead.

★ Old Town Guest House
B&B $$

(☑800-290-6423, 435-649-2642; www.old-townguesthouse.com; 1011 Empire Ave; r incl breakfast $169-199; ✳ @ 🛜) Grab the flannel robe, pick a paperback off the shelf and snuggle under a quilt on your lodgepole-pine bed or relax in the hot tub on the large deck at this comfy in-town B&B. The host will gladly provide space for your gear and give you the lowdown on the area's great outdoors.

Park City Peaks
HOTEL $$

(☑800-333-3333, 435-649-5000; www.parkcitypeaks.com; 2121 Park Ave; r $149-249; ✳ @ 🛜 ♒) Hobnob with junior bobsledders and other US team hopefuls who stay at this hotel between downtown and Olympic Park. December through April, breakfast is included with the cushy contemporary rooms.

Sky Lodge
LUXURY HOTEL $$$

(☑888-876-2525, 435-658-2500; www.theskylodge.com; 201 Heber Ave; ste $400-1000; ✳ @ 🛜 ♒) The urban-loft-like architecture containing the chic Sky Lodge suites both complements and contrasts with the three historic buildings that house the property's stellar restaurants. You can't be more stylish, or more central, if you stay here.

St Regis Deer Valley
LUXURY HOTEL $$$

(☑866-932-7059, 435-940-5700; www.stregisdeervalley.com; 2300 Deer Valley Dr E; r $700-1300; ✳ @ 🛜 ♒) You have to ride a private funicular just to get up to the St Regis. So whether you're lounging by the outdoor fire pits, dining on an expansive terrace or peering out over your room's balcony rail, the views are sublime. The studied elegant rusticity here is the height of Deer Valley's luxury lodging.

🍴 Eating

Park City is not known for cheap eats, but it does have exceptional upscale dining; Deer Valley (p372) has some of the best resort restaurants. Pick up the menu guide put out by Park City Magazine (www.parkcitymagazine.com) for more. Note that from April through November restaurants reduce hours and may take extended breaks. Reservations are required for all top end ($$$) establishments.

Java Cow Coffee & Ice Cream
CAFE $

(402 Main St; dishes $3-8; ☉7am-10pm; 🛜) Enjoy a scoop of site-made ice cream like Moo-ana (with organic banana chunks) along with your Ibis coffee at this always lively cafe. Sandwiches and crepes, too.

Uptown Fare CAFE $
(227 Main St; sandwiches $6-11; ⊙11am-3pm) Comforting house-roasted turkey sandwiches and homemade soups are served at this cozy cafe hidden below Treasure Mountain Inn.

★**Silver Star Cafe** NEW AMERICAN $$
(www.thesilverstarcafe.com; 1825 Three Kings Dr; breakfast & small plates $9-14, dinner mains $15-20; ⊙8am-9pm) We can't decide if it's the inventive, hearty Western dishes or the perfect, out-of-the-way mountain-base location that first hooked us. Either way, we love kicking back on the sunny patio aprés ski or enjoying the singer-songwriter showcases.

Good Karma FUSION $$
(www.goodkarmarestaurants.com; 1782 Prospector Ave; breakfast $7-12, mains $12-22; ⊙7am-10pm) 🍴 Whenever possible, local and organic ingredients are used in the Indo-Persian meals, with an Asian accent. You'll recognize the place by the Tibetan prayer flags flapping out front.

Vinto ITALIAN $$
(www.vinto.com; 900 Main St, Summit Watch Plaza; dishes $8-17; ⊙11am-10pm Mon-Sat, 4-9pm Sun) Minimalist surrounds are suitably stylish for Main St. But the wood-fired pizzas and light, fresh Italian dishes, surprisingly, won't break your bank.

Riverhorse on Main NEW AMERICAN $$$
(🗷435-649-3536; http://riverhorseparkcity.com; 540 Main St; brunch $25-35, dinner mains $35-45; ⊙5-10pm Mon-Thu, 5-11pm Fri & Sat, 11am-2:30pm & 5-10pm Sun) Consistently one of the town's top performers, garnering numerous awards for its upscale American dishes such as pistachio-covered Utah trout. Live music nightly in winter.

Wahso ASIAN $$$
(🗷435-615-0300; www.billwhiterestaurantgroup.com/wahso.html; 577 Main St; mains $30-50; ⊙5:30-10pm Wed-Sun) Engagingly exotic. A see-and-be-seen crowd frequents this sophisticated Indochine fusion restaurant.

🍷 Drinking & Nightlife

Main St is where it's at, with half a dozen or more bars, clubs and pubs. In winter, there's action nightly – even restaurants have music. Outside peak season, the scene is weekends-only. For listings, see www.thisweekinparkcity.com.

ROBERT REDFORD'S SUNDANCE RESORT

Wind your way up narrow and twisting Hwy 92, for a truly special experience at Robert Redford's **Sundance Resort** (🗷800-892-1600, 801-225-4107; www.sundanceresort.com; 9521 Alpine Loop Rd, Provo; r $199-500; 🕸). 🍴 Even if a night's stay at this elegantly rustic, ecoconscious wilderness getaway is out of reach, you can have a stellar meal at the Treehouse Restaurant or deli, attend an outdoor performance at the amphitheater or watch pottery being made (and sold) at the art shack. Skiing, hiking and spa services are also on site. Just walking the grounds is an experience. The resort is 30 miles south of Park City and 50 miles southeast of SLC.

High West Distillery & Saloon BAR
(703 Park St; ⊙11am-10pm, tours 3pm & 4pm) A former livery and Model A–era garage is home to Park City's own microdistillery. Take a tour, sample some rye, order a whiskey lemonade and stay for supper.

No Name Saloon & Grill BAR
(447 Main St; ⊙11am-1am) There's a motorcycle hanging from the ceiling, Johnny Cash's 'Jackson' playing on the stereo and a waitress who may or may not be lying about the history of this memorabilia-filled bar.

ℹ Information

Library (🗷435-615-5600; http://parkcitylibrary.org; 1255 Park Ave; ⊙10am-9pm Mon-Thu, 10am-6pm Fri & Sat, 1-5pm Sun; 🕸) Free wi-fi and internet stations for use.
Main Street Visitor Center (🗷435-649-7457; 528 Main St; ⊙10am-7pm Mon-Sat, noon-6pm Sun) Small desk inside the busy Park City Museum.
Visitor Information Center (🗷800-453-1360, 435-649-6100; www.visitparkcity.com; 1794 Olympic Pkwy; ⊙9am-6pm; 🕸) Vast visitor center with a coffee bar, terrace and incredible views of the mountains near Olympic Park. Visitor guides available online.

ℹ Getting There & Around

Park City Transportation (🗷800-637-3803, 435-649-8567; www.parkcitytransportation.com) and **Canyon Transportation** (🗷800-255-1841; www.canyontransport.com) both run shared-van service ($40 one-way) and private-charter vans (from $100 for one to three people) to/from Salt Lake City airport. The latter also has ski transfers (from $50) that will take you from Park City to Salt Lake City resorts.

PC-SLC Connect (bus 902) takes you from central Salt Lake to the **Park City Transit Center** (www.parkcity.org; 558 Swede Alley). No need for a car once you get to Park City. The excellent transit system covers the town: accessing the historic district, Kimbell Junction and all three ski resorts. The free buses run one to six times an hour from 8am to 11pm (reduced frequency in summer). There's a downloadable route map online.

Northeastern Utah

Most people head northeast to explore Dinosaur National Monument, but this rural, oil-rich area also has some captivating wilderness terrain. All towns are a mile above sea level.

Vernal

As the closest town to Dinosaur National Monument, it's not surprising that Vernal welcomes you with a large pink dino-buddy. Since oil and gas production in the region has expanded, and the monument is fully operational after many dormant years, new things are popping up in town all the time.

The informative film at the **Utah Field House of Natural History State Park Museum** (http://stateparks.utah.gov; 496 E Main St; ⊙9am-5pm Mon-Sat; 🏃) is a great all-round introduction to Utah's dinosaurs. Interactive exhibits, video clips and, of course, giant fossils are wonderfully relevant to the area.

Don Hatch River Expeditions (☑435-789-4316, 800-342-8243; www.donhatchrivertrips.com; 221 N 400 East; 1 day adult/child $99/76) offers rapid-riding and gentler float trips on the nearby Green and Yampa Rivers.

Chain motels are numerous along Main St, but they book up with local workers – so don't expect a price break. **Holiday Inn Express & Suites** (☑435-789-4654; www.vernalhotel.com; 1515 W Hwy 40; r incl breakfast $100-170, ste $130-200; 🅿🛜🏊) has the most amenities, and **Econo Lodge** (☑435-789-2000; www.econolodge.com; 311 E Main St; r $69-99) will do in a bargain pinch. For something different, try **Landmark Inn & Suites** (☑888-738-1800, 435-781-1800; www.landmark-inn.com; 301 E 100 S; motel r incl breakfast $129-169, B&B $80-100; 🛜),

which has both an upscale motel and an off-site inn.

Backdoor Grille (87 W Main St; mains $5-8; ⊙11am-6pm Mon-Sat) makes fresh sandwiches and cookies, which are great to take on a picnic; you can also pick up a hiking guide at the associated bookshop. For dinner, the **Porch** (www.facebook.com/theporchvernal; 251 E Main St; lunch $8-12, dinner $14-22; ⊙11am-2pm & 5-9pm Mon-Fri, 5-9pm Sat) is the place to go for Southern US favorites. **Don Pedro's Mexican Family Restaurant** (http://klcyads.com/don-pedros; 3340 N Vernal Ave; dishes $8-15; ⊙11am-2pm & 5-10pm), north of town, serves festive meals from south of the border.

Vernal Chamber of Commerce (☑800-477-5558; www.dinoland.com; 134 W Main; ⊙9am-5pm Mon-Fri) provides information on the entire region, including numerous driving-tour brochures for area rock art and dino tracks.

Dinosaur National Monument

Straddling the Utah–Colorado state line, **Dinosaur National Monument** (www.nps.gov/dino; off Hwy 40; 7-day per vehicle $10; ⊙24hr) protects one of North America's largest dinosaur fossil beds, discovered here in 1909. Though both state's sections are beautiful, Utah has the bones. Don't miss the **Quarry Exhibit** (9am to 4pm), which is an enclosed, partially excavated wall of rock with more than 1600 bones protruding – quite the sight to see.

In summer, you will have to take a shuttle to see the quarry and hours may be extended a little; out of season you may be required to wait until a ranger-led caravan of cars is scheduled to drive up. From below the quarry parking lot, follow the Fossil Discovery Trail (2.2 miles round-trip) to see a few more giant femurs and such sticking out of the rock. The rangers' interpretive hikes are highly recommended. Plus there's easily-accessible Native American rock art to see on the Utah side.

In Colorado, the Canyon Area is at a higher elevation – with some stunning overlooks – but is closed to snow until late spring. Both sections have numerous hiking trails, interpretive driving tours (brochures for sale), Green or Yampa river access and campgrounds ($8 to $15 per tent and RV site). The Quarry portion of the park is 15 miles northeast of Vernal, UT, on Hwy 149. The Canyon Area is roughly 30 miles farther east, outside Dinosaur, CO.

There are two visitor centers: the Quarry Visitor Center (⊘8am-6pm mid-May–late Sep, 9am-5pm late Sep–mid-May) and, in Colorado, the Canyon Area Visitor Center (☑970-374-3000; www.nps.gov/dino; Dinosaur, CO; ⊘9am-5pm Jun-early Sep, 10am-4pm Sat & Sun only mid-April–May).

Flaming Gorge National Recreation Area

Named for its fiery red sandstone, this gorge-ous park has 375 miles of reservoir shoreline, part of the Green River system. Area resort activities at Red Canyon Lodge (☑435-889-3759; www.redcanyonlodge.com; 790 Red Canyon Rd, Dutch John; cabins $115-145) include fly-fishing, rowing, rafting and horseback riding, among others. Its pleasantly rustic cabins have no TVs. Flaming Gorge Resort (☑435-889-3773; www.flaminggorgeresort.com; 155 Greendale/Hwy 191, Dutch John; r $90-120, ste $120-160) has similar water-based offerings and rents motel rooms and suites. Both have decent restaurants.

Get general information at www.flaminggorgecountry.com and contact the USFS Flaming Gorge Headquarters (☑435-784-3445; www.fs.fed.us/r4/ashley; 25 W Hwy 43, Manila; ⊘8am-5pm Mon-Fri) for the public camping lowdown. The area's 6040ft elevation ensures pleasant summers – daytime highs average about 80°F.

Moab & Southeastern Utah

Snow-blanketed peaks in the distance provide stark contrast to the red-rock canyons that define this rugged corner of the Colorado Plateau. For 65 million years water has carved serpentine, sheer-walled gorges along the course of the Colorado and Green Rivers. Today these define the borders of expansive Canyonlands National Park (p378). At nearby Arches National Park (p377), erosion sculpted thousands of arches and fin rock formations. Base yourself between the parks in Moab, aka activity central – a town built for mountain biking, river running and four-wheel driving. In the far southeastern corner of the state, Ancestral Puebloan sites are scattered among remote and rocky wilderness areas and parks. Most notable is Monument Valley, which extends into Arizona.

Green River

The 'World's Watermelon Capital,' the town of Green River offers a good base for river running on the Green and Colorado Rivers. The legendary one-armed Civil War veteran, geologist and ethnologist John Wesley Powell first explored these rivers in 1869 and 1871. Learn about his amazing travels at the extensive John Wesley Powell River History Museum (www.jwprhm.com; 885 E Main St; adult/child $3/1; ⊘8am-7pm Apr-Oct, 8am-4pm Nov-Mar), which also has exhibits on the Fremont Indians, geology and local history. The museum serves as the local visitor center.

Outfitters Holiday Expeditions (☑800-624-6323, 435-564-3273; www.holidayexpeditions.com; 10 Holiday River St; day trip adult/child $195/175) and Moki Mac River Expeditions (☑800-284-7280, 435-564-3361; www.mokimac.com; day trip $160) run one-day rafting trips in Westwater Canyon, as well as multiday excursions.

Family-owned, clean and cheerful, Robbers Roost Motel (☑435-564-3452; www.rrmotel.com; 325 W Main St; s $35, d $45; ❉ 🛜 🐾) is a motorcourt budget-motel gem. Otherwise, there are numerous chain motels where W Main St (Business 70) connects with I-70. Residents and rafters alike flock to Ray's Tavern (25 S Broadway; dishes $8-26; ⊘11am-10pm), the local beer joint, for the best hamburgers and fresh-cut French fries in Southeastern Utah.

Green River is the only stop in the area on the daily *California Zephyr* train run by Amtrak (☑800-872-7245; www.amtrak.com; 250 S Broadway) to Denver, CO ($90, 10¾ hours). Green River is 182 miles southeast of Salt Lake City and 52 miles northwest of Moab.

Moab

Southeastern Utah's largest community (population 5093) bills itself as the state's recreation capital, and... oh man, does it deliver. Scads of rafting and riding (mountain bike, horse, 4WD...) outfitters here make forays into surrounding public lands. Make this your base, too, and you can hike Arches or Canyonlands National Parks during the day, then come back to a comfy bed, a hot tub and your selection of surprisingly good restaurants at night. Do note that this alfresco adventure gateway is not a secret: the town is mobbed, especially during spring and fall events. If the traffic irritates you, remember that you can disappear into the vast surrounding desert in no time.

🏃 Activities

The Moab visitor center puts out several brochures on near-town rock art, hiking trails, driving tours, etc. It also keeps a list of the numerous area outfitters that offer half-day to multiday adventures (from $60 for a sunset 4WD tour to $170 for a white-water day on the river) that include transport, the activity and, sometimes, meals. Book ahead.

Outfitters

Sheri Griffith Expeditions   RAFTING
(☑ 800-332-2439; www.griffithexp.com; 2231 S Hwy 191; day trip $170) Highly rated rafting outfitter; some multisport adventures.

Poison Spider Bicycles   MOUNTAIN BIKING
(☑ 800-635-1792, 435-259-7882; www.poison-spiderbicycles.com; 497 N Main St; per day rental $45-70) Mountain- and road-bike rentals and tours; superior advice and service.

Farabee's Jeep Rental &
Outlaw Tours   ADVENTURE SPORTS
(☑ 877-970-5337; www.farabeesjeeprentals.com; 1125 S Highway 191; per day Jeep rental $150-225) Four-wheel-drive rentals, self-drive and fully guided off-road Jeep tours.

Moab Desert Adventures   ADVENTURE SPORTS
(☑ 877-765-6622, 435-260-2404; www.moabde-sertadventures.com; 415 N Main St; half-/full-day $165/285) Top-notch climbing tours scale area towers and walls; canyoneering and multisport packages available.

Red Cliffs Lodge   HORSEBACK RIDING
(☑ 866-812-2002, 435-259-2002; www.redcliffs-lodge.com; Mile 14, Hwy 128; half-day $80) Daily half-day trail rides offered; advanced, open-range rides also available.

🛏 Sleeping

Most lodgings in town have bike storage facilities and hot tubs to soothe sore muscles. Despite having an incredible number of motels, the town does fill up; reservations are highly recommended March through October. Rates drop significantly in the off-season.

Individual **BLM campsites** (www.blm.gov/utah/moab; tent & RV sites $10-12; ⊙year-round) in the area are first-come, first-served. In peak season, check with the Moab Information Center to see which sites are full.

Adventure Inn   MOTEL $
(☑ 866-662-2466, 435-259-6122; www.adventureinnmoab.com; 512 N Main St; r incl breakfast $80-105; ⊙Mar-Oct; ❄🐾) A great little indie motel, the Adventure Inn has spotless rooms (some with refrigerators) and decent linens, as well as laundry facilities.

Cali Cochitta   B&B $$
(☑ 888-429-8112, 435-259-4961; www.moab-dreaminn.com; 110 S 200 East; cottages incl breakfast $135-170; ❄🐾) Make yourself at home in one of the charming brick cottages a short walk from downtown. A long wooden table on the patio provides a welcome setting for community breakfasts.

Sunflower Hill   INN $$
(☑ 800-662-2786, 435-259-2974; www.sunflower-hill.com; 185 N 300 East; r incl breakfast $165-225; ❄🐾🐾) Relax amid the manicured gardens of a rambling 100-year-old farmhouse and an early-20th-century home. All 12 guest quarters have a sophisticated country sensibility.

Gonzo Inn   MOTEL $$
(☑ 800-791-4044, 435-259-2515; www.gonzoinn.com; 100 W 200 South; r incl breakfast Apr-Oct $160-180; ❄@🐾🐾🐾) Brushed metal-and-wood headboards, concrete shower stalls and colorful retro patio furniture spruce up this desert-colored adobe motel.

Sorrel River Ranch   LODGE $$$
(☑ 877-359-2715, 435-259-4642; www.sorrelriver.com; Mile 17, Hwy 128; r $420-530; ❄@🐾) Southeast Utah's full-service luxury lodge, set on 240 acres along the banks of the Colorado River, was originally an 1803 homestead. Horseback riding, spa services and gourmet restaurant on site.

🍴 Eating

There's no shortage of places at which to fuel up in Moab, from backpacker coffeehouses to gourmet dining rooms. Pick up the *Moab Menu Guide* (www.moabmenuguide.com) at area lodgings. Some restaurants close earlier, or on variable days, from December through March.

Love Muffin   CAFE $
(www.lovemuffincafe.com; 139 N Main St; dishes $6-8; ⊙7am-2pm; 🐾) The largely organic menu at this vibrant cafe includes imaginative sandwiches, breakfast burritos and egg dishes such as 'Verde,' with brisket and slow-roasted salsa.

Milt's   BURGERS $
(356 Mill Creek Dr; dishes $5-10; ⊙11am-8pm Mon-Sat) A classic 1954 burger stand with fresh-cut fries and oh-so-thick milkshakes.

Miguel's Baja Grill   MEXICAN $$
(www.miguelsbajagrill.com; 51 N Main St; mains $14-24; ⊙5-10pm) Dine on fish tacos or fajitas, and sip margaritas, in the sky-lit breezeway patio lined with brightly painted walls.

Cowboy Grill   AMERICAN $$
(☑435-259-2002; http://redcliffslodge.com; Mile 14, Hwy 128, Red Cliffs Lodge; breakfast & lunch $10-16, dinner $14-28; ⊙6:30-10am, 11:30am-2pm & 5-10pm) Incredible Colorado River sunset views are to be had from the patio or behind the huge picture windows here. The hearty meat and seafood dishes aren't bad either.

★**Sabuku Sushi**   FUSION $$$
(☑435-259-4455; http://sabakusushi.com; 90 E Center St; rolls $12-18, small plates $14-19; ⊙5-10pm Tue-Sun) Such impossibly fresh sushi is especially impressive this far into the desert. Try inventive rolls and small plates such as elk *tataki* (like carpaccio, with an Asian twist).

Desert Bistro   SOUTHWESTERN $$$
(☑435-259-0756; http://desertbistro.com; 36 S 100 West; mains $20-50; ⊙5:30-10pm Mar-Nov) Stylized preparations of game and seafood are the specialty at this welcoming white-tablecloth restaurant. Great wine list, too

🛍 Shopping

Look for art and photography galleries – along with T-shirt and Native American knickknacks – near the intersection of Center and Main Sts.

Arches Book Company &
Back of Beyond   BOOKS
(83 N Main St; ⊙9am-8pm; 🛜) Excellent, adjacent indie bookstores with extensive regional selection, including guides and maps.

ℹ Information

Most businesses and services, including fuel and ATMs, are along Hwy 191, also called Main St in the center of town.

BLM (Bureau of Land Management; ☑435-259-2100; www.blm.gov/utah/moab) Public-land phone and internet assistance only.

Grand County Public Library (www.moablibrary.org; 257 E Center St; per hr free; ⊙9am-8pm Mon-Fri, to 5pm Sat) Easy 15-minute internet; register for longer access.

Moab Information Center (www.discovermoab.com; cnr Main & Center Sts; ⊙8am-7pm Mon-Sat, 9am-6pm Sun) Excellent source of information on area parks, trails, activities, camping and weather; big bookstore, too. Free brochures also available online.

ℹ Getting There & Around

Great Lakes Airlines (☑800-554-5111; www.flygreatlakes.com) has regularly scheduled flights from **Canyonlands Airport** (CNY; www.moabairport.com; off Hwy 191), 16 miles north of town via Hwy 191, to Denver, CO, and Prescott, AZ.

Moab Luxury Coach (☑435-940-4212; www.moabluxurycoach.com) operates van service to and from SLC ($160 one-way, 4¾ hour) and Grand Junction ($90 one-way, 3¾ hour). **Roadrunner Shuttle** (☑435-259-9402; www.roadrunnershuttle.com) and **Coyote Shuttle** (☑435-260-2097; www.coyoteshuttle.com) offer on-demand Canyonlands Airport, hiker-biker and river shuttles.

Moab is 235 miles southeast of Salt Lake City, 150 miles northeast of Capital Reef National Park.

Arches National Park

One of the Southwest's most gorgeous parks, **Arches** (☑435-719-2299; www.nps.gov/arch; Hwy 191; 7-day per vehicle $10; ⊙24hr, visitor center 7:30am-6:30pm Mar-Oct, 9am-4pm Nov-Feb) boasts the world's greatest concentration of sandstone arches – more than 2000, ranging from 3ft to 300ft wide at last count. Nearly one million visitors make the pilgrimage here, just 5 miles north of Moab, every year. Many noteworthy arches are easily reached by paved roads and relatively short hiking trails; much of the park can be covered in a day. To avoid crowds, consider a moonlight exploration, when it's cooler and the rocks feel ghostly.

Highlights include **Balanced Rock**, oft-photographed **Delicate Arch** (best captured in the late afternoon), spectacularly elongated **Landscape Arch** and popular **Windows Arches**. Reservations are necessary for the twice-daily ranger-led hikes into the maze-like fins of the **Fiery Furnace**; book at least a few days in advance – in person or online at www.recreation.gov.

Because of water scarcity and heat, few visitors backpack, though it is allowed with free permits (available from the visitor center). Advance reservations are a must for the

SOUTHWEST MOAB & SOUTHEASTERN UTAH

NEWSPAPER ROCK RECREATION AREA

This tiny, free recreation area showcases a single large sandstone rock panel packed with more than 300 petroglyphs attributed to Ute and Ancestral Puebloan groups during a 2000-year period. It's about 12 miles along Hwy 211 from Hwy 191, en route to the Needles section of Canyonlands National Park (8 miles further).

scenic Devils Garden Campground (☑877-444-6777; www.recreation.gov; tent & RV sites $20), 18 miles from the visitor center. Dates book up far in advance for stays from March to October. No showers, no hook-ups.

Canyonlands National Park

Red-rock fins, bridges, needles, spires, craters, mesas, buttes – Canyonlands (www.nps.gov/cany; 7-day per vehicle $10, tent & RV sites without hookups $10-15; ☺24hr) is a crumbling, decaying beauty, a vision of ancient earth. Roads and rivers make inroads into this high-desert wilderness stretching 527 sq miles, but much of it is still untamed. You can hike, raft and 4WD here but be sure that you have plenty of gas, food and water. Cataract Canyon offers some of the wildest white water in the West (find outfitters in Moab and Green River).

The canyons of the Colorado and Green Rivers divide the park into separate districts. The Island in the Sky district offers amazing overlooks. The visitor center (☑435-259-4712; Hwy 313, Canyonlands National Park; ☺visitor center 8am-6pm Mar-Oct, 9am-4pm Nov-Feb) is 32 miles northwest of Moab. Our favorite short hike there is the half-mile loop to oft-photographed Mesa Arch, a slender, cliff-hugging span framing a picturesque view of Washer Woman Arch and Buck Canyon. Drive a bit further to reach the Grand View Overlook trail; the path follows the canyon's edge and ends at a praise-your-maker precipice. Wilder and more far-flung, the Needles section is ideal for backpacking and off-roading. To reach the visitor center (☑435-259-4711; Hwy 211; ☺8am-6pm Mar-Oct, 9am-4:30pm Nov-Feb), follow Hwy 191 south and Hwy 211 west, 40 miles from Moab. Both sections have small, basic campgrounds (no

showers) that are available first-come, first served.

In addition to normal entrance fees, advance-reservation permits ($10 to $30) are required for backcountry camping, 4WD trips and river trips. For more, contact the Backcountry Reservations Office (☑435-259-4351; http://www.nps.gov/cany/planyourvisit/backcountrypermits.htm; Canyonlands National Park).

Dead Horse Point State Park

Tiny but stunning Dead Horse Point State Park (www.stateparks.utah.gov; Hwy 313; park day-use per vehicle $10, tent & RV sites $20; ☺park 6am-10pm, visitor center 8am-6pm Mar-Oct, 9am-4pm Nov-Feb) has been the setting for numerous movies, including scenes from *Mission Impossible II* and *Thelma & Louise*. Located en route to the Needles Section of Canyonlands NP, the park is an easy stop off Hwy 313. Mesmerizing views are worth the detour: look out at red-rock canyons rimmed with white cliffs, the Colorado River, Canyonlands and the distant La Sal Mountains. The 21-site campground has limited water (bringing your own is highly recommended); no showers, no hookups. Reserve ahead.

Bluff

One hundred miles south of Moab, this tiny tot town (population 258) makes a comfortable, laid-back base for exploring the desolately beautiful southeastern corner of Utah. Bluff sits surrounded by redrock and public lands near the junction of Hwys 191 and 162, along the San Juan River. The settlement was founded by Mormon pioneers in 1880. Other than a trading post and a couple of places to eat or sleep, there's not much town.

For backcountry tours that access rock art and ruins, hire Far Out Expeditions (☑435-672-2294; www.faroutexpeditions.com; half-day from $125) to lead a day or multiday hike into the remote region. A rafting trip with Wild Rivers Expeditions (☑800-422-7654; www.riversandruins.com; 101 Main St; day trip adult/child $175/133), a history and geology-minded outfitter, also includes ancient site visits.

The hospitable Recapture Lodge (☑435-672-2281; www.recapturelodge.com; Hwy 191; r incl breakfast $70-90; ❉@☎≋) is a rustic, cozy place to stay. Owners sell maps and know the region inside and out; you can follow trails from here to the river. Also nice are the spacious log rooms at the **Desert Rose Inn** (☑888-475-7673, 435-672-2303; www.desert-roseinn.com; Hwy 191; r $105-119, cabins $139-179; ❄@🛜).

Artsy **Comb Ridge Coffee** (www.comb-ridgecoffee.com; 680 S Hwy 191; dishes $3-7; ⏱7am-5pm Tue-Sun, varies Nov-Feb; ☑) serves espresso, muffins and sandwiches inside a timber and adobe cafe. For lunch and dinner, the organic-minded **San Juan River Kitchen** (www.sanjuanriverkitchen.com; 75 E Main St; mains $14-20; ⏱5:30-10pm Tue-Sat) offers regionally sourced, inspired Mexican American dishes.

Hovenweep National Monument

Beautiful, little-visited **Hovenweep** (www.nps.gov/hove; Hwy 262; park 7-day per vehicle $6, tent & RV sites $10; ⏱park dusk-dawn, visitor center 8am-6pm Jun-Sep, 9am-5pm Oct-May), meaning 'deserted valley' in the Ute language, contains impressive towers and granaries that are part of prehistoric Ancestral Puebloan sites. The Square Tower Group is accessed near the visitor center; other sites require long hikes. The campground has 31 basic, first-come, first-served sites (no showers, no hookups). The main access is east of Hwy 191 on Hwy 262 via Hatch Trading Post, more than 40 miles northeast of Bluff.

Monument Valley

Twenty-five miles west from Bluff, after the village of **Mexican Hat** (named for an easy-to-spot sombrero-shaped rock), Hwy 163 winds southwest and enters the Navajo Indian reservation. Thirty miles south, the incredible mesas and buttes of **Monument Valley** rise up. Most of the area, including the tribal park with a 17-mile unpaved driving loop circling the massive formations, is in Arizona (p357).

Natural Bridges National Monument

Fifty-five miles northwest of Bluff, this really remote **monument** (www.nps.gov/nabr; Hwy 275; park 7-day per vehicle $6, tent & RV sites $10; ⏱24hr, visitor center 8am-6pm May-Sep, 9am-5pm Oct-Apr) protects a white sandstone canyon (it's not red!) containing three impressive and easily accessible natural bridges. The oldest, the Owachomo Bridge, spans 180ft but is only 9ft thick. The flat 9-mile Scenic Drive loop is ideal for overlooking. The

campground has 13 basic sites (no showers, no hookups) that are available on a first-come, first-served basis. There is some primitive overflow camping space, but be aware that there are no services before Blanding (40 miles east).

Zion & Southwestern Utah

Local tourist boards call it 'color country,' but the cutesy label hardly does justice to the eye-popping hues that saturate the landscape. The deep-crimson canyons of Zion, the delicate pink-and-orange minarets at Bryce Canyon, the swirling yellow-white domes of Capitol Reef – the land is so spectacular that located here are three national parks and the gigantic Grand Staircase-Escalante National Monument (GSENM).

Capitol Reef National Park

Not as crowded as its fellow parks but equally scenic, **Capitol Reef** (☑435-425-3791, ext 4111; www.nps.gov/care; cnr Hwy 24 & Scenic Dr; admission free, 7-day scenic drive per vehicle $5, tent & RV sites $10; ⏱24hr, visitor center & scenic drive 8am-6pm Apr-Oct, to 4:30pm Nov-Mar) contains much of the 100-mile Waterpocket Fold, created 65 million years ago when the earth's surface buckled up and folded, exposing a cross-section of geologic history that is downright painterly in its colorful intensity. Hwy 24 cuts grandly through the park, but

> ### ℹ ELEVATION MATTERS
>
> As elsewhere, southern Utah is generally warmer than northern Utah. But before you go making any assumptions about weather, check the elevation of your destination. Places less than an hour apart may have several thousand feet of elevation – and 20°F temperature – difference.
>
> ➡ St George (3000ft)
> ➡ Zion National Park – Springdale entrance (3900ft)
> ➡ Cedar Breaks National Monument (10,000ft)
> ➡ Bryce National Park Lodge (8100ft)
> ➡ Moab (4026ft)
> ➡ Salt Lake City (4226ft)
> ➡ Park City (7100ft)

make sure to take the scenic drive south, which passes through orchards – a legacy of Mormon settlement. In season, you can freely pick cherries, peaches and apples, as well as stop by the historic Gifford Farmhouse to see an old homestead and buy fruit-filled minipies. The shady, green campground (no showers, no hookups) is first-come, first-served; it fills early spring through fall.

Torrey

Just 15 miles west of Capital Reef, the small pioneer town of Torrey serves as the base for most national park visitors. In addition to a few Old West–era buildings, there are a dozen or so restaurants and motels.

Western-themed on the outside, Austin's Chuckwagon Motel (☑ 435-425-3335; www.austinschuckwagonmotel.com; 12 W Main St; r $75-85, cabins $135; ⊙ Mar-Oct; ❋ 🐾 🛏 ❋) has nice, clean, slightly characterless guest rooms on the inside. Note that budget digs are over the general store, where you can grab supplies or sandwiches.

Dressed with country elegance, each airy room at the 1914 Torrey Schoolhouse B&B (☑ 435-633-4643; www.torreyschoolhouse.com; 150 N Center St; r incl breakfast $118-148; ⊙ Apr-Oct; ❋ 🐾) has a story to tell. (Butch Cassidy may have attended a town dance here.) After consuming the full gourmet breakfast, laze in the garden or the huge 1st-floor lounge before you head out hiking.

Whenever possible, Capitol Reef Cafe (☑ 435-425-3271; www.capitolreefinn.com; 360 W Main St; breakfast & lunch $6-12, dinner $16-22; ⊙ 7am-9pm Apr-Oct) uses local and organic ingredients in its meals. Homemade pies are a hit, but so are healthier dishes like trout. At this writing, the renowned local restaurant, Cafe Diablo (☑ 435-425-3070; http://cafediablo.net; 599 W Main St; lunch $10-14, dinner $22-40; ⊙ 11:30am-10pm mid-Apr–Oct; 🐾) was undergoing an ownership change.

If you want to explore further or find local outfitters, contact the Wayne County Travel Council (☑ 800-858-7951, 435-425-3365; www.capitolreef.org; cnr Hwys 24 & 12; ⊙ noon-7pm Mon-Sat Apr-Oct).

Boulder

Though the tiny outpost of Boulder (www.boulderutah.com), population 227, is just 32 miles south of Torrey on Hwy 12, you have to cross over Boulder Mountain to get there. The area is so rugged and isolated that a paved Hwy 12 didn't connect through until 1985. From here, the attractive Burr Trail Rd heads east across the northeastern corner of the Grand Staircase-Escalante National Monument, eventually winding up on a gravel road that leads either up to Capital Reef or down to Bullfrog Marina on Lake Powell.

To explore area canyons and rock art, consider a one-day (pet-friendly) trek with knowledgeable Earth Tours (☑ 435-691-1241; www.earth-tours.com; trips per person from $150; ⊙ Mar-Oct; 🐾). The small but excellent Anasazi State Park Museum (www.stateparks.utah.gov; Main St/Hwy 12; admission $5; ⊙ 8am-6pm Mar-Oct, 9am-5pm Nov-Apr) curates artifacts and a Native American site inhabited from AD 1130 to 1175. Get information on area public lands inside the museum, at the GSENM Interagency Desk.

Rooms at Boulder Mountain Lodge (☑ 435-335-7460; www.boulder-utah.com; 20 N Hwy 12; r $110-175; ❋ @ 🐾) are plush, but it's the 15-acre wildlife sanctuary setting that's unsurpassed. An outdoor hot tub with mountain views is a particularly soothing spot to bird-watch. The lodge's destination restaurant, Hell's Backbone Grill (☑ 435-335-7464; http://hellsbackbonegrill.com; 20 N Hwy 12, Boulder Mountain Lodge; breakfast $8-12, lunch $12-18, dinner $18-27; ⊙ 7:30-11:30am & 5-9:30pm Mar-Oct) serves soulful, earthy preparations of regionally inspired and sourced cuisine. Book ahead.

Organic vegetable tarts, eclectic burgers and scrumptious homemade desserts at Burr Trail Grill & Outpost (http://burrtrailgrill.com; cnr Hwy 12 & Burr Trail Rd; dishes $8-18; ⊙ grill 11am-2:30pm & 5-9:30pm, outpost 7:30am-8pm Mar-Oct; 🐾) rival dishes at the more famous Hell's Backbone Grill nearby. You'll also find a coffee shop and a gallery.

Grand Staircase-Escalante National Monument

The 2656-sq-mile Grand Staircase-Escalante National Monument (GSENM; www.ut.blm.gov/monument; ⊙ 24hr) FREE covers more territory than Delaware and Rhode Island combined. It sprawls between Capitol Reef National Park, Glen Canyon National Recreation Area and Bryce Canyon National Park. The nearest services, and GSENM visitor centers, are in Boulder and Escalante on Hwy 12 in the north, and Kanab on US 89 in the south. Otherwise, infrastructure is minimal, leaving a vast, uninhabited canyonland full of 4WD roads that call to adventurous travelers who have the time, equipment and knowledge to explore. Be warned: this waterless region was so inhospitable that it was the last to be mapped in the continental US.

A 6-mile round-trip to the falls at **Lower Calf Creek** (Mile 75, Hwy 12; day use $2, tent & RV sites $7; ☺day use dawn-dusk), between Boulder and Escalante, is the most accessible and most used trail in the park. The 13 popular creekside campsites (no showers, no hookups) fill fast; no reservations taken.

Escalante

This national monument gateway town of 792 people is the closest thing to a metropolis for miles and miles. It's a good place to base yourself – or to stock up and map it out – before venturing into the adjacent GSENM. The **Escalante Interagency Office** (☑435-826-5499; www.ut.blm.gov/monument; 775 W Main St; ☺8am-4:30pm daily Apr-Sep, Mon-Fri Oct-Mar) is a superb resource center with complete information on all monument and forest service lands in the area. Escalante is 30 slow and windy miles from Boulder and 65 from Torrey, near Capital Reef National Park.

Escalante Outfitters & Cafe (☑435-826-4266; www.escalanteoutfitters.com; 310 W Main St; ☺8am-9pm) is a traveler's oasis: the bookstore sells maps, guides, camping supplies – and liquor(!). The pleasant cafe is the place for homemade breakfast, pizzas and salads. It also rents out tiny, rustic cabins ($45) and mountain bikes (from $35 per day). Long-time area outfitter **Excursions of Escalante** (☑800-839-7567; www.excursionsofescalante.com; 125 E Main St; full-day from $145; ☺8am-6pm) leads canyoneering, climbing and photo hikes; it, too, has a cafe on site.

There are a number of decent lodgings in town, including **Canyons Bed & Breakfast** (☑866-526-9667, 435-826-4747; www.canyonsbnb.com; 120 E Main St; r incl breakfast $135-165; ▣🐾) with upscale cabin-rooms that surround a shady courtyard, and the **Circle D Motel** (☑435-826-4297; www.escalantecircledmotel.com; 475 W Main St; r $65-75; ▣🐾🐕), an older-but-updated budget motel with a friendly proprietor and a full-service restaurant.

Kodachrome Basin State Park

Dozens of red, pink and white sandstone chimneys highlight this colorful **state park** (☑435-679-8562; www.stateparks.utah.gov; off

Cottonwood Canyon Rd; day-use per vehicle $6, tent & RV sites with/without hookups $25/16; ☺day use 6am-10pm), named for its photogenic landscape by the National Geographic Society. Some of the developed campsites (showers available) at the campground can be reserved online. Horseback riding and cabin concessions also on-site.

Bryce Canyon National Park

The Grand Staircase, a series of steplike uplifted rock layers elevating north from the Grand Canyon, culminates at this rightly popular **national park** (☑435-834-5322; www.stateparks.utah.gov; Hwy 63; 7-day vehicle pass $25, tent & RV sites without hookups $15; ☺24hr; visitor center 8am-8pm May-Sep, to 4:30pm Oct-Apr) in the Pink Cliffs formation. It's full of wondrous sorbet-colored pinnacles and points, steeples and spires, and totem-pole-shaped 'hoodoo' formations. The 'canyon' is actually an amphitheater eroded from the cliffs. From Hwy 12, turn south on Hwy 63; the park is 50 miles southwest of Escalante.

Rim Road Scenic Drive (8000ft) travels 18 miles, roughly following the canyon rim past the visitor center, the lodge, incredible overlooks (don't miss **Inspiration Point**) and trailheads, ending at **Rainbow Point** (9115ft). From early May through early October, a free shuttle bus runs (8am until at least 5:30pm) from a staging area just north of the park to as far south as **Bryce Amphitheater**.

The park has two camping areas, both of which accept some reservations through the park website. **Sunset Campground** is bit more wooded, but is not open year round. Coin-op laundry and showers are available at the general store near **North Campground**. During summer, remaining first-come sites fill before noon.

The 1920s **Bryce Canyon Lodge** (☑877-386-4383, 435-834-8700; www.brycecanyon-forever.com; Hwy 63, Bryce Canyon National Park; r & cabins $175-200; ☉Apr-Oct; @) exudes rustic mountain charm. Rooms are in modern hotel-style units, with up-to-date furnishings, and thin-walled duplex cabins with gas fireplaces and front porches. No TVs. The lodge **restaurant** (☑435-834-8700; Bryce Canyon National Park; breakfasts $6-12, lunch & dinner $18-40; ☉7-10:30am, 11:30am-3pm & 5:30-10pm Apr-Oct) is excellent, if expensive.

Just north of the park boundaries, **Ruby's Inn** (☑435-834-5341; www.rubysinn.com; 1000 S Hwy 63; r $115-170, tent sites $26-55, RV sites with hookups $35-60; ✳@⊚≋) is a town as much as it is a resort complex. Choose from several motel lodging options, plus a campground, before you take a helicopter ride, watch a rodeo, admire Western art, wash laundry, shop for groceries, fill up with gas, dine at one of several restaurants and then post a letter about it all.

Eleven miles east of the park on Hwy 12, the small town of **Tropic** (www.brycecanyoncountry.com/tropic.html) has additional food and lodging.

Kanab

At the southern edge of Grand Staircase-Escalante National Monument, vast expanses of rugged desert surround remote Kanab (population 3564). Western filmmakers made dozens of films here from the 1920s to the 1970s, and the town still has an Old West movie-set feel to it.

The **Kanab GSENM Visitor Center** (☑435-644-1300; www.ut.blm.gov/monument; 745 E Hwy 89; ☉8am-4:30pm) provides monument information; **Kane County Office of Tourism** (☑800-733-5263, 435-644-5033; www.kaneutah.com; 78 S 100 East; ☉9am-7pm Mon-Fri, to 5pm Sat) focuses on town and movie sites. John Wayne, Maureen O'Hara and Gregory Peck are a few Hollywood notables who slumbered at the somewhat-dated **Parry Lodge** (☑888-289-1722, 435-644-2601; www.parrylodge.com; 89 E Center St; r 70-125; ✳⊚≋🐾).

A colorful, retro-cool style pervades all 13 rooms at **Quail Park Lodge** (☑435-215-1447; www.quailparklodge.com; 125 N 300 W; r $115-159; ✳@⊚≋🐾), a refurbished 1963 motorcourt motel. Stay there, then eat downtown at **Rocking V Cafe** (www.rockingvcafe.com; 97 W Center St; lunch $9-14, dinner $15-29; ☉11:30am-10pm; ☑), where fresh ingredients star in dishes such as buffalo tenderloin and curried quinoa.

Zion National Park

Entering **Zion National Park** (www.nps.gov/zion; Hwy 9; 7-day per vehicle $25; ☉24hr; Zion Canyon visitor center 8am-7:30pm Jun-Aug, closes earlier rest of year) from the east along Hwy 9, the route rolls past yellow sandstone and **Checkerboard Mesa** before reaching an impressive gallery-dotted tunnel and 3.5 miles of switchbacks going down in red-rock splendor. More than 100 miles of park trails here offer everything from leisurely strolls to wilderness backpacking and camping.

If you've time for only one activity, the 6-mile **Scenic Drive**, which pierces the heart of Zion Canyon, is it. From April through October, taking a free shuttle from the visitor center is required, but you can hop off and on at any of the scenic stops and trailheads along the way. The famous **Angels Landing Trail** is a strenuous, 5.4-mile vertigo-inducer (1400ft elevation gain, with sheer drop-offs), but the views of Zion Canyon are phenomenal. Allow four hours round-trip.

For the 16-mile backpacking trip down through the **Narrows** (June to September only), you need a hiker shuttle (book through Zion Adventure Company (p383) and a backcountry permit from the visitor center, which in season requires advance reservations available on the park website. You can get part of the experience by walking up from **Riverside Walk** 5 miles to **Big Springs**, where the canyon walls narrow and day trips end. Remember, in either direction, you're hiking *in* the Virgin River for most of the time.

Reserve far ahead and request a riverside site in the cottonwood-shaded **Watchman Campground** (☑for reservations 877-444-6777; www.recreation.gov; Hwy 9, Zion National Park; tent sites $16, RV sites with hookups $18-20) by the canyon. Adjacent **South Campground** (Hwy 9, Zion National Park; tent & RV sites without hookups $16; ☉early Mar-Oct) is first-come, first-served only. Together these two campgrounds have almost 300 sites.

Smack in the middle of the scenic drive, rustic **Zion Lodge** (☑435-772-7700, 888-297-2757; www.zionlodge.com; Zion Canyon Scenic Dr; r $185, cabins $195, ste $225; ✳@⊚) has 81 well-appointed motel rooms and 40 cabins with gas fireplaces. All have wooden porches with stellar red-rock cliff views, but no TVs. The lodge's full-service dining room, **Red Rock Grill** (☑435-772-7760; Zion Canyon Scenic Dr, Zion Lodge; breakfast & sandwiches $8-14, dinner $18-30; ☺6:30-10:30am, 11:30am-3pm & 5-10pm Mar-Oct, hours vary Nov-Feb), has similarly amazing views. Just outside the park, the town of Springdale offers many more services.

Note that you must pay an entrance fee to drive on public Hwy 9 through the park, even if you are just passing through. Motorhome drivers are also required to pay a $15 escort fee to cross through the 1.1-mile Zion-Mt Carmel tunnel at the east entrance.

Springdale

Positioned at the main south, entrance to Zion National Park, Springdale is a perfect little park town. Stunning red cliffs form the backdrop to eclectic cafes, restaurants are big on organic ingredients, and artist galleries are interspersed with indie motels and B&Bs.

In addition to hiking trails in the national park, you can take outfitter-led climbing, canyoneering, mountain biking and 4WD trips (from $140 per person, per half-day) on adjacent BLM lands. All the excellent excursions from Zion Rock & Mountain Guides (☑435-772-3303; www.zionrockguides.com; 1458 Zion Park Blvd; ☺8am-8pm Mar-Oct, hours vary Nov-Feb), including family trips, are private; solo travelers may be able to save money by joining an existing group through Zion Adventure Company (☑435-772-1001; www.zionadventures.com; 36 Lion Blvd; ☺8am-8pm Mar-Oct, 9am-noon & 4-7pm Nov-Feb). Both offer Narrows outfitting and have hiker/biker shuttles; the latter also offers river tubing in summer.

Springdale has an abundance of good restaurants and nice lodging options. The updated motorcourt rooms at Canyon Ranch Motel (☑866-946-6276, 435-772-3357; www.canyonranchmotel.com; 668 Zion Park Blvd; r $99-119, apt $120-140; ❈❞❅) ring a shady lawn with picnic tables and swings. Five flower-filled acres spill down to the Virgin River bank at Cliffrose Lodge (☑800-243-8824, 435-772-3234; www.cliffroselodge.com; 281 Zion Park Blvd; r $159-189; ❈❞❅).

Of the area B&Bs, Zion Canyon B&B (☑435-772-9466; www.zioncanyonbandb.com; 101 Kokopelli Circle; r incl breakfast $135-185; ❈❞) is the most traditional, serving a full, sit-down repast. We like the Red Rock Inn (☑435-772-3139; www.redrockinn.com; 998 Zion Park Blvd; cottages incl breakfast $127-132; ❈❞) for its individual, upscale cottages and pastry-chef-quality goodies delivered to your door. The owners' creative collections of art and artifact enliven the 1930s bungalow that is Under the Eaves Inn (☑435-772-3457; www.undertheeaves.com; 980 Zion Park Blvd; r incl breakfast $110-160, ste $185; ❈❞); the morning meal is a gift certificate to a local restaurant.

For a coffee and *trés bonnes* crêpes – both sweet and savory – make Meme's Cafe (www.facebook.com/memescafezion#!; 975 Zion Park Blvd; dishes $6-10; ☺7am-9pm) your first stop of the day. It also serves paninis and waffles, and in season has live music and barbecues on the patio. In the evening, the Mexican-tiled patio with twinkly lights at Oscar's Cafe (www.cafeoscars.com; 948 Zion Park Blvd; breakfast & burgers $10-15, dinner mains $16-30; ☺8am-10pm) and the rustic Bit & Spur Restaurant & Saloon (www.bitandspur.com; 1212 Zion Park Blvd; mains $16-28; ☺5-10pm daily Mar-Oct, 5-10pm Thu-Sat Nov-Feb) are local-favored places to hang out, eat and drink.

Zion Canyon Visitors Bureau (☑888-518-7070; www.zionpark.com) does not have a physical office; research or request a town guide online. A free Springdale menu magazine, available at local lodgings, comes out every spring.

St George

Nicknamed 'Dixie' for its warm weather and southern location, St George (population 75,561) is popular with retirees. This spacious Mormon town, with an eye-catching temple and pioneer buildings, is a possible stop between Las Vegas (120 miles) and Salt

SOUTHWEST ZION & SOUTHWESTERN UTAH

IF YOU HAVE A FEW MORE DAYS: CEDAR CITY & BREAKS

At 10,000ft, the summer-only road to Cedar Breaks National Monument (☑435-586-0787; www.nps.gov/cebr; Hwy 148; 7-day per person $4; ☺24hr, visitor center 9am-6pm mid-Jun–mid-Oct) is one of the last to open after winter snow. But it's worth the wait for the amazing amphitheater overlooks that rival those of Bryce Canyon. Nearby Cedar City (www.scenicsouthernutah.com) is known for its four-month-long Shakespeare Festival and an abundance of B&Bs. The town is on I-15, 52 miles north of St George and 90 miles west of Bryce Canyon; the national monument is 22 miles northeast of the town.

Lake City (304 miles) – or en route to Zion National Park. The 15,000-sq-ft collection of in-situ dino tracks and exhibits at Dinosaur Discovery Site (www.dinotrax.com; 2200 E Riverside Dr; adult/child $6/3; ◎10am-6pm Mon-Sat) are worth a detour.

Nearly every chain motel known to man is represented somewhere in St George; they're your best bet if you're looking for lodging cheaper than what's available 40 miles (one hour) east in Springdale. Best Western Coral Hills (☑800-542-7733, 435-673-4844; www.coralhills.com; 125 E St George Blvd; r incl breakfast $80-139; ❀@🛜❄) is walking distance from downtown restaurants and historic buildings. Two lovely, late-1800 houses contain Seven Wives Inn (☑800-600-3737, 435-628-3737; www.sevenwivesinn. com; 217 N 100 West; r & ste incl breakfast $99-185; ❀@🛜❄), a B&B with a small, central swimming pool.

The Utah Welcome Center (☑435-673-4542; http://travel.utah.gov; 1835 S Convention Center Dr, Dixie Convention Center; ◎8:30am-5:30pm), off I-15, addresses statewide queries.

NEW MEXICO

SOUTHWEST ALBUQUERQUE

It's called the Land of Enchantment for a reason. The play of sunlight on juniper-speckled hills that roll to infinity; the traditional Hispanic mountain villages with pitched tin roofs atop old adobe homes; the gentle magnificence of the 13,000ft Sangre de Cristo Mountains; plus volcanoes, river canyons and vast high desert plains beneath an even vaster sky – the beauty sneaks up on you, then casts a powerful spell. The culture, too, is alluring, with silhouetted crosses topping historic mud-brick churches, ancient and living Indian pueblos, chili-smothered enchiladas, real-life cowboys and a vibe of otherness that makes the state feel like it might be a foreign country.

The legend of Billy the Kid lurks around every corner. Miracle healings bring flocks of faithful pilgrims to Chimayo. Bats plumb the ethereal corners of Carlsbad Caverns. Something crashed near Roswell...

Maybe New Mexico's indescribable charm is best expressed in the captivating paintings of Georgia O'Keeffe, the state's patron artist. She herself exclaimed, on her very first visit: 'Well! Well! Well!...This is wonderful! No one told me it was like this.'

But seriously, how could they?

History

People roamed the land here as far back as 10,500 BC, but by Coronado's arrival in the 16th century, pueblos (Native American villages) were the dominant communities. Santa Fe was crowned the colonial capital in 1610, after which Spanish settlers and farmers fanned out across northern New Mexico, and missionaries began their often violent efforts to convert the area's Puebloans to Catholicism. Following a successful revolt in 1680, Native Americans occupied Santa Fe until 1692, when Diego de Vargas recaptured the city.

In 1851 New Mexico became US territory. Native American wars, settlement by cowboys and miners and trade along the Santa Fe Trail further transformed the region, and the arrival of the railroad in the 1870s created an economic boom.

Painters and writers set up art colonies in Santa Fe and Taos in the early 20th century. In 1943 a scientific community descended on Los Alamos and developed the atomic bomb. For the past few years, New Mexico has been hit hard by drought.

ℹ Information

Where opening hours are listed by season (not month), readers should call first, as hours can fluctuate based on weather, budgets or for no reason at all.

New Mexico Route 66 Association (www.rt66nm.org) Information on the famous path through the state.

New Mexico State Parks Division (☑888-667-2757; www.emnrd.state.nm.us/SPD) Info on state parks, with a link to camping reservations.

Public Lands Information Center (☑877-851-8946; www.publiclands.org) Camping and recreation information.

Albuquerque

This bustling crossroads has a sneaky charm, one based more on its locals than big-city sparkle. The citizens here are proud of their city, and folks are more than happy to share history, highlights and must-try restaurants – which makes the state's most populous city much more than a dot on the Route 66 map.

Centuries-old adobes line the lively Old Town area, and the shops, restaurants and bars in the hip Nob Hill zone are all within easy walking distance of each other. Ancient petroglyphs cover rocks just outside town while modern museums explore space and nuclear energy. There's a distinctive and vibrant mix of university students, Native Americans, Hispanics, gays and lesbians. You'll find square dances and yoga classes flyered with equal enthusiasm, and ranch hands and real-estate brokers chowing down at hole-in-the-wall taquerias and retro cafes.

Albuquerque's major boundaries are Paseo del Norte Dr to the north, Central Ave to the south, Rio Grande Blvd to the west and Tramway Blvd to the east. Central Ave is the main artery (aka old Route 66) – it passes through Old Town, Downtown, the university and Nob Hill. The city is divided into four quadrants (NW, NE, SW and SE), and the intersection of Central Ave and the railroad tracks just east of Downtown serves as the center point of the city.

◉ Sights

⊙ Old Town

From its foundation in 1706 until the arrival of the railroad in 1880, the plaza was the hub of Albuquerque; today Old Town is the city's most popular tourist area.

Also in the Old Town are **San Felipe de Neri Church** (www.sanfelipedeneri.org; Old Town Plaza; ⊙7am-5:30pm daily, museum 9:30am-4:30pm Mon-Sat), built in 1793, ¡Explora! (p386) and the **New Mexico Museum of Natural History & Science** (www.nmnaturalhistory.org; 1801 Mountain Rd NW; adult/child $7/4; ⊙9am-5pm; ⓓ).

★**American International Rattlesnake Museum** MUSEUM
(www.rattlesnakes.com; 202 San Felipe St NW; adult/child $5/3; ⊙10am-6pm Mon-Sat, 1-5pm Sun May-Sep, 11:30am-5:30pm Mon-Fri, 10am-6pm Sat, 1-5pm Sun, Sep-May) From eastern diamondback to rare tiger rattlers, you won't find more types of live rattlesnakes anywhere else in the world. Once you get over the freak-out factor, you'll be amazed not just by the variety of vipers but by the intricate beauty of their colors and patterns. Hopefully you'll never see them this close in the wild! Weekday hours are a little longer in summer.

Albuquerque Museum of Art & History MUSEUM
(www.cabq.gov/museum; 2000 Mountain Rd NW; adult/child $4/1; ⊙9am-5pm Tue-Sun) Conquis-

tador armor and weaponry are highlights at the Albuquerque Museum of Art & History, where visitors can study the city's tricultural Native American, Hispanic and Anglo past. Works by New Mexico artists also featured.

⊙ Around Town

The University of New Mexico (UNM) area has loads of good restaurants, casual bars, offbeat shops and hip college hangouts. The main drag is Central Ave between University and Carlisle Blvds. Just east is trendy Nob Hill, a pedestrian-friendly neighborhood lined with indie coffee shops, stylish boutiques and patio-wrapped restaurants.

★**Indian Pueblo Cultural Center** MUSEUM
(IPCC; ☎505-843-7270; www.indianpueblo.org; 2401 12th St NW; adult/child $6/3; ⊙9am-5pm) Operated by New Mexico's 19 pueblos, the Indian Pueblo Cultural Center is a must for contextualizing the history of northern

SOUTHWEST ALBUQUERQUE

New Mexico. Appealing displays trace the development of Pueblo cultures, exhibit customs and crafts, and feature changing exhibits.

National Museum of Nuclear Science & History
MUSEUM

(www.nuclearmuseum.org; 601 Eubank Blvd SE; adult/child & senior $8/7; ⊙ 9am-5pm; 🚻) Exhibits examine the Manhattan Project, the history of arms control and the use of nuclear energy as an alternative energy source. Docents here are retired military, and they're very knowledgeable.

Petroglyph National Monument
ARCHAEOLOGICAL SITE

(www.nps.gov/petr; ⊙ visitor center 8am-5pm) 🏃 More than 20,000 rock etchings are found inside the Petroglyph National Monument northwest of town. Stop by the visitor center (on Western Trail at Unser Blvd) to determine which of three viewing trails – in different sections of the park – best suits your interests. For a hike with great views but no rock art, hit the Volcanoes trail. Note: smash-and-grab thefts have been reported at some trailhead parking lots, so don't leave valuables in your vehicle. Head west on I-40 across the Rio Grande and take exit 154 north.

Sandia Peak Tramway
CABLE CAR

(www.sandiapeak.com; Tramway Blvd; vehicles $1, adult/youth 13-20yr/child $20/17/12; ⊙ 9am-8pm Wed-Mon, from 5pm Tue Sep-May, 9am-9pm Jun-Aug) The 2.7-mile Sandia Peak Tramway starts in the desert realm of cholla cactus and soars to the pines atop 10,378ft Sandia Peak in about 15 minutes. The views are huge and that's what you're paying for at the restaurant at the top.

🏃 Activities

The omnipresent Sandia Mountains and the less-crowded Manzano Mountains offer outdoor activities, including hiking, skiing (downhill and cross-country), mountain biking, rock climbing and camping. For information and maps, head to the Cibola National Forest office (📷 505-346-3900; 2113 Osuna Rd NE; ⊙ 8am-4:45pm Mon-Fri) or the Sandia Ranger Station (📷 505-281-3304; 11776 Hwy 337, Tijeras; ⊙ 8am-4:30pm Mon-Fri), off I-40 exit 175 south, about 15 miles east of Albuquerque.

Sandia Crest National Scenic Byway
DRIVING, HIKING

(I-40 exit 175 north) Reach the top of the Sandias via the eastern slope along the lovely Sandia Crest National Scenic Byway, which passes numerous hiking trailheads. Alternatively, take the Sandia Peak Tramway or Hwy 165 from Placitas (I-25 exit 242), a dirt road through Las Huertas Canyon that passes the prehistoric dwelling of Sandia Man Cave.

Sandia Peak Ski Park
SKIING/CYCLING

(📷 505-242-9052; www.sandiapeak.com; lift tickets adult/child $50/40; ⊙ 9am-4pm Dec-Mar & Jun-Sep) Sometimes the snow here is great, other times it's lame, so check before heading up. The ski area opens on summer weekends and holidays (June to September) for mountain bikers. You can rent a bike at the base facility ($58 with $650 deposit) or ride the chairlift to the top of the peak with your own bike ($14). Drive here via Scenic Byway 536, or take the Sandia Peak Tramway (skis are allowed on the tram, but not bikes).

Discover Balloons
BALLOONING

(📷 505-842-1111; www.discoverballoons.com; 205c San Felipe NW; adult/under 12yr $160/125) Sev-

---

ALBUQUERQUE FOR CHILDREN

The gung-ho ¡Explora! (www.explora.us; 1701 Mountain Rd NW; adult/child $8/4; ⊙ 10am-6pm Mon-Sat, noon-6pm Sun; 🚻) will captivate your kiddies for hours. From the lofty high-wire bike to the leaping waters to the arts-and-crafts workshop, there's a hands-on exhibit for every type of child (don't miss the elevator). Not traveling with kids? Check the website to see if you're in town for the popular 'Adult Night.' Typically hosted by an acclaimed local scientist, it's become one of the hottest tickets in town.

The teen-friendly New Mexico Museum of Natural History & Science (p385) features an Evolator (evolution elevator), which transports visitors through 38 million years of New Mexico's geologic and evolutionary history. The new Space Frontiers exhibit highlights the state's contribution to space exploration, from ancient Chaco observatories to an impressive, full-scale replica of the Mars Rover. The museum also contains a Planetarium (adult/child $7/4) and the 3-D IMAX-screened DynaTheater (adult/child $10/6).

eral companies will float you over the city and the Rio Grande, including Discover Balloons. Flights last about an hour, and many are offered early in the morning to catch optimal winds and the sunrise.

Tours

From mid-March to mid-December, the Albuquerque Museum of Art & History (p385) offers informative, guided Old Town walking tours (⊙ 11am Tue-Sun, Mar-Dec). They last 45 minutes to an hour and are free with museum admission.

Festivals & Events

Gathering of Nations Powwow   CULTURAL
(www.gatheringofnations.com; ⊙ April) The biggest Native American powwow in the world, with traditional music, dance, food, crafts and the crowning of Miss Indian World.

International Balloon Fiesta   FIESTA
(www.balloonfiesta.com; ⊙ early Oct) Some 800,000 spectators are drawn to this weeklong event. The highlight is the mass ascension, when more than 500 hot-air balloons launch nearly simultaneously.

Sleeping

Route 66 Hostel   HOSTEL $
(✆ 505-247-1813; www.rt66hostel.com; 1012 Central Ave SW; dm $20, r from $25; P❀🐾) Clean, fun and inexpensive, this place is simple and has a good travelers' vibe. A kitchen, library and outdoor patio are available for its guests to use.

Hotel Blue   HOTEL $
(✆ 877-878-4868; www.thehotelblue.com; 717 Central Ave NW; r incl breakfast $60-99; P❀@🐾🐾) Well positioned beside a park and Downtown, the art-deco 134-room Hotel Blue has Tempurpedic beds and a free airport shuttle. Bonus points awarded for the good-sized pool and 40in flat-screen TVs.

★ Andaluz   BOUTIQUE HOTEL $$
(✆ 505-242-9090; www.hotelandaluz.com; 125 2nd St NW; r $160-290; P❀@🐾) Albuquerque's best hotel will wow you with style and attention to detail, from the dazzling lobby – where six arched nooks with tables and couches offer alluring spaces to talk and drink in public-privacy, to the Italian-made hypoallergenic bedding. The restaurant is one of the best in town, and there's a beautiful guest library and a rooftop bar. The hotel is so 'green' you can tour its solar water-

heating system – the largest in the state. You'll get big discounts if you book online.

Mauger Estate B&B   B&B $$
(✆ 800-719-9189, 505-242-8755; www.maugerbb.com; 701 Roma Ave NW, cnr 7th St NW; r incl breakfast $99-195, ste $160-205, townhouse $129-195; P🐾🐾) This restored Queen Anne mansion (Mauger is pronounced 'major') has comfortable rooms with down comforters, stocked fridges and freshly cut flowers. Kids are welcome and there's one dog-friendly room complete with Wild West decor and a small yard ($20 extra).

Böttger Mansion   B&B $$
(✆ 505-243-3639, 800-758-3639; www.bottger.com; 110 San Felipe St NW; r incl breakfast $104-179; P❀@🐾) A friendly and informative proprietor gives this well-appointed Victorian-era B&B an edge over some tough competition. The eight-bedroom mansion, built in 1912, is close to Old Town Plaza, top-notch museums and several in-the-know New Mexican restaurants. The honeysuckle-lined courtyard is a favorite with bird-watchers. Famous past guests include Elvis, Janis Joplin and Machine Gun Kelly.

Eating

★ Frontier   NEW MEXICAN $
(www.frontierrestaurant.com; 2400 Central Ave SE; mains $3-11; ⊙ 5am-1am; 🐾🐾) An Albuquerque tradition, the Frontier boasts enormous cinnamon rolls, addictive green-chili stew, and the best huevos rancheros ever. The food and people-watching are outstanding, and students love the low prices on the breakfast, burgers and Mexican food.

Flying Star Café   AMERICAN $
(www.flyingstarcafe.com; 3416 Central Ave SE; mains $6-12; ⊙ 6am-11pm Sun-Thu, to midnight Fri &Sat; 🐾🐾🐾) With seven constantly packed locations, including a branch at Juan Tabo Blvd (4501 Juan Tabo Blvd NE; ⊙ 6am-10pm Sun-Thu, 6am-11pm Fri & Sat; 🐾), this is the place to go for creative diner food made with regional ingredients, including homemade soups, main dishes from sandwiches to stir-fries, and yummy desserts. There's something here for everyone.

Golden Crown Panaderia   BAKERY $
(✆ 505-243-2424; www.goldencrown.biz; 1103 Mountain Rd NW; mains $5-20; ⊙ 7am-8pm Tue-Sat, 10am-8pm Sun) Who doesn't love a friendly neighborhood bakery? Especially one with gracious staff, fresh-from-the-oven

bread and pizza, fruit-filled empanadas, smooth coffee and the frequent free cookie. Call ahead to reserve a loaf of quick-selling green-chili bread. Go to the website to check out the 'bread cam.'

Annapurna   INDIAN $

(www.chaishoppe.com; 2201 Silver Ave SE; mains $7-12; ⊙ 7am-9pm Mon-Fri, 8am-9pm Sat, 10am-8pm Sun; 🚭🍴) For some of the freshest, tastiest health food in town, grab a seat in the bright, mural-covered walls of Annapurna. The delicately spiced ayurvedic dishes are all vegetarian or vegan, but they're so delicious that even carnivores will find something to love.

Artichoke Café   MODERN AMERICAN $$$

(🗷 505-243-0200; www.artichokecafe.com; 424 Central Ave SE; lunch mains $10-16, dinner mains $19-30; ⊙ 11am-2:30pm Mon-Fri, 5-9pm daily, to 10pm Fri & Sat) Voted an Albuquerque favorite many times over, this place takes the best from Italian, French and American cuisine and serves it with a touch of class.

🍷 Drinking & Entertainment

Popejoy Hall (www.popejoypresents.com; Central Ave, at Cornell St SE) and the historic **KiMo Theatre** (www.cabq.gov/kimo; 423 Central Ave NW, downtown) are the primary venues for big-name national acts, local opera, symphony and theater. To find out what's happening in town, grab a free copy of the weekly *Alibi* or visit www.alibi.com. Most of Albuquerque's trendy cafes and bars are found in the Nob Hill/UNM districts, though a few good ones are downtown.

Satellite Coffee   CAFE

(2300 Central Ave SE; ⊙ 6am-11pm; 🚭) Don't be put off by the hip, space-age appearance. The staff is welcoming and seats are filled with all manner of laptop-viewing, java-swilling locals. There are eight locations scattered across town; also try the one in **Nob Hill** (3513 Central Ave NE, Nob Hill).

Anodyne   BAR

(409 Central Ave NW; ⊙ 4pm-1:30am Mon-Fri, 7pm-1:30am Sat, 7-11:30pm Sun) Anodyne is a huge but cozy space with 10 red pool tables, wood ceilings, plenty of overstuffed chairs, more than 100 bottled beers. You'll find a diverse crowd where everyone belongs.

Kelly's Brewery   BREWERY

(www.kellysbrewpub.com; 3222 Central Ave SE; ⊙ 8am-10:30pm Sun-Thu, to midnight Fri & Sat)

Grab a seat at a communal table then settle in for a convivial night of people-watching and house-brewed pints at this former Ford dealership and gas station. On warm spring nights, it seems everyone in town is chilling on the sprawling patio.

Launch Pad   LIVE MUSIC

(www.launchpadrocks.com; 618 Central Ave SW, downtown) Indie, reggae, punk and country bands rock the house most nights (though not at the same time). Look for the spaceship on Central Ave. Right next door is the **El Rey Theater** (www.elreytheater.com; 620 Central Ave SW, downtown), another longtime favorite for live music.

🛍 Shopping

For eclectic gifts, head to Nob Hill, east of the university. Park on Central Ave SE or one of the college-named side streets, then take a stroll past the inviting boutiques and specialty stores.

Palms Trading Post   ARTS & CRAFTS

(1504 Lomas Blvd NW; ⊙ 9am-5:30pm Mon-Fri, 10am-5:30pm Sat) If you're looking for Native American crafts and informed salespeople who can give you advice, come here.

Silver Sun   JEWELRY

(116 San Felipe St NW; ⊙ 10am-4:30pm) Just south of the plaza, Silver Sun is a reputable spot for turquoise and silver, where you can sometimes see the smiths at work.

Mariposa Gallery   ART & CRAFTS

(www.mariposa-gallery.com; 3500 Central Ave SE, Nob Hill) Beautiful and funky arts, crafts and jewelry, mostly by regional artists.

ℹ Information

EMERGENCY & MEDICAL SERVICES

Police (🗷 505-764-1600; 400 Roma Ave NW)
Presbyterian Hospital (🗷 505-841-1234, emergency 505-841-1111; 1100 Central Ave SE; ⊙ emergency 24hr)
UNM Hospital (🗷 505-272-2411; 2211 Lomas Blvd NE; ⊙ emergency 24hr) Head here if you don't have insurance.

INTERNET ACCESS

Lots of restaurants and cafes have wi-fi.
Main Library (🗷 505-768-5141; 501 Copper Ave NW; ⊙ 10am-6pm Mon & Thu-Sat, 10am-7pm Tue & Wed; 🚭) Free internet access after purchasing a $3 SmartCard. Wi-fi available for free but must obtain access card.

POST

Post Office (201 5th St SW; ⊙9am-4:30pm Mon-Fri)

TOURIST INFORMATION

Albuquerque Convention & Visitors Bureau (www.itsatrip.org; Albuquerque International Airport; ⊙9:30am-8pm Sun-Fri, to 4:30pm Sat) At the lower-level baggage claim.

Old Town Information Center (☑505-243-3215; www.itsatrip.org; 303 Romero Ave NW; ⊙10am-5pm Oct-May, to 6pm Jun-Sep)

USEFUL WEBSITES

Albuquerque.com (www.albuquerque.com) Attractions, hotels and restaurants.

City of Albuquerque (www.cabq.gov) Information on public transportation, area attractions and more.

❶ Getting There & Around

AIR

Albuquerque International Sunport (☑505-244-7700; www.cabq.gov/airport; 2200 Sunport Blvd SE) is New Mexico's main airport and most major US airlines fly here. Cabs to Downtown cost $20 to $25; try **Albuquerque Cab** (☑505-883-4888; www.albuquerquecab.com).

BUS

The **Alvarado Transportation Center** (100 1st St SW, cnr Central Ave) houses **ABQ RIDE** (☑505-243-7433; www.cabq.gov/transit; 100 1st St SW; adult/child $1/35, day pass $2), the public bus system. It covers most of Albuquerque from Monday to Friday and hits the major tourist spots daily. Most lines run until 6pm. ABQ RIDE Route 50 connects the airport with downtown (last bus at 8pm Monday to Friday, limited service Saturday). Check the website for

maps and exact schedules. Route 36 stops near Old Town and the Indian Pueblo Cultural Center.

Greyhound (☑800-231-2222, 505-243-4435; www.greyhound.com; 320 1st St SW) serves destinations throughout New Mexico. **Sandia Shuttle** (☑888-775-5696; www.sandiashuttle.com; one-way/return $28/48; ⊙8:45am-11:45pm) runs daily shuttles from the airport to many Santa Fe hotels, while **Twin Hearts Express** (☑575-751-1201; www.twinhearts-expresstransportation.com) runs a shuttle service from the airport to northern New Mexico destinations, including Taos and surrounding communities.

TRAIN

The *Southwest Chief* stops daily at Albuquerque's **Amtrak station** (☑800-872-7245, 505-842-9650; 320 1st St SW; ⊙10am-5pm), heading east to Chicago ($173, 26 hours) or west through Flagstaff, AZ ($91, five hours), to Los Angeles, CA (from $114, 16½ hours).

A commuter line, the **New Mexico Rail Runner Express** (www.nmrailrunner.com), shares the station, with eight departures for Santa Fe weekdays (one-way/day pass $8/9), four on Saturday and three on Sunday, though weekend service may be discontinued. The trip takes about 1½ hours.

Along I-40

Although you can zip between Albuquerque and Flagstaff, AZ, in less than five hours, the national monuments and pueblos along the way are well worth a visit. For a scenic loop, take Hwy 53 southwest from Grants, which leads to all the following sights except Acoma. Hwy 602 brings you north to Gallup.

SCENIC DRIVES: NEW MEXICO'S BEST

Billy the Kid National Scenic Byway This mountain-and-valley loop (www.billyby-way.com) in southeastern New Mexico swoops past Billy the Kid's stomping grounds, Smokey Bear's gravesite and the orchard-lined Hondo Valley. From Roswell, take Hwy 380 west.

High Road to Taos The back road between Santa Fe and Taos passes through sculpted sandstone desert, fresh pine forests and rural villages with historic adobe churches and horse-filled pastures. The 13,000ft Truchas Peaks soar above. From Santa Fe, take Hwy 84/285 to Hwy 513 then follow the signs.

NM Highway 96 From Abiquiu to Cuba, this little road wends through the heart of Georgia O'Keeffe country, beneath the distinct profile of Cerro Pedernal, then passing Martian-red buttes and sandstone cliffs striped purple, yellow and ivory.

NM Highway 52 Head west from Truth or Consequences into the dramatic foothills of the Black Range, through the old mining towns of Winston and Chloride. Continue north, passing the Monticello Box – where Geronimo finally surrendered – and emerging onto the sweeping Plains of San Augustin before reaching the bizarre Very Large Array.

Acoma Pueblo

The dramatic mesa-top 'Sky City' sits 7000ft above sea level and 367ft above the surrounding plateau. One of the oldest continuously inhabited settlements in North America, this place has been home to pottery-making people since the later part of the 11th century. Guided tours (adult/senior/child $23/20/15; ⊘ hourly 9:30am-3:30pm Apr-early Nov, check online or call for winter schedule) leave from the visitor center (☑ 800-747-0181; www.acomaskycity.org; ⊘ 9am-5pm Apr-early Nov; check online or call for winter opening hours) at the bottom of the mesa and take two hours, or one hour just to tour the historic mission. From I-40, take exit 102, which is about 60 miles west of Albuquerque, then drive 12 miles south. Call ahead to make sure it's not closed for ceremonial or other reasons.

El Morro National Monument

The 200ft sandstone outcropping at this monument (www.nps.gov/elmo; admission free; ⊘ 9am-5pm, last trail entry 4pm) **FREE**, also known as 'Inscription Rock,' has been a travelers' oasis for millennia. Thousands of carvings – from petroglyphs in the pueblo at the top (c 1275) to elaborate inscriptions by the Spanish conquistadors and the Anglo pioneers – offer a unique means of tracing history. It's about 38 miles southwest of Grants via Hwy 53.

Zuni Pueblo

The Zuni are known worldwide for their delicately inlaid silverwork, which is sold in stores lining Hwy 53. Check in at the visitor center (☑ 505-782-7238; www.zunitourism.com; 1239 Hwy 53; tours $10; ⊘ 8:30am-5:30pm Mon-Fri, 10:30am-4pm Sat, noon-4pm Sun) for information, photo permits and tours of the pueblo, which lead you among stone houses and beehive-shaped adobe ovens to the massive Our Lady of Guadalupe Mission, featuring impressive kachina murals. The Ashiwi Awan Museum & Heritage Center (www.ashiwi-museum.org; Ojo Caliente Rd; admission by donation; ⊘ 9am-5pm Mon-Fri) displays early photos and other tribal artifacts.

The friendly, eight-room Inn at Halona (☑ 800-752-3278, 505-782-4547; www.halona.com; Halona Plaza; r from $79; P ⊛), decorated with local Zuni arts and crafts, is the only place to stay on the pueblo. Its breakfasts rank with the best of any B&B in the state.

Gallup

Not just a classic Route 66 town, Gallup also serves as the Navajo and Zuni peoples' major trading center, making it one of the best places in New Mexico to buy top-quality Native American art and crafts at fair prices. You'll find many trading posts, pawnshops, jewelry stores and crafts galleries in the historic district.

The town's lodging jewel is El Rancho (☑ 505-863-9311; www.elranchohotel.com; 1000 E Hwy 66; r from $85; P ⊛ ⊛ ⊛). Many of the great actors of the 1940s and '50s stayed here. El Rancho features a superb Southwestern lobby, a restaurant, a bar and an eclectic selection of simple rooms. There's wifi in the lobby. Most chain hotels are found along Route 66, west of the town center.

Santa Fe

Walking among the historic adobe neighborhoods or even around the tourist-filled plaza, there's no denying that Santa Fe has a timeless, earthy soul. Founded around 1610, Santa Fe is the second-oldest city and oldest state capital in the USA. It's got the oldest public building and throws the oldest annual party in the country (Fiesta). Yet the city is synonymous with contemporary chic, and boasts the second-largest art market in the nation, gourmet restaurants, great museums, spas and a world-class opera.

At 7000ft, it's also the highest state capital in the US, sitting at the base of the Sangre de Cristo range, a conveniently fantastic place to hike, mountain bike, backpack and ski.

Cerrillos Rd (I-25 exit 278), a 6-mile strip of hotels and fast-food restaurants, enters town from the south; Paseo de Peralta circles the center of town; St Francis Dr (I-25 exit 282) forms the western border of downtown and turns into Hwy 285, which heads north toward Los Alamos and Taos. Most downtown restaurants, galleries, museums and sights are within walking distance of the plaza, the historic center of town.

◉ Sights

Art enthusiasts coming for the weekend may want to arrive early on Friday to take advantage of the evening's free admission policies at many museums.

MUSEUM OF NEW MEXICO

The Museum of New Mexico administers four (or five, depending on how you count them) unique and excellent museums around town. Admission is free for children 16 and under. Adults can buy a four-day pass with entry into all four (or five) museums for $20. Two (or three) are at the plaza, two are on Museum Hill.

Museum of International Folk Art (www.internationalfolkart.org; 706 Camino Lejo; adult/child $9/free, free 5-8pm Fri summer; ⊙10am-5pm, closed Mon Sep-May) The galleries here, on Museum Hill, are at once whimsical and mind-blowing – featuring the world's largest collection of traditional folk art. Try to hit the incredible folk-art market, held each July.

Museum of Indian Arts & Culture (www.indianartsandculture.org; 710 Camino Lejo; adult/child $9/free, free Fri 5-8pm in summer; ⊙10am-5pm, closed Mon Sep-May) On Museum Hill, this is one of the most complete collections of Native American arts and crafts – and a perfect companion to the nearby Wheelwright Museum.

Palace of the Governors (☑505-476-5100; www.palaceofthegovernors.org; 105 W Palace Ave; adult/child $9/free; ⊙10am-5pm, closed Mon Oct-May) On the plaza, this 400-year-old abode was once the seat of the Spanish colonial government. It displays a handful of regional relics, but most of its holdings are now shown in an adjacent exhibit space called the **New Mexico History Museum** (113 Lincoln Ave), a glossy, 96,000-sq-ft expansion. One ticket works for both.

New Mexico Museum of Art (www.nmartmuseum.org; 107 W Palace Ave; adult/child $9/free; ⊙10am-5pm, closed Mon Sep-May) Just off the plaza, there are more than 20,000 pieces of fine art here, mostly by Southwestern artists.

⭐**Georgia O'Keeffe Museum**   MUSEUM
(☑505-946-1000; www.okeeffemuseum.org; 217 Johnson St; adult/child $12/free; ⊙10am-5pm, to 7pm Fri) Possessing the world's largest collection of her work, the Georgia O'Keeffe Museum features the artist's paintings of flowers, bleached skulls and adobe architecture. Tours of O'Keeffe's house in Abiquiu require advance reservations.

Canyon Rd   GALLERIES
(www.canyonroadarts.com) The epicenter of the city's upscale art scene, more than 100 galleries, studios, shops and restaurants line this narrow historic road. Look for Santa Fe School masterpieces, rare Native American antiquities and wild contemporary work. The area positively buzzes with activity during the early-evening art openings on Fridays, and especially on Christmas Eve.

Wheelwright Museum of the American Indian   MUSEUM
(www.wheelwright.org; 704 Camino Lejo; ⊙10am-5pm Mon-Sat, 1-5pm Sun) FREE In 1937, Mary Cabot established the Wheelwright Museum of the American Indian, part of Museum Hill, to showcase Navajo ceremonial art. While its strength continues to be Navajo exhibits, it now includes contemporary Native American art and historical artifacts as well.

St Francis Cathedral   CHURCH
(www.cbsfa.org; 131 Cathedral Pl; ⊙8:30am-5pm) Houses the oldest Madonna statue in North America.

Shidoni Foundry   GARDENS, GALLERY
(www.shidoni.com; 1508 Bishop's Lodge Rd, Tesuque; ⊙9am-5pm Mon-Sat;) Five miles north of the plaza; outdoor sculpture garden (open dawn to 5pm), indoor gallery and an on-site glass-blowing studio (open 9am to 5pm). On Saturdays, watch the artisans do huge bronze pours in the workshop ($5).

Loretto Chapel   CHURCH
(www.lorettochapel.com; 207 Old Santa Fe Trail; admission $3; ⊙9am-5pm Mon-Sat, 10:30am-5pm Sun) Famous for its 'miraculous' spiral staircase that appears to be supported by thin air.

🏃 Activities

The **Pecos Wilderness** and **Santa Fe National Forest**, east of town, have more than 1000 miles of hiking trails, several of which lead to 12,000ft peaks. The popular and scenic **Winsor Trail** starts at the Santa Fe Ski Basin. Summer storms are frequent, so prepare for hikes by checking weather reports. For maps and details, contact the Public Lands Information Center. If mountain

Santa Fe

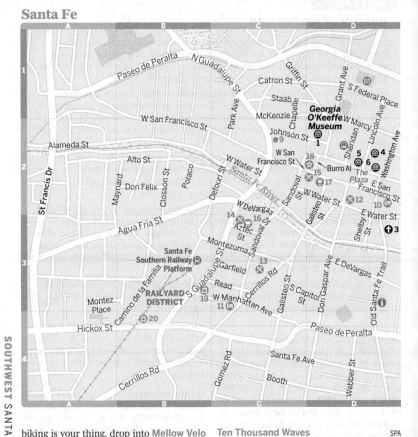

biking is your thing, drop into **Mellow Velo** (☑ 505-995-8356; www.mellowvelo.com; 132 E Marcy St; rentals per day from $35; ⊙ 9am-5:30pm Mon-Sat), which rents bikes and has loads of information about regional trails.

Busloads of people head up to the Rio Grande and Rio Chama for white-water river running on day and overnight adventures. Contact **Santa Fe Rafting Co** (☑ 505-988-4914; www.santaferafting.com; ⊙ Apr-Sep) and stay cool on trips through the Rio Grande Gorge (half-day/full day $65/99), the wild Taos Box (full day $110) or the Rio Chama Wilderness (three days $595).

Ski Santa Fe   SKIING
(☑ 505-982-4429, snow report 505-983-9155; www.skisantafe.com; lift ticket adult/child $66/46; ⊙ 9am-4pm late Nov-Apr) A half-hour drive from the plaza up Hwy 475, you'll find the second-highest ski area in the USA. When the powder is fresh and the sun is shining, it's as good as it gets.

Ten Thousand Waves   SPA
(☑ 505-982-9304; www.tenthousandwaves.com; 3451 Hyde Park Rd; communal tubs $24, private tubs per person $31-51; ⊙ noon-10:30pm Tue, 9am-10:30pm Wed-Mon Jul-Oct, reduced hours Nov-Jun) The Japanese-style 10,000 Waves, with landscaped grounds concealing eight attractive tubs in a smooth Zen design, offers waterfalls, cold plunges, massage and hot and dry saunas. Call to reserve private tubs.

⚖ Courses

Santa Fe School of Cooking   COOKING
(☑ 505-983-4511; www.santafeschoolofcooking.com; 125 N Guadalupe St; classes $75-98; ⊙ 9:30am-5:30pm Mon-Fri, 9:30am-5pm Sat, noon-4pm Sun) If you develop a love for New Mexican cuisine, try cooking lessons here. Classes, including hands-on green and red chili workshops, are typically between two and three hours long.

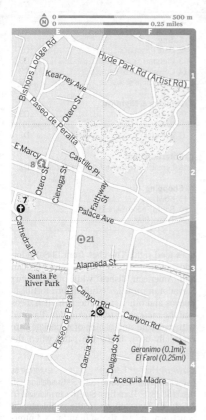

N
0 — 500 m
0 — 0.25 miles

Hyde Park Rd (Artist Rd)
Bishops Lodge Rd
Kearney Ave
Paseo de Peralta
Otero St
E Marcy
Castillo Pl
Otero St
Cienega St
Faithway St
Palace Ave
Cathedral Pl
Alameda St
Santa Fe River Park
Paseo de Peralta
Canyon Rd
Canyon Rd
Garcia St
Delgado St
Geronimo (0.1mi);
El Farol (0.25mi)
Acequia Madre

8
7
21
2

🎭 Festivals & Events

★ **Spanish Market**   CULTURAL

(www.spanishcolonial.org; ⊙late Jul) Traditional Spanish colonial arts, from *retablos* (paintings on wooden panels) and *bultos* (wooden carvings of religious figures) to handcrafted furniture and metalwork, make this juried show an artistic extravaganza.

★ **Santa Fe Indian Market**   CULTURAL

(www.swaia.org) Typically held the weekend after the third Thursday in August, this event draws the country's finest Native American artisans to the plaza – and tens of thousands of visitors.

★ **Santa Fe Fiesta**   CULTURAL

(www.santafefiesta.org; ⊙early Sep) Two weeks of events, including concerts, dances, parades and the burning of Zozobra (Old Man Gloom).

🛏 Sleeping

Cerrillos Rd is lined with chains and independent motels. There's camping in developed sites in Santa Fe National Forest and Hyde State Park on Hwy 475, the road to the ski basin; for more information, go to the Public Lands Information Center (p384).

Silver Saddle Motel   MOTEL $

(☑505-471-7663; www.santafesilversaddlemotel. com; 2810 Cerrillos Rd; r winter/summer from $45/62; P🅿⊛@🛜🐾) Shady wooden arcades outside and rustic cowboy-inspired decor inside, including some rooms with attractively tiled kitchenettes. For a bit of kitsch, request the Kenny Rogers or Wyatt Earp room. Probably the best value in town.

Rancheros de Santa Fe Campground   CAMPGROUND $

(☑505-466-3482; www.rancheros.com; 736 Old Las Vegas Hwy; tent/RV sites/cabins $25/41/49; ⊙Mar-Oct; 🛜🐾) Super-friendly, this wooded campground is 7 miles southeast of town. Enjoy hot showers, cheap morning coffee and evening movies.

Santa Fe Motel & Inn   HOTEL $$

(☑505-982-1039; www.santafemotel.com; 510 Cerrillos Rd; r $89-155, casitas $129-169; P🅿⊛@🛜🐾) It's the aesthetic and technological attention to detail that make this downtown-adjacent motel a great pick. Bright tiles, clay sunbursts, LCD TVs and a welcoming chili pepper carefully placed atop your towels are just a few memorable pluses. Savor hot breakfasts on the kiva-anchored patio.

El Rey Inn   HOTEL $$

(☑505-982-1931; www.elreyinnsantafe.com; 1862 Cerrillos Rd; r incl breakfast $105-165, ste from $150; P🅿⊛@🛜🐾) A highly recommended classic courtyard hotel, with super rooms, a great pool and hot tub, and even a kids' playground scattered around 5 acres of greenery. The inn recycles and takes a lot of green-friendly steps to conserve resources. Most rooms have air con.

★ **La Fonda**   HISTORIC HOTEL $$$

(☑800-523-5002; www.lafondasantafe.com; 100 E San Francisco St; r/ste from $140/260; P🅿⊛@🛜🐾) Claiming to be the original 'Inn at the end of the Santa Fe Trail,' here in one form or another since perhaps 1610, La Fonda has always offered some of the best lodging in town. Freshly renovated in 2013, the hotel blends modern luxury with folk-art touches; it's authentic, top-shelf Santa Fe style.

Santa Fe

✗ Eating

★ San Marcos Café
NEW MEXICAN $

(☑505-471-9298; www.sanmarcosfeed.com; 3877 Hwy 14; mains $7-10; ⊙8am-2pm; 🐾) About 10 minutes' drive south on Hwy 14, this spot is well worth the trip. San Marcos has a down-home feeling and the best red chili you'll ever taste. The whole place is connected to a feed store, giving it some genuine Western soul – and turkeys and peacocks strut and squabble outside. The pastries and desserts – especially the bourbon apple pie – sate any sweet tooth. Make reservations on weekends.

Horseman's Haven
NEW MEXICAN $

(4354 Cerrillos Rd; mains $8-12; ⊙8am-8pm Mon-Sat, 8:30am-2pm Sun; 🐾) Hands down the hottest green chili in town! (The timid should order it on the side). Service is friendly and fast, and the enormous 3-D burrito might be the only thing you need to eat all day.

Cleopatra's Cafe
MIDDLE EASTERN $

(www.cleopatrasantafe.com; 418 Cerrillos Rd, Design Center; mains $6-14; ⊙11am-8pm Mon-Sat; 🛜) Makes up for lack of ambience with taste and value – big platters of delicious kebabs, hummus, falafel and other Middle Eastern favorites. It's inside the Design Center.

Tia Sophia's
NEW MEXICAN $

(210 W San Francisco St; mains $7-10; ⊙7am-2pm Mon-Sat, 8am-1pm Sun; 🖉🐾) Arguably the best New Mexican food downtown.

Tune-Up Café
INTERNATIONAL $$

(www.tuneupsantafe.com; 1115 Hickox St; mains $7-14; ⊙7am-10pm Mon-Fri, from 8am Sat & Sun; 🐾) This local favorite is casual, busy and does food right. The chef, from El Salvador, adds a few twists to classic New Mexican and American dishes, while also serving Salvadoran *pupusas* (stuffed corn tortillas), huevos and other specialties. The fish tacos and the *mole colorado enchiladas* (flavored with red chili and a hint of chocolate) are especially tasty. Enjoy the patio when the weather allows.

Cowgirl Hall of Fame
BARBECUE $$

(www.cowgirlsantafe.com; 319 S Guadalupe St; mains $8-18; ⊙11am-11pm Sun-Thu, to midnight Fri & Sat; 🐾) Two-step up to the cobblestoned courtyard and try the salmon tacos, butter-nut-squash casserole or the BBQ platter – all served with Western-style feminist flair. Youngsters are welcomed, with an outdoor play yard and buckets of coloring crayons to draw on the lengthy kids' menu. It also has a perennially popular bar with live music and attached pool hall.

★ Cafe Pasqual's
INTERNATIONAL $$$

(☑505-983-9340; www.pasquals.com; 121 Don Gaspar Ave; breakfast & lunch mains $9-17, dinner mains $16-30; ⊙7am-3pm & 5:30-9pm; 🖉🐾) Sante Fe's most famous breakfast, for good reason.

Geronimo
MODERN AMERICAN $$$

(☑505-982-1500; www.geronimorestaurant.com; 724 Canyon Rd; mains $30-45; ⊙5:45-10pm Mon-Thu, to 11pm Fri & Sat) Housed in a 1756 adobe, Geronimo is among the finest and most romantic restaurants in town. The short but diverse menu includes fiery sweet chili and honey-grilled prawns and peppery elk tenderloin with applewood-smoked bacon.

SOUTHWEST SANTA FE

🍸 Drinking & Entertainment

You'll also find live music and good drinking most nights at the Cowgirl Hall of Fame (p394).

★ 317 Aztec
CAFE
(317 Aztec St; ⊗8am-10pm Mon-Sat; 🛜) Even with new owners, the former Aztec Cafe remains our pick for best local coffeehouse and juice/smoothy bar, with its colorful indoor art space and outdoor patio. The food is great (and healthy) too!

Evangelo's
BAR
(200 W San Francisco St; ⊗midday-1:30am Mon-Sat, to midnight Sun) There's foot-stompin' live music nightly at Evangelo's. The sounds of rock, blues, jazz and Latin combos spill into the street.

Bell Tower Bar
BAR
(100 E San Francisco St; ⊗3pm-sunset Mon-Thu, 2pm-sunset Fri-Sun May-Oct, closed rest of yr) At La Fonda hotel, ascend five floors to the newly renovated Bell Tower and watch one of those patented New Mexico sunsets.

★ El Farol
TRADITIONAL DANCE, LIVE MUSIC
(www.elfarolsf.com; 808 Canyon Rd; ⊗11am-midnight Mon-Sat, 11am-11pm Sun) As much a restaurant as a bar, El Farol specializes in tapas ($8), live music, world-class flamenco and the ambience of Santa Fe's oldest cantina.

★ Santa Fe Opera
OPERA
(☑505-986-5900; www.santafeopera.org; Hwy 84/285, Tesuque; backstage tours adult/child $5/free; ⊗late Jun-late Aug, backstage tours 9am Mon-Fri Jun-Aug) You can be a decked-out socialite or show up in cowboy boots and jeans; it doesn't matter. Opera fans (and those who've never attended an opera in their lives) come to Santa Fe for this alone: an architectural marvel, with views of wind-carved sandstone wilderness crowned with sunsets and moonrises, and at center stage internationally renowned vocal talent performing masterworks of aria and romance.

Lensic Performing Arts Theater
PERFORMING ARTS
(☑505-984-1370; www.lensic.com; 211 W San Francisco St) For live performances and movies, see what's doing at the Lensic Performing Arts Center. This beautifully renovated 1930s movie house is the city's premier venue for performing arts. Continuing its film history, it also holds $5 classic-movie screenings.

🛍 Shopping

Offering carved howling coyotes, turquoise jewelry and fine art, Santa Fe attracts shoppers of all budgets. Head to the sidewalk outside the Palace of the Governors to buy Indian jewelry direct from the craftspeople who make it.

★ Santa Fe Farmers Market
MARKET
(☑505-983-4098; 55yd west of Guadalupe St, Paseo de Peralta; ⊗7am-noon Sat & Tue Apr-Nov; 🚼) Don't miss this market at the redeveloped rail yard. Free samples and a festive mood make for a very pleasant morning.

Pueblo of Tesuque Flea Market
MARKET
(Hwy 84/285; ⊗8am-4pm Fri-Sun Mar-Nov) This outdoor market a few minutes' drive north of Santa Fe at Tesuque Pueblo offers deals on high-quality rugs, jewelry, art and clothing.

Kowboyz
CLOTHING
(www.kowboyz.com; 345 W Manhattan Ave) This secondhand shop has everything you need to cowboy up. Shirts are a great deal at $10 each; the amazing selection of boots, however, demands top dollar. Movie costumers looking for authentic Western wear often come in here.

Travel Bug
MAPS
(www.mapsofnewmexico.com; 839 Paseo de Peralta; ⊗7:30am-5:30pm Mon-Sat, 11am-4pm Sun; 🛜) A huge selection of guidebooks, maps and travel gear, plus travel slide shows on Saturdays.

ℹ Information

EMERGENCY & MEDICAL SERVICES
Police (☑505-955-5000; 2515 Camino Entrada)
St Vincent's Hospital (☑505-983-3361; 455 St Michael's Dr) Has 24-hour emergency care.

INTERNET ACCESS
Santa Fe Public Library (☑505-955-6781; 145 Washington Ave) Reserve up to an hour of free access.
Travel Bug (☑505-992-0418; 839 Paseo de Peralta; 🛜) Free wi-fi and internet access from on-site terminals.

POST
Post office (120 S Federal Pl)

TOURIST INFORMATION
New Mexico Tourism Bureau (☑505-827-7440; www.newmexico.org; 491 Old Santa Fe Trail; ⊗8am-5pm) Has brochures, a hotel

CHIMAYO

Twenty-eight miles north of Santa Fe is the so-called 'Lourdes of America' – El Santuario de Chimayo (www.elsantuariodechimayo.us; ⊙ 9am-5pm Oct-Apr, to 6pm May-Sep), one of the most important cultural sites in New Mexico. In 1816, this two-towered adobe chapel was built where the earth was said to have miraculous healing properties – even today, the faithful come to rub the *tierra bendita* – holy dirt – from a small pit inside the church on whatever hurts; some mix it with water and drink it. During holy week, about 30,000 pilgrims walk to Chimayo from Santa Fe, Albuquerque and beyond, in the largest Catholic pilgrimage in the USA. The artwork in the *santuario* is worth a trip on its own. Stop at Rancho de Chimayo (☑505-984-2100; www.ranchodechimayo.com; County Rd 98; mains $8-18; ⊙ 8:30-10:30am Sat & Sun, 11:30am-9pm daily, closed Mon Nov-Apr) afterward for lunch or dinner.

reservation line, free coffee and free internet access.

Public Lands Information Center (☑505-438-7542; www.publiclands.org; 301 Dinosaur Trail; ⊙ 8:30am-4pm Mon-Fri) Tons of maps and information on exploring New Mexico's National Forests, Parks and Monuments, wilderness areas, and other public lands. Just south of the intersection of Cerillos Rd and I-25.

Useful Websites

New Mexican (www.santafenewmexican.com) Daily paper with breaking news.

SantaFe.com (www.santafe.com) Listings for upcoming concerts, readings and openings in northern New Mexico.

Santa Fe Information (www.santafe.org) Official online visitors' guide.

Santa Fe Reporter (www.sfreporter.com) Free alternative weekly; culture section has thorough listings of what's going on.

ⓘ Getting There & Around

A few commercial airlines fly daily between **Santa Fe Municipal Airport** (SAF; ☑505-955-2900; wwwsantafenm.gov; 121 Aviation Dr) and Dallas, Denver, Los Angeles, and Phoenix; historically, these routes have been added and cut with surprising frequency, so check to make sure they are all still active. Many more flights arrive at and depart from Albuquerque (one-hour drive south of Santa Fe).

Sandia Shuttle Express (☑888-775-5696; www.sandiashuttle.com) runs between Santa Fe and the Albuquerque Sunport ($28). **North Central Regional Transit** (www.ncrtd.org) provides free shuttle bus service to Espanola, where you can transfer to shuttles to Taos, Los Alamos, Ojo Caliente and other northern destinations. Downtown pickup/drop-off is on Sheridan St, a block northwest of the plaza.

The **Rail Runner** (www.nmrailrunner.com) commuter train has multiple daily departures for Albuquerque – with connections to the airport

and the zoo. The trip takes about 1½ hours. Weekend service may be discontinued. **Amtrak** (☑800-872-7245; www.amtrak.com) stops at Lamy; buses continue 17 miles to Santa Fe.

Santa Fe Trails (☑505-955-2001; www.santafenm.gov; one-way adult/child $1/free, day pass $2) provides local bus services. If you need a taxi, call **Capital City Cab** (☑505-438-0000; www.capitalcitycab.com).

If driving between Santa Fe and Albuquerque, try to take Hwy 14 – the Turquoise Trail – which passes through the old mining town (now art-gallery town) of Madrid, 28 miles south of Santa Fe.

Around Santa Fe

Pueblos

North of Santa Fe is the heart of Puebloan lands. Eight Northern Indian Pueblos (www.enipc.org) publishes the excellent and free *Eight Northern Indian Pueblos Visitors Guide,* available at area visitor centers. Its annual arts-and-crafts show is held in July; check the ENIPC website for exact dates and location.

Eight miles west of Pojoaque along Hwy 502, the ancient San Ildefonso Pueblo (☑505-455-3549; per vehicle $10, camera/video/ sketching permits $10/20/25; ⊙ 8am-5pm) was the home of Maria Martinez, who in 1919 revived a distinctive traditional black-on-black pottery style. Stop at the Maria Poveka Martinez Museum (⊙ 8am-4pm Mon-Fri) FREE and browse the shops of the exceptional potters (including Maria's direct descendants) who work in the pueblo today.

Just north of San Ildefonso, on Hwy 30, Santa Clara Pueblo is home to the Puye Cliff Dwellings (☑888-320-5008; www.puyecliffs.com; tours adult/child $20/18; ⊙ hourly 9am-

5pm May-Sep, 10am-2pm Oct-Apr), where you can visit Ancestral Puebloan cliffside and mesa-top ruins.

Las Vegas

Not to be confused with the glittery city to the west in Nevada, this Vegas is one of the loveliest towns in New Mexico and one of the largest and oldest towns east of the Sangre de Cristo Mountains. Its eminently strollable downtown has a pretty Old Town Plaza and some 900 historic buildings listed in the National Register of Historic Places. Its architecture is a mix of Southwestern and Victorian.

Built in 1882 and carefully remodeled a century later, the elegant Plaza Hotel (800-328-1882, 505-425-3591; www.plazahotel-nm.com; 230 Old Town Plaza; r incl breakfast from $89; P ❉ @ 🛜 ❉) is Las Vegas' most celebrated and historic lodging. Choose between Victorian-style, antique-filled rooms in the original building or bright, modern rooms in a newer adjoining wing.

Right on the plaza, you can get your chile fix at El Encanto Restaurant (1816 Plaza; mains $5-9; 6am-2pm), your caffeine fix at World Treasures Travelers Cafe (1814 Plaza St; snacks $3-6; 7:30am-4:30pm Mon-Sat; 🛜), and your ice cream fix at the soda fountain at Plaza Drug (178 Bridge St; 8am-6pm Mon-Sat).

From the plaza, Hot Springs Blvd leads 5 miles north to Gallinas Canyon and the massive Montezuma Castle; once a hotel, it's now the United World College of the West. Along the road there, you can soak in a series of natural hot-spring pools. Bring a swimsuit and test the water – some are scalding hot! Don't miss the Dwan Light Sanctuary (admission free; 6am-10pm) FREE on the school campus, a meditation chamber where prisms in the walls cast rainbows inside.

Ask for a walking-tour brochure from the visitor center (800-832-5947; www.lasvegas-newmexico.com; 500 Railroad Ave; 9am-5pm).

Los Alamos

The top-secret Manhattan Project sprang to life in Los Alamos in 1943, turning a sleepy mesa-top village into a busy laboratory of secluded brainiacs. Here, in the 'town that didn't exist,' the first atomic bomb was developed in almost total secrecy. Today you'll encounter a fascinating dynamic in which

souvenir T-shirts emblazoned with atomic explosions and 'La Bomba' wine are sold next to books on pueblo history and wilderness hiking.

You can't actually visit the Los Alamos National Laboratory, where lots of classified cutting-edge research still takes place, but you can visit the well-designed, interactive Bradbury Science Museum (www.lanl.gov/museum; 1350 Central Ave; 10am-5pm Tue-Sat, 1-5pm Sun & Mon) FREE, which covers atomic history and includes new exhibits on security technology. A short film traces the community's wartime history and reveals a few fascinating secrets. The small but interesting Los Alamos Historical Museum (www.losalamoshistory.org; 1050 Bathtub Row; 10am-4pm Mon-Fri, from 11am Sat, from 1pm Sun) FREE is on the nearby grounds of the former Los Alamos Ranch School – an outdoorsy school for boys that closed when the scientists arrived.

Grab a bite with local braniacs at the Coffee House Cafe (www.thecoffeebooth.com; 723 Central Ave; mains $6-12, pizzas $21-30; 6am-8pm Tue-Fri, 7am-3pm Sat, 8am-3pm Sun, 6am-3pm Mon), opposite Smith's supermarket.

Bandelier National Monument

Ancestral Puebloans dwelt in the cliffsides of beautiful Frijoles Canyon, now preserved within Bandelier (www.nps.gov/band; per vehicle $12; visitor center 9am-4:30pm, park to dusk; 🐾). The adventurous can climb ladders to reach ancient caves and kivas used until the mid-1500s. There are also almost 50 sq miles of canyon and mesalands offering scenic backpacking trails, plus camping at Juniper Campground (campsites $12), set among the pines near the monument entrance. Note that between 9am and 3pm, from the end of May to mid-October, you need to take a shuttle bus to Bandelier from the White Rock Visitor Center, along Hwy 4.

Abiquiu

The tiny community of Abiquiu (sounds like 'barbecue'), on Hwy 84 about 45 minutes' drive northwest of Santa Fe, is famous because the renowned artist Georgia O'Keeffe lived and painted here from 1949 until her death in 1986. With the Chama River flowing through farmland and spectacular rock landscape, the ethereal setting continues to attract artists, and many live and work in

Abiquiu. O'Keeffe's adobe house is open for limited visits, with one-hour **tours** (☑505-685-4539; www.okeeffemuseum.org; tours $35-45) offered on Tuesday, Thursday and Friday from March to November, and Tuesday through Saturday from June to October, often booked months in advance.

A retreat center on 21,000 Technicolor acres that obviously inspired O'Keeffe's work (and was a shooting location for the movie *City Slickers*), **Ghost Ranch** (☑505-685-4333; www.ghostranch.org; US Hwy 84; suggested donation $3; ⛺) has hiking trails, a **dinosaur museum** (suggested donation $2; ⊙9am-5pm Mon-Sat, 1-5pm Sun) and offers horseback rides (from $50), including instruction for kids four and up ($30). Basic **lodging** (tent sites $19, RV sites $22-29, dm incl breakfast $50, r without/with bathroom incl breakfast from $70/80) is available, too.

The lovely **Abiquiú Inn** (☑888-735-2902, 505-685-4378; www.abiquiuinn.com; US Hwy 84; RV sites $18, r $110-150, casitas from $179; P✿☎) is a sprawling collection of shaded faux-adobes. Its spacious casitas have kitchenettes, and wi-fi is available in the lobby and the on-site restaurant, **Cafe Abiquiú** (breakfast mains under $10, lunch & dinner mains $10-20; ⊙7am-9pm). The lunch and dinner menu includes numerous fish dishes, from chipotle honey-glazed salmon to trout tacos.

Ojo Caliente

At 140 years old, **Ojo Caliente Mineral Springs Resort & Spa** (☑800-222-9162, 505-583-2233; www.ojospa.com; 50 Los Baños Rd; r $139-169, cottages $179-209, ste $229-349; ✿☎) is one of the country's oldest health resorts – and Pueblo Indians were using the springs long before then! Fifty miles north of Santa Fe on Hwy 285, the newly renovated resort offers 10 soaking pools with several combinations of minerals (shared/private pools from $18/40). In addition to the pleasant, if nothing special, historic hotel rooms, the resort has added 12 plush, boldly colored suites with kiva fireplaces and private soaking tubs, and 11 New Mexican–style cottages. Wi-fi is available in the lobby. The on-site **Artesian Restaurant** (breakfast mains $5-10, lunch mains $9-12, dinner mains $16-28; ⊙7:30am-11am, 11:30am-2:30pm & 5-8:30pm Sun-Thu, to 9pm Fri & Sat) prepares organic and local ingredients with aplomb.

Taos

Taos is a place undeniably dominated by the power of its landscape: 12,300ft snow-capped peaks rise behind town; a sage-speckled plateau unrolls to the west before plunging 800ft straight down into the Rio Grande Gorge; the sky can be a searing sapphire blue or an ominous parade of rumbling thunderheads so big they dwarf the mountains. And then there are the sunsets...

Taos Pueblo, believed to be the oldest continuously inhabited community in the United States, roots the town in a long history with a rich cultural legacy – including conquistadors, Catholicism and cowboys. In the 20th century, Taos became a magnet for artists, writers and creative thinkers, from DH Lawrence to Dennis Hopper. It remains a relaxed and eccentric place, with classic adobe architecture, fine-art galleries, quirky cafes and excellent restaurants. Its 5000 residents include Bohemians, alternative-energy aficionados and old-time Hispanic families. It's rural and worldly, and a little bit otherworldly.

◉ Sights

The Museum Association of Taos offers a pass for $25 to five museums: Harwood Museum of Art, Taos Historic Museums, Millicent Rogers Museum and Taos Art Museum & Fechin Institute.

★**Millicent Rogers Museum**　MUSEUM (www.millicentrogers.org; 1504 Millicent Rogers Rd; adult/child $10/2; ⊙10am-5pm, closed Mon Nov-Mar) Filled with pottery, jewelry, baskets and textiles, this has one of the best collections of Native American and Spanish Colonial art in the US.

Harwood Foundation Museum　MUSEUM (www.harwoodmuseum.org; 238 Ledoux St; adult/child $10/free; ⊙10am-5pm Tue-Sat, noon-5pm Sun) Housed in a historic mid-19th-century adobe compound, the Harwood Museum of Art features paintings, drawings, prints, sculpture and photography by northern New Mexico artists, both historical and contemporary.

Taos Historic Museums　MUSEUM (www.taoshistoricmuseums.org; each museum adult/child $8/4; ⊙10am-5pm Mon-Sat, midday-5pm Sun) Taos Historic Museum runs two houses: **Blumenschein Home** (www.taoshistoricmuseums.org; 222 Ledoux St; adult/child $8/4), a trove of art from the 1920s by the Taos Society of Artists, and **Martínez Hacienda** (708 Hacienda Way, off Lower Ranchitos Rd), a 21-room colonial trader's former home from 1804.

Taos Art Museum & Fechin Institute · MUSEUM
(www.taosartmuseum.org; 227 Paseo del Pueblo Norte; adult/child $8/free; ⊙10am-5pm Tue-Sun, shorter hours in winter) The home of Russian-born artist Nicolai Fechin, the house itself is worth just as much of a look as the collection of paintings, drawings and sculptures.

San Francisco de Asís Church · CHURCH
(St Francis Plaza; ⊙9am-4pm Mon-Fri) Four miles south of Taos in Ranchos de Taos, the San Francisco de Asís Church, famed for the angles and curves of its adobe walls, was built in the mid-18th century but didn't open until 1815. It's been memorialized in Georgia O'Keeffe paintings and Ansel Adams photographs. Hours are not really fixed, and the church may be open on Saturday. Mass is held three times on Sunday morning, once in Spanish.

Rio Grande Gorge Bridge · BRIDGE, CANYON
At 650ft above the Rio Grande, the steel Rio Grande Gorge Bridge is the second-highest suspension bridge in the US; the view down is eye-popping. For the best pictures of the bridge itself, park at the rest area on the western end of the span.

Earthships · ARCHITECTURE
(www.earthship.com; US Hwy 64; self-guided tours $7; ⊙10am-4pm) Just 1.5 miles west of the bridge is the fascinating community of Earthships, with self-sustaining, environmentally savvy houses built with recycled materials that are completely off the grid. You can also stay overnight in one.

🏃 Activities

During summer, white-water rafting is popular in the Taos Box, the steep-sided cliffs that frame the Rio Grande. Day-long trips begin at around $100 per person; contact the visitor center for local outfitters, where there's also good info about hiking and mountain-biking trails.

Taos Ski Valley · SKIING
(www.skitaos.org; half-/full-day lift ticket $64/77) With a peak elevation of 11,819ft and a 2612ft vertical drop, Taos Ski Valley offers some of the most challenging skiing in the US and

TAOS PUEBLO

Built around AD 1450 and continuously inhabited ever since, the streamside Taos Pueblo (☎505-758-1028; www.taospueblo.com; Taos Pueblo Rd; adult/child $10/free, photo or video permit $6; ⊙8am-4:30pm) is the largest existing multistoried pueblo structure in the US and one of the best surviving examples of traditional adobe construction. Dances held at the pueblo during the Pow-Wow (in July) and San Geronimo Day (September) are open to the public; call or check the website for exact dates. The pueblo closes for 10 weeks around February to March.

yet remains low-key and relaxed. The resort now allows snowboarders on its slopes.

🛏 Sleeping

Sun God Lodge · MOTEL $
(☎575-758-3162; www.sungodlodge.com; 919 Paseo del Pueblo Sur; r from $55; P❄🐾🛜🏊) The hospitable folks at this well-run two-story motel can fill you in on local history as well as the craziest bar in town. Rooms are clean – if a bit dark – and decorated with low-key Southwestern flair. Located 1.5 miles south of the plaza, it's one of the better budget choices in town.

Abominable Snowmansion · HOSTEL $
(☎575-776-8298; www.snowmansion.com; 476 Hwy 150, Arroyo Seco; tent sites $22, dm $27, r without/with bathroom $50/55, tepee $55; P🐾🛜🏊) About 9 miles northeast of Taos, this well-worn and welcoming hostel is a cozy mountainside alternative to central Taos. A big, round fireplace warms guests in winter, and kitschy tepees are available in summer.

★ Earthship Rentals · BOUTIQUE HOTEL $$
(☎505-751-0462; www.earthship.com; US Hwy 64; earthship $145-305; 🛜🏊) Experience an off-grid overnight in a boutique-chic, solar-powered dwelling. A cross between organic Gaudí architecture and space-age fantasy, these sustainable dwellings are put together using recycled tires, aluminum cans and sand, with rain catchment and gray-water systems to minimize their footprint. Half-buried in a valley surrounded by mountains, they *could* be hastily camouflaged alien vessels – you never know.

Historic Taos Inn
HISTORIC HOTEL **$$**

(☑ 575-758-2233; www.taosinn.com; 125 Paseo del Pueblo Norte; r $75-275; P✳🕸) Even though it's not the plushest place in town, it's still fabulous, with a cozy lobby, a top-notch restaurant, heavy wooden furniture, a sunken fireplace and lots of live local music at its famed Adobe Bar. Parts of this landmark date to the 1800s – the older rooms are actually the nicest.

🍴 Eating

Michael's Kitchen
NEW MEXICAN **$**

(www.michaelskitchen.com; 304c Paseo del Pueblo Norte; mains $7-16; ⊘ 7am-2:30pm Mon-Thu, to 8pm Fri-Sun; 🍴) Great breakfasts, freshly made pastries and tasty New Mexican fare. Go for the stuffed sopapilla! Then try to walk...

El Gamal
MIDDLE EASTERN **$**

(www.elgamaltaos.com; 12 Doña Luz St; mains $7-12; ⊘ 9am-5pm Sun-Wed, to 9pm Thu-Sat; 🕸☑🍴) Vegetarians rejoice! Here's a fabulous meatless Middle Eastern menu. There's a big kids' playroom in back, plus a pool table and free wi-fi.

Taos Pizza Out Back
PIZZA **$**

(www.taospizzaoutback.com; 712 Paseo del Pueblo Norte; whole pies $13-29; ⊘ 11am-10pm May-Sep, to 9pm Oct-Apr; ☑🍴) Warning: these pizza pies may be cruelly habit-forming. This place uses organic ingredients and serves epicurean combos such as a Portabella Pie with sun-dried tomatoes and gorgonzola. Slices are the size of a small country.

Taos Diner
DINER **$**

(www.taosdiner.com; 908 Paseo del Pueblo Norte; mains $4-14; ⊘ 7am-2:30pm; 🍴) It's with some reluctance that we share the existence of this marvelous place, a mountain-town diner with wood-paneled walls, tattooed waitresses, fresh-baked biscuits and coffee cups that are never less than half-full. This is diner grub at its finest, prepared with a Southwestern, organic spin. Mountain men, scruffy jocks, solo diners and happy tourists – everyone's welcome here. We like the Copper John's eggs with a side of green chili sauce. There's another branch south of the plaza.

★ Love Apple
ORGANIC **$$**

(☑ 575-751-0050; www.theloveapple.net; 803 Paseo del Pueblo Norte; mains $13-22; ⊘ 5-9pm Tue-Sun) Housed in the 19th-century-adobe Placitas Chapel, the understated rustic-sacred atmosphere is as much a part of this only-in-New-Mexico restaurant as the food is. From the veggie lasagne to the grilled antelope with couscous, every dish is made from organic or free-range regional foods. Make reservations!

★ Trading Post Cafe
INTERNATIONAL **$$$**

(☑ 575-758-5089; www.tradingpostcafe com; Hwy 68, Ranchos de Taos; lunch mains $8-14, dinner mains $15-32; ⊘ 11am-9pm Tue-Sat) A longtime favorite, the Trading Post is a perfect blend of relaxed and refined. The food, from paella to pork chops, is always great. Portions of some dishes are so big you should think about splitting a main course – or if you want to eat cheap but well, get a small salad and small soup. It'll be plenty!

🍸 Drinking & Entertainment

Adobe Bar
BAR

(125 Paseo del Pueblo Norte, Historic Taos Inn; ⊘ 11am-11pm) Everybody's welcome in 'the living room of Taos.' And there's something about it: the chairs, the Taos Inn's history, the casualness, the tequila. There's a streetside patio in summer, an indoor kiva fireplace in winter, plus top-notch margaritas and an eclectic lineup of live music all year round.

KTAO Solar Center
LIVE MUSIC

(www.ktao.com; 9 Ski Valley Rd; ⊘ bar from 4pm) Watch the DJs at the 'world's most powerful solar radio station' while hitting happy hour at the solar center bar. It's also a happenin' live-music venue for grooving local or big-name bands. There's even a play area for kids on the grassy lawn.

Alley Cantina
LIVE MUSIC

(121 Terracina Lane; ⊘ 11:30am-11pm) It's a bit-cooler-than-thou, but maybe 'tude happens when you inhabit the oldest building in town. Catch live rock, blues, hip-hop or jazz almost nightly.

🛍 Shopping

Taos has historically been a mecca for artists, demonstrated by the huge number of galleries and studios in and around town. Indie stores and galleries line the John Dunn Shops (www.johndunnshops.com) pedestrian walkway linking Bent St to Taos Plaza. Here you'll find the well-stocked Moby Dickens Bookshop (www.mobydickens.com; 124A Bent Street; ⊘ 10am-6pm) and the tiny but intriguing G Robinson Old Prints & Maps

(124D Bent St; ☺11am-5pm), a treat for cartography geeks.

Just east of the Plaza, pop into El Rincón Trading Post (114 Kit Carson Rd; ☺10am-5pm) and Horse Feathers (109 Kit Carson Rd; ☺10:30am-5:30pm) for classic Western memorabilia.

❶ Information

Taos.org (www.taos.org) Great resource for visitors, with easy-to-navigate links.

Taos Visitor Center (☑575-758-3873; Paseo del Pueblo Sur, Paseo del Cañon; ☺9am-5pm; ☎)

Wired? (705 Felicidad Lane; ☺8am-6pm Mon-Fri, 8:30am-6pm Sat & Sun, shorter hours weekends in winter) Funky coffee shop with computers ($7 per hour). Free wi-fi for customers.

❶ Getting There & Away

From Santa Fe, take either the scenic 'high road' along Hwys 76 and 518, with galleries, villages and sites worth exploring, or follow the lovely unfolding Rio Grande landscape on Hwy 68.

North Central Regional Transit (www.ncrtd.org) provides free shuttle-bus service to Espanola, where you can transfer to Santa Fe and other destinations. **Twin Hearts Express** (☑800-654-9456; www.twinhearts-expresstransportation.com) will get you to Santa Fe ($40) and the Albuquerque airport ($50).

Northwestern New Mexico

Dubbed 'Indian Country' for good reason – huge swaths of land fall under the aegis of the Navajo, Pueblo, Zuni, Apache and Laguna tribes – this quadrant of New Mexico showcases remarkable ancient Indian sites alongside solitary Native American settlements and colorful geological badlands.

Farmington & Around

The largest town in New Mexico's northwestern region, Farmington makes a convenient base from which to explore the Four Corners area. The visitors bureau (☑505-326-7602; www.farmingtonnm.org; 3041 E Main St, Farmington Museum at Gateway Park; ☺8am-5pm Mon-Fri) has more information.

Shiprock, a 1700ft-high volcanic plug that rises eerily over the landscape to the west, was a landmark for the Anglo pioneers and is a sacred site to the Navajo.

An ancient pueblo, Salmon Ruin & Heritage Park (www.salmonruins.com; adult/child $3/1; ☺8am-5pm Mon-Fri, 9am-5pm Sat & Sun; from noon Sun Nov-Apr) features a large village built by the Chaco people in the early 1100s. Abandoned, resettled by people from Mesa Verde and again abandoned before 1300, the site also includes the remains of a homestead, petroglyphs, a Navajo hogan and a wickiup (a rough brushwood shelter). Take Hwy 64 east 11 miles toward Bloomfield.

Fourteen miles northeast of Farmington, the 27-acre Aztec Ruins National Monument (www.nps.gov/azru; adult/child $5/free; ☺8am-5pm Sep-May, to 6pm Jun-Aug) features the largest reconstructed kiva in the country, with an internal diameter of almost 50ft. A few steps away, let your imagination wander as you stoop through low doorways and dark rooms inside the West Ruin. In summer, rangers give early-afternoon talks about ancient architecture, trade routes and astronomy.

About 35 miles south of Farmington along Hwy 371, the undeveloped Bisti Badlands & De-Na-Zin Wilderness is a trippy, surreal landscape of strange, colorful rock formations, especially spectacular in the hours before sunset; desert enthusiasts shouldn't miss it. The Farmington BLM office (☑505-564-7600; www.nm.blm.gov; 6251 College Blvd; ☺7:45am-4:30pm Mon-Fri) has information.

The lovely, three-room Silver River Adobe Inn B&B (☑800-382-9251, 575-325-8219; www.silveradobe.com; 3151 W Main St, Farmington; r $115-175; ❄☎) offers a peaceful respite among the trees along the San Juan River.

Managing to be both trendy *and* kid-friendly, the hippish Three Rivers Eatery & Brewhouse (www.threeriversbrewery.com; 101 E Main St, Farmington; mains $8-26; ☺11am-9pm; ❧) has good steaks, pub grub, and its own microbrews. It's the best restaurant in town by a mile.

Chaco Culture National Historic Park

Featuring massive Ancestral Puebloan buildings set in an isolated high-desert environment, intriguing Chaco (www.nps.gov/chcu; per vehicle/bike $8/4; ☺7am-sunset) contains evidence of 5000 years of human occupation. In its prime, the community at Chaco Canyon was a major trading and ceremonial hub for the region – and the city the Puebloan people created here was masterly in its layout and design. Pueblo Bonito is four stories tall and may have had 600 to 800 rooms and kivas. As well as taking the self-guided loop tour, you can hike various backcountry trails. For stargazers, there's the Night Skies program offered Tuesday, Friday and Saturday evenings April through October.

The park is in a remote area approximately 80 miles south of Farmington. Gallo Campground (campsites $10) is 1 mile east of the visitor center. No RV hook-ups.

Chama

Nine miles south of the Colorado border, Chama's Cumbres & Toltec Scenic Railway (575-756-2151; www.cumbrestoltec.com; adult/child from $89/49; late May–mid-Oct) is the longest (64 miles) and highest (over the 10,015ft-high Cumbres Pass) authentic narrow-gauge steam railroad in the US. It's a beautiful trip, particularly in September and October during the fall foliage, through mountains, canyons and high desert. Lunch is included and on many trips kids ride free. See the website for details on trip options.

Northeastern New Mexico

East of Santa Fe, the lush Sangre de Cristo Mountains give way to vast rolling plains. Dusty grasslands stretch to infinity and further – to Texas. Cattle and dinosaur prints dot a landscape punctuated with volcanic cones. Ranching is an economic mainstay, and on many roads you'll see more cows than cars.

The Santa Fe Trail, along which pioneer settlers rolled in wagon trains, ran from New Mexico to Missouri. You can still see the wagon ruts in some places off I-25 between Santa Fe and Raton. For a bit of the Old West without a patina of consumer hype, this is the place.

Cimarron

Cimarron once ranked among the rowdiest of Wild West towns; it's name even means 'wild' in Spanish. According to local lore, murder was such an everyday occurrence in the 1870s that peace-and-quiet was newsworthy, one paper going so far as to report:

'Everything is quiet in Cimarron. Nobody has been killed in three days.'

Today, the town is quiet, luring nature-minded travelers who want to enjoy the great outdoors. Driving here to or from Taos, you'll pass through gorgeous Cimarron Canyon State Park, a steep-walled canyon with several hiking trails, excellent trout fishing and camping.

You can stay or dine (restaurant mains $7 to $20) at what's reputed to be one of the most haunted hotels in the USA, the 1872 St James (888-376-2664; www.exstjames.com; 617 Collison St; r $85-135;) – one room is so spook-filled that it's never rented out! Many legends of the West stayed here, including Buffalo Bill, Annie Oakley, Wyatt Earp and Jesse James, and the front desk has a long list of who shot whom in the now-renovated hotel bar. The authentic period rooms make this one of the most historic-feeling hotels in New Mexico.

Capulin Volcano National Monument

Rising 1300ft above the surrounding plains, Capulin (www.nps.gov/cavo; admission per vehicle $5; 8am-4pm) is the most accessible of several volcanoes in the area. From the visitor center, a 2-mile road spirals up the mountain to a parking lot at the crater rim (8182ft), where trails lead around and into the crater. The entrance is 3 miles north of Capulin village, which itself is 30 miles east of Raton on Hwy 87.

Southwestern New Mexico

The Rio Grande Valley unfurls from Albuquerque down to the bubbling hot springs of funky Truth or Consequences and beyond. Before the river hits the Texas line, it feeds one of New Mexico's agricultural treasures: Hatch, the so-called 'chili capital of the world.' The first atomic device was detonated at the Trinity Site, in the bone-dry desert east of the Rio Grande known since Spanish times as the Jornada del Muerto – Journey of Death.

To the west, the rugged Gila National Forest is wild with backpacking and fishing adventures. The mountains' southern slopes descend into the Chihuahuan Desert that surrounds Las Cruces, the state's second-largest city.

Truth or Consequences & Around

An offbeat joie de vivre permeates the funky little town of Truth or Consequences, which was built on the site of natural hot springs in the 1880s. A bit of the quirkiness stems from the fact that the town changed its name from Hot Springs to Truth or Consequences (or 'T or C') in 1950, after a popular radio game show of the same name. Publicity these days comes courtesy of Virgin Galactic CEO Richard Branson and other space-travel visionaries driving the development of nearby Spaceport America, where wealthy tourists will launch into orbit sometime soon. Spaceport tours (⌨575-740-6894; www.ftstours.com; adult/under 12yr $59/29; ☺9am & 1pm Fri & Sat, 9am Sun) include a look at the launch site and mission control.

About 60 miles north of town, sandhill cranes and Arctic geese winter in the 90 sq miles of fields and marshes at Bosque del Apache National Wildlife Refuge (www.fws.gov/southwest/refuges/newmex/bosque; per vehicle $5; ☺dawn-dusk). There's a visitor center and driving tour. The Festival of the Cranes is held in mid-November.

🛏 Sleeping & Eating

Many local motels double as spas.

★Blackstone Hotsprings   BOUTIQUE HOTEL $
(⌨575-894-0894; www.blackstonehotsprings.com; 410 Austin St; r $75-135; P❄🐾) Blackstone embraces the T or C spirit with an upscale wink, decorating each of its seven rooms in the style of a classic TV show, from the *Jetsons* to the *Golden Girls* to *I Love Lucy*. Best part? Each room comes with its own hot-spring tub or waterfall. Worst part? If you like sleeping in darkness, quite a bit of courtyard light seeps into some rooms at night.

Riverbend Hot Springs   BOUTIQUE HOTEL $
(⌨575-894-7625; www.riverbendhotsprings.com; 100 Austin St; r from $70; ❄🐾) Former hostel Riverbend Hot Springs now offers more traditional motel-style accommodations – no more tepees – from its fantastic perch beside the Rio Grande. Rooms exude a bright, quirky charm, and several units work well for groups. Private hot-spring tubs are available by the hour (guest/nonguest $10/15), as is a public hot-spring pool (guest/nonguest free/$10).

Happy Belly Deli   DELI $
(313 N Broadway; mains $2-8; ☺7am-3pm Mon- Fri, 8am-3pm Sat, 8am-noon Sun) Draws the morning crowd with fresh and filling breakfast combos.

★Café Bellaluca   ITALIAN $$
(www.cafebellaluca.com; 303 Jones St; lunch mains $8-15, dinner mains $13-38; ☺11am-9pm Mon, Wed & Thu, to 10pm Fri & Sat, to 8pm Sun) Earns raves for its Italian specialties; pizzas are amazing.

Las Cruces & Around

The second-largest city in New Mexico, Las Cruces is home to New Mexico State University (NMSU), but there's surprisingly little of real interest for visitors.

⊙ Sights

For many, a visit to neighboring Mesilla (aka Old Mesilla) is the highlight of their time in Las Cruces. Wander a few blocks off Old Mesilla's plaza to gather the essence of a mid-19th-century Southwestern town of Hispanic heritage.

★New Mexico Farm & Ranch Heritage Museum   MUSEUM
(www.nmfarmandranchmuseum.org; 4100 Dripping Springs Rd; adult/child $5/2; ☺9am-5pm Mon-Sat, noon-5pm Sun; 🚻) This terrific museum in Las Cruces has more than just engaging displays about the agricultural history of the state – it's got livestock! There are daily milking demonstrations and an occasional 'parade of breeds' of beef cattle, along with stalls of horses, donkeys, sheep and goats. Other demonstrations include blacksmithing (Friday to Sunday), spinning and weaving (Wednesday), and heritage cooking (call for schedule).

White Sands Missile Test Center Museum   MUSEUM
(www.wsmr-history.org; Bldg 200, Headquarters Ave; ☺8am-4pm Mon-Fri, 10am-3pm Sat) FREE About 25 miles east of Las Cruces along Hwy 70 (look for the White Sands Missile Range Headquarters sign), White Sands has been a major military testing site since 1945, and it still serves as an alternative landing site for the space shuttle. Look for the crazy outdoor missile park. Since it's on an army base, everyone entering over the age of 18 years must show ID, and the driver might have to present car registration and proof of insurance.

EAVESDROPPING ON OUTER SPACE

Past the town of Magdalena on Hwy 60 is the **Very Large Array** (VLA; www. nrao.edu; off Hwy 52; ⊙8:30am-sunset) **FREE** radio telescope facility, a complex of 27 huge antenna dishes sprouting like giant mushrooms in the high plains. At the visitor center, watch a short film about the facility and take a self-guided walking tour with a window peek into the control building. It's 4 miles south of Hwy 60 off Hwy 52.

🛏 Sleeping

★**Lundeen Inn of the Arts**   B&B $$
(📞505-526-3326; www.innofthearts.com; 618 S Alameda Blvd, Las Cruces; r incl breakfast $80-125, ste $99-155; P❋❋🛜) In Las Cruces, Lundeen Inn of the Arts, a large turn-of-the-19th-century Mexican territorial-style inn, has seven guest rooms (all unique), genteel hosts, an airy living room with soaring ceilings (made of pressed tin) and impressive freshly made breakfasts.

🍴 Eating

Nellie's Café   NEW MEXICAN $
(1226 W Hadley Ave; mains $5-8; ⊙8am-2pm Tue-Sun) A favored local New Mexican restaurant, great for breakfast and lunch. Cash only.

La Posta   NEW MEXICAN $$
(www.laposta-de-mesilla.com; 2410 Calle de San Albino; mains $8-15; ⊙11am-9pm) The most famous restaurant in Old Mesilla, in a 200-year-old adobe, may at first raise your doubts with its fiesta-like decor and touristy feel. But the New Mexican dishes are consistently good, portions are huge and service is prompt.

ℹ Information

Las Cruces Visitors Bureau (📞575-541-2444; www.lascrucescvb.org; 211 N Water St; ⊙8am-5pm Mon-Fri)

ℹ Getting There & Away

Greyhound (📞575-524-8518; www.greyhound. com; 800 E Thorpe Rd, Chucky's Convenience Store) buses traverse the two interstate corridors (I-10 and I-25). Daily destinations include Albuquerque ($29, 3½ hours), Roswell ($52, four hours) and El Paso ($12.60, one hour).

Silver City & Around

The spirit of the Wild West still hangs in the air here, as if Billy the Kid himself – a former resident – might amble past at any moment. But things are changing, as the mountain-man/cowboy vibe succumbs to the charms of art galleries, coffeehouses and gelato. (One word of caution when strolling through downtown Silver City – look carefully before you step off the sidewalk. Because of monsoonal summer rains, curbs are higher than average, built to keep the Victorian and the brick and cast-iron buildings safe from quick-rising waters.)

Silver City is also the gateway to outdoor activities in the **Gila National Forest**, which is rugged country suitable for remote cross-country skiing, backpacking, camping, fishing and other activities.

Two hours north of Silver City, up a winding 42-mile road, is **Gila Cliff Dwellings National Monument** (www.nps.gov/gicl; admission $3; ⊙trail 9am-4pm, visitor center to 4:30pm), occupied in the 13th century by Mogollons. Mysterious and relatively isolated, these remarkable cliff dwellings are easily accessed from a 1-mile loop trail and look very much as they would have at the turn of the first millennium. For **pictographs**, stop by the Lower Scorpion Campground and walk a short distance along the marked trail.

Weird rounded monoliths make the **City of Rocks State Park** (www.nmparks.com; Hwy 61; day-use $5, tent/RV sites $8/10) an intriguing playground, with great camping among the formations; there are tables and fire pits. For a rock-lined gem of a spot, check out campsite 43, the Lynx. Head 24 miles northwest of Deming along Hwy 180, then 3 miles northeast on Hwy 61.

For a smattering of Silver City's architectural history, overnight in the 22-room **Palace Hotel** (📞575-388-1811; www.silvercitypalacehotel.com; 106 W Broadway; r from $51; ❋🛜). Exuding a low-key, turn-of-the-19th-century charm (no air con, older fixtures), the Palace is a great choice for those tired of cookie-cutter chains. On the corner, the lofty **Javalina** (201 N Bullard St; pastries from $2; ⊙6am-9pm Mon-Thu, to 10pm Fri & Sat, to 7pm Sun; 🛜) offers coffee, snacks and wi-fi in a comfy, come-as-you-are space.

Downtown offers a variety of eateries, including the deservedly popular **Diane's Restaurant & Bakery** (📞575-538-8722; www. dianesrestaurant.com; 510 N Bullard St; lunch $8-10, dinner $15-30; ⊘ 11am-2pm & 5:30-9pm Tue-Sat, 11am-2pm Sun) and the Peace Meal Cooperative (www.peacemealcoop.com; 601 N Bullard St; mains $6-10; ⊘ 11am-7pm Wed-Mon; ⏶) build-your-own burrito bar. For a real taste of local culture, head 7 miles north to Pinos Altos and the Buckhorn Saloon (⏰575-538-9911; www.buckhornsaloonandoperahouse.com; Main St, Pinos Altos; mains $10-39; ⊘ 5-9pm Mon-Sat), where the specialty is steak and there's live music most nights. Call for reservations.

ℹ Information

The **visitor center** (⏰575-538-3785; www.silvercity.org; 201 N Hudson St; ⊘ 9am-5pm Mon-Fri, 10am-2pm Sat & Sun) and the **Gila National Forest Ranger Station** (⏰575-388-8201; www.fs.fed.us/r3/gila; 3005 E Camino Del Bosque; ⊘ 8am-4:30pm Mon-Fri) have area information. To learn about the town's contentious mining history, watch the blacklisted 1954 movie *Salt of the Earth*.

Southeastern New Mexico

Two of New Mexico's greatest natural wonders are tucked down here in the arid southeast – mesmerizing White Sands National Monument and magnificent Carlsbad Caverns National Park. This region is also home to some of the state's most enduring legends: aliens in Roswell, Billy the Kid in Lincoln and Smokey Bear in Capitan. Most of the lowlands are covered by hot, rugged Chihuahuan Desert, but you can escape to cooler climes by driving up to higher altitudes around the popular forested resort towns such as Cloudcroft and Ruidoso.

White Sands National Monument

Slide, roll and slither through brilliant, towering sand hills. Sixteen miles southwest of Alamogordo (15 miles southwest of Hwy 82/70), gypsum covers 275 sq miles to create a dazzling white landscape at this crisp, stark monument (www.nps.gov/whsa; adult/under 16yr $3/free; ⊘ 7am-9pm Jun-Aug, to sunset Sep-May). These captivating windswept dunes are a highlight of any trip to New Mexico. Don't forget your sunglasses – the sand is as bright as snow!

Spring for a $17 plastic saucer at the visitor center gift store then sled one of the back dunes. It's fun, and you can sell the disc back

for $5 at day's end (no rentals to avoid liability). Check the park calendar for sunset strolls and occasional full-moon bike rides (adult/under 16 years $5/2.50), the latter best reserved far in advance. Backcountry campsites, with no water or toilet facilities, are a mile from the scenic drive. Pick up one of the limited permits ($3, issued first-come, first-served) in person at the visitor center at least one hour before sunset.

Alamogordo & Around

Alamogordo is the center of one of the most historically important space- and atomic-research programs in the country. The four-story New Mexico Museum of Space History (www.nmspacemuseum.org; Hwy 2001; adult/child $6/4; ⊘ 9am-5pm; ⏶) has excellent exhibits on space research and flight. Its Tombaugh IMAX Theater & Planetarium (adult/child $6/4.50; ⏶) shows outstanding science-themed films on a huge wraparound screen.

Numerous motels stretch along White Sands Blvd, including Best Western Desert Aire Hotel (⏰575-437-2110; www.bestwestern.com; 1021 S White Sands Blvd; r from $78; ✳@🛜🏊), with standard-issue rooms and suites (some with kitchenettes), along with a sauna. If you'd rather camp, hit Oliver Lee State Park (www.nmparks.com; 409 Dog Canyon Rd; tent/RV sites $8/14), 12 miles south of Alamogordo. Grab some grub at the friendly Pizza Patio & Pub (2203 E 1st St; mains $7-15; ⊘ 11am-8pm Mon-Thu & Sat, to 9pm Fri; ⏶), which has pizzas, pastas, big salads and pitchers or pints of beer on tap.

Cloudcroft

Pleasant Cloudcroft, with turn-of-the-19th-century buildings, offers lots of outdoor recreation, a good base for exploration and a low-key feel. Situated high in the mountains, it provides welcome relief from the lowlands heat to the east. For good information on hiking trails, free maps of forest roads, and topo maps for sale, go to the Lincoln National Forest Ranger Station (4 Lost Lodge Rd; ⊘ 7:30am-4:30pm Mon-Fri). High Altitude (⏰575-682-1229; www.highaltitude.org; 310 Burro Ave; ⊘ 10am-5:30pm Mon-Thu, to 6pm Fri & Sat, to 5pm Sun) rents mountain bikes and has maps of local fat-tire routes.

The Lodge Resort & Spa (⏰888-395-6343; www.thelodgeresort.com; 601 Corona Pl; r from $125; @🛜🏊) is one of the Southwest's best historic hotels. Rooms in the main Bavarian-style hotel are furnished with period and Victorian pieces. Within the lodge, **Rebecca's** (📞575-682-3131; Lodge Resort & Spa, 601 Corona Pl; mains $8-36; ☉7-10am, 11:30am-2pm & 5:30-9pm), named after the resident ghost, offers by far the best food in town.

Ruidoso

Downright bustling in summer and big with racetrack bettors, resorty Ruidoso (it means 'noisy' in Spanish) has an utterly pleasant climate thanks to its lofty and forested perch near Sierra Blanca (12,000ft). It's spread out along Hwy 48 (known as Mechem Dr or Sudderth Dr), the main drag.

◉ Sights & Activities

To stretch your legs, try the easily accessible **forest trails** on Cedar Creek Rd just west of **Smokey Bear Ranger Station** (📞575-257-4095; 901 Mechem Dr; ☉7:30am-4:30pm Mon-Fri year-round, plus Sat in summer). Choose from the USFS Fitness Trail or the meandering paths at the Cedar Creek Picnic Area. Longer day hikes and backpacking routes abound in the White Mountain Wilderness, north of town. Always check fire restrictions around here – it's not unusual for the forest to close during dry spells.

Ski Apache   SKIING
(www.skiapache.com; lift ticket adult/child $51/33) The best ski area south of Albuquerque. It's 18 miles northwest of Ruidoso on the slopes of beautiful Sierra Blanca Peak (about 12,000ft). To get there, take exit 532 off Hwy 48.

Ruidoso Downs Racetrack   HORSE RACING
(www.raceruidoso.com; Hwy 70; grandstand seats free; ☉Fri-Mon late May-early Sep) Serious horse racing happens here.

Hubbard Museum of the American West   MUSEUM
(www.hubbardmuseum.org; 26301 Hwy 70; adult/child $6/2; ☉10am-4:30pm; 🖈) Displays Western-related items, with an emphasis on Old West stagecoaches, Native American artifacts and, well, all things horse.

🛏 Sleeping & Eating

Numerous motels, hotels and cute little cabin complexes line the streets. There's plenty of primitive camping along forest roads on the way to the ski area.

Sitzmark Chalet   HOTEL $
(📞800-658-9694; www.sitzmark-chalet.com; 627 Sudderth Dr; r from $60; ❋🐾📶) This ski-themed chalet offers 17 simple but nice rooms. Picnic tables, grills and an eight-person hot tub are welcome perks.

Upper Canyon Inn   LODGE $$
(📞575-257-3005; www.uppercanyoninn.com; 215 Main Rd; r/cabins from $79/119; 📶) Rooms and cabins range from simple good values to rustic-chic luxury.

Cornerstone Bakery   BREAKFAST $
(www.cornerstonebakerycafe.com; 359 Sudderth Dr; mains under $10; ☉7am-2pm; 🖉) Stay around long enough and this eatery may become your touchstone. Everything on the menu, from the omelets to croissant sandwiches, is worthy, and the piñon-flavored coffee is wonderful.

Café Rio   PIZZA $
(2547 Sudderth Dr; mains $8-25, cash only; ☉11:30am-8pm, closed Wed off-season; 🖉🖈) Friendly service isn't the first description that leaps to mind at this scruffy pizza joint, but oh…take one bite of a pillowy slice and all will be forgiven.

☆ Entertainment

Flying J Ranch   VARIETY
(📞888-458-3595; www.flyingjranch.com; 1028 Hwy 48; adult/child $27/15; ☉from 5:30pm Mon-Sat late May-early Sep, Sat only to mid-Oct; 🖈) Circle the wagons and ride over about 1.5 miles north of Alto for a meal. This 'Western village' stages gunfights and offers pony rides with its cowboy-style chuckwagon.

ℹ Information

The **chamber of commerce** (📞575-257-7395; www.ruidoso.net; 720 Sudderth Dr; ☉8am-4:30pm Mon-Fri, 9am-3pm Sat) has visitor information.

Lincoln & Capitan

Fans of Western history won't want to miss little Lincoln. Twelve miles east of Capitan along the **Billy the Kid National Scenic Byway** (www.billybyway.com), this is where the gun battle that turned Billy the Kid into a legend took place. The whole town is beautifully preserved in close to original form and the main street has been designated the **Lincoln State Monument** (www.nmmonuments.org/lincoln; adult/child $5/free; ☉8:30am-4:30pm); modern influences (such

CARLSBAD CAVERNS NATIONAL PARK

Scores of wondrous caves hide under the hills at this unique **national park** (☑575-785-2232, bat info 505-785-3012; www.nps.gov/cave; 3225 National Parks Hwy; adult/child $6/free; ☺caves 8:30am-5pm late May-early Sep, 8:30am-3:30pm early Sep-late May; 🅿), which covers 73 sq miles. The cavern formations are an ethereal wonderland of stalactites and fantastical geological features. From the **visitor center** (☺8am-5pm late May-early Sep) you can ride an elevator, which descends the length of the Empire State Building in under a minute, or take a 2-mile subterranean walk from the cave mouth to the Big Room, an underground chamber 1800ft long, 255ft high and more than 800ft below the surface. If you've got kids (or are just feeling goofy), plastic caving helmets with headlamps are sold in the gift shop.

Guided tours (☑877-444-6777; www.recreation.gov; adult $7-20, child $3.50-10) of additional caves are available, and should be reserved well in advance. Wear long sleeves and closed shoes; it gets chilly.

The cave's other claim to fame is the 300,000-plus Mexican free-tailed bat colony that roosts here from mid-May to mid-October. Be here by sunset, when they cyclone out for an all-evening insect feast.

as neon-lit motel signs, souvenir stands, fast-food joints) are not allowed.

Buy tickets to the historic town buildings at the **Anderson-Freeman Museum**, where you'll also find exhibits on Buffalo soldiers, Apaches and the Lincoln County War. Make the fascinating **Courthouse Museum** your last stop; this is the well-marked site of Billy's most daring – and violent – escape. There's a plaque where one of his bullets slammed into the wall.

For overnights, the **Ellis Store Country Inn** (☑800-653-6460; www.ellisstore.com; Hwy 380; r incl breakfast $89-129) offers three antique-filled rooms (complete with wood stove) in the main house; five additional rooms are located in a historic mill on the property. From Wednesday to Saturday the host offers an amazing six-course dinner ($75 per person), served in the lovely dining room. Perfect for special occasions; reservations recommended.

A few miles west on the road to Capitan, **Laughing Sheep Farm and Ranch** (☑575-653-4041; www.laughingsheepfarm.com; Hwy 380; mains $10-35; ☺5-9pm Thu-Sat; 🅿) raises sheep, cows and bison – along with vegetables and fruit – then serves them up for dinner. The dining room is comfortable and casual, with a play-dough table and an easel for kids and live music each night it's open. Comfortable cabins with hot tubs are rented by the night from $130.

Like Lincoln, cozy Capitan is surrounded by the beautiful mountains of **Lincoln National Forest**. The main reason to come is

so the kids can visit **Smokey Bear Historical State Park** (118 W Smokey Bear Blvd; adult/child $2/1; ☺9am-5pm), where Smokey (yes, there actually was a real Smokey Bear) is buried.

Roswell

If you believe 'The Truth Is Out There', then the Roswell Incident is already filed away in your memory banks. In 1947 a mysterious object crashed at a nearby ranch. No one would have skipped any sleep over it, but the military made a big to-do of hushing it up, and for a lot of folks, that sealed it: the aliens had landed! International curiosity and local ingenuity have transformed the city into a quirky extraterrestrial-wannabe zone. Bulbous white heads glow atop the downtown streetlamps and busloads of tourists come to find good souvenirs.

Believers and kitsch-seekers must check out the **International UFO Museum & Research Center** (www.roswellufomuseum.com; 114 N Main St; adult/child $5/$2; ☺9am-5pm), displaying documents supporting the cover-up as well as lots of far-out art and exhibitions. The annual **Roswell UFO Festival** (www.roswellufofestival.com) beams down in early July, with an otherworldly costume parade, guest speakers, workshops and concerts.

Ho-hum chain motels line N Main St. About 36 miles south of Roswell, the **Heritage Inn** (☑575-748-2552; www.artesiaheritage-inn.com; 209 W Main St, Artesia; r incl breakfast from $119; ✳ @ 🛜 🛁) in Artesia offers 11 Old West–style rooms and is the nicest lodging in the area.

For simple, dependable New Mexican fare, try **Martin's Capitol Cafe** (110 W 4th St; mains $7-15; ⊙6am-8:30pm Mon-Sat); for American eats, **Big D's Downtown Dive** (www.bigdsdowntowndive.com; 505 N Main St; mains $7-10; ⊙11am-9pm) has the best salads, sandwiches and burgers in town.

Pick up local information and have your picture snapped with an alien at the **visitors bureau** (📋575-624-6860; www.seeroswell.com; 912 N Main St; ⊙8:30am-5:30pm Mon-Fri, 10am-3pm Sat & Sun; 🛜).

The **Greyhound Bus Depot** (📋575-622-2510; www.greyhound.com; 1100 N Virginia Ave) has buses to Carlsbad ($30, 1½ hours) and El Paso, TX, via Las Cruces ($52, four hours).

Carlsbad

Travelers use Carlsbad as a base for visits to nearby Carlsbad Caverns National Park and the Guadalupe Mountains. The **Park Service office** (📋575-885-8884; 3225 National Parks Hwy; ⊙8am-4:30pm Mon-Fri) on the south edge of town has information on both.

On the northwestern outskirts of town, off Hwy 285, **Living Desert State Park** (www.nmparks.com; 1504 Miehls Dr, off Hwy 285; adult/child $5/3; ⊙8am-5pm Jun-Aug, 9am-5pm Sep-May) is a great place to see and learn about desert plants and wildlife. There's a good 1.3-mile trail that showcases different habitats of the Chihuahuan Desert, with live antelopes, wolves, roadrunners and more.

Most of Carlsbad lodging consists of chain motels on S Canal St or National Parks Hwy. The top value is the **Stagecoach Inn** (📋575-887-1148; 1819 S Canal St; r from $50; ✳🛜✳), with clean rooms, a pool, and a good on-site playground for kids. The best accommodation in town is the new, luxurious **Trinity Hotel** (📋575-234-9891; www.thetrinityhotel.com; 201 S Canal St; r from $169-219; ✳🛜), a historic building that was originally the First National Bank; the sitting room of one suite is inside the old vault! The restaurant here is Carlsbad's classiest.

The perky **Blue House Bakery & Cafe** (609 N Canyon St; mains $4-8; ⊙6am-noon Mon-Sat) brews the best coffee in this quadrant of New Mexico and specializes in breakfasts and pastries. For country-style dinner, hit the lip-smackin' good **Red Chimney Pit Barbecue** (www.redchimneypitbarbecue.com; 817 N Canal St; mains $7-15; ⊙11am-2pm & 4:30-8:30pm Mon-Fri), where you're sure to get your fill.

For other in-the-know advice, visit the **chamber of commerce** (📋575-887-6516; www.carlsbadchamber.com; 302 S Canal St; ⊙9am-5pm Mon, 8am-5pm Tue-Fri).

Greyhound (📋575-628-0768; www.greyhound.com; 3102 National Parks Hwy) buses depart from the Shamrock gas station inside Food Jet South, heading only to El Paso ($52, three hours) and Lubbock, TX ($52, four hours).

Understand Western USA

Western USA Today

The big news in the West? The citizens of Colorado and Washington voted to legalize the recreational use of marijuana in 2012, and a Supreme Court decision in 2013 allowed same-sex marriage to continue in California. Economically, the region is still recovering from the recession. There is also a sense of climate-related unease, which stems from ongoing drought across the Southwest, cataclysmic floods in Colorado and devastating fires across the entire region.

Best in Print

The Grapes of Wrath (John Steinbeck; 1939) Dust Bowl migrants travel west to California.

Desert Solitaire (Edward Abbey; 1968) Essays about the Southwest and industrial tourism by no-holds-barred eco-curmudgeon.

Bean Trees (Barbara Kingsolver; 1988) Thoughtful look at motherhood and cross-cultural adoption in Tucson.

Into the Wild (Jon Krakauer; 1996) Alexander Supertramp wanders across the West in search of meaning.

Best Films

Stagecoach (1939)
Sunset Boulevard (1950)
Butch Cassidy & the Sundance Kid (1969)
Chinatown (1974)
One Flew Over the Cuckoo's Nest (1975)
The Shining (1980)
Thelma & Louise (1991)
Boyz n the Hood (1991)
Sideways (2004)
The Hangover (2009)
127 Hours (2010)

It's All About Politics...

In recent years the most high-profile political issue in California has been same-sex marriage. The state Supreme Court struck down a constitutional ban against same-sex marriage in 2008, but, later that year, the voter-backed Proposition 8 again limited marriage to a union between a man and a woman. In 2013, federal courts ruled that Prop 8 was unconstitutional. A subsequent appeal of this ruling to the US Supreme Court was denied on jurisdictional grounds, and same-sex marriages have resumed in the state.

In the fall of 2012 residents of Colorado and Washington voted to legalize the recreational use of marijuana. Colorado voters passed Amendment 64, which allowed for the limited possession and use of marijuana by anyone 21 years of age and older, and rules for the cultivation and sale of recreational pot in Colorado were adopted in September 2013. Regulations for recreational use are expected by the end of 2013 (and may vary by locality); marijuana stores could open in early 2014. A similar initiative was passed in Washington. The federal government has indicated that it will not challenge these state laws, which are in conflict with federal laws.

Illegal immigration remains a hot-button issue, and border-patrol agents have a very visible presence in southern Arizona, where their green-and-white SUVs are a common sight on rural roads. Arizona has also passed a stringent anti-immigration law, requiring police officers to ask for ID from anyone they suspect of being in the country illegally. Challenges to the law, known as SB 1070, are making their way through the court system.

...Fire & Water...

Although the exact causes are unclear – climate change, residential development, government policy – the West has been hard hit by forest fires. In June 2013, nineteen members of the Granite Mountain Hotshots, an elite team of firefighters, were killed during the devastating Yarnell fire in central Arizona, and 27 homes were lost. The Rim Fire that same year, in and around Yosemite National Park, ripped across more than 250,000 acres, making it the third-largest fire in California since the 1930s. In 2011, the Las Conchas Fire burned more than 244 sq miles near Los Alamos, New Mexico.

But fire isn't the only natural foe in the West these days. A 10-year drought has left water levels in Lake Mead extremely low. At the other extreme, severe flooding in September 2013 affected a 4500-sq-mile area across Colorado's Front Range, killing at least six, leaving hundreds missing, and destroying roads and homes.

...& Money

Fiscal woes are still affecting states across the West, and legislatures have been slashing their budgets accordingly. In Arizona, California and Utah, state parks have been especially hard hit; in Arizona, many state parks are operating on a five-day schedule. Nevada's unemployment rate hit 12% in the spring of 2011, which was higher than the national average.

Moving Forward

The recession marches on but so does technological development, and the tributes describing the accomplishments of Apple co-founder and California native Steve Jobs show just how far and how quickly. California's innovations are myriad: PCs, iPods, Google. But Northern California holds more than Silicon Valley – it's also the site of a burgeoning biotech industry. In the Pacific Northwest, the Seattle area is headquarters for Microsoft, Nintendo and Amazon.com. Branches of Intel, Tektronix and Google support Oregon's 'Silicon Forest.'

In the Southwest, Richard Branson's Virgin Galactic plans to send civilian 'astronauts' into space from the new Spaceport in central New Mexico. At the Grand Canyon, ecofriendly initiatives are gaining traction, including a park-and-ride shuttle from Tusayan and a bicycle rental service. Online retail giant Zappos is relocating its headquarters to downtown Las Vegas and revitalizing the scruffy blocks near Fremont St. Environmentally, Colorado leads the way, with progressive clean-energy standards, legislated incentives for residents to use clean energy, and significant growth in solar-energy jobs.

POPULATION (US):
317 MILLION

AREA (US):
3.79 MILLION SQ MILES

GDP (US): **15.9 TRILLION**

UNEMPLOYMENT (US): **7.3%**

if USA were 100 people

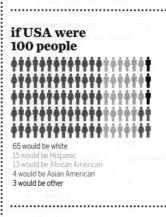

65 would be white
15 would be Hispanic
13 would be African American
4 would be Asian American
3 would be other

belief systems
(% of population)

51 Protestant
24 Roman Catholic
21 Other
2 Jewish
2 Mormon

population per sq mile

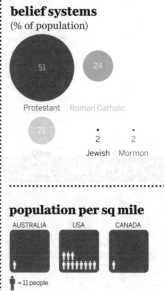

AUSTRALIA   USA   CANADA

≈ 11 people

History

History is up close, personal and willing to be engaged in the West. The downtown plaza in Santa Fe, once the terminus of the Santa Fe Trail, still buzzes with visitors. Temple Sq, dating from the mid-1800s, remains a gathering place for Mormons in Salt Lake City. Abandoned mining towns share their weathered secrets. As you'll soon discover, the explorers and settlers who came before – Native American hunters, Spanish conquistadors, East Cast fortune hunters, Mormon pioneers, Asian entrepreneurs – left stubborn reminders of their existence and their dreams.

From gunslingers and prospectors to Native Americans ancient and contemporary, www.desertusa.com deals the goods on the people and places that call (and have called) the Southwestern desert home.

The first inhabitants of this region actually arrived from the west, crossing the Bering Strait between modern-day Russia and Alaska about 20,000 years ago. These hardy souls flowed south, splitting into diverse communities that adapted as required by the weather and surrounding landscapes. The Spanish arrived in the Southwest in the 1540s, looking for the Seven Cities of Gold. Missions and missionaries followed in the 1700s as the Spanish staked their claim along the California coast.

The Spanish, as well as the British and Americans, were soon searching for the Northwest Passage, an east–west water route, but President Thomas Jefferson eventually scooped this endeavor with the Louisiana Purchase in 1803. His emissaries, Meriwether Lewis and William Clark, marched west from St Louis to explore America's newest holding, opening the door for a wave of pioneers.

An estimated 400,000 people trekked west across America between 1840 and 1860, lured by tales of gold, promises of religious freedom and visions of fertile farmland. The 'Wild West' years soon followed with ranchers, cowboys, miners and entrepreneurs staking claims and raising hell. Law, order and civilization arrived, hastened by the telegraph, the transcontinental railroad and a continual flow of new arrivals who just wanted to settle down and enjoy their piece of the American pie.

This goal became harder to accomplish in the arid West because lack of water limited expansion. The great dam projects of the early 1900s tempered the water problem and allowed for the development of cities – Los Angeles, Las Vegas, Phoenix – in places where cities didn't necessarily belong.

TIMELINE >	20,000–40,000 BC >	8000 BC >	7000 BC–AD 100 >
	The first peoples to the Americas arrive from Central Asia by migrating over a wide land bridge between Siberia and Alaska (when sea levels were lower than today).	Widespread extinction of ice-age mammals including the woolly mammoth, due to a warming climate and cooperative hunting. People begin to hunt smaller game and gather native plants.	'Archaic period' marked by nomadic hunter-gatherer lifestyle. By the end of this period, corn, beans and squash and permanent settlements are well established.

The West took on a more important economic and technological role during WWII. Scientists developed the atomic bomb in the secret city of Los Alamos. War-related industries, such as timber production and work at naval yards and airplane factories, thrived in the Pacific Northwest and California. After the war, industry took on new forms, with Silicon Valley's dot-com industry drawing talented entrepreneurs to the Bay area in the 1990s. The film industry still holds strong in Los Angeles, but tax incentives have drawn filmmakers to other western enclaves, particularly New Mexico.

Today, the West has been forced to take a closer look at the effects of rapid growth. Immigration, traffic, extended drought conditions, dropping water levels and environmental concerns grab headlines and affect people's way of life. The continuing allure of the West will depend on how these issues are tackled.

Cliff Dwellings

Mesa Verde National Park, NM

Bandelier National Monument, NM

Gila Cliff Dwellings National Monument, NM

Montezuma Castle National Monument, AZ

Walnut Canyon National Monument, AZ

HISTORY THE FIRST AMERICANS

The First Americans

Western America's earliest inhabitants crossed the Bering Strait more than 20,000 years ago. When Europeans arrived, approximately two to 18 million Native American people lived north of present-day Mexico and spoke more than 300 languages.

Pacific Northwest

In the Pacific Northwest, early coastal inhabitants went out to sea in pursuit of whales or sea lions, or depended on catching salmon and cod and collecting shellfish. On land they hunted deer and elk while gathering berries and roots. Food was stored for the long winters, when free time could be spent on artistic, religious and cultural pursuits. The construction of ornately carved cedar canoes led to extensive trading networks that stretched along the coast.

Inland, a regional culture based on seasonal migration developed among tribes. During salmon runs, tribes gathered at rapids and waterfalls to net or harpoon fish. In the harsh landscapes of Oregon's southern desert, tribes were nomadic peoples who hunted and scavenged in the northern reaches of the Great Basin desert.

California

By 1500 AD more than 300,000 Native Americans spoke some 100 distinct languages in the California region. Central-coast fishing communities built subterranean roundhouses and saunas, where they held ceremonies, told stories and gambled for fun. Northwest hunting communities constructed big houses and redwood dugout canoes, while the inhabitants of southwest California created sophisticated pottery and developed irrigation systems that made farming in the desert possible.

1300	1492	1598	c 1600
The entire civilization of Ancestral Puebloans living in Mesa Verde, CO, abandons the area, possibly due to drought, leaving behind a sophisticated city of cliff dwellings.	Italian explorer Christopher Columbus 'discovers' America, eventually making three voyages to the Caribbean. He names the indigenous inhabitants 'Indians,' mistakenly thinking he'd reached the Indies.	A large force of Spanish explorers, led by Don Juan de Onate, stops near present-day El Paso, TX, and declares the land to the north New Mexico for Spain.	Santa Fe, America's oldest capital city, is founded. The Palace of Governors is the only remaining 17th-century structure; the rest of Santa Fe was destroyed by a 1914 fire.

Native Americans in California had no written language but observed oral contracts and zoning laws.

Within a century of the arrival of Spanish colonists in 1769, California's Native American population was decimated to 20,000 by European diseases, conscripted labor regimes and famine.

The Southwest & Southern Colorado

Those Who Came Before, by Robert H and Florence C Lister, is an excellent source about the prehistory of the Southwest and the archaeological sites of its national parks and monuments.

Archaeologists believe that the Southwest's first inhabitants were hunters. The population grew, however, and wild game became extinct, forcing hunters to augment their diets with berries, seeds, roots and fruits. After 3000 BC, contacts with farmers in what is now central Mexico led to the beginnings of agriculture in the Southwest.

By about AD 100, three dominant cultures were emerging in the Southwest: the Hohokam of the desert, the Mogollon of the central mountains and valleys, and the Ancestral Puebloans – formerly known as the Anasazi.

The Hohokam lived in the deserts of Arizona, adapting to desert life by creating an incredible river-fed irrigation system. They also developed low earthen pyramids and sunken ball courts with earthen walls. By about 1400, the Hohokam had abandoned their villages. There are many theories on this tribe's disappearance, but the most likely involves a combination of factors including drought, overhunting, conflict among groups and disease.

The Mogollon culture settled near the Mexican border from 200 BC to AD 1400. They lived in small communities, often elevated on isolated mesas or ridge tops, and built simple pit dwellings. Although they farmed, they depended more on hunting and foraging for food. Around the 13th or 14th century, the Mogollon had probably been peacefully incorporated by the Ancestral Puebloan groups from the north.

The Ancestral Puebloans inhabited the Colorado Plateau, also called the Four Corners area. This culture left the richest archaeological sites and ancient settlements that are still inhabited in the Southwest. Their descendants live in Pueblo Indian communities in New Mexico. The oldest links with the Ancestral Puebloans are found among the Hopi tribe of northern Arizona. The mesa-top village of Old Oraibi has been inhabited since the 1100s, making it the oldest continuously inhabited settlement in North America.

The Europeans Arrive

Francisco Vasquez de Coronado led the first major expedition into North America in 1540. It included 300 soldiers, hundreds of Native American guides and herds of livestock. It also marked the first major violence between Spanish explorers and the native people.

1787–91

The Constitutional Convention in Philadelphia draws up the US Constitution. The Bill of Rights is later adopted as constitutional amendments articulating citizens' rights.

1803

Napoleon sells the Louisiana Territory to the US for $15 million, thereby extending the boundaries of the new nation from the Mississippi River to the Rocky Mountains.

➜ Rocky Mountain National Park (p259), Colorado

The expedition's goal was the fabled, immensely rich Seven Cities of Cibola. For two years, it traveled through what is now Arizona, New Mexico and as far east as Kansas. Instead of gold and precious gems, the expedition found adobe pueblos, which they violently commandeered. During the Spaniards' first few years in northern New Mexico, they tried to subdue the pueblos, with much bloodshed. The Spanish established Santa Fe as the capital around 1610. The city remains the capital of New Mexico today, the oldest capital in what is now the USA.

When 18th-century Russian and English trappers began trading valuable otter pelts from Alta California, Spain concocted a plan for colonization. For the glory of God and the tax coffers of Spain, missions would be built across the state, and within 10 years these would be going concerns run by local converts.

Spain's missionizing plan was approved in 1769, and Franciscan Padre Junípero Serra secured support to set up *presidios* (military posts) alongside several missions in northern and central California in the 1770s and '80s. Clergy relied on soldiers to round up conscripts to build missions. In exchange for their labor, Native Americans were allowed one meal a day (when available) and a place in God's kingdom – which came much sooner than expected due to the smallpox the Spanish brought with them. In the Southwest, more than half of the pueblo populations were decimated by smallpox, measles and typhus.

In 1680, during the Pueblo Revolt, the northern New Mexico Pueblos banded together to drive out the Spanish after the latter's bloody campaign to destroy Puebloan ceremonial objects. The Spanish were pushed south of the Rio Grande and the Pueblo people held Santa Fe until 1682.

HISTORY LEWIS & CLARK

Lewis & Clark

After President Thomas Jefferson bought the Louisiana Territory from Napoleon in 1803 for $15 million, he sent his personal secretary, Meriwether Lewis, west to chart North America's western regions. The goal was to find a waterway to the Pacific while exploring the newly acquired Louisiana Purchase and establishing a foothold for American interests. Lewis, who had no training for exploration, convinced his good friend William Clark, an experienced frontiersman and army veteran, to tag along. In 1804, the 40-member party, called the Corps of Discovery, left St Louis.

The expedition fared relatively well, in part because of the presence of Sacagawea, a young Shoshone woman married to a French-Canadian trapper who was part of the entourage. Sacagawea proved invaluable as a guide, translator and ambassador to the area's Native Americans. York, Clark's African American servant, also softened tensions between the group and the Native Americans.

The party traveled some 8000 miles in about two years, documenting everything they came across in their journals. Meticulous notes were made about 122 animals and 178 plants, with some new discoveries being made along the way. In 1805 the party finally reached the mouth of the

Anasazi, a Navajo word meaning 'enemy ancestors,' is a term to which many modern Pueblo Indians object; it's no longer used.

1803–06	1811	1841	1844
President Jefferson sends Meriwether Lewis and William Clark west. Guided by Shoshone tribeswoman Sacagawea, they trailblaze from St Louis, Missouri, to the Pacific Ocean and back.	Pacific Fur Company mogul John Jacob Astor establishes Fort Astoria, the first permanent US settlement on the Pacific Coast. He later becomes the country's first millionaire.	Wagon trains follow the Oregon Trail, and by 1847 over 6500 emigrants a year are heading West, to Oregon, California and Mormon-dominated Utah.	First telegraph line is inaugurated with the phrase 'What hath God wrought?' In 1845, Congress approves a transcontinental railroad, completed in 1869. Together, telegraph and train open the frontier.

Columbia River and the Pacific Ocean at Cape Disappointment and bedded down for the winter nearby, thus establishing Fort Clatsop.

Lewis and Clark returned to a hero's welcome in St Louis in 1806.

Westward, Ho!

As the 19th century dawned on the young nation, optimism was the mood of the day. With the invention of the cotton gin in 1793 – followed by threshers, reapers, mowers and later combines – agriculture was industrialized, and US commerce surged. The 1803 Louisiana Purchase doubled US territory, and expansion west of the Appalachian Mountains began in earnest.

Exploiting the West's vast resources became a patriotic duty in the 1840s – a key aspect of America's belief in its Manifest Destiny. New York editor John O'Sullivan, echoing the expansionist credo of President James Polk, urged Americans to 'overspread the continent allotted by providence for the free development of your yearly multiplying millions.' During the early territorial days, movement of goods and people from the East to the West was very slow. Horses, mule trains and stagecoaches represented state-of-the-art transportation at the time.

One of the major routes was the Oregon Trail. Spanning six states, it sorely tested the families who embarked on this perilous trip. Their belongings were squirreled away under canvas-topped wagons, which often trailed livestock. The journey could take up to eight months, and by the time the settlers reached eastern Oregon their food supplies were running on fumes. Other major routes included the Santa Fe Trail and the Old Spanish Trail, which ran from Santa Fe into central Utah and across Nevada to Los Angeles in California. Regular stagecoach services along the Santa Fe Trail began in 1849; the Mormon Trail reached Salt Lake City in 1847.

The arrival of more people and resources via the railroad led to further land exploration and the frequent discovery of mineral deposits. Many Western mining towns were founded in the 1870s and 1880s; some are now ghost towns like Santa Rita while others like Tombstone and Silver City remain active.

Eureka!

Real estate speculator, lapsed Mormon and tabloid publisher Sam Brannan was looking to unload some California swampland in 1848 when he heard rumors of gold flakes found near Sutter's Mill, 120 miles from San Francisco. Figuring this news should sell some newspapers and raise real estate values, Brannan published the rumor as fact. Initially the story didn't generate excitement. So Brannan ran another story, this time verified by Mormon employees at Sutter's Mill who had sworn him

You can follow the Lewis and Clark expedition on its extraordinary journey west to the Pacific and back again online at www.pbs.org/lewisandclark, featuring historical maps, photo albums and journal excerpts.

Among the provisions recommended for those traveling the Oregon Trail were coffee (15lb per person), bacon (25lb per person), 1lb of castile soap, citric acid to prevent scurvy and a live cow for milk and emergency meat.

1846–48	1847	1849	1859
The battle for the West is waged with the Mexican-American War. The war ends with the 1848 Guadalupe-Hidalgo treaty that gives most of present-day Arizona and New Mexico to the USA.	Mormons fleeing religious persecution in Illinois start arriving in Salt Lake City; over the next 20 years more than 70,000 Mormons will head to Utah via the Mormon Pioneer Trail.	After the 1848 discovery of gold near Sacramento, an epic cross-country gold rush sees 60,000 'forty-niners' flock to California's Mother Lode. San Francisco's population explodes to 25,000.	The richest vein of silver ever discovered in the USA, the Comstock Lode, is struck in Virginia City, NV, which quickly becomes the most notorious mining town in the Wild West.

to secrecy. Brannan reportedly kept his word by running through the San Francisco streets, brandishing gold entrusted to him as tithes for the Mormon church, shouting, 'Gold on the American River!'

Other newspapers hastily published stories of 'gold mountains' near San Francisco. By 1850, the year California was fast-tracked for admission as the 31st state, its non-native population had ballooned from 15,000 to 93,000. Most arrivals weren't Americans, but Peruvians, Australians, Chileans and Mexicans, with some Chinese, Irish, native Hawaiian and French prospectors.

The Long Walk & Apache Conflicts

For decades, US forces pushed west across the continent, killing or forcibly moving whole tribes of Native Americans who were in their way. The most widely known incident is the forceful relocation of many Navajo in 1864. US forces, led by Kit Carson, destroyed Navajo fields, orchards and houses, and forced the people into surrendering or withdrawing into remote parts of Canyon de Chelly. Eventually, they were starved out. About 9000 Navajo were rounded up and marched 400 miles east to a camp at Bosque Redondo, near Fort Sumner in New Mexico. Hundreds of Native Americans died from sickness, starvation or gunshot wounds along the way. The Navajo call this 'The Long Walk,' and it remains an important part of their history.

The last serious conflicts were between US troops and the Apache. This was partly because raiding was the essential path to manhood for the Apache. As US forces and settlers moved into Apache land, they became obvious targets for the raids that were part of the Apache way of life. These continued under the leadership of Mangas Coloradas, Cochise, Victorio and, finally, Geronimo, who surrendered in 1886 after being promised that he and the Apache would be imprisoned for two years and then allowed to return to their homeland. As with many promises made during these years, this one, too, was broken.

Even after the wars were over, Native Americans were treated like second-class citizens for many decades. Non-Native Americans used legal loopholes and technicalities to take over reservation land. Many children were removed from reservations and shipped off to boarding schools where they were taught in English and punished for speaking their own languages or behaving 'like Indians' – this practice continued into the 1930s.

The Wild West

Romanticized tales of gunslingers, cattle rustlers, outlaws and train robbers fuel Wild West legends. Good and bad guys were designations in flux – a tough outlaw in one state became a popular sheriff in another.

The cry 'Geronimo!' became popular for skydivers after a group of US Army paratroopers training in 1940 saw the movie *Geronimo* (1939) one night, then began shouting the great warrior's name for courage during their jumps.

Best Old West Towns
Bisbee, AZ
Tombstone AZ
Silverton, CO
Lincoln, NM
Virginia City, NV

1861–65	1864	1881	1882
American Civil War erupts between North and South. The war's end on April 9, 1865, is marred by President Lincoln's assassination five days later.	Kit Carson forces 9000 Navajo to walk 400 miles to a camp near Fort Sumner. Hundreds of Native Americans die from sickness, starvation and gunshot wounds along 'The Long Walk.'	In 1881, Wyatt Earp, his brothers Virgil and Morgan, and Doc Holliday, kill Billy Clanton and the McLaury brothers in a blazing gunfight at the OK Corral in Tombstone, AZ.	Racist sentiment, particularly in California (where over 50,000 Chinese immigrants had arrived since 1848) leads to the Chinese Exclusion Act, the only US immigration law to exclude a specific race.

Gunfights were more frequently the result of mundane political struggles in emerging towns than storied blood feuds. New mining towns mushroomed overnight, playing host to rowdy saloons and bordellos where miners would come to brawl, drink and gamble.

Legendary figures Billy the Kid and Sheriff Pat Garrett, both involved in the infamous Lincoln County War, were active in the late 1870s. Billy the Kid reputedly shot and killed more than 20 men in a brief career as a gunslinger – he himself was shot and killed by Garrett at the age of 21. In 1881, Wyatt Earp, along with his brothers Virgil and Morgan, and Doc Holliday, shot dead Billy Clanton and the McLaury brothers in a blazing gunfight at the OK Corral in Tombstone – the showdown took less than a minute. Both sides accused the other of cattle rustling, but the real story will never be known.

Riders and swift horses were the backbone of the Pony Express (1860–61). They carried letters between Missouri and California in an astounding 10 days!

Water & Western Development

Americans began to think about occupying the area between the coasts. The lingering image of the Great American Desert, a myth propagated by early explorers, had deterred agricultural settlers and urban development. Though the western interior was not a desert, water was a limiting factor as cities such as Denver began to spring up at the base of the Front Range.

The struggle for an adequate supply of water for the growing desert population marked the early years of the 20th century, resulting in federally funded dam projects such as the 1936 Hoover Dam and, in 1963, the Glen Canyon Dam and Lake Powell. Water supply continues to be a key challenge in this region.

Reforming the Wild West

On November 7, 1893, Colorado became the first US state – and one of the first places in the world – to grant women the right to vote.

When the great earthquake and fire hit San Francisco in 1906, it signaled change for California. With public funds for citywide water mains and fire hydrants siphoned off by corrupt bosses, there was only one functioning water source in San Francisco. When the smoke lifted, one thing was clear: it was time for the Wild West to change.

While San Francisco was rebuilt at a rate of 15 buildings per day, California's reformers set to work on city, state and national politics, one plank at a time. Californians concerned about public health and trafficking in women pushed for passage of the 1914 statewide Red Light Abatement Act. Mexico's revolution from 1910 to 1921 brought a new wave of migrants and revolutionary ideas, including ethnic pride and worker solidarity. As California's ports grew, longshoremen's unions coordinated a historic 83-day strike in 1934 along the entire West Coast that forced concessions for safer working conditions and fair pay.

1919	1938	1945	1946
The Grand Canyon becomes the USA's 15th national park, and a dirt road to the North Rim is built from Kanab. The park was visited by 4.4 million people in 2007.	Route 66 becomes the first cross-country highway to be completely paved, including more than 750 miles across Arizona and New Mexico. The Mother Road is officially decommissioned in 1984.	The first atomic bomb is detonated in the ironically named Jornada del Norte (Journey of Death) Valley in southern New Mexico, which is now part of the White Sands Missile Range.	The opening of the glitzy Flamingo casino in Las Vegas sparks a mob-backed building spree. By the fabulous '50s, Sin City has reached its first golden peak.

At the height of the Depression in 1935, some 200,000 farming families fleeing the drought-stricken Dust Bowl in Texas and Oklahoma arrived in California, where they found scant pay and deplorable working conditions at major farming concerns. California's artists alerted middle America to the migrants' plight, and the nation rallied around Dorothea Lange's haunting documentary photos of famine-struck families and John Steinbeck's harrowing fictionalized account in his 1939 novel *The Grapes of Wrath*.

WWII & the Atomic Age

Los Alamos

In 1943, Los Alamos, New Mexico, then home to a boys' school perched on a 7400ft mesa, was chosen as the top-secret headquarters of the Manhattan Project, the code name for the research and development of the atomic bomb. The 772-acre site, accessed by two dirt roads, had no gas or oil lines and only one wire service, and it was surrounded by forest.

Isolation and security marked every aspect of life on 'the hill.' Not only was resident movement restricted and mail censored, there was no outside contact by radio or telephone. Perhaps even more unsettling, most residents had no idea why they were living in Los Alamos. Knowledge was on a 'need to know' basis; everyone knew only as much as their job required.

In just under two years, Los Alamos scientists successfully detonated the first atomic bomb at the Trinity site, now White Sands Missile Range.

> The Denver Mint struck and minted its first gold and silver coins on February 1, 1906. It is the largest producer of coins in the world. The mint was robbed of $200,000 in broad daylight on 18 December, 1922.

CALIFORNIA'S CIVIL RIGHTS MOVEMENT

When 110,000 Japanese Americans along the West Coast were ordered into internment camps by President Roosevelt in 1942, the San Francisco–based Japanese American Citizen's League immediately filed suits that advanced all the way to the Supreme Court. These lawsuits established groundbreaking civil-rights legal precedents, and in 1992 internees received reparations and an official letter of apology for internment signed by President George HW Bush.

Adopting the nonviolent resistance practices of Mahatma Gandhi and Martin Luther King Jr, labor leaders César Chávez and Dolores Huerta formed United Farm Workers in 1962 to champion the rights of underrepresented immigrant laborers. While civil-rights leaders marched on Washington, Chávez and Californian grape pickers marched on Sacramento, bringing the issue of fair wages and the health risks of pesticides to the nation's attention. When Bobby Kennedy was sent to investigate, he sided with Chávez, bringing Latinos into the US political fold.

1947	1963	1973
An unidentified object falls in the desert near Roswell. The government first calls it a crashed disk, then a day later a weather balloon, and mysteriously closes off the area.	The controversial Glen Canyon Dam is finished and Lake Powell begins, eventually covering up ancestral Native American sites and stunning rock formations but creating 1960 miles of shoreline and a boater fantasyland.	The debut of the MGM Grand in 1973 signals the dawn of the corporate-owned 'megaresort,' and sparks a building bonanza along Las Vegas' Strip that's still going strong.

RICHARD CUMMINS / GETTY IMAGES ©

➡ Flamingo (p319), Las Vegas

After the US detonated the atomic bomb in Japan, the secret city of Los Alamos was exposed to the public. The city continued to be cloaked in secrecy, however, until 1957, when restrictions on visiting were lifted.

Changing Workforce & New Industries

California's workforce permanently changed in WWII, when women and African Americans were recruited for wartime industries and Mexican workers were brought in to fill labor shortages. Contracts in military communications and aviation attracted an international elite of engineers, who would launch California's high-tech industry. Within a decade after the war, California's population had grown by 40%, reaching almost 13 million.

The Oscar-winning *There Will Be Blood* (2007), adapted from Upton Sinclair's book *Oil!*, depicts a Californian oil magnate and was based on real-life SoCal tycoon Edward Doheny.

The war also brought economic fortune to the Pacific Northwest, when the area became the nation's largest lumber producer and both Oregon's and Washington's naval yards bustled, along with William Boeing's airplane factory. The region continued to prosper through the second half of the 20th century, attracting new migrations of educated, progressively minded settlers from the nation's east and south.

Hollywood & Counterculture

In 1908, California became a convenient movie location for its consistent sunlight and versatile locations, although its role was limited to doubling for more exotic locales and providing backdrops for period-piece productions. But gradually, California began stealing the scene in movies and iconic TV shows with waving palms and sunny beaches.

Chinatown (1974) is the fictionalized yet surprisingly accurate account of the brutal water wars that were waged to build both Los Angeles and San Francisco.

Not all Californians saw themselves as extras in *Beach Blanket Bingo,* however. WWII sailors discharged for insubordination and homosexuality in San Francisco found themselves at home in North Beach's bebop jazz clubs, bohemian coffeehouses and City Lights Bookstore. San Francisco became the home of free speech and free spirits, and soon everyone who was anyone was getting arrested: Beat poet Lawrence Ferlinghetti for publishing Allen Ginsberg's epic poem *Howl,* comedian Lenny Bruce for uttering the F-word onstage, and Carol Doda for going topless. When Flower Power faded, other Bay Area rebellions grew in its place: Black Power, gay pride and medical marijuana clubs.

But while Northern California had the more attention-grabbing counterculture from the 1940s to '60s, nonconformity in sunny Southern California shook America to the core. In 1947, when Senator Joseph McCarthy attempted to root out suspected communists in the movie industry, 10 writers and directors who refused to admit communist alliances or to name names were charged with contempt of Congress and barred from working in Hollywood. The Hollywood Ten's impassioned defenses of the Constitution were heard nationwide, and major Hollywood play-

1980	1995	2000	2008
Mt St Helens blows her top, killing 57 people and destroying 250 homes. Her elevation is cut from 9677ft to 8365ft, and where a peak once stood, a mile-wide crater is born.	Amazon, one of the first major companies to sell products online, is launched in Seattle. Originally started as a bookseller, it will not become annually profitable until 2003.	Coloradans vote for Amendment 20 in the state election, which provides for dispensing cannabis to registered patients. A proliferation of medical marijuana clinics ensues over the next decade.	California voters pass Proposition 8, which banned gay marriage. Federal courts ruled the law unconstitutional. In 2013, the US Supreme Court did not take up an appeal; same-sex marriages resumed.

ers boldly voiced dissent and hired blacklisted talent until California lawsuits put a legal end to McCarthyism in 1962.

On January 28, 1969, an oil rig dumped 200,000 gallons of oil into Santa Barbara Channel, killing dolphins, seals and some 3600 shore birds. The beach community organized a highly effective protest, spurring the establishment of the Environmental Protection Agency.

Geeking Out

When California's Silicon Valley introduced the first personal computer in 1968, advertisements breathlessly gushed that Hewlett-Packard's 'light' (40lb) machine could 'take on roots of a fifth-degree polynomial, Bessel functions, elliptic integrals and regression analysis' – all for just $4900 (about $29,000 today). Hoping to bring computer power to the people, 21-year-old Steve Jobs and Steve Wozniak introduced the Apple II at the 1977 West Coast Computer Faire with unfathomable memory (4KB of RAM) and microprocessor speed (1MHz).

By the mid-1990s, an entire dot-com industry boomed in Silicon Valley with online start-ups, and suddenly people were getting their mail, news, politics, pet food and, yes, sex online. But when dot-com profits weren't forthcoming, venture funding dried up, and fortunes in stock options disappeared on one nasty Nasdaq-plummeting day: March 10, 2000. Overnight, 26-year-old vice-presidents and Bay Area service-sector employees alike found themselves jobless. But as online users continued to look for useful information and one another in those billions of web pages, search engines and social media boomed.

Meanwhile, California biotech has been making strides. In 1976, an upstart company called Genentech cloned human insulin and introduced the hepatitis B vaccine. California voters approved a $3 billion bond measure in 2004 for stem-cell research, and by 2008 California had become the biggest funder of stem-cell research and the focus of Nasdaq's new Biotech Index.

Twenty-year-old artist and vagabond Everett Ruess explored the Four Corners region in the early 1930s. He disappeared under mysterious circumstances outside of Escalante, UT, in November 1934. Read his evocative letters in the book *Everett Ruess: A Vagabond for Beauty*.

2008	2010	2012	2013
Barack Obama is elected President of the United States, the first African American to hold the office.	Arizona passes controversial legislation requiring police officers to ask for identification from anyone they suspect of being in the US illegally. Immigration rights activists call for a boycott of the state.	New Mexico and Arizona, the 47th and 48th states to join the Union, celebrate their Centennials.	In California, same-sex marriages – which were banned by Proposition 8 – resume after a US Supreme Court decision.

The People

Who lives in the West? If you believe the headlines, it's angry Arizonans up-in-arms about illegal immigration, gay couples marrying in San Francisco, hair-pulling housewives in Orange County and pot-smoking deadbeats in Colorado. And, according to *Portlandia* comedy sketches, Portland brims with bike-riding, organic-obsessed hipsters who want to put a bird on everything. Are these accurate depictions? Yes and no. The headlines may reflect some regional attitudes, but most folks are just trying to go about their lives with as little drama as possible.

Regional Identity

Key Sports Websites

Baseball
www.mlb.com

Basketball
www.nba.com

Football
www.nfl.com

Hockey
www.nhl.com

Nascar
www.nascar.com

Soccer
www.mlssoccer.com

The cowboy has long been a symbol of the West. Brave. Self-reliant. A solitary seeker of truth, justice and a straight shot of whiskey. The truth behind the myth? Those who settled the West were indeed self-reliant and brave. But they had to be. In that harsh and unforgiving landscape, danger was always a few steps behind opportunity. As the dangers dissipated, however, and settlers put down roots, the cowboy stereotype became less accurate. Like the red-rock mesas that have weathered into new and varying forms over the years, the character of the populace has also evolved. Stereotypes today, accurate or not, are regionally based, and the residents of Portland, San Diego, Santa Fe and Phoenix are perceived very differently from one another.

California

Californians are stereotyped as laid-back, health-conscious, eco-aware, self-absorbed and open-minded. The stats behind the stereotypes? According to the the National Oceanic and Atmospheric Administration (NOAA), more than 25.5 million Californians lived in a coastal shoreline county in 2010 – the highest number for any coastal state. The state's southern beaches are sunniest and most swimmable, thus Southern Cali-

THE SPORTING LIFE

Westerners cherish their sports, whether they're players themselves or just watching their favorite teams. Here's a breakdown of the West's professional teams by sport.

National Football League AFC West: Denver Broncos, Oakland Raiders, San Diego Chargers; NFC West: Arizona Cardinals, San Francisco 49ers, Seattle Seahawks

National Basketball Association Western Conference Pacific: Golden State Warriors, LA Clippers, LA Lakers, Phoenix Suns, Sacramento Kings; Northwest: Denver Nuggets, Portland Trailblazers, Utah Jazz

Women's National Basketball Association LA Sparks, Phoenix Mercury, Seattle Storm

Major League Baseball American League: LA Angels, Oakland Athletics, Seattle Mariners; National League: Arizona Diamondbacks, Colorado Rockies, LA Dodgers, San Diego Padres, San Francisco Giants

fornia's inescapable associations with surf, sun and prime-time TV soaps like *Baywatch* and *The OC*. Self-help, fitness and body modification are major industries throughout California, successfully marketed since the 1970s, while exercise and good food help keep Californians among the nation's fittest. Yet some cities in California collect millions of tax dollars from medical marijuana dispensaries – Oakland alone took in $1.4 million in tax revenue from them in 2011. According to surveys, 45% of the state was believed to be likely to vote Democratic and 32% to vote Republican, with 19% considered independents. Environmentally, Golden Staters have zoomed ahead of the national energy-use curve in their smog-checked cars; more hybrid cars are sold here than in any other state.

California's adult prison population reached a peak in 2006 at 163,000; that number declined to 144,000 prisoners by the fall of 2011.

Pacific Northwest

And what about folks living in Washington and Oregon? Tree-hugging hipsters with activist tendencies and a penchant for latte? That's pretty accurate, actually. Many locals are proud of their independent spirit, profess a love for nature and, yes, will separate their plastics when it's time to recycle. They're a friendly lot and, despite the common tendency to denigrate Californians, most are transplants themselves. Why did they all come here? Among other things, for the lush scenery, the good quality of life and the lack of pretension that often afflicts bigger, more popular places. Primping up and putting on airs is not a part of Northwestern everyday life, and wearing Gore-Tex outerwear to restaurants, concerts or social functions will rarely raise an eyebrow.

The Rocky Mountain States

Still looking for that Western cowboy? Start here. Ranching is big business in these parts, and the solitary cowboy – seen riding a bucking bronco on the Wyoming license plate – is an appropriate symbol for the region. It takes a rugged individualist to scratch out a living on the lonely, windswept plains – plains that tend to leave big-city travelers feeling slightly unmoored.

Politically, the northern Rockies – Wyoming, Montana and Idaho – skew conservative, although you will find pockets of liberalism in the college and resort towns. Wyoming may have been the first territory to give women the right to vote, in 1869, but this nod to liberal thinking has been overshadowed by Wyoming's association with former vice president Dick Cheney, the divisive Republican who was a six-term congressman from the state. In addition to ranching, the other big industry in Wyoming is energy.

Colorado is the West's most recognizable swing state. For every bastion of liberalism like Boulder there's an equally entrenched conservative counterpart like Colorado Springs.

The Phoenix Suns protested Arizona's new immigration law in 2010 by changing the team's name on their jerseys to 'Los Suns' (that's Spanglish) for one game.

Southwest

The Southwest has long drawn stout-hearted settlers – Mormons, cattle barons, prospectors – pursuing slightly different agendas than those of the average American. A new generation of idealistic entrepreneurs has transformed former mining towns into New Age art enclaves and Old West tourist attractions. Scientists flocked to the empty spaces to develop and test atomic bombs and soaring rockets. Astronomers built observatories on lonely hills and mountains, making the most of the dark skies and unobstructed views.

In recent years high-profile governmental efforts to stop illegal immigration have impacted the laid-back vibe, at least in the southern reaches of Arizona. The anti-immigration rhetoric isn't common in day-to-day conversation, but heightened press coverage of the most vitriolic comments, coupled with a heavy Border Patrol presence, does cast a pall over

MARRIAGE: EQUAL RIGHTS FOR ALL

Forty thousand Californians were already registered as domestic partners when, in 2004, San Francisco Mayor Gavin Newsom issued marriage licenses to same-sex couples in defiance of a California same-sex marriage ban. Four thousand same-sex couples promptly got hitched. The state ban was nixed by California courts in June 2008, but then Proposition 8 passed in November 2008 to amend the state's constitution and prohibit same-sex marriage. Civil-rights activists challenged the constitutionality of the proposition, and federal courts eventually ruled that the law unconstitutionally violated the equal protection and due process clauses. In 2013, the US Supreme Court did not take up an appeal and same-sex marriages resumed in the Golden State.

the otherwise sunny landscape. Other regions of the Southwest, for the most part, have taken a more inclusive approach.

Population & Multiculturalism

California, with 38 million residents, is the most populous state in the entire US. More than 30% of the USA's Asian American population currently lives in California, and the state's Latino population, currently 14.1 million, is expected to become California's majority ethnic group by 2020. Latino culture is deeply enmeshed with that of California, and most residents see the state as an easygoing multicultural society that gives everyone a chance to live the American Dream. The state has an estimated 2.5 million undocumented immigrants.

Colorado, Arizona and New Mexico all have large Native American and Hispanic populations. These residents take pride in maintaining their cultural identities through preserved traditions and oral history lessons. Generally, Southwestern states have developed and retained a live-and-let-live philosophy, although relations between Arizona and Mexico, which share a 350-mile border, have been strained since the Arizona state legislature passed a controversial law in 2010 requiring police officers to ask for identification from anyone they suspect of being in the country illegally.

> It's no myth. Colorado really does average 300 days of sun annually, and more than 411,000 people rafted down Colorado rivers in 2012.

Religion

Although Californians are less churchgoing than the American mainstream, and one in five Californians professes no religion at all, it remains one of the most religiously diverse states. About a third of Californians are Catholic, due in part to the state's large Latino population, while another third are Protestants. But there are also more than one million Muslims statewide, and LA has the second-largest Jewish community in North America. About 2% of California's population identifies as Buddhist.

About a quarter of Pacific Northwesterners have no religious affiliation. Those who are religious tend to adhere to Christianity, Judaism or the Mormon Church. Asian Americans have brought Buddhism, Hinduism, Sikhism and Islam, and New Age spirituality isn't a stranger here.

The Southwest has its own anomalies. In Utah, 62% of the state's population identifies as Mormon. The church stresses traditional family values, and drinking, smoking and premarital sex are frowned upon. Family and religion are also core values for Native Americans and Hispanics throughout the Southwest. For the Hopi, tribal dances are such sacred events that they are mostly closed to outsiders. And, although many Native Americans and Hispanics are now living in urban areas, working as professionals, large family gatherings and traditional customs are still important facets of daily life.

> In September 2013, more than 61,100 euphoric souls descended upon the Nevada desert for Burning Man, an annual camping extravaganza, art festival and rave where freedom of expression, costume and libido are all encouraged.

Native Americans

The indigenous people of the West are extremely diverse, with unique customs and beliefs molded in part by the landscapes they inhabit. They follow equally diverse paths, as they inherit a legacy left by both their ancestors and outside cultures. Some may be weavers living on reservations, others may be web designers living in Phoenix. Some plant corn and squash, others seek to harvest the sun in solar-energy farms. Some are medicine men, some are surgeons. One stereotype does not fit all.

More than 5 million Native Americans (full and part-Indian) from more than 556 recognized tribes reside in the US and speak 175 languages. California has the largest Native American population in the country, with Arizona and New Mexico ranking third and fifth respectively. The Navajo tribe is the largest western tribe, second only to the Cherokee nationwide.

One of the best museums devoted to Southwest Native American life and culture is Phoenix's Heard Museum.

Culturally, tribes today grapple with questions about how to prosper in contemporary America while protecting their traditions from erosion and their lands from further exploitation, and how to lift their people from poverty while maintaining their sense of identity and the sacred.

The Tribes

Most of the major western tribes are located in the Southwest. Well-known tribes with large reservations in Arizona include the Navajo, the Hopi and the Apache. Two smaller Arizona tribes, the Hualapai and the Havasupai, live on reservations beside the Grand Canyon. New Mexico's tribes are clustered in 19 pueblos located in the north-central region of the state.

Apache

The Southwest has three major Apache reservations: New Mexico's Jicarilla Apache Reservation and Arizona's San Carlos Apache Reservation and Fort Apache Reservation, home to the White Mountain Apache tribe. All the Apache tribes descend from Athabascans who migrated from Canada around 1400. They were nomadic hunter-gatherers who became warlike raiders, particularly of Pueblo tribes and European settlements, and they fiercely resisted relocation to reservations.

The most famous Apache is Geronimo, a Chiricahua Apache who resisted the American takeover of native lands until he was finally subdued by the US Army with the help of White Mountain Apache scouts.

The People by Stephen Trimble is a comprehensive and intimate portrait of Southwest native peoples, filled with Native American voices and beautiful photos.

Havasupai

The Havasupai Reservation abuts Arizona's Grand Canyon National Park beneath the canyon's South Rim. The tribe's one village, Supai, can only be reached by an 8-mile hike or a mule or helicopter ride from road's end at Hualapai Hilltop.

Havasupai (hah-vah-*soo*-pie) means 'people of the blue-green water,' and tribal life has always been dominated by the Havasu Creek tributary of the Colorado River. Reliable water meant the ability to irrigate fields, which led to a season-based village lifestyle. The deep Havasu Canyon also protected them from others; this extremely peaceful people basically avoided Western contact until the 1800s. Today, the tribe relies on tourism, and Havasu Canyon's gorgeous waterfalls draw a steady stream of visitors. The tribe is related to the Hualapai.

Hopi

The Hopi Reservation occupies more than 1.5 million acres in the Navajo Reservation. Most Hopi live in 11 villages at the base and on top of three mesas jutting from the main Black Mesa; Old Oraibi, on Third Mesa, is considered (along with Acoma Pueblo) the continent's oldest continuously inhabited settlement. Like all Pueblo peoples, the Hopi are descended from the Ancestral Puebloans (formerly known as Anasazi).

For decades, traditional Navajo and Hopi have thwarted US industry efforts to strip mine sacred Big Mountain. Black Mesa Indigenous Support (www.supportblackmesa.org) tells their story.

Hopi (*ho*-pee) translates as 'peaceful ones' or 'peaceful person,' and perhaps no tribe is more renowned for leading such a humble, traditional and deeply spiritual lifestyle. The Hopi practice an unusual, near-miraculous technique of 'dry farming'; they don't plow, but plant seeds in 'wind breaks' and natural water catchments. Their main crop has always been corn (which is central to their creation story).

Hopi ceremonial life is complex and intensely private, and extends into all aspects of daily living. Following the 'Hopi Way' is considered essential to bringing the life-giving rains, but the Hopi also believe it fosters the wellbeing of the entire human race. Each person's role is determined by their clan, which is matrilineal. Even among themselves, the Hopi keep certain traditions of their individual clans private.

The Hopi are skilled artisans; they are famous for pottery, coiled baskets and silverwork, as well as for their ceremonial kachina (spirit) dolls.

ETIQUETTE

When visiting a reservation, ask about and follow any specific rules. Almost all tribes ban alcohol, and some ban pets and restrict cameras. All require permits for camping, fishing and other activities. Tribal rules may be posted at the reservation entrance, or visit the tribal office or the reservation's website.

When you visit a reservation, you are visiting a unique culture with perhaps unfamiliar customs. Be courteous, respectful and open-minded, and don't expect locals to share every detail of their lives.

Ask First, Document Later

Some tribes restrict cameras and sketching entirely; others may charge a fee, or restrict them at ceremonies or in certain areas. *Always ask before taking pictures or drawing.* If you want to photograph a person, ask permission first; a tip is polite and often expected.

Pueblos Are Not Museums

The incredible adobe structures are homes. Public buildings will be signed; if a building isn't signed, assume it's private. Don't climb around. Kivas are nearly always off limits.

Ceremonies Are Not Performances

Treat ceremonies like church services; watch silently and respectfully, without talking, clapping or taking pictures, and wear modest clothing. Powwows are more informal, but remember: unless they're billed as theater, they are for the tribe, not you.

Privacy & Communication

Many Native Americans are happy to describe their tribe's general religious beliefs, but not always or to the same degree, and details about rituals and ceremonies are often considered private. Always ask before discussing religion and respect each person's boundaries. Also, Native Americans consider it polite to listen without comment; silent listening, given and received, is another sign of respect.

Hualapai

The Hualapai Reservation occupies around 1 million acres along 108 miles of the Grand Canyon's South Rim. Hualapai (*wah*-lah-pie) means 'people of the tall pines.' Because this section of the Grand Canyon was not readily farmable, the Hualapai were originally seminomadic, gathering wild plants and hunting small game.

Today, forestry, cattle ranching, farming and tourism are the economic mainstays. The tribal headquarters are in Peach Springs, AZ, which was the inspiration for 'Radiator Springs' in the animated movie *Cars*. Hunting, fishing and rafting are the reservation's prime draws, but the Hualapai have recently added a unique tourist attraction, Skywalk.

The Hopi Arts Trail spotlights artists and galleries on the three mesas that are the heart of the Hopi reservation. For a map, as well as a list of artists and galleries, visit www.hopiartstrail.com.

Navajo

Nationwide, there are about 300,000 Navajo, making it the USA's second-largest tribe after the Cheroke. The **Navajo Reservation** (www.discover navajo.com) is by far the largest and most populous in the US. Also called the Navajo Nation and Navajoland, it covers 17.5 million acres (over 27,000 sq miles) in Arizona and parts of New Mexico and Utah.

The Navajo were feared nomads and warriors who both traded with and raided the Pueblos and who fought settlers and the US military. They also borrowed generously from other traditions: they acquired sheep and horses from the Spanish, learned pottery and weaving from the Pueblos, and picked up silversmithing from Mexico. Today, the Navajo are renowned for their woven rugs, pottery and inlaid silver jewelry, as well as for their intricate sandpainting, which is used in healing ceremonies.

In the Pacific Theater during WWII, Navajo 'code talkers' sent and received military messages in the Navajo's Athabascan tongue, which is notoriously complex. Japan never broke the code, and the code talkers were considered essential to US victory.

Pueblo

New Mexico contains 19 Pueblo reservations. Four reservations lead west from Albuquerque: Isleta, Laguna, Acoma and Zuni. Fifteen pueblos fill the Rio Grande Valley between Albuquerque and Taos: Sandia, San Felipe, Santa Ana, Zia, Jemez, Santo Domingo, Cochiti, San Ildefonso, Pojoaque, Nambé, Tesuque, Santa Clara, Ohkay Owingeh (or San Juan), Picuris and Taos.

These tribes are as different as they are alike. Nevertheless, the term 'pueblo' (Spanish for 'village') is a convenient shorthand for what these tribes share: all are believed to be descended from the Ancestral Puebloans and to have inherited their architectural style and their agrarian, village-based life – often atop mesas.

Pueblos are unique among Native Americans. These adobe structures can have up to five levels, connected by ladders, and are built with varying combinations of mud bricks, stones, logs and plaster. In the central plaza of each pueblo is a kiva, an underground ceremonial chamber that connects to the spirit world. A legacy of missionaries, Catholic churches are prominent in the pueblos, and many Pueblos now hold both Christian and native religious beliefs.

Arts

Native American art nearly always contains ceremonial purpose and religious significance; the patterns and symbols are woven with spiritual meaning that provides an intimate window into the heart of the people.

In addition to preserving their culture, contemporary Native American artists have used sculpture, painting, textiles, film, literature and performance art to reflect and critique modernity since the mid-20th century, especially after the civil-rights activism of the 1960s and cultural renaissance of the '70s. *Native North American Art* by Janet Berlo and Ruth Phillips offers a superb introduction to North America's varied indigenous art – from pre-contact to postmodernism.

Not all pueblos have websites, but available links and introductions to all are provided by the Indian Pueblo Cultural Center (www.indianpueblo.org).

By purchasing arts from Native Americans themselves, visitors have a direct, positive impact on tribal economies, which depend in part on tourist dollars. Many tribes run craft outlets and galleries, usually in the main towns of reservations. The **Indian Arts & Crafts Board** (www.iacb. doi.gov) lists Native American–owned galleries and shops state-by-state online – click on 'Source Directory of Businesses.'

N Scott Momaday's Pulitzer Prize–winning *House Made of Dawn* (1968), about a Pueblo youth, launched a wave of Native American literature.

Pottery & Basketry

Pretty much every Southwest tribe has pottery and/or basketry traditions. Originally, each tribe and even individual families maintained distinct styles, but modern potters and basket makers readily mix, borrow and reinterpret classic designs and methods.

Pueblo pottery is perhaps most acclaimed of all. Initially, local clay determined color, so that Zia pottery was red, Acoma white, Hopi yellow, Cochiti black and so on. Santa Clara is famous for its carved relief designs, and San Ildefonso for its black-on-black style, which was revived by world-famous potter Maria Martinez. The Navajo and Ute Mountain Utes also produce well-regarded pottery.

Pottery is nearly always synonymous with village life, while more portable baskets were often preferred by nomadic peoples. Among the tribes who stand out for their exquisite basketry are the Jicarilla Apache (whose name means basket maker), the Kaibab-Paiute, the Hualapai and the Tohono O'odham. Hopi coiled baskets, with their vivid patterns and kachina iconography, are also notable.

Navajo Weaving

Navajo legend says that Spider Woman taught humans how to weave, and she seems embodied today in the iconic sight of Navajo women patiently shuttling handspun wool on weblike looms, creating the Navajo's legendary rugs (originally blankets), so tight they hold water. Preparation of the wool and sometimes the dyes is still done by hand, and finishing a rug takes months (occasionally years).

Authentic Navajo rugs are expensive, and justifiably so, ranging from hundreds to thousands of dollars. They are not average souvenirs but artworks that will last a lifetime, whether displayed on the wall or the floor. Take time to research, even a little, so you recognize when quality matches price. To learn about Navajo rugs, visit www.gonavajo.com.

Silver & Turquoise Jewelry

Jewelry using stones and shells has always been a native tradition; silverwork did not arrive until the 1800s, along with Anglo and Mexican contact. In particular, Navajo, Hopi and Zuni became renowned for combining these materials with inlaid-turquoise silver jewelry. In addition to turquoise, jewelry often features lapis, onyx, coral, carnelian and shells.

Authentic jewelry is often stamped or marked by the artisan, and items may come with an Indian Arts & Crafts Board certificate; always ask. Price may also be an indicator: a high tab doesn't guarantee authenticity, but an absurdly low one probably signals trickery. A crash course can be had at the August Santa Fe Indian Market (p393).

Western USA Cuisine

The term 'Western cuisine' is bit of a misnomer. Food served in the western part of the United States can't be slotted into one neat category because regional specialties abound. Half the fun of any trip is digging into a dish that has cultural and agricultural ties to a region, from hearty steaks in southern Arizona or green chile enchiladas in New Mexico, to grilled salmon in the Pacific Northwest. And let's not forget San Diego's messy but delicious fish tacos.

Staples & Specialties

Breakfast

Morning meals in the West, as in the rest of the country, are big business. From a hearty serving of biscuits and gravy at a cowboy diner to a quick Egg McMuffin at the McDonald's drive-thru window or lavish Sunday brunches, Americans love their eggs and bacon, their waffles and hash browns, and their big glasses of orange juice. Most of all, they love that seemingly inalienable American right: a steaming cup of morning coffee with unlimited refills.

Lunch

After a mid-morning coffee break, an American worker's lunch hour affords only a sandwich, quick burger or hearty salad. The formal 'business lunch' is more common in big cities like Los Angeles, where food is not necessarily as important as the conversation.

Dinner

Americans settle in to a more substantial weeknight dinner, usually early in the evening, which, given the workload of so many two-career families, might be takeout (eg pizza or Chinese food) or prepackaged meals cooked in a microwave. Desserts tend toward ice cream, pies and cakes. Some families still cook a traditional Sunday-night dinner, when relatives and friends gather for a big feast, or grill outside and go picnicking on weekends.

Quick Eats

Fast-food restaurants with drive-thru windows are ubiquitous across the West, and you'll usually find at least one beside a major highway exit. Eating a hot dog from a street cart or a taco from a roadside truck is a

Must-Try Regional Specialties

Fish tacos
(San Diego, CA)

Frito pie (NM)

Green chile cheeseburgers (NM)

Navajo tacos (northeastern AZ)

Sonoran dogs (Tucson, AZ)

Rocky Mountain oysters (CO)

BREAKFAST BURRITOS

There is one Mexican-inspired meal that has been mastered in the West: the breakfast burrito. It's served in diners and delis in Colorado, in coffee shops in Arizona and beach-bum breakfast joints in California. In many ways, it is the perfect breakfast – cheap (usually under $6), packed with protein (eggs, cheese, beans), fresh veggies (or is avocado a fruit?), hot salsa (is that a vegetable?) and rolled to go in paper and foil. Peel it open like a banana and let the savory steam rise into your olfactories.

convenient option in downtown business districts. Don't worry about health risks – these vendors are usually supervised by the local health department. At festivals and county fairs, pick from cotton candy, corn dogs, candy apples, funnel cakes, chocolate-covered frozen bananas and plenty of tasty regional specialties. Farmers markets often have more wholesome, affordable prepared foods.

California

Owing to its vastness and variety of microclimates, California is truly America's cornucopia for fruits and vegetables, and a gateway to myriad Asian markets. The state's natural resources are overwhelming, with wild salmon, Dungeness crab and oysters from the ocean; robust produce year-round; and artisanal products such as cheese, bread, olive oil, wine and chocolate.

Starting in the 1970s and '80s, star chefs such as Alice Waters and Wolfgang Puck pioneered 'California cuisine' by incorporating the best local ingredients into simple yet delectable preparations. The influx of Asian immigrants, especially after the Vietnam War, enriched the state's urban food cultures with Chinatowns, Koreatowns and Japantowns, along with huge enclaves of Mexican Americans who maintain their own culinary traditions across the state. Global fusion restaurants are another hallmark of California's cuisine scene.

North Coast & the Sierras

San Francisco hippies headed back to the land in the 1970s for a more self-sufficient lifestyle, reviving traditions of making breads and cheeses from scratch and growing their own *everything* (note: farms from Mendocino to Humboldt are serious about No Trespassing signs). Hippie-homesteaders were early adopters of pesticide-free farming, and innovated hearty, organic cuisine that was health-minded yet satisfied the munchies.

On the North Coast, you can taste the influence of wild-crafted Ohlone and Miwok cuisine. In addition to fishing, hunting game and making bread from acorn flour, these Native Northern Californians also tended orchards and carefully cultivated foods along the coast. With such attentive stewardship, nature has been kind to this landscape, yielding bonanzas of wildflower honey and blackberries. Alongside traditional shellfish collection, sustainable caviar and oyster farms have sprung up along the coast. Fearless foragers have identified every edible plant from Sierra's wood sorrel to Mendocino sea vegetables, though key spots for wild mushrooms remain closely guarded local secrets.

San Francisco Bay Area

San Francisco has more restaurants per capita than any other metropolitan area in the US. In 2011, SF was home to 3588 restaurants – meaning there was one for every 227 people. In addition to restaurants, there were 200 or so licensed food trucks and 29 farmers markets.

Some city novelties have had extraordinary staying power, including ever-popular *cioppino* (Dungeness crab stew), chocolate bars invented by the Ghirardelli family, and sourdough bread, with original gold-rush-era mother dough still yielding local loaves with that distinctive tang. Dim sum is Cantonese for what's known in Mandarin as *xiao che* (small eats) or *yum cha* (drink tea), and there are dozens of places in San Francisco where you'll call it lunch.

Mexican, French and Italian food remain perennial local favorites, along with more recent SF ethnic food crazes: *izakaya* (Japanese bars serving small plates), Korean tacos, *banh mi* (Vietnamese

The hottest dining craze on wheels: food trucks. From crab-cake tacos to red-velvet cupcakes, there's no telling what kind of creative, healthy, gourmet, decadent or downright bizarre twist on 'fast food' you'll find. You'll chase down the trucks in Los Angeles, Portland and Las Vegas.

sandwiches featuring marinated meats and pickled vegetables on French baguettes) and *alfajores* (Arabic-Argentine crème-filled shortbread cookies).

SoCal

Los Angeles has long been known for its big-name chefs and celebrity restaurant owners. Robert H Cobb, owner of Hollywood's Brown Derby Restaurant, is remembered as the namesake of the Cobb salad (lettuce, tomato, egg, chicken, bacon and Roquefort). Wolfgang Puck launched the celebrity-chef trend with the Sunset Strip's star-spangled Spago in 1982.

For authentic ethnic food in Los Angeles, head to Koreatown for flavor-bursting *kalbi* (marinated barbecued beef short ribs), East LA for tacos *al pastor* (marinated, fried pork), and Little Tokyo for ramen noodles made fresh daily.

Further south, surfers cruise Hwy 1 beach towns from Laguna Beach to La Jolla in search of the ultimate wave and quick-but-hearty eats like breakfast burritos and fish tacos. And everybody stops for a date shake at Ruby's Crystal Cove Shake Shack south of Newport Beach.

Pacific Northwest

The late James Beard (1903–85), an American chef, food writer and Oregon native, believed foods prepared simply, without too many ingredients or complicated cooking techniques, allowed their natural flavors to shine. This philosophy has greatly influenced modern Northwest cuisine. Pacific Northwesterners don't like to think of their food as trendy or fussy, but at the same time, they love to be considered innovative, especially when it comes to 'green,' hyperconscious eating.

Farmland, Wild Foods & Fish

The diverse geography and climate – a mild, damp coastal region with sunny summers and arid farmland in the east – foster all types of farm-grown produce. Farmers grow plenty of fruit, from melons, grapes, apples and pears to strawberries, cherries and blueberries. Veggies thrive here too: potatoes, lentils, corn, asparagus and Walla Walla sweet onions, all of which feed local and overseas populations.

Many wild foods thrive, especially in the damper regions, such as the Coast Range. Foragers seek the same foods once gathered by local Native American tribes – year-round wild mushrooms, as well as summertime fruits and berries.

With hundreds of miles of coastline and an impressive system of rivers, Northwesterners have access to plenty of fresh seafood. Depending on the season, specialties include razor clams, mussels, prawns, albacore tuna, Dungeness crab and sturgeon. Salmon remains one of the region's most recognized foods, whether it's smoked or grilled, or in salads, quiches and sushi.

For LA's most brutally honest foodie opinions, check www.laweekly.com and www.la.eater.com.

Some Pacific species have been overfished to near-extinction, disrupting local aquaculture. For best options, good choices, and items to avoid on local seafood menus, reference Monterey Bay Aquarium's Seafood Watch (www.montereybayaquarium.org/cr/seafoodwatch.aspx).

SLOW, LOCAL, ORGANIC

The 'Slow Food' movement, along with renewed enthusiasm for eating local, organically grown fare, is a leading trend in American restaurants. The movement took off in America in 1971 courtesy of chef Alice Waters at Berkeley's Chez Panisse. Recently, farmers markets have been popping up all across the country and they're great places to meet locals and take a big bite out of America's cornucopia of foods, from heritage fruit and vegetables to fresh, savory and sweet regional delicacies.

WESTERN USA CUISINE STAPLES & SPECIALTIES

The Southwest

Diners, grab your steak knives and unbutton your fat pants because the food in Arizona, New Mexico, Utah, southern Colorado and Las Vegas doesn't have time for the timid. Sonoran hot dogs, green chile cheeseburgers, huevos rancheros, juicy steaks and endless buffets – moderation is not a virtue.

Two ethnic groups define Southwestern food culture: the Spanish and the Mexicans, who controlled territories from Texas to California until well into the 19th century. While there is little actual Spanish food today, the Spanish brought cattle to Mexico, which the Mexicans adapted their own corn-and-chile-based gastronomy to make tacos, tortillas, enchiladas, burritos, chimichangas and other dishes made of corn or flour pancakes filled with everything from chopped meat and poultry to beans. In Arizona and New Mexico, a few Native American dishes are served on reservations and at tribal festivals. Steaks and barbecue are always favorites on Southwestern menus, and beer is the drink of choice for dinner and a night out.

For a cosmopolitan foodie scene, visit Las Vegas, where top chefs from New York City, LA and even Paris are sprouting satellite restaurants.

Steak & Potatoes

Have a hankerin' for a juicy slab of beef with a salad, baked potato and beans? Look no further than the ranch-filled Southwest, home to intimate chophouses, family-friendly steak restaurants and trail-ride cookouts. In Utah, the large Mormon population influences culinary options. Here, good, old-fashioned American food like chicken, steak, potatoes, vegetables, homemade pies and ice cream prevail.

Mexican & New Mexican Food

Mexican food is often hot and spicy. If you're sensitive, test the heat of your salsa before dousing your meal. In Arizona, Mexican food is of the Sonoran type, with specialties such as *carne seca* (dried beef). Meals are usually served with refried beans, rice and flour or corn tortillas; chiles are relatively mild. Tucsonans refer to their city as the 'Mexican food capital of the universe,' which, although hotly contested by a few other places, carries a ring of truth. Colorado restaurants serve Mexican food, but they don't insist on any accolades for it.

New Mexico's food is different from, but reminiscent of, Mexican food. Pinto beans are served whole instead of refried; *posole* (a corn stew) may replace rice. Chiles aren't used so much as a condiment (like salsa) but more as an essential ingredient in almost every dish. *Carne adobada* (marinated pork chunks) is a specialty.

If a menu includes red or green chile dishes and sauces, it probably serves New Mexican–style dishes. The state is famous for its chile-enhanced Mexican standards. The town of Hatch, New Mexico, is particularly known for its green chiles.

Native American Food

Modern Native American cuisine bears little resemblance to that eaten before the Spanish conquest, but it is distinct from Southwestern cuisine. Navajo and Indian tacos – fried bread usually topped with beans, meat, tomatoes, chile and lettuce – are the most readily available. Chewy *horno* bread is baked in the beehive-shaped outdoor adobe ovens (*hornos*) using remnant heat from a fire built inside the oven, then cleared out before cooking.

Not all chiles are picked – those left on the plant are allowed to mature to a deep ruby red, then strung on the *ristras* which adorn walls and doorways throughout the Southwest.

Kim Jordan founded Fort Collins–based New Belgium brewery with ex-husband Jeff Lebesch in 1991. Today she is the company's CEO, and New Belgium – famous for its Fat Tire microbrews – is the 7th-largest brewery in the country. The company is regularly named one of the best work environments in the US.

Most other Native American cooking is game-based and usually involves squash and locally harvested ingredients like berries and piñon nuts. Though becoming better known, it can be difficult to find. Your best bets are festival food stands, powwows, rodeos, Pueblo feast days and casino restaurants.

Drinks

Work-hard, play-hard Americans are far from teetotalers. About 66% of Americans drink alcohol, with the majority preferring beer to wine.

Beer

Beer is about as American as Chevrolet, football and apple pie. According to a Gallup poll, about 39% of Americans drink beer on a regular basis, while 35% of Americans regularly drink wine. Liquor trails the other two, with only 22% of Americans consuming liquor every week.

Craft & Local Beer

Today, beer aficionados sip and savor beer as they would wine, and some urban restaurants even have beer 'programs,' 'sommeliers' and cellars. Microbrewery and craft-beer production is rising meteorically, accounting for 12% of the domestic market in 2012. In recent years it's become possible to 'drink local' all over the West as microbreweries pop up in urban centers, small towns and unexpected places. They're particularly popular in gateway communities outside national parks, including Moab, Flagstaff and Durango.

A microbrewery sells most of its beer off site. A brewpub sells most of its beer on site, and typically there's a restaurant attached.

Wine

There are more than 7000 wineries in the US today, and 2010 marked the first year that the US actually consumed more wine than France. To the raised eyebrows of European winemakers, who used to regard Californian wines as second class, many American wines are now even (gulp!) winning prestigious international awards. In fact, the nation is the world's fourth-largest producer of wine, behind Italy, France and Spain.

Wine isn't cheap in the US, but it's possible to procure a perfectly drinkable bottle of American wine at a liquor or wine shop for around US$10 to US$12.

BEER GOES LOCAL

In outdoorsy communities across the West, the neighborhood microbrewery is the unofficial community center – the place to unwind, swap trail stories, commune with friends and savor seasonal brews. Here are a few of our favorites:

Beaver Street Brewery (p344) Flagstaff, AZ.

Four Peaks Brewing Company (p341) Tempe, AZ.

Kelly's Brewery (p388) Albuquerque, NM.

Great Divide Brewing Company (p253) Denver, CO.

Steamworks Brewing (p280) Durango, CO.

Snake River Brewing Co (p294) Jackson, WY.

North Coast Brewing Co (p160) Fort Bragg, CA.

Amnesia Brewing (p221) Portland, OR.

Pike Pub & Brewery (p196) Seattle, WA.

San Diego has so many good ones that we've prepared a separate list; see p102.

Wine Regions

Today almost 90% of US wine comes from California, and Oregon and Washington wines have achieved international status.

Without a doubt, the country's hotbed of wine tourism is in Northern California, just outside of the Bay Area in the Napa and Sonoma Valleys. As other areas – Oregon's Willamette Valley, California's Central Coast and Arizona's Patagonia region – have evolved as wine destinations, they have spawned an entire industry of bed-and-breakfast tourism that goes hand in hand with the quest to find the perfect Pinot Noir.

There are many excellent 'New World' wines that have flourished in the rich American soil. The most popular white varietals made in the US are Chardonnay and Sauvignon Blanc; best-selling reds include Cabernet Sauvignon, Merlot, Pinot Noir and Zinfandel.

California's latest and greatest wines and wine-making trends are covered by *Wine Enthusiast*'s West Coast editor, Steve Heimoff, on his blog: http://steveheimoff.com.

Margaritas

In the Southwest it's all about the tequila. Margaritas are the alcoholic drink of choice, and synonymous with this region, especially in heavily Hispanic New Mexico, Arizona and southwestern Colorado. Margaritas vary in taste depending on the quality of the ingredients used, but all are made from tequila, a citrus liquor (Grand Marnier, Triple Sec or Cointreau) and either fresh-squeezed lime or premixed Sweet & Sour.

Margaritas are either served frozen, on the rocks (over ice) or straight up. Most people order them with salt. Traditional margaritas are lime flavored, but the popular drink comes in a rainbow of flavors – best ordered frozen.

Favorite Vegetarian Eateries

Lovin' Spoonfuls
(Tucson, AZ)

Macy's
(Flagstaff, AZ)

Greens
(San Francisco, CA)

Veggie Grill
(West Hollywood, CA)

Coffee

America runs on caffeine, and the coffee craze has only intensified in the last 25 years. Blame it on Starbucks. The world's biggest coffee chain was born amid the Northwest's progressive coffee culture in 1971, when Starbucks opened its first location across from Pike Place Market in Seattle. The idea, to offer a variety of roasted beans from around the world in a comfortable cafe, helped start filling the American coffee mug with more refined, complicated (and expensive) drinks compared to the ubiquitous Folgers and diner cups of joe. By the early 1990s, specialty coffee houses were springing up across the country.

Independent coffee shops support a coffee-house culture that encourages lingering; think free wi-fi and comfortable seating. That said, when using free cafe wi-fi, remember: order something every hour, don't leave laptops unattended, and deal with interruptions graciously.

Arts & Architecture

Western American art is marked by a unique merging of personality, attitude and landscape: the take-it-or-leave-it cow skulls in Georgia O'Keeffe paintings; the prominent shadows in an Ansel Adams' photograph of Half Dome; the gonzo journalism of Hunter S Thompson in the sun-baked Southwest; even Nirvana's grunge seems inseparable from its rainy Seattle roots. The landscape is a presence; beautiful yet unforgiving.

Literature

California is the most populous state in a region that has long inspired novelists, poets and storytellers.

Social Realism

Arguably the most influential author ever to emerge from California was John Steinbeck, who was born in Salinas in 1902. His masterpiece of social realism, *The Grapes of Wrath,* tells of the struggles of migrant farm workers.

Playwright Eugene O'Neill took his 1936 Nobel Prize money and transplanted himself to near San Francisco, where he wrote the autographical play *Long Day's Journey into Night.*

Upton Sinclair's *Oil!,* which inspired Paul Thomas Anderson's movie *There Will Be Blood,* was a muckraking work of historical fiction with socialist overtones.

Pulp Noir & Mysteries

In the 1930s, San Francisco and Los Angeles became the capitals of the pulp detective novel. Dashiell Hammett *(The Maltese Falcon)* made San Francisco's fog a sinister character. The king of hard-boiled crime writers was Raymond Chandler, who thinly disguised his hometown of Santa Monica as Bay City.

Since the 1990s, a renaissance of California crime fiction has been masterminded by James Ellroy *(LA Confidential),* Elmore Leonard *(Jackie Brown)* and Walter Mosley *(Devil in a Blue Dress),* whose Easy Rawlins detective novels are set in South Central LA's impoverished neighborhoods.

But not all detectives work in the cities. Tony Hillerman, an enormously popular author from Albuquerque, wrote *Skinwalkers, People of Darkness, Skeleton Man* and *The Sinister Pig.* His award-winning mystery novels take place on the Navajo, Hopi and Zuni Reservations.

Movers & Shakers

After the chaos of WWII, the Beat Generation brought about a provocative new style of writing: short, sharp, spontaneous and alive. Based in San Francisco, the scene revolved around Jack Kerouac *(On the Road),* Allen Ginsberg *(Howl)* and Lawrence Ferlinghetti, the Beats' patron and publisher.

Joan Didion nailed contemporary California culture in *Slouching Towards Bethlehem,* a collection of essays that takes a caustic look at 1960s

In Northern California, professional hell-raiser Jack London grew up and cut his teeth in Oakland. He turned out a massive volume of influential fiction, including tales of the late-19th-century Klondike Gold Rush.

The National Cowboy Poetry Gathering (www. westernfolklife. org) – the bronco of cowboy poetry events – is held in January in Elko, Nevada. Ropers and wranglers have waxed lyrical here for more than 25 years.

flower power and the Haight-Ashbury district. Tom Wolfe also put '60s San Francisco in perspective with *The Electric Kool-Aid Acid Test,* which follows Ken Kesey's band of Merry Pranksters.

In the 1970s, Charles Bukowski's semi-autobiographical novel *Post Office* captured down-and-out downtown LA, while Richard Vasquez's *Chicano* took a dramatic look at LA's Latino barrio.

Hunter S Thompson, who committed suicide in early 2005, wrote *Fear and Loathing in Las Vegas,* set in the temple of American excess in the desert; it's the ultimate road-trip novel, in every sense of the word.

Eco-Warriors & Social Commentators

Edward Abbey, noted for his strong environmental and political views, created the thought-provoking and seminal works of *Desert Solitaire* and *The Journey Home: Some Words in Defense of the American West.* His classic *Monkey Wrench Gang* is a comic fictional account of real people who plan to blow up Glen Canyon Dam before it floods Glen Canyon.

Wallace Stegner's western-set novel *Angle of Repose* won the Pulitzer Prize in 1972. His book of essays *Where the Bluebird Sings to the Lemonade Springs* discusses the harmful consequences of the mythologizing of the West. Former Tucsonian Barbara Kingsolver published two novels with Southwestern settings, *The Bean Trees* and *Animal Dreams.* She shares her thoughts about day-to-day life in the Southwest in a series of essays in *High Tide in Tucson.*

Cheryl Strayed's bestselling memoir *Wild* traces her long-distance solo hike on the Pacific Coast Trail after her mother's death. Reese Witherspoon, whose production company bought the movie rights, is playing the lead. Filming began in the fall of 2013.

Music

Much of the American recording industry is based in Los Angeles, and SoCal's film and TV industries have proven powerful talent incubators. Indeed, today's troubled pop princesses and *American Idol* winners are only here thanks to the tuneful revolutions of all the decades of innovation that came before, from country folk to urban rap.

Rockin' Out

The first homegrown rock-and-roll talent to make it big in the 1950s was Richie Valens, whose 'La Bamba' was a rockified version of a Mexican folk song. When Joan Baez and Bob Dylan had their Northern California fling in the early 1960s, Dylan plugged in his guitar and played folk rock. When Janis Joplin and Big Brother & the Holding Company developed their shambling musical stylings in San Francisco, folk rock splintered into psychedelia. Meanwhile, Jim Morrison and the Doors and the Byrds blew minds on LA's famous Sunset Strip. The epicenter of LA's psychedelic rock scene was the Laurel Canyon neighborhood, just uphill from the Sunset Strip and the legendary Whisky a Go Go nightclub.

Wanna hear the next break-out indie band before they make it big? Tune into the 'Morning Becomes Eclectic' show on Southern California's KCRW (www.kcrw.com) radio station for live in-studio performances and musician interviews. Listen online, download KCRW's free podcasts or buy the mobile app.

Rap & Hip-Hop Rhythms

Since the 1980s, LA has been a hotbed for West Coast rap and hip-hop. Eazy E, Ice Cube and Dr Dre released the seminal NWA (Niggaz With Attitude) album, *Straight Outta Compton,* in 1989. Death Row Records, cofounded by Dr Dre, has launched megawatt rap talents including Long Beach bad boy Snoop Dog and the late Tupac Shakur, who launched his rap career in Marin County and was fatally shot in 1996 in Las Vegas in a suspected East Coast/West Coast rap feud.

Throughout the 1980s and '90s, California maintained a grassroots hip-hop scene closer to the streets in LA and in the heart of the black power movement in Oakland. In the late 1990s, the Bay Area birthed underground artists like E-40 and the 'hyphy movement,' a reaction against the increasing commercialization of hip-hop. Also from Oakland, Michael Franti & Spearhead blend hip-hop with funk, reggae, folk, jazz and rock stylings into messages for social justice and peace. Meanwhile, during the late '90s and early 2000s, Korn from Bakersfield and Linkin Park from LA County combined hip-hop with rap and metal to popularize 'nu metal.'

Grunge & Indie Rock

Grunge started in the mid-1980s and was heavily influenced by cult group the Melvins. Distorted guitars, strong riffs, heavy drumming and gritty styles defined the unpolished musical style. Grunge didn't explode until the record label Sub Pop released Nirvana's *Nevermind* in 1991, skyrocketing the 'Seattle Sound' into mainstream music. True purists, however, shunned Nirvana for what they considered selling out to commercialism while overshadowing equally worthy bands like Soundgarden and Alice in Chains. The general popularity of grunge continued through the early 1990s, but the very culture of the genre took part in its downfall. Bands lived hard and fast, never really taking themselves seriously. Many eventually succumbed to internal strife and drug abuse. The final blow was in 1994, when Kurt Cobain – the heart of Nirvana – committed suicide.

A few western cities are especially connected with indie music. Seattle was the original stomping grounds for Modest Mouse, Death Cab for Cutie and the Postal Service. Olympia, WA, has been a hotbed of indie rock and riot grrls. Portland, OR, has boasted such diverse groups as folktronic hip-hop band Talkdemonic, alt-band the Decemberists and multi-genre Pink Martini, not to mention the Shins – originally from Albuquerque, NM – the Dandy Warhols, Blind Pilot and Elliot Smith.

You can see the handwritten lyrics of Nirvana singer/songwriter Kurt Cobain (born in Aberdeen, WA) at the Experience Music Project in the Seattle Center.

Film

From the moment movies – and later TV – became a dominant entertainment medium, California took center stage in the world of popular culture. In any given year some 40 TV shows and scores of movies use California locations, not including all of those shot on SoCal studio backlots.

The Industry

The movie-making industry grew out of the humble orchards of Hollywoodland, a residential neighborhood of Los Angeles, where entrepreneurial moviemakers, many of whom were European immigrants, established studios in the early 1900s. German-born Carl Laemmle built Universal Studios in 1915, selling lunch to curious guests coming to watch the magic of moviemaking; Polish immigrant Samuel Goldwyn joined with Cecil B DeMille to form Paramount Studios; and Jack Warner and his brothers, born to Polish parents, arrived a few years later from Canada.

LA's perpetually balmy weather meant that most outdoor scenes could be easily shot there. Fans loved early silent-film stars like Charlie Chaplin and Harold Lloyd, and the first big Hollywood wedding occurred in 1920 when Douglas Fairbanks wed Mary Pickford, becoming Hollywood's first de facto royal couple. The silent-movie era gave way to 'talkies' after 1927's *The Jazz Singer,* a Warner Bros musical starring Al Jolson, premiered in downtown LA, ushering in Hollywood's glamorous Golden Age.

Hollywood & Beyond

From the 1920s, Hollywood became the industry's social and financial hub, but only one major studio, Paramount Pictures, stood in Hollywood proper. Most movies have been shot elsewhere around LA, from Culver City (at MGM, now Sony Pictures), to Studio City (at Universal Studios) and Burbank (at Warner Bros and later at Disney).

ARTS & ARCHITECTURE FILM

Top Film Festivals

AFI Fest
(www.afi.com)

Outfest
(www.outfest.org)

San Francisco International Film Festival
(www.sffs.org)

Sundance Film Festival
(www.sundance.org)

Telluride Film Festival
(www.telluridefilm festival.org)

Seattle International Film Festival
(www.siff.net)

Today's high cost of filming has sent location scouts outside the state. During his two terms as governor of New Mexico (2002–10), Bill Richardson wooed production teams to the state by offering a 25% tax rebate on expenditures. His efforts helped inject more than $3 billion into the economy. Film and TV crews have also moved north to Canada, often shooting in Vancouver, Toronto and Montréal.

Western Films

Though many westerns have been shot in SoCal, a few places in Utah and Arizona have doubled as film and TV sets so often that they have come to define the American West. In addition to Utah's Monument Valley, first popularized by director John Ford in *The Stagecoach*, movie-worthy destinations include Moab for *Thelma and Louise* (1991), Dead Horse Point State Park for *Mission Impossible: 2* (2000), Lake Powell for *Planet of the Apes* (1968) and Tombstone for the eponymous *Tombstone* (1993). Scenes in *127 Hours*, the film version of Aron Ralston's harrowing time trapped in Blue John Canyon in Canyonlands National Park, were shot in and around the canyon.

The Small Screen

The first TV station began broadcasting in Los Angeles in 1931. Through the following decades, iconic images of LA were beamed into living rooms across America in shows such as *Dragnet* (1950s), *The Beverly Hillbillies* (1960s), *The Brady Bunch* (1970s), *LA Law* (1980s), *Baywatch*, *Melrose Place* and *The Fresh Prince of Bel-Air* (1990s), through to teen 'dramedies' *Beverly Hills 90210* (1990s) and *The OC* (2000s), the latter set in Newport Beach, Orange County. If you're a fan of reality TV, you'll spot Southern California starring in everything from *Top Chef* to the *Real Housewives of Orange County*.

Southern California has also been a versatile backdrop for edgy cable-TV dramas, from Showtime's *Weeds*, about a pot-growing SoCal widow, to TNT's cop show *The Closer*, about homicide detectives in LA, and FX's *The Shield*, which fictionalized the City of Angels' police corruption.

But SoCal isn't the only TV backdrop. Former *X-Files* writer Vince Gilligan brought more of his off-beat brilliance to the small screen in 2008 with the premiere of *Breaking Bad*. Set and shot in sun-baked Albuquerque, the Emmy-winning drama traces the rise and fall of chemistry-teacher-turned-meth-dealer Walter White and his hard-luck assistant Jesse Pinkman.

Some exterior shots for David Lynch's quirky *Twin Peaks* were shot in Snoqualmie and North Bend, WA. Because of tax incentives, Vancouver, BC, has long been a popular shooting location for television production companies. Many of their shows, from the *X-Files* to *Battlestar Galactica* to *Fringe*, are actually set somewhere else.

Architecture

Westerners have adapted imported styles to the climate and available materials, building cool, adobe-inspired houses in Tucson and fog-resistant redwood-shingle houses in Mendocino.

Spanish Missions & Victorian Queens

The first Spanish missions were built around courtyards, using materials that Native Americans and colonists found on hand: adobe, limestone and grass. Many missions crumbled into disrepair as the church's influence waned, but the style remained practical for the climate. Early California settlers later adapted it into the rancho adobe style, as seen at El Pueblo de Los Angeles and in San Diego's Old Town.

In Albuquerque, *Breaking Bad* fans can visit Twisters (4257 Isleta Blvd), which doubled as Gus Fring's Los Pollos Hermanos. For dessert, Rebel Donut (www.rebeldonut.com; 400 Gold Ave) sells a Blue Sky doughnut with blue sugar crystals – a nod to Walter White's blue meth.

In 1915, newspaper magnate William Randolph Hearst commissioned California's first licensed female architect Julia Morgan to build his Hearst Castle – a mixed blessing, since the commission would take Morgan decades, and require careful diplomacy through constant changes and a delicate balancing act among Hearst's preferred Spanish, Gothic and Greek styles.

During the mid-19th-century gold rush, California's nouveau riche imported materials to construct grand mansions matching European fashions, and raised the stakes with ornamental excess. Many millionaires favored the gilded Queen Anne style. Outrageous examples of Victorian architecture, including 'Painted Ladies' and 'gingerbread' houses, can be found in such Northern California towns as San Francisco, Ferndale and Eureka.

Many architects rejected frilly Victorian styles in favor of the simple, classical lines of Spanish colonial architecture. Mission revival details are restrained and functional: arched doors and windows, long covered porches, fountains, courtyards, solid walls and red-tiled roofs.

Arts-and-Crafts & Art Deco

Simplicity was the hallmark of the arts-and-crafts style. Influenced by both Japanese design principles and England's Arts and Crafts movement, its woodwork and handmade touches marked a deliberate departure from the Industrial Revolution. SoCal architects Charles and Henry Greene and Bernard Maybeck in Northern California popularized the versatile one-story bungalow, which became trendy at the turn of the 20th century. Today you'll spot them in Pasadena and Berkeley with their overhanging eaves, terraces and sleeping porches harmonizing indoors and outdoors.

In the 1920s, the international art deco style took elements from the ancient world – Mayan glyphs, Egyptian pillars, Babylonian ziggurats – and flattened them into modern motifs to cap stark facades and outline streamlined skyscrapers, notably in LA and downtown Oakland. Streamline moderne kept decoration to a minimum and mimicked the aerodynamic look of ocean liners and airplanes, as seen at LA's Union Station.

A few years later master architect Frank Lloyd Wright was designing homes in the Romanza style, following the principle that for every indoor space there's an outdoor space, and this flowing design is best exhibited in LA's Hollyhock House, constructed for heiress Alice Barnsdale. His part-time home and studio in Scottsdale, AZ, Taliesin West, complements and showcases the surrounding desert landscape.

Postmodern Evolutions

Architectural styles have veered away from strict high modernism, and unlikely postmodern shapes have been added to the landscape. Richard Meier made his mark on West LA with the Getty Center, a cresting white wave of a building atop a sunburned hilltop. Canadian-born Frank Gehry relocated to Santa Monica. His billowing, sculptural style for LA's Walt Disney Concert Hall winks cheekily at shipshape Californian streamline moderne. Renzo Piano's signature inside-out industrial style can be glimpsed in the sawtooth roof and red-steel veins on the Broad Contemporary Art Museum extension of the Los Angeles County Museum of Art.

San Francisco has lately championed a brand of postmodernism by Pritzker Prize–winning architects that magnifies and mimics California's great outdoors, especially in Golden Gate Park. Swiss architects Herzog & de Meuron clad the MH de Young Memorial Museum in copper, which will eventually oxidize green to match its park setting. Nearby, Renzo Piano literally raised the roof on sustainable design at the LEED platinum-certified California Academy of Sciences, capped by a living garden.

Visual Arts

Although the earliest European artists were trained cartographers accompanying Western explorers, their images of California as an island show more imagination than scientific rigor. This mythologizing tendency continued throughout the gold-rush era, as Western artists alternated

---

ARTS & ARCHITECTURE VISUAL ARTS

Jim Heimann's *California Crazy & Beyond: Roadside Vernacular Architecture* is a romp through the zany, whimsical world of California, where lemonade stands look like giant lemons and motels are shaped like tipis.

Art in Out-of-the-Way Places

ART IN NEW MEXICO

Both Taos and Santa Fe have large and active artist communities considered seminal to the development of Southwestern art. Santa Fe, the third-largest art market in the US, is a particularly good stop for those looking to browse and buy art and native crafts. More than 100 of Santa Fe's 200 galleries line the city's Canyon Rd. Native American vendors sell high-quality jewelry and crafts beside the plaza; Friday art walks begin at 5pm. Serious collectors can also take a studio tour or drive the bucolic High Rd, a low-key scenic byway between Santa Fe and Taos that swings by galleries, historic buildings and an art market.

between caricatures of Wild West debauchery and manifest-destiny propaganda urging pioneers to settle the golden West. The completion of the transcontinental railroad in 1869 brought an influx of romantic painters, who produced epic California wilderness landscapes.

In the early 1900s, homegrown colonies of California impressionist plein-air painters emerged, particularly at Laguna Beach and Carmel-by-the-Sea. In the Southwest, Georgia O'Keeffe (1887–1986) painted stark Southwestern landscapes that are exhibited in museums throughout the world.

Photographer Pirkle Jones saw expressive potential in California landscape photography after WWII, while San Francisco native Ansel Adams' sublime photographs had already started doing justice to Yosemite. Adams founded Group f/64 with Edward Weston from Carmel and Imogen Cunningham in San Francisco. Berkeley-based Dorothea Lange turned her unflinching lens on the plight of Californian migrant workers in the Great Depression and Japanese Americans forced to enter internment camps in WWII. Glass blowing is a specialty of the Puget Sound area, led by artisans from the Pilchuk School. Washington-born artist Dale Chihuly, acclaimed for his blown-glass creations, can be found in more than 200 galleries worldwide.

As the postwar American West became crisscrossed with freeways and divided into planned communities, Californian painters captured the abstract forms of manufactured landscapes. In San Francisco, Richard Diebenkorn and David Park became leading proponents of Bay Area Figurative Art, while San Francisco sculptor Richard Serra captured urban aesthetics in massive, rusting monoliths resembling ship prows and industrial Stonehenges. Pop artists captured the ethos of conspicuous consumerism, through Wayne Thiebaud's gumball machines, British émigré David Hockney's LA pools and, above all, Ed Ruscha's studies of SoCal pop culture. In San Francisco, artists showed their love for rough-and-readymade 1950s Beat collage, 1960s psychedelic Fillmore posters, earthy '70s funk and beautiful-mess punk, and '80s graffiti and skate culture.

Today's contemporary art scene brings all these influences together with muralist-led social commentary, an obsessive dedication to craft and a new-media milieu that embraces cutting-edge technology. LA's Museum of Contemporary Art puts on provocative and avant garde shows, as does LACMA's Broad Contemporary Art Museum and the Museum of Contemporary Art San Diego, which specializes in post-1950s pop and conceptual art. To see California-made art at its most experimental, browse the SoCal gallery scenes in downtown LA and Culver City, then check out independent NorCal art spaces in San Francisco's Mission District and the laboratory-like galleries of SOMA's Yerba Buena Arts District.

Photography buffs can plan their California trip around the top-notch SFMOMA in northern California, where the superb collection runs from early Western daguerreotypes to experimental postwar Japanese photography, and LA's Getty Center, with more than 100,000 images.

Landscapes & Wildlife

Crashing tectonic plates, mighty floods, spewing volcanoes, frigid ice fields: for millions and millions of years, the American West was an altogether unpleasant place. But from this fire and ice sprang a kaleidoscopic array of stunning landscapes bound by a common modern trait: an undeniable ability to attract and inspire explorers, naturalists, artists and outdoor adventurers. And for travelers? This is the place to finally use the good camera.

Read Marc Reisner's *Cadillac Desert: The American West and Its Disappearing Water* for a thorough account of how exploding populations in the West have utilized every drop of available water.

The Land

As Western novelist and essayist Wallace Stegner noted in his book *Where the Bluebird Sings to the Lemonade Springs*, the West 'is actually half a dozen subregions as different from one another as the Olympic rainforest is from Utah's slickrock country, or Seattle from Santa Fe.' The one commonality in Stegner's view? The aridity of the region. Aridity, he writes, sharpens the brilliance of the light and heightens the clarity of the air in most of the West. It also leads to fights over water rights, a historic and ongoing concern.

California

The third-largest state after Alaska and Texas, California covers more than 155,000 sq miles.

According to the US Geological Survey, the odds of a magnitude 6.7 or greater earthquake hitting California in the next 30 years is 99.7%.

Geology & Earthquakes

California is a complex geologic landscape formed from fragments of rock and earth crust scraped together as the North American continent drifted westward over hundreds of millions of years. Crumpled coast ranges, the downward-bowing Central Valley and the still-rising Sierra Nevada are evidence of gigantic forces exerted as the continental and ocean plates crush together.

About 25 million years ago the ocean plates stopped colliding and instead started sliding against each other, creating the massive San Andreas Fault. Because this contact zone doesn't slide smoothly, but catches and slips irregularly, it rattles California with an ongoing succession of tremors and earthquakes.

The state's most famous earthquake in 1906 measured 7.8 on the Richter scale and demolished San Francisco, leaving more than 3000 people dead. The Bay Area made headlines again in 1989 when the Loma Prieta earthquake (7.1) caused a section of the Bay Bridge to collapse. Los Angeles' last 'big one' was in 1994, when the Northridge quake (6.7) caused parts of the Santa Monica Fwy to fall down, making it the most costly quake in US history – so far.

Many of the Southwest's common flowers can be found in *Canyon Country Wildflowers* by Damian Fagan.

The Coast to the Central Valley

Much of California's coast is fronted by rugged coastal mountains that capture winter's water-laden storms. San Francisco divides the Coast Ranges roughly in half, with the foggy North Coast remaining sparsely populated, while the Central and Southern California coasts have a balmier climate and many more people.

A fully hydrated giant saguaro can store more than a ton of water.

In the northernmost reaches of the Coast Ranges, nutrient-rich soils and abundant moisture foster forests of giant trees. On their eastern flanks, the Coast Ranges subside into gently rolling hills that give way to the 450-mile-long Central Valley, an agricultural powerhouse producing more than 250 different types of crops – from nuts to fruits and vegetables – valued at more than $17 billion a year.

PLANTS OF THE WEST

The presence of many large mountain ranges in the West creates a remarkable diversity of niches for plants. One way to understand the plants of this region is to understand life zones and the ways each plant thrives in its favored zone.

In the Southwest, at the lowest elevations, generally below 4000ft, high temperatures and a lack of water create a desert zone where drought-tolerant plants such as cacti, sagebrush and agave survive. Many of these species have small leaves or minimal leaf surface area to reduce water loss, or hold water like a cactus to survive long hot spells.

At mid-elevations, from 4000ft to 7000ft, conditions cool a bit and more moisture is available for woody shrubs and small trees. In much of Nevada, Utah, northern Arizona and New Mexico, piñon pines and junipers blanket vast areas of low mountain slopes and hills. Both trees are short and stout to help conserve water.

Nearly pure stands of stately, fragrant ponderosa pine are the dominant tree at 7000ft on many of the West's mountain ranges. In fact, this single tree best defines the Western landscape and many animals rely on it for food and shelter; timber companies also consider it their most profitable tree. High mountain, or boreal, forests composed of spruce, fir, quaking aspen and a few other conifers are found on the highest peaks in the Southwest. This is a land of cool, moist forests and lush meadows with brilliant wildflower displays.

Incredibly diverse flowers appear each year in the deserts and mountains of the Southwest. These include desert flowers that start blooming in February, and late summer flowers that fill mountain meadows after the snow melts or pop out after summer thunderstorms wet the soil. Some of the largest and grandest flowers belong to the Southwest's 100 or so species of cacti.

Southern California's desert areas begin their peak blooming in March, with other lowland areas of the state producing abundant wildflowers in April. As snows melt later at higher elevations in the Sierra Nevada, Yosemite National Park's Tuolumne Meadows is another prime spot for wildflower walks and photography, with peak blooms usually in late June or early July.

In the Pacific Northwest, the wet and wild west side of the Cascade Range captures most rain clouds coming in from the ocean, relieving them of their moisture and creating humid forests full of green life jostling for space. The dry, deserty east side – robbed of rains by the tall Cascades – is mostly the stomping grounds for sagebrush and other semi-arid-loving vegetation, although there are lush pockets here and there, especially along the mountain foothills.

When it comes to trees, California is a land of superlatives: the tallest (coast redwoods approaching 380ft), the largest (giant sequoias of the Sierra Nevada over 36ft across at the base) and the oldest (bristlecone pines of the White Mountains that are almost 5000 years old). The giant sequoia, which is unique to California, survives in isolated groves scattered on the Sierra Nevada's western slopes, including in Yosemite, Sequoia and Kings Canyon National Parks.

Mountain Highs

On the eastern side of the Central Valley looms the world-famous Sierra Nevada. At 400 miles long and 50 miles wide, it's one of the largest mountain ranges in the world and is home to 13 peaks over 14,000ft. The vast wilderness of the High Sierra (lying mostly above 9000ft) presents an astounding landscape of glaciers, sculpted granite peaks and remote canyons. The soaring Sierra Nevada captures storm systems and drains them of their water, with most of the precipitation over 3000ft falling as snow. These waters eventually flow into half a dozen major river systems that provide the vast majority of water for San Francisco and LA as well as farms in the Central Valley.

California claims both the highest point in the contiguous US (Mt Whitney; 14,505ft) and the lowest elevation in North America (Badwater, Death Valley; 282ft below sea level) – plus they're only 90 miles apart, as the condor flies.

The Deserts & Beyond

With the west slope of the Sierra Nevada capturing the lion's share of water, all lands east of the Sierra crest are dry and desertlike, receiving less than 10 inches of rain a year. Surprisingly, some valleys at the eastern foot of the Sierra Nevada are well watered by creeks and support a vigorous economy of livestock and agriculture.

Areas in the northern half of California, especially on the elevated Modoc Plateau of northeastern California, are a cold desert at the western edge of the Great Basin, blanketed with hardy sagebrush shrubs and pockets of juniper trees. Temperatures increase as you head south, with a prominent transition as you descend from Mono Lake into the Owens Valley east of the Sierra Nevada. This southern hot desert (part of the Mojave Desert) includes Death Valley, one of the hottest places on earth.

The Southwest

Extremely ancient rocks (among the oldest on the planet) exposed in the deep heart of the Grand Canyon show that the region was underwater two billion years ago. Younger layers of rocks in southern Utah reveal that this region was continuously or periodically underwater. About 286 million years ago, near the end of the Paleozoic era, a collision of continents into a massive landmass known as Pangaea deformed the earth's crust and produced pressures that uplifted the ancestral Rocky Mountains. Though this early mountain range lay to the east, it formed rivers and sediment deposits that began to shape the Southwest.

The sequence of oceans and sand ended around 60 million years ago as North America underwent a dramatic separation from Europe, sliding westward over a piece of the earth's crust known as the East Pacific Plate and leaving behind an ever-widening gulf that became the Atlantic Ocean. The East Pacific Plate collided with the North American Plate. This collision, named the Laramide Orogeny, resulted in the birth of the modern Rocky Mountains and uplifted an old basin into a highland known today as the Colorado Plateau. Fragments of the East Pacific Plate also attached themselves to the leading edge of the North American Plate, transforming the Southwest from a coastal area to an interior region increasingly detached from the ocean.

On the evening of July 5, 2011, a mile-high dust storm with an estimated 100-mile width enveloped Phoenix after reaching speeds of more than 50mph. Visibility dropped to between zero and one-quarter of a mile. There were power outages, and Phoenix International Airport temporarily closed.

In contrast to the compression and collision that characterized earlier events, the earth's crust began stretching in an east–west direction about 30 million years ago. The thinner, stretched crust of New Mexico and Texas cracked along zones of weakness called faults, resulting in a rift valley where New Mexico's Rio Grande now flows. These same forces created the stepped plateaus of northern Arizona and southern Utah.

During the Pleistocene glacial period, large bodies of water accumulated throughout the Southwest. Utah's Great Salt Lake is the most famous remnant of these mighty ice-age lakes. Basins with now completely dry, salt-crusted lakebeds are especially conspicuous on a drive across Nevada.

For the past several million years the dominant force has probably been erosion. Not only do torrential rainstorms readily tear through soft sedimentary rocks, but also the rise of the Rocky Mountains generates large, powerful rivers that wind throughout the Southwest, carving mighty canyons in their wake. Nearly all of the contemporary features in the Southwest, from arches (Arches National Park has more than 2500 sandstone arches) to hoodoos, are the result of weathering and erosion.

Geographic Makeup of the Land

The Colorado Plateau is an impressive and nearly impenetrable 130,000-sq-mile tableland lurking in the corner where Colorado, Utah, Arizona and New Mexico join. Formed in an ancient basin as a remarkably coherent body of neatly layered sedimentary rocks, the plateau has remained relatively unchanged even as the lands around it were compressed, stretched and deformed by powerful forces.

Perhaps the most powerful testament to the plateau's long-term stability is the precise layers of sedimentary rock stretching back two billion years. In fact, the science of stratigraphy – the reading of earth history through its rock layers – stemmed from work at the Grand Canyon, where an astonishing set of layers have been laid bare by the Colorado River cutting across them. Throughout the Southwest, and on the Colorado Plateau in particular, layers of sedimentary rock detail a rich history of ancient oceans, coastal mudflats and arid dunes.

Edward Abbey shares his desert philosophy and insights in his classic *Desert Solitaire: A Season in the Wilderness*, a must-read for desert enthusiasts and conservationists.

Landscape Features

The Southwest is jam-packed with remarkable rock formations. One reason for this is that the region's many sedimentary layers are so soft that rain and erosion readily carve them into fantastic shapes. But not any old rain; it has to be hard, fairly sporadic rain, as frequent rain would wash the formations away. Between rains there have to be long arid spells that keep the eroding landmarks intact. The range of colors derives from the unique mineral composition of each rock type.

Geology of the Grand Canyon

Arizona's Grand Canyon is the best-known geologic feature in the Southwest and for good reason: not only is it on a scale so massive it dwarfs the human imagination, but it also records two billion years of geologic history – a huge amount of time considering the earth is just 4.6 billion years old. The canyon itself, however, is young, a mere five to six

UNIQUE LANDSCAPE FEATURES IN THE SOUTHWEST

Badlands Crumbling, mineral-filled soft rock; found in the Painted Desert at Petrified Forest National Park, at Capitol Reef National Park or in the Bisti Badlands.

Hoodoos Sculptured spires of rock weathered into towering pillars; showcased at Bryce Canyon National Park and Arches National Park.

Natural Bridges Formed when streams cut through sandstone layers; three bridges can be seen at Natural Bridges National Monument.

Goosenecks Early-stage natural bridges formed when a stream U-turns across a landscape; visible from Goosenecks Overlook at Capitol Reef National Park.

Mesas Hulking formations of layered sandstone where the surrounding landscape has been stripped away; classic examples can be found at Monument Valley (and) on the Arizona–Utah border.

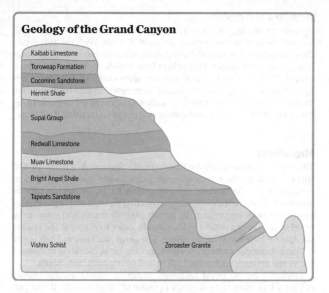

Geology of the Grand Canyon

Kaibab Limestone
Toroweap Formation
Coconino Sandstone
Hermit Shale
Supai Group
Redwall Limestone
Muav Limestone
Bright Angel Shale
Tapeats Sandstone
Vishnu Schist
Zoroaster Granite

million years old. Carved by the powerful Colorado River as the land bulged upward, the 277-mile-long canyon reflects the differing hardness of the 10-plus layers of rocks in its walls. Shales, for instance, crumble easily and form slopes, while resistant limestones and sandstones form distinctive cliffs.

The layers making up the bulk of the canyon walls were laid during the Paleozoic era, 542 to 251 million years ago. These formations perch atop a group of one- to two-billion-year-old rocks lying at the bottom of the inner gorge of the canyon. Between these two distinct sets of rock is the Great Unconformity, a several-hundred-million-year gap in the geologic record where erosion erased 12,000ft of rock and left a huge mystery.

Pacific Northwest

From 16 to 13 million years ago, eastern Oregon and Washington witnessed one of the premier episodes of volcanic activity in earth's history. Due to shifting stresses in the earth's crust, much of interior western North America began cracking along thousands of lines and releasing enormous amounts of lava that flooded over the landscape. On multiple occasions, so much lava was produced that it filled the Columbia River channel and reached the Oregon coast, forming prominent headlands like Cape Lookout. Today, the hardened lava flows of eastern Oregon and Washington are easily seen in spectacular rimrock cliffs and flat-top mesas.

Not to be outdone, the ice ages of the past two million years created a massive ice field from Washington to British Columbia – and virtually every mountain range in the rest of the region was blanketed by glaciers.

Wildlife

Although the staggering numbers of animals that greeted the first European settlers are now a thing of the past, it is still possible to see wildlife thriving in the West in the right places and at the right times of year.

Visit www.publiclands.org for a one-stop summary of recreational opportunities on government-owned land in the Southwest, regardless of managing agency. The site also has maps, a book index, links to relevant agencies and updates on current restrictions and conditions.

Reptiles & Amphibians

On a spring evening, canyons in the Southwest may fairly reverberate with the calls of canyon tree frogs or red-spotted toads. With the rising sun, these are replaced by several dozen species of lizards and snakes that roam among rocks and shrubs. Blue-bellied fence lizards are particularly abundant in the region's parks, but visitors can always hope to encounter a rarity such as the strange and venomous Gila monster. Equally fascinating are the Southwest's many colorful rattlesnakes. Quick to anger and able to deliver a painful or toxic bite, rattlesnakes are placid and retiring if left alone.

Pages of Stone: Geology of the Grand Canyon & Plateau Country National Parks & Monuments by Halka and Lucy Chronic provides an excellent introduction to the Southwest's diverse landscape.

Birds

Migrations

There are so many interesting birds in the Southwest – home to 400 species – that it's the foremost reason many people travel to the region. Springtime is a particularly rewarding time for bird-watching here as songbirds arrive from their southern wintering grounds and begin singing from every nook and cranny. In the fall, sandhill cranes and snow geese travel in long skeins down the Rio Grande Valley to winter at the Bosque del Apache National Wildlife Refuge. The Great Salt Lake in Utah is one of North America's premier sites for migrating birds, including millions of ducks and grebes stopping each fall to feed before continuing south.

California lies on major migratory routes for more than 350 species of bird, which either pass through the state or linger through the winter. This is one of the top birding destinations in North America. Witness, for example, the congregation of one million ducks, geese and swans at the Klamath Basin National Wildlife Refuge Complex every November. During winter, these waterbirds head south into the refuges of the Central Valley, another area to observe huge numbers of native and migratory species.

California Condors & Bald Eagles

With a 9ft wingspan, the California condor looks more like a prehistoric pterodactyl than any bird you've ever seen. Pushed to the brink of extinction, these unusual birds – which fed on the carcasses of mastodons and saber-toothed cats in prehistoric days – are staging a minor comeback at the Grand Canyon. After several decades in which no condors lived in the wild, a few pairs are now nesting on the canyon rim. The best bet for spotting them is Arizona's Vermilion Cliffs. In California, look skyward as you drive along the Big Sur coast or at Pinnacles National Monument.

The Pacific Northwest is a stronghold for bald eagles, which feast on the annual salmon runs and nest in old-growth forests. With a 7.5ft wingspan, these impressive birds gather in huge numbers in places like Washington's Upper Skagit Bald Eagle Area and the national wildlife refuges in the Klamath Basin region in northern California and southern Oregon. In California, bald eagles have regained a foothold on the Channel Islands, and they sometimes spend winter at Big Bear Lake near LA. At their low point, only two or three breeding pairs nested in Colorado, but that number has increased by eight or nine each year, and in 2011 there were more than 100 nests. Anywhere from 400 to 1000 bald eagles spend winter in the state.

An estimated nine million free-tailed bats once roosted in Carlsbad Caverns. Though reduced in recent years, the evening flight is still one of the premier wildlife spectacles in North America.

Mammals

Many of the West's most charismatic wildlife species – grizzlies, buffalo, prairie dogs – were largely exterminated by the early 1900s. Fortunately, there are plenty of other mammals still wandering the forests and deserts. At the very least, if you keep your eyes open, you'll see some mule deer or a coyote.

Bears

The black bear is probably the most notorious animal in the Rockies. Adult males weigh from 275lb to 450lb; females weigh about 175lb to 250lb. They measure 3ft high on all fours and can be over 5ft when standing on their hind legs.

Black bears also roam the Pacific Northwest, the Southwest and California. They feed on berries, nuts, roots, grasses, insects, eggs, small mammals and fish, but can become a nuisance around campgrounds and mountain cabins where food is not stored properly.

The grizzly bear, which can be seen on California's state flag, once roamed California's beaches and grasslands in large numbers, eating everything from whale carcasses to acorns. Grizzlies were particularly abundant in the Central Valley. The grizzly was extirpated in the early 1900s after relentless persecution. Grizzlies are classified as an endangered species in Colorado, but they are almost certainly gone from the state; the last documented grizzly in Colorado was killed in 1979. In 2010, scientists estimated there were 603 grizzlies wandering the Yellowstone National Park area. A recent study suggests that the introduction of wolves to Yellowstone may be helping the grizzly population there – wolves eat elk, leaving more berries for the grizzlies.

In 1990, the northern spotted owl was declared a threatened species, barring timber industries from clear-cutting certain old-growth forests. The controversy sparked debate all across the Pacific Northwest, pitting loggers against environmentalists.

Elk

About 2350 elk roam across Rocky Mountain National Park, with a resident herd of about 1700. Mature elk bulls may reach 1100lb, and cows weigh up to 600lb. Both have dark necks with light tan bodies. Like bighorn sheep, elk were virtually extinct around Estes Park by 1890, wiped out by hunters. In 1913 and 1914, before the establishment of the park, people from Estes Park brought in 49 elk from Yellowstone. The population increase since the establishment of Rocky Mountain National Park is one of the National Park Service's great successes.

Among the Pacific Northwest's signature animals is the Roosevelt elk, whose eerie bugling courtship calls can be heard each September and October in forested areas throughout the region. Full-grown males may reach 1100lb and carry 5ft racks of antlers. During winter, large groups gather in lowland valleys and can be observed along the Spirit Lake Memorial Highway in Mt St Helens National Volcanic Monument. Olympic National Park is home to the world's largest unmanaged herd of Roosevelt elk.

California's mountain forests are home to an estimated 25,000 to 35,000 black bears, whose fur actually ranges in color from black to dark brown, cinnamon and even blond.

Bighorn Sheep

Rocky Mountain National Park is a special place: 'Bighorn Crossing Zone' is a sign you're unlikely to encounter anywhere else. From late spring through summer, groups of up to 60 sheep – typically only ewes and lambs – move from the moraine ridge north of the highway across the road to Sheep Lakes in Horseshoe Park. Unlike the big under-curving horns on mature rams, ewes grow swept-back crescent-shaped horns that reach only about 10in in length. The Sheep Lakes are evaporative ponds ringed with tasty salt deposits that attract the ewes in the morning and early afternoon after lambing in May and June. In August they rejoin the rams in the Mummy Range.

Pronghorn Antelope

The open plains of eastern Oregon and Washington are the playing grounds of pronghorn antelope, curious-looking deer-like animals with two single black horns instead of antlers. Pronghorns belong to a unique antelope family and are only found in the American West, but they are more famous for being able to run up to 60mph for long stretches – they're the second-fastest land animal in the world.

Environmental Issues

Growth in the West has come with costs. In the Pacific Northwest, the production of cheap hydroelectricity and massive irrigation projects along the Columbia have led to the near-irreversible destruction of the river's ecosystem. Dams have all but eliminated most runs of native salmon and have further disrupted the lives of remaining Native Americans who depend on the river. Logging of old-growth forests has left ugly scars. Washington's Puget Sound area and Portland's extensive suburbs are groaning under the weight of rapidly growing population centers.

Ongoing controversies in the Southwest include arguments about the locations of nuclear power plants and the transport and disposal of nuclear waste, notably at Yucca Mountain, 90 miles from Las Vegas. A 2013 headline in the *Las Vegas Review-Journal* summed it up by saying 'No end in sight for Yucca legal fights.'

Water distribution and availability continue to be concerns throughout the region. In an arid landscape like the Southwest, many of the region's most important environmental issues revolve around water. Drought has so severely impacted the region that researchers have warned that 110-mile-long Lake Mead has a 50% chance of running dry by 2021, leaving an estimated 12 to 36 million people in cities from Las Vegas to Los Angeles and San Diego in need of water.

Construction of dams and human-made water features throughout the Southwest has radically altered the delicate balance of water that sustained life for countless millennia. Dams, for example, halt the flow of warm waters and force them to drop their rich loads of life-giving nutrients. These sediments once rebuilt floodplains, nourished myriad aquatic and riparian food chains, and sustained the life of ancient endemic fish that now flounder on the edge of extinction. In place of rich annual floods, dams now release cold waters in steady flows that favor the introduced fish and weedy plants that have overtaken the West's rivers.

In August of 2013, there were more than 50 large wildfires burning across Western states, in Arizona, California, Idaho, Montana, Nevada, Oregon, Washington and Wyoming. Evidence indicates that Western fires are occurring more frequently and are more intense than previously. The reasons? Scientists are looking at three factors. The first is global warming, which may be contributing to the extended Western drought. The dry conditions are exacerbated by low snow packs. Another factor may be increased development, leading more people – and potential fire-starters – to the forest. Finally, the long-running forestry practice of fire suppression may have allowed the build-up of more underbrush, which later ignites and fuels the fire.

Salmon-conservation efforts include protecting populations around the entire Pacific Rim from the Russian Far East to northern California. Learn more at www.wildsalmoncenter.org.

Survival Guide

Directory A–Z

Accommodations

Exceptional picks are marked with a ★ icon throughout this book, but every property recommended meets a certain baseline standard for quality within its class. Accommodations are listed in budget order.

Rates

➡ Rates in this book are categorized as **$** (under $100), **$$** ($100 to $200) or **$$$** (over $200). Unless noted, rates do not include taxes, which average more than 10%.

➡ Generally, midweek rates are lower except in hotels geared toward weekday business travelers. These hotels lure leisure travelers with weekend deals.

➡ Rates quoted are for high season: June to August everywhere except the deserts and mountain ski areas, where December through April are busiest.

➡ Demand and prices spike higher around major holidays and for festivals, when some properties may impose multiday minimum stays.

Discounts

➡ Discount cards and auto-club membership may get you 10% or more off standard rates at participating hotels and motels.

➡ Look for freebie ad magazines packed with hotel and motel discount coupons at gas stations, travel centers, highway rest areas and tourist offices.

➡ You might get a better deal by booking through discount-travel websites like **Priceline** (www.priceline.com), **Hotwire** (www.hotwire.com) or **Hotels.com** (www.hotels.com). For last-minute deals in larger cities, try the Hotel Tonight app.

➡ Bargaining may be possible for walk-in guests without reservations, especially during off-peak times.

B&Bs

In the USA, many B&Bs are high-end romantic retreats in restored historic homes that are run by personable, independent innkeepers who serve gourmet breakfasts. These B&Bs often take pains to evoke a theme – Victorian, rustic, Cape Cod – and amenities range from merely comfortable to indulgent. Rates normally top $100, and the best run $200 to $300. Some B&Bs have minimum-stay requirements, some exclude young children and many exclude pets.

European-style B&Bs also exist: these may be rooms in someone's home, with plainer furnishings, simpler breakfasts, shared baths and cheaper rates. These often welcome families.

B&Bs can close out of season and reservations are essential, especially for top-end places. To avoid surprises, always ask about bathrooms (whether shared or private). B&B agencies are sprinkled throughout this guide. Also check listings online:

Bed & Breakfast Inns Online (www.bbonline.com)

BedandBreakfast.com (www.bedandbreakfast.com)

BnB Finder (www.bnbfinder.com)

Camping

Most federally managed public lands and many state parks offer camping. First-come, first-served 'primitive' campsites offer no facilities; overnight fees range from free to under $10. 'Basic' sites usually provide toilets (flush or pit), drinking water, fire pits and picnic tables; they cost $5 to $15 a night, and some or all may be reserved in advance.

BOOK YOUR STAY ONLINE

For more accommodations reviews by Lonely Planet authors, check out http://lonelyplanet.com/hotels/. You'll find independent reviews, as well as recommendations on the best places to stay. Best of all, you can book online.

'Developed' campsites, usually in national or state parks, have nicer facilities and more amenities: showers, barbecue grills, RV sites with hookups etc. These run $12 to $45 a night, and many can be reserved in advance.

Camping on most federal lands – including national parks, national forests, Bureau of Land Management (BLM) and and so on – can be reserved through **Recreation.gov** (☏877-444-6777, international 518-885-3639; www.recreation.gov). Camping is usually limited to 14 days and can be reserved up to six months in advance. For some state-park campgrounds, you can make bookings through **ReserveAmerica** (☏national campgrounds 877-444-6777; www.reserveamerica. com). Both websites let you search for campground locations and amenities, check availability and reserve a site, view maps and get driving directions online.

Private campgrounds tend to cater to RVs and families (tent sites may be few and lack atmosphere). Facilities may include playgrounds, convenience stores, wi-fi access, swimming pools and other activities. Some rent camping cabins, ranging from canvas-sided wooden platforms to log-frame structures with real beds, heating and private baths. **Kampgrounds of America** (KOA; ☏406-248-7444; www.koa. com) is a national network of private campgrounds with a full range of facilities. You can order KoA's free annual directory (shipping fees apply) or browse its comprehensive campground listings and make bookings online.

Dude Ranches

Most visitors to dude ranches today are city-slickers looking for an escape from a fast-paced, high-tech world. These days you can find anything from a working-ranch experience (smelly chores and 5am wake-up calls included) to a Western Club

Med. Typical week-long visits start at over $100 per person per day, including accommodations, meals, activities and equipment.

While the centerpiece of dude-ranch vacations is horseback riding, many ranches feature swimming pools and have expanded their activity lists to include fly-fishing, hiking, mountain biking, tennis, golf, skeet-shooting and cross-country skiing. Accommodations range from rustic log cabins to cushy suites with Jacuzzis and cable TV. Meals range from family-style spaghetti dinners to four-course gourmet feasts.

Arizona Dude Ranch Association (☏520-823-4277; www.azdra.com)

Colorado Dude & Guest Ranch Association (☏866-942-3472; www.coloradoranch. com)

Dude Ranchers' Association (☏866-399-2339, 307-587-2339; www.duderanch.org)

Hostels

In the West, hostels are mainly found in urban areas in the Pacific Northwest, California and the Southwest.

Hostelling International USA (☏240-650-2100; www. hiusa.org) runs more than 50

hostels in the US; 19 of them are in California. Most have gender-segregated dorms, a few private rooms, shared baths and a communal kitchen. Overnight fees for dorm beds range from about $23 to $40. HI-USA members are entitled to small discounts. Reservations are accepted (you can book online) and advised during high season, when there may be a three-night maximum stay.

The USA has many independent hostels not affiliated with HI-USA, particularly in the Southwest. For online listings:

Hostels.com (www.hostels. com)

Hostelworld.com (www. hostelworld.com)

Hostelz.com (www.hostelz. com)

Hotels

Hotels in all categories typically include in-room phones, cable TV, alarm clocks, private baths and a simple continental breakfast. Many midrange properties provide microwaves, hairdryers, internet access, air-conditioning and/or heating, swimming pools and writing desks, while top-end hotels add concierge services, fitness and business centers,

---

WHAT'S THE BLM?

The **Bureau of Land Management** (www.blm.gov) is a Department of Energy agency that oversees more than 245 million surface acres of public land, much of it in the West. It manages its resources for a variety of uses, from energy production to cattle grazing to overseeing recreational opportunities. What does that mean for you? Outdoor fun, as well as both developed camping and dispersed camping. Generally, when it comes to dispersed camping on BLM land, you can camp wherever you want as long as your campsite is at least 900ft from a water source used by wildlife or livestock. You cannot camp in one spot longer than 14 days. Pack out what you pack in and don't leave campfires unattended. Some regions may have more specific rules, so check the state's camping requirements on the BLM website and call the appropriate district office for specifics.

spas, restaurants, bars and higher-end furnishings.

Even if hotels advertise that children 'sleep free,' cots or rollaway beds may cost extra. Always ask about the hotel's policy for telephone calls; all charge an exorbitant amount for long-distance and international calls, but some also charge for dialing local and toll-free numbers.

Lodges

Normally situated within national parks, lodges are often rustic looking but are usually quite comfy inside. Rooms generally start at $100, but can easily be double that in high season. Since they represent the only option if you want to stay inside the park without camping, many are fully booked well in advance. Want a room today? Call anyway – you might be lucky and hit on a cancellation. In addition to on-site restaurants, they also offer touring services.

Motels

Motels – distinguished from hotels by having rooms that open onto a parking lot – tend to cluster around interstate exits and along main routes into town. Some remain smaller, less-expensive 'mom and pop' operations; a light continental breakfast is sometimes included; and amenities might top out at a phone and a TV (maybe with cable). However, motels often have a few rooms with simple kitchenettes.

Although many motels are of the cookie-cutter variety, these can be good for discount lodging or when other options fall through. For deals, pick up free coupon books at visitor centers, rest areas and travel centers. At an independent motel, if the lot isn't full and you're not afraid to move on, try negotiating your rate at the counter.

Don't judge a motel solely on looks. Facades may be faded and tired, but the proprietor may keep rooms spotlessly clean. Of course, the reverse could also be true. Try to see your room before you commit.

Resorts

Luxury resorts really require a stay of several days to be appreciated and are often destinations in themselves. Start the day with a round of golf or a tennis match, then luxuriate with a massage, swimming, sunbathing and drinking. Many are now kid friendly, with extensive children's programs.

Customs Regulations

For a complete and current list of US customs regulations, visit the official portal for **US Customs and Border Protection** (www.cbp.gov).

Duty-free allowance per person is typically as follows:

⇒ 1L of liquor (provided you are at least 21 years old)

⇒ 100 cigars and 200 cigarettes (if you are at least 18)

⇒ $200 worth of gifts and purchases ($800 if a returning US citizen)

⇒ If you arrive with $10,000 in US or foreign currency, it must be declared.

There are heavy penalties for attempting to import illegal drugs. Other forbidden items include drug paraphernalia, firearms, lottery tickets, items with fake brand names, and most goods made in Cuba, Iran, Myanmar (Burma) and most of Sudan. Any fruit, vegetables or other food or plant material must be declared (whereby you'll undergo a time-consuming search) or left in the bins in the arrival area.

Discount Cards

America the Beautiful Interagency Annual Pass (http://store.usgs.gov/pass; $80) Admits four adults and all children under 16 years old for free to all national parks and federal recreational lands (eg USFS, BLM) for one year. It can be purchased online or at any national park entrance station. US citizens and permanent residents 62 years and older are eligible for a lifetime **Senior Pass** ($10), which grants free entry and 50% off some recreational-use fees like camping, as does the lifetime **Access Pass** (free to US citizens or permanent residents with a permanent disability). These passes are available in person or by mail.

American Association of Retired Persons (AARP; ☑888-687-2277; www.aarp.org; annual membership $16) Advocacy group for Americans 50 years and older offers member discounts (usually 10%) on hotels, car rentals and more.

American Automobile Association (AAA; ☑877-428-2277; www.aaa.com; annual membership from $48) Members of AAA and its foreign affiliates (eg CAA, AA) qualify for small discounts (usually 10%) on Amtrak trains, car rentals, motels and hotels, chain restaurants, shopping, tours and theme parks. People over 65 (sometimes 55, 60 or 62) often qualify for the same discounts as students; any ID showing your birth date should suffice as proof of age.

International Student Identity Card (ISIC; www.isic.org; up to $22) Offers savings on airline fares, travel insurance and local attractions for full-time students. For non-students under 26 years of age, an **International Youth Travel Card** (IYTC; $22) grants similar benefits. Cards are issued by student unions, hostelling organizations and travel agencies.

Student Advantage Card (☑877-256-4672; www.studentadvantage.com; $23) For international and US students, offers 15% savings on Amtrak and Greyhound, plus discounts of 10% to 20% on some airlines and chain shops, hotels and motels.

Electricity

AC 110/120V is standard; buy adapters to run most non-US electronics.

120V/60Hz

Embassies & Consulates

International travelers who want to contact their home country's embassy while in the US should visit **Embassy.org** (www.embassy.org), which lists contact information for all foreign embassies in Washington, DC. Most countries have an embassy for the UN in New York City. Some countries have consulates in other large cities; look under 'Consulates' in the yellow pages, or call local directory assistance.

Food

Top choices throughout this book are marked with a ★ icon, and restaurants are listed by price category (budget, midrange, top end). Within each category restaurants are listed in order of author recommendation. In reviews, restaurant prices usually refer to an average main course

at dinner and are categorized as **$** (under $10), **$$** ($10 to $20) or **$$$** (over $20). These prices don't include drinks, appetizers, desserts, taxes or tip. Note the same dishes at lunch will usually be cheaper, maybe even half-price. Many Utah restaurants are closed on Sunday.

Gay & Lesbian Travelers

GLBT travelers will find lots of places where they can be themselves without thinking twice. Beaches and big cities typically are the most gay-friendly destinations.

Hot Spots

You will have heard of San Francisco, the happiest gay city in America, and what can gays and lesbians do in Los Angeles and Las Vegas? Hmmm, just about anything. In fact, when LA or Vegas gets to be too much, flee to the desert resorts of Palm Springs.

Attitudes

Most major US cities have a visible and open GLBT community. In this guide, many cities include a section that describes the city's best GLBT offerings.

The level of acceptance varies across the West. In some places, there is absolutely no tolerance whatsoever, and in others acceptance is predicated on GLBT people not 'flaunting' their sexual preference or identity. In rural areas and extremely conservative enclaves, it's unwise to be openly out, as violence and verbal abuse can sometimes occur. When in doubt, assume locals follow a 'don't ask, don't tell' policy. Same-sex marriage, a hotly debated topic, is now legal in a handful of states.

Resources

Advocate (www.advocate.com) Gay-oriented news website

reports on business, politics, arts, entertainment and travel.

Gay Travel (www.gaytravel.com) Online guides to dozens of US destinations.

GLBT National Help Center (⌨888-843-4564; www.glbtnationalhelpcenter.org; ⊙1-9pm PST Mon-Fri, 9am-2pm PST Sat) A national hotline for counseling, information and referrals.

National Gay & Lesbian Task Force (www.thetaskforce.org) National activist group's website covers news, politics and current issues.

OutTraveler (www.outtraveler.com) Has useful online city guides and travel articles to various US and foreign destinations.

Purple Roofs (www.purpleroofs.com) Lists gay-owned and gay-friendly B&Bs and hotels nationwide.

Health

Healthcare & Insurance

➡ Medical treatment in the USA is of the highest caliber, but the expense could kill you. Many healthcare professionals demand payment at the time of service, especially from out-of-towners or international visitors.

➡ Except for medical emergencies (call ⌨911 or go to the nearest 24-hour hospital emergency room, or ER), phone around to find a doctor who will accept your insurance.

➡ Keep all receipts and documentation for billing and insurance claims and reimbursement purposes.

➡ Some health-insurance policies require you to get pre-authorization for medical treatment before seeking help.

➡ Overseas visitors with travel health-insurance policies may need to contact a call center for an assessment by phone before getting medical treatment.

➤ Carry any medications you may need in their original containers, clearly labeled. Bring a signed, dated letter from your doctor describing all medical conditions and medications (including generic names).

Environmental Hazards

ALTITUDE SICKNESS

➤ Visitors from lower elevations undergo rather dramatic physiological changes as they adapt to high altitudes.

➤ Symptoms, which tend to manifest during the first day after reaching altitude, may include headache, fatigue, loss of appetite, nausea, sleeplessness, increased urination and hyperventilation due to overexertion.

➤ Symptoms normally resolve within 24 to 48 hours.

➤ The rule of thumb is, don't ascend until the symptoms descend.

➤ More severe cases may display extreme disorientation, ataxia (loss of coordination and balance), breathing problems (especially a persistent cough) and vomiting. These folks should descend immediately and get to a hospital.

➤ To avoid the discomfort characterizing the milder symptoms, drink plenty of water and take it easy – at 7000ft, a pleasant walk around Santa Fe can wear you out faster than a steep hike at sea level.

DEHYDRATION, HEAT EXHAUSTION & HEATSTROKE

➤ Take it easy as you acclimatize, especially on hot summer days and in Southern California's deserts.

➤ Drink plenty of water. One gallon per person per day minimum is recommended when you're active outdoors.

➤ Dehydration (lack of water) or salt deficiency can cause heat exhaustion, often characterized by heavy sweating, pale skin, fatigue, lethargy, headaches, nausea, vomiting, dizziness, muscle cramps and rapid, shallow breathing.

➤ Long, continuous exposure to high temperatures can lead to possibly fatal heatstroke. Warning signs include altered mental status, hyperventilation and flushed, hot and dry skin (ie sweating stops).

➤ Hospitalization is essential. Meanwhile, get out of the sun, remove clothing that retains heat (cotton is OK), douse the body with water and fan continuously; ice packs can be applied to the neck, armpits and groin.

HYPOTHERMIA

➤ Skiers and hikers will find that temperatures in the mountains and desert can quickly drop below freezing, especially during winter. Even a sudden spring shower or high winds can lower your body temperature dangerously fast.

➤ Instead of cotton, wear synthetic or woolen clothing that retains warmth even when wet. Carry waterproof layers (eg Gore-Tex jacket, plastic poncho, rain pants) and high-energy, easily digestible snacks like chocolate, nuts and dried fruit.

➤ Symptoms of hypothermia include exhaustion, numbness, shivering, stumbling, slurred speech, dizzy spells, muscle cramps and irrational or even violent behavior.

➤ To treat hypothermia, get out of bad weather and change into dry, warm clothing. Drink hot liquids

(no caffeine or alcohol) and snack on high-calorie food.

➤ In advanced stages, carefully put hypothermia sufferers in a warm sleeping bag cocooned inside a wind- and waterproof outer wrapping. Do not rub victims, who must be handled gently.

Insurance

Getting travel insurance to cover theft, loss and medical problems is highly recommended. Some policies do not cover 'risky' activities such as scuba diving, motorcycling and skiing, so read the fine print. Make sure the policy at least covers hospital stays and an emergency flight home.

Paying for your airline ticket or rental car with a credit card may provide limited travel accident insurance. If you already have private health insurance or a homeowner's or renter's policy, find out what those policies cover and only get supplemental insurance. If you have prepaid a large portion of your vacation, trip cancellation insurance may be a worthwhile expense.

Worldwide travel insurance is available at www. lonelyplanet.com/travel -insurance. You can buy, extend and claim online anytime – even if you're already on the road.

Internet Access

This guide uses an internet icon (@) when a place has a net-connected computer for public use and a wi-fi icon (🛜) when it offers wireless internet access, whether free or fee-based.

➤ Internet cafes listed typically charge $6 to $12 per hour for online access.

➤ With branches in most cities and towns, **FedEx Office** (☑ 800-463-3339; www. fedex.com) offers internet access at self-service computer workstations (30¢ per minute) and sometimes free wi-fi, plus digital-photo printing and CD-burning stations.

➹ Wi-fi hot spots (free or fee-based) can be found at major airports; many hotels, motels and coffee shops (eg Starbucks); and some tourist information centers, RV parks (eg KOA), museums, bars, restaurants (including chains such as McDonalds and Panera Bread) and stores (eg Apple).

➹ Free public wi-fi is increasing and even some state parks are now wi-fi enabled.

➹ Public libraries have internet terminals, but online time may be limited, advance sign-up required and a nominal fee charged for out-of-network visitors. Increasingly libraries offer free wi-fi access.

➹ If you're not from the US, remember that you will need an AC adapter for your laptop, plus a plug adapter for US sockets; both are available at larger electronics shops, such as **Best Buy** (☏888-237-8289; www. bestbuy.com).

Legal Matters

In everyday matters, if you are stopped by the police, remember that there is no system of paying traffic or other fines on the spot. Attempting to pay a fine to an officer is frowned upon at best and may result in a charge of bribery. For traffic offenses, the police officer or highway patroller will explain the options to you. There is usually a 30-day period to pay a fine. Most matters can be handled by mail.

If you are arrested, you have a legal right to an attorney, and you are allowed to remain silent. There is no legal reason to speak to a police officer if you don't wish, but never walk away from an officer until given permission to do so. Anyone who is arrested is legally allowed to

make one phone call. If you can't afford a lawyer, a public defender will be appointed to you free of charge. Foreign visitors who don't have a lawyer, friend or family member to help should call their embassy; the police will provide the number upon request.

As a matter of principle, the US legal system presumes a person innocent until proven guilty. Each state has its own civil and criminal laws, and what is legal in one state may be illegal in others.

Driving
In all states, driving under the influence of alcohol or drugs is a serious offense, subject to fines and even imprisonment.

Drugs
Recreational drugs are prohibited by federal and most state laws. Washington and Colorado voters recently voted to allow recreational marijuana use, but the regulatory framework is still being determined. It is still illegal to smoke in public in either state. Some states, such as California and Alaska, treat possession of small quantities of marijuana as a misdemeanor, though it is still punishable with fines and/or imprisonment. The federal government recently indicated it won't challenge state laws that have legalized marijuana, but pot use still remains illegal under the federal Controlled Substances Act.

Possession of any illicit drug, including cocaine, ecstasy, LSD, heroin, hashish or more than an ounce of pot, is a felony potentially punishable by lengthy jail sentences. For foreigners, conviction of any drug offense is grounds for deportation.

Money
ATMs
➹ ATMs are available at most banks, shopping malls, airports and grocery and convenience stores.

➹ Expect a minimum surcharge of $2 to $3 per transaction, in addition to any fees charged by your home bank. Some ATMs in Las Vegas may charge $5 to withdraw cash.

➹ Most ATMs are connected to international networks and offer decent foreign-exchange rates.

➹ Withdrawing cash from an ATM using a credit card usually incurs a hefty fee and high interest rates; check with your credit-card company for a PIN number.

Cash
Most people don't carry large amounts of cash, relying instead on credit cards, debit cards and ATMs. Some businesses refuse to accept bills over $20.

Credit Cards
Major credit cards are almost universally accepted. In fact, it's almost impossible to rent a car, book a room or buy tickets over the phone without one. A credit card may also be vital in emergencies. Visa, MasterCard and American Express are the most widely accepted.

Moneychangers
➹ You can exchange money at major airports, some banks and all currency-exchange offices such as **American Express** (☏800-528-4800; www. americanexpress.com) or **Travelex** (☏877-414-6359; www.travelex.com). Always inquire about rates and fees.

➹ Outside big cities, exchanging money may be a problem, so make sure you have a credit card and sufficient cash on hand.

Taxes
➹ Sales tax varies by state and county, with state sales taxes ranging from zero in Montana to 7.5% in California

➹ Hotel taxes vary by city.

Tipping

Tipping is *not* optional. Only withhold tips in cases of outrageously bad service.

Airport skycaps & hotel bellhops $2 per bag, minimum $5 per cart

Bartenders 10% to 15% per round, minimum $1 per drink

Concierges Nothing for simple information, up to $20 for securing last-minute restaurant reservations, sold-out show tickets etc

Housekeeping staff $2 to $4 daily, left under the card provided; more if you're messy

Parking valets At least $2 when handed back your car keys

Restaurant staff & room service 15% to 20%, unless a gratuity is already charged

Taxi drivers 10% to 15% of metered fare, rounded up to the next dollar

Traveler's Checks

Traveler's checks have pretty much fallen out of use. Larger restaurants, hotels and department stores will often accept traveler's checks (in US dollars only), but small businesses, markets and fast-food chains may refuse them. Visa and American Express are the most widely accepted issuers of traveler's checks.

National & State Parks

Before visiting any national park check out its website, using the navigation search tool on the NPS home page (www.nps.gov). On the Grand Canyon's website (www.nps.gov/grca), you can download the seasonal newspaper, *The Guide*, for the latest information on prices, hours and ranger talks. There is a separate edition for both the North and South Rims.

At the entrance of a national or state park, be ready to hand over cash (credit cards may not always be accepted). Costs range from nothing at all to $25 per vehicle for a seven-day pass. If you're visiting several parks in the Southwest, you may save money by purchasing the America the Beautiful annual pass ($80).

Due to ongoing fiscal woes, many state governments across the West have slashed their budgets for state parks. Parks in Arizona, California and Utah have been particularly hard hit. In Arizona some state parks have begun operating on a five-day schedule, closed Tuesdays and Wednesdays. Before visiting a state park, check its website to confirm current status.

Opening Hours

The following times are an indication of business hours; exact hours are listed in reviews:

Banks	8:30am-4:30pm Mon-Thu, to 5:30pm Fri (and possibly 9am-noon Sat)
Bars	5pm-midnight Sun-Thu, to 2am Fri & Sat
Nightclubs	10pm-2am Thu-Sat
Post offices	9am-5pm Mon-Fri
Shopping malls	9am-9pm
Stores	10am-6pm Mon-Sat, noon-5pm Sun
Super-markets	8am-8pm, some open 24hr

Photography & Video

Print film can be found at specialty camera shops. Digital camera memory cards are widely available at chain retailers such as Best Buy and Target.

Some Native American tribal lands prohibit photography and video completely; when it's allowed, you may be required to purchase a permit. Always ask permission if you want to photograph someone close up; anyone who then agrees to be photographed may expect a small tip.

For more advice on picture-taking, consult Lonely Planet's *Guide to Travel Photography*.

Post

For 24-hour postal information, including post office locations and hours, contact the **US Postal Service** (USPS; ☎800-275-8777; www.usps.com), which is reliable and inexpensive.

For sending urgent or important letters and packages either domestically or overseas, **Federal Express** (FedEx; ☎800-463-3339; www.fedex.com) and **United Parcel Service** (UPS; ☎800-742-5877; www.ups.com) offer more expensive door-to-door delivery services.

Postal Rates

At the time of writing, the postal rates for 1st-class mail within the USA were 46¢ for letters weighing up to 1oz (20¢ for each additional ounce) and 33¢ for postcards. In 2013 the US Post Office introduced the $1.10 Global Forever stamp, which is good for any 1oz letter going anywhere in the world.

Sending & Receiving Mail

If you have the correct postage, you can drop mail weighing less than 13oz into any blue mailbox. To send a package weighing 13oz or more, go to a post office.

Mail can usually be sent to you c/o General Delivery at any post office that has its own zip code. Mail can usually be held up to 30 days before it's returned to sender; you might ask the sender to write 'Hold for Arrival' on the envelope.

Public Holidays

On the following national public holidays, banks, schools and government offices (including post offices) are closed, and transportation, museums and other services operate on a Sunday schedule. Holidays falling on a weekend are usually observed the following Monday.

New Year's Day January 1

Martin Luther King Jr Day Third Monday in January

Presidents' Day Third Monday in February

Memorial Day Last Monday in May

Independence Day July 4

Labor Day First Monday in September

Columbus Day Second Monday in October

Veterans Day November 11

Thanksgiving Fourth Thursday in November

Christmas Day December 25

During spring break (March and April), high school and college students get a week off from school. For students of all ages, summer vacation runs from June to August.

Telephone
Cell Phones

➧ You'll need a multiband GSM phone in order to make calls in the US. Popping in a US prepaid rechargeable SIM card is usually cheaper than using your network.

➧ SIM cards are sold at telecommunications and electronics stores. These stores also sell inexpensive prepaid phones, including some airtime.

➧ If you don't have a compatible phone, you can buy an inexpensive, no-contract (prepaid) phone with a local number and a set number of minutes that can be topped up at will. Electronics stores such as Radio Shack and Best Buy sell these phones.

Dialing Codes

➧ US phone numbers consist of a three-letter area code followed by a seven-digit local number.

➧ When dialing a number within the same area code, use the seven-digit number; however, some places now require you to dial the entire 10-digit number even for a local call.

➧ If you are calling long distance, dial ☑1 plus the area code plus the phone number.

➧ Toll-free numbers begin with 800, 866, 877 or 888 and must be preceded by 1.

➧ For direct international calls, dial ☑011 plus the country code plus the area code (usually without the initial '0') plus the local phone number.

➧ For international call assistance, dial ☑00.

➧ If you're calling from abroad, the country code for the US is 1 (the same as Canada, but international rates apply between the two countries).

Payphones & Phonecards

➧ Where payphones still exist, they are usually coin-operated, although some may only accept credit cards (eg in national parks).

➧ Local calls usually cost 35¢ to 50¢ minimum.

➧ For long-distance calls, you're usually better off buying a prepaid phonecard, sold at convenience stores, supermarkets, newsstands and electronics stores.

TIPS FOR SHUTTERBUGS

➧ If you have a digital camera, bring extra batteries and a charger.

➧ For print film, use 100 ASA film for all but the lowest light situations; it's the slowest film, and will enhance resolution.

➧ A zoom lens is extremely useful; most SLR cameras have one. Use it to isolate the central subject of your photos. A common composition mistake is to include too much landscape around the person or feature that's your main focus.

➧ Morning and evening are the best times to shoot. The same sandstone bluff can turn four or five different hues throughout the day, and the warmest hues will be at sunset. Underexposing the shot slightly (by a half-stop or more) can bring out richer details in red tones.

➧ When shooting red rocks, a warming filter added to an SLR lens can enhance the colors of the rocks and reduce the blues of overcast or flat-light days. Achieve the same effect on any digital camera by adjusting the white balance to the automatic 'cloudy' setting (or by reducing the color temperature).

➧ Don't shoot into the sun or include it in the frame; shoot what the sunlight is hitting. On bright days, move your subjects into shade for close-up portraits.

Time

➡ The US date system is written as month/day/year. Thus, the 8th of June, 2008, becomes 6/8/08.

➡ Daylight Saving Time pushes the clocks ahead an hour. It runs from the second Sunday in March to the first Sunday in November.

➡ Arizona does not observe daylight-saving time; during that period it's one hour behind other Southwestern states. The Navajo Reservation, which lies in Arizona, New Mexico and Utah, does use daylight-saving time. The Hopi Reservation, which is surrounded by the Navajo Reservation in Arizona, follows the rest of Arizona.

Tourist Information

State tourism offices are listed in the Information section at the start of each regional chapter, while city and county visitor information centers are listed throughout.

Any tourist office worth contacting has a website, where you can download free travel e-guides. They also field phone calls; some local offices maintain daily lists of hotel room availability, but few offer reservation services. All tourist offices have self-service racks of brochures and discount coupons; some also sell maps and books.

State-run 'welcome centers,' usually placed along interstate highways, tend to have materials that cover wider territories, and offices are usually open longer hours, including weekends and holidays.

Many cities have an official convention and visitor bureau (CVB); these sometimes double as tourist bureaus, but since their main focus is drawing the business trade, CVBs can be less useful for independent travelers.

Keep in mind that, in smaller towns, when the local chamber of commerce runs the tourist bureau, their lists of hotels, restaurants and services usually mention only chamber members; the town's cheapest options may be missing.

Similarly, in prime tourist destinations, some private 'tourist bureaus' are really agents who book hotel rooms and tours on commission. They may offer excellent service and deals, but you'll get what they're selling and nothing else.

PRACTICALITIES

Newspapers & Magazines

➡ National newspapers: *New York Times*, *Wall Street Journal*, *USA Today*

➡ Western newspapers: *Arizona Republic*, *Denver Post*, *Seattle Times*, *Los Angeles Times*, *San Francisco Chronicle*

➡ Mainstream news magazines: *Time*, *US News*, *World Report*

Radio & TV

➡ Radio news: National Public Radio (NPR), lower end of FM dial

➡ Broadcast TV: ABC, CBS, NBC, FOX, PBS (public broadcasting)

➡ Major cable channels: CNN (news), ESPN (sports), HBO (movies), Weather Channel

Video Systems

➡ NTSC standard (incompatible with PAL or SECAM)

➡ DVDs coded for Region 1 (US and Canada only)

Weights & Measures

➡ Weight: ounces (oz), pounds (lb), tons

➡ Liquid: ounces (oz), pints, quarts, gallons

➡ Distance: feet (ft), yards (yd), miles (mi)

Travelers with Disabilities

If you have a physical disability, the USA can be an accommodating place. The Americans with Disabilities Act (ADA) requires that all public buildings, private buildings built after 1993 (including hotels, restaurants, theaters and museums) and public transit be wheelchair accessible. However, call ahead to confirm what is available. Some local tourist offices publish detailed accessibility guides.

Telephone companies offer relay operators, available via teletypewriter (TTY) numbers, for the hearing impaired. Most banks provide ATM instructions in Braille, and via earphone jacks for hearing-impaired customers. All major airlines, Greyhound buses and Amtrak trains will assist travelers with disabilities; just describe your needs when making reservations at least 48 hours in advance. Service animals (guide dogs) are allowed to accompany passengers, but bring documentation.

Some car-rental agencies – such as Budget and Hertz – offer hand-controlled vehicles and vans with wheelchair lifts at no extra charge, but you must reserve them well in advance. **Wheelchair Getaways** (☑800-642-2042; www.wheelchairgetaways. com) rents accessible vans throughout the USA. In many cities and towns, public buses are accessible to wheelchair riders; just let the driver know that you need the lift or ramp.

Many national and some state parks and recreation areas have wheelchair-accessible, paved, graded dirt or boardwalk trails. The website for the **Rails-to-Trails Conservancy** (www.traillink.com) lists wheelchair-accessible hikes by state.

US citizens and permanent residents with permanent disabilities are entitled to a free 'America the Beautiful' Access Pass, which gives free entry to all federal recreation lands (eg national parks).

Some helpful resources for travelers with disabilities:

Access-Able Travel Source (www.access-able. com) General travel website with useful tips and links.

Access Northern California (www.accessnca.com) Extensive links to accessible-travel resources, publications, tours and transportation.

Access San Francisco (www.sanfrancisco.travel/ accessibility/San-Francisco-Access-Guide.html) Free downloadable accessible travel info (somewhat dated, but still useful).

Accessing Arizona (www.accessingarizona.com) Up-to-date information about wheelchair-accessible activities in Arizona.

Disabled Sports USA (☑301-217-0960; www.disabledsportsusa.org) Offers sports and recreation programs for those with disabilities and publishes *Challenge* magazine.

Flying Wheels Travel (☑877-451-5006, 507-451-5005; www.flyingwheelstravel. com) A full-service travel agency, highly recommended for those with mobility issues or chronic illness.

Mobility International USA (☑541-343-1284; www. miusa.org) Advises on mobility issues, but primarily runs an educational exchange program.

Moss Rehabilitation Hospital (☑215-663-6000; www. mossresourcenet.org/travel. htm) Extensive links and tips for accessible travel.

Society for Accessible Travel & Hospitality (SATH; ☑212-447-7284; www.sath.org) Advocacy group provides general information for travelers with disabilities.

Splore (☑801-484-4128; www.splore.org) Offers accessible outdoor adventure trips in Utah.

Visas

Warning: all of the following information is highly subject to change. US entry requirements keep evolving as national security regulations change. All travelers should double-check current visa and passport regulations *before* coming to the USA.

The **US State Department** (☑visa questions 202-663-1225, main switchboard 202-647-4000; www.travel. state.gov) maintains the most comprehensive visa information, providing downloadable forms, lists of US consulates abroad and even visa wait times calculated by country. For more information on entering the USA, see p461.

Visa Applications

Apart from most Canadian citizens and those entering under the Visa Waiver Program, all foreign visitors will need to obtain a visa from a US consulate or embassy abroad. Most applicants must schedule a personal interview, to which you must bring all your documentation

and proof of fee payment. Wait times for interviews vary, but afterward, barring problems, visa issuance takes from a few days to a few weeks.

Your passport must be valid for at least six months after the end of your intended stay in the USA. You'll need a recent photo (2in by 2in), and you must pay a nonrefundable $160 processing fee, plus in a few cases an additional visa issuance reciprocity fee. You'll also need to fill out the online DS-160 nonimmigrant visa electronic application.

Visa applicants are required to show documents of financial stability (or evidence that a US resident will provide financial support), a round-trip or onward ticket and 'binding obligations' that will ensure their return home, such as family ties, a home or a job. Because of these requirements, those planning to travel through other countries before arriving in the USA are generally better off applying for a US visa while they are still in their home country, rather than while on the road.

VISA WAIVER PROGRAM

Currently under the Visa Waiver Program (VWP), citizens of the following countries may enter the USA without a visa for stays of 90 days or fewer: Andorra, Australia, Austria, Belgium, Brunei, Czech Republic, Denmark, Estonia, Finland, France, Germany, Greece, Hungary, Iceland, Ireland, Italy, Japan, Latvia, Liechtenstein, Lithuania, Luxembourg, Malta, Monaco, the Netherlands, New Zealand, Norway, Portugal, San Marino, Singapore, Slovakia, Slovenia, South Korea, Spain, Sweden, Switzerland, Taiwan and the UK.

If you are a citizen of a VWP country, you do not need a visa *only if* you have a passport that meets current US standards *and* you have gotten approval from the

Electronic System for Travel Authorization (ESTA) in advance. Register online with the Department of Homeland Security at https://esta.cbp.dhs.gov at least 72 hours before arrival; once travel authorization is approved, your registration is valid for two years. The fee, payable online, is $14.

Visitors from VWP countries must still produce at the port of entry all the same evidence as for a nonimmigrant visa application. They must demonstrate that their trip is for 90 days or fewer, and that they have a round-trip or onward ticket, adequate funds to cover the trip and binding obligations abroad.

Entering the USA

As of April 2013, the arrival/departure record form (form I-94), that was once required of all visitors, is no longer used. The information is now typically gathered electronically from travel records for those who arrive by air or sea. The paper form is still used at land borders (www.cbp.gov). You will be asked to fill out the US customs declaration, which is usually handed out on the plane. Complete it before you approach the immigration desk. For the question 'US Street Address' give the address where you will spend the first night (a hotel address is fine).

No matter what your visa says, US immigration officers have an absolute authority to refuse admission to the USA or to impose conditions on admission. They will ask about your plans and whether you have sufficient funds; it's a good idea to list an itinerary, produce an onward or round-trip ticket and have at least one major credit card. Don't make too much of having friends, relatives or business contacts in the USA; the immigration official may decide that this will make you more likely to overstay. It also helps to be neatly dressed and polite.

The Department of Homeland Security's registration program, formerly called **US-VISIT** (www.dhs.gov/us-visit), is now the Office of Biometric Identity Management (OBIM). At US visa-issuing posts, biometric information is collected and checked against a watch list. This information is checked upon entry into the US (www.dhs.gov/us-visit-traveler-information). For most visitors (excluding, for now, most Canadian and some Mexican citizens) fingerprints are taken; the process takes less than a minute.

Short-Term Departures & Reentry

→ It's temptingly easy to make trips across the border to Canada or Mexico, but upon return to the USA, non-Americans will be subject to the full immigration procedure.

→ Always take your passport when you cross the border.

→ If your immigration card still has plenty of time on it, you will probably be able to reenter using the same one, but if it has nearly expired, you will have to apply for a new card, and border control may want to see your onward air ticket, sufficient funds etc.

→ Citizens of most Western countries will not need a visa to visit Canada, so it's really not a problem at all to pass through on the way to Alaska.

→ Travelers entering the USA by bus from Canada may be closely scrutinized. A round-trip ticket that takes you back to Canada will most likely make US immigration feel less suspicious.

→ Mexico has a visa-free zone along most of its border with the USA, including the Baja Peninsula and most of the border towns, such as Tijuana and Ciudad Juárez. You'll need a Mexican visa or tourist card if you want to go beyond the border zone.

Women Travelers

→ Women traveling alone or in groups should not expect to encounter any particular problems in the USA. In terms of safety issues, single women need to practice common sense.

→ When first meeting someone, don't advertise where you are staying, or even that you are traveling alone. Americans can be eager to help and even take in solo travelers. However, don't take all offers of help at face value. If someone who seems trustworthy invites you to his or her home, let someone (eg hostel or hotel manager) know where you're going. This advice also applies if you go for a hike by yourself. If something happens and you don't return as expected, you want to know that someone will notice and know where to begin looking for you.

→ Some women carry a whistle, mace or cayenne-pepper spray in case of assault. If you purchase a spray, contact a police station to find out about local regulations. Laws regarding sprays vary from state to state; federal law prohibits them being carried on planes.

→ If you are assaulted, consider calling a rape-crisis hotline before calling the police, unless you are in immediate danger, in which case you should call 911. Be aware that not all police have much sensitivity training or experience assisting sexual assault survivors, whereas rape-crisis-center staff will tirelessly advocate on your behalf and act as a link to other community services, including hospitals and the police. Telephone books have listings of local rape-crisis centers, or contact the 24-hour **National Sexual Assault Hotline** (☎800-656-4673; www.rainn.org). Alternatively, go straight to a hospital emergency room.

Transportation

GETTING THERE & AWAY

Flights and tours can be booked online at www.lonely-planet.com/bookings.

Entering the USA

If you are flying into the US, the first airport where you land is where you must go through immigration and customs, even if you are continuing on the flight to another destination. Fingerprints are taken and biometric information is checked upon entry into the US (www.dhs.gov/us-visit-traveler-information). See p459 for more information on visa requirements and entering the USA.

Passports

➡ Under the Western Hemisphere Travel Initiative (WHTI), all travelers must have a valid machine-readable passport (MRP) when entering the USA by air, land or sea.

➡ The only exceptions are for most US citizens and some Canadian and Mexican citizens traveling by land or sea who can present other WHTI-compliant documents (eg pre-approved 'trusted traveler' cards). For details, check www.getyouhome.gov.

➡ All foreign passports must meet current US standards and be valid for at least six months longer than your intended stay.

➡ MRP passports issued or renewed after October 26, 2006 must be e-passports (ie have a digital photo and integrated chip with biometric data). If your passport was issued before October 26, 2005, it must be 'machine readable' (with two lines of letters, numbers and <<< at the bottom); if it was issued between October 26, 2005, and October 25, 2006, it must be machine readable and also must include a digital photo.

➡ For more information, consult www.cbp.gov/travel.

Air

Airports

The western USA's primary international airports:

Los Angeles International Airport (LAX; ☏310-646-5252; www.lawa.org/lax; 1 World Way; ☏) California's largest and busiest airport, located 20 miles southwest of downtown LA, near the coast.

San Francisco International Airport (SFO; www.flysfo.com) Northern California's major hub, 14 miles south of downtown, on San Francisco Bay.

Seattle-Tacoma International (SEA; www.portseattle.org/Sea-Tac) Known locally as 'Sea-Tac.'

CLIMATE CHANGE & TRAVEL

Every form of transport that relies on carbon-based fuel generates CO_2, the main cause of human-induced climate change. Modern travel is dependent on airplanes, which might use less fuel per kilometer per person than most cars but travel much greater distances. The altitude at which aircraft emit gases (including CO_2) and particles also contributes to their climate change impact. Many websites offer 'carbon calculators' that allow people to estimate the carbon emissions generated by their journey and, for those who wish to do so, to offset the impact of the greenhouse gases emitted with contributions to portfolios of climate-friendly initiatives throughout the world. Lonely Planet offsets the carbon footprint of all staff and author travel.

Major regional airports with limited international service (most have wi-fi access – check the website):

Albuquerque International Sunport (☑505-244-7700; www.cabq.gov/airport; 2200 Sunport Blvd SE) Serving Albuquerque and all of New Mexico.

Denver International Airport (DEN; ☑303-342-2000; www.flydenver.com; 🛜) Serving southern Colorado; if you rent a car in Denver, you can be in northeastern New Mexico in four hours.

LA/Ontario International Airport (ONT; www.lawa.org/welcomont.aspx) In Riverside County, east of LA.

McCarran International Airport (LAS; ☑702-261-5211; www.mccarran.com; 5757 Wayne Newton Blvd; 🛜) Serves Las Vegas, NV, and southern Utah. Las Vegas is 290 miles from the South Rim of Grand Canyon National Park and 277 miles from the North Rim.

Mineta San José International Airport (SJC; ☑408-501-0979; www.sjc.org) In San Francisco's South Bay.

Oakland International Airport (OAK; ☑510-563-3300; www.oaklandairport.com) In San Francisco's East Bay.

Palm Springs International Airport (PSP; ☑760-323-8299; www.palmspringsairport.com; 3400 E Tahquitz Canyon Way) In the desert, east of LA.

Portland International Airport (PDX; ☑503-460-4234; www.flypdx.com; 7000 NE Airport Way) About 12 miles from downtown Portland, OR.

Salt Lake City International Airport (SLC; www.slcairport.com; 776 N Terminal Dr) Serving Salt Lake City and northern Utah; a good choice if you're headed to the North Rim and the Arizona Strip.

San Diego International Airport (SAN; ☑619-400-2404; www.san.org; 3325 N Harbor Dr) Four miles northwest of downtown.

Sky Harbor International Airport (☑602-273-3300; http://skyharbor.com; 3400 E Sky Harbor Blvd; 🛜) Serving Phoenix and the Grand Canyon, it's one of the 10 busiest airports in the country. Phoenix is 220 miles from the South Rim of Grand Canyon National Park and 335 miles from the North Rim.

Tucson International Airport (☑520-573-8100; www.flytucson.com; 7250 S Tucson Blvd) Serving Tucson and southern Arizona.

Vancouver International Airport (YVR; www.yvr.ca) Located 6 miles south of Vancouver, on Sea Island; between Vancouver and the municipality of Richmond.

Security

➡ To get through airport security checkpoints (30-minute wait times are standard), you'll need a boarding pass and photo ID.

➡ Some travelers may be required to undergo a secondary screening, involving hand pat-downs and carry-on luggage searches.

➡ Airport security measures restrict many common items (eg pocket knives) from being carried on planes. Check current restrictions with the **Transportation Security Administration** (TSA; ☑866-289-9673; www.tsa.gov).

➡ Currently, TSA requires that all carry-on liquids and gels be stored in 3.4oz or smaller bottles placed inside a quart-sized clear plastic zip-top bag. Exceptions, which must be declared to checkpoint security officers, include medications.

➡ All checked luggage is screened for explosives. TSA may open your suitcase for visual confirmation, breaking the lock if necessary. Leave your bags unlocked or use a TSA-approved lock like **Travel Sentry** (www.travelsentry.org).

Land

Border Crossings

➡ It is relatively easy crossing from the USA into Canada or Mexico; it's crossing back into the USA that can pose problems if you haven't brought your required documents. Check the ever-changing passport and visa requirements with the **US Department of State** (☑1888 407 4747; http://travel.state.gov) beforehand. **US Customs and Border Protection** (www.cbp.gov) tracks current wait times at every Mexico border crossing.

➡ Some borders are open 24 hours, but most are not.

➡ Have your papers in order, be polite and don't make jokes or casual conversation with US border officials.

➡ At research time, drug cartel violence and crime were serious dangers along the US–Mexico border. See the box, opposite, for more information.

Bus

➡ US-based **Greyhound** (☑800-231-2222, international customer service 214-849-8100; www.greyhound.com) and **Greyhound Mexico** (☑01-800-010-0600; www.greyhound.com.mx) have cooperative service, with direct buses between main towns in Mexico and the US.

➡ Northbound buses from Mexico can take some time to cross the US border, as US immigration may insist on checking every person on board.

➡ **Greyhound Canada** (☑800-661-8747; www.greyhound.ca) routes between Canada and the US may require transferring buses at the border.

Car & Motorcycle

➡ If you're driving into the USA from Canada or

Mexico, bring your vehicle's registration papers, liability insurance and driver's license; an international driving permit (IDP) is a good supplement, but not required.

➡ If you're renting a car or motorcycle, ask if the agency allows its vehicles to be taken across the Mexican or Canadian border; chances are it doesn't.

To/from Canada

➡ Canadian auto insurance is typically valid in the USA, and vice versa.

➡ If your papers are in order, taking your own car across the US–Canada border is usually quick and easy.

➡ On weekends and holidays, especially in summer, border-crossing traffic can be heavy and waits long.

➡ Occasionally the authorities of either country decide to search a car *thoroughly*. Remain calm and be polite.

To/from Mexico

➡ Very few car-rental companies will let you take a car from the US into Mexico.

➡ Unless you're planning an extended stay in Tijuana, taking a car across the Mexican border is more trouble than it's worth. Instead take the trolley from San Diego or leave your car on the US side and walk across.

➡ US auto insurance is not valid in Mexico, so even a short trip into Mexico's border region requires you to buy Mexican car insurance, available for around $25 per day at most border crossings, as well as from

AAA (☎800-874-7532; www. aaa.com).

➡ For a longer driving trip into Mexico beyond the border zone or Baja California, you'll need a Mexican *permiso de importación temporal de vehículos* (temporary vehicle import permit).

➡ Expect long border-crossing waits, as security has tightened in recent years.

➡ See Lonely Planet's *Mexico* guide for further details, or call Mexico's **tourist information number** (☎800-446-3942) in the USA.

Train

➡ **Amtrak** (☎800-872-7245; www.amtrakcascades.com) operates the daily *Cascades* rail service with thruway bus service between Vancouver, BC, in Canada and Seattle, WA.

➡ **VIA Rail** (☎888-842-7245; www.viarail.ca) also serves Vancouver, BC, with routes running north and east across Canada.

➡ US/Canadian customs and immigration inspections happen at the border, not upon boarding.

➡ From Seattle, Amtrak's *Coast Starlight* connects south to numerous destinations in California en route to LA.

➡ Currently, no train service connects Arizona or California with Mexico.

GETTING AROUND

Air

The domestic air system is extensive and reliable, with dozens of competing airlines, hundreds of airports and thousands of flights daily. Flying is usually more expensive than traveling by bus, train or car, but it's the best option if you're in a hurry.

CROSSING THE MEXICAN BORDER

The issue of crime-related violence in Mexico has been front and center in the international press in recent years. Nogales, Arizona, for example, is safe for travelers, but Nogales, Mexico is a major locus for the drug trade and its associated violence. Travelers should also exercise extreme caution in Tijuana. We cannot safely recommend crossing the border for an extended period until the security situation changes. You're fine for day trips, but anything past that may be risky.

The State Department recommends that travelers visit its **website** (http://travel.state.gov/travel/cis_pa_tw/cis/cis_970.html) before traveling to Mexico. Here you can check for travel updates and warnings and confirm the latest border-crossing requirements. Before leaving, US Citizens can sign up for the **Smart Traveler Enrollment Program** (STEP; http://step.state.gov/step/) to receive email updates.

US citizens returning from Mexico must present a US passport or passport card and enhanced driver's license or a trusted traveler card (either NEXUS, SENTRI, FAST or Global entry cards). US and Canadian children under age 16 can also enter using their birth certificate, a Consular Report of Birth Abroad, Naturalization Certificate or Canadian Citizenship Card. All other nationals must carry their passport and, if needed, visas for entering Mexico and reentering the US. Regulations change frequently, so get the latest scoop at www.cbp.gov.

TRAVELING TO ALASKA & HAWAII

Alaska

At the northwest tip of North America lies the USA's 49th state, Alaska. It's the biggest state by far, and home to stupendous mountains, massive glaciers and amazing wildlife. Mt McKinley (the continent's highest peak) is here, as are huge numbers of humpback whales and bald eagles. See Lonely Planet's *Alaska* guide for details.

The majority of visitors to Alaska fly into **Ted Stevens Anchorage International Airport** (ANC; www.dot.state.ak.us/anc; ☎). **Alaska Airlines** (☑800-252-7522; www.alaskaair. com) has direct flights to Anchorage from Seattle, Chicago, Las Vegas and Los Angeles. It also flies between many towns within Alaska, including daily north-/southbound flights year-round through southeast Alaska, with stops at all main towns including Ketchikan and Juneau. **Delta** (☑800-221-1212; www.delta.com) offers direct flights from Minneapolis while **US Airways** (☑800-428-4322; www.usairways.com) and **United** (www.united.com) fly nonstop from Phoenix. **JetBlue** (www.jetblue.com) offers nonstop flights from Seattle. There are also nonstop flights from Seattle to Juneau.

By ferry it takes almost a week on the **Alaska Marine Highway** (AMHS; ☑800-642-0066; www.dot.state.ak.us/amhs/pubs/), which connects Bellingham, WA, with more than 12 towns in southeast Alaska. The complete trip (Bellingham to Haines; $353 one way, 2½ to three days) stops at ports along the way and should be reserved in advance. Alaska Marine Highway ferries are equipped to handle cars ($462 one way), but space must be reserved months ahead.

The Alaska–Canada Military Hwy is today the Alcan (the Alaska Hwy). This 1390-mile road starts at Dawson Creek in British Columbia and ends at Delta Junction (northeast

Airlines in the Western USA

Overall, air travel in the USA is very safe (much safer than driving on the nation's highways); for comprehensive details by carrier, check out **Airsafe.com** (www.airsafe. com).

The main domestic carriers in the West:

Alaska Airlines (☑800-252-7522; www.alaskaair.com) Serves Alaska and the western US, with flights to the East Coast and Hawaii.

American Airlines (☑800-433-7300; www.aa.com) Nationwide service.

Delta Air Lines (☑800-221-1212; www.delta.com) Nationwide service.

Frontier Airlines (☑800-432-1359; www.flyfrontier.com) Denver-based airline with nationwide service, including to Alaska.

Hawaiian Airlines (☑800-367-5320; www.hawaiianair.com) Serves the Hawaiian islands and the West Coast, plus Las Vegas and Phoenix.

JetBlue Airways (☑800-538-2583; www.jetblue.com) Nonstop connections between eastern and western US cities, plus Florida, New Orleans and Texas.

Southwest Airlines (☑800-435-9792; www.southwest.com) Service across continental USA.

Spirit Airlines (☑801-401-2200; www.spiritair.com) Florida-based airline; serves many US gateway cities.

United Airlines (☑800-864-8331; www.united.com) Nationwide service.

US Airways (☑800-428-4322; www.usairways.com) Nationwide service.

Virgin America (☑877-359-8474; www.virginamerica.com) Flights between East and West Coast cities and Las Vegas.

Bicycle

Regional bicycle touring is popular. It means coasting over winding back roads (because bicycles are often not permitted on freeways), and calculating progress in miles per day, not miles per hour. Cyclists must follow the same rules of the road as automobiles, but don't expect drivers to respect your right of way. Wearing a helmet is mandatory for riders under 18 years of age in California and many western cities.

Some helpful resources for cyclists:

Adventure Cycling Association (www.adventure-cycling.org) Excellent online resource for purchasing bicycle-friendly maps and long-distance route guides.

Better World Club (☑866-238-1137; www.betterworldclub.com) Annual membership ($40, plus $12 enrolment fee) entitles you to two 24-hour emergency roadside pickups with transportation to the nearest bike-repair shop within a 30-mile radius.

Rental & Purchase

➡ You can rent bikes by the hour, the day or the week in most cities and major towns.

➡ Rentals start from around $20 per day for beach

of Anchorage); in between it winds through the vast wilderness of northwest Canada and Alaska. The driving distance between Seattle and Anchorage is about 2250 miles.

Hawaii

Floating all by itself more than 2500 miles off the California coast, Hawaii enjoys a unique sense of self, separate from the US mainland. On its islands you can hike across ancient lava flows, learn to surf and paddleboard, snorkel with green turtles or kayak to your own deserted island. The primary islands are O'ahu; Hawai'i, the Big Island; Maui; Lana'i; Moloka'i and Kaua'i. No matter the adventure or the island, encounters with nature are infused with the Hawaiian sensibilities of *aloha 'aina* and *malama 'aina* – love and care for the land. See Lonely Planet's *Hawaii* guide for details.

About 99% of visitors to Hawaii arrive by air, and the majority of flights – both international and domestic – arrive at **Honolulu International Airport** (HNL; ☎808-836-6411; http://hawaii.gov/hnl; 300 Rodgers Blvd) on O'ahu. In Maui, the **Kahului Airport** (OGG; ☎808-872-3830; www.hawaii.gov/ogg; 1 Kahului Airport Rd) is about 25 minutes from Kihei and 45 minutes from Lahaina.

Most cruises to Hawaii include stopovers in Honolulu and on Maui, Kaua'i and the Big Island. Cruises usually last two weeks, with fares starting at around $100 per person per day. Popular cruise lines include **Holland America** (☎877-932-4259; www.hollandamerica.com), **Princess** (☎800-774-6237; www.princess.com) and **Royal Caribbean** (☎866-562-7625; www.royalcaribbean.com).

---

cruisers, and up to $40 or more for basic mountain bikes; ask about multiday and weekly discounts.

➡ Most rental companies require a credit-card security deposit of several hundred dollars.

➡ Buy new models from specialty bike shops, sporting-goods stores and discount-warehouse stores, or used bicycles from notice boards at hostels, cafes and universities.

➡ To buy or sell used bikes, check online bulletin boards like **Craigslist** (www.craigslist.org).

Transporting Bicycles

➡ If you tire of pedaling, some local buses and trains are equipped with bicycle racks.

➡ Greyhound transports bicycles as luggage (surcharge $30 to $40), provided the bicycle is disassembled and placed in a box ($10, available at some terminals).

➡ Most of Amtrak's *Cascades, Pacific Surfliner, Capital Corridor* and *San Joaquin* trains feature onboard racks where you can secure your bike unboxed; try to reserve a spot when making your ticket reservation (surcharge $5 to $10).

➡ On Amtrak trains without racks, bikes must be put in a box ($15) and checked as luggage (fee $10). Not all stations or trains offer checked-baggage service.

➡ Before flying, you'll need to disassemble your bike and box it as checked baggage; contact the airline directly for details, including applicable surcharges (typically $50 to $100, sometimes more).

Boat

There is no river or canal public transportation system in the West, but there are many smaller, often state-run, coastal ferry services. Most larger ferries will transport private cars, motorcycles and bicycles.

Off the coast of Washington, ferries reach the scenic San Juan Islands. Several of California's Channel Islands are accessible by boat, as is Catalina Island, offshore from Los Angeles. On San Francisco Bay, regular ferries operate between San Francisco and Sausalito, Larkspur, Tiburon, Angel Island, Oakland, Alameda and Vallejo.

Bus

➡ **Greyhound** (☎800-231-2222, international customer service 214-849-8100; www.greyhound.com) is the major long-distance bus company, with routes throughout the USA and Canada. To improve efficiency and profitability, Greyhound has recently stopped service to many small towns; routes generally trace major highways and stop at larger population centers. To reach country towns on rural roads, you may need to transfer to local or county bus systems; Greyhound can usually provide their contact information.

➡ Most baggage has to be checked in; label it loudly and clearly to avoid it getting lost. Larger items, including skis, surfboards and bicycles, can be transported, but there may be an extra charge. Call to check.

➡ The frequency of bus services varies widely. Despite the elimination of many tiny destinations, nonexpress Greyhound buses still stop every 50 to 100 miles to pick up passengers. Long-distance buses stop for meal breaks and driver changes.

➡ Greyhound buses are usually clean, comfortable and reliable. The best seats are typically near the front away from the bathroom. Limited onboard amenities include freezing air-con (bring a sweater) and slightly reclining seats; select buses have electrical outlets and wi-fi. Smoking on board is prohibited.

➡ Many bus stations are clean and safe, but some are in dodgy areas. Some towns have just a flag stop. If you are boarding at one of these, pay the driver with exact change.

Costs

➡ For lower fares, purchase tickets seven to 14 days in advance. Round-trip travel may be cheaper and the price may vary depending on the day of the week you are traveling.

➡ Discounts (on unrestricted fares only) are available for seniors aged 62 and over (5%), students (20%) with a Student Advantage Card, and up to 50% off for two family members with the purchase of one full-price fare. Check the website for details about discounts for active military personnel, and dependents and veterans.

➡ Special promotional discounts are often available on the Greyhound website, though they may come with restrictions or blackout periods. The Discovery Pass, which allowed for unlimited travel, has been discontinued.

Reservations

➡ Greyhound bus tickets can be bought over the phone or online. You can print tickets at home or pick them up at the terminal using 'Will Call' service (bring photo ID).

➡ Seating is normally first-come, first-served. Greyhound recommends arriving an hour before departure to get a seat.

➡ Travelers with disabilities who need special assistance should call ☎800-752-4841 (TDD/TTY ☎800-345-3109) at least 48 hours before traveling; there are limited spaces for those in wheelchairs, although wheelchairs are also accepted as checked baggage. Service animals, such as guide dogs, are allowed on board.

Car & Motorcycle

A car allows maximum flexibility and convenience, and it's particularly helpful if you want to explore rural America and its wide-open spaces.

Automobile Associations

For 24-hour emergency roadside assistance, free maps and discounts on lodging, attractions, entertainment, car rentals and more:

American Automobile Association (AAA; ☎800-874-7532; www.aaa.com) Add-on coverage for RVs and motorcycles, and reciprocal agreements with some international auto clubs (eg CAA in Canada, AA in the UK) – bring your membership card from home.

Better World Club (☎866-238-1137; www.betterworldclub.com) Ecofriendly alternative supports environmental causes and also offers cyclists emergency roadside assistance.

Driver's License

➡ Foreign visitors can legally drive a car in the USA for up to 12 months using their home driver's license. However, an international driving permit (IDP) will have more credibility with US traffic police, especially if your home license doesn't have a photo or isn't in English. Your automobile association at home can issue an IDP, valid for one year, for a small fee. Always carry your home license together with the IDP.

➡ To drive a motorcycle in the USA, you will need a valid US state motorcycle license. International visitors need a drivers' permit from their home country, or an IDP specially endorsed for motorcycles.

Insurance

➡ Before renting a car, check your auto-insurance policy from home or your travel-insurance policy to see if

USEFUL BUS ROUTES

SERVICE	PRICE ($)	DURATION (HR)
Las Vegas–Los Angeles	60	5-7
Los Angeles–San Francisco	59-65	7½-12
Phoenix–Tucson	18	2
Seattle–Portland	30-33	4
Denver–Salt Lake City	101-105	10-12¼

ROAD DISTANCES (MILES)

	Denver	Grand Canyon National Park (South Rim)	Las Vegas	Los Angeles	Phoenix	Portland	San Francisco	Santa Fe	Seattle
Grand Canyon National Park (South Rim)	68								
Las Vegas	750	270							
Los Angeles	1020	485	270						
Phoenix	825	215	285	375					
Portland	1260	1330	1020	965	1335				
San Francisco	1270	790	570	380	750	635			
Santa Fe	395	455	635	850	530	1450	1145		
Seattle	1330	1365	1165	1135	1500	175	810	1545	
Yellowstone National Park	530	810	670	950	920	795	1000	820	875

TRANSPORTATION CAR & MOTORCYCLE

you're already covered and what is covered. Your policy probably includes liability protection but, if not, expect to pay about $7 to $14 per day for liability insurance. Insurance against damage to the car itself, called Collision Damage Waiver (CDW) or Loss Damage Waiver (LDW), costs another $20 to $40 per day; you may be required to pay the first $100 to $500 for any repairs. Some credit cards cover this, provided you charge the entire cost of the car rental to the card. If there's an accident you may have to pay the rental-car company first and then seek reimbursement from the credit-card company. Check your credit card's policy carefully before renting.

Rental

CAR

➡ To rent your own wheels, you'll typically need to be at least 25 years old, hold a valid driver's license and have a major credit card, not a check or debit card. A few companies may rent to drivers under 25 but over 21 for a surcharge (around $15 to $25 per day). If you don't have a credit card, you may occasionally be able to make a large cash deposit instead.

➡ With advance reservations, you can often get an economy-sized vehicle with unlimited mileage from around $30 per day, plus insurance, taxes and fees. Weekend rates are usually more economical. Airport locations may have cheaper rates but higher fees; if you get a fly-drive package, local taxes may be extra when you pick up the car. City-center branches may offer free pick-ups and drop-offs.

➡ Rates generally include unlimited mileage (check the mileage cap), but expect surcharges for additional drivers and one-way rentals. Some rental companies let you pay for your last tank of gas upfront; this is rarely a good deal.

Major international car-rental companies:

Alamo (☎877-222-9075; www.alamo.com)

Avis (☎800-331-1212; www.avis.com)

Budget (☎800-527-0700; www.budget.com)

Dollar (☎800-800-3665; www.dollar.com)

Enterprise (☎800-261-7331; www.enterprise.com)

Hertz (☎800-654-3131; www.hertz.com)

National (☎877-222-9058; www.nationalcar.com)

Thrifty (☎800-847-4389; www.thrifty.com)

You might get a better deal by booking through discount-travel websites such as **Priceline** (www.priceline.com) or **Hotwire** (www.hotwire.com), or by using online travel-booking sites, such as **Expedia** (www.expedia.com), **Orbitz** (www.orbitz.com) or **Travelocity** (www.travelocity.com). You can also compare rates across travel sites at **Kayak** (www.kayak.com).

A few major car-rental companies (including Avis, Budget, Enterprise, Hertz and Thrifty) offer 'green' fleets of hybrid or biofueled rental cars, but they're in short supply. Reserve well in advance. Also try **Simply Hybrid** (☎323-653-0011,

888-359-0055; www.simply hybrid.com) in Los Angeles, which offers free delivery and pick-up from some locations with a three-day minimum rental; or **Zipcar** (☎866-494-7227; www.zipcar.com), which is available in California (Los Angeles, San Diego and the San Francisco Bay area) and Denver, Portland and Seattle. This car-sharing club charges usage fees (per hour or daily), and includes free gas, insurance (damage fee of up to $750 may apply) and limited mileage. Apply online (foreign drivers are OK). Annual membership is $60, and the application fee $25.

To compare independent car-rental companies, try **Car Rental Express** (www.carrentalexpress.com), which is especially useful for finding cheaper long-term rentals. Independent companies that may rent to drivers under 25:

Rent-a-Wreck (☎877-877-0700; www.rentawreck.com) Minimum rental age and surcharges vary by location.

Super Cheap Car Rental (www.supercheapcar.com) Normally surcharge for drivers aged 21 to 24; daily fee applies for drivers aged 18 to 21.

MOTORCYCLE & RECREATIONAL VEHICLE (RV)

If you dream of cruising across America on a Harley, **EagleRider** (☎888-900-9901; www.eaglerider.com) has offices in major cities nationwide and rents other kinds of adventure vehicles, too. Motorcycle rental and insurance are expensive.

Companies specializing in RV and camper rentals:

Adventures on Wheels (☎800-943-3579; www.wheels9.com)

Cruise America (☎800-671-8042; www.cruiseamerica.com)

Happy Travel Campers (☎800-370-1262; www.camperusa.com)

Fueling Up

Many gas stations in the West have fuel pumps with automated credit-card pay screens. Most machines ask for your zip code. For foreign travelers, or those with cards issued outside the US, you'll have to pay inside before pumping gas. Tell the clerk how much money you'd like to put on the card. If there's still cash left, go back inside and have the difference refunded to the card.

Road Conditions & Hazards

➡ Road hazards include potholes, commuter traffic, wandering wildlife and distracted and enraged drivers.

➡ Where winter driving is an issue, many cars are fitted with steel-studded snow tires; snow chains are sometimes required in mountain areas. Driving off-road, or on dirt roads, is often forbidden by rental-car companies, and it can be very dangerous in wet weather.

➡ In deserts and range country, livestock sometimes grazes next to unfenced roads. These areas are signed as 'Open Range' or with the silhouette of a steer. Where deer and other wild animals frequently appear roadside, you'll see signs with the silhouette of a leaping deer. Take these signs seriously, particularly at night.

For nationwide traffic and road-closure information, visit www.fhwa.dot.gov/traffic info/index.htm.

For current road conditions within a state, call ☎511. From outside a state, try the following:

Arizona (☎888-411-7623; www.az511.com)

California (☎800-427-7623; www.dot.ca.gov)

Colorado (☎303-639-1111; www.cotrip.org)

Idaho (☎888-432-7623; http://511.idaho.gov/)

Montana (☎800-226-7623; www.mdt.mt.gov/travinfo/)

Nevada (☎877-687-6237; www.nvroads.com)

New Mexico (☎800-432-4269; http://nmroads.com)

Oregon (☎503-588-2941; www.tripcheck.com)

Utah (☎866-511-8824; www.commuterlink.utah.gov)

Washington (☎800-695-7623; www.wsdot.com/traffic/)

Wyoming (☎888-996-7623; www.wyoroad.info)

Road Rules

➡ Cars drive on the right-hand side of the road.

➡ The use of seat belts and child safety seats is required in every state. Most car-rental agencies rent child safety seats for around $12 per day, but you must reserve them when booking.

➡ In some states, motorcyclists are required to wear helmets.

➡ On interstate highways, the speed limit is sometimes raised to 75mph. Unless otherwise posted, the speed limit is generally 55mph or 65mph on highways, 25mph to 35mph in cities and towns and as low as 15mph in school zones (strictly enforced during school hours). It's forbidden to pass a school bus when its lights are flashing.

➡ When emergency vehicles (ie police, fire or ambulance) approach from either direction, pull over safely and get out of the way. In an increasing number of states, it is illegal to talk on a handheld cell (mobile) phone or text while driving; use a hands-free device or pull over to take your call or text message.

➡ The maximum legal blood-alcohol concentration for

SCENIC TRAIN ROUTES

Historic locomotives chug through mountain ranges and other scenic landscapes across the west. Most trains run in the warmer months only, and they can be extremely popular, so book ahead.

Cumbres & Toltec Scenic Railroad (☑575-756-2151; www.cumbrestoltec.com; adult/child from $89/49; ⊙late May–mid-Oct) Living, moving museum from Chama, NM, into Colorado's Rocky Mountains.

Durango & Silverton Narrow Gauge Railroad (☑970-247-2733, toll-free 877-872-4607; www.durangotrain.com; adult/child return from $85/51; ⊙departure at 8am, 8:45am & 9:30am) Ends at historic mining town Silverton in Colorado's Rocky Mountains.

Mount Hood Railroad Winds through the scenic Columbia River Gorge outside Portland, OR.

Skunk Train (☑707-964-6371; www.skunktrain.com; adult/child from $20/10) Runs between Fort Bragg, CA, on the coast, and Willits, further inland, passing through redwoods.

Grand Canyon Railway (☑928-635-4253, 800-843-8724; www.thetrain.com; round trip adult/child from $75/45) Vintage steam and diesel locomotives with family-oriented entertainment runs between Williams, AZ, and Grand Canyon National Park.

Also worth riding is Pikes Peak Cog Railway, an 8.9-mile track outside Colorado Springs that climbs from a canyon to above the timberline.

---

drivers is 0.08%. Penalties are very severe for 'DUI' – driving under the influence of alcohol and/or drugs. Police can give roadside sobriety checks to assess if you've been drinking or using drugs. If you fail, you will then be required to take a breath test, urine test or blood test to determine the level of alcohol or drugs in your body. Refusing to be tested is treated the same as if you'd taken the test and failed.

➡ In some states it is illegal to carry 'open containers' of alcohol in a vehicle, even if they are empty.

USEFUL TRAIN ROUTES

SERVICE	PRICE ($)	DURATION (HR)
Los Angeles–Flagstaff	70	10½
Los Angeles–Oakland/San Francisco	61	11¼
San Francisco/Emeryville–Salt Lake City	97	17
Seattle–Oakland/San Francisco	104	23

Local Transportation

Except in cities, public transport is rarely the most convenient option, and coverage to outlying towns and suburbs can be sparse. However, it is usually cheap, safe and reliable.

Airport Shuttles

Shuttle buses provide inexpensive and convenient transport to/from airports in most cities. Most are 12-seat vans; some have regular routes and stops (which include the main hotels) and some pick up and deliver passengers 'door to door' in their service area.

Costs average $15 to $22 per person.

Bicycle

Some cities are more amenable to bicycles than others, but most have at least a few dedicated bike lanes and paths, and bikes can usually be carried on public transportation.

Bus

Most cities and larger towns have dependable local bus systems, though they are often designed for commuters and provide limited service in the evening and on weekends. Costs average about $2 per ride. Limited routes in tourist areas may be free.

Subway & Train

The largest systems are in Los Angeles and the San Francisco Bay Area. Other cities may have small, one- or two-line rail systems that mainly serve downtown.

Taxi

➡ Taxis are metered, with flag-fall fees of $2.50 to $5, plus $2 to $3 per mile. Credit cards may be accepted.

➡ Taxis may charge extra for baggage and/or airport pick-ups.

➡ Drivers expect a 10% to 15% tip, rounded up to the next dollar.

➡ Taxis cruise the busiest areas in large cities, but elsewhere you may need to call a cab company.

Train

Amtrak (☎800-872-7245; www.amtrak.com) operates a fairly extensive rail system throughout the USA. Fares vary according to the type of train and seating (eg reserved or unreserved coach seats, business class, sleeping compartments). Trains are comfortable, if a bit slow, and are equipped with dining and lounge cars on long-distance routes.

Amtrak routes in the West:

California Zephyr Daily service between Chicago and Emeryville (from $163, 52 hours), near San Francisco, via Denver, Salt Lake City, Reno and Sacramento.

Coast Starlight Travels the West Coast daily from Seattle to LA (from $115, 35 hours) via Portland, Sacramento, Oakland and Santa Barbara; wi-fi may be available.

Southwest Chief Daily departures between Chicago and LA (from $169, 44 hours) via Kansas City, Albuquerque, Flagstaff and Barstow.

Sunset Limited Thrice-weekly service between New Orleans and LA (from $205, 48 hours) via Houston, San Antonio, El Paso, Tucson and Palm Springs.

COSTS

➡ Purchase tickets at train stations, by phone or online. Fares depend on the day of travel, the route, the type of seating etc. Fares may be slightly higher during peak travel times such as summer. Round-trip tickets cost the same as two one-way tickets.

➡ Usually seniors over 62, veterans with a Veterans Advantage Card and students with an ISIC or Student Advantage Card receive a 15% discount, while up to two children aged two to 15 who are accompanied by an adult get 50% off. AAA members save 10%. Special promotions can become available anytime, so check the website or ask.

RESERVATIONS

Reservations can be made from 11 months in advance up to the day of departure. Space on most trains is limited, and certain routes can be crowded, especially during summer and holiday periods, so it's a good idea to book as far in advance as you can.

TRAIN PASSES

➡ Amtrak's **USA Rail Pass** (www.amtrak.com) is valid for coach-class travel for 15 ($439), 30 ($669) or 45 ($859) days; children aged two to 15 pay half-price. Actual travel is limited to eight, 12 or 18 one-way 'segments,' respectively. A segment is *not* the same as a one-way trip; if reaching your destination requires riding more than one train, you'll use multiple pass segments.

➡ Purchase rail passes online; make advance reservations for each travel segment.

➡ For travel within California, consider the seven-day California Rail Pass (adult/child $159/$80).

Behind the Scenes

SEND US YOUR FEEDBACK

We love to hear from travelers – your comments keep us on our toes and help make our books better. Our well-traveled team reads every word on what you loved or loathed about this book. Although we cannot reply individually to postal submissions, we always guarantee that your feedback goes straight to the appropriate authors, in time for the next edition. Each person who sends us information is thanked in the next edition – the most useful submissions are rewarded with a selection of digital PDF chapters.

Visit **lonelyplanet.com/contact** to submit your updates and suggestions or to ask for help. Our award-winning website also features inspirational travel stories, news and discussions.

Note: We may edit, reproduce and incorporate your comments in Lonely Planet products such as guidebooks, websites and digital products, so let us know if you don't want your comments reproduced or your name acknowledged. For a copy of our privacy policy visit lonelyplanet.com/privacy.

OUR READERS

Many thanks to the travelers who used the last edition and wrote to us with helpful hints, useful advice and interesting anecdotes: Erika Hellin, Georgina Pitts, Rudolf Rolelofsen, Stefan Zinte

AUTHOR THANKS

Amy C Balfour

Big thanks to my friends and experts in the Southwest, with special kudos to BLM maestro Chris Rose for his invaluable Nevada insights and Elvis knowledge. Thanks also to Justin Shepherd, Tracer Finn, Jim Christian, Alex Amato, Mike Roe, Catrien van Assendelft, Lewis Pipkin, Sara Benson, Dan Westermeyer and fellow adventurers Sandee McGlaun, Lisa McGlaun, Paul Hanstedt and Grand Canyon power walker Karen Schneider.

Sandra Bao

Thanks to my husband Ben Greensfelder, who kept our home (mostly) intact while I was off researching. Kudos to my top-notch coordinating authors on the Pacific Northwest (whose information I adapted for this book), Celeste Brash and Brendan Sainsbury. A big hug to commissioning editor Suki Gear – thanks for the gig and best of luck in your coming life adventures. And finally, I could not have done this book without the support of my parents and brother.

Michael Benavav

Big thanks to Suki for convincing me to drive to all the little corners of this state that I love, and for her pitch-perfect blend of professionalism and humor. Also to Kelly and Luke, who always let me go, and always let me come back.

Greg Benchwick

Special thanks to my friend and commissioning editor Suki, my coordinating author and the rest of the Lonely Planet team.

Sara Benson

Thanks to Suki Gear, Sasha Baskett, Alison Lyall, Regis St Louis and everyone at Lonely Planet for making this book happen. I'm grateful to everyone I met on the road, from park rangers to beer geeks and foodies, who generously shared their local expertise. Big thanks to my Golden State friends and family, especially the Picketts, Starbins and Boyles. Jonathan, you kept on driving, even when you didn't know exactly where we'd end up – thank you.

Alison Bing

Heartfelt thanks to Lonely Planet guidebook mastermind Suki Gear, managing editor Sasha Baskett, and co-author and fellow adventurer John Vlahides; to intrepid research companions Sahai Burrowes, Haemin Cho, Lisa Park,

Yosh Han, Rebecca Bing, Tony Cockrell and Akua Parker; but above all to Marco Flavio Marinucci, who made a Muni bus ride into the trip of a lifetime.

Celeste Brash

Thanks to my family for helping me research beaches and mountains some days, and getting on at home without me on others. To old friends who I found scattered across Washington: Oliver Irwin, Kati Halmos Jones, Dan Jones, the Forster family and Jackie Capalan-Auerbach. And to new friends I made: too many to mention!

Lisa Dunford

So many kindred spirits on the Utah road – thanks to all, including Karla Player for the beautiful craftsmanship. Karen and John, it was great having a chat. And I'm so glad I got to reconnect with my friend Trista Kelin Rayner; wishing her and daughter Mechelle all the best.

Carolyn McCarthy

I'm indebted to the good people of the Rocky Mountains. Special thanks to Lance and his Ouray friends for the bed and BBQ, Melissa and Steve for the Billings grand tour, the amazing Jones in Steamboat and Jennifer in Crested Butte. Richard and Rachel were the best drivers and companions. Thanks to Coraline, for steadfast motoring, and the generous Conan Bliss. Virtual beers go out to Regis St Louis, Greg Benchwick and Chris Pitts for being great to work with.

Brendan Sainsbury

Thanks to all the untold bus drivers, tourist info volunteers, restaurateurs, coffee baristas and indie punk rockers who helped me during my research. Special thanks to my wife Liz and seven-year-old son Kieran for their company on the road.

ACKNOWLEDGMENTS

Climate map data adapted from Peel MC, Finlayson BL & McMahon TA (2007) 'Updated World Map of the Köppen-Geiger Climate Classification', Hydrology and Earth System Sciences, 11, 1633¬44.

Illustration pp136-7 by Michael Weldon.

Cover photograph: Monument Valley, Arizona–Utah, Alan Copson/AWL.

THIS BOOK

This 2nd edition of Lonely Planet's *Western USA* guidebook was researched and written by Amy C Balfour, Sandra Bao, Michael Benanav, Greg Benchwick, Sara Benson, Alison Bing, Celeste Brash, Lisa Dunford, Carolyn McCarthy, Chris Pitts and Brendan Sainsbury. Amy, Michael, Sara, Alison, Lisa, Carolyn and Brendan also contributed to the previous edition, along with Andrew Bender, Nate Cavalieri, Sarah Chandler, Bridget Gleeson, Beth Kohn, Bradley Mayhew, Andrea Schulte-Peevers and John A Vlahides. This guidebook was commissioned in Lonely Planet's Oakland office, and produced by the following:

Commissioning Editor Suki Gear

Coordinating Editors Katie O'Connell, Martine Power

Senior Cartographer Alison Lyall

Book Designer Wendy Wright

Associate Product Directors Sasha Baskett, Angela Tinson

Senior Editors Catherine Naghten, Karyn Noble

Assisting Editor Kate James

Assisting Layout Designer Virginia Moreno

Cover Research Naomi Parker

Thanks to Brendan Dempsey, Ryan Evans, Larissa Frost, Briohny Hooper, Genesys India, Jouve India, Indra Kilfoyle, Chad Parkhill, Trent Paton, Alison Ridgway, Dianne Schallmeiner, Lyahna Spencer, John Taufa, Amanda Williamson, Juan Winata

Index

Map Pages **000**
Photo Pages **000**

482

NOTES

NOTES

Map Legend

Sights

- Beach
- Bird Sanctuary
- Buddhist
- Castle/Palace
- Christian
- Confucian
- Hindu
- Islamic
- Jain
- Jewish
- Monument
- Museum/Gallery/Historic Building
- Ruin
- Sento Hot Baths/Onsen
- Shinto
- Sikh
- Taoist
- Winery/Vineyard
- Zoo/Wildlife Sanctuary
- Other Sight

Activities, Courses & Tours

- Bodysurfing
- Diving
- Canoeing/Kayaking
- Course/Tour
- Skiing
- Snorkeling
- Surfing
- Swimming/Pool
- Walking
- Windsurfing
- Other Activity

Sleeping

- Sleeping
- Camping

Eating

- Eating

Drinking & Nightlife

- Drinking & Nightlife
- Cafe

Entertainment

- Entertainment

Shopping

- Shopping

Information

- Bank
- Embassy/Consulate
- Hospital/Medical
- Internet
- Police
- Post Office
- Telephone
- Toilet
- Tourist Information
- Other Information

Geographic

- Beach
- Hut/Shelter
- Lighthouse
- Lookout
- Mountain/Volcano
- Oasis
- Park
- Pass
- Picnic Area
- Waterfall

Population

- Capital (National)
- Capital (State/Province)
- City/Large Town
- Town/Village

Transport

- Airport
- BART station
- Border crossing
- Boston T station
- Bus
- Cable car/Funicular
- Cycling
- Ferry
- Metro/Muni station
- Monorail
- Parking
- Petrol station
- Subway/SkyTrain station
- Taxi
- Train station/Railway
- Tram
- Underground station
- Other Transport

Note: Not all symbols displayed above appear on the maps in this book

Routes

- Tollway
- Freeway
- Primary
- Secondary
- Tertiary
- Lane
- Unsealed road
- Road under construction
- Plaza/Mall
- Steps
- Tunnel
- Pedestrian overpass
- Walking Tour
- Walking Tour detour
- Path/Walking Trail

Boundaries

- International
- State/Province
- Disputed
- Regional/Suburb
- Marine Park
- Cliff
- Wall

Hydrography

- River, Creek
- Intermittent River
- Canal
- Water
- Dry/Salt/Intermittent Lake
- Reef

Areas

- Airport/Runway
- Beach/Desert
- Cemetery (Christian)
- Cemetery (Other)
- Glacier
- Mudflat
- Park/Forest
- Sight (Building)
- Sportsground
- Swamp/Mangrove

Sara Benson

California After graduating from college in Chicago, Sara jumped on a plane to San Francisco with just one suitcase and $100 in her pocket. She has bounced around California ever since, in between stints living in Asia and Hawaii and working as a national-park ranger. The author of 55 travel and nonfiction books, Sara summited Sierra Nevada peaks, uncovered the Lost Coast and survived Death Valley while researching this guide. Follow her adventures online at www.indietraveler.blogspot.com and @indie_traveler on Twitter.

Alison Bing

California Over 15 years in San Francisco, Alison has done everything you're supposed to do in the city and many things you're not, including falling in love on the Haight St bus and quitting a Silicon Valley day job to write 43 Lonely Planet guidebooks and commentary for magazines, mobile guides and other media. Join further adventures as they unfold on Twitter @AlisonBing.

Celeste Brash

Pacific Northwest Locals have a hard time believing it, but the beauty of the Pacific Northwest is what coaxed Celeste back to the US after 15 years in Tahiti. She was thrilled to explore and imbibe the treasures of her new backyard, hike snowy peaks, look for orcas, and get in touch with her cowboy and Indian roots for this book. Find out more about Celeste and her award-winning writing at www.celestebrash.com.

Lisa Dunford

Southwest As one Brigham Young's (possibly thousands of) great-great-granddaughters, Lisa was first drawn to Utah by ancestry. But it's the incredible red rocks that have kept her coming back for 10 years. She feels at home hiking through pinkish sand around Zion or Arches until her shoes are permanently stained, rounding a bend and being accosted by purple-, crimson- and rose-colored cliffs. Lisa co-authored Lonely Planet's *Zion & Bryce Canyon National Parks*.

Carolyn McCarthy

Rocky Mountains Carolyn fell for the Rockies as an undergraduate at Colorado College, where she spent her first break camping in a blizzard in the Sangre de Christo Range. For this title she sampled craft beers, tracked wolves and heard even more Old West ghost stories. Carolyn has contributed to over 20 Lonely Planet titles, specializing in the American west and Latin America, and has written for *National Geographic, Outside, Lonely Planet Traveller* and other publications.

Christopher Pitts

Rocky Mountains Chris first drove west on a family road trip across the US and instantly fell in love with Colorado's star-studded nights. After four years at Colorado College, he decided to move up to Boulder for grad school – but only after mastering Chinese. Fifteen years, several continents and two kids later, he finally made it to the end of what is normally a 90-minute drive. Chris currently divides his time between writing, dad-dom and exploring Colorado's wilder corners. Visit him online at www.christopherpitts.net.

Brendan Sainsbury

Pacific Northwest An expat Brit from Hampshire, England, now living near Vancouver, Canada, Brendan is a Nirvana-loving, craft-beer-appreciating, outdoors-embracing, art-admiring, bus-utilizing coffee addict who had no problem finding like-minded souls in Seattle. He's been writing Lonely Planet guides for the last nine years and collecting notes on Seattle since 2009. He is the author of Lonely Planet's current guide to Seattle, and has contributed to numerous US titles.

OUR STORY

A beat-up old car, a few dollars in the pocket and a sense of adventure. In 1972 that's all Tony and Maureen Wheeler needed for the trip of a lifetime – across Europe and Asia overland to Australia. It took several months, and at the end – broke but inspired – they sat at their kitchen table writing and stapling together their first travel guide, *Across Asia on the Cheap*. Within a week they'd sold 1500 copies. Lonely Planet was born.

Today, Lonely Planet has offices in Melbourne, London and Oakland, with more than 600 staff and writers. We share Tony's belief that 'a great guidebook should do three things: inform, educate and amuse'.

OUR WRITERS

Amy C Balfour

Coordinating Author, Southwest Amy has hiked, biked, skied and gambled her way across the Southwest. In Arizona she enjoyed a return trip to Phantom Ranch, hiking down the South Kaibab Trail from the South Rim and back up on the Bright Angel. Amy has authored or co-authored more than 15 books for Lonely Planet and has written for *Backpacker, Every Day with Rachael Ray, Redbook, Southern Living* and *Women's Health*.

Sandra Bao

Pacific Northwest Sandra has lived in Buenos Aires, New York and California, but Oregon has become her final stop. Researching the Beaver state has been a highlight of Sandra's 14-year-long authoring career with Lonely Planet, which has covered four continents and dozens of guidebooks. She's come to appreciate the wondrous beauty of her home state, how much it has to offer both travelers and locals and how friendly people can be in tiny towns in the middle of nowhere.

Michael Benanav

Southwest Michael came to New Mexico in 1992, fell under its spell, and moved to a village in the Sangre de Cristo foothills where he still lives. Since then, he's spent years exploring the state's mountains, deserts and rivers as a wilderness instructor. Aside from his work for Lonely Planet, he's authored two nonfiction books and writes and photographs for magazines and newspapers. Check out his work at www.michaelbenanav.com.

Greg Benchwick

Rocky Mountains A Colorado native, Greg's been all over the Centennial State. He has taught skiing in Vail, walked through fire-pits in campsites across the state and attended journalism school in Boulder. He calls Denver's Highlands home.

OVER PAGE MORE WRITERS

Published by Lonely Planet Publications Pty Ltd
ABN 36 005 607 983
2nd edition – Apr 2014
ISBN 978 1 74220 742 1
© Lonely Planet 2014   Photographs © as indicated 2014
10 9 8 7 6 5 4 3 2 1
Printed in China